GEORGE WASHINGTON DUKE

NOTABLE
SOUTHERN FAMILIES

Compiled by
ZELLA ARMSTRONG

Six Volumes in Three

Volumes III-IV

GENEALOGICAL PUBLISHING CO., INC.
BALTIMORE   1974

Originally Published
Chattanooga, Tennessee

Volume I —1918
Volume II —1922
Volume III—1926
Volume IV—1926
Volume V —1928
Volume VI—1933

Reprinted
Six Volumes in Three
Genealogical Publishing Co., Inc.
Baltimore, 1974

Library of Congress Cataloging in Publication Data

Armstrong, Zella, comp.
    Notable southern families.

    Vol. 5 compiled by J. P. C. French and Z. Armstrong; v. 6 compiled
by J. P. C. French.
    Reprint of the 1918-33 ed. published by Lookout Pub. Co., Chattanooga.
    CONTENTS: v. 1-2. Armstrong. Banning. Blount. Brownlow. Calhoun.
Deaderick. Gaines. Howard, Key. Luttrell, Lyle. McAdoo, McGhee. Mc-
Millan. Phinizy. Polk. Sevier. Shields. Stone. Turnley. VanDyke. Bean.
Boone. Borden. Bryan. Carter. Davis. Donaldson. Hardwick. Haywood.
Holiday. Hollingsworth. Houston. Johnston. Kelton. Magill. Rhea. Montgomery. Shelby. Vance. Wear. Williams. 1 v.—v. 3-4, Armstrong, "Trou-
per." Cockrill. Duke. Elston. Lea. Park. Parkes. Tunnell. The Sevier family.
1 v.—v. 5-6. The Crockett family and connecting lines. The Doak family.
1 v.
    1. Southern States—Genealogy. I. French, Janie Preston (Collop)
1877- II. Title.
CS69.A852   929.2'0973   72-531
ISBN 0-8063-0508-8

NOTICE

This work was reproduced from the original edition by the photo-offset
process. The uneven image evident in the reprint is characteristic of the
original typography. This shortcoming notwithstanding, our printer has
made every effort to produce as fine a reprint of the original edition as
possible.

Genealogical Publishing Co., Inc.

Made in the United States of America

To my father and mother
John MacMillan Armstrong
and
Martha Turnley Armstrong
This book is affectionately dedicated

FOREWORD

THE Southern States were settled by three great waves of emigration—Cavalier, Scotch-Irish and Huguenot. These types retain their characteristics to this day, perhaps, largely, because groups of relatives friends and neighbors settled in one section and gave a dominant tinge in creed, church and custom. The sons and daughters of these families married, and creed and custom grew stronger from year to year. Thus the Scotch-Irish, a people of Scotch origin, though living in Ireland for many years before the American emigration, settled in many parts of Virginia, North and South Carolina, and what is now East Tennessee, in great numbers and impressed their Presbyterian faith upon their posterity.

In the chapters of this book examples will be given of each of these groups—Cavalier, Scotch-Irish and Huguenot.

The early history of several of these Southern families is here presented, being published, at least in collected form, for the first time. The compiler takes no credit for authorship, as genealogy is not a science of invention. The facts, however, are clearly stated, and in the case of each family, each line may be brought down to the present time from the earliest settler in America.

The Colonial, Revolutionary, 1812 and War Between the States record of each family is set forth succinctly. Little space has been given to tradition, though many traditions in the families mentioned are interesting and doubtless could be followed up and proved. Many histories have been consulted and many family documents studied, only reliable records being used.

Though the chief endeavor of these chapters is to show the Colonial or Revolutionary soldier and his posterity, a brief line of his progenitors is given in some cases, as the origin of the name and family is always interesting.

Hundreds of histories, court records and family documents have been examined in the preparation of this volume

While scores of friends and descendants of the families have contributed valuable material, special credit must be given to Miss Lucy M. Ball who prepared the complete Turnell record, to Mrs. Sesseler Hoss who prepared the Cockrill record, to Miss Frances Powell Otkin who collected much of the Lea data, to Elston Luttrell who prepared the complete Elston record, and to Roy H. Parks who collected much of the Parks data and to Mrs. Alexander M. Barrow whose interest in the history of her ancestor, Col. James Armstrong was the inception of the Armstrong chapter.

Appreciation is also hereby expressed for generous assistance from Benjamin Newton Duke, Miss Kate White, Miss Augusta Bradford, Mrs. William Sawyer; Mrs. John T. Moore, A. P. Foster, Francis Armstrong, Mrs. Luther Allen, Mrs. William Egbert, Miss Aileen Benson and many others who helped in research or preparattion of material.

Contents

NOTABLE
SOUTHERN FAMILIES

Volume III

Armstrong

Colonel James "Trooper" Armstrong

GENERAL ROBERT ARMSTRONG

ARMSTRONG—COLONEL JAMES
"TROOPER" ARMSTRONG

T HE family of Armstrong derives its name from the following circumstance. An ancient King of Scotland had his horse killed under him in battle. Fairbairn, his armor-bearer, immediately grasped the King by the thigh and set him on another horse. For this assistance at such a critical moment, the King rewarded him with lands upon the border, and to perpetuate the memory of so important a service, as well as the manner in which it was performed, the King gave him the appelation Armstrong and assigned him for a crest an armed arm and hand grasping a leg in armor. This is the left hand.

The hero of the exploit, "Siward the Armstrong," Earl of Northumberland, first of the name and ancestor of the renowned Border family of Armstrong, was one of those stalwart figures who will never pass away from the pages of history and tradition. In his physical strength and prowess, wit and wisdom, loftiness of character, defiance of death and danger he was remarkable. He was undoubtedly a Christian, for he built the minster of York, but he reminds us of those old heroes of the Edda, from whom his ancestors were said to have descended. He acquired honor for England by his successful conduct of the only foreign enterprise undertaken during the reign of Edward the Confessor. (Johannes Brinston, Saxe Gramatieur, George Stephens). Duncan, King of Scotland, was a prince of gentle disposition, and lacked the genius for governing so turbulent a country as Scotland, and one so infested by the intrigues and animosities of the great Macbeth. Siward embraced, by Edward's orders, the protection of the distressed royal family. He marched an army into Scotland, and, having defeated Macbeth in battle restored Malcolm, Duncan's son, to the throne of his ancestors. This service, added to his former connection with the royal family of Scotland, brought great accession to the authority of Siward in the North.

Soon after his return from this campaign he was attacked by a fatal disorder. As he felt his end approaching he said to his attendants: "Lift me up that I may die on my legs like a soldier, not couching like a cow. Dress me in my coat of mail, cover my head with my helmet, put my shield on my left arm and my battle axe in my right hand that I may die under arms."

1

Ingulf's record of his death reads as follows:

"In the year of our Lord 1056, Siward the brave Earl of Northumberland, departed this life and was buried in the cloister of the monastery of Saint Mary, which he had built without the walls of the city of York."

Siward was a Dane and he was much beloved by his Northumbrians, who were chiefly of a Danish extraction.

Siward married twice. His son by the first wife, called Young Siward in "Macbeth," was killed by Macbeth in the battle of Dunsinmore. Siward married for his second wife Aelfled, daughter of Alfred Earl of Northumberland and through her, acquired that title and great authority. The Northumberlands were of Danish extraction and rejoiced at being ruled by the great Earl who was of Danish blood. His son by Aelfled succeeded to the title and his daughter by Aelfled married David I, King of Scotland.

Here is a list of the different forms of Siwadr's name: In the Irish records he was called the Strong, in the Terwinney records he was called Fayborn and the Armstrong; in old manuscripts brought over by Armstrongs to North Carolina from Londonderry, Ireland, in 1711, he was called the Strong.

In the old records the names most frequently given to the Armstrongs are Rolland, Goeffry and Robert, all showing the ancient Nordic extraction, Robert is the name most frequently used in every branch of the family to this day.

From Siward the Strong Arm the Armstrong clan is descended. The ancient border family grew and flourished and though, in the years and centuries that followed they roamed afar, even as Siward himself roamed from his native land, they retained the spirit of Siward and were always bold, courageous, war-like and high principled.

Their adventures in the history of the Border are many and interesting. They fought in every war and after their emigration to America they participated in every war undertaken by the United States, from Indian fighting before the Revolution to the present time.

In the fifteenth century, Thomas Armstrong, fifth lord of Maingerton, had four sons, of whom the eldest, Alexander Armstrong was the sixth Lord. He had seven sons. Thomas the eldest succeeded and was Seventh Lord Maingerton, but the second son was called John Ahmstrong, of Gilnockie. All the Armstrongs in Ireland in the seventeenth century are descended from him, and all the American Armstrongs, (who trace through the Scotch-Irish clan). He was Robin Hood of the Border, and the stories of his exploits run through all Scottish literature. Sir Walter Scott makes frequent references to him.

All descendants whose names are recorded in the following article are eligible to societies of the Revolution, the Mexican War, War of 1812 and the War Between the States. It is an interesting fact that in the War Between the States, in which the Armstrongs of the Southern Clan fought on each side of the great conflict, that one Regiment of Tennesseeans was made up largely of Armstrongs and their kin, and that every officer was an Armstrong by name. Siward the Strong Arm therefore must be sleeping peacefully in his tomb after his eight centuries to think that his descendants continue the game.

To return, however, to Siward's immediate posterity. In the time of James the First of England, great bodies of land in the Province of Ulster, Ireland, were forfeit to the crown in consequence of the rebellion of Tyrone and Tirconnell and these lands were offered to the Scotch and English people for settlement.

Thousands of the Border Scots, including many Armstrongs, old Siward's descendants, accepted the offer and went to the new land. It was estimated in 1638 that there were forty thousand Scotchmen in Ulster.

These are the people who became known subsequently as the Scotch-Irish, though they had in most instances not a drop of Irish blood. A hundred years or more they lived in Ulster and then early in seventeen hundred emigration to America began.

COLONEL JAMES ARMSTRONG CALLED TROOPER

Colonel James Armstrong, called "Trooper" Armstrong, is first mentioned in American history June 6th, 1777, in Abingdon, Virginia. He was already widely known as "Trooper Armstrong." Later he moved, like the Robert Armstrong family, from Virginia to Tennessee. It is not known whether Trooper Armstrong was related closely to the Armstrongs who were descendants of Robert Armstrong, I, but the connection was intimate and they had emigrated from the same district in Ireland, so it is evident that some tie of friendship and possibly of close blood relation existed. Robert Armstrong's family emigrated much earlier, although they had not been in the Tennessee section more than a few years before we have the first definite evidence of Trooper Armstrong's presence in Tennessee. This is Dr. J. G. Ramsay's account in the "Annals of Tennessee" of the Holston Treaty, Governor Blount's Council with the Cherokees at White's Fort, now Knoxville, July, 1791.

Dr. Ramsey in describing this event says: "Governor Blount received and entertained the Chieftains and head warriors with signal attentions and ceremonials. The treaty ground was at the foot of Water Street, where the governor appeared in full dress. He wore a sword and military hat and acted throughout the occasion the polite and accomplished gentleman, the dignified officer and courteous negotiator. He remained seated near his marquee, under and surrounded by tall trees which then shaded the banks of the Holston, his officers, civil and military, stood near him, uncovered and respectful. On this occasion James Armstrong was arbiter elegantarium. One of the interpreters introduced each chief to Armstrong, who then presented him to the governor, announcing each chief by his aboriginal name.

"James Armstrong, alias Trooper Armstrng, was the ancestor of General Robert Armstrong, the hero of Emuckfaw and other battles in the Creek War, and at present the editor of the Washington Union. The father (James Armstrong) had seen service in Europe, and was familiar with foreign etiquette and acquitted himself on this occasion much to the satisfaction of both governor and the Indians. The latter are always pleased with ceremony and forms."

Colonel James (Trooper) Armstrong resided some years in Virginia before he arrived in Tennessee to serve as a chief aid to

Governor Blount in 1791. His daughter, Ann Armstrong, married John McCormick in Abingdon, Virginia, and they continued to reside there for several years. Indeed, Trooper Armstrong himself, while he seems to have taken up land in the new settlement, kept his residence in Abingdon, Virginia, for several years. He was trustee in 1778 and seems to have continued in his office as trustee until about 1802, when an election was held in Abingdon to replace the trustees, Matthew Willoughby, who had died, and Colonel James Armstrong, who had removed from the town. Yet in "Americana" his son, General Robert Armstrong, is given as born in Tennessee in 1790.

Several references to Colonel James Armstrong in connection with his son-in-law. John McCormick are given in Virginia history and at least one in Summer's South West Virginia mentions his nick-name "Trooper," as the formal name given to an alley, which probably lay near his property.

This item from Summers, page 625, is: "June 6, 1777, William Edmiston, Robert Armstrong, Robert Preston and Robert Campbell, terming themselves trustees for the town of Abingdon, met at Christopher Acklin's in said town and proceeded to business and surveyed a part of said town, namely, the inner lots, after which the board adjourned until the next day, the 7th of June, 1777, on which day the trustees ordered an alley to be laid off, one pole wide, adjoining the lower end of the lots on the South side of Main Street, and that a street be laid off, three poles wide, ten poles from said alley, and that the land between the alley and the street be laid off in half-acre lots, and that the said street be known by the name Trooper's Alley."

Colonel Armstrong before emigrating to America was an officer in the Enniskillen Dragoons and derived his soubriquet "Trooper" from this circumstance. Colonel James Armstrong married about 1782, Susan Wells, daughter of Charles Wells, founder of Wellsburg, West Virginia. It is possible that her mother was named Ann Tevis. Colonel Armstrong and his wife died about 1817. They were buried on what is now known as the Brice Farm in Knox County on Flat Creek, about fifteen miles from Knoxville. In a deed to this property executed December 5, 1818, the heirs to James Armstrong have signed their names. This list was copied for me by R. A. J. Armstrong, surveyor of Knox County, and a descendant of Robert Armstrong I. The list of signatures agrees with a list of children given by Dr. James Park, authority on Knoxville history and genealogy, with two exceptions. In the names signed to the deed is Joshua Armstrong, heir of James. His name is not given by Dr. Park, but Dr. Park mentions John Armstrong, whose name is not signed. However, Dr. Park expressly says John Armstrong died early, so that accounts for the lack of his signature in 1818.

Colonel James Armstrong purchased this property from Francis Maybury, of Knox County, January 22, 1801, paying "twenty hundred pounds current money of Virginia." The land aggregated 2180 acres.

The children of Colonel James (Trooper) Armstrong and Susan Wells Armstrong, from the combined list given by Dr Park and given to me by R. A. J. Armstrong as signed to the 1818 deed:

I. Francis Armstrong
II. Nancy (Ann) Tevis Armstrong
II. Jane Crozier Armstrong
IV. Robert Armstrong
V. William Armstrong
VI. Joshua Armstrong
VII. John Armstrong

(These names are not given in order of birth.

I FRANCIS ARMSTRONG

Francis Wells Armstrong, son of Col. James Armstrong and Susan Wells Armstrong was born about 1783. He entered West Point where he graduated and served in the United States Army. He was the inventor of the Derringer pistol, by the authority of Dr. Park. Dr. Park adds, "My brother William Park and Hugh L. McClung were with Francis Armstrong when he gave the pattern of the pistol to Derringer." William Park was a brother-in-law to Francis Armstrong, having married Jane Crozier Armstrong.

Francis Armstrong married Ann Willard of Baltimore and Washington, who was a Catholic. He died a few years after the marriage, perhaps about the year 1840, and later his widow married General Persifer Smith. After General Smith's death she entered a convent and became a Mother Superior.

Francis Armstrong was Government agent to the Indians and was in the Indian Territory, now Oklahoma, when his son Francis Crawford Armstrong was born (1835.) President Jackson gave him this Appointment.

Francis Armstrong and Anne Willard Armstrong had at least one son:

Francis Crawford Armstrong, who was born in 1835 in the Indian Territory. The fact that his father and his step-father were Army Officers inclined him to a military career and he became one of the most distinguished officers of the Confederate Army. In 1854 when he was just twenty years of age he accompanied his step-father General Persifer Smith, on an expedition of United States Troops to New Mexico.

He married about 1865, Maria Walker, of Memphis, daughter of General Knox Walker. They had one child, a daughter, Isabel Arm.-

strong, now Mrs. Isabel Armstrong Barklie, of Wayne, Pennsylvania, who furnishes the following brief biography of her father:

General Frank C. Armstrong was born in the Indian Territory, in 1835. His father, Frank Wells Armstrong, Captain in the United States Infantry and afterwards appointed United States Marshall of Alabama by President Jackson, and afterwards appointed by General Jackson to move the Indians from Alabama and Tennessee to the Indian Territory where he resided from 1830 until his death in 1839. General Frank C. Armstrong was Captain in the second dragoons, being appointed a Lieutenant in the United States Army to accompany General Albert Sidney Johnson on his expedition to Utah, and at the outbreak of the war he was the youngest Captain in the army. At the outbreak of the war he was stationed at Fort Leavenworth. Going with his company to Washington, he tendered his resignation to the War Department and joined the Confederate Army. He was assigned to the army of the West and became a Brigadier General, and served with Gen. Forrest in his great campaigns with great distinction. He became assistant Commissioner of the Indian affairs under President Cleveland, and later served on the Dawes Commision from 1893-1898. He died at Bar Harbor in September, 1909, being survived by a daughter, Isabel, who was first married to J. Dundas Lippincott, of Philadelphia, and later to Archibald Barklie, of New York. General Armstrong was married in 1863 to Maria Polk Walker, of Columbia, Tennessee, great niece of President Polk. His second wife, who survived him, was Charlotte Combs, of St. Mary's County, Maryland, the widow of Kilty MacSherry, Lieutenant in the United States Navy. General Armstrong's mother was Anne M. Willard, of St. Mary's County, Maryland.

II NANCY (ANN TEVIS ARMSTRONG

Nancy (Ann) Tevis Armstrong, daughter of Colonel James Armstrong and Susan Wells Armstrong was born————. Dr. Park refers so her as Ann but she signed the deed in 1818 "Nancy". She married in Abingdon, Virginia, John McCormick, and had one child, a daughter, Susan Wells McCormick.

Sustn Wells McCormick, only child of Ann Armstrong McCormick and John McCormick, was born————. She married Luke Lea. Luke Lea was born January 24, 1783. Their marriage took place about 1810. They had eight children, namely:

1. James Armstrong Lea
2. John McCormick Lea
3. Frank Wells Lea
4. William Park Lea
5. Ann E. Lea
6. Susan Lea

7. Lavinia Lea

8. Margaret Lea

1. James Armstrong Lea, son of Susan Wells McCormick Lea and Luke Lea married ——————.

2. John McCormick Lea, son of Susan Wells McCormick Lea and Luke Lea was born in Knoxville, December 25, 1818. He married Elizabeth Overton in Memphis, Tennessee, in 1845. Elizabeth Overton Lea died September 13, 1890. They had children:

a. Overton Lea

b. Robert Lea

c. Luke Lea

Of these:

Overton Lea, born——,died 1903, married Ella Cocke and had four children, namely:

Overton Lea, Jr.

Laura Lea.

Luke Lea.

Elizabeth Lea.

Overton Lea, Jr., died unmarried.

Laura Lea, daughter of Overton Lea and Ella Cocke Lea, married William Clendenning Robertson and has four children Eva Lea Robertson, who married Harold Hinton and lives in Paris; Ella Lea Robertson who married Thomas Meek Carothers and has one child, Mildred Ragon Carothers; William Clendenning Robertson, Jr., and Laura Lea Robertson.

Luke Lea, son of Overton Lea and Ella Cocke Lea, was born in 1879. He was Senator from Tennessee and during the World War commanded a regiment and served abroad for the entire period of the War. He married twice. His first wife was Mary Louise Warner, daughter of Percy Warner, by whom he had two sons, Luke Lea Jr., and Percy Warner Lea. Mary Louise Warner Lea died during the War, while her husband was in France. Several years later Col. Luke Lea married her sister, Percy Warner. Col. Luke Lea and Percy Warner Lea have a daughter, Mary Louise Lea.

Elizabeth Lea, the second daughter of Overton Lea and Elizabeth Cocke Lea married J. O. Fordock.

(3) Francis Wells Lea, son of Susan Wells McCormick and Luke Lea was born———— He married Rebecca Callaway Donohue.

(4.) William Park Lea, son of Susan Wells McCormick Lea and Luke Lea was born————. He married Ellen McCallie.

(5.) Ann E. Lea, daughter of Susan Wells McCormick Lea and Luke Lea was born————.

6. Susan Lea, daughter of Susan Wells McCormick Lea and Luke Lea, was born ——————. She married Thomas H. Callaway.

Susan Jane Lea Callaway and Thomas H. Callaway had eleven children as follows:

a. Joseph Callaway.
b. Luke Lea Callaway.
c. Lucy Callaway.
d. Benjamin Callaway.
e. Thomas H. Callaway, Jr.
f. Susan Callaway.
g. James Callaway.
h. Margaret Callaway.
i. John Lea Callaway.
j. Annie Barnard Callaway.
k. Frank E. Callaway.

Of the foregoing.

a.   Joseph Callaway, son of Susan Jane Lea Callaway and Thomas H. Callaway, born September 16, 1847, died September 1, 1890, married Julia Anderson , May, 1870. They had two children, Susan Lea Callaway and Joseph Jacques Callaway.

b.   Luke Lea Callaway, son of Susan Jane Lea Callaway and Thomas H. Callaway, was born May 19, 1850, died August 7, 1921. He married first Caroline Johnson and had two children, namely, Thomas H. Callaway and Lucy Callaway, and married second Caledonia Montgomery and had six children, namely, Benjamin Callaway, Hettie Callaway, Flora Callaway, Ida Callaway, Inez Callaway and Frances Callaway.

c.   Lucy Callaway, daughter of Susan Jane Lea Callaway and Thomas H. Callaway, was born June 25, 1852, died November 5, 1871. She married James A. Johnson, of Madisonville, Tenn., December 16, 1870.

d.   Benjamin Callaway, son of Susan Jane Lea Callaway and Thomas H. Callaway, was born May 13, 1855, died April 15, 1913. He married Maggie Thompson. They had five children, namely: Luke Callaway, Campbell Callaway, John Callaway, Robert Callaway.

e.   Thomas H. Callaway, Jr., son of Susan Jane Lea Callaway Thomas H. Callaway, was born June 17, 1857, died October 25, 1889. He married first Carrie Coleman, of Atlanta, November 10, 1880, and had one child, Carrie Coleman Callaway, and married second Susan McEnery, of Louisiana, in 1887. They had one child, Lea McEnery Callaway.

f.   Susan Callaway, daughter of Susan Jane Lea Callaway and Thomas H. Callaway, was born August 6, 1859, died March 18, 1862.

g.   James H. Callaway, son of Susan Jane Lea Callaway and Thomas H. Callaway, was born September 11, 1861, died September 16, 1920. He married Lula Harrison and had nine children, namely:

Joseph Callaway, Eizabeth Callaway, Annabelle Callaway, Thomas Callaway, Henry Callaway, James Callaway, Jr., Lula Callaway, Merrick Callaway and Lea Callaway.

h. Margaret Callaway, daughter of Susan Jane Lea Callaway and Thomas H. Callaway, was born April 15, 1863. She married James Burch Carson September 6, 1862, and had six children, namely: James Gray Carson, Thomas Callaway Carson, Robert Lea Carson, Joseph Armstrong Carson, John McCormick Carson and susan Barnard Carson.

i. John Lea Callaway, son of Susan Jane Lea Callaway and Thomas H. Callaway, was born September 23, 1865. He married Florence Newton, of Atlanta, June 16, 1892. They had three children, namely: Newton Callaway, Frank Callaway and John Lea Callaway, Jr.,

j. Annie Barnard Callaway, daughter of Susan Jane Lea Callaway and Thomas H. Callaway, was born October 4, 1867. She married Dr. H. Gray Hutchinson, of Atlanta, October 23, 1893.

k. Frank Callaway, son of Susan Jane Lea Callaway and Thomas H. Callaway, was born June 24, 1870. He died January, 1873.

(7) Lavinia Lea, daughter of Susan Wells McCormick Lea and Luke Lea was born————. She married three times, first John Calvin Henderson and second Samuel Smith and third Joseph Ernest. By her first marriage she had one child, Susan Wells Henderson.

Susan Wells Henderson married David M. Nelson anl had four children, Ann Stuart Nelson, who married R. R. Evans, lives in Griffin, Georgia, and has one child Minnie Evans, who married first Hugh L. Bayley and had two children, Hugh L. Bayley Jr., and Robert Evans Bayley and married second Hamilton Fish, of New Orleans; Thomas R. Nelson, who lives in Chicago; Luke Lea Nelson, who lives in St. Louis; Inez Nelson, who married Thomas Deaderick and had one son who died in infancy.

8. Margaret Lea, daughter of Susan Wells McCormick Lea and Luke Lea was born in 1831. She married Henry Benton Henegar. Their handsome homestead in Charleston, Tennessee, is still standing. They had four children.

Edward Henegar
Ann Henegar
Lucy Henegar
Lavinia Henegar

Lucy Henegar married William B. Allen, of Charleston, Tennessee and has one daughter, Margaret E. Allen.

Lavinia Henegar married Luther D. Campbell of Cleveland, Tennessee.

Ann Henegar married George T. White, of Chattanooga, Tennessee, and had three children: Edward White who died young; Benton White, who married Harriet Bauman; and Margaret Lea White, who married Gardner Bright and has two children, Ann Henegar Bright and George T. Bright, born August, 1924.

Edward Henegar married Mamie McMillan, of Knoxville. (See McMillan Family, Volume I, Notable Southern Families). They had six children: Margaret Henegar, who died young; Anne Henegar, who married Matthew Thomas and has two daughters, Mary Henegar Thomas and Barbara Thomas; Mamie Henegar, who married Edward John McMillan and has one child, Nancy Alexander McMillan; Herbert Hall Henegar, who married Josephine Kendall; Martin Condon Henegar; and Henry Benton Henegar.

III—JANE CROZIER ARMSTRONG

Jane Crozier Armstrong, daughter of Colonel James (Trooper) Armstrong and Susan Wells Armstrong, was born ——————————. She married about 1810, William Park. He was born about —————————————. He died in 1846. Jane Crozier Armstrong Park died in 1848. Their children were:

1. Robert Park, died in infancy.
2. Susan Wells Park.
3. Ann Eliza Park.
4. Sophia Moody Park.
5. Mary Jane Park.
6. Naomi Park, born 1821, died young.

Of the foregoing:

1. Robert Park, died young.

2. Susan Wells Park, born August 31 ,1812, married Dr. Leonidas Baker in 1829, and after his death married James C. Moses, leaving children by both marriages. She died March 6, 1839.

3. Ann Eliza Park, born 1816, died March 6, 1839. She married in 1839, James Houston Armstrong, of the Robert Armstrong, I, family. She had three sons:

a. Frank Armstrong, who married Lazinka E. Martin, and left one daughter, Mry Armstrong.

b. Robert Armstrong who never married.

c. William Park Armstrong, married Alice Isbell (see Howard family) and lived in Selma, Alabama. They had four children, William Park Armstrong, Jr., (who married Rebekah Purvis and has William Park Armstrong, III, George Purvis Armstrong, Ann Elizabeth Armstrong and Jane Crozier Armstrong), Houston Churchwell Armstrong, (married Mina Lamar Cary and has Houston Churchwell Armstrong, Jr., Alice Isbell Armstrong and Mina Cary Armstrong); Margaret Armstrong, (who married Ainslee Power Ardagh and lives in Canada. They have Margaret Ardagh, Ainslee Power Ardagh, Jr., Alice Ardagh, Kathleen Ardagh and Edith Ardagh), and Anne E. Armstrong, (who married Thomas Stoo Johnson and lives in New Orleans).

4. Sophia Moody Park, born June 5, 1817, died 1898. She married in 1837, George W. Churchwell.

5. Mary Jane Park, born 1819, died 1844 unmarried.

6. Naomi Park, born 1821. Died young.

IV—ROBERT ARMSTRONG

Robert Armstrong, son of Colonel James (Trooper) Armstrong and Susan Wells Armstrong, was born in 1790, in Tennessee, according to Americana. He died in Washington, D. C., February 23, 1854. He was an artillery captain in the war with the Creek Indians in 1813, being badly wounded at Talladega. He is called by Dr. Ramsay and others the Hero of the Enotochapko. At the Battle of New Orleans, January 8, 1815, he was chief in command of the American artillery, and during the second Seminole War, 1835-1837, he was a Brigadier-General. He was a close friend and loyal supporter of General Jackson, who appointed him Postmaster of Nashville during his administration. A descendant says he was Postmaster-General during Jackson's administration, but I do not find this fact recorded in biographies of him.

General Robert Armstrong was Commander-in-Chief of Artillery at the battle of New Orleans. General Jackson gave General Armstrong his sword. General Armstrong in his will requested that the sword be presented to the United States and at his death Senator Thomas Hart Benton, of Missouri, represented the Armstrong family and made the speech of presentation on the floor of the United States Senate.

He was candidate for Governor of Tennessee in 1837. In 1845 he was appointed consul to Liverpool by President Polk. He remained in this office for seven years. When he returned to America he made his home in Washington, where he was owner and editor of the Washington Union. During this period of his life he was the confidential advisor of President Polk. He died February 23, 1854. He married Margaret D. Nichols, of Nashville, June 9, 1814, and had several children, among them:

1. Robert Armstrong, Jr.

2. Eleanor Armstrong.

1. Robert Armstrong, Jr., son of General Robert Armstrong and Margaret D. Nichols Armstrong, was born ——————. He married ————————. He served in the army of the Confederacy.

2. Eleanor Armstrong, daughter of General Armstrong and Margaret D. Nichols Armstrong, was born ——————. She lived in Nashville. She married Joseph Vaulx and had five children:

a. Margaret Vaulx, who married George Crochett and had a son, Joseph Vaulx Crochett;

b. Catherine Vaulx, who is unmarried;

c. Martha Vaulx, who married Robert Cowan and has a son, Robert Cowan, Jr., and a son and daughter who died in infancy.

In 1919 Miss Catherine Vaulx, granddaughter of General Robert Armstrong, presented his portrait to the Tennessee Historical Society and in connection with the ceremonies several interesting addresses were made. The Tennessee Historical Magazine for July, 1919, Vol. V, No. 2, gives full details of the event and repeats from a number of 1888, a sketch of the life of General Armstrong written by Dr. J. H. Calendar, the distinguished historian. This is full of valuable and interesting data, as Dr. Calendar knew General Armstrong well. I therefore quote this sketch in full:

"The eminent artist of this city, Mr. George Dury, has recently completed for the family a portrait of the late General Robert Armstrong, for many years a distinguished citizen of this state and a resident of this city. More than the period of a generation has elapsed since his death, and the term 'the late' we use, will only be significant to the minds of the older people who remember him as a conspicious figure in this community and a prominent actor in the civil and military history of the State and the Nation. Many of these who have examined the portrait have pronounced it an admirable likeness and a work of art which will add to the reputation of the painter. In due time it will probably be presented to the Tennessee Historical Society to take its place in the galaxy of those who have conferred renown on the state and a brief record of his life will be interesting to his surviving contemporaries and instructive to the younger generation.

"General Robert Armstrong was the son of 'Trooper' Armstrong, of Virginia, a valiant soldier of the War of the Revolution, noted for his superb figure and great physical strength, as well as his skill and enterprise and a partisan fighter in the struggle of that period in Virginia and the Carolinas. His son, who inherited in a great degree these personal characteristics, was born in Abingdon, Virginia, September 28, 1792. The father removed with his family early in the present century to Knox County, Tennessee, where decendants still reside. Beside the subject of this memoir, two brothers, Major Frank Armstrong and Major William Armstrong, were men of high character, employed in the Indian service of the United States government in the South West, both of them serving as superintendent of the Indian territory after the removal of the tribes west of the Mississippi River. They were beloved by the red men for their justice and humane treatment and their service was recognized by the Government as of great value.

"Robert Armstrong's education was chiefly attained at school at his native place at Abingdon, but before its completion and in his twentieth year he returned to Tennessee and was made Lieutenant of a company of volunteer artillery and soon joined the command of General Andrew Jackson, engaged in what is known as the Creek War. At the battle of Enotochapko, January 24, 1814, one of the decisive engagements of the war, he displayed conspicious courage and qualities as an officer, arresting a formidable movement of the Indian forces, and, by the report of General Jackson, turning the fortunes of the day. He was wounded severely and carried the missile through life, at times suffering greatly from its effects. His gallantry endeared him to his commander, and he was appointed to his staff and was his aide-de-camp at the battle of New Orleans. The following year at the conclusion of hostilities he became a citizen of Nashville. On June 9, 1814, he married Margaret D., daughter of Josiah Nichol, a leading merchant. His daughter, the widow of Joseph Vaulx who died in 1878, a resident of this city, ,survives him.

"In 1829 he was apointed Post Master of Nashville and held the office for sixteen years. In 1836, while in this position, he was made Brigadier-General of the Tennessee Mounted Volunteers and commanded them when sent by the United States Government against the Seminole Indians in Florida. This was a brief campaign and ended in the battle of Wahoo Swamp, in which the Indians were defeated. Politically he was a warm adherent of President Jackson and the measures of his eventful administration, and in 1837, after his return from Florida, was the candidate for Governor of Tennessee against Governor Newton Cannon, who represented that portion of the people of the state who had become alienated from the Jackson influence under the lead of Hugh L. White and John Bell. In this contest he was defeated. Upon the advent of Mr. Polk to the Presidency in 1854, he was appointed United States Consul to Liverpool, one of the most important positions in the foreign service, which he held until 1849. Before his departure for Europe in the spring of 1845 and a few months before the death of General Jackson, he was the honored recipient at the hands of his old commander of the sword worn by the latter at the battle of New Orleans, as a testimonial of his personal friendship and his estimation of General Armstrong's military service. This sword, after General Armstrong's death, was formally presented, in 1855, by his family to the United States Government, and is deposited in the Archives of the War Department. In 1851 General Armstrong and Major Andrew W. Donelson, of Tennessee, became proprietors of the Washington Union Newspaper and shortly thereafter General Armstong became the sole poprietor and in this capacity was made printer for the National House of Repesentatives.

"In January, 1855, his remains were removed to Nashville for final interment, which was conducted under the direction of a committee of prominent citizens appointed at a public meeting; the civic orders and military bodies generally formed the funeral escort and his body lies in the Nashville Cemetery.

"Born amidst the warm and recent memories of the Revolutionary struggles for the independence of the country and an enthusiastic and gallant supporter in his manhood's prime in the War of 1812, the virtue of patriotism shown conspiciously in General Armstrong's character and was admired by all in later life even when his temperment made him a stern, unbending partisan in a period of acrimonious political controversy never exceeded in this country and in which he bore a noble part.

"Ardent in his convictions, unequalled in courage and devoted in attachments, he maintained the esteem and friendship of his fellow-citizens through confidence inspired by his candor and honorable dealings not less than by his kindness of heart and graciousness of manner, and he was at all times personally popular with men of all classes.

"He was imposing and dignified in carriage, commanding respect, and bore himself with credit in every sphere in which he figured.

"He died in his sixty-third year, when shadows falling from the West were growing long in an active and exciting life and had perhaps no personal enemies but instead a great group of loving friends."

V—WILLIAM ARMSTRONG

William Armstrong, son of Colonel James (Trooper) Armstrong and Susan Wells Armstrong was born about 1800. He married Nancy Irwin, in Nashville, July 1, 1823. Nancy Irwin Armstrong was born in 1804 and died September 28, 1836.

William Armstrong bought a plantation in Arkansas near Pine Bluff. This plantation now is owned by his granddaughter, Mrs. Alexander Barrow.

Colonel William Armstrong participated in the Battle of New Orleans. He was appointed by President Andrew Jackson as superintendent of Indian affairs. He conducted the Chickasaws and Choctaws from their lands in Mississippi and Alabama to the Indian Territory. He died June 12, 1847, in the Choctaw territory.

The children of William Armstrong and Nancy Irwin Armstrong were:

1. Mary Elizabeth Armstrong.

2. James Trooper Armstrong.

3. David Irwin Armstrong.

4. Margaret Armstrong, born 1829.

5. Susan Wells Armstrong.

6. Nancy Irwin Armstrong.

7. Francis Armstrong.

1. Mary Elizabeth Armstrong, daughter of William Armstrong and Nancy Irwin Armstrong, was born June 25, 1825. She married William Cooke, June 8, 1841, and died shortly after her marriage, leaving no children.

2. James Trooper Armstrong, son of William Armstrong and Nancy Irwin Armstrong, was born October 28, 1825. He married June 4, 1850, Matilda Porter Green, born January 9, 1830, died January 19, 1895, Nashville, Tennessee. He served in the Confederate Army and died July 4, 1873. They had six children. This branch of the family lives in Columbus, Mississippi.

a. William Armstrong, son of James Trooper Armstrong and Matilda Porter Green Armstrong, was born November 19, 1852.

b. Robert Wells Armstrong, son of James Trooper Armstrong and Matilda Porter Green Armstrong, was born September 2, 1854.

c. James Trooper Armstrong, Jr., son of James Trooper Armstrong and Matilda Porter Green Armstrong, was born in Bedford County, Tennessee, November 21, 1857. He married Sarah Frances Irwin, October 5, 1887. Their children are:

Francis Irwin Armstrong, born June 25, 1888; Lady Mary Armstrong, born June 1, 1890; Caro Irwin Armstrong, born March 17, 1893; James Trooper Armstrong, born September 27, 1895; William Lindly Armstrong, born October 8, 1898; Sarah Frances Armstrong, born in Lowndes County, Mississippi, February 4, 1902; Penelope Porter Armstrong, born in Lowndes County, Mississippi, December 6, 1907.

d. Francis Wells Armstrong, son of James Trooper Armstrong and Matilda Porter Armstrong, was born in Jefferson County, Arkansas, May 26, 1860.

e. Penelope Porter Armstrong, daughter of James Trooper Armstrong and Matilda Armstrong, was born in Jefferson County, Arkansas, December 17, 1861.

f. Woods Irwin Armstrong, son of James Trooper Armstrong and Matilda Porter Armstrong, was born in Lowndes County, Mississippi, October 8, 1870 .

3. David Irwin Armstrong, son of William Armstrong and Nancy Irwin Armstrong, was born August 9, 1827. He married Elizabeth Cockrill, in Nashville, January 18, 1854. He died October 3, 1880.

They had one child:

Annie McDonald Armstrong. She married Alexander M. Barrow. They had six children: Alexander M. Barrow, Jr., Effie Cockrill Barrow, who married Henry Trulock and left one child, Anne Barrow Trulock; Sterling Cockrill; Armstrong Barrow; Junius Barrow, who married Marsilite Hilburn; and Wylie Aylett Barrow, who married Jean Hart.

4. Margaret Armstrong, daughter of William Armstrong and Nancy Irwin Armstrong, was born———.She married June 19, 1851, Spain. They had one son, John Shelby Barrow, Jr., who married, Spain. They had one son, John Shelby Barrow, Jr., who married 1873, Lucy Claibourne, of Nashville.

5. Susan Wells Armstrong, daughter of William Armstrong and Nancy Irwin Armstrong, born 1829, died unmarried, August 30, 1848.

6. Nancy Irwin Armstrong, daughter of William Armstrong and Nancy Irwin Armstrong, was born———. She married February 23, 1858, William Alexander Percy, of Greenville, Miss. She died June 24, 1897.

They had several children:

a. LeRoy Percy, now United States Senator.

b. Fannie Percy.

c. Lady Percy, who married C. J. McKinney and lives in Knoxville.

d. William Armstrong Percy, who lives in Memphis.

e. Walker Percy.

a. LeRoy Percy, born in Washington County. Misssissippi, November 9, 1861, son of Col. William Alexander Percy and Nancy Irwin Armstrong Percy, married Camille Bourges, December, 1883. He was elected United States Senator in 1919.

b. Walker Percy, born November 8, 1864, died 1917, son of Colonel William Alexander Percy and Nancy Irwin Armstrong Percy, married Mary Pratt DeBardeleben, of Birminghm, April 17, 1888. They had children, Leroy Percy II, Ellen Percy, deceased. LeRoy Percy married and has three children; Ellen Percy married Matthew H. Murphy and has one child.

7. Frank Wells Armstrong, son of William Armstrong and Nancy Irwin Armstrong, was born————. He died unmarried May 6, 1868, at the home of his first cousin, Mrs. Eleanor Armstrong Vaulx, daughter of General Robert Armstrong, in Nashville.

VI—JOSHUA ARMSTRONG

Joshua Armstrong, son of Colonel James (Trooper) Armstrong and Susan Wells Armstrong, was born ————. He is not mentioned by Dr. Park in referring to the children of Trooper Armstrong, but his name is signed December 18, 1818, to the deed to the home place of James Armstrong, as one of the heirs of said James Armstrong.

VII—JOHN ARMSTRONG

John Armstrong, son of Colonel James (Trooper) Armstrong and Susan Wells Armstrong ,was born ————————. He is mentioned by Dr. Park as one of the sons, but his name does not appear among the signatures to the deed in 1818. Dr. Park, however, states that John Armstrong served in the United Army and died quite early.

Cockrill

COCKRILL

JOHN COCKRILL THE EMIGRANT

JOHN COCKRILL the emigrant was of Scotch parentage, though born in Wales about 1740. He came to America with Braddock's command but did not return to England with the remnants of that ill fated company, preferring to make his home in the new settlement. He settled in Richmond County, Va., where he became a large planter.

In October of 1756 he enlisted with Captain Henry Harrison's company in response to the call of Governor Dinwiddie for volunteers in the French and Indian Wars. In the record of his enlistment he is described as being five feet eleven inches tall and with brown hair and eyes. He is further said to have been a man of good education and pleasing appearance and manner.

He was twice married, the name of his first wife being unknown but by that marriage he had one son, Simon, from whom the Missouri Cockrills are descended. His second wife was a Miss Fox of the famous family of that name. To the second wife was born John Junior, who is commonly called Major John Cockrill to distinguished him from his father, John the Emigrant.

MAJOR JOHN COCKRILL

Major John Cockrill was born in Virginia, Dec., 19, 1757. He died at Nashville, Tennessee, April 11, 1837.

He served in the command of Colonel William Russell and was sent to Wautauga in June of 1776. The following winter he joined under Brigadier McIntosh and continued in the service until 1779, when he followed James Robertson to the Bluff settlement on the Cumberland, afterwards Nashville. From Nashville he returned to the older settlement and accompanied the Adventurer Flotilla on its long and adventurous trip. It was probably on this trip that the romance that had its colmination in the marriage of Ann Robertson Johnston and Major John Cockrill, began. She was the widowed sister of James Robertson and accompanied his family to the new settlement with her three daughters. She was a woman of more than the average education and on her arrival at the new settlement soon organized both Sunday and day school, being the first teacher at that place.

Both Major John and his wife Ann Robertson Cockrill were granted lands by the precmption act of 1784 for "Meritorious services to the Cumberland settlements." Major John built his home at what

21

is now Cedar street, Nashville. This was the first brick house built in Nashville and was still standing and occupied in 1915.

Children of Major John and Ann R. Cockrill:

John III
Ann
Sterling
James Robertson
Mark Robertson
Susanna
Sara
Martha

JOHN COCKRILL III

Was born at Nashville July 8, 1781 and died at Tuscumbia Ala., in 1814. He was thrice married but had issue by his first wife only. She was Elizabeth Harding Underwood, daughter of Thomas and Jane Farrar Harding and widow of Alexander Underwood.

Their children were:

Sterling
Eliza Minerva
Washington Jefferson
Granville
Alfred Madison
Tennessee V.
Valeria
John Pike
Elizabeth Underwood

ANN COCKRILL

Married Drury Pulliam and had issue;

Eliza Cheeves
Ann Robertson
Sara
Martha
John Cockrill
Belinda
Mary Jane
Benjamin Graves
Elijah Robertson
Luther Rice
Carolina Tennessee

JAMES ROBERTSON COCKRILL

Was twice married and had children by both marriages.
Children of James Robertson Cockrill and Sara Jones Cockrill:
William Goodloe
Edward Iredell

Mark
Rufus Sterling
Martha M.
Louisa
Mary Ann
John Robertson

Children of James Robertson and Sallie Young Cockrill:

Sallie Young.
James Harvey.
Julia.

MARK ROBERTSON COCKRILL

Mark Robertson Cockrill was born December 2, 1788. To him Tennessee owes much for his consistent efforts at the betterment of the live stock of the state. He was internationally known as an authority on sheep. His flock of Merino sheep was second to none in breeding, and his contention that Tennessee grass produced the finest wool and hair in the world seems to have been supported by the gold medals, still in the possession of his descendants, won by his wool exhibits both in London and in France. He was also interested in horses and imported numbers of them both from England and Canada.

He married Susan Collingsworth, daughter of Edmund Collingsworth and Alice Thomspon Collingsworth, and granddaughter of David and ———— Fox Cockrill Collingsworth. Alice Thompson was the daughter of James or Jacon, as he is sometimes called, who with his wife and another daughter were murdered by the Indians. Alice Thompson was carried into captivity and after eighteen months was ransomed by traders for eight hundred pounds of deer hides. She was then returned to Nashville by way of Knoxville.

Children of Mark Robertson and Susan Collingsworth Cockrill:
Julia A.
Almira Jane.
George.
Alexander
Benjamin.
James Robertson.
Daniel W.
Mark Stirling
Henrietta

MARTHA COCKRILL

Married first Alexander Jones, brother of Gov. James C. Jones and had issue;

A. Sidney.
Married second Robert C. Thompson and had issue;
Robert Emmett
John Cockrill
Mary Bell Catherine.

FIFTH GENERATION.

STERLING ROBERTSON COCKRILL (JOHN III, JOHN II; JOHN I)

Married Anna H. McDonald, daughter of James Mcdonald and Elizabeth Aylett Moore in 1833. Issue;
Robert Emmett
Elizabeth Harding
Effie
Henrietta
James McDonald
Amanthis
Valeria
Sterling R.

ELIZA COCKRILL (JOHN III; JOHN II; JOHN I)

Married Robert Blackwell Malone and had issue;
John Lewis Malone.

GRANVILLE COCKRILL (JOHN II, JOHN I)

Married Maria Louise Turner and had issue:
Sterling
Mary Louise
Sara Elizabeth
John LaForce
Washington Pike
Granville

TENNESSEE V. COCKRILL (JOHN III; JOHN I)

Married John D. Newell and had issue:
Augusta
Valeria
Ella
John Edward
Belle

VALERIA COCKRILL (JOHN III ETC.)

Married William Rose and had issue:
John Fielding
Tennessee Virginia
Adella E.

William Washington
Henrietta Cockrill
Harding Meredith
Tennessee V.
Granville Pike
Sara Louise

WILLIAM COOLIDGE COCKRILL (JAMES; JOHN II; JOHN I;)

Married Sara Louise Gholston and had issue:
James B.
Sara Ann
Mark Apple White
Martha
Susan C.
After the death of Sara Louise, William G. Cockrill married
Amanda P. McMillan and had issue.
Curtis Cowart
Elizabeth Goodloe
Amanda Louisa
Robert Edward
John
Mark Rufus
Samuel J.

EDWARD COCKRILL (JAMES; JOHN II; JOHN I;)

Married Josephine Young and had issue:
James Oscar b. 1832
Sara J.
Leonidas L.
Tennessee A.
William Goodloe
Joseph Edward

LOUISA C. COCKRILL (JAMES; JOHN II; JOHN I)

Married John Sutton and had a large family.

SALLIE YOUNG COCKRILL (JAMES; JOHN III; JOHN I)

Married Charles H. Hill and had issue:
Barbara
Charles Henry

JAMES HENRY COCKRILL (JAMES; JOHN II; JOHN I)

Married Martha Haynie and had issue:
James T.
Elizabeth Clay
Sallie Melinda

ALMIRA JANE COCKRILL (MARK ROBERTSON; JOHN II;

Married Willia'n Evans Watkins IV, son of William Evans Watkins and Matilda Howett Watkins on Feb., 2, 1842, and had issue:
Mark Robertson
Irene
William Evans V.
Matilda

BENJAMIN F. COCKRILL (MARK ROBERTSON ETC.)

Married Sallie Foster and had issue:
Cornelia
Sallie
Susan
Benjamin F. Jr.
Jeanette
Ellen

JAMES COCKRILL (MARK ROBERTSON ETC.)

Married——————— and had issue:
Susie
Henrietta
Mark
James
Louisa

MARK STERLING COCKRILL (Mark Robertson, etc.)

Married Mary Hill Goodloe and had issue:
Harriet Turner.
Mark Sterling.
Calvin Goodloe.
David Short.
Jane Watkins.
Mary Hill.

HENRIETTA COCKRILL (Mark Robertson, etc.)

Married Albert Gallatin Ewing, son of Orville and Matilda Williams Ewing, and had the following issue:
Rowena.
Albert G., Jr.
Susan.
Mark C.
Orville.
Mary.
Milbrey.
Henrietta.

Robertson C.
Edgar.
Margaret.
For descendants of this branch see Ewing genealogy.

ROBERT EMMETT COCKRILL (Sterling R., John II, etc.)

Married Eliza McGavock and had issue:
Sterling Robertson.
Robert Emmett, II.

ELIZABETH HARDING COCKRILL (Sterling R., etc.)
Married William L. Nicholl and had issue:
Henry.

STERLING R. COCKRILL, JR. (STERLING R.)

Married Mary Ashley Freeman and had issue:
Ashley.
Annie McDonald.
Sterling III.
Mary Freeman.
Emmet.
Garlow.
Freeman.

MARTHA JANE COCKRILL (WILLIAM GOODLOE, ETC.)

Married Constantine Scales Hamner and had issue:
James Edward, married Kate Harris.
Lennie Elizabeth, married Frank Farquirl.
John Decatur.

SUSAN CAROLINE (WILLIAM GOODLOE, ETC.)

Married Ralph Stegall and had issue:
William Alexander.
Fannie Garner.

AMANDA L. COCKRILL (WILLIAM GOODLOE, ETC.)

Married John Stanley and had issue:
John Cockrill Stanley.

CURTIS C. COCKRILL (WILLIAM GOODLOE, ETC.)

Married Joshua McMillan and had issue:
Lester.
Mabel.

JOHN COCKRILL (WILLIAM GOODLOE, ETC.)

Married Ida Ballew and had issue:
Ruby.
Lula.

SARAH JOSEPHINE COCKRILL (EDWARD IREDELL, ETC.

Married J. Clark Culbreth on April 12, 1868, and had issue:
J. C. Farrar.
Mary Josephine.
John Edward.
Charles Goodloe.

WILLIAM GOODLOE COCKRILL (EDWARD IREDELL, ETC.)

Married Laura J. Mays in 1867 and had issue:
Jessie, married W. H. Parker.
Josephine.
Lucian.
Willie Ellen.
Elizabeth Womble.
Curtis Edward.

SALLIE COCKRILL (BENJ. F., ETC.)

Married Irby Morgan and had issue:
Cornelia, married Edwin Murray.
Sarah, married B. H. Perrin.
Benjamin Cockrill, married Maybelle Cosby.
Julia, married James Ratcliffe.

SUSAN COCKRILL (BENJAMIN F., ETC.)

Married E. W. Foster and has issue:
Ellen Cockrill married Joseph Coronado, of Costa Rica.
Robert.

BENJAMIN F. COCKRILL, JR.

Married Willie Christian and had issue:
Ben F. III.
William, married Hazel Brandon.
Daisy.
Martha.
Susan.
Archie.
Vernon.

JEANNETTE COCKRILL (BENJ. F., I, ETC.)

Married Oliver Shields and had issue:
George, married Nell Wright.

Jamie.
Sara.
Ben, married Louise Scrygley.

HARRIET COCKRILL (MARK STIRLING, ETC.)

Married Ed. Hicks and had issue:
Mary Hill.
Edward, Jr.
Mark.
Ben.

MARY HILL (MARK S., ETC.)

Married Duncan Kenner and has issue:
Evelina.
Mary Hill.

Duke

BENJAMIN NEWTON DUKE

DUKE

THE Duke family is of Norman origin, the name deriving from titular designation. As a surname it is among the most ancient of those borne by English families. It appears in the Domesday Book and is continually chronicled during the reigns of the Norman Kings following the making of the great document which means so much to historians and genealogists.

The Family of Duke acquired many estates in England and held positions of importance. Descendants of the Dukes who distinguished themselves under the Royal banner in the civil conflicts became allied by marriage with the Royal house. Edward Duke of that period was rewarded by Charles II with Knighthood and a Baronetage for his allegiance.

As early however as King Richard I the Dukes were occupying positions of trust. In the fourth and fifth years of Richard I, Peter Duke was Sheriff of London, serving in the time of King John.

Peter's son was Roger Duke and strange to say he also became Sheriff of London, which they must have thought by that time was the family office. Roger was Sheriff in the time of Henry III, and after he had served one year as sheriff he was made Mayor of London. London was even then a very great city. Roger served as its Mayor for four years, the twelfth, thirteenth, fourteenth and fifteenth years of the reign of Henry III.

Roger Duke's son Walter Duke established himself in Brampton in the time of Edward III. He was from this period known as Walter Duke of Brampton and did homage for his land in Shadingfield. His son, named for his father, Roger Duke, continued to reside on the family estate. For many generations thereafter the family is associated with Brampton and Shadingfield, though they continue to increase their property.

Roger Duke's eldest son and heir was Robert, who held the land in the time of Henry VI. Robert's eldest son and heir was John Duke. He married Joan, daughter and heiress of Spark of Astacton, County Suffolk. They had a son, Thomas Duke, Esquire, of Brampton. He married twice, first an heiress of the house of Woodwell. His second wife was Margaret, daughter and heiress of Henry Baynard, Esquire, of Speckshall, County of Suffolk. Thomas Duke's son and heir was William Duke, who married Thomasine, daughter of Sir Edmund Jenny, of Knottishall, Suffolk. They had a son, George Duke.

George Duke married Anne, daughter of Sir Thomas Blenner-hattet, Knight of Fronshell.

George and Anne Duke had at least two sons, George and Edward. Edward the eldest son and heir, known as Edward of Brampton and Shadingfield, added to the family estate by purchasing Benhall in Suffolk. He married Dorothy, daughter of Sir Ambrose Jermyn, Knight, of Rosbrook, Suffolk. Edward died in 1598. He named his son Ambrose Duke for the grandfather (Sir Ambrose Jermyn). He is known as Ambrose Duke of Benhall. He married Elizabeth, daughter of Bartholomew Calthorpe, Esquire, of Suffolk. She was a co-heir to her father's estate. Ambrose Duke died in 1610 and Elizabeth his wife died in the following year. Their son was Sir Edward Duke of Benhall, Brampton and Worlingham. He was Knighted by Charles II, and later was made baronet by the same monarch. He married Ellen, daughter and co-heir of John Panton, Esquire, of Brunslip, Denbligh. They had several children, among them, Sir John Duke, Baronet, their eldest son and heir. Thereafter the English family traces through his line. Another son was Col. Henry Duke from whom the American family comes.

COLONEL HENRY DUKE

Col. Henry Duke founder of the Duke family in America was a native of County Suffolk, England, and was born about the middle of the seventeenth century. He was the son of Sir Edward Duke and Ellen Panton Duke. At the time Henry Duke reached his majority Virginia was attracting the younger sons of scores of English families and he evidently followed the popular tide of emigration. He seems to have arrived possessed of some means since he almost immediately began to acquire extensive estates. He was affiliated with the military forces and held the rank of Captain and later Colonel. He was a member of the Governor's Royal Council. He was a member of the House of Burgesses and he was Sheriff at Jamestown and Justice. He left many thousands of acres in his estate at his death in 1714. He married Lydia Hansford, daughter of Charles Hansford.

He named his son and heir, Henry Duke and he was too a member of the House of Burgesses. He did not long survive his father as his death took place less than four years later. His widow Elizabeth Duke was named as administratrix of his estate January 18, 1718. Elizabeth, the widow, was before marriage Elizabeth Cliveures, of Huguenot ancestry. They had among other children Henry Duke the Third and Cliveures Duke. Cliveures Duke became the ancestor of the Virginia line. Henry Duke the Third held estates in Louisa County, Virginia, adjoining his brother Cliveurs Duke. He married Ann——————.

MAJOR HENRY DUKE THE FOURTH

Henry Duke the Third and Ann————Duke had among other children Henry Duke the Fourth. He moved to North Carolina shortly before the War of the Revolution and settled in Orange County. Deeply interested in the cause of the Colonies he enlisted immediately upon the call for soldiers. He held the rank first of Captain and later of Major in the Continental line. He married before the Revolution Susannah————.

TAYLOR DUKE

Major Henry Duke the Fourth and Susannah Duke had among other children Taylor Duke. He was born in Orange County, North Carolina about 1770. He died 1867. He was a member of the State Militia and was Deputy Sheriff. He married Dicey Jones. They had ten children, among them Washington Duke.

WASHINGTON DUKE

Washington Duke, son of Taylor Duke and Dicey Jones Duke was born near Bahama, Orange County, North Carolina, December twentieth, 1820. He received the name of the first president. Reaching maturity he rented a small farm, married early in life, and for four years worked his rented farm. Then he purchased a small place, gradually adding to his property until in 1860 he owned three hundred acres.

He opposed the withdrawal of the Southern States from the Union of States, but when North Carolina decided to withdraw he at once proved his patriotism and allegiance to his state. He offered his service to North Carolina and served with conspicuous bravery until the close of the War Between the States.

Washington Duke served on guard duty at Camp Holmes and was later transferred to the Confederate Navy, serving on board ship in the Charleston Harbor. He was again transferred, this time being assigned to the Artillery and placed in Battery Brook, which was part of the defense of Richmond until that city surrendered. On the retreat from Richmond, Washington Duke fell prisoner to the Union Army and was sent to Libby Prison.

In a few weeks peace was declared and the prisoners were released. The Federal Government releasing him, sent him as far as Newbern, N. C. The remaining distance to his home, one hundred and forty miles, he walked. His sole possessions at that period of his life were his farm, or what might be left of it, two blind mules and a silver fifty cent peace which he had secured in exchange for a Confederate five dollar bill.

The story of his success from that apparently hopeless beginning when he was already nearly fifty years of age is one of the romances of American history.

Returning to his little farm and his small family he determined to win from the land sustenance for himself and children. He was a widower and his children, three sons and a daughter, had been cared for during his absence by their grand parents.

He began the cultivation of tobacco, and his three sons, though young, shared labor with him. The out put of his farm was taken care of in a single building in 1865. He later removed the business to Durham and can be truly said to have made the name of Durham famous as well as his own. It was not long until Duke of Durham became a name, almost a title one might say, known throughout the world.

Washington Duke was a sincere and earnest church member and a liberal supporter of Church work. He became deeply interested in Trinity College, which at that time was going through a trying period in its history. His first gift was eighty-five thousand dollars, a sum which he increased in three years time to half a million dollars. The Duke family has continued the support of this splendid institution and North Carolina owes to the Dukes a boundless debt of gratitude in that they preserved the college when failure threatened it and continued to up-hold it.

Trinity College however was not the only beneficence of Washington Duke. In 1892 he paid the entire debt on an old, well established female college in North Carolina when he learned that the college was facing difficulties. A few years later he established the Southern Conservatory of Music at Durham, donating the site and constructing large buildings for it. In these and many unrecorded gifts he displayed his love for his native state as well as his interest in educational advantages for young people.

He lived to a splendid old age surrounded by devoted friends and a most adoring family. The death of his only daughter, who had been his confidant and comfort through all her years and in a sense the administratrix of his many charitles, saddened his later years. In the early part of 1905 he sustained a fall in which his hip was injured and he died May 8, 1905, leaving a colossal fortune and a good name.

He married twice, both wives dying early in life. He first married Mary C. Clinton of Orange County North Carolina. The marriage took place in 1844. She died in 1847, leaving two children: Sidney T. Duke, who died at fourteen years of age, and Brodie Leonidas Duke.

Washington Duke married for his second wife Artelia Roney of Alamance County, North Carolina. The marriage took place December ninth 1852. She died six years later, August 10, 1858. She left three children:

Mary Elizabeth Duke who married Robert E. Lyon of Durham and died in 1893.

Benjamin N. Duke.

James B. Duke.

BRODIE LEONIDAS DUKE

Brodie Leonidas Duke, the eldest surviving son of Washington Duke, married Martha MacMannen. They had three children, namely;

Mabel Duke.

Pearl Duke.

Lawrence Duke.

Mabel Duke married Rivers Goodall of Durham and has one daughter, Mabel Duke Goodall.

Pearl Duke married Judge Nathan L. Bachman of Chattanooga and has one daughter, Martha Dulaney Bachman.

Lawrence Duke is not married. He makes his home in New York.

Brodie Duke married for his second wife Minnie Woodward of Gadsden, Alabama. They had one son Woodward Duke who died young.

BENJAMIN NEWTON DUKE

Benjamin N. Duke, son of Washington Duke and Artelia Roney Duke was born in Orange County, North Carolina April 27, 1855. He attended town and county schools in his youth and at an early age began to aid his father, when Washington Duke returned from the War Between the States without fortune and apparently without prospect. Besides his interest in the Tobacco Company, which they built up and the American Tobocco Company, which they were largely instrumental in forming, Benjamin N. Duke and his brother James B. Duke, the only brother now surviving, have immense interests in other organizations. James B. Duke is President of the Southern Power Company of which Benjamin Duke is Vice President. His benefactions have been many and generous, his modesty preventing a list of institutions and the amount which he has given. He is a member of the Methodist Episcopal Church, South. The interests of the church have always been warmly and generously supported by him.

Mr. Duke's greatest philanthropy is his gifts to Trinity College. He has given to its development large sums of money from time to times as the college needed it. But dollars do not measure his interest in it. By his efforts with others, by his advice to those who have had its destiny in hand, by his continual interests in all the progress it has made, by his openly affirmed confidence in its methods of instruction, and by many other actions, he has been a source of strength to it which he himself little suspects. There is no part of its life in which he has not shown an appreciative interest. He has watched its development to a college standing, he has become enthusiastic over its athletic interests, he has encouraged by appreciative words its professors who have sought to spread its influence among scholars, he has taken deep interest in beautification of its grounds, he has fulfilled at some inconvenience to his private affairs the duties of a college trustee, and all he has done cheerfully.

Socially he is charming and gracious, entertaining with a warm hospitality in which he is ably assisted by his wife. He was unanimously elected president of the North Carolina Society of New York and served the organization with ability.

He married Sarah Pearson Angier, of Durham, North Carolina, daughter of M. A. Angier, one of the distinguished citizens of Durham. The marriage took place February 21, 1877.

They had three children namely:

George Washington Duke, named for his grand father, died young. Angier Buchanan Duke, born December 8, 1884. Mary Lillian Duke.

Angier Buchanan Duke married April 2, 1915, Cordelia Biddle, daughter of Mr. and Mrs. Anthony J. Drexel Biddle, of Philadelphia. They had two sons, Angier Buchanan Duke, junior, and Anthony Newton Duke. Angier Buchanan Duke died September 3, 1923.

Mary Lillian Duke married June 16, 1916, the brother of her brother's wife, Anthony J. Drexel Biddle, junior. They have two children, Mary Duke Biddle and A. J. Drexel Biddle, III.

JAMES BUCHANAN DUKE

James Buchanan Duke, son of Washington Duke and Artelia Roney Duke, was born near Durham, North Carolina, December 23, 1856. Like so many of America's most successful men, the early life of Mr. Duke began under circumstances apparently unfavorable to success. His mother died when he was but two years of age and his father answered the call to arms for the Confederate Army when the youngest son was but seven years old. Leaving his children in the care of an aged relative and making an effort to provide for their upkeep by the sale of his farm on terms, Washington Duke did all that was in his power to properly care for his little family during his absence.

After peace was declared Washington Duke returned to find that the entire district had been impoverished by the heavy hand of war, both armies having used the surrounding territory as a camping ground.

Washington Duke and his sons began to cultivate tobacco in North Carolina and the tobacco produced by his cultivation and care was the finest grade possible. At first they could not obtain more than the necessities of life from the sale of the tobacco, but as conditions gradually improved, prosperity attended upon their labors and after a short lapse of time, the Dukes determined upon the manufacture of tobacco for the market. Although he was the youngest of them all, James Buchanan Duke shared in the labors of the family, displaying even at this early age the grit and determination and indefatigable energy which has placed him in the front rank of American Princes of Industry.

The early education of James B. Duke was received in such schools as he could attend and was later supplemented by a course at the New Garden School, Guilford County, S. C. (now Guilford College).

It was not long before the remarkable initiative of James B. Duke in developing new avenues for activity made him a leader in pushing the fortunes of the family. At the age of less than twenty years he was in charge of the factory which had been established at Durham, purchasing the raw product and directing its development throughout every stage of its manufacture into a finished article. He was also salesman for the factory's output, traveling and selling throughout the South and West, disposing of the entire output of the factory on every trip. The business grew rapidly and soon the small factory in which the business begun was a large and well built structure. And yet though the business was prosperous James B. Duke voluntarily practiced rigorous economy in order that he might turn every dollar back into the enterprise.

In 1878 the firm consisted of Washington Duke, his sons, Brodie L., Benjamin N., and James B. Duke, and George W. Watts, the later having been taken into the firm. The principal output of the factory at this time was smoking tobacco. In 1883, at the instance of James B. Duke, the firm determined to enter the cigarette field and it was forr first successfully introducing the machine-made cigarette and then he carried out the extension of the business to New York. The fight which he successfully made against great odds, lack of sufficient capital and the heavy opposition of competitors is one of the romances of American business. To Mr. Duke also goes the credit for first successfully introducing the machine made cigarette and within a few years the Duke plant which had been the smallest producer in the country was controlling nearly half the business.

Between the years of 1885 and 1890 the dominant personality of James B. Duke became nationally known. He became a recognized leader in his selective line; and was acknowledged a Merchant prince in New York.

With the vision which has characterized his entire career James B. Duke saw greater possibilities for the tobacco trade and in 1890 The American Tobacco Company was formed, merging many of the principal tobacco companies of that day and capitalizing for the amount of twenty-five million dollars. James B. Duke was president of the company. As the years passed the American Tobacco Company extended its boundaries beyond the United States and America and a great demand for American tobacco was found in foreign fields. The British Tobacco interests made a violent fight against the encroachment and without loss of time, James B. Duke went to London, bought over the largest of the British tobacco companies and on their own grounds staged a brilliant trade war with the British tobacco interests.   He won the fight fairly, openly, quickly.

In 1911 the American Tobacco Company was dissolved under a mandate from the United States Supreme Court and the company resolved into the original sub-divided companies from which it had been formed.   The business of the companies when separated, however, continued as prosperous as before.

After the dissolution of the American Tobacco Company, Mr. Duke retired from office of the president and gave a very large portion of his time to the British American Tobacco Company, from which he recently resigned as chairman of the board of directors.

James B. Duke has also been actively interested in other industries, among them being the Southern Power Company, a corporation formed to supply power for North Carolina and South Carolina cotton mills, lighting plants, railways and for countless other utilitarian purposes. Mr. Duke is president of the corporation and a member of the directorate.

Interested not only in the development of commercial interests in the south, Mr. Duke has given large sums of money to the educational institutions. Trinity College at Durham, North Carolina, the college dear to his father has been the recipient of countless gifts at his hands and he and his brother Benjamin N. Duke have heavily endowed it. A few years ago James B. Duke gave another million dollars to Trinity College.   Another gift of James Duke and Benjamin N. Duke has been the Memorial Hall erected and presented to Guilford College in the memory of the only sister of the Duke brothers. These are only a few of the many benefactions of James B. Duke to public welfare.

James B. Duke married, July 23, 1907, Mrs. Nannie Lee Holt Inman, of Atlanta, Georgia.   They have one child:

Doris Duke, born November 22, 1912.

THE DUKE TRUST

Establishment of a trust for charitable and educational purposes in North and South Carolina embracing properties valued at at least $40,000,000 was announced in December, 1924, by James Buchanan Duke.   Among the securities thus set aside are about three-fourths of Mr. Duke's holdings in the Southern Power System, the income of

JAMES BUCHANON DUKE

which during the next few years will aggregate approximately $2,000,000 a year.

The trust will be administered by fifteen trustees, who will constitute a self-perpetuating body.

The trustees first are directed and empowered to expend not exceeding $6,000,000 in acquiring lands and in erecting and equipping thereon buildings/ "in the state of North Carolina to be known as Duke University," but with the provision that if Trinity College, at Durham, North Carolina, should change its name to Duke University this sum should be spent in expanding and extending Trinity College.

The trust then provides that twenty per cent of the income shall be retained each year and added to ,the principal until such fund has aggregated $80,000,000. After this percentage has been set aside the other 80 per cent is to be divided as follows:

Thirty-two per cent to Duke University, for all purposes of the university.

Thirty-two per cent. for maintaining and securing hospitals, primarily in the states of North Carolina and South Carolina, on the plan of paying to the hospitals a sum not exceeding $1 per day for each free bed occupied and in assisting in building and equipping hospitals.

Ten per cent. for the benefit of white and colored orphans in North and South Carolina.

Six per cent. for assisting in building Methodist Episcopal churches in the sparsely settled rural districts of North Carolina.

Four per cent. for assistting in maintaining Methodist Episcopal churches in the sparsely settled \rural districts of North Carolina.

Two per cent. for pensioning superannuated preachers and widows and orphans of deceased preachers who have served in North Carolina conferences.

Five per cent. to Davidson College, Davidson, N. C.   Davidson is a Presbyterian institution.

Five per cent. to Furman University, Greenville, S. C.   Furman is a Baptist university.

Four per cent. to Johnson C. Smith University, Charlotte.   Johnson C. Smith University formerly was known as Biddle University, and is a negro school.

The trustees named by Mr. Duke include Mrs. James B. Duke, Somerville, N. J.; George G. Allen, William R. Perkins, William B. Bell, Anthony J. Drexel Biddle, junior, Walter C. Parker and Alexander H. Sands, junior, of New York; William S. Lee, Charles I. Burkholder, Norman A. Cocke and Edwin C. Marshall, Charlotte, and Benjamin E. Geer, Greenville, South Carolina.

Recalling that he has for years been engaged in developing waterpower resources of North Carolina and South Carolina, Mr.

Duke, in a statement set out in the indenture for the guidance of the trustees, said that "my ambition is that the revenues of such developments shall administer to the social welfare, as the operation of such developments is administering to the economic welfare of the communities which they serve." He then commends to the trustees the securities of the Southern Power System as the prime investment for the funds of the trust, and, advises the trustees not to change such investments unless urgently necessary.

"I recognize that education, when conducted along sane and practical, as opposed to dogmatic and theoretical, lines, is, next to religion, the greatest civilizing influence," says Mr. Duke's statement, in giving his reason for creating Duke University. He asks that a faculty assuring the university "a place of real leadership in the educational world" be secured, and that courses be arranged primarily for training preachers, teachers, lawyers ,and physicians.

Hospitals have been selected as another means of distributing the income of the trust because, according to ,the statement, they not only minister to the comfort of the sick, but increase "the efficiency of mankind" and prolong human life.

Orphans are included in the trust, Mr. Duke's statement to the trustees says, "in an effort to help those who are unable to help themselves." He adds that in his opinion, however, "nothing can take the place/ of a home and its influences," adding that "every effort should be made to safeguard these wards of society."

The choice of supernnuated ministers and rural churches of the Methodist churches is made as "a very fertil and neglected field for useful help in religious life, in order to assist "by way of support and maintenance in those cases where the head of the family, through devoting his life to the religious service of his fellow man, has been unable to accumulate for his declining years and for his widow and children, and assisting in building and maintenance of churches in the rural districts where the people are not able to do this properly themselves."

In conclusion, he says;

"I have endeavored to make provision in some measure for the needs of mankind along physical, mental and spiritual lines, largely confining the benefaction to those sections served by these waterpower developments (the Southern Power System). I might have extended this aid to other charitable objects and to other sections, but my opinion is that so doing would probably be productive of less good by reason of attempting too much.   I therefore urge the trustees to seek to administer well the trust hereby committed to them within the limits set and to this end that in at least one meeting each year this indenture be read to the assembled trustees."

DUKE UNIVERSITY

The directors and trustees of Trinity College met early in January, 1925, to consider Mr. Duke's generous offer. They voted unanimously to change the name of Trinity College to Duke University and to accept Mr. Duke's splendid endowment. The University which has already been of much help in North Carolina and surrounding states through the already munificent gifts of the Duke family, will be enabled to widen its sphere of influnce and to take even higher rank among the institutions of learning in America.

Elston

ELSTON

THE Elstons are an old Welsh family in Cardeganshire, Wales. Their history dates back to a remote period. The present representatives of the family there are wealthy mine owners.

The first emigrants of the name coming to America were three brothers who came from Cardeganshire to New York in about 1760. It is thought that one of the three settled in New York, and spelled his name Alston instead of Elston, and from him is descended the very numerous and important family bearing that name to the present day.

Another of the brothers, probably named Jo or Jonathan, left New York about the time of the Revolution, and joined General Greene's army in the south. Some of his descendants are now living in the South.

The third emigrant brother was named William Elston. He settled in New Jersey at or near Elizabeth and reared a family there. One of his sons, also named William Elston, went south and finally settled in Smith County, Tennessee. He reared a family there, and his descendants are widely scattered. One of his sons, Elias Elston, being among the eldest, was born in New Jersey. He afterwards went to North Carolina, married there, then lived a few years in Tennessee and went to Missouri in 1818 and settled there. He became the progenitor of the family now living in Missouri.

David Elston, another son of William Elston of Wales, was born probably in Wales, about 1745. He raised a family in New Jersey. About 1786 he moved to Wilkes County, North Carolina, and lived there about six years. Then (about 1792) he moved his entire family to the new state of Kentucky, and lived there the remainder of his life.

John Elston, son of David Elston, was born October 8, 1775, in or near Elizabeth, New Jersey. He lived with his father until about 23 years of age. We find him in 1794-95 driving beef cattle from Kentucky into Ohio for the use of General Wayne's army. About 1798 he and his younger brother, Allen Elston, went to the new or western portion of South Carolina, afterwards called the Pendleton District. Here they accumulated considerable property. Here also in 1801 John Elston married Elizabeth Clark, a daughter of Major William H. Clark and granddaughter of Governor John Sevier of Tennessee.

47

Elizabeth Clark was born in South Carolina July 20, 1787. Her father, Major William H. Clark, was one of the first settlers of upper S. C. He married Elizabeth Sevier, daughter of Gov. John Sevier, and by her had (1) Sarah Hawkins Clark, (2) Elizabeth Clark, born July 20, 1787, married John Elston, 1801; (3) Ruth Clark, married to Allen Elston; and (4) John Sevier Clarke. Major William H. Clark married a second wife, Ruth Goodwin, February 14, 1792, and by her had four children: (1) John Clark, born Nov. 5, 1792; (2) Oliver Clark, born October 9, 1794; (3) Sevier Clark, born Sept. 11, 1797; and (4) Sabra Clark, born March 3, 1799. Major Clark died in Hall County, Georgia, June 4, 1843. His widow. Ruth Goodwin Clark, was granted a pension on her application executed April 2, 1844.

John Elston and Elizabeth Clark Elston reared a family of eleven children, the first six born in Pendleton District, South Carolina, and the last five born in Habersham County, Georgia. They lived near the South Carolina and Georgia line on the Tugaloo River, first on the South Carolina side in what was then the Pendleton District, later Oconee County, until 1815-16, then on the Georgia side in Habersham County until 1834, at which date they moved to the Creek nation and settled in the upper Choccolocco valley in Benton (afterwards Calhoun) County, Alabama. Five of their children, namely, Sevier, William, John Clark, Ruth and Martha, came with them to Alabama.

The children of John and Elizabeth Clark Elston were eleven in number, as follows:

1. Allen Elston, born May 25, 1802.
2. Sally Elston, born August 8, 1805.
3. Neaty Elston, born June 29, 1807.
4. Nancy Elston, born September 16, 1809.
5. Sabra Elston, born April 8, 1812.
6. Sevier Elston, born December 27, 1814.
7. William Elston, born April 6, 1817.
8. Elizabeth Elston, born October 23, 1819.
9. John Clark Elston, born July 4, 1822.
10. Ruth Elston, born July 18, 1825.
11. Martha Elston, born April 17, 1831.

John Elston and his sons were among the pioneer settlers of old Benton County, Alabama. They bought and entered large plantations of valuable land around the old Corn Grove postoffice in the upper Choccolocco Valley. John Elston died July 11, 1853, just seven days after signing his last will and testament. His wife Elizabeth died November 11, 1845. They lie buried side by side in the family burying ground on the Allen Elston home place near the house. Several of their children and grandchildren are also buried there.

I—ALLEN ELSTON

Allen Elston, the eldest child of John Elston and Elizabeth Clark Elston, and grandson of David Elston, of New Jersey, was born in Pendleton District, South Carolina, May 25, 1802. He married Martha Humphreys of the same place in 1822. Martha Humphreys was born in South Carolina October 23, 1806. They emigrated to the Choccolocco valley in Alabama about 1836, and settled in Benton (now Calhoun) County, near the Corn Grove postoffice. Here he developed a large plantation alongside his father and brothers, and here he lived out his days in comfort if not affluence. He owned many black slaves whom he treated humanely. He was all his life a leading citizen of the community and was greatly esteemed by all. He was a high-toned Christian gentleman of the antebellum type. He died May 21, 1879, aged 77 years, and was laid to rest in the family burying ground on the place and near his house.

Martha Humphreys Elston, wife of Allen Elston, died January 2, 1855. Mr. Elston afterwards married a second wife, Mrs. Minerva Gibson, of Fayetteville, Tennessee, November 8, 1857. There were no children by this marriage. The children of Allen Elston by his first wife, Martha Humphreys Elston, were ten in number, as follows:

1. Nancy Elston, born June 23, 1823.
2. Sabra Elston, born May 6, 1825.
3. Martha Elizabeth Elston, born June 8, 1827.
4. William Clark Elston, born March 6, 1829.
5. Sarah Elston, born June 17, 1831.
6. John Humphreys Elston, born June 18, 1835.
7. Kitty Hudson Elston, born October 31, 1837.
8. Susan Frances Elston, born February 14, 1840.
9. Eva Borders Elston, born Septeber 18, 1842.
10. Ann W. Elston, born October 24, 1844; died in infancy.

For further account of these see later.

II—SALLY (OR SARAH) ELSTON EDDINS

Sally Elston, second child of John Elston and Elizabeth Clark Elston, was born in Pendleton district, South Carolina, August 5, 1805. Her name is written "Sally" in the family Bible, but in her father's will she is mentioned as Sarah. She married James Eddins, of Franklin County, Georgia; died in Pickens District, South Carolina, in 1831 or 1832, leaving four daughters and one son. James Eddins afterwards married Salina Trimmer, of Toxaway Creek, South Carolina, and moved to Pickens County, Alabama, in 1835. He died December 22, 1877.

III—NEATY ELSTON DENMAN

Neaty Elston, the third child of John Elston and Elizabeth

Clark Elston, was born in Pendleton District, South Carolina, June 29, 1807. She was married to Blake Denman near Cherokee Mountain, Habersham County, Ga. They lived there several years and then moved to Alabama and settled on a farm near Jacksonville. Here she died about 1852. Blake Denman died at the same place about 1886. They had seven or more children, whose names are not known.

IV—NANCY ELSTON

Nancy Elston, fourth child of John and Elizabeth Clark Elston, was born September 16, 1809. She is supposed to have died young.

V—SABRA ELSTON YOWELL

Sabra Elston, fifth child of John Elston and Elizabeth (Clark) Elston, was born in Pendeleton dist., S. C., April 8, 1812. She was married to James Allen Yowell, of Lincoln County, Tennessee. They had perhaps nine or ten children. She died there 1855-60.

VI—SEVIER ELSTON

Sevier Elston, sixth child of John Elston and Elizabeth (Clark) Elston, was born in Pendleton dist., S. C., December 27, 1814. Migrated to Alabama with his father in 1834. He married in S. C., Miss Elizabeth B. Davis, of Pickens dist., in 1847. They settled in Benton County, with others of the family, and acquired large agricultural interests. They had an only son, Harvey Davis Elston, born August 3, 1861, died July 11, 1869. Sevier Elston was postmaster at Corn Grove postoffice from 1842 to 1852. He died September 26, 1885.

VII—WILLIAM ELSTON

William Elston, seventh child of John Elston and Elizabeth (Clark) Elston, was born in Habersham County, Georgia, April 6, 1817; came to Alabama with his parents in 1834. He married there Miss Jane Worthington near White Plains, Calhoun County, Alabama, 18—. Had one daughter, Eleanor Elston, and an infant that died young. He died in 1854 of pneumonia. In 1857 his widow Jane and daughter Eleanor went out to Texas with some relatives. There Mrs. Elston married a second husband, name not known, and then a third named Broadus. They were yet living there in Burleson County, in 1881. The daughter Eleanor (later spoken of as Annie Elizabeth) married twice in Texas; 1st to A. Judson Jones, of Virginia. 2nd in 1879 to William Elston Taylor, her half-cousin from Talladega, Ala., he being a grandson of Allen Elston, Sr., of S. C. There were two sons by this union: (1) William Elston Taylor, Jr. (2) Andrew Law Taylor.

VIII—ELIZABETH (ELSTON) WEIR

Elizabeth Elston, eighth child of John Elston and Elizabeth (Clark) Elston, was born in Habersham County, Georgia, October 23, 1819. Was married to Dr. John R. Weir, of Blount County, Tenn., in about 1835. Had several children. About 1842 moved to Washington County, Texas. Elizabeth died there April 20, 1851. Dr. Weir also died there in 1878-9. Two or three of their children were living in Texas in 1881. We find the following record of some of the children in the family Bible of John Elston, Mrs. Weir's father: (1) Mary Weir, born July 17, 1836, (2) Cullen Weir, born March 27, 1838. (3) Third child born February 26, 1840.

IX—JOHN CLARK ELSTON

John Clark Elston, ninth child of John Elston and Elizabeth (Clark) Elston, was born at Owl Swamp, in Habersham County, Ga., July 4, 1822. Moved with his parents to Alabama in 1834. He married January 21, 1846, Selina Jones, of Pendleton dist., S. C., a first cousin of James M. Jones, husband of his niece Nancy Elston. They lived in Benton (Calhoun) County, Alabama, till about 1869, then went to Johnson County, Texas, where he died March 19, 1896, Grandview postoffice. They had four children. For record of these and the grandchildren see later.

X—RUTH (ELSTON) MATTISON

Ruth Elston, tenth child of John Elston and Elizabeth (Clark) Elston, was born in Habersham County, Georgia, July 18, 1825. Migrated with parents to Alabama in 1834. Was married to Glover Mattison, in Alabama, about 1838. Reared four children. They moved to Denton County, Texas, in about 1866, and Ruth (Elston) Mattison died there July 8, 1870. Two of her children were living there in 1881. We have no further record of the chilrren.

XI—MARTHA (ELSTON) HOLLINGSWORTH

Martha Elston, eleventh child of John Elston and Elizabeth (Clark) Elston was born in Habersham County, Georgia, April 17, 1831. Came to Alabama in 1834; was married at home about 1846 to Stephen P. Hollingsworth, of Rusk County, Texas, and they went at once to Texas to make their home there, settling in Johnson County. Mr. Hollingsworth died there in the fall of 1879. Mrs. Hollingsworth was living there in 1881. They had three children.

CHILDREN OF ALLEN AND MARTHA (HUMPHREYS) ELSTON OF CALHOUN COUNTY, ALABAMA

I—NANCY (ELSTON) JONES

Nancy (Elston) Jones, daughter and first child of Allen and Martha (Humphreys) Elston, was born in Pendleton dist., S. C., July

23, 1823; came with her parents to Alabama in 1836; was married
to James Martin Jones, of Tennessee, July 3, 1838. They lived a
few years in Petersburg, Tennessee; then came to Benton (now Calhoun) County, Alabama, and lived out their days in this county.
James Martin Jones was born in Maury County, Tennessee, September 12, 1812; died in Jacksonville, Alabama, January 16, 1875, and
was buried in Oxford, Alabama. Nancy (Elston) Jones died in Jacksonville, December 28, 1875, and was buried in Oxford cemetery. The
children of this couple were seven in number. For further account of
the children see later.

II—SABRA (ELSTON) HAYS

Sabra (Elston) Hays, daughter and second child of Allen and
Martha (Humphreys) Elston, was born in Pendleton dist., S. C.,
May 6, 1825; came to Alabama with her parents in 1836; was married February 11, 1841, in Tennessee, to John B. Hays of that state
while on a visit to her sister, Nancy Jones. John Hays was born Nov.
28, 1816. They settled at White Plains, Alabama. John Hays died
April 9, 1863. Mrs. Hays died Sept., 26, 1886. They had nine children
as follows all born at White Plains:

1. Martha J. Hays, born January 14, 1842.
2. Allen A. Hays, born August 7, 1843.
3. Clifton C. Hays, born Dec. 6, 1845.
4. Infant daughter, born and died in 1847.
5. Alice V. Hays, born July 22, 1849.
6. Clara C. Hays, born December 24, 1852.
7. John Knox Hays, born March 4, 1855.
8. James W. Hays, born January 28, 1858.
9. Addie L. Hays, born Nov. 9, 1862.

III—MARTHA ELIZABETH (ELSTON) 1, DENDY; 2, DOYLE; 3, LUTTRELL

Martha Elizabeth (Elston) 1, Dendy; 2, Doyle; 3, Luttrell;
third child of Allen and Martha (Humphreys) Elston, was born in
Pendleton dist., S. C., June 8, 1827. She moved to Alabama with her
parents in 1836. Was married at home February 25, 1847, to James
W. Dendy, of South Carolina. They had two children, one of
whom died in infancy. The other child, James Allen Dendy, was born
May 27, 1848; went out to Texas when a young man and reared a
family there; was still living there in 1918 near Weatherford. James
W. Dendy (the husband and father) was born March 21, 1823, and was
a first cousin to his wife Martha E. Elston, their mothers being sisters. He was drawn into the Confederate States Army and sent to
Richmond, Virginia, where he died May 4, 1863.

Mrs. Martha E. (Elston) Dendy married in 1869 a second husband, Dr. James A. Doyle, a widower with several grown children. They lived in Fort Madison, Oconee County, S. C., until Mr. Doyle's death about 1887. Mrs. Doyle then went to live with her son, James Allen Dendy, in Texas, where she remained until 1898. She then went to Oxford, Ala., where she was married to her widowed brother-in-law, Harvey W. Luttrell. They lived happily there until his death which occurred July 26, 1899. She again returned to Texas to make her home with her son, James A. Dendy, near Weatherford. Here she died October 8, 1916, aged 89 years. She had no children by second and third marriages.

IV—WILLIAM CLARK ELSTON

William Clark Elston, son and fourth child of Allen and Martha (Humphreys) Elston, was born in Pendleton District, S. C., March 6, 1829; came to Benton County, Ala., with the family in 1836. He married Adline Findley, of Benton County, Alabama, in 1848. Adline was born Nov. 23, 1829. They moved to Arkansas in 1870 and settled in the Red River Valley near the Texas line. Here the mother Adline died February 19, 1877. Mr. Elston later moved over into Oklahoma, leaving most of his children (now grown up) in Arkansas and Louisiana. He died in Oklahoma in 1899.

The children of William Clark and Adline (Findley) Elston were nine in number, six sons and three daughters. The sons came to be very successful business men in and around Shreveport, La. For for further account of these see later.

V—SARAH (ELSTON) BOWLING

Sarah (Elston) Bowling, daughter of Allen and Martha (Humphreys) Elston, was born in S. C. June 17, 1831; came to Alabama with her parents in 1836. She married February 25, 1847, Dr. William E. Bowling of Georgia. They settled near the Corn Grove postoffice where they lived out their lives. Dr. Bowling was a farmer, school teacher and practicing physician. He died March 6. 1899. His wife died June 4, 1904. The children of this union were six in number. For further account of them and their offspring see later.

VI—JOHN HUMPHREYS ELSTON

John Humphreys Elston, son and sixth child of Allen and Martha (Humphreys) Elston, was born in S. C. June 18, 1835. He lived on the old home place with his father all his life. He was a leading and highly esteemed citizen and served in the Confederate States army in the War Between the States. He married Mollie Reagan, of Talladega County, Alabama, about 1876. They had two children: 1, Janie Elston, daughter, born March 16, 1878. 2, Louie Elston, son, born November 9, 1879. In the year 1880 Mr Elston went on a tour through Texas and died there May 10, 1880.

VII—KITTY HUDSON (ELSTON) HUDSON

Kitty Hudson (Elston) Hudson, daughter and seventh child of Allen and Martha (Humphreys) Elston, was born in Benton County, Alabama, October 31, 1837. She was married to J. Gip Hudson at home in 1868. She died November 5, 1874, leaving two or three small children.

VIII—SUSAN FRANCES (ELSTON) LUTTRELL

Susan Frances (Elston) Luttrell, daughter and eighth child of Allen and Martha (Humphreys) Elston, was born in Benton County, Alabama, February 14, 1840. She grew up intellectually active and was favored with good academic education. Her religious and moral ideals were high. She moved in cultured and refined circles of society. She was married December 14, 1856, to Harvey Wilkerson Luttrell, formerly of Knox County, Tennessee, but then of Oxford, Alabama. They lived in and near Oxford to the end of their lives. Mrs. Luttrell died at Oxford April 25, 1897. Mr Luttrell died same place July 26, 1899. The children of this union were eleven as follows:

1. Corrie Luttrell, dau. born April 1, 1858.
2. Oscar F. Luttrell, son, born June 14 1859.
3. Elston Luttrell, son, born May 26, 1861.
4. Chester M. Luttrell, son, born October 8, 1862.
5. Bruce F. Luttrell, son, born July 13, 1868.
6. Rush Luttrell, son, born December 7, 1870.
7. A son, not named, born Jan. 14, 1872. Died 1872.
8. Katie Luttrell, dau., born July 4, 1875. Died 1875.
9. Marcy Luttrell, son, born January 16, 1877.
10 and 11. Frank and Fred Luttrell, twin sons, born March 28, 1879. Frank died Aug. 24, 1879. Fred died Aug. 14th, 1879.

For further account of these children see later.

IX—EVA BORDERS (ELSTON) DeARMAN

Eva Borders (Elston) DeArman, daughter and ninth child· of Allen and Martha (Humphreys) Elston, was born in Benton (later Calhoun) County, Alabama, September 12, 1842. She was married to James T. DeArman of the same county December 24, 1865. They lived out their lives in this county at different locations. Mrs. De-Arman died in Anniston, Ala., February 10, 1905. Mr. DeArman died same place a few years later. Of this union there were six children, as follows:

1. Alma Newell DeArman, daughter, born Nov. 14, 1866.
2. Cleff Elston DeArman, son, born June 21, 1869.
3. Kittie Turnipseed DeArman, dau., born July 20. 1872

4. Louie DeArman, son, born October 31, 1876.

5. Retha DeArman, daughter, born July 9, 1878.

6. Pearl DeArman, daughter, born May 15, 1883.

For further account of these children see later.

X—ANN W. ELSTON

Ann W. Elston, daughter and last child of Allen and Martha (Humphreys) Elston, was born in Benton County, Alabama, October 24, 1844; died March 9, 1845.

CHILDREN OF JOHN CLARK ELSTON AND SELINA (JONES) ELSTON

1. Mary (Elston) Keith, daughter and first child, was born in 1847-8; was married to a Mr. Keith; died in Tennessee.

2. Roxie Carolina (Elston) Snow, daughter, and second child, was born August 14, 1849. She married in Oxford, Alabama, Nov. 26, 1868, Clark Snow, youngest son of Dudley and Priscilla (Moung-er) Snow, of Oxford. Here also they lived out their days. Roxie died in Oxford July 4th, 1909. Clark Snow died July 19th, 1919. They had seven children. See below for account of the children.

3. Brazora (Elston) Heath, daughter, born————; was married to Chester Heath. Died in Cleburne, Texas; left children, one of them Arthur Heath of Artesia, New Mexico.

4. John Jabez Elston, son, born at Corn Grove December 24, 1853. Died January 24, 1856. Burried on the Allen Elston home place.

CHILDREN OF ROXIE CAROLINA (ELSTON) SNOW AND CLARK SNOW, OF OXFORD, ALABAMA

1. Kate Corinne Snow, daughter, born in Oxford, Alabama, Jan. 28, 1870; was married to Thomas Daniel Jackson June 17, 1896; died June 10, 1915. She left one daughter Joyce Elston Jackson born Dec. 5, 1904.

2. Ada Elston Snow, daughter, born December 8, 1871; was married to Charles Caleb Morgan November 17, 1897. To this union were born two sons: 1, Marechal Clark Morgan; 2, Norman Snow Morgan.

3. Ruth Snow, daughter, born in Oxford, Alabama, February 17, 1876; was married to Samuel Hallman December 15, 1910. Residence Oxford, Alabama. No children.

4. Julius Fane Snow, son, born March 22, 1878. Died January 13, 1879.

5. Maxie Snow, daughter, born July 19, 1879; was married to Joe L. Montgomery January 4, 1920.

6. Norman Lee Snow, son, born June 7, 1883. Not married.

7. Mary Winnifred Snow, daughter, born October 11, 1885; was married to James N. Griffin December 19, 1907. To this union one son Jim Snow Griffin, born January 25, 1918.

CHILDREN OF NANCY (ELSTON) JONES AND JAMES MARTIN JONES

1. Mary Elizabeth (Jones) Hames,, daughter and first child, was born in Petersburg, Tennessee, April 18, 1843. Was married in Jacksonville, Ala., in 1866, to Captain William M. Hames and is yet living there. Had six children. Captain Hames died Feb. 8, 1908.

2. Joseph A. Jones, son, born in Alabama April 28, 1845. Married and had family of several children. Residence, Birmingham Ala.

3. Abner Gregory Jones, son, born in Alabama December, 1846. Died September 16, 1863.

4. Rowena (Jones) McClurkin, daughter, born 1848. Was married November 6, 1866, to James McClurkin. He lived near Oxford, Ala. for a number of years and raised a family of seven children. Husband died and she now lives in Jacksonville, Florida. The seven children are:

a. Curtis McClurkin, son, born 1867. Died in Anniston, Ala.

b. Joseph J.McClurkin, son, born December 10, 1868.

c. Burt McClurkin, son, born October 25, 1870.

d. Florence McClurkin, daughter, born August 30, 1875. Died——.

e. Walter McClurkin, son, born 1877.

f. Avery McClurkin, son, born October, 1881.

g. George P. McClurkin, son, born ——. Died————.

5. Mattie (Jones) Lester, daughter, born December 1, 1851. Was married February 4, 1885, to a Mr. Lester. Died in Jacksonville, Ala.

6. Alice (Jones) Camp, daughter, born December 2, 1862. Married.

7. Walter Jones, son, born June 1, 1864. Died in Anniston.

POSTERITY OF WILLIAM CLARK ELSTON AND ADLINE (FINDLEY) ELSTON OF ALABAMA

(1) FANNIE LEE (ELSTON) 1, HARRIS; 2, HARRIS

Fannie Lee (Elston) 1, Harris; 2, Harris, daughter and first child, was born in Alabama, in 1849; was married to Walter Harris, of Texas, and to this union were born two children, George and Walter C. Walter Harris died and then his widow Fannie Lee married a second husband, George Harris, brother of her first husband, and to this union was born one daughter Golda. The mother died in Texas about 1878. For account of these children see page—— of this Volume.

(2) (3) (4) (5) HENRY WORD ELSTON, WALTER ELSTON, HORACE ELSTON AND MARTHA ELSTON, four children of William Clark Elston are all mentioned as having died in childhood.

(6) JOSEPH WALKER ELSTON

Joseph Walker Elston, son, born in Alabama November 3,

1860. Went to Arkansas with his father's family about 1870. When reaching maturity began service as station agent with the V.S.&P. Railway in Louisiana. Was in this service a number of years and also engaged in mercantile business and was quite successful. He married at Haughton, La, December 8, 1886, Emily Ogilvie Moore, a school teacher from Georgia. To this union were born in Haughton, La., nine children. See page——— of this Vilume for account of children. The father later moved to Shreveport, La., and prospered in business with his brothers-in-law until the family jointly were possessed of several large river bottom plantations, oil land, an interest in one of the city banks, and the commercial business of Elston, Prince & McDade, (wholesale grocers and cotton factors) and seventeen producing oil wells, all located in the vicinity of Shreveport. Joseph W. Elston died September 16, 1922.

(7) PERCY PELHAM ELSTON

Percy Pelham Elston, son, born in Alabama, March 30, 1867. Lived most of his life in Haughton and Shreveport, La., where he was associated with his brothers in business. Died in 1898 at the age o 31. Was never married.

(8) ROSA PEARL (ELSTON), 1, ALLEN; 2, PRINCE

Rosa Pearl (Elston), 1, Allen; 2, Prince; daughter, born Jan., 5, 1870. She married first Pleasant D. Allen, of New Orleans, a railway trainman, and by him had two sons, Lawrence Elston and Joseph William. Mr. Allen was killed in a railway accident. Rosa Pearl later married a second time Joseph Wilson Prince. No children by this union. They lived on their two-thousand-acre plantation a few miles from Shreveport, La. For account of the Allen children see later.

(9) CHARLES H. ELSTON

Charles H. Elston, son, born April 5, 1873. Married Mamie Boone, and to this union was born one son, Charles Joseph Elston, April 21, 1898, at Doyline, La., and he married Peggy Eva Green February 18, 1921, and had one son.

CHILDREN OF FANNIE LEE (ELSTON) HARRIS

1. George Harris, son, by first husband Walter Harris, was born in Texas.
2. Walter Campbell Harris, born in Texas__———; married and had four children: (1) Fannie Lee Harris; (2) Juanita Harris; (3) Margaret Harris; (4) Walter Campbell Harris, Jr.
3. Golda Harris, daughter by second husband George Harris, born in Texas———; m. George Frank Brooks and had two daugh-

ters: (1) Fannie Lee Brooks; (2) Margaret Brooks. The mother
Golda (Harris) Brooks died in Temple, Texas.

CHILDREN OF JOSEPH WALKER ELSTON OF LA.

1 Julia Moore Elston, daughter, born in Haughton, La., Sept.
26, 1887. Married Buford Dean Battle in Shreveport, La., Aug. 27,
1919.

2. Dudley Clark Elston, son, born February 13, 1889. Married first
Myrtle Lawrence April 29, 1907. To this union were born three
children: (1) Ruth Elston, b. July 27, 1909. (2) Dudley Clark Elston,
Jr., b. April 4, 1911. (3) Paul Lawrence Elston, b. June 7, 1912. Dud-
ley Clark Elston married a second wife Una Lee Harrell, and to this
union have been born three children: (1) Joseph Harrell Elston, b.
September 28, 1918. (2) Robert Douglas Elston, b. March 2. 1921. (3)
Evelyn Claire Elston, b. January 28, 1923.

3. Ethel Earl Elston, daughter, born at Haughton, La., September
12, 1890. Was married to Ross E. McDade May 24, 1911, and to this
union have been born three daughters: (1) Ethel Elston McDade, (2)
Emily Sarah McDade, (3) Juliet Adeline McDade.

4. Parks Moore Elston, son, born at Haughton, La., January 26,
1892. Married Lucy Nicholson, and to this union have been born three
daughters: (1) Eleanor Earle Elston, b. May 7, 1917. (2) Ethel
Lemerle Elston, b. January 5, 1920. (3) Dorothy Lilian Elston, b.
March 28, 1922.

5. Joseph Walker Elston, Jr., son, born at Haughton, La., Nov.,
9, 1894. Married Wilhelmina McDade. She was born January 22, 1893.
To this union have been born four children: (1) Margaret Lindsey
Elston, b. July 12, 1917. (2) Joseph Walker Elston (III), b. Nov.,
22, 1919. (3) Mamie Elizabeth Elston, b. November 19, 1921. (4)
Wilhelmina Elston, b. September 4, 1923.

6. William Word Elston, son, born December 27, 1894. Not married.

7. Robert Lee Elston, son, born February 15, 1897. Not married.

8. Harry Paul Elston, son, born July 15, 1899. He finished his
education with A. B. degree at Washington University, St. Louis,
Missouri, in 1923. Married Mildred Gibbons of St. Louis April 22, 1924.
She was raised in London, England, and came to St. Louis with her
parents in 1919. H. P. Elston is one of the managing heads of the
large wholesale grocery and cotton business of Elston, Prince & Mc-
Dade, of Shreveport, La.

9. Emily Elizabeth Elston, daughter and last child of Joseph
Walker Elston, Sr., and Emily O. (Moore) Elston, was born in
Haughton, La., September 5, 1901. She was married June 12, 1924, to
Floyd Reynolds Hodges. Residence, Shreveport, La.

CHILDREN OF ROSA PEARL (ELSTON) 1, ALLEN

1. Lawrence Elston Allen, son, born in New Orleans, Nov., 12 1897. Not married. Lives in California.

2. Joseph William Allen, son, born in New Orleans Jan., 11, 1904. Married Mildred Love January 3, 1923, at Shreveport. Resides in California.

CHILDREN OF SARAH (ELSTON) BOWLING AND DR. WM. E BOWLING OF CALHOUN COUNTY, ALABAMA

(1) MARTHA ELIZABETH BOWLING BARKER, the first child, was born December 29, 1847; was married to Abiah Morgan Barker September 26, 1865, in Alabama, but went at once to Texas, where the family afterward lived. She died in DeLeon, Texas, in 1922; husband yet living there in 1924, age 81. Their cihldren were five in number as follows:

a. George Ephraim Barker, b. July 20, 1866, married Cora Womble. Has several children and grandchildren. Residence, Waco, Texas.

b. Alban Eustace Barker, b. March 5, 1868. Married and has children. Residence, DeLeon, Texas (1924).

c. William Barker, b. September 26, 1869. Married and has children. Residence, DeLeon, Texas (1924).

d. Mollie Barker, b. —————. Married first a Ross; second a Hammett. Residence, DeLeon, Texas (1924).

e. Evan Barker, b. —————. Residence, DeLeon, Texas.

(2) GEORGE W. BOWLING, son, b. June 29, 1849. Died April 1861.

(3) VIRGINIA CUNNINGHAM (BOWLING) EVANS, third child born October 10, 1850; was married to Josephus M. Evans, October 19, 1871. They lived at Heflin, Alabama. The mother died there January 8, 1919. The children of this union were nine in number as follows:

a. Lena Georgia Evans, b. July 18, 1872: was married to W. Jack Vaughn November 24, 1892; Has two children. Residence, Heflin, Alabama.

b. Ewell Kirkham Evans, son, b. December 1873; d. 1875.

c. Jesse Evans, son, b. September 20, 1875; married Susie Belle Ingram, of Opelika, Alabama, December 23, 1902; has four children; residence Anniston, Alabama.

d. William Evans, son, b. 1877; died young.

e. Alex Olin Evans, son, b. July 23, 1880; married Minnie Lee Harris January 1, 1907; died March 30, 1914; had one child that died young.

f. Cynthia Elston Evans, daughter, b. February 11, 1883; died May 1, 1885.

g. Martin Josephus Evans, son, b. March 14, 1885; residence, Heflin, Alabama.

h. George Bismarck Evans, son, b. October 3, 1887; married Onnie Lou Black October 8, 1913; one child; wife died 1920. Residence, Heflin, Alabama.

i. Bruce Knox Evans, son, b. March 5, 1890; married Nellie Mae Grant November 3, 1914; one son; residence Anniston, Alabama.

(4) CYNTHIA BORDERS (BOWLING) WRIGHT, fourth child, was born Sept. 7, 1856; was married to Eli Martin Wright Dec. 17, 1874. Mr. Wright died within a few years. She died at Heflin, Ala., 1919. The children were two, as follows:

1. Lizzie Martin Wright, daughter, born July 9, 1880; married Ulysses Vaughn; has two children, Ruth and Martin. Lives at Heflin, Ala.

2. Elijah Allen Wright, son, born 1882; married —————. Wife deceased. Two children, Flora and Allen. Residence, Heflin, Ala.

(5) SALLY JACKSON (BOWLING) FAULKNER, fifth child, was born December 10, 1861. Was married January 30, 1879, to John Thomas Faulkner. Residence, (1924) 1801 Copeland Avenue N, Birmingham, Ala. J. T. Faulkner was born in Cobb County, Ga., Feb. 7, 1856, and died in Birmingham March 23, 1912. The children of this union were eleven in number, as follows:

1. John Thomas Faulkner, Jr., born and died November, 1879.

2. Maud Virginia Faulkner, da., b. May 26, 1861; died May 28, 1882.

3. Thomas Byron Faulkner, son, b. April 9, 1883; married Katherine Gossett Dec. 2, 1906; one son, Thos. B., Jr., b. Oct. 12, 1909

4. Sarah Blanche Faulkner, da., b. Dec. 12, 1886, was married May 12, 1909, to Walter Douglas Miles; has one da., Sallie Blanche, b. April 29, 1916.

5. William Ralph Faulkner, son, twin to Blanche, b. Dec. 12, 1886; married Nov. 20, 1910, Margaret Kathleen Saunders; has one da., May Christine, b. Aug. 12, 1912.

6. Jacob L. Faulkner, son, b. July 26, 1889. Not married.

7. Frank Elston Faulkner, son, b. Oct. 10, 1891; married April 2, 1910, Dora Williams; has one da., Hazel, b. Nov. 26, 1911.

8. May Faulkner, da., b. May 6, 1894; died Nov. 30, 1898.

9. Ruth Elizabeth Faulkner, da., b. May 20, 1896; was married June 10, 1916, to Melvin D. Jones; has one da., Dorothy Elizabeth, b. Mar. 23, 1919.

10. Fred L. Faulkner, son, b. Mar. 4, 1900; married Nov. 10, 1920, Louise S. Collins, of Biringham, Ala.

11. George Randolph Faulkner, son and last child, b. Nov. 16, 1902.

(6) WILLIAM BISMARCK BOWLING, son and last child of Sarah Elston and Dr. William E. Bowling, was born in Calhoun Co., Ala., Sept 24, 1870. Received high school education. Taught school, studied law, was elected to Congress several terms and is now (1924) serving. Married June 2, 1896, at LaFayette, Ala., Frances Steele Collins, whose parents were from London, Eng. Their children are four in number, as follows:

1. George Randolph Bowling, son, b. March 7, 1897; married Dec. 7, 1922, Sally Susan Dowdell; has one son, George Randolph. Bowling, Jr., b. May 12, 1924. Residence, LaFayette, Ala.

2. Marion Elston Bowling, da., b. Mar. 28, 1899; married to George Luckie Jenkins June 12, 1824. Residence, LaFayette, Ala.

3. Sarah Frances Bowling, da., b. Jan 18, 1901; not married.

4. Elizabeth Bowling, da., died in infancy, 1904

CHILDREN OF SUSAN FRANCES (ELSTON) LUTTRELL AND HARVEY WILKERSON LUTTRELL, OF CALHOUN CO., ALA.

(1) CORRIE LUTTRELL SOWELL, daughter and first child, was born in Oxford, Ala., April 1, 1858. Was married to Charles L. Sowell, of Brewton, Ala., Oct. 22, 1885. Died May 8, 1903. Had no children.

(2) OSCAR FOWLER LUTTRELL, son, b. June 14, 1859. In 1889 he and others organized the Bank of Brewton, at Brewton, Ala., and he served as cashier of this institution for a period of twenty-four years. He married April 12 ,1893, Mollie Magill Oden, daughter of John P. Oden of Syllacauga, Ala. He died in Brewton, Ala., July 23, 1922. The children were four in number, all sons, as follows:

1. A son, not named, born May 20, 1895. Died in infancy.

2. John Oden Luttrell, born Sept. 10, 1896. Married. Residence, Denver, Colorado (1924).

3. Oscar Forney Luttrell, born June 13, 1899. Married in Atlanta, Ga., Aug. 23, 1922, Eliza M. Fariss. Residence, Atlanta.

4. Frank Alex Luttrell, born Dec. 16, 1901. Not married. Lives with his mother in Brewton, Ala.

(3) ELSTON LUTTRELL, third child, born near Oxford, Ala., May 26, 1861. Married in Florida July 15, 1886, Lucy Barber, daughter of James L. and Ellen M. Barber, of Kentucky. Lived some years in Oxford, Ala. Later located in Brewton, Ala., where he has

since been engaged in mercantile business. The children of this union are five in number, as follows:

1. Randolph Luttrell, son, born in Oxford, Ala., May 29, 1888. Married Georgia Binion, daughter of J. T. Binion, of Dothan, Ala., July 4, 1907. Residence, Brewton, Ala., since 1897. The children of this union are: 1, Lucile Luttrell, born July 9, 1909. 2, Randolph Binion Luttrell, born March 26, 1912. 3, Joe Bell Luttrell, born March 1, 1918. 4, Clarence Reid Luttrell, born Feb. 1, 1923.

2. Corrie Luttrell, daughter, born in Oxford, Ala., June 7, 1889. Married Clarence M. Reid, of Fort Deposit, Ala., Dec. 16, 1908. Residence, 509 Finley Avenue, Montgomery, Ala. They have only one child, Lucy Olivia Reid, born Dec. 2, 1911.

3. Annie Laurie Luttrell, daughter, born in Oxford, Ala., December 15, 1891. Married in Brewton, Ala., Aug. 25, 1908, to William Marshall Strong. The children of this union are four: 1, Laurie Barber Strong, born June 23, 1916. 2, George Elston Strong, born Jan. 29, 1918. 3, Lutie May Strong, born Jan. 20, 1920. 4, Marshall Rush Strong, b. June 3, 1923.

4. Harvey Haynes Luttrell, born near Brewton, Ala., April 19, 1894. Served in the World War 1918-19. Married Mary Jane Adams, daughter of John A. Adams, in Montgomery, Ala., Sept. 24, 1919. Residence, Montgomery Ala. No children.

5. Alton Luttrell, born near Brewton, August 24, 1895. Died July 21, 1896.

(4) CHESTER McAULEY LUTTRELL, son, born Oct. 8, 1862. Followed mercantile pursuits all his life. Married October 5, 1886, Augusta Harwell, Oxford, Alabama. Present residence, Bradford, Pennsylvania. Their children are four in number, all daughters, as follows:

1. Juliet Luttrell, born July 31, 1887. Was married to Rev. Royal K. Tucker, of Mobile, Alabama, 1908. Residence (1924) Louisville, Kentucky. They have five children, all girls. (1) Lacl Tucker, born March 28, 1909. (2) Ruth Tucker, born April 21, 1911. (3) Lucile Tucker, born October 29, 1912. (4) Juliet Tucker, born November 20, 1914. (5) Royal Leigh Tucker, born December 10, 1919.

2. Kattie May Luttrell, born January 18, 1900. Was married to Dr. Ernest E. Tucker, of Mobile, Alabama, ————. Residence (1924) New York City. They have two children: (1) Ernest Tucker, born March 20, 1921. (2) Katherine Tucker, born December 12, 1922.

3. Elizabeth Lynn Luttrell, born March 9, 1893. Was married to Lowell S. Langworthy, of Bradford, Pennsylvania, ————. There they yet live and have three children: (1) Mary Lynn Langworthy, born October 20, 1915. (2) Richard Langworthy, born May 21, 1919. (3) Lucile Langworthy, born October 20, 1921.

4. Ethel Lucile Luttrell, born April 28, 1898. Not married. Lives with her sister Katie May Tucker in New York City.

(5) BRUCE FRANCIS LUTTRELL, son, born near Oxford, Ala., July 13, 1868. Married at Evergreen, Alabama, August 4, 1896, Lena Crumpton, daughter of B. H. Crumpton. Has followed mercantile pursuits and is at present located in Tampa, Florida. The children are nine in number, as follows:

1. Suelston Luttrell, daughter, born July 26, 1897. Married October 10, 1920, to Charles A. Barker. Residence, Philadelphia Pa.

2. Ralphine Luttrell, born January 28, 1899. Married July 22, 1915, to Ellis H. Till. No children. Residence, Tampa, Forida.

3. Rush Luttrell, son, born January 17, 1900. Died July 28, 1900.

4. Lucy Grace Luttrell, daughter, born September 12, 1901. Married December 16, 1918, to J. H. Fisher, of Virginia. Has one daughter, Bernadette, born April 1, 1921. Residence, Tampa, Florida.

5. Marcie Luttrell, daughter, born August 3, 1903. Married in Tampa, Florida, June 29, 1921, to Willis W. Henderson. Has two children: (1) Dorothy, born 1922. (2) Geraldine, born 1923.

6. Bruce Luttrell, Jr., son, born August 6, 1905. Not married.

7. Boardman Luttrell, son, born November 28, 1906.

8. Ernestine Luttrell, daughter, born August 17, 1908. Married in Tampa, Florida, May 10, 1924, to Barney Tapp, of Tampa.

9. Lena Luttrell, daughter, born December 25, 1912.

(6) RUSH LUTTRELL, son, born near Oxford, Ala., December 7, 1870. Spent his life in railroad train service. Married in Calera, Alabama, Lutie Blevins. Died May 13, 1924. No children.

(7) A son, not named, born January 4, 1872. Died July, 1872.

(8) KATIE LUTTRELL, daughter, born July 4, 1875. Died August 18, 1875.

(9) MARCY LUTTRELL, son, born January 16, 1877. Was an electrical and mechanical engineer. Electrocuted by accident in Selma, Alabama, December 14, 1903. Not married.

(10 & 11) FRANK and FRED LUTTRELL, twin sons, born March 28, 1879. Fred died August 14, 1879. Frank died August 24, 1879.

CHILDREN AND GRANDCHILDREN OF EVA BORDERS (ELSTON) DeARMAN AND JAMES T. DeARMAN OF CALHOUN COUNTY, ALABAMA

(1) ALMA NEWELL (DeARMAN) BORDERS, daughter, born Nov. 14, 1866. Was married to William C. Borders, Jan. 23, 1884. Died June 14, 1891, in Anniston, Alabama. She had two children, as follows:

1. Sam J. Borders, son, born June 14, 1885. He is an R. F. D. mail carrier and resides at DeArmanville, Alabama.

2. Salie Borders, daughter, born May 2, 1887; was married —— —— to W. O. Chitwood. Residence, DeArmanville, Ala.

(2) CLEFF ELSTON DeARMAN, son, born June 21, 1869. Married Lucy Methvin, of Senoia, Ga., December 28, 1898. Cleff Elston died April 28, 1901, and his wife Lucy died April, 1911. They had no children.

(3) KITTIE TURNIPSEED (DeARMAN) METHVIN, daughter, born July 20, 1873. Was married to D. R. Methvin, of Senoia, Ga., December 27, 1894. Present residence, Anniston, Alabama. There were six children to this union, as follows:

1. Eva Lucile Methvin, born October 4, 1895. Married a Mr. Dye. Residence Anniston, Alabama.

2. D. T. Methvin, born August 12, 1897.

3. Cleff Leon Methvin, born September 26, 1899. Married and resides in Anniston, Alabama.

4. Roy Methvin, born April 22, 1901.

5. Paul Methvin, born September 3, 1903.

6. Kittie Ruth Methvin, born October 14, 1909.

(4) LOUIE JONES DeARMAN, son, born October 31, 1876. Married Ida Rosila Brightmon, of Anniston, Ala., June 27, 1899. Residence Fairfield, Alabama. Their children are seven in number as follows:

1. Hubert Pryor DeArman, born October 29, 1900.

2. Evelyn Louise DeArman, born September 18, 1902; was marred to James Newton Smith, February 15, 1922; has one son, James Newton Smith, (Jr.) born October 3, 1924.

3. Cleff Elston DeArman, (Jr.) born December 15, 1904.

4. Retha Gertrude DeArman, born November 3, 1906.

5. Ida Margaret DeArman, born April 6, 1911.

6. Louie Jones DeArman, (Jr.) born April 6, 1911. (Twin).

7. Virginia Loraine DeArman, born June 29, 1913.

(5) RETHA EVELYN (DeARMAN) McCLURKIN, daughter, born July 9, 1878. Was married to James Walter McClurkin, Anniston, Alabama, April 4, 1906. They reside in Anniston and have four children as follows:

1. James Avery McClurkin, born June 7, 1907.

2. Evelyn Pearl McClurkin, born May 31, 1910.

3. Louie Walter McClurkin, born January 14, 1918.

4. Sarah Retha McClurkin, born May 10, 1918.

(6) PEARL (DeARMAN) OWENS, daughter, born **May 15, 1883**; married December 20, 1910, to Foster Pierce Owens, of Heflin, Alabama. They now reside at Heflin and have three children as follows:

1. Foster Pierce Owens (Jr.), born August 25, 1913.
2. Retha Eva Owens, born November 18, 1916.
3. Annie Pearl Owens, born January 14, 1920.

FAMILY OF ALLEN ELSTON, SR., OF SOUTH CAROLINA AND ALABAMA

Allen Elston, one of the younger sons of David Elston, of **New Jersey**, was born in Eizabeth, New Jersey, January 13, 1782. He naturally followed the fortunes of his father's family in their migrations, first to Wilkes County, North Carolina, then to Tennessee and Kentucky. The father David Elston seems to have finally located in Kentucky near Lexington, possibly then embraced in "The State of Franklin", and to have lived out his life there. But the two sons, John and Allen, in about 1798, being then 24 and 16 years of age respectively, went on further southward and settled in upper South Carolina, in Pendleton District, on the Georgia line. We find these two brothers and their families lived quite close together for several succeeding generations. About 1815 John Elston crossed over the line into Habersham County, Georgia, Allen Elston may have done likewise. They both developed large and valuable agricultural and mercantile interests. Later they decided to try their fortunes further west and in a yet newer country. Accordingly in 1833, "the year the stars fell," Allen Elston moved to the Creek nation and located in the Choccolocco valley in Talladega County. His brother, John Elston, followed him in 1834 and located in the same valley in Benton county. Here their good fortunes followed them. Allen and his sons amassed valuable agricultural and mercantile properties and all lived out their lives in this county. The father, Allen Elston, Sr., died December 9th, 1868, at nearly 87 years of age.

Allen Elston (Sr.) of South Carolina, son of David Elston of New Jersey, as best we can determine from the evidence before us, which however is not absolutely conclusive, married in South Carolina, a first wife who was Ruth Clark, a daughter of Major William Clark and Elizabeth Sevier, daughter of Governor John Sevier. We have no record of any children by this marriage, and the probabilities are that Ruth did not live long after the marriage. Allen married a second wife, Mrs. Annie Blair Terrell, a widow with one daughter, Elizabeth Terrell. This daughter afterwards married William Johnson and had children, one of them Harriet Johnson, who married Charles J. Cooper, of Oxford, Ala., and had a large family. Mrs. Annie Blair (Terrell) Elston is spoken of as a relative of Franklin P. Blair. She was evidently not old at the time of her second marriage. The eleven children mentioned in the family Bible of Allen Elston, Sr., are supposed to all belong to the wife Annie Blair.

Mrs. Porter King, of Atlanta, thinks that her grandfather, Allen Elston, Sr., came to Alabama direct "from the state of Franklin." But members of the John Elston branch seem clear and positive in the conviction that Allen lived in South Carolina, some years as a close neighbor to his brother, John, and moved from there to Alabama in 1833-34.

CHILDREN OF ALLEN ELSTON, SR., OF SOUTH CAROLINA AND ALABAMA

1. Johnathan Lynn ("Jot") Elston, son, born probably about 1815. Died in Talladega, Alabama, in 1887. Was never married. Held offices of trust in the county for a number of years.

2. James Elston, born ————. Followed a successful commercial career. Died ————. Probably never married.

3. Joseph Terrell Elston, son, born ————. Never married.

4. William Elston, son, born ————. Is thought to have married a Miss Cunningham and had two children. Died ————.

5. David Elston, son, born ————. Was a prosperous farmer and merchant in partnership with his brothers. Died about 1850-53. Not married.

6. Netie Caroline Elston, daughter, born January 16, 1823. Married David Hamilton Ramsen (or Remson), of Talladega, Alabama, January 6, 1842. There were eight children by this union: (1) Charles Freeman Remsen, born April 30, 1843; died January 20, 1920. (2) Seaborn Remsen, born 1845; died 1862. (3) Hamilton Remsen, born 1847; married Mattie Best December 5, 1878; died December 12, 1896; left one son. (4) Allen Elston Remsen, born 1849; married Dora Bicham August 27, 1874; died 1907; had one son. (5) Mary Remsen, born 1851; died 1856. (6) Fannie Nannie Remsen, born ————; died in infancy. (7) David Murry Remsen, born September 1, 1861; married Agnes Cunningham April 16, 1884; had five children. (8) Carrie Elston Remsen, born April 3, 1865; married November 21, 1883, to Porter King, of Atlanta, Ga.; had four children. Residence, 696 Peachtree Street, Atlanta.

7. Oliver Allen Elston, Sr., son, born ————. Married Elizabeth Bush, of Calhoun County . Had three daughters and one son. He died in 1857-58. The children are: (1) Alice Elston, married John M. Huey, of Talladega, had several children. (2) Annie Blair Elston, married N. S. McAfee, of Talladega; had no children. (3) Carrie Elston; never married; died in 1914 (4) Oliver Allen Elston, Jr., only son, born in 1857. He and his Uncle "Jot" Elston were for some years the only male representatives of the Elston

name in this branch of the family, and they both died childless; hence the name has now ceased in this branch. Oliver was trained up in the cotton brokerage business in Mobile by his uncle, Albert P. Bush, and was accounted a most exemplary and able business man. He was chosen as the first cashier of the First National Bank of Anniston at its organization and was most highly esteemed by the patrons of that institution. He died in Talladega October 5, 1884, age 27. Never married.

8. **Mary Frances** Elston, daughter, born September 19, 1834. Was married January 17, 1855, to Dr. William Taylor, of Talladega. They had an only son, William Elston Taylor, born June 14, 1856. The mother died May 27, 1857. Dr. William Taylor was born August 18, 1824, in Tennessee, and died April 7, 1907, in Talladega. The son, William Elston Taylor, after growing up, went out to Texas in 1877 and married there in 1879 his half-cousin, Eleanor Elston, daughter of William Elston, of Calhoun County, Alabama. Two sons were born to this union: (a) William Elston Taylor, Jr.; (b) Andrew Law Taylor. In 1884 he returned to Alabama, and on December 25, 1891, married a second wife, Ida Alexander, of Mobile. They reside at 32 Lee Street, Mobile. No children by this union.

9, 10, 11. Mention is made of three sons of Allen Elston, Sr., of South Carolina, and his wife, Annie Blair Elston, who died in infancy. No names or dates given.

Lea

LEA

The Virginia-North Carolina-Tennessee family of Lea is of English extraction. The date assigned for coming to the United States is 1740. The emigrants consisted of two brothers, James and William Lea, and a near relation, John C. Lea The exact relationship of John C. Lea to William and James Lea is not certain, some of the descendants claiming the three as brothers. In any case, they all traced to John Lea, of Lea Hall, Cheshire, England.

The three Leas settled first in Virginia, going in a few years, however, to a point in North Carolina, afterwards called for them, Leasburg. This movement was made in 1749 or 1750. There they established and built an English Church but afterwards became converts to the Baptist denomination. Tradition is authority too, for the statement that the three emigrants decided to adopt each a different spelling of his name, one spelling his name Lee, one Leigh, while the eldest brother retained Lea as they had spelled the name in England.

The Leas of Tennessee are descended from the oldest of the three Emigrants, James Lea. He was born in 1718. He emigrated to America about 1740. His will was made in Orange County, North Carolina. It mentions wife Anne and appoints his three sons, William, John and Major Lea as executors. The will was proved in Caswell County Court, North Carolina March, 1792.

James Lea was born in 1718. He died June 2, 1788. He married Anne Tolbert. They had several children, among them:

I. Luke Lea

II. Major Lea

III. William Lea

IV. John Lea

V. Isabelle Lea

VI. Nancy Lea

VII. ———— Lea, a daughter.

Of the daughters there seems little record, though Isabelle Lea married Captain John Herndon Graves; Nancy Lea, married Paul Hernlson or Henderson and the third daughter is said to have married ———— Green.

I Luke Lea

Luke Lea, son of James Lea, the Emigrant, and Anne Tolbert Lea, was born December 26, 1739. This was probably before his parents left England. He became a Baptist minister. He moved in 1790 to Grainger County, Tennessee, and Lea Springs bears his name. While still in Caswell County, North Carolina he married, May 4, 1759, Elizabeth Wilson born November 26, 1739. He lived until 1813.

They had twelve children:

1. James Lea, born April 3, 1760
2. William Lea, born February 1, 1762
3. Joseph Lea, born February 4, 1764 died young
4. John Lea, born February 24, 1765, died young
5. Mary Elizabeth Lea, born July 31, 1767
6. Joseph Lea, born May 13, 1769
7. Major Lea, born April 21, 1771, married Lavinia Jarnagin
8. John Lea, born March 8, 1773, married Ann Roddy
9. Zachariah Lea, born January 18, 1776 married Sabrina Clay
10. Jefferson Lea, born November 30, 1777
11. David Lea, born December 2, 1779, married Nancy Clay
12. Luke Lea, junior, born January 24, 1783, married Susan Wells McCormick.

James Lea

1. James Lea, son of Luke Lea and Elizabeth Wilson Lea, was born April 3, 1760, died April 7, 1823 and is buried in Mount Vernon burying ground Amite, Miss. He married Elizabeth Roddy who was born 1767 and died 1823.

Their children were:

a. George Roddy Lea, born 11-10-1796 died 3-1-1869 married 1-22-1824, Nancy Paul, b. 1-15-1825, d. 10-7-1869 Amite County, Miss.

b. Dr. Squire Lea, born 1786 near Knoxville, Tennessee. Married in 1814, first Eliza Nelson of Wheeling, Va. second Elizabeth Devall.

Dr. Squire Lea was a surgeon in U. S. Army. Died of wound received in duel with Dr. Harney, also Surgeon in Army. Duel fought on plantation on Bayou Manchac, La.

c. Alexander Lea, born ———— died ———— married Mary Ann May.

d. Franklin Lea no issue

e. Sarah Ann Lea, no issue, married Judge Samuel H. Harper

f. Cecilia Lea, born 5-6-1789, died 4-28-1819, married 2-27-1809 Amite County, Miss., Dr. William Lattimore, b. 2-9-1774, d. 4-3-1843

William Lea

2. William Lea, son of Luke Lea and Elizabeth Wilson Lea, was born February 21, 1762. I have very little record of him. He was an early settler in Kingston, Roane County, Tennessee. He was a Commissioner to locate Anderson, the County seat of Clinton County, Tennessee. on or after 1801.

Joseph Lea

3. Joseph Lea, son of Luke Lea and Elizabeth Wilson Lea, was born February 4, 1764 and died in infancy.

John Lea

4. John Lea, son of Luke Lea and Elizabeth Wilson Lea was born February 24, 1765. He died in infancy.

Mary Elizabeth Lea

5. Mary Elizabeth Lea, daughter of Luke Lea and Elizabeth Wilson Lea, was born July 31, 1767. Of her I have no record.

Joseph Lea

6. Joseph Lea, son of Luke Lea and Elizabeth Wilson Lea, was born May 13, 1769. He was the second child bearing this name the first having died young. He married in Tennessee Mrs. Sartin, a widow with one child, John Sartin, who married Margaret Barnes and settled in Pike County, Miss.

Their children were:
    a. Major Lea
    b. Barton Lea, married Matilda Burkhead
    c. Noble Lea
    d. Luke Lea
    e. Elizabeth Lea
    f. Elceba Lea married Wiley P. Harris of Jackson, Miss.
    g. Lavinia Lea, born 1808 married in 1828 Joseph Newsom.

Major Lea

7. Major Lea, son of Luke Lea and Elizabeth Wilson Lea, was born May 21, 1771. He died July 16, 1822 in Grainger County, Tennessee. He is buried near Lea Springs, Tennessee. He married November 17, 1793 in Jefferson County, Tennessee Lavina Jarnagin born October 2, 1770. She died March 17, 1849 in Grainger County, Tennessee.

Their children were:

a. Pryor Lea (Judge), b. 8-13-1794 Tenn. d. 9- -1880 Goliad, Tex married first Maria Kennedy, issue 3, married second Minerva Heard, married third, Mrs. Mary Perkins.

b. Dr. William Wilson Lea, b. 4-9-1796, d. 2-14-1878 Fulton, Tennessee. Married 12-21-1821 Eliza Augusta Lewis, married second 1854 Mrs. Martha Newton Corprew.

    c. Anderson Lea b. 2-4-1798, d. 1807

    d. Thomas Jarnagin Lea, b. 11-11-1799, d. 10-6-1838.   Married 1822 Mary Carper Talbot

    e. John Hampton Lea, b. 10-12-1801, married Eliza Ann Martin

    f. Cynthia Lea, b. 8.31-1803, d. 7-31-1890, married 2-2-1838 Rev. Elihu Millikan

    g. Harmon Graves Lea, b. 8-24-1805, d. 2- -1887, married 10-2-1827 Johanna Shields

    h. Cecilia Lea, b. 5-2-1807, d. 6- -1807

    i. Albert Miller Lea, b. 7-23-1808, d.———— 1891, married first Ellen Shoemaker, married second Catherine Davey Heath

    j. Luke Lea, b. 11-16-1810 married Mary Mayrant Smith

    k. James Lea, b. 5-22-1814, d. 7-7-1814.

John Lea

8. John Lea, son of Luke Lea and Elizabeth Wilson Lea, was born March 8, 1773. He was the second son to bear that name the other having died in infancy. John Lea was sheriff of Grainger County, Tennessee 1804-1806. He died in 1830. He married Anne Roddy.

Their children were:

    a. Pleasant Miller Lea, born ————, died 1866 Bradley County, Tennessee, married 1831 Martha H. Cravens,

    b. Thomas Lea
    c. John Lea, died in youth
    d. James Lea
    e. Luke Lea
    f. Franklin Lea, born, died 1835, Missouri

    g. Susan Lea, married in 1834, Jesse Roddy of Rhea County, Tennessee.

    h. Isaac Lea, married Minerva Saunders, Bradley County, Tennessee.

Zachariah Lea

9. Zachariah Lea, son of Luke Lea, senior, and Elizabeth Wilson Lea, was born, January 15, 1776, died February 5, 1845 in Amite County, Mississippi, married January 19, 1802, Sabrina Clay (daughter of James Clay and Margaret Muse) born January 14, 1783, died August 11, 1802. Their marriage license was issued in Rutledge, Tennessee.

They had ten children:

    a. Elizabeth Wilson Lea, daughter of Zachariah Lea and Sabrina Clay Lea, was born November 22, 1802, in Granger County,

Tennessee died in Amite County, Mississippi January 6, 1878.   She married twice, first, John Firth; married second, John Everett.

b. Isabella (called Elceba Lea, daughter of Zachtriah Lea and Sabrina Clay Lea, was born March 1, 1805 in Granger County, Tennessee. She died December 22, 1877 in Summit, Miss.   Married twice, first Hon. Jehu Wall; second Richard Bates.   She had no children.

c. Lucinda Clay Lea, daughter of Zachariah Lea and Sabrina Clay Lea, was born in Granger County, Tennessee, March 1, 1805, died December 17, 1886 in Amite County, Miss.   She married John Richmond.

d. Hampton Muse Lea, son of Zachariah Lea and Sabrina Clay Lea was born October 5, 1810 in Amite County, Miss., died in Amite County.

e. Alfred Mead Lea, son of Zachariah Lea and Sabrina Clay Lea, married Elizabeth Garner.

f. Nancy Lea, daughter of Zachariah Lea and Sabrina Clay Lea, married Aaron Robinson.

g. Wilford Zachariah Lea, son of Zachariah Lea and Sabrina Clay Lea, was born December 27, 1815 in Amite County, Miss. He died December 20, 1806 in Amite County, Miss.   He married January 27, 1842, Rachel Powell, born July 6, 1819, died March 10, 1904.

h. James Everett Lea, son of Zachariah Lea and Sabrina Clay Lea, was born July 28, 1819, in Amite County, Miss, died April 25, 1878 in Amite County, Miss.   He married January 15, 1846, Frances Powell, born August 22, 1827, died February 12, 1886.

i. Iverson Green Lea, son of Zachariah Lea and Sabrina Clay Lea.

j. Margaret A. Lea, daughter of Zachariah Lea and Sabrina Clay Lea, died at twenty, unmarried.

Jefferson Lea

10. Jefferson Lea, son of Luke Lea and Elizabeth Wilson Lea was born November 30, 1777.   He died December 25, 1830 in Mississippi.   He married September 21, 1709 in Jefferson County, Tennessee, Elizabeth Farley.   Their children were:

a. Jefferson Lea, junior, born August 17, 1800, died 1863

b. Caswell Lea, born March 31, 1801

c. Matilda Lea, born December 1, 1803 married in 1825

d. ———— Lea, born ———— unmarried

e. Sheppard Lea, born April 20, 1808

f. Maria Lea, born August 3, 1812, married Oliver Garner

g. Tennessee Lea, born April 20, 1815, married James Tate

    h. Latimore Lea, born April 9, 1818

    i. Rowan Lea, born March 10, 1819, married Maria Bazoon

    j. Lavinia Lea, born January 21, 1822, married John Travis.

David Lea

    11. David Lea, son of Luke Lea and Elizabeth Wilson Lea was born December 2, 1770, died December 5, 1844.   He married, February 2, 1802, Nancy Clay, born January 22, 1780 died October 13, 1858.

    They had twelve children:

    a. Margaret Muse Lea, born January 2, 1803, married Agrippa Gayden

    b. Wesley Wilson Lea, born November 17, 1804, died June 24, 1861, unmarried.

    c. Wilson Dixon Lea, born January 28, 1807, died May 4, 1849, married May 14, 1833, Virginia Caroline Kemp

    d. Winchester Muse Lea, born August 11, 1809, died November 21, 1809

    e. Landon Ludwell Lea, born October 16, 1810, died July 8, 1890. Married twice, first, Emily Robinson, September 8, 1836; second, Charlsey Jane Edwards, November 9, 1845.

    f. Martha Melissa Lea, born February 18, 1813, died September 19, 1813.   She married twice, first, William McMatthews; second John W. Courtney.

    g. James Monroe Lea, born May 16, 1815.   Died at Oakland College, Miss.

    h. Robert Montgomery Lea, born October 7, 1817, died August 30, 1855; married Letty Edwards.

    i. Mary Reed Lea, born February 6, 1820, died September 14, 1884.   Married Thomas Gordon, first and married second, Samuel Lee.

    j. David Clay Lea, born November 4, 1821.   Died October 4, 1847.   Married September 10, 1843.   Married Nancy Edwards.

    k. Julia Clay Lea, born October 16, 1823, died December 5, 1840, unmarried.

    l. Charles Clinton Lea, born November 12, 1827, died at Oakland College, Mississippi.

Luke Lea

    12. Luke Lea, junior, son of Luke Lea and Elizabeth Wilson Lea, was born in Surry County, North Carolina, January 26, 1782. He moved with his father to the new country afterwards Tennessee, in 1790, and when he attained his majority he was elected clerk of the House of Representatives.   He served in the Creek and Seminole War, under General Jackson.   He was elected to Congress.

He was appointed Indian Agent by President Taylor. He was killed by being thrown from his horse, July 17, 1851. He married Susan Wells McCormick the only child of Ann Armstrong McCormick and John McCormick. Their marriage took place about 1810. They had eight children, namely:

1. James Armstrong Lea

2. John McCormick Lea

3. Francis Wells Lea

4. William Park Lea

5. Ann E. Lea

6. Susan Lea

7. Lavinia Lea

8. Margaret Lea

9. ———— a son Luke Lea, junior died in youth.

1. James Armstrong Lea, son of Susan Wells McCormick Lea and Luke Lea died unmarried in Mexican War.

2. John McCormick Lea, son of Susan Wells McCormick Lea and Luke Lea was born in Knoxville, December 25, 1818. He married Elizabeth Overton in Memphis, Tennessee, in 1845. Elizabeth Overton Lea died September 13, 1890. They had Children:

a. Overton Lea

b. Robert Lea

c. Luke Lea

Of these:

Overton Lea, born ————, died 1903, married Ella Cocke and had four children, namely:

Overton Lea, Jr.

Laura Lea.

Luke Lea.

Elizabeth Lea.

Overton Lea, Jr., died unmarried.

Laura Lea, daughter of Overton Lea and Ella Cocke Lea, married William Clendenning Robertson and has four children Eva Lea Robertson, who married Harold Hinton and lives in Paris; Ella Lea Robertson who married Thomas Meek Carothers and has one child, Mildred Ragon Carothers; William Clendenning Robertson, Jr., and Laura Lea Robertson.

Luke Lea, son of Overton Lea and Ella Cocke Lea, was born in 1879. He was Senator from Tennessee and during the World War commanded a regiment and served abroad for the entire period of the War. He married twice. His first wife was Mary Louise Warner, daughter of Percy Warner, by whom he had two sons, Luke Lea Jr., and Percy Warner Lea. Mary Louise Warner Lea died during the War, while her husband was in France. Several years later Col. Luke Lea married her sister, Percy Warner. Col. Luke Lea and Percy Warner Lea have a daughter, Mary Louise Lea.

Elizabeth Lea, the second daughter of Overton Lea and Elizabeth Cocke Lea married J. O. Fordock.

(3) Francis Wells Lea, son of Susan Wells McCormick and Luke Lea was born————.He married Rebecca Callaway Donohue.

(4.) William Park Lea, son of Susan Wells McCormick Lea and Luke Lea was born ————. He married Ellen McCallie. Some records say he married Kate McCallie.

(5.) Ann E. Lea, daughter of Susan Wells McCormick Lea and Luke Lea was born————. She married James Bernard.

6. Susan Lea, daughter of Susan Wells McCormick Lea and Luke Lea was born ————. She married Thomas Howard Callaway.

Susan Jane Lea Callaway and Thomas Howard Callaway had eleven children as follows:

a. Joseph Callaway.

b. Luke Lea Callaway.

c. Lucy Callaway.

d. Benjamin Callaway.

e. Thomas H. Callaway, Jr.

f. Susan Callaway.

g. James Callaway.

h. Margaret Callaway.

i. John Lea Callaway.

j. Annie Barnard Callaway.

k. Frank E. Callaway.

Of the foregoing.

a.   Joseph Callaway, son of Susan Jane Lea Callaway and Thomas H. Callaway, born September 16, 1847, died September 1, 1890, married Julia Anderson , May, 1870. They had two children, Susan Lea Callaway and Joseph Jacques Callaway.

b. Luke Lea Callaway, son of Susan Jane Lea Callaway and Thomas H. Callaway, was born May 19, 1850, died August 7, 1921. He married first Caroline Johnson and had two children, namely, Thomas H. Callaway and Lucy Callaway, and married second Caledonia Montgomery and had six children, namely, Benjamin Callaway, Hettie Callaway, Flora Callaway, Ida Callaway, Inez Callaway and Frances Callaway.

c. Lucy Callaway, daughter of Susan Jane Lea Callaway and Thomas H. Callaway, was born June 25, 1852, died November 5, 1871. She married James A. Johnson, of Madisonville, Tenn., December 16, 1870.

d. Benjamin Callaway, son of Susan Jane Lea Callaway and and Thomas H. Callaway, born June 17, 1857, died October 25, 1889. He married Maggie Thompson. They had four children, namely: Luke Callaway, Campbell Callaway, John Callaway, Robert Callaway.

e. Thomas H. Callaway, Jr., son of Susan Jane Lea Callaway Thomas H. Callaway, was born June 17, 1857, died October 25, 1889. He married first Carrie Coleman, of Atlanta, November 10, 1880, and had one child, Carrie Coleman Callaway, and married second Susan McEnery, of Louisiana, in 1887. They had one child, Lea McEnery Callaway.

f. Susan Callaway, daughter of Susan Jane Lea Callaway and Thomas H. Callaway, was born August 6, 1859, died March 18, 1862.

g. James H. Callaway, son of Susan Jane Lea Callaway and Thomas H. Callaway, was born September 11, 1861, died September 16, 1920. He married Lula Harrison and had nine children, namely: Joseph Callaway, Eizabeth Callaway, Annabelle Callaway, Thomas Callaway, Henry Callaway, James Callaway, Jr., Lula Callaway, Merrick Callaway and Lea Callaway.

h. Margaret Callaway, daughter of Susan Jane Lea Callaway and Thomas H. Callaway, was born April 15, 1863. She married James Burch Carson September 6, 1862, and had six children, namely: James Gray Carson, Thomas Callaway Carson, Robert Lea Carson, Joseph Armstrong Carson, John McCormick Carson and Susan Barnard Carson.

i. John Lea Callaway, son of Susan Jane Lea Callaway and Thomas H. Callaway, was born September 23, 1865. He married Florence Newton, of Atlanta, June 16, 1892. They have three children, namely: Newton Callaway, Frank Callaway and John Lea Callaway, Jr.,

j. Annie Barnard Callaway, daughter of Susan Jane Lea Callaway and Thomas H. Callaway, was born October 4, 1867. She married Dr. H. Gray Hutchinson, of Atlanta, October 23, 1893.

k. Frank Callaway, son of Susan Jane Lea Callaway and Thomas H. Callaway, was born June 24, 1870. He died January, 1873.

(7) Lavinia Lea, daughter of Susan Wells McCormick Lea and Luke Lea was born————. She married three times, first John Calvin Henderson and second Samuel Smith and third Joseph Ernest. By her first marriage she had one child, Susan Wells Henderson.

Susan Wells Henderson married David M. Nelson anl had four children, Ann Stuart Nelson, who married R. R. Evans, lives in Griffin, Georgia, and has one child Minnie Evans, who married first Hugh L. Bayley and had two children, Hugh L. Bayley Jr., and Robert Evans Bayley and married second Hamilton Fish, of New Orleans; Thomas R. Nelson, who lives in Chicago; Luke Lea Nelson, who lives in St. Louis; Inez Nelson, who married Thomas Deaderick and had one son who died in infancy.

8. Margaret Lea, daughter of Susan Wells McCormick Lea and Luke Lea was born in 1831. She married Henry Benton Henegar. Their handsome homestead in Charleston, Tennessee, is still standing. They had four children.

Edward Henegar

Ann Henegar

Lucy Henegar

Lavinia Henegar

Lucy Henegar married William B. Allen, of Charleston, Tennessee and has one daughter, Margaret E. Allen.

Lavinia Henegar married Luther D. Campbell of Cleveland, Tennessee.

Ann Henegar married George T. White, of Chattanooga, Tennessee, and had three children: Edward White who died young; Benton White, who married Harriet Bauman; and Margaret Lea White, who married Gardner Bright and has two children, Ann Henegar Bright and George T. Bright, born August, 1924.

Edward Henegar married Mamie MacMillan, of Knoxville. (See MacMillan Family, Volume I, Notable Southern Families). They had six children: Margaret Henegar, who died young; Anne Henegar, who married Matthew Thomas and has two daughters, Mary Henegar Thomas and Barbara Thomas; Mamie Henegar, who married Edward John MacMillan and has two children, Nancy Alexander MacMillan and Helen Briscoe MacMillan; Herbert Hall Henegar, who married Josephine Kendall; Martin Condon Henegar; and Henry Benton Henegar.

II Major Lea

Major Lea, son of James Lea and Ann Tolbert Lea, was born 1741. He died November 19, 1843 being over one hundred years old, in Powell's Valley near Cumberland Gap, Tennessee. He was a magistrate in Grainger County, Tennessee, in 1796. Major is a name and not a title and it is repeated many times in the family. Major Lea married Elizabeth Herndon.

Major Lea and Elizabeth Herndon Lea had several children, among them:

1. Herndon Lea

2. Abner Lea

3. Major Lea, junior

Of these:

Herndon Lea

1. Herndon Lea, son of Major Lea and Elizabeth Herndon Lea, was born in 1765. He was given his mother's name of Herndon. He married Fannie Hightower and had a son Eppa Lea, born April 11, 1792 in Caswell County, N. C. He moved to Jefferson County, Tennessee with his parents in 1806 and to Anderson County near Clinton in 1839. He married ———— ———— and had a son, Gideon B. R. Lea, who married Mrs. Nannie Tunnell, born, Cox, October 13, 1870, in Anderson County, Tennessee. Mrs. Tunnell Lea was born March 11, 1840, Anderson County, Tennessee, married William C. Tunnell, September 25, 1861. He was born March 17, 1831, the son of Samuel and Sarah (MacKamey) Tunnell. William C. and Fannie Cox Tunnell, had one son, Samuel, born October 20, 1862, who is Cashier of Oliver Springs, Tennessee, bank. William C. Tunnell died shortly after or before his son was born.

Abner Lea

2. Abner Lea, son of Major Lea and Elizabeth Herndon Lea, was born about 1770. He married Mary Dodson.

Major Lea, junior

3. Major Lea, junior, son of Major Lea and Elizabeth Herndon Lea was born February 26, 1775. He died August 8, 1821. He married in Jefferson County, Tennessee, about 1800, Rhoda Jarnagin, who was born January 26, 1778 and died December 21, 1852 near Cleveland, Tennessee. Their children were:

a. Caswell Lea, born August 21, 1802.

b. Alfred Lea, born February 15, 1804.

c. Herndon Houston Lea, born November 25, 1805.

d. Pleasant John Graves Lea, born November 6, 1807.

    e. Anna Jarnagin Lea, born December 22, 1809.

    f. William Pinckney Lea, born May 17, 1812.

    g. Preston Jarnagin Lea, born October 20, 1814.

    h. Eliza Adaline Lea, born October 12, 1817.

    i. Pryor Newton Lea, born March 14, 1820.

VI Nancy Lea

Nancy Lea, daughter of James Lea and Anne Tolbert Lea was born about 1737.   She married 1754, Paul Haralson, son of Peter Haralson and his wife ———— Chambers Haralson.   Peter Haralson died about 1750 and after his death his sons moved to Orange County, N. C. and settled on Hyco River.

Nancy Lea Harlason and Paul Harlason had thirteen children, eight sons and five daughters, but I know the names of only two sons.

    1. Herndon Haralson

    2. Jonathon Haralson

Of these:

Herndon Haralson

Herndon Haralson, son of Nancy Lea Haralson and Paul Haralson, was born October 12, 1757.   He died May 27, 1847.   He was Deputy Surveyor, County of Caswell, N. C. 1777-1780.   He organized a Volunteer Company and joined the Army under General Greene.   He moved to Tennessee in 1820.   He married Mary Murphey, born March 13, 1771, died September 13, 1847.   Their children were:

    a. Archibald Haralson, born July 5, 1792.

    b. Jonathon Haralson, born February 12, 1794.

    c. Herndon Haralson, born January 20, 1796.

    d. Paul Haralson, born June 20, 1798.

    e. Green Lea Haralson, born July 27, 1800.

    f. Betsy Murphey Haralson, born August 2, 1802.

    g. William Henry Haralson, born September 2, 1805.

    h. James Madison Haralson, born April 3, 1807.

    i. Jane Ann Haralson, born November 6, 1809.

    j. Mary Herndon Haralson, born July 7, 1813.

    k. John Haywood Haralson, born June 24, 1817.

Jonathon Haralson

2. **Jonathon Haralson,** son of Nancy Lea Haralson and Paul Haralson was born about 1759. He lived and died near Greensboro, Georgia. He married twice. By his first wife ——— ——— he had two sons, Vincent Haralson and Herndon Haralson, Jr. By his second wife, Clara Browning Culberson Haralson he had three sons. William Browning Haralson, (born June 10, 1799, died May 22, 1879), Kinoheon Lea Haralson, (moved from La Grange, Georgia to Brownsville, Texas and thence to Austin, Texas), and Hugh A. Haralson, (who represented the State of Georgia for twelve years in Congress. The County of Haralson in Georgia is named for him.)

Fannie Heaslip Lea

Fannie Heaslip Lea, born October 30, 1884, the story writer, who married H. P. Agee, of Honolulu, is a daughter of James John Lea, who married Louis Skillman and a great-granddaughter of Dr. S. Squire Lea, born 1786 near Knoxville, who married first, Miss Eliza Nelson, of Wheeling, Virginia and second Elizabeth Devalland, a great-granddaughter of James Lea, who married Elizabeth Roddy and a great-great-grandfather of the Reverend Luke Lea, who married Elizabeth Wilson.

Park

PARK

This family originating in Southern France took the name Parc. Members of this family fled from France to Scotland and subsequently to the north of Ireland at the time of the massacre of St. Bartholomew and later at the Revocation of the Edict of Nantes. The spelling Parc yielded to Park and descendants of th's family have never recognized any other spelling, since that first change was made. The descendants of the Huguenot family of Parc remained in Ireland for many generations, always adhering vigorously to the Protestant cause. Ultimately many of the family emigrated to America, where they cling presistently to the name without an e and without an s.

They emigrated from Ireland to Pennsylvania as many of the North of Ireland Protestant families did. From that point the tide of emigration drifted South, some to South Carolina, some to South Western Virginia and eventually to North Carolina and Tennessee. In 1722 Joseph Park, son of Arthur Park of Donegal County, Ireland, supposedly of the Huguenot strain, emigrated to West Chester County, Pennsylvania. His wife was Mary, his daughter was Mistress Ann Noble, and his sons were John, Joseph, junior, and Samuel. It is said they all served in the Revolution and it is certain that John served as a Lieutenant and that his son was also in the War and that he died of wounds received. John the son had moved to South Carolina. It is significant that the Calhouns, who also had a daughter married to a Noble, had emigrated from County Donegal, Ireland, had settled first in Pennsylvania and later in South Carolina. John Park is said to have many descendants in South Carolina and in Georgia.

The distinguished Park family of Tennessee comes without a doubt through the French Parc, the Huguenot family which fled to Ireland from Southern France at the time of the Massacre of Saint Bartholomew or later at the Revocation of the Edict of Nantes.

It is of this family that the late Dr. James Park of Knoxville, is descended.

Andrew Park of County Donegal, Ireland, is the first ancestor, of whom we have record, of the Tennessee family. He may have been a son or grand-son of Arthur Park who was living in Donegal in 1700.   The names in the families of both are similar and every indication points to close kinship.   Andrew Park was born in County Donegal about 1720.   He had a son Robert Park, born about 1740.   Robert Park married Nancy Aiken about the year 1762.

Their home was Balleighan, Manor Cunningham, County Donegal, Ireland.

Their children were:

Andrew Park, junior

Robert Park, junior

Joseph Park

James Park, born April 14, 1770

William Park

Nathan Park

Elizabeth Park

Nancy Park

The information concerning this family was gathered by the late Dr. James Park, of Knoxville.   He secured the foregoing information from Ireland by correspondence and printed a brief pamphlet for private circulation among his kinspeople.   The matter has been rearranged but is all substantially Dr. Park's.

Concerning the foregoing children of Robert Park and Nancy Aiken Park.

ANDREW PARK, JUNIOR

Andrew Park, junior, son of Robert Park and Nancy Aiken Park, was born in County Donegal, Ireland, about 1765.   He married Jean Henderson, of Bellyholly, September 15, 1796.   They had three daughters, Mary Park, Nancy Park and Peggy Park and one son Robert Park who died at the age of twenty-one.   Peggy Park married Robert McKinley and had two daughters.   Andrew Park, junior, and his family did not emigrate to America but remained in County Donegal, Ireland.

ROBERT PARK, JUNIOR

Robert Park, junior, son of Robert Park and Nancy Aiken Park was born about 1767.   He emigrated to America about 1793.   He located in Boonsboro, Md., and married Mary ————.   He had a son Robert Park, III, who arrived in Knoxville, Tennessee, to join relatives and there married Evelina Mason, daughter of John Mason. Robert Park, III, and Elizabeth Mason Park had four children, two daughters and two sons.   He moved with his family to Alabama where he died.   Robert Park, junior, the emigrant, had a daughter

———————— Park, who married ———————— Miller.   They had a son,
Park Miller, who was in Knoxville between 1840 and 1850.

JOSEPH PARK

Joseph Park, son of Robert Park and Nancy Aiken Park was
born in County Donegal about 1768.   He emigrated to America
about 1793, settling first in Lexington, Virginia.   He moved to
Rogersville, Tennessee, and later to Nashville where he died
unmarried.

JAMES PARK

James Park, son of Robert Park and Nancy Aiken Park, was
born in County Donegal, Ireland, April 14, 1770.   He is the
ancestor of a large and interesting family and will be written of
fully at the close of the paragraphs relating to his brothers and
sisters.

WILLIAM PARK

William Park, son of Robert Park and Nancy Aiken Park, was
born in County Donegal, Ireland, about 1772.   He emigrated to
America with his brother James Park in 1796.   They stopped for a
time in Baltimore where they had kinsmen, John Kennedy, father it
is supposed of John Pendleton Kennedy, and others.   They then went
to Chambersburg, Pennsylvania, where they stayed a while.   Finally
they moved to Knoxville, Tennessee, where they entered the
mercantile business and lived the remainder of their lives.   William
Park married about 1810 Jane Crozier Armstrong, daughter of
Colonel James Armstrong known as Trooper Armstrong.   William
Park was an elder in the Presbyterian church.   He died August 31,
1846.   Jane Crozier Armstrong Park died 1848.

William Park and Jane Crozier Armstrong had six children,
namely:

(1.)   Robert Park, who died in infancy.

(2.)   Susan Wells Park, born August 31, 1812, who married Dr.
Leonidas Baker in 1829 and after his death married James C. Moses,
leaving children by both marriages.   She died March 9, 1894.

(3.)   Ann Elizabeth Park, born 1816, married in 1839 James
Houston Armstrong (not related to her grandfather, Colonel James
(Trooper) Armstrong).   She had three sons, William Park
Armstrong, who married Alice Isbell and lived in Selma, Alabama;
Robert Armstrong, who never married; and Frank Armstrong, who
married Lazinka White and had one daughter May Armstrong.   For
the history of these Armstrongs see Notable Southern Families
Volume I.   Ann Eliza Park Armstrong died March 6, 1886.

(4.)   Sophia Moody Park, born June 5, 1817, married 1837
George W. Churchwell and died May 1898.

(5.)   Mary Jane Park, born 1819, died 1844, unmarried.

(6.)   Naomi Park, born 1821.   Died young.

NATHAN PARK

Nathan Park, son of Robert Park and Nancy Aiken Park, was born in Donegal County, Ireland, about 1774.   He emigrated to America in 1798 and arrived in Knoxville to   join   his   brothers William and James Park in the same year.   He died unmarried in 1818.

ELIZABETH PARK

Elizabeth Park, daughter of Robert Park and Nancy Aiken Park was born in County Donegal, Ireland, about 1776.   She married James Culbert.   She did not emigrate but her   oldest child did emigrate to America.   She had seven children. Mathew Culbert, her oldest child came to the United States in 1830.   He went to Knoxville, Tennessee, Winchester and Fayetteville and later to Alabama where he died unmarried.   Some of the daughters of James Culbert and Elizabeth Park Culbert also emigrated to   America   and   were visited several times by Dr. James Park in the period between 1843 and 1846.

NANCY PARK

Nancy Park, daughter of Robert Park and Nancy Aiken Park was born in County Donegal, about 1778.   She married James Armour and had four sons and two daughters.   She did   not   emigrate   to America.

Before taking up the history of James Park, son of Robert Park and Nancy Aiken Park, we quote from Dr. Park's pamphlet.   He says:

"Their connections in Ireland were with the Campbells, Kennedys, Alexanders, Duchanahs, Blackwoods, Reids, Tarens, Harris, Fisks, Stuarts and others.   How these connections came about I only know in part.   Patrick Campbell, son of Hugh, near Ramelton, married Margaret Park, sister of Robert Park, of Balleighan, and aunt of James and William Park, of Knoxville.   Hugh and Andrew Campbell, sons of Patrick and Margaret Campbell, came to the United States before 1800, and located in Rodgersville, Tennessee, where Hugh married and died without issue.

"Andrew Campbell moved to Middle Tennessee, married Mary Caldwell, of Shelbyville, who bore him two sons—William P. and John.   She died and he then married Jane   Campbell,   of   the Virginia and East Tennessee Campbells, and they had four children,

Arthur, Margaret, Elizabeth and Jane. William P. Campbell reared a family in Williamson County, Tennessee. Margaret marr:ed John Marshall, of Franklin, Tennessee. John settled in Louisville, Kentucky, and Arthur went to Mississippi, and a son of his, William A. Campbell, lives in Columbus, Mississippi. Others of the Campbell connection, Patrick, William S. and Andrew, brothers, came over and settled in Williamson County, Tennessee, about 1839, and John, another brother, came over in 1853 with his family. These Campbells are in Williamson and Davidson Counties, and Memphis, Tennessee, Little Rock, Arkansas, Mobile, and other places.

"Robert Buchanan, a cousin of the Parks, lived with them in Knoxville about 1805-1810, then went to Nashville, where he married Elizabeth Turley. He died in 1829, leaving two daughters—Maggie and Sallie. Maggie died unmarried. Sallie married Thomas Plater, January, 1851, and four children were born to them, viz.: Elizabeth, Eveline, Roxbury and Thomas, all of whom are deceased, except Elizabeth, who married E. S. Gardner, :n Nashville. Mr. Gardner died January 26, 1901, leaving her with a son—E. S. Gardner, junior, who was born June 5, 1872.

"Old letters from Andrew Park and his sisters in Ireland to my father, which are in my possession speak of 'Uncle John Kennedy,' 'Cousin John Kennedy, of Baltimore,' 'Aunt Harris' family,' 'Uncle John Tarens,' 'Cousin John Fisk,' 'Cousin William Stuart, of Glencoe,' but I do not know how the connections came.

"As to Alexander connection with the Park family I only know that the Alexander clan in Rockbridge County, Virginia, (including the Reverend Doctor Archibald Alexander, of Princeton, New Jersey,) claimed kinship with the Knoxville Park family. Mrs. Elizabeth Mc-Clung, of Stanton, Virgin:a, (who was a sister of Doctor Alexander, and knew my uncles, Joseph and William Park, told me, in 1846, of the connection between the two famil:es. Since that I have learned that an Archibald Alexander, of Scotland, emigrated to Ireland with his family, including three sons, and settled in Manor Cunningham, Donegal County, and Archibald Alexander, born in Manor Cunningham, February 4, 1708, married his cous:n, Margaret Park, December 31, 1734; and a Thomas Alexander, son of Archibald, the Scotch emigrant, married a sister of Joseph Park, who, I suppose, was my father's great-grand-father, and among the early Park settlers in Donegal."

JAMES PARK

James Park, son of Robert Park and Nancy A:ken Park was born in Balleighan, Manor Cunningham, County Donegal, Ireland, April 14, 1770. It is by the exact date of his birth preserved in h:s family Bible that the birth dates of his brothers and s:sters are predicated.   He emigrated to the United States in 1796 with his brother William Park.   They stopped for a short while in Baltimore, where they had kinsmen, then went to Chambersburg, Pa., for a period and finally settled in Knoxville, Tennessee, in 1798. They entered the mercantile business.   They were both elders in the Presbyterian church.   February 23, 1804, James Park was married to Sophia Moody by the Reverend Samuel Carrick, founder and first Pastor of the Presbyterian Church in Knoxville.

Sophia Moody was born in Wilmington, Delaware, April 2, 1780. Her sister had married Thomas Brown who settled in Knoxville about 1797 and Sophia Moody had come to Knoxville with her sister and brother-in-law.   They lived on what is now Kingston Pipe two miles from Knoxville.   James Park owned property adjoining Thomas Brown's place and when he was wounded by some people who had taken adverse possession he was taken to the home of Mr. and Mrs. Brown and was nursed by Mrs. Brown and Miss Moody.   When he recovered he married Miss Sophia Moody.

Their children were:

1.   Nancy Aiken Park

2.   Andrew Park

3.   William Park

4.   Sophia Moody Park

5.   Eliza Park

6.   Mary Park

7.   Harriet Park

8.   Joseph Park

9.   Margaret Park

10.   Jane Park

11.   James Park

12.   Carrick White Park.

Nancy Aiken Park

Nancy Aiken Park, daughter of James Park and Sophia Moody Park, was born in Knoxville, December 7, 1804.   She married October 25, 1821, Charles Andrew Carrick White, born December 22, 1797, son of Hugh Lawson White and Elizabeth Carrick White. Charles Andrew Carrick White died January 18, 1826, Nancy Aiken White died February 23, 1826.   Their children were:

(1.)   Sophia Elizabeth White, born August 6, 1822.
(2.)   Hugh Lawson White, born March 27, 1824.
(3.)   James Park White, born December 24, 1825.

Of the foregoing:

(1.) Sophia Elizabeth White, born August 6, 1822, died June 19, 1850, married September 28, 1841, Robert Craighead (died September 30, 1884). They had four children:

a. James Park Craighead, born January 6, 1841, died March 26, 1888.

b. Elizabeth Lawson Craighead, born May 12, 1846, died in infancy.

c. Hugh Lawson Craighead, born October 26, 1848, died January 5, 1904. Married June 19, 1878, Elizabeth Lea Overton.

(2.) Hugh Lawson White, born March 27, 1824, died May 12, 1843. He was just nineteen and was, I presume, unmarried, as I do not find any other information regarding him in Dr. Park's notes.

(3.) James Park White, born December 24, 1825, died December 27, 1826.

Andrew Park

Andrew Park, son of James Park and Sophia Moody Park was born in Knoxville March 2, 1896. He died February 2, 1871. He married April 22, 1830, Amanda Morgan. She died in St. Louis December 25, 1901.

William Park

William Park, son of James Park and Sophia Moody Park was born in Knoxville December 14, 1807. He died November 24, 1895. He married Sarah J. Crockett (a daughter of Franklin T. Crockett), October 26, 1836. William Park died in Columbia, Tennessee November 24, 1895. Sarah J. Crockett Park died in Columbia, February 18, 1879. Their children were:

(1.) James Park, born February 25, 1837, died January 24, 1873.

(2.) Samuel Crockett Park, born August 2, 1839.

(3.) Frances Bland Park, born October 28, 1841.

(4.) William Park, junior, born March 16, died in infancy.

(5.) Helen Dudley Park, born January 30, 1848, died in infancy.

(6.) Sallie Park, born August 1, 1849, died in infancy.

(7.) William Park, junior, (second of name) born January 21, 1851, died March 4, 1899.

(8.) Virginia Dudley Park, born December 20, 1852.

(9.) Madeleine Park, born October 13, 1854.

(10.) Marshall Park, born October 26, 1859, died in infancy.

Of the foregoing:

(1.) James Park, son of William Park and Sarah J. Crockett Park, born February 25, 1837, died January 24, 1873.

(2.) Samuel Crockett Park, son of William Park and Sarah J. Crockett Park was born August 2, 1839 died October 8, 1896.

(3. Frances Bland Park, daughter of William Park and Sarah J. Crockett Park, born October 28, 1841, died young.

(4.) William Park, junior, son of William Park and Sarah J. Crockett Park, born March 16, 1846, died in infancy.

(5.) Helen Dudley Park, daughter of William Park and Sarah J. Crockett Park, born January 30, 1848, died in infancy.

(6.) Sallie Park, daughter of William Park and Sarah J. Crockett Park, born August 1, 1849, died in infancy

(7.) William Park, junior, (second child given this name) son of William Park and Sarah J. Crockett Park was born January 21, 1851. He died March 4, 1899. He married October 6, 1880, Eva Lytle of Murfreesboro. Their children:

a. Madeleine Park, born December 13, 1882 (who married James Cason November 19, 1902 and has a son John Favor Cason, born March 23, 1906).

b. Sarah Park, born January 14, 1885, married Charles Twinum of Chattanooga and has one child, a daughter.

c. Ridgely Dashiel Park, born August 23, 1887.

(8.) Virginia Dudley Park, daughter of William Park and Sarah J. Crockett Park, was born December 21, 1852. She died——. She married John J. Vertrees of Nashville June 16, 1886. They had a son.

a. John J. Vertrees, junior, born March 19, 1887.

(9.) Madeleine Park, daughter of William Park and Sarah J. Crockett Park, was born October 13, 1854. She died ——————. She married N. B. Sheperd, Columbia, Tennessee August 21, 1891.

(10.) Marshall Park, son of William Park and Sarah J. Crockett Park, was born October 26, died in infancy.

Sophia Moody Park

Sophia Moody Park, daughter of James Park and Sophia Moody Park was born in Knoxville November 7, 1808. She died April 30, 1894. She married George McNutt White (son of Moses White) November 29, 1827. George McNutt White died in Knoxville December 1884.

Their children were:

(1.) Nancy Park White

(2. Moses White

(3.) Sophia Moody White, died young

(4.) Isabella McNutt White

(5.) Naomi Jane White, died young

(6.) James Park White

(7.) Hugh White

(8.) Margaret White

(9.) Sophia Moody White (second child of name)

(10.) Amanda Morgan White

(11.) George McNutt White, junior

(12.) Andrew Park White

(13.) Carrick White

Of the foregoing:

(1.) Nancy Park White, daughter of Sophia Moody Park White and George McNutt White was born, August 13, 1828. She died December 27, 1898. She married November 18, 1847, Albert G. Welcker (died May 4, 1868).

a. Mary Elizabeth Welcker, born September 23, 1848, died in infancy.

b. Sophia White Welcker, born February 5, 1850, died in infancy.

c. Katherine Welcker, born October 23, 1851, died November 24, 1872. She married William J. McNutt, January 18, 1872 and had one child, Katherine Welcker McNutt, born November 14, 1872. Katherine Welcker McNutt married February 8, 1893, R. P. Johnson and had three children namely: Ellen Armstrong Johnson, born November 28, 1893; William McNutt Johnson, born October 21, 1896; and Margaret Houseley Johnson, born January 5, 1902.

d. George Henry Welcker, born December 9, 1853, died in infancy.

e. Isabella Clinton Welcker, born January 9, 1857. She married Edward E. MacMillan January 5, 1882. They had four children namely: Elizabeth MacMillan born ——— died young; Margie Belle MacMillan, born ——— (married Hal Bartlett Mebane January 10, 1905 and has two sons, Edward MacMillan, born _____ and Hal Bartlett Mebane, junior, born ———); Edward John MacMillan, born ———, (married Mamie Henegar ——— and has two children, Nancy Alexander MacMillan and Helen Briscoe Mac-Millan); and Helen MacMillan, born ——— (married Lucian Briscoe).

f. Albert G. Welcker, junior, born January 16, 1858, died in infancy.

(2.) Moses White, son of George McNutt White and Sophia Moody Park White was born, December 19, 1829.

(3.) Sophia Moody White, daughter of George McNutt White and Sophia Moody Park White was born, October 26, 1831. She died young.

(4.) Isabella McNutt White, daughter of George McNutt White and Sophia Moody Park White was born, July 30, 1833.

(5.) Naomi Jane White, daughter of George McNutt White and Sophia Moody Park White was born, January 11, 1835. She died young.

(6.) James Park White, son of George McNutt White and Sophia Moody Park White was born, June 23, 1837. He died July 2, 1906. He married, June 14, 1868, Harriet Walker.

Their children were:

a. David Walker White, born July 27, 1869, died ————. He married Mary D. Sparks, February 8, 1902.

b. George McNutt White, junior, born February 6, 1871, married June 23, 1904, Annie McKamey, their son James McKamey White was born September 9, 1905.

c. Lucy D. White, born February 9, 1874, married March 2, 1892, Howell B. Trapp. They have seven children namely: Kathleen Trapp, born April 13, 1894; Harry McTeer Trapp, born October 24, 1895; Clyde Howell Trapp, born December 5, 1897; Marion Trapp, born February 28, 1899; Fredrick Chalmers Trapp, born October 14, 1900; George White Trapp, born March 22, 1903; and Claude Jeter Trapp, born October 25, 1905.

d. James Park White, junior, born October 3, 1878, married September 7, 1900, Isabella French. They had a daughter Rida French White, born August 13, 1901.

(7.) Hugh White, son of George McNutt White and Sophia Moody Park White was born, February 22, 1839. He died April 2, 1871.

(8.) Margaret White, daughter of George McNutt White and Sophia Moody Park White, was born April 1, 1841. She died ——— She married July 25, 1865, S. A. McDermott. He died May 24, 1897.

Their children:

a. Jane McDermott, born July 27, 1867

b. Sophia White McDermott, born May 5, 1872, married December 22, 1902, W. F. Stark. They have two children, William McDermott Stark, born August 16, 1894 and Margaret Stark, born May 25, 1900.

c. Gussie McDermott, born July 19, 1874, married October 7, 1903, W. W. Prater. They have a daughter, Margaret Jane McDermott Prater, born, October 25, 1905.

d. Nellie M. McDermott, born January 31, 1800.

(9.) Sophia Moody White, daughter of George McNutt White and Sophia Park White was born, January 13, 1843. She died January 13, 1902.

(10.) Amanda M. White, daughter of George McNutt White and Sophia Moody Park White was born September 4, 1844. She died ————. She married July 5, 1869, Joseph T. McTeer. He died January 6, 1904.

Their children were:

a. Margaret McTeer, born October 31, 1870, died October 30, 1904. She married December 14, 1893, Charlton P. Brooke. They had two children, Joseph T. McTeer Brooke, born December 31, 1896, died in infancy and Charlton P. Brooke, junior, born January 23, 1898.

b. Charles McTeer, born September 10, 1873.

c. George White McTeer, born April 12, 1876.

d. Moody McTeer, born March 3, 1878, died November 6, 1892.

e. Joseph T. McTeer, junior, born August 5, 1881, married June 8, 1905, Minnie K. McClung.

(11.) George McNutt White, Jr., son of George McNutt White and Sophia Moody Park White was born August 26, 1846, died———— married July 5, 1871, Mary Kennon Martin.

Their children:

a. Lazinka White, born————, died January 9, 1907, married Thomas C. Pollock and had a son Robert Armstrong Pollock, born October 1, 1894.

b. Andrew P. White, Junior, born ————, married September 10, 1903, Jennie C. Churchman.

(12.) Andrew Park White, son of George McNutt White and Sophia Moody Park White was born June 8, 1848, died————. He married November 10, 1874, Juliet M. Park.

Their children were:

a. Isabel White, born January 3, 1876, married October 30, 1895, Joseph Ernest Briscoe. They have no children.

b. Juliet White, born October 24, 1877, married October 10, 1899 Charles W. Metcalf, Jr. They have two children, Juliet Metcalf, born October 14, 1902 and Charles W. Metcalf III, born December 8, 1905.

(13.) Samuel Carrick White, son of George McNutt White and Sophia Moody Park White was born March 2, 1850. He died January 9, 1852.

ELIZA PARK

Eliza Park, daughter of James Park and Sophia Moody Park, was born in Knoxville, September 22, 1811. She married Charles H. Coffin January 4, 1837. She died in Walnut Ridge, Ark., June 16, 1874. Charles Coffin died June 18, 1855.

Their children were:

(1.) James Park Coffin.

(2.) Charles Coffin, Jr., died in infancy.

(3.) Charles Coffin, Jr., died young.

(4.) Hector Coffin.

(g.) William Coffin, died young.

(6.) Ann Eliza Coffin, died young.

(7.) Margaret Coffin, died young.

(8.) Samuel Carrick Coffin, died young.

(1.) James Park Coffin, son of Charles H. Coffin and Eliza Park Coffin was born September 22, 1828. He died ———. He married November 3, 1862, S. Lucy Lyons. She died March 8, 1887.

Their children were:

a. Charles H. Coffin, born October 29, 1863, married December 5, 1888 Nettie B. Maxfield.

b. Maxwell Coffin, born September 12, 1865, married June 2, 1897 Annie McDonald Cockrell and had three children: Margaret McDonald Coffin, born February 16, 1898, died in infancy; Mary Coffin, born December 8, 1899; Maxwell Coffin, Jr., born December 18, 1903, died in infancy.

c. Jessie Coffin, born November 22, 1867, married April 9, 1890 James B. Fitzhugh. They had four children namely: Lucy Fitzhugh, born April 9, 1891; a son born and died December 7, 1894; Margaret Coffin Fitzhugh, born September 18, 1896, died in infancy; and Virginia Stuart Fitzhugh, born July 20, 1907.

(2.) Charles Coffin son of Eliza Park Coffin and Charles H. Coffin, died in infancy.

(3.) Charles H. Coffin, a second child by that name, son of Eliza Park Coffin and Charles H. Coffin died in infancy.

(4.) Hector Coffin, son of Eliza Park Coffin and Charles H. Coffin, born April 15, 1844, died ———, married Alice Jones of Memphis, October 13, 1875.

Their children:

a. **Alice E.** Coffin, born August 25, 1876, married November 28, 1900 William F. Smith, Jr. They had two children, Alice Coffin Smith born, April 2, 1903 and Sarah Falconer Smith, born January 8, 1905.

b. Margaret Coffin, born August 18, 1884.

c. Rosa Sadler Coffin, born June 26, 1880, married November 4, 1904, Lieut. Troup Miller, U. S. Army. Their child, Troup Miller, Jr., born August 25, 1905, died in infancy.

d. Ella Jones Coffin, born February 1, 1822.

e. Hector Coffin, Jr., born December 24, 1883.

f. Carrie Coffin, born November 18, 1885, died young.

g. Lizzie Coffin, born January 5, 1889, died in infancy.

h. Carrie Coffin, born January 21, 1891.

(7.) Margaret Coffin, daughter of Eliza Park Coffin and Charles H. Coffin, born February 19, 1852, died September 2, 1900. She married April 8, 1873, Dr. Zaphney Orto. They lived in Pine Bluff, Ark.

Their children:

a. Eliza Orton, born January 9, 1874, married April 21, 1897, Walter N. Trulock. Their child, Walter N. Trulock, Jr., was born in Pine Bluff, Ark., February 7, 1898.

b. Carson Orton, born January 11, 1879.

c. Charles Hector Orton, born August 11, 1880.

d. Allen Zaphney Orton, born February 15, 1883.

e. Mattie Orton, twin born August 12, 1885,

f. Margaret Orton, twin born August 12, 1885, died in infancy.

g. James Park Coffin Orton, born March 1, 1887, died in infancy.

h. Wilbur Orton, born February 10, 1890.

Mary Park

Mary Park, daughter of James Park and Sophia Moody Park, was born in Knoxville, August 25, 1813. She was twin to Harriet Park. Mary Park married October 13, 1833, George W. English. He died in 1834, one year after their marriage. They had one child, Georgiana W. English.

Mary Park married January 31, 1843, William S. Kennedy who died March 26, 1878. Mary Park Kennedy died November 23, 1900. She had seven children by her second husband.

Her children were:

(1.)   Georgiana W. English.

(2.)   Sarah Kennedy.

(3.)   Sophia Park Kennedy.

(4.)   John M. Kennedy.

(5.)   Harriet Park Kennedy, died young.

(6.)   Samuel B. Kennedy.

(7.)   James Park Kennedy.

(8.)   William S. Kennedy, died young.

(1.) Georgiana W. English, daughter of Mary Park English and George W. English, born October 13, 1834, married Thomas E. Oldham June 1, 1853.   Their children were:

a   Carrick Park Oldham, born March 26, 1854, married December 16, 1878, Lillie E. Giddens.   Their children were: Georgia Gertrude Oldham born November 29, 1880; Lena Oldham, born June 12, 1882, died in infancy; William Giddens Oldham, born May 9, 1883; Carrick Park Oldham, Jr., born August 17, 1884, twin to Thomas Oldham; Thomas Oldham, born August 17, 1884, died in infancy; Floyd Galt Oldham, born August 21, 1886.

b. Lula Oldham, born January 2, 1856, married James V. Fulkerson November 14, 1874.   They had twelve children namely: Alice Armstrong Fulkerson, born ————, (married Sidney Garland Kent August 15, 1901 and had three children, Clarence Armstrong Kent, Sidney Garland Kent, Jr., and Mildred Adelaide Kent), Margaret Virginia Fulkerson, born August 25, 1877, (married Oscar H. Tedford January 10, 1906 and has Lula Oldham Tedford, born January 31, 1907). Lula Oldham Fulkerson born July 6, 1879; Floyd Hurt Fulkerson, born July 8, 1881; Thomas Oldham Fulkerson, born May 26, 1883; Georgiana English Fulkerson, born February 6, 1885; James Lyons Fulkerson, born June 16, 1886; Francis Marion Fulkerson, born October 31, 1887; Arthur Youmans Fulkerson, born December 10, 1889; Samuel Vance Fulkerson, born June 1, 1892; Naomi White Fulkerson, born November 13, 1893; and Abram Fulkerson, born October 7, 1895.

c. Mary Kennedy Oldham, born March 7, 1858, married November 13, 1879, W. T. Mann.   They had three children: Ernest K. Mann, born July 17, 1881 (who married Katie Seay and had three children, William T. Mann, Jr., Alice Mann and Earnest K. Mann, Jr.); Edward Oldham Mann, born September 11, 1882; and Lillian Oldham Mann, born April 14, 1898.

d. Margaret Welcker Oldham, born February 13, 1860.

e. William Oldham, born October 1, 1861, married June 7, 1887, Nellie Dallas, they had one child Julia H. Oldham, born January 14, 1889.

f. Richard Wilson Oldham, born September 26, 1863, married December 6, 1888, Alice Wagin. They had five children: Albert Owens Oldham born August 22, 1889, died in infancy; Richard Wilson Oldham, born January 30, 1894; Thomas Edward Oldham, born August 4, 1896; Marie Lucille Oldham, born August 31, 1899; and Lesley Myers Oldham, born June 30, 1904.

g. Sallie Oldham, born January 29, 1866, married November 3, 1885, T. J. Youmans. They had five children: Moultrie Youmans, born November 30, 1886; Herschel Youmans born August 6, 1889; Sallie Youmans, born June 12, 1892; and Ruth Youmans, born September 12, 1897.

h. Julia Knight Oldham, born January 21, 1868, married October 11, 1887, J. C. Helner. Their child Fritz Helner was born June 12, 1888.

i. Edward Oldham, born March 25, 1870, married October 14, 1894, Ella J. McCampbell.

j. George English Oldham, born November 21, 1872, married October 26, 1899, Julia E. Clark. Their children: Herman Jones Oldham, born April 27, 1901 and George Edward Oldham, born May 15, 1904.

k. Lillian Oldman born February 6, 1875, married July 19, 1894, Herman Jones. Their children: Herman Jones, junior, born, February 16, 1898; Rhoda Shields Jones born March 20, 1902; and Cecil Heiner Jones, born February 14, 1906.

(2) Sarah Kennedy, daughter of Mary Park English Kennedy and William S. Kennedy was born November 27, 1843. She died— ————. She married Edward F. May, July 8, 1867 who died October 20, 1887.

They had children:

a. Mary Kennedy May, born April 23, married October 16, 1888, James Dixon McCarty and lives in Atlanta, Ga. Their children are: James Dixon McCarty, junior, born March 19, 1900; Edwin Forest McCarty, born November 24, 1891; Helen McCarty, born October 5, 1896; William Anderson McCarty, born December 8, 1901; and Mary McCarty, born September 15, 1906.

b. Honora May, born August 19, 1871.

c. William Kennedy May, born February 19, 1873, married Ethel E. Reid, July 2, 1901.

(3.) Sophia Park Kennedy, daughter of Mary Park English Kennedy, and William S. Kennedy was born August 8, 1845 died —— ——. She married Dr. Thomas C. Hunter, who died October 8, 1880.

Their child was:

a. William Kennedy Hunter.

(4.) John M. Kennedy, son of Mary Park English Kennedy and William S. Kennedy was born January 7, 1847, died——. He married December 25, 1876, Maria L. Ramsey.

Their children were:

a. Mary Kennedy, born February 8, 1872

b. Paul Kennedy, born October 12, 1879.

c. Cornelius Kennedy, born January 10, 1881.

d. William S. Kennedy, born July 8, 1882.

e Bettie Breck Kennedy, born March 18, 1884

f. Anna Humes Kennedy, born August 31, 1885.

g. Frank Ramsey Kennedy, born November 16, 1886.

h. Jean Kennedy, born January 5, 1888.

i. Helen Kennedy, born April 6, 1889.

j. John Harrison Kennedy, born August 8, 1890, died August 24, 1906.

k. Margaret Kennedy, born May 26, 1892, died in infancy.

l. Almon Brooks Kennedy, born August 25, 1893.

m. Juliet Hazen Kennedy born August 18, 1895.

n. Elizabeth Washington Kennedy, born October 26, 1896.

(5.) Harriet Park Kennedy, daughter of Mary Park English Kennedy and William S. Kennedy was born October 14, 1848. She died young.

(6.) Samuel B Kennedy, son of Mary Park English Kennedy and William S. Kennedy was born, July 1, 1850; died September 22, 1897.

(7.) James Park Kennedy, son of Mary Park English Kennedy and William S. Kennedy was born November 1, 1854; died January 7, 1898.

(8.) William S. Kennedy, junior, son of Mary Park English Kennedy and William S. Kennedy was born, September 28, 1858. He died young.

Harriet Park

Harriet Park, daughter of James Park and Sophia Moody Park was born in Knoxville August 25, 1813.   She was a twin to Mary Park.   Harriet Park died March 1, 1899.   She never married.

Joseph Park

Joseph Park, son of James Park and Sophia Moody Park was born in Knoxville January 15, 1816.   He died October 14, 1816.

Margaret Park

Margaret Park, daughter of James Park and Sophia Moody Park was born in Knoxville October 10, 1817.   She died March 10, 1892. She married December 6, 1843, James M. Welcker who died September 18, 1758.

They had one child:

(1.)   Elizabeth Sophia Welcker, born October 11, 1844.   She married December 6, 1870, Carolinus Turner, who died —————.
She married for her second husband Henry C. Chambers of Chattanooga by whom she had no children.

The children of Elizabeth Sophia Welcker Turner:

a.   Margaret Park Turner, born July 11, 1872, died July 12, 1872.

b.   Carolinus Turner born, December 17, 1875, (who married Elizabeth Cooly.   He died in Chattanooga and had no children).

Jane Park

Jane Park, daughter of James Park and   Sophia   Moody   Park was born in Knoxville October 5, 1819.   She died in Rome, Georgia, May 21, 1897.   She married Langdon Bowie September 28, 1841. He died in Savannah, Georgia, July 27, 1870.

Their children were:

(1.)   Langdon Bowie, junior.

(2.)   Sophia Park Bowie

(3.)   Rosa Bowie

(4.)   Eliza Wardlaw Bowie.

(5.)   James Park Bowie.

(6.)   Susan W. Bowie.

(1.)   Langdon Bowie, junior, son of Jane   Park   Bowie   and Langdon Bowie was born in Charleston, South Carolina, September 30, 1842, died—————.   He married October 24, 1877, Hattie Wurts in Rome, Georgia.

Their children:

a. William Wurts Bowie, born August 29, 1879.

b. Langdon Bowie, III, born August 9, 1881.

c. Hamilton Gray Bowie, born April 20, 1883.

(2.) Sophia Park Bowie, daughter of Jane Park Bowie and Langdon Bowie was born in Charleston, South Carolina, February 19, 1844.

(3.) Rosa Bowie, daughter of Jane Park Bowie and Langdon Bowie, was born in Charleston, South Carolina December 9, 1845; died ————. She married Charles S. Kingsberry, Rome, Georgia, January 7, 1875.

a. Janie Park Kingsberry, born December 9, 1875, married April 12, 1902, Dr. Robert M. Harbin, of Rome, Georgia. They have two children: Robert M. Harbin, junior born February 16, 1903, and Rosa Kingsberry Harbin, born May 31, 1906.

b. Mary Kingsberry, born June 9, 1878.

c. Rosa Bowie Kingsberry, born October 13, 1881.

d. Charles S. Kingsberry, junior, born 1884.

(4.) Eliza Wardlaw Bowie, daughter of Jane Park Bowie and Langdon Bowie was born in Charleston, South Carolina, August 20, 1847; died ————. She married June 25, 1872, in Rome, Georgia, W. W. Gammon.

Their children:

a. Adelaide Aiken Gammon, born April 3, 1873, married June 16, 1895, H. D. Cothran. Their children are: Adelaide Cothran, born November 11, 1897; H. D. Cothran, junior, born May 19, 1899; and Lillie Bowie Cothran, born July 20, 1902.

b. Langdon Bowie Gammon, born July 25, 1874.

c. Jane Bowie Gammon, born April 8, 1876, died in infancy.

d. Sophia Bowie Gammon, born November 16, 1877, died young.

e. Evelyn Aiken Gammon born June 11, 1880, died young.

f. W. M. Gammon, junior, born September 11, 1881.

g. Rosa Gammon, born May 16, 1883.

h. Lillie Wardlaw Gammon, born November 12, 1885.

i. Sallie Fuller Gammon, born November 20, 1887, died young.

j. William G. Gammon, born December 6, 1888. died in infancy.

k. Isabel Martin Gammon, born January 1, 1893.

(5) James Park Bowie, son of Jane Park Bowie and Langdon Bowie, was born in Charleston, South Carolina, September 16, 1853 died ————. Married October 26, 1880, Fannie P. Freeman.

Their children:

a. Frank Freeman Bowie, born October 25, 1881.

b. Janie Park Bowie, born February 12, 1884. Married April 19, 1905, Charles Caperton. They have two children: Frances Caperton born November 7, 1906, and ———————— Caperton.

c. Susie Terhune Bowie, born April 17, 1888.

d. Adaleen Bowie, born January 5, 1895.

e. Sidney Bowie, born January 19, 1889.

(6) Susan W. Bowie, daughter of Jane Park Bowie and Langdon Bowie was born in Charleston, South Carolina, April 15, 1865, died ————. Married Cornelius Terhune, Rome, Georgia, October 5, 1882.

Dr. James Park

James Park, junior, son of James Park and Sophia Moody Park was born in Knoxville, September 18, 1822. He became a famous Presbyterian minister and served the church into which he was almost born, since his father and two of his uncles were elders and all of his people communicants, the First Presbyterian Church of Knoxville, as its minister for more than fifty years. He deserves an extended notice in this family history for his own great distinction and attainments as well as for the fact that it is due to his painstaking endeavor that the facts concerning the family are known to the present generation. He prepared and had printed for private circulation a pamphlet containing the names and dates of the birth, marriage and death of all members of his family. He married, May 27, 1847, Phebe C. Alexander, of Lexington, Virginia.

Phebe Caruthers Alexander Park, died in Knoxville, July 28, 1908. She was the daughter of William H. Alexander and Juliet Caruthers Alexander and was born in Rockbridge County, Virginia, January 2, 1825.

The children of James Park and Phebe Caruthers Alexander Park were:

(1.) Sophia Moody Park.

(2.) John Preston Park.

(3.) Juliet M. Park.

(4.)   Sarah Caruthers Park.

(5.)   Mary Park.

(6.)   James Welcker Park.

(7.)   William Alexander Park.

(8.)   Harriet Park.

(9.)   Andrew Park.

(1.)   Sophia Moody Park, daughter of Dr. James Park and Phebe C. Alexander Park, was born April 20, 1848.   She died April 26, 1886.   She married John M. Brooks, November 12, 1868.

Their children were:

a   James Park Brooks, born September 18, 1869.

b.   Alma Brooks, born June 24, 1871, died November 19, 1900. She married John T. Watson, October 26, 1892.

c.   Joseph A. Brooks, born July 18, 1878, died May 19, 1880.

d.   John M. Brooks, junior, born October 1, 1881.

e.   Robert Craighead Brooks, born December 11, 1882.

(2)   Dr. John Preston Park, son of Dr. James Park and Phebe C. Alexander Park, born February 23, 1851, died October 31, 1907. He married December 3, 1884, Eva Sevier.

Their children were: James Sevier Park, born November 14, 1885, and Edward Caruthers Park, born April 5, 1890.

(3.)   Juliet M. Park, daughter of Dr. James Park and Phebe C. Alexander Park was born January 27, 1853.   She died ————.

(4.)   Sarah Caruthers Park, daughter of Dr. James Park and Phebe C. Alexander Park was born in Knoxville April 6, 1855.   She lives in Rome, Georgia.   She married February 24, 1881, Benjamin Isbell Hughes, (died 1922).

Their children:

a.   Benjamin Isbell Hughes, junior, born April 25, 1885, married Frances Halterwanger and has two children, Sarah B. Hughes and Juliet Caruthers Hughes.

b.   John Francis Hughes, born December 27, 1886.

c.   Phebe Alexander Hughes, born January 2, 1889; married Capers Simmonds and has one child, Sarah Jane Simmonds.

d.   Park Hughes, born February 21, 1891.

e.   Sophy Park Hughes, born November 12, 1892.

f.   Lucius Graham Hughes, born December 12, 1893.

g. Sarah Elizabeth Hughes, born November 20, 1898. Married Lieut. William Wade, United States Navy, and has one child.

(6.) James Welcker Park, son of Dr. James Park and Phebe C. Alexander Park, was born September 3, 1859. He died October 11, 1902. He married Fannie M. Mitchell, November 21, 1888.

Their children:

a. Katherine Douglas Park, born August 22, 1889, married Tomlinson Ragsdale.

b. Lillie Mitchell Park, born April 6, 1898, married Martin Sims Read. They have two children.

(7.) William Alexander Park, son of Dr. James Park and Phebe C. Alexander Park, was born March 17, 1863. He married for his first wife, November 23, 1887, Fannie R. House (she died June 12, 1893).

Their children:

a. William House Park, born September 30, 1888.

b. Phebe Alexander Park, born January 2, 1890.

c. Fannie House Park, born May 19, 1893.

William Alexander Park married September 21, 1897, for his second wife Emily L. Gettys.

Their children:

d. Emily Ann Park, born July 10, 1898.

e. Katherine Zimmerman Park, born February 3, 1902.

(5.) Mary Park, daughter of Dr. James Park and Phebe C. Alexander Park, was born November 26, 1856, died ————. Married Thomas E. Howell, November 25, 1880. They lived in Rome, Georgia; Thomas Howell born March 18, 1845, died March 18, 1895.

Their children:

a. Juliet Howell, born May 12, 1883, married Robert William Graves April 7, 1904, (died 1922).

Their children are: Robert William Graves, junior, born February 8, 1905 and Juliet Graves, born 1911.

b. Mary Howell, born Rome, Georgia, January 21, 1886, married William Egbert (born 1884) lives in Chattanooga, Tennessee.

c. Anne Howell, born, Rome, Georgia October 25, 1887, married 1915 Dr. Robert Olin Simmonds and has two children: Robert Olin Simmonds, junior, and Eloise Simmonds.

d. Robert Hugson Howell, born, Rome, Georgia, May 9, 1889. Married Miss Miller in 1912 and had one child who died young.

e. John Chesley Howell, born Rome, Georgia, March 27, 1891, died in infancy.

f. Harriet Park Howell, born Rome, Georgia, February 14, 1893. Married William Welch and has one child, Mary Park Welch.

(8.) Harriet Park, daughter of Dr. James Park and **Phebe** Caruthers Alexander Park was born, March 3, 1865.   She **lives in** Chicago.   She married June 6, 1888 William I. Thomas.

Their children:

a. William Alexander Thomas, born January 3, 1890.

b. Edward Brown Thomas, born July 29, 1891.

c. Robert Craighead Thomas, born October 19, 1892, **died in** infancy.

d. Dorothy Thomas, born May 16, 1895, died in infancy.

e. Madeline Thomas, born August 9, 1897, died in infancy.

(9.) Andrew Park, son of Dr. James Park and Phebe **Caruthers** Park, was born January 17, 1868, died —————.

Carrick White Park

Carrick White Park, son of James Park and Sophia Moody **Park,** was born in Knoxville, October 2, 1826.   He died in **Knoxville,** September 28, 1890.   He married December 8, 1859, Ann **Deadrick.**

Their children were:

(1.) David Deadrick Park,

(2.) Elizabeth Sophia Park.

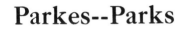

Parkes--Parks

PARKES--PARKS

Parkes, Parks, Parke and Park, all are forms of one family name, said however, to have two distinct derivations. One derivation is credited to the name Peter, through its various curruptions, Pyrke, Perk, Purkis, Perkins and Peterkin. The original families assuming the name probably lived near the Royal Park in which case it is a place name, or they were descendants of a Master of the Parke, as in the case of that loyal follower of William the Conquerer, Thomas de Parke. Thomas was rewarded for certain deeds of loyalty by large grants of land and a baronetage and the place and perquisites of Master of the Royal Parke. He was also Master of the Hunt for the Conqueror.

Sir Thomas de Parke had a long line of successors and six hundred years later a direct descendant, Sir Robert de Parke, came to America. This was in 1630. He abandoned his title, although many of the emigrants of noble birth continued to use titles until the Revolution automatically made all citizens of equal distinction. Sir Robert de Parke, however, became Mr. Robert Parke shortly after his arrival in America.

Sir Thomas de Parke, whose descendant, Sir Robert de Parke, settled in Connecticutt, had two other emigrant descendants, close kin to Sir Robert de Parke, whose emigration is dated 1630. About the same year a de Parke settled in Virginia.

Daniel Parke, of Shirley, England, a near relative of Sir Robert, was vesteryman of Williamsburg Church in Virginia, in 1676. He had a son, Daniel Park, who married Jane, daughter of Phillip Ludwell and had two daughters, Lucy Parke, who married Colonel William Byrd and Frances Parke, who married John Custis.

This is the family of which Daniel Parke Custis was a member. It was the widow of Daniel Parke Custis, the lovely Martha Dandridge Custis, who became the literal First Lady of our Land, Madame George Washington.

A Thomas de Parke, or Parkes was living in Virginia in 1670, and he is the ancestor of the family which this article gives in full. From the time of Thomas de Parke, in Virginia, 1670, members of this family seem to use their personal discretion in spelling the name. They use or omit the e or the s or both, so that literally four forms.

Parke, Parkes, Park and Parks are in use by close kinsmen.   So far no one has considered reassuming the prefix de used by their ancestors for so many centuries, as the tendency has been to shorten the name, but I shall not be surprised at any moment to find "de Parkes" on the modern family tree.

Descendants of Thomas Parkes of Virginia

In the year 1670 Thomas Parkes was living in Virginia.   He is the progenitor of a large family some members of which adhere to the spelling Parkes while others have dropped the e, some have dropped the s, and others have dropped both letters.

Thomas Parkes living in Virginia in 1670 had among other children or grandchildren:

1.   John Parkes.

2.   Thomas Parkes, junior.

John Parkes of Virginia

John Parkes, son or grandson of Thomas Parkes of Virginia, was probably born in Virginia.   He married and had seventeen children, ten of whom were sons.   The youngest child was George Parkes.   He had descendants in Memphis, among them E. M. Parkes who contributed this information to the family records.   He stated that some of the sons of John Parkes settled in North Carolina and in the territory known as Tennessee, some remained in Virginia and one son went to Georgia, becoming the ancestor of the Georgia Parkes.   E. M. Parkes stated that in 1840 he went from Memphis to Philadelphia to study medicine and that enroute he stopped in Wilkes County, North Carolina, to visit relatives and there learned the foregoing facts and some other information which is incorporated in this article.

Thomas Parkes, junior, of Virginia

Thomas Parkes, junior, of Virginia son or grandson of Thomas Parkes of Virginia may have been the eldest son in his family as he bears the family name of Thomas.   He was born probably in Virginia.   He married and moved to Wilkes County, North Carolina.   He had six children all of whom were sons namely:

1.   John Parkes.

2.   Thomas Parkes III.

3.   Reuben Parkes.

4.   Aaron Parkes.

5.   Ambrose Parkes.

6.   William Parkes.

1. John Parkes, son of Thomas Parkes, junior, was born about
————. He moved to what is now Tennessee.

2. Thomas Parkes III, son of Thomas Parkes, junior, remained
in Wilkes County, North Carolina, and his descendants are in that
district now.

3. Reuben Parkes, son of Thomas Parkes, junior died in
Tennessee.

Aaron Parkes' Descendants

4. Aaron Parkes, son of Thomas Parkes, junior, was born about
1765. He settled near Fayetteville, Tennessee. He married Ona
Dotson. They had twelve children:

    a. William Parkes.

    b. John Parkes.

    c. Thomas Parkes.

    d. Fannie Parkes.

    e. Aaron Parkes, junior.

    f. Ambrose Parkes.

    g. Robert Parkes.

    h. (a daughter) Parkes.

    i. Woodruff Parkes.

    j. Joel Dotson Parkes.

    k. Fielden Parkes.

    l. Parthenia Parkes.

Of the foregoing:

(a.) William Parkes, son of Aaron Parkes, died in Lincoln
County, Tennessee, leaving nine children, among them: Aaron Parkes
(who married ————Thurston). Joel Parkes, called Red Joel (who
married ———— ———— and has Frank Parkes and Sallie Parkes who
lived in Fayetteville).

(b.) John Parkes, son of Aaron Parkes, went to Fort Anderson
County, Texas.

(c.) Thomas Parkes, son of Aaron Parkes, died in Lincoln
County, Tennessee. He had children, among them: William Parkes
(who went to Waxahachie, Texas, and had five daughters,) Aaron
Parkes who married ———— ———— and went to Texas,) Jesse W.
Parkes (who died in Lincoln County, Tennessee, leaving two sons,
Thomas Parkes and Mathew Parkes) Tennie Parkes. (who married
———— ————), Mary Parkes, Martha Parkes, Sallie Parkes,
and (a son) Parkes (who married ———— ————).

(d.)   Fannie Parkes, daughter of Aaron Parkes, married ———
Boaz.   She died in Lincoln County, Tennessee.   She had children,
Edward Boaz of Lincoln County, Sallie Boaz (who died unmarried),
Parthenia Boaz, (who died unmarried.)   and   Betsey   Boaz,   (who
married ——— Broadway).

(e.)   Aaron Parkes, junior, son of Aaron   Parkes,   went   to
Arkansas and died there.   He left daughters.

(f.)   Ambrose Parkes, son of Aaron Parkes, and twin to Aaron
Parkes, junior, died young unmarried.

(g.)   Robert Parkes, son of Aaron Parkes, married and went to
Fayetteville, Arkansas.   He had a number of children among them
several sons who were killed in the Confederate Service.

(h.)   ——— Parkes, daughter of   Aaron   Parkes,   married
——— Boaz.   They moved to Illinois to live   before   the   War
Between the States.

(i.)   Woodruff Parkes. born in North Carolina in 1799, son of
Aaron Parkes, married Dovie Cashion.   Their children were: Joel
Dotson Parkes, (who married Emma 'Puckette Hudson and had Joel
Dotson Parkes, junior and Elizabeth Parkes); William C. Parkes,
Aaron T. Parkes, Woodruff Parkes, junior, Joseph F. Parkes and
Jennie Parkes, (who married W. E. Pitts and left   one   child
Woodruff Pitts who lives in Nashville)

(j.)   Joel Dotson Parkes, son of Aaron Parkes, died in Texas,
unmarried. He left considerable property and a suit concerning it
proves the relationship of members of this family.

(k.   Fielden Parkes, son of Aaron Parkes, married ———
Johnson.   He moved to Arkansas, Texas and Missouri.

(1.)   Parthenia Parkes, daughter of Aaron Parkes, married
James Rorax and moved to Illinois.   She had two sons, William
Rorax and Joel Rorax.

5.   Ambrose Parkes, son of Thomas Parkes, junior, was born
about ———.

6.   William Parkes, son of Thomas Parkes, junior, "went west"
to quote E. M. Parks who secured a great deal of information in
1840 in Wilkes County while on a visit to relatives.   "Went West"
does not however mean passed away, as it   is   used   in   modern
phrasing, it means merely that he emigrated to some western point
unknown to the family biographer at the time.

Ambrose Parkes

Ambrose Parkes, first of that name on   record , the   son   of
Thomas Parkes, junior, was probably   born   in   Wilkes   County,
North carolina, where he lived many years.   He was born possibly

about the year 1765. From the time of his marriage however the information is clear as family records have been kept with care and handed down from generation to generation.

He married Frances Isbell, daughter of Livingston Isbell and Anne Martin Isbell. For the Isbell family see Volume I. Notable Southern Families. The marriage took pace some time previous to 1790, when Ambrose Parkes is given in Wilkes County in the North Carolina census as the head of a family with four in family including two males under sixteen (presumably sons) two females (presumably wife and one daughter) and three slaves showing that he was fairly prosperous. It is on record in the family annals that later when his daughters were grown and married he gave to each of them a slave and to each of his sons a male slave. Roy H. Parkes, of Lynchburg, Tennessee remembers distinctly the slave "King David" who was given to Martin Livingston Parkes.

He gave to his daughter, Martha Parkes, who married Benjamin Isbell a slave named Milly. Millcy survived her young mistress many years and was a faithful servant to her children and children's children. She is remembered by the surviving grandchildren as a very capable person and the "boss" of the other negroes on the plantation.

Ambrose Parkes and Frances Isbell Parkes moved about the time their children were grown, to Tennessee where several of the sons and daughters had settled and later went on to Missouri where they probably both died. They were living there in 1837, from that date, however, I have no further record of them.

They had ten children namely:

1. Martin Livingston Parkes.

II. Thomas Lodge Dennis Parkes.

III. James Parkes.

IV. Hastings Parkes.

V. Susan Parkes.

VI. Cynthia Parkes.

VII. Martha Parkes.

VIII. Polly Parkes.

IX. Allen Waller Parkes.

X. Ambrose Lee Parkes.

Some of the foregoing information was given to me by Martha Parkes' daughters, Miriam Isbell Turnley and Missouri Isbell McMillan. Missouri Isbell McMillan says she received information from her aunt Prudence Isbell Carleton in 1861. She says "My mother (Martha Parkes Isbell) had brothers who had settled at or near Lynchburg, Tennessee.   Some of the family moved to the State of Missouri and that is how I came to be named Missouri.   When I was the youngest child (1837) mother received a letter from grand-mother telling her that she was coming to Middle Tennessee (from Missouri) for a visit and for her to meet her there.   For some reason, mother felt she could not leave home, and she wrote that she could not go.   But after the letter was written she grieved so much that my father had her get ready and with babe (myself, Missouri) nurse, Frances and Martin (my sister and brother) took the carriage and made the trip; but on reaching there late one evening, found her mother gone.   She had left that morning.   She never saw her mother again.   Sister Frances told me about this trip shortly before her death."

Thus it will be seen that in 1837, the year of Missouri Isbell's birth, Frances Isbell Parkes was living and made the trip from her home in Missouri to Tennessee and return.   It is believed that she died shortly after this date.   She was then between sixty and seventy years of age.   Her husband Ambrose Parkes was a few years older.

Martin Livingston Parkes

Martin Livingston Parkes, son of Ambrose Parkes and Frances Isbell Parkes bears family names showing descent from Livingston and Martin. (Frances Isbell was the daughter of Livingston Isbell and his wife Anne Martin Isbell.)   Martin Livingston Parkes was born in Wilkes County, North Carolina, August 26, 1793.

The following information was furnished by Roy H. Parkes of Lynchburg, Tennessee.

I.   Martin Livingston Parkes, son of Ambrose Parkes and his wife, Frances Isbell Parkes, was born August 26, 1793 in Wilkes County, North Carolina; emigrated to what is now Moore County (then Lincoln County) Tennessee about the year 1819; married Susannah B. Smith, daughter of William Smith, a Revolutionary Soldier, May 18, 1819.   Martin Livingston Parkes, the son, served in the War of 1812.   He was enrolled at Wilkesboro, North Carolina, September 18, 1812, in Captain Lee's Company, Colonel Wilborn's Tenth Regiment, North Carolina militia.   Martin Livingston Parkes, 1st, and his wife, Susannah B., had the following named children:

(1.)   William Smith Parkes, a son, born April 18, 1820; married Elizabeth McQueen; died at Woodville, Texas, August 3, 1911, leaving four children.

(2.)   Dr. Ambrose Lee Parkes, a son, born July 20, 1822, died in Bedford County, Tennessee, near the village of Flat Creek, July 15, 1891, leaving sons and daughters as follows:

(a.) Andrew, a son.

(b.) Lee, a son, who resides in Kansas City, Mo.

(c.) Maria, a daughter, who married Jake Kiser.

(d.) Harriett, a daughter, who married G. Kimery.

(e.) Laura, a daughter, who married Joe Kimery.

(f.) Dennis, a son, who resides in Saint Louis (at 6023 Columbus Avenue).

(g.) Kate, a daughter, who married Frank Hix.

(3.) Thomas Lodge Dennis Parkes, 2nd, son of Martin Livingston Parkes, 1st, was born in 1823; married Rebecca Gray; died in Moore County, Tennessee, November 30, 1900.

(4.) Martin Livingston Parkes, 2nd, a son of Martin Livingston Parkes, 1st, born May 17, 1831, was twice married, his first wife being Elizabeth Edens, daughter of Alex. and Cincinnati Edens; and his second wife being Elizabeth's sister, Sophronia Edens; died at Lynchburg, Tennessee, March 5, 1917. The children of Martin Livingston Parkes, 2nd, were:

(a.) Morris Newton Parkes, 2nd, a son, who resides at Mulberry, Tennessee.

(b.) Thomas Parkes, a son, who resides at Meadville, Pa.

(c.) James Parkes, a son.

(d.) Fannie (Parkes) West, a daughter, who married Sim West and resides at Huntland, Tennessee.

(e) Luther Parkes.

(f.) A. Wilson Parkes.

(g.) Birdie Parkes, a daughter, married D. S Evans, whose children are: Charles and Felix, sons; and Mary, a daughter, wife of Jack Bobo; and Ophelia, a daughter, wife of Lem Motlow—all of whom are residents of Lynchburg, Tennessee.

(h.) Ida, a daughter, who married Mack Motlow, and resides at Chattanooga, Tennessee.

(i.) Emma, a daughter, who married Til Reynolds and resides at Huntland, Tennessee.

(j.) Effie, a daughter, who married Buckner Reynolds and resides at Huntland, Tennessee.

(k.) Mary, a daughter, who married Rufus F. Wagoner of Moore County, Tennessee, moved to Missouri and died there. Her children are Martin and George W., sons and Mary, a daughter, wife of Ilah Dance of Selma, Alabama.

(1.) Martin Alexander, nicknamed "Rudd," a son, who married Cynthia Brazier, and died in 1891, leaving two daughters.

5. Martha Jane, a daughter of Martin Livingston Parkes, 1st, born October 21, 1834; married Alex. Timmons; died in Moore County, Tennessee, in 1879.

6. Dr. Albert Henderson Parkes, son of Martin Livingston Parkes, 1st, born October 11, 1836; married Mary Elizabeth Keller, daughter of Dr. J. A. Keller, a soldier in the Mexican War; died in Moore County, Tennessee, March 6, 1890, leaving the following named children: Laura M. and Susan B., daughters, and Albert H. Parkes, son, all of Lynchburg, Tennessee.

7. Morris Newton Parkes, 1st, son of Martin Livingston Parkes, 1st, born January 19, 1839; married Frances Womack, daughter of Elisha Womack; died at Lynchburg, Tennessee, March 4, 1916. His children were: Charles, a son; Lena, a daughter, who married George E. Raby, all of whom reside at Lynchburg; Mary Ann, a daughter, who married William H. Dance, of Huntland, Tennessee; and John B , a son who died in Fort Worth, Texas, leaving one son, Frank, who resides in Chicago, Illinois.

8. Milton C. Parkes, son of Martin Livingston Parkes, 1st, born in 1843, married Delphia Cain, died in 1923.

One daughter of Martin Livingston Parkes, 1st, Susan Bird born January 18, 1833, died unmarried about the year 1850.

Thomas Lodge Dennis Parkes

II. Colonel Thomas Lodge Dennis Parkes, 1st, a son of Ambrose Parkes and his wife, Frances (Isbell) Parkes, was born in North Carolina in the year ————; he married Elizabeth, a daughter of William Smith, and sister of Susannah B. Parkes, wife of Martin Livingston Parkes, 1st. Colonel Parkes (he was probably a colonel of militia) died in Lynchburg, Tennessee, in January 1849 (his will was probated in the County Court at Fayetteville, Tennessee, February, 1849; the last codicil to the will is dated January 9, 1849). He had the following named chidren: William and James, sons, who moved to and died at Shawneetown, Illinois; Ann, a daughter, who married A. M. (Alvin) Dean; Martin, a son; Polly, a daughter, and Susan, a daughter.

James Parkes

III. James Parkes, son of Ambrose Parkes and Frances Isbell Parkes was born in Wilkes County, North Carolina.

Hastings Parkes

IV. Hastings Parkes, son of Ambrose Parkes and Frances Isbell Parkes, was born in Wilkes County, North Carolina, about————. After living in Moore County, Tennessee, for a short while he settled in Missouri, at St. Genévieve, it is believed.

Susan Parkes

V. Susan or Susie Parkes, daughter of Ambrose Parkes and Frances Isbell Parkes, was born in Wilkes County, North Carolina, about ———————. She married Green Hubbard. They both died in Moore County, Tennessee. She is buried in the Smith cemetery on the farm of Lem Motlow.

Cynthia Parkes

VI. Cynthia Parkes, daughter of Ambrose Parkes and Frances Isbell Parkes, was born in Wilkes County, North Carolina, about——. She married ——————— Barnes.

Martha Parkes

VII. Martha Parkes, daughter of Ambrose Parkes and Frances Isbell Parkes was born in Wilkes County, North Carolina.

Martha Parkes was born April 6, 1799. She married in Wilkes County, February 17, 1818, Benjamin Isbell. They were cousins. It is believed that both the Isbell and Parkes families were members of the King's Creek Baptist Church which was destroyed by fire a number of years ago when all its records burned. It will be noted that her marriage took place the year that her brother Martin Livingston Parkes, removed to Moore County, Tennessee. In 1821, three years after their marriage Benjamin Isbell and Martha Parkes Isbell removed to Tennessee, settling in McMinn County, near Athens. She died July 15, 1840, when she was only forty-one years of age and is buried on the farm in McMinn County. She had eleven children, five sons and six daughters.

The children of Martha Parkes Isbell and Benjamin Isbell were:

1. Miriam Isbell married Mathew J. Turnley.

2. Thomas Martin Isbell married Sarah Ann Terry.

3. Frances Discretion Isbell married John Hughes.

4. Martha Ann Isbell married Robert Houston MacMillan.

5. Mary Louise Isbell married Richard Hampton.

7. Sarah Elizabeth Isbell married Jesse Gaut.

8. Benjamin Howard Isbell died unmarried.

9. John William Isbell died unmarried.

10. Lucinda Missouri Isbell married Robert Houston MacMillan.

11. Dennis Rowan Isbell married Emma Callaway.

These lines can be traced in full in Volume I. Notable Southern Families in the Howard and Isbell Chapters.

Allen Waller Parkes

IX.   Allen Waller Parkes, son of Ambrose Parkes and Frances Isbell Parkes, was born in Wilkes County, North Carolina, March 18, 1797; married Fannie Miller, daughter of John and Elizabeth Miller January 12, 1822.   He emigrated to Tennessee in 1826 and settled in Lynchburg in what was then Lincoln County, but is now Moore County Tennessee.   He died at Lynchburg, November 18, 1884.   His wife was born May 17, 1802 and died in Lynchburg January 6, 1877.

Their children were: Frances Ann Parkes (1823-1890), Louise Elizabeth Parkes, (1825-1861), Annis Marilda Parkes (1838-1900), daughters, and Rufus Burton Parkes (1827-1897), a son.

Frances Ann Parkes married Williamson Haggard (1813-1883) and had the following children: Allen Luther Haggard (1842-1904) who married Sallie Nicks (1845-1898), and had the following children: Nannie Elizabeth who married J. A. Fuller;   Fannie   Belle;   and Gertrude, who married Robert Giles; Harvey Haggard who married Etta Ivy; Virginia Frances Haggard who married Samuel Tilford and had one child, Katie who married Joseph Gunn; Susan Belle Haggard, who married Jessie Harris; Laura Haggard who married P. J. O'Reilly.

Annis Marilda Parkes was twice married.   Her first husband was William R. Collins by whom she had   one   child, Fannie, a daughter, who married Thomas Benton Manning.   Mrs. Manning has one son, John S., who married Rebecca Knight.   After the death of her first husband, Annis Marilda married John F. Piant.

Louise Elizabeth Parkes married William R. Shaw and had one child, Marion.

Rufus Burton Parkes, son of Allen Waller Parkes and his wife, Fannie Miller Parkes, was born May 5, 1827; married Emily Jane Rountree, daughter of James L. Rountree and his wife, Musadora Flack Rountree.   James L. Rountree was a son of Thomas Roundtree, founder of Lynchburg, Tennessee, and his wife, Sarah.   Rufus Burton Parks was the first of this line of the Parkes family to drop the "e" from his name.   He died at Lynchburg September 21, 1897. He had four children to live to maturity, namely: Rufus Alonzo, a son; Alice A., a daughter; Edwin Lee, a son; and May, a daughter.

Rufus Alonzo Parks married Susan A. Holt, daughter of Jordan C. Holt, junior, and his wife, Jane Phelps Holt, grand-daughter of Brittain Phelps, an original settler of what is   now   Moore   (then Lincoln) County, Tennessee.   Their children are: Roy H. Parks, a son, married to Eva Colsher, daughter of William H. Colsher and Susan M. Edens Colsher, and whose children are: Roy H., junior, Robert, Jack and Nell, the latter the oldest, who   married   Lacey Hobbe, and whose children are Charles Edwin and William C., sons;

Pearl, a daughter, who married George D. Bobo, and whose children are: Jean, Roy, Marvin, Floy, Gladys, Lila, Dixon Billie and Sammie Lee; Harry R. Parks, who married Bessie Dance, daughter of Dr. E. M. Dance and granddaughter of Dr. S. E. H. Dance and his wife, Miriam Berry Dance, and whose child is Edwina, a daughter; Margaret, a daughter who married George F. Waggoner, and who died in Denver, Colorado; Lexie Logue Parks, a son, who resides at Tampa, Florida. He married Mary Adams, and has one child, Mary, a daughter; Rufus Burton Parks, 2nd, who married Stella Couser, daughter of Robert Couser, and who has one child, Betty Sue, a daughter; Marion, a daughter, who married Thomas W. Pitts, and whose children are: William, a son, Margaret and Lou, daughters.

Alice A. Parks married L. J. Robertson, son of Loderick Robertson, and their children are: William L., who married Jonie Holt; Charles R.; Eugene L.; A. Boone, who married Edna Banks; Albert D., who married Leria Marrow; May, who married H. Dies; Nellie, who married Alan Pamphlin; Rufus Burton; and Wilma.

Edwin L. Parks was twice married, his first wife being Nannie Allen and his second, Urman Foster. He has the following children: Emma, who married Thomas Baxter; Annie, who married A. D. Harbin; Alice, who married P. A. Stowers; and Carl.

May Parkes married Thomas A. Hays, and their children are: Parks, Brownie, Harold and Lorena.

Ambrose Lee Parkes

X. Ambrose Lee Parkes, 1st, son of Ambrose Parkes and his wife, Frances Isbell Parkes, was born in the year ————— in North Carolina; after his marriage to Eleanor E. Watts he moved to Missouri and resided in that state until 1846 when he removed to Lynchburg, Tennessee, where he and his wife died about 1850. The children of Ambrose Lee and his wife, Eleanor Watts Parkes were:

1. Missouri, a daughter, who married W. M. Watts.

(2.) Mary, a daughter, who first married J. J. Watts and after his death, T. J. Creel.

(3.) Marcus L., a son, now dead, whose children are (a) Eugene, (b.) Lafayette, (c) Thomas H., sons; and (d.) Ellen Caroline, (e.) Virginia C., (f.) Mary S., and (g.) Emily E., wife of J. L. Miller, daughters.

(4.) Thomas H., a son, born in Missouri October 19, 1840; settled with his parents in Lynchburg, Tennessee, in 1846; and on the death of his parents went to Alexandria County, North Carolina, where they lived until 1858 when he returned to Lynchburg; was married in 1869 to Emily A. M. Taylor, daughter of John H. Taylor and granddaughter of Woody B. Taylor, one of the first settlers of what is now Moore County, Tennessee.   Thomas H. died April 27, 1891; his widow died in August, 1922.   Their children are:

(a.)   John Lee, a son, resident of Nashville.

(b.)   William K., a son, of Lynchburg, Tennessee.

(c.)   Minnie, a daughter, who married O. R. Brittain and resides at Franklin, Tennessee.

(d.)   Emma, a daughter, who married James N. Daniel, and resides at Lynchburg, Tennessee.

*(e.)   Harry T., a son, who resides at Fayetteville, Tennessee.

*(Harry T.'s name is as given, and not Thomas H. junior, as given in Goodspeed's history).

(f.)   Nellie, a daughter, who died in infancy.

The Parks Family in Williamson County, Tennessee

John Parks, born February 5, 1785, and Andrew B. Parks, his brother, born March 20, 1793, and their mother, were among the first settlers in Williamson County, Tennessee, located near Franklin. John Parks married Susan Neely, and their descendants live near Spring Hill, Tennessee.   Andrew B. Parks was twice married, his first wife being Rhoda Neely, by whom   he   had   ten   children, namely: Sally Jane Parks, a daughter, born July 10, 1822, married Samuel House and had several children; Stephen S. V. Parks, a son, born April 5, 1824, married Mary Halfacre; Susan Frances Parkes, a daughter, born May 13, 1826; John Washington Parks, a son, born June 15, 1828, married and moved to Maury County; James Adams Parks, a son, born March 30, 1830, married Miss Sine Dereberry and moved to Maury County; Mary Elizabeth Parks, a daughter, born May 25, 1833, married a Sweeney and moved to Houston, Texas; Andrew B. Parks, junior, born March 21, 1835, died unmarried; William F. Parks, a son, born July 28, 1838, died unmarried.   Two other children died young and unmarried.

Andrew B. Parks next married Elizabeth Gibson Barnett, and to this union three children were born, to wit: Sophronia, a daughter, and Margaret, a daughter, neither of whom were ever married; and Joseph B. Parks, a son, who married Addie Sweeney, and had three children, namely: Walter J. Parks, a son, Estelle Parks, a daughter and Mary Elizabeth Parks, a daughter, who married T. Y. English.

John Parks and Andrew B. Parks belonged to a family of nine children, and belong to the North Carolina branch of   the   Parks family.   The brothers and sisters of John and Andrew B. Parks, as given in the Bible records in possession of the family of Andrew B. Parks, are as follows: Frances Parks, born February 9, 1772; Reuben Parks, born December 19, 1773; Nancy Parks, born December 24, 1775; Clacy Parks, born November 24, 1779; Minney Parks, born February 5, 1785; Benjamin Parks, born January 22, 1788; and Sary Parks, born November 1, 1790.

Tunnell

TUNNELL

Though there have been several families of this name in Virginia the most prominent has been that which settled in Spotsylvania County, spread to Fairfax County, to North Carolina and Tennessee, and now has representatives in many states and several foreign countries.

The family name in France was Tonnelier, a surname derived from an occupation, meaning barrel maker or cooper. Several years after the revocation of the Edict of Nantes a progenitor of the Virginia Tunnell family fled his native France and sought refuge in England. Kinsmen, who also fled their homeland to escape religious persecution, settled on the Elbe in Germany. There some assumed the spelling Tunell, while others changed to Kiecer, the German equivalent for the name. It is said that some of the German Tunnells went to Sweden and some of these changed to the spelling Thunnell. There are descendants of the German and Swedish branches in Minnesota and Illinois while there are people in Indiana and Florida who use the French spelling, Tonnelier.

Guillaum Tonnelier, born about 1675 in France, with his wife, whose name in unknown, and a son, a babe in arms, settled near Scarbrough, North Riding, Yorkshire, England in 1702 or 1703. The name was there Anglicized to Tunnel. Guillaume Tunnel and wife died in England.

Wiliam Tunnel, son of Gullaume Tonnelier (or Tunnel), born 1702 or 1703, in France, went with his parents to Yorkshire, England. He married Lady Ann Howard of Yorkshire. The title of "Lady Ann" clung to her to the day of her death. They were married in England but the date is not known. About 1736 they emigrated to the English Colonies in America and settled near Fredricksburg, Virginia. Later they moved to Fairfax County and lived some distance from Herndon but not far from the falls of the Potomac. William Tunnel died December 28, 1787, it is thought in Loudon County, Virginia and was buried in Fairfax County. "Ann Tunnell departed this life February 18, 1814 supposed to be one hundred and four years old". (Bible record) She died at the home of her son, the Rev. William Tunnell, near Robertsville, Anderson County, Tennessee. After she had celebrated the centennial of her birth she forded the Clinch River on horseback.

127

About 1740 two brothers of William Tunnel crossed to America. These were John Tunnel, who lived in Accomac County, Virginia, and in Delaware, who is said to have married a widow, "Lady Scarbrough," and James Tunnel, who went to North Carolina.

The names of four sons of William and Lady Ann Howard Tunnel are known. There may have been other children who died in infancy. The four sons were clergymen. It is said that two, William and Stephen, were patriots of the War for American Independence. Many of this blood have been distinguished in times past and numerous members are holding positions of prominence at the present.

Robert Tunnel, son of William and Ann Howard Tunnel, was born 1747 Fredricksburg, Virginia. He is said to have married and moved to North Carolina. No further details.

William Tunnel, son of William and Ann Howard Tunnel, was born 1751 Spotsylvania County, Virginia and died August 16, 1814 near Robertsville, Tennessee. He married Mary Maysey (Bible spelling).

Stephen Tunnel, son of William and Ann Howard Tunnel, was born 1753 Spotsylvania County, Virginia and died 1828 Tompkinsville, Kentucky. He married Kezia Money.

John Tunnel, son of William and Ann Howard Tunnel, was born 1755 near Fredricksburg, Virginia and died June 1790, at Sweet Springs, Virginia, now in West Virginia. He was not married.

This record is designed to record and preserve the lines of descent from William Tunnel, born 1751, and Stephen Tunnel, born 1753. The double "l" ending of the name was assumed by William and Stephen and their families.

PART ONE
WILLIAM TUNNELL

William Tunnell, son of William and Ann Howard Tunnel, was born 1751 and "departed this life on the 16th of August about sunrise, 1814, in the sixty-third year of his age". (Bible record). His death occured shortly after death of his wife and mother. He was a Baptist minister. He married Mary Maysey December 9, 1771 in Fairfax County, Virginia. "Mary Tunnell departed this life April 6, about sunrise, 1814, in the sixty-first year of her age." (Bible record). She died near Robertsville, Tennessee. Little is known of the Maysey family, of English origin. A descendant of Mrs. Tunell says her family name was Mey Ley. She had a sister or half-sister, Betsy Maysey, who died unmarried near Robertsville, Tennessee. She had a brother or half-brother, Charles Maysey, who lived at Jacksboro, Tennessee in 1810, who later moved to Hamilton County, Tennessee. It is said that he and his sons served in the Mexican War. William and Mary Tunnell lived in Virginia until 1788 when they moved to North Carolina. According to the first federal census, 1790, they were living in Rutherford County, North Carolina. The family name is given in the census as Tunnill. In February 1792 they moved to near the present town of Robertsville, Tennessee. The plantation on which they lived and died is now owned by one of their descendants. They had seven sons, one of whom died young; sixteen grandsons bearing the name Tunnell and of these seven died unmarried. Although names of four thousand of their descendants are known there are at the present time, less than two hundred males bearing the name of Tunnell. In Anderson County Tennessee descendants unto the seventh generation are living and it may be said that the Tunnell family tree is a forest.

In a Bible, which once belonged to Lady Ann Howard Tunnell, and valued highly by its present owner, Mrs. George Ball, of Jacksonville, Illinois, are the following entries, names and dates of births of children of William and Mary Maysey Tunnell.

A. John Tunnel b. February 23, 1773.

B. William Tunnel b. November 14, 1774.

C. Caty Tunnel b. January 31, 1777.

D. Nancy Tunnel b. December 27, 1779.

E. Lettice Tunnel b. February 26, 1781.

F. Robert Tunnel b. December 14, 1782.

G. Betsy Tunnel b. April 5, 1785.

H. James Tunnel b. May 22, 1787.

I. Polly Tunnel b. February 26, 1789.

J. Calvin Tunnel b. October 4, 1791.

K. Luther Tunnel b. September 26, 1793.

L. Stephen Tunnel b. October 19, 1795.

M. Sally Tunnel b. July 29, 1799.

John Tunnell

A. John Tunnell, son of William and Mary Maysey Tunnel, and namesake of his uncle the Rev. John Tunnll, beloved pioneer Methodist minister in Amerira, was born February 23, 1773 in Fairfax County, Virginia, and died July 11, 1826 near Robertsville, Tennessee. In 1788 he moved, with his parents to North Carolina, and in February, 1792 to near Robertsville, Tennessee. He married Nancy Ann Worthington b March 1746 Baltimore, Mdl d January 3, 1821 Knoxville, Tennessee gives her name as Weatherington. She was born June 10, 1784 and was one of the twin daughters of Samuel Worthington (b. March. 1746 Baltimore, Md.; d. January 3, 1821 Anderson County, Tennessee and Elizabeth (Carney) Worthington b April 30, 1754; d October 22, 1850, Anderson Cousty, Tennessee.) Nancy Tunnell survived her husband and died in Anderson County, Tennessee. The Worthington family settled at Burrville, now known as Clinton, Tennessee, and another daughter, Elizabeth, and a son, James, married into the Tunnell family. Ch. b. nr. Robertsville, Tennessee.

I. Sally Tunnell b. March 15, 1802.

II. Polly Tunnell b. November 23, 1803.

III. Elizabeth Ann Tunnell b. November 29, 1805.

IV. Margaret Ann Tunnell b. May 31, 1808.

V. Maria Louisa Tunnell b. March 10, 1810.

VI. Emerine Engleton Tunnell b. May 19, 1812.

VII. William Valentine Tunnell b May 3, 1814.

VIII. Samuel Jasper Tunnell b. September 9, 1816.

IX. Jesse Worthington Teunnell b. August 29, 1818.

X. John Calvin Tunnell b. November 17, 1820.

XI. Martin Luther Tunnell b. February 12, 1822.

XII. Nancy Adeline Tunnell b. November 25, 1826.

Of the foregoing:

I. Sally Tunnell, daughter of John and Nancy Worthington Tunnell, was b March, 15, 1802 and d about 1850. Her home was near Carlinville, Ill. for many years. She m. first, Absalom Smith Aug. 3, 1830 Greene Co., Ill. (d abt 1836); and m second, ———— Sturdiville. Children:

One. Nancy Smith b May 28, 1831.

Two. John Calvin Smith b 1833.

Three. Sarah Smith b 1835.

Four. Elizabeth Sturdiville b abt 1838.

Five. Mary Sturdiville b 1840.

Of these:

One. Nancy Smith b May 28, 1831, in Ill., d Jan. 24, 1873, Butler Mo.; m Flemiel J. Hughes Mar. 19, 1850 (b Sept. 15, 1824; d Sept. 8, 1869 Butler, Mo.) and had: (a) William Thomas Hughes b Feb. 24, 1851; d June 16, 1916 Helena, Mont. (m Anna C. Adams Nov. 5, 1886 Vernango, Neb. and had 1. Ada Elizabeth Hughes b July 26, 1888 Denver, Col.; d Oct. 8, 1890 Denver; 2. Edith V. Hughes b July 22, 1891 Blanchard, Iowa; m Bert G. Wiley May 20, 1912 Helena, Mont. (b Sept. 15, 1885 Coffeyville, Kas.; of Los Angeles, Calif.) and had. (aa) Anita Alene Wiley b Mar. 27, 1913 Helena, Mont.; (bb) Deloris Nancy Wiley b Feb. 16, 1917 Helena, Mont.; 3. Edwin Hughes b Aug. 5, 1893 North Platte, Neb.; served in World War; unmarried; with Northern Pacific R. R.; 4. Elmer B. Hughes b Oct. 26, 1896 Omaha, Neb.; unmarried, with Los Angeles Electric R. R. Co.; 5. Homer Hughes b Nov. 19, 1899 Bozeman, Mont.; d Jan. 22, 1904); (b) Sarah E. Hughes b Jan. 22, 1853; d Oct. 27, 1854; (c) Nancy J. Hughes b Oct. 27 1855; d Sept. 11, 1864; (d) Mary Alice Hughes b Sept. 8, 1858; d June 15, 1890 North Platte, Neb. (m Thomas Botts June 1884 North Platte, (d Aug. 1885 North Platte) and had no ch.); (e) Cordelia Ann Hughes b May 29, 1861; d Nov. 15, 1873; (f) George Edwin Hughes b Dec. 12, 1863 near Carlinville, Ill; d April 23, 1917 Oregon (m Nellie A. Caldwell Sept. 3, 1890, Albany, Ore. and had an only ch.; 1. Roy Hughes b abt 1892, radio operator, unmarried); (g) Laura Emma Hughes b Dec. 30, 1866; d May 18, 1867; (h) Ada Elizabeth Hughes b Oct. 21, 1868 Butler, Mo., of Hope, Idaho (m Frank L. Putney Jan. 25, 1887 Ogalala, Neb. (b Apr. 24, 1856 Conneaut, O.) and had; 1. May Marie Putney b Dec. 12, 1889, of Ashton, Ida.; m Charles H. Powell Dec. 21, 1918 at Pocatello, Idaho and had no ch.; 2. Jennie Alice Putney b July 16, 1891, of Triangle, Ida. m William Hagberry Dec. 12, 1909 at Ashton, Ida., ranchman, and had; (aa) Leonard Hagberry b Sept. 26, 1910 Ashton, Ida.; (bb) Convin Hagberry b Aug. 14, 1912 Wyo.; (cc) Ernest Hagberry b Oct. 14, 1915 Ashton, Ida.; 3. Mable Putney b Sept. 16,

1894, m Archie Merle Truesdell Feb. 5, 1917 Ashland, Neb. (b Dec. 13, 1886, Prof. Mathematics United States Government College in Alaska) and had ch. b Gary, Ind ; (aa) Lola Agnes Truesdale b Nov. 25, 1917; (bb) Floyd Harold Truesdale b Aug. 16, 1919.

Two. John Calvin Smith b 1833 in Ill.; d 1875; married Elizabeth T. Shelton 1868 (b 1845 Pike Co., Ill.) and had an only ch.; (a) Simeon Cal Cecil Smith.

Three. Sarah Smith b 1835 in Ill.; d aft. 1873 Calif.; m Jacob Worrel (d aft 1873 Calif.) and had several ch., including; (a) William Worrel; (b) Lawrence Worrel.

Four. Elizabeth Sturdiville b abt 1838; dead; married Alexander Baker and had; (a) William Baker; (b) Robert Baker; (c) George Baker. Alexander Baker married a second time and lived near Kansas City.

Five. Mary Sturdiville b 1840; d abt 1860; m Alexander Molen, a nephew of her sister's husband, Alexander Baker, and had an only ch., a dau. who d in inf.

II. Polly Tunnell, dau of John and Nancy Worthington Tunnell, was born Nov. 23, 1803 and died Oct. 26, 1804.

III. Elizabeth Ann Tunnell, dau of John and Nancy Worthington Tunnell, was b Nov. 29, 1806 and d Oct. 1, 1870 near Carlinville, Ill. She married Isaac White Julian Nov. 25, 1830 Anderson Co., Tenn. (d Nov. 25, 1879 near Carlinville, Ill.) and had ch b Anderson Co., Tennessee.

One. Stephen Lafayette Julian b Jan. 29, 1832.

Two. William Valentine Julian b Jan. 21, 1834.

Three. Jesse Worthington Julian b Sept. 25, 1837.

Four. Nancy Catherine Julian b Sept. 27, 1840.

Five Sarah Elizabeth Ann Julian b Oct. 31, 1845.

Of these:

One. Stephen Lafayette Julian b Jan. 29, 1832; d May 19, 1863; served in the Union Army and died in service; m Mary Elizabeth Bagby Sept. 7, 1854 in Mo. (d Aug., 1904 Arlington, Kan., who m second, C. H. Reynolds 1872 Macoupin Co., Ill.) and had; (a) Dr. Isaac Berry Julian b Mar. 17, 1858, of Salina, Kan. (m first, Clara Maze Nov. 15, 1883 Brookville, Kan., who d July 12, 1898 Junction City, Kan. and had; 1. Arthur William Julian b Sept. 11, 1884 Arlington, Kan., of Omaha, Neb., m Mable Lewis and had no ch.; and m second, Margaret Ann Scarlett Mar. 15, 1899 Abilene, Kan. (b April 1869 Ohio; d June 25, 1902 Salina, Kan.) and had; 2, Mildred Bera Julian b Nov. 23, 1899, of Joplin, Mo., m Mark Hergenreder Aug. 1921 Salina, Kan. and had; (aa) June Marie Hergenreder b

June 24, 1924 Joplin, Mo.; 3. Gladys Marie Julian b Mar. 6, 1902 Ellis, Kan., of Rockford, Ill. m Norton Edward Burt July 1920 Chicago, Ill., and had; (aa) Betty Eloise Burt b Nov. 10, 1921 Rockford, Ill.; (bb) Norton Julian Burt b June 10, 1924 Dubuque, Iowa; and m third, Laura Sebina Martin June 26, 1923 Omaha, Neb.); (b) Dorinda Julian b abt 1860; d Aug. 18, 1872 Macoupin Co., Ill.; (c) William Worthington Julian b 1863 Rolla, Mo., of Arlington, Kan. (m first, Ella Post at Stockville, Neb. (b 1868 Ottumwa, Iowa; d Apr. 20, 1921 Arlington, Kan.) and had; 1. Claud Julian b Sept. 10, 1890; d 1890; 2. Clare Everett Julian b Sept. 13, 1891; d Mar. 25, 1913 Kansas City, Mo.; 3. Irene Bonita Julian b Feb. 11, 1893, of Ellis, Kan., m Quincy Bates Yaple Apr. 10, 1911 Kingman, Kan. and had; (aa) Julian Dudley Yaple b Feb. 1915 Arlington, Kan.; (bb) Ida Bernice Yaple b Aug. 11, 1917 Arlington, Kan.; d Apr. 18, 1921 Ellis Kan.; (cc) Gloyce Edward Yaple b October 1, 1919 Arlington, Kan.; (dd) Claire Eugene Yaple b Nov. 4, 1923 Ellis, Kan ; (ee) Alice Audene Yaple b Nov. 25, 1924 Ellis, Kan. W. W. Julian m second, Nellie Reece).

Two. William Valentine Julian b Jan. 21, 1834; d Feb. 24, 1863. He was a Union soldier and died in service; unmarried.

Three. Jesse Worthington Julien b Sept. 25, 1837; d Dec. 19, 1873 near Carlinville, Ill.; married Clara Jane Wheeler Nov. 8, 1866 Butler, Ill. (b Jan. 9, 1848 near Carlinville. Ill; (a) William Newton Julian b Oct. 2, 1867, of Los Angeles, Calif. (m Nellie Emma Cochran Nov. 24, 1892 Winfield, Kan. (b Aug. 12, 1871 near Columbus, Kan.) and had; 1. Laird Newton Julien b Mar. 15, 1894 near Dexter, Kan , of Vernon, Calif., m Laura Ostrander Mar. 12, 1915 (b May 30, 1894) and had; (aa) Laird Newton Julian the Second, b Sept. 17, 1917 Hominy, Okla ; (bb) Devere Julien b Apr. 20, 1920 San Bernardino, Calif.; 2. Eunice Julien b Dec. 30, 1896 near Blackwell, Okla., of Tulsa, Okla., m Arthur Brock Sept. 21, 1923 Sapulpa, Okla. (served in Rainbow Division in World War; 3. Clara E. Julien b Sept. 8, 1899 near Blackwell, Okla., of Shawnee, Okla., m J. Corbett Hardin Oct. 14, 1922 Shawnee, Okla. (b Sept. 17, 1899 Alabama); 4. Lorene Julien b July 12, 1902 near Blackwell, Okla., of Shawnee, Okla., m Dunk Bleecker Sept. 4, 1920 Shawnee, Okla. (b Dec. 25, 1901 Miss.) and had; (aa) James Newton Bleecker b July 1, 1921; 5. Ruth Julien b Oct. 18, 1904 Lone Wolf, Okla); (b) Cora Jessie Julien b Oct. 19, 1869, of Burden, Kan. (m Dr. John J. A. Manser May 6, 1896 Burden, Kan. (b April 8, 1863 Gracin Co., West Va.) and had ch b Burden, Kan.; 1. Marie Manser b June 12, 1897, m Emory James Giblin June 12, 1923 Burden, Kan.; 2. Julien Garfield Manser b Mar. 20, 1905; 3. Helen Manser b Jan 7, 1908); (c) Grace Truman Julien b Nov. 24, 1871; d Dec. 5, 1872 near Carlinville, Ill. Clara Jane Wheeler married second, Willoughby McMillan Corn Nov. 1877 Litchfield, Ill., who d Apr. 30, 1902 Eaton, Kan.)

Four. Nancy Catherine Julien b Sept. 27, 1840, of Eudora, Mo.; married Samuel J. Nash Dec. 24, 1912 Marshfield, Mo.

Five. Sarah Elizabeth Julien b Oct. 31, 1845; d May 19, 1870 near Carlinville, Ill.; unmarried.

IV. Margaret Ann Tunnell (Peggy Ann) was the second child of John and Nancy Worthington Tunnell to bear the name Ann. She was born May 28, 1808 and died Jan. 12, 1872 Pittsfield, Ill. She married first, James Parks June 15, 1830, who was born June 15, 1802 and died Dec. 5, 1843. On Sept. 22, 1848 she married Peyton Cornwell   Ch:

One. John Love Parks b May 8, 1831.

Two. Nancy Catherine Parks b June 27, 1832.

Three. William Thompson Parks b Apr. 17, 1835

Four. Mary Ann Parks b Dec. 28, 1837.

Five. West Parks b June 1, 1841.

Six. James Worthington Parks b June 23, 1842.

Seven. William Lucius Cornwell b June 23, 1849.

Of these:

One. John Love Parks b May 8, 1831; d in inf.

Two. Nancy Catherine Parks b June 27, 1832; d July 17, 1901 Oregon City, Ore., dau Isaac Benjamin and Louisa (Frost) Kauffman, June 2, 1825 East Windsor, Conn.; d May 12, 1904 Oregon City, Ore., son of David Bissell) and had ch. b Pittsfield, Ill.; (a) William Edwin Bissell b Nov. 23, 1852; unmarried, of Santa Cruz, Cal f.; (b) Mary Sylvia Bissell b Apr. 1854; d 1864 Pike Co., Ill.; (c) Laura Emma Bissell b Dec. 22, 1856; d Dec. 6 1903 Portland, Ore. (m Henry Sitten Sept. 4, 1875 Detroit, Ill and had 1. Mary Eden Sitten b Sept. 15, 1877; d 1887 Alma, Neb.; 2 Helen Bell Sitten b Aug. 17, 1880, m ——— Kail and had two children; 3. William Arthur Sitton b June 25, 1884 with Merchants Transportation Co., Tacoma, Wash); (d) Nellie May Bissell b Sept. 7 1868, of Santa Cruz. Cal. m Weldon M. Shank Sept. 6. 1893 and had no ch; (e) James Harvey Bissell b March 12, 1871; d May 4, 1924 Canby, Ore (m first, Winifred Elsie Kauffman May 6 1895 San Francisco, Calif. (b Dec. 18, 1876 near Oregon City, Ore., dau Isaac Benjamin and Louisa (Frost) Kauffman, and a step niece of Alfred Bissell) and had ch b Canby,; Ore. 1. Catherine Daphne Bissell b Jan. 21, 1897, of Portland, Ore., m Roland Myrle Hewitt Dec. 24, 1916 Sacremento, Calif. and had; (aa) Gene Myrle Hewitt b Apr. 13, 1921 Portland, Ore; 2. Muriel Maud Bissell b Dec 21, 1900. of Portland, Ore. m Archie R. Averill Oct. 24, 1920 (served in A. E. F. in France during World War) and had; (aa) Addison Rodgers Averill b June 15, 1922 Portland, Ore.; d July 17,

1922 Portland, Ore.; 3, Laura Pauline Bissell b Oct. 30, 1906, of Portland, Ore. James Harvey Bissell married Mrs. Mable Clifford Feb. 2, 1924 at Canby, Ore.).

Three. William Thompson Parks b Apr. 17, 1835; d in inf.

Four. Mary Ann Parks b Dec. 28, 1837; d June 2, 1870 Greenfield, Ill.; m George W. Coonrod Feb. 18, 1858 Meredosia, Ill, (b Sept. 3, 1827 Wayne Co., Ill., d Aug. 21, 1888 Greenfield, Ill. (son of the Rev. Stephen (b 1798 Ky.; d 1872 Ill.) and Claudis (Lee) /Coonrod) and had: (a) Arthur George Coonrod b Jan. 6, 1859 Greenfield, Ill.; d Jan. 8, 1903 Greenfield, Ill.; m Clara Culver Sept. 17, 1885 at Humbolt, Kan. and had no ch. Clara Culver Coonrod m George Melvin and lives Greenfield, Ill.; (b) Louis Parks Coonrod b Oct. 5, 1860 Greenfield, Ill.; lumberman, of Spokane, Wash. (m Margaret F. Ross May 28, 1902 Stronghurst, Ill. and had an only child; 1. Louis Ross Coonrod b Feb. 15, 1915); (c) Catherine Elizabeth Coonrod b Apr. 17, 1863 Greenfield, Ill; d Oct. 8, 1864 Greenfield, Ill.; (d) Mary Emma Coonrod b July 12, 1865 Carrollton, Ill.; d Feb. 27, 1895 Ramsey, Ill. (m George Morrison Feb. 6, 1889 Colorado Spring, Col. and had; 1, Margie Morrison b Aug. 13, 1890 Ramsey, Ill., of Chicago, Ill., m Clifford Russell Coffeen June 28, 1914 Decatur, Ill. and had: (aa) James Arthur Coffeen b Nov. 1, 1917 Indianapolis; (bb) Ruth Coffeen; 2, Mildred Morrison b Apr. 27, 1892 Ramsey, Ill. of Detroit, Mich., m George Edward Fleck June 22, 1916 Clinton, Ill. and had; (aa) Dorothy Jane Fleck b Sept. 27, 1919 Detroit, Mich.; 3. Merrill Morrison b Feb. 2, 1895 Ramsey, Ill.; d Mar. 5, 1895 Ramsey, Ill. George Morrison married the second time); (e) Helen Gertrude Coonrod b Dec. 24, 1868 Carrollton, Ill; d Feb. 22, 1922 Assumption, Ill.; buried Greenfield, Ill. (m Dr. Noah Allen Crouch Aug. 20, 1890 Greenfield, Ill. (b May 16, 1864 Hettick, Ill., son of John Crouch (b 1822 Jonesboro, Tenn.; d 1903 Greenfield, Ill.) and Margaret Ruth Galloway Crouch (b 1827 Sullivan Co., Tenn; d 1873 Hettick, Ill.; m 1849 Sullivan Co, Tenn.) and Greenfield, Ill.; 2. Wilbur Allen Crouch b Sept. 1896 Chesterfield, Ill. with Crowell Publishing Co., Springfield, Ill., m Louise Potts June 5 1921 Lowder, Ill. (b Aug 27, 1900 Lowder, Ill. and had: (aa) Howard Lee Crouch b May 19, 1922; (bb) Louis Allen Crouch b Sept. 27, 1923; 3. Louis Arthur Crouch b Sept. 10, 1902 Chesterfield, Ill.; d June 12, 1912 Assumption, Ill.; buried Greenfield, Ill.; 4. Murice Lee Chouch b Oct. 7, 1907 Assumption, Ill. (George W. Coonrod married second, Mattie E. Nutting 1871, who survived him).

Five. West Parks b June 1, 1841; d in inf.

Six. James Worthington Parks b 1840; d Sept. 1864; unmarried; served as private in Company G. 99th Ill. Reg. in War Between the States.

Seven. William Lucius Cornwell, second to bear the name of William, b June 23, 1849; d 1851.

V. Maria Louisa Tunnell, daughter of John and Nancy Worthington Tunnell, spent her entire life in Anderson Co., Tenn. She was born Mar. 18, 1810 and died Aug. 26, 1851. She married William Scarbrough Freels, son of Isaac and Nancy Freels, Oct, 10, 1833 Anderson Co, Tenn. He was born Oct. 6, 1807 and died March 4, 1886; was chairman of Anderson Co. Court for many years and a prosperous planter. Aug. 11, 1870 W. S. Freels married Susan Caroline Rather, who died July 27, 1901. Children of Maria Louisa Tunnell Freels b near Scarboro, Tenn:

One. John Tunnell Freels b Aug. 26, 1834.

Two. Isaac Clark Freels b Apr. 3, 1836.

Three. William Jasper Freels b Mar. 14, 1838.

Four. James Newton Freels b June 1, 1840.

Five. Jesse McDonald Freels b Oct. 13, 1842.

Six. Nancy Jane Freels b May 17, 1845.

Seven. Sarah England Freels b June 4, 1848.

Eight. Elijah M. Freels b May 15, 1851.

Of these:

One. John Tunnell Freels b Aug. 26, 1834; d Jan. 19, 1911, Anderson Co , Tenn.; m Sarah E. Holt, dau. of Austin and Nancy Holt, July 31, 1855 Anderson Co., Tenn. (d at Scarboro, Tenn. after 1911), and had children born Freels' Bend, Clinch River, Anderson Co., Tenn.; (a) Maria Louisa Freels b Dec. 5, 1856, unm., of Fountain City, Tenn.; (b) William Austin Freels b May 27, 1858, of Edgemoor, Tenn. (m Annie B. Holloway, dau. of Henry and Lou Scarborough Holloway, Oct. 1, 1880 Scarboro, Tenn. (b May 21, 1862) and had ch. born Freels' Bend, Clinch River, Anderson Co., Tenn.; 1. Laura Grace Freels b Jan. 17, 1882; m Colonel Morgan Duncan Dec. 4, 1904 Scarboro, Tenn. and had (aa) Ruth Irene Duncan b Oct. 7, 1905 Edgemoor, Tenn.; (bb) Annie Lois Duncan b Feb. 21, 1908 Edgemoor; d June 25, 1908; (cc) Roscoe Franklin Duncan b Mar. 5, 1911; (dd) Willie Mae Duncan b July 4, 1912 Knoxville, Tenn.; (ee) Mary Marjorie Duncan b June 25, 1915 Knoxville, Tenn.; (ff) Colonel Morgan Duncan, Jr. b Aug. 25, 1921 Madisonville, Tenn.; (gg) Barbara Dorrace Duncan b and d Aug. 25, 1924; 2. Samuel E. Freels b Jan. 15, 1883, farmer; m Alma Belle Nichols Jan. 27, 1923 at Greenfield, Iowa. (b Feb. 19, 1898 Holden, Mo.) and had; (aa) Anna Madeane Freels b Nov. 13, 1923 Scarboro, Tenn.; 3. James Allen Freels b July 4, 1885; farmer; m Clara Etta Duncan June 19, 1912 Clinton, Tenn. (d Sept. 1912); 4. Sallie L. Freels b Oct. 14, 1888; m John Boyd Jones Jan. 3, 1912, Scarboro, Tenn. and had ch. b near Edgemoor, Tenn.; (aa) Jonnie Clarice Jones b June 17, 1913; (bb) Anna Ruth Jones b Mar. 6, 1915; (cc) James Edward Jones b

Apr. 20, 1917; (dd) Laura Elizabeth Jones b Oct. 7, 1919; (ee) Sallie Gene Jones b Jan. 15, 1922; 5. William Austin Freels Jr. b July 18, 1891; mail carrier; served in World War from Sept. 1, 1918 to Jan. 1, 1919; m Evelyn L. Qualls Sept. 15, 1917 Anderson Co., Tenn. (b July 18, 1889 Clinchport, Va.) and had ch. b Scarboro, Tenn.; (aa) Evelyn Louise Freels b Nov. 5, 1918; (bb) William Austin Freels, the Third, b Nov. 29, 1920; (cc) Annie Margaret Freels b Feb. 14, 1922; 6. John Clyde Freels b July 25, 1894; served in World War Over Seas; m Elizabeth Anna Crudgington May 10, 1918 (b Nov. 2, 1897) and had; (aa) Clara Clyde Freels b Mar. 24, 1919; (bb) Robert Crudgington Freeels b Feb. 27, 1921; 7. Leonard Albert Freels b Aug. 23, 1897; clerk, Knoxville, Tenn.; m Helen Lee Patrick May 28, 1924 Maryville, Tenn. (b Dec. 31, 1904); 8. Nora Gene Freels b Oct. 2, 1901, of Oliver Springs, Tenn.; m Arthur Frank Lockett, merchant, Mar. 27, 1924 Clinton, Tenn. (b Sept. 18, 1898); (c) Samuel Clark Freels b Mar. 24, 1860, of Alaska; m ——— ——— (d June 12, 1921 Los Angeles, Calif.) and had; 1. William Pershing Freels; 2. dau. b June 12, 1921; (d) Nancy Jane Freels b Dec. 16, 1871, of Knoxville, Tenn. (m Emilas De Marcas 1886 Anderson Co., Tenn., and had; 1. Mary Freels De Marcas, of Fountain City, Tenn.; m Henry Clark 1922 Knoxville, Tenn. and had one child.)

Two. Isaac Clark Freels b Apr. 3, 1836; d 1890 Anderson Co., Tenn ; m Anna Adelia Morris Nov. 26, 1868, Anderson Co. (b Oct. 1849, of Knoxville, Tenn.) and had ch. b Anderson Co., Tenn.; (a) William Morris Freels b Jan. 19, 1870 (m Rena F. Cobb Nov. 17, 1893 and had: 1. Alice Almira Freels b Aug. 9, 1894; 2. Nellie Ann Freels b Feb. 22, 1896; 3. William Guthrue Freels b July 30, 1898); (b) Adelia Mason Freels b Nov. 3, 1871 (m William Billingsley Feb. 4, 1896 and had 1. Roy McDonald Billingsley b Feb. 19, 1897; d Feb. 20, 1897; 2. Laura Elizabeth Billingsley b Aug. 19, 1898; 3. Henrietta Billingsley; 4. Ernest Billingsley; 5. Anna Grace Billingsley; 6. William Franklin Billingsley); (c) Jesse Tunnell Freels b Feb. 26, 1873 (m Nancy Copeland and had; 1. Arthur Thurman Freels; 2. Raymond Freels; 3. John Isaac Freels; 4.Mary Freels); (d) Elbert Anderson Freels b Apr. 6, 1877 (m Annie B. Diggs and had; 1, Samuel Elwood Freels b Sept. 6, 1902. Anna Mary Freels b Sept. 5, 1902; 3. Essie Mae Freels b Aug. 15, 1906; 4. John Henry Freels b May 26, 1909); (e) Nancy Maria Freels b Dec. 21, 1874; d Aug. 9, 1875; (f) Ernest Clayton Freels b Feb. 20, 1879 (m Flora L. Dunlap Nov. 18, 1906); (g) James Laurence Freels b Apr. 19, 1881; m Eva Tallent Feb. 10, 1906; (h) Manly Clark Freels b Dec. 26, 1884; (i) Oliver Abernethy Freels b Nov. 22, 1886; d Aug. 5, 1887; (j) Suda Jane Freels b Jan. 10, 1888; (k) John Edward Freels b Jan. 29, 1890; d July 1, 1890. Record of 1909.

Three. William Jasper Freels b May 14, 1838; served in C. S. A. and was killed in battle. He was not married.

Four. James Newton Freels b June 1, 1840; d Feb. 11, 1908, Scarboro, Tenn.   On Feb. 14, 1862 he enlisted in the Federal Army and was Second-Lieut. of Co. H. of 13th Regt. of Tenn.   In june 1865 was promoted to a First Lieutenancy.   He married first, Julia Ann Hoskins July 3, 1870 Anderson Co., Tenn. (b Sept. 28, 1849 Anderson Co.; d Jan. 30, 1888 Anderson Co., dau of   George P. and   Mary (Parker) Hoskins) and had ch. b Scarboro, Tenn.; (a) Mary Jane Freels b Oct. 2, 1871, of Harriman, Tenn. (m E. T. McKinney Sept. 6, 1893 (d Feb. 10, 1920 Harriman, Tenn.) and had ch b Harriman, Tenn.; 1. Jesse Leonard McKinney b Sept. 17, 1894; 2. Julia Grace McKinney b Mar. 17, 1897: 3. Mary Phoebe McKinney b Apr. 2. 1902); (b) Martha Maria Freels b June 7, 1873, of Knoxville, Ill. (m Robert Alexander Russell June 8, 1904 Anderson Co., Tenn. and had; 1. Julia Hope Russell b Feb. 29, 1908 La Follette, Tenn.); (c) Margaret Alice Freels b Nov. 17, 1874; d June 24, 1875; (d) William Jasper Freels b Aug. 10, 1876, unmarried; (e) Augusta May Freels b Aug. 5, 1878, of Harriman, Tenn. (m Dr. Rowland Hustler Fowlkes June 8, 1910 Harriman, Tenn. and had ch. b Harriman, Tenn.; 1. Robert Freels Fowlkes b Mar. 3, 1912; 2. Charles Cleveland Fowlkes b Dec. 26, 1914); (f) Stella Washington Freels b Jan. 2, 1880, of La Follette, Tenn.; 1. Allen Meredith Riggs, Jr., b Dec. 14, 1904; Scarboro, Tenn. (d Apr. 1, 1922 La Follette, Tenn.) and had ch. b La Lollette, Tenn.; 1. Allen Meredith Riggs, Jr., b Dec. 14, 1904; 2. Robert Freels Riggs b May 18, 1907; 3. James Washington Riggs b June 10, 1910; 4. William McDonald Riggs b Sept. 28, 1915); (g) Sallie McDonald Freels b Apr. 20, 1882, of Oklahoma City, Okla. (m Chester Earl Crew Dec. 20, 1906 Scarboro, Tenn. (d Oct. 7, 1916 Knoxville, Tenn.) and had ch. b Knoxville; 1. Evalyn Lyons Crew b Sept. 28, 1908; 2. Chester Earl Crew, Jr., b Nov. 29, 1910; (h) James Cleveland Freels b Feb. 3, 1885, druggist, Morristown, Tenn. (m Aileen Fisher July 23, 1919 Morristown, Tenn. and had ch. b Morristown, Tenn.; 1. Charlotte Freels b Sept. 15, 1920; 2. Mary Nelson Freels b Dec. 25, 1923); (i) Samuel Fisher Freels b Oct. 31, 1887 of United States Navy (m Daisy Waymouth at Seattle, Wash.) James Newton Freels married a sister of his first wife, Frances Hoskins Yount, May 11, 1891 Clinton, Tenn. (b Sept, 1863; d May 11, 1896 Scarboro, Tenn.) and had; (j) Wade Clifton Freels b Mar. 10, 1892; unmarried; engineer, Detroit, Mich.; (k) Esther Frances Freels b Dec. 62, 1893, of Oklahoma City, Okla. (m Dr. George Hamilton Gillen Feb. 22, 1916 La Follette, Tenn. and had; 1. Frances Rosaline Gillen b Feb. 17, 1917 South Pittsburg, Tenn.; 2. Joseph Newton Gillen b Apr. 27, 1924 Oklahoma City, Okla ; (1) Victor Boyd Freels b July 31, 1895; unmarried; druggist, Kingsport, Tenn.

Five.   Jesse McDonald Freels b Oct. 13, 1842; d Mar. 29, 1915 East St. Louis, Ill.   He attended Tenn. Univ. at Knoxville and grad. from Amherst College 1871; in 1874 was valedictorian in law school

of Iowa Univ.   In Aug. 1874 he entered upon the practice of law in
E. St. Louis.   Of him "The Bench and Bar of Illinois" says, in part,
he has served as counsel on some of the most celebrated cases that
have been tried in southern Illinois, where his masterly arguments,
sound logic and clear reasoning are unmistakable evidence of his
skill and ability. He has always avoided criminal cases, making a
specialty of corporation and other branches of the civil law." In
Feb. 1862 he enlisted in the Federal Army and was assigned to Co.
E. Third Tenn. Vol. Inf., participating in the leading battles with
his regiment, including the engagements at Richmond and Perryville,
Ky.; Resaca, Ga. and those of the Atlanta campaign under command
of Generals Thomas and Sherman.   Later his regiment returned to
Nashville where the Union troops succeeded in defeating Gen. Hood.
In one battle in which he participated his brother, William Jasper
Freels, who was a soldier in the C. S. A. lost his life. Judge Jesse
M. Freels married first, his second cousin, Alice Tunnell, Nov. 15,
1882 near Plainview, Ill.   She was born Aug. 16, 1857 near
Plainview, Ill. and died Oct. 23, 1886 near Plainview.   She was the
daughter of John and Elizabeth (Brown) Tunnell and granddaughter
of Calvin and Jane (Addair) Tunnell. By this marriage there were
two children.   Judge Jesse Freels married Mary Isabelle Baker, a
relative of his first wife, Dec. 13, 1888 at Red Banks, North Carolina.
Mary Isabelle Baber, of E. St. Louis, Ill., b May 10, 1861 Robeson
Co., N. C. daughter of Angus Sellars Baker (b Feb. 7, 1814 Robeson
Co., N. C ; d Sept. 12, 1883) and Harriet McEahern Baker (b Nov. 23,
1830 Robeson Co., N. C ; d Mar. 16, 1920 Jacksonville, Fla.; m Feb. 2,
1860, A. S. Baker, son of Archibald Baker (b 1769 Moore Co., N. C.;
d 1842) and Catherine McCullum Baker.   Children of Judge Jesse M.
Freels b E. St. Louis, Ill.; (a) Dr. Arthur McDonald Freels b Sept.
12, 1883, of Denison, Texas; served as Capt. in Medical Corps from
Aug. 1918 to Mar. 1920; (m Frances Edna Saunders Dec. 28, 1911
Denison, Texas and had ch. b Denison, Tex.; 1. Jesse Saunders Freels
b Oct. 16, 1912; 2, Frances Edna Freels b Apr. 16, 1914; 3, Alice
Mary Freels b Aug 27, 1922); (b) Alice Tunnell Freels b Apr. 9,
1886, of Washington, D. C. (m Conrad Rutherford Smith, of
Charleston, W. Va., Oct. 14, 1914, E. St. Louis, Ill. (b Mar. 10, 1883
Roanoke, Va; d Aug. 10, 1920 Washington D. C.) and had no ch.;
(c) Jesse Baker Freels b Sept. 18, 1889; d Feb. 15, 1893; (d.) John
William Freels b Dec. 27, 1893, of E. St. Louis, Ill.; unmarried;
Assistant States Attorney E. St. Louis served in World War; was
commissioned in regular army from first training camp at Ft.
Sheridan, 1917, and served in 57th Inf. becoming regimental
adjudant, then on on division staff 15th Division; now Capt. of Inf.
Reserve Corps; (e) Mary Isabelle Freels, the Second, b Dec. 17, 1895,
of Jacksonville, Fla. (m Lieut. George Logan Rosborough June 18,
1919 E. St. Louis, Ill. (b Windsor, Fla., son of John and Mary King
Rosborough) and had; 1. George Logan Rosborough the Second, b

May 14, 1922 in Jacksonville, Fla.); (f) Archibald James Freels b **Jan.** 11, 1901; unmarried; Ensign in U. S. Navy; graduated from U. S. Naval Acadamy June 1924.

Six. Nancy Jane Freels b May 17, 1845; d May 24, 1913 Knoxville, Tenn. She m Samuel Black Oct. 31, 1867 Scarboro, Tenn. (b Mar. 29, 1844 Anderson Co., Tenn.; d Feb. 10, 1894 near Scarboro, Tenn., son of John Black (b Sept. 1781) who served in War of 1812). Samuel Black enlisted in Co. H First Tenn. Federal Inf. which he served till the organization of Third Inf. when he was promoted to Lieut. of Co. C. and was discharged from service Feb. 29, 1865. Ch. b near Clinch River, Anderson Co., Tenn.; (a) son b and d Sept. 20, 1868; (b) Joseph McDonald Black b Aug. 28, 1869; unmarried; attorney, Denver, Colo.; (c) John Black b Feb.28, 1871; d Mar. 26, 1912 Denver Colo ; unmarried; (d) William Black b Mar. 24, 1873; d Oct. 1, 1923 Knoxville, Tenn; a number of years he practiced law in Knoxville; (e) Maria Tunnell Black b Feb. 23, 1875; d Aug. 21, 1909 Knoxville, Tenn. (m Jacob T. Mary Sept. 15, 1908 and had no children); (f) Bettie Tilden Black b Oct. 18, 1876, of Stockton, Calif. (m Otis E. Brown Sept. 30, 1915 San Francisco, Calif. and had; 1. Jessie Tunnell Brown b Aug. 3, 1916.)

Seven. Sarah England Freels b June 4, 1848; d Sept. 20, 1891 Scarboro, Tenn. She married Dr. Robert J. Lockett Dec. 31, 1868 (d 1875 Scarboro, Tenn.) and had ch b Scarboro, Tenn.; (a) Sarah Alice Lockett b Sept. 23, 1869; d abt May 1915 Knoxville, Tenn. m first, Clarence Kent Sept. 7, 1879 (d July 8, 1904) and had; 1. Mary Garland Kent b June 27, 1898, of Macon, Ga.; m Charles Edward Wright Mar. 26, 1920; 2. Robert Clarence Kent b June 27, 1898; and m second, D. J. Davis May 30, 1910); (b) Mary J. Lockett b Oct. 4, 1871; d Mar. 8, 1901, Knoxville, Tenn.; unmarried; (c) Dr. William Robert Lockett b Nov. 14, 1873, of Ft. Stanton, New Mexico (m Gertrude Rook Oct. 11, 1904 Knoxville, Tenn. and had; 1. William Robert Lockett, Jr., b June 2, 1906 Knoxville, Tenn.); Sarah England Freels Lockett m Dr. Henry Thomas Fisher, who d 1915 Knoxville, Tenn.

Eight. Elijah M Freels b and d May 15, 1851.

VI. Emmeran Engleton Tunnell, dau of John and Nancy Worthington, was born May 19, 1812 and died in Texas, of yellow fever, which disease claimed her two sons. About 1830 she married William Williams in Tenn. and had;

One. Hosea Williams b abt 1832; d in Texas.

Two. Calvin Williams b abt 1835; d in Texas; m ——— ——— and had at least one child; (a) Calvin Williams, Jr., who lived in Texas in 1880.

VII. William Valentine Tunnell, son of John and Nancy Worthington Tunnell, was born May 3, 1814 and died Oct. 16, 1862 Macoupin Co, Ill. He m Tirgah Rhoads July 5, 1838 (b Aug. 5, 1817; d Apr. 1, 1859 Macoupin Co., Ill, dau of Samuel Vanmeter Rhoads). Their three older ch. b Greene Co., Ill.; others in Macoupin Co., Ill.;

One. Franklin Tunnell b Oct. 3, 1839.

Two. John Luther Tunnell b May 7, 1841.

Three. Margaret Ann Tunnell b Sept. 19, 1843.

Four. Frances Jane Tunnell b June 24, 1845. .

Five Dorinda Tunnell b Mar. 28, 1847.

Six. Samuel Tunnell b June 20, 1849.

Seven. Nancy Tunnell b Sept. 6, 1851.

Eight Wiand Tunnell b Sept. 8, 1853.

Nine Mary Eleanor Tunnell b June 4, 1855.

Of these:

One. Franklin Tunnell b Oct. 3, 1839; d Oct. 31, 1839 Greene Co., Ill.

Two. John Luther Tunnell b May 7, 1841; d Oct. 15, 1914 Ozark, Mo.; m Nancy Annie Pettijohn May 3, 1872 Greene Co., Mo. (living at Ozark, Mo., dau of John M. and Margarette A. (Wilson) Pettijohn) and had ch. b Ozark, Mo.; (a) William Thaddeus Tunnell b Mar. 28, 1873, restaurant keeper Ozark, Mo. (m Margaret Shikey Oct. 20, 1915 Springfield, Mo. and had no ch.; (b) Clyde Tunnell b Dec. 2, 1874 (m Mary Vaughn Sept. 23, 1903 and had; 1. Vaughn Tunnell b Aug. 12, 1904); (c) Royce B. Tunnell b Jan. 4, 1879, restaurant keeper, Springfield, Mo. m Madge Park; (d) Lynn Tunnell b Aug. 30, 1883; unmarried; clerk, Ozark, Mo.

Three. Margaret Ann Tunnell b Sept. 19, 1843, whose home was in Portland, Ore.; d Aug. 7, 1925 at Rogersville, Mo. while on a visit m Felix Grundy Haycraft July 10, 1873 Fulton, Mo. (b Apr. 23, 1844 Macoupin Co., Ill.; d Apr. 26, 1915, son of Isaac Van Meter Haycraft) and had ch. b Wichita, Kan.; (a) Verne Isaac Haycraft b Sept. 11, 1874; salesman, Wichita, Kan. (m Sarah Lavinia Wood June 20, 1909 (b Oct. 1887 Pittis Co., Mo., dau of Newton Wood) and had: 1. Dora Eloise Haycraft b Apr. 26, 1911 Wichita, Kan.); (b) Dora Emily Haycraft b Sept. 21, 1876, of Portland, Ore. (m Paul E. Graham, merchant, July 26, 1903 (b Apr. 3, 1873, son of James R. Graham) and had: 1. Zoa Margaret Graham b July 14, 1905 Wichita, Kan; 2. Dora Eleanor Graham b Aug. 30, 1911 Wichita, Kan.

Four. Frances Jane Tunnell b June 24, 1845; d Mar. 29, 1869 Macoupin Co., Ill.; unmarried.

Five Dorinda Tunnell b Mar. 28, 1847; d Jan. 15, 1873 Macoupin Co., Ill.; unmarried.

Six. Samuel Tunnell b June 20, 1849 near Carlinville, Ill, of Dallas, Tex.; m Mary Jane Candler Dec. 25, 1873 Chesterfield, Ill. (b Jan. 20, 1856 Macoupin Co., Ill ; d Dec. 11, 1922 Dallas, Tex., dau of Cant and Millicent (Holliday) Candler) and had; (a) Horace Luther Tunnell b Feb. 3, 1875 Chesterfield, Ill.; d Feb. 6, 1879 Chesterfield; (b) William C. Tunnell b Dec. 12, 1877 Chesterfield; d Jan. 20, 1879 Chesterfield; (c) Nellie Tunnell b Aug. 5, 1879 near Carlinville, Ill., of Hutchinson, Kan. (m Benjamin J. Yowell July 25, 1900 Red Bud, Kan. (b Nov. 7, 1874 near Carlinville, Ill., son of John J. (b July 12, 1846 near Carlinville, Ill.) and Sarah Ann (Wyer) Yowell, (b Mar. 36, 1850 Fulton Co., Ill.) and had; ch b Wichita, Kas., save youngest b Cotulla, Tex.; 1. Benjamin Winchester Yowell b May 9, 1901 m Faye M McReynolds Aug. 23, 1924 Colorado Springs, Col. (b Jan. 24, 1904 Grant City, Mo., dau J. H. and Ella McReynolds); 2. Theodore Ross Yowell b Aug. 23, 1901; 3. Nellie Brook Yowell b Sept. 16, 1903 m Earl E. Roberts Dec. 9, 1923 Liberal, Kan. (b May 24, 1900, son of Sherman and Nellie M. (Shipley) Roberts) and had; (aa) Virginia Lee Roberts b Sept. 26, 1924; 4. Thelma Rick Yowell b Jan. 19, 1905; d Apr. 8, 1905. Dan O'Leary Yowell b Oct. 5, 1906; d Aug. 30, 1909 Wichita, Kan.; 6. Patricia Adelle Yowell b May 10, 1908; 7. Cleo Carol Yowell b Oct. 12, 1909; 8. Roberta Lenorr Yowell b Feb. 14, 1912); (d) Minnie Millicent Tunnell b Dec. 26, 1881 near Garden Plains, Kan.; d Jan. 7, 1900 DeSoto, Mo.; (e) Chester S. Tunnell b Nov. 10, 1883 near Garden Plains, Kan.; Baptist minister, of Portland, Ore. (m Helen L. Tutt Nov. 1, 1910 in Mo. and had; 1, Chester Leonard Tunnell b June 30, 1912; 2. Georgia Helen Tunnell b July 24, 1914); (f) Nora Margaret Tunnell b Oct. 10, 1887 Wichita, Kan.; of Dallas, Tex. (m Robert J. Ross Nov. 18, 1914 Dallas, Tex, and had; 1. Margaret Ross b Aug. 16, 1915 Dallas, Texas.)

Seven. Nancy Tunnell b Sept. 6, 1851; d Oct. 20, 1851 in Macoupin Co., Ill.

Eight. Wiand Tunnell b Sept. 8, 1853, of Tunnell and Son, Rodgersville Roller Mill. Co., Rogersville, Mo.; m Susie Chestnut Mar. 9, 1879 Ozark, Mo. (b Jan. 29. 1859, dau of William and Martha Chestnut) and had children born Ozark, Mo.; (a) Clara Tunnell b June 10, 1880 m ———— Thomas and had: 1. John Wiand Thomas; (b) Harold Tunnell b Mar. 28, 1883 (m Myrtle Beatie June 6, 1906 (b Dec. 9, 1886) and had; 1. Maurine Tunnell b May 14, 1907; 2. Claiborne Tunnell b July 1, 1908; d Feb. 17, 1920; 3. Mary Tunnell b July 11, 1911; 4. Mildred Tunnell b Dec. 22, 1914).

Nine. Mary Eleanor Tunnell b June 4, 1855; d Sept. 9, 1925 at Portland, Ore. m Samuel Lorenzo Berryman June 22, 1873 in lMacoupin Co., Ill. who served in Co. F. 123rd Ill. Inf. in the War Between the States; d 1908 Chesterfield, Ill ; and had an only child; (a) William Claude Berryman b Sept. 21, 1874 Chesterfield, Ill ; d Jan. 22, 1892 Chesterfield, Ill.

VIII. Samuel Jasper Tunnell, son of John and Nancy Worthington Tunnell, was born Sept. 9, 1816 and died Mar. 1, 1882 in Mo. He married Cornelia Estill 1850 in Mo. (d Nov. 6, 1918 Cedar Co., Mo.) and had children born Dade Co., Mo.

One. Nancy Matilda Tunnell b Oct. 14, 1851.

Two. William Franklin Tunnell b Aug. 4, 1853.

Three. Robert Worthington Tunnell b Nov. 5, 1856.

Four. James Estill Tunnell b Apr. 2, 1858.

Five. Sarah Elizabeth Tunnell b Nov. 3, 1861.

Six. Fannie Margaret Tunnell b Apr. 11, 1864.

Seven. Cornelia Colfax Tunnell b Jan. 7, 1869.

Of these:

One. Nancy Matilda Tunnell b Oct. 14, 1851; unmarried, of Stockton, Mo.

Two. William Franklin Tunnell b Aug. 4, 1853; farmer, Aldrich, Mo.; m A. L. Fanning Nov. 3, 1881 and had: (a) Nora D. Tunnell b Mar. 23, 1883 m first, Ben Griffin Sept. 1902 (d Dec. 20, 1914) and had: 1. Carrie Griffin b June 6, 1904; 2. Jesse Griffin b June 24, 1907; and m second, William A. Hays Oct. 10, 1917 and had; 3. Martha Helen Hays b Dec. 22, 1918); (b) Lena May Tunnell b Mar. 12, 1885; d June 2, 1914; (c) H. G. Tunnell b June 5, 1887; farmer, Aldrich, Mo. (m Ida Lantrip Dec. 25, 1907 and had; 1. Quinton Tunnell b Feb. 16, 1909; 3. Floris Tunnell b June 1, 1911; 3. Carl Tunnell b Oct. 1916; 4. Mazie Tunnell b 1920); (d) Ivy G. Tunnell b May 26, 1889 (m Earnest Tefertiller May 26, 1907 and had; 1. Vivian Tefertiller b Dec. 21, 1909); (e) Charles R. Tunnell b Oct. 18, 1893; farmer, Aldrich, Mo. (m Mable Taylor and had: 1. Gula Tunnell b Feb. 5, 1917; 2. Hulda Tunnell b July 4, 1919; 3. Etalue Tunnell b Oct. 16, 1924); (f) William B. Tunnell b Mar. 31, 1896, of Dadeville, Mo.; served in World War; m Clara M. Davis; (g) Eunice O Tunnell b June 28, 1905.

Three. Robert Worthington Tunnell b Nov. 5, 1856; farmer, Stockton, Mo.; m Martha Bullen Jan. 13, 1883 (b Sept. 10, 1853; d Aug. 27, 1897 Jasper, Mo.) and had: (a) Lewis E Tunnell b July 4, 1884, of White City, Kan., who married and had; 1, Annabell Tunnell b Apr. 4, 1922 near Dadeville, Mo.; (b) Leslie Ivan Tunnell b Sept 5, 1888 near Dadeville, Mo.; d June 24, 1890 near Dadeville.

Four. James Estill Tunnell b Apr. 2, 1851, of Miami, Okla.; m Laura Smith Jan. 10, 1881 and had; (a) Iley Bennis Tunnell b Dec. 29, 1881, of Miami, Okla. (m Nellie Tafner Dec. 22, 1906 and had; 1. Pauline Tunnell; 2. Marvin Tunnell; 3. Harold Tunnell); (b) William Edgar Tunnell b Mar. 6, 1883, of Miller, Mo. (m Ida Todd and had; 1, Fern Tunnell; 2. Opal Tunnell; 3. Homer Tunnell; 4. Blaine Tunnell; 5. Howard Tunnell); (c) Laura Belle Tunnell b Jan. 19, 1885 m H. H. Haynie; (d) Jewel Virginia Tunnell b Mar. 6, 1888 m L. L. Fallis; (e)Frank Hartford Tunnell b Nov. 8, 1890, of Miami, Okla. (m Edith Taylor and had; 1. Frank Leonard Tunnell b Jan. 10, 1924); (f) Clara Pearl Tunnell b Dec. 9, 1893 (m Blaines S. Taylor and had; 1. Virginis Taylor; 2. Blaine Taylor; 3. Howard Taylor); (g) Flossie Mable Tunnell b Mar. 28, 1896 m W. D. Barger; (h) Margie Marie Tunnell b Jan. 28, 1898 m L. L. Hall; (i) Harry Jackson Tunnell b July 17, 1900 (m Leah Nickelson and had; 1. Gladys Tunnell; 2. Harriett Tunnell); (j) Lake Freta Tunnell b Jan. 19, 1903 m W. W. Henry; (k) James Carl Tunnell b July 17, 1906.

Five. Sarah Elizabeth Tunnell b Nov. 3, 1861, of Stockton, Mo. m W. F. Adams Sept. 1, 1917.

Six. Fannie Margaret Tunnell b Apr. 11, 1864, of Fair Play, Mo.; m James Lynrh Mar. 10, 1895 Dade Co., Mo. (b Oct. 25, 1866 Stockton, Mo.) and had; (a) William Samuel Lynch b Sept. 30, 1896; unmarried, of Stockton Mo.; (b) James Elmer Lynch b Nov. 4, 1898; d Aug. 3, 1901.

Seven. Cornelia Colfax Tunnell b Jan. 7, 1869, of Fair Play, Mo.; m James Thomason Sept. 9, 1894 and had; (a) Roy B. Thomason b Sept. 12, 1896; (b) James L. Thomason b Dec. 24, 1900, (c) Herbert Thomason b Feb. 11, 1902; (d) Cornelia A. Thomason b Nov. 12, 1906; (e) Silvia L. Thomason b. Feb. 14, 1910.

IX. Jesse Worthington Tunnell, son of John and Nancy Worthington Tunnell, was born Aug. 29, 1818 and died Dec. 3, 1901 in Cincinnatti, Arkansas. He married Polly Ann England Aug. 6, 1840 Anderson Co., Tenn. (b Jan. 26, 1822 Anderson Co., Tenn.; d 1905 Washington Co., Ark) and had children born in Missouri.

One. John Sevier Tunnell b 1842.

Two. Alfred Noble Tunnell b 1843.

Three. Nancy Ames Tunnell b June 27, 1845.

Four. James M. Tunnell b 1847.

Five. Barton Luther Tunnell b 1849.

Six. Mary Tunnell b Sept. 2, 1851.

Seven. Martha Isabelle Tunnell b 1853.

Eight. Sarah Ann Tunnell b 1855.

Nine.   Samuel Marion Tunnell b 1855.

Ten.   Jesse Smith Tunnell b 1859.

Eleven   Robert Worthington Tunnell b 1861.

Twelve.   Bathsheba Ellen Tunnell b 1863.

Thirteen.   Ibera Scott Tunnell b 1866.

Of these:

One.   John Sevier Tunnell b 1842; d 1863 Chillicothe, Mo; unmarried.

Two.   Alfred Noble Tunnell b 1843; d 1858 Sullivan Co., Mo.

Three.   Nancy Ames Tunnell b June 27, 1845, of Eureka, Kan.;
m John Cicero Clopton, Dadeville, Mo. (deceased) and had; (a)
William Horace Clopton b 1868; d small; (b) Ella Mae Clopton b
Sept. 16, 1870, of Atwater, Calif. (m N. A. Neil and had; 1. Ivan
Neil; 2. Royal Neil, of Kansas City; 3. Shirley Neil, of Carthage, Mo.;
4. Cora Neil, of Aldrich, Mo. m ———— Mallicoat; 5. Osa Neil m ————
— ————; (c) Harry Clopton b Sept. 14, 1872, of Stockton, Mo. (m
Desta M. Meredith Aug. 28, 1892 and had; Mertie Alma Clopton b
Dec 29, 1893, of Carthage, Mo.; m James A. Richardson and had;
(aa) James Richardson, Jr.; (bb) Paul Franklin Richardson; (cc)
Carl Edward Richardson; (dd) Wilbur Lee Richardson; 2. Willie
Odessa Clopton b Aug. 11, 1896, of Carthage, Mo.; m H. C. Stark
and had; (aa) Katherine June Stark; (bb) Winifred Marie Stark;
(cc) Barbara Jean Stark; 3. Bernie Wilbur Clopton b June 26, 1901;
4. Ada Irene Clopton b Mar. 6, 1905 m Donald Paynher June 28, 1924;
5. Gladys Lucile Clopton b Nov. 22, 1907; 6 Paul Meredith Clopton
b Dec. 1, 1911); (d) Mattie Jane Clopton b Dec. 9, 1874; d Jan. 10,
1876; (e) Robert Ira Clopton b abt 1876; d abt 1886; (f) Mary
Elnora Clopton; (g) Maud Elva Clopton, of Eureka, Kan. m W. T.
Meredith; (h) Maggie Clopton b Sept. 13, 1882; d Mar. 28, 1909; (i)
John Oral Clopton, of Eldorado Springs, Mo. (m Birdie Heller and
had; 1. Pauline Clopton; 2. Muriel Clopton; 3. Gete (?) Clopton);
(j) Jessie Clopton b June 6, 1887, of Cedar Springs, Mo. m Claud
Neely and had five children).

Four.   James M. Tunnell b 1848; d 1849.

Five.   Barton Luther Tunnell b 1849; d 1872 Cave Springs, Mo.;
unmarried.

Six.   Mary Tunnell b Sept. 2, 1851 Mercer Co., Mo., of Summers,
Ark.; m first, E. L. Sheridan 1875 and had; (a)   Edward   Leonard
Sheridan b Oct. 11, 1877; d 1920; and m second, J. E. Brand 1886
Grand View, Tex. and had; (b) Samuel Claud Brand b May 7, 1889
Grand View; d Jan. 7, 1890 Grand View.

Seven.   Martha Isabelle Tunnell b 1853, of Manitou, Col. in 1913;
m ———— Ramey at Ft. Dodge, Kan.

Eight. Sarah Anna Tunnell b July 7, 1855; m Daniel Clayton
Rook Dec. 21, 1871 (b Oct. 4, 1850) and had ten children, all living
1924; (a) Fred Rook b Oct. 14, 1872, of Porterville, Calif. (m Belle
Vance, of Dadeville, Mo. 1906 and had; 1. Rex Rook; 2. Elmo Rook;
3. Leon Rook); (b) Nancy Ellen Rook b Aug. 4, 1874, of College
Place, Wash. (m N. J. Perkins, of Dadeville, Mo. and had; 1. Homer
Perkins, Missionary in Japan, married and had one child; 2. Blanche
Perkins; 3. Ida Perkins; 4. Jewel Perkins; 5. Tex Perkins; 7. James
Perkins); (c) Oren H. Rook b June 14, 1876. of Spokane, Wash. (m
Nellie Gail Wetzel 1912 and had no ch.); (d) Arthur Rook b Mar. 15,
1878, of Huntington, Ore. (m Pearl Moudy, of Caldwell,' Idaho and
had no \ch.); (e) Stella Rook b June 30, 1880, of Lamar, Col. (m
Elbert Perkins, of Dadeville, Mo. 1900 and had; 1. Bernice Perkins
m George Batdarf 1918 Lamar, Col. and had; (aa) Dwayne Batdarf;
(bb) Dale Batdarf; (cc) Elbert Franklin Batdarf; 2. Gail Perkins
m Gay Walker 1922 Bristol, Col.; 3. Sam Perkins; 4. Joe Perkins;
5. Wanda Perkins m Walter Stussex 1924; 6. Helen Perkins; 7. Fern
Perkins; 8. Allie Maxine Perkins; 9. Elbert Rook Perkins; 10. Stella
Lee Perkins); (f) J. Buckner Rook b Aug. 23, 1882, of Dadeville,
Mo. (m Mecie Friend 1907 Dadeville, Mo. and had; 1. Lowell Bryon
Rook; 2. Dwayne Clayton Rook; 3. Thayes Elton Rook); (g) Lloyd
Rook b Nov. 12, 1885, of Greenfield, Mo. m Alta Wilkinson 1916
Greenfield, Mo. and had no ch.; (h) Buel Rook b Sept. 7, 1889, of
Greenfield, Mo. (m Ola May Fitzpatrick 1914 Lockwood, Mo. and
had; 1, Cleo Wayne Rook; 2, John Clayton Rook); (i) Fern J. Rook
b Mar. 13, 1897, of Greenfield, Mo. m Frank Poe 1916 Greenfield and
had no ch.; (j) Creed C. Rook b July 29, 1901; unmarried, Everton,
Mo.

Nine. Samuel Marion Tunnell b 1857, of Summers, Ark.; m
Sarah Jones 1897 Cincinnatti, Ark. and had no children.

Ten. Jesse Smith Tunnell b 1859, of Summers, Ark; m Lizzie
Dean Parks 1899 Cincinnatti, Ark. and had; (a) Mary Kate Tunnell
b Oct. 21, 1900; (b) Dean Parks Tunnell (daughter) b Jan. 25, 1905;
(c) Jesse Ewell Tunnell b May 11, 1911.

Eleven. Robert Worthington Tunnell b 1861; m first Emma D.
Mason 1889 Cincinnatti, Ark. (d 1896) and had; (a) Jesse Rhea
Tunnell b 1894, of Clarksdale, Arizona; and m second, Cora Raper
1899.

Twelve. Bathsheba Ellen Tunnell b 1863; d 1865 near Quincy, Ill.

Thirteen Ibera Scott Tunnell b 1866 Dade Co., Mo., of Summers,
Ark.; m Robert Burton 1903 Cincinnatti, Ark. and had; (a) James
Samuel Burton b Dec 19, 1905 Springvale, Ark.; (b) Jewel Ruth
Burton b Oct. 1, 1908 Springvale, Ark.; (c) Robert Clark Burton b
July 20, 1913 Summers, Ark.

X. John Calvin Tunnell, son of John and Nancy Worthington Tunnell, was born Nov. 17, 1820 and d Apr. 17, 1848 Campbell Station, Tenn.   He married Nancy Jane Roberts, dau of John and Martha (Mangrum) Roberts Nov. 16, 1843 Anderson Co., Tenn. and had ch b Anderson Co.   Nancy Jane Roberts Tunnell married Pleasant M. Freels (b Oct. 25, 1827; d Aug. 3, 1877, half-brother of William Scarborough Freels who married Maria Louisa Tunnell) Apr. 8, 1852.

One.   Martha Ann Tunnell b Nov. 17, 1844 .

Two.   Sarah Jane Tunnell b June 18, 1846.

Three.   John Lafayette Tunnell b Feb. 23, 1848.

Of these:

One.   Martha Ann Tunnell b Nov. 17, 1844; d Anderson Co., Tenn.; m John H. Hale May 28, 1865 Anderson Co., Tenn. and had ch. l in that county; (a) Olive Hale b Feb. 5, 1872, of Grand Junction, Col.; (m Joseph F. Key May 29, 1893 Anderson Co., Tenn. and had ch. b Knox Co., Tenn.; 1, Frank Key b July 18, 1895; 2, Woodie L. Key b Nov. 8, 1896 m Olive Barnard Apr. 9, 1920 and had; (aa) Virginia Marie Key b July 18, 1922; 3, Sadie F. Key b Jan. 3, 1900; 4, William O. Key b July 30, 1901; 5, Joseph E. Key b July 12, 1904; 6, Neta Mae Key b July 14, 1906; 7, Roy E. Key b July 4, 1908; 8, Ross Key b Oct. 2, 1911; 9, Martha B. Key b Sept. 22, 1913; 10, Daisy Beatrice Key b May 8, 1915); (b) William Tunnell Hale b June 17, 1874, of Edgemoor, Tenn. (m Sallie Pearl Wals Aug. 16, 1900 Bonham, Tex. (b Jan. 21, 1883 Bonham, Tex; d Mar. 18, 1923 Edgemoore, Tenn.) and had ch. b Anderson Co., Tenn.; 1, E. L. Hale b Mar. 1, 1902; 2, Mattie L. Hale b July 14, 1904 m Ray Bowman Oct. 25, 1923; 3. J. E Hale b Oct. 13, 1906; 4, W. O. Hale b Dec. 22, 1908; 5, W. H. Hale (daughter) b Dec. 25, 1910; 6, Edna L. Hale b Nov. 25, 1917; 7, Teddy Carter Hale b Sept. 5. 1919); (c) Samuel McLain Hale; (d) Ida Florence Hale m ———— Hudson.

Two.   Sarah Jane Tunnell b June 28, 1846; d in int, in Anderson Co., Tenn.

Three.   John Lafayette Tunnell b Feb. 23, 1848; m Lucretia M. Ellis Apr. 11, 1870 Anderson Co., Tenn. and had several children including; (a) Charles Tunnell; (b) Joe Tunnell.

XI. Martin Luther Tunnell, son of John and Nancy Worthington Tunnell, was born Feb. 24, 1824 and died Sept. 29, 1903 Santa Maria, Calif.   He married Salina Haskins May 11, 1848 Anderson Co., Tenn. She was born Apr. 4, 1824 and died Feb. 5, 1903 Santa Maria, Calif ; dau of John (b Apr. 27, 1783) and Margaret Haskins (b May 10, 1793). They left Anderson Co., Tenn. and crossed the plains to Calif. in 1852 and settled near Ukiah where they lived until 1867 when they moved to Santa Maria.   Their son G. R. Tunnell lives on their farm.   Children;

One.   John Lafayette Haskins Tunnell b Nov. 18, 1850.

Two.   Frank Marion Tunnell b Apr. 18, 1853.

Three.   Eliza Jane Tunnell b Dec. 30, 1854.

Four.   Thomas Jasper Tunnell b Nov. 18, 1856.

Five.   James Monroe Tunnell b Jan. 13, 1859.

Six.   William Tunnell b Feb. 5, 1861.

Seven.   Martin Luther Tunnell, Jr., b July 11, 1863.

Eight.   George Robert Tunnell b Dec. 18, 1865.

Nine.   Henry Clay Tunnell b Sept. 5, 1867.

Ten.   Nellie Anna Tunnell b Santa Maria, Calif.

Of these;

One.   John Lafayette Haskins Tunnell b Nov. 18, 1850; d abt 1917 Santa Maria, Calif.; m Ella Cook Sept. 5, 1879 and had; (a) Theray Zoe Tunnell, of San Luis Obispo, Calif. (m Thomas F. Delaney and had no ch.) (b) Charles Tunnell (m .——————— ——————— and had; 1, Byron Tunnell); (c) Theron Tunnell, of Fullerton, Calif. (m Alta ——————— and had a son b 1922).

Two.   Frank Marion Tunnell b Apr. 18, 1853, of Los Olives, Calif. m Emma Angeline Hopper Oct. 19, 1875 and had; (a) Fred Francis Tunnell b Oct. 14, 1876, of Santa Maria, Calif. (m Cora Hartley Sept. 5, 1900 and had; 1, Laverne Francis Tunnell b Aug. 2, 1903; 2, Muriel Violet Tunnell b Oct. 18, 1907; 3. James Tunnell b Dec. 27, 1909); (b) Elbert Jefferson Tunnell b Oct. 10, 1878; unmarried, Los Olives, Calif.; (c) Elsie Evangeline Tunnell b Aug. 8, 1881, of San Luis Obispo, Calif. (m Lemuel Thompson Mar. 17, 1902 and had; 1, Eugene Clifford Thompson b May 25, 1906); (d) Myrtle Helen Tunnell b Sept. 30, 1884, of San Jose, Calif. (m George Thorpe Sept. 19, 1904 and had; 1, Claire Elane Thorpe b Mar. 8, 1908); (e) Mable Claire Tunnell b Dec. 15, 1886 m Bert Hardison June 30, 1909; (f) Raymond Tunnell b Oct. 6, 1889, unmarried, Los Olives, Calif; (g) Gertrude Ferrel Tunnell b Sept. 27, 1891 (m first, James Richard Torrence May 21, 1911, and second, Chris Sorenson and had two ch); (h) Sadie Mildred Tunnell b Aug. 18, 1893; (i) Russell Dewey Tunnell b Mar. 18, 1895, of Gavista, Calif. m Marie Pointer Dec. 18, 1922 Santa Barbara, Calif.; (j) Sybil Sanderson Tunnell b May 22, 1900, unmarried.

Three.   Eliza Jane Tunnell b Dec. 30, 1854, of Santa Maria, Calif.; m first, John Hopper Jan. 25, 1872 and had no children. She m William Hobson abt 1878 and had; (a) Frank Hobson died small; (b) Ethel Hobson (b Oct. 1881 married Regnaldo Olivera abt 1898 and second, Louis Holt and had no issue by either marriage.

Four. Thomas Jasper Tunnell b Nov. 18, 1856; d Mar. 6, 1924 Santa Maria, Calif.; m Mary Jane Bradley Nov. 28, 1879 (b Jan. 21, 1859 South Wingfield, Derbyshire, Eng., of Santa Maria, Calif.) and had children b Santa Maria, Calif.; (a) Annie Elizabeth Tunnell b Sept. 11, 1880 (m Jesse James Guthrie July 5, 1910 Santa Barbara, Calif. (d Mar. 24, 1919 San Francisco, Calif.) and had ch b Santa Maria, Calif.; 1. Mary Ellen Guthrie b Sept. 6, 1912; 2. Jesse James Guthrie, Jr. b Oct 30, |1915; 3. Thomas Arthur Guthrie b Mar. 6, 1917); (b) Lola Tunnell b Dec. 31, 1881; d Mar. 3, 1883 Santa Maria, Calif.; (c) Arthur William Tunnell b Aug. 11, 1883; d Jan. 29, 1919 Sisquoc, Calif. (m Rosa Flores May 6, 1907 San Luis Obispo, Calif., who died a few days before her husband, Jan. 13, 1919) and had ch b Sisquoc, Calif.; 1. William Ernest Tunnell b Mar. 14, 1908; 2. Clarence Willard Tunnell b Nov. 20, 1909); (d) Sadie Tunnell b Nov. 26, 1893; d June 12, 1895 Santa Maria; (e) Ida May Tunnell b Oct 6, 1896, unmarried, of Santa Maria, Calif.; (f) Thomas Dewey Tunnell b Nov. 29, 1898, of Santa Maria; m Mary Kathleen Hourihan Dec. 31, 1924 Santa Maria; (g) Ellen Anona Tunnell b Jan. 10, 1904, m Tony Brass and had no children.

Five. James Monroe Tunnell b Jan. 13, 1859; d Jan. 2, 1904; unmarried.

Six. William Tunnell b Feb. 5, 1861, of Santa Maria, Calif.; m Fannie Davis abt 1882 and had; (a) Roy Tunnell m Ann Murdock and had no ch.; (b) Teen Tunnell m Chester Martin and had; 1. Adela Patrice Martin; 2 Bobbie Martin; (c) Veda Tunnell m Alec Dalessi and had; 1. Billy Dalessi.

Seven. Martin Luther Tunnell, Jr. b July 11, 1863, of Big Creek, Calif.; m Florence ———— (deceased) and had an only child; (a) Paul Tunnell b abt 1897.

Eight. George Robert Tunnell b Dec. 18, 1865, of Santa Maria, Calif.; m Ellen Kortner Oct 4, 1905 San Luis Obispo, Calif. (b Sept. 1880) and had; (a) son b and d July 1906; (b) Teresa Salina Tunnell b Oct 14, 1907 Santa Maria, Calif.; (c) George Curtis Tunnell b Jan 8, 1910 San Francisco.

Nine. Henry Clay Tunnell b Sept. 5, 1867, of Santa Maria, Calif. m Fannie Stowell Nov. 10, 1908 and had no children.

Ten. Nellie Ann Tunnell, of San Francisco, Calif.; m first, Thomas Sedgwick and had an only child; (a) Neal Willard Sedgwick b Jan. 2, 1896 Santa Maria, Calif.; d Dec. 1918, unmarried, and m second, Charles C. Shattuck Oct. 1907 and had no children by this marriage.

XII. Nancy Adeline Tunnell, dau of John and Nancy Worthington Tunnell, was born Nov. 25, 1826 and died Dec. 10, 1909 near

Troup, Tex.   She married Ampton (or Armstead) B. Norman July 16, 1847 Knox Co., Tenn. (d Apr. 4, 1891 near Troup, Tex.) and had ch. b near Troup, Texas.

One.   Maggie Norman b Apr. 28, 1848.

Two.   Lafayette Norman b Sept. 25, 1850.

Three   Mary C. Norman b Feb. 12, 1852.

Four.   Sallie L. Norman.

Five.   Ophelia Norman.

Six.   T. Douglas Norman.

Seven.   Octavia Norman.

Eight.   William Norman.

Nine.   Luther Tunnell Norman b Sept. 10, 1872.

Of these:

One.   Maggie Norman b Apr. 28, 1848; d Feb. 24, 1915 Troup, Texas; m Rufus Smith Aug. 3, 1865 (b may 7, 1843; d Dec. 13, 1908) and had ch b Troup Texas; (a) Mary Lee Oney Smith b Sept. 19, 1866 (m John A. Kelton Nov. 15, 1889 and had 1. John Kelton); (b) Rosa Lee Smith b Jan. 23, 1869; (c) Lula Lee Smith b Mar. 30, 1871 (m S. M. McKay Oct. 1895 Troup, Tex. and had; 1. Nathile McKay; 2. Leon McKay); (d) Ella Mae Smith b Jan. 10, 1877 (m Charlie Farley Nov. 15, 1899 Troup, Tex. and had; 1. Carmel Farley m D. O. Elliott and had (aa) D. O. Elliott, Jr.; 2. Frank Farley b Aug. 1, 1905; 3. Billy Farley); (e) Brown Etheldrew Smith b Nov. 2, 1874, of Troup, Tex. (m Virginia Estella Jackson Feb. 10, 1901 and had; 1. Doris O'Rella Smith b June 10, 1905; 2. Douglas William Smith b July 16, 1910); (f) Charlie Smith b Mar. 7, 1880; d Aug. 14, 1884; (g) Mamie Smith b Sept. 1, 1882; d at New Orleans, La. (m Valara Keasler Jan. 22, 1901 and had; 1. Theodore Keasler); (h) Belle Smith b Apr. 28, 1886; m Roland Borders Dec. 7, 1906; (i) Lester Kelton Smith b Jan. 3, 1890 (m Oma Parker and had; 1. Rufus Parker Smith).

Two.   Lafayette Norman b Sept. 25, 1850; d Jan. 6, 1906; m Ada Carlisle Oct 7, 1900 near Troup, Tex. (deceased) and had; (a) Euna Norman b Dec. 1904.

Three.   Mary C. Norman b Feb. 12, 1852; d Feb. 18, 1888; m—— Coupland Feb 19, 1873 and had; (a) Tom A. Coupland, of Troup, Texas; (b) Ed Coupland.

Four.   Sallie L. Norman b in Texas d June 10, 1910 (m R. N. Morris Mar. 12 1885 and had; (a) Greg Morris, of Troup, Texas; (b) Bob Morris.

Five. Ophelia Norman, of Conroe, Tex.; m J. L. M, Pyrtle Dec. 20, 1875 and had; (a) Stayton Pyrtle; (b) John Pyrtle; (c) Aldin Pyrtle.

Six. T. Douglas Norman died unmarried.

Seven. Octavia Norman died July 26, 1870.

Eight. William Norman died June 9, 1891.

Nine. Luther Tunnell Norman b Sept 10, 1872, of Troup, Tex.; m Uta Munn Dec. 3, 1897 and had; (a) Evangelina Norman (m Will O. Ogletree); (b) Luther Tunnell Norman Jr. (m Vertie Freeze Sept. 1923 and had; 1, ————Norman (b 1924); (c) Mary Beth Norman; (d) Nancy Mae Norman; (e) Helen Norman.

WILLIAM TUNNELL

B. William Tunnell, third of the name in direct line of definite record, son of William and Mary Maysey Tunnell, was born Nov. 14, 1774 Fairfax Co., Va. and died June 14 1861 near Robertsville, Tenn. after a married life of over sixty years. He went, with his parents, to North Carolina in 1788 and to near Robertsville, Tenn. Feb. 1792. He was a Colonel in the War of 1812 and commanded a regiment of Tennessee Volunteers at New Orleans, Jan. 8, 1815. His brother, James, was a Captain and, it is said, his brothers-in-law, James Roberts and James Worthington, were under his command. Vines Hicks, who later married the oldest daughter of William Tunnell, and his four brothers, served under him. He was, for many years, prominent in political circles, serving in the House of Representatives of Tennssee in the Thirteenth, Fourteenth, Six- teenth, and Twenty-first assembly. He married Elizabeth Worthing- ton Aug. 29, 1797 near Robertsville, Tenn. She was born Oct. 1, 1781 and died 1862 near Robertsville, Tenn. She was the daughter of Samuel and Eilzabeth Carney Worthington, and a sister of Nancy Worthington, who married John Tunnell; and of James Worthington, who married Lettice Tunnell. The farm on which Col. William Tunnell and wife spent their married life, and on which their children were born, is now owned by a great grandson, Oscar Tunnell.

I Betsey Tunnell b 1799

II Margaret Tunnell b about 1802-3

III Samuel Tunnell (b Jan. 16, 1805

IV Nancy Tunnell b 1807

V Caty Tunnell b Jan. 3, 1809

VI Zerelda Tunnell b Apr. 20, 1811

VII Sarah Tunnell b Nov. 1, 1813

VIII John Tunnell b Apr. 26, 1816

IX James Monroe Tunnell b Feb. 26, 1818

X Jesse Tunnell b 1820

XI Thomas Tunnell b Sept. 3, 1828

Of the following;—

I. Betsy Tunnell, dau of William and Elizabeth Worthington Tunnell, was born in 1799 and died Nov. 10, 1876 near White Hall, Ill. ater a married life of fifty-nine years. On July 3, 1817 she married in Anderson Co., Tenn. near Robertsville, Vines Hicks. Their honeymoon journey was a trip to their new home in the then Illinois Territory. Vines Hicks and Calvin Tunnell, uncle of Betsy Tunnell Hicks, "spliced teams" and moved to near Edwardsville, Illinois Territory in 1817.   Here Vines   joined   the   Rangers "the pioneer militiamen who rode over the prairies keeping track of desperadoes and hostile Indians and trying to make the country safe for settlers."   After Feb. 1819 Vines Hicks and little family moved to what is now Woodville township, Greene Co., Ill. sw of Carrollton, Ill. and remained a year or more. They moved to near White Hall, Ill. where the remainder of life was spent. There was a band of Indians living only a short distance from the Hicks family.

Vines Hicks was born Feb. 4, 1788 near Richmond, Va., on the James River and died two months after celebrating the one hundredth anniversary of his birth; on April 15, 1888 near White Hall, Ill. He was one of the fourteen children of David and Nancy (Thomas) Hicks, who lived to be grown and was of a family remarkable for its number and longevity. Nancy, wife of David Hicks, died Dec. 11, 1834, aged 66, according to inscription on her tombstone, near White Hall, Ill. His gradfather was Aaron Hicks, who was born in Va.   Vines Hicks and four brothers, Joseph, Merritt, Dibden and George Hicks enlisted, from Anderson Co., Tenn. in the Second War with the British, under Colonel Tunnell and Captain James Tunnell, and were on the oak sentineled Chalmette battlefield at New Orleans, under General Jackson on Jan. 8, 1815. Vines Hicks was also a soldier in the Black Hawk War.

Children of Vines and Betsy Tunnell Hicks were born in Illinois, first in Madison Co., near Edwardsville; second near Carrollton, Ill. then in Madison Co., now Greene Co. and others near White Hall, Ill.   They not only celebrated fifty years of marital happiness but three of their children celebrated golden wedding anniversaries.

One. Nancy Hicks b July 2, 1818.

Two. William Hicks b Dec. 21, 1820.

Three. John Hicks b Mar. 24, 1823.

Four. Calvin Hicks b Sept. 10, 1825.

Five. Eliza Hicks b Jan. 26, 1828.

Six. Elizabeth Hicks b Dec. 4, 1830.

Seven. Luther Hicks b Apr. 2, 1832.

Eight. Vines Hicks, the Second, b Sept. 26, 1835.

Nine. Samuel Francis Marion Hicks b Apr. 10, 1838.

Of these;—

One. Nancy Hicks, dau of Vines and Betsy Tunnell Hicks, b
July 2, 1818; d about 1856 near Donnelson, Ill.; married John Ash,
Greene Co., Ill. (b Feb. 24, 1813 Kentucky d Jan. 1, 1889 near Litch-
field, Ill.) John Ash married a second time. Children;

a Sarah Ann Ash b 1843

b Mary Ash b abt 1845.

c Andrew Jackson Ash, twin of Mary

d Elizabeth Ash b about 1847

e William Russell Ash b June 28, 1849

f Vernetta Ash b Feb. 6, 1853

Of these;—

a. Sarah Ann Ash b 1843 near Donnelson, Ill. June 1910 Columbus, Kan. m John Andrew Brigg 1865 (b 1843 near Litchfield,
Ill.; d 1903 Columbus, Kan) and had; 1, Minnie Alice Briggs b
June 15, 1866 Litchfield, Ill., of Spokane, Wash., m Roland Burnap
Jenkins Feb. 18, 1885 Columbus, Kan. (b Aug. 12, 1861 near Butler,
Ill., son of Charles Washington and Camilla (Burnap) Jenkins, latter
a descendant of Col. Steward, prominent in Alaskan affairs) and had
ch b near Butler, Ill.; (aa) Sarah Camilla Jenkins b Feb. 14, 1788,
m the Rev. Otto Aamerial Bremer July 1914, Charleston, Ill. (pastor
of Univ. English Lutheran Church Seattle, Wash) and had five ch.,
John Roland Bremer b Feb. 12, 1916 Boakland, Md); d Jan. 26, 1921
Spokane, Wash.; Alice Minnie Bremer b Mar. 5, 1917 Spokane;
David Henry Bremer b Nov. 12, 1919 Spokane; Otto Amos Bremer b
Oct. 25, 1922 Spokane; and John Spethar Bremer b June '26, 1924
Seattle; (bb) Alice Jenkins b Aug. 18, 1891; d Oct. 10, 1917 Prescott,
Arizona; buried Hillsboro, Ill., m the Rev. Frank A. Lindhorst m Dec.
24, 1916 Charleston, Ill. and had no children The Rev. F. A. Lindhorst
m second Alice Miller; (cc) Irene Jenkins b Aug. 13, 1893, unmarried,
of Seattle, Wash.; (dd) Charles Burnap Jenkins b Nov. 14, 1895, real
estate agent, Spokane, Wash., served two years in World War, with
8 months service in France with Field Hospital Division 345, m
Eilzabeth McNutt Aug. 5, 1919 Charleston, Ill. and had no children; 2,
Charles Hall Briggs b Apr. 12, 1868, grocer, Columbus, Kan., m
Stella Rittenhouse and had; (aa) Bessie Briggs; (bb) Roscoe

Briggs; (cc) Mabel Briggs; (dd) Camilla Briggs; (ee) Clifford Briggs,, some of whom are married and have families; 3, John Putman Briggs b Jan. 7, 1870, of Miami, Okla. m first, Tessie Burnap, at Butler, Ill. and had; (aa) Gretta Briggs; (bb) Wilbur Briggs; and m second————— —————; 4, Mary Vernetta Briggs b Aug. 13, 1871 Butler, Ill., m Charles H. Norvell, Butler, Ill., a farmer, and had, (aa) Muriel Norvell, m Ellis Duff; (bb) George Norvell, m Bessie Cress and had ch; (cc) Mary Norvell, m Kenneth Smalley; (dd) Frank Norvell; (ee) Claud Norvell; (ff) Hubert Norvell; 5, Joseph Franklin Briggs b Apr. 16, 1874, of Columbus, Kan., m Florence Effie Johnson Jan. 18, 1906 Neodosha, Kan. (b Apr. 18, 1887 Fall River, Kan.; d Apr. 11, 1917) and had no ch.; 6 Julia Anne Briggs b Feb. 7, 1876 Montgomery Co., Ill. of Columbus, Kan., m Harry Newton Mahaffey Sept. 21, 1898 Columbus, Kan.; engineer, prominent in political affairs of his town, having served as mayor and on city council; b Feb. 25, 1873 Vermillion Co., Ill., son of Robert and Mary Mahaffey) and had; ch b Columbus; (aa) Harold Robert Mahaffey b Apr. 24, 1903, unmarried; (bb) Lelia Margurite Mahaffey b July 13, 1905; 7, Jerome Mordecai Briggs b Jan. 1, 1878 unm., of Columbus, Kan.; 8. Stephen Robert Briggs b Apr. 16, 1880, of Parsons, Kan., m ————— ————— and had two daughters; 9. Lavanchie Iola Briggs b Aug. 24, 1883 Hillsboro, Ill., of Columbus, Kan., m Elmer A. Albin Apr. 2, 1908 Girard, Kan. (b Sept. 19, 1876 Salina, Kan. and had ch b Columbus, Kan.; (aa) Edgar Ageselans Albin b Dec. 17, 1908; (bb) John Coleman Albin b Apr. 29, 1912; (cc) Richard Gordon Albin b Oct. 22, 1920; 10. George Burnap Briggs b June 29, 1887 Kan., of Pittsburg, Kan., m first, ————— —————, and had; (aa) Mable Briggs; (bb) George Burnap Briggs, the second; and m second ————— —————; 11. Edith Ora Briggs b Mar.6, 1889 Kan., unm., of New York City.

b. Mary Ash b abt 1845; d 1907 St. Louis, Mo.; m Robert Hill and had; 1. Charles Hill, of Greenville, Ill., who m twice; 2. William Hill, unm., of Greenville, Ill.; 3. Margaret Hill, deceased, m ————— Semon and had; (aa) Roy Semon, of St. Louis; (bb) Frank Edward Semon, served overseas in World War, of Detroit, Mich.; 4. Bertha Hill, d in state of Washington, m ————— Davis.

c. Andrew Jackson Ash, twin to Mary Ash, died in inf.

d. Elizabeth Ash b abt 1847; d in inf.

e. William Russell Ash b June 28, 1849 White Hall, Ill.; d. Jan. 1, 1923 Quincy, Ill.; served in Union Army in War Between the States; m Rebecca Clark, dau of Isaiah and Elizabeth (Johnson) Clark, Aug. 17, 1875 White Hall, Ill. (b Mar. 10, 1852 Murfreesboro, Tenn.) and had; 1. Ada M. Ash b Nov. 2, 1878 Hillview, Ill., of Alton, Ill., m William Arthur Bigham, son of Edward and Laura Bigham, Nov. 4, 1896 Donnelson, Ill. (b Mar. 5, 1875 Sorento, Ill.)

and had ch b Donnelson, Ill.; (aa) Blanche Bigham b Sept. 1, 1898, m W. A. Crislip Mar. 24, 1918 Altamont, Ill., of Moran, Tex. and had two ch. b Moran, Tex.; William Alvy Crislip b May 3, 1919 and James Crislip b Jan. 11, 1923; (bb) Laura Bigham b Apr. 21, 1904, unm., Alton, Ill.; (cc) Dalph Bigham b Apr. 26, 1909; 2. Clarence Emmet Ash b Nov. 25, 1883 White Hall, Ill. of Roxana, Ill., m Mary Suthard Feb. 11, 1920 St. Louis, Mo.; 3, William Alva Ash b Nov. 7, 1886 White Hall, Ill., of Guthrie, Okla., m Jewel Zook Aug. 9, 1909 Buffalo, Kan. and had; (aa) George Rickard Ash b July 3, 1915 Des Moines, Ia.; (bb) Rebecca Jane Ash b Aug. 11, 1917 Hayes, Kan.; 4. Florence Elizabeth Ash b Jan. 14, 1890 Hillsboro, Ill., m Daniel Jenkins Jan. 24, 1907 Charleston, Ill., of Peking, Ill. and had; (aa) Mildred Jenkins b Nov. 11, 1912 Carlinville, Ill.; (bb) Daniel Jenkins, Jr., b Aug. 31, 1915 Pekin, Ill.

f. Vernetta Ash b Feb. 6, 1853 Greene Co., Ill.; d Feb. 25, 1922 near Litchfield, Ill.; m August Bollman May 22, 1878 Litchfield, Ill. ('b Feb. 29, 1848 Hamburg, Germany, son of August Bollman (b Apr. 18, 1881 Hamburg; d Mar. 1, 1870 St. Louis, Mo.) and Dorothea Upsonchurch Bollman (b Dec. 10, 1807 Germany; d Jan. 30, 1884 Litchfield, Ill.) and had ch b near Litchfield, Ill.; 1. Emory Francis Bollman b May 6, 1879, farmer, Rush Springs, Okla., m Laura Belle Whitney 1905 Rush Springs, Okla. and had; (aa) Harold Bollman; (bb) John Bollman; (cc) Joseph Bollman; (dd) Bennie Bollman; 2, Samuel Bollman b Jan. 29, 1881; 3. Minnie Dorothy Bollman b Oct. 27, 1883; d Mar. 21, 1919 near Litchfield, Ill. m Clarence Edwards Nov. 12, 1906 St. Louis, Mo. and had ch b Coffeen, Ill; (aa) Murice Edwards b 1908; (bb) Evelyn Edwards b 1910; (cc) Honora Edwards b 1915 and two others who died. Clarence Edwards m second time and lives Charleston, Ill.; 4. August Newton Bollman b Apr. 18, 1886, unm., with auto service station, Gillespie, Ill.; 5. Ida May Bollman b May 30, 1888, of Gillespie, Ill., m Arthur Edward Crites July 24, 1912 Litchfield, Ill. (b Feb. 13, 1883 Sullivan, Ill., with auto service station) and had an only ch.; (aa) Anita Margaret Crites b Aug. 6, 1913 Barnesville, Ohio.

Two. William Hicks, son of Vines and Betsy Tunnell Hicks, b Dec. 21, 1820; d Aug. 6, 1903 near White Hall, Ill.; married first, Luraney Bigham, dau of Josiah and Jane (Bussell) Bigham, Mar. 25, 1839 Greene Co., Ill. (b Nov. 6, 1821 McMinn Co., Tenn.; d Sept. 17, 1897 near White Hall, Ill.) and had seven ch. b near White Hall, Ill.; and married second a cousin, Talitha Hicks, dau of James Hicks, at Terre Haute, Ind. (b Jan. 1, 1841; d Mar. 3, 1881) and had four ch.

Children, by first marriage:

a. Isham Hicks b July 21, 1843.

b. Elizabeth Jane Hicks b Dec. 2, 1845.

c. Cordelia Angeline Hicks b Dec. 28, 1847.

d. William Henry Hicks b Dec. 2, 1849.

e. Andrew J. Hicks b Dec. 1, 1854.

f. Laura Adelia Hicks b July 17, 1858.

g. Luther M. Hicks b Jan. 20, 1861.

Children by second marriage:

h. Wilbur Tarra Hicks b July 13, 1866.

i. Lucy Hicks b Apr. 1, 1868.

j. Sarah Hicks b 1871.

k. Addi Belle Hicks b Nov. 9, 1879.

Of these;

a. Isham Hicks b July 21, 1843; d June 24, 1923 near White
Hall, Ill., m first, Emma Brown, dau of Elias Brown, Apr. 1864
White Hall, Ill. (b 1850 Greene Co. Ill.; d Oct. 2, 1883 Warren Co.,
Mo.) and had 1. Frank Hicks b Feb. 1, 1865, of Drake, Ill., m
Lucretia Ballard Dec. 27, 1888 Greene Co., Ill (b Sept. 9, 1870 near
White Hall, Ill) and had; (aa) Uel Hicks b May 20, 1892, of Alton,
Ill. m. Rose Smith Feb. 18, 1909 Manchester, Ill., and had; Glea
Hicks b Oct. 18, 1910, Ruth Hicks b Aug. 24, 1912, Frank Hicks b
Sept. 9, 1916 and Lowell Hicks b Jan. 29, 1919; (bb) Orville Hicks
b Oct. 9, 1895, m Marie Carter and had; Evaline Hicks b Feb. 13,
1921, Wayne Hicks b July 17, 1923; (cc) Harley Hicks b Jan. 30,
1897, m Louise Rufe May 30, 1919 Greene Co., Ill. (b July 15, 1897
St. Louis, Mo.) and had; Harley LaVerne Hicks b Aug. 22, 1923;
(dd) Lowell Hicks b Oct. 24, 1901; (ee) Alta Hicks b Dec. 29, 1904,
m Loverett March Oct. 1921 and had; Junior March b Sept. 25, 1923;
(ff) Stella Hicks b Apr. 18, 1906; (gg) Kenneth Hicks b Dec. 1, 1908;
(hh) Hazel Hicks b June 11, 1911; (ii) Zelma Hicks b Aug. 14, 1914;
2. Charles Hicks b June 7, 1867 Greene Co., Ill., of Hillview, Ill , m
Addie Carter Dec. 30, 1891 Greene Co., Ill. (b June 8, 1865) and had
ch b Greene Co., Ill ; (aa) Bessie Hicks b Oct. 11, 1893, m Roy B.
Brady (b May 22, 1893) and had; Mary Alice Brady; (bb) Rose Hicks
b July 2, 1895, m Augustus Townill Feb. 4, 1914 and had, Ralph
Townill b Feb. 21, 1915; (cc) Dewey Hicks b Apr. 23, 1899; (dd)
Gladys Hicks b June 2, 1902, 3 Edward Elias Hicks b June 10, 1873
Greene Co., Ill., of Lodi, Tex., m Berdie Alma Ford Mar. 15, 1905 Lodi,
Tex. (b Sept. 2, 1881, Lodi, Tex., dau Spencer and Florence (Chandler)
Ford) and had ch b Lodi, Tex.; (aa) Edward Ford Hicks b Apr. 30,
1906; (bb) Helen Lorene Hicks b Apr. 16, 1908; (cc) Alice Odessa
Hicks b July 22, 1910; (dd) Mabel Florence Hicks b Mar. 22, 1913;
(ee) Emma Lucille Hicks b Apr. 2, 1915; (ff) Charles William Hicks
b Aug. 21, 1917; (gg) Lois Estelle Hicks b May 17, 1920; (hh) Ray

Chandler Hicks b Nov. 19, 1922; 4, Dessie Fannie Hicks b Oct. 27, 1875, of White Hall, Ill., m a relative, Charles Troy Hicks, son of Luther and Olivia (Hosack) Hicks, g-s Vines and Betsy Tunnell Hicks, Mar. 19, 1893 Drake, Ill. See record of Luther Hicks; 5, Otis Hicks b 1876; d Jan. 14, 1916 Manilla, Ark., m Oma Lawson 1903) d May 1917 Manilla, Ark.) and had; (aa) Virgil Hicks b Dec. 1906; (bb) Cladie Hicks b 1908; d 1912; 6, Emery Hicks b Sept. 9, 1883, m Frances Zabriskie Nov. 1904 in Kan. and had; (aa) Orville Hicks b June 1, 1906 McLouth, Kan.; (bb) Harold Wilson Hicks b Jan. 25, 1908 Greene Co., Ill.; 7. son, twin with Emery Hicks b and d Sept. 9, 1883. Isham Hicks, b July 21, 1843, m second, Josephine Selson Feb. 18, 1885 Nevada, Mo. (b 1864) and had; 8, Rudolph Hicks b Feb. 3, 1887 Greene Co., Ill., ticket agent, Drake, Ill., m Lydia Garner May 21. 1909 (b July 23, 1894) and had ch b Greene Co., Ill.; (aa) Naomi Hicks b Mar. 14, 1910; (bb) Violet Hicks b Sept. 15, 1915; (cc) Clara Hicks b Mar. 21, 1921; 9, Florence Hicks b Mar. 4, 1889 Nevada, Mo., m Charles Crabtree, son of Joel Crabtree, June 26, 1904 Greene Co., Ill. and had ch b Greene Co.; (aa) Beatrice Crabtree b Mar. 16, 1905 m Morrell Boone Dec. 24, 1921 Greene Co., Ill. and had Richard Boone b July 13. 1923; (bb) Arrawanna Crabtree b Nov. 29, 1906; d Dec. 18. 1906; (cc) Bernice Crabtree b Sept. 16, 1909; (dd) Nava Crabtree b Jan. 18, 1912; (ee) Neva Crabtree, twin with Nava Crabtree, b Jan. 18, 1912 (ff) Wanna Crabtree b June 28, 1924.

b.   Elizabeth Jane Hicks b Dec. 2, 1845, of White Hall, Ill., m James Nichols Nov. 2, 1869 Greene Co., Ill. (b Sept. 1851 Marion Co., Ill.; d Mar. 10. 1914 Greene Co., Ill.) and had; 1, Alva Fay Nichols b Nov. 27, 1870 Macoupin Co., Ill. d Aug. 27. 1913 White Hall, Ill., m Ella Akers 1891 Macoupin Co., Ill. and had ch b Greene Co., Ill.; (aa) Edith Nichols b Jan. 9, 1892, of Drake, Ill., m Don Leach May 17, 1911 Greene Co., Ill. (b 1884, son Luke Leach (b May 8, 1847 Anderson Co., Tenn.; d Apr. 17, 1915 Drake, Ill.) and Orlena Jane Farmer Leach (b Jan. 29, 1854 Anderson Co., Tenn ; married Nov. 29, 1868 Anderson Co., Tenn., dau of William and Mary (Sellens) Farmer) and had 5 children b Greene Co., Ill., Philander Leach b Dec. 2, 1912, Lydia Leach b Nov. 1, 1914, Orlena Leach b Dec. 17, 1916, Maude Leach b Feb. 7, 1919 and Clara Jane Leach b Jan. 25, 1923; d Mar. 25, 1923; (bb) Roy Nichols b Nov. 3, 1894 White Hall, Ill., m Mabel Roberts Sept. 1915 and had; Eugene Nichols b 1916; Wayne Nichols b 1918 and Nita Nichols b 1920; (cc) Esther Nichols b Feb. 27, 1896; d June 28, 1924 Greene Co., Ill., m Russell Wyatt July 26, 1916 and had; Grover Wyatt b Feb. 12, 1917, Mary Helen Wyatt b Nov. 27. 1919 and Ruby Wyatt b July 28, 1922; (dd) Calvin Nichols b Apr. 8, 1898, unmarried; (ee) Laura Helen Nichols b June 8, 1903, of Patterson, Ill., m Perry Dawdy Feb. 16, 1921 and had; Margaret Dawdy b Feb. 7, 1922; (ff) Francis Nichols b 1905; 2, Virgil Nichols b Oct. 1, 1872 Macoupin Co., Ill., of Wood River, Ill, m first George McCarvle Jan. 2, 1900; (d Apr. 17, 1909) and had; (aa) Ruth Nichols b

Jan 15, 1901, m J. P. King June 2, 1919 Wood River, Ill., and had ch. b. Wood River, Ill., J. P. King, Jr., b Apr. 16, 1920 and William Frederick King b Nov. 3, 1921; (bb) Georgine Nichols b Mar. 18, 1909 Greene Co., Ill. Virgil Nichols, b Oct. 1, 1872, m second, Vena Chirn Aug. 22, 1910 Greene Co., Ill. and had; (cc) Pauline Nichols b Sept. 26, 1911 Bluffs, Ill.; (dd) Anabell Nichols b Mar. 17, 1916 Wood River, Ill. 3, Loodie Nichols b Oct. 4, 1874 Macoupin Co., Ill., of Murrayville, Ill., m Charles Hodges Crist, a descendant of Elder William Brewster (b Sept. 15, 1870, son of Jacob and Eliza (Wales) Crist; g-s David and Maria (Jackson) Crist, same Harmon and Lydia (Andrews) Wales; ggs Moses Crist; same Ira and Katie (Moon) Wales. Ira Wales of the Brewester family. Acknowledgement is here made for Mrs. Crist's assistance in preparing record of Betsy Tunnell Hicks. Children b in Greene Co., Ill.; (aa) Myrtle Mae Crist b July 9, 1849 of Silverdale, Wash., m William Peter Byl Aug. 21, 1915 Twin Falls, Idaho (b Dec. 17, 1893 Holland; came to America in 1909) and had, William Gerrett Byl b June 30, 1916 Spokane, Wash., and Ralph Elbert Byl b Oct. 20, 1921 Cassia Co., Idaho; (bb) Lucile Crist b May 5, 1896, of Twin Falls, Idaho, m Earland Flower Apr. 3, 1920 Twin Falls, Idaho, and had, Jaunita Flower b May 21, 1921 Twin Falls, Idaho, Harriet Flower b Jan. 4, 1923 Utah, and Lorene Ethel Flower b Oct. 27, 1924 Twin Falls, Idaho; (cc) James Jacob Crist b Jan. 21, 1902 ,unmarried; (dd) Charles Davis Crist b Nov. 6, 1903; unmarried; 4, William Harvie Nichols b Nov. 3, 1876, m Edith Edwards Feb. 16, 1902 Greene Co., Ill. (b Aug. 13, 1883) and had 4 children b Greene Co., Ill., the 5th at Mexico, Mo.; (aa) Juna Mae Nichols b Sept. 22, 1903; (bb) Lynn Nichols b Apr. 1, 1906; (cc) Harland Nichols b Nov. 15, 1908; (dd) Avis Nichols b Dec. 11, 1911; (ee) Ora Nichols b June 15, 1916; 5, James Oscar Nichols b Nov. 19, 1879 in Kansas, m Clara Pinkerton and had; (aa) Clarence Nichols b 1904; (bb) Gladys Nichols b Dec. 9, 1912; 6, Arlie Leroy Nichols b Aug. 14, 1883 Cass Co., Mo.; d May 2, 1907; buried White Hill, Ill. unmarried.

c. Cordelia Angeline Hicks b Dec. 28, 1847: d June 8, 1919 sw of Farmersville, Ill.; married Benjamin Archibald Stead (b 1877 (d Aug. 30, 1923 sw of Farmersville, Ill., son of David Stead (b Nov. 29, 1829 Yorkshire, Eng.; d Dec. 18, 1915 near Girard, Ill.) and Mary Ann (Boston) Stead; gs of Benjamin and Martha (Taylor) Stead, natives of Yorkshire, Erg., and of Beverly and Elizabeth (Boston) Boston; ggs of Benjamin Stead, of Yorkshire, Eng.) and had only one child; 1, Norman D. Stead b June 2, 1879, farmer near Farmersville, Ill., m Katie Murphy Apr. 6, 1904 Clayton, Mo. (b July 1, 1887) and had ch b on same farm on which he was born and on which he lives; (aa) Olen Walter Stead b May 28, 1905; (bb) John Benjamin Stead b Jan. 18, 1907; (cc) Earl Lloyd Stead b Mar. 3, 1909.

d William Henry Hicks b Dec. 9, 1849, of White Hall, Ill., married first, Emma Hawn 1876 (d May 27, 1877) and had; 1, Emery

Hicks b May 27, 1877, of Manchester, Ill., m Mary McGinnis and had ch b Greene Co., Ill.; (aa) Jaunita Hicks b May 1905; Zelda Hicks b July 1913. William Henry Hicks b Dec. 9, 1849, m second, Amanda Thunderbolt Apr. 3, 1878 Springfield, Ill. (b Nov. 15, 1856) and had; 2, Earl Hicks b Oct. 2, 1881 Greene Co. farmer, White Hall, Ill., m Lena Whitesides, dau of William and Emma Whitesides, and ch b Greene Co., (aa) William Hicks b Dec. 1908; (bb) Earlmond Hicks b Dec. 1915; (cc) Mildred Hicks b June 1917.

e Andrew J. Hicks b Dec. 1, 1854; d Sept. 1856.

f Laura Adelia Hicks b July 17, 1858; d Jan. 15, 1921 Kansas City; buried White Hall, Ill.; m Charles Edward Hogg Sept. 11, 1879 Harrisonville, Mo., (b Dec. 18, 1856 Collinsville, Ill.) and had an only child; 1, Laura Elma Hogg b Oct. 11, 1894 Kansas City, of Olathe, Kan., m Henry C. Farber Oct. 15, 1919 Kansas City (b July 3, 1891 Neligh, Neb) and had ch b Olathe, Kan.; (aa) Laura Henrietta Hogg b Sept. 26, 1920; (bb) Louise Adelia Hogg b Sept. 21, 1922.

g Luther M. Hicks b Jan. 20, 1861; d Sept. 1888 Greene Co., Ill.; m Lucy Roberts, dau of Isham and Artimesa (Baird) Roberts; Feb. 20, 1881 (b 1862 Greene Co., Ill.; d Nov. 1, 1925 near White Hall, Ill.) and had; 1, Norval Hicks b July 23, 1882 Greene Co , Ill., of White Hall, Ill., m Alma Anderson Dec. 31, 1906 and had; (aa) Norma C Hicks b Mar. 1908; (bb) Richard Hicks b July 1910; (cc) Ruth Hicks b July 22, 1921; 2 , Robert Hicks b Mar. 26, 1887, of White Hall, Ill., m Bessie Wilkerson Jan. 5, 1911 and has no ch. Lucy Roberts Hicks married second, Robert Hudson June 5, 1890.

h Wilbur Tarra Hicks b July 13, 1866 Terre Haute, Ind., of "The Hicks Press," Chicago, Ill., m Ruth Baxter, dau of Nathan and Rachel W. Baxter, Oct. 27, 1898 Winchester, Ill. (b Jan. 26, 1880) and had no ch.

i Lucy Hicks b Apr. 1, 1868 near White Hall, Ill.; m Rufus E. Converse, son of Jeremiah and Lovinia (Corey) Converse, 1888 and had ch including; 1, Ed Converse, of Palmyra, Ill.

j Sarah Hicks b 1871 Scottville, Ill.; d 1892 Patterson, Ill.; unm;

k Addie Belle Hicks b Nov. 9, 1877 Scottville, Ill.; m William Riley Ambrose, son of Benjamin F. and Lucinda (Howard) Ambrose, Feb. 16, 1896 Greene Co., Ill. and had ch.

Three. John Hicks, son of Vines and Betsy Tunnell Hicks, b Mar. 24, 1823; d Mar. 15, 1881 near Patterson, Ill. /He married Lucinda Smith Sept. 9, 1855 Greene Co., Ill. (b in Tenn.; d June 25, 1829 Los Angeles, Calif.) and had ch b near Patterson, Ill.; (a) Jane Hicks b July 17, 1857; d Nov. 1883 (m John Hale, whose first wife was her younger sister, in 1878, who d June 1883 and had; 1, Nona

Hale b Dec. 1878; d Oct. 17, 1901 Palmyra, Ill., m James Beasley 1895 and had three ch, all of whom d in inf. James Beasley married a second time and lives at Medora, Ill.; 2, Doy Hale b Aug. 11, 1881, of Los Angeles, Calif., m Edith Besanceney Oct. '24, 1901 and had (aa) Linton Hale b Nov. 5, 1902; (bb) Marguerite Hale b May 14, 1904); (b) Minerva Hicks b June 23, 1859; d 1877; (m John Hale 1876, who d June 1883 and had one ch; d in inf); (c) William Thomas Hicks b June 6, 1862; d '1863; (d) Samuel Francis Hicks b June 22, 1864; d June 1884, unm; (e) John Calvin Hicks b Jan. 20, 1867; (g) Vines Lewis Hicks b Aug. 4, 1872; d Mar. 21, 1891 (m Lucy J. McCollister Oct. 28, 1888' (b Oct. 24, 1869) and had; 1, Bessie Hicks b Mar. 23, 1890; d Aug. 1890. Lucy J. McCollister Hicks m second, Oscar Taylor Sept. 10, 1895); (h) Minnie Florence Hicks b Mar. 11, 1875; d Nov. 1884; (i) Cora Frances Hicks b Aug. 13, 1878; d Jan. 1899 Roodhouse, Ill. (m Robert Peebles, son of Maurce de Lafayette and Mary (Moore Peebles, July 4, 1897, who d Dec. 3, 1911 and had no ch.) Mrs. Lucinda Hicks, who sent this record, outlived all her children and grandchildren save one.

Four. Calvin Hicks, son of Vines and Betsy Tunnell Hicks, was born Sept. 10, 1825 near White Hall, Ill. and died Jan. 23, near White Hall; married Catherine Martin (b July 1909 near White Hall) and had an only child; (a) Marcus Lafayette Hicks b Oct. 3, 1855 near Roodhouse, Ill.; d Oct. 22, 1917, m Emma Greene and had no children.

Five. Eliza Hicks, dau of Vines and Betsy Tunnell Hicks, b Jan. 26, 1828 near White Hall, Ill.; d White Hall; married Noah M. Stone, Greene Co., Ill. (b Quincy, Ill.) and had ch b Greene Co., names may not be in order of birth; (a) William Alfred Stone, died Apr. 1922, (m Rebecca Denham and had; 1, Flora Stone d in inf.; 2, Mannie Stone b 1874, of White Hall, Ill., m William Baird May 18, 1892 and had; (aa) Albert Baird b Mar. 15, 1893; 3, Fred Stone b 1876, m Henrietta Myres; 4, Leora Stone, of St. Louis, Mo., m Charles Runion; 5, Fannie Stone, m Arthur Dumon; 6, Edward Stone, of St. Louis, Mo., m ————; 7, Verna Stone; 8, Norma Stone); (b) Robert Stone died about 1905 near White Hall, Ill. (m Jane Morgan and had; 1, Sam Stone; 2, Nellie Stone; 3, Noah Stone; 4, Henry Stone; 5, Riley Stone; 6, Joe Stone); (c) Martha Jane Stone died 1901 (m David Wyatt, son of Thomas and Nancy (Denham) Wyatt (b 1841 White Hall; d 1922) and had; 1, Louis Webster Wyatt b 1873, of Roodhouse, Ill., m Alice Watt and had; (aa) Willis Wyatt; (bb) Russell Wyatt; 2, Cora Frances Wyatt b 1875, of Roodhouse, Ill., m Walter Bartlett and had; (aa) Lewis J. Bartlett, m Mattie Hudson and had 4 ch, James Henry Bartlett, Walter David Bartlett, Bertha Mae Bartlett and Robert Cleveland Bartlett, (bb) Mamie Ethel Bartlett, m Klenn Stanley Gilmore and had 4 ch. Helen Geneva Gilmore, Lucille Marie Gilmore, Walter Odis Gilmore and Blanch Lavern Gilmore; (cc) Irene Estelle Bartlett, m George Emmett Barber and had no ch; (dd) Lelia Effie Bartlett, m Charles Henry Wells and had, Virginia Lee Wells; (ee) Frank Donald Bartlett, a veteran of World war with overseas service, m May Annie Miller and had, Nell Rose Bartlett; (ff) Walter David Bartlett, unm; (gg) Dorothy Hazel Bartlett, unm.; 3, Stella Wyatt b 1877, m Thomas F. Rendell and had; (aa) Electa Rendell); (l) Angie Stone, died Bloomington, Ill. (m Matt Carleton and had; 1, Winifred Carleton; 2, Ethel Carleton; 3, Ada Carleton; , Eliza Carleton; 5, Edward Carleton; 6, Manfred Carleton); (e) Katie Stone (m first, Ed Howard and had; 1, Claude Howard; 2, Frank Howard; 3, Stanley Howard; 4, Winona Howard; and m second,——— Frankenburg and had no issue; (f) Jessie Stone, of Pekin, Ill. (m Curtis Wilkerson, uncle of Bessie Wilkerson who m Robert Hicks, and had; 1, Thurman Wilkerson; 2, Earl Wilkerson; 3, Edith Wilkerson; 4, Estelle Wilkerson; 5, Ruth Wilkerson).

Six. Elizabeth Hicks, dau of Vines and Betsy Tunnell Hicks, b Dec. 4, 1830 near White Hall, Ill.; d May 11, 1903, near White Hall; married first, Joshua Roberts Nov. 13, 1845 (d May 13, 1849) and had ch b near White Hall; (a) Rebecca E. Roberts b Dec. 24, 1846; d in inf.; (b) Joshua Roberts Jr. b Dec. 31, 1849; d in inf.; and married second, Andrew Lewis McConnell June 27, 1860 (d July 21, 1901) and had ch b near White Hall; (c) Mary Frances McConnell b July 28, 1863; d Mar. 27 1917 White Hall (m Charles C. Withrow, son of S. J. and Esther (Crampton) Withrow (b Mar. 15, 1861 Schuyler Co., Ill., of White Hall) and had ch b White Hall, Ill.; 1, E. Grover Withrow b Jan. 10, 1885; d June 10, 1907 near Mexico, Mo., unm; 2, S. Louis Withrow b Feb. 28, 1887 of Wilder, Mass., m Ruth Edgerton April 1915 in Mass. and had; (aa) Mary Jane Withrow b Jan. 11, 1918 Malta, Mont.; (bb) Charles James Withrow b Apr. 27, 1922 West Springfield, Mass.; 3, Horace Withrow b Sept. 7, 1889, served in World war, of old Mexico, m Louise Tenney Feb. 7, 1921 and had no ch; (d) Eliza Jane McConnell b Feb. 8, 1865, of Drake, Ill. (m Joseph Schutz, son of Matthew and Christine Schutz, 1881 Greene Co., Ill. (d Aug. 1922 near White Hall, Ill.) and had ch b near White Hall, Ill. 1, Hattie E. Schutz b 1886, m Charles Reveal Sept. 17, 1899 Greene Co., Ill. and had ch born near White Hall, Ill. (aa) Norma Reveal b Sept 1902; (bb) Kenneth Reveal b Aug. 1904; (cc) George Reveal b Feb. 1907; (dd Oren Reveal b Mar. 1911; (ee) Leo Reveal b Apr. 1913; (ff) Woodrow Reveal b Mar. 1914; (gg) and (hh), Velma Reveal and Zelma Reveal, twins, b Mar. 1917; (ii) Opal Reveal b Oct. 1919; (jj) Ellene Reveal b Mar. 1921; (kk) Wilma Reveal b Aug. 1922; 2, Harry Schultz b 1888, m Ethel Ashlock and had; (aa) Veta Schultz b 1908; 3, Ada F. Schultz b 1890, of Louisiana, Mo., m first, Otis Leonard and had (aa) Mary Leonard b 1910; (bb) Ada May Leonard b 1911; (cc) John Otis Leonard b 1912; and m second, A. J. Marsh Apr. 1925 Louisiana, Mo ; 4, George E. Schutz b 1892, m Minnie Buckholt and had; (aa) Marvel Schutz b 1912;

(bb) Margaret Schutz b 1913; (cc) Gilbert Schutz b 1914; (dd) George Edward Schutz b May 1924; 5, Charles L. Shutz b 1894, unm; 6, Mary Cora Ann Schutz b 1896, m Lonnie Moore and had no ch; 8, Claude A. Schutz b 1898, of Farber, Mo., m Cecil Painter and had; (aa) Lloyd Schutz; (bb) Mabel Schutz; (cc) Phyllis Schutz; (dd) Gerald Schutz; (ee) Lottie Mae Schutz; (ff) child b May 1924; 8, C. W. Schutz b 1899, unm, of East Moline, Ill.; 9, Marcus L. Schutz b 1901, m Ruby Hitch an had; (aa) Georgia M. Schutz b, 1922; 10, Edith May Schutz b 1906, m John Farmer, son of Harvey Farmer; 11, Joseph O. Schutz b 1908); (e) George Gideon McConnell b Nov. 14, 1866; d July 21, 1899 Seattle, Wash., (m Annie M. Prichard, dau William and Amanda (Ball) Prichard) June 12, 1892 Greene Co., Ill.; (f) Samuel Vines McConnell b Feb. 18, 1868 (m Cora Crabtree, dau Chester and Martha (Hudson) Crabtree, Sept. 13, 1888 Greene Co., Ill. (d July 16, 1922 Roodhouse, Ill. and had; 1, George Emmett McConnell; 2, Alta McConnell; 3, Martha McConnell); (g) Thomas Calvin McConnell b May 29, 1871, of Roodhouse, Ill., m Helen Lucy Hudson, dau Robert and Lucy (Roberts) Hicks Hudson, Aug. 25, 1920 and had no ch.; (h) Charles Lewis McConnell b Apr. 11, 1884; d young (i) John Luther McConnell b Feb. 2, 1886, farmer, Roodhouse, Ill. (m Pearl F. Allen, dau Alonzo and Sana (Howard) Allen, July 19, 1903 and had; 1, Harold McConnell b July 14, 1908).

Seven. Luther Hicks, son of Vines and Betsy Tunnell Hicks, b Apr. 2, near White Hall, Ill.; d Dec, 19, 1915 Orlando, Florida; buried White Hall, Ill.; married first, Olivia Hosack Feb. 6, 1868 Winchester, Ill. (b Oct. 17, 1853 near Alsey, Ill., who m second, Mr. Coates and lives Marchester, Ill.) and had an only child; (a) Charles Troy Hicks b Dec. 4, 1870 near White Hall, Ill., general manager Drake Clay Products Co., of White Hall, Ill. (m first, Lillie Mae Coates, dau of William and Elizabeth (Watt) Coates, Jan. 21, 1891 White Hall, Ill.) and had; 1, Edith Estel Hicks b and d same day; and m second, Dessie Fannie Hicks, Mar. 19, 1893 (b Oct. 27, 1875, dau of Isham and Emma (Brown) Hicks; g-d William and Luraney (Bigham) Hicks) and had; 2, Edith G. Hicks b Sept. 22 1894, m Kenyon W. Morrow and had no ch; 3, Estel E. Hicks b Mar. 7, 1896 Alva, Okla., of Columbus, Ohio, m Marshall Smith and had; (aa) Marshall Smith Jr.; (bb) Dessie Smith; 4, Eva N. Hicks b Mar. 26, 1897 Drake, Ill., of East Alton, Ill. m Leslie L. Ricks Dec. 24, 1914 Greene Co., Ill. and had; (aa) Clifton Ricks; (bb) Theda Ricks; 5, Beatrice Hicks b Mar. 17, 1904 near White Hall, Ill., of White Hall, m David Giger Luther Hicks b Apr. 2, 1832, married second, Ella Chorn, a twin daughter of John and Elizabeth (Martin) Chorn, Dec. 8, 1881 near Carrollton, Ill. (b 1861; d May 5, 1916 Carrollton, Ill.) and had an only child by this marrage; (b) Clifton Hicks b Mar. 4, 1886 near White Hall, Ill.; d Feb. 6, 1903.

Eight. Vines Hicks, the second, son of Vines and Betsey Tunnell Hicks was born Sept. 26, 1835 near White Hall, Ill. He is a retired farmer living Barr township, Macoupin Co., Ill. near Greenfield, Ill. He married Nancy Rhodes, dau of Alden and Sarah (Morrow) Rhodes, Feb. 28, 1860 Greene Co., Ill. She was born Aug. 13, 1839 near Bradshaw's Mound, Greene Co., Ill. and died June 21, 1917 Scottville, Ill. after a married life of fifty-seven years. Their home for many years, was near Scottville, Ill. Childern; (a) Sarah Elizabeth Hicks b Apr 12, 1861 near Athensville, Ill., of Scottville. (m Owen Cline, son of Ruben and Diana (Cady) Cline; gs David and Sarah (Mills Cline) Macoupin Co., Ill. (b July 23, 1851 Washington Co., Ohio; d Apr. 23, 1916 Scottville, Ill.) and had; 1. Lucreta Mae Cline b Mar. 21, 1880, m James Martin Emmons and had; (aa) Blanche Mae Emmons b June 21, 1909 Scottville, Ill.; d Apr. 27, 1911 Bluffs, Ill.; (bb) Dorothy Gladys Emmons b Jan. 15, 1911 Winchester, Ill.; (cc) Carless Alden Emmons b Jan. 2, 1913 Bluffs, Ill.; d Jan. 10, 1913; (dd) James Samuel Emmons b Nov. 29, 1914 Exeter, Ill.; d Apr. 9, 1922 Jacksonville, Ill.; (ee) Raymond Alexander Emmons b Oct. 28, 1916 Bluffs, Ill; 2 Vines Ruben Cline b Dec. 5, 1881; unmarried (b) Robert Rudolph Hicks b Dec. 6, 1863; d Dec. 5, 1881; (c) Samuel Francis Marion Hicks b Feb. 5, 1867, farmer, near Greenfield, Ill., served on board of supervisors of Macoupin Co., Ill. a number of years (m Ella Mitchell Sept. 25, 1895 Springfield, Ill. (b Dec. 1, 1867 near Athensville, Ill., dau of Jackson Gates Mitchell (b Aug. 21, 1838 Greene Co., Ill.; d Feb. 19, 1914 Greene Co.) and Sarah Elizabeth Hubbell Mitchell (b Nov. 17, 1845 Menard Co., Ill.; d June 2, 1911); (granddau. Anderson and Elizra (Whitlock) Mitchell, of Justus and Nancy (Smiley) Hubbell)and had ch b Macoupin Co., Ill.; 1, Stanley Orin Hicks b July 1, 1896; d Jan. 29, 1918 Colorado Springs, Col; buried Palmyra, Ill.; 2, Ira Mitchell Hicks b June 15, 1898, unmarried

3, Georgiana Gabrella Hicks b Apr. 12, 1901, unmarried; 4, Vera Nancy Hicks b Nov. 29, 1906); (d) Lucretia Iona Hicks b Mar. 21, 1869; d Apr. 9, 1904; unmarried; (e) Jane Mary Hicks b Aug. 21, 1871; d Jan. 19, 1901, unmarried; (f) Georgiana Gabrella Hicks b Aug. 9, 1873; d Nov. 12, 1891, unmarried; (g) Alden Rhodes Hicks b Jan. 21, 1876, unmarried, of Twin Falls, Idaho; grad. Leland Stanford Univ. A. B. 1901; Univ. of Chicago, L. D., 1903; practiced law Lewiston, Idaho 1905-1909, since which time he has practiced his profession as attorney of Twin Falls County, and was a member of the House of Representatives, from that county, 1915-1916; (h) Beatrice Cordelia Hicks b Mar. 25, 1879, of Waverly, Ill. (m first Abram Moses Bull Jan. 16, 1901 (b Sept. 9, 1875 Morgan Co., Ill.; d Nov. 13, 1919 Jacksonville, Ill.; buried near Scottville, Ill., son of Solomon (b Mar. 14, 1832 Roxboro, N. C.; d Jan. 31,1914 Eureka Springs, Ark.; buried near Franklin, Ill.) and Elizabeth (Seymour) Bull (b Morgan Co., Ill.; d 1923, Jacksonville, Ill.); gs Moses and Elizabeth (Fuller) Bull, of William and Elizabeth Seymour) and had no children; and m second, William Edward Swift, Mar. 1, 1921

Sullivan, Ill. (son of William (d 1898) and Anna Louise (Ward Swift (b Feb. 1847; d June 17, 1925 Waverly, Ill., m 1867) and had no issue by this marriage.)

Nine. Samuel Francis Marion Hicks, son of Vines and Betsy Tunnell Hicks, was born Apr. 10, 1838 near White Hall, Ill. and died Apr. 5, 1917 on the farm on which he spent his life, the farm which his parents settled on abt 1821 or 2.   He was a prominent farmer. He m first, Fannie Martin, a sister of his brother Calvin's wife, Feb. 23, 1863, who died Jan. 23, 1867, and had; (a) daughter b and d Feb. 23, 1866.   He m second, Fannie Patterson, dau of Lemuel J. and A. E. (Hume) Patterson, Nov. 28, 1870 (b Jan. 25, 1852 Patterson, 27, 1877; (c) Ida Mae Hicks b Jan. 1, 1876, of Roodhouse, Ill, m lived for 53 years) and had; (b) Frank Hicks b Sept. 7, 1871; d Oct. 27, 1877; (c) Ida Mae Hicks b Jan. 1, 1876, of Roodhouse, Ill., m first, C. Leslie Taylor, son of Alfred and Teraisa (Edwards) Taylor, in Greene Co., Ill. and had 1, Cecile Taylor b May 20, 1893, of Roodhouse, m George Byron Roodhouse, son of W. C. and Love Zila (Hosford) Roodhouse, Apr. 19, 1913 Greene Co., Ill. and had ch. b Roodhouse, Ill.; (aa) Katherine Elizabeth Roodhouse; (bb) Fannie Isabel Roodhouse; (cc) Byron Lemuel Roodhouse b 1919; (dd) William Franklin Roodhouse; (ee) Edward Clair Roodhouse; 2, Kenneth Taylor b June. 21, 1894, served in World War, m Georgia Nagle and had; (aa) William Alfred Taylor; (bb) Stuart Samuel Taylor); Ida Mae Hicks m second, John Roy McLamar May 14, 1913 Clayton, Mo. (b 1881; d Jan. 23 1919 near White Hall, Ill.) and m third, William E. Landman June 1921 Greene Co., Ill.; (d) Lemuel Hicks b May 26, 1879, unmarried, of White Hall, Ill.; (e) Harry Hicks b Dec. 2, 1883; d Mar. 14, 1894; (f) Louis Hicks b July 6, 1888, unmarried, of White Hall, Ill.

II.   Margaret Tunnell, dau of William and Elizabeth Worthington, was born abt 1802 or 1803 and died at Shelbyville, Ind.   She married first, Hiram T. Aldridge, who d abt Nov. 1831 Shelbyville, Ind., and had five children.   She married second, David Montgomery Jan. 22, 1835 Shelby Co., Ind., who died Shelby Co , Ind. and had three ch.

One. Hiram T. Aldridge, junior.
Two. Jackson C. Aldridge.
Three. William W. Aldridge, died abt Sept. 1846 Shelby Co., Ind.
Four. Dewitt C. Aldridge, died abt Sept. 11, 1835 Shelby Co., Ind.
Five. Elizabeth Ann Aldridge, died abt Jan. 24, 1838 Shelby Co.
Six. James K. Polk Montgomery.
Seven. John L. Montgomery.
Eight. Margaret Ann Montgomery.
Of these;
Six. James K. Polk Montgomery, d abt 1910 Greenfield, Ind.
Seven. John L. Montgomery, died abt 1871; married Mary Reid

Jan. 1, 1862 and had; (a) McClellan Montgomery d in inf.; (b) Mamie Montgomery, d abt 1891 Arlington, New Jersey; (c) John L Montgomery, of Arlington, N. J.; (e) Horace Montgomery, of Shelbyville, Indiana, Sec. and Treas. of The Monte Glove Co.

Eight.   Margaret Ann Montgomery, died at |Peabody, Kansas; married first, William Laningham June 6, 1844, who died; and second, ————— Rieter, who died; and third ————— Kamp.

III   Samuel Tunnell, son of William and Elizabeth Worthington Tunnell, was born Jan. 16, 1805 and died June 26, 1886 Anderson Co., Tenn.   He married first, Sarah McKamey, dau of John and Pol'y (McKamey) McKamey, 1830 in Anderson Co., Tenn. (b Mar. 24, 1804 Anderson Co., 'd abt 1860 Anderson Co.) and had three ch.; and married second, Mary Charlotte (Butler) Hutson, widow of George Hutson, Sept. 3, 1867 Anderson Co., Tenn.   Two daughters of George and Mary Butler Hutson, Lizzie Hutson and Anne Hutson, married into the Tunnell family.   Ch. b Anderson Co., Tenn.

One.   William C. Tunnell b Mar. 17, 1831; joined the Texas Rangers abt 1860 and d 1862; married Fannie Cox, dau of John Cox, Sept. 25, 1861 Anderson Co., Tenn. (b Mar. 11, 1840 Anderson Co.) and had an only ch ; (a) Samuel Tunnell b Oct. 20, 1862, unmarried, cashier of Oliver Springs, Tenn. Bank, who owns the farm on which the ¡Rev. Wiliam and Mary Maysey Tunnel! settled in Feb. 1792. Fannie Cox Tunnell m second, Gideon B. R. Lea Oct. 13, 1870 Anderson Co., Tenn.   He was son of Eppa Lea b Apr. 11, 1792 Caswell Co., N. C.; d Oct. 5, 1885 Anderson Co., Tenn , of the prominent N. C. and Tenn. Lea family whose family history Miss Frances Powell Otken, McComb, Miss. has traced.

Two.   Po'ly Ann Tunnell b Aug. 24, 1833; d Aug. 6, 1876 Anderson Co., Tenn.; unm.

Three.   John McKamey Tunnell b Feb. 23, 1836; d 1863 unm.

IV.   Nancy Tunnell, dau of William and Elizabeth Worthington Tunnel , was born 1807 and d 1893 Mercer Co., M.   She married first Joseph Ga'braith,, abt 1830, Anderson Co., Tenn. (d abt 18b5 Anderson Co.) and second, Francis McConnell, 1854.   Ch. b near Andersonville, Tenn.

One.   William Tunnell Gailbraith b Oct. 27, 1833; d Oct. 6, 1896 Mercer Co , Mo.; married Nancy S. Oliver Apr. 18, 1854 Anderson Co., Tenn. (b Jan. 10, 1833; d July 28, 1910 Platte City, Mo) and had ch b Mo., first two Mercer Co., others Platte City; (a) Mary E. Galbraith b Feb. 27. 1855, of Camden Point, Mo , m ————— Boyd; (b) Nancy F. Galbraith b Aug. 31, 1856, of Birmingham, Mo., m W. T. Dickinson.; (c) Josephine Galbraith b Sept. 7, 1858; d Mar. 24, 1864 Platte Co.. Mo.; (d) Charles H. Galbraith b Aug . 22, 1861, unm., of Platte City, Mo ; (e) Saral L. Ca'braith b Oct. 2, 1864, m ————— Killeher and had no ch. (f) Samuel O. Galbraith b May 20, 1866, of Le Loup, Kan. (m Florence Hiatt 1892 and had; 1, Charles Clifford Galbraith b 1894; d Sept, 29, 1918 Great Lakes Training Station,

Chicago; unm.; 2, Julia Galbraith b 1900, of Le Loup, Kan., m Harry
M. Hoover Nov. 22, 1920 and had; (aa) Margaret Hoover b Jan. 24,
1925 Le Loup, Kan.); (g) Malinda J. Galbraith b Feb. 21, 1873, of
Camden Point, Mo. (m ——— ——— and had; 1, Nancy Jane Galbraith
b Oct. 8, 1900; 2, William Gray Galbraith b May 11, 1903.)

Two. Samuel Galbraith b abt 1835, moved to Platte Co., Mo.
1857; soldier in War Between the States; d in Libby prison, 1863;
unm.

Three. John Thomas McConnell.

Four. Mary Elizabeth McConnell.

V. Caty (Kitty) Tunnell, dau of William and Elizabeth Worthington Tunnell, was born Jan. 3, 1809 and died Oct. 5, 1866 near
White Hall, Ill. She married William Marlin Farmer, junior, Dec.
19, 1833 Anderson Co., Tenn. (b Oct. 7, 1809; d Aug. 19, 1853 near
White Hall, Ill., son of William Marlin and Mary (Selens) Farmer.
W. M. Farmer, junior, and 4 brothers moved from Halifax Co.,Va.
to Anderson Co., Tenn.   Children:

One. William Henry Farmer b Mar. 26, 1835.

Two. Elizabeth Mary Farmer b Nov. 17, 1836

Three. Luke Martin Farmer b Oct. 13, 1838.

Four. Zerelda Jane Farmer b May 1, 1841.

Five. John Tunnell Farmer b Apr. 9, 1843.

Six. Thomas Washington Farmer b Dec. 17, 1845.

Seven. Sarah Ann Farmer b Nov. 15, 1848.

Eight. Catherine Massa Farmer b Apr 28, 1851.

Of these;

One. William Henry Farmer b Mar. 26, 1835; d Greene Co.,
Ill.; married Elizabeth Emaline Allen Apr. 10, 1856 Greene Co., Ill.
(d Dec. 15, 1907) and had ch b near White Hall, Ill.; (a) Mary
Catherine Farmer b Jan. 5, 1857, of Roodhouse, Ill. (m Alfred T.
Steelman Apr. 8, 1875 Greene Co., Ill. and had ch b near White Hall,
Ill.; 1, Julian Catherine Steelman b Mar. 22, 1876; d Apr. 5, 1899
Greene Co., Ill., m Edward Hamon May 2, 1894 and had; (aa) Charles
A. Hamon b Apr. 30, 1895, m Margaret Brackett and had, Gerald
Edmond Hamon and Wayne Alfred Hamond; 2 Effie Matilda Steelman
b Sept. 25, 1878, unm., of Roodhouse, Ill.; 3, George Wesley Steelman
b May 30, 1881, m first, Emma Hawk Dec. 29, 1903 (d Mar. 20, 1906)
and had; (aa) Buell Lee Steelman b Oct. 7, 1904 and m second,
Dollie Boston, in Greene Co., Ill. and had; (bb) Mildred May Steel-
man; (cc) Dorothy Ilene Steelman; (dd) Wayne Thomas Steelman;
(ee) Glenn Boston Steelman; 4, William A. Steelman b Jan. 17, 1883,
m Ollie Mitchell in Greene Co., Ill. and had; (aa) Rishard Ashley
Steelman; 5, Lillie B. Steelman b Dec. 17, 1885, of St Louis, Mo., m
Dr. Charles Fredrick Sherwin and had; (aa) Mary Evaline Sherwin;
(bb) Charles Steelman Sherwin); (b) Andrew Jackson Farmer b
Sept. 14, 1858 d same day, near White Hall, Ill.; (c) Aletha Jane
Farmer b Sept. 8, 1859; d May 9, 1894 near White Hall, Ill., unm;

(d) William Marlin Farmer b Sept. 1, 1861, unm.; (e) George
Washington Farmer b Apr. 20, 1864; d Feb. 15, 1882; (f) Sarah Ann
Farmer b Feb. 28, 1866, of Pearl, Ill. (m first, John M. Pepperdine,
son of William S. and Pricilla (Angelo) Pepperdine, Dec. 31, 1886
and had ch. b Greene Co., Ill ; 1, George Thomas Pepperdine b Sept
3, 1888; d Aug. 16, 1908 near White Hall, Ill.; 2, Cora May Pepper-
dine b Sept. 19, 1890; d Aug. 26, 1908 near White Hall; 3, Lydia
Jane Pepperdine b Nov. 26, 1892; d Apr. 3, 1906 near White Hall; 4,
Harold Alfred Pepperdine b Jan. 10, 1895; d June 7, 1896 near White
Hall; 5, Dora Bell Pepperdine b Oct. 6, 1898, unmarried; 6, Cecil
Henry Pepperdine b Oct. 16, 1900; d June 5, 1903 near White Hall.
Sarah Ann Farmer m second, Charles Pruitt;)(g) James Marlin
Farmer b Jan 9, 1868, of White Hall, Ill. (m Hester Martin, dau of
James and Eliza (Harwood) Martin, Apr. 12, 1903 Greene Co., Ill.,
and had ch b near White Hall; 1, William Alfred Farmer b Dec. 24,
1904; 2, Harold Marlin Farmer b Aug. 14, 1908); (h) James Henry
Farmer, second by name of James, b Dec. 22, 1870; d July 17, 1871;
(i) Fannie Alice Farmer b May 13, 1873; d Nov. 6, 1874; (j) Thomas
Edgar Farmer b Sept. 16, 1877, of Royal Oak, Mich. (m first, Daisy
A March, dau of Rudolph and Martha (Arnold) March, Sept. 22,
1901, Roodhouse, Ill.; and had; 1, Daisy Elizabeth Farmer b Nov 19,
1903 Burtonview, Ill.; d Feb. 9, 1904 Burtonview, Ill.; 2, Nelie Malinda
Farmer b Oct. 14, 1906 Easton, Ill.; and m second, Bertha B. Short
Oct. 1, 1917 and had; 3, Florence Elizabeth Farmer b June 17, 1917
Detroit, Mich.; 4, Alice Evelyn Farmer b Feb. 21, 1921 Berkley, Mich.;
5, Marlin Thomas Farmer b Nov. 14, 1923 Berkley, Mich.)

Two. Elizabeth Mary Farmer b Nov. 17, 1836; d Feb. 1, 1866
Greene Co., Ill.; married Andrew F. Fry, son of George and Milly
(Crouse) Fry, (d Sept. 9, 1866) and had ch b Greene Co., Ill.; (a)
George Martin Fry b Oct. 1860, who m ———— ———— in Mo.; (b)
Mary Catherine Fry b 1863 who m ———— ———— in Mo.; (c) Andrew
Franklin Fry b Jan. 23, 1866; d Sept 9, 1866.   A F. Fry m second
———— Ballard and moved to Mo. abt 1868.

Three. Luke Martin Farmer b Oct. 13, 1838; d Nov. 12, 1903
Pyulapup, Wash.; married Elizabeth Coates, Dec. 23, 1866 Greene
Co., Ill., now of Seattle, Wash., (dau of John Coates (b 1799 S. C.; d
Mar. 4, 1876 Greene Co., Ill.) and Elizabeth Owdom Coates (b N. C.;
d 1849, Greene Co., Ill.) and had; (a) Charles Jasper Farmer b Oct.
14, 1867; d Feb. 19, 1887 Downs, Kan.; (b) Gracie Catherine Farmer
b May 19, 1873 Roodhouse, Ill., of Seattle, Wash. (m Elmer J. Coffman Mar. 7, 1891 Pyuapup, Wash., and had; 1, Elvan Coffman b Nov.
3, 1894 Pyulapup, Wash.); (c) Jessie Lee Farmer b Apr. 2, 1876
Roodhouse, Ill., (m James J. Clark Mar. 25, 1895 Pyuapup, Wash.,
and had; 1, Hazel Iona Clark b Feb. 8, 1897, m Richard L. Talbot
Sept. 8, 1915 Tacoma, Wash. and had; (aa) Richard L. Talbot, junior,
b June 24, 1917 Pyulapup); (d) Clifton Clark Farmer b Apr. 3, 1885,
(m Jessie Ellen Taylor Feb. 13, 1907 Pyulapup, Wash. and had; 1,

La Varne Maud Farmer b Jan. 8, 1908 Pyulapup; 2, Elaine Gertrude Farmer b Dec. 19, 1911 Auburn, Wash.)

Four.   Zerelda Jane Farmer b May 1, 1841; d Sept. 13, 1866; married Chester Coates, son of John and Martha (Owdom) Coates, 1863 (d 1866) and had; (a) Lawrence Washington Coates b Aug. 19, 1865; d Apr. 20, 1876.

Five.   John Tunnell Farmer b Apr. 9, 1843; d Jan. 28, 1901 in Colorado; unmarried.

Six.   Thomas Washington Farmer b Dec. 17, 1845; d Jan. 28, 1909 White Hall, Ill.; unmarried.

Seven.   Sarah Ann Farmer b Nov. 15, 1848, of Roodhouse, Ill.; married James Linville Bandy, son Robert and Nancy (Taylor) Bandy, Mar. 19, 1868 (d Feb. 26, 1902) and had an only ch.; (a) Oscar Elmer Bandy b Sept. 20, 1872 Greene Co., Ill., (m Florence Liddie Dunham Apr. 8, 1894 Scott Co., Ill. and had ch b Greene Co., Ill.; 1, Floyd Ellsworth Bandy b May 23, 1895; d Nov. 1, 1914; 2, Robert Linville Bandy b June 23, 1899.)

Eight.   Catherine Massa Farmer b Apr. 28, 1851, of White Hall, Ill.; married Philander F. Floyd, son of Henry and Mary (Mc-Collister) Floyd, Aug. 28, 1876 (b Nov. 3, 1852) and had no children. Thanks are due Mrs. Floyd for the record of Caty Tunnell Farmer.

VI.   Zerelda Tunnell, dau of William and Elizabeth Worthington Tunnell, was born Apr 20, 1811 and died Sept. 18, 1875 Sebastian Co., Ark.   She married Capt. John Cunningham McKamey, son of John and Polly (McKamey) McKamey, Jan. 1, 1839 Anderson Co., Tenn.   He was born 1809 in Anderson Co., Tenn., and died 1854 while on a prospecting trip near Little Rock, Ark.   Children;

One.   William Tunnell McKamey b Dec. 22, 1839.

Two.   Isabella McKamey b Sept. 13, 1841.

Three.   John Samuel Monroe McKamey b Mar. 2, 1849.

Of these;

One.   William Tunnell McKamey b Dec. 22, 1839; d Apr. 28, 1871 near Hartford, Ark.   He entered C. S. A., from Clinton, Tenn. and served four years, first in the 19th Tenn. Inf., afterwards in Thomason's Legion of Sharpshooters and was wounded in service.   He married Mattie Rillian Oct. 1868 Hartford, Ark. (d abt 1873) and had no children.

Two.   Isabella McKamey b Sept. 13, 1841, of Taft, Tex.; married William Robertson Spessard, son of William and Delaney (Leach) Spessard, Sept. 12, 1867 Anderson Co., Tenn. (b June 2, 1844; d Mar. 22, 1880) and had; (a) Alice Spessard b Aug, 20, 1868, of Taft, Tex. (m Daniel Timothy Lippard Mar. 3, 1887 in Tex. and had; 1, Stella Lippard b Nov. 7, 1891, of Taft, Tex., m Urie G. Miller June 1920 Sinton, Tex.; 2, Huberta Lippard b Feb. 18, 1902); (b) William McKamey Spessard b Oct. 18, 1870, ranchman, Taft, Tex. (m Cora Bryant Jan. 15, 1896 Ft. Worth, Tex. and had; 1, Rowena Spessard b Nov. 18, 1896; 2, W. Bryant Spessard b June 22, 1899 at Gregory,

Tex.; 3, Esther Spessard b Mar. 18, 1902 Angelita, Tex.; 4, Fanny Wilson Spessard b Aug. 17, 1910 Angelita, Tex.); (c) Nancy Ellen Spessard b Feb. 25, 1873; d Mar. 27, Huntington, Ark. (m Jeff Bass and had; 1, Drucie Bell Bass, of Valier, Ill., m Harry Ingle Sims abt 1919 Huntington, Ark. and had; (aa) Jimmie Jefferson Bass b Mar. 27, 1922); (d) Mary Esther Spessard b Sept. 14, 1875, of Taft, Tex. (m Eugene Hodges Dec. 23, 1902 Gregory, Tex. and had ch b Gregory; 1, Eugene Hodges, junior, b Nov. 13, 1904; 2, Robert Hodges b Feb. 14, 1906; 3, Loraine Hodges b Feb 25, 1908; 4, Le Moyne Hodges b Nov. 1, 1912; 5, Mary Esther Hodges b Aug. 21, 1915); (e) John Franklin Spessard b Jan. 18, 1877; d Jan. 25, 1878 Huntington Co., Ark.; (f) Robert Lee Spessard b Dec. 11, 1878 Huntington Co., Ark.; d Oct. 10, 1879; (g) Ada Spessard b Aug. 15, 1880 Huntington Co., Ark.; d Mar. 8, 1881 Huntington Co., Ark.

Three. John Samuel Monroe McKamey b Mar. 2, 1849 Roane Co., Tenn d Sept. 16, 1916 Gregory, Tex. in 1890 where he became one of the most prominent citizens of that part of Texas. He was banker, merchant and cotton buyer. He married Sarah Rebecca Bonham, dau of Absalom T. and Eliza J. (McClure) Bonham, Nov. 20, 1873 Sebastian Co., Ark. (b Nov. 20, 1852, now of Gregory, Tex.) and had ch. b near Salem, Sebastian Co., Ark ; (a) Inez Bonham McKamey b Oct. 19, 1874, of Gregory, Tex. (m first, Alamo Cedric Priday, Nov. 21, 1897 Waco, Tex. and had; 1, Dr. Alamo Cedric Priday b Jan. 21, 1898 Waco, Tex.; 2, Inez Morella Priday b Jan. 14, 1901 Gregory, Tex., of Rockdale, Tex, m James L. Coleman Sept. 19, 1923 and had; (aa) James L. Coleman, junior, b July 17, 1924 Corpus Christi, Tex.; 3, Quinton Murice Priday b Jan. 19, 1902, of Gregory, Tex. Inez B. McKamey m second, Roy Willis, and had no issue by this marriage) ;(b) Isabella May McKamey b July 28, 1876, of Dallas, Tex. (m Rhea Miller June 6, 1900 Gregory, Tex. (b June 28, 1874) and had; 1, Truman Rhea Miller b Mar. 1, 1904 Corpus Christi, Tex.; 2, Billie Fred Miller b Mar. 13, 1909 Gregory, Tex.; 3, Sara Bess Miller b Oct 30, 1911 Gregory, Tex.); (c) John William McKamey b Aug. 3, 1878, ranchman, of Port Lavaca, Tex. (m Maude Elizabeth Todd Nov. 6, 1901 (b Sept. 6, 1882) and had; 1, Glenn Ethelbert McKamey b Oct. 3, 1905; 2, Riva May McKamey b May 5, 1908; 3, Lynn Worth McKamey b June 7, 1910 Port Lavaca, Tex.; d May 1, 1911 Port Lavaca, Tex.; 4, Ivy Lurline McKamey b Aug. 14, 1912 Port Lavaca, Tex.; 5, Maida Maurine McKamey b Sept. 14, 1914 Port Lavaca, Iris Lynn McKamey b Sept. 18, 1917); (d) Myrtle Eliza McKamey b Feb. 18, 1880, of Austin, Tex. (m Robert Houston Hamilton Jan. 17 1900 and had; 1, Robert Houston Hamilton, the second, b Sept. 12, 1906 Corsicana,Tex.; 2, Helen Hamilton b Oct. 20, 1908 Waco, Tex.; 3, Theresa Hamilton b July 29, 1911 Gregory, Tex ; 4, Mary Gail Hamilton b Mar. 31, 1920 Port Lavaca, Tex. R. H. Hamilton b Dec. 25, 1873 near Corsicana, Tex. For several years he taught at Baylor University. He is now judge of the court of criminal appeal at

Austin, Tex.); (e) Tunnell Absalom McKamey b Oct. 17, 1891, ranch-
man, Gregory, Tex. (m Lillian Russell McConnico June 27, 1907 near
Corsicana, Tex. (b July 4, 1888) and had; 1, Kenneth Grayson Mc-
Kamey b May 25, 1910 Gregory, Tex.); (f) Ivy Marcella McKamey b
Dec. 20, 1883, Osteopath, of Dallas, Tex.); (m Ernest Eugene Mc-
Annelly August. 22, 1909 Gregory, Tex. (b July 22, 1881 Devine, Tex.;
d July 26, 1916 Dallas, Tex. and had no children).

VII.   Sarah Tunnell, dau of William and Elizabeth Worthington
Tunnell, was born Nov. 1, 1813 and died Mar. 24, 1893 near Roberts-
ville, Tenn., having spent her entire life n ithe same neighborhood.
She married William Peak, son of Jacob Peak, 1835, Anderson Co.,
Tenn. (b Jan. 1, 1812; d June 14, 1864) and had ch b near Roberts-
ville, Tenn.

   One.   Elizabeth Mary Peak b June 14, 1836.
   Two.   Nancy Margaret Ann Peak b Jan. 19, 1838.
   Three.   Zerelda Kizziah Peak b Sept. 22, 1839.
   Four.   William Henry Harrison Peak b Apr. 1, 1841.
   Five.   Sarah Catherine Rhoda Jane Peak b Nov. 11, 1842
   Six.   Amanda Isabel Peak b Dec. 4, 1844.
   Seven.   Byrd Peak b Dec. 17, 1846.
   Eight.   Jacob Peak b Oct. 4, 1848.
   Nine.   E. M. M. P. H. W. (Milly) Peak b Nov. 29, 1850.
   Ten.   James Wesley Peak b Mar. 2, 1853.
   Eleven.   John Abner Peak b June 2, 1855.
   Of these;
   One   Elizabeth Mary Peak b June 14, 1836; d abt 1870 Anderson
Co., Tenn.; m George Monger Nov. 3, 1853 Anderson Co. and had no
ch.

   Two.   Nancy Margaret Ann Peak b Jan. 19, 1838; d May 18,
1864 Anderson Co., Tenn.; m Noble Johnson Oct. 19, 1854 Anderson
Co., Tenn. (b Oct. 15, 1829 Anderson Co, Tenn d May 28, 1919
Anderson Co., Tenn. son of Craven S. (b Dec. 31, 1797 Knox Co.,
Tenn., d Apr. 16, 1881 near Clifton, Tenn.) and Jane (Lynort) Johnson
(b Sept. 15, 1798 Penn.; d Mar. 22, 1880 Anderson Co., Tenn; gs
Kinzie Johnson, who lived in Anderson Co., and on whose farm
Noble Johnson lived). Noble Johnson enlisted 1862 with Co. K. with
Capt. Butler of Thomas' Legions of Indians and Highlanders of the
C. S. A. Ch. b near Clinton, Tenn.; (a) William Craven Johnson b
Aug. 4, 1855; d Feb 18, 1862; (b) John Calvin Johnson b Mar. 14,
1858, of Andersonville, Tenn. (m Maggie J. Shinliver 1879 Anderson
Co. (b Dec. 26, 1857 Anderson Co., dau of Charles and Talitha Shin-
liver) and had ch b Anderson Co.; 1, William J Johnson b July 11,
1880, m Mattie McCrackin, of Clyde, N. C., July 9, 1904 and had ch
b Knoxville, Tenn.; (aa) Lois M. Johnson b May 19, 1905; (bb)
Vaughn Johnson b Oct. 18, 1907; (cc) Albert Sidney Johnson b Jan.
4, 1909; (dd) Helen Sophia Johnson b July 19, 1910; 2, C Oscar
Johnson b Sept. 22, 1886, of Los Angeles, Calif., m Rosa Lee Long,

of Morristown, Tenn., Sept. 15, 1910 and had; (aa) Ralph Milton
Johnson b Sept. 18, 1912; 3, Bertha Ellen Johnson b July 22, 1888; d
Oct. 18, 1888; 4, Alma Ethel Johnson b Aug. 22, 1889, m O. E.
Miller Dec. 25, 1908 and had; (aa) Grace May Miller b Nov, 25, 1910;
(bb) Carl P. Miller b Jan. 15, 1912); (c) Gilbert Wane Johnson b
Nov. 14, 1859, of Cleveland, Tenn. (m Mary Hancock, dau of William
and Nancy (Davis) Hancock, Dec. 26, 1880 Bradley Co., Tenn. (b
Dec. 27, 1855 Bradley Co.) and had ch b Bradley Co; 1, Ida Mae
Johnson b Dec. 14, 1881, m Arthur Murray Mar. 23, 1905 Bradley Co.,
and had ch b in that county; (aa) Scott Murray; (bb) Gilbert Wane
Murray; (cc) Claude Murray; (dd) Gertrude Murray; (ee) Clarence
Murray; (ff) Ada Murray; 2, Deally Bell Johnson b Feb. 9, 1883; d
Apr. 20, 1898; 3, Nancy Jane Johnson b Mar. 6, 1885, m Absalom
Butcher Nov. 27, 1909 Chattanooga, Tenn.; 4, Mamie Johnson b
Mar. 3, 1887; 5, Leona Johnson b Sept. 8, 1888; 6, Margarette Ann
Johnson b Oct. 1, 1889; d Aug. 23, 1908 Bradley Co., Tenn.; 7,
William Robert Johnson b Mar 2, 1891; 8, Gilbert Wane Johnson,
Jr. b Mar. 13, 1892; d Apr. 30, 1892 Bradley Co ; 9, Jessie Lee Nora
Johnson b Mar. 21, 1893; 10, Julia B. Johnson b Nov. 19, 1894; 11,
John Calvin Johnson b Apr 21, 1899); (d) Sarah E izabeth Johnson
b Aug. 8, 1861; d June 11, 1862 Anderson Co., Tenn ; (e) Mary Ann
Johnson b Nov. 8, 1863, of Edgemoor, Tenn. (m Henry French John-
son, though of same surname not related, son of Elijah and Rosana
(French) Johnson, Sept. 7, 1882 Anderson Co., Tenn. (b Apr. 10,
1861 Knox Co., Tenn.) and had ch b Anderson Co , Tenn.; 1, Joseph
Byrd Johnson b June 11, 1883; d May 19, 1908, unm.; 2, John Noble
Johnson b Nov. 30, 1884, of Jersey City, N. J., m first, Lizzie Mc-
Carthy Jan. 21, 1909 Chicago, Ill., who died July 24, 1915 in the
Eastland disaster, Chicago, and had; (aa) Evelyn Elizabeth Johnson
b Sept. 1909 Chicago, Ill.; and m second, Rosa McGoldrick, 1923;
3, Evelyn Johnson b Aug 20, 1886, m Clarence Walters Apr. 19, 1908
(b Dec. 1, 1883 Va.) and had ch b Anderson Co., Tenn ; (aa) William
Fletcher Walters b July 1, 1909; (bb) John Thomas Walters b Oct.
22, 1913; (cc) Herbert Franklyn Walters b Dec. 29, 1918; 4, Henry
Laurence Sanford Johnson b Feb. 17, 1888, of Chicago, Ill., m Olga
Thorson Mar. 25, 1914 Chicago, Ill. and had; (aa) Walter Laurence
Johnson b Sept 30, 1915; (bb) Bettie Ann Johnson b Apr. 27, 1921).

Three. Zerelda Kizziah Peak b Sept. 22, 1839; d July 31, 1876
Decatur, Tenn.; m David Alexander Gallaher, Jr., son of David
Alexander Gallaher, native of Scotland, 1858 Robertsville, Tenn. (b
Sept. 22, 1834 Kingston, Tenn.; d Dec. 6, 1893 Decatur, Tenn.) and
had; (a) James Acton Gallaher b July 17, 1859 Cleveland, Tenn , of
Reedley, Calif., (m Susan Elizabeth Boggess Nov. 17, 1878 Decatur,
Tenn. (b Aug. 31, 1863 Decatur, Tenn.; d July 24, 1908 Reedley,
Calif.) and had ch b Decatur, Tenn.; 1, Charles King Gallaher b Oct.
29, 1879, m Arvy Able Jan. 1905 Decatur, Tenn. and had no ch.; 2,
David Thomas Gallaher b May 31, 1881 d July 7, 1882 Decatur, Tenn ;

3, James Frank Gallaher b Apr. 23, 1883 d Mar. 10, 1919 San Fran-
cisco, Calif., unm.; 4, Lizzie Kizzie Gallaher b Oct. 4, 1884, of Reedley,
Calif., m Perrie Hixon Stewart Aug. 14, 1902 Decatur, Tenn. (b Nov,
20, 1881) and had; (aa) Sam Gallaher Stewart b May 4, 1903
Decatur, Tenn.; (bb) Jessie Rose Stewart b Feb. 24, 1906 'Reedley,
Calif.; (cc) Rebecca Stewart b Jan. 20, 1908 Reedley, Calif.; (dd) J.
A. Stewart b Dec. 31, 1909 Reedley, Calif.; 5, Lucy Kate Gallaher b
Sept. 3, 1886, Decatur, Tenn., of Fresno, Calif., m Will Neil and had;
(aa) Frankie Neil b June 9, 1906; (bb) 'Sue Neil; 6, John Boggess
Gallaher b Dec. 19, 1889 Decatur, Tenn., of Reedley, Calif., m
Georgie B. Snooks 1908 Fresno, Calif. (b Mar. 17, 1891 Ohio d Aug.
9, 1924 Reedley, Calif.) and had; (aa) Lucile Gallaher b Aug. 28,
1909 Reedley, Calif.; 7, Emma May Gallaher b Dec 4, 1891; d Oct.
21, 1902 Decatur, Tenn.; 8, Hattie Lou Gallaher b July 21, 1894, of
Sanger, Calif. m Clyde Rohrer 1915 Reedley, Calif. and had; (aa)
Dorothy Rohrer b Aug. 15, 1917 Colton, Calif.; 9, William A. Gallaher b Aug. 22, 1897, of Oregrande, Calif., m Lola Nunaly May 20,
1921 Fresno, Calif. James Acton Gallaher m second, Dora Belle
Goodner, 1910 Fresno, Calif.); (b) David Peak Gallaher b Mar. 17,
1861; d Jan. 25, 1862 Decatur, Tenn.; (c) Fredrick Gallaher b Dec.7,
1862; d 1920 Colfax, Calif. (m Florence Mitchell at Fresno, Calif.
and had a son who d in inf.); (d) Emily Gallaher b Mar. 1, 1865, of
Colfax, Calif. (m Baxter Fowler and had; 1, Houston Fowler, m twice
but had no ch.; 2, Grace Fowler, of Berkley, Calif., m —————
Wood and had (aa) Laurence Wood; 3, David Fowler, d at 13); (e)
Dr. Augustus Gallaher b Jan. 20, 1867; d 1912 Decatur, Tenn. (m
Elizabeth Fritts 1899 Decatur, Tenn and had; 1, Eva Gallaher b
1900; 2, Stella Gallaher b 1902; 3, Minnie May Gallaher; 4, Emma
Gallaher; 5, Fritts Gallaher; all of whom live Sweetwater, Tenn);
(f) Charles Gallaher b Sept. 23, 1868; d Aug. 26, 1869 Decatur, Tenn.;
(g) Eugene Gallaher b Mar. 6, 1870; d young; (h) Claude Gallaher
b Nov. 24, 1871, of St. Albany, Ala. (m twice and had three ch., all
of whom are married); (j) William Peak Gallaher b Apr. 7, 1874,
unm, of Calif. David Alexander Gallaher Jr. m second, Mary E.
Taft).

Four. William Henry Harrison Peak b Apr. 1, 1841; d Nov. 23,
1878 Anderson Co., Tenn.; m Julia Jennings Dec. 18, 1872 and had an
only ch.; (a) Mary Tunnell Peak b Aug. 3, 1875; d June 21, 1876.

Five. Sarah Catherine Rhoda Jane Peak b Nov. 11, 1842, of
Clinton, Tenn.; married a relative, Jesse Brown Worthington, Sept. 8,
1860 Anderson Co., Tenn. (b Jan. 14, 1839 Anderson Co, Tenn.; d
June 29, 1906 near Clinton, Tenn., son of Jesse Worthington (b Apr.
22, 1794; d May 3, 1879 Anderson Co., Tenn.) and Nancy Galbraith
Worthington (b Nov. 16, 1798; d Oct 29, 1874 m 1822); grandson
Samuel Worthington (b Mar. 1846 near Baltimore, Md.; d Jan. 3,
1821 Anderson Co, Tenn.) and Elizabeth Carney Worthington (b Apr.
30, 1754; d Oct. 22, 1830 Anderson Co, Tenn.; m 1774) and had ch b.

near Clinton, Tenn.; (a) Sam Worthington b June 17, 1861 (m Alice
Steele Sept. 27, 1883 and had; 1, Della Worthington b Feb. 17, 1885;
2, Carrie Elizabeth Worthington b Feb. 21, 1887; 3, Mary Hazel
Worthington b Apr. 23, 1890; 4, Joseph L. Worthington b May 29,
1892; 5, Maud Worthington b Apr. 14, 1895; 6, Nancy Jane Worthington b May 26, 1898; 7, Lucille Worthington b Mar. 16, 1900; 8,
Edith Worthington b Feb. 14, 1903; 9, Claud Worthington b Sept. 14,
1907; d Jan. 10, 1908); (b) Robert Worthington b Nov. 28, 1863; d
unm.; (c) James Worthington b and d Jan. 13, 1868; (e) John C.
Worthington, twin with Thomas C. Worthington, b Jan. 13, 1868; d
Jan. 21, 1868; (f) Ada Worthington b Aug. 1, 1869; d Aug. 2, 1869;
(g) Millie Worthington b Aug. 2, 1870; d Aug. 13, 1870; (h) Eddie
Worthington b Nov. 19, 1871; d May 26, 1891; (i) Byrd Worthington
b Oct. 12, 1874; d Oct. 14, 1874; (j) Mary Elizabeth Worthington b
Nov. 21, 1875; d Nov. 27, 1875; (k) Nancy Worthington b Apr. 8,
1877; d Apr. 16, 1877; (l) Jesse King Worthington b June 1, 1878
(m Martha Braden Nov. 1, 1896 and had; 1, Sam Worthington b
June 21, 1897; 2, Robert Worthington b June 1, 1898; 3, Ed Carney
Worthington b Jan. 7, 1903; 4, Era Worthington b Apr. 15, 1908);
(m) Malinda Byrd Worthington b Aug. 21, 1881 (m Henry Duncan
Feb. 15, 1900 and had; 1, Acton Duncan b Dec. 1900; 2, Ada Duncan
b 1908); (n) Sarah Roberson Worthington b Mar. 6, 1884, unm., of
Clinton, Tenn.)

Six.   Amanda Isabel Peak b Dec. 4, 1844; d Sept. 1882 Anderson
Co., Tenn.; m Joseph L. Pyatt, Dec. 7, 1871 Anderson Co., Tenn. and
had; (a) Mollie Pyatt, of Clinton, Tenn. (m William Hightower and
had; 1, Stella Hightower; 2, Ed Hightower; 3, Sam Hightower; 4,
Frank Hightower; 5, Vera Pearl Hightower; 6, John Hightower,
deceased); (b) John Pyatt, of Edgemoor, Tenn. (m Annie Goldstein
and had; 1, James Pyatt; 2, Ralph Pyatt; 3, Sam Pyatt); (c) Sallie
Pyatt, of Edgemoor, Tenn. (m James Hackworth and had; 1, Orin
Hackworth; 2, Annie Joe Hackworth); (d) Sam Pyatt, who d unm.;
(e) Dora Pyatt, of Knoxville, Tenn. (m B. Frank Wilson and had; 1,
Bernard Wilson; 2, Joe Wilson; 3, Grace Wilson).

Seven.   Byrd Peak b Dec. 17, 1846; m Mary Glover and had; (a)
Sallie Peak, d young; (b) son d young.

Eight.   Jacob Peak b Oct. 4, 1848; d May 29, 1899 Anderson Co.,
Tenn.; m his first cousin, Nancy M. Tunnell, dau of Thomas and
Bashaba (England) Tunnell, Dec. 21, 1876 (b Nov. 25, 1856 Anderson
Co., Tenn.; d Aug. 18, 1893 Anderson Co., Tenn.) and had; (a) Julia
Peak died Aug. 1906; (b) Daisy Peak, of San Franscisco, Calif., m
D. B. Kelley; (c) William Peak, of Hoquiam, Wash.; (d) Grace Peak
of Springfield, Ore., m Joe Stalcup; (e) Jesse Peak b Dec. 20, 1888, of
Nashville, Tenn., m Elizabeth Myrtle Hunt June 29, 1912 Nashville,
Tenn.

Nine.   Milly Peak b Nov. 29, 1850.   Her name merits a sentence
of its own for it was Easter Minerva Melceny Parthena Hannah

Woods Peak.   She d May 1885.   She m Dr. James A. King (once of Atlanta, Ga.) and had; (a) Minnie King, of Dayton, Tenn., m —— —— ——; (b) Charles King; (c) Will King.

Ten.   James Wesley Peak b Mar. 2, 1853, of Edgefield, South Carolina; m Julia Peak Jan. 3, 1884 (b Oct. 10, 1853; deceased) and had; (a) Willie Hill Peak b May 26, 1885; d Sept. 1, 1885; (b) Morage Peak b Jan. 10, 1887, of Troy, S. C., m Willie Perrin Sullivan, dau of William and Mary (Royal) Sullivan; (c) Nellie May Peak b Nov. 5, 1889; d June 26, 1890; (d) James William Peak b Dec. 31, 1890; (e) Annie Hortense Peak b Aug. 23, 1892, of Anderson, S. C., m the Rev. Patrick H. Bussey, Edgefield, S. C.; (f) Mary Royall Peak, b Mar. 28, 1894, of Greenwood, S. C., m A. F. Pinson, who served with A. E. F. in France, Dec. 27, 1921; (g) Florence Adams Peak b Jan. 16, 1896, of Heath Springs, S. C., m G. Otis Nobley, who served overseas in 30th Division, June 5, 1917; (h) Sallie Perrin Peak b June 24, 1898, of Sumter, S. C., m David H. Britton June 24, 1919; (i) Willie Peak b Sept. 15, 1900 (daughter); (j) Edward Furman Peak b July 4, 1905.

Eleven.   John Abner Peak b June 2, 1855, of Clinton, Tenn.; m first Sabra Scarborough; m second, Lizzie Hutson, (d near Roberts-ville, Tenn.) a sister of Anne Hutson who m his first cousin, John R. Tunnell and m third, his cousin, Margaret R. Garner, dau Hugh and Carney Elizabeth Worthington Garner; gd Jesse and Nancy Galbraith Worthington; ggd Samuel and Elizabeth Carney Worthington, Sept. 21, 1879 and had; (a) Clyde W. Peak b Aug. 1883, of Clinton, Tenn., m Voleria Lee and had ch (b) Clarence Peak, d young.

VIII.   John Tunnell, son of William and Elizabeth Worthington Tunnell, was born Apr. 26, 1816 and died Aug. 30, 1887 not far from where he was born.   He was a prominent planter in Anderson Co., Tenn.   He married first, Talitha Wood of Beaver Creek Valley, the dau of Clement and Hannah (Aldridge) Wood, Feb. 11, 1841, who died Jan. 16, 1882.   About 1884 he married Julia Jones, who survived him.   Children, all by first marriage, b near Clinton, Tenn.

One.   Hannah Elizabeth Tunnell b Apr. 22, 1842.
Two.   Parthena Melissa Tunnell b Apr. 6, 1845.
Three.   Sarah Ann Tunnell b June 14, 1847.
Four.   Margaret Minerva Tunnell b June 22, 1848.
Five.   Harriet Jane Tunnell b Sept. 12, 1849.
Six.   William Clement Wood Tunnell b Feb. 24, 1853.
Seven.   John Calvin Tunnell b May 3, 1855.
Eight.   Nancy Catherine Tunnell b Feb. 13, 1858.
Nine.   Mratha Adelia Tunnell b Jan. 31, 1860.
Ten.   Mary Evaline Tunnell b Oct. 10, 1861.
Eleven.   Julia Emarine Tunnell b Dec. 1, 1863.
Twelve.   Jesse Thomas Tunnell b Sept. 17, 1867.
Of these:
One.   Hannah Elizabeth Tunnell b Apr. 22, 1842; d Apr. 3, 1889

in Tenn ; married Samuel Tillery Jan. 15, 1860 Anderson Co., Tenn., and had; (a) John M. Tillery b Nov. 17, 1860, once of Harriman, Tenn. (m Bertha Bishop Apr. 15, 1896 and had; 1, Mildred Tillery b Nov. 26, 1898; 2, Eula May Tillery b Feb. 23, 1901); (b) Samuel L. Tillery b Apr. 10, 1865; d July 17, 1865; (c) daughter b and d Oct. 3, 1866; (d) Edward Tillery b Oct. 7, 1867, of Powell's Station, Tenn. (m Margaret Lewis Oct 10, 1889 and had; 1, Jessie Augusta Tillery b Sept. 18, 1890; 2, Acton Tillery b Nov. 23, 1892; 3, Odessa Tillery b Nov. 1, 1894; 4, Julia Tillery b June 12, 1898); (e) Laura Tillery b Dec. 9, 1870 (m J. Edward Groner Apr. 23 1896 and had; 1, Margaret Groner b July 5, 1897; 2, Irene Groner b June 3, 1905).

Two. Parthena Melissa Tunnell b Apr. 6, 1845; d Apr. 30, 1919 Knoxville, Tenn.; married John L A. Sterchi June 28, 1860 (b Sept. 1, 1838 Berne Switzerland; d Nov. 15, 1914 Knoxville, Tenn.; son of Francois Henry Sterchi, b Sept. 10, 1797 Berne, Switzerland, d Aug. 17, 1883 Anderson Co., Tenn., and Wilhelmina Giroud Sterchi, b Mar. 8, 1817 Switzerland; d Feb. 1, 1874). Ch., with exception of second one, b in Tenn All the sons and son-in-law, with one exception, are in the furniture business. (a) William Henry Sterchi b Aug. 28, 1862 Knox Co., Tenn., of Knoxville, Tenn.; president of American National Bank; president of Knoxville Outfitting Co. and Knoxville Mattress Co., (m Nina Blackmer June 20, 1887 and had; 1, Horace Earl Sterchi b Aug. 19, 1889, furniture dealer, Knoxville, Tenn., m Ethel Austin June 5, 1909 Knoxville, Tenn. and had; (aa) William Austin Sterchi b June 9, 1911 Knoxville; 2, John Calvin Sterchi b Jan. 17, 1893, furniture dealer, Knoxville, Tenn , m Mattie M. Duncan Oct 27, 1913 and had ch b Knoxville; (aa) William Frederic Sterchi b Aug 25, 1914; (bb) Nina Marie Sterchi b May 26, 1917; (aa) Martha Duncan Sterchi b May 18, 1920; d July 26, 1921; 3, William Jennings Sterchi b July 17, 1900, m Lockie Parks May 24, 1920 Bristol, Va.-Tenn.; 4, Irene Belle Sterchi b Feb. 11, 1902; d Jan. 1, 1903 Knoxville; 5, Charles F. Sterchi b Sept. 26, 1903, m Elizabeth Trainurs Mar. 3, 1922 and had; (aa) Charles Fredrick Sterchi b Dec. 11, 1922; 6, Nina May Sterchi b Oct. 30, 1905; d July 1924); (b) John Calvin Sterchi b Jan 25, 1865 near Carrollton, Ill., of San Antonio, Tex. (m first, Martha Ida Pilleaux, Sept. 28, 1887, who died July 20, 1911 Chattanooga, Tenn.; and m second, Margaret Mickler, 1918. Ch. by first marriage; 1, Lena Mae Sterchi b Mar. 5, 1889, of Chattanooga, Tenn., m John O. Fowler Sept. 1909, Knoxville, Tenn., furniture dealer, and had ch b Chattanoogo, Tenn.; (aa) John Fowler b May 1911; (bb) Calvin Fowler b Sept. 1912; (cc) Charlotte Fowler b Jan. 1914; (dd) Mary Fowler; (ee) James Sterchi Fowler b July 1924; 2, Bessie Lee Sterchi b Nov. 27, 1890, unm., of Chattanooga, Tenn ; 3, Callie Marguerite Sterchi b July 25, 1892; d 1895 Knoxville, Tenn.; 4, John Wallace Sterchi b May 31, 1894, furniture dealer, m Althea Miller 1915 and had (aa) Althea Sterchi b 1916 Chattanooga; 5, Robert Thomas Sterchi b June 22, 1896, m Georgia McConnell 1919

Chattanooga and had; (aa) Bettie Ellen Sterchi b Mar. 26, 1921; 6, Ruth Sterchi b Nov. 15, 1899, m Harold Parkhurst Street Apr. 12, 1921 Chattanooga and had (aa) Harold Parkhurst Street, Jr., b Mar. 18, 1922; 7, Rose Sterchi twin of Ruth Sterchi, b Nov. 15, 1899; d 1900 Chattanooga; 8, Helen Sterchi b May 30, 1901, m Hubert Rutland Apr 29 1924 San Antonio, Tex.; 9, Martha Ida Sterchi b Sept. 30, 1904, unm.); (c) James Gilbert Sterchi b June 23, 1867, of Knoxville, Tenn., president of the Sterchi Furniture Co. operating a dozen stores in the South (m Gertha Karnes Oct. 12, 1897 and had an only ch.; 1, James Gilbert Sterchi, the second, b Feb. 13, 1901, unm., with Sterchi Brothers Company); (d) Wilhelmina Sterchi b Feb. 20 1870. of Knoxville, Tenn. (m William N. Smith Sept 2, 1890 and had; 1, Mabel P. Smith b Apr. 1, 1892, of Cumberland Gap, Tenn., m Dr. Luther Fuson May 20, 1912; 2, James W. Smith b Aug. 14, 1894; 3, Grace Alberta Smith b Mar. 6, 1897, m Howard Logan Oct. 13, 1919 Knoxville, Tenn. and had; (aa) William Newton Logan h Aug. 16, 1921; 4, Bertha Louise Smith b Oct. 28, 1899, m Capt. Carroll Holmes and had; (aa) Margaret Holmes b Oct. 21, 1920; (bb) David Carroll Holmes b Mar. 22, 1924; 5, John Raymond Smith b Jan. 18, 1902); (e) Edna Susan Sterchi b May 14, 1873, of Knoxville, Tenn. (m Charles K. Vance May 4, 1898 and had ch. b Knoxville ; 1, Margaret P. Vance b Sept. 13, 1899; d June 7, 1916; 2, John Sterchi Vance b Oct. 24, 1901; d Sept. 8, 1917; 3, Nora Elizabeth Vance b Sept. 8, 1904, m James Albert Burkhart, a furniture dealer 'and had; (aa) Margaret Evelyn Burkhart b Nov. 16, 1923; 4, James William Vance b Dec. 17, 1908; 5, Ruth Edna Vance b Apr. 24, 1916); (f) Mary Elizabeth Sterchi b Jan. 7, 1876, of Knoxville (m Bruce Gentry Apr. 7, 1895 and had ch b Knoxville; 1, John Albert Gentry b Jan. 29, 1896, m Julia E. Russell July 30, 1919 and had; (aa) Dorotha May Gentry b Oct. 13, 1920; (bb) Mary E. Gentry b Jan. 9, 1924; 2, Nellie May Gentry b Jan. 21, 1898; d Aug. 29, 1900; 3, Robert Calvin Gentry b Apr. 16, 1901; 4, Mildred E. Gentry b Apr. 22, 1903, of Bristol, Va.-Tenn., m William C. Wood Nov. 27, 1921 Knoxville and had; (aa) Gertrude Elizabeth Wood b Sept. 1, 1922 Bristol; 5, Edna Elizabeth Gentry b July 17, 1906); (g) Bertha Sterchi b June 6, 1878, of Knoxville, Tenn. (m William A. Tallant Dec 27, 1899, chief electrician for Southern Railway, and had ch b Knoxville; 1, John William Tallant b Jan. 10, 1902; 2, Vera Blanche Tallant b Dec. 30, 1903, m Claude Ledgerwood, Oct. 11, 1924, Knoxville, Tenn.); (h) Robert E. Lee Sterchi b Dec. 19, 1880, of Knoxville (m Josie E. Reed June 14, 1905 and had ch b Knoxville; 1, Eleanor Lee Sterchi b Apr. 13, 1906; 2, Reed Sterchi b Feb. 3, 1908; 3, Robert Hugh Sterchi b Apr. 1911; 4, Elizabeth Sterchi b Dec. 8, 1913; 5, Parthena Fay Sterchi b Feb. 26, 1918; 6 Frances Rebecca Sterchi b June 26, 1923); (i) Louis Augustus Sterchi b July 3, 1884, of Bristol, Va.-Tenn.; m Bessie Knight Watkins Oct. 10, 1905 Knoxville, and had no children; (J) Ida Louise Sterchi b Oct. 16, 1886 (m Eugene Haun Jan. 1, 1906 and had ch. b Knoxville; 1, Thelma Parthenia Haun b Mar. 23, 1907; 2, Louis Eugene Haun b Apr. 21, 1916).

Three. Sarah Ann Tunnell b June 14, 1847; d July 14, 1847.

Four. Margaret Minerva Tunnell b June 22, 1848; d July 6, 1848.

Five. Harriet Jane Tunnell b Sept. 12, 1849; d Mar.17, 1907 Fountain City, Tenn.; married John M. Harris Dec. 1, 1870 and had no children. John M. Harris m second, 1910 Miss Frazier, sister of former U. S. Senator, J. B. Frazier of Tenn.

Six. William Clement Wood Tunnell b Feb. 24, 1853; d July 6, 1895 (m Etura Wieland Dec. 27, 1877 (deceased) and had; (a) Mabel E. Tunnell b Oct. 8, 1878 (m Roy Scott Mar. 21, 1900 and had; 1, Helen Tunnell Scott b Apr. 4, 1901; 2, Walter Tunnell Scott b Jan. 6, 1903); (b) Walter Clarence Tunnell b Feb. 19, 1882, of Knoxville, Tenn. (m Mary Clotworthy July 16, 1914 and had; 1, William Tunnell b May 19, 1915 and two other sons).

Seven. John Calvin Tunnell b May 3, 1855; married Harriett Grilles Mar. 18, 1877 and had; (a) Frank Tunnell b Feb. 20, 1878; d Sept. 13, 1891; (b) Ethelyn Tunnell b July 17, 1880; d July 9, 1903.

Eight. Nancy Catherine Tunnell b Feb. 13, of)Greenfield, Ill.; married John Marion Linder, son of Isham and Sarah (Vaughn) Linder, Dec. 23, 1875 Anderson Co., Tenn. (b Jan. 12, 1825 nr. Carrollton, Ill.; (a) son b and d Dec. 7, 1877; (b) Jesse Tunnell Linder b Nov. 13. 1880 of Greenfield, Ill. (m Ruth Wilhite Sept. 19, 1907 Greenfield, Ill., dau of Samuel M. (b 1840; d Dec. 20, 1918 Vero, Florida) and Mary E. (Hembrough) Wilhite, and had; 1, son b and d May 1, 1908 Claremore, Okla.; 2, John Marion Linder b 1911 Greenfield, Ill.); (c) Etna Tunnell Linder b Mar. 27, 1892; d Apr. 16, 1920 St. Louis, Mo. buried Greenfield, Ill. (m Luther C. Valentine Jan. 9, 1913 Greenfield, Ill., son of Harvey (b Apr. 11, 1842 Greenfield, Ill.; d Mar. 25, 1917 Greenfield, Ill.) and Sarah B. (Cameron) Valentine, and had an only child; 1, Clarabelle Valentine b Dec. 1913. John Marion Linder married first, Louisa Elvira Tunnell, Jan. 5, 1862. See record of Luther and Louisa (Parks) Tunnell).

Nine. Martha Adelia Tunnell b Jan. 31, 1860; d June 10, 1860.

Ten. Mary Evaline Tunnell b Oct. 10, 1861, of Fountain City, Tenn.; married Calloway Clapp Mar. 19, 1882 and had; (a) Arthur Clapp b Jan. 26, 1883; (b) Eula May Clapp b Oct. 25, 1885; (c) Hattie Clapp b Feb. 4, 1890; (d) Jessie Clapp b May 20, 1895; (e) Mary Clapp b Feb. 25, 1898, (f) Evelyn Clapp b Aug. 15, 1905.

Eleven. Julia Emarine Tunnell b Dec. 1, 1863; d Sept. 9, 1887, unmarried.

Twelve. Jesse Thomas Tunnell b Sept. 17, 1867, of Powells Station, Tenn., served thirty years in the regular army and enlisted for war work during World War; married, Oct. 1922, a widow, Mrs. Monday whose maiden name was Weaver and had; (a) John Tunnell b Sept. 3, 1923; (b) son, d in inf.

IX.   James Monroe Tunnell, son of William and Elizabeth Worthington Tunnell, was born Feb. 26, 1818 and died July 3, 1850 Hartville,
Mo.   He married Cynthia Cross July 2, 1840 near Clinton, Tenn., who,
died. Apr. 7, 1865 Hartville, Mo.   Children b \Hartville, 'Mo.
    One.   William Brittain Tunnell b Apr. 3, 1841.
    Two   Mary E. Tunnell b Mar. 12, 1843.
    Three.   Sarah Louise Tunnell b Aug. 14, 1846.
    Four.   Maretta Tunnell b Jan. 27, 1848.
    Five.   Dorthula Tunnell b Oct. 25, 1850.
Of these:
    One.   Dr. William Brittain Tunnell b Apr. 3, 1841; d Dec. 13,.
1904 Chitwood, Mo , attended Union Medical College; served as Union
soldier in the War Between the States; married Mary Elizabeth Car-
son, Oct. 2, 1866 St. Louis, Mo. She was born Aug. 2, 1843 Jacksonville,
Ill., and lives Tulsa, Okla. (She was dau of James Kendall Carson (d
Feb. 1856 Perry, Ill.) and Elizabeth B. Walker Carson, married Nov.
15, 1838 Exeter, Ill., born Oct. 7, 1816 Va.); granddau. Andrew Thomas
Carson from County Down, Ireland, and Catherine Chancellor Kendall
Carson (b Sept. 11, 1785 Shenandoah Co., Va.; d Nov. 22, 1869; arrived
Jacksonville, Ill. 1824, known as "Mother" Carson, first nurse in cen-
tral Illinois.) Children; (a) Frederick Scott Tunnell b Aug. 21, 1867
Hartville, Mo.; d Apr. 19, 1896, unm., Puerto Barrios, Guatamala,
Central America; (b) Roy Eugene Tunnell b Aug. 2, 1871 Golden City,
Mo.; d April 3, 1874 Lead Hill, Ark.; (c) Lily Virginia Tunnell b
July 13, 1875 Hartville, Mo., of Tulsa, Okla. (m Dr. Charles Ira
Trimble, son of William Jefferson and Martha Jane (Brixey) Trimble,
Apr. 11, 1894 Seymour, Mo. (b Oct. 4, 1872 Waldo, Mo.) and had; 1,
Iris Penelope Trimble b Jan. 21, 1897 Seymour, Mo., m Thomas Loraine
Johnson April 11, 1916 West Plains, Mo. and had; (aa) Virginia
Estelle Johnson b Feb 3, 1917; (bb) Iris Johnson b Sept. 3, 1920; 2,
Joe Tunnell Trimble b Sept. 30, 1903 West Plains, Mo.); (d) Charles
Kingsley Tunnell b Feb. 2, 1878 Hartville, Mo.; d Mar. 25, 1878 Hart-
ville, Mo.; (e) Retta Louisa Dorthula Tunnell b Oct. 4, 1879 Hart-
ville, Mo.; d Dec. 18, 1902 Dover, Okla., unm.
    Two.   Mary E. Tunnell b Mar. 12, 1843; d June 6, 1844 Hartville
Mo.
    Three.   Sarah   Louise   Tunnell   b   Aug.   14,   1846;   d Jan. 24,
1920 Ontario, Calif.; married Capt. John P. Robertson, son of James
Campbell and Frances C. (Robinette) Robertson, Nov. 8, 1866 Hartville, Mo.; d May 14, 1900 Ontario, Calif. (m Martin Van Buren
McQuigg 1886 Seymour, Mo., and had; 1, Frank Robertson McQuigg
b Sept. 21, 1887 Mt. Grove, Mo , broker, Pasadena, Calif., m Sarah
Gertrude Elstun Apr. 16. 1909 Los Angeles, Calif.; 2, Harry Martin
McQuigg b 1891 near Ontario, Calif., of Pasadena; 3, Clara McQuigg
b Jan. 25, 1897 near Ontario, Calif., of Pasadena. M. V. McQuigg
married second Annie Woods 1907 Pasadena, Calif.); (b) Hattie Wilson Robertson b June 3, 1869 Hartville, Mo.; d Sept. 15, 1901 Long

Beach, Calif. (m John F. Horsley Sept. 1896 Ontario, Calif., florist of Los Angeles, and had; 1, Frederick Robertson Horsley b June 1897 Ontario, Calif., of San Francisco, m Mary Welsh Jan. 20, 1913 Ontario, Calif.); (c) Maude Robertson b Aug. 13, 1871 Hartville, Mo., of Tipton, Calif. (m Nicholas Abraham Cavanaugh (b Nov. 21, 1865 Elmira, Canada; d July 1, 1925) and had; 1, Beth Cavanaugh b Aug. 23, 1893 Ontario, Calif., of Tipton, Calif., m first, Robert Edward Davis, July 8, 1915 Tipton, Calif. and second Charles Burk, Oct. 4, 1924; 2, John Leonard Cavanaugh b Jan. 10, 1896 m Florence Lorraine Moore Oct. 20, 1921 and had; (aa) Kathleen Cavanaugh b Dec. 9, 1923 Los Angeles, Calif.; 3, Muriel Cavanaugh b Oct. 18, 1898 Ontario, Calif.; d Oct. 6, 1914 Ontario, Calif.); Thula Robertson b May 8, 1876 Webster Co., Mo., of Prescott, Ariz. (m Arthur B. Fox 1898 Ontario, Calif., banker, and had; 1, Evelyn Fox b 1898 Los Angeles, of Oakland, Calif., m George Wescott Miller Dec. 27, 1914 Denver, Col. and had; (aa) George Wescott Miller, the second b Nov. 27, 1915 Pheonix, Ariz.; 2, Gladys Fox b 1899 San Fransisco, m Walter Alexander Nickerson May 8, 1920 and had; (aa) Nancy Fox Nickerson b June 6, 1921 New York City); (e) William James Robertson b Feb. 5, 1879 Webster Co., Mo., d 1901 Ontario, Calif,; (f) Edith Maretta Robertson b July 25, 1881 Webster Co., Mo.; d 1912, unm. Ontario, Calif.; (g) Opal Frances Robertson b Apr. 11, 1883 Seymour, Mo., unm., of Ontario Calif.; (h) Blanche Louise Robertson b Aug. 28, 1885 Seymour, Mo. (m first, Chester Laurance 1911 Pheonix. Ariz. (d Dec. 12, 1912); and m second, John Winthrop Barnes, Colonel of U. S. Infantry, Aug. 13, 1917 at Long Beach, Calif., of Los Angeles, Calif.)

Four.   Maretta Tunnell b Jan. 27, 1848, of Mountain Grove, Mo.; married James Campbell Robertson Jr., brother of Capt. John P. Robertson, Jan. 30, 1868 Hartville, Mo. and had; (a) Cora Robertson b 1869 Hartville, Mo., of Mountain Grove, Mo. (m Arthur Collier and had; 1, Grace Collier; 2, Louise Collier; 3, Paul Collier; 4, Frank Collier; 5, Dan Collier); (b) Eva Robertson, of Mountain Grove, Mo.; (c) Minnie Robertson b 1873; d July 22, 1910, unm.; (d) Charles Robertson; (e) Ethel Robertson, died young; (f) Annie Robertson died Mar. 15, 1921; (g) Mayme Robertson, of Mountain Grove, Mo.

Five.   Dorthula Tunnell b Oct. 25, 1850; d Dec. 9, 1889; married Dr. W. C. Wilson May 25, and had an only child; (a) Edward Wilson. lost in the earthquake San Francisco, California.

X.   Jesse Tunnell, son of William and Elizabeth Worthington Tunnell, was born Sept. 3, 1828 and died Nov. 10, 1914 near present town of Marlow.   His entire life was spent on 'the farm on which he was born.   He married Bashaba England Nov. 10, 1849 Anderson Co., Tenn.) (d June 6, 1898 Anderson Co., Tenn.) and had;

One.   Mary Elizabeth Tunnell b Dec. 2, 1850.

Two.   William Tunnell b Mar. 8, 1853.

Three.   Hannah Tunnell b Jan. 20, 1855.

Four.   Nancy Tunnell b Nov. 25, 1856.

Five. James Calvin Tunnell b Oct. 30, 1863.

Six. John Robert Tunnell b Oct. 30 1867.

Seven Samuel Tunnell b June 12, 1870.

Of these;—

One. Mary Elizabeth Tunnell b Dec. 2, 1850; d Nov. 18, 1886; married Alfred Edward Roberts Aug. 8, 1867 (b Nov. 17, 1846; d Nov. 8, 1923 Ashdown, Ark., son of Nelson Roberts) and had ch b Robertsville, Tenn.; (a) William Roberts b Sept. 18, 1868; d July 19, 1891 Lebanon, Ore. (m ——— and had one child); (b) Henry Roberts b abt 1870; d May 16, 1918 Oliver Springs, Tenn. (m Rosie Newbill and had; 1, Grace Burnette Roberts b Aug. 1907, of Chattanooga, Tenn.); (c) Laura Roberts b Jan. 29, 1872, of Robertsville, Tenn., m Luke Kesterson, son of William Kesterson, July 26, 1896, and had no ch.; (d) Mary Roberts b Nov. 11, 1874; d June 24, 1904 Marlow, Tenn. (m Will Taylor July 19, 1891 (b Oct. 31, 1871; d (Feb. 7, 1904 Coal Creek, Tenn.) and had; 1, Ethel Taylor b Apr. 26, 1892 Coal Creek; d July 2, 1892; 2, Curtis Taylor b July 3, 1893 Coal Creek; d Jan. 2, 1895 Coal Creek; 3, Lavinia Taylor b Sept. 5, 1895 Woodridge, Tenn., of East Lake, Tenn., m ——— Landreth; 4, Charles Taylor b Sept. 27, 1897 Wooldridge, Tenn.; 5, Beulah Taylor b Sept. 1, 1900; 6 Marion Taylor b June 15, 1903 Indian Mountain, Tenn., m Sylvia Vandergriff Oct. 14, 1922 and had; (aa) Helen Elizabeth Taylor b Jan. 11, 1924. Alfred Edward Roberts married second, Elizabeth Smith, now of Okla. City, Okla.

Two. William Tunnell b Mar. 8, 1853; d July 29, 1854.

Three. Hannah Tunnell b Jan. 20, 1855; d at Kemp, Indiana Territory; married James Hooks and had ch., several of whom were born Anderson Co., Tenn., (a) Jessie Hooks; (b) May Hooks; (c) Vic Hooks; (d) Percy Hooks; (e) Henrietta Hooks.

Four. Nancy Tunnell b Nov. 25, 1856; d Aug.. 18, 1893 Robertsville, Tenn.; married her first cousin, Jacob Peak, son of William and Sarah (Tunnell) Peak, Dec. 21, 1876. For ch see record William and Sarah Tunnell Peak.

Five. James Calvin Tunnell b Oct. 30, 1863; d Nov. 20, 1892 Anderson Co., Tenn.; married Belle Wilson, dau of Thomas and Missouri Wilson, at Oliver Springs, Tenn. (died Dec. 12, 1916 Roane Co. Tenn.) and had an only child; (a) Oscar Tunnell b Sept. 10, 1886 at Oliver Springs, Tenn., of Clinton Tenn., living on farm owned by his great-grandparents, William and Elizabeth (Worthington) Tunnell; married a distant relative, Mollie England, Nov. 26, 1906 Anderson Co. (b Aug. 3, 1890 near Oliver Springs, Tenn., dau of James and Rhoda Elizabeth (Butler) England; g-d of Fred and Mary (McKamey) England) and had ch b near Marlow, Tenn.; 1, Blanche Loriene Tunnell b June 5, 1909; 2, James Thomas Tunnell b July 26, 1912; 3, William Laurence Tunnell b June 13, 1920; 4, Rhoda Faith Tunnell b July 6, 1923.

Six. John Robert Tunnell b Oct. 30, 1867, of Oliver Springs,

Tenn.; married Annie Huston abt 1904 Anderson Co., Tenn. and had an only child; (a) John Roosevelt Tunnell b abt 1906. Annie Huston, dau of George and Charlotte (Butler) Huston, the latter marrying, for second husband, Samuel Tunnell, uncle of John Robert Tunnell.

Seven. Samuel Tunnell b June 12, 1870; d Apr. 17, 1892; married Maude Wren and had no children.

CATY TUNNELL COULTER

C. Caty Tunnell, oldest daughter of William and Mary Maysey Tunnell, was born Jan. 31, 1777 in Fairfax Co., Virginia and died Sept. 12, 1826, it is thought in Rhea Co., Tenn. In 1788 her parents moved to North Carolina and in 1792 to near Robertsville, Anderson Co., Tenn. She married James Coulter in 1794, near Robertsville and they lived in different places in Tenn., "on Holston River," "in Sequatchie Valley" and at one time near her brother, Robert Tunnell, near Harrison, Hamilton Co., Tenn. About 1829 James Coulter, with his children, save eldest, moved to Cane Hill, Ark. and he died there in 1850. Names of children may not be in order of birth.

I. Thomas Coulter b June 25, 1795.
II. Polly Coulter b abt 1797.
III. James Coulter b abt 1800
IV. Elizabeth Coulter b abt 1802.
V. Anna Coulter b Jan. 21, 1804 Rhea County., Tenn.
VI. Infant, unnamed, b and d abt 1806.
VII. Lavinia Coulter b abt 1808.
VIII. Margaret Coulter b 1811.
IX. Marian Coulter b Sept. 23, 1813.
X. Ruth Coulter b abt 1815.
XI. Alexander Coulter b abt 1817.
XII. Lettice Coulter b abt 1819.
XIII. Rebecca Coulter b abt 1821.
XIV. Infant, unnamed, b and d abt 1822.
XV Jemima Coulter b abt 1824.

I. Thomas Coulter, son of James and Caty Tunnell Coulter, was born June 25, 1795 and died May 14, 1876 Hamilton Co., Tenn. He married Rebecca Parks Apr. 26, 1815 (b 1796; d Jan. 1880) and had ch b Sale Creek, Tenn.
Of the following:-

One. Thomas Jefferson Coulter b Apr. 15, 1816.
Two. James P Coulter b Oct. 24, 1817.
Three. Margaret Coulter b abt 1819.
Four. Ruth Coulter b abt 1821.
Five. Caty Coulter b abt 1823.
Six. Robert Coulter b abt 1825.
Seven. John Jerome Coulter b Mar. 17, 1827.
Eight. Milo Coulter b abt 1830.
Of these;—
One Thomas Jefferson Coulter b Apr. 15, 1816; d abt 1885; mar-

ried first, Joanna Gamble 1840 (d abt 1845) and had ch b Sale Creek, Tenn.; (a) Elizabeth S. Coulter b Mar. 24, 1842; (b) Margaret Coulter b Sept. 10, 1843 (m ———— Williams and had one dau); (c) Minerva Coulter b Feb. 23, 1845; d in Tenn. (m ———— Martin and had one dau); 1, Maggie Martin m ———— Williams and had two sons. Thomas Jefferson Coulter married Jane P. McDonald 1847 (Sept. 25, 1821; d Jan. 1896) and had; (d) Thomas B. 'Coulter b Dec. 5, 1848; (e) Kitty Jane Coulter b Aug. 7, 1850; (f) Mary C. Coulter b May 6, 1852; (g) James M. Coulter b Nov. 17, 1856, of Carmen, Okla. (m M. E. Kerskner and had; 1, D. Gertie Coulter b Mar. 27, 1882 in Hanna Co., Kan., m ———— Patterson; 2, Fannie E. Coulter b July 21, 1883 m W. E. Dewitt Dec. 1898 and had; (aa) Maggie Dewitt b Dec. 15, 1899; (bb) Sidney Dewitt b Jan. 8, 1904; (cc) Raymond F. Dewitt b Apr. 2, 1911; 3, Ernest Coulter b Mar. 19, 1885 m Anna McCray Nov. 28, 1905 and had; (aa) Everett E. Coulter b June 1, 1907; (bb) Harold E. Coulter b May 22, 1909; (cc) Bertha A. Coulter b May 23, 1911; (dd) Clyde R. Coulter b May 10, 1913; 4, H. M. Coulter b July 1, 1887; 5, W. L. Coulter b Sept. 8, 1889; 6, Catherine J. Coulter b Dec. 10, 1891 m Akine McCray Feb. 12, 1911 and had; (aa) Lloyd McCray b and d June 12, 1912; 7, Ruth R. Coulter b Mar. 14, 1894 Reno Co., Kan.; 8, J. T. Coulter b Aug. 26, 1896; 9, M. A. Coulter b Feb. 24, 1899 Alfafa Co., Okla.; 10, R. H. Coulter b Feb. 2, 1901; 11, L. S. Coulter b July 16, 1903; 12, Dollie E. Coulter b Feb. 2, 1907); (h) William L. Coulter b June 14, 1860; (i) Ruth A. Coulter b Aug. 8, 1863; (j) Robert Jerome Coulter b Aug. 1, 1868 (m Susan Jones Dec. 28, 1898 (d July 13, 1902) and had; 1, Robert Jones Coulter b Dec. 10, 1899; 2, Elizabeth Coulter b Apr. 23, 1902. Robert Jerome Coulter m Alpha Albin Aug. 18, 1903 and had; 3, Millard Lewis Coulter b July 14, 1904).

Two.   James P. Coulter b Oct. 24, 1817; d July 14, 1864 Sale Creek, Tenn.; married Nancy A. McDonald, dau James and Kitty Mc Donald, Feb. 5, 1839 Sale Creek, 'Tenn. (b May 1821 Hamilton Co., Tenn.; d July 29, 1910 Dayton, Tenn.) and had ch b Rhea Co., Tenn.; (a) Amanda J. Coulter b June 5, 1840, of Cleveland, Tenn. (m J. N. Aiken Nov. 14, 1861 Georgetown, Tenn. (d 1892) and had; 1, Samuel J. Aiken b Jan 25, 1866; d July 1901 Cleveland, Tenn., m Carrie Webb (d Apr. 1923 Knoxville, Tenn.) and had; (aa) J. N. Aiken, the second, b Feb. 21, 1899, associate editor of "Virginian Pilot", Norfolk, Va., unmarried; (bb) Carolyn Aiken b Mar. 4, 1900, teacher in Porto Rico, unmarried; (cc) Samuel Aiken b Oct 6, 1901, teacher in Porto Rico, unmarried; 2, Paul Aiken b May 13, 1867; d 1889 Cleveland, Tenn., unmarried; 3, Mary Teuton Aiken b June 2, 1869 (deceased); 4, Ruth Aiken b Nov. 5, 1870, of Cleveland, Tenn., unmarried; 5, Grace Aiken b Mar. 4, 1872; d 1915 Cleveland, Tenn., unmarried; 6, Martha Ann Aiken b Apr. 27, 1875, of Knoxville, Tenn., m ———— ———— July 22, 1914, 7, Amanda Coulter Aiken b Dec. 26, 1880; d Feb. 1, 1905, Cleveland, Tenn.); (b) Alexander Coulter

b Sept. 6, 1842; d Apr. 12, 1862 in Kansas; (c) Adolphus J. Coulter
b Apr. 22, 1845; d Chattanooga, Tenn. (m Louisa Lodemia Holman
July 15, 1868 (b 1850, dau of Burton and Sallie (Worthington)
Hutcheson Holdman; granddau Samuel and Mary (Murfree) Worth-
ington; g-granddau Samuel and Elizabeth (Carney) Worthington)
and had ch b Sale Creek, Tenn.; 1, Samuel Alexander Coulter b May
11, 1869, of Chattanooga, Tenn., m a relative, Mary Virginia Thatcher
Oct. 12, 1892 Soddy, Tenn. (b May 8, 1873 Soddy, Tenn., dau Samuel
Seldon and Margaret Cyrena (Coulter) Thatcher; granddau John
Jerome and Arabell (Hickman) Coulter; g-granddau Thomas and
Rebecca (Parks) Coulter) and had; (aa) Frank Coulter b Dec. 17,
1893 Soddy, Tenn., unmarried; (bb) Claud Thatcher Coulter b Nov.
14, 1895 Soddy, Tenn., unmarried, served over seas in World War;
(cc) Lorena Madge Coulter b Sept. 17, 1898 Sale Creek, Tenn. m Ira
Franklin Templeton, of Chattanooga Oct. 6, 1923; (dd) Mike Coulter
b Jan. 29, 1901 Sale Creek, Tenn, unmarried, served over seas in
World War; (ee) Lee Chester Coulter b Mar. 8, 1904 Sale Creek,
Tenn; 2, James Lafayette Coulter b Mar. 17, 1871, of Sale Creek.,
Tenn. m Alwen Price Feb. 5, 1902 and had; (aa) Carlton Coulter b
Feb. 14, 1903; (bb) child, deceased; 3, Edna Earl Coulter b Sept. 19,
1873; d Oct. 26, 1876; 4, Sarah Ann Gertrude Coulter b May 28, 1881,
m W. H. List Feb. 19, 1902 and had; (aa) Aleen List b Oct. 30, 1905;
(bb) Martha Helen List b Nov. 19, 1908; 5, Claude Coulter b Nov. 26,
1883; d July 14, 1884; 6, Carrie Edith Coulter b June 1, 1889, of
Pratt City, Ala. m Thomas Guilliam Sept. 19, 1910 and had; (aa)
Carrie Louise Guilliam b Sept. 5, 1911); (d) Margaret T. Coulter b
Oct. 10, 1847; d May 26, 1869 Sale Creek, Tenn.; (e) Emily A. Coulter
b Apr. 19, 1850; d Oct. 11, 1856 Sale Creek, Tenn.; (f) John Parks
Coulter b Dec. 18, 1852; d Chattanooga, Tenn. (m Jane Hickman Sept.
5, 1874); (g) Luke Lee Coulter b Jan. 14, 1856, of Spring City, Tenn.
(m Arragine Abel Sept. 8, 1880); (h) Robert Tate Coulter b Aug.
14, 1858; d in Colorado (m Mary Hixson Apr. 24, 1879 and had; 1,
James W. Coulter b Sept. 10, 1882; 2, Coy H. Coulter b Apr. 4, 1886;
3, Eugenia Coulter b July 16, 1887); (i) Mary Marcella Coulter b
Aug. 24, 1861, of Cleveland, Tenn. (m Frank H. Abel, son of White-
house Abel, Mar. 30, 1884 and had; 1, Hettie G. Abel b Jan. 3, 1885
Dayton, Tenn.; d Sept. 23, 1885; 2, Mary M. Abel b May 14, 1887, of
Cleveland, Tenn., m Neil Varnell Nov. 18, 1910 and had; (aa) John
Franklin Varnell b July 9, 1911; (bb) Robert Wayne Varnell b June
26, 1913; (cc) Sam Neil Varnell b Dec. 18, 1921; (dd) Gilbert Varnell
b June 4, 1923; 3, Paul Abel b Apr. 4, 1890; served in France in the
79th Division in World War; m ——— ———; 4, Raleigh R. Abel b
June 28, 1892, m ——— ——— and had ch b Cleveland, Tenn.;
(aa) Walter Abel b Aug. 17, 1916; (bb) Dorothy Abel b July 30, 1918;
(cc) Glen W. Abel b Mar. 11, 1923; 5, Buford F. Abel b July 26,
1897 Dayton, Tenn.; served in Coast Artillery in World War, m

————— ————— and had; (aa) Mary Hill Abel b July 22, 1921;
(bb) Franklin Abel b Sept. 23, 1922).

Three. Margaret Coulter b abt 1819; d Texas; married Charles Hutcheson in Tenn. and had no children.

Four. Ruth Coulter b abt 1821; d 1907 near Arlington, Texas.; m I. Lafayette Hutcheson and had ch including; (a) Albert Hutcheson (b) Margaret Hutcheson; (c) Kitty Hutcheson; (d) James Hutcheson; (e) Emma Hutcheson; (f) Mary Hutcheson; (g) William Hutcheson.

Five. Caty Coulter b abt 1823, lived within a stone's throw of the old Coulter home in Tenn. and died there. She married John R. Hickman and had an only child; (a) Minerva Tennessee Hickman (d bef 1907) (m James Nelson and had two children, who lived Coulterville, Tenn).

Six. Robert Coulter b abt 1825; d in Texas; married Amanda Clift, aunt of William Joseph Clift who m Malinda Arbell Thatcher of the Coulter family, and moved to Texas before 1871. Among the ch were; (a) William Coulter; (b) Rebecca Coulter; (c) Thomas Coulter, who visited Tenn. abt 1890; (d) James Coulter; (e) Brooks Coulter; (f) Joseph Coulter; (g) Robert Coulter; (h) Elizabeth Coulter; (i) Mary Ann Coulter.

Seven. John Jerome Coulter b Mar. 17, 1827; d Dec 22, 1909 Soddy, Tenn.; lived many years at Coulterville, Tenn., which was named for him. He married Arabell Hickman May 15, 1849 (b Nov. 22, 1826; d Jan. 23, 1863) and had ch b Soddy, Tenn.; (a) George W. Coulter b July 25, 1850; d Apr. 17, 1908 Tex. (m ————— McKnight, in Tex. and had; 1, Leslie Coulter, of Arlington, Tex ; 2, Charles Coulter); (b) Margaret Cyrena Coulter b Dec. 19, 1852, of Coulterville, Tenn. (m Samuel Seldon Thatcher Dec. 23, 1868 Coulterville, Tenn. (b Feb. 3, 1847 Knoxville, Tenn., son of Samuel Seldon Thatcher Sr.) and had; 1, Malinda Arbell Thatcher b Aug. 2, 1871 Soddy, Tenn. m William Joseph Clift Dec. 30, 1890 Soddy, Tenn. (b 1862; farmer, Soddy, Tenn.) and had an only child; (aa) Attie Mae Clift b Apr. 24, 1895 Soddy, Tenn., of Wheelwright, Ky., m Samuel Norwood Hall Oct. 21, 1916 Soddy, Tenn. and had, Sarah Lynn Hall b July 11, 1917 Fleming, Ky., Samuel Norwood Hall, the second, b Nov. 2, 1919 Chattanooga, Tenn., Alma Elizabeth Hall b Aug. 15, 1921 Chattanooga; 2, Mary Virginia Thatcher b May 8, 1873 Soddy, Tenn., of Chattanooga, Tenn. m a cousin, Samuel Alexander Coulter Oct. 12, 1892 Soddy, Tenn. (see record of James P. and Mary (McDonald) Coulter for record); 3, William Craighead Thatcher b Aug. 11, 1875 Soddy, Tenn.; d Jan. 30, 1913 Dante, Va., m Laura Angeline Hall Sept. 12, 1894 Soddy, Tenn. (b Nov. 14, 1871 Soddy, Tenn.) and had ch b Soddy, Tenn.; Seldon Thatcher b July 1, 1895, served as Sergeant of Co. D. 56th Engineers, with overseas service in World War, m Pearl McGill, at Bakewell, Tenn. and had ch b Bakewell, Tenn.; Laura Margaret Thatcher and William Seldon Thatcher; (bb) Lillie Lorena Thatcher b Aug. 30, 1897, of Mr. Vernon, Ohio, m Angle B. Pastor

Dec. 23, 1917 Chattanooga and had no ch.; (aa) Stella Bell Thatcher b Apr. 8, 1900, of N. Y., m Frank R. Folley at Rossville, Ga. and had ch. b N. Y., Thatcher Folley, Richard Frank Folley, Joseph Warren Folley; (dd) Lucile Thatcher b Jan. 25, 1902, of Soddy, Tenn., m George R. Reese Apr. 1920 Rossville, Ga. and had ch b Soddy, Tenn; George Roberts Reese b Aug. 15, 1921, Betty Jane Reese b Aug. 17, 1923; (ee) Willie Lee Thatcher b Aug. 24, 1904; d June 29, 1905 Soddy, Tenn.; (ff) James Douglas Thatcher b June 18, 1906; (gg) Laura Mae Thatcher b June 10, 1909; (hh) Charles Lewis Thatcher b Mar. 3, 1912; 4, John Coulter Thatcher b Sept. 4, 1877, farmer, Soddy, Tenn., m Lottie Scybert Nov. 9, 1904 (b Mar. 27, 1884 Sale Creek, Tenn.) and had ch b Soddy, Tenn.; (aa) Lottie Louise Thatcher b Apr. 21, 1908; (bb) John Clift Thatcher b Feb. 11, 1910; 5, Infant b and d Feb. 4, 1879 Soddy, Tenn.; 6, Anna Lee Thatcher b Mar. 14, 1880 Soddy, Tenn., m Samuel Gamble Hutcheson Aug. 9, 1900 Coulterville, Tenn. (b Mar. 1, 1878 Coulterville) and had ch b near Coulterville; (aa) Edna Mae Hutcheson b May 25, 1901, m ———— Camp (deceased) and had one ch., Harold Camp b Aug. 24. 1921; (bb) Margaret Adelia Hutcheson b Aug. 16, 1903; (cc) Brudos Leland Hutcheson b Nov. 16, 1905; (dd) Elba Louise Hutcheson b Nov. 15, 1907; (ee) Rena Lin Hutcheson b July 14, 1910; d Nov. 21, 1921; (ff) Charles Pat Hutcheson b July 4. 1913; (gg) Geneva Virginia Hutcheson b Oct. 8, 1916; 7, Charles Lewis Thatcher b Dec. 19, 1882 Coulterville, Tenn., of Falling Water, Tenn.. m Ruby Frank Selcer Oct. 9, 1911 (b Apr. 3, 1886 Falling Water, Tenn.) and had ch b Chattanooga; (aa) Charles Lewis Thatcher, Jr. b Sept. 14, 1914; (bb) Ruby Mildred Thatcher b Sept. 10, 1919; 8, Samuel Seldon Thatcher the Third, b Dec. 19, 1885 Soddy, Tenn., of Chattanooga, m Lizzie Worley Dec. 30, 1908 Soddy, Tenn. (b July 16, 1887 Soddy) and had; (aa) Vivian May Thatcher b Apr. 30. 1910; (bb) Margaret Helen Thatcher b 1914; (cc) Samuel Seldon Thatcher, the Fourth, b June 14. 1923 Chattanooga; 9. Robert Walker Thatcher b July 4, 1888 Coulterville, Tenn., of Chattanooga, m Sarah Jane Marsh July 1, 1914 (b Sept. 30, 1896 Soddy. Tenn.) and had; (aa) Roberta Thatcher; (bb) L'llian Thatcher; (cc) Virginia Thatcher; (dd) ———— Thatcher (dau); 10, Infant b Aug. 26, 1890; d Sept. 4, 1890; 11, George W. Thatcher b Oct. 13. 1894 Coulterville, Tenn., unmarried, farmer, served overseas in World War; (c) E. V. Coulter (called Jennie) b Jan. 29, 1855; d Mar. 5, 1904 (m Elijah Bell Jan. 25. 1880 Coulterville, Tenn. (now of Dal'as, Tex.) and had; 1, Lillian Bell b 1882 Coulterville, Tenn. of Dallas, Tex., m Robert T. Meador Mar. 7, 1907 and had ch b Dal'as, Tex.; (aa) Robert Franklin Meador; (bb) Virginia Louise Meador b Sept. 11. 1910; (cc) Lillian Margaret Meador b Sept. 19, 1912; 2, Frances Bell b Sept. 10, 1886 Arlington, Tex , of Dallas, Tex. m Thomas Wren Nov. 27, 1912; 3. Winifred Bell b Dec. 30. 1887; 4, John Russell Bell b Sept. 25, 1891 Dallas, Tex., m Duanna McAdams Nov. 5, 1912; 5, Pearl Bell d in inf.; 6, Ruby Bell d in inf.); (d) Arvah L.

Coulter b Jan. 6. 1858; d May 24, 1880 Tenn. (m Abner Bell Sept. 1879 and had; 1, Stella Bell b May 11. 1880 m ———— Gill and lived Ooltewah, Tenn.); (e) Robert L. Coulter b Aug. 18, 1860; d Feb. 18, 1904. unmarried.

Eight. Milo Coulter b abt 1830; d abt 1905 Arlington, Tex.; unmarried.

II. Polly Coulter, dau of James and Caty Tunnell Coulter, was born abt 1797 and died abt 1850 in Cedar Co., Mo. She married in Tenn., Abram Mitchell (b Jan. 28, 1789; d Feb. 5, 1870 Renick, Mo., son of the Rev. Jesse and Elizabeth (Hushing) Mitchell) and had the following ch. whose names may not be given in order of birth.

One. James H. Mitchell b May 16. 1817

Two. Elizabeth Mitchell b May 16, 1819.

Three. Stephen Alexander Mitchell b Mar. 1. 1821.

Four. Baxter Mitchell b abt 1823.

Five. John Mitchell b abt 1826.

Six. Abram Mitchell Jr. b abt 1830.

Seven. Catherine Mitchell b abt 1835.

Eight. Thomas Coulter Mitchell b Feb. 2, 1836.

Nine. Louise Mitchell.

Ten. Anne Mitchell.

Of these;

One. James H. Mitchell b May 16, 1817 Hamilton Co., Tenn.; d Dec. 10, 1891 Cook Co., Tex.; m Julia F. Lilburn, dau of Andy Lilburn, 1839 in Mo. (b June 4, 1820 Tenn.; d abt 1900) and had ch b Cedar Co., Mo.; (a) John W. Mitchell b Dec. 7, 1840; d Feb. 1872, unmarried; (b) Russell Mitchell b Sept. 2, 1843; d Sept. 1884 Okla.; (c) Abe J. Mitchell b Jan. 27, 1848; d Apr. 3, 1912 Gerty, Okla. (m Eliza Winton and had no ch.); (d) Amanda J. Mitchell b Oct. 3, 1850, lived a number of years at Gerty, Okla. (m John W. Givens Aug. 28, 1868 Grayson Co., Tex. (b Jan. 4, 1837 Ray Co., Mo., son of Isaac and Catherine Givens) and had ; 1, J. I. Givens b June 18, 1870, m Dora Wallas Dec. 24, 1895 and had; (aa) Jesse Givens b Oct. 10, 1899; d 1901; (bb) Carl Givens b Oct. 14, 1901; (cc) Corin Givens b Dec. 5, 1902; (dd) Alogene Givens b Feb. 5, 1905, (ee) James M. Givens b Oct. 2, 1911; 2, Aaron Givens b Feb. 28, 1872; d Mar. 4, 1872; 3, Mabel Givens b May 3, 1874, m J. B. Welch Sept. 1, 1891, and had; (aa) Herman Welch b Jan. 16, 1893; (bb) Bryan Welch b Nov. 16, 1895; (cc) Jewell Welch b July 18, 1907; (dd) Bruce Welch, deceased; 4, Abe Givens b Dec. 14, 1876; d Nov. 8, 1901; m Lidie Cutner and had; (aa)Leila Givens; (bb) Maupin Givens, deceased; 5, Beulah Givens b Aug. 31, 1881, m F. C. Russell Jan. 30, 1900 Hughes Co., Okla. and had; (aa) Clyde Russell b Dec. 12, 1901; (bb) Leroy Russell b Sept. 30, 1906, deceased; 6, John Oliver Givens b July 24, 1882, m W. Rodgers Oct. 2, 1904 and had; (aa) Rodger Lee Givens; 7, Gilbert Givens b Jan. 25, 1885, m Myrtle Cash Dec. 29, 1907 and had; (aa) Ray Givens b Aug. 6, 1911; 8, Julia Givens b July 14, 1888 Grayson

Co., Tex.; 9, Merritt Givens b Apr. 19, 1891 Grayson Co.; 10, Marvin Givens b Oct. 10, 1893 Grayson Co.); (e) Thomas Mitchell b 1853; d 1867 Boone Co., Mo.; (f) Sallie Mitchell b Mar. 10, 1856; d Oct. 8, 1908 Whitesboro, Tex. (m James R. Crabtree Dec. 10, 1880 Cook Co., Tenn. and had ch.); (g) James Mitchell b Sept. 20, 1858 (m Mary Seaton 1881 Grayson Co., Tex. and had; 1, Roby Mitchell; 2, Corrin Mitchell; 3, Ganes Mitchell; 4, James Mitchell, Jr.)

Two. Elizabeth Mitchell b May 16, 1819 Hamilton Co., Tenn.; d July 13, 1887; m Alexander Givens 1839 Cane Hill, Ark. (b Sept. 14, 1813 Mo.; d Nov. 6, 1879 Tex.; and had; (a) James Givens b July 25, 1841; d Oct. 1867. Soldier in C. S. A., Co. F. Third Mo. Cav. (m Adeline Johnson 1865 and had; 1, Melvina Givens b Apr. 1866; d 1883; 2, James Givens b Oct. 1868, of Tex.); (b) William Givens b June 18, 1843; d abt 1865 Little Rock, Ark., served in Co. F. Third Mo. Cav. C. S. A.; (c Mary A. Givens b Nov. 3, 1845 Dade Co., Mo., of Minco, Okla., (m W. Wilson Nov. 15, 1866 Whitesboro, Tex. (b Jan 3, 1840 Dade Co., Mo., served in Co. F. Third Mo. Cav. C. S. A.) and had; 1, Anna Wilson b Mar. 16, 1868, of Tabler, Okla., m Marion Morrow and had (aa) Clayton Morrow; (bb) Clifton Morrow; (cc) Bertha Morrow; (dd) Arthur Morrow; (ee) Bernice Morrow; (ff) Bernardine Morrow; 2, Dora Wilson b Sept. 14, 1870; d Oct. 14, 1877; 3, Mollie Wilson b May 10, 1873; d Nov. 6, 1904 Rush Springs, Okla., m Tip Worsam at Maysville, Okla. and had; (aa) Ethel Worsam; (bb) Cullen Worsam; d bef. 1914; (cc) Willie Worsam, deceased; (dd) Eula Worsam; (ee) Arthur Worsam; (ff) Raymond Worsam; 4, Sammy Wilson b Apr. 4, 1874; d Oct. 9, 1877; 5, Oscar Wilson b Mar. 3, 1877; d Oct. 9, 1877, same day as his brother and five days before his sister Dora; 6, Arthur Wilson b Sept. 23, 1878, of Minco, Okla., m Auga Paschal Sept. 30, 1905 and had; (aa) Bernice Wilson b. 1907; (bb) Alma Wilson b 1909; (cc) Artie Wilson b 1911; 7, Della May Wilson b June 23, 1881; d Sept. 17, 1905 Rush Springs, Okla. m Uriah Smith 1904; 8, Callie Wilson b Feb. 15, 1887, of Hydro, Okla., m Harry Taylor Dec. 23, 1908 and had; (aa) Howard Taylor b Dec. 5, 1910; (bb) Glen Taylor b Apr. 18, 1913); (d) Thomas Baxter Givens b Nov. 11, 1855 in Mo., of Roff, Okla. (m Anna Louise Hayter Feb. 14, 1878 and had; 1, Walter Thomas Givens b Nov. 1, 1878 m Florence Hunt Roff Dec. 20, 1903 and had; (aa) Frank Givens b Oct. 21, 1904; (bb) Pauline Givens b Sept. 21, 1907; (cc) Margurite Givens b Aug. 18, 1900; (dd) Bernardine Givens b Aug. 18, 1911; 2, Hattie May Givens b Feb. 6, 1881 Gordonville, Tex.; 3, John Elmer Givens b Mar. 31, 1883 Gordonville, Tex.; d Sept. 29, 1905 Roff, Okla.; 4, Roy Lee Givens b July 27, 1887 Mannsville, Ind. Ter.; 5, Sarah Effie Givens b Dec. 14, 1891 Mannsville, Ind. Ter.; d Oct. 5, 1905; 6, James Guy Givens b June 28, 1893; d July 3, 1893; 7, Cecil Hayter Givens (Sam) b July 1, 1895 Mannsville, Ind. Ter.); (e) Myra Givens b Sept. 5, 1858; d May 3, 1912 Dallas, Tex. (m Chesley Cundiff (d abt 1910) and had; 1, Ada

Cundiff, of Dallas, Tex., m ———— Smith, Grayson Co., Tex.; 2, John Cundiff; 3, James Cundiff; 4, Homer Cundiff).

Three. Stephen Alexander Mitchell b Mar. 1, 1821 Hamilton Co., Tenn.; d May 23, 1906 near Elliot, Mo.; married first, Louise Lilburn, sister of Julia Lilburn, Nov. 21, 1843 (b Oct. 2, 1824 Rhea Co., Tenn. d Aug. 22, 1867 Renick, Mo.) and had ch b Cedar Co., Mo.; (a) Elizabeth J. Mitchell b Sept. 26, 1844; d Feb. 3, 1865; (bb) James Russell Mitchell b Jan. 17, 1846; d Dec. 9, 1854; (c) Mary Louise Mitchell b May 23, 1848, of Highbee, Mo. (m Isham Powell, son Golson and Mary (Coulter) Powell, of Boyle Co., Ky.; grandson Thomas Coulter, Feb. 24, 1870 Renick, Mo. (d Dec. 31, 1921) and had ch b near Renick, Mo.; 1, Lula Powell b Nov. 16, 1875, m James Milton Terrill Oct. 6, 1908 and had no ch.; 2, Henry Powell b Dec. 8, 1877, m Melissa Lewis Sept. 30, 1900 and had; (aa) Frank Collins Powell b Aug. 5, 1904); (d) Julia C. Mitchell b Oct. 6, 1850; d May 20, 1856; (e) Thomas Asbury Mitchell b Oct. 2, 1852; d June 20, 1854; (f) Rebecca A. Mitchell b Feb. 11, 1856 (m Grannison Goin Oct. 4, 1877 Renick, Mo. and had; 1, Gertrude Goin, of Moberly, Mo., m Buford Hulen and had; (aa) Elizabeth Hulen; 2, James Goin, d unm.; child deceased); (g) Laura V. Mitchell b Oct. 23, 1859; d Feb. 11, 1910 Moberly, Mo. (m Ammon H. Shearer Feb. 10, 1881 Renick, Mo. and had; 1, Bessie V. Shearer, of Moberly, Mo., m Ernest Pattison and had (aa) Virginia Pattison m J. D. Hammett; and others; 2, Bertie A. Shearer, of Moberly, Mo., m Maude Bradley and had; (aa) Juanita Shearer; 3, Merle Shearer, Principal of Kansas City school, m Helen Miller and had one child; 4, Juanita Shearer, d young; 5, Reba Shearer, of Kansas City, Mo.; 6, Lucille Shearer, of Michigan City, Ind., m Barney Engle and had two children, one dead); (h) Jefferson Alexander Mitchell b Aug. 16, 1861; d Aug. 27, 1882. Stephen Alexander Mitchell married second, Sarah Toalson (d Aug. 27, 1882) and had; (i) Minnie B. Mitchell b Mar. 17, 1870 Renick, Mo., of Kansas City (m Lan Ingersoll and had; 1, Frank Ingersoll; 2, Iola Ingersoll).

Four. Baxter Mitchell b abt 1825; d young. He lived in Oregon and Calif.

Five. John Mitchell b abt 1826; d 1861 near Humansville, Mo.; married Harriet Rule and had; (a) Robin Mitchell; (b) Gines Mitchell; (c) James Mitchell.

Six. Abram Mitchell Jr. b abt 1830. He lived in Oregon and Calif. and is said to have married and had children.

Seven. Catherine Mitchell b abt 1835; d abt 1870; married Dr. Dudley and had one son b 1855, who d 1857.

Eight. Thomas Coulter Mitchell b Feb. 2, 1836, who lived 1912 Springfield, Mo. He married first, Bettie Gilbert at Linden, Mo. and had one son, who went to South America. He married second, ————, in Tex. He had eight children living 1912, including; (a) John M., of Springfield, Mo.; (b) Harry Mitchell; (c) Jane M. Mitchell; (d) Lee Mitchell; (e) Sue Mitchell.

Nine. Louisa Mitchell, died abt 1855, unmarried.

Ten. Ann Mitchell died unmarried.

III. James Coulter Jr., son of James and Caty Tunnell Coulter, was born abt 1800 and died abt 1840. He married Mary Moore and had;

One. Ellen Coulter d in inf.

Two. John Coulter, d 1850 Cane Hill, Ark., unmarried.

Three. Amy Coulter b abt 1836, lived in Belton, Bell Co., Tex. She married Robert Cox 1855 and had two children.

IV. Elizabeth Coulter, dau James and Caty Tunnell Coulter, was born abt 1802 and d 1854 Cane Hill, Ark. She married Thomas Galbraith abt 1851 and had no children. After her death Thomas Galbraith moved back to Tenn.

V. Anna Coulter, dau of James and Caty Tunnell Coulter, was born Jan. 21, 1804 Rhea Co., Tenn. and died Oct. 8, 1865 Washington Co., Ark. She married James Bryant Russell Dec. 6, 1827 (b Feb. 22, 1803 Rhea Co., Tenn.; d Aug. 16, 1899 Arkansas) and had;

One. Mary Catherine Russell b Mar. 23, 1829.

Two. Elizabeth Ann Russell b Aug. 20, 1830.

Three. Alta Russell b Sept. 11, 1835.

Four. James McGrady Russell b Feb. 17, 1837.

Five. George Thomas Russell b Nov. 15. 1838.

Six. Samantha Russell b Jan. 14, 1840.

Seven. Samuel Plyant Russell b Sept. 22, 1844.

Of these;

One. Mary Catherine Russell b Mar. 23, 1829 Tenn.; d in Ark; married John James May on Feb. 1, 1844 Cane Hill, Ark. (d Feb. 10, 1857) and had ch b Cane Hill, Ark.; (a) Jesse Thomas May b May 27, 1845; d Feb. 19, 1865 while serving as a soldier in the War Between the States; (b) William Anderson May b July 17, 1847; d bef. 1918 (m Kate Boynton June 3, 1891 and had; 1, Russell May b Mar. 4, 1892, of Little Rock, Ark., m Victoria Norberry and had two children; William Anderson May Jr. b June 17, 1899, unmarried); (c) John Anna May b Mar. 19, 1849; d Apr. 4, 1849.

Two. Elizabeth Ann Russell b Aug. 20, 1830 Tenn.; d Mar. 23, 1909 Bentonville, Ark.; married James Terrill Craig June 19, 1851 Cane Hill, Ark. (b Dec. 22, 1818 Tenn.; d Mar. 23, 1895 Bentonville, Ark.) and had ch. b Cane Hill, Ark.; (a) Charles Russell Craig b Mar. 29, 1854 real estate dealer of Bentonville, Ark. m Charlotte E. Reding Mar. 27, 1876 and had ch, b Bentonville, Ark.; 1, James Reding Craig b May 8, 1878, with N. Y. Life Ins. Co., Fayetteville, Ark., m Mabel Bedford June 18, 1903 Paris, Tex. (b Dec. 14, 1884 Paris, Tex.) and had; ch. b Bentonville, Ark.; (aa) Charles Bedford Craig b May 11, 1904; (bb) Lillian Ruth Craig b Dec. 2, 1906; (cc) James Russell Craig b Mar. 24, 1908; (dd) Edwin Martin Craig b Mar. 13, 1909; (ee) George William Craig b Dec. 20, 1913; 2, Carrie May Craig b July 9, 1880; d Dec. 6, 1904 Bentonville, Ark.; m Edwin F. Jackson and had; (aa) Charlotte Jackson, of Fayetteville, Ark. m Roy Elliott and had no ch.; (bb) Craig Jackson, unmarried, of Rogers, Ark.; 3, Edward Mathis Craig b May 12, 1883, real estate dealer, Bentonville, Ark., m Ela Black 1910 and had ch. b Bentonville; (aa) Joe Craig b 1914; (bb) Eliza Ann Craig b 1916; 4, Ethel Moore Craig b Oct. 3, 1886, of Tarkio, Mo., m John Capp Feb. 1918 and had; (aa) Craig Capp b. 1909; (bb) Charlotte Capp b 1911; (cc) Joe Capp b 1913; (dd) Frank Capp b 1916; 5, Annie M. Craig b July 2, 1888, of Bentonville, Ark., m E. Pickens Apr. 15, 1907 (cashier Benton County National Bank and had; (aa) William C. Pickens b Apr. 8, 1910; (bb) Ann Pickens b Jan. 8, 1917; (cc) Martha Pickens b May 15, 1923); (b) Edward Albert Craig b Nov. 5, 1860; d at San Antonio, Tex. (m Winnie McDaniel Jan. 14. 1884 (now of Kansas City, Mo.) and had; 1, Bess Craig, of Kansas City, m Herbert Dierks, manager Dierks Lumber Co., and had no ch.; 2, John Craig, of Idabell, Okla., m ————— ————— and had; (aa) John Craig Jr. b 1910; (bb) Margaret Craig b 1912; (cc) Elizabeth Craig, twin of Margaret Craig b 1912; (c) George McGrady b Sept. 17, 1862 Cane Hill, Ark. President of Merchants National Bank, Port Arthur, Tex. (m Jane Alice Taliaferro Sept. 14, 1886 Bentonville, Ark. (b Sept. 21, 1868 Bentonville, Ark. dau Charles Dickinson and Jane Adeline (Dickson) Taliaferro, natives of Tenn.) and had children b Bentonville, Ark; 1, Bennette Craig b Mar. 25, 1888, of Buffalo, N. Y., m Edward Bennett Germain, President Dunlap Tire and Rubber Co., and had; (aa) Edward Bennett Germain, the second, b Mar. 1, 1916 Boston, Mass.; 2, Louise Berry Craig b Sept. 27, 1890, of Port Arthur, Tex., m Ernest Dean Dorchester Jr. May 3, 1916 and had; (aa) Craig Dorchester, daughter, b Nov. 13, 1918 Port Arthur, Tex.; (bb) Ernest Dean Dorchester, the third, b Apr. 2, 1923, Waxahachie, Tex.; 3, George Taliaferro Craig b Oct. 26, 1892; d June 1, 1924, m Martha Halse Oct. 13, Buffalo, N. Y. and had; (aa) Jack Bennett Craig b Nov. 13, 1919, Buffalo, N. Y.); (d) John Samuel Craig b Feb. 3, 1867; d Mar. 1, 1869 Cane Hill, Ark.

Three. Alta Russell b Sept. 11, 1835 Cane Hill, Ark; d Dec. 11, 1918 Cane Hill, Ark.; married Rev. John Thomas Buchanan Oct. 29, 1861 (b Mar. 27, 1836; d Mar. 7, 1910) and had ch b Cane Hill, Ark.; (a) Marietta Buchanan b Aug, 16, 1862; d Dec. 14, 1918; m Capt. John Truesdale McClellan June 16, 1894 (d 1920 Cane Hill, Ark.) and had no ch.; (b) James Isaac Buchanan b Nov. 28, 1865; d Nov. 29, 1865; (c) Naomi Anne Buchanan b Sept. 14, 1868, of Lincoln, Ark. (m George Hiram Bell Dec. 25, 1894 Batesville, Ark. (b May 20, 1872, farmer, son of Judge J. J. and Sarah Ann (Banks) Bell; gs Robert Scott Bell, of Ky., for years a missionary to the Choctaw Indians) and had; 1. Aileen Bell b Apr. 16, 1896 Batesville, Ark., of Portersville, Calif., m Ira R. Elliott, a rancher, Sept. 29, 1917 Fayetteville, Ark. and had; (aa) Virginia Elliott b Sept. 27, 1918; (bb) Elizabeth Elliott b Apr. 1921; 2, John Irvin Bell b Oct. 22, 1898 at Whitesboro,

Tex., unmarried, farmer, Fayetteville, Ark.; 3, Mary Catherine Bell
b Jan. 12, 1902 Searcey, Ark., of Wood River, Ill., m Roy A. Carson
Feb. 23, 1924, with Standard Oil Co.; b, Sarah Alta Bell b Apr. 26,
1905; 5, Joseph Scott Bell b Aug. 13, 1908).

Four. James McGrady Russell b Feb. 17, 1837 Cane Hill, Ark.,
of Elmer, Okla.; married Mary R. Bellar July 20, 1859 (b Oct. 4,
1840; d Feb. 14, 1902 Bellforte, Ark.) and had ch b Cane Hill, Ark.;
(a) William Campbell Russell b Dec. 22, 1861, farmer, of Elmer,
Okla. (m Mrs. Jennie Stultz 1903 and had 1, Mildred Russell b
Muskagee, Okla., of Wilmington, Tex., m Mikie Summers Dec. 1922;
2, Margaret Russell); (b) Ewert Edward Russell b Jan. 16, 1869,
Jeweler and Optometrist, of Altus, Okla. (m Ellen Baucum Sept. 18,
1893 and had ch b Altus, Okla.; 1, Wylie Bryant Russell b Nov. 17,
1895, of Altus, Okla., served in World War, m Inez Earl Nov. 30,
1923; 2, James McGrady Russell, the second, b Jan. 15, 1897, of Altus,
Okla., served in World War, m Della Gould and had; (aa) Vivian
Russell b Oct. 4, 1914; (bb) James McGrady Russell, the third, b Apr.
22 1916; (cc) Loyd Ewert Russell b Mar. 1920; (dd) C. Fay
Russell b Mar. 1922; 3, Vivian Russell b May 11, 1898; d June 6,
1899; 4, Lanier W. Russell b Jan. 8, 1900, of Altus, Okla., served in
World War, m Juanita Cox and had; (aa) Virginia Russell b June 13,
1919 Altus, Okla.; (bb) Ella Mae Russell b July 1922 Altus, Okla.;
5, Forest Ewert Russell b Dec. 9, 1910); (c) Ola Russell b May 24,
1871, of Elmer, Okla. (m A. C. Harral Feb. 24, 1892 Cane Hill, Ark.,
(b May 19, 1861; d Sept. 4, 1896) and had; 1, Velma Beatrice
Harral b Mar. 11 1893, of Olusta, Okla., m John McKinzie and had;
(aa) Mary McKinzie b Feb. 1916; (bb) Jim David McKinzie b Sept.
1, 1923; 2, James Asa Harral b Sept. 19, 1895, unmarried, Elmer,
Okla); (d) ———— Russell (daughter unnamed) b Feb. 23, 1875; d
Apr. 6, 1875 Cane Hill, Ark.; (e) Nona Russell b July 15, 1876, of
Altus, Okla. (m Walter Wright Sept. 18, 1899 Altus, Okla. (b Jan. 27,
1871 Tenn., merchant) and had ch b Altus, Okla.; 1, Audrey Hope
Wright b Apr. 29, 1902; 2, Adron Russell Wright b Jan. 1, 1905; 3,
Dorothea Irene Russell b Oct. 24, 1908.

Five. George Thomas Russell b Nov. 15, 1838 Ark.; deceased;
married Sarah Hagood Dec. 28, 1875 (d 1903) and had; (a) Charles
Hagood Russell b Jan. 13, 1877; (b) James McGrady Russell b 1879;
(c) Mary G. Russell b 1888, of Fort Worth, Tex., m Fred Browning.

Six. Samantha Russell b Jan. 14, 1840 Ark.; d June 21, 1905
Morrow, Ark.; married George W. Morrow Dec. 7. 1865 (b May 2,
1842, of Lincoln, Ark.) and had ch b Morrow, Ark.; (a) Annie
Elizabeth Morrow b July 1, 1867, of Atkinson, Neb., m T. M. Elder
Apr. 9, 1923; (b) William Robert Morrow b Apr. 9, 1869 (m
Lucretia Baucum, sister of Ellen Baucum, Sept. 6, 1892 and had ch
b Altus, Okla.; 1, Floyd Wilson Morrow b June 25, 1895, of Fredrick,
Okla., served in World War, m Vida Hale Aug. 23, 1921 Altus, Okla.
and had; (aa) Floyd Wilson Morrow Jr., b Apr. 25, 1922 Altus, Okla.;

(bb) Thomas Franklin Morrow b Sept. 22, 1923 Frederick, Okla.; 2, Samantha Elizabeth Morrow b Aug. 23, 1897, of Hoffman. Okla., m William Hobart Lewis June 5, 1919 Okla. City and had; (aa) Joy Elizabeth Lewis b Apr. 14, 1920 Boynton, Okla.; (bb) Florence June Lewis b July 21, 1921 Haskell, Okla.; (cc) William, Hobart Lewis Jr. b Oct. 20, 1922 Haskell, Okla.; 3, Glenn Elmer Morrow b Mar. 9, 1902, served in Navy during World War, m Daisy Little Morrow Mar. 9, 1924 Frederick, Okla.; 4, Raymond Acey Morrow b 1904; d in inf ; 5, Gladys Irene Morrow b Mar. 27, 1906; d Dec. 6, 1918 Altus, Okla.); (c) Maggie May Morrow b Oct. 1, 1870; d Oct. 22, 1908; (d) Estella Jane Morrow b Oct. 21, 1872, unmarried, of Morrow, Ark.; (e) Hugh Oscar Morrow b Dec. 6, 1876, of Morrow, Ark. (m Mary Cole June 5, 1904 and had ch b Morrow, Ark.; 1, Hugh Otho Morrow b June 25, 1905; 2, Nannie Elizabeth Morrow b Mar. 30, 1908; 3, Samuel Wilson Morrow b Oct. 24, 1908; 4, Ruben Cole Morrow b Aug. 31, 1912; 5, Kenneth Sydney Morrow b Apr. 13, 1916); (f) Ena Russell Morrow b Aug. 7, 1879; d July 17, 1903 (m Charles Crozier Sept. 21, 1902 and had twin daughters; 1, Margie Ena Cozier b July 14, 1903, unmarried, of Morrow, Ark.; 2, Nannie Russell Crozier, twin of Margie Ena Crozier b July 14, 1903; d Aug. 1, 1903).

Seven. Samuel Plyant Russell b Sept. 22, 1844, of Cane Hill, Ark. married Eliza Yates Mar. 7, 1867 (d abt 1908) and had; (a) Alice Eliza Russell b Mar. 7, 1868, of Cane Hill, Ark. (m Samuel McCulloch and had; 1, Bertha McCulloch b 1899; 2, Lila McCulloch; 3, Hazel McCulloch 4, Lacy McCulloch (son) 5, Myrtle McCulloch); (b) Ollie Russell, of Cane Hill, Ark. (m Tennie Casnahan and had; 1, Conrad Russell; 2, Gordon Russell).

VI. Infant child of James and Caty Tunnell Coulter was born about 1806 and died in infancy.

VII. Lavinia Coulter, dau of James and Caty Tunnell Coulter, was born about 1808. She died at age of eighteen, unmarried.

VIII. Margaret Coulter, dau of James and Caty Tunnell Coulter, was born about 1811 in Tenn. and died June 10, 1863 Rusk, Cherokee Co, Tex. She married William M. Munkers 1831 Cane Hill, Ark. (b 1812; d July 18, 1877, Cherokee Co, Tex.) They moved to Texas in the eighteen forties. The surname, Munkers appears as Monkers, Monkres and Monkress among descendants. William M. Munkers, or Monkers, married second, Minerva (Mc-Knight) Spraggins and lived Jacksonville, Tex. Children;

One. Elizabeth Jane Monkers b Dec. 29, 1832.

Two. Alexander Monkers b 1834.

Three. Missouri Monkers b Mar. 25, 1837.

Four. Tennessee Monkers b 1839.

Five. James Henry Monkers b 1842.

Six. Samuel Harris Monkers b Aug. 9, 1844.

Seven. Robert Pope Monkers b Aug. 7, 1846.

Eight. Charles William Monkers b Nov. 18, 1847.

Nine. Margaret Ruth Monkers b May 25, 1853.

Of these;

One. Elizabeth Jane Monkers b Dec. 29, 1832; Cane Hill, Ark; d Feb. 26, 1901 Tyler, Tex.; married Harrison Crawford Stout, son of John and Jane (Kirby) Stout, Feb. 3, 1848 Cane Hill, Ark. (b July 25, 1825 East Tenn.; d Aug. 1894 Rusk, Tex.) and had ch b in Texas; (a) Mary Stout b 1851; d in inf. Nacoydoches Co., Tex.; (b) Angela Stout b 1854; d in inf. Cherokee Co., Tex.; (c) William R. Stout b Aug. 8, 1856; d Dec. 14, 1920 Dallas, Tex. (m first, Mary Bascom Jarratt May 22, 1879 (b July 16, 1860 Craft, Tex.; d Jan. 7, 1906 Craft, Tex.) and had ; 1, Ed Stout b Mar. 3, 1880 Rusk, Tex. (deceased) m Kate ———— and had; (aa) Mary Stout b Jan. 4, 1906 Denison, Tex.; (bb) Ruth Stout b Oct. 3, 1908; 2, Harry Grady Stout, for a number of years on battleship "South Dakota," m ———— aft 1918, of Everett, Wash. William R. Stout m second, Eudora Burdick Feb. 20, 1907 Dallas, Tex. (b Aug. 9, 1877 Waller Co., Tex., now of Washington, D. C.); (d) Martha Baldwin Stout b Dec. 4, 1858; d Mar. 8, 1919 Mt. Pleasant, Tex. (m Jefferson Earley Shook July 13, 1873 (d Apr. 15, 1923 Wichita Falls, Tex.) and had; 1, Jefferson Shook b Feb. 3, 1875 Nacoydoches, Tex., newsdealer, Ft. Worth, Tex., m Sinia Morris June 16, 1896 Rusk, Tex., and had; (aa) Mary Kate Shook b 1899; (bb) Earley M. Shook b Dec. 21, 1901; 2, William Harrison Shook b Jan. 13, 1877, attorney, Rusk, Tex. m Daisy Tittle June 26, 1901 and had; (aa) W. H. Shook b June 27, 1902, unmarried, Los Angeles, Calif.; (bb) John Louis Shook b May 23, 1908; (cc) Virginia Shook b Jan. 10, 1912; (dd) Samuel Philip Shook b Mar. 13, 1915; 3, Wyatt Blasingame Shook b Nov. 18, 1882 Rusk, Tex., with Hollis Post Herald, Hollis, Okla., m Olive Montgomery Hardwick Nov. 18, 1902 and had; (aa) Hardwick Blasingame Shook b Nov. 4, 1903 Overton, Tex.; (bb) Wyatt Baldwin Shook b Nov. 9, 1906 Overton, Tex.; (cc) Thomas Early Shook b Dec. 23, 1910 Shreveport, La.; (dd) Maynard Everett Shook b Sept. 6, 1913 Overton, Tex.; (ee) Buford Oliver Shook b Feb. 23, 1917 Shreveport, La.; (ff) William Cameron Shook b Apr. 20, 1923 Childress, Tex.; 4, Winona Shook b Oct. 26, 1886 Batesville, Tex., of Wichita Falls, Tex., m Milton T. Harbison July 26, 1905 Rusk, Tex. and had; (aa) Milton T. Harbison, the second, b Nov. 19, 1906; d Dec. 3, 1906; (bb) Katheryne Harbison b Aug. 31, 1908; (cc) Emily Eudora Harbison b Dec. 28, 1913 Pittsburg, Tex.; (dd) Robert Hardison b May 2, 1916; (ee) Edna May Harbison b Oct. 5, 1918 Arlington, Tex.; (ff) Frank Harbison b Nov. 11, 1921; 5, May Shook b May 1, 1889 Jacksonville, Tex., m Carter Hill Fitts Oct. 1907 Jacksonville, Tex. and had ch. b Rusk, Tex.; (aa) Daisy May Fitts b Sept. 11, 1908; (bb) Thomas Shook Fitts b Jan. 4, 1910; (cc) James Hill Fitts b Aug. 27, 1913; (dd) Herbert Milburn Fitts b June 15, 1917; (ee) Joseph Early Fitts b Apr. 2, 1919); (e) John W. Stout b 1864; d in inf.; (f) Samuel Thomas Stout b Dec. 2, 1865; d Dec. 19, 1891 Tyler, Tex., (m ————

———— and had; 1, James Bennett Stout, in charge of daily news
paper of steamship Leviathan); (g) Richard Orton Stout b Dec. 3,
1875; d 1895 Rusk, Tex. (m Ada Findley and had no children).

Two. Alexander Monkers b 1834; d in inf.

Three. Misouri Monkers b Mar. 25, 1837; d after 1913 Jacksonville, Tex. She was twice married; first to W. Henderson Mills abt
1859, who d Nov. 7, 1867, and second to Pat Murry abt 1872, who d
bef 1913. Three children by first marriage and two by last marriage
b in Rusk Co., Tex.; (a) Margarte Belton Mills b Oct. 5, 1860 (m S. G.
Barton Dec. 24, 1882 Cherokee Co., Tex.; farmer Brownsboro, Tex.
and had; 1, Jeannette Barton b Oct. 23, 1883 Brownsboro, Tex., m
first, W. L. Darden Jan. 20, 1901 near Opelika, Tex. (d Apr. 10, 1909
near Mars, Tex.) and had ch b near Mars, Tex.; (aa) Walter Alfred
Darden b Dec. 1, 1901; (bb) Bessie Annie Darden b Oct. 15, 1903;
(cc) Maggie Elizabeth Darden b Sept. 18, 1905; (dd) William
Garrett Darden b Dec. 24, 1907; and m second, A. A. Darden, half-
brother of her first husband, Apr. 19, 1913 (d Aug. 20, 1920) and had
ch b near Leagueville, Tex.; (ee) Frankie May Cooie Darden b Jan.
21, 1915; (ff) Horton Mills Darden b Feb. 3, 1917; (gg) Jim Darden
b Aug. 23, 1920; 2, Daughter b Jan. 17, 1885 near Brownsboro; d Feb.
10, 1885 near Brownsborn; 3, Minnie Lee Barton b Feb. 7, 1887 near
Jacksonville, Tex., m E. L. Jordan Dec. 3, 1902 near Brownsboro, Tex.
and had; (aa) Bessie Agnes Jordan b Apr. 10, 1905, m Archie B.
Crawford Mar. 26, 1922 near Brownsboro, Tex. and had Archie Leroy
Crawford b Feb. 19, 1923; (bb) Josie Belton Jordan b Nov. 16, 1906;
(cc) James Gordon Jordan b Oct. 25, 1908; (dd) Virgil Frank Jordan
b Oct. 24, 1910; (ee) Fred Elmer Jordan b Mar. 25, 1913; (ff) Minnie
Ola Jordan b May 23, 1915; (gg) Iva Edith Jordan b Apr. 26, 1917;
(hh) Pearlie Frances Jordan b Dec. 11, 1919; (ii) Nellie Erline Jordan
b May 12, 1922; (jj) daughter b Dec. 19, 1924; 4, Annie May Barton
b May 20, 1889 near Jacksonville, Tex., m E. V. Fowler Feb. 2, 1913
near Brownsboro, Tex. and had ch b Murchison, Tex.; (aa) Herman
Wesley Fowler b May 12, 1914; (bb) Hazel Jewel Fowler b Apr. 22,
1916; (cc) Frankie Vera Fowler b Sept. 1, 1918; (dd) daughter b and
d Feb. 26, 1922; (ee) Margaret Evelia Fowler b Jan. 10, 1924; 5,
Frank Mills Barton b July 11, 1893 Thackerville, Okla., m Fannie
Carver Feb. 4, 1923 near Brownsboro, Tex.); (b) Frank Mills b May 8,
1863, of Jacksonville, Tex. (m first. Alice Harriett ———— (d Dec.
16, 1910) and had second Ethel Vandergriff and had no children);
(c) Will Mills b Nov. 24, 1866 unmarried, of Jacksonville, Tex.; (d)
Walter P. Murry b Nov. 25 1873 near Jacksonville, Tex. (m Mollie
Causey Sept. 15, 1902 near Jacksonville, Tex. and had; 1, Will Mills
Murry b July 27, 1903, m Pearl Vosick Nov. 10, 1923 Tyler, Tex.; 2,
Joe Francis Pope Murry b Aug. 13, 1907; 3, Eunice Murry b Mar.
30, 1909; 4, Walter Lee Murry b May 11, 1911; 5, Goldie May Murry
b July 12, 1913; 6, Dessie Belton Murry b Dec. 8, 1915); (e) Linnie
Murry b Dec. 6, 1876 near Craft, Tex.; d June 29, 1879.

Four.   Tennessee Monkers b 1838, lived for a number of years at Eldorado, Okla. and d Dec. 1924.   She m first, Anderson Long, 1857 (d 1861) and had three children; m second, W. Mitchell 1864 (d 1870) and had one son; and m third, I. N. Langston 1871 and had two children (a) William H. Long b 1858; d 1862; (b) James A. Long b July 16, 1860 (m Carrie West 1897 Thackerville, Okla.); (c) Charles P. Long, twin of James A. Long, b July 16, 1860, unm. in 1913; (d) George W. Mitchell b Dec. 17, 1869; d Mar. 11, 1902 (m Nettie Myers abt 1890 Thackersville, Okla. and had; 1, Jameh Mitchell; 2, Essie Mitchell; 3, Clyde Mitchell; 4, John Mitchell); (e) Bonnie E. Langston b Mar. 31, 1872; d Sept. 19, 1872; (f) John Langston b Nov. 21, 1874; d July 8, 1909 (m first, Cora Rose and had an only child; 1, Ray Langston d young; and m second, Cassie ———— and had three children, two dying in infancy).

Five.   James Henry Monkers b 1842, of Tipton, Okla.; married Rachel Burk and had; (a) Jane Monkers; (b) Frank Monkers; (c) Sam Monkers, deceased; (d) Maggie Monkers; (e) J. P. Monkers; (f) Viola Monkers.

Six.   Samuel Harris Monkers b Aug. 9, 1844 Russellville, Ark.; d Dec. 17, 1913 Tishimingo, Okla.; married Mattie Dunnica, dau John and Elizabeth J. (Ferguson) Dunnica, Dec. 26, 1866 Rusk Co., Tenn. (b July 21, 1848 Cherokee Co., Tex.; d Mar. 22, 1881 Bryan, Tex.) and had; (a) Leona Monkers b Sept. 21, 1867 Rusk, Tex., of Dustin, Okla. (m George M. Mayes Sept. 17, 1884 on Texas side of Red River, near Thackervllie, Okla. and had 1, James Mayes b Nov. 16, 1886, of Dustin, Okla., m Susan Peavy Jan. 27, 1907 and had; (aa) Thelma Mayes; (bb) Arlyn Mayes; (cc) Leona Mayes; (dd) Willard Mayes; (ee) Alva Mayes; (ff) Alma Jean Mayes; 2, Maud Mayes b Mar. 5, 1891, m Newton Taff Dec. 17,1913 and had; (aa) Homer Taff; (bb) Maurice Taff; (cc) Merle Taff; (dd) Hayward Taff); (b) Jane Monkers b 1869 Cherokee Co., Tex.; d May 1, 1891 Thackerville, Okla. (m Boland P. Edwards and had; 1, Robert Edwards b Apr. 30, 1890 Thackerville, Okla., who married 1913); (c) William T. Monkers b abt 1872 Kaufman Co., Tex.; unmarried; (d) Emma Monkers b abt 1874 Rusk Co., Tex.; d Nov. 13, 1916 Tishmingo, Okla. (m Cage Edwards, brother of Boland P. Edwards, at Thackerville, Okla. (d Dec. 1918) and had; 1, Leona Edwards m Charles McSwain; 2, Lela Edwards m Fred Grimes; 3, Kate Edwards; 4, Roy Edwards; 5. Willie Edwards; 6, Maud Edwards; 7, Lloyd Edwards; 8, Charles Edwards; 9, Harold Edwards and two others d in infancy); (e) Redmond Monkers b Mar. 19, 1877 near Jacksonville, Tex., of Wichita Falls, Tex. (m his cousin, Bessie Guinn, dau of Philleo Pericles and Margaret Ruth Monkers) Guinn, Jan. 10, 1907, and had an only child; 1, Raymond D. Monkers b Aug. 26, 1909 Gainesville, Tex.)

Seven.   Robert Pope Monkres b Aug. 7, 1846, of Centerview, Mo.; married first Susie Mitchell abt 1867 Rusk, Tex. (d Jan. 25, 1899), and second ———— Storms and had ch. by first marriage; (a) Ector

Monkers b Dec. 4, 1869 Cherokee Co., Tex., of Chickasaw, Okla. (m Emma Monroe and had; 1, Edgar Monkres; 2, William Monkres, served in the World War, wounded in service; 3, Newton Monkres; 4, Herschel Monkres; 5, Virgie Monkres; 6, Bernice Monkres; 7, Lassie Monkres); (b) Samuel T. Monkres b Apr. 19, 1872 Cherokee Co., Tex., of Margaret, Tex. (m Eula Jones and had; 1, Oney Monkres; 2, Claudie Monkres; 3, Ruby Monkres; 4, Thomas Monkres; 5, Juanita Monkres; 6, Drake Monkres; 7, Incley Monkres; 8, Charles Monkres; 9, Helen Monkres; 10, Hulen Monkres); (c) William P. Monkres b Dec. 25, 1873 Cherokee Co., Tex., of Margaret, Tex. (m Lizzie Myers and had; 1, Rena Monkres; 2, Lucian Monkres; 3, Joe Monkres; 4, Jewell Monkres; 5, Kenneth Monkres; 6, James Monkres); (d) James Monkres b May 25, 1876 Cherokee Co., Tex., m Edith Curtis and had no children; (e) Lucian Monkres b Mar. 12, 1879 Cherokee Co., Tex., of Tulsa, Okla., m Anna Jinks and had no children; (f) Lela Monkres b Mar. 21, 1881 Indian Territory, of Tulsa, Okla. (m Benn Paul and had; 1, Mabel Paul; 2, Virgil Paul); (g) Buddie Monkres b June 10, 1884 Indian Terr.; d in inf.; (h) Charles Monkres b June 10, 1884, twin with Buddie Monkres, of Margaret, Tex. (m Zula Scott and had; 1, Lou Monkres; 2, Lea Monkres; 3, Ovis Monkres; 4, Weldon Monkres; 5, Lottie Monkres); (i) Lula Monkres b July 28, 1886, of Red Fork, Okla. (m Lon Scaggs and had no children).

Eight.   Charles William Monkers b Nov. 18, 1847; d Nov. 22, 1872 Cherokee Co., Tex.; married Vetura Evaline Staton, dau T. J. and Martha (Thomason) Staton, 1867 (b Apr. 6, 1852 near Valley Head, Ala.; d June 20, 1912 Jacksonville, Tex.) and had ch b Jacksonville, Tex.; (a) Virgil Pope Monkers, who adopted spelling of Monkress. b Aug. 1, 1868 Jacksonville, Tex.; d Nov. 11, 1921 Jacksonville, Tex. (m Lavinia Albritton aft. Dec. 1913); (b) son b Oct. 14, 1870; d June 15, 1871; 3, Charlie Parlie Monkress b Nov. 17, 1872, of Glendale, Calif. (m first W. H. G. Brady and had no ch.; and second C. B. Case).

Nine.   Margaret Ruth Monkers b May 25, 1853 near Jacksonville, Tex. d May 17, 1894 New Birmingham, Tex.; married Philleo Pericles Guinn, son of Robert and Sarah Jane Guinn, Mar. 20, 1873 Rusk Co., Tex. (b Dec. 3, 1849) and had ch. b Rusk, Tex.; (a) Thomas Guinn b May 24, 1875, of Rusk, Tex. (m first, Emma Sterling Aug. 1, 1895 New Birmingham, Tex. (d Feb. 14, 1904) and had ch b Rusk, Tex.; 1, Willie Ruth Guinn b Aug. 20, 1896, m first Elmer Gabbert Nov. 1914 Wichita Falls, Tex. (d Mar. 25, 1920 Altus, Okla.); and m second, Henry Maness Dec. 1923, Rusk, Tex. and had no issue by either marriage; 2, Ralph Leslie Guinn b May 31, 1899, of Rusk, Tex., m Goldie Howard Oct. 4, 1920 and had; (aa) Tom Howard Guinn b Dec. 22, 1921; 3, Paul Sterling Guinn b Apr. 19, 1902, unmarried. Thomas Guinn m second Bettie Perkins 1909 and had; 4, Margaret Elizabeth Guinn b Feb. 9, 1913); (b) Tennie Guinn b Oct. 26, 1876; d Mar. 28, 1884; (c) Bessie Guinn b Apr. 20, 1880, of Wichita Falls, Tex. (m her cousin, Redmond Monkers, son of Samuel Harris and

Mattie (Dunnica) Monkers; (d) Lula Guinn b Feb. 19, 1885; d Apr. 27, 1886; (e) Allie Guinn b Feb. 9, 1888; d Aug. 1, 1891.   Philleo Pericles Guinn m second, Mary Clay May 19, 1895 New Birmingham, Tex.

IX.   Marian Coulter, dau of James and Caty Tunnell Coulter, was born Sept. 23, 1813 in Tenn. and d abt 1870 Fayetteville, Ark. She married John Lewis abt 1832 Cane Hill, Ark. (b July 1, 1807 in Tenn.; d Dec. 7, 1861) and had;

One.   William M. Lewis b Sept. 23, 1833.

Two.   J. A. Lewis b May 22, 1835.

Three.   Virginia Lewis b Nov. 12, 1837.

Four.   Josephine Lewis b Feb. 19, 1840.

Five.   Margaret Catherine Lewis b June 14, 1843.

Six.   John Marion Lewis b June 1, 1847.

Of these;

One.   William M. Lewis b Sept. 23, 1833 (lived 1912 Cane Hill, Ark.) married first, a cousin, Caroline Wright, dau of Maurice and Ruth (Coulter) Wright, Dec. 31, 1856 (d Oct. 3, 1857); and second, Mary E. Reed Feb. 5, 1868 at Fayetteville, Ark., and had; (a) William Lewis b 1869; d 1869; (b) Mary Josephine Lewis b Jan. 1, 1870, of Gravette, Ark. (m Dr. G. A. Hughes Nov. 21, 1895 Cane Hill, Ark., and had; 1, Reginald Othello Hughes b Mar. 7, 1897, d Apr. 30, 1912 Gravette, Ark.; 2, Lillian Venetta Hughes b May 14, 1899; 3, Lewis Hurley Hughes b Feb. 24, 1902; 4, Lena Elizabeth Hughes b Mar. 4, 1904; 5, Margaret Louise Hughes b Mar. 29, 1906); (c) Margaret Catherine Lewis b Oct. 5, 1872, unm. 1914; (d) John Reed Lewis b May 25, 1875, of Cane Hill, Ark. (m Laura Lacy McCulloch Jan. 18, 1898 Cane Hill, Ark. and had; 1, Velma Lewis b May 1890); (e) Elizabeth May Lewis b Aug. 17, 1877, of Siloam Springs, Ark. (m first John W. Shepherd Oct. 2, 1901 and had no ch.; and second, Ollie Reed).

Two.   J. A. Lewis b May 22, 1835; d 1855, unmarried.

Three.   Virginia Lewis b Nov. 12, 1837; d aft 1850; married first Ezekiel Phillips abt 1855 (d abt 1860) and second, Colonel Milton Lake and had no issue by either marriage.

Four.   Josephine Lewis b Feb. 19, 1840; d Oct. 23, 1890; married William Mitchell Dec. 1, 1858 (d Ark.) and had; (a) Jennie Mitchell b Aug. 1, 1866; m Albert E. Leach Oct. 13, 1901; (b) James Mitchell b July 19, 1868; (c) William Ezekiel Mitchell b Aug. 24, 1870, m Laura Iva Leach Jan. 14, 1903; (d) Mary Kate Mitchell b Aug. 22, 1872, m David Stewart Oct. 13 1901; (e) John Maurice Mitchell b Aug. 31, 1878 d Jan. 27, 1912; (f) Nannie Joe Mitchell b July 15, 1881, m Joshua Kirby Jan. 10, 1910; (g) Lizzie Annie Mitchell b Jan. 11, 1885, m William Irvin Linkart May 9, 1906.

Five.   Margaret Catherine Lewis b June 14, 1843; married Sam Smithson (deceased) and had; (a) Josephine Smithson, m John Cope and had no children; (b) Jessie Smithson, who d May 13, 1900.

Six.   John Marion Lewis b June 1, 1847.

X.   Ruth Coulter, daughter of James and Caty Tunnell Coulter, was born abt 1815 in Tenn. and d Aug. 8, 1862 Cane Hill, Ark. She married Maurice Wright, abt 1835, in Ark., who d Cane Hill, and had ch. b Washington Co., Ark.

One.   Elizabeth Wright b Sept. 26, 1836.

Two.   Caroline Wright b abt 1838.

Three.   Robert B. Wright b Nov. 1839.

Four.   Maurice Wright, Jr. b Jan. 14, 1845.

Five.   Laura Wright b Oct. 2, 1846.

Of these;

One.   Elizabeth Wright b Sept. 26, 1836; d Aug. 30, 1896 Hoopeston, Ill.   She moved to Iroquois Co. abt 1866.   She married Dr. Arthur T. Crozier May 12, 1859 Cane Hill, Ark. (b Aug. 9, 1833; d Sept. 3, 1891 Iroquois Co. Ill., son of Dr. Hugh Crozier (b Oct. 22, 1810) and Mary Oliver Crozier) and had; (a) Minnie Crozier b July 27, 1861 Cane Hill, Ark.; d Nov. 6, 1917 Hoopeston, Ill. (m Dr. Finlep P. Johnson Sept. 6, 1885 Iroquois, Ill. (b Mar. 4, 1856 Mazon, Ill., son of Matthew Johnson (b June 27, 1821 Uniontown, Pa.; d Apr. 20, 1902) and Mary J. Preston Johnson (b Sept. 6, 1824; d Oct. 29, 1904; m Apr. 14, 1842), and had 1, Arthur Maurice Johnson b Dec. 15, 1886, in Indiana, unmarried; 2, Nellie M. Johnson b Nov. 20, 1891 Iroquois, Ill.; d July 23, 1897 Hoopeston, Ill.; 3, Harold Crozier Johnson b Dec. 31, 1903 m Muriel Ellerman Aug. 28, 1923 Peoria, Ill. (b Apr. 5, 1904 Hoopeston, Ill., dau Fred H. and Gertrude Ellerman); (b) Robert Maurice Crozier b Mar. 1, 1864 Iroquois, Ill.; d Apr. 21, 1864; (c) Arthur May Crozier b Dec. 16, 1866 Iroquois, Ill., of Olton, Texas.

Two. Caroline Wright b abt 1838; d Oct. 3, 1857 Washington Co. Ark.   She married her first cousin, William M. Lewis, Dec. 31, 1856 (b Sept. 23, 1833, son of John and Marian (Coulter) Lewis) and had no ch.

Three.   Robert B. Wright b Nov. 1839; d Mar. 31, 1923 in Tex.; married Annie Barton Nov. 8, 1890 (d Sept. 1917) and had no children.

Four.   Maurice Wright, Jr., b Jan. 14, 1845; d Jan. 11, 1911; married Sarah J. Wolf 1877, now of Forestburg, Tex. and had ch b Wise Co., Tex., save one; (a) Robert Dean Wright b Nov. 13, 1878 (m Bertha Davis Oct. 1905 and had; 1, Grady Wright b 1906; 2, Gladys Wright b 1908; 3,Minis Wright b 1910; 4, Addie May Wright b 1912; 5, Evelyn Wright b 1914); (b) George Albert Wright b Oct. 22, 1880, of Forestburg, Tex.; (c) Leonard Earl Wright b July 10, 1883 (m Belle Vick Aug. 1903 and had; 1, John Maurice Wright b 1904, m Ella Burchard Aug. 1924; 2, Emmett Wright b 1906; 3, Terrell Wright b 1908; 4, Stanley Wright b 1912; 5, Novella Wright b 1914); (d) Fred Wright b June 5, 1887 (m Dorothy Casey Apr. 1917 and had; 1, Garvin Wright b 1918); (e) Myrtle Anna Wright b June 21, 1889; d Feb. 4, 1911 (m D. L. Buck Mar. 1910 and had; 1, Robert M. Buck b Jan. 1911, of Beaumont, Tex); (f) Esther Beatrice Wright b Sept. 21,

1891 (m J. R. Buck Dec. 1918 and had; 1, Melvin Buck b 1912; 2, J.
D. Buck b 1914; 3, Lila May Buck b 1916; 4, Jake R. Buck b 1918;
5, Vera May Buck b 1920); (g) Gertrude Wright b Aug. 8, 1893, m
L. L. Freeman Jan. 1922; (h) Arnold T. Wright b Aug. 5, 1895 (m
Zora Dye Jan. 1923 and had; Arnold T. Wright, the second, b Dec.
1923); (i) Melissa Wright b Dec. 5, 1898 (m S. B. Thompson Jan.
1916 and had; 1, Margaret Sue Thompson b Nov. 1917).

Five. Laura Wright b Oct. 2, 1846, of Ardmore, Okla.; married
first Benn Miller, in Ark. (d abt 1867) and had; (a) Ida Miller b Jan.
19, 1865, of Abernathy, Tex. (m James E. Fitzgerald Feb. 28, 1886
Sunset, Tex. and had; 1, Avie Laura Fitzgerald b Mar. 28, 1887, m
Warren R. Brown Dec. 23, 1908 Abernathy, Tex. (d Dec. 23, 1919) and
had; (aa) Edgar Mae Brown (son) b Oct. 30, 1909 Abernathy, Tex.;
d Jan. 20, 1917; (bb) Bernice Neal Brown (son) b July 8, 1911; (cc)
Cathryn Elizabeth Brown b Sept. 23, 1913; (dd) Warren Richard
Brown b Nov. 10, 1915; (ee) George Leland Brown b Apr. 8, 1918;
2, John Nelson Fitzgerald b Sept. 12, 1889 Sunset, Tex., m Frances
Roberson Dec. 24, 1912 Petersburg, Tex. and had; (aa) Claudie
Evelyn Fitzgerald b Oct. 22, 1914; (bb) Georgie Rhea Fitzgerald b
Aug. 23, 1916; (cc) John Nelson Fitzgerald. the second, b May 10,
1919; 3, Mattye Viola Fitzgerald b Apr. 30, 1892 Hale Center, Tex.,
m J. W. Sorey June 14, 1919 Dallas, Tex. and had; (aa) J. W. Sorey,
Jr. b Oct. 4, 1920 Wichita Falls, Tex.; (bb) Sylvia Sue Sorey b Nov.
8, 1923 Los Angeles, Calif.; 4, George Washington Fitzgerald b Sept.
29, 1895 Hale Center, Tex.; volunteered for service in the World War
July 1917; landed in France April 1918; wounded in action at Chateau
Thierry July 23, 1918 and d in Base Hospital No. 31, on Aug. 1, 1918;
body brought to America and interment made July 2, 1921 Abernathy,
Tex.; 5, Christina McIntosh Fitzgerald b Jan. 5, 1902 Hale Center,
Tex.; 6, son b and d same day, abt 1904; 7, son b and d same day, abt
1905; 8, James Robert Fitzgerald b Apr. 26, 1906 Abernathy, Tex.;
9, Henrietta Lee Fitzgerald b Apr. 16, 1908 Abernathy, Tex.; 10,
Minnie Mae Fitzgerald b Nov. 2, 1910). Laura Wright Miller married
George Herron 1877 Wise Co., Tex. (b Dec. 24, 1834 Germany; d
Ardmore, Okla.) and had; (b) Joe Herron b Jan. 12, 1881 Wise Co.,
Tex., plumber, of Ardmore, Okla. (m Anna Balthrop 1901 Wise Co.,
Tex. and had; 1, Alta Gladys Herron b 1904 Earl, Okla.; 2, Mittie
Eva Herron b and d 1903 Ardmore, Okla.; 3, Geneva Jo Herron b
1913 Ardmore, Okla.; 4, Juanetta Herron b 1916 Ardmore); (c)
Marvin Herron b Aug. 8, 1882 Carter Co., Tex., farmer, Scipio, Okla.
(m Beatrice Whitson 1902 and had; 1, Bonnie Herron b 1903 Ardmore,
Okla.; 2, Ruby Herron b 1906 Ardmore; d 1909); (d) Lawrence
Herron b May 6, 1886 Wise Co., Tex., farmer, Scipio, Okla. (m Ollie
Cothran 1904 and had an only ch.; 1, Everett Herron b 1906); (e)
Dovie Herron b Feb. 17, 1891 Carter Co., Okla.; d 1918 Carter Co.,
Okla. (m Roscoe Foster 1907 and had; 1, Wilmore Foster b 1908; 2,

George Foster b and d 1909; 3, Ruth Paul Foster (daughter) b 1912; 4, Roscoe Foster, Jr., b 1914; d 1917).

XI. Alexander Coulter, son of James and Caty Tunnell Coulter, was born abt 1817 and died abt 1835. He was not married.

XII. Lettice Coulter, dau of James and Caty Tunnell Coulter, was born about 1819 in Tenn. and died in the 1850's in Ark. She married Jacob Moyers and had ch b Cane Hill, Ark. Names may not be in order of birth.

One. Catherine Moyers.

Two. James Moyers.

Three Mary Emeline Moyers.

Four. William Alexander Moyers b Apr. 9, 1844.

Of these;

One. Catherine Moyers died at 16 in Arkansas.

Two. James Moyers d in the early 1870's in Tex., unmarried.

Three. Mary Emeline Moyers died 1875; married David Moore, who d 1867, and had; (a) Annie Moore; (b) Willie Moore.

Four. William Alexander Moyers b Apr. 9, 1844; d June 13, 1903; married first, Lauretta Ernest Graves Apr. 1, 1880 Blue Ridge, Tex., (b Jan. 30, 1848 Dalton, Ga.; d Oct. 21, 1888 Blue Ridge, Tex.) and had ch b Blue Ridge, Tex.; (a) Mary Katherine Moyers b May 3, 1881, unmarried, of Blue Ridge, Tex.; (b) Lillian Camille Moyers b Nov. 5, 1882; d Aug. 24, 1918 (m Samuel Russell Dickinson July 18, 1905 Anna, Tex., now of Chambersville, Tex. and had ch b Malissa, Tex.; 1, William Raymond Dickinson b July 22, 1906; 2, Cora Ernest Dickinson b July 31, 1908; 3, Samuel Winfrey Dickinson b Oct. 22, 1910; 4, Charles Russell Dickinson b June 16, 1912; 5, Mary Katherine Dickinson b Jan. 31, 1914; 5, Ruby Elizabeth Dickinson b May 8, 1916; 7, Lillian Grace Dickinson b Aug. 20, 1918; d Nov. 1918); (c) Sallie Graves Moyers b Nov. 17, 1884, of Blue Ridge, Tex. (m Paul Alexander Copeland Apr. 22, 1903 Blue Ridge, Tex. and had ch b Blue Ridge; 1, Willie Meree Copeland b Feb. 16, 1904; 2, Mildred Graves Copeland b Dec. 18, 1907; 3, James Hoyt Copeland b Nov. 19, 1909). William Alexander Moyers married second, Margaret Ann Smith Feb. 5, 1891 Albany, Ky. and had ch b Blue Ridge, Tex., (d) Lauretta Alma Moyers b Mar. 28, 1893, of Farmersville, Tex. (m Roger Mills Hendrix Nov.6, 1910 Blue Ridge, Tex. and had ch b Blue Ridge; 1, Rodger Elwyn Hendrix b Aug. 6, 1911; 2, James Moyers Hendrix b July 31, 1914; 3, Philip Eugene Hendrix b May 3, 1917); (e) Zelma Maurine Moyers b Apr. 17, 1895, of Blue Ridge, Tex. (m Roy W. McCarley Aug. 1914 and had; 1, Von Roy McCarley b June 22, 1915; 2, Gwyneth Latane McCarley b Feb. 28, 1917; 3, Billy Noyce McCarley b Apr. 9, 1919); (f) Vivian Juanita Moyers b Dec. 22, 1897, of Dallas, Tex. (m William Lloyd Manning June 18, 1924 Blue Ridge, Tex.) (g) Letitia Janie Moyers b Aug. 11, 1900, unmarried; (h) William Alexander Moyers, the second, b Aug. 4, 1903, of Farmersville, Texas.

XIII. Rebecca Coulter, dau of James and Caty Tunnell Coulter, was born a'bt 1821 in Tenn. and died June 1856 Cane Hill, Ark. She married Richard Kirby, at Cane Hill, Ark, (b Greene Co., Tennessee; d Dec. 1867 Cane Hill, Ark.; son of Christopher and Betsy Kirby, natives of Virginia, and grandson of Richard Kirby) and had ch b Cane Hill, Ark.;

One. Christopher Kirby b Mar. 10, 1846.

Two. Thomas H. Kirby b Apr. 20, 1848.

Three. Anna Kirby.

Four. William A. Kirby.

Five. Alta Kirby.

Of these;

One. Christopher Kirby b Mar. 10, 1846, of Westville, Okla.; married Mary Irwin Dec. 7, 1870 Cane Hill, Ark. (b July 7, 1846 Armour City, Ireland)ᵻ and had; (a) James Harry Kirby b Oct. 1, 1871 (m Jessie Brogden Feb. 14, 1899 and had; 1, Louie Kirby b Sept. 13, 1906) (b) Lillian Roberta Kirby b Oct. 20, 1872 (m L. S. Watson Dec. 1897 and had; 1, Lillian Watson b Oct. 10, 1898; 2, Christine Watson b Aug. 30, 1902; 3, Robert Watson, and others); (c) Bessie Kirby b June 26, 1874; (d) Margaret Dickson Kirby b Sept. 25, 1875; d Aug. 1876; (e) Frank Irwin Kirby b Dec. 11, 1876 (m Lyde M. Parish Dec. 20, 1905 and had; 1, John Christopher Kirby b Apr. 7, 1908); (f) Robert D. Kirby b Feb. 7, 1878; (g) Mary Lacy Kirby b Mar. 8, 1886 (m T. C. Jones Dec. 21, 1905 and had; 1, Margaretta Jones b Apr. 22, 1907; 2, Bessie Jones b Jan. 22, 1912; 3, Thomas Christopher Jones b July 25, 1915).

Two. Thomas H. Kirby b Apr. 20, 1848; d Oct. 24, 1913 Cane Hill, Ark.; married Rebecca Virginia Ashley Jan. 20, 1870 Independence, Mo. (d July 10, 1920 Cane Hill, Ark.) and had ch b Cane Hill, Ark.; (a) the Rev. W. F. Kirby b Sept. 20, 1871, pastor of U. S. A. Church Sherman, Tex. (m Lula Cole Dec. 23, 1895 and had; 1, Burney Kirby b 1896, m ———— ———— and had 2 ch., Jennie Mae Kirby b 1898, unmarried; 3, Mary Lou Kirby, of Shrevesport, La., m ———— Northcott and had one child; 4, Irene Kirby, of Arlington, Tex., m ———— Brittallas and had one child; 5, Landrith Kirby, unmarried); (b) Annie Laura Kirby b Jan. 16, 1873; d Sept. 1908 Prague, Okla. (m ———— Chambers and had; 1, Clarence Chambers; 2, Rosa Lee Chambers; 3, Everett Chambers); (c) Alice Mae Kirby b Mar.5, 1874, of Denison, Tex. (m William Glenn Knox Feb. 5, 1896 (d June 20, 1908 Wynnewood, Okla.) and had only ch.; 1, ———— Knox, m Gordon Campbell b 1922); (d) Jessie Clifford Kirby b June 20, 1876; d 1900 Cane Hill, Ark. (m ———— Brewster 1898 and had; 1, Lillian Brewster (d Apr. 12, 1922 Los Angeles, Calif.) who m ———— Foote); (e) Henry Lee Kirby b July 5, 1879; d Apr. 22, 1898 Norman, Okla.; (f) Charles T. Kirby b Feb. 28, 1881, of Cane Hill, Ark. (m Mattie Morgan McCleur 1905 and had; 1, Genevieve

Kirby b 1906; 2, Thomas Grant Kirby b 1908; 3, Norman Kirby b 1910; 4, Robert Kirby b 1915; 5, Dorothy Kirby b 1917).

Three. Anna Kirby died abt 1885 in Ark.; married Aurelius James abt 1879 and had; (a) Alta Cornelius James b Aug. 9, 1880 (m G. Jones and had a son b bef. 1912); (b) John M. James b July 11, 1882, once of Morrow, Ark.

Four. William Kirby, of Onyx, Ark.; married ———— Irvin, sister of his brother's wife, Mary Irvin, and had; (a) James Kirby, of Westville, Okla., m Hester Brogden; (b) Frank Kirby, m ———— ————; (c) Robert Kirby; (d) Bird Kirby, m ———— Watson; (e) Elizabeth Kirby; (f) Mollie Krby, m ———— Jones.

Five. Alta Kirby died at Cane Hill, Ark. She m Alexander E. Andrews 1874 Cane Hill, Ark. and had no children.

XIV. Infant child of James and Caty Tunnell Coulter was born abt 1822 and d in infancy, unnamed.

XV. Jemina Coulter, called Dick, dau of James and Caty Tunnell Coulter, was born abt 1824 and d 1888 Cane Hill, Ark. She married Robert Moore, who also died 1888 at Cane Hill, Ark. and had ch b Cane Hill, Ark.

One. Martha Moore, unmarried, Cane Hill, Ark.

Two. Elizabeth Moore; died Feb. 23, 1908 Cane Hill, Ark., unmarried.

Three. Kate Moore, unmarried, of Cane Hill, Ark.

Four. Caroline Moore b Jan. 30, 1855, of Cane Hill, Ark.; married Frank Braley Mar. 30, 1887 Cane Hill, Ark. and had; (a) Kathleen Braley b Mar. 6, 1893 (only child) (m Clyde Foley 1917 Cane Hill, Ark. and had; 1, Ruth Foley b Oct. 6, 1920 Clyde, Ark.)

Five. May Moore died Jan. 1902 Ft. Smith, Ark.; married Boudont Griffith, Cane Hill, Ark. (d Ft. Smith) and had; (a) Anna Griffith, died at Ft. Smith, Ark. (m ———— ———— and had one childchild); (b) Marguerite Griffith, of Ft. Smith, Ark. (m a relative, Theodore Griffith and had; 1, Winifrid Griffith b Dec. 17, 1916).

D. Nancy Tunnell, dau of William and Mary Maysey Tunnell, was born Dec. 27, 1779 Fairfax Co., Va. and died young. She was living in Rutherford County, North Carolina, in 1790.

LETTICE TUNNELL WORTHINGTON

E. Lettice Tunnell, dau of William and Mary Maysey Tunnell, was born Feb. 26, 1781 in Fairfax Co., Va. She moved, with her parents to N. C. and later to near Robertsville, Anderon Co., Tenn. Here she married, 1799, James Worthington, son of Samuel and Elizabeth (Carney) Worthington, and survived her husband. James Worthington was born July 11, 1799 and died Nov. 13, 1813, it is said at Fort Strother. He was a soldier in the War of 1812.

The surname of Worthington is, like many other family names, derived from the locality where the first known progenitor of the family resided.   The name is credited with being from three Saxon words;— Wearth-in-tomn, i. e. Farm-in-town.   "The Worthington family," says Burke's Landing Gentry, "of ancient English origin possessed estates in Devonshire and Lancaster¡ in England prior to 1236 A. D. "It is a name as old as any in England and by some is said to have originally been spelt "Weorthington"; and translated into modern English has the meaning of "the descendants of the men who settled the place".   Records at Knoxville show the spelling "Weatherington" while the family used Worthington.

No history of Anderson Co., Tenn. would be completed with out mention of the Worthington family.   Samuel Worthington is spoken of in "Historical Counties of Tenn." in connection with the erection of Anderson Co.   He was at Burrville, now Clinton, Tenn. in the early 1790's.   He was born Mar. 1746 near Baltimore, Md.; moved to Va., later to Tenn. and died Jan. 21, 1821 Anderson Co., Tenn. He married Elizabet Carney in 1774, who was born Apr. 30, 1754 and died Oct. 20, 1830 Anderson Co., Tenn.

Children of James and Lettice Tunnell Worthington born in Anderson Co., Tenn.

I.   Samuel Worthington b May 27, 1800.
II.   William Worthington b Dec. 22, 1801.
III.   Mary Worthington b Feb. 2, 1804.
IV.   Betsey Worthington b 1805.
V.   Thomas Worthington b June 11, 1808.
VI.   Catherine Worthington b May 10, 1810.
Of the foregoing;

I.   Samuel Worthington, son of James and Lettice Tunnell Worthington, was born May 27, 1800 and died May 1832 in Texas. He was a surveyor and aided in survey of state of Tex.   He married Polly Barnes 1823 in McMinn Co., Tenn. (b Apr. 5, 1805 Tenn. d Nov. 4, 1866 near Bentonville, Ark.)Their children were born in Warren Co. Tenn.

One.   James Worthington b June 27, 1824.
Two.   Sally Worthington b Oct. 15, 1826.
Of these:

One.   Dr. James Worthington b June 27, 1824; d Mar. 4, 1871 in Ark.; married Nancy Faulkner, dau of Asa Faulkner, July 21, 1846 McMinnville, Tenn. (b Nov. 6, 1826 Tenn.; d June 20, 1910 Ada, Okla.) and had; (a) Mary Worthington b Aug 14, 1847 Trenton, Ga.; (b) Annie Worthington b July 2, 1849 Trenton, Ga., of Linn Creek, Mo. (m Joseph M. Farmer Dec. 21. 1871, near Bentonville, Ark. and had ch b near Linn Creek, Mo.; 1, James Farmer b Feb. 5, 1875; d Feb. 15, 1875; 2, Asa Farmer b Dec. 2, 1877, m Ethel Corns July 18, 1902 and had; (aa) son b and d Mar. 1910; 3, Thomas Farmer b Nov. 12, 1880, m Phlllis Lodge Dec. 25, 1907 and had; (aa) son b and d Sept. 1910; (bb) Edwin Farmer b Aug. 11, 1912; 4, Elza Farmer b Aug. 27, 1884, m Hazel Britton Feb. 14, 1905 and had; (aa) Margaret Farmer

b Nov. 12, 1910; 5, Herman Farmer b Aug. 21, 1887, m Floe Jackson
Oct. 14, 1909 and had; (aa) Ivan Farmer b July 18, 1910; 6, Ella
Farmer b Apr. 27, 1892; 7, Emil Farmer b June 3, 1895); (c) Elizabeth Worthington b July 18, 1851 Trenton, Ga.; d before 1910, m
John M. Conklin Feb. 1872 and had children; (d) Augusta Worthington b Jan. 20, 1854 Trenton, Ga.; d Jan 24, 1855 Trenton, Ga.; (e)
son, unnamed b Dec. 13, 1855 Trenton, Ga.; d Sept. 29, 1856 Pelham,
Tenn.; (f) Josephine Worthington b June 3, 1857 Pelham, Tenn., m
M. M. Grantham near Bentonville, Ark.; (g) Florence Worthington
b Apr. 2, 1859 Pelham, Tenn., once of Ada, Okla. (m J. Calvin Robertson, son of Joseph and Amy T. (Retherford) Robertson, June 5, 1887
near Bentonville, Ark. (b May 17, 1860 Mo.) and had; 1, Josephine
Robertson b Aug. 10, 1888 Oday, Mo.; d Nov. 5, 1910 Ada, Okla.,
unmarried; 2, Albinus Robertson b Nov. 10, 1889 Bentonville, Ark.;
3, John Robertson b Dec. 22, 1892 Bentonville, Ark.; d Apr. 26, 1893
Marsden, Okla.; 5, Mabel Robertson b Sept. 3, 1894 Marsden, Okla.
6, Bryan Robertson b Aug. 29, 1896 Marsden, Okla.; 7, Pearl Robertson b Aug. 24, 1900 Marietta, Okla.); (h) Emma Worthington b June
25, 1861 near Smithville, Tenn.; d Sept. 22, 1878; (i) daughter, unnamed, b and d July 17, 1863 near Paris, Tex.; (j) Samuel Worthington b Aug. 5, 1864 near Paris, Tex.; d Mar. 20, 1867 near Bentonville,
Ark.; (k) Asa Worthington b Nov. 4, 1866 near Bentonville, Ark.; d
1888 near Bentonville; (l) Thomas G. Worthington b Mar. 13, 1870
near Bentonville, Ark., m Musa Louis abt 1890 in Indian Territory
and moved to Calif.

Two. Sally Worthington b Oct. 15, 1826; d Aug. 16, 1904
Decatur, Tex.; married Dr. William Renshaw Dec. 23, 1847 in Tenn.
(b Mar. 9, 1822; d May 20, 1887 Tex. Children; (a) James Addison
Renshaw b Oct. 21, 1848, of Decatur, Tex. (m Lizzie Perrin Mar. 23,
1869 Denton Co., Tex. (b Dec. 19, 1851 Lincoln Co., Ky.) and had ch b
Decatur, Tex.; 1, Lute Renshaw b Feb. 16, 1870; d Nov. 27, 1890; 2,
Ella Renshaw b Feb. 2, 1872, of Decatur, Tex., m Shelby Hoyle 1893
Decatur, Tex. and had ch b Decatur; (aa) Archie Hoyle b Aug. 8,
1894, served in U. S. Navy from Mar. 1918 until June 1919, m Doris
Faith July 8, 1923 and had Elizabeth Hoyle b Apr. 15, 1924; (bb)
Cecil Hoyle b Jan. 2, 1897, m Bessie Van Meter July 1918 and had
Cecil Bryan Hoyle b June 1919 and Basil Hoyle b July 1921; (cc)
Ruth Hoyle b July 21, 1905; 3, ———— Renshaw b and d same day
1873; 4, Will Renshaw b Dec. 1, 1874, farmer, Decatur, Tex., m Anna
Mecasky Oct. 1903 and had ch b Decatur, Tex.; (aa) Mildred Renshaw
b Aug. 1904, of Dallas, Tex., m Aubery Ingram Oct. 1923; (bb)
Weldon Renshaw b Jan. 1906; (cc) James Addison Renshaw b Feb.
1913; (dd) Marco Renshaw b May 1915, 5, Gordon Renshaw b Jan.
30, 1877, grocer, Decatur, Tex., m Laura Sandusky Dec. 1906 Decatur,
Tex. and had; (aa) Dannah Marie Renshaw b July 1910; (bb) Theodore Gordon Renshaw b May 1912; (cc) John Renshaw b Feb. 1914;
6, Ethel Renshaw b Mar. 4, 1880, unmarried, of San Antonio, Tex.;

7, George Renshaw b 1881; d 1886; 8, Eugene Renshaw b 1884; d
1889; 9, Edgar Renshaw b July 1885, farmer, Decatur, Tex., m first,
Alice Arnett 1907 and had; (aa) Warren Renshaw b Nov. 1908; and
m second, Willie Mae Padgett Aug. 1918 and had; (bb) Fay Renshaw
b June 1919; (cc) Ruth Renshaw b Mar. 1921; 10, Sallie Renshaw b
1887, m Herbert Wilson 1909, mechanic, Denton, Tex. and had ch b
Decatur, Tex., save youngest; (aa) Eugene Wilson b Oct. 1910; (bb)
Ben Wilson b May 1912; (cc) Woodrow Wilson b Oct. 1914; (dd)
Bernice Wilson b Oct. 1916; (ee) John Joyce Wilson b May, 1918;
(ff) Doris Wilson b Nov. 1922 Denton, Tex.; 11, Hallie Renshaw b
July 1889, m Jesse Vandiver Apr. 1912 and had; (aa) Martha Elizabeth Vandiver b Mar. 19, 1915; 12, Charles Renshaw b Jan. 28, 1892;
d Nov. 28, 1914 Decatur, Tex.; 13, Gladys Renshaw b Jan 12, 1895,
of Los Angeles, Calif., m John Travers Hunsaker Mar. 21, 1921 Los
Angeles and had; (aa) John Renshaw Hunsaker b Oct. 31, 1923 Los
Angeles, Calif.); (b) Luther Renshaw b 1850, of Decatur, Tex.,
married —————— —————— and had children; (c) Eva Dorinda Renshaw b Feb. 16, 1854; d Apr. 23, 1923 Ft. Worth, Tex. (m John Washington Hogg, son of Joseph Lewis and Lucinda (McMath) Hogg; and
grandson of Thomas Hogg and Elisha McMath, Dec. 26, 1872 Decatur,
Tex. (b Mar. 20, 1848 Rusk, Tex.; d Nov. 3, 1912 Decatur, Tex. promi-
nent in civil and political affairs of his county) and had ch b Decatur,
Tex.; 1, Joseph Lewis Hogg, the second, b Feb. 5, 1875; d Dec. 12,
1875; 2, Eva Velma Hogg b Mar. 15, 1877, of Ft. Worth, Tex., m Dr.
Charles Briggs Simmons May 23, 1900 Decatur Tex. and had ch b
Decatur, Tex.; (aa) Maurine Simmons b Apr. 4, 1901, m Dr. Frank
Sackett Schoonover Feb. 9, 1922 Ft. Worth, Tex. and had Ann
Maurine Schoonover b Nov. 1923 Ft. Worth, Tex.; (bb) Mary Frances
Simmons b Nov. 24, 1906; 3, Julia Maud Hogg b Nov. 14, 1881, un-
married, of Decatur, Tex.; 4, Eugenia Josephine Hogg b Jan. 2, 1884,
of Decatur, Tex., m first, William Furman Greathouse May 2, 1906
Decatur, Tex. (deceased) and had; (aa) John Furman Greathouse b
July 14, 1907 Decatur, Tex.; (bb) William Hogg Greathouse b Mar.
11, 1910 Dallas, Tex.; (cc) Charles Simmons Greathouse b Sept. 26,
1913 Dallas, Tex. and m second, Jess Alfred Brown Oct. 23, 1917
Decatur, Tex. and had ch b Decatur, Tex.; (dd) Alf Brown b Dec. 15,
1918; (ee) Eva Elizabeth Brown b Dec. 28, 1923; 5, Willie Davis
Hogg (daughter) b Sept. 17, 1888; d June 12, 1889 Decatur, Tex.);
(d) Alice Renshaw b Jan. 10, 1856 (m first, Adam Gordon and had;
1, Emma Gordon, who d young; and m second John R. Ray and had;
2, Willie Prince Ray; 3, Jonnie May Ray); (e) Hattie Renshaw b Oct.
17, 1857 (m first, M. L. Gordon 1875 (d 1876) and had; 1, Ella
Gordon b 1875; d Dct. 16, 1899; and m second, R. H. Beall Aug. 5,
1878 and had ch b in Tex.; 2, Sarah Dorinda Beall b July 2, 1879, m
Rufus Starnes and had; (aa) Gill Starnes; 3, Mary Alice Beall b Dec.
5, 1881, m W. A. Bowen and had; (aa) Capas Bowen; (bb) Harold
Bowen; 4, Lillie Beall b Feb. 16, 1883, m C. C. Meek Apr. 1911 and

had; (aa) ———— Meek; 5, Lena Beall, twin with Lillie Beall, b
Feb. 16, 1883; d July 13, 1883; 6, William J. S. Beall b Apr. 10, 1886;
d July 24, 1912, m Ethel Cartwright Aug. 1906 and had three ch. who
d in inf.; 7, Dr. John Renshaw Beall b Aug. 28, 1888;, 8, Robert
Farrah Beall b May 1, 1891; 9, Ewin Beall b Apr. 19,, 1893; 10,
Charles Thompson Beall b Dec. 1, 1895; 11, Laurence James Beall b
June 25, 1898; 12, Agnes Embrey Beall b Mar. 3, 1904); (f) Charles
Franklin Renshaw b Jan. 7, 1860; d Nov. 3, 1888 (m Rhoda ————
and had; 1, Dell Renshaw, deceased; 2, Frank Renshaw. Rhoda ————
————Renshaw m second ———— Hawk and lives Chico, Tex.); (g)
Eugenia Bell Renshaw b Aug. 12, 1861; d Lakeport, Calif. (m James
Wright and had; 1, Minnie Wright; 2, Logan Wright; 3, Walter
Wright); (h) Sarah Josephine Renshaw b Mar. 7, 1863, of Boulder,
Colorado (m W. H. Bulloch Aug. 7, 1879 (b Nov. 11, 1850 Sherman,
Tex., attorney) and hal ch b Decatur, Tex.; child b Dec. 1, 1881; d
Dec. 4, 1881; 2, Bessie Bulloch b Jan. 11, 1883; d Oct. 25, 1883; 3,
Sallie Bulloch b Aug. 20, 1885; d Oct. 20, 1893; 4, John Randolph
Bulloch b Feb. 15, 1888, of McKinney, Tex., m Bernice Hadden Dec.
8, 1908 Sherman, Tex. and had; (aa) James Randolph Bulloch b
July 15, 1910; (bb) Robert Bulloch b 1912; (cc) Leslie Bulloch b Dec.
25, 1919; 5, William Bulloch b June 12, 1891, electrician U. S. Army,
Ft. Sam Houston, Texas; 6, Eugene Bulloch b Jan 28, 1895; 7, Irene
Bulloch b Jan. 7, 1899, m Clarence Gillbough Mar. 1, 1924 Omaha,
Neb.; 8. Margaret Bulloch b May 19, 1902, m Christopher Garbarina
Dec. 23, 1923, attorney, Boulder, Col. and had; (aa) Harold Louis
Garbarina b Oct. 8, 1924; 9, Lucile Bulloch, twin with Margaret
Bulloch, b May 18, 1902, unmarried); (i) William Samuel Worthing-
ton Renshaw b Oct. 29, 1864, of Bridgeport, Tex (m Lena Kenny Oct.
9, 1889 and had ten children); (j) Dr. John Renshaw b Mar. 3, 1867,
of Los Angeles, Calif m Anna Calhoun and had no children); (k)
Mary Emma Renshaw died in inf.

II. William Worthington, son of James and Lettice Tunnell
Worthington, was born Dec. 22, 1801 and died Apr. 15, 1875 Van
Buren Co , Tenn. He married his first cousin, Betsey Worthington,
dau of Samuel and Mary (Murfree) Worthington, granddau Samuel
and Elizabeth (Carney) Worthington, Dec. 21, 1828, Bledsoe Co.,
Tenn. (b abt 1802; d Sept. 3, 1891 Van Buren Co., Tenn.) and had ch
b Van Buren Co., Tenn.

One. Mary Worthington b Oct. 13, 1829.

Two. Lodemia Worthington b June 22, 1831.

Three. James Worthington b Nov. 5, 1833.

Four. Sarah Worthington b 1836.

Five. Samuel Worthington b Apr. 17, 1839.

Six. Margaret Robertson Worthington b 1841.

Seven. William Thomas Worthington b Sept. 10, 1844.

Eight. Lettice Angeline Worthington b Feb. 8, 1847.

Of these;

One. Mary Worthington (Polly), dau William and Betsey

(Worthington) Worthington, b Oct. 13, 1829; d abt 1890 Spencer, Tenn.; m first, William Parker, son of Arthur L. and Eleanor (Ballard) Parker, in Van Buren Co. (d V. B. Co.) and m second, William Moffitt in V. B. Co. and had no issue by either marriage.

Two. Lodemia Worthington, dau William and Betsey (Worthington) Worthington, b June 22, 1831; d Oct. 12, 1912 near Spencer, Tenn.; married Arthur Parker, a Baptist minister, son of Arthur L. and Eleanor (Ballard) Parker, 1849 Spencer, Tenn. (d Sept. 1, 1901 near Spencer, Tenn.) and had ch b near Spencer, Tenn.

(a) William Worthington Parker b Mar. 24, 1851.
(b) Mary Ellen Parker b Nov. 25, 1852.
(c) Samuel J. Parker b July 1, 1854.
(d) Elizabeth Catherine Parker b July 26, 1856.
(e) Arthur James Parker b 1858.
(f) Urcie Lodemia Parker b Oct. 21, 1862.
(g) Theodocia Parker b Dec. 12, 1865.
(h) Lenora Belle Parker b Nov. 27, 1873.
Of these;

(a) Dr. William Worthington Parker b Mar. 24, 1851, of Napier Tenn., m first, Violet Sparkman Apr. 28, 1869 Spencer, Tenn. (b May 10, 1851 near Spencer, Tenn.; d May 10, 1908 Smithville, Tenn., dau of Billie and Preshia (Nichols) Sparkman; g-d of Hardie Sparkman) and had; 1, Dr. William Byron Parker b Dec. 30, 1872 near Spencer, Tenn., who enlisted in Medical Corps 1918 and won the gold leaf of Major and is in the government service at Washington, D. C. He m Novella West Aug. 26, 1903 Smithville, Tenn. and had no ch.; 2, Dr. Arthur Otis Parker b July 16, 1883 Dibrell, Tenn., of North Alexandria, Tenn., m Florrie Bratten Jan. 9, 1907 Liberty, Tenn. (b Jan. 17, 1884 Liberty, Tenn.) and had ch b Smithville, Tenn.; (aa) Violet Bratten Parker b Aug. 11, 1908; (bb) Annie Will Parker b Nov. 22, 1911. Dr. William Worthington Parker m second, Georgia Hopps Dobbs Mar. 1915 Nashville, Tenn. (b Apr. 2, 1876 Jessup, Ga., dau Judge R. B. and Cora (Bryant) Hopps). Dr. W. W. Parker and sons conducted a Medical Journal for several years at Smithville, Tenn.

(b) Mary Ellen Parker b Nov. 25, 1852, of McMinville, Tenn., m first, George Johnson, son of Rowan and Jane (Hill) Johnson and had no children; and m second, George Washington Trogden Aug. 7, 1876 Warren Co., Tenn. (b Aug. 3, 1851; d June 12, 1879 Van Buren Co., Tenn., son of Abraham and Lucinda (Haston) Trogden; g-s David L. and Margaret Haston) and had one daughter; and m third, Solomon Sparkman Aug. 7, 1881 (b Apr. 14, 1844; d Dec. 3, 1920, son of Jackie Sparkman (b 1794 Van Buren Co.) and Vina McElroy Sparkman (b 1802; d 1888). Solomon Sparkman married first, Burke Gribble and had a daughter by that marriage, Ada Sparkman, who married Dr. A. James Parker, brother of Mary Ellen Parker). Children of Mary Ellen Parker Sparkman b Van Buren Co., Tenn.

Children; 1, Maggie Lee Trogden b Aug. 23, 1877, (m Ewin Fergus Chambers, son of James Allen and Artimisha (Tosk) Chambers, Dec. 22, 1892 (b Jan. 6, 1875 Van Buren Co., farmer McMinnville, Tenn.) and had ch b Van Buren Co., Tenn.; (aa) James Allen Chambers b Oct. 2, 1893, teacher, McMinnville, Tenn., served in World War, m Elizabeth Bell Sept. 10, 1922 and had Harry Gordon Chambers b Sept. 7, 1924; (bb) Eliza Edna Chambers b Feb. 14, 1896, m Frank B. Jones Sept. 8, 1912 Van Buren Co.; teacher, Fort Worth, Tex. and had Charles Frederick Rogers b June 14, 1913 and Bertha Pearl Rogers b May 25, 1924; (cc) Flora Ethel Chambers b Jan. 16, 1898, m Byron Loyd Caten Feb. 3, 1915 Van Buren Co., of Ft. Worth, Tex. and had Willowdean Caten b Jan. 23, 1916 and Maggie Veneta Caten b Mar. 18, 1921; (dd) Minnie Bell Chambers b Apr. 6, 1902, of McMinnville, Tenn., m John Bell Mar. 25, 1922; (ee) William Solomon Chambers b July 7, 1904, machinist, Muncie, Indiana; (ff) Reta Lodell Chambers, twin, b May 19, 1909; (gg) Leta Bell Chambers twin of Reta Lodell Chambers, b May 19, 1909; (hh) Mildred Josephine Chambers b June 28, 1912); 2, Lodemia Ursaline Sparkman b Aug. 23, 1882 (m Eliza Russell 1900, farmer, McMinnville, Tenn.) and had; (aa) Alberta Russell b 1905; (bb) Collie Russell b 1907; (cc) Otto Katell Russell b 1909); 3, Collie Fredward Sparkman b July 30, 1885, of Salt Lake City, Utah (m Rosemary Carnavon, dau of Robert and Cecelia (McIntire) Carnarvon, Dec. 31, 1914 N. Y. (b Apr. 27, 1895 Edinburg, Scotland) and had ch b Bryan, Tex.; (aa) Wilford Cecil Sparkman b Oct. 26, 1915; (bb) Lorna Doone Sparkman b Sept. 16, 1917. Dr. Sparkman took his B. Pd degree 1908 Valpariaso; M. A. 1911 Clark Univ., Mass.; PhD 1914 N. Y. Univ.; studied summer of 1913 Jena University, Germany. He was Supt. Del Rio, Tex. Schools 1908-10; teacher of Spanish DeWitt Clinton H. S. in N. Y. 1914-15; Asst. Prof. Romance Language A & M College, Tex. 1915-17; Inst. Romance Language Indiana U. 1917-18; Asst. Prof. Spanish at Purdue U. 1918-20; member of American Commission of Education to Peru Jan. 1920 to Jan. 1922; Asst. Prof. French Mississippi Univ. Feb. 1922 to June 1922; Asst. Prof. Romance Languages Univ. of Utah since Sept. 1923. He is the author of "Industral Spanish" and "Primer Curso de Ingles" Mrs. Sparkman and children died during the family's residence in Salt Lake) 4, Minnie Ethel Sparkman b Apr. 18, 1888, of Quebeck, Tenn., (m a relative, James Maybry, Mar. 7, 1904 (b Mar. 18, 1878, son of William Thomas Worthington and Catherine (Martin) Maybry; g-s Thomas and Catherine (Worthington) Maybry. See record of Catherine Worthington for children); 5, Emma Lector Sparkman b July 17, 1891, of McMinnville, Tenn. (m Dr. Titus Floyd Page Dec. 25, 1907 and had ch b McMinnville; (aa) Lois Maxin Page b July 22, 1909; (bb) Jonnie Bell Page b Aug. 24, 1912; (cc) Mary Joe Page b Aug. 12, 1914; (dd) Ruby Evelyn Page b May 12, 1916; (ee) Thomas Floyd Page b Apr. 20, 1918 (ff) Harold Page b July 19, 1922); 6,

Edward Clifton Sparkman b Jan. 28, 1895, farmer, Van Buren Co., Tenn. (m Ethel Miller 1915 Van Buren Co., and had four children).

(c) Samuel J. Parker b July 1, 1854; d Sept. 28, 1879 near Spencer, Tenn.; unmarried.

(d) Elizabeth Catherine Parker b July 26, 1856; d Oct. 16, 1907; married Isham Haston Jr. Nov. 25, 1877 Van Buren Co., Tenn. (b Dec. 16, 1852, of Spencer, Tenn., son of Isaac Haston (b Mar. 29, 1827) and Elizabeth (Sparkman) Haston (b Sept. 28, 1827); grandson George W. and Berthena (Goddard) Sparkman; of David and Margaret (Roddy) Haston) and had; 1, Horace Haston b Mar. 9, 1879; d May 18, 1915 Quebeck, Tenn., m a distant relative, Willie Sparkman, dau of Reed and Randa (Holder) Sparkman; g-d of Hardie and Mary (Coffey) Sparkman, Feb. 24, 1901 Quebeck, Tenn. and had ch b Quebeck, Tenn.; (aa) Harold Haston b Dec. 15, 1902, m Margaret Smith of Nashville, Tenn.; (bb) Harry Haston b Aug. 5, 1905; (cc) Clara Bell Haston b Sept. 25, 1908; (dd) Willie Reed Haston b Oct. 7, 1911. Willie Sparkman Haston m second, William Kiser and lives Nashville, Tenn.; 2, Della Haston b Nov. 6, 1881, of Sparta, Tenn., m Charlie Druett Dec. 8, 1905 and had; (aa) Arabell Druett b Mar. 14, 1907; (bb) Catherine Druett b Dec. 14, 1908; 3, Arie Belle Haston b Jan. 19, 1884, of Winston-Salem, N. C., m I. A. Austin June 24, 1908 and had; (aa) I. A. Austin Jr.; (bb) Elizabeth Austin; (cc) Margaret Austin; 4, Arthur Haston b June 29, 1886 White Co., Tenn., unmarried, of Sparta, Tenn.; 5, Isham Haston, the third, b Oct. 20, 1888 White Co., Tenn., unmarried, of Sparta, Tenn.; 6, Bettie Haston b Oct. 6, 1892, of Spencer, Tenn., m John Lewis and had; (aa) Janette Lewis; (bb) Lillian Lewis; (cc) Sterling Lewis; 7, Roy Haston b June 21, 1899 White Co., Tenn., of Jacksonville, Florida m Sarah Yent June 28, 1922 and had; (aa) Nancy Haston b in Florida. Isham Haston Jr. b Dec. 16, 1852, m second, Emma (Steakley) McElroy Nov. 7, 1909 Sparta, Tenn.

(e) Dr. Arthur James Parker b 1858; d 1914 Hollis, Okla.; married Ada Sparkman, dau of Solomon and Burke (Gribble) Sparkman; g-d of Jackie and Vina (McElroy) Sparkman, and had; 1, and 2, twins, b and d same day, in Spencer, Tenn.; 3, Flora Parker b abt 1893 Spencer, Tenn. d June 13, 1909 Bruceville, Tex. Ada (Sparkman) Parker m second, Mal Reeves.

(f) Ursie Lodemia Parker b Oct. 21, 1862; d Sept. 7, 1884 near Spencer, Tenn.; unmarried.

(g) Theodocia Parker b Dec. 12, 1865; d Aug. 14, 1904 near Spencer, Tenn.; married Sam Johnson Sept. 25, 1890 near Spencer, Tenn. (b Apr. 10, 1867 near Spencer, Tenn., son of Dr. F. M. and Winnie (Sparkman) Johnson; grandson Billie and Preshia (Nichols) Sparkman. Winnie Sparkman a sister of Violet Sparkman who m Dr. W. W. Parker, brother of Theodocia Parker. Dr. F. M. Johnson, son of Squire and Lavinia (Hill) Johnson. Squire Johnson, brother of Rowan Johnson, whose son, George Johnson, m Mary Ellen Parker, sister of Theodocia Parker. Lavinia Hill was a sister of Jane Hill, who married Rowan Johnson. Sam Johnson, married, second, Lela Whatley July 12, 1908 Mt. Calm, Tex. and lives Dallas, Tex. Ch. of Sam and Theodocia Parker Johnson; 1, Vesta Johnson b Sept. 27, 1891 near McMinnville, Tenn., of Bone Cave, Tenn. who furnished data on Sparkman-Worthington families, m Bill Rogers Sept. 23, 1916 McMinnville, Tenn. and had; (aa) Ernesteen Rogers b Dec. 22, 1917 McMinnville, Tenn.; (bb) Sammie Rogers b Dec. 1, 1919 near Bone Cave, Tenn.; (cc) Janett Rogers b Jan. 29, 1921; 2, Lenora Johnson b May 8, 1893 near Alledo, Tex., of Sparta, Tenn., m Brown Passons July 16, 1919 Dallas, Tex. and had; (aa) Brownie Passons b Aug. 9, 1920 near Sparta, Tenn.; (bb) Christine Passons b Sept. 26, 1921 near Sparta; (cc) Douglas Passons b Aug. 28, 1924 Bone Cave, Tenn.; 3, Kenneth Johnson b Feb. 3, 1895 near Spencer, Tenn., of Dallas, Tex., served in World War; 4, Herman Johnson b Jan. 17, 1897, near Spencer, Tenn., farmer, Dallas, Tex., m Sadie Lyons 1918 Seymour, Tex. and had; (aa) James Dallas Johnson b July 8, 1920 Dallas, Tex.; 5, Sylvester Johnson b Dec. 23, 1898 near Spencer, Tenn.; 6, Dema Johnson b Apr. 10, 1902 near Spencer; d Sept. 24, 1908 near Spencer; 7, son b and d May 1904 near Spencer, Tenn.

(h) Lenora Belle Parker b Nov. 27, 1873, of Chattanooga, Tenn. married Edmond Clark Angel Oct. 7, 1914 Spencer, Tenn. (b Sept. 10, 1873, jeweler, son of John Wesley Angell (b Sept. 20, 1844 St. Joe, Mo.; d July 20, 1914 Spring City, Tenn.) and Mary Barnard Angell (b Sept. 21, 1841; d May 22, 1916) and had no children.

Three. James Worthington, son of William and Betsy (Worthington) Worthington, b Nov. 5, 1833, lived near Spencer, Tenn., and d Mar. 16, 1908. He served in both houses of the General Assembly of Tenn. He m Emma Clenny abt 1884 (b Sept. 1844; d Jan. 12, 1901) and had an only child; (a) Dr. William Clinton Worthington b Sept. 1, 1885, with Veterans Bureau, Indianapolis, served overseas in World War, m Stella Lewis, of Spencer, Tenn. and had; 1, Gordon Worthington b 1908; 2, Louis Worthington b 1917.

Four. Sarah Worthington, dau of William and Betsey (Worthington) Worthington, b 1837; d Mar. 24, 1915 Knoxville, Tenn.; married first, William Templeton in Van Buren Co., Tenn. and had; (a) Willie Templeton who died shortly after her marriage to Hiram Dodd. Sarah Worthington married second, Solomon Sparkman, son of Bryant and ———— (Holland) Sparkman, in Van Buren Co., Tenn. and had ch b in that county (b) Mary Sparkman, of Quebeck, Tenn. (m first, Richard Moore, and had ch. b Van Buren Co., Tenn.; 1, Alba Moore b Nov. 15, 1877, of Carrollton, Tex., m James Seamans (b Apr. 3, 1875) and had ch. b Van Buren Co., Tenn. save youngest; (aa) Louisa Seamans b Jan. 15, 1898, of Carrollton, Tex., m Vernie Brake at Farmer's Branch, Tex. and had; James Eldon Brake b May 11, 1914 and Clovia Lavern Brake b Oct. 5, 1924; (bb) Recie Seamans b Oct. 6, 1900, m Carl Pearson at Coppell, Tex. and had; Reba Joy

Pearson b July 9, 1923; (cc) Tessie Seamans b Apr. 25, 1905; (dd) Ray E. Seamans b Sept. 20, 1907; (ee) J. P. Seamans b Nov. 27, 1911; 2, Patrick Moore b 1881; d Oct. 12, 1918 Jacksonville, Tex., m ——————— ——————— and had; (aa) Patsy C. Moore b Jan. 1919 Jacksonville, Tex.; 3, Octa Moore, of Chicago, Ill., m Jacob Beasley 1905 and had (aa) Geneva Beasley b 1907; (bb) Bud Beasley b 1910; 4, Enzie Moore died May 29, 1924 Chicago, Ill., m William Schofield and had no children.   Mary Sparkman Moore married second, Thomas Ward and had; 5, Titus Ward; 6, John Ward); (c) Sam Sparkman b abt 1847; d 1919 Mansfield, Tex. (m Lydia Johnson and had; 1, Arthur Sparkman of U. S. Army; 2, Clarence Sparkman b Feb. 25, 1890 Cleburne, Tex.; 3, Hubert Sparkman b July 8, 1892 Carrollton, Tex.; 4, Nora Sparkman b June 3, 1894; 5, Minnie Sparkman b 1896; 6, William Sparkman b 1897; 7, Ted Sparkman b Aug. 1900); (d) Tom Sparkman died, unmarried, Gatesville, Tex.; (e) Martha Sparkman (Dossie) deceased (m a relative, Dent Sparkman, son of Reed Sparkman by his first marriage, to Phoebe Denton; g-s Isaac Denton and Jackie Sparkman (1794-1882) by his first wife, ——————— (Nicely) Sparkman and had; 1, Will Sparkman; 2, John Sparkman; 3, Floyd Sparkman; 4, Sarah Sparkman; 5, Emma Sparkman, m Demps Van).

Five.   Samuel Worthington, son of William and Betsey (Worthington) Worthington, b Apr. 17, 1839, of Creek, Tenn.; served four years to a day in the War Between the States; married Sarah Jane Neal, dau. of William and Elizabeth Neal, Aug. 17, 1865 Van Buren Co., Tenn. (b Jan. 15, 1846) and their married life of sixty years has been spent in Van Buren Co., Tenn.   Children; (a) William Joseph Worthington b Sept. 21, 1866, farmer, (m first, Jennie (Stewart) Tibbs June 30, 1895 White Co., Tenn.; d Jan. 8, 1897 Van Buren Co.; and m second, Nannie Baldwin May 13, 1900 Van Buren Co. and had ch b Van Buren Co.; 1, Pearl May Worthington b July 24, 1905; 2, Willie Worthington b May 30, 1910; 3, Emma Lucille Worthington b Feb. 5, 1913; 4, Isham Burnett Worthington b Aug. 13, 1916; 5, Ruth Anna Lee Worthington b Mar. 14, 1924); (b) Mary Elizabeth Worthington b Aug. 30, 1869 (deceased) (m George Henry Kell Apr. 4, 1889 and had ch b Van Buren Co.; 1, Charles Kell b Mar. 28, 1890, m Myrtle Green in Warren Co., Tenn. and had one child; 2, Oscar Kell b Aug. 26, 1891, m Edna Rogers in Van Buren Co., and had four ch b Van Buren Co.; 3, Chester Kell b Mar. 27, 1893, m Lula Rogers in Van Buren Co. and had one child; 4, George Kell b June 7, 1895, m Jerusha Hillis in Van Buren Co. and had one child; 5, Emmett Kell b Dec. 13, 1897, m Ova Simmons in Warren Co. and had two ch. 6, Victor Kell b Jan. 11, 1903; d Aug. 19, 1904; 7, Neal Kell b June 7, 1907); (c) Emma Worthington b Oct. 3, 1871; d Feb. 24, 1921 Van Buren Co. (m James Monroe Walling Dec. 10, 1893 Ban Buren Co., Tenn. and had ch b in that county; 1, Eston Vertrees Walling b Sept. 11, 1895; 2, Elmer Neal Walling b Jan. 13, 1900, m Mary Belle Stubblefield; 3, Roy Fleming Walling b Sept. 6, 1904); (d) Lola Bell

Worthington b Oct. 12, 1873, of Spencer, Tenn. (m Richard Russell Apr. 15, 1900 and had; 1, Mary Louise Russell b Mar. 16, 1903, m Walter Masmahan Aug. 17, 1924 Van Buren Co.; 2, Richard Neal Russell b Apr. 25, 1907; d May 30, 1907; 3, Ella B. Russell b May 14, 1908; 4, Emma Lucile Russell b Feb. 22, 1912); (e) Dema Worthington b Apr. 7, 1876 (m W. F. Johnson Jan. 21, 1900 Van Buren Co., Tenn. and had; 1, Janie Gladys Johnson b June 14, 1902 Van Buren Co., m Lester McCoy May 26, 1923 and had a child b Van Buren Co.); (f) Samuel Worthington, Jr. b Mar. 3, 1878, unmarried, farmer, Creek, Tenn.; (g) Sarah Angeline Worthington b Dec. 4, 1880; d July 15, 1885; (h) John Worthington b Feb. 15, 1883, farmer, Creek, Tenn., m Ella Bouldin Oct. 2, 1910 Van Buren Co., Tenn.; (i) Maggie Worthington b Feb. 15, 1888 (m Pearl Shokley Dec. 24, 1908, farmer Van Buren Co., Tenn., and had ch b Van Buren Co.; 1, Lewis Edwin Shockley b May 22, 1910; 2, Janie Lee Shockley b Feb. 6, 1913; 3, Loyd Buren Shockley b Sept. 30, 1915).

Six. Margaret Robertson Worthington, dau of William and Betsey (Worthington) Worthington, b June 5, 1841; d Oct. 20, 1897 near Spencer, Tenn.; married first, James K. Hillis Nov. 6, 1856 Van Buren Co., Tenn. (b Apr. 25, 1835; d Apr. 25, 1877) and had nine children; and married second, A. Jesse Evans, son of James and Mary Evans, Feb. 28, 1879 near Spencer, Tenn. (b Aug. 24, 1851; d Sept. 12, 1910) and had two children; all ch. b Van Buren Co., Tenn.; (a) Elizabeth Hillis b Nov. 28, 1859, of Dallas, Tex. (m Jonah Dodson and had ch b Laurelburg, Tenn., save youngest, all of Dallas, Tex.; 1, James R. Dodson b Sept. 6, 1880, unmarried; 2, William Samuel Dodson b Dec. 2, 1882, m Enlen Vogel Dec. 26, 1916 and had; (aa) Glenn Dodson; (bb) Cecil Dodson; 3, Ella Dodson b Sept. 14, 1885, m first, James Hunt, 1904; and second, J. M. Rich 1914; 4, George Roy Dodson b May 18, 1890, m Iva Lee Zachary Jan. 7, 1913 (b Aug. 10, 1895) and had; (aa) John Bert Dodson b May 27, 1915; 5, Jonah Worthington Dodson b Aug. 10, 1893, unmarried; 6, Byron Smith Dodson b May 19, 1896, served as Sergeant overseas in World War, m Lela Farless Aug. 21, 1921 (b Mar. 3, 1906) and had; (aa) Evelyn Norma Dodson b Apr. 23, 1922; 7, Edward Felix Grundy Dodson b Jan. 1, 1899, unmarried; 8, Fannie Laura Belle Dodson b June 3, 1905 Addison, Tex., m Andrew B. Martin Dec. 22, 1922); (b) James Worthington Hillis b Oct. 17, 1861, of Morrison, Tenn. (m first, Mollie Hambrick; and m second, Tina Martin and had ch by both marriages); (c) Mary Hillis b Jan. 10, 1864; d in inf.; (d) William Hillis b Mar. 16, 1866, of Farmer's Branch, Tex. (m first Dora Hambrick and had no issue; and m second, Ada Farless and had no issue; and m third, Jennie Templeton and had; 1, William Kenneth Hillis, deceased, who served in World War; 2, Dora Hillis, of Detroit, Mich., m Carl Evans and had; (aa) William Evans; (bb) Carl Evans, Jr.; (cc) Charles Evans; 3, James Farless Hillis, m Laura E. Graham, and perhaps an other); (e) Margaret Lodemia Hillis b May 20, 1868 (m William or

Erwin Lisenbee and had; 1, daughter m Frank Davis; 2, Alice Lisenbee, of Moody, Okla., m ————— Hines; 3, daughter who m —————
—————; 4, daughter who m ———— ————; 5, Madge Lisenbee;
6, Bob Lisenbee; 7, Dutch Lisenbee; 8, Macon Lisenbee); (f) Emma
Hillis b Aug. 8, 1870, of McMinnville, Tenn. (m Arthur P. Evans Jan.
10, 1889 and had; 1, James Murphy Evans b Dec. 24, 1889, m Ada
Graves; 2, Joseph Leslie Evans b May 18, 1892, m Helen Brady and
had; (aa) Lois Evans b Nov. 1, 1917; (bb) Dorothy Joe Evans b Oct.
10, 1919; (cc) Darrell Evans b Jan. 14, 1921; 3, Thomas Harold Evans
b Jan. 22, 1895, m Nannie McGee 1916 (d 1918) and had; (aa)
Arnold Evans b Aug. 7, 1917; 4, George Avery Evans b Mar. 2, 1897,
m Gertie McGregor Jan. 13, 1918 and had; (aa) Eva Evans b Oct. 10,
1918; (bb) Carmon Evans b June 8, 1921; (cc) Myrtle Evans b Dec.
24, 1923; 5, Clyde Etter Evans b June 28, 1899, m Mytrle Farless;
6, Avis Velma Evans b Apr. 2, 1901, m A. B. Crouse Dec. 10, 1922; 7,
Artie Evans b June 13, 1905, m Bus Bloomberg Oct. 9, 1924; 8, Emmett
Hills Evans b July 12, 1908; 9, William Vogle Evans b Jan. 15,
1910); (g) Laura Hillis b July 4, 1873, of McMinnville, Tenn. (m
Richmond Curtis and had; 1, Luther Hillis Curtis b Oct. 13, 1899,
unmarried assistant cashier First National Bank, McMinnville, Tenn.;
2,Emmet Lee Curtis, b Nov. 11, 1903, m William V. Farless Mar. 20,
1923; 4, Elizabeth Curtis b Dec. 13, 1906; 5, Margaret Virginia Curtis
b Feb. 20, 1916); (h) Eva Hillis b Oct. 14, 1875; d 1912 Proctor, Okla.
(m William Hambrick and had; 1, Ira Hambrick; 2, Vestal Hambrick;
3, Heston Hambrick; 4, Avis Hambrick, all of Waureka, Okla.); (i)
Mary Hillis b Jan. 20, 1864; d June 1864; (j) Sallie Evans b Jan. 1,
1880, of Newmarket, Ala. (m Elzie Luther Davis July 9, 1899 (b
May 8, 1876) and had ch. six of whom were born near Laurelburg,
Tenn.; 1, Sophia Davis b Aug. 5, 1900, m Marion Lee Hillis Jan. 31,
1920 and had; (aa) David Elzie Robert Hillis b July 15, 1921; (bb)
Maggie Lee Elna Hillis b Dec. 18, 1922; (cc) Arthur Leo Thomas
Hillis b Aug. 16, 1924; 2, Effie Davis b Sept. 21, 1902; 3, Willie E.
Davis b Nov. 19, 1904; 4, Arthur T. Davis b June 30, 1908; 5, Jessie
Davis b June 17, 1910; 6, Margaret E. Davis b Aug. 8, 1916; 7, Emma
L. Davis b Apr. 19, 1919; 8, Luther M. Davis b May 22, 1924 at New-
market, Ala.); (k) Belle Evans b Feb. 25, 1886, of Addison, Tex. (m
A. Rector Atkins Aug. 3, 1905 Addison, Tex. and had ch b Addison;
1, Annie Atkins b Aug. 30, 1906; 2, Hazel Atkins b Mar. 27, 1911; 3,
Margaret Atkins b Dec. 8, 1913; 4, Dorothy Fay Atkins b June 2,
1919).

    Seven. William Thomas Worthington, son of William and Betsey
(Worthington) Worthington, b Sept. 10, 1844; d May 30, 1922 Gatesville, Tex.; married Elizabeth Neal, sister of Sarah Jane Neal, July
3, 1867 Spencer, Tenn. and had ch b near Gatesville, Tex.; (a) James
Murphy Worthington b Apr. 12 1868 (m Annie Cummings (d May 5,
1922) and had; 1, Rosa Elizabeth Worthington b June 7, 1895; d Sept.
2, 1895; 2, Charles Herman Worthington b Dec. 27, 1896, served in
World War; 3, Jennings Bryan Worthington b June 19, 1900; d Oct.

2, 1900; 4, Samuel Murphy Worthington b Nov. 2, 1905); (b) Josephine Worthington b Oct. 9, 1869; d Sept. 19, 1888; (c) Francis Marion Worthington b Nov. 2, 1871, farmer, Gatesville, Tex. (m Lelia Bell Bashan Aug. 15, 1895 and had; 1, Alla Ibera Worthington b June 5, 1897, m Ed Anderson; 2, James Byron Worthington b Oct. 24, 1898, rancher, Clovis, New Mexico; 3, son b Oct. 10, 1900; d Nov. 4, 1900; 4, Marion Dennis Worthington b Sept. 30, 1901, served with Army of Occupation in Germany; 5, Leora Worthington b Apr. 14, 1908; 6, Winifred L. Worthington b Sept. 3, 1910); (d) Angeline Worthington b Oct. 9, 1873; d Oct. 3, 1900; (e) William Thomas Worthington, Jr. b Oct. 2, 1875, farmer, Gatesville, Tex. (m first, Minnie Dodson Dec. 24, 1903 (d Mar. 24, 1919) and had ch b Gatesville, Tex.; 1, Raymond Worthington b Jan. 10, 1905; 2, Clyde Paxton Worthington b Sept. 23, 1910; 3, Naomi Belle Worthington b Sept. 2, 1916; and m second, Alice Truss May 16, 1920 (b Mar. 5, 1887 Paige, Tex.) and had; 4, Rozell May Worthington b Nov. 16, 1921); (f) Isabel Worthington b Oct. 10, 1877, of Evant, Tex. (m William A. Shaw Aug. 1912 and had; 1, Nettie Shaw b Dec. 2, 1913; 2, Mary Shaw b Aug. 6, 1917; 3, Olive Belle Shaw b Jan. 1918); (g) Joseph Samuel Worthington b Oct. 17, 1870; d July 4, 1923 (m Ida Barrett at Evant, Tex. and had; 1, Neal Worthington; 2, Lyman Worthington; 3, Floyd Worthington); (h) Kate Worthington b Sept. 16, 1881; d Mar. 3, 1916 Gatesville, Tex. (m William White Nov. 25, 1906 Mound, Tex. and had ch b Mound, Tex.; 1, Walden White b Dec. 29, 1907; 2, Katie Lea White b Mar. 3, 1910); (i) Robert Lea Worthington b Nov. 10, 1885, of Houston, Tex. (m Nettie Beck and had; 1, Carl Worthington b Jan. 1913; 2, Orville Worthington; 3, Opal Worthington).

Eight. Lettice Angeline Worthington, dau of William and Betsey (Worthington) Worthington, b Feb. 8, 1847; d Mar. 22, 1866; unmarried.

III. Mary Worthington, daughter of James and Lettice Tunnell Worthington was birn Feb. 20, 1804 and died Sept. 9, 1880 in Warren Co., Tenn.; married James English Rawlings, son of Michael and Agnes (English) Rawlings 1821 in Tenn. (b Feb. 7, 1801; d a few days before his wife, Sept. 1, 1880 Warren Co., Tenn.) and had ch b Warren Co., Tenn.

One.   Eliza Rawlings b Dec. 20, 1822.
Two.   Asiel Rawlings b Dec. 24, 1824.
Three.   daughter b 1826; d in inf.
Four.   William Worthington Rawlings b Jan. 13, 1828.
Five.   Catherine Rawlings b Oct. 16, 1830.
Six..   Mary Lettice Rawlings b Aug. 14, 1835.
Seven.   James Rawlings b July 2, 1838.
Eight.   Margaret Rawlings b Oct. 5, 1842.
Nine.   Thomas Rawlings b Feb. 13, 1845.
Ten.   Nathan Rawlings b Dec. 18, 1847.
Eleven.   Samuel Andrew Rawlings b June 14, 1849.

Of these;

One. Eliza Rawlings b Dec. 20, 1822; d Oct. 2, 1903 Gonzales, Tex.; married William Rhodes in Warren Co., Tenn. (b Nov. 13, 1807 N. C.; d Nov. 19, 1879 DeWitt Co., Tex.) and had ch b Warren Co., Tenn. They moved to Texas 1874; (a) Arminda Rhodes b abt 1856; d Gonzales, Tex, (m Warren Gordon 1877 DeWitt Co., Tex. and had; 1, Isaac Gordon, m ———— ———— and had ch.; 2, Warren Gordon Jr., m ———— ———— and had ch.); (b) Mary Rhodes b abt 1858; d abt 1893 Guadalupe Co., Tex. (m Alfred Lawlm, a veteran of C. S. A., Apr 1. 1875 DeWitt Co., Tex. (d at Austin, Tex.) and had; 1, William Lawlm, deceased; 2, James Charles Lawlm b May 15, 1879 De Witt Co., Tex., m first, Hilda Dockery 1912 Wrightsboro, Tex. and had; (aa) James Charles Lawlm the second, b Mar. 15, 1915; and m second, Jody Mangum and had; (bb) Nancy Josephine Lawlm b Feb. 21, 1920, Humble, Tex.; (cc) Lola Frances Lawlm b Oct. 28, 1921 Humble, Tex.; 3, Mary Elizabeth Lawlm b Nov. 27, 1881 Brady, Tex. of Leesville, Tex., m J. A. Dawe Dec. 18, 1901 Gonzales, Tex. and had; (aa) Ruth Elizabeth Dawe b Oct. 26, 1902, m L. O. Lott Oct. 30, 1924 Leesville, Tex.; (bb) James Arthur Dawe b Feb. 1, 1907 Wrightsboro, Tex.; (cc) Dorothy Dawe b Apr. 15, 1909 Wrightsboro, Tex; 4, Lola Bell Lawlm b July 23, 1885 Kerrville, Tex., m John Parr Nov. 6, 1901 Gonzales, Tex. and had; (aa) Thelma Parr b Dec. 20, 1905; (bb) Irma Parr b May 1, 1908; (cc) Beulah Parr b Oct. 8, 1910; (dd) Luella Parr b May 2, 1914; (ee) Hazel Parr b Sept. 17, 1917; (ff) Stella Parr b Jan. 5, 1920; (gg) Ruby Parr b Apr. 20, 1922; 5, Lillie Josephine Lawlm b Dec. 30, 1887 Guadalupe Co., Tex., of Gonzales, Tex., m Joe B. Dunning May 6, 1908 Gonzales, Tex., petroleum engineer, and had an only child; (aa) Sarah Murphy Dunning b Feb. 23, 1909 Gonzales, Tex.; 6, Robert Lee Lawlm b Oct. 1, 1889, m Claudie Elizabeth Turner 1912 and had; (aa) Janie Marie Lawlm b Nov. 25, 1923); (c) Eugenia Rhodes b abt 1860; d at Brady, (cc) Robert Wallice Lawlm b Oct. 3, 1919; (dd) William Alfred Lawlm b Nov. 25, 1923); (c) Eugenia Rhodes b abt 1860; d at Brady Tex. (m W. O. Placker 1880 Gonzales, Tex. and had four ch; (d) James Rhodes b 1861; d 1883 Kerrville, Tex.; (e) Margaret Rhodes b abt 1863; d Ft. McCarrett, Tex. (m L. H. Placker, brother of W. O. Placker, 1879 De Witt Co., Tex.; (f) Thomas Rhodes b 1866, farmer, Gonzales, Tex. (m Willie (Floyd) Evans and had ch b near Gonzales, Tex.; 1, William Claude Rhodes b Feb. 8, 1898, m Mamie Hyatt Oct. 24, 1923; 2, Uba Clyde Rhodes b Feb. 24. 1899, m Delia Deberry July 14, 1923; 3, Sallie Rhodes b Apr. 28, 1901, m A. E. Shelton Aug. 12, 1923; 4, Homer Rhodes b Dec. 4, 1904; d Aug. 20, 1920 Gonzales, Tex.; 5, Demonsthenses Rhodes b Nov. 25, 1906; 6, Eula Rhodes b July 29, 1909).

Two. Asiel Rawlings b Dec. 24, 1824; d abt June 1826 Warren Co., Tenn.

Three. Daughter, unnamed, b 1826; d in inf., Warren Co., Tenn.

Four. William Worthington Rawlings b Jan. 13,1828; d June 14, 1920 Corvallis, Ore.; married Anna Rettie Thomas Jan. 25, 1857 Warren Co.. Tenn. (b, Dec. 14, 1835; d Oct. 3, 1909 Medford, Ore.). They moved to Ark. 1884 and to Everett, Wash. 1900 and to Oregon in 1903. Ch. b Warren Co., Tenn.; (a) William Thomas Rawlings b Nov. 1, 1865, engineer of Pine Bluff, Ark. (m first. Isadora Spark- man, dau of Elvin Sparkman, Sept. 21, 1884 Warren Co., Tenn. (b Mar. 4, 1865; d Nov. 24, 1887 Madison Co., Ark.) and had; 1. Benjamin Franklin Rawlings b May 10, 1886 Carroll Co., Ark., machinist, of Pine Bluff, Ark., m Sarah Richards Jan. 7, 1912 Ashley Co., Ark. and had; (aa) Dorothy Rawlings b Mar. 27, 1914 Pine Bluff, Ark. W. T. Rawlings m second, Sarah Jessie Barlow June 10, 1894, Wilmot, Ark. (b Jan. 19, 1875 Ashley Co., Ark., dau George and Margaret Barlow) and had ch b Ashley Co.; 2, Mervin Rawlings (daughter) b Aug. 20, 1895; d July 24, 1904; 3, George Worthington Rawlings b July 26, 1897; 4, James Tilden Rawlings b Dec. 14, 1901; 5, Lois Rawlings b June 28, 1904); (b) James Lewis Rawlings b July 18, 1867, of Chicago, Ill. in 1901; (c) Martha Catherine Rawlings b Jan 12, 1873, of Lindon, Colorado (m William Fritts, son of Charles and Mary Fritts, Sept. 18, 1887 Drake's Creek, Ark. (b 1865 Ark.) and had ch b Drake's Creek, Ark.; 1, Isa Ann Fritts b Jan. 4. 1890; d Nov. 29, 1918 Thorney, Ark., m John Dunaway Sept. 15. 1907 Drake's Creek and had ch. save youngest, b Drake's Creek; (aa) William Clyde Dunaway b Sept. 16, 1908; (bb) son b and d 1911; (cc) Gertie Opal Dunaway b Feb. 26, 1913; (dd) Gladys Genevieve Dunaway b Oct. 1914; (ee) Betah Mildred Dunaway b Mar. 15, 1916; (ff) Daughter b Feb. 1918; d Mar. 1918 Thorney, Ark.; 2, Asa Calvin Fritts b 1892, of Lindon, Col., m Sarah Elizabeth Sims Nov. 25, 1917 Fayetteville, Ark. and had; (aa) Jasper Lee Fritts b Dec. 3, 1918 Wesley, Ark; (bb) Ella Marie Fritts b Oct. 16, 1921 Lindon, Col.; (cc) Myrtle Elizabeth Fritts b Oct. 12, 1924 Lindon, Col.; 3, Ernest Earl Fritts b Mar. 27, 1896, served in Army from June 15, 1917 to June 15, 1919; in marine corps from Mar. 12, 1920 for a year; re-enlisted Aug. 1922; stationed in California); (d) Samuel Tilden Rawlings b Nov. 18, 1876, with lumber company, Corvallis, Ore. (m Dora Elizabeth Hankins, Mar. 23, 1896 Thompson, Ark. (b Nov. 24, 1875) and had; 1, Ella Bertha Rawlings b Feb. 24, 1897 Thompson, Ark., unmarried, with Y. W. C. A. San Francisco, Calif.; 2, Everett Bryan Rawlings b Jan. 22, 1899 Tecumseh, Okla., carpenter, of Medford, Ore., m Vernie Yantes Sept. 1922 Albany, Ore. (b 1901 in Kan.) and had; (aa) Margaret Ilene Rawlings b July 18, 1923 Venonio, Ore.; 3, Oliver Clark Rawlings b Sept. 16, 1900 Drake's Creek, Ark., in clerical work, Roseburg, Ore., m Alice Poor Sept. 26, 1923 Ashland, Ore.; 4, Clarence Ray Rawlings b Oct. 24, 1902 Everett, Wash., of Corvallis, Ore., m Vivian Gould June 6, 1923 Corvallis, Ore. (b 1901) and had; (aa) Carolyn J. Rawlings b 1924; 5, Samuel Lloyd Rawlings b Aug. 13, 1905 Medford, Ore.; 6, Alice

Adelia Rawlings b Aug. 23, 1907 Medford; d Sept. 10, 1909 Medford; 7, Earl Washington Rawlings b Mar. 14, 1915 Medford, Ore.)

Five. Catherine Rawlings b Oct. 16, 1830; d abt 1919 Dublin, Tex.; married King O'Neal (d 1893 Pikeville, Tenn.) and had b b Pine Bluff, Warren Co., Tenn.; (a) A. Sam O'Neal b Nov. 28, 1853; d bef. 1910, once of Ft. Worth, Tex.; (b) J. Kink O'Neal b Sept. 11, 1855, of Dublin, Tex., m ———— Barnes; (c) Mary Esther O' Neal b 1857; (d) Wiley O'Neal b Jan. 13, 1861, m Laura White and had no ch.; (e) William O'Neal b 1863, of Dublin, Tex. (m Electra Hancock and had; 1, Ty O'Neal; 2, Eugenia O'Neal); (f) Albert Sidney Johnston O'Neal b abt 1866, m Cora Moore and had ch.; (g) Charlie O'Neal, once of Chattanooga, Tenn.

Six. Mary Lettice Rawlings b Aug. 14, 1835; d June 20, 1920 Quebeck, Tenn.; married Louis Chappell Mason Sept. 30, 1898 (b Feb. 22, 1832 Elbert Co., Ga.; d Mar. 3, 1913 near Quebeck, Tenn., son of William and ———— (Penn) Mason; g-s of William Mason). Louis C. Mason married first, Cynthia Caroline Roberts Feb. 16, 1845, who was a first cousin of mother of Mary Lettice Rawlings.

Seven. James Rawlings b July 2, 1838; d 1845 Warren Co., Tenn.

Eight. Margaret Rawlings b Oct. 5, 1842; d Sept. 7, 1880, in the same week with her parents; unmarried.

Nine. Thomas Rawlings b Feb. 13, 1845; wounded at Battle of Stone River Dec. 31, 1862 and d Jan. 20, 1863; unmarried.

Ten. Nathan Rawlings b Dec. 18, 1847; d June 20, 1849 Warren Co., Tenn.

Eleven. Samuel Andrew Rawlings b June 14, 1849, of Allen, Tex.; married Mary Owen, dau of Richard and Martha Jane Owen, Nov. 6, 1873 Warren Co., Tenn. (b Mar. 3, 1856 Kellysburg, Penn.) and had; (a) Nancy Agnes Rawlings b June 25, 1878 Warren Co., Tenn., of Allen, Tex. (m Bryant Carroll Dec. 7, 1898 Collin Co., Tex. and had ch b Allen, Tex.; 1, Birdella Carroll b Dec. 16, 1901, m Marion A. Sykes Dec. 3, 1921 Allen, Tex. and had; (aa) Elsie Ruth Sykes b May 16, 1924; 2, Roy Carroll b Apr. 28, 1903; 3, Lula Carroll b Nov. 5, 1905; 4, Alice Carroll b Dec. 22, 1907; 5, Mildred Carroll b June 27, 1909; 6, Alma Carroll b June 26, 1911; 7, Fred Carroll b Feb. 2, 1913; 8, Eldran Douglass Carroll b Feb. 13, 1923); (b) William Andrew Rawlings b Aug. 19, 1883 in Cherokee Nation, of Allen, Tex. (m Minnie Malone Aug. 9, 1911 Collin Co., Tex. and had ch b Allen, Tex.; 1, Nora Isabella Rawlings b June 4, 1912; 2, Nellie Rawlings b Oct. 7, 1913; 3, Edgar Ray Rawlings b May 9, 1916; 4, Dorothy Lee Rawlings b Mar. 26, 1918; 5, Ruby Inez Rawlings b Nov. 21, 1922); (c) Charles Clarence Rawlings b Dec. 5, 1885 in Cherokee Nation, of Frisco, Tex. (m Pearl Beck Nov. 23, 1908 and had ch b Allen, Tex.; 1, Austin Rawlings b June 24, 1911; 2, Oveta Rawlings b Mar. 22, 1914; 3, Eugene Rawlings b May 15, 1917; 4, Omer Rawlings b June 28, 1918; 5, Clarence Rawlings b May 15, 1921) (d) Hiram Joseph Rawlings b Mar. 31, 1888 Crawford Co.,

Ark., of Weston, Tex. (m Coy Thompson Dec. 1918 and had; 1, Ernest Roy Rawlings b Dec. 31, 1919 McKenney, Tex.; 2, Ruth Rawlings b Nov. 23, 1921 Allen, Tex.); (e) John Octavus Rawlings b Apr. 22, 1891 Collins Co., Tex.; d Feb. 7, 1917 Allen, Tex. (m Alta J. C. Smith Nov. 22, 1913 and had; 1, Arthur Samuel Rawlings b Aug. 1, 1914; 2, John Herschel Rawlings b Oct. 15, 1917); (f) Etta Elizabeth Rawlings b Feb. 7, 1894 Collin Co., Tex., of Lampasas, Tex. (m J. H. Phares Nov. 15, 1913, McKinney, Tex.; 2, Myrtle Agnes Phares b Jan. 19, 1916 Fitzhugh, Okla.; 3, Helen Janet Phares b May 30, 1917 Henryetta, Okla.; 4, Roy Andrew Phares b Dec. 29, 1918 Ada, Okla.; 5, Michael Duane Phares b Oct. 8, 1920 Lula, Okla.; 6, Olena Phares b June 6, 1922 Tupelo, Okla.); (g) Claude Lee Rawlings b Apr. 16, 1898 Collin Co., Tex., of Frisco, Tex. (m Vernie Irene Lermond Oct. 6, 1917 and had; 1, Floyd Lee Rawlings b Sept. 4, 1918 McKinney, Tex.; 2, Claude J. E. Rawlings b July 25, 1920 Celina, Tex.; 3, Pauline E. Rawlings b Aug. 19, 1923, Frisco, Tex.).

IV. Betsy Worthington, dau of James and Lettice Tunnell Worthington, was born 1805 and died abt 1828 in Warren Co., Tenn. She married Andrew Rawlings, brother of James English Rawlings, abt 1820 in Tenn. and had an only child, b in Warren Co., Tenn.

One. Asahel Rawlings b Sept. 1, 1821; was living, in May 1831, at Mt. Airy, Bledsoe Co., Tenn. with a friend of his parents, Nancy Ingram. He moved to Tex. and d May 4, 1864 near Palestine, Texas. He married first ———— ————, in Tenn., who died Oct. 5, 1843 in Tenn., leaving a daughter a few hours old. He married second, Nancy Jane Cox, in Tenn. (b Oct. 15, 1825 near Cumberland Gap, Tenn.; d Sept. 27, 1875 near Palestine, Tex. The mother of Nancy Jane Cox was, before her marriage, Polly Galbraith). Children; (a) Mary Ann Rawlings b Oct. 5, 1843 in Tenn.; d 1886 Wills Point, Tex. (m Rufus Nelson Smith near Palestine, Tex., who d Gonzales Co., Tex. and had; 1, Minnie Smith, m Hudson Kee and lived near Moulton, Tex.; 2, Bell Smith; 3, Nettie Smith; 4, Mattie Smith; 5, Helen Smith); (b) Sarah Elizabeth Rawlings b June 5, 1846 Bosier Parish, La., of Mineral Wells, Tex. (m first John Echols 1864 (d 1866); and m second, John N. Daves Sept. 21, 1868 (d Jan. 12, 1878) and had; 1, William A. Daves b Mar. 28, 1870, of Newlin, Tex., m ———— ———— Dec. 5, 1889 and had; (aa) Jesse Daves b Nov. 7, 1890, of Mt. Dora, N. M., m first ———— ———— 1906 and had; Elmer Daves b Dec. 30, 1907 and a son d in inf.; and m second ———— ———— and had three ch.; (bb) Hilda Daves b Dec. 7, 1892, of Clayton, New Mexico, m ———— Denham Apr. 1, 1907 and had no ch.; (cc) Birdie Daves b Jan. 10, 1895; d Mar. 1, 1923, m ———— Johnson Jan. 20, 1910 and had 3 sons and 1 dau.; (dd) Lena Daves b Oct. 20, 1896, m first ———— Prieskorn and had a dau b Oct. 22, 1916; and m second, ———— ———— and had a dau b Aug. 4, 1919; (ee) John Daves b Sept. 1, 1900, of Mt. Dora, N. M., m ——— ——— May

6, 1916 and had 2 sons and 1 dau.; (ff) Jim Davis b Feb. 16, 1902, of
Mt. Dora, N. M., m ————— ————— Jan. 10, 1920 and had a dau b
Feb. 16, 1922; (gg) Jack Daves b Nov. 10, 1905, of Mt. Dora, N. M.,
m ————— ————— Jan. 21, 1925; (hh Rena Daves b Oct. 18, 1906, of
Newlin, Tex,; (ii) Viola Wilson Daves b Apr. 3, 1909, of Wichita
Falls, Tex., m —————. ————— Apr. 19, 1925; (jj) Mary Daves b Mar.
29, 1911; (kk) Earl Daves b Feb. 7, 1915; (ll) Alvin Daves b Mar. 21,
1917); 2, Rodolphus D. Daves b Sept. 21, 1872 Henderson Co., Tex.,
of Mt. Dora, N. M. (m Lula May Rockett and had; (aa) Susie Daves
b Feb. 1, 1892 Leon Co., Tex., of Mt. Dora, N. M. m Ben Davis Mar.
16, 1909 and had; Othel Davis b Dec. 12, 1911, Opal Davis b Sept. 13,
1912, and H. T. Davis b Nov. 19, 1921; (bb) James Robert Daves b
Sept. 16, 1899 Childress Co., Tex., of Quay, N. M., m Pearl Ford Oct.
14, 1916 and had; Oleta Daves b Aug. 23, 1917 d Apr. 2, 1921, Floyd
F. Daves b Jan. 20, 1920 and Frank Daves b June 21, 1922; (cc)
Infant b Sept. 28, 1904 Harmon Co., Okla.; d Oct. 5, 1904; (dd)
Eddie F. Daves b Oct. 8, 1907 Harmon Co., Okla.; (ee) Ardie Daves
b Jan. 22, 1909 Harmon Co., Okla.; (ff) Alvin G. Daves b Sept. 10,
1911 Harmon Co., Okla.; (gg) Jewell Daves b Jan. 3, 1914 Union Co.,
N. M. Sarah Elizabeth Rawlings b June 5, 1846, m third, Thomas
Jason Bedgood July 22, 1880 (d Feb. 22, 1882) and had; 3, Sallie
Janson Bedgood b Apr. 27, 1882, m first, J. O. Shumake June 12, 1896
Athens, Tex. and had an only ch.; (aa) Bennie Martin Shumake b Dec.
21, 1899, m Viola Martin Nov. 1, 1924 El Paso, Tex. (b Nov. 22, 1896)
and m second, Arthur Berry Mar. 30, 1909 Whitt, Tex, and had no ch);
(c) Reason Monroe Rawlings b Dec. 15, 1849 Bosier Parish, La.; d
Dec. 19, 1891 nr Palestine, Tex. (m Beuna Vista ————— abt 1876 (b
May 22, 1859; d Apr. 25, 1880 nr Palestine, Tex.) and had three sons;
1, J. M. Rawlings b June 1, 1852; d Apr. 24, 1869; 2, W. N. Rawlings
b Sept. 6, 1854; d Feb. 1, 1872, unmarried; 3, R. T. Rawlings b June
1, 1852 Bosier Parish, La.; d Apr. 24, 1869 nr Palestine, Tex., un-
married; (e) William Newton Rawlings b Sept. 6, 1854 Bosier Parish,
La.; d Feb. 1, 1872 near Palestine, Tex.; d Feb. 20, 1880 nr Palestine,
Tex., unm.; (g) Eliza Torrence Rawlings b Oct. 24, 1860 nr Palestine,
Tex.; d Aug. 23, 1901 nr Childress, Tex. (m Frank Williams, nr
Palestine, Tex. (b Feb. 22, 1856 Ala.) and had; 1, Floyd McEntire
Williams b Jan. 30, 1886 Palestine, Tex., of Del Rio, Tex., m Rose E.
Woods Feb. 3, 1903 Childress, Tex. and had; (aa) William Francis
Williams b Oct. 11, 1905; (bb) Charles Odell Williams b Mar. 1907;
(cc) Rachel Jane Williams b June 20, 1908; (dd) Dollie Dave
Williams (daughter); 2, Stella Tunnell Williams b Jan. 24, 1888
Palestine, Tex., of Baggs, Wyoming, m William H. Morrow, son of
Marion and Rebecca Morrow, Jan. 1, 1906 Arlie, Tex. and had (aa)
William Wesley Morrow b Nov. 25, 1906; (bb) Artie Velmo Morrow
(son) b May 4, 1908; (cc) Loyd Chester Morrow b Nov. 8, 1909, all
b nr Childress, Tex.; 3, Jewell Beatrice Williams b Jan. 17, 1890
Naches, Tex., of Hollis, Okla., m Robert W. Worrell Jan. 8, 1907
Childress, Tex. (m Mar. 5, 1886 Mo.) and had ch. b Hollis, Okla.,
save second b at Olympus, Tex.; (aa) Glenn Roy Worrell b Oct. 14,

1907; (bb) Hugh Leroy Worrell b Aug. 16, 1909; (cc) Loys Efton Worrell July 26, 1911; (dd) Lynn Doyle Worrell b Oct. 19, 1913; (ee) R. B. Worrell b Oct. 26, 1915; (ff) James Orvill Worrell b Mar. 6, 1919; (gg) Teresa Pauline Worrell b Mar. 22, 1921; 4, Sam Robert Williams b Dec. 24, 1891 Childress, Tex., of Archer City, Tex., m Era Idel Bearden Apr. 22, 1918 Wichita Falls, Tex. and had; (aa) Lois Adeline Williams b May 5, 1920 Electra, Tex.; (bb) Robert Archibald Williams b Apr. 25, 1922 Burkburnett, Tex.; (cc) Sam Andrew Williams b Dec. 26, 1924 Archie City, Tex.; 5, William Francis Williams b Dec. 9, 1894 Olympus, Tex.; d Mar. 5, 1925 Del Rio, Tex., served in World War, m Nina Bell Fisher June 1920 and had; (aa) A. J. Williams b Apr. 14, 1921; 6, Eva Irene Williams b Nov. 16, 1896 Olympus, Tex., of North Uvalde, Tex., m James Roy Coston June 20, 1917 Montell, Tex. and had; (aa) Hattie Lee Coston b Sept. 12, 1918; (bb) James Roy Coston, the second, b Nov. 24, 1919; (cc) Phoebe Adelle Coston; (dd) Hugh Martin Coston b Nov. 15, 1924; 7, Bessie Mae Williams b Jan. 8, 1898 Olympus, Tex., of Del Rio, Tex., m Ernest Phaxton Dec. 27, 1919 Edna, Tex. and had; (aa) Mabel Phaxton b Sept. 22, 1920 Edna, Tex.; (bb) Jack Phaxton b Dec. 31, 1921 Montell, Tex.; (cc) Charles William Phaxton b Apr. 15, 1924 Montell, Tex. Frank Williams married second, Sarah Elizabeth Brannan and lives Montell, Tex.).

V. Dr Thomas Worthington, son of James and Lettice Tunnell Worthington, was born June 11, 1808 and died Nov. 14, 1888 Pittsfield, Illinois. A County history says of him; "He is a lineal descendant of the Worthington and Calvert (Baltimore) families, both eminent in the early annals of the state of Maryland. Although his birthplace was on southern soil and he was a slave holder by inheritance, he was convinced of the fundemental injustice of the institution of slavery and was largely influenced by the conviction in his removal to Ill. He was a man of broad capacity and high culture and as a physician and surgeon enjoyed an enviable reputation. Originally a staunch Whig he was elected as such from Pike County to the State Senate, serving in the 13th and 14th General Assemblies. His political zeal lent added impetus to the organization of the Republican party in Ill. and he was a delegate to the first Republican convention held in the state, 1856, in Bloomington. He was a soldier in the Black Hawk War. In 1837 he settled in Pittsfield, Ill., where, for many years, he practised his profession. During the latter years of his life he devoted much time to the study of geology and was instrumental in organizing an Archaeological Society. He was one of the ablest and most distinguished citizens not only of Pittsfield but of the state of Ill." He married Amelia J. Long (called Minna), Jan. 19, 1837. She was born Jan. 19, 1819 Baltimore, Md. and died Feb. 9, 1881 Pittsfield, Ill., the dau of Colonel Kennedy Long (b 1763; d 1821, in command of the 27th Md. Regt. in War of 1812) and wife, Elizabeth Kennedy Long (b 1779; d 1859; married 1797). Colonel

Kennedy Long was the son of Andrew Long, a Captain of Penn. troops in Revolutionary War. Elizabeth Kennedy was the dau of Andrew Kennedy (b 1751 in Ireland; d 1811 Philadelphia, who served in Penn. line in the Revolution) and wife, Elizabeth Potts Kennedy. Elizabeth Potts, the dau of Ezekiel Potts (b Jan. 30, 1708, a member of Provincial Assembly 1728-29-30) and wife, Barbara Vodges Potts. Ezekiel Potts the son of David and Alice (Croasdale) Potts, who were forbears of ex-President Theodore Roosevelt. See Potts Family, by Thomas Maxwell Potts. Children of Dr. Thomas Worthington b Pittsfield, Ill., save Thomas, Jr., who was born at Spencer, Tenn., while his parents were there visiting relatives.

One. William Baker Worthington b Aug. 30, 1838.

Two. Emily Worthington b Nov. 13, 1839.

Three. James Kennedy Worthington b Sept. 1, 1842.

Four. Elizabeth Worthington b May 28, 1844.

Five, George Balfour Worthington b Jan. 15, 1846.

Six. Mary Katherine Worthington b Mar. 5, 1848.

Seven. Thomas Worthington, Jr., b June 8, 1850.

Eight. John Gremshaw Worthington b Dec. 26, 1852.

Nine. Laura Helen Worthington b Jan. 29, 1855.

Ten. Andrew Kennedy Worthington b Aug. 25, 1859.

Of these;

One. William Baker Worthington b Aug. 30, 1838; d Jan. 7, 1839 Pittsfield, Ill.

Two. Emily Worhington b Nov. 13, 1839; d Apr. 14, 1903; unmarried.

Three. James Kennedy Worthington b Sept. 1, 1842; d Aug. 12, 1889 Kirkwood, Mo.; served as Union soldier in the War Between the States; married Harriet Elizabeth Sneed, dau of Rev. Samuel K. and Rachel O. (Crosby) Sneed, Apr. 6, 1871, Kirkwood, Mo. (b 1842; d Aug. 28, 1907 Forest Park University, St. Louis, Mo.) Mrs. Worthington succeeded in obtaining the first temperance law for the state of Mo. in 1883. She was at the time of her death, Vice Pres. of Forest Park Univ., an institution founded by her sister, Mrs. Anna Sneed Cairns, in 1861, its President for many years. Older ch. of James Kennedy and Harriet Elizabeth (Sneed) Worthington b Pittsfield, Ill. and those who have died are buried at Kirkwood, Mo.; (a) James Alexander Worthington b Apr. 5, 1872 (m Grace Mae Slinkard May 1, 1901 Kirkwood, Mo. and had ch. including; 1, Grace Alexander Worthington b Feb. 12, 1902 Denver, Col.; 2, Harriet Elizabeth Worthington b July 9, 1904 nr Argo, Col.; 3, Anna Earle Worthington b June 28, 1907 St. Louis, Mo.; 4, Helen Mary Worthington b Mar. 22, 1909 St. Louis, Mo.); (b) Samuel Sneed Worthington b Nov. 29, 1873; d Oct. 30, 1899 Leadville, Col.; (c) Arthur Thomas Worthington b Nov. 10, 1875; (d) Anna Emily Worthington b Sept. 5, 1877; d May 6, 1898 Colorado Springs, Col.; unmarried; (e) Jesse Kennedy Worthington b Oct. 27, 1880; (f) Harriet Elizabeth Worthington b Feb. 25, 1884

Kirkwood, Mo.; (g) Frank Edward Worthington b May 15, 1887; d Aug. 15, 1890 Kirkwood, Mo.

Four. Elizabeth Worthington b May 28, 1844; d Feb. 19, 1873 Pittsfield, Ill.; married Alexander F. Mirrilees, a native of Aberdeen, Scotland, Dec. 3, 1869 Pittsfield, Ill. and had an only child; (a) Margaret Ronald Mirrilees b Sept. 30, 1871 Pittsfield, Ill., of Spokane, Wash., m Lydell Baker Sept. 30, 1898 Pittsfield, Ill. and had no ch.

Five. George Balfour Worthington b Jan. 15, 1846; d Apr. 5, 1895 Barry, Ill.; married Hanna Morrison Criswell Oct. 17, 1867 Pittsfield, Ill.; (b Mar. 23, 1848 Alleghany, Penn.; d Mar. 28, 1920 Jacksonville, Ill.; buried Pittsfield, Ill. She was the dau of James and Letitia (Hull) Criswell; granddau Robert and Mary (Hamilton) Criswell, who were married in Ireland, came to America 1818 and settled in Penn. and g-g-dau James Criswell of Upper Anhagalt on Bum Dale Donegal, nr Londonnerry, Ireland. Letitia Hull, the dau of John and Sarah (Carnahan) Hull; g-d Serg. John and Jane (Hastings) Hull; g-g-d Thomas and Martha (Marshall) Carnahan. Ch. of George B. and Hannah (Criswell) Worthington b Pittsfield, Ill.; (a) Paul Worthington b July 19, 1868; d 1896 Montery, Mexico, unmarried; (b) Minna Worthington b Aug. 28, 1870, of Jacksonville, Ill. (m Dr. Albyn Lincoln Adams, June 11, 1896 Pittsfield, Ill. (b Apr. 13, 1865 Pine Hill, Ontario, Canada, son of James W. (b 1838; d July 21, 1924 Chicago, Ill.) and Lee (Bowman) Adams; g-s Thomas and Mary (McGill) Adams; of Benjamin and Mary (Clemens) Bowman). Dr. Adams has devoted his attention to diseases of the eye, ear, nose and throat and has served as Oculist and Aurist for the State Sshool for the Deaf and State School for the Blind. Ch. b Jacksonville, Ill.; 1, Albyn Worthington Adams b Mar. 5, 1897, salesman, Sergeant in World War with overseas service, member of the First corps artillery on Chateau Thierry front; m Helen Candee June 11, 1924 St. Louis, Mo. and had (aa) Henry Allyn Adams b Sept 11, 1925 St. Louis; 2, Helen Wilcox Adams b Sept. 9, 1899; d Dec. 17, 1921 Denver, Col., buried Jacksonville, Ill., m Robert Vorhees Shoemaker June 12, 1920 Springfield, Ill. and had no chidren. R. V. Shoemaker m second, Mary Virginia Leech Nov. 1924; 3, Mary Katherine Graham Adams b Oct. 7, 1900; d July 21, 1901; 4, Albyn Lincoln Adams the second, b May 5, 1902; d Sept. 1903; 5, George Worthington Adams b Nov. 22, 1905; 6, Minna Margaret Adams b Aug. 27, 1913); (c) Helen Morrison Worthington b Jan. 21, 1873; d 1902 Chicago, Ill. (m Major Holman G. Purinton, of U. S. A., June 24, 1899 Jacksonville, Ill. and had no children); (d) George Mirrilees Worthington b Feb. 14, 1875; d July 4, 1875 St. Louis, Mo.; (e) Robert Kennedy Worthington b Apr. 7, 1876, unmarried.

Six. Mary Katherine Worthington b Mar. 5, 1848; d Sept. 27, 1917 Denver, Col.; married Dr. John W. Graham June 24, 1884 Pittsfield, Ill. (b May 24, 1843 Westmoreland Co., Penn.; d Feb. 14, 1908 Denver, Col.; son of Andrew Graham (b 1805; d 1859) and wife, Jane

White (Brown) Graham (b 1805; d 1890), and had no children.

Seven. Thomas Worthington, Jr., b June 8, 1850 Spencer, Tenn.; d Feb. 15, 1922 Jacksonville, Ill. After completing his education he practised law in Baltimore, Md. and Pittsfield, Ill. and located in Jacksonville, in 1892. He served as minority representative in the State Legislature from the district comprising Brown, Calhoun and Pike Counties. From 1901 to 1905 he served as U. S. District Attorney for Southern Ill. His specialty was in drainage laws and in this field he built an enviable reputation. He was an officer of the Ill. Bar Association; member of Board of Trustees of Illinois College for 17 years and was prominent in legal, political, literary and religious circles. He married the daughter of his law partner, Miriam Morrison, Nov. 16, 1892 Jacksonville, Ill. (b 1854 Jacksonville, Ill.; d Aug. 2, 1923 Jacksonville, Ill.) and had an only child; (a) Isaac Lafayette Morrison Worthington b Sept. 12, 1893, Jacksonville, unmarried, attorney, Jacksonville, Ill. Miriam Morrison, the dau of Isaac Lafayette and Anna Rebecca (Tucker) Rapalje Morrison, who were m July 27, 1853 Jacksonville, Ill. I. L. Morrison b Jan. 20, 1826 Barren Co., Ky.; d Feb. 27, 1901 Jacksonville, Ill., a leader af the Bar and of the Republican party which he assisted in organizing as a member of its first state convention; three times a member of legislature; the son of John C. Morrison (b Va.; d 1841 Barren Co., Ky.; served in Indian wars) and Elizabeth (Wellborn) Morrison. Anna Rebecca Tucker Rapalje the dau of Jonathan and Miriam (Weeks) Tucker. Miriam Weeks a descendant of Francis Weeks one of the four men who, with Roger Williams, signed the purchase of Providence Plantation.

Eight. John Grimshaw Worthington b Dec. 26, 1852, of Kansas City, Kansas; married Jessamine Matthews Mar. 29, 1881 Chicago, Ill. (b June 20, 1858) and had an only child; (a) Julian Mathews Worthington b July 19, 1884 Chicago, Ill.; d Jan. 7, 1919 Chicago, Ill., m Ruth Simmons and had no children.

Nine. Laura Helen Worthington b Jan. 29, 1855, of Colorado Springs, Col.; married William Theodora Gauss June 24, 1875 Pittsfield, Ill. W. T. Gauss b July 1, 1851 Chariton Co., Mo., son of Charles William and Louisa Aletta (Fallenstein Gauss. Charles William Gauss b Oct. 23, 1813 Goettingen; d Aug.23, 1879 St. Louis, Mo., son of the celebrated mathematician and astronomer, Carl Friedrich Gauss, (b Apr. 30, 1777 Braunschweig; d Feb. 23, 1855 Goettingen) and Minnie (Waldeck) Gauss (d Sept. 12, 1831 Goettingen). Louisa Aletta Fallenstein b Apr. 20, 1813 Levern, Prussia; d Sept. 15, 1883 St. Louis, Mo. dau of Henry and Charlotte (Bessell) Fallenstein and a descendant of Jobst von Bessell, ennobled by Emperor Maximillian 1494. Ch. of W. T. and Laura Helen (Worthington) Gauss b St. Louis, Mo.; (a) Carl Friedrich Gauss b Oct. 19, 1878, of Littleton, Col. (m Mrs. Ann P. Griffith Dec. 12, 1914 Colorado Springs, Col. (b Feb, 21, 1879) and had no ch.; (b) Helen Worthington Gauss b Apr. 9, 1881, of Colorado Springs,Col., unmarried, who assumed the name of Helen at death of her sister; (c) Theodore Worthington Gauss b Sept. 4, 1884, of Colorado Springs, Col. (m Gladys Olivia Robinson Sept. 25, 1913 St. Joseph, Mo. (b Apr. 27, 1888) and had ch b Colorado Springs; 1, Theodore Worthington Gauss, the second, b July 12, 1914; 2, Robert Parker Gauss b June 16, 1918; (d) Helen Worthington Gauss, third child to receive name of Worthington, b July 18, 1887; d Feb. 8, 1889 St. Louis, Mo.

Ten. Jesse Worthington b June 30, 1857; d Aug. 24, 1859.

Eleven. Dr. Andrew Kennedy Worthington, second child to have middle name of Kennedy, b Aug. 25, 1859; unmarried, of Denver, Colorado.

VI. Catherine Worthington, dau of James and Lettice Tunnell Worthington, was born May 18, 1810 and died 1860 in Warren Co., Tenn. She married Thomas Maybry, Sept. 15, 1830, nr McMinnville, Tenn. (b Apr. 18, 1804; d 1861 Warren Co., Tenn.) and had ch b Warren Co., Tenn.

One. Frances Ann Maybry Sept. 16, 1831.

Two. Mary Caroline Maybry b Oct. 10, 1832.

Three. William Thomas Worthington Maybry b Oct. 13, 1836.

Four. Melchizedek Hill Maybry b Feb. 19, 1839.

Of these;

One. Frances Ann Maybry b Sept. 16, 1831; d Apr. 20, 1920; married Sidney Crowder, son of Richard and Mary (Easthem) Crowder, Nov. 18, 1851 Warren Co., Tenn. (b 1828 Sparta, Tenn.; d Dec. 12, 1885 Cooper, Tex.) They moved from Warren Co., Tenn. to near Honey Grove, Tex., and later to Hopkins, Tex. After her husband's death Mrs. Crowder spent part of her time at Durant, Okla. Names of ch. may not be given in order of birth; (a) Mary Catherine Crowder b Jan. 25, 1853 Tenn., of Cooper, Tex.; (m Thomas J. Craig July 21, 1870 Delta Co., Tex. and had ch b Cooper, Tex.; 1, Dillard L. Craig b Oct. 12, 1873; d Dec. 21, 1903; 2, Emma V. Craig b Nov. 26, 1878, m J. R. Cook Nov. 20, 1898 and had; (aa) Willie Lester Cook b Sept. 21, 1899 Lamar Co., Tex.; 3, Mattie Catherine Craig b Mar. 3, 1882; d May 29, 1905; 4, Fannie Craig b May 31, 1884, m O. W. Harrison Dec. 21, 1901 and had; (aa) Floy Harrison b Dec. 6, 1902 Delta Co., Tex.; (bb) Catherine Craig Harrison b Mar. 25, 1911 Amarillo, Tex.; 5, Evely May Craig b Jan. 3, 1887, m E. P. Woodard June 10, 1908 Ft. Worth, Tex. and had; (aa) Edgar Poe Woodard b Sept. 7, 1910 Stanton, Tex.; 6, Jessie Alma Craig b Sept. 6, 1888, m Oscar Tidwell Jan. 14, 1912 and had; (aa) Beryl Tidwell b Nov. 25, 1912; 7, Thomas Broden Craig b June 20, 1893); (b) William Reps Crowder b Apr. 19, 1854 Tenn.; d 1873 Gatesville, Tex. (m Mattie Harrison abt 1874 Gatesville, Tex., who d in Ark. and left no children; (c) Hickson Bluchers Crowder b Apr. 9, 1858 Tenn., of Katy, Tex. (m first, Laura Early Nov. 22, 1883 Cooper, Tex. (b Sept. 25, 1858 Hendersonville, Ky.; d Sept. 9, 1893 Commerce, Tex., dau of J. M.

Early) and had ch b Cooper, Tex.; 1, Reps Crowder b Oct. 15, 1885, m Myrtle Caughey Dec. 1906 Durant, Okla. and had; (aa) Alyne Crowder b Jan. 25, 1908 Waller, Tex.; (bb) Helen Crowder b Feb. 1909 Waller, Tex.; (cc) Beatrice Crowder b Mar. 1910 Waller, Tex.; (dd) James M. Crowder b at Katy, Tex.; (ee) Blucher Crowder b at Katy, Tex.; 2, James Crowder b Dec. 31, 1887; d Dec. 24, 1917, m Minerva Morgan Mar. 13, 1913 Hempstead, Tex. and had no ch. Hickson Blucher Crowder m second, Edna Stapleton, dau S. Stapleton, Aug. 22, 1896 Hempstead, Tex. (b Jan. 1, 1868 Columbus, Tex.) and had ch b Waller, Tex.; 3, Hickson Blucher Crowder Jr. b June 29, 1897, of Wortham, Tex., m Phebe Cole and had, (aa) Hickson Blucher Crowder, the third; (bb) John Cole Crowder; 4, Sidney Crowder, twin, b Jan. 6, 1899, oil driller, Tampico, Mexico, 5, Edna Francis Crowder (son) twin of Sidney Crowder, b Jan. 6, 1899; 6, Richard Crowder b Dec. 7, 1900, of Katy, Tex., m Mayme Ruskey Dec. 7, 1923 and had; (aa) Richard Crowder Jr. b Sept. 22, 1924 Alvin, Tex.; 7, John Crowder b Sept. 4, 1903, of Durant, Okla.; 8, Wallace Crowder b Sept. 21, 1907; 9, Lucile Crowder b Jan. 6, 1909. Two sons of H. B. Crowder saw service in World War, one wounded); (d) Thomas Sidney Crowder b June 23, 1860, of Stanton, Tex. (m Susannah Wynn and had; 1, Byrd Crowder, m ——— Pratt; 2, Myrtle Crowder, of Cooper, Tex., m ——— Pratt; 3, Hiram Crowder, m ——— ———; 4, Ethel Crowder; 5, Raynor Crowder; 6, Winnie Crowder); (e) Lem Crowder died 1869; (f) C. Richard Crowder b 1866 Cooper, Tex., of Durant, Okla. (m Rena Beal and had; 1, Fronia Crowder b Dec. 3, 1886 Cooper, Tex., of Klondyke, Tex., m W. M. McBride and had; (aa) Wirten (?) McBride; (bb) Arbery McBride; (cc) Dovie McBride; 2, Mary Catherine Crowder b Nov. 27, 1898 Durant, Okla.; m Jack Kelley; 3, John F. Crowder b Sept. 6, 1903 Durant, Okla.; d Sept. 12, 1903; 4, Frances Crowder b Nov. 15, 1905 Durant, Okla.); (g) John Crowder b May 9, 1869 in Tex.; d in Okla. (m Sophia Nelson and had; 1, Mary Susan Crowder, m Frank Anderson; 2, Laura Crowder, m Lem Ferguson and had; (aa) Lillie Angie Ferguson; 3, John Crowder Jr.; (h) Bedford Crowder died in inf.; (i) Fannie Crowder died Jan. 29, 1906 Roswell, N. M. (m Joseph Deiss (d abt 1919 Amerillo, Tex.) and had an only ch.; 1, Nellie Deiss b 1898, of San Diess, Calif., m Dr. Boyd. Joseph Deiss m second ——— bef. 1910 and lived then Twin Falls, Idaho).

Two. Mary Caroline Maybry b Oct. 10, 1832; d 1875 Warren Co., Tenn.; unmarried.

Three. William Thomas Worthington Maybry b Oct. 13, 1836; d Feb. 15, 1890 Van Buren Co., Tenn.; married Catherine Martin, dau Jacob and Nellie Martin, Dec. 29, 1868 (b Apr. 12, 1841 Warren Co., Tenn.; d Mar. 5, 1923 nr Quebeck, Tenn.) and had; (a) Thomas Jackson Maybry b Oct. 21, 1869 Warren Co., Tenn., of Walling, Tenn. (m Sallie Gardiner, dau of John and Mary Gardiner, Dec. 23, 1903 White Co., Tenn. and had ch b nr Quebeck, Tenn.; 1, Leta Maybry b

May 9, 1905, m Eston Fisher Aug. 26, 1923 White Co., Tenn.; 2, John Maybry b Aug. 1, 1907; 3, Nolan Maybry b July 13, 1909; 4, Linville Maybry b Feb. 13, 1912; d Quebeck, Tenn.; 5, Walter Maybry; 6, Harold Maybry; 7, Charles Maybry died Quebeck, Tenn.); (b) Jacob Edgar Maybry b Nov. 15, 1871 Warren Co., Tenn., of Farmer's Branch, Tex. (m Daisy Moore in Van Buren Co., Tenn., and had; 1, Ivan Maybry b V. B. Co., Tenn.; 2, William Maybry b V. B. Co., m ———— ————; 3, Estol Maybry b V. B. Co.; 4, Landiss Maybry b Tex.; 5, Lila Bell Maybry b Tex.; J. O. Maybry b Tex.); (c) Floren Reps Maybry b Mar. 20, 1873 Warren Co., Tenn.; d Aug. 20, 1873; (d) William Warren Maybry b Jan. 24, 1875 Warren Co., Tenn.. unm., of Quebeck, Tenn.; (e) James Worthington Maybry b Mar. 18, 1878 Van Buren Co., Tenn., of Quebeck, Tenn. (m a relative, Minnie Ethel Sparkman, Mar. 7, 1904 V. B. Co., Tenn. (b   Apr.   18,   1888,   dau Solomon and Mary Ellen (Parker) Johnson Trogden Sparkman; granddau Jackie and Vina (McElroy) Sparkman; of Rev. Arthur L. and Lodemia (Worthington) Parker; g-g-d William   and   Betsey (Worthington) Worthington) and had; 1, Herschel Maybry b Dec. 8, 1904 V. B. Co., Tenn.; 2, Clifton Maybry b Apr. 13, 1907, m Joe E. Goldston Sept. 23, 1923; 3, Bertram Maybry b June 22, 1909 Quebeck, Tenn.; 4, Earl Maybry, twin; and 5, Ernest Maybry, twin with Earl, b Oct. 21, 1911 in New Mexico; 6, Hugh Maybdy b   May   5,   1915 Quebeck, Tenn; 7, Miron Maybry (dau) b abt 1917 Quebeck, Tenn.; 8, J. W. Maybry b Sept. 20, 1920 Quebeck, Tenn; 9, Mildred Maybry b abt 1922 Quebeck, Tenn.); (f) Elizabeth May Maybry b May 14, 1880, unmarried, of Quebeck, Tenn.

Four.   Melchizedek Hill Maybry b Feb. 19, 1839; d May 19, 1839.

ROBERT TUNNELL

F.   Robert Tunnell, son of William and Mary Maysey Tunnell, was born Dec. 14, 1782 Fairfax Co., Virginia.   At the age of six he moved to North Carolina with his parents and   in   1792   to   near Robertsville, Tenn.   He married Elizabeth Johnson abt 1802 and they lived in Knox Co., Tenn. a number of years, then moved to Hamilton Co., Tenn.   He was Indian Agent, and served in War of 1812 and is said to have been in seven battles.   In 1847 Robert Tunnell and wife were returning to Tenn. from a visit with daughters near Nacoydoches, Tex. and were murdered by Indians "on the state line road between Arkansas and Indian Nation", according to grandchildren.   It is said their three sons died without issue.   Names may not be given in order of birth.

I.   Matilda Tunnell b Dec. 21, 1805.

II.   Susan Tunnell b abt 1807.

III.   Eliza Tunnell b Jan. 22, 1810.

IV.   James Tunnell b abt 1812.

V.   Noble Tunnell b abt 1814.

VI.   William Tunnell b abt 1817.

VII.   Mary Louise Tunnell b July 1819.

VIII.   Harriet N. Tunnell b Nov. 15, 1821.

IX. Emily Jane Mortimer Tunnell b May 30, 1824.
X. Nancy Tunnell b Aug. 6, 1828.
Of the foregoing;
I. Matilda Tunnell, dau of Robert and Elizabeth Johnson Tunnell, was born Dec. 21, 1805 Knox Co., Tenn. and died Feb. 5, 1871 Rusk Co., Texas. She married William Reagan abt 1825. He was born Aug. 1, 1794 and died Oct. 8, 1867 Rusk Co., Tex., the son of James and Betty (Cook) Reagan; grandson John and Mary Reagan, of Knoxville, Tenn. See "History of Sweetwater Valley' by Lenoir, for Reagan history. William Reagan was the first tax collector for Rusk Co., Tex. Children;
One. Eliza Adeline Reagan b Oct. 1, 1826.
Two. James H. Reagan b Dec. 8, 1829.
Three. Amanda Melvina Reagan b Jan. 23, 1831.
Four. Robert William Reagan b Dec. 26, 1833.
Five. Caroline Matilda Reagan b Sept. 4, 1836.
Six. Noble Marion Reagan b Mar. 22, 1839.
Seven. Mary Emily Reagan b Feb. 24, 1841.
Eight. Helen Jane Reagan b Apr. 24, 1845.
Nine. Harriet Albina Reagan b Aug. 16, 1849.
Of these;
One Eliza Adeline Reagan b Oct. 1, 1826 in Tenn.; d Mar. 26, 1899 in Tex., married Captain Francis Marion Rust, in Tex. (b Va.; d Tex.) and had; (a) Lizzie Alice Rust b 1842; d 1893 (m Sam Houston Bromley (b 1839; d 1905) and had; 1, William Bromley b Nov. 20, 1872, m Etta Johnson and had; (aa) Robert Bromley; (bb) Cleda Bromley; 2, Alleta Estella Bromley b Jan. 8, 1875, of San Antonio, Tex., m Hugh Thomas Davis and had; (aa) Louis Irby Davis b Nov. 10, 1897; (bb) Darthula Davis b May 2, 1900; (cc) Beryl Davis b May 15, 1902, m R. B. Beckcom and had Hugh Warren Beckcom b June 4, 1923; (dd) Robert Bervey Davis b Feb. 26, 1910; (ee) Alleta Davis b Oct. 25, 1911; 3, Drayton Bromley b Sept. 15, 1878; 4, Vera Bromley, died at thirteen months; 5, Adaline Bromley b Oct. 25, 1884; d 1901;) (b) Matilda Rust b Rust Co., Tex., of Abilene, Tex. (m James E. McDavid and had; 1, Edna McDavid, of Abilene, Tex. (m ————and had a son; 2, Beulah McDavid, unmarried; 3, Vera McDavid, m ———— Hardin; 4, Julian McDavid m ———— and had ch; 5, Marion McDavid, m ———— (d 1922) and had ch.; b, Roy McDavid, m ——— ——·—— ; 7, Glen McDavid, of Electra, Tex., m ——— ———— and had ch.; and others); (c) Albert Rust, b Rust Co., Tex., d at age of 5; (d) Robert William Rust b Mar. 24, 1859 Little Rock, Ark., of Drumright, Okla., lived in Texas from 1865 to 1915 (m Minnie Hull, of Henderson, Tex., Dec. 1886 (b Feb. 1869; d Oct 17, 1912) and had; 1, Lucile Rust b Sept. 17 1888; d Dec. 8, 1903 Brownwood, Tex., 2, Hubert Clifford Rust b Sept. 19, 1890, of Drumright, Okla., m Anna Whallon July 21, 1923 (b Dec. 13, 1903) and had; (aa) Wanda Rust b Aug. 20, 1924; 3, Adelle Rust b Oct. 24, 1893, of San Antonio, Tex., m James W. Davis and had; (aa) James

W. Davis Jr. 4, Roy Martin Rust b Mar. 10, 1897, of Drumright, Okla., m Jewel Steel Mar. 24, 1918 (b July 23, 1898) and had; (aa) Jessie Belle Rust b July 19, 1919; (bb) Geraldine 'Rust b June 23, 1923; 5, Lois Rust b Aug. 6, 1899, m Guy Lesley and 'had; (aa) Guy Lesley Jr. died at 18 months; (bb) Paul Forest Lesley; 6, Robert Wilfred Rust b Dec. 12, 1901, of San Antonio, Tex., m Ura Williams;) (e) Alberta Rust b 1861, of Fort Worth, Tex., '(m Lynn Holloman 1889 (deceased) and had; 1, Alberta Lynn Holloman, m first W. Cull McDaniels Oct. 11, 1907 (d Mar. 24, 1919) and had; (aa) Francis Freeman McDaniels b Nov. 8, 1908 Crandall, Tex., of U. S. Army, stationed in Honolulu; and m. second, James Joiner Oct. 10, 1922;) (f) Noble M. Rust b 1864, of Ft. Worth, Tex. (m first, Jennie Florence 1886 (b 1873; d Apr. 21, 1900) and had; 1, Alberta Rust b Oct, 30, 1887; d 1889; 2, Tillie Rust b July 13, 1888, m Carol Jenkins and had; (aa) Ruby Jenkins b 1908; (bb) Lovie Jenkins b 1910; (cc) Florence Jenkins b 1912; (dd) Mildred Jenkins b 1914; (ee) Clarence Jenkins b 1920; (hh) Harold Jenkins b 1922; 3, Ernest Rust b Apr. 13, 1890, m Novette Ellis and had no ch.; 4, Carrie Rust b Jan. 16, 1892, m Gus Bramlett and had; (aa) Ernest Bramlett; (bb) Fay Bramlett; (cc) Etta Bramlett; 5, Edith Rust b 1894, m Ed Huckelby 1914 and had; (aa) Edwin Huckelby b 1916; (bb) Harold Huckelby b 1920; 6, Copeland Rust b 1896, m Ethel Howard 1916 and had; (aa) Georgia Ellen Rust; (bb) Lowell Rust; (cc) Noble Lee Rust and others; 7, Jimmie Rust b Apr. 21, 1900, m Marvin McElvaney 1918 and had; (aa) Mary Frances McElvaney; (bb) Junior McElvaney. Noble M. Rust, b 1864 m second, Mrs. Etta Davidson and had; 8, Buell Rust, d young; 9, Marian Rust, d young; 10, Noble Marion Rust b 1915); (g) James Edwin Rust b in Tex. (m Bell Hardin and had; 1, Alvin Rust; 2, Nolan Rust; 3, Armond Rust; 4, Verna Rust; 5, Mable Rust; perhaps others).

Two   James H. Reagan b Dec. 28, 1828 Tenn.; d 1862 nr Jacksonville, Tex.; married Sarah Dodson and had children, including; (a) Robert Reagan; (b) Clarence Reagan.

One   Eliza Adeline Reagan b Oct. 1, 1826 in Tenn.; d Mar. 26, 1899 in Tex.; m Capt. Francis Marion Rust in Tex. (b Va.; d Tex.) and had; (a) Lizzie Alice Rust b about 1842; d in Tex. 1893; (m Sam Houston Bromley in London, Tex. (d abt 1918 Ft. Worth, Tex.) and had; 1, Leta Bromley; of San Antonio, Tex., m ——— Davis and had children; 2, William Bromley; 3, Drayton Bromley; 4, Addie Bromley and perhaps others); (b) Matilda Rust b Abt 1855 Rust Co., Tex., or Abilene, Tex. (m James E. McDavid and had; 1, Edna McDavid, of Abilene, Tex., m ——— ——— and had a son; 2, Beulah McDavid, unmarried; 3, Vera McDavid, m ——— Hardin; 4, Julian McDavid, m ——— ——— and had ch.; 5, Marion McDavid, m ——— ——— ——— (d 1922 and had ch.; 6, Roy McDavid, m ——— ——— ———; 7, Glen McDavid, of Electra, Tex., m ——— ——— and had ch.; and others); (c) Albert Rust died at 5; (b) Robert William Rust b Mar. 24, 1859 Little Rock, Ark., of Drumright, Okla., lived in

Texas from 1865 to 1915 (m Minnie Hull, of Henderson, Tex. Dea.
1886 (b Feb. 1869; d Oct. 17, 1912) and had; 1, Lucile Rust b Sept.
17, 1888; d Dec 8, 1903 Brownwood, Tex.; 2, Hubert Clifford Rust
b Sept. 19, 1890 of Drumright, Okla., m Anna Whallon July 21, 1923
(b Dec. 13, 1903) and had; (aa) Wanda Rust b Aug 20, 1924; 3,
Adelle Rust b Oct. 24, 1893, of San Antonio, Tex., m James W.
Davis and had; (aa) James W. Davis Jr.; 4, Roy Martin Rust b Mar.
10, 1897, of Drumright, Okla., m Jewel Steele Mar. 24, 1918 (b July
23, 1898) and had; (aa) Jessie Belle Rust b July 19, 1919; (bb)
Geraldine Rust b June 23, 1923; 5, Lois Rust b Aug. 6, 1899, m
Guy Lesley and had; (aa) Guy Lesley Jr. died at 18 months; (bb)
Paul Forest Lasley; 6, Robert Wilfred Rust b Dec. 12, 1901, of San
Antonio, Tex., m Ura Williams); (a) Alberta Rust b 1861, of Ft.
Worth, Tex. (m Lynn Holloman 1889 (deceased and had; 1, Alberta
Lynn Holloman 1889 (deceased) and had; 1, Alberta Lynn Holloman,
m first W. Cull McDaniels Oct. 11, 1907 (d Mar 24, 1919) and had;
(aa) Francis Freeman McDaniels b Nov. 8, 1908 Crandall, Tex., of
U. S. Army, Stationed in Honolulu; and m. second, James Joiner Oct.
10, 1922); (f) Noble M. Rust b 1864, of Ft. Worth, Tex. (m first
Jimmie Florence 1886 (b 1873; d Apr. 21, 1900) and had; 1, Albert
Rust b Oct. 30, 1887; d 1889; 2, Tillie Rust b July 13, 1888, m Carol
Jenkins and had; (aa) Ruby Jenkins b 1908; (bb) Lovie Jenkins b
1910; (cc) Florence Jenkins b 1912; (dd) Mildred Jenkins b 1914; (ee)
Clarence Jenkins b 1916; (ff) Jack Jenkins b 1918; (gg) Bernice
Jenkins b 1920; (hh) Harold Jenkins b 1922; 3, Ernest Rust b Apr. 13,
1890, m Novette Ellis and had no ch.; 4, Carrie Rust b Jan. 16, 1892,
m Gus Bramblett and had; (aa) Ernest Bramblett, (bb) Fay Bramb-
lett; (cc) Etta Bramblett; 5, Edith Rust b 1894, m Ed Huckelby 1914
had (aa) Edwin Huckelby b 1916; (bb) Harold Huckelby b 1920; 6,
Copeland Rust b 1896, m Ethel Howard 1916 and had; (aa) Georgia
Ellen Rust; (bb) Lowell Rust; (cc) Noble Lee Rust and others; 7,
Jimmie Rust b Apr. 21, 1900, m Marvin McElvaney 1918 and had;
(aa) Mary Frances McElvaney; (bb) Junior McElvaney. Noble M.
Rust, b 1864, m second, Mrs. Etta Davison and had; 8, Buell Rust
died young; 9, Marian Rust, died young; 10, Noble Marion Rust b
1915.); (g) James Edwin Rust b in Tex. (m Bell Hardin and had; 1,
Alvin Rust; 2, Nolan Rust; 3, Armond Rust; 4, Verna Rust; 5, Mable
Rust; perhaps others).

Two   James H. Reagan b Dec. 28, 1828 Tenn.; d 1862 nr Jacksonville, Tex.; married Sarah Dodson and had children, including; (a)
Robert Reagan; (b) Clarence Reagan.

Three   Amanda Melvina Reagan b Jan. 23, 1831 Knox Co.,
Tenn.; d Oct. 10, Cleburne, Texas; married Lucious Drayton Smith,
son of Saul and Talitha (Dobson) Smith, June 10, 1854 Rusk Co., Tex.
(b Buncombe Co., N. C.; b Mar. 19, 1898 Somerville Co, Tex.) and
had; (a) Talitha Helen Smith b Aug. 20, 1855 Rusk Co., Tex.; d Apr.
7, 1916 Glen Rose, Tex. (m Rev. Oscar Addison, son of Samuel and

Sarah Addison, Dec. 18, 1879 (b Nov 24, 1820 Baltimore, Md.; d Oct. 12, 1898 near Somerville, Tex.) and had no children); (b) Charles Byron Smith b May 10, 1857 Glenfawn, Tex., of Tulsa, Okla. (m Lizzie Dalton at Cleburne, Tex. and had; 1; Vida Smith b Cisco, Tex., of Tulsa, Okla., m Charles Gilmore, Muskogee, Okla. (served in World war; on a ship that was sunk by submarine in English channel) and had ch. b Tulsa, Okla.; (aa) Charles Gilmore, the second; (bb) David Gilmore; 2, Bascom Smith b Pecos, Tex., of Washington, D. C., who was educated at Annapolis and on a battleship in the danger zone during the World war, m Mildred Cameron, Washington, D. C. and had one daughter; 3, Lois Smith b Dec. 1894 Pecos, Tex., unmarried, of Tulsa, Okla.; 4, Charles Buckley Smith b 1897, mechanical engineer, of Dallas, Tex., who was a cadet in University of Oklahoma during the war; 5, Ruth Smith b 1901 Pecos, Tex. unmarried, of Tulsa, Okla.; 6, Douglas Smith b 1903 Muscogee, Okla.); (c) Jessie Reagan Smith b Oct. 1, 1861 Parker Co., Tex., of Huntsville, Tex. (m William Oscar Glasscock, son of Henley and Melvina (Stevens) Glasscock, Aug. 28, 1822 Caddo Grove, Tex. (July 5, 1846 Hamilton, Ala.; d July 3, 1924 Alvin, Tex., who "answered the call of his beloved Southland and enlisted in the Confederate army") and had; 1, Oscar Reagan Glasscock b June 3, 1883 Ladonia, Tex., of Conroe, Tex., m Kate Martin Sept. 16, 1903 Alvin, Tex. and had; (aa) Oscar Gilbert Glasscock b 1904 Alvin, Tex., of Harlinger, Tex.; (bb) Mary Kate Glasscock b abt 1905; d 1905; (cc) Cecil Gordon Glasscock b 1907 in Louisiana; (dd) Lucian Bryan Glasscock b 1909 Louisiana; (ee) Agnes Louise Glasscock b 1911 Alvin, Tex.; 2, Jesse Melvin Glasscock b Sept. 13, 1885 Ladonia, Tex., of Pheonix, Ariz., m Althea Davenport in San Saba Co., Tex. and had; (aa) Melba Glasscock b Mar. 6, 1912 San Saba Co., Tex.; 3, Nathaniel William Glasscock b June 21, 1888 Ladonia, Tex., of Moran, Tex., m Lena Gambling in San Saba Co., and had; (aa) Ranston Glasscock b Oct. 12, 1910; 4, Charles Glasscock b Feb. 8, 1890 Milburn, Tex.; d May 25, 1900 Milburn, Tex.; 5, Enoch Marvin Glasscock b Nov. 28, 1891 Milburn, Tex., of Angleton, Tex., county superintendent of schools, m Mabel Rairight June 21, 1914 Alvin, Tex., and had no ch.; 6, Helen Louise Glasscock b Dec. 14, 1893 Milburn, Tex., of Huntsville, Tex., m E. C. McCurdy Feb. 12, 1920 Alvin, Tex., and had; (aa) Helen Frances McCurdy b Apr. 2, 1921 Houston, Tex.; (bb) E. C. McCurdy b Feb. 19, 1923 Conroe, Tex.; 7, Maynard Arthur Glasscock b May 1, 1896 Milburn, Tex., m Vera Martin Nov. 13, 1918 San Antonio, Tex., and had ch b Houston, Tex.; (aa) Maynard Glasscock b Nov. 1919; (bb) Dalton Glasscock b Aug. 26, 1922; 8, Luke Gradon Glasscock b Sept. 8, 1900 Milburn, Tex.; d May 28, 1910); (d) Carolyn Lavinia Smith b Rusk Co., Tex., of Cisco, Tex. (m first, Eli Charnic Cox Apr. 20, 1881 Johnson Co., Tex. (b Mar. 31, 1883 Ladonia, Tex.) and had; 1, Paul Drayton Cox b Jan. 10, 1882 Landonia, Tex.; d Apr. 16, 1883 Landonia, Tex.; and m second, George Langston, son of John and Cynthia (Truitt) Langston, Jan. 31, 1893 Citra, Florida (b Feb. 5,

1860 Rusk Co., Tex., with the T. & P. R. R.) and had; 2, Joyce Langston b Oct. 3, 1895 Cisco, Tex., of Los Angeles, Calif., m Paul Schmitz, son of Albert and Kate (Gaston) Schmitz, June 28, 1920 San Francisco, Calif. (b Mar. 5, 1894, manufacturer) and had; (aa) Paul Schmitz, the second, b Feb. 27, 1925 Los Angeles, Calif. In 1906 Mrs. Langston wrote and published the "History of Eastland County, Texas." "Since 1921 she has served as State Chairman of Peace in the T. F. W. C. and her work in this office is written in the annals of federated work, for during her office she organized the peace pledge, now adopted by the state federation and by many other organizations throughout the country. The pledge is the essence of all human relationship, yet is so concise and simple that its real depth may be preceived instantly — 'Before I speak or act in retaliation I will try a peaceful solution of every difficulty.' This pledge has received the endorsement of the National Council for Prevention of Wars. Modestly disclaiming any credit for the idea she says that the words would be effective regardless of their originator, yet her zealous efforts in placing this simple remedy before the many organizations of the country have been very worthwhile and praiseworthy work and as such have received the greatful consideration of a peace loving state and nation. She also designed the peace pin"); (e) Nathaniel Wilson Smith b May 11, 1865 Marystown, Tex., of Houston, Tex. (m Lola Berry at Greenville, Tex., and had; 1 Gladys Smith; 2, Violet Smith; 3, Dorothy Smith); (f) Louisana Albina Smith of Ft. Worth, Tex. (m Bion E. Prickett, Marystown, Tex., and had; 1, Paul Smith Prickett b Sept. 21, 1899, cadet in A. & M. College last year of World war; 2, Bion Langston Prickett b Nov. 12, 1905; 3, Benjamin Prickett b Sept. 5, 1909); (g) Adeline Melva Smith b Oct. 21, 1870, of Cleburne, Tex. (m William W. Ransone June 19, 1902 Cisco, Tex. and had; 1, Reuben Key Ransone b July 22, 1903 Cleburne, Tex.; 2, Lady George Ransone b Oct. 16, 1906); (h) Mary Kate Smith b Dec. 22, 1871; d at two; (i) Annie Drayton Smith b Jan. 23, 1873; d Nov. 8, 1910 Cisco, Tex. (m William H. Key at Cisco, Tex. (d Sept. 12, 1903 Jacksonville, Tex.) and had; 1, Lucile Thelma Key b July 9, 1899 Dublin, Tex., of Jacksonville, Tex., m O. Looney 1920 Jacksonville, Tex. and had; (aa) James Key Looney b Dec. 3, 1923. William Key m second, Pearl Looney); (j) Minnie Lee Smith, of Center Point, Tex., (m Richard D. Wills and had; 1, Archie Lou Wills died when 16 at Center Point, Tex.)

Four. Robert William Reagan b Dec. 26, 1833; d Oct. 26, 1858, unmarried.

Five. Caroline Matilda Reagan b Sept. 4, 1836 in the old Stone Fort at Nacoydoches, Tex.; d Feb. 29, 1912 San Antonio, Tex.; married first, James J. Bagley Jan. 13, 1859 Rusk Co., Tex. and had; (a) James Robert Bagley b Apr 6, 1860, of Terrill, Hot Wells, San Antonio, Tex., m ———— ————; (b) Noble Reagan Bagley b July 5, 1862, of Old Colony Club, New York, m ———— ————. Caroline

Matilda Reagan m second, her first cousin, Robert Tunnell Cannon, May 19, 1867 Rusk Co., Tex. (b Feb. 24. 1836 Old Dallas, nr Chattanooga, Tenn.; d June 20, 1916 San Antonio, Tex., son of Benjamin Bartlett and Eliza Tunnell Cannon. See record of B. B. and Eliza Tunnell Cannon for descendants.

Six. Dr. Noble Marion Reagan b Mar. 22, 1839 Rusk Co., Tex.; d May 8, 1893 Joshua, Tex.; unmarried.

Seven. Mary Emily Reagan b Feb. 24, 1841 Rusk Co., Tex.; d Feb. 1, 1877 Corsiciana, Tex.; married Douglas J. Cater, son of William G. and Beatnah T. (Greening) Cater, May 22, 1866 (b Mar. 27, 1841 Sparta, Ala., attorney, San Antonio, Tex.) and had; (a) Clint Cater b abt 1867; d Apr. 22, 1870; (b) Rufus Cater b abt 1869; d Feb. 23, 1875; (c) Clyde Cater b abt 1872; d Nov. 4, 1875.

Eight. Helen Jane Reagan b Apr. 24, 1845 Rusk Co., Tex.; d Sept. 30, 1854 Rusk Co., Tex.

Nine. Harriet Albina Reagan b Aug. 16, 1849 nr Glenfawn, Tex.; d Aug. 17, 1900 Jacksonville, Tex.; married Charles Lewis Nunnally, son of Archie and Caroline (Spence) Nunnally, Dec. 16, 1869 (b Apr. 3, 1837 Milton, N. C.; d Mar. 26, 1913 Jacksonville, Tex.) and had ch b in Tex. (names may not be in order of birth); (a) Guy Reagan Nunnally b Jan. 26, 1872 nr Glenfawn, Tex., city tax assessor, Jacksonville, Tex. (m ———— ———— Sept. 1909 and had; 1, Dorothy Nunnally b Sept. 14, 1913; 2, Guy Reagan Nunnally b July 7, 1917; 3, James Edgar Nunnally b Apr. 20, 1924); (b) Charles Lewis Nunnally b Apr. 1873; d Dec. 17, 1919 (m Maud Evans and had; 1, Carrie Lee Nunnally b Aug. 13, 1907; 2, Willie Virginia Nunnally (deceased); (c) Carrie Estella Nunnally (m R. Mims and had; 1, Robert Mims b abt 1913); (d) Edmund Lee Nunnally, teacher, San Angelo, Tex. (m Jessie Kropp and had; 1, Edmund Lee Nunnally the second b 1912); (e) Robert Bruce Nunnally b Jan. 26, 1880 (m Kate Woods and had; 1, Robert Bruce Nunnally the second b 1912; 2, Reagan Wood Nunnally b 1915); (f) Marion Diehl Nunnally (m Anna Lee Barber and had; 1, Marion Diehl Nunnally the second; 2, Mary Frances Nunnally); (g) Daisy Nunnally, d in inf.; (h) Percy Nunnally, d in inf.; (i) Lawrence Nunnally, d in inf.

II. Susan Tunnell, daughter of Robert and Elizabeth Johnson Tunnell, was born abt 1807 Knox Co., Tenn. and died aft. 1830, Tenn. She married, in Tenn. a Mr. Johnson, whose first name is thought to have been Richard. Their children b in Tenn. may not be given in order of birth.

One. Susan Johnson is said to have married ———— Hart and moved to Missouri.

Two. Emily Johnson.

Three. Robert T. Johnson (known as Dick) b abt 1829. It is said he went to California as a "49-er" and that he was one of the pioneer orange growers near Los Angeles. It is thought he died unmarried. No further details on family of Susan Tunnell Johnson.

III.   Eliza Tunnell, daughter of Robert and Elizabeth Johnson Tunnell, was born Jan. 22, 1810 Knox Co., Tenn. and died June 9, 1847 Rusk Co., Texas.   Her marriage is recorded in the Bible of her father-in-law in this wise; "Benjamin Bartlett Cannon, eldest son of Zachariah and Elizabeth Cannon (before marriage Elizabeth Edgar) and Eliza Tunnell, third daughter of Robert and Elizabeth Tunnell (before marriage Elizabeth Johnson) were married on the third day of April 1828, by Samuel Fleming, Esq. in the house of Robert Tunnell, Knox Co., Tenn. Benjamin Bartlett Cannon was born Mar. 13, 1801 Jefferson Co., Tenn., and died Sept. 8, 1859 at San Augustine, Tex., while organizing a Masonic lodge.   He was one of the U. S. Commissioners who moved the' Indians from Tenn. and Georgia to Indian Territory 1835.   He was a member of the Fourth and Fifth legislatures of Tex. elected from Cherokee Co.   He introduced sundry bills and resolutions; among them one to establish a system of common schools, introduced Jan. 13, 1853.   He was known as "Free-School Cannon".   Children;

One.   Elizabeth Cannon b Feb. 15, 1829.

Two.   Mary Cannon b June 30, 1831.

Three.   Zachariah Henderson Cannon b June 6, 1833.

Four.   Robert Tunnell Cannon b Feb. 24, 1836.

Five.   Harriet Matilda Willoughby Cannon b June 4, 1838.

Six.   James Harrison Cannon b Nov. 24, 1840.

Seven.   Benjamin Bartlett Cannon Jr. b Oct. 12, 1843.

Eight.   George Douglas Riley Cannon b Mar. 4, 1846.

Of these;

One.   Elizabeth Cannon b Feb. 15, 1829 Knox Co., Tenn.; d Oct. 2, 1841 Harrison, Hamilton Co., Tenn.

Two.   Mary Cannon b June 30, 1831 Dallas, Hamilton Co., Tenn.; d 1893 Rusk, Tex; married ———— Mitchell and had; (a) James G. Mitchell, unmarried 1913; (b) Ben Mitchell, d unmarried; (c) Harriet Mitchell died 1891 (m ———— Mathis and had an only child that died young; (d) Mary Mitchell d 1893, unmarried.

Three.   Zachariah Henderson Cannon b June 6, 1833 Dallas, Hamilton Co., Tenn.; d Mar. 30, 1860 nr Seguin, Tex.; unmarried.

Four.   Robert Tunnell Cannon b Feb. 24, 1836 Dallas, Hamilton Co., Tenn.; d June 20, 1916 San Antonio, Tex; married his cousin, Caroline Matilda (Reagan) Bagley, dau of William and Matilda (Tunnell) Reagan, May 19, 1867 Rusk Co., Tex. (b Sept. 4, 1836 at the Fort at Nacoydoches, Tex.; d Feb. 29, 1912 San Antonio, Tex.) and had; (a) Zachariah William Cannon b June 20, 1868, real estate dealer, San Antonio, Tex. (m Gertrude Sanders July 22, 1891 Orange, Tex. (dau of Jabez Elisha and Eliza Jane (Laird) Sanders; grand-dau Jabez and Nancy (Russell) Sanders, of Abraham and Christine (Bean) Laird; great-g-d Daniel and Tamar (Weeks) Sanders, of Samuel (b Grayson Co., Va.) and Elizabeth (Doty) Russell, of Jacob and Matilda (Holcomb) Laird, of John and Winnie (Youngblood) Bean; g-g-gd Philip Russell) and had; 1, Violet Cannan b June 16, 1892 Orange, Tex., of San Antonio, Tex., m Robert Grant Coulter Feb. 18, 1922 San Antonio, Tex. (b Sept. 19, 1890; Capt. in the 90th Division during World War; of firm Cadwalder-Coulter Payne Advertising Agency; son of Charles Alvin (b June 15, 1859) and Lucy J. (Brown) Coulter (d Oct. 27, 1896 Brackenridge, Col.); g-s of Robert King Coulter (b Sept. 22, 1822; d Oct. 10, 1904 La Salle, Ill.) and wife, Mary E. Alliner Coulter (b June 2, 1826 Brownsville, Penn.); g-g-s Nicholas R. Brown (b Oct. 6, 1818; d Apr. 3, 1901 Peru, Ill.) and wife Hannah Pike (Kilborn) Brown (b May 30, 1825; d Oct. 17, 1877); 2, Leone Lillian Cannon b Jan. 11, 1894 Orange, Texas., of Uruguay, m George Pierce Collier Apr. 9, 1919 New York (served Over Seas in World War as Capt. of 90th Division; manager of Singer co., Montevedea, Uruguay; son of W. W. Collier (b Dec. 2, 1863 Rusk, Tex.) wife, Ella Patterson) Collier (d 1890); grandson Thomas Pierce Collier (b 1819 Huntsville, Ala., d Waco, Tex., of same Pierce ancestry as the fourteenth President of the United States) and wife, Susan Anna (Lewis) Collier (b 1823 Rome, Ga.; Waco, Tex.); g-g-s of Jonathan Collier and wife, Jane (Scholtze) Collier; of Lotspeich and Jane (Peyton) Lewis, of Va.) and had; (aa) George Pierce Collier the second b Feb. 1, 1920 Philadelphia, Penn.; (bb) Robert Patterson Collier b Aug. 6, 1924 San Antonio, Tex.; 3, George Noble Cannon b Nov. 1, 1897 Logansport, La., attorney, San Antonio, Tex; served as First Lieut. in Aerial service Over Seas in World War and was wounded; m Frances Post Nov. 6, 1923 Haskell, Tex.; 4, Robert Benton Cannon b Apr. 3, 1899 nr Overton, Tex., auditor in government service, San Antonio, Tex., unmarried; 5, Hazel Eliza Cannon b Oct. 2, 1901 nr Overton, Tex., m John Bachman Lee Greer July 16, 1921 San Antonio, Tex. (served as Ensign in Navy during World war; of Greer Farrell Insurance Co., Waco, Tex.) and had; (aa) John Bachman Lee Greer, the second, b Oct. 20, 1923 Waco, Texas. Acknowledgement is here made for the valuable assistance rendered by Mrs. Gertrude Sanders Cannon in preparing record of the family of Robert and Elizabeth Johnson Tunnell); (b) Ethel Matilda Cannon b Mar. 25, 1870; d Feb. 26, 1875; (c) Carrie May Cannon b Oct. 6, 1874 Old London, Rusk Co., Tex. (m W. H. Taliaferro Feb. 24, 1901 Rusk Co., Tex. (b Apr. 13, 1869 nr Rome, Ga., son of Dickerson Taliaferro Jr., of Va.) and had; 1, Noble Edge Taliaferro b Apr. 22, 1905 Overton, Tex.; 2, Robert Newell Taliaferro b June 17, 1904 Overton, Tex.; 3, William Herbert Taliaferro b May 16, 1908 Old London, Rusk Co., Tex.; d Jan. 27, 1913 San Antonio, Tex.; 4, Cecil Glen Taliaferro b Mar. 11, 1911 San Antonio, Tex.; 5, Roy Reagan Taliaferro b Jan. 12, 1914 San Antonio, Tex.); (d) Mollie Cannon b Oct. 9, 1877 Old London, Tex. (m W. H. Claiborne Nov. 1912 San Antonio, Tex. (b Sept. 1874 East Tenn.) and had; 1, Carrie Marie Claiborne b Feb. 11, 1915; d Oct. 11, 1920 Huntsville, Tex.; 2, Martha

Lee Claiborne, twin with Carrie Marie Claiborne, b Feb. 11, 1915; 3, W. H. Claiborne, the second, b Sept. 11, 1920 Huntsville, Tex.)

Five. Harriet Matilda Willoughby Cannon b June 4, 1838 Dallas, Hamilton Co., Tenn.; d in Texas; married James T. Deckerd (d 1866 Palestine, Tex.) and had ch b Rusk Co., Tex.; (a) Julia Deckerd, of Dallas, Tex., m John Patton; (b) William David Deckerd b 1859, of Rusk, Tex. (m Dolly Ridley June 7, 1888 and had ch b Rusk, Tex.; 1, Jim Oleta Deckerd b Apr. 6, 1889, m Marshall D. McCord Apr. 16, 1909 and had; (aa) Edward Deckerd McCord b Apr. 4, 1910; (bb) David McCord b Aug. 28, 1912; (cc) James McCord b Nov. 16, 1920; (dd) Helen Katheryne McCord b July 11, 1922; 2, Julia Deckerd b Nov. 8. 1890, m John McDonald Feb. 23, 1908 Rusk, Tex. and had ch b Rusk, Tex.; (aa) Virginia Eloise McDonald b May 15, 1910; (bb) Lucille Deckerd McDonald b Apr. 4, 1913; d Sept. 22, 1915; (cc) Rose Mildred McDonald b Mar. 31, 1921; 3, Belle Deckard b Aug. 30, 1892, m Tom H. Singleton, the second b Mar. 11, 1918; 4, May Deckerd b Mar. 3, 1895, m W. Elmer Pate Sept. 18, 1919 Rusk, Tex. and had; (aa) Ulysses Francis (daughter) b Sept. 13, 1918; 6, John Iby Deckerd b June 3, 1903).

Six. James Harrison Cannon b Nov. 24, 1840 "in the vicinity of the town of Harrison, Tenn." (Bible record); d Jan. 4, 1914 Rusk Co., Tex.; unmarried.

Seven. Benjamin Bartlett Cannon Jr. b Oct. 12, 1843 Harrison, Tenn.; d May 20, 1924 Arlington, Texas; married Margaret Amanda Knight, dau of O. W. Knight, Dec. 7, 1876 Dallas, Tex. (b Aug. 24, 1856, now of El Paso, Tex.) and had ch b Jacksonville, Texas, save one; (a) Bessie Rena Cannon, of El Paso, Tex. (m Rufus Parker March in 1908 and had; 1, Martha Margaret March b 1909; 2, Rufus Parker March Jr. b 1913); (b) Benjamin Bartlett Cannon, the third, b July 4, 1879, of Webster Groves, Mo., regional directon Glidden Co. St. Louis, m Estelle Ham 1911 and had; 1, Benjamin Bartlett Cannon, the Fourth, b July 6, ———; 2, George Ham Cannon b Nov. 3, ——— 3, Margaret Adelaide Cannon b Aug. 7, ———); (c) Epps Knight Cannon b Mar. 16, 1881, salesman, unmarried, Arlington, Tex.; (d) Edward Lee Cannon b Oct. 30, 1883, salesman, St. Joe, Tex., m Ardella Cannon Nov. 1923, who, though bearing same surname is not a relative; (e) Arch R. Cannon b June 12, 1885, salesman, Arlington, Tex. (m Zorah Hatton and had; 1, James Benjamin Cannon); 6, Frank F. Cannon b July 14, 1894 Weatherford, Tex., unmarried, salesman, St. Louis, Mo.; and two daughters and a son who died in inf.

Eight. George Douglas Riley Cannon b Mar. 4, 1846 Harrison, Tenn.; "died on board the boat between the Muscle Shoals and Florence, Alabama on the 4th of April 1847 and was buried in the burying ground at Florence, Ala." (Bible record). The parents were moving to Texas and the mother died shortly after the arrival at her sister's, Mrs. William Reagan.

IV. James Tunnell, son of Robert and Elizabeth Johnson Tunnell,

was born abt 1812.   He was one of the fifty-two citizens of Chattanooga, Tenn. when the town was organized in 1838.   It is thought
he died before 1845, unmarried.

V.   Noble Tunnell, son of Robert and Elizabeth Johnson Tunnell, was born abt 1814, Knox Co., Tenn.   His father wrote a brother,
Calvin Tunnell, May 1, 1845 from Harrison, Tenn., "our son, N. J.
Tunnell, has moved to Newton Co., Mo., the nearest post office to him
in Bentonville, Arkansas."   Noble J. Tunnell had first cousins, the
Coulters, at Cane Hill, Ark. and visited them, took sick and abt 1846
returned to Tenn.

VI.   William Tunnell, son of Robert and Elizabeth Johnson
Tunnell, was born abt 1817.   In 1845 his father wrote "William has
gone down the river for some time.   I look for him back in a few
weeks."   It is said William Tunnell went to Calif. to his nephew,
Dick Johnson and that he was in Rusk Co., Tex. in the 1850's to visit
his sisters.

VII.   Mary Louise Tunnell, dau of Robert and Elizabeth Johnson
Tunnell, was born July 1819 Knox Co., Tenn. and died Mar. 2, 1880 nr
Tompson, Tex.   She married Dr. William Woolwine abt 1834 in Tenn.
(b June 14, 1814 Christiansburg, Va.; d May, 1870 Rusk Co., Tex.)
They moved from nr Chattanooga, Tenn., to Rusk Co., Tex., and he
practised medicine a number of years at Caledonia, Tex.   Children;

One.   Margaret Woolwine b 1836.
Two.   Maria Louise Woolwine b 1840.
Three.   son b 1842; d in inf.
Four.   Harriet Matilda Woolwine b Apr. 1, 1844.
Five.   Nancy Emily Woolwine b Apr. 18, 1846.
Six.   Virginia Tennessee Woolwine b Dec. 31, 1848.
Seven.   son b abt 1850; d in inf.
Eight.   Louemma Douthit Woolwine b Apr. 8, 1853.
Nine.   Gulia Elma Woolwine b Jan. 18, 1856.
Ten.   son b Dec. 1857; d in inf.
Eleven.   Henrietta Letitia Woolwise b July 6, 1859.
Of these;

One.   Margaret Woolwine b 1836 in Tenn.; d 1859 in Tex.; married Oliver Branch, in Tex. and had; (a) Laura Branch (m James Carroll in Nacoydoches Co., Tex. and had at least one child; 1, ————
Carroll, who m Lee Cotton and had at least one child, a son, of Sils-
bee, Tex., 1924); (b) Mary Emily Branch died Nacoydoches, Tex., m
Sam Davis and had children.

Two.   Maria Louise Woolwine b 1840 in Tenn.; d 1879 in Tex.;
married first, Lucian Polk, who d during the War Between the States,
and had; (a) William Polk, died small; (b) Charles Woolwine Polk.
She m second, John Keating and had; (c) Mollie Keating; (d) Arthur
Keating, of County Line, Tex., (e)   Minnie   Keating;   (d)   Arthur
Tex., m ———— Gilbreath.

Three.   Son b 1842 in Tenn.; d in infancy, in Tenn.
Four.   Harriet Matilda Woolwine b Apr. 1, 1844 Caledonia, Tex.;
d Nov. 27, 1923 Tipson, Tex.; married Rev. George N. Weaver Nov. 2,

1865 (b Nov. 9, 1844 Calloway Co., Ky.) and had; (a) William Woolwine Weaver b Aug. 3, 1866 Center, Tex.; carpenter; Clarksburg, Calif. (m Letitia Hardage 1888 (d 1902) and had; 1, Floyd Weaver, of Cleburne, Tex; 2, Clyde Weaver, of Richardson, Tex.; 3, Homer Weaver, deceased; 4, Zannie Weaver, of Cleburne, Tex.; 5, Max Weaver, of Cleburne, Tex.; 6, Harold Weaver, deceased; 7, Mason Weaver); (b) Elbert Newton Weaver b Oct. 28, 1869 Center, Tex., of Los Angeles, Calif. (m Nellie Wallace June 2, 1900 and had ch b Timpson, Tex.; 1, Harriet Lynett Weaver b Apr. 1902; 2, Elbert Wallace Weaver b Mar. 6, 1908; d 1910 Timpson, Tex.; 3, Nellie Vesta Weaver b Aug. 1911); (c) Minnie Lee Weaver b Aug. 1, 1872 Timpson, Tex., of Dallas, Tex. (m Jim Frank Rhodes Dec. 23, 1893 and had ch b Timpson, Tex.; 1, Mable Olin Rhodes b Sept. 15, 1894; 2, Cyril Weaver Rhodes b Nov. 6, 1895, m ———— ————; 3, Gladys Rhodes b Mar. 1895, of Dallas, Tex., m John West Morton· 4, Emma Evelyn Rhodes b Mar. 1899, of San Antonio, Tex., m W. H. Fuller; 5, Inez Rhodes b Mar. 1902, of Dallas, Tex., m Jack Jones; 6, Frank Rhodes b Oct. 1905; 7, Vida Rhodes b Oct. 1907; 8, Walton Rhodes b 1910; 9, Edmund Rhodes b 1912, deceased); (d) Herman R. Weaver b Mar. 14, 1874 Timpson, Tex., of Merryville, La. (m Anna Lyttleton Sept. 1902 and had ch b Timpson, Tex.; 1, Lyttleton Weaver b Jan. 7, 1906; 2, Elizabeth Weaver b Aug. 1911); (e) Carrie Cannon Weaver b July 31, 1878 Timpson, Tex., of San Augustin, Tex. (m Edward Boone Brackett Jr. b June 15, 1905 Timpson, Tex.; 2, Harriet Carolyn Vivian Brackett b Mar. 12, 1911 Woodson, Tex.); (f) Mytt Weaver, twin, b Dec. 20, 1882 Timpson, Tex., of Timpson (m T. Pierce Whiteside Sept. 1906 Timpson and had ch b there; 1, Helen Maurine Whiteside b Aug. 1907; 2, Russell Errett Whiteside b Aug. 1910; 3, Blanche Whiteside b 1916; 4, Rudolph Emerson Whiteside b 1918); (g) Mae Weaver, twin of Mytt Weaver, b Dec. 20, 1882, of Timpson, Tex. (m James A. Arnold May 1908 Breckenridge, Tex., and had; 1, James A. Arnold Jr. b Apr. 1909 Crockett, Tex.); (h) Raymond A. Weaver b July 22, 1889 Timpson, Tex., of Arlington, Tex. (m Blanche Haynes 1911 and had 1, Dorothy Rae Weaver b 1912 Breckenridge, Tex.; 2, Camille Weaver b 1914 Timpson, Tex.; 3, Mary Jane Weaver b 1920 Arlington, Tex.)

Five. Nancy Emily Woolwine b Apr. 6, 1846 nr Mt. Enterprise, Tex., of Timpson, Tex.; married William H. Evans 1864 Rusk Co., Tex. (b 1833 N. C.; d 1878 Tex.) and had ch b Tex.; (a) Estella Evans b 1865; d June 19, 1922 Akens, Tex., (m Dr. Robert Boothe and had; 1, Edwin Boothe, salesman, Nacoydoches, Tex., m Annie Rhodes and had; (aa) R. E. Boothe b 1912; (bb) Thomas Boothe; (cc) Bryan Boothe; (dd) Barham Boothe; 2, Vera Boothe, m John Hargis and had; (aa) Ruth Hargis; (bb) Marguerite Hargis; (cc) John Hargis Jr.; (dd) Estilla Hargis); (b) Marietta Evans b 1869 (m W. H. Emmons (d Dec. 1919) and had; 1, Willie Mae Emmons, m Lee Weaver and had; (aa) Lucile Weaver; 2, Henrietta Emmons, of Houston, Tex., m

Bernard Hooper and had; (aa) May Helen Hooper; 3, Durward Emmons b 1900, of Beaumont, Tex., m ———— ————; 4, Jessie Emmons, m A. Strasden); (c) Zachariah Evans b 1870 of Long View, Tex. (m Lillie Renshaw and had; 1, Lena Evans m H. O. Day, of San Marcos, Tex.; 2, Thomas Evans); (d) William Woolwine Evans died Nov. 2, 1822 Timpson, Tex. (m Nora Avery and had; 1, Dumah Evans b Jan. 23, 1900· Avery Evans b Dec. 27, 1903; 3, Paul Evans b Sept. 6, 1906; 4, Mary Evans b June 16, 1910; 5, Sarah Evans b Apr. 12, 1912.

Six. Virginia Tennessee Woolwine b Dec. 31, 1848 Rusk Co., Tex., of Center, Tex., and Shrevesport, La., was given a name in honor of the native states of her parents. She married Samuel W. Weaver son of George and Elizabeth (Freeland Weaver, July 30, 1867 Logansport, La. (b Jan. 20, 1834 Murray Co., Tenn.; d May 4, 1902 Timpson, Tex.) and had; (a) Ernest Weaver b Jan. 25, 1869 Center, Tex., land and timber commissioner of Center, Tex. (m Delaney (Whitson) Weaver, dau of Joe and Mary Whitson, Dec. 20, 1908 Center, Tex. (b July 15, 1879; d Apr. 7, 1923 Center, Tex.) and had; 1, Damon Weaver b Nov. 12, 1909 Timpson, Tex.; 2, Louise Weaver b Aug. 14, 1912 Waterman, Tex.; 3, Ray Weaver b June 13, 1914 Timpson, Tex.; 4, Earl Weaver b Oct. 28, 1916 Timpson, Tex.); (b) Noble Weaver b June 4, 1870 Center, Tex., with Pickering Lumber Co., Center, Tex. (m Ida Whitson, sister of Delaney Whitson); (c) Vernon Forsyth Weaver b Mar. 30, 1872 Center, Tex., in Wholesale grocery business, Center, Tex. (m Bunyan Dillon); (d) Robert Tunnell Weaver b Oct. 4, 1874 Center, Tex.; d Sept. 12, 1897 Rusk Co., Tex. (m Delaney Whitson, dau Joe and Mary Whitson (b July 15, 1879; d Apr. 7, 1923 Center, Tex.) and had; 1, Robert Weaver b Nov. 5, 1897 nr Timpson, Tex.; d Nov. 14, 1918 Longview, Tex., m Bernie Baron and had; (aa) Robert Weaver the third, b abt 1917); (e) Tolbert Fanning Weaver b Sept. 5, 1876 Timpson, Tex., Evangelist of Houston, Tex. (m Elizabeth Crews at Woodville, Tex. and had; 1, Tolbert Weaver. The President of the Christian Ministers Association of Houston, Tex. says of Rev. T. F. Weaver "we know him to be a preacher of marked ability, true to the world and persuasive. Rich experience has proven that he is gifted in the high art of soul winning. During the years of his pastorate in our city he has done an outstanding work for the Kingdom; he has exemplified the highest type of Christian living and service. All who meet him readily become his friends and feel that their lives are enriched by his exceptionally fine spirit, high ideals and loyal helpfullness"); (f) Ada Lucille Weaver b Sept. 29, 1878 Timpson, Tex., of Shrevesport, La., whose songs of a religious nature may appropriately be used in her brother's ecclesiastical work, (m John Emory Wilmore at Timpson, Tex. (b Jan. 1, 1879 Lexington, Va. with Standard Oil Co. Shrevesport, La.) and had ch b Longview, Tex.; 1, Emory Wilmore b Nov. 9, 1909; 2, Carlton Wilmore b Nov. 18, 1914); (g) Woolwine Douthit Weaver b July 1, 1880 Timpson, Tex., in wholesale grocery business, Center, Tex.

(m Bessie Canada at Port Arthur, Tex., and had; 1, Leonard Weaver; 2, Glenn Weaver); (h) Marion Martin Weaver b Apr. 5, 1888, in wholesale grocery business, Center, Tex. (m Stella Scruggs, in Miss. and had; 1, Malvolm Weaver; 2, Martin Weaver).

Eight. Louemma Douthit Woolwine b Apr. 8, 1853 Rusk Co. Tex., of Timpson, Tex.; married first, John Forsyth Sept. 8, 1870 Center, Tex. (b 1849 Tenn.; d 1874, soldier in the War Between the States) and had two children. She married second, Charles S. Haden 1877 Rusk Co., Tex. (d Dec. 1906) and had ten children; all b in or near Timpson, Tex.; (a) Ella Forsyth b July 12, 1871; d Nov. 14, 1908; (b) Jonnie Forsyth (daughter) b 1874; d 1876; (c) Antoinette Haden b Sept. 21, 1878 (m E. W. Victory Apr. 1906 Shrevesport, La. (d May 1910) and had; 1, Charlton Douglas Victory b July 1908 Timpson, Tex.); (d) Charles Clinton Haden, twin, b June 5, 1881 Timpson, Tex., electrician of Timpson, Tex. (m first, Birdie Harkrider Aug. 22, 1905 (d 1920) and had; 1, Martha Haden b 1908; 2, Lucile Haden b 1911; and m second, Cecil McEntire and had; 3, Charles McEntire Haden); (e) Wesley Woolwine Haden, twin of Charles Clinton Haden, b June 5, 1881, Christian minister (m Lillian Denard Nov.4, 1903 and had; 1, Denard Haden b 1908; 2, Rachel Haden b 1914); (f) Beulah Benton Haden b Aug. 10, 1883 Timpson, Tex.; d Sept. 24, 1914 (m Aber Collins Nov. 1901 and had; 1, Thomas Haden Collins b 1903; 2, Helen Miller Collins b 1907); (g) Sudie Roache Haden b May 29, 1885, Timpson, Tex., of Houston, Tex., m W. M. Ross 1907; (h) Daniel D. Haden b Sept. 13, 1887; d Mar. 11, 1910, unmarried.; (i) Clyde S. Haden b May 20, 1890, pharmacist, m Vesta Smith Nov. 21, 1907 and had no ch.; (j) Thomas Tunnell Haden b Sept. 17, 1892, unmarried, theatre manager, Timpson, Tex.

Nine. Gulia Elma Woolwine b Jan. 18, 1856 Rusk Co., Tex., of Clarksburg, Calif.; married first, James Reagan Vaught, son of Dr. James and Nancy(Tunnell) Vaught, Apr. 9, 1874 Nacoydoches Co., Tex. (b Apr. 13. 1851 Rusk Co., Tex.; d Jan. 1, 1914 nr Ragley, Tex); and second, L. Houston Weaver, son of George and Elizabeth (Freeland) Weaver. Children; (a) Charles Vaught b Feb. 23, 1875 Nacoydoches Co., Tex. farmer; unmarried; (b) Florence Vaught b Jan. 5, 1877 Nacoydoches Co. Tex., of Clarksburg, Calif. (m first, Everett Weaver Dec. 31, 1895 Panola Co., Tex. and had; 1, Lee Weaver b Feb. 19, 1896 Panola Co., Tex., veteran of World War, singer, of New York; and m second, Ernest Ellington Jan. 13, 1921 in Calif.); (c) Robert Rains Vaught b Mar. 28, 1883 Panola Co., Tex.; d Jan. 24, 1919 (m Jennie Guthrie Feb. 4, 1905 Panola Co. (b Aug. 24, 1884) and had; 1, Lenora Vaught b Dec. 5, 1906 Gary, Tex., of Coleman, Tex., m Marvin Kempt Jan. 7, 1923; 2, Elva Vaught b Aug. 2, 1909 Gary, Tex.; 3, Clarice Vaught b Aug. 22, 1911 Gary, Tex.; 4, Rachel Vaught b Nov. 2, 1913 Gary, Tex.; 5, Robert Vaught b Sept. 25, 1915; 6, William Vaught b May 18, 1919 Smith Co., Tex.); (d) Lula Vaught b Nov. 4, 1886 Rusk Co., Tex., of Omen, Tex., (m Dr. Sheldon Ferguson Nov.

20, 1907 Shrevesport, La. and had no ch.); (e) Norman Vaught b Jan. 1, 1888; d June 11, 1918 in training camp at Camp Travis, San Antonio, Tex.

Eleven. Henrietta Letitia Woolwine b July 6, 1859 Rusk Co., Tex., of Timpson, Tex.; married William Henry King, son of George and Irene (Williams) King, (b Jan. 20, 1851 Shelby Co., Tex.) and had ch. save one, Price, b Shelby Co., Tex.; (a) Mary Irene King b Mar. 6, 1877, of Timson, Tex. (m T. J. Herrington, a contractor and had ch b Shelby Co., Tex.; 1 Herbert Herrington b Oct. 27, 1894, served in World War, of Shrevesport, La., m Nadina Nelson and had; (aa) Wanda Fay Herrington b 1923; 2, Guy Herrington b Mar. 14, 1899, with Southern Pacific, Dibrell, Tex., m Rachel Cooper and had; (aa) Charles Wayne Herrington b 1921; (bb) Chrystelle Herrington b 1924; 3, Thelma Irene Herrington b July 18, 1900; 4, Willie James Herrington b July 14, 1908); (b) Della Mae King b May 16, 1880 Shelby Co., Tex., of Lafkin, Tex., (m W. T. Denard, foreman of Gulp Pipe Line Co., and had ch b Shelby Co.; 1, Mable Loraine Denard b Mar. 3, 1906; 2, Marguerite Denard b Jan. 1, 1910; 3, Doris Denard b Aug. 15, 1914; 4, Barbara Denard b Oct. 30, 1918); (c) Woolwine King b May 3, 1882 Shelby Co., Tex.; d July 9, 1918 Beaumont, Tex. (m first, Addie Strode (d Mar. 27, 1907) and had 1, Addie Mozelle King b June 29, 1903, of Nacoydoches, Tex., m Elton Hartsfield, a salesman; 2, Annie Estelle King b Apr. 10, 1905; d Feb. 28, 1913 Timpson, Tex.; and m second, Nettie Moye and had; 3, Billie Maurine King b Nov. 23, 1912); (d) William Howard King b July 5, 1886, furniture dealer, Port Arthur, Tex. (m Cornelia Chatwin, of Los Angeles, Calif., and had; 1, Howard King b Mar. 16, 1914 Beaumont, Tex.; Audrey King b May 26, 1918); (e) Charles Hubbard King b Dec. 15, 1887, planter, Rusk Co., Tex. (m Laura Cubbins and had ch b Rusk Co.; 1, Billie King (daughter) b Sept. 26, 1914; 2, Laverne King b Jan. 20, 1920); (f) Amanda King b Jan. 6, 1892 (m Louis Tinkle, merchant, San Antonio, Tex., and had; 1, Louis Tinkle Jr. b June 22, 1916, Tyler, Tex.; d June 8, 1923 San Antonio, Tex.; 2, David Tinkle b May 30, 1921 San Antonio); (g) Price King b Oct. 22, 1893 Nacoydoches Co., Tex., manager furniture store, Beaumont, Tex. (m Gatling Hunter, of Merryville, La., and had; 1, Virginia Lee King b Apr. 1, 1916 Shelby Co., Tex.); (h) Ruth King b Jan. 6, 1895 (m John Marion Britt, 1920, agent S. P. R. R., Timpson, Tex. and had no children).

VIII. Harriet N. Tunnell, dau of Robert and Elizabeth Johnson Tunnell, was born Nov. 15, 1821 Knox Co., Tenn. and died Feb. 4, 1899 Corsicana, Tex. She married Rev. William Harle, son of Baldwin and Isabella (Miller) Harle, who were married Feb. 13, 1800 Blount Co., Tenn., and grandson of Colonel Baldwin Harle, Feb. 7, 1837 in Tenn. He was born Mar. 8, 1812 in Tenn. and died Jan. 11, 1863 in Tex. They moved to Rusk Co., Tex. about 1846. Children;

One. Robert Baldwin Harle b Feb. 13, 1838.

Two. James Leonard Harle b Sept. 11, 1841.
Three. William F. Harle b Apr. 17, 1845.
Four. Emma Adeline Harle b Aug. 23, 1848.
Five. Florence Adella Harle b Sept. 1, 1852.
Six. Angie Harle b Apr. 26, 1855.
Seven. Isabelle Elizabeth Harle b Feb. 28, 1857.
Of these;
One. Robert Baldwin Harle b Feb. 13, 1838, lived many years in Corsicana, Tex.; d Mar. 18, 1911; married first, Emma T. Brown, Feb. 21, 1867 (b Aug. 23, 1870) Robertson Co., Tex) and had; (a) Carie Harle b July 6, 1870, of Los Angeles, Calif., m C. H. Nix. He m second, Mrs. Ella Patton, Mar. 1878, Corsicana, Tex. and had; (b) Clyde Harle; (c) Earle Harle, of Ft. Worth, Tex.; (d) Lottie Harle.
Two. James Leonard Harle b Sept. 11, 1841 Tenn.; d Apr. 22, 1901, unmarried. He was county judge of Navarro Co., Tex. and was one mayor of Corsicana.
Three. William F. Harle b Apr. 17, 1845; d Oct. 1903; married Emma Jane Powell June 30, 1874 and had; (a) Leonard Harle, of San Antonio, Tex.; (b) John Harle; (c) William Harle; (d) Sydney Harle; (e) Angie May Harle.
Four. Emma Adeline Harle b Aug. 23, 1848 Rusk Co., Tex.; d Sept. 25, 1869 Rusk Co., Tex.; unmarried.
Five. Florence Adella Harle b Sept. 1, 1852 Rusk Co., Tex.; d July 27, 1895, Corsicana, Tex.; unmarried.
Six. Angie Harle b Apr. 26, 1855 Rusk Co., Tex., of El Paso, Tex.; married Marion Martin Oct. 22, 1877 Corsicana, Tex., son of James and Elizabeth (Cofield) Martin) and had; (a) Marion Martin Jr., b Dec. 27, 1880, of El Paso, Tex. (m Elizabeth Alberta Scott Jan. 26, 1910 (b Jan. 23, 1885 Freestone Co., Tex.) and had; 1, Angie Elizabeth Martin b May 14, 1919 Corsicana, Tex.); (b) May Martin b May 29, 1883; d Oct. 2, 1896 Corsicana, Tex.; (c) Frank Martin b Sept. 14, 1885; d Jan. 30, 1916, unmarried, Corsicana; and others who died in infancy. In 1859 Marion Martin was elected to the State Senate and took a conspicious place among workers of that body and opposed secession. In 1875 he was delegate to the Constitutional Convention. He was a member of the 16th and 17th senates and in 1882 was elected Lieut. Governor of his adopted state, Texas.
Seven. Isabelle Elizabeth Harle b Feb. 28, 1857 Rusk Co., Tex.; d Oct. 15, 1875, Corsicana, Tex.; unmarried.
IX. "Emily Jane Mortimer Tunnell, sixth daughter of Robert and Elizabeth (Johnson) Tunnell, was born in Knox Co., Tenn. on the 30th day of May 1824", so reads the record in the Cannon Bible. She died Feb. 8, 1865 in Texas. She married James Wyley Harle, son of Baldwin and Isabella (Miller) Harle (married Feb. 13, 1800 Blount Co., Tenn.); and grandson of Colonel Baldwin Harle, and of David Miller, a relative of Mary (Ball) Washington, mother of the first President of the United States. She married Feb. 6, 1865 in Texas. James Wyle Harle was born Sept. 12, 1814 in Tenn. and died May 26, 1869 in Texas. Their ch were born near Nacoydoches, Tex.
One. Child born and died June 11, 1856.
Two. Child, twin with "One", born and died June 11, 1856.
Three. Angie McFarland Harle b Aug. 28, 1857.
Four. Bascom Harle b July 18, 1859.
Five. Matilda Reagan Harle b July 27, 1861.
Six. Matilda McFarland Harle b July 28, 1863.
Seven. Yelberson Harle b Aug. 5, 1864.
Of these;
Three Angie McFarland Harle b Aug. 28, 1857, of Kilgore, Tex.;

married first, John Milton McDavid Nov. 8, 1882 (b Mar. 3, 1842; d Feb. 1885) and had; (a) Grover Cleveland McDavid b Aug. 11, 1884 nr Overton, Tex., druggist of Timpson, Tex. (m Ewing McKay May 1906 and had; 1, Finis Eugene McDavid b Jan. 13, 1907).   Angie McFarland Harle married second, William A Mullikin Apr. 26, 1888 and had; (b) Bonnie Laura Mullikin b Jan. 7, 1889, of Moonshine Hill, Tex. (m Joe J. Parker Aug. 23, 1922 and had; 1, Joe Parker b May 8, 1923); (c) Willie Mullikin b Feb. 25, 1890; d Aug. 23, 1892; (d) Beulah Florida Mullikin b July 28, 1891, of Houston, Tex. (m James Irl Laird Dec. 27, 1917 and had; 1, Joe Alex Laird b Oct. 3, 1918; 2, Emily Ruth Laird b Mar. 21, 1921; 3, Margaret Elizabeth Laird b July 13, 1922); (e) Hayne Dickson Mullikin b Mar. 6, 1893, unmarried, of Houston, Tex.; (f) Angie Mary Mullikin b Jan. 19, 1896, of Kilgore, Tex. (m James Romy Elliott Apr. 12, 1915 and had; 1, James McFarland Elliott b Jan. 31, 1919.

Four.   Bascom Harle b July 18, 1859; d Nov. 24, 1897 Logansport, La.; married Sue Ella McDavid, dau of Robert and Frances Christina McDavid, Nov. 18, 1889 Fountainhead, Tex. (b Aug. 11, 1872 Overton, Tex.; d July 23, 1903 Timpson, Tex.) and had; (a) James Wiley Harle b Aug. 11, 1890, manager manufacturing department Gulf Refining Co., Port Arthur, Tex.; served in World War with 36th Co. 165 D. B. Camp Travis, Tex. (m Mable Alma Stark, dau of James Burrough and Sallie Mae (House) Stark, Mar. 20, 1924 (b Nov. 17, 1905 Saratoga, Tex.) and had twin sons; 1, James Burrough Harle b Dec. 1, 1924 Port Arthur, Tex; 2, Wiley Bascom Harle b Dec. 1, 1924 Port Arthur, Tex.); (b) Francis Marion Harle b Aug. 8, 1892, druggist of Port Author, Tex., served in World War with 36th Division, landed at Brest on his birthday, Aug. 8, 1918, went into action in relief of units of Second Division on night of Oct. 6th, was attached to French Army under command of Gen. Gouraurd, wounded Oct. 8th at Medah Farm, Mount Branc, lost right arm and was discharged from service Mar. 29, 1919.   He m Ethel Latham, dau of Jonathan M. and Emma Latham, Mar. 22, 1920 (b Dec. 5, 1894 Jacksonville, Florida) and had; 1, Oliver Latham Harle b Jan. 31, 1921 Port Arthur, Tex.; 2, Wilma Ann Harle b Jan. 25, 1925 Port Arthur, Tex.); (c) Wilma Bascom Harle b Jan. 5, 1895, of San Diego, Calif. (m William LeRoy Garth Dec. 23, 1914 (b Sept. 17, 1893 Dubuque, Iowa; physician and surgeon, son of Dr. James William and Esther (Tyrrell) Garth and grandson Dr. Thomas Garth) and had; 1, William LeRoy Garth, the second, b Sept .26, 1915 Tulsa, Okla.; 2, Wilma Harle Garth b May 23, 1918 Beaumont, Tex.); (d) Robert Yelberson Harle b Aug. 24, 1896, auditor, Port Arthur, Tex., served as First Lieut. 358th Inf. and 79th Inf. in the 90th Div., with over seas service (m Frances Ellen Caldwell, dau James Pearce and Frances Ellen (Schofield) Caldwell, Jan. 1, 1919 Coleman, Tex. (b Mar. 22, 1897 San Marcos, Tex.) and had ch b Port Arthur, Tex.; 1, Joe Pearce Harle b Nov. 12, 1919; 2, Samuel Neil Harle b July 31, 1924).

Five.   Matilda Reagan Harle b Aug. 27, 1861; d small.

Six.   Matilda McFarland Harle b July 28, 1863; married William McDavid Nov. 8, 1882 Henderson, Tex. (b Aug. 11, 1857, brother of John McDavid who married her sister) and had ch. b nr Overton, Tex.; (a) Angie Maude McDavid b Sept. 8, 1883; d Oct. 30, 1901 Overton, Tex.; (b) Mary Elliott McDavid b Dec. 3, 1884, of Grand Junction, Colorado (m Ben H. Simpson July 29, 1912 Salt Lake City, Utah and had; 1, Marion Simpson b Sept. 21, 1917 Glade Park, Col.; 2, Allen McDavid Simpson b Feb. 19, 1920 Glade Park, Col.; 3, Julian Erle Simpson b Jan. 7, 1923 Grand Junction, Col.); (c) Bascom Erle McDavid b Nov. 6, 1886, in mercantile business Overton, Tex., m

Delia Wherry Hill May 10, 1911; (d) James Allen McDavid b Dec. 9, 1888, organized a Company at Abilene, Tex. Aug. 1917, was First Lieut. of 142nd Inf. and died at Camp Bowie, Ft. Worth, Tex., May 8, 1918; (e) Nina Alma McDavid b Mar. 14, 1891 (m Kos Rogers Dec. 25, 1916 Overton, Tex. and had ch b Overton, Tex.; 1, Agnes Eloise Rogers b Sept. 16, 1920; 2, William Harle Rogers b July 22, 1922); (f) Agnes Emily McDavid b Feb. 6, 1893, unmarried; (g) Daisie Merle McDavid b Jan. 30, 1897; d Nov. 20, 1897; (i) Linnie Fay McDavid b Nov. 30, 1898, of Yancey, Tex., m Polk Childress Jr. Dec. 15, 1923 Ft. Worth, Tex.; (j) Bertha Elva McDavid b Dec. 7, 1900, unmarried; (k) Grace Eloise McDavid b Mar. 14, 1905.

Seven. Yelberson Harle b Aug. 5, 1864, of San Marcos, Tex.; married Hester Pearl ——— and had no children.

X. Nancy Tunnell, dau of Robert and Elizabeth Johnson Tunnell was born Aug. 6, 1828 in Tenn. ("Cumberland mountain region") and died Sept. 19, 1907 Garrison, Tex. Her middle name has been given as both Jane and Judson. She married Dr. James B. Vaught abt 1850 Rusk Co., Tex. (b Jan. 10, 1816 Jackson Co., Ala.; d Jan. 12, 1879 nr Nacoydoches, Tex.) and had ch b Nacoydoches Co., Tex.

One. James Reagan Vaught b Apr. 13, 1851.
Two. William Meigs Vaught b Aug. 18, 1857.
Three. Zachariah Cannon Vaught b May 28, 1859.
Four. Thomas Garrett Vaught b Aug. 16, 1862.
Five. Robert Tunnell Vaught, twin, b Aug. 16, 1862.
Of these;

One. James Reagan Vaught b Apr. 13, 1851; d Jan. 1914 nr Ragley, Tex.; married first, his cousin, Gulia Elma Woolwine, dau of Dr. William and Mary Louise (Tunnell) Woolwine, Apr. 9, 1874 Nacoydoches Co., Tex. (b Jan. 18, 1856 Rusk Co., Tex.) For children see record of Mary Louise Tunnell Woolwine. James Reagan Vaught married second, Martha (Moore) Hensley Franklin, of Timpson, Tex., and had; (f) Dolly Vaught, deceased; (g) Lola Vaught, twin with Dolly Vaught, of Mt. Enterprise, Tex. (m Ell Robinson and had three children, one of whom is dead); (h) Zack Vaught (m first, Mrs. Omie Hudson; and second, Clara Vaught and had no issue by either marriage); (i) J. B. Vaught (m May Jones and had one child); (j) Susie Vaught, of Timpson, Tex., m Joe Thompkins and had no children.

Two. William Meigs Vaught b Aug. 18, 1857; d abt 1869.
Three. Zachariah Cannon Vaught b May 28, 1859; d Mar. 2, 1920 nr Nacoydoches, Tex; married Millie Militia Swift at Melrose, Tex. (b Oct. 5, 1859; d Dec. 30, 1897 nr Garrison, Tex.) and had ch b nr Nacoydoches, Tex.; (a) Edith Vaught b June 1, 1884, (m first, Loren Jones (b Aug. 26, 1888; d May 23, 1910 nr Nacoydoches, Tex.) and had; 1, Tassie Jones b Feb. 2, 1911; and m second, Lou Phillips and had no issue); (b) Nannie Ida Vaught b May 26, 1886; d Feb. 29, 1908, unmarried; (c) Dora Vaught b July 14, 1888; d Mar. 4, 1906 Miller's Mill, Tex.; (d) Ruth Vaught b Jan. 7, 1892; d Apr. 27, 1892 Appelby, Tex.; (e) Valeria Vaught b July 1895 (m Henry Cox (b July 5, 1885) and had no children); (f) James Henry Vaught b Dec. 25, 1897; d Oct. 30, 1904.

Four. Thomas Garrett Vaught b Aug. 16, 1862, sheriff, Nacoydoches, Tex.; married Dora Pounds, dau of D. T. and E. C. Pounds, Apr. 26, 1885 in Tex. (b May 27, 1867 nr Center, Tex.) and had ch b nr Garrison, Tex.; (a) Jesse Arlington Vaught b Aug. 27, 1886; d May 27, 1889 nr Garrison Tex.; (b) Essie May Vaught b Nov. 26, 1888; d Jan. 18, 1919, (c) Thomac Clyde Vaught b Jan. 7, 1890, jeweler, Port Arthur, Tex., m Mable Hedrick May 13, 1922; (d) Leo Garrett Vaught b June 26, 1892, unmarried with an income tax firm,

Washington, D. C.; (e) Lillian Vaught b Oct. 17, 1895, unmarried; (f) Elva Lynn Vaught b Feb. 14, 1899, unmarried, salesman, Houston, Texas.

Five. Robert Tunnell Vaught, twin with Thomas Garrett Vaught, b Aug. 16, 1862; d very young.

BETSEY TUNNELL ROBERTS

G. Betsey Tunnell, daughter of William and Mary Maysey Tunnell, was born Apr. 1, 1785 Fairfax Co., Va. and died 1830 nr Pine Bluff, Warren Co., Tenn. When three years old she moved, with her parents, to North Carolina and in Feb. 1792 to nr Robertsville, Tenn. She married James Roberts in the spring of 1815, shortly after his return from the War 1812. He was born Dec. 29, 1793 Mecklenburg Co., N. C. and died Mar. 4, 1844 Warren Co., Tenn. He was at the Battle of New Orelans, Jan. 8, 1815. He was the son of Ruben and Mary Milly (Ashor) Roberts, married Aug. 1785 in N. C. They moved to Anderson Co., Tenn. and the town of Robertsville was named for the family. Reuben Roberts was born Jan. 4, 1744 Birmingham, Eng.; and d Dec. 24, 1844 nr Pine Bluff, Tenn., after celebrating the centennial of his birth. He came to America about 1750 and served in the Revolution. He enlisted at Hillsboro, N. C. 1775 and participated in battles of Brandywine, White Horse, Germantown, King's Mountain and Guilford. Mary Milly Ashor was born Orleans, France and died Warren Co., Tenn. Reuben Roberts was son of John Roberts who lived and died in Birmingham, England. James Roberts married second, abt 1853, Martha Allison, in Warren Co., Tenn., who died July 3, 1853. The farm on which James and Betsey Tunnell Roberts lived in Warren Co., was later the property of their daughter, Elmina McGiboney and the latter's son was living on the farm in 1908. Children.

I. Margaret Elmina Roberts b Apr. 19, 1816.
II. Amanda Melvina Roberts b Mar. 27, 1818.
III. James Monroe Roberts b Feb. 20, 1820.
IV. Sarah Eliza Roberts b Jan. 29, 1822.
V. Cynthia Caroline Roberts b June 19, 1825.
VI. William Luther Roberts b Apr. 18, 1827.

Of the foregoing;
I. Margaret Elmina Roberts, daughter of James and Betsey Tunnell Roberts, was born Apr. 19, 1816 Carter Co., Tenn. and died Mar. 5, 1876 Warren Co., Tenn. She married William McGiboney Feb. 20, 1845 Warren Co., Tenn. (b May 12, 1819 Guilford Co., N. C.; d Jan. 15, 1895 Rock Island, Tenn., son of Daniel (b 1790 Guilford Co., N. C.; d 1865 White Co., Tenn.) and Elizabeth (Allison) McGiboney (b 1792 Guilford Co., N. C.; d 1872 Warren Co., Tenn.) Ch. b Warren Co., Tenn.

One. Martha Elizabeth McGibony b Sept. 24, 1849.
Two. James David McGiboney b Oct. 22, 1850.
Three. William Tunnell McGiboney b Aug. 17, 1852.
Four. Mary Caroline McGiboney b Dec. 7, 1854.
Five. Sarah Catherine McGiboney b Jan. 29, 1857.
Six. John Monlone McGiboney b Dec. 12, 1858.

Of these;
One. Martha Elizabeth McGiboney b Sept. 24, 1849.
Two. James David McGiboney b Oct. 22, 1850, of Roland, Tenn.; m Sarah Howard Feb. 13, 1876 Putnam Co., Tenn. (b Sept. 20, 1848; D. Sept. 2, 1902, dau Robert and Nancy Howard) and had ch b Rock Island, Tenn.; (a) Robert William McGiboney b Dec. 5, 1876; farmer, Rock Island, Tenn. (m first, Josie E. Martin Dec. 6, 1895 Warren Co., Tenn. (b Nov. 23, 1878; d Nov. 1906, dau Sampson and Annie Martin)

and had ch b Rock Island, Tenn.; 1, Lola Ather McGiboney b Oct. 10, 1896 m James Baker b Oct. 29, 1912 and had ch. b nr Campaign, Tenn.; (aa) Grady Baker b Mar. 24, 1914; (bb) John Baker b Oct. 24, 1916; (cc) Malchus Baker b Aug. 31, 1919; (dd) Luverna Baker b Sept. 5, 1922; 2, Catherine Drusilla McGiboney b Mar. 26. 1898, m Ota Payne Oct. 3, 1917, farmer, Rock Island, Tenn. and had; (aa) Laurence Roy Payne b Aug. 15, 1918; (bb) R. J. Payne b Jan. 20, 1920; (cc) Josie May Payne b Oct. 15, 1922; (dd) Viola Bell Payne b Sept. 12, 1923; d Oct. 11 1923; 3, James Clinton McGiboney b Nov. 8, 1899; 4, Luther Sampson McGiboney b Nov. 15, 1901; farmer, Rowland, Tenn., m Mildred Grace Wallace Nov. 12, 1922 Warren Co., Tenn. (b July 15, 1905) and had; (aa) Marian Opal McGiboney b Oct. 26, 1924; 5, Sally May McGiboney b Dec. 15. 1903, m Henry Stipes Apr. 20, 1924; 6. Willie McGiboney b Feb. 2, 1906; d Jan. 1, 1908. Robert William McGiboney m Millie Baker Jan. 1, 1908 Walling, Tenn. (b Feb. 2, 1886, dau John and Cynthia Baker) ard had; 7, Cynthia Lou McGiboney b Nov. 2, 1908; d June 21, 1909; 8, Omar Cephas McGiboney b Oct. 8, 1910; 9, Ivora McGiboney b Mar. 5, 1913; 10, Orion David McGiboney b Sept. 21, 1920); (b) Clarence Leander McGiboney b Aug. 15, 1880; d Oct. 16, 1903 Rock Island, Tenn.; unmarried; (c) Allen Cephas McGiboney b Dec. 15, 1886 (m Luella Martin, sister of Josie Martin, Aug. 1906 nr Rock Island, Tenn., who d Feb. 1908.

Three. William Tunnell McGiborey b Aug. 17, 1852; d Jan. 6, 1918 El Paso, Ark.; m first, Mattie Clark Jan. 11, 1885 Warren Co., Tenn. (b Aug. 10, 1857; d Feb. 3, 1886) and had; (a) Glenara McGiboney b Jan. 2, 1886 (m first, Ernest Kimbrel Oct. 10. 1905 and had; 1, Leaton Kimbrel b Aug. 11, 1906; and m second, Frank Brackenridge Feb. 8, 1913 and had; 2, Thomas Brackenridge b Mar. 12, 1916; 3, Hallie Brackenridge b Mar. 24, 1922). William Tunnell McGiboney m second, Millie Gribble Aug. 26, 1888 White Co., Tenn. (b Aug. 22, 1866; d July 12, 1902) and had; (b) Parthenia McGiboney b June 7, 1890 (m John Aclin Dec. 14, 1910 Ward, Ark. and had; 1, Cantrum Aclin b Oct. 7, 1911; 2, Roy Aclin b Feb. 28, 1913; 3, Martha Aclin b Apr. 24, 1916; 4, Lloyd Aclin b Aug. 21, 1920); (c) Elmina McGiboney b Oct. 31, 1891 (m Emro Adams Dec. 4, 1910 El Paso, Ark. and had; 1, Alfred Adams b June 15, 1912; 2, Hugh Adams b July 14, 1914); (d) Alma McGiboney b July 10, 1894, of El Paso, Ark. (m Rena Burns Sept. 16, 1915 (d July 4, 1918) and had; 1, Marjorie McGiboney b Apr. 17, 1917; 2, Christine McGiboney b June 18, 1918); (e) Olna McGiboney b Dec. 25, 1895 (m Iva Berg Sept. 26, 1920 and had; 1, Odessa McGiboney b June 14, 1921; 2, Hoy McGiboney b Apr. 9, 1923); (f) Amelia McGiboney b June 6, 1898 (m Henry Gann Oct. 12, 1918 El Paso, Ark. and had; 1, Zelma Gann b Jan. 1, 1920; 2, Bernice Gann b Dec. 21, 1922); (g) Ozella McGiboney b July 23, 1900 (m Morris Quick Jan. 27, 1918 White Co., Ark. and had; 1, daughter b and d Dec. 17, 1918; 2, Nelson Quick b Nov. 19, 1919; 3, Nolin Quick b Mar. 19, 1922; 4, Wanon Quick b July 9, 1924). William Tunnell McGiboney m third, Grace Evars Nov. 16, 1914. Grace Evans McGiboney m Iron Neal Sept. 28, 1921.

Four. Mary Caroline McGiboney b Dec. 7, 1854; d June 1, 1919 Hammonsville, Ark.; married a relative, John Wesley Roberts Nov. 3, 1869 Warren Co., Tenn. (b Oct. 16, 1849 McMinnville, Tenn.; d Feb. 8, 1912 Hammonsville, Ark.; son of James and Elizabeth (McCormic) Roberts; grandson of Reuben Roberts) and had ch. b Warren Co., Tenn., (a) William James Roberts b Apr. 12, 1872; d Nov. 8, 1891 White Co., Ark.; (b) Viola Lucretia Roberts b Mar. 7, 1880; d May 17, 1892 White Co., Ark.; (c) Leroy Clifford Roberts b Jan.

13, 1887, cotton gin operator, Mt. Vernon, Ark. (m first, Johnie Belle Stewart Oct. 8, 1905 White Co., Ark. and had; 1, Laney James Roberts b Nov. 1, 1906 Hammonsville, Ark.; 2, Mary Lucile Roberts b Sept. 14, 1908, Hammonsville, Ark.; and m second, Marie Gunter Nov. 7, 1917 Vilonia, Ark. and had; 3, Alice Awana Roberts b Oct. 1, 1920, Hammonsville, Ark.

Five.   Sarah Catherine McGiboney b Jan. 29, 1857; d Jan. 31, 1916 nr Rock Island, Tenn.; married John Haynes Mar. 7, 1878 and had; (a) Carroll Hayes b July 18, 1879, d Aug. 2, 1906, unmarried, at Nashville, Tenn; buried Pine Bluff, Tenn.; (b) Luther Hayes b Mar. 30, 1881; d Apr. 15, 1882 White Co., Tenn.; (c) Dillard Hayes b Feb. 20, 1883, m Anna Stepp 1924 Gowanda, N. Y.; (d) Ezra Hayes b Feb. 17, 1885 farmer, unmarried, Rock Island, Tenn.; (e) Virgie Ethel Hayes b Aug. 31, 1890; d Mar. 7, 1923 McMinnville, Tenn. (m Clarence Joab Clark Dec. 20, 1907 (b Dec. 12, 1882, farmer of Sparta, Tenn.) and had ch.; 1, Dillard Eastley Clark b Aug. 11, 1912 Campaign, Tenn.; 2, Zora Maye Clark b Oct. 18, 1917 Clear Lake, Collin Co., Tex.; 3, John Thomas Clark b Apr. 7, 1921 Clifty, Tenn. Clarence Joab Clark m second, Etta Kell Mar. 23, 1924); (f) Horace Hayes b Jan. 30, 1888; d June 3, 1892 White Co., Tenn.

Six.   John Monlone McGiboney b Dec. 12, 1858, of Dibrell, Tenn. married Bertie Clark Oct. 8, 1882 (b Mar. 30, 1856 White Co., Tenn., dau Thomas (b 1826 N. C.) and Nancy (Parker) Clark (b 1832 Van Buren Co., Tenn.) and had; (a) Eva McGiboney b Aug. 30, 1833 (m William M. Paris and had; 1, William Paris; 2, Robert Paris); (b) Thomas McGiboney b Mar. 30, 1885) m Audra Carter and had; 1, Eva Carter McGiboney; 2, John Thomas McGiboney; 3, James Clark McGiboney); (c) John McGiboney b July 5, 1886 who was a member of the 57th General Assembly of Tenn.; m Maude Byrd and had; 1. Nell McGiboney; 2, Roberta McGiboney.

II.   Amanda Melvina Roberts, dau of James and Betsey Tunnell Roberts, was born Mar. 27, 1818 nr Clinton, Tenn. and died 1840 Warren Co., Tenn.; unmarried.

III.   James Monroe Roberts, son of James and Betsey Tunnell Roberts, was born Feb. 20, 1820 Clinton, Tenn. and died Sept. 10, 1838, Warren Co., Tenn.; unmarried.

IV.   Sarah Eliza Roberts, dau of James and Betsey Tunnell Roberts, was born Jan. 29, 1823 Clinton, Tenn. and died Mar. 15, 1842 Warren Co., Tenn.; unmarried.

V.   Cynthia Caroline Roberts, daughter of James and Betsey Tunnell Roberts, was born June 19, 1825 Warren Co., Tenn. and died Apr. 20, 1897 nr Quebeck, Tenn.   She married Louis Chappell Mason Feb. 16, 1845 Warren Co., Tenn. (b Feb. 22, 1825 Elbert Co., Georgia; d Mar. 3, 1913 nr Quebeck, Tenn.; son of William and ———— (Penn) Mason; grandson William Mason, of England). Louis C. Mason married second, a relative of his first wife, Mary Lettice Rawlings Sept. 30, 1898 (b Aug. 14, 1835 Warren Co., Tenn.; d June 20, 1920 Quebeck, Tenn.; dau James English and Mary Worthington Rawlings and grand dau of James and Lettice Tunnell Worthington). Children of Louis C. and Cynthia Caroline Roberts Mason, save youngest, born nr Pine Bluff, Warren Co., Tenn.

One.   Martha Elizabeth Mason b Jan. 2, 1846.

Two.   Amanda M. Mason b Apr. 21, 1848.

Three.   James Calvin Mason b Dec. 23, 1849.

Four.   William Thomas Mason b Apr. 8, 1852.

Five.   Luther Zebidee Mason b July 7, 1854.

Six.   Frances Elvira Mason b Oct. 14, 1856.

Seven.   John Kelly Mason b Jan. 10, 1859.

Eight. Milton Lafayette Mason b June 27, 1861.

Nine. Eustace Cosmo Mason b Feb. 7, 1868.

Of these;

One. Martha Eizabeth Mason b Jan. 2, 1846; d Sept. 25, 1860 nr Pine Bluff, Tenn.

Two. Amanda M. Mason b Apr. 21, 1848; d Nov. 24, 1868 White Co., Tenn.

Three. James Calvin Mason b Dec. 23, 1849; d Jan. 6, 1915 nr Walling, Tenn.; m Almeda Moore July 12, 1872 Walling, Tenn. (b Sept. 12, 1853, dau of Matison and Elizabeth (Cole) Moore) and had ch b nr Walling, Tenn.; (a) Levander Casto Mason b May 15, 1874; farmer, Walling, Tenn. (m Daisy Moneyham, dau Thomas and Charity Moneyham Jan. 5, 1896 White Co., Tenn. and had ch. b White Co., Tenn.; 1, Chlora Euzena Mason b Feb. 16, 1897, of Sparta, Tenn., m John Vass Snodgrass, son of John Snodgrass, May 25, 1921 Walling, Tenn. (veteran of World War with over seas service; circuit clerk White Co., Tenn.) and had; (aa) Cora Daisy Joyce Snodgrass b May 30, 1923 White Co., Tenn.; 2, Terry Ezra Mason b May 11, 1901, of Dinuba, Calif.; bank clerk; m Pearl Gillem June 1, 1924 Dinuba, Calif.; 3, Raymond Levan Mason b Jan. 17, 1910; 4, James Thomas Mason b Mar. 21, 1914); (b) Cynthia Elizabeth Mason b Nov. 22, 1875 (m Indiminion Benjamin Moore, son of Losson and Nancy (Cantrell) Moore, Oct. 17, 1897 White Co., Tenn. (member 1913 of General Assembly of Tenn.) and had an only ch.; 1, Eaton Lee Moore b Nov. 9, 1906); (c) Louis Parker Mason b Aug. 17, 1878, farmer, Walling, Tenn. (m Sudie Bossom, dau of James and Amanda Bossom) Nov. 20, 1900 White Co., Tenn. and had ch. b White Co.; 1, Etral May Mason b Sept. 27, 1901, of Akron, Ohio, m Kerlee Helton Jan. 26, 1922 Walling, Tenn. and had; (aa) Robert Lee Helton b Nov. 16, 1922; 2, Era Almeda Mason b Jan. 30, 1903, of Walling, Tenn., m Hill Rascoe Dec. 25, 1920 Walling, Tenn. and had; (aa) Fred Hill Rascoe b Oct. 11, 1921; (bb) Helen Winona Rascoe b Mar. 25, 1924; 3, Karl Parker Mason b Oct. 3, 1905; 4, Musetta Toutloff Mason b Nov. 30, 1908; 5, Lloyd Wilson Mason b Nov. 28, 1917); (d) Amanda Jane Mason b Feb. 8, 1884, of Quebeck, Tenn. (m first, Spencer Holder, son of John Holder, Dec. 25, 1901 White Co., Tenn. and had ch. b White Co.; 1, John Calvin Holder b Dec. 8, 1902, with International Harvester Co., Birmingham, Ala., m Robbie Annie Salter Aug. 13, 1924 Birmingham, Ala.; 2, Jesse Douglass Holder b Jan. 23. 1904, with International Harvester Co. Chattanooga, Tenn.; 3, Elizabeth Louise Holder b Aug. 28, 1908. Amanda J. Mason m second, a cousin, Arthur Overton Mason, son of John Kell and Celia Chrisholm Mason, Dec. 11, 1916, McMinnville, Tenn. and had no ch. by this marriage.

Four. William Thomas Mason b Apr. 8, 1852; d Dec. 8, 1903 White Co., Tenn. nr Walling; married Jane Carder Feb. 23, 1876 nr Walling, Tenn. (b 1859; d Apr. 13, 1920) and had ch b nr Walling, Tenn.; (a) Mount C. Mason b Jan. 16, 1877, farmer, Quebeck, Tenn. (m Eva Denton, dau Spencer and Armeda (Hutchins) Denton) July 27, 1898 White Co., Tenn. and had ch b White Co., Tenn.; 1, Vernie Mason b July 10, 1899, m Eddie Phifer and had; (aa) Charles Frederick b July 27, 1918; (bb) Sue Evaline b Jan. 18, 1920; (cc) Maud Ellen b Jan. 30, 1922; (dd) Ray Cathleen b Oct. 26, 1923; 2, Spencer Mason b July 6, 1900; d 1903 White Co., Tenn.; 3, William Mason b Mar. 23, 1902, m Myrtle Randa Holder, dau of William Reed and Alice Houston (Hendley) Holder, gd of Simpson and Mary (Underwood Hlder, and had; (aa) Quentin Austin Mason b Feb. 19, 1923; 4, Louis Ray Mason b Mar. 5, 1904; 5, Wayman Mason b Feb. 23,

1906; 6, Elbert Lee Mason b Feb. 8, 1908; 7, Erma Armeda Mason b May 18, 1912; 8, Eva Jane Mason, twin of Erma Armeda Mason, b May 18, 1912; 9, Eston Huston Mason b May 6, 1914; 10, Nannie Bell Mason b June 22, 1916; 11, Richard Denton Mason b Sept. 4, 1918); (b) Mary Ova Mason b Aug. 10, 1879; d in inf.; (c) Martha Mason b Jan. 14, 1881, unmarried, Walling, Tenn; (d) Kelly Mason b Feb. 6, 1883, farmer, Walling, Tenn. (m Mollie Jane Dodson Nov. 26, 1911 White Co., Tenn. and had ch b nr Walling; 1, Millie Mason b 1913; 2, William Mason b 1916); (e) William Fredrick Mason b Dec. 7, 1884, of Louisville, Ky. (m a relative, Ethel Patton, July 24, 1905 and had; 1, Thomas Mason b Aug. 31, 1906; 2, Lowell Ida Mason b Nov. 6, 1908; 3, Robert Lee Mason b May 1911; 4, ——— Mason); (f) Lucy Mason died a few days after birth; (g) Emmet Mason b Feb. 23, 1887, farmer, Walling, Tenn. (m Lela Mae Rowland Dec. 25, 1910 White Co., Tenn. and had ch b White Co.; 1, Beecher John Mason b Nov. 18, 1911; 2, Emma Mae Mason b Feb. 13, 1914; 3, Melba E. Mason b May 5, 1917; 4, Leroy Earl Mason b Aug. 26, 1922); (h) Oliver Floyd Mason b Nov. 1, 1891; d Sept. 9, 1902; (i) Dorman Mason b May 29, 1894, with International Harvester Co. Chattanooga, Tenn. m Annie Mae Jernigan Apr. 15, 1917 Mt. Pisgan (b Aug. 2, 1894) and had ch b nr Walling; 1, Jonnie Belle Mason b Jan. 14, 1918; 2, Sarah Estelle Mason b Jan. 31, 1919; 3, Joel Casto Mason b Mar. 13, 1921); (j) Everett Mason b Jan. 29, 1897, unmarried; (k) John Mason b May 7, 1899, unmarried; (l) Dillon Mason b Feb. 14, 1902 (m Cassie Mai Pettit and had; 1, Floyd Thomas Mason b Oct. 25, 1922; 2, Anna Christine Mason b Nov. 1, 1923).

Five. Luther Zebidee Mason b July 7, 1854; d July 26, 1907, Justin, Texas; married Miranda Holder, dau A. Jackson Holder, 1873 Van Buren Co., Tenn. (b Aug. 13, 1850 Van Buren Co., Tenn.; d June 8, 1908 Justin, Tex.) and had; (a) Lewis Spencer Mason b June 29, 1874; d Oct. 15, 1876; (b) Frances Jane Mason b Dec. 31, 1875; d Nov. 5, 1891 Quebeck, Tenn.; (c) Andrew Jackson Mason b Apr. 5, 1878 Van Buren Co., Tenn.; farmer, Justin, Tex. (m Lizzie Lentz, dau of D. C. and M. L. Lentz, Dec. 2, 1900 (b Jan. 29, 1878 Justin, Tex.) and had ch b Justin, Tex.; 1, Rena Mason b Feb. 28, 1902; d May 18, 1902 Justin, Tex.; 2, Una Lee Mason b Sept. 20, 1903; 3, Ina Mason b Mar. 4, 1905; 4, son b Oct. 29, 1906; d Oct. 30, 1906; 5, daughter b Mar. 27, 1909; d May 2, 1909; 6, Andrew J. Mason b Nov. 8, 1911; 7, Dorris Lentz Mason b July 12, 1918); (d) Albert Mason b Jan. 30, 1880 White Co., Tenn.; d Mar. 20, 1899 Justin, Tex.; (e) Cynthia Mason b Mar. 30, 1883 White Co., Tenn.; d Apr. 11, 1883 White Co., Tenn.; (f) Allen Mason b Sept. 19, 1884; farmer, Roanoke, Tex. (m Alma Peterson, dau N. F. and Christine Peterson, Dec. 22, 1907 Roanoke, Tex. and had; 1, Leroy Zebidee Mason b June 14. 1912); (g) Dora Mason b Apr. 26, 1887 Roanoke, Tex., of Sebring, Ohio (m F. M. Thompson June 17. 1917 Justin, Tex. and had; 1, Clyde Andrew Thompson b July 28, 1918 Sebring, O.) (h) Emma Mason b May 26, 1892 Roanoke, Tex.; d Mar. 3, 1896 Justin, Tex.

Six. Frances Elvira Mason b Oct. 14, 1856; d 1867.

Seven. John Kelly Mason b Jan. 10, 1859; d May 25, 1924 Quebeck, Tenn.; married Celia Chisholm, dau of Overton and Celia (Hash) Chisholm, Dec. 14, 1882 White Co., Tenn. (b May 13, 1856 nr Walling, Tenn. and had ch b White Co., Tenn.; (a) Lela Etha Mason b Oct. 1, 1883, of Walling, Tenn. (m Charles Denton, son of Spencer and Armenda (Hutchins) Denton, May 30, 1903 White Co.. Tenn. (b Sept. 5, 1881 nr Quebeck. Tenn.; farmer) and had ch b White Co., Tenn.; 1, Charles Conrad Denton b May 29, 1904; farmer, Quebeck, Tenn. m Edna Davis 1923; 2, Carl Mason Denton b May 14, 1906; 3, Eustace

Kelly Denton b Nov. 28, 1908; d Oct. 11, 1910; 4, Juanita Josephine
Denton b July 30, 1912, 5, Elizabeth Jesseline Denton b June 26,
1915; 6, Melba Edna Denton b Nov. 6, 1919; d Nov 1, 1920; 7, Samuel
Leonard Denton b Oct. 22, 1921); (b) Joseph I Chappell Mason b
Mar. 7, 1886, farmer, Spencer, Tenn. (m Maude Walling Jan. 8, 1917
nr Gillentine, Tenn. (b Dec. 23, 1892) and had; 1, daughter b and d
Jan. 1, 1918; 2, William Lonnie Mason b Dec. 1, 1919; 3, James
Kelly Mason b Oct. 19, 1921); (c) Arthur Overton Mason b Dec. 12,
1887; farmer, Quebeck, Tenn. m a cousin, Amanda Jane (Mason)
Holder, dau of James Calvin and Almeda (Moore) Mason, Dec. 11,
1916 McMinnville, Tenn. and had no ch.); (d) Elmer Zebidee Mason b
Feb. 3, 1891; unmarried, farmer, Quebeck, Tenn.
    Eight.   Milton Lafayette Mason b June 27, 1861; d 1868.
    Nine.   Dr. Eustace Cosmo Mason b Feb. 7, 1868 nr Quebeck,
Tenn., of Russellville, Arkansas; married Vernon Cooper, daughter
John S. and Belle (High) Cooper, Apr. 24, 1913 Nashville, Tenn. and
had an only child; 1, John Cooper Mason b June 17, 1914 nr Quebeck,
Tenn.   Dr. Mason was one of the first in White Co., Tenn. to enlist
for service in the World War.   He entered service as First Lieut.
Medical Reserve Corps July 31, 1917 and was sent to Camp Funston.
From Sept. 11, to Mar. 15, 1919 he was Asst. Surgeon 432nd
F. A. Student Army Training Corps, Camp Rollo, Mo.   Instructor
of enlisted men of Medical Corps at Ft. Leavenworth, Kan.   He is
now in Reserve Medical Corps., as Capt.   Acknowledgement is here
made for valuable assistance rendered by Dr. Mason in preparing
the record of Betsey Tunnell Roberts and some of the Worthington
records.
    VI.   William Luther Roberts, son of James and Betsey Tunnell
Roberts, was born Apr. 18, 1827 Warren Co., Tenn. and died Apr. 19,
1863.   He was a soldier in the war Between the States and was
fatally wounded at Murfreesboro, Tenn.   He married Luck Blackburn 1853 in Warren Co., Tenn. (d Oct. 1880) who married second,
—— McWhirter.   Children b Warren Co., Tenn.
    One.   John P. Roberts b Apr. 16, 1854.
    Two.   James Monroe Roberts b Oct. 16, 1856.
    Three.   George Caswell Roberts b Nov. 1858.
    Four.   Samuel Roberts b Oct. 12, 1860.
    Five.   William Parker Roberts b Aug. 1863.
    Of these;
    One.   John P. Roberts b Apr. 16, 1854; d Sept. 17, 1924 Connor,
Ark.; married Lou J. Dunlap Oct. 13, 1876. Their two older ch b
Warren Co., Tenn. others in Ark; (a) Sallie Porcia Roberts b Sept. 6,
1877, of Rudd, Ark. (m William Deweese July 28, 1892 and had; 1,
Erton Deweese b Jan. 29, 1894 m Elizabeth Ray and had; (aa) Bruce
Deweese; (bb) Bettie Deweese 2, Albert Deweese b Apr. 29, 1896; 3,
Ota Deweese b Feb. 11, 1898 m Oscar Hammons 1916 and had; (aa)
Cline Hammons b 1920; (bb) Helen Hammons b 1922; 4, Lou Dew-
eese b June 11, 1901 m Ray Littrell and had; (aa) Rex Littrell; 5,
Pearl Deweese b Oct. 15, 1904 m Jay Hammons and had; (aa) Jay
Clark Hammons; 6, Wayman Deweese b Jan. 2, 1906; 7, Grady
Deweese b Nov. 19, 1911; 8, Dannie Deweese b 1918); (b) Dr. David
Carson Roberts b Feb. 11, 1880, of Fayetteville, Ark. (m first Jewel
Wilson Dec. 29, 1904 (d Oct. 13, 1909) and had; 1, Raymond Roberts
b Nov. 24, 1905; and m second, Etta Ray Dec. 22, 1910 and had 2,
Ray Roberts b Jan. 27, 1912; 3, Roberta Lou Roberts b labt 1918; 4,
Jimmie Roberts b abt 1921); (c) Vicia Ann Roberts b Nov. 2, 1882,
of Rudd, Ark. (m William Miller June 25, 1897 and had; 1, Vinnie
Miller b Mar. 25, 1898 m Claud Seitz and had; (aa) Clyde Seitz; (bb)

Lucie Seitz; (cc) Lavern Seitz; 2, Chloe Miller b Nov. 29, 1899 m Macum Jones; 3, Denvie Miller b Aug. 6, 1901; d Aug. 22, 1902; 4, Ruby Miller b Oct. 9, 1904 m Frank Ussery; 5, Margie Miller b Sept. 7, 1908; 6, Parker Miller b June 15, 1911; 7, Tom Miller b 1913; 8, Lou Miller b abt 1917; 9, Janette Miller b abt 1922); (d) Lucy Emma Roberts b Nov. 23, 1884, of Connor, Ark. (m Tim Deweese Sept. 29, 1904 and had; 1, Kate Deweese b Feb. 8, 1911; 2, Ruby Deweese b abt 1920); (e) Hallie Calesta Roberts b Jan. 25, 1887 (m Crump Fancher Feb. 1906 (d Jan. 29, 1910) and had; 1, Dick Fancher b May 5, 1907; 2, William Fancher b Oct. 5, 1909); (f) William Parker Roberts b Apr. 22, 1890, of Connor, Ark. (m Vinnie Howard Mar. 3, 1912 and had; 1, Howard Roberts b abt 1914; 2, Hallene Roberts b abt 1918); (g) Edna Jewell Roberts b Feb. 27, 1892, of Twin Falls, Idaho (m Ralph Qualls and had; 1, Clifford Qualls b Apr. 29, 1909 Connor, Ark.; 2, Helen Qualls b June 17, 1912; 3, Blanche Qualls b 1915; 4, John Alexander Qualls b 1918; 5, Betty Qualls b 1923); (h) Fannie Lee Roberts b Dec. 12, of Twin Falls, Idaho (m Clarence Rector Dec. 29, 1910 and had; 1, Lena Rector b Sept. 13, 1911 Zurich, Kan.; 2, Ruth Rector b Feb. 2, 1916; 3, Reta Rector b Aug. 20, 1920); (i) Jay Palmer Roberts b Jan. 22, 1896, clergyman, Valley Spring, Ark. (m Sue Sisco May 17, 1915 and had; 1, Eugene Roberts b Jan. 17, 1917; 2, Keith Roberts b Nov. 27, 1918; 3, John W. Roberts b Oct. 7, 1923); (j) Ruth Mable Roberts b Jan. 30, 1898, of Dry Fork, Ark. (m Lester Owens Oct. 16, 1918 and had; 1, Lester Owens Jr., b Feb. 25, 1921; 2, Maxine Owens b Apr. 23, 1922); (k) Henry Clay Roberts b Aug. 4, 1900, of Connor, Ark. (m Avo Grigg Oct. 3, 1923 and had; 1. Lou Roberts b July 17, 1924); (l) John Bradley Roberts b Nov. 23, 1906.

Two. James Monroe Roberts b Oct. 16, 1856; d Jan 10, 1873.

Three. George Caswell Roberts b Nov. 1858; unmarried, Rowland, Tenn.

Four. Samuel Roberts b Oct. 12, 1860; d Sept. 6, 1881 (m Myra Gribble July 15, 1877 and had; (a) Dora Roberts b June 10, 1878; (b) Lela Roberts b Sept. 14, 1880; d Apr. 1883.

Five. William Parker Roberts b Aug. 1863, of Port Lavaca, Tex.; married Hattie Louise Haltman and had; (a) Edward Clemon Roberts b Apr. 8, 1882 Rowland, Tenn of Texas City, Tex. (m Amy Forrest Webb Sept. 29, 1907 Dot, Tex. and had; 1, Ray Weldon Roberts b Oct. 8, 1908 Cego, Tex.; 2, Forrest Edward Roberts b Feb. 15, 1910 Cego, Tex.; 3, Naomi Aileen Roberts b July 10, 1914 Texas City; 4, Vera Ella Roberts b Nov. 16, 1915 Texas City; 5, Clarence William Roberts b Sept. 23, 1919 Texas City; 6, Kenneth Webb Roberts b Aug. 26, 1922 Texas City); (b) Eliza Jane Roberts b 1884 Carroll Co., Ark., of Port Lavaca, Tex. (m John Jackson at Cego, Texas and had; 1, Gladys Irene Jackson b 1907 Cego, Tex.; 2, Ruby Inez Jackson b 1909 San Marcos, Tex.; 3, Lillian Lucille Jackson b 1912 San Marcos, Tex.); (c) Lucy S. Roberts b 1886 Rudd, Ark., of Port Lavaca, Tex. (m Walter M. Jackson at Cego, Tex. and had ch. b Cego, Tex.; 1, Willie Edna Jackson b 1907; 2, Nellie Ernestine Jackson; 3, Clara Ruth Jackson; 4, William Marvin Jackson; 5, Fred Warner Jackson; 6, Neba Jackson; 7, Joyce Louise Jackson; 8, Betty Jean Jackson); (d) Lula May Roberts b 1888 Moody, Tex., of Port Lavaca, Tex. (m Thomas Spencer Upchurch at Cego, Tex. and had two ch. both dead); (e) Elbert D. Roberts b 1890 Pendleton, Tex., of Port Lavaca (m Blanch Clark, at Port Lavaca and had; 1, James Melverd Roberts b 1923 Port Lavaca); (f) Ellis M. Roberts b 1893 Pendleton, Tex., of Port Lavaca (m Clara Woods, at Port Lavaca and had ch b Port Lavaca; 1, Melvered Ovella Roberts b 1918; 2, Ellis Wayman Roberts;

3, Joe A. Roberts; 4, Thomas Spencer Roberts); (g) Beadie Roberts b 1895 Pendleton, Tex., of Texas City, Tex. (m Prince Earle Bruner at Port Lavaca and had; 1, Dorothy Louise Bruner b 1922 Port Lavaca, Tex.; 2, Prince Earle Bruner Jr., b Nov. 6, 1924 Texas City, Tex.); (h) William Malverd Roberts b Sept. 17, 1897 Cego, Tex., of Port Lavaca, Tex. (m [Abbie Pierson at Port Lavaca, Tex. and had no children); (i) Thelma Roberts b 1899 Cego, Tex., of Texas City, Tex. (m H. S. Kee at Port Lavaca and had ch b Port Lavaca; 1, Marjorie Imogene Kee b 1918; 2, Bernice Maurine Kee b 1920; 3, Hasting S. Kee b 1922).

JAMES TUNNELL

H. James Tunnell, son of William and Mary Maysey Tunnell, was born May 22, 1787 Fairfax Co., Va and died Sept. 17, 1826 nr Carrollton, Ill. at the home of his brother, Calvin, whom he was visiting. He went with his parents to North Carolina in 1788 and in Feb. 1792 to nr Robertsville, Tenn. He was a Captain in the Second War with the British. He married Dicy Hauskins, dau of Elisas Hauskins, in the fall of 1813 in Tenn. They moved, about 1816, to the then Illinoise Territory and settled at Edwardsville. Dicy Hauskins Tunnell married second, Thomas Ray, Oct. 23, 1826 Madison Co. Ill. and died July 4, 1848 Edwardsville, Ill. Children;

    I. Nancy Tunnell b Feb. 2, 1815.
    II. Wililam West Tunnell b Feb. 23, 1824.

Of the foregoing;
    1. Nancy Tunnell, only dau of Jarem and Dicy Hauskins Tunnell, was born Feb. 2, 1815 Anderson Co., Tenn. and died on her ninety-third birthday, Feb. 2, 1908 Alhambra, Ill, on the farm she went to as a bride 67 years before. She married Levi Harnsberger Dec.2, 1841 Madison Co., Ill. (b 1811 Rockingham Co., Va.; reared in Trigg Co., Ky.; moved to Alhambra 1831; d June 9, 1890 Alhambra, Ill.) and had ch b Alhambra, Ill.

    One. Maria Josephine Harnsberger b Sept. 2, 1842; d Mar. 18, 1844.

    Two. Mary Jane Harnsberger b Nov. 4, 1849, of Los Angeles, Calif.; married Harry E. Wood Feb. 29, 1880 Alhambra, Ill, who d Mar. 23, 1889 St. Jacobs, Ill., and had ch b St. Jacobs, Ill.; (a) Hattie L. Wood b Mar. 1, 1881, of Los Angelese, Calif. (m Robert Wallace Mar. 23, 1901 Alhambra, Ill. and had; 1, Robert Harrison Wallace b Apr. 10, 1903 Clinton, Ill.; 2, Royal Wallace b Lowell, Ind.; 3, Jessica Wallace b Lowell, Ind.); (b) Harrison Wood b May 1888 St. Jacobs, Ill.; d Nov. 1888 St. Jacobs, Ill.

    Three. William Augustus Harnsberger b Sept. 7, 1851, of Kansas City, Mo.; married Frank Harlam Dec. 22, 1897 Kansas City, and had no ch.

    Four. Dr. Charles Eugene Harnsberger b Mar. 6, 1854; d Aug. 4, 1924, Alhambra, Ill.; married Valeria Stephenson, dau of Dr. Robert and Lucy Jane (Stepp) Stephenson, Feb. 22, 1893 nr Alhambra (b Apr. 29, 1869) and had; (a) Pogue Eugene Harnsberger b Nov. 9, 1895 on farm on which his father was born, of Alhambra, Ill., soldier in World War, married Sadie Haring, dau of Augustus and Louise (Schauffner) Haring, Apr. 13, 1918 Louisville, Ky. (b July 3, 1899 Alhambra, Ill.) and had ch b Alhambra, Ill., 1, Eugene Harrison Harnsberger b Feb. 16, 1919; 2, Robert Augustus Harnsberger b Oct. 23, 1921.

    II. William West Tunnell, only son of James and Dicky Haushins Tunnell, was born Feb. 23, 1824 Edwardsville, Ill. and died Oct. 7, 1865 Edwardsville, Ill. He married Letitia McKee Feb. 7, 1850 Madison Co., Ill. She was born Jan 8, 1833 and died Jan. 4, 1874

Edwardsville, Ill. and was the dau of Robert McKee (b Jan. 18, 1795) and Nancy Cornelison McKee, (b Dec. 2, 1804).   Children b Edwardsville, Ill.

One.   Robert Ferdinand Tunnell b Jan. 8, 1851, retired merchant Edwardsville, Ill.; married Mary Elizabeth Ottilia Springer, dau of Frederic and Sophia (Thurman) Springer, Feb. 23, 1882 Madison Co., Ill. (b Mar. 7, 1856) and had ch b Edwardsville, Ill.; (a) son b and d Dec. 14, 1883; (b) Sophia Letitia Tunnell b Feb. 14, 1885, unm., of Edwardsville, Ill.; (c) Robert Ferdinand Tunnell, the second, b Aug. 5, 1887, attorney, unm., of Edwardsville, Ill.; (d) Ella Julia Tunnell b Nov. 18, 1889, unm., of Edwardsville, Ill.; (e) William West Tunnell b Sept. 27, 1891; d Dec. 30, 1907 Edwardsville, Ill.

Two.   Emily Jane Tunnell b Jan. 22, 1853; d Oct. 28, 1865 Madison Co., Ill.

Three.   Ella Frances Tunnell b Sept. 22, 1854; d Sept. 24, 1909 while on a visit in Edwardsville, Ill.; married Allen McDowell Ghost, for years a prominent realtor of Denver, Col., son of Phllip and Katherine (McDowell) Ghost, Dec. 23, 1874 Madison Co., Ill.   He was born Apr. 12, 1844 Venango Co., Penn. and died June 23, 1913 Denver, Col. and was buried at Edwardsville, Ill.   There was an only child of this marriage; (a) Genevieve Ghost b June 29, 1878 Denver, Col., of Denver who married Elmer Ellsworth Whitted, son of John D. and Susan (Watson) Whitted, June 1903 Denver, Col. and had no children.   E. E. Whitted b Apr. 11, 1860 Williamsburg, Ind., attorney, Denver, Col.

Four.   James Ewing Tunnell b Apr. 16, 1856; d Apr. 22, 1912; married Elizabeth Evans, dau of Robert Boyd and Elizabeth Jane (Hendricks) Evans, Oct. 14, 1880 Madison Co., Ill. (b Oct. 15, 1859 Booneville, Mo., now of Denver) and had; (a) James Evans Tunnell b Mar. 14, 1883, of Denver, Col. (m Mary Carolyn Laning Jan. 11, 1905 Norwalk, Ohio, and had; 1, James Evans Tunnell, the second, b Oct. 14, 1905 Edwardsville, Ill.; 2, Mary Ruth Tunnell b Feb. 16, 1908 Edwardsville, Ill.; 3, Genevieve Tunnell b Aug. 1, 1919 Denver, Col.); (b) Katherine Tunnell b June 20, 1887, unm., of Denver, Col.

Five.   Edward McKee Tunnell b Nov. 2, 1858; d Apr. 2, 1872 Madison Co., Ill.

Six.   Charles William Tunnell b Aug. 30, 1860, in Y. M. C. A. work during World War; married first, Jennie Springer, Oct. 5, 1887, who died Sept. 8, 1911; and second, Maude Gregory, Dec. 1, 1923 (b Feb. 21, 1883, dau of Thomas Beverly Gregory b Sept. 20, 1859 Brooklyn, Ind. and Ida Sturdevant Gregory, b Apr. 18, 1860 Bolivar, Mo.).   No issue by either marriage.

Seven.   Alice Letitia Tunnell b Aug. 10, 1863; d Oct. 29, 1865 Madison Co., Ill.

Eight.   Frank West Tunnell b Aug. 24, 1864; d Oct. 4, 1910 Edwardsville, Ill.; married Alice Baird, dau of Robert George and Ann Mara (Kinder) Baird, Sept. 4, 1895 Madison Co., Ill (b Mar. 15, 1872 nr Edwardsville, of Edwardsville) and had ch b Edwardsville, Ill.; (a) Robert West Tunnell b Oct. 21, 1896, unm., of Edwardsville, Ill. served in World War; enlisted July 1918 and sent to Camp Hancock, Augusta, Ga.; in Officers Training Camp Aug. 1918; injured in training and was in hospital until Jan. 1919, when he was honorably discharged; attorney; (b) son born Mar. 25, 1898; (c) Frank West Tunnell, the second, b July 14, 1903, attorney, unm., of Edwardsville, Ill.; (d) Virginia Louise Tunnell b July 20, 1908.

POLLY TUNNELL LEIB

I.   Polly Tunnell, dau of William and Mary Maysay Tunnell, was born Feb. 26, 1789 in North Carolina and Oct. 2, 1820 in Tenn. She married Daniel Leib, son of John Leib, of Anderson Co., Tenn.

It is said there were children of this marriage, though names are not known.   Daniel Leib married second, Barbara ——— and is said to have had a daughter, Serilda Leib.   Daniel Leib moved to Ill. and lived in that part of Greene Co., Ill., which is now Morgan Co., and he was one of the county commissioners when Morgan Co. was formed in 1821.   His name appears on a deed made 1823 in the same county.   He moved to Arkansas about 1830 or earlier and it is said one of his sons held a state office there.   No further details.

CALVIN TUNNELL

J. Calvin Tunnell, son of William and Mary Maysay Tunnell, was born Oct. 4, 1791 in North Carolina and died Apr. 7, 1867 nr Carrollton, Ill.   His parents moved to nr Robertsville, Tenn, Feb 1792.   Here he married Jane Addair Aug. 25, 1811.   They left the Valunteer State, in 1817, in company with Vines Hicks, a veteran of the War of 1812, and his wife, Betsy Hicks, a daughter of Colonel William Tunnell, and came to Edwardsville, a frontier settlement in the Illinois Territory.   On Feb. 14, 1819 Calvin Tunnell moved his family to the home he had built, nr present town, of Carrollton, Ill., in that part of Maddison Co. which was later embraced in Greene Co. and on the land he entered from the government, he and his wife dwelt until death.   They are buried on their farm now owned by a daughter-in-law, Mrs. Laura A. Tunnell.   They were the second permanent white settlers north of Macoupin Creek although a number of pioneers followed soon after.   It is said the first religious service held in the county was that conducted in their home.   Calvin Tunnell was a Baptist and preached in the earlier part of his pioneer life. He was a member of the Ninth General Assembly, 1834-35 and of the Fourteenth General Assembly, 1844-46.   He also served as probate judge for four years, having been elected in 1839.

Jane Addair was born July 28, 1795 in West Va. and died Aug. 30, 1858 nr Carrollton, Ill.   She was the dau of Thomas Addair (b abt 1775; d abt 1840) and Betsy Kirby Addair (b Mar. 1777; d 1860 Blount Co., Tenn.)   Her maternal grandparents were Richard and Sarah Kirby, both of whom were born in 1749, who moved from Yadkin country of N. C. to nr Rockford Co., Tenn., where they died; he Apr. 30, 1811 and she Apr. 5, 1826.

Three of the children of Calvin and Jane Tunnell were born Anderson Co., Tenn., Sally near Edwardsville, Ill. and the others two miles from Carrollton, Ill.

I.   James Tunnell b Aug. 24, 1812.
II.   William Albertus Tunnell b Sept. 3, 1814.
III.   Daniel Leib Tunnell b Oct. 30, 1816.
IV.   Sally Tunnell b Oct. 5, 1818.
V.   Polly Tunnell b Mar. 25, 1820.
VI.   Eliza Jane Tunnell b Nov. 9, 1821.
VII.   Luther Tunnell b Dec. 5, 1824.
VIII.   Nancy Tunnell b Jan. 6, 1826
IX.   John Tunnell b Jan. 6, 1828.
X.   Elizabeth Tunnell b Jan. 20, 1831.
XI.   Franklin Witt Tunnell b Feb. 6, 1832.
XII.   Calvin Witt Tunnell b June 4, 1833.
XIII.   Andrew Jackson Tunnell b June 28, 1837.
XIV.   Elvira Adeline Tunnell b Aug. 22, 1839.
Of the foregoing;

I.   James Tunnell, son of Calvin and Jane Addair Tunnell, was born Aug. 4, 1812 Anderson Co., Tenn. and died Nov. 3, 1812 Anderson Co., Tenn.

II.   William Albertus Tunnell, son of Calvin and Jane Addair

Tunnell, was born Sept. 3, 1814 Anderson Co., Tenn. and died Aug. 14, 1865 Greenfield, Ill. He married Mary Jane Allen, July 15, 1847 nr Greenfield, Ill. She was born Oct. 25, 1828 White Hall, Ill. and died Jan. 24, 1864 Greenfield, Ill., the dau of George Washington Allen, founder of town of Greenfield (b May 15, 1801 Tenn.; d Jan. 17 1865 Greenfield, Ill.) and Caroline Henderson Allen; granddau of Zachariah Allen of Tenn. Caroline Henderson b Oct. 13, 1808 nr Circleville, O.; d Apr. 5, 1894 Greenfield, Ill., the dau of James and Mary (White) Henderson, said to be first settlers north of Apple Creek, Greene Co., Ill. James Henderson b Mar. 9, 1783 N. J..; d July 25, 1849 nr White Hall, Ill., son of Edward Henderson. Mary White b Oct. 25, 1785 Penn. d Aug. 9, 1849 nr White Hall, Ill, the dau of Thomas and Amy (McGee) White, the latter a dau of James and Mercy (Shreve) White. Children of W. A. and Mary Jane Tunnell b Greenfield, Ill.

One. Emma Tunnell b Apr. 7, 1848.
Two. Allen Morse Tunnell b Sept. 15, 1849
Three. Newton Tunnell b Apr. 22, 1851.
Four. Effie Tunnell b June 5, 1859.
Five. Mary Tunnell b Mar. 9, 1863.
Of these;
One. Emma Tunnell b Apr.7, 1848; d May 4, 1919 Rock Island, Ill.; married Edward Dennel Sweeney Oct. 27, 1894 Rock Island, Ill. E. D. Sweeney b Aug. 13, 1833 Newcastle, Del.; d Sept. 14, 1910 Rock Island, Ill.; celebrated the fiftieth anniversary of his admission to the Bar of Illinois a month before his death; son of Miles Sweeney (b Nov. 29, 1803) and Ann Dennell Sweeney (b Jan. 6, 1806 Manchester, England).

Two. Allen Morse Tunnell b Sept. 15, 1849; d Oct. 9, 1894 Fairbury, Neb.; married Mary Ann Williams Sept. 13, 1873 Greenfield, Ill. She was born Dec. 6, 1851 and died —— Roseburg, Ore., dau of Mildton and Elmira Adeline (Edwards) Williams; gd of William White Williams (b July 7, 1791 N. C.; d Dec. 28, 1884 Greenfield, Ill.) and Lydia Williams, married Jan. 14, 1811 Ky.; ggdau David and Elmira (Edwards of Vermont). Children; (a) Adeline Maude Tunnell b Oct. 14, 1874 Morgan Co., Ill., of Medford, Ore. (m Herbert Newton Edwards, a descendant of David and Elmira Edwards, Nov. 7, 1906 Mobile, Ala., and had no ch.); (b) Edward Lynn Tunnell b Apr. 21, 1883 Fairbury, Neb.; d June 18, 1921 Medford, Ore., unmarried; (c) Stewart Tunnell b June 14, 1885 Fairbury, Neb.; d Aug. 27, 1885 Neb.

Three. Newton Tunnell b Apr. 22, 1851; d May 22, 1881 Fairbury, Neb.; married Maria Caswell, dau of Valentine and Maria (Burton) Caswell; gdau Capt. Josia Caswell, Oct. 24, 1876 Greenfield, Ill., who died Mar. 4, 1900, and had ch b Fairbury, Neb; (a) William Albertus Tunnell b Nov. 2, 1877; d Oct. 4, 1892 Fairbury, Neb.; (b) Ross Augustus Tunnell b Aug. 25, 1879, of Oak Grove, Ala. (m Eliza Vaughn Oct. 23, 1907 Mobile, Ala. and had ch b Mobile; 1, Ross Augustus Tunnell the second, b Nov. 30, 1908; 2, James Tunnell b and d Feb. 18, 1910; 3, Elizabeth Vaughn Tunnell b July 5, 1914; 4, Richard McClellan Tunnell b Oct. 19, 1917; 5, Willian Newton Tunnell b Sept. 20, 1923)

Four. Effie Tunnell b June 5, 1859, unm., of Rock Island, Ill.
Five. Mary Tunnell b Mar. 9, 1863; d Aug. 5, 1863 Greenfield, Illinois.

III. Daniel Leib Tunnell, son of Calvin and Jane Addair Tunnell, was born Oct. 30, 1816 Anderson Co., Tenn. and died Sept. 28, 1899 McPherson, Kan. He married Polly Witt Sept. 2, 1835 Greene Co., Ill. She was born Feb. 6, 1815 nr Witt's Foundry, Tenn. and died

Apr. 29, 1891 McPherson, Kan. ; She was the dau of Harmon Witt (b Nov. 16,1788 nr Witt's Foundry, Tenn.; d Dec. 21, 1830 Pope Co., Ill.) and Mariam Skeen Witt (b Nov. 10, 1790; d Aug. 28, 1838 nr Carrallton, Ill.) and granddau Elijah Witt, b 1753, who moved from Halifax Co., Va. to nr present town of Witt's Foundry, Tenn. 1782; same of John and Catherine (White) Skeen; ggdau Charles and Lavinia (Harbour) Witt, of Halifax Co., Va.   Ch. of Daniel L. Tunnell;
One.   William Calvin Tunnell b Oct. 18, 1836.
Two.   Mary Catherine Tunnell b Sept. 20, 1838.
Three.   Luther Benton Tunnell b Jan. 3, 1841.
Four.   Miriam Eveline Tunnell b Jan. 29, 1843.
Five.   Jane Elizabeth Tunnell b Mar. 31, 1848.
Six.   Pryor Dulaney Tunnell b Dec. 9, 1851.
Of these;
One.   William Calvin Tunnell b Oct. 18, 1836 nr Carrollton, Ill. d Jan. 14, 1925 Sapulpa, Okla.; married Cleora Crane Feb. 5, 1862 (b Mar. 13, 1842; d Dec. 13, 1923 Sapulpa, Okla., after a married life of sixty years; dau of Carmen and Harriet Melissa (Colby) Crane; gdau of Luther and Hannah Crane.   Cleora Crane first cousin of Emeline (Nix) Scandrett, whose dau, Laura Scandrett, married A. J. Tunnell, uncle of W. C. Tunnell.   Children;
a.   Emma Jane Tunnell b Jan. 24, 1863 nr Plainview, Ill.; d Nov. 9, 1911 Cogar, Okla.; married first, Charles A. Northrup July 18, 1879 (b Aug. 1, 1856) and had; 1, Dollie E. Northrup b Nov. 29, 1879; d July 26, 1880; 2, Henry C. Northrup b and d Aug. 26, 1880; 8, Susan Arullia Northrup b Aug. 13, 1882; 4, Treba Albirtie Northrup b Nov. 14, 1883; d Aug. 26, 1884; 5, John William Wesley Northrup b Mar. 4, 1886; d July 26, 1886; and married second, Charles B. Bay Sept. 22, 1903 El Reno, Okla. (b Jan. 7, 1864 Cumberland, O.) and had; 6, Robert Orlando Bay b Aug. 7, 1907 Cogar, Okla., of Los Angeles, Calif.; 7, Owen Bay, died Cogar, Okla.
b.   Henry Jackson Tunnell b Jan. 8, 1864 nr Plainview, Ill.; d Aug. 5, 1921 nr Buffalo, Okla. (m Lucy Harrington Oct. 5, 1891 Great Bend, Kan. (b Sept. 25, 1871 Princeton, Mo., now of Enid, Okla.) and had; 1, Roy Jackson Tunnell b Oct. 28, 1892 Conway, Kan., of Denver, Col., m Myrtle M. Darbro Sept. 11, 1922 Woodward, Okla. (b Feb. 22, 1904 Selmon, Okla., dau John Darbro) and had; (aa) Roy Jackson Tunnell, the Second, b July 4, 1923 Buffalo, Okla.; (bb) Dorothy Ione Tunnell b May 3, 1925, Enid, Okla.; 2, Charles Tunnell b Apr. 15, 1894; d Apr. 16, 1894; 3, Clara Ellen Tunnell b July 3, 1895, of Laverne, Okla., m J. R. Cowsar and had; (aa) Hugh Cowsar b Dec. 3, 1912 Buffalo, Okla.; (bb) Harold Cowsar b Jan. 22, 1915 Buffalo, Okla. (cc) Floyd Cowsar b July 10, 1916 Newark, Tex.; (dd) Hazel Cowsar b Sept. 27, 1918 Newark, Tex,; (ee) John H. Cowsar b Sept. 26, 1920 Newark, Tex.; (ff) Ileen Cowsar b Sept. 15, 1922 Buffalo, Okla.; (gg) Ethel Cora Cowsar b Sept. 3, 1924 Laverne, Okla.; 4, Mary Catherine Tunnell b Dec. 18, 1898 Exline, Iowa; d Oct. 7 1899 Exline; 5, Pansy Tunnell b Dec. 9, 1905 Buffalo, Okla, of Enid, Okla.; 6, Opal Tunnell b Mar. 21, 1910 Bison, Okla.)
c.   Anna Evaline Tunnell b June 26, 1864 nr Plainview, Ill., of Sapulpa, Okla. (m first, Loren A. Gates Feb. 5, 1881 (b Oct. 4, 1855; d Nov. 1, 1898) and had; 1, May Bell Gates b Nov. 27, 1882 nr Conway, Kan., of Sapulpa, Okla., m James Mongold June 1907 St. Louis, Mo. and had; (aa) Goldie Mongold, m ——— Anderson Oct. 28, 1924; (b Carl Mongold; (cc) Minnie Mongold; (dd) Helen Mongold; (ee) James Mongold; (ff) W. P. Mongold; 2, Milo Harson Gates b Sept. 19, 1894, of Aurora, Kan., m Hazel ——— and had an only ch.; (aa) Loren Gates b abt 1912; 3, Cleora Harriet Gates b Apr. 10, 1886

Republic Co., Kan., of Grafton, Ill., m Oscar McCalla 1902 South Enid, Okla. and had; (aa) Loren Alerander McCalla b Dec. 27, 1902 Dow, Ill., unm., minister, of Riverside, Calif.; (bb) Dorothy Estelle McCalla b Oct. 6, 1904, Dow, Ill., unm.; (cc) Albert John McCalla b Nov. 12, 1906 nr Elsah, Ill.; (dd) Cecil Wallace McCalla b Jan. 7, 1909 nr Elsah, Ill.; (ee) Hazel May McCalla b Jan. 12, 1911; (ff) Rosella June McCalla b Sept. 27, 1913; (gg) Pearson Leonard Mc-Calla b Apr. 26, 1919 nr Ogence, Wis.; (hh) Marvin Paul McCalla b July 31, 1918 Alton, Ill; (ii) Claretta Loraine McCalla b Aug. 20, 1921 Alton, Ill.; (jj) Maurice Addison McCalla b Sept. 11, 1923 nr Dow, Ill.; all living; 4, Marshall Gates b Mar. 3, 1888 Kan.; d Mar. 12, 1888; 5, Lottie Pearl Gates b Oct. 26, 1890 Ames, Kan.; d fall of 1918, m Louis Henley, 1911, now of Sapulpa, Okla. and had; (aa) Floyd Henley b Oct. 27, 1912; (bb) ———— Henley (son); (cc) ———— Henley (daughter); 6, Minnie Lizzie Gates b Feb. 10, 1892 Clyde, Kan., of Sapulpa, Okla., m John McIntyre 1921 Kan. and had no ch.; 7, Rosie Ella Gates b Nov. 16, 1893 Bradford, Kan., of Boise, Idaho, m Carl Hinkson in Boise, Ida. and had; (aa) Ellen Hinkson b June 1910; (bb) Harold Hinkson; (cc) Carl Hinkson Jr.; 8, Hattie Gates b Nov. 30, 1895 Macon Co., Mo.; d Dec. 18, 1896; 9, Ada Reem Gates b Nov. 16, 1897 nr Economy, Mo., of Calif., m Earl Red, in Twin Falls, Ida. and had; (aa) son; (bb) daughter; (cc) son b Nov. 30, 1924. Anna E. Tunnell m second, Wes Reed Dec. 25, 1900 (b Aug. 15, 1840) and had; 10, Hattie Myrtle Reed b Aug. 12, 1902; d Sioux Falls, S. D., m Frank Taylor and had an only ch.; 11, Dora Reed b Aug. 5, 1904, of Supulpa, Okla., m her half-sister's widower, Lewis Henley and had; (aa) and (bb) twins, dead; (cc) dau b and d 1923; (dd) dau b Dec. 2, 1924; 12, Laurence Reed, twin, b Aug. 30, 1906, of Sapulpa, Okla.; 13, Florence A. Reed, twin, b Aug. 30, 1906, of Sioux Falls, S. D., m Edward Breen.   Anna E. Tunnell m third, Fred Walters, at Sioux Falls, S. D., who d 1924 Sapulpa, Okla.)

    d.   Amanda Catherine Tunnell b Aug 19, 1867, of St. Joe, Mo. (m Benjamin Scott Blake Mar. 4, 1885 (b Dec. 18, 1862) and had an only ch.; 1, Jerry M. Blake b Aug. 3, 1891, m Edith Ferguson Oct. 25, 1908 (b May 10, 1888) and had; (aa) Alice M. Blake b Dec. 23, 1909).

    e.   Calvin Witt Tunnell b May 2, 1869, of Dawson, Okla. (m Susie A. Harrington, sister of Lucy Harrington, Nov. 16, 1890 (b Dec. 24, 1875; d Aug. 23, 1924 Dawson, Okla.) and had; 1, Mary Ethel Tunnell, of Lakin, Kan., m Grover B. Smith, at Garden City, Kan. and had; (aa) James Albert Smith b Aug. 11, 1911 Holcomb, Kan.; (bb) Bessie Urene Smith b Dec. 26, 1912 Holcomb, Kan.; (cc) Lena May Smith b July 10, 1914 Deerfield, Kan.; (dd) Edna Ruth Smith b Jan. 3, 1916 Lakin, Kan.; (ee) Walter Richard Smith b Sept. 29, 1917 Lakin, Kan.; (ff) Helen Marie Smith b Jan. 11, 1919 Lakin, Kan.; (gg) Loyd Smith b July 5, 1925.; 2, Bertha Ellen Tunnell b July 1, 1894, of Williamsburg, Kan., m A. Lawson Miskimon and had; (aa) Wesley Edgar Miskimon; (bb) Forest Olin Miskimon; (cc) Morton Loyd Miskimon; (dd) Everett Earl Miskimon; 3, Charles Albert Tunnell b Aug. 1, 1896; d Sept. 16, 1896; 4, Lewis Alfred Tunnell b Aug. 30, 1897, m Lena Wise and had three ch.; 5, Luther Edward Tunnell b Dec. 30, 1899, of Buffalo, Okla. m Mary Watts and had two ch.; 6, Edith May Tunnell b June 29, 1902; d abt 1921 Albuquerque, N. Mex., m Arthur Wise, brother of Lena Wise, and had one child that died in inf. 7, Theodore Roosevelt Tunnell b Nov. 19, 1904; 8, Loyd Harrison Tunnell b May 29, 1908 Kibby, Okla.; 9, Glen Bertie Tunnell b abt 1910; 10, Willie Tunnell b abt 1913; 11, Hazel Tunnell b abt 1915).

    f.   Caroline Tunnell b June 24, 1871; d Sept. 8, 1872.

g. Mary E. Tunnell b Dec. 11, 1872; d Apr. 23, 1914 Cogar, Okla. (m William Hack July 30, 1890 (b Oct. 20, 1853, of Pittsburg, Kan.) and had; 1, Etta L. Hack b Dec. 13, 1891 in Kan., m first, John M. Doane (d Jan. 18, 1918 Davenport, Okla.); and second, T. J. Marks Feb. 18, 1919 (d Oct. 27, 1919 Tulsa, Okla.); and third, George Shrimp Jan. 2, 1921, and had a daughter, Ruth Helen, of Drumright, Okla.; 2, Clara Elizabeth Hack b Sep. 17, 1893 Kan.; d Sep. 27, 1920, m William Thompson Feb. 10, 1920 and had no ch.; 3, Charles Thomas Hack b Dec. 25, 1895 in Mo., of Tomkawa, Okla., m Martha Taylor June 1919 and had; (aa) Mildred Hack b Mar. 9, 1923; 4, Alvina Irene Hack b Nov. 10, 1897 Glencoe, Okla.; d Aug. 13, 1916 Cedar Grove; m Harry Hart July 1, 1914 and had (aa) Lula Hart b June 9, 1915; d July 25, 1916; (bb) Ilene Hart b June 29, 1916; d July 26, 1916; 5, George Franklin Hack b Feb. 6, 1900 Glencoe, Okla.; d Sept. 1, 1923 Pittsburg, Kan., unmarried; 6, Asa Tillman Hack b May 31, 1902, of Towkawa, Okla., m Laura Taylor, sister Martha Taylor, Nov. 24, 1923; 7, David Arthur Hack b Oct. 27, 1903; d Dec. 25, 1903; 8, Edwin Elliott Hack b Sept. 29, 1904, unm., of Drumright, Okla. 9, Harriet Melissa Hack b Mar. 23, 1907, of Pittsburg, Kan., m Earl Spencer Aug. 30, 1924 Pittsburg, Kan.; 10, Joseph Luther Hack b Mar. 2, 1909; 11, James Levi Hack b Apr. 1, 1911).

h. Ida May Tunnell b Dec. 27, 1873, of St. Joe, Mo. (m William A. Blake May 29, 1890 and had; 1, Estella Salaka Blake b Nov. 12, 1891 Wier City, Kan.; 2, Horace Wesley Blake b Feb. 23, 1894 Cherokee, Kan.; 3, Thomas Buster Blake b May 3, 1896 St. Joe, Mo.; 4, Charles Peter Blake b Nov. 21, 1898 Maysville, Mo.; 5, Mable Gertrude Blake b Mar. 4, 1901 St. Joe, Mo.; d Mar. 7, 1902 St. Joe; 6, Everett Allison Blake b Aug. 4, 1902 St. Joe; d Dec. 26, 1902 St. Joe; 7, Henry Franklin Blake b Apr. 29, 1904; 8, Pearl Florence Crysta. B ake b Apr. 7, 1907 St. Joe; 9, Odessia Gladys Blake b June 11, 1909 St. Joe.)

i. James Herbert Tunnell b May 6, 1876, of St. Joe, Mo. (m ——— ———, who died 1924).

j. John Luther Tunnell b Mar. 27, 1878, of Randlett, Okla (m Maggie Ada Smith Nov. 7, 1909 (b Oct. 2, 1884) and had; 1, Lemuel Grady Tunnell b Dec. 10, 1910; 2, Olive Elizabeth Tunnell b Feb. 2, 1914; 3, Virgie Lee Tunnell b June 9, 1916; 4, Chester Tunnell b Dec. 23, 1918; 5, Martha Pearl Tunnell b Mar. 22, 1922; 6, Frank Tunnell b June 4, 1923).

k. William Thomas Tunnell b Oct. 13, 1879 nr McPherson, Kan. of Buffalo, Okla. (m Emily Iva Large Feb. 10, 1904 in Iowa. (b May 12, 1886 Iowa) and had an only ch.; 1, Ermal Otis Tunnell b Jan. 21, 1905).

l. Teletha Polly Tunnell b Aug. 17, 1881; d May 1, 1905 Douglas, Okla. (m Theodore Malzahn Feb. 19, 1899 Exline, Iowa and had; 1, Lester Malzahn b Nov. 1899; d in inf.; 2, Everett Malzahn b Oct. 1901 d in inf.)

m. David Franklin Tunnell b Aug. 10, 1884, (m Martha Johnson Feb. 5, 1909 (b Mar. 10, 1890) and had no ch.

Two. Mary Catherine Tunnell b Nov. 9, 1838 nr Carrollton, Ill. d Nov. 6, 1873 nr Conway, Kan.; married Emanuel W. Young Sept. 28, 1856 in Ill. (b Jan. 27, 1830; d Dec. 28, 1896 Trinidad, Col.) and had ch b nr Plainview, Ill., all of whom but one d McPherson Co., Kan.; (a) Edwin Young b Dec. 28, 1857; d Aug. 5, 1885, unmarried; (b) Lucy H. Young b Mar. 5, 1860; d Mar. 5, 1882, unmarried; (c) Emma Young b Dec. 15, 1861; d July 22, 1898 Trinidad, Col. (m Fred Minns (d Nov. 1918 Marquette, Kan.) and had ch b nr McPherson, Kan.; 1, Agnes Blanch Minns b Dec. 24, 1882, of Kansas City,

Mo., m Clarence Lester bef. Sept. 1906 (b Jan. 28, 1877) and had; (aa)
Ruby Lester; (bb) Frederick Lester; (cc) Edith Lester; 2, Floyd
Minns, died Aug. 5, 1885; 3, Chester Nelson Minns b June 5, 1886, of
La Junta, Col., m Helen Horchheimer Sept. 4, 1920 Cheraw, Col. and
had ch b Marquette, Kan.; (aa) Phyllis Elaine Minns b Feb. 13, 1922;
(bb) Marie Minns b Feb. 1923; 4, Ralph Frederick Minns b Mar. 28,
1889, unm., d in Brest, France Feb. 5, 1918, buried Arlington, Va.,
enlisted in Nebraska and served in First Co. Vet. Hospital 18, 5,
Mary Minns b Sept. 5, 1891, of Russell, Kan., m Joe Huston after
June 1906 and had; (aa) Sidney Huston; (bb) Vivian Huston; (cc)
Laverne Huston; (dd) Earl Huston; (ee) Max Huston; (ff) Ralph
M. Huston; 6, Paul Minns b Dec. 9, 1893, served five years in Co. D.
137th Inf., enlisted McPherson, Kan., of McPherson, m Frieda Fisher
and had; (aa) Lester Minns; (bb) Pauline Minns; (cc) Deloris May
Minns; 7, Fred Minns died July 1, 1896); (d) Mary Young, twin, b
Jan. 15, 1863; d Feb. 21, 1885, unmarried; (e) Martha Young, twin
of Mary Young, b Jan. 15, 1863; d Feb. 11, 1882, unmarried; (f)
Nelson Young b Feb. 12, 1866; d July 15, 1885, unmarried; (g)
Josephine Young b July 25, 1872; d Mar. 25, 1895, unmarried.

Three. Luther Benton Tunnell b Jan. 3, 1841 nr Carrollton, Ill.,
retired farmer, McPherson, Kan.; served in the War Between the
States; enlisted in Sidney Hull's Co. F. 122nd Ill. Regt. Aug. 15,
1862; discharged from service July 15, 1865 Mobile, Ala. He married
first, Adeline Jane King, Aug. 24, 1865. She was born Feb. 15, 1843
Montgomery, Ala. and died Dec. 2, 1903 McPherson, Kan., the dau of
Samuel P. and Elizabeth (Sawyer) King; gdau John and Elizabeth
(Bailey) Sawyer; ggdau John and Sarah (Grouch) Sawyer. He mar-
ried second, Rosetta Susan Risinger Ruble, Aug. 24, 1905 McPherson,
Kan. (b June 13, 1864 Ripley Co., Ind., dau of David and Catherine
(Maddox) Risinger). Children:

a. Felix Oscar Tunnell b Sept. 21, 1866 nr Plainview, Ill.; d
Aug. 1867 nr Plainview, Ill.

b Miles Leib Tunnell b Nov. 8, 1867 east of Virden, Ill., of Mc-
Pherson, Kan. (m Matilda Jane Davis Jan. 1, 1891 Kan. and had ch
b nr McPherson, Kan.; 1, Ella May Tunnell b Jan. 23, 1892, m Emmitt
Nelson All, son of Daniel Vorice All (b 1862 Terre Haute, Ind.) and
Maggie McGlaughlin All (b 1859 Darlington, England), Feb. 23, 1910
McPherson, Kan. (b 1885 Elyria, Kan.) and had; (aa) Roma Alene All
b Jan. 6, 1911 Elyria, Kan.; (bb) Marvin Delbert All b Nov. 3, 1914
Elyria, Kan.; (cc) Gilbert Verlyn All b Feb. 18, 1917 nr McPherson,
Kan.; 2, Russell Delbert Tunnell b Sept. 18, 1894 nr McPherson, Kan.,
of Kiowa, Kan., served in World War; inducted in U. S. A. June 24,
1918, left Long Island Nov. 2, 1918; landed Brest, France Nov. 9,
1918; left Brest Jan. 4, 1919; landed Long Island Jan 17, 1919; discharged at Camp Knox, Ky. Feb. 17, 1919; m Naomi Ruth Wright
Sept. 12, 1917 McPherson, Kan. and had; (aa) Bettie Dee Tunnell b
Oct. 19, 1920 Windom, Kan.)

c. Ele Ora Tunnell b July 8, 1869 east of Virden, Ill.; d July
13, 1925 McPherson, Kan. (m Nettie E. Langdon May 22, 1890 nr Mc-
Pherson, Kan. and had ch b nr McPherson, Kan.; 1, Guy Earl Tunnell
b Apr. 30, 1891, served in World War, with overseas service, in Co. D.
137th Inf. 35th Div., returned to America July 5, 1919; 2, Hazel Irene
Tunnell b July 24, 1894, m Earl Claytor Feb. 14, 1914 and had; (aa)
Edith Louise Claytor b Oct. 21, 1916; 3, Maude Rose Tunnell b July
25, 1896, of McPherson, Kan., m first, Ernest Buehre, Mar. 9, 1918
Camp Funston, Kan. (b Aug. 10, 1895 Ellis, Kan., killed on War's
crimson battlefield. in the Argonne Oct. 1, 1918. He served in Supply
Co. 89th Div. at Camp Funston and was transferred to 140th Inf.

35th Div..) Maud Tunnell m second, John Henry Buehre, brother of Ernest Buehre, June 17, 1919 Ellsworth, Kan. and had; (aa) child b Mar. 1920; d at one day; (bb) Bernice Buehre b Feb. 21, 1921 Salina, Kan.; (cc) Ruth May Buehre b May 9, 1923 nr McPherson, Kan.; 4, Lillian Addie Tunnell b Dec. 11, 1897; d Jan. 11, 1901; 5, child b and d June 12, 1902; 6, Vivian Luther Tunnell b Dec. 25, 1903; 7, Ora La-Verne Tunnell b Nov. 7, 1909).

    d. Ella Belle Tunnell b May 20, 1873 nr Hutchinson, Kan.; d Dec. 19, 1887 nr McPherson, Kan.

    e. George Thomas Tunnell b Oct. 24, 1876 nr Hutchinson, Kan. for a number of years Sec. of The Empire Zinc Co., of Denver, Col., transferred to New York Office 1920, of Yonkers, N. Y. (m Edith Augusta Blunt Aug. 21, 1904 Kansas City, Mo. and had ch b Denver, Col.; 1, Robert Gordon Tunnell b Apr. 28, 1907; 2, Madeline Jean Tunnell b Jan. 24, 1910. Edith A. Blunt b June 4, 1881 Chicago, Ill., dau of George Green Blunt (b Jan, 16, 1848 Mason Co., Ill.; deceased) and Alice Estella Phelps Blunt (b Aug. 9, 1852); gdau Robert Chambers Blunt (b Jan. 11, 1826; d May 18, 1866) and Mary Jane Trailor Blunt (b Aug. 26, 1827); same William G. Phelps (b Feb. 5, 1829 O.; d in Neb.) and Martha A. Russell Phelps; ggdau Thomas Fisher Blunt (b July 14, 1800 Md.; d Sept. 6, 1881 Ky.) and Sinia Alderson Blunt (b 1795 Hart Co., Ky.); same Jesse Trailor Jr., in War af 1812, and Obedience Blankenship Trailor; same Ralph Rudolphus Phelps (b Sept. 17, 1789 Vermont; d Feb. 26, 1831 Ohio) and Catherine King Phelps (b Staunton, Va.; d in Ky.) same James Russell Jr. and Charity Smith Russell (b Sept. 20, 1807 N. Y.; d Mar. 11, 1876).

    f. Eda E. Tunnell b Apr. 13, 1879 nr Hutchinson, Kan.; d Apr. 17, 1879.

    g. Wesley Benton Tunnell b Aug. 26, 1882 nr Hutchinson, Kan. d July 27, 1886 nr Hutchinson, Kan.

    Four. Miriam Evaline Tunnell b Jan. 29, 1843 nr Plainview, Ill. d Mar. 3, 1873 nr Plainview, Ill.; married John William Armour abt 1867 and had no ch. J. W. Armour lived for many years nr Meldora, Ill.

    Five. Jane Elizabeth Tunnell b Mar. 31, 1848 nr Plainview, Ill. d Apr. 13, 1870; married Francis Marion Ragan Oct. 7, 1866 and had an only child, a son b 1868, who died in inf.

    IV. Sally Tunnell, dau of Calvin and Jane Addair Tunnell, was born Oct. 5, 1818 nr Edwardsville, Ill. and died Dec. 17, 1818 nr Edwardsville.

    V. Polly Tunnell, dau of Calvin and Jane Addair Tunnell, the second white child born north of Macoupin Creek in the present Greene Co., Ill., was born Mar. 25, 1820 and died Jan. 23, 1902 on the farm she had lived since her marriage to Randolph Witt, Aug. 18, 1836, six miles sw of Carrollton, Ill. Randolph Witt was born Dec. 30, 1810 nr Witt's Foundry, Tenn. and died June 24, 1884 sw of Carrollton, Ill. He was the son of Eli and Nancy (McNealy) Witt, who were married July 17, 1806 nr Witt's Foundry, Tenn., then in Jefferson Co. Eli Witt was born Aug. 15, 1785 on the farm on which his children were born in that part of Tenn. then known as The State of Franklin. He served in the Second War with the British; participated in the battle of Horseshoe; moved, with his family, to Greene Co., Ill. 5 miles sw of Carrollton, arriving there Dec. 9, 1829; died east of Carrollton Oct. 15, 1851. Nancy McNealy was born May 14, 1790 and died Oct. 17, 1860 nr Carrollton, Ill. Eli Witt was the son of Captain Elijah Witt, b 1755 in Va., who d 1802 nr Witt's Foundry, Tenn.; gson of Charles and Lavinia (Harbour) Witt, of Halifax Co., Va. in 1771. The father of Charles Witt was William Witt, one of the

French refugees from Pays d' Aunis, La Rochelle, who in 1699, with his wife settled at Manakintowne, about 15 mi. from Richmond, Va. The Huguenot Society of the Founders of Manakin in the Colony of Virginia was founded and organized by a descendant of William Witt, Mrs. Mary Latham Norton, of San Francisco, who is the National President of the society. Children;

> One. Andrew Jackson Witt b Dec. 14, 1837.
> Two. John Calvin Witt b Feb. 19, 1842.
> Three. William Tunnell Witt b Jan. 14, 1844.
> Four. Jane Elizabeth Witt b Feb. 14, 1847.
> Five. Elzina Witt b July 2, 1851.
> Of these;

One. Andrew Jackson Witt b Dec. 14, 1837; d Feb. 8, 1902 on the farm on which he was born, his death being the third to occur in the family within sixteen days. He was buried at Girard, Ill. He married Frances Ball Apr. 23, 1863 nr Virden, in Macoupin Co., Ill. She was born Apr. 11, 1837 nr Talybont, Breconshire, Wales and died at the Methodist parsonage, Carrollton, Ill. Jan. 1, 1917. She was buried at Girard, Ill. She was the dau of Richard McLothlin Ball (b abt 1800 at the "Yatt" home, still standing, in the parish of old Radnor, Radnorshire, Wales; crossed to America and settled at Virden, Ill. 1854, where he died Aug. 15, 1856) and Maria Evans Ball. Richard M. Ball, the son of William Ball (b abt 1756 Herefordshire, England; d in Wales) and Arabelle McLothin Ball, the dau of Richard McLothlin, of Scotland. Maria Evans was born May 6, 1804 Rutland, Radnorshire, Wales; emigrated to America, on the sailing vessel "Aurora," with several of her children, to join her husband; arrived at Virden, Ill. Dec. 11, 1855. She died Mar. 18, 1893 nr Girard, Ill. and was the dau of Thomas and Mary (Ball) Evans and gdau of William Evans. Mary Ball Evans was distantly related to William Ball, b abt 1756. Two brothers of Frances Ball Witt, John Ball and George Ball, married sisters of A. J. Witt, Jane E. Witt and Elzina Witt, while a sister of Frances Ball Witt, Ann Ball married Calvin Tunnell, an uncle of A. J. Witt. A nephew of Frances Ball Witt, George Lewis Lloyd, married Florence Tunnell, first cousin of A. J. Witt. With the exception of ten years, 1890 to 1900 spent in Virden, Ill., A. J. Witt and wife spent on their farm nr Farmersville, Ill., a portion of the town situated on their land. Ch. b nr Farmersville, Ill.; (a) Arabelle Jane Witt b Mar. 21, 1864; d Aug. 7, 1882 Farmersville, unm.; (b) Newton Randolph Witt b Feb. 27, 1867; d Apr. 30, 1887 Farmersville, unm.; (c) Annie Mary Witt b Feb. 1, 1873; d May 29, 1915, unm., Farmresville; (d) Maria Irene Witt b Feb. 5, 1876, of Beardstown, Ill. (m Rev. Charles Spence Boyd Aug. 17, 1904 Farmersville and had no children. He was b Dec. 29, 1874 Washington, Ohio, son of James Scott and Mary Eleanor Spence Boyd (b 1843; d May 12, 1924 Cambridge, O.); gs John and Susan (Scott) Boyd; same James and Harriet (Saltsgaver) Spence. Rev. C. S. Boyd deeply and vitally interested in anything pertaining to Methodism entered the Central Illinois Conference 1901, with first pastorate at Farmersville. Succeeding pastorates; Morrisonville, Bloomington circuit, Downs, Arthur, Carrollton, Leroy, Springfield for six years, and Beardstown); (e) Henry Jackson Witt b June 3, 1880, farmer, Farmersville, Ill. (m Ethel May Scott Aug. 26, 1908 Elizabeth City, New Jersey and had ch b Farmersville, Ill.; 1, Charles Jackson Witt b Aug. 8, 1909; 2, Walter Henry Witt b Apr. 20, 1911; 3, Frances Lydia Witt b June 25, 1913; 4, Mable Scott Witt b Aug. 12, 1917; 5, Robert Newton Witt b May 26, 1921. Ethel M. Scott b Mar. 15, 1882 Elizabeth City, N. J., dau of Charles Winfield Scott (b

Feb. 11, 1846) and Lydia Emmet DeGroff Scott (b Nov. 24, 1847);
gdau Charles Scott (b Jan. 10, 1815 England; d 1885 N. J.) and
Rachel Williams Scott (b June 7, 1817 Elizabeth City, N. J.; d N. J.);
same Christopher H. DeGroff (b Apr. 25, 1815; d;) and Eleanor
Patterson Latimer DeGroff; ggdau David and Hannah (Whitehead)
Williams; same Josiah and Anna (Shear) DeGroff; same Johiel and
Abigail (Hoover) Latimer.

Two.   John Calvin Witt b Feb. 19, 1842; d Oct. 17, 1842.

Three.   William Tunnell Witt b Jan. 14, 1844; d Jan 29, 1902.
His entire life was spent on the farm on which he was born.   He
was never married.

Four. Jane Elizabeth Witt b Feb. 14, 1847; d Oct. 2, 1917 Farm-
ersville, Ill.; married John Ball, son of Richard M. and Maria (Evans)
Ball, Oct. 16, 1867 nr Carrollton, Ill.   He was born Oct. 19, 1842 nr
Talybont, Breconshire, Wales and died Apr. 4, 1914 Farmersville, Ill.
From their marriage until their removal to Farmersville, Ill. in 1907,
they lived east of Girard, Ill.   In 1892 he organized the bank of
John Ball & Co., Farmersville, Ill., known now as The Farmersville
State Bank, and was its president until his death.   Ch. b e of
Girard, Ill.; (a) Clarence Henry Ball b Aug. 30, 1869, farmer, Van-
dalia, Ill. (m Margie Smetters May 3, 1899 Chicago, Ill. and had 1,
Frederick Newton Ball b Jan. 19, 1902 Harvel, Ill., unm., teacher,
Vandalia, Ill.; 2, John Allen Ball b Dec. 26, 1903 Farmersville,
Ill., unm., salesman, St.Louis, Mo.; 3, Clarence Elbert Ball b June
27, 1908 E. St. Louis, Ill.; d Jan. 23, 1909 E. St. Louis, Ill.; buried
Farmersville; 4, Helen Elizabeth Ball b Apr. 16, 1911 Luoraxa, Ark.
Margie Smetters dau of Daniel and Nancy Jane (Hartley) Smetters
latter b 1843 Mt. Sterling, Ill.; d Oct. 12, 1919 Chicago, Ill., dau of Eli
and Mary (Buchanan) Hartley); (b) Elbert Witt Ball b Aug. 28, 1872,
cashier Farmersville State Bank. Farmersville, Ill. (m Metta Olivia
Simonson Dec. 26, 1901 east of Farmersville and had an only child;
1, Amy Elberta Ball b Aug. 27, 1902 on the farm which was her
father's birthplace as well as her own, of Girard, Ill., m Ross P.
Bonnett, farmer son of David and Florence (Jordan) Bonnett, Sept.
16, 1921 Peoria, Ill. and had ch b e of Girard, Ill.; (aa) Elizabeth
Louise Bonnett b June 10, 1922; (bb) Elbert David Bonnett b Jan.
26, 1924.   Metta O. Simonson b Mar. 30, 1873 nr Farmersville, Ill.,
dau of Mical Simonson (b June2, 1829 Norway; came to America
Aug. 1, 1849; d Feb. 21, 1870 nr Farmersville, Ill.) and Elvira Steidley Simonson (b Feb. 29, 1836 Xenia, O.; d Oct. 2. 1899 nr Farmersville, Ill., m July 18, 1869 Girard, Ill.); gdau Simon Simonson
(b 1790 Norway; came to America Aug. 1, 1849; d Jan. 1851 Spring-
field, Ill.) and Kjersten (Salveson) Gjerluldson Simonson (b 1788; d
1841 Norway; married 1814 Norway); same Joseph B. Steidley (b
Mar. ., 1801 Md.; d Jan. 2, 1861 Palmyra, Ill.) and Elvira Rowland
Steidley (b Feb. 28, 1807 Shenandoah Valley, Va.; d Mar. 7, 1849
Palmyra, Ill.; married Dec. 13, 1827). Elvira Rowland dau of
Samuel Rowland); (c) Agnes Elzina Ball b June 9, 1875, of Girard,
Ill. (m Castellar Michael Simonson, farmer, son of Mical and Elvira
Steidley Simonson, Oct. 16, 1904 nr Girard, Ill. and had ch b n e of
Farmersville, Ill.; 1, Margaret Simonson b Jan 12, 1908; 2, Robert
Ball Simonson b Aug. 16, 1910; 3. Richard Castellar Simonson b Sept.
11, 1915.   C. M. Simonson b June 25, 1877 nr Farmersville, Ill.
served in the Phillipines during the Spanish-American War); (d)
Allen Jackson Ball b Aug. 24, 1878, farmer, Girard, Ill. (m Flora
Agnes Gilman, Sept. 19, 1906 Springfield, Ill. and had ch b on same
farm on which the father has always lived; 1, Kenneth Eugene Ball
b Dec. 18, 1905; 2, Leland Duane Ball b Oct. 6, 1917; 3, Dale Ball,

twin, b Dec. 27, 1922; 4, Donald Ball, twin, b and d Dec. 27, 1922. Flora Agnes Gilman b June 24, 1885 nr Farmersville, Ill, dau of Charles (b in Brunswick, Germany) and Christina (Hantla) Gilman); (e) Amy Jane Ball b Aug. 16, 1886, of Farmersville, Ill. (m Dr. Karl Lowell Hayes Sept. 14, 1916 Pleasant Plains, Ill. and had an only ch.; 1, John Joseph Hayes b Aug. 17, 1919 Farmersville, Ill. Dr. K. L. Hayes b May 3, 1882 Sangamon Co., Ill., served as Lieut. in Medical Corps in World War; son Joseph W. (d Sept. 14, 1915 Pleasant Plains, Ill.) and Fannie M. (Pierce) Hayes (d Dec. 11, 1918 Pleasant Plains, Ill.); gs Augustus Hayes, b Lancaster, Penn.)

Five. Elzina Witt b July 2, 1851, of Jacksonville, Ill.; married George Ball Feb. 17, 1876 nr Carrollton, Ill.   He is a retired farmer and was born Sept. 12, 1846, nr Talybont, Breconshire, Wales, eighth and youngest son of Richard M. and Maria (Evans) Ball.   From their marriage until 1897, when they moved to Jacksonville, Ill., their home was east of Girard, Ill.   Children; (a) Effie Elzia Ball b Feb. 21, 1877, of Jacksonville, Ill. (m Eber G. Moore, Jan. 8, 1898 Jacksonville, Ill. (b Jan. 24, 1864 Athens, O.; d Apr. 2, 1917 Chicago, Ill.; buried Jacksonville) and had; 1, daughter b and d Oct. 11, 1898 Jacksonville; 2, Edna Irene Moore b Sept. 21, 1899 Jacksonville; d Oct. 21, 1899 Jacksonville; 3, daughter b and d July 31 1900 Jacksonville; 4, Lucy Mary Moore b July 9, 1906 Chicago, Ill., of Jacksonville, Ill.); (b) Lucy Mary Ball b May 26, 1879. unm., of Jacksonville, Ill., compiler of Tunnell record and National Historian of Founders of Manakin Huguenot Society; (c) Frederick William Ball b Nov. 3, 1881; d Oct. 25, 1901 Jacksonville. Ill., unm.; buried Girard, Ill.   To George and Elzina Witt Ball and to the memory of their son this record of the Tunnell family is affectionately dedicated.

VI.   Eliza Jane Tunnell, dau of Calvin and Jane Addair Tunnell, was born Nov. 9, 1821 and died Mar. 20, 1898 Lawson, Mo.   She married Pryor Dulaney Witt, (son of Eli and Nancy (McNealy) Witt, gs of Elijah Witt; ggs Charles and Lavinia (Harbour) Witt of Halifax Co., Va.; ggs William Witt, one of the founders of Manikintowne, Va. 1699) Mar. 12, 1840 nr Carrollton, Ill.   He was born Dec. 30, 1816 nr Witt's Foundry, Tenn. and died Jan. 28, 1881 nr Lawson, Mo. Children b nr Carrollton, Ill.

One.   Nancy Jane Witt b Oct. 2, 1841.

Two.   Mary Louisa Witt b Oct. 14, 1844.

Three.   William Worth Witt b May 1, 1848.

Four.   Emily Elizabeth Witt b Jan. 3, 1853.

Of these;

One.   Nancy Jane Witt b Oct. 2, 1841; d Apr. 29, 1874 in Mo.; married Pleasant Moss Robinette Mar. 27, 1862 Montgomery Co., Ill. He was born Feb. 9, 1840 and married second, Nannie Claflin, and lives Lawson, Mo. Ch.; (a) Mary Effie Robinette b Mar. 16, 1863 in Macoupin Co., Ill. east of Virden, of Perry, Okla. (m Reuben Cornelius Farris Mar. 31, 1881 Lawson. Mo. (b Mar. 31, 1860 Williamsburg, Ky.. son of John Hansford, b Apr. 19, 1832 Knox Co., Ky., and Amanda Melvina Eastin Farris, b Nov. 8, 1832 Madison Co., Ky.) and had ten ch b Lawson, Mo., others Waukomis, Okla.; 1, Ruby Farris b Oct. 5, 1882; d Oct. 29, 1918 Kansas City, Mo., m F. O. Milnes May 16, 1915 Kansas City, and had; (aa) Helen Louise Milnes b 1917; 2. Nina Farris b Oct. 6, 1883, of Oklahoma City, Okla., m Frank McMillen Sept. 3. 1912 Colorado Springs. Col.; 3, Moss Hansford Farris b Aug. 1, 1886 of Perry. Okla., m Mary Ella Dagley Oct. 24, 1915 Lawson, Mo. and had; (aa) Mary Louise Farris; (bb) Thelma Bernice Farris: (cc) Lelah Alice Farris; (dd) Betty Frances Farris; 4, Pearl Edna Farris b July 15, 1888, m Orville Lee Taylor Nov. 11,

1915, Pawhuska, Okla. and had; (aa) George Farris Taylor; (bb) Joe Warren Taylor; 5, Neva Louis Farres b July 22, 1890, of Oklahoma City, m Clem Vern Dodge Sept. 26, 1910 Enid, Okla. and had (aa) Clem Dodge; 6, Florence Emma Farris b Oct. 12, 1892, m J. Carl Williams Jan. 18, 1914 Sapulpa, Okla.; 7, Howard Cornelius Farris b May 22, 1894, of Pawhuska, Okla., served in World War, m Grace Pearl Smith Feb. 5, 1921 Pawhuska; 8, Ernest Witt Farris b Oct. 21, 1896, served in World War, unmarried, of Pawhuska; 9, Helen Effie Farris b Aug. 31, 1899, unm., of Oklahoma City; 10, Nancy Ruth Farris b July 29, 1901, unm., of Oklahoma City; 11, Margaret Amanda Farris b July 29, 1904 Waukomis, Okla., unm., of Oklahoma City; 12, Harriet Inez Farris b May 1907; 13, Marvin Ball Farris b Feb. 24, 1910); (b) Pleasant Orson Robinette b Nov. 23, 1864, of Cameron, Mo. (m Mary Claflin July 1887 Mo. and had; 1, Nancy Ethel Robinette b Apr. 25, 1888, m ——— ——— who d soon after marriage; 2, Leon Morris Robinette b June 30, 1891); (c) William Jefferson Robinette b Feb. 24, 1867, of Lawson, Mo. (m first, Emma Hart, Aug. 22, 1889, who d Lawson, Mo. and had; 1, Clyde Robinette b July 30, 1891; 2, Harold Robinette b Feb. 26, 1895; and married second, ——— ——— and had one son); (d) Maurice Witt Robinette b July 6, 1869, of Missoula, Mont. (m Vitta Whitseet May 27, 1894 and had; 1, Glenn Robinette b Jan. 29, 1895, m ——— ——— and had; 1, ——— Robinette); (e) Jane Louis Robinette b June 17, 1872, of Kansas City, Mo. (m Lute Vivion Feb. 4, 1891 and had two ch.; 1, Cleda Vivion b Jan. 31, 1892; 2, ——— Vivion (son) b June 1911 Kansas City, Mo.)

Two. Mary Louisa Witt b Oct. 14, 1844, of Lawson, Mo.; married James Lowe Smith Mar. 26, 1863 Bois D'Arc township, Montgomery Co., Ill. (b Sept. 2, 1840 Knoxville, Tenn.; d May 16, 1897 Lawson, Mo., son of John Houston Smith (b Apr. 8, 1813; d Oct. 7, 1846) and Catherine Lowe Smith (July 25, 1810; d Jan. 1, 1847) and had five ch. b Montgomery Co., Ill., others nr Lawson, Mo.; (a) Walter Edwin Smith b Dec. 1864, unm., of Lawson, Mo.; (b) Mattie Smith b Apr. 1, 1866, of Fort Collins, Col. (m Edward Donohoo, son of William and Sarah Elizabeth Donohoo, Dec. 11, 1890 Lawson, Mo. and had ch b Lawson, Mo.; 1, daughter b Aug. 9, 1892; d Oct. 25, 1892; 2, Mildred Frances Donohoo b Des. 9, 1894 of Casper, Wyoming, m Robert Morris Hancock Sept. 9, 1921 Denver, Col; 3, James Ellsworth Donahue b July 4, 1899 of Fort Collins, Col., m Mable Leerskov Dec. 9, 1920 Brush, Col. and had; (aa) Janet Marilyn Donahue b Jan. 8, 1925; 4, Elizabeth Donohoo b May 28, 1902; d July 20, 1902); (c) Lettie Jane Smith b Jan. 5, 1867, of Kansas City, Mo. (m Thomas J. Campbell, son of William and Salina Campbell, Jan. 9, 1890 Plattsburg, Mo. and had; 1, Lillian Ruth Campbell b Dec. 9, 1891 nr Lawson, Mo., m Harvey J. Haney May 2, 1915 Plattsburg, Mo.; 2, James Herbert Campbell b May 18, 1893 nr Lathrop, Mo., m Sarah Elizabeth Woner Dec. 10, 1913 Lathrop, Mo. and had (aa) Richard Kenneth Campbell b July 24. 1915 Lathrop, Mo.; (bb) Virginia Louise Campbell b Nov. 8, 1918 Lawson, Mo.; (cc) James Audley Campbell b June 26, 1924 Kansas City, Mo.); (d) Lillie Smith b Dec. 26, 1869, of Denver, Col. (m Ben Kemper, son of John Quincy Adams and Adelaide (Smith) Kemper, Jan. 14, 1897 Lawson, Mo. and had; 1, Lynn Smith Kemper b May 28, 1899 Cameron, Mo., m Mary Elizabeth Baker Sept. 30, 1922 Pueblo, Col. and had (aa) son b 1925; 2, Laurence Benjamin Kemper b Nov. 24, 1900 St. Joe, Mo.; d Oct. 28, 1921 nr Fort Morgan, Col., unm.); (e) Mary Emma Smith b Oct. 14, 1872, of Alamosa, Col. (m Clement Leonard Smith, son of Addison and Catherine Smith, Dec. 24, 1890 Lawson, Mo. and had ch b nr

Lawson; 1, Chester Clement Smith b Oct. 12, 1891, m Clarice Hightower May 3, 1912 Colorado Springs, Col.; 2, Mary Victoria Smith b Dec. 26, 1892; 3, Carrie Purl Smith b Dec. 17, 1896, m Richard Wesley Hauser May 8, 1912 Kansas City, Mo. (d Mar. 23, 1916 nr Excelisor Springs, Mo.) and had; (aa) Carolyn Hauser b May 11, 1914 nr Excelsior Springs; 4, Ralph Leonard Smith b Sept. 19, 1898, m Laura Ann Spencer Sept. 12, 1923 Alamosa, Col.; 5, Florence Emma Smith b Feb. 25, 1900, m Irvin Merchant Aug. 18, 1923 Kansas City, Mo.; 6, Lenora Jane Smith b Mar. 21, 1902, m George Naylor Nov. 14, 1923 Kansas City, Mo. and had (aa) John Addison Naylor b Sept. 4, 1924 Kansas City; 7, Edith Frances Smith b Nov. 25, 1905); (f) William Dulaney Smith b Mar. 17, 1874, nr Lawson, Mo., unm., of Calif.; (g) Katherine Smith b Apr. 25, 1876, of Turney, Mo., m James Ernest Williams, son of Thomas J. and Mary Orcelia Williams, Mar. 5, 1902 Lawson, Mo. and had ch b nr Cameron, Mo.; 1, Helen Meredith Williams b Dec. 21, 1906; 2, James Laverne Williams b Mar. 1911); (h) Nell Smith b Oct. 25, 1879, unm., of Lawson, Mo.; (i) Grace Smith b Oct. 7, 1881; d Mar. 20, 1912 Denver, Col., buried Lawson, Mo., unm.; (j) Ethel Smith b Apr. 25, 1883; d Aug. 31, 1883; (k) Edith Smith b Aug. 14, 1884, of Excelsior Springs, Mo. (m Reuben Shouse, son of James Officer and Elizabeth Shouse, Nov. 12, 1901, and had ch b nr Lawson, Mo.; 1, Lucille Shouse b Nov. 29, 1902, m David William Smallwood Sept. 27, 1921 Liberty, Mo. and had; (aa) Jean Marie Smallwood b July 28, 1922 Kansas City, Mo.; 2, James Estill Shouse b Sept. 2, 1908); (l) Beatrice Smith b Oct. 26, 1886, of Los Angelese, Calif. (m first, Morris Chauncey Bidwell, July 6, 1902 Lawson, Mo. and had an only child; 1, Marian Louise Bidwell b June 25, 1903 Norborne, Mo., unm.; and m second, Caleb Benjamin Guinn, son of Isaac and Mary Jane Guinn, Sept. 10, 1923 Kansas City, Mo.)

Three. William Worth Witt b May 1, 1848; d Dec. 7, 1878 nr Lawson, Mo., unm.

Four. Emily Elizabeth Witt b Jan. 3, 1853; d July 24, 1897 Lawson, Mo.; married Chester Bethel, Jan. 4, 1874 nr Lawson, Mo. He was born June 17, 1847 and died Jan. 6, 1922 Spokane, Wash., son of Bluford and Nancy (Seymour) Bethel. He married second, Florence Moberly, 1899 Plattsburg, Mo. Ch. b nr Lawson, Mo.; (a) Nancy Alice Bethel b Oct. 9, 1874, of Hamburg, Ark. (m Frank Titus, son of John Harrison and Lavinia Elizabeth Titus, July 17, 1900 Lawson, Mo. (b Sept. 26, 1871) and had first three ch b nr Lawson, others at Hamburg, Ark.; 1, Helen Elizabeth Titus b Apr. 21, 1901, unm.; 2, Virginia Louise Titus b Dec. 9, 1902, unm.; 3, Frank Bethel Titus b Jan. 9, 1904; 4 John Myron Titus b Mar. 17, 1905; 5, Mary Ellen Titus b May 15, 1907; 6, William Harrison Titus b Oct. 20, 1910; d Mar. 26, 1912; 7, Ruth Frances Titus b Nov. 15, 1917); (b) Mary Effie Bethel b Feb. 5, 1881, of Spokane, Wash. (m James William Dawkins June 5, Salt Lake City, Utah. They have given their name to and are rearing two adopted children; 1, Mary Elizabeth Dawkins b Mar. 25, 1918; 2, Helen Louise Dawkins b Jan. 15, 1923); (c) Flora Eliza Bethel b Mar. 30, 1886; d July 18, 1917 Spokane, Wash. (m Ralph Hubert Zercher 1912 Couer d' Aline, Idaho and had; 1, William Henry Zercher b July 23, 1913 Spokane, Wash.)

VII. Luther Tunnell, son of Calvin and Jane Addair Tunnell, was born Dec. 5, 1824 and died Sept. 8, 1838.

VIII. Nancy Tunnell, dau of Calvin and Jane Addair Tunnell, was born Jan. 6, 1826 and died Mar. 10, 1907 nr Newbern, Va. She married a relative, George Summers, whose home was in Pulaski Co., Va., Feb. 10, 1847 nr Carrollton, Ill. He was born Mar. 19, 1814 in Ohio

and died Feb. 1, 1881 nr Newbern, Va., son of George Summers, who
died before 1835 Anderson Co., Tenn., and Susanne Addair Summers
(b 1789; d Oct. 2, 1865 Pulaski Co., Va.) Susanne Addair was a half-
sister of Jane Addair.   Children b Pulaski Co., Va.
   One.   Mary Jane Summers b Mar. 21, 1848.
   Two.   William Calvin Summers b Nov. 11, 1849.
   Three.   George Washington Summers b Sept. 8, 1851.
   Four. Margaret Ann Summers b Nov. 5, 1853.
   Five. John Robert Summers b Apr. 26, 1855.
   Six.   Emma Josephine Summers b Dec. 15, 1857.
   Seven.   James Elbert Summers b June 7, 1861.
   Eight.   Pryor DeWitt Summers b June 21, 1864.
   Nine.   Nannie Tunnell Summers b Apr. 8, 1868.
   Of these;
   One.   Mary Jane Summers b Mar. 21, 1848, of Ward West Vir-
ginia; married John Grafson Cecil, the Third, Sept. 28, 1876 Pulaska
Co., Va. (b Dec. 8, 1846; d July 29, 1917 Newbern, Va., son of John
Grayson Cecil, junior, and Linnie (Mitchell) Cecil; gson Rev. John
Grayson Cecil, senior, of the English Cecil family; and gson of Rev.
Zachariah Mitchell), and had ch. b Pulaski Co. Va.; (a) George Lee
Cecil b Sept. 30, 1877, of Spears Fork, W Va., m Emily (Spencer,
Townsend May 29, 1919 and had no ch.; (b) Josie Blanche Cecil b
Sept. 1. 1879; d Dec. 5, 1917 Newbern, Va. (m James Marvin Cecil. son
of William B. and Mollie (Trollinger) Cecil; gson John and Ellen
(Trinkle) Cecil; same John and Mary (Wygal) Trollinger, Feb. 16,
1897 Princeton, W. Va., (d Apr. 3, 1914 Dublin, Va.) and had; 1,
John Paul Cecil b Jan. 10, 1901, druggist, Blue Field, W. Va., m
Mildred Whietsell and had; (aa) Jacqueline Palmer Cecil b Sept. 8,
1923; 2, Lewis Cecil b Aug. 19, 1903, of Dublin, Va.); (c) Fred Tun-
nell Cecil b Oct. 16. 1881, unm., of Ward, W. Va.; (d) Harry Grayson
Cecil b Nov. 11, 1883; d Nov. 13, 1915 Greenup, Ky. (m Julia A. Pratt
1914 Greenup, Ky., now of Portsmouth, O. and had 1, Lattie Elizabeth
Cecil b June 27, 1915 Maysville, Ky.); (e) Mary Lattie Cecil b Dec.
9, 1885, of Princeton, W. Va. (m Kellie W. McClaugherty Feb. 22,
1905 Princeton, (real estate dealer, son of Dr. Walace and Lucretia
(Peck) McClaugherty, and had ch b Princeton; 1, Blanche Earnestine
McClaugherty b July 27, 1906; 2. Thomas Richard McClaugherty b
Sept. 4, 1908; 3. Walace McClaugherty b Mar. 3, 1912); (f) Frank
Summers Cecil b May 6, 1888, unm., of Logan, W. Va.; served in
World War; in 1911 and 1912 served in regular army; stationed at
Ft. Mott, N. J. and Ft. Slocum, N. Y.
   Two.   William Calvin Summers b Nov. 11, 1849, unm.
   Three.   George Washington Summers, b Sept. 8, 1851, farmer,
Snowville, Va.; married Salome Meredith, dau of Jeremiah Crockett
and Sarah Meredith, Aug. 24, 1876 Pulaski Co., Va. (b Sept. 16, 1849
Snowville, Va.) and had ch b nr Snowville, Va.; (a) Cephas Glenn
Summers b June 9, 1877, merchant and farmer, Snowville, Va. (m
Sadie Van Pelt dau of Newton Brown Van Pelt and Virginia Van Pelt,
Oct. 25. 1899 Harper's Ferry, Va. (b May 25, 1879) and had ch b
Snowville, Va.; 1, Margaret Belvidere Summers b Sept. 23, 1900; 2,
Eloise Virginia Summers b Dec. 3, 1901; 2, Janice Meredith Summers
b Aug. 19. 1903; 4, Nellie Steele Summers b May 14, 1905; 5, Lucy
Kathleen Summers b June 24, 1906; 6, George Summers, the Third, b
June 10, 1910; 7, Mary Glenn Summers b Apr. 28, 1919, all of Snow-
ville, Va., none married); (b) Dr. Forest Tunnell Summers b Dec. 27,
1878, unm., of Snowville, Va.; served as First Lieut. in Medical
Corps at Ft. Oglethorpe, Ga. and Camp Green. N. C. and Overseas;
(c) Nellie Steele Summers b June 10, 1883; d Oct. 21, 1891 Snow-

ville, Va.; (d) Roy Linder Summers b Jan. 12, 1886; d Sept. 16, 1897 Snowville, Va.

Four. Margaret Ann Summers b Nov. 5, 1853; d Feb. 28, 1854.

Five. John Robert Summers b Apr. 26, 1855; d Mar. 5, 1900 Pulaski Co., Va.; married Corilda Cecil, dau of Sebastian and Marinda Cecil, Jan. 27, 1878 Pulaski, Va. (b 1862 Pulaski Co., Va., now of Roanoke, Va.) and had; (a) Fletcher Cecil Summers b Aug. 28, 1879, m Ollie Pulley Carter, in Okla. and had no ch.; (b) Robert Clyde Summers b Apr. 15, 1881, of Roanoke, Va. (m Daphne Howard and had; 1, Robert Howard Summers b Sept. 1905; 2, Ralph Tunnell Summers b July 1907; 3, Nellie Virginia Summers; b, Daphne Summers; 5 and 6, twins, Claudine Summers and Raymond Summers b 1918); (c) Lewis Clark Summers b Aug. 6, 1882 Pulaski Co. Va., of Roanoke, Va. (m Birdie Lucas in Montgomery Co., Va. and had; 1, Lewis Clark Summers, the second, b at Wichita Falls, Tex.); (d) Grover Cleveland Summers b Feb. 28, 1884, unm; (e) Grace Virginia Summers b July 3, 1882 nr Mahaska, Kan., of Roanoke, Va. (m Frank Palmer, Salem, Va. and had ch b Blackstone, Va.; 1, Frances Palmer b Dec. 1914; 2, Mary Lucile Palmer b 1920); (f) Jackson Claud Summers b Nov. 12, 1887 Kan., of Roanoke, Va. (m Mary Lois Mador and had; 1, Jackson Summers b July 5, 1920 Wichita Falls, Tex.; 2, Mary Lois Summers b July 28, 1921 Wichita Falls, Tex.; 3, Leo Julian Summers b Feb. 28, 1923 Roanoke, Va.; 4, Harold Cornelius Summers b May 5, 1924 Roanoke, Va.); (g) Mary Emma Summers b July 12, 1889, m Hubert C. Downey at Culpeper, Va. and had no ch.; (h) Lucile Elizabeth Summers b Mar. 12, 1892, of Roanoke, Va., m Stergis Allen 1923 Roanoke, Va.; (i) Guy Grayson Summers b Oct. 3, 1894, unm., served in World War with overseas service.

IX. John Tunnell, son of Calvin and Jane Addair Tunnell, was born Jan. 6, 1828 and died Aug. 18, 1890 Carlinville, Ill. He was a prominent farmer of Plainview, Ill. for many years. He married Elizabeth Catherine Brown Aug. 15, 1854 nr Plainview, Ill. She was born Mar. 16, 1832 nr Elkton, Tenn. and died Dec. 29, 1885 nr Plainview, Ill. She was the dau of Peter Brown (b June 8, 1801 N. C.; d Aug. 31, 1864 Plainview, Ill.) and Catherine Baker Brown (b July 8, 1799 Robeson Co., N. C.; d Feb. 1, 1892 Paola, Kan.); granddau of Samel and Flora (McMillan) Brown; same of Archibald (b 1769 Moore Co., N. C.) and Catherine (McCollum) Baker. Children b nr Plainview, Ill.

One. Baker Adair Tunnell b Nov. 12, 1855.
Two. Alice Tunnell b Aug. 16, 1857.
Three. William Howard Tunnell b July 27, 1859.
Four. Clara Tunnell b Dec. 23, 1861.
Five. Mary Tunnell b Mar. 25, 1864.
Six. Newell Summers Tunnell b Nov. 10, 1866.
Seven. Estella Tunnell b Jan. 28, 1869.
Eight. Albertus Tunnell b May 12, 1871.
Nine. John Alfred Tunnell b May 2, 1872.
Ten. Lucius Brown Tunnell b Oct. 26, 1874.
Eleven. Florence Tunnell b July 29, 1877.

Of these;
One. Baker Adair Tunnell b Nov. 12 1855; d Oct. 23, 1856.
Two. Alice Tunnell b Aug. 16, 1857; d Oct. 23, 1886 nr Plainview, Ill.; married a kinsman, Jesse McDonald Freels, Nov. 15, 1882 nr Plainview, Ill. (b Oct. 13, 1842 Anderson Co., Tenn.; d Mar. 29, 1915 E. St. Louis, Ill., son of William Scarbrough and Maria L. (Tunnell) Freels; gs John and Nancy (Worthington) Tunnell) and had ch b E. St. Louis, Ill.; (a) Dr. Arthur McDonald Freels b Sept.

12, 1883, of Denison, Tex., served as Captain in Medical Corps during World War (m Frances Edna Saunders Dec. 28, 1911 Denison, Tex, and had ch b Denison; 1, Jessie Saunders Freels b Oct. 16, 1912; 2, Frances Edna Freels b. Apr. 16, 1914; 3, Alice Mary Freels b Aug. 27, 1922); (b) Alice Tunnell Freels b Apr. 9, 1886, of Washington, D. C., m Conrad Rutherford Smith Oct. 14, 1914 E. St. Louis, Ill. (b Mar. 10, 1883 Roanoke, Va.; d Aug. 9, 1920 Washington, D. C.) and had no ch.   Jesse McDonald Freels married second, Mary Isabelle Baker Dec. 13, 1888 Red Banks, N. C.   See record John and Nancy (Worthington) Tunnell.

Three.   William Howard Tunnell b July 27, 1859; d July 24, 1886 nr Plainview, Ill., an attorney; married two weeks before his death, July 10, 1886 nr Plainview, Ill., Jennie Pearl Reagan, who died Aug. 1891 Greencastle, Ind.

Four.   Clara Tunnell b Dec. 23, 1861; d Sept. 6, 1865.

Five.   Mary Tunnell b Mar. 25, 1864, of Carlinville, Ill.; married Arthur Boyle Mar. 21, 1888 nr Plainview, Ill.   He is a retired farmer and was born Apr. 1, 1856 Burton. N. J., the son of William Boyle (b 1815; d 1881 Macoupin Co., Ill.) and Margaret (McPhillips) Boyle (b 1827; d 1863 Macoupin Co., Ill.)   No children.

Six.   Newell Summers Tunnell b Nov. 10, 1866; d Dec. 6, 1924 Gregory, Tex.   For several years he was a member of the firm of Duncan and Tunnell, Cape Town, South Africa.   He married first, Nellie Inez Mason, dau of Alfred H. and Inez (Phillips) Mason, Sept. 9, 1895 Cape Town, South Africa (b Sept. 9, 1880 Battle Creek, Mich.; d July 6, 1907 Blocksburg, Calif.) and had; (a) John Lester Tunnell b Aug. 26, 1897 Cape Town, South Africa, proprietor Leghornville, Gregory, Tex.   Of his war record a Carlinville, Ill. paper stated; "this young man was a marine in the sixth regiment and participated in all the big American battles, Chateau Thierry, Belleau Wood, Slossons, San Mihiel and Champaign.   He was a batallion runner and his duty was to carry messages to headquarters.   He was in the second battle of the Marne.   He was among those decorated with the Croix de Guerre.   He wears a red cord on his right arm and shoulder for Legion of Honor, that is for eleven citations for gallantry under fire and gold service chevrons for long service in the trenches and gold wound stripes."   He married Latta Esterle Cook Nov. 9, 1919 Sinton, Tex. and had; 1, Nellie Virginia Tunnell b Oct. 20, 1920 Gregory, Tex.; 2, Lewy Joe Tunnell b Mar. 11, 1924 Portland, Tex.; d Oct. 16, 1924 Gregory, Tex.; (b) Dr. Philips Jackson Tunnell b Feb. 17, 1899 Cape Town, South Africa, of Lomo Linda, Calif. (m Ethel Anneta Hare June 2, 1922 (b Dec. 24, 1903 Los Angeles, Calif., dau of Rev. Stephen Hare, b 1869 New Zealand, and Mary Hoar Hare, b 1871 Petaluma, Calif.) and had; 1, Philips Jackson Tunnell the second, b Oct. 3, 1923 Los Angeles, Calif.); (c) Dr. Alfred Mason Tunnell b June 28, 1902 Cazenovia, New York, of Calif., m Doris May Bradbury, dau of William Clifton and Clara (Snow) Bradbury, Nov. 22, 1923 Lodi, Calif.; (d) Katherine Adair Tunnell b and d same day, 1907, Eureka, Calif.   Newell S. Tunnell married second, Lucile Howard, dau of John and Celia (Prater) Howard, Oct. 6, 1912 Corpus Christi, Tex. (b Feb. 11, 1888 Grand Prairie, Tex., now of Gregory, Tex.) and had; (e) John Wesley Tunnell, second by name of John, b Apr. 2, 1914 Dallas, Tex.; (f) Newell Howard Tunnell b Mar. 26, 1915 Gregory, Tex.; (g) William Franklin Tunnell b May 20, 1921 Gregory, Tex.

Seven.   Estella Tunnell b Jan. 29, 1869, of McCune, Kan.; married William Benjamin Trabue b June 15. 1898 Plainview, Ill. and had; (a) Benjamin Tunnell Trabue b May 25, 1899 nr Dorchester, Ill., m ——— 1, Ruth Marie b 1926; (c) Lucius Boyl Trabue b Apr. 10,. 1903 nr Dorchester, Ill., unm.; (d) Elizabeth Martha Trabue b Aug. 18, 1918 Brookins, S. D.; (e) Joseph Adair Trabue b Oct. 21, 1910. W. B. Trabue b Oct. 29, 1854, son of Joseph Haskins Trabue (b 1825; d 1882) and Martha A. Parks Trabue; gson James and Mary (Harlan) Parks; same Haskins Trabue (b 1790 Va., d 1860 Ill.) and Olympia Wilson Trabue. Haskins Trabue, son of Stephen and Jane (Haskins) Trabue; gs John James and Olympia (Dupuy) Trabue Olympia Dupuy dau of Count Bartholomew Dupuy, b 1654 Saimtgua, France, who settled Manakin-Towne, Va. (See Huguenot Bartholomew Dupuy and his Descendants.)

Eight.   Albertus Tunnell b May 12, 1871; d May 14, 1871.

Nine.   John Alfred Tunnell b May 2, 1872, mail carrier, Hornsby, Ill.; married Florence Matilda Barnstable Feb. 6, 1896 nr Carlinville, Ill. (dau of Thomas and Alta Virginia (Ling) Barnstable, the latter b Dec. 1, 1848 Westonzoland, Eng.; d Aug. 10, 1916 nr Hornsby, Ill.) and had; (a) Harrold Barnstable Tunnell, twin, b /Sept. 17, 1898 Alton, Ill. attorney, Litchfield, Ill., served in World War; m Dorothy Mae Goff, Jan. 26, 1926; (b) Howard McCullum Tunnell, twin of Harold Barnstable Tunnell, b Sept. 17, 1898, served in World War, farmer, unm., Hornsby, Ill.; (c) Lucius Baker Tunnell b Oct. 29, 1909 nr Hugoton, Kan.; (d) Ada Virginia Tunnell b Apr. 20, 1918 nr Hornsby, Ill.

Ten.   Lucius Brown Tunnell b Oct. 26, 1874, ranchman, Gridley, Calif.; served in Spanish-American War, with B. Troop Fourth Cav. and was stationed at Naic, P. I. Jan. 1901; married Stella May Peck Sept. 10, 1907 Kennett, Calif. and had no children.

Eleven.   Florence Tunnell b July 29, 1877, of Springfield, Ill.; married George Lewis Lloyd Nov. 11, 1916 St. Louis, Mo. and had an only child; (a) Eleanor Margaret Lloyd b Apr. 29, 1920 St. Louis, Mo.   G. L. Lloyd b Mar. 9, 1865 Verden. Ill., with Franklin Life Insurance Co., Springfield, Ill., the son of Thomas Lloyd (b May 1, 1816 England; d July 23, 1867 Virden, Ill.) and Arabella Ball Lloyd (b Aug. 3, 1827 Merthyr Tydfil, Wales; d Oct. 22, 1910 Springfield, Ill., married at Abergavenny Wales).   Thomas Lloyd and wife came to Virden, Ill. 1857 on sailing vessel "City of Rome".   Arabella Lloyd , the dau of Richard M. and Maria (Evans) Ball.

X.   Elizabeth Tunnell, dau of Calvin and Jane Addair Tunnell, was born Jan. 20, 1830 and died Dec. 30, 1874 nr Carrollton, Ill.   She married a kinsman, Ezekiel Hiram Summers Feb. 10, 1847 nr Carrollton, Ill.   There was a double wedding ceremony for her sister, Nancy, married, at the same time, George Summers, brother of E. H. Summers.   E. H. Summers was born in Ohio and died Jan. 29, 1903 Mahaska, Kan.   He married second, Amanda (Stickles) Aldridge, in Kan., who survived him.   Shortly after the double ceremony the participants all left for their new home in Pulaski Co., Va.   E. H. Summers had lived in Pulaski Co., Va. and later in Anderson Co., Tenn. but was living in Pulaski Co., Va. at time of his marriage.   In Mar. 1868 E. H. Summers and family moved to nr Carrollton, Ill.   Children b Pulaski Co., Va.

One.   Susan Jane Summers b Jan. 12, 1848.

Two.   Charlotte Elizabeth Summers b Nov. 26, 1849.

Three.   James Tunnell Summers b Apr. 12, 1851.

Four.   Sarah Adeline Summers b Aug. 18, 1854.

Five.   Charles Henry Summers b Apr. 25, 1857.

Six.   Ann Elizabeth Summers b June 24, 1859.

Seven.   Nancy Mary Summers b Aug. 2, 1863.

Eight.   Wade Temple Summers b May 23, 1865.

Nine. Jackson Lewis Summers b Aug. 17, 1867.
Of these;
One. Susan Jane Summers b Jan. 12, 1848; d Dec. 27, 1910 Carrollton, Ill.; married Daniel Thatcher Ozbun Apr. 7, 1875 nr Carrollton, Ill.) son of Benjamin Ozbun (b Nov. 18, 1810 Summer Co., Tenn.; d July 18, 1885 nr Carrollton, Ill.) and Nancy Ann (McCool) Ozbun (b Aug. 10, 1817; d Greene Co., Ill. O: gs of Bartholomew Ozbun (b Mar. 10, 1776; d in Ill.) and Elizabeth (Abbott) Ozbun (b Aug. 26, 1817; d May 22, 1805). Ch. b nr Carrollton, Ill.; (a) Charles Uen Ozbun b Feb. 22, 1876, of Carrollton, Ill. (m Lula P. Smith, dau Joel Smith, Jerseyville, Ill. and had ch b Greene Co., Ill.; 1, Keith Ozbun b July 1917; d Nov. 16, 1908; 2, Clyde Leroy Ozbun b Apr. 22, 1909); (b) Alice Elzina Ozbun b Oct. 23, 1878, of Carrollton, Ill. (m Horace Walter Foreman Apr. 22, 1899 nr Carrollton, Ill., and had; 1, Lenora May Foreman b Feb. 15, 1900 Quincy, Ill.; d Feb. 16, 1900; 2, Horace Ozbun Foreman b July 5, 1905 Carrollton, Ill.; 3, Ralph Tunnell Foreman b Oct. 31, 1907 Carrollton, Ill.; 4, Daniel Josephus Foreman b Dec. 26, 1916 Carrollton, Ill. H. W. Foreman b July 5, 1871 Bois D'Arc, Montgomery Co., Ill., city clerk, has served several years as deputy county clerk and for four years county treasurer of Greene Co. He is son of Dr. Josephus Foreman (b Nov. 8, 1844 Pike Co., Ill.; d Dec. 24, 1914 Patterson, Ill.) and Sarah Adeline (Peebles) Foreman (b July 9, 1851; d Sept. 30, 1915 Patterson, Ill.; gs David Foreman (b 1771; d July 18, 1856) and Mary Elizabeth (Watson) Foreman; same of Abraham and Narcissus (Glynn) Peebles. H. W. and Alice Foreman have furnished data on several branches of the Tunnell family); (c) Jackson Lee Ozbun b Feb. 6, 1881 d July 30, 1902 nr Carrollton, Ill., unm.; (d) Allen Tunnell Ozbun b Nov. 5, 1885; d July 8, 1886; (e) Elmer Calvert Ozbun b Sept. 3, 1889, of Louisville, Ky., served as Sergeant in World War at Camp Taylor from Greene Co., Ill. (m first, Lula Estella Wood Jan. 5, 1911 nr White Hall, Ill., (b Apr. 30, 1892; d Oct. 23, 1918 nr White Hall, Ill., dau Wilson and Julia (Cannedy) Wood, and had; 1 Edna May Ozbun b Sept. 11, 1912 nr Carrollton, Ill.; and m second, Mayme Carolina (Garies) Schwenker, dau of Gustav and Louisa Schwenker, Mar. 16, 1919 Jefferson Co., Ky. and had ch b Louisville, Ky.; 2, Dorothy Laverne Ozbun b Mar. 28, 1920; 3, Elberta Alice Ozbun b May 29, 1923).

Two. Charlotte Elizabeth Summers b Nov. 25, 1849; d Feb. 5, 1919 Carrollton, Ill.; married Uen Linder Nov. 4, 1873 at home of aunt in Pulaski Co., Va. (b Apr. 30, 1845 nr Carrollton, Ill.; d July 20, 1917 Carrollton, Ill; son of Isham Linder (b Aug. 3, 1802; d Greene Co., Ill.) and Sarah (Vaughn) Linder, b June 20, 1809; gs of Jacob Linder, b nr Abingdon, Va., who m Dicy Wood, of N. C., in Anderson Co. Tenn. 1798. Sarah Vaughn, the dau of Joshua Vaughn). Ch. b nr Daum, Ill.; (a) Clyde Linder b Apr. 2, 1877, who has been with the Greene Co. State Bank, of Carrollton, Ill. since 1898 (m Grace Seely, dau of A. S. and Lora (Hubbard) Seely; gdau William and Martha (Kline) Hubbard; ggdau Isaac and Sarah Kline, Sept. 10, 1900 nr White Hall, Ill. and had an only child; 1, Stewart Seely Linder b Oct. 29, 1901 Carrollton, Ill., of Chicago, Ill., m Ruth Bridgewater, dau of Frank Bridgewater, at Waukegan, Ill. and had; (aa) Betty Lynette Linder b Apr. 1925 White Hall, Ill.); (b) Ralph Linder b July 16, 1882, undertaker, Kane, Ill. (m Charlotte Reinicke, dau of William C. and Emily (Siegle) Reinicke; gd Gottleib and Charlotte Siegle; same William and Christina Reinicke, May 2, 1905 Kane, Ill. and had no ch.); (c) Porter Linder b Oct. 25, 1884, of Calif. (m Ethel Schafer Reed, dau of L. W. Reed, gd Joel G. and Harriet Reed,

Oct. 11, 1911 St. Louis, Mo., and had no ch.)

Three.   James Tunnell Summers b Apr. 12, 1851 nr Newbern, Va., retired farmer, Mahaska, Kan.; married Martha Ann Witt, niece of his sister's husband, Uen Linder, July 17, 1876 nr Carrollton, Ill. She was born May 4, 1854 nr Carrollton, Ill., dau of Daniel M. Witt (b Oct. 18, 1827 Jefferson Co., Tenn.; d Oct. 8, 1893 Carrollton, Ill.) and Dicy (Linder) Witt (died Sept. 4, 1904 Mahaska, Kan.) gdau Eli and Nancy (McNealy) Witt.   J. T. and Martha Witt Summers had an only child; (a) Walter Lewis Summers b Nov. 1874 nr Carrollton, Ill., merchant, Mahaska, Kan. (m first, Philobena Christina Knauff, Dec. 24, 1896 nr Mahaska, Kan. (b Dec. 14, 1878 nr Ft. Madison, Iowa; d Oct. 1, 1917 nr Mahaska, Kan.) and had; 1, Leona Goldie Summers b Feb. 2, 1900 nr Mahaska, of Mahaska, m Pearl Ginn Oct. 14, 1918 Mahaska (b Mar. 13, 1898 Republic Co., Kan.) and had; (aa) George Lewis Ginn b Oct. 6, 1920 nr Mahaska, Kan.; 27, ——— Summers, (son) b and d same day.   Walter L. Summers m second, Edith Braddock Feb. 15, 1919 Emporia, Kan. (b Sept. 25, 1882, dau of J. T. and Lois Braddock, and had ch b Mahaska, Kan.; 3, James Lewis Summers b Apr. 26, 1920; 4, Betty Lois Summers b Nov. 9, 1921. J .T. Summers, wife and son moved to Washington Co., Kan. Feb. 1876.

Four.   Sarah Adeline Summers b Aug. 18, 1854; d Dec. 12, 1856 nr Newbern, Va.

Five.   Charles Henry Summers b Apr. 25, 1857; d Apr. 10, 1879 nr Carrollton, Ill., unm.

Six.   Ann Elizabeth Summers b June 24, 1859; d Apr. 5, 1876 nr Carrollton, Ill., unm.

Seven.   Nancy Mary Summers b Aug. 2, 1863; d Aug. 20, 1863.

Eight.   Wade Temple Summers b May 23, 1865 nr Dublin, Va., of Mahaska, Kan.; married Sarah Elizabeth Wheeler, Sept. 16, 1886 Washington Co., Kan. (b Dec. 5, 1866 Minn., dau Henry and Elizabeth Wheeler, both of whom were born in state of New York) and had ch. b Washington Co., Kan.; (a) Guy L. Summers b Sept. 2, 1887 (m Alta M. Coonrod June 19, 1912 Republic Co., Kan. (b Apr. 30, 1894 Washington Co., Kan., dau Charles and Cynthia Coonrod) and had ch b Washington, Co., Kan.; 1, Doris Summers b Apr. 22, 1913; 2, Leroy Summers b July 13, 1915); (b) Rozella Summers b Feb. 25, 1889 (m Guy Spears Apr. 21, 1909 Washington Co., Kan. (b Mar. 15, 1886 Washington Co.) and had ch b Washington Co.; 1, Henry Temple Spears b May 6, 1910; 2, Vera Marie Spears b June 2, 1911; 3, Ruby Spears b Mar. 23, 1913); (c) Beulah Summers b Oct. 1, 1891 (m Harley H. Coonrod, brother of Alta M. Coonrod, June 21, 1911 Washington Co., Kan (b Mar. 1, 1890 Iroquois, Ill.) and had ch b Washington Co., Kan.; 1, Harry Jackson Coonrod b Oct. 25, 1912; 2, Harold Coonrod b Nov. 20, 1919); (d) Bessie Luella Summers b Sept. 17, 1893 (m Harrt T. Short Feb. 3, 1915 Mahaska, Kan. (b Nov. 8, 1889) and had ch b Washington Co., Kan.; 1, Victor Leon Short b Oct. 13, 1916, dead; 2, Luella M. Short b Sept. 24, 1919; d Oct. 28, 1919; 3, Marguerite M. Short b Mar. 5, 1921); (e) Ralph Eugene Summers b Dec. 25, 1898 (m Lola Reesor June 9, 1918 Fairbury, Neb. and had; 1, Ernest E. Summers b Oct. 30, 1919 Washington Co., Kan.); (f) Roy Summers b July 21, 1904 unm.

Nine.   Jackson Lewis Summers b Aug. 17, 1867 nr Newbern, Va., unmarried, of Mahaska, Kan.

XI.   Franklin Witt Tunnell, son of Calvin and Jane Addair Tunnell, named for Hon. Franklin Witt, was born Feb. 6, 1832 and died June 30, 1832.

XII.   Calvin Witt Tunnell, son of Calvin and Jane Addair Tunnell, and second child named for Hon. Franklin Witt, was born June 4, 1833 and died June 29, 1881 east of Virden, Montgomery Co., Ill. He married first, Susan Parker, Mar. 22, 1860 Greene Co., Ill. (b Jan. 22, 1835 Greene Co., Ill.; d Nov. 29, 1860 of Virden, Ill., dau of Jacob W. and Mary (Ludwig) Parker). He married second, Ann Ball, Feb. 23, 1862 nr Virden, in Macoupin Co., Ill. She was born Mar. 11, 1839 nr Talybont, Wales and died Oct. 4, 1873 e of Virden, in Montgomery Co., Ill. There were five children of this marriage. He married third, Sarah Maria Hoagland, Aug. 12, 1877 Raymond, Ill. She was born Jan. 19, 1849 Jersey City, New Jersey, the dau of William Van Fleet and Sarah (Beekman) Hoagland, and lives in Virden, Ill. There were two sons. Ch b in Montgomery Co., Ill., e of Virden.

One. Henry Andrew Tunnell b Dec. 4, 1862.
Two. Agnes Tunnell b July 13, 1865; d Aug. 24, 1865.
Three. James Tunnell b Dec. 30, 1866.
Four. Evans Adair Tunnell b July 11, 1868.
Five. Susan Jane Tunnell b Jan. 19, 1871.
Six. James Calvin Tunnell b June 12, 1878.
Seven. Frederick Van Fleet Tunnell b Mar. 24, 1880.
Of these;

One. Henry Andrew Tunnell b Dec. 4, 1862, of Gandy, Neb., cashier Gandy Bank; married Sarah Eva Johnson, dau of Elmer and Elizabeth (Bennett) Johnson, Apr. 12, 1893 Gandy, Neb. (b July 17, 1862 Macoupin Co., Ill.; d Nov. 10, 1900 nr Gandy, Neb.) and had ch b nr Gandy; (a) Ann Elizabeth Tunnell b Jan. 1, 1894; d Aug. 4, 1895 Gandy, Neb.; (b) Curtis Albert Tunnell b Sept. 22, 1896, farmer, Gandy, Neb., m Nellie Freels Oct. 1, 1919 and had no ch.; (c) Howard Adair Tunnell b Apr. 30, 1899, unm., farmer, Gandy, Neb.

Two. Agnes Tunnell b July 13, 1865; d Aug. 24, 1865.
Three. James Tunnell b Dec. 30, 1866; d Sept. 23, 1873.
Four. Evans Adair Tunnell b July 11, 1868; d Aug. 16, 1868.
Five. Susan Jane Tunnell b Jan. 19, 1871, of Girard, Ill.; married Frank George Wood May 2, 1898 Shelbyville, Ill. and had an only child; (a) Isabel Frances Wood b Apr. 16, 1902, unm. Frank G. Wood b Apr. 9, 1868, attorney of Girard, Ill. and county judge of Macoupin Co., Ill., the son of George W. Wood (b Feb. 28, 1834; d Feb. 7, 1877 Girard, Ill.(and Isabella P. Eastham Wood (b Nov. 29, 1829 nr Danville, Kentucky; d Apr. 1, 1890 Girard, Ill.; m Feb 14, 1853); gson William Wood (b Oct. 1794 Knox Co., Tennessee; d Jan. 2, 1858 Texas) and Polly Cox Wood (b Sept 15, 1795 Ky.; d Dec. 19, 1863 Knox Co., Illinois; m Feb. 2, 1814 Madison Co., Ill.); same James Eastham (b Ky.; d 1852 Louisville, Ky.) and Nancy Helm Eastham (b Nov. 1, 1799; d Aug. 1883 Girard, Ill.; m 1822); ggson George Cox (b S. C.; d 1819 Auburn, Ill.) and Joanne Hubbard Cox; same Edward Eastham (b 1773 Culpepper Court House, Va.; d 1821) and Ann Thornton Eastham (b Dec. 25, 1776 Va.; d 1840); same George Helm (b Aug. 22, 1747 Va.; d July 9, 1821 Lincoln Co., Ky., Revolutionary soldier) and Frances Coppage Helm (b Aug. 7, 1761; d Oct. 6, 1857 nr Danville, Virginia);gggson Zachariah Eastham, Revolutionary soldier of Culpepper Co., Va.; same George Thornton, Revolutionary soldier of Caroline Co., Va. (b Nov. 18, 1752; d Aug. 30, 1853) and Margaret Stanley Thornton; same of Meredith Helm, junior (b 1724; d 1804 nr Winchester, Va., Colonel in Revolution) and Ann Calmes Helm; gggggson Meredith Helm, senior, who d 1768 Frederick Co., Va.; same Anthony Thornton, junior (b 1726) and Sarah Taliaferro Thornton (b 1728); same of a French Marquis, the Marquis de la Calmes, of a French Huguenot family, who m Winifred Waller

gggggson Anthony Thornton senior (b 1695; d 1751 Stafford Co., Va. and Winifred Presley Thornton; same of John Taliaferro, who was Lieut. of Rangers against the Indians and in the House of Burgesses in 1699, who m Sarah Smith; same of Leonard Helm ggggggson of Colonel Peter Presley, of Northumberland Co., Va., member of the House of Burgesses, and Winifred Griffin Presley; same of Robert Taliaferro (1635-1700) who m a granddau of Lieut.-General Grymes of Cromwell's army; same of Francis Thornton (1651-1826) and Alice Savage Thornton. The families of Eastham, Helm, Calmes, Thornton, Taliaferro and Presley were of the "F. F. V's". Their militant as well as civil history is meritorious. The Thornton line may be traced as far as 1313. "The Invincibles" trace the lineage of Alice Savage for more than twenty generations. Here one may wander to the very thrones of kings and queens of Europe.

Six. James Calvin Tunnell, second child to bear the name of James, b June 12, 1878, farmer, of Virden, Ill.; married Ida May Pottorf, dau of James and Samantha Jane (Bledsoe) Pottorf, Nov. 1906 in Montgomery Co., Ill. and had ch b Montgomery Co., Ill. (a) Mary Evelyn Tunnell b Nov. 6, 1907; (b) Alberta May Tunnell b Mar. 24, 1910; (c) Helen Latavon Tunnell b Aug. 1912; (c) Clifford Tunnell b Apr. 5, 1917.

Seven. Frederick Van Fleet Tunnell b Mar. 24, 1880, of Virden, Ill.; married Lillian Lister, dau of William and Ann (Day) Lister, in Macoupin Co., Ill. and had; (a) Beulah Evelyn Tunnell b Oct. 24, 1902, of Springfield ,Ill., m Ralph Filburn, son of Ben Filburn, June 6, 1925 Springfield, Ill.; (b) Frederick Calvin Tunnell b Sept. 24, 1904, unm., Virden, Ill.; (c) Essie Lucille Tunnell b Jan. 21, 1907, of Virden, Ill. (m William J. Smith Jr., who d Mar. 4, 1925 Springfield, Ill. and had; (aa) Harold Edwin Smith); (d) Geraldine Marie Tunnell b Oct. 16, 1915.

XIII. Andrew Jacson Tunnell, son of Calvin and Jane Addair Tunnell, was born June 28, 1837 and died May 30, 1906. His entire life was spent on the farm on which his parents settled in Feb. 1819. He married first, Caroline Purl, Sept. 19, 1861 nr Carrollton, Ill. She was born June 15, 1841 Indiana and died Feb. 14, 1899 nr Carrollton, Ill., the dau of Thomas Purl (b Dec. 15, 1812 Bedford Co., Penn.; d Feb. 21, 1891 nr Carrollton, Ill.) and Mary Anne (Purl) Purl). He married second, Laura Alice Scandrett June 22, 1904 nr Rockbridge, Ill. She was born Nov. 7, 1861 nr Rockbridge, Ill. and now lives on the farm on which she was born. Her parents were Charles Sayer Scandrett junior, (b Aug. 16, 1827 Worchester, Eng. emigrated to America and settled in Greene Co., Ill. 1836; d Mar. 1, 1902 Rockbridge, Ill.) and Sarah Emiline Nix Scandrett (b 1833; d Mar. 7, 1873 nr Rockbridge, Ill.) C. S. Scandrett the son of Charles Sayer Scandrett, senior (b 1805 London, Eng.; d 1897 Rockbridge, Ill.) and Elizabeth Strickland Papps Scandrett (b 1804; d Greene Co., Ill.) Sarah Emeline Nix, the dau of Elias Nix (died Rockbridge, Ill.) and Nancy Crane Nix (b 1813 Ohio; d 1901 Rockbridge, Ill.) and gdau Luther and Hannah Crane and ggdau of Benjamin Crane, a Revolutionary soldier. There was no issue by either marriage of A. J. Tunnell.

XIV. Elvira Adeline Tunnell, dau of Calvin and Jane Addair Tunnell was born Aug. 22, 1839 and died Nov. 7, 1909 nr Plainview, Ill. She married first, Daniel Parker, brother of her sister-in-law, Susan Parker Tunnell, Nov. 12, 1857 nr Carrollton, Ill. He was born Oct. 12, 1833 and died Nov. 26, 1860, the son of Jacob W. Parker(b June 1801 W. Va.; d July 26, 1871 Greene Co., Ill.) and Mary Ludwig Parker (b May 1801 West Va.; d July 1867 Greene Co., Ill.) There were two children by his marriage. Elvira A. Tunnell married second,

John Lyons, Jan 25, 1864 Greene Co., Ill.   He was born Apr. 29,
1829 in north Ireland and died Aug. 15, 1910 nr Plainview, Ill., son
of Thomas and Mary A. (Taggert) Lyons; gs Robert and Fannie
(Fulton) Lyons, of Scotch-Irish lineage; same John and Jane Taggert.
The six children by second marriage b nr Plainview, Ill.
    One. Mary Eugenia Parker b Nov. 26, 1858.
    Two. Henry Lewis Parker b Sept. 30, 1860.
    Three. Thomas C. Lyons b June 25, 1865.
    Four. Robert Newton Lyons b Nov. 2, 1867.
    Five. James Lyons b May 31. 1871.
    Six. Elvira Lyons b Sept. 13, 1873.
    Seven. John Lyons b May 13, 1878.
    Eight. Luther Tunnell Lyons b Apr. 27, 1880.
    Of these;
    One. Mary Eugenia Parker b Nov. 26, 1858; married first, John
Caywood Mar. 3, 1878 Macoupin Co., Ill. and had; (a) Charles Cay-
wood b 1879; d in inf.; (b) Mary Elvira Caywood b Aug. 15, 1881, of
Bunker Hill, Ill. (m Frank Groves and had; 1, Frances Groves b Dec.
17, 1897, m Paul Jaynes Feb. 15, 1918 Shipman, Ill. and had; (aa)
Arvesta Jaynes; (bb) Eleanor Jaynes b Sept. 1923; 2, Howard Groves
b Apr. 21, 1900, unm.; 3, Orville Groves b Sept. 15, 1902, m Pauline
Baker Aug. 1, 1922 and had; (aa) Orville Franklin Groves b July 1,
1923; 4, Clifford Groves b Nov. 11, 1904, unm.; 5, Myrtle Groves b
Apr. 12, 1907; 6, Hattie Groves, deceased; 7, Charles Groves
deceased); (c) Hettie Caywood b 1883; d in inf.   Mary Eugenia
Parker married second, Rufus Ward, 1904.
    Two. Henry Lewis Parker b (Sept. 30, 1860 nr Plainview, Ill.,
of East Alton, Ill.; married Carrie Lyon Coriell, dau of Peter and
Henrietta (Martin) Coriell, Apr. 4, 1887 Plainview, Ill. (b July 28,
1863 Plainview, Ill.) and had; (a) Gace Tunnell Parker b Feb. 21,
1888, of East Alton, Ill. (m Theodore J. Malsen Aug. 26, 1908 and had
1, Erwin Parker Malsen b Apr. 23, 1909; 2, Edwin Nelson Malsen b
Feb. 12, 1911; 3, Russell Joseph Malsen b Jan. 28, 1921); (b) Jessie
Coriell Parker b July 23, 1890, of E Alton, Ill. (m first, Russell W.
Ford July 3, 1908 (d Aug. 18, 1918) and second, Fred Rampenthal
Oct. 8, 1922 and had no ch.); (c) Henry Lewis Parker, the second, b
Jan. 7, 1894, of E. Alton, Ill. (m Gladys Worthy May 3, 1917 and had;
1,Douglas Wayne Parker b Jan. 31, 1918; 2, Russell Bernard Parker
b Aug. 27, 1920; 3, Verna Mae Parker b Dec. 29, 1922); (d) Ralph
Coriell Parker b July 19, 1896, of E. Alton, Ill., m Sarah Hullette
Sept. 28, 1920 and has no ch., (e) Theodore John Parker b Sept. 30,
1898, of E. Alton (m Arline Putt July 28, 1917 and had; 1, Richard
Coriell Parker b Jan. 29, 1918; 2, Theodore John Parker, the second, b
Oct. 9, 1919; 3, Kay Austin Parker b June 3, 1924): (f) Robert Ells-
worth Parker b Mar. 30, 1903, unm., of E. Alton, Ill.
    Three. Thomas C. Lyons b June 25, 1865; d Sept. 24, 1865.
    Four. Robert Newton Lyons b Nov. 2, 1867; d Oct. 24, 1893; mar-
ried Jessie Coriell, sister of Carriel Coriell, June 8, 1890 Plainview,
Ill. (b Aug. 26, 1870 Plainview, Ill.) and had; (a) Walter Raymond
Lyons b Jan. 6, 1891, unm., of St. Louis, Mo.; (b) Frederick Archer
Lyons b July 23, 1893, of St. Louis, Mo. (m Lelia Hass Sept. 29, 1914
(b Sept. 16, 1893) and had; 1, Robert Frederick Lyons b Apr. 29,
1915; 2, Leland Mayo Lyons b July 18, 1916; 3, Iva Evelyn Lyons b
Sept. 22, 1917).
    Five. James Lyons b May 31, 1871; d Feb. 1912 Shipman, Ill.;
married Ida May Jones Sept. 24, 1895 nr Plainview, Ill., who d Oct.
22, 1896 nr Plainview, Ill.   There were no ch. of this marriage.
    Six. Elvira Lyons b Sept. 13, 1873, of Macoupin Co., Ill.

Seven.   John Lyons Jr. b May 13, 1878; d July 15, 1878.
Eight.   Luther Tunnell Lyons b Apr. 27, 1880; d July 13, 1880.

LUTHER TUNNELL

K. Luther Tunnell, son of William and Mary Maysey Tunnell, was born Sept. 26, 1793 near Robertsville, Tenn. and died Aug. 3, 1865 Greenfield, Ill. He was the third brother to move to Illinois. On Oct. 14, 1819 he was a member of a jury, in Anderson Co.; Tenn., to lay off a road.   Soon after he moved to Green Co., Ill., settling east of Carrollton.   He married Louisa Parks Nov. 22, 1825 in Greene Co., Ill., who died May 17, 1850 near Greenfield, Ill.   It is worthy of note that not a single descendant of Luther Tunnell bears the name of Tunnell.   Children b east of Carrollton, Ill.

   I.   Nancy Adeline Tunnell b 1827.
   II.   William Tunnell b June 12, 1829
   III.   Mary Jane Tunnell b Oct. 21, 1831.
   IV.   Rebecca Emmeran Tunnell b Jan. 3, 1834.
   V.   Martha Tunnell b Feb. 11, 1836.
   VI.   Louisa Elvira Tunnell b Sept. 9, 1838.
   VII.   John Calvin Tunnell b Jan. 26, 1841.
   VIII.   Malvina Catherine Tunnell b Nov. 19, 1843.
   IX.   Minerva Virginia Etna Tunnell b Mar. 20, 1846.
   Of the foregoing;
   I.   Nancy Adeline Tunnell, dau of Luther and Louisa Parks Tunnell was born 1827 and died, abt 1840, in Greene Co., Ill.
   II.   William Tunnell, son of Luther and Louisa Parks Tunnell, was born June 12, 1829 and died Mar. 10, 1867 Scottville, Ill.; married Harriet Eliza Booker, dau of Richard M. and Harriett E. (Le-Marr) Booker, Sept. 29, 1853 Greenfield, Ill. (b Jan. 6, 1836 Green-field, Ill.; d Mar. 21, 1856 Alton, Ill.) and had an only child;
   One.   Louisa Virginia Tunnell b Aug. 1, 1854 nr Greenfield, Ill. of Scottville, Ill.; married first, Cyrus Augustus Crouch, son of Thomas and Julia (McAfee) Crouch, Sept. 29, 1873 Girard, Ill. (Nov. 11, 1849 Tenn.; d Oct. 1912 Humphreys, Mo.) and had; (a) Harry Clyde Crouch b Aug. 8, 1876 Lindley, Mo., of King Hill, Idaho (m Pearl Atridge, June 1906 Salt Lake City, Utah and had ch b Salt Lake City; 1, Mary Louisa Crouch b May 4, 1907; 2, June Wilbur Crouch b Sept. 11, 1909; 3, Dorothy Ellen Crouch b Sept. 11, 1912. Harry Clyde Crouch m Wendella Cragum June 3, 1923 Salt Lake City, Utah and had; 4, Wendell Harry Crouch b May 5, 1924); (b) William Tunnell Crouch b July 2, 1879 Lindley, Mo., of Galt, Mo., m Adah Jaynes abt 1912 at Osgood, Mo. and had no children; (c) Kitty Wells Crouch b June 17, 1887 Lindley, Mo., of Alexander, Ill., m William Fred Neal, a banker, Aug. 6, 1910 and had no children; (d) Jessie Lee Crouch b May 5, 1889 Harris, Mo.; d Apr. 22, 1893 Harris, Mo. Louisa Virginia Tunnell married second, Everett E. Booker, merchant, Scottville, Ill, on Oct. 1901 Keokuk, Iowa (b Nov. 8, 1854 Eminence, Ky., son of Frank Booker, brother of Harriett Eliza Booker Tunnell and Martha Booker.
   III.   Mary Jane Tunnell, dau of Luther and Louisa Parks Tunnell, was born Oct. 21, 1831 and died Dec. 4, 1902 Kansas City, Mo. She married William Sargent Gobble, son of Sargent Gobble, Dec. 24, 1856 Greenfield, Ill.   He was born Jan. 1, 1835 Carrollton, Ill. and died Feb. 7, 1903 Kansas City, Mo.   Their sons assumed the spelling Goble.   Children, save youngest, born Scottville, Ill.
   One.   Lillie Alena Gobble b May 2, 1858, of Venice, Calif.; married first, Herman Gotthelf May 19, 1879 Jacksonville, Ill. (b Jan. 4, 1857; d Jan. 8, 1916 Kansas City, Mo.); and m second, Max Kahn, at Topeka, Kan. (d Apr. 11, 1918 Kansas City) and had no ch.

Two. Edna Virginia Gobble b July 16, 1866, of Kansas City, Mo. married Jacob Earl Kuhn Jan. 1 1898 Kansas City, Mo. (b Dec. 25, 1871 Wilkesbarre, Penn., son of John and Elizabeth (Weaver) Kuhn, and had no ch.

Three. William Eugene Goble b Apr. 18, 1869; d July 2, 1922 Kansas City, Mo.; married Katherine McClintock and had no ch.

Four. Nellie Grace Gobble b Feb. 16, 1872, of Colorado Springs, Col.; married James Edmund Williams Apr. 28, 1895 Kansas City, Mo. (b Jan. 6, 1865 East St. Louis, Ill.; d July 9, 1924 Kansas City, son of Travis A. Williams (b Apr. 24, 1835 N. C.) and Ellen R. Wilborn Williams (b Mar. 29, 1841; d May 5, 1923), and had ch b Kansas City; (a) James Edmund Williams Jr. b Feb. 20, 1897, of Kansas City, m Agnes Hubbard June 15, 1923 St. Joe, Mo.; (b) Harry Kahn Williams b Dec. 24, 1899, of Kansas City, m Wilma Lucile Thompson July 19, 1922 St. Joe, Mo.

Five. Claude Tunnell Goble b Oct. 9, 1874 Girard, Ill., of Los Angeles, Calif.; married Margaret Tipton June 8, 1916 Topeka, Kan., dau of Franklin Pierce Tipton (b Dec. 17, 1852) and Amanda Caroline Throgmartin Tipton (b July 7, 1858) and had; (a) Mary Jane Gloria Goble b Jan. 30, 1922 San Antonio, Tex.

IV. Rebecca Emmeran Tunnell, dau of Luther and Louisa Parks Tunnell, was born Jan. 9, 1834 and died Aug. 15, 1862 nr Carrollton, Ill. She married Robert Preston McKnight Sept. 2, 1857 nr Carrollton, Ill. He was born Jan. 14, 1829 Bean Station, Tenn. and died Sept. 29, 1915 St. Louis, Mo. He was a "49-er"; going from Scottville, Ill. to Calif. 1849 but returning to his home three years later. He served four years in the War Between the States, first as Lieut. of Co. D. Fourteenth Ill. Inf. He was brevetted Major, for efficient service, before the close of the war. Children b Greenfield, Ill.

One. Harry Price McKnight b Mar. 4, 1859, of St. Louis, Mo., married Ida Mae Cann, at Geneso, Ill., and had no children.

Two. Jessie Will McKnight b Nov. 14, 1861, of St. Louis, Mo.; married Henry M. Gotthelf, brother of Herman Gotthelf, Nov. 24, 1879 Jacksonville, Ill. and had ch., oldest b Jacksonville, others at Virden, Ill.; (a) Emma C. Gotthelf b Sept. 1, 1880, of St. Louis, Mo. (m first, John D. Evans July 29, 1900 St. Louis (d July 14, 1917 St. Louis) and had an only child; 1, Evelyn Emma Evans b Mar. 5, 1901 and m second, Fred J. Pfunder Aug. 23, 1924 St. Louis, Mo.); (b) Harry Gotthelf b and d Mar. 29, 1883; (c) Herbert M. Gotthelf b June 12, 1884 m Myrtle Dodd, of Terra Haute, Ind., Jan. 1, 1905, and had no ch.; (d) Robert Price Gotthelf b Jan. 5, 1886, unm., of St. Louis, Mo., (e) Lynn Ethel Gotthelf b Dec. 10, 1889, of St. Louis, Mo. (m William Behrens June 22, 1910 St. Louis, Mo., and had an only child; 1, Dorothy Evelyn Behrens b Oct. 17, 1912 St. Louis); (f) Esther Geraldine Gotthelf b Jan. 9, 1895 (m William Paxton Morrison, of El Reno, Okla., June 7, 1914 and had ch b El Reno, Okla.; 1, William Paxton Morrison Jr. b Oct. 8, 1915; 2, David John Morrison b Aug. 20, 1917).

V. Martha Tunnell, dau of Luther and Louis Parks Tunnell, was born Feb. 11, 1836 and died May 1914 Girard, Ill. She married Edmund Mills Cooper Aug. 30, 1855 Greene Co. Ill. He was born Nov. 25, 1831 Christain Co., Ky. and died June 4, 1910 Girard, Ill. They moved from Greene Co., Ill. to Girard, Ill. 1864. He was son of Edmund Landrum Cooper (b Sept. 24, 1799 Lawrence Co., Va; d Greenfield, Ill. shortly after celebrating his one hundredth birthday) and Mary Mills Perry Cooper. Children;

One. Frederic Eugene Cooper b Mar. 3, 1859 Greene Co., Ill.; d Jan. 26, 1899 Van Buren, Ark.; married Jennie Elvira Shive, dau of

Rufus Washington and Serilda (Markert) Shive, July 3, 1890 Austin, Ark. (b May 14, 1865 Miss., now of Corpus Christi, Tex.) and had ch b Van Buren, Ark.; (a) Mary Julia Cooper b May 23, 1891, of Corpus Christi, Tex., unm.; (b) Albert Everett Cooper b Jan. 26, 1893, of Corpus Christi, Tex., unm., who was in Border Service with the Seventh New York in 1916; in 1918 second Lieut. Aide-de-camp in France; 1919 soldier student Oxford University; 1920-24 Instructor Adjunct Prof. Math. Engineering Department, University of Texas; Ph D degree 1925; (c) Frederick Eugene Cooper, the second, b Mar. 16, 1895; d in inf. Van Buren, Ark.; (d) Edmund Luther Cooper, b Sept. 27, 1897, of Corpus Christi, Tex., unm.

Two. Charles Ardeen Cooper b Apr. 2, 1861 Greene Co., Ill., of New York City 1919; married Addie Ketchell (d bef. 1919 N. Y.) and had; (a) Edmund Luther Cooper b abt 1889, of N. Y. City. m —— ——; (b) Frank Everett Cooper b abt 1891 (m —— —— at Miami, Florida 1912 and had; 1, Mary Julia Cooper b 1913 N. Y.); (c) Charles Ardeen Cooper Jr. b abt 1893, m —— —— abt 1916 N. Y.; (d) child b abt 1917 in Cuba; d in inf.; (e) Harry Cooper b abt 1904. C. A. Cooper lived at one time Bois D'arc township, Montgomery Co., Ill.; and for short time in Cuba.

Three. E. Everett Cooper b Dec. 4, 1863; unmarried, of Girard, Ill. and Van Buren, Ark.

Four. Frank Tunnell Cooper b 1871 Girard, Ill.; d 1871 Girard.

Five. William Cooper b 1876 Girard, Ill.; d 1876 Girard, Ill.

VI. Louisa Elvira Tunnell, dau of Luther and Lousia Parks Tunnell, was born Sept. 9, 1839 and died Jan. 9, 1875 nr Greenfield, Ill. She married John Marion Linder Jan. 6, 1862 Greene Co., Ill. He was born Jan. 12, 1835 nr Carrollton, Ill. and died July 12, 1919 Greenfield, Ill., the son of Isham Linder (b Aug. 13, 1802; d Jan. 1892 Carrollton, Ill.) and Sarah Vaughn Linder (b June 20, 1809 Madison Co., Ill.; d Greene Co., Ill. who were married Aug. 25, 1825 Greene Co., Ill.) and grandson of Jacob Linder, b nr Abingdon, Va., who m Dicy Wood, of N. C. 1798 in Anderson Co., Tenn. gs of Joshua Vaughn. John Marion Linder married second, a relative, who was also relative of Louisa Elvira Tunnell, Nancy Catherine Tunnell Dec. 23, 1875 Anderson Co., Tenn. For record of last marriage see record Colonel William and Elizabeth Worthington Tunnell. Children of John M. and Louisa E. Tunnell Linder;

One. Minnie Cordelia Linder b May 1, 1864 nr Virden, in Macoupin Co., Ill.; d Nov. 12, 1921 Alton, Ill.; married George Andrew Olbert, son of Capt. George W. and Malvina V. (Barr) Olbert, Sept. 29, 1881 nr Greenfield, Ill. (b Sept. 24, 1856 (and had; (a) James Howard Olbert b Jan. 24, 1887 Bois D'Arc, Montgomery Co., Ill.; d Apr. 8, 1887; (b) Balfour Lockwood Olbert b June 30, 1889 nr Carlinville, Ill., of East Alton, Ill., m Isabel Alice Bare, dau of William R. and Sylvia May (Simpson) Bare, Aug. 27, 1919 nr Carrollton, Ill. (b Dec. 21, 1894) and had no ch.; (c) John William Olbert b Apr. 17, 1891 nr Barr, Ill., of Chicago, Ill. (m Lena Giller, dau of George Giller, Jan. 14, 1915 St. Louis, Mo. (b Oct. 20, 1894) and had; 1, John William Olbert, the second, b Mar. 4, 1918 Greenfield, Ill.; d Dec. 11, 1920 Grenada, Miss.; 2, Jean Catherine Olbert b Jan. 21, 1922 Grenada, Miss.) George A. Olbert, realtor of Summer Haven, Florida, m second, Alice Virginia Bryant Dec. 14, 1923 St. Augustine, Fla.

Two. Walter Louis Linder b Sept. 1, 1868, undertaker, Springfield, Ill.; married Anna G. Marrell, dau William and Emeline (Goode) Marrell, Feb. 17, 1897 Palmyra, Ill. (b Jan. 4, 1879 Palmyra, Ill.) and had an only child; (a) Fayne Louise Linder b Mar. 14, 1899 (m George P. Swope Jan. 26, 1918 Springfield, Ill. and had; 1, Constance

Swope b Aug. 21, 1918 Palmyra, Ill.; d Oct. 8, 1918).

VII. John Calvin Tunnell, son of Luther and Louisa Jarks Tunnell, was born Jan. 26, 1841 and died Feb. 9, 1897 Boulder, Col. He married Martha Elizabeth Fales Nov. 21, 1865 Carrollton, Ill. She was born July 8, 1847 nr Carrollton, Ill. and died Sept. 1, 1907 Sterling, Col. She was dau of Warren Fales (b 1814 Mass.; d 1867) and Hannah Elizabeth Barber Fales (b 1815 Vt.; d 1857). Ch. b nr Carrollton, Ill.;

One. William Luther Tunnell b Oct. 2, 1867; d Sept. 8, 1920 Chillicothe, Mo.; married Alice Lee Jones Oct. 4, 1892 Chillicothe, Mo and had an only child; (a) Mary Ellen Tunnell b Aug. 5, 1895, of Denver, Col. (m first, Walter Jay Gould Dec. 21, 1917 Chillicothe, Mo. (b Aug. 4, 1892 Wheeling, Mo.; d Mar. 15, 1918 Brest, France, soldier in World War) and m second, Arthur W. Lineberry June 17, 1922 Kansas City and had; 1, Virginia Lee Lineberry b Sept. 19, 1924 Denver, Col.)

Two. Maria Desdemona Tunnell b Oct. 9, 1869; d Dec. 24, 1874.

Three. Warren Fales Tunnell b Aug. 24, 1871; d Sept. 7, 1892 Boulder, Col.; unmarried.

Four. Emma Irene Tunnell b June 3, 1874; d Sept. 26, 1876.

Five. Adelaide Louise Tunnell b June 24, 1878, of Peyton, Col. married Abraham L. Loban Jan. 7, 1904 Boulder, Col. and had; (a) Elizabeth Loban b Mar. 22, 1905 Boulder, Col.; (b) Homer Stanton Loban b Mar. 10, 1907 Boulder, Col.; (c) Dorothy Marguerite Loban b Oct. 7, 1908 Boulder, Col.; (d) Genevieve Loban b Sept. 19, 1910 Boulder, Col. (e) Irene Loban b Nov. 16, 1912 Elbert, Col.; (f) Florence Loban b Nov. 6, 1914 Elbert, Col.; (g) Clyde Tunnell Loban b Sept. 19, 1916 Boulder, Col.; (h) Edgar Fales Loban b July 7, 1918 Elbert, Col.

Six. Georgia Tunnell b Sept. 20, 1883, of Denver, Col.; married David A. Barthclow Sept. 26, 1906 Boulder, Col. and had; (a) Adelaide Bartholow b Nov. 9, 1909; (b) Warren Fales Bartholow b Dec. 20, 1913 Sterling Col.

VIII. Melvina Catherine Tunnell, dau of Luther and Louisa Parks Tunnell, was born Nov. 19, 1843 and died Feb. 22, 1875 Carrollton, Ill. She married Isham M. Linder, junior, Sept. 4, 1865 Greene Co., Ill He was born May 24, 1839 Greene Co., Ill,; d Apr. 30, 1926 Carrollton, Ill.; and married second, Adaline C. Doolittle Sept. 21, 1876 (b Feb. 17, 1850; d Mar. 3, 1908). He is a brother of John M. Linder, who married Louisa Elvira Tunnell. Children;

One. Finice Ardeen Linder b Oct. 2, 1867 nr Carrollton, Ill., of Carrollton; married first, Mary Doyle, dau of John and Elizabeth (Miller) Doyle, Nov. 28, 1888 Greene Co., Ill. (b July 9, 1869 Greene Co., Ill.; d June 7, 1900 Greene Co., Ill.) and had ch b Greene Co.; (a) Ione Linder b June 27, 1894, of Jacksonville, Ill. (m Dr. Carl Ellsworth Black, the second. (son of Dr. Carl Ellsworth and Bessie McLaughlin Black; gson of Dr. Greene Vardeman and Jane (Coughenour) Black; same of Rev. James and Frances (Kirby) McLaughlin), Dec. 23, 1918 Carrollton, Ill. and had ch b Jacksonville, Ill.; 1, Carl Ellsworth Black, the Third, b May 19, 1920; 2, Ardeen Black (daughter) b Aug. 3, 1922; 3, Mary Elizabeth Black b and d Mar. 25, 1924); (b) Isham Doyle Linder b July 14, 1897, of Carrollton, Ill.; served with Marines in World War overseas, (m Grace Wiseman, dau of A. J. Wiseman, Sept. 3, 1922 Jerseyville, Ill. and had; 1, Isham Wiseman Linder b Feb. 14, 1924 Jacksonville, Ill.) Finice A. Linder married second, Annie Stout. dau of Elisha and Lucia E. (Converse) Stout, Apr. 15. 1903 White Hall, Ill. and had ch b Carrollton, Ill.; (c) Lucia Ardeen Linder b Jan. 6, 1904; (d) Child b and d Oct. 28, 1905.

Two. Elsie Annora Linder b May 19, 1874 in Carrollton; d Oct. 11, 1874.

IX. Minerva Virginia Etna Tunnell, dau of Luther and Louisa Parks Tunnell, was born Mar. 20, 1846 and lives St. Augustine, Fla. She married Ed Bailey June 12, 1867 Greene Co., Ill. (b Mar. 10, 1834 Philadelphia; d May 2, 1902 St. Augustine, Fla.) and had an only child; (a) Clyde Tunnell Bailey b Jan. 8, 1871 Girard, Ill., of Chicago, Ill. (m Henrietta Elizabeth Cunningham, dau of John S. and Harriet Bell (Ginn) Cunningham, Oct. 7, 1896 Mattoon, Ill. and had; 1, Elizabeth Ginn Bailey b Mar. 9, 1903 Chicago, Ill., m Judge Alfor M. Eberhardt Nov. 18, 1924 Chicago, Ill.; (b) Clyde Tunnell Bailey, the Second, b Mar. 9, 1906).

L. Stephen Tunnell, son of William and Mary Maysey Tunnell, was born Oct. 19, 1795 and "Departed this life July 11 About an hour by Sun in the morning 1815 in the twentieth year of his age". (Bible record). He died nr Robertsville, Tenn.; unmarried.

SALLY TUNNELL MILLER

M. Sally Tunnell, daughter of William and Mary Maysey Tunnell, was born July 29, 1799 nr Robertsville, Anderson Co., Tenn and died July 21, 1874 Greenfield, Illinois. She married James William Wellington Miller Sept. 20, 1820 (b July 21, 1798; d Aug. 16, 1838 Warren Co., Tenn.) It is said the town of Campaign, Tenn is built on land they owned. In 1845 Sally Tunnell Miller moved, with her family, to Greene Co., Ill.; she being the fourth child of her parents to move to Illinois. Children born near Rock Island, Tenn.

I. Polly Miller b July 13, 1822.
II. Abram Worthington Miller b Dec. 25, 1824.
III. James Calvin Miller b Nov. 25. 1826.
IV. Eliza Jane Miller b Apr. 20, 1829.
V. Wilson McKamey Miller b Apr. 16, 1831.
VI. Martha Elizabeth Miller b June 11, 1833.
VII. Cyrus Jasper Miller b Sept. 16, 1835.
V III. Sarah Adeline Miller b Dec. 3, 1838.

Of the foregoing;
I. Polly Miller dau of J. W. W. and Sally Tunnell Miller, b July 13, 1822; d Apr. 4, 1906 Greenfield, Ill.; m Albert Smith, Greene Co., Ill. (d about 1890) and had no children.

II. Abram Worthington Miller, son of J. W. W. and Sally Tunnell Miller. b on Christmas day 1824; d Greenfield, Ill. He m first, Margaret Smith (sister of Albert Smith) and had;

One. John Miller b abt 1841 Greenfield, Ill. who enlisted in the Union Army and was killed at Mobile, Ala. in battle. A. W. Miller married second, Mrs. Harriet (Lemar) Booker (the mother-in-law of his first cousin, William Tunnell) and had,

Two. Albert Miller d in inf.

III. James Calvin Miller, son of J. W. W. and Sally Tunnell Miller, b Nov 25, 1826; d Jan. 18, 1884 nr Hettick, Ill. He m Mary N. Jones Aug. 27. 1848 (b July 2, 1827; d Sept. 4, 1887 nr Hettick, Ill.) and had ch. b nr Greenfield, Ill.

One. Frances Ann Miller b July 6. 1849; d Sept. 10, 1854.

Two. Sarah Miller b Mar. 25, 1851, of Hettick, Ill.; m Smith Sutton Feb. 6. 1873 nr Hettick (b Mar. 5. 1845; d Aug. 8, 1910) and had ch. b nr Hettick Ill · (a) James Sutton b Nov. 16. 1873; d Nov. 13, 1879; (b) Mary Sutton b Feb. 20, 1876, of Deertrail, Col. (m George A. Thompson and had; 1. Orval Thompson, of Los Angeles, Calif.; 2. Dolan Thompson m William Self and had; (aa) Ralph Self; 3, Harold Albert Thompson of Deertrail, Col.; 4. Mable Thompson; 5. Elsie Thompson; 6, James Thompson); (c) Albert Sutton b Nov.

12, 1878, Hettick, Ill. (m Goldy Patterson and had; 1, Bonny Pauline Sutton; 2, Leroy Sutton· 3, Velma May Sutton; 4, Frieda May Sutton); (d) Thomas Sutton b Dec. 11, 1880; d Sept. 24, 1881; (e) Theodore Sutton b Feb. 20, 1889; d Dec. 15, 1920 Hettick, Ill. (m Prudence Lula Tennhill and had; 1, Lillian Sutton; 2, Madeline Sutton).

Three.   Rachel Miller b Nov 12, 1853; d Nov. 9, 1854.

Four.   Cyrus Jasper Miller b Nov. 26, 1855; retired farmer, Hettick, Ill.; m Alice Crouch Oct. 28, 1880 nr Hettick (b Sept. 3, 1856 Sullivan Co., Tenn., dau John and Mary Ruth (Caloway) Crouch; sister of Dr. Noah Allen Crouch whose wife, Helen Coonrod was of Tunnell family (sse record John and Nancy Worthington Tunnell). Ch. b nr Hettick, Ill.; (a) James Allen Miller, farmer, of Virden, Ill. (m Pearl Alderson Aug. 17, 1910 and had; 1, Clara Alice Miller b Sept. 5 1911; 2, Helen Virginia Miller b June 5, 1914 Lowder, Ill.; 3, Barbara Miller b Sept. 16, 1917 Virden, Ill.); (b) Julia Miller, of Los Angeles, Calif. (m Claude Powell June 19, 1906 and had; 1, Glenn Morris Powell b May 22, 1907; 2, Charles Hugh Powell b Mar 15, 1910; 3, Willard Powell b Oct. 17, 1914; 4, Samuel Powell b Mar. 16, 1918); (c) Elsie Miller b Apr. 18, 1884, of Palmyra, Ill. (m Albert Ross Apr. 12, 1906 nr Palmyra and had no children).

Five.   John Abram Miller b Nov. 12, 1859; d small.

Six.   William Wellington Miller b Apr. 10, 1862, farmer, Hettick, Ill.; m Sarah Bragg Apr. 27, 1893 and had ch. b nr Hettick; (a) Calvin Miller b Mar. 19, 1894; d Apr. 15, 1895; (b) Everett Miller b June 6, 1895; d small; (c) Teddy Miller b 1897, of Alton, Ill.; (d) Edgar Miller of Alton. Ill.; (e) Mamie Miller (m Vernie Calhoun and had; 1, Katherine Irene Calhoun; 2, William Taylor Calhoun; 3, Earl Calhoun; 4, Mable Lucile Calhoun); (f) George Miller; (g) Lucille Miller; (h) Elmo Miller.

IV.   Eliza Jane Miller dau of J. W. W and Sally Tunnell Miller, b Apr. 20, 1829; d June 2, 1907 Greenfield, Ill. She m David Liles Aug. 10, 1848 Greene Co., Ill. (b Aug. 12, 1824 Greene Co., Ill. d Dec. 24, 1904 Greenfield, Ill., son of George Washington and Bettie (Austin) Liles) and had ch. b Greenfield, Ill.

One.   Mary Elizabeth Liles b Sep. 4, 1849; d July 6, 1851.

Two.   Mary Ann Liles, second by name of Mary, b Oct. 29, 1851, of Greenfield, Ill.; m Edward J. Stock Oct. 28, 1869 Greenfield, (b Oct. 11, 1844, Philadelphia, Pa.; d June 1907 Greenfield, son of Frederick and Christina Fay (Kohler) Stock) and had on only child; (a) Nine Stock b Apr. 19, 1871, of Greenfield, Ill; m Ben M. Kincaid 1849 (son of William Lynn and Amanda Mason Kincaid (b Aug. 22, 1839 nr Lancaster, Ky.; d Nov. 4, 1924 Greenfield, Ill., dau of Dr. George and Elizabeth Mason) and had no children.

Three.   Etna Jane Liles b Jan. 1, 1854, of Eldorado, Kansas; m Fred Stock Jan. 11, 1871 Greenfield, Ill. (b May 31, 1847 Philadelphia, Pa.; d Aug. 18, 1817 Greenfield, Ill., son of Frederick and Christina Fay (Kohler) Stock) and had on only child; (a) Fred Liles Stock b Oct. 30, 1875 Greenfield, Ill., of Eldorado, Kas. (m Rose C. Farrow Nov. 1895 Greenfield, Ill. (b Dec. 25, 1873 Medora, Ill.) and had; 1, Paul Lile Stock b July 10, 1898 Greenfield; m Hazel Bernice Willaby Nov. 19, 1924 (b Dec. 12, 1901 Toronto, Kas.); 2, Natalia Virginia Stock b Aug 20, 1899 Greenfield; m Charles Blackburn May 1, 1920 Eldorado, Kas. (b Sept. 12, 1900 Waynesburg, Pa.) and had; (aa) Constance Ann Blackburn b Sept. 17, 1921 Eldorado, Kas.; 3, Frederick C. Stock b May 31, 1902, Greenfield; 4, Donald William Stock b Jan. 19, 1909 St. Louis, Mo.; 5, Finice Farrow Stock b Mar. 22, 1911 St. Louis, Mo.)

Four.   Rebecca Emerson Liles b Feb. 24, 1856; d small.

Five. Eliza Douglas Liles b Aug. 20, 1857, of Carbondale, Ill.
m John Wahl May 8, 1879 and had ch. b Greenfield, Ill.; (a) Malcon
Leonard Wahl b May 6, 1880, farmer, Centerton. Ark. (m Eula Roach
May 23, 1912 Greenfield, Ill. and had; 1, Jack Wahl b July 31, 1921
Centerton, Ark.); (b) Harold Liles Wahl b July 31, 1882, conductor on
I. C. R. R., Carbondale, Ill.; (c) Ruby Estelle Wahl b Oct. 1, 1888 of
Cookshire, Quebeck, Canada (m James Andrew Frasier, manufacturer,
and had; 1, Gloria Elaine Frasier b Aug. 9, 1909 Cookshire, Canada.
     V. Wilson McKamey Miller, son of J. W. W. and Sally Tunnell
Miller, b Apr. 16, 1831; d in infancy.
     VI. Martha Elizabeth Miller, dau. of J. W. W. and Sally Tun-
nell Miller, b June 11, 1833; d Dec. 16, 1892 nr Wrights, Greene Co.,
Ill. She m John Doyle Mar. 16, 1859 Greene Co., Ill. (b Apr. 19,
1834 Greene Co., Ill.; d May 14, 1916 nr Wrights. Lll.. a first cousin
of Lorenzo Doyel who married Sarah Adeline Miller,) and had ch.
b nr Wrights, Ill.;
     One. Thomas Doyle b Feb. 9, 1863, of Carrollton, Ill., former
county clerk of Greene Co.; m Catherine Geery Mar. 16, 1886 Greene
Co., Ill. (b Jan. 9, 1864 White Hall, Ill., dau of Abraham and Elizabeth Geery) and had ch. b Greene Co.; (a) Meda Lee Doyle b Sept.
19, 1889, of Carrollton, Ill., (m Albert L. Dowdall Jan. 21, 1920
Carrollton, Ill. (b June 12, 1891; d Dec. 28, 1922 Jacksonville, Ill.,
son of W. Frank and Jennie (Robinson) Dowdall) and had no ch.;
(b) Freda B. Doyle b Oct. 25, 1891, of Carrollton, Ill. (m Delbert
Perry Driver Apr. 22, 1920 Carrollton, Ill. and had; 1, Vivian Lucile
Driver b May 17, 1921 Jacksonville, Ill. Delbert P. Driver, farmer, b
June 8, 1890, Carrollton, Ill., son of Robert Perry (b Mar. 12, 1844
Greene Co., Ill.) and Mary Alice (Purl) Driver (b June 15, 1861,
Greene Co., Ill.; g-s Thomas Purl (b Dec. 15, 1812 Bedford Co., Penn.;
d Feb. 21, 1891 nr Carrollton, Ill.) and Violet (Jones) Driver (b Dec.
15, 1821 Centerville, Ind.; d 1871). Thomas Purl m first, a relative,
Mary Anne Purl and they were parents of Caroline Purl who married
Andrew Jackson Tunnell. See record Calvin and Jane Addair
Tunnell.
     Two. Alice Doyle b Oct. 24, 1860, of Wrights, II.; m David
Johnson 1881 and had; (a) Maud Johnson b Mar. 7, 1884 (m Virgil
Staat and had several ch.); (b) Ethel Johnson b Dec. 26, 1888 (m
———— Thaxton and had ch.); (c) Elmer Johnson b July 14, 1890;
(d) Earl Johnson b Jan. 1892; m ———— ————; (e) Helen Johnson
b Sept. 18, 1894; m ———— ———— and had ch.; (f) Mary Johnson b
Dec. 26, 1896; m ———— and had ch.
     Three. Mary Doyle b July 9, 1869; d June 7, 1900; m her second
cousin, Finice Ardeen Linder. See record of Luther and Louisa
(Parks) Tunnell.
     Four. J. Frank Doyle b Feb. 11, 1866; farmer, Wrights. Ill; for
a number of years member of the county board of Supervisors; m
Dora Short Dec. 25, 1888 Greene Co., Ill. and had ch. b nr Wrights,
Ill.; (a) Ralph Wilbur Doyle b Dec. 1889; (b) Edith Doyle b Jan. 16,
1891; (m Grant Melvin and had; 1, John Melvin); (c) Zella Doyle b
Sept. 1892 (m E. M. Mosier Jan. 1910 Virginia, Ill. and had ch.) (d)
Martha Doyle m Ward Burton; (e) Finice L. Doyle.
     VII. Cyrus Jasper Miller, son of J. W. W. and Sally Tunnell
Miller, b Sept. 16, 1835; d Mar. 28, 1908 in Mo. He m Sarah Garrett
1856 (d Apr. 6, 1898) and had ch. one born in Ill., others in Mo.
     One. John Alonzo Miller b Sept. 1857; d June 17, 1890; un-
married.
     Two. Annetta Ann Miller b 1858; m Joe Stover and had; (a)
Jennie Stover m ———— Ardinger and had; 1, Charles Ardinger; (b)

Rog G. Stover, of Springfield, Ill. (m ———— ———— and had; 1,
Stover; 4, Robert Stover; 5, Edgar Stover; 6, Agnes Stover; 7, Vesta
Carl Cecil Stover; 2, Florence Stover b July 29, 1907; 3, Frances
Stover); (c) Earl Stover; (d) Fannie Stover; (e) Will Stover; (f)
Carl Stover; (g) Charles Stover.

Three. Eliza Miller b May 6, 1860; m William Miller Dec. 25,
1879 and had; (a) Sarah Elizabeth Miller b July 18, 1880; d Mar. 24,
1881; (b) William Delaine Miller b Nov.-17, 1881; d Mar. 24, 1882;
(c) John Allen Miller b July 5, 1882; m Mary E. Clark; (d) Alice
Mae Miller b Feb. 18, 1889 (m Claude A. Hickok Mar. 21, 1906 and
had; 1, Elmer Claude Hickok b Mar. 17, 1907); (e) Monte C. Miller
b Sept. 13, 1893; d May 14, 1894; (f) Nina Gertrude Miller b Nov. 24,
1896; (g) Lora Bell Miller b Oct. 4, 1901.

Four. William Albert Miller b Aug. 16, 1862; farmer, Cross
Timbers, Mo.; m Mary Taylor Mar. 18, 1890 Paola, Kas. and had; (a)
Clarence Lloyd Miller b Jan. 24, 1891 Parker, Kas.; farmer, Hermitage, Mo. (m Dollo Boyd Apr. 16, 1913 and had ch. b Hermitage, Mo;
1, Otis Owen Miller b Jan. 30, 1914; 2, Warren G. Miller b May 16,
1922); (b) Xina Hazel Miller b June 29, 1893 Parker, Kas., of Bowling Green, Mo. (m Orie Sparks Aug. 22, 1922); (c) lla Vee Miller b
Mar. 5, 1894, Parker, Kas.; of Kansas City, Mo. (m Weyet Duncan
Dec. 17, 1915 and had; 1, Thelma Loretta Duncan b July 25, 1917
Hickory Co., Mo.; d Aug. 19, 1920); (d) Neva Lynn Miller b Mar. 2,
1896 Greenfield, Ill.; of Corning, Mo. (m Elmer H. Harpham May 21,
1918 and had; 1, Charlotte Marie Harpham b May 16, 1920 Kirks-
ville, Mo.; 2, Mary Emma Harpham b July 13, 1922 Warrensburg,
Mo.); (e) Fred Liles Miller b Feb. 3, 1902; farmer, Cross Timbers,
Mo,; unmarried.

Five. Mary Ellen Miller b abt 1864, of Greenfield, Mo.; m Frank
Probst and had; (a) Lula Probst; (b) Minnie Probst; (c) Albert
Probst b Mar. 5, 1889 Greenfield, Ill. (m ———— ———— and had; 1,
Denzell Probst b Sept. 30, 1913; 2, Norman Probst b Nov. 1, 1915; 3,
Frances Probst b Mar. 22, 1919; 4, Clarabell Probst b May 23, 1922;
5, Harlan Lee Probst b Nov. 29, 1923); (d) Harrison Probst, died
young; (e) Wesley Probst, of Guam Islands; (f) Fred Probst, of Kansas City, Mo.; m ———— ————; (g) Frank Probst; (h) Basel Probst
d young.

Six. Fannie Adeline Miller b abt 1866, of Orrick, Mo.; m first,
Louis Starr and had; (a) Goldier Starr; and m second, John Head
and had ch., including; (b) Helen Head.

Seven. Maggie Miller b July 4, 1868; m Herbert Allen Aug. 19,
1897 and had; (a) Mary Elizabeth Allen b Apr. 25, 1898; (b) Marguerite Allen b May 9, 1899; d Aug. 29, 1899; (c) LeRoy Allen b June
12, 1900.

Eight. Sarah Elizabeth Miller b abt 1870; d small.

Nine. Ida Mae Miller b Nov. 8, 1872; m George W. Schaffer
Dec. 25, 1903 (b Feb. 21, 1860) and had no ch.

Ten. Bert Miller b abt 1874; d at 21.

Eleven. James Miller b June 13, 1876.

Twelve. Clem Miller b abt 1878; d at 3.

VII'. Sarah Adeline Miller, daughter of J. W. W. and Sally Tunnell Miller, was born Dec. 3, 1838, and lives (1925) Macon, Georgia.
She m Lorenzo Doyle Mar. 26, 1857 Greenfield, Ill. He was born Feb.
9, 1836 Greenfield, Ill. and died Nov .19, 1879 Atlandic, Iowa and was
buried at Wrights, Ill. He was the son of John and Matilda (Brown)
Doyle. Children.

One. Rufus Doyle b June 15, 1859 Greenfield, Ill.; d Oct. 18,
1880; unmarried.

Two.   Harry Doyle b and d Sept. 2, 1869, Nilwood, Ill.

Three.   Addie Doyle b 1873 Atlantic, Iowa, of Macon, Ga.; m first Rev. Absalom Alexander Benfield Aug, 15, 1899 Greenfield, Ill. (b Dec. 10, 1870 Oxfordshire, England; d Aug. 17, 1906 Hoopeston, Ill; son of Eli and Mary Ann (Rylands) Benfield) and had no children.   Addie Doyle m second, John Talbot Davison Dec. 18, 1912 Macon, Ga. (b Nov. 8, 1861 Ala. retired, for twenty five years treasurer for wholesale grocery; son of James and Nancy (Mackey) Davison.

Four.   John Albert Dovel b Dec. 9, 1874 Atlantic, Iowa; d Dec. 5, 1900; m Loretta Mullery Jan. 19, 1898 (b Mar. 18, 1880 St. Louis, Mo., of Greenfield, Ill.; dau of Peter Richard and Maggie (Condon) Mullery) and had ch b Meldora, Ill.; (a) Albert Richard Doyel b Jan. 2, 1899, advertising manager, Connellsville, Penn.; m Henrietta McMillan May 28, 1923 Washington, D. C. (b May 28, 1902 Cedarville, O., dau of William R. McMillard, who d Sept. 1924, Monmouth, Ill.); (b) Lorenzo Mullery Doyel b Sept. 15, 1901, of Macon, Ga.; (c) Aileen Margaret Doyel b Feb. 27, 1903, of Greenfield, Ill.; m Darrell Prentice Hamilton Jan. 3, 1925 Carrollton, Ill.   D. A. Hamilton, salesman, b June 23, 1899, son of Harley Warren (b Sept. 18, 1875) and Edith Ostrom (Allen) Hamilton (b Nov. 18, 1876); gs Hiram Balmannah and Frances Levonia (Griswold) Hamilton; same Luther Prentice and Jane Ann (Ostrom) Allen; ggs Henry Joel and Caroline (Hunt) Hamilton; of Franklin and Philena (Kidder) Griswold; of George W. and Caroline (Henderson) Allen; of Isaac Roberts and Deborah Ann (Wooley) Ostrom.)

PART TWO

Stephen Tunnell, son of William and Ann Howard Tunnell, was born 1753 Spotsylvania Co., Va. and died 1828 Tompkinsville, Ky. He was a Methodist minister and inherited the horse, from his brother, Rev. John Tunnell, which had taken the latter over a vast territory during his ministerial career.   He served in the Revolution and participated in the battle of Long Island.   His wife, Kezia Money, whom he married 1776 in Georgetown, Maryland, died 1836 Morgan Co., Ill. (RMT)   She was of a Huguenot family of the eastern shore of Maryland.   They lived in Va. until 1788 when they moved to Washington Co., Tenn. and it is said they lived at one time in Greene Co.   Several of their ch were born in Va. while the others were born in Upper East Tennessee.   Five of their sons were ministers.   They had an only daughter, who married and, like her mother, was the mother of ten sons and one daughter.   There are many descendants who bear the name as names of four thousand are known. Names of the ch may not be in order of birth.

A.   James Tunnell b 1777.
B.   William Tunnell b abt 1779.
C.   Nancy Tunnell b abt 1782.
D.   Perry Tunnell b abt 1787.
E.   John Tunnell.
F.   Stephen Tunnell b Mar. 4, 1790.
G.   Nicholas Money Tunnell b Apr. 30, 1892.
H.   Wesley Tunnell b abt 1794.
I.   Jesse Tunnell b abt 1798.
J.   Martin Luther Tunnell.
K.   David Tunnell b Nov. 25, 1800.

JAMES TUNNELL

A.   James Tunnell, eldest child of Stephen and Kezia Money Tunnell, was born 1777 near Fredericksburg, Va. and died abt 1865 at the home of a step-son, named Campbell, near Robertsville, Tenn.

He moved, with his parents, in 1788 to Washington Co., Tenn.   He married first, Jane Ball 1796 and settled on Beach Creek, Hawkins Co., Tenn.   She was born abt 1780 and died in Hawkins Co., Tenn. She was the dau of Moses and Mary (Harden) Ball; Moses Ball, of Penn., and one the pioneer settlers in Hawkins Co.   James Tunnell married second, a widow, Mrs. Campbell.

James Tunnell was a Baptist minister.   For fifty years he was a member of Double Springs Church.   Of him Rev. J. J. Burnett in his book "Tennessee's Pioneer Baptist Preachers" says; "he was not a 'Primitive or Old School' Baptist, but like some of them would sing out his sermons, I have been told, after the approved fashion and popular and effective style of preaching in many parts of the country of that day.   Dr. Broadus used to say that the 'sing-song' habit of some of the dear old men was a by-product of out of door speaking and being retsful to the 'overstrained' vocal chords, was natural."

Children of Rev. James Tunnell, all by first marriage, were born on Beach Creek, Hawkins Co., Tenn.   Names may not be in order of birth.

1. John Tunnell b June 7, 1797 or 1798.
II. Spencer Tunnell b abt 1800.
III. Jane Tunnell b Mar. 13, 1805.
IV. Wesley Tunnell b 1807.
V. James Tunnell b Sept. 8, 1809.
VI. Kizzie Tunnell.
VII. Jesse Tunnell b abt 1814.
VIII. Isaac Tunnell b 1816.
Of the foregoing;

I.   John Tunnell, son of James and Jane Ball Tunnell, was born June 9, 1797, or 1798, and died Mar. 8, 1868 Galt, Mo.   He married Elizabeth Charles Sept. 24, 1818, on her seventeenth birthday Hawkins Co., Tenn.   She was born Sept. 24, 1801 and died May 7, 1877 Galt, Mo.   They moved to Mo. 1844.   All their children, save youngest, b Hawkins Co., Tenn.   Six sons served as soldiers in the War Between the States.

One.   Jacob Charles Tunnell b Dec. 13, 1821; d 1864; soldier; married first, Sarah Woods Mar. 12, 1843 Greene Co., Tenn., ceremony performed by his grandfather, Rev. James Tunnell. No children.   He married second, Susanah Ellis Sept. 1844 (marriage license granted Sept. 9, 1844) and his grandfather, Rev. James Tunnell was the officiating clergyman at this wedding.   Children; (a) Josiah Tunnell b abt 1845 or 1846 in Tenn.; d 1864 Chattanooga, Tenn.; soldier in the War Between the States; unm.; (b) David C. Tunnell, died in southern Mo., m ———— ———— and had no ch.; (c) Stephen Tunnell b in Sullivan Co., Mo.; dead (m Sarah Smedley abt 1879, who d 1908, in Mo. and had; 1, Edith Tunnell; 2, Ellen Tunnell); (d) Jesse Tunnell b Sullivan Co., Mo.

Two.   James Wiley Tunnell b Sept. 14, 1823; d Apr. 8, 1908 Fairview, Kan.; served in the Union Army; moved to Grundy Co. Mo. 1844 and to Kansas 1887 ;married first, Pauline (Winters) Payton Sept. 30, 1851 (d Sept. 6, 1861 Galt, Mo.) and had ch b nr Galt, Mo. (a) Sarah E. Tunnell b June 28, 1853; d in nifancy.; (b) Nannie A. Tunnell b Dec. 2, 1855, of Milam, Mo. (m H. T. Knight May 1881 Milam, Mo. and had ch b Milam; 1, Herbert Lee Knight b May 26, 1882, of Milam, Mo., m Edna Stanforh May 23, 1905 Milam, Mo. and had ch b Milam; (aa) Eleanor Fay Knight; (bb) Alice Lee Knight; (cc) Rose Knight; (dd) Dean Knight; (ee) Mary Knight; (ff) Irma Knight; (gg) Paul Knight; (hh) Ruth Knight; 2, Lula Fay Knight b Feb. 14, 1885, county superintendent of schools, Sullivan Co., Mo.);

(c) Marticia Alice Tunnell b Jan. 20, 1857, of Fairview, Kan. (m first, John J. Crooks Mar: 11, 1877 Trenton, Mo. (d Mar. 24, 1879) and had; 1, Albert Crooks b May 5, 1878; d Mar. 22, 1879; and m second, James B. Allison Oct. 26, 1882 Hiawatha, Kan. and had; 2, James McCandless Allison b Aug. 17, 1884 Hiawatha, Kan., m Bessie M. Wilson Apr. 6, 1904 and had ch b nr Fairview, Kan.; (aa) James Ivan Allison b July 4, 1905; (bb) Charles Loren Allison b Mar. 28, 1907; (cc) Edith Wilferene Allison b Jan. 10, 1910; (dd) Mary Eleanor Allison b Feb. 17, 1915; (ee) Bessie Ruth Allison b Mar. 4, 1919; (ff) Vivian Fay Allison b Jan. 15, 1922); (d) John F. Tunnell b Mar. 20, 1861; d June 20, 1886, unmarried.   James Wiley Tunnell b Sept. 14, 1823 married second, Mary Ann Chase Johnson June 15, 1864 (d Jan. 1, 1915 Fairview, Kan.) and had; (e) Mary Pink Tunnell b Dec. 2, 1865 Grundy Co., Mo.; d May 20, 1903 Brownell, Kan. (m; William Henry Jordan Jan. 5, 1891 Wakeeney, Kan. and had; 1, Mary Emma Jordan b Feb. 20, 1892, of Sabetha, Kan., m Walter A. Shipman Sept. 5, 1912 and had ch b Sabetha, Kan,; (aa) Freddie William Shipman b Nov. 2, 1913; (bb) Norman Barton Shipman b Feb. 8, 1919; 2, Wilma Alice Jordan b June 30, 1898, m Leslie E. Hampton Dec. 4, 1918 Powhatan, Kan. and had; (aa) Lervy Sylvester Hampton b Feb. 10, 1922; 3, Marticia Pink Jordan b Apr. 17, 1903, m Maurice Neilson Aug. 11, 1921 Topeka, Kan. and had; (aa) Harlow Dean Neilson b Feb. 22, 1924); (f) Henry Edgar Tunnell b May 7, 1870, of Ellis, Kan., m Cora Johnson Feb. 18, 1893, who d Feb. 22, 1909 and had no children.

Three.   Darkey Jane Tunnell b Sept. 22, 1825; d abt 1849; unm.

Four.   John Wesley Tunnell b Oct. 9, 1827; d at Galt, Mo.; served in Union Army; married first, Polly Wilson, abt 1846, who d in Mo. and had several ch., including (a) Alfred Sawyer Tunnell, of Galt, Mo.; (b) Martha Tunnell, dead, m first, ——— Semon and second——— Martin.   J. W. Tunnell m second, Sarah J. King and had two daughters, Polly and Bessie.

Five.   Stephen Senter Tunnell b Nov. 29, 1829; d Oct. 31, 1913 Osgood, Mo.; married Elizabeth Callihan 1853 in Mo. / (b Apr. 11, 1830; d Oct. 29, 1916 Osgood, Mo.) and had thirteen ch, three of whom died same day of birth; (a) Mary Jane Tunnell b 1855 Wintersville, Mo., of Larned , Kan. (m John Henry Edson 1879 (b July 30, 1851 Eaton, Ohio; d 1923 Larned, Kan.) and, like her mother had 13 ch., including; 1, Matilda E. Edson b 1881 Wintersville, m Ellis Patrick 1895 Dawn, Mo. and had; (aa) Parker Clendenden Patrick b 1896, m Ona Todd and had; Gertrude Patrick b 1915 and Gala Patrick b 1917; (bb) Elsie May Patrick b 1898; d 1913 Minneapolis, Minn.; 2, Stephen Franklin Edson b 1883 Wintersville, Mo.; d 1884; 3, James Alfred Edson b 1885 Wintersville, Mo., m Agnes Fulton 1919 Larned, Kan.; 4, Mary Alda Edison b 1886 Osgood, Mo., d Larned, Kan., m Andrew D. Hill (b 1887 Rogers, Kan.) and had ch., oldest b Osgood, Mo., others Larned, Kan.; (aa) Myrtle Amber Hill b June 16, 1907; (bb) Fay Claudy Hill b Sept. 1, 1913; (cc) John W. Hill b Nov. 19, 1915; (dd) Maudie Marie Hill b Sept 17, 1920; (ee) Bettie Lee Hill b May 6, 1923; 5, William Senter Edson b 1888 Osgood, m Hattie Fulton (1895 Burdett, Kan) and had ch b Burdett, Kan.; (aa) William Leonard Edson b Feb. 27, 1913; d Oct. 30, 1915 ;(bb) Ruby Jane Edson b Jan. 19, 1915; 6, John Henry Edson, the Second, b 1890 Osgood. Mo., m Hattie Myers (b Nov. 15, 1898) and had ch. oldest b King Cilty, Mo., others Larned, Kan.; (aa) Mary Ellen Edson b Oct. 17, 1915; (bb) Wilbur Franklin Edson b May 9, 1918; d Apr. 8, 1919; (cc) and (dd), twins, Ray Leon Edison and Fay Levon Edison b Apr. 29, 1920; 7, Eva Ella Edson b 1891 Osgood, Mo.; d 1891; 8, Iva Myrlle Edson b 1893 Chillicohte, Mo.; d 1894; 9, Maudie Lutishia Edson b 1895 Chillicothe, m a relative, George Tunnell 1913, in Mo. (b May 28, 1886, son of Josiah R. and Catherine (Rush) Tunnell; gs George White and Mary (Callihan) Tunnell) See record of G. W. Tunnell for children; 10, Winchel Dewey Edson b 1898 Chillicothe, Mo.; d 1899; 11, Truby Jane Edson b 1900 Utica, Mo., m, Fred Garver and had; (aa) Jack Eugene Garver b June 11, 1921 Larned, Kan.); (b) Martha Ann Tunnell b 1857; d July 1924 (m William Ellis and had five ch., including; 1, Alda Ellis, m Wilbur Barnett and had 5 ch.; 2, Ida Ellis, of Ava, Mo. m ———— Kennen and had 2 ch.,); (c) Sarah Frances Tunnell b 1859; d 1909 (whose son married and had six ch.); (d) Celia Catherine Tunnell b 1861, d small; (e) Minerva Elizabeth Tunnell b 1863; d small; (f) Nancy Emeline Tunnell b 1865 (m John Doolin and had 7 ch., including; 1, Albert Doolin, of Osgood, Mo., m ———— ———— and had 8 ch.; 2, Nora Doolin, of Osgood, Mo., m ————' Moore and had 5 ch.; 3, Clella Doolin, m ———— Taylor and had 3 ch.; 4, Lizzie Doolin; 5, Jessie Doolin; 6, Wayne Doolin, m ———— ———— and had one ch.); (g) Lutitia Alice Tunnell b Oct. 8, 1866 Osgood, Mo., of Harris, Mo. (m John Nida and had; 1, Mary Almeda Nida b Jan. 17, 1887, m first, William M. Ralls Nov. 19, 1904 and had; (aa) William Clifton Ralls b Sept. 25, 1905 Osgood, Mo., of Creston, Iowa., m Pauline McKee Apr. 9, 1923 and had; Marylyn Jean Ralls b Oct. 30, 1924 Creston, Ia.; (bb) Bertha Eunice Ralls Oct. 15, 1907, m Wade Brassfield June 14, 1924. Mary Almedia Nida m second, Crove A. Johnson Oct. 2, 1911 and had ch b nr Osgood, Mo.; (cc) Nellie Margaret Johnson b Dec. 25, 1912; (dd) Helen Lutitia Johnson b Oct. 18, 1915; (ee) Gladys Elvesta Johnson b Mar. 3, 1918; (ff) Ceca Bernice Johnson b Apr. 18, 1920; (gg) Ursia Elton Johnson b Sept. 19, 1922; (hh) Eunice Wineva Johnson b Oct. 15, 1924; 2, William Henry Nida b Mar. 20, 1889, m Eva Brassfield Feb. 27, 1912 and had ch b Osgood, Mo.; (aa) Charlie Everett Nida b June 21, 1913; (bb) Waldon Henry Nida b May 4, 1918; (cc) Venna Louise Nida b Nov. 26, 1921; 3, Alta Ray Nida b Feb. 1, 1892, m Verge Johnson Aug. 23, 1910 and had ch b Osgood, Mo.; (aa) Wiletta May Johnson b Mar. 1, 1912; (bb) Bertha Colene Johnson b Dec. 14, 1914; (cc) Joseph Sylvester Johnson b Mar. 4, 1918; (dd) Evelyn Beatrice Johnson b Feb. 18, 1920; (ee) Willford Clyde Johnson b Nov. 24, 1921; (ff) Donald Woodean Johnson b Oct. 2, 1924; 4, Nellie May Nida b Apr. 17, 1894, of Wichita, Kan., m Fred Shepherd Feb. 27, 1911 Ottumwa, Ia. and had; (aa) Thelma Elvestie Shepherd b July 20, 1912 Ottumwa, Ia.; (bb) Ronald Clyde Shepherd b Apr. 30, 1916 Wichita, Kan.; (cc) Doris Juletta Belle Shepherd b Ottumwa, Kan.; 5, Dollie Elvestie Nida b Jan. 12, 1897 Spickard, Mo., of Wichita, Kan., m Frank Ballinger Aug. 24, 1916; 6, Ida Lutitia Nida b Oct. 15, 1899 Osgood, Mo.; d Mar. 9, 1901; 7, Amos Clyde Nida b Dec. 8, 1901 Osgood, Mo., of Wichita, Kan., m Anna Humphreys Dec. 24, 1923 and had; (aa) Donna Moreen Humphreys b Mar. 3, 1925); (h) John Alexander Tunnell, died young, unm.; (i) William Allen Tunnell, d small; 10, Lucy Josephine Tunnell, m John Boyer).

Six. Samuel Patten Tunnell b Feb. 25, 1832; d July or Aug. 1915 Livingston, Montana; moved to Mo. when quite young; crossed the plains to Calif. 1861; lived at one time in Utah, another in Calif. He married Mary Jane Vencill Nov. 27, 1856 Galt, Mo. (b Aug. 1, 1840; d years ago at Nevada, Mo. and had; (a) Reece Williamson Tunnell b Dec. 30, 1857 in Mo.; d Sept. 21, 1914 Calgary, Canada, m Irene Ryerson and had no ch,; (b) Elizabeth Jane Tunnell b Nov. 21, 1859 in Mo.; d in early childhood in Calif.; (c) Nevada Tunnell b Feb. 16, 1862 in Calif.; d small; (d) Mary Frances Tunnell b Feb. 7,

1867 in Calif., of Livingston, Montana (m Woodson Hodges Apr. 12, 1893 Livingston, Mont, (d Mar. 24, 1924) and had; 1, Roy Hodges b Feb. 9, 1894, unm. served in World War; 2, Aubery Patten Hodges b Apr. 25, 1896, unm., served in World War; 3, Montana Francis Hodges b Nov. 15, 1898); (d) Stresley Tunnell b Jan. 7, 1869 in Calif., of Billings, Mont. m Mary Cunningham abt 1915 and had no ch.; (e) Laura Bell Tunnell b Aug. 25, 1870, of Big Timber, Mont. (m William Perry Dutton and had ch b Big Timber, Mont.; 1, Walter Cottle Dutton b Mar. 31, 1892, of Livingston, Mont., m Agnes Annie Michels Sept. 6, 1924 and had; (aa) Walter Arthur Dutton b June 17, 1925; 2, Vivian Merlin Dutton b July 24, 1895, of Livingston, Mont., m Manila Celia Pechiett July 19, 1918; 3, Beulah Bell Dutton b Sept. 11, 1897, of San Bernardino, Calif., m Cligord Bruce Wylie Feb. 4, 1920; 4, Vesta Pearl Dutton b July 6, 1899, of Los Angeles, Calif., m Frank A. Podach Aug. 1922 and had; (aa) Vyonne Pearl Podach b Oct. 24, 1923; 5, Dimple Dutton b May 12, 1902, m Noah Thomas Ball Oct. 25, 1922; 6, Herbert Perry Dutton b Sept. 18, 1904, m Aletha Alice Walters June 11, 1923 and had; (aa) son b Mar. 18, 1925; 7, Glenn William Dutton b July 28, 1906; d Jan. 6, 1918; 8, Sabra Laura Dutton b Oct. 21, 1909; 9, Helen Irene Dutton b May 20, 1913).

Seven. Elizabeth Mary Tunnell b Feb. 1, 1834; d in Kansas; married first, John Erwin 1871 and had three sons, all of whom died within three weeks of each other, all under ten years; and married second, Ben Malone and had no ch by second marriage.

Eight. George White Tunnell b Dec. 7, 1835, of Springfield, Mo.; lived for thirty-one years in Sullivan Co., Mo., then moved to Kansas; served in the War Betwen the States; married three times; first, Mary Callihan, sister of Elizabeth Callihan, Jan. 9, 1857 in Mo. (b Feb. 17, 1832 in Ill.; d in Mo.); married second, Mary E. Taylor Mar. 30, 1890 and married a third time, abt 1923. Children, all by first marriage, b Sullivan Co., Mo.; (a) Celia Elizabeth Tunnell b Dec. 31, 1857; d Aug. 3, 1909 Emporia, Kan. (m James Thomas Ford June 9, 1879 (b Feb. 20, 1850 Trenton, Mo.; d July 19, 1922 Emporia, Kan.) and had ch b in Kan.; 1, Mary Ellen Ford b Feb. 18, 1880 Ellis, Kan., of Emporia, Kan., m Albert B. Whipple Nov. 27, 1901 Emporia, Kan. and had ch b Emporia; (aa) Ralph Leroy Whipple b Dec. 3, 1903, m Maude More Dec. 29, 1923 and had, Lotus Lorine Whipple b Jan. 29, 1925 Emporia, Kan.; (bb) Frances Elizabeth Whipple b Aug. 29, 1909; (cc) Ivan Whipple b Sept. 27, 1912; (dd) Inez Irene Whipple b May 22, 1915; (ee) Florence Hazel Whipple b Mar. 24, 1918; 2, Sarah Elizabeth Ford b Sept. 26, 1882 Ellis, Kan., m Charles J. Buck July 4, 1924 (d Nov. 27, 1924) and had; (aa) Charles Russell Buck b Apr. 7, 1925 Emporia, Kan.; 3, Effie Ann Ford b Oct. 18, 1884 Brownell, Kan., of Topeka, Kan., m Allie Stouder Feb. 1903 and had ch b Emporia, Kan.; (aa) James Harold Stouder b Nov. 14, 1903; (bb) Eleanor Margarette Stouder b Nov. 26, 1906; (cc) Ruth Elizabeth Stouder b Aug. 10, 1909. Effie Ann Ford m second, Victor Plants and had no ch. 4, William Thomas Ford b Feb. 10, ——, Brownell, Kan.; d at three weeks; 5, James Franklin Ford b July 14, 1888 Brownell, Kan.; d Oct. 31, 1901 Emporia, Kan.); (b) Lydia Tunnell b Feb. 13, 1860; d Oct. 23, 1888 Sullivan Co., Mo. m Samuel Stokesberry Feb. 4, 1876 Sullivan Co., Mo. and had ch b Sullivan Co.; 1, Mary B. Stokesberry b Jan. 24, 1877, m Joseph Steward and had one ch.; 2, Maggie Stokesberry b Sept. 9, 1878, of McCracken, Kan., m Arthur Lawson and had; (aa) Oliver Samuel Lawson b Mar. 22, 1903; (bb) Lloyd Stanley Lawson b Oct. 17, 1904; d Mar. 27, 1912; (cc) Allene Caroline Lawson b Feb. 21, 1906; (dd) Gail Kimbal Lawson b Oct. 18, 1907; (ee) Opal Gwendolyn Lawson b May 26, 1913; 3, Arthur

Stokesberry b Sept. 17, 1880, Free Methodist minister of Osgood, Mo., m May Leonard and had no ch.; 4, Bertha Stokesberry b Nov. 15, 1882; d 1896; 5, Lillie May Stokesberry b May 24, 1886, dead; 6, G. Harvey Stokesberry b Oct. 10, 1888; d May 1920 Hays, Kan., was in regular army and served in Battery B. First Field Artillery, in World War, m —————— ——————, now of New York, and had; (aa) Anna Stokesberry); (c) Josiah Roten Tunnell b Jan. 13, 1862, president Mountain View. Mo. Bank (m first, Catherine Rush July 16, 1882 (d Apr. 6, 1889 and had; 1, Jessie Tunnell b Apr. 26, 1883, m Leslie Hardwick Oct. 1901 and had; (aa) Hazel Hardwick; (bb) Walter Hardwick; (cc) Pauline Hardwick; (dd) Sylvia Hardwick; 2, Zelma Tunnell b Aug. 18, 1884, m Charles Fawcett 1904 Emporia, Kan. and had; (aa) Catherine Fawcett b Apr. 30, 1905, m —————— —————— 1924; (bb) Lucy Fawcett b Oct. 12, 1907; d Aug. 1911; (cc) Paul Fawcett b Oct. 30, 1909; 3, George Tunnell b May 28. 1886 in Kan., m a relative, Maudie Lutishia Edison 1913 Mo. (b 1895 Chillicothe, Mo., dau John Henry and Mary Jane (Tunnell) Edson; gd of Stephen Senter and Elizabeth (Callihan) Tunnell) and had; (aa) Glen Henry Tunnell b Oct. 1, 1915 Brownell, Kan.; (bb) Peggy Louise Tunnell b Apr. 28, 1922 Larned, Kan.; 4, Lula Tunnell b Aug. 16, 1888, m W. L. Barringer May 1908 and had; (aa) Maybell Ruth Baringer b Jan. 18, 1911; d Jan. 23, 1923.   Josiah Roten Tunnell b Jan. 13 1862 married second, Mary E. Taylor, Mar. 30, 1890 and had no issue by this marriage.

Nine. Delay Fletcher Tunnell b Jan. 7, 1839; died in the War Between the States.

Ten. Josiah Roten Tunnell b Mar. 1, 1843; died in the War Between the States.

Eleven. William Harrison Tunnell b Aug. 8, 1846; d Aug. 1918 Iowa married Chris Bailey 1870 in Mo. and had; (a) Frank Tunnell, died unm. Kearney, Neb.; (b) Roten Tunnell, of Kearney, Neb.; (c) Lee Tunnell; (d) Grace Tunnell.

II. Spencer Tunnell, son of James and Jane Ball Tunnell, was born abt 1800 and died in Greene Co., Tenn., probably in the early thirties.   He married Rhoda English, dau of Alexander English, who married, for second husband, William Brandon.   She died in Mo. Ch. b in Greene Co., Tenn., may not be in order of birth.

One. Milton Tunnell b May 19, 1825; served as Union soldier in the War Between the States, in 44th Mo. Inf., Co. K.; married first, Elizabeth Gray Walker May 18, 1843 Greene Co., Ill. (b Apr. 28, 1826; d June 24, 1850 Greene Co., Tenn. and had 3 ch.; and married second Anna Eliza Philips Nov. 3, 1850 Greene Co., Tenn. (b in Tenn.; d Trenton, Mo.) and had 5 ch.; (a) Mary Catherine Tunnell b Aug. 12, 1845 of Trenton, Mo.; went to Mo. 1881 (m Rev. Joab Holloway Dec. 27, 1885 Trenton, Mo., who d Mar. 31, 1901; and m second, Rev. Charles H. Cash Oct. 21, 1903 Trenton, Mo., who d 1917, and had no issue by either marriage); (b) Harriet Atwood Newell Tunnell b Dec. 4, 1847; d July 21, 1884 Greene Co., Tenn. (m Henry McNeece, in Tenn. (d 1866 Greene Co., Tenn.) and had an only child; 1, Alice McNeece b July 22, 1865 Greene Co., Tenn., of Limestone, Tenn., m A. J. Williams and had ch b Greene Co., Tenn.; (aa) Mary Adeline Williams b May 8, 1885, m Buford Dobbins and had 2 ch b Greene Co., Tenn., Kathleen Dobbins and Olevia Dobbins; (bb) Kate Elizabeth Williams b June 16, 1887, m Edwin Parker and had 4 ch b Greene Co., Tenn.; J. A. Parker, Roy Parker, Hugh Parker and Georgia Marie Parker; (cc) Walter Franklin Williams b Nov. 9, 188_, of Iowa, m Kate Parker and had 2 ch b Iowa, Lucile Williams and Leona Williams; (dd) Oscar Lee Williams b Oct. 26, 1891, m Mary Parker and had 3 ch b Greene Co., Tenn., J. W. Williams, James

Williams and Edna Pauline Williams; (ee) Marion Ernest Williams
b May 15, 1894, m Emma Guinne and had no ch.; (ff) Vernie Clyde
Williams b Jan. 11, 1897; d Aug. 25, 1898; (gg) Letha Odell Williams
b Sept. 8, 1900, m Ruble Shanks and had 3 ch b Greene Co., Tenn.,
A. J. Shanks, Thelma Nadine Shanks and Dennis Earl Shanks; (hh)
Derrel Delmo Williams b Oct. 27, 1903, m Edith Draine and had,
Sylvia Williams b Greene Co., Tenn.; (ii) Huble Earl Williams b
Sept. 7, 1909); (c) son, unnamed, b and d June 10, 1850; (d) Manford
Tunnell b June 26, 1854 nr Nevada, Mo., of Trenton, Mo. (m first,
Millie Burtin 1876 Sullivan Co., Mo. (d July, 4, 1908) and had; 1,
David Wilbur Tunnell b Nov. 5, 1878 Reger, Mo., of Trenton, Mo., m
first, Bessie Elwood Nov. 23, 1902 and had; (aa) Daisy Lorraine
Tunnell b Jan. 31, 1904 Trenton, Mo., of Wichita, Kan., m William F.
Donaldson Mar. 22, 1921 Newton, Kan. and had one ch., Anna Jeane
Donaldson b Mar. 19. 1923; (bb) Vernon Elwood Tunnell b Aug. 11,
1905; and m second, Mattie C. Springer Aug. 23, 1908 Milan, Mo.; 2,
Emma Jane Tunnell b Mar. 10, 1881 nr Trenton, Mo.; d Nov. 16, 1918
Tulasona, Tex., m John Joslin, Little Rock, Ark. and had no ch.; 3,
William Tunnell b 1883 Humphreys, Mo.; d July 1884; Manford Tun-
nell m second, Ollie Dennison Oct.' 15, 1922); (e) Elizabeth Jane
Tunnell, of Collins, Mo. (m J. E. Burt and had 4 rh., two of whom
are dead); (f) Rhoda Evaline Tunnell, of Newton, Kan. (m Jake
Brown and had 2 ch.); (g) James Spencer Tunnell b Apr. 2, 1863 nr
Lindley, Mo., of Valley Junction, Iowa. (m Emma Jane Redding Dec.
22, 1883 Trenton, Mo. and had ch b Trenton, Mo.; 1, Sylvia Grace
Tunnell b June, 3, 1885, m Barton Lester Jones Oct. 9, 1912 Valley
Junction; Ia. and had no ch.; 2, Clarence James Tunnell b May 28,
1887, m Elsie Grace Weisler Nov. 24,,1914 Valley Junction, Ia. and
had; (aa) Eugene Tunnell b Sept. 5, 1916; 3, Charles Richard Tunnell b Oct. 3, 1889, m Marie Hattield Feb. 9, 1919 Des Moines, Ia. and
had no ch.); (h) John Tunnell d at 7 or 8.

Two. John Tunnell died on his way home from the War Between
the States, at Knoxville, Tenn. He married Thuriza Williams Sept.
30, 1844 Greene Co., Tenn., who d in Tenn. and had ch. b Jearlds-
town, Greene Co., Tenn. Names may not be in order of birth; (a)
Leanah Tunnell b abt 1846, m John Barnett, of Greene Co. Tenn.; (b)
Rhoda Tunnell b abt 1850; d 1924 Hawkins Co., Tenn. (m a relative,
Fletcher Tunnell, son of Wesley and Rebecca (Ball) Tunnell; gs
Rev. James and Jane (Ball) Tunnell. See record of Wesley Tunnell); (c) Amanda Jane Tunnell, deceased (m Hale White and had;
1, George White; 2, John White; both of whom are married and have
families, at Rheatown, Tenn.); (d) Margarent Ann Tunnell, deceased
(m a relative, John Bernard, (son of John and Pop (Ball) Bernard;
gs Wesley and Nancy (Bailey) Ball; ggs Moses and Mary (Harden)
Ball) and had ch b Hawkins Co., Tenn.; 1, Ruby K. Bernard (son),
of Van Hill, Tenn; 2, Leanah Bernard; 3, Fannie Bernard; 4, ——
Bernard (son); all unm.); (e) James Buchanan Tunnell b Sept. 28,
1858, of English, West Va. (m a relative, Patience Lucas (b July 26,
1859, dau of Solomon P. and Mary Jane (Tunnell) Lucas; gd Wesley
and Rebecca (Ball) Tunnell; ggd of Rev. James and Jane (Ball) Tunnell) and had; 1, William Harrison Tunnell b Dec. 23, 1876 Van Hill,
Tenn., of English, W. Va., m Jennie Rosnoke July 31, 1897 nr Rosnoke, Va. and had; (aa) Nelson Miles Tunnell b June 27, 1898 nr Rosnoke, Va.; (bb) Bertha May Tunnell b June 2, 1901 Finney, Va.; (bb)
Carson Tunnell b Apr. 24, 1903 Glamorgan, Va.; (dd) Ethel Tunnell
b June 21, 1905 Norton, Va.; (ee) Millard Tunnell b Aug. 17, 1907
Norton, Va.; (ff) Glenn C. Tunnell b Dec. 2, 1909 Norton, Va.; (gg)
Edwin Duke Tunnell b Apr. 1, 1913 Norton, Va.; (hh) Theodore R.

Tunnell b June 20, 1916 English, W. Va.; d Feb. 22, 1919; 2, Hugh
N. Tunnell b Oct. 22, 1879 Van Hill, Tenn.; deceased; m Cecila Rosnoke 1901 nr Rosnoke, Va. and had; (aa) Harrison Tunnell; (bb)
Virgie Tunnell; (cc) Alfa Tunnell; (dd) George Tunnell; '(ee) Clarence Tunnell; 3, Leora Tunnell b Sept. 18, 1881 Van Hill, Tenn.; d
1913, m Porter Carver (d same year as wife) and had; (aa) Bessie
Carver, of English, W. Va.; (bb) Hazel Carver, m —— Palmer;
(cc) Julian Carver; (dd) J. B. Carver; 4, Richard Tunnell b Oct. 22
1883 Van Hill, Tenn., m Lillie Madison at Norton, Va.; 5, Albert
Tunnell b Nov. 12, 1885 Van Hill, Tenn., of Osaka, Va., m twice and
had several ch.; 6, Lillie May Tunnell b May 1, 1889 Wayland, Va.,
of New Hall, W. Va., m Doc W. Beavers of English, W. Va. and had
ch.; 7, Isaac Tunnell, twin, b Mar. 29, 1892 Wayland, Va., deceased;
8, Bart B. Tunnell, twin of Isaac, b Mar. 29, 1892, of Bluefield, W.
Va., m May Witten at Tazwell, Va. and had two ch.; 9, Dockey Tunnell b Feb. 7, 1894 nr Cleveland, Va.; 10, Rufus Tunnell b June 29,
1896 nr Finney, Va., served in World War, with 13 months service in
France, m —— ——); (f) George McClellan Tunnell, deceased
(m Julia Calet and had 1, Charles Tunnell, of Johnson City, Tenn.;
2, Robert Tunnell, of Johnson City; 3, 4 and 5, daughters, who are
dead); (g) Emily Catherine Tunnell, died very young; (h) Spencer
Tunnell, died young.

Three. Alexander Tunnell married Eliza Myers Mar. 3, 1843
Greene Co., Tenn. No record.

Four. —— Tunnell, daughter, d in inf.

II.. Jane Tunnell, dau of James and Jane Ball Tunnell, was born
Mar. 13, 1805 and died June 2, 1867 Russell Co., Va. She married
James Ball, presumably a relative, the son of John Wesley Ball, abt
1821 in Hawkins Co., Tenn. He was born Apr. 24, 1806 Russell Co.,
Va. and died Jan. 30, 1883 in same county. James Ball married sec-
ond, Celia Fleather Sykes. Some ch. of Jane Tunnell Ball b Russell
Co., Va.; and others Buchanan; names may not be in order of birth.

One. Cynthia Ball, died Russell Co., Va.; m first, Albert Lester
and second, David Tiller.

Two. Celia Ball, died Russell Co., Va.; m a relative, Noah Ball,
son of George and Catherine Ball.

Three. Nancy T. Ball died when abt 20, unm.

Four. Rebecca Ball b Jan. 8, 1828; d May 10, 1872 Russell Co.,
Va.; married John W. Ball, brother of Noah Ball above, who was b
June 17, 1822 and died Dec. 26, 1908. He m second, Annie Whitt.
Ch. of Rebecca (Ball) Ball b in Va.; (a) Haskew Ball b Aug. 28, 1844,
of Va. (m Cynthia Hurt Sept. 24, 1868 (b May 14, 1853; d June 5,
1892) and had; 1, A. C. Ball b Aug. 29, 1869, of Honaker, Va., m Ida
Gertrude Miller Jan. 31, 1894 and had; (aa) Bert E. Ball b Dec. 31,
1894, of Norton, Va., m Carrie M. Smith May 10, 1916 and had 3 ch.,
Esther Louise Ball, Helen Marjorie Ball and Harry Thomas Ball; (bb)
Grace E. Ball b Dec. 30, 1896, m E. W. Hurt June 28, 1919 and had,
Eugene Kelso Hurt b and d Mar. 27, 1921; (cc) Edgar L. Ball b Apr.
27, 1898, of Chihowee, Va., m Hannah Powers Aug. 28, 1922 and had,
Edgar Ross Ball b May 14, 1925; d May 19, 1925; (dd) Gladys Dorne
Ball b Apr. 6, 1902, of Gainsville, Florida, m Ross E. Jeffries Aug. 16,
1922 Louisville, Tenn.; 2, A. R. Ball b Aug. 1, 1871, of Gardner's, Va.,
m Jettie Harris, who is dead; 3, Corrie A. Ball b Feb. 14, 1874, of
Blackford, Va., m W. E. Mutter; 4, Alonzo F. Ball b Oct. 2, 1876; d
Sept. 17, 1881; 5, Elbert W. Ball b Nov. 22, 1876, of Gardner's, Va.,
m Myrtle Fletcher; 6. Mary E. Ball b July 1883; d in inf.; 7, Eunice
P. Ball b Aug. 3, 1885, of King's Mountain, m Dr. W. D. Laswell; 8,
Arthur H. Ball b July 31, 1887; d at 16); (b) Jasper Ball b Dec. 20,

1846; d in inf.; (c) Catherine Jane Ball b June 24, 1848 (m Moses Hurt May 5, 1867, who d Jan. 9, 1918 Gardner's, Va., and had; 1, Haskew Hurt, of Somerset, Ky., m Georgiana Barrett and had; (aa) Claude Hurt, of Somerset, Ky., m Fordie Mulkey and had no ch,; (bb) Maggie Myrtle Hurt, dead; (cc) Pearl Hurt, of Honaker, Va., m Clyde Beamer and had, Clyde Beamer, Jr.; (dd) Garnett Hurt; (ee) Luther Hurt; (tf) Janyce Catherine Hurt, of Somerset, Ky., m Lee Sweeney and had one ch.; (gg) Nettie Hurt, of Dayton, O., m Frank Newel; (hh) Paul Hurt; (ii) Russell Hurt; (jj) Ella Hurt; (kk) Georgia Lee Hurt; 2, John Hurt, of Gardner's, Va., m Nannie Seavor and had; (aa) Rev. E. W. Hurt m Grace Ball and had one ch. dead; (bb) Ethel Hurt; (cc) Rubye Hurt; (dd) Tyler Hurt; (ee) Onslo Hurt; (ff) Clarence Hurt; (gg) Carbaugh Hurt; (hh) Emory Hurt; (ii) Aaron Hurt; (jj) Nannie Hurt; (kk) Mary Hurt; (li) Fannie Hurt; 3, Eddie L. Hurt (daughter), unm., of Gardner's Va.; 4, Ida Jane Hurt, of Honaker, Va., m Leonard Owens and had; (aa) Albert A. Owens (deceased); (bb) Alden Owens (deceased); (cc) Eula Owens, of Honaker, Va., m Olus Combs and had no ch.; (dd) Aurelia Owens, (deceased); (ee) Grace Owens, m Ernest Jackson and had 2 ch.; (ff) Elizabeth Owens; 5, Myrtle Hurt, unm., of Gardner's, Va.; 6, Dora Hurt, of Corbin, Ky., m Samuel Harris Parrott and had no ch.; 7, Lula Hurt, unm. of Gardner's, Va.; 8, Mollie Hurt, of Bluefield, W. Va., m Everett Lemons and had no ch.; 9, William Hurt, deceased; 10, Fannie Hurt, of Bluefield, W. Va., m O. L. Dye and had; (aa) Carl Dye; (bb) Thelma Dye; (cc) Harry Lee Dye; 11, Bess Hurt, of Gardner s, Va., m Nathaniel Burchfield and had; (aa) William Nathaniel Burchfield); (d) George W. Ball b Feb. 7, 1852, unm.; (e) Noah Ball b Feb. 2, 1855, d in inf.; (f) Mary E. Ball b Oct. 5, 1856, of Davenport, Va., m T. A. Smith Jan. 30, 1882; (h) Martha Jane Ball b Oct. 12, 1862; d abt 1882; (i) Frank C. Ball b Jan. 18, 1866, m ———— ———— and had ch.; (j) C. R. Ball b Feb. 7, 1868, of Davenport, Va., m ———— ———— and had ch.)

Five. Spencer Tunnell Ball, b Mar. 10, 1844; d July 12, 1921 Russell Co., Va.; married first, Lucinda C. Fuller (b May 12, 1844; d Sept. 6, 1922 Lewis Center, Ohio) and had; (a) James B. Ball, of Lewis Center, O., m Evaline Cox and had ch., some of whom are married; (b) Bonapart Ball, of Davenport, Va., m Mary McFarlaine and had 6 ch., three married; (c) Ira R. Ball b Feb. 14, 1871, of Council, Va. (m Mary Fletcher Jan. 30, 1895, who d Jan. 11, 1914, and had; 1, Laura A. Ball b Oct. 31, 1895; 2, Frank P. Ball b Aug. 4, 1897; 3, Corrie Ball b Apr. 11, 1899; d July 11, 1899; 4, Charlie W. Ball b Apr. 10, 1900; 5, Ruther Ellis Ball b Feb. 8, 1902; 6, Washington Irving Ball b Oct. 16, 1903; 7, Ezra T. Ball b Sept. 9, 1905; 8, Dollie M. Ball b Sept. 1, 1907; 9, Ada A. Ball b Mar. 29, 1909; 10, Gracie E. Ball b July 4, 1911; 11, Earl Ball b Jan. 8, 1914; d Jan. 8, 1914, same day as his mother); (d) Harvey G. Ball, dead, married first, Celina Kindrick (dead) and m second, Catherine Compton, (dead) and third, Fanny Tiller and had several children, one of whom is Mrs. Dewey Ratliff, of Grundy, Va.) Spencer T. Ball married second, Nancy Lester and had; (e) Christopher Columbus Ball, of Harmond, Va.. m Mary Davis ; no nad large family, some ch. married; (f) Grover Ball, unm., of Kimball, W. Va.; (g) Guy Ball, of Kimball, W. Va., m ———— ———— and had 2 ch.; (h) Matt P. Ball, of Davenport, Va., m Bessie Perkins and had several ch.; (i) Phebe Ball (dead), m Henry Tiller and had one child. Henry Tiller m second time and lives Duty, Va.; (j) Chloe Ball (dead), m Walker Tiller and had 3 ch.); Spencer T. Ball married third, Cynthia McGraw and had; (k) Glen Ball; (l) Ethel Ball; (m) Flossie Ball.

Six. Martha Ball married George W. Tiller.

Seven. Mary Ball, who at one time lived nr Coal Creek, Pike Co., Ky.; married Sam Burnett and had; (a) Nancy Jane Burnett; (b) Rebecca Burnett; (c) Eliza Burnett; (d) John Burnett.

Eight. John George Ball b Aug. 23, 1848, deceased; married Nancy A. Tiller, sister of George W. Tiller and dau of David Tiller, Oct. 20, 1867 (b Apr. 14, 1851; deceased) and had ch b Buchanan Co., Va.; (a) Rohasia Seymour Ball b Nov. 6, 1868, of Davenport, Va. (m Alola Duty and had; 1, Elbert Ball; 2, Alta Ball; 3, Martin Ball; 4, Henry Ball; 5, McKinley Ball; 6, Luther Ball; 7, Paul Ball; 8, Grace Ball; 9, Leona Ball; 10, Alola Ball; 11, ch. dead; 12, ———— Ball); (b) Evans W. Ball b Sept. 21, 1870; d in inf.; (c) Victoria V. Ball b Mar. 26, 1873; d in inf.; (d) Louis L. Ball b June 21, 1876, of Parksville, Ky. (m Rosa Womplar and had; 1, Loy L. Ball b Apr. 22, 1902 Buchanan Co., Va., m ———— and had a dau b Oct. 20, 1924 Boyle Co., Ky.; 2, Bertha M. Ball b Feb. 10, 1904 Boyle Co., Ky.; 3, Cora Ball b July 19, 1906 Boyle Co. Ky.; 4, Viola Mae Ball b Sept. 10, 1910 Jefferson Co., Tenn.; 5, Roy S. Ball b Feb. 15, 1913 Jefferson Co., Tenn.; 6, Herbert M. Ball b May 1, 1915 Jefferson Co., Tenn.; 7, Clarence Ball b Jefferson Co., Tenn.; 8, Golda G. Ball b July 1, 1922 Boyle Co., Ky.; 9, Beulah May Ball b Nov. 21, 1924 Boyle Co. Ky.); (e) Sarah Jane Ball b Sept. 30, 1878, of Morristown, Tenn. (m Jesse Davis in Buchanan Co., Va. and had; 1, Clara Davis, m John McKinney; 2, Eura Davis, both girls b Buchanan Co., Va.); (f) Ellen A. Ball b Apr. 30, 1880; d 1907; (g) Larkin S. Ball b Feb. 21, 1883; d in inf.; (h) Ora Ball b Aug. 20, 1884, of Russell Co., Va. (m Jake Wilson in Buchanan Co. and had; 1, Myrtle Wilson; 2, Gladys Wilson; 3, Willard Wilson; 4, Leonard Wilson; 5, Dewey Wilson; 6, Beauty May Wilson; 7, Dora Wilson, and others, all b Buchanan Co.); (i) Dora Ball b Mar. 25, 1887, of Morristown, Tenn. (m ———— Sykes and had; 1, James Larkin Sykes died 1905 Buchanan Co., Va.; 2, Dollie Sykes b Nov. 10, 1906, m Sherman Lawson 1923 Morristown, Tenn.; 3, Earnest Sykes b Jan. 1, 1909; 4, Cecil E. Sykes b Feb. 9, 1911; 5, Della Sykes b Feb. 18, 1913; 6, Gladys Sykes b May 31, 1915); (j) Minnie Ball b Apr. 13, 1891, of Morristown, Tenn. (m B. D. Fullington, in Tenn. and had; 1, Effie Fullington; 2, Walden Fullington, dead; 3, Bessie May Fullington; 4, Charlie Fullington; 5, S. E. Fullington; 6, Annie Mary Fullington, dead); (k) Winnie Ball b Dec. 12, 1893, of Morristown, Tenn. (m George Harton and had; 1, George Lee Harton; 2, John William Harton).

IV. Wesley Tunnell, son of James and Jane Ball Tunnell, was b 1807 and died Mar. 1872 on Beech Creek, Hawkins Co., Tenn. He married Rebecca Ball, dau of John Ball of Russell Co., Va. She was born Mar. 10, 1810 nr Honaker, Va. and died abt 1897 Hawkins Co., Tenn. Children b Hawkins Co., Tenn.

One. Mary Jane Tunnell b Sept. 11, 1829.
Two. John Tunnell b abt 1831.
Three. Spencer Tunnell b 1834.
Four. Isaac Tunnell b 1836.
Five. Eliza Tunnell b Oct. 31, 1838.
Six. James Harvey Tunnell b Mar. 25, 1842.
Seven. Martha Tunnell b abt 1844.
Eight. David Carter Tunnell b Oct. 18, 1848.
Nine. William Fletcher Tunnell b 1850.
Ten. Daughter, twin of William Fletcher.
Of these;

One. Mary Jane Tunnell b Sept. 11, 1829; d after 1871 Hawkins Co., Tenn.; married Solomon P. Lucas abt 1849 Hawkins Co.,

Tenn. (b Mar 11, 1825; d at Van Hill, Tenn.) and had ch b Van Hill, Tenn.

    a. John W. Lucas b May 11, 1850; d 1923 Van Hill, Tenn.; married first, Betsy Kelly and had; 1, Cora Lucas, m Walter Moore; Charles Lucas, m first, Callie Hawkins, and second, Phoebe Strong; 3, James Lucas, m Cordie Hawkins. John W. Lucas married second, Sarah (Cook) Andes, sister of Mrs. Alexander Lucas and Mrs. John Rhoten Tunnell, and had; 4, Emma Lucas; 5, Elsie Lucas; 6, Melvin Lucas.

    b. Dr. Spencer T. Lucas b June 26, 1852; d Mar. 21, 1925 Jefferson City, Tenn.; married Maigaret Patience White Sept. 15, 1880 Hawkins Co., Tenn. and had ch b Hawkins Co.; 1, Reuben A. Lucas b June 6, 1881; 2, Addie Lucas b Nov. 22, 1883; 3, Novella J. Lucas b Oct. 15, 1885; 4, Bertha E. Lucas b Feb. 17, 1887; 5, Clara M. Lucas b July 31, 1890; 6, Dama Lucas b June 13, 1892; 7, Isma P. Lucas b Oct. 22, 1894; 8, Solomon S. Lucas b Apr. 8, 1897; 9, Anna M. Lucas b Mar. 24, 1900; 10, Charles M. Lucas b Apr. 6, 1902; several of whom are married and have families.

    c. Rebecca Jane Lucas b Mar. 13, 1854; d nr Van Hill, Tenn., a few days after deaths of her brothers, William and Harve Lucas. She was unmarried.

    d. Mary Elizabeth Lucas, twin with Rebecca Jane Lucas, b Mar. 13, 1854; d Oct. 30, 1900 nr Baileyton, Tenn.; married Solomon Dalton, Hawkins Co., Tenn, who d Mar. 27, 1914, and had ch b Hawkins Co., Tenn.; 1, Thomas Dalton b May 19, 1875; d Jan. 25, 1878; 2, W. Eckel Z. Dalton b May 23, 1883; d Apr. 18, 1903 in U. S. A. in Phillipines; 3, Agnes Dalton b Mar. 4, 1885, of Lebanon, Kan., m G. W. Annis; 4, Bertha Dalton b Dec. 19, 1888, of Baileyton, Tenn., m ——— Luster and had; (aa) Mildred Luster b Sept. 10, 1917; (bb) Charles Luster b Nov. 9, 1919; 5, Charles Dalton b Apr. 1, 1891, of Greeneville, Tenn., m ——— ——— and had; (aa) Gilbert Dalton b Apr. 20, 1917; (bb) Leland Dalton b Apr. 10, 1922; 6, Rebecca Dalton b Jan. 12, 1894, unm., of Greeneville, Tenn.

    e. Alexander K. Lucas b Apr. 19, 1856, of Baileyton, Tenn. for many years but now of Greene Co., Tenn.; married Mary Jane Cook, dau of George and Jane Cook, and sister of Sarah Cook Andes Tunnell and Julia Cook Tunnell, and had; 1, Bessie Lucas, m Bud Malone; 2, Baxter Lucas, unm.; 3, Major Lucas, unm.

    f. Nancy Ann Lucas b Oct. 19, 1857; d nr New Hope, Tenn.; married Samuel Burrell and had; 1, Rebecca Burrell; 2, Gilbert Burrell; 3, Mollie Burrell; 4, Hela Burrell, of Baileyton, Tenn., m John Ball.

    g. Patience Lucas b July 26, 1859, of English, West Va.; married a relative, James Buchanan Tunnell, son of John and Thuriza (Williams) Tunnell; gs Spencer and Rhoda (English) Tunnell; ggs James and Jane (Ball) Tunnell. See record of John and Thuriza Williams Tunnell.

    h. James Harve Lucas b Aug. 20, 1861; d 1882 a few weeks after his brother William; married a cousin, Rebecca Tunnell, 1881 Van Hill, Tenn., (dau of Spencer and Martha Jane (Ball) Tunnell; gdau Wesley and Rebecca (Ball) Tunnell; same John and Rebecca (Kelly) Ball of Hardin Co., Ky.; ggdau James and Jane (Ball) Tunnell; same Wesley and Nancy (Bailey) Ball on Beach Creek, Hawkins Co., Tenn.; gggdau Moses and Mary (Harden) Ball) and had no issue. Rebecca Tunnell m second, ——— Anderson; and third, Mark P. Myers and lives Greeneville, Tenn.

    i. William J. Lucas b July 8, 1864; d 1882 nr Van Hill, Tenn. unm

j. George W. Lucas b Jan. 22, 1867; married first, a relative, Sarah Ball, dau of John and Pattie (Morelock) Ball; gd John Ball and ggdau Moses and Mary (Harden) Ball, and had; 1 Roy Lucas; and married second, Mary Matthews and had several children.

k. Nettie Armincie Lucas b July 7, 1869, of Burem, Tenn.; married William R. Dykes, brother of Alice Dykes, and had ch b Hawkins Co., Tenn; 1, Carson Dykes, m a relative, Roxie Jones, who d Hawkins Co., dau of I. N. and Serelda Tunnell Jones; gdau John and Alys Hale Tunnell; ggdau Wesley and Rebecca Ball Tunnell; gggdau James and Jane Ball Tunnell; ggggdau Moses and Mary Harden Ball, and had children; 2, Mary Dykes, deceased; m Claude Dykes; 3, Elsie Dykes, m ――― Bradshaw; 4, Gilbert Dykes; 5, Eldridge Dykes; 6, Debbie Dykes.

l. Frank M. Lucas b July 30, 1871, of Missouri; married Alice Dykes, sister of W. R. Dykes, and had; 1 Mina Lucas; 2, Patrick Lucas; 3, Lucy Lucas.

Two. John Tunnell b abt 1831; nr Van Hill, Tenn.; married Alys Hale abt 1850 Hawkins Co., Tenn. (b 1836; d Van Hill, Tenn.) and had ch b Hawkins Co., Tenn. (a) Elbert Tunnell b 1852; d abt 1891 Hawkins Co., Tenn., unm.; (b) James Wesley Tunnell b 1854; d Mar. 5, 1925 Hawkins Co., Tenn.; lived on Spencer Ball farm which was entered by his ancestor, Moses Ball, and where he lived and died and was buried; married a relative. Rebecca Lucas. 1874, Hawkins Co., Tenn. (b 1854, dau Kelly and Nancy (Ball) Lucas; gdau Wesley and Nancy (Bailey) Ball; ggdau Moses and Mary (Harden) Ball) and had ch b Hawkins Co., Tenn.; 1, Essie Tunnell b 1876, of Van Hill, Tenn., m Patrick K. Lawson 1896, (b 1872) and had ch b Van Hill, Tenn.; (aa) James Carl Lawson b 1897; (bb) Christie Bell Lawson b 1902; (cc) Vestal Opal Lawson b 1904, all unmarried; 2, Paul Tunnell b 1886 d 1887; 3, Sylvia Tunnell b Feb 16, 1891; d Apr. 29, 1915 Van Hill, Tenn., m John Ammos (b 1886) and had; (aa) Sylvia Ammos b 1915; (c) Serelda Tunnell b 1856, living on part of the old Spencer Ball farm nr Baileyton, Tenn. (m Isaac N. Jones b 1852) and had: ch b Hawkins Co.. Tenn.; 1, John Jones b July 23, 1872, m Phema Dykes in Sullivan Co., Tenn. (b 1874 and had; (aa) Roy Jones b 1879; (bb) Huval Jones b 1900; (cc) Ray Jones b 1903; (dd) Delmer Jones b 1906; (ee) Izetta Jones b 1909; 2, David Jones b Aug. 23, 1875 Etta Baskette in Greene Co., Tenn and had; (aa) Dencil Jones b 1906; (bb) Harris Jones b 1908; (cc) Clara Mae Jones b 1923; 3. Carrie Jones b July 6, 1877; d Apr. 4, 1911 Greeneville, Tenn.; 4, Eva Jones b Sept. 13, 1879; 5, Addie Jones b Sept. 6, 1881, m Charlie Bernard and had: (aa) Grace Bernard b 1903; (bb) Earl Bernard b 1904; (cc) Rex Bernard; (dd) Edith Bernard; (ee) Helen Bernard; (ff) Coy Berrard; 6 Charles Jones b Aug. 13, 1883, m Roxie Lucas, a relative thru both Ball and Tunnell families, in Hawkins Co.. Tenn. (b Oct. 3, 1892, dau of John and Lucinda (White) Lucas; gdau George W. and Eliza (Tunnell) Lucas; ggdau Kelley and Nancy (Ball) Lucas; same Wesley and Rebecca (Ball) Tunneli; gggdau Wesley and Nancy (Bailey) Ball; same of James and Jane (Ball) Tunnell; ggggdau Moses and Mary (Harden) Ball), and had; (aa) Gladys Jones b 1912; (bb) Drexel Jones b 1914; (cc) Rex Jones b 1916; (dd) Marie Jones b 1920; (ff) Boneta Jones b 1923; 7, Gilbert Jones b Aug. 7. 1886; d 1904 Van Hill, Tex.; 8, Roxie Jones b 1889; d Oct. 16, 1922 Hawkins Co. Tenn., m a relative, Carson Dykes, (son of William R. and Nettie Armincie (Lucas) Dykes; gs Solomon and Mary Jane (Tunnell) Lucas; ggs Wesley and Rebecca (Ball) Tunnell; gggs James and Jane (,Ball) Tunnell; ggggs Moses and

Mary (Harden) Ball) and had; (aa) Lester Dykes b 1917; (bb) Chester Dykes b 1918: 9, Mona Jones b Aug. 13, 1893; 10, May Jones b Nov. 2, 1885, m John Simpson in Hawkins Co., Tenn., and had; (aa) Cecil Simpson b 1917; (bb) Norma Simpson b 1922; 11, Nettie Jones b Mar. 4, 1898, m Arthur Morelock and had (aa) Thelma Morelock b 1918; (bb) Reva Morelock b 1923; 12, Stella Jones b Nov. 18, 1901); (d) John Rhoten Tunnell b 1860, lives on old John Tunnell farm, nr Baileyton, Tenn. (m Julia Cook, dau George and Jane Cook, 1887 and had ch b Hawkins Co., Tenn.; 1, Laura May Tunnell b Nov. 28,C 1888; d Mar. 10, 1889; 2, Luther Harrison Tunnell b Aug. 12, 1890, m Pearl Ball and had (aa) Texie Ray Tunnell; (bb) Charles Orville Tunnell; (cc) Lela Vestal Tunnell; (dd) Spencer Roat Tunnell; (ee) Clarence Reece Tunnell; 3, Luna Robert Tunnell b Jan. 28, 1893, m Bonnie Gardner (dau Emerson and Mollie (Jones) Gardner; gdau Wiley and Polly (Weems) Gardner; same of Elbert and Ruthy Jane (McLain) Tunnell Jones; ggdau James and Annie (Myers) Gardner; gggdau John Gardner) and had ch b nr Van Hill, Tenn.; (aa) Attie Clover Tunnell; (bb) Tommy Ralph Tunnell; (cc) Coy Cecil Tunnell; (dd) Julia Mollie Lara Maud Tunnell; (ee) Dewey Robert Tunnell; 4, Coy Cecil Tunnell b Aug. 16, 1896, killed in France Oct. 17, 1918, body interred Hew Hope, Hawkins Co., Tenn., unm.; 5, Tilman Horace Tunnell b July 31, 1898; 6, James Oscar Tunnell b Feb. 28, 1901; 7, Leta Emily Alice Jane Tunnell b Nov. 5, 1905; 8, Charles Wayland Tunnell b Apr. 28, 1910).

Three. Spencer Tunnell b 1834; d abt 1857 in Mo.; married Martha Jane Ball, a second cousin, dau of John W. (b 1808) and Rebecca (Kelly) Ball, gdau Wesley and Nancy (Bailey) Ball; ggdau Moses and Mary Harden) Ball, in 1852, who was born Apr. 1838 and who d Mar. 1, 1908 Greeneville, Tenn., having married, for second husband, Garrett Jones, 1867. Spencer and Martha Jane Ball Tunnell had an only child; (a) Rebecca Tunnell b Oct. 31, 1856 Van Hill, Tenn., of Greeneville, Tenn. (m first. her first cousin, James Harvey Lucas, 1881 Van Hill, Tenn. (b Aug. 20, 1861 Hawkins Co., Tenn.; d 1882 Van Hill, Tenn., the son of Solomon and Mary Jane (Tunnell) Lucas; and m second, —— Anderson, 1896 Greene Co., Tenn., who died 1900; and m third, Mark P. Myers Apr. 19, 1908 Greene Co., Tenn. and had no issue.

Four. Isaac Tunnell b 1836; d Oct. 25, 1871 Hawkins Co., Tenn.; married Ruthia Jane McClain abt 1856 (b May 16, 1831; d June 6, 1901)Rutha Jane McClain Tunnell married second, Elbert Jones and had an only child, Mollie Jones, who married Edgar D. Gardner and their dau, Bonnie Gardner married Luna Robert Tunnell (b Jan. 28, 1893). son of John Rhoten Tunnell. Children of Isaac and Jane McLain Tunnell b in Hawkins Co., Tenn.

(a) Harrison Tunnell b May 23, 1857, deceased, (m Mollie Weems and had; 1, Ruthie Tunnell, m Sam Luster and had five ch.; 2, Cora Tunnell, m Chris Woods; 3, Nancy Tunnell, m Pent McClain; 4, Rhonie Tunnell, unm.; 5, Gracie Tunnell, m —— Bumgarden; 6, Patience Tunnell; 7, Katherine Tunnell; 8, Tilman Tunnell; 9, Mazie Tunnell. Mollie Weems Tunnell married second "Dock' Manness and third, Jacob Luster, of Baileyton, Tenn.); (b) Wesley Tunnell b Feb. 24, 860, of White Pine, Tenn. (m Malinda Dyer and had ch b Hawkins Co., Tenn.; 1, Bob Tunnell, m a relative, Turffa Richards (b Nov. 6, 1887) and had; (aa) Gib Tunnell b Nov. 6, 1907; (bb) Cubert C. Tunnell b Sept. 19, 1909: (cc) Elmer Tunnell; (dd) Alvis Tunnell; (ee) Teddy Tunnell; (ff) Hurlow Tunnell; (gg) Heiskell Tunnell b Feb. 1, 1923; 2, Harrison Tunnell; 3, Gus Tunnell, of Leadvale, Tenn.; 4, Myrtle Tunnell; 5, Dannie Tunnell; 6, Caroline Tunnell, m W. E.

Earley and had; (aa) Raymond Earley; (bb) Bessie Earley; (cc)
Mattie Lou Early; (dd) Douglas Early; (ee) Floy Early; 7, Lucinda
Tunnell, of Morristown, Tenn., m Hugh Richards and had; (aa)
Stella Richards; (bb) Bart Richards; (cc) ———— Richards); (c)
Cora Tunnell b Feb. 20, 1863, of Bismarck, Mo. (m Thomas David-
son and had; 1, Carrie Davidson, dead; 2, Sherman Davidson, dead;
3, Charlie Davidson; 4, Emmet Davidson, m ———— ————; 5, Hya-
cinth Davidson, m ———— ————; 6, Kenneth Davidson, unm.); (d)
Rebecca Anna Tunnell b Oct. 28, 1865, of Persia, Tenn. (m J. Samuel
Richards (b Apr. 10, 1866) and had ch b Hawkins Co., Tenn.; 1,
Turffa Richards b Nov. 6, 1887, m Bob Tunnell, son of Wesley and
Malinda (Dyer) Tunnell; gs Isaac and Rutha Jane (McClain) Tunnell,
and had ch b Hawkins Cᵒ Tenn.; 2, Isaac Richards b Feb. 22, 1893,
m first, ———— ———— and had; (aa) Keller Richards b Sept. 19,
1913; (bb) Lena Pearl Richards b Oct. 15, 1917; (cc) S. B. Richards b
Apr. 10, 1920; and m second, ———— ————, and had; (dd) Annie
Richards b Oct. 16, 1922; 3, Elbert J. Richards b Jan. 9, 1894; 4,
Nancy C. Richards b Jan. 28, 1897; d Aug. 28, 1918, m G. W. Rich-
ards, who d Mar. 21, 1920, and had; (aa) Gracie Lee Richards b Oct.
3, 1915; 5, William Richards b June 12, 1900, unm.; 6, Rubert Rex
Richards b July 31, 1903; 7, Robert Lee Richards b Nov. 13, 1905; 8,
Sallie Ann Richards b Sept. 8, 1908); (e) Caroline Tunnell b Aug. 6,
1868, of Baileyton, Tenn. (m first, Harve Morelock and had no ch.;
and m second, Rufus Burns, (d Oct. 15, 1910) and had ch b Van Hill,
Tenn., Mary Burns b Sept. 19, 1889, of Midway, Tenn., m first, Edgar
E. Gardner June 14, 1906 (b Sept. 19, 1889; d Dec. 10, 1914, son of
Newton and ———— (Tate) Gardner; gs James and Annie (Myers)
Gardner; ggs John Gardner) and had; (aa) Mildred Lee Gardner b
June 13, 1908; (bb) Shular Gardner b May 5, 1911; and m second,
Rufus Low and had; (cc) Carmal Low b Nov. 24, 1915; (dd) Georgie
Low b Sept. 7, 1917; (ee) Orbin Low b June 2, 1920; (ff) Mary
Lucile Low b Aug. 25, 1923; 2 Lillie Burns b Nov. 19, 1891, m Rufus
K. Gardner, first cousin of Edgar E. Gardner who m Mary Burns, the
son of Wiley and Polly (Weems) Gardner; gs James and Annie
(Myers) Gardner; ggs John Gardner, and had; (aa) Mary Gardner;
(bb) Helen Gardner; (cc) Charles Brooks Gardner; 3, Charlie
Burns b Sept. 27, 1894, m Lily Luster and had; (aa) Dannie Burns;
(bb) Stella Beatrice Burns; 4, Thomas Burns b Jan. 4, 1898, unm. and
perhaps another); (f) Melissa Tunnell b Sept. 30, 1872 of Knoxville,
Tenn. (m Will Edmonds and had; 1, Bessie Edmons, m Buster
Stephens; 2, Ethel Edmonds died 1924, m Charles Wilson; 3, Delanew
Edmonds, dead, m Jim Miller; 4, Fred Edmonds, m ———— ————; 5,
Roxie Edmonds, m ———— ————; 6, Mable Edmonds m ————
————; 7, Rachel Edmonds.

Five. Eliza Tunnell, called Louisa by some, b Oct. 31, 1838; d
Hawkins Co., Tenn.; married George W. Lucas, first cousin of Solo-
mon Lucas, who married Mary Jane Tunnell, sister of Eliza. G. W.
Lucas died Hawkins Co., Tenn. He was a relative of his wife, being
the son of Kelly and Nancy (Ball) Lucas; gs Wesley and Nancy
(Bailey) Ball; ggs Moses and Mary (Harden) Ball. Children b
Hawkins Co., Tenn.; (a) Rebecca Jane Lucus b 1870, of Baileyton,
Tenn. (m first, Tom Arnold, who died, and had; 1, Emma Arnold
b Sept. 28. 1892: and m second, Frank Feagins and had; 2, Palmer
Feagins; 3, Charlie Feagins); (b) John Lucas b 1873, living on the
old Lucas place nr Van Hill, Tenn. (m Lucinda White and had; 1,
Roxie Lucas b Oct. 3, 1892, m a relative Charles Jones, son of Isaac
and Serelda (Tunnell) Jones; gs John and Alys (Hale) Tunnell; ggs
Wesley and Rebecca (Ball) Tunnell, and had ch.; 2, Tom Lucas b

Dec. 3, 1894, m Ethel Feagins and had ch.; 3, Bonnie Lucas b Nov.
9, 1896; 4, Mona Lucas b June 29 1898; 5, George Lucas b Aug. 6,
1906; 6, Clyde Lucas b Nov. 24, 1910); (c) Allie Lucas b 1875, of
Baileyton, Tenn. (m first, Lena Poe (d Hawkins Co., Tenn.) and had;
1, Bonnie Lucas, m John Mowl; 2, Clyde Lucas; and m second,
Mahala Spears, niece of Lena Poe; and m third, ——— Mullins.   No
issue save by first marriage).

Six.   James Harvey Tunnell b Mar. 25, 1842; d July 10, 1925, nr
Persia, Tenn.   He served as Lieut. in the Union Army in the War
Between the States.   He married first, Sallie Bruner, abt 1861,
Greene Co., Tenn., who died in Tex. and had no children.   He mar-
ried second, Sallie Caldwell, dau of Thomas and Maria (Bussell)
Caldwell, abt 1863 Hawkins Co., Tenn., who died Apr. 16, 1864 nr
Persia, Tenn., leaving a son.   He married third, a sister of his
second wife, Maria Caldwell, Aug. 15, 1869 Hawkins Co., Tenn. (b
Jan. 31, 1849; d Apr. 4 1918 nr Persia, Tenn.) and had ch. b Hawkins
Co., Tenn.; (a) Thomas W. Tunnell b Apr. 1, 1864, of Hawkins Co.,
Tenn. (m first, Malinda Jane McCannis, dau of John and Maria Mc-
Cannis (or McAmis), Aug. 27, 1882 Hawkins Co., Tenn. (b Apr. 3,
1864 Greene Co., Tenn.) and had; 1, Mattie E. Tunnell b Dec. 29,
1883 Hawkins Co., Tenn., of Knoxville, Tenn., m John Wesley Legg,
Dec. 9, 1900 Hamblen Co., Tenn, and had no ch.   J. W. Legg b June
23, 1879 Hawkins Co., Tenn., son of George Washington (b Oct. 13,
1857; d Jan. 26, 1907) and Amanda Elizabeth (Grigger) Legg, b Dec.
26, 1861; gs John Wesley and Matilda (Davis Legg; ggs Samuel
Legg).   Thomas W. Tunnell m second, Tina Morelock and had ch b
Hawkins Co., Tenn.; 2, Joseph Dewey Tunnell, died in Hawkins Co.;
3, Robert Ray Tunnell, died in Hawkins Co.; 4, Charles Tunnell, died
in Hawkins Co.; 5, Effie Mae Tunnell; 6, Ada Tunnell; 7, Roy Tun-
nell); (b) Sarah Cordelia Tunnell b Jan. 29, 1872, unm., of Persia,
Tenn.; (c) John David Tunnell b Feb. 22, 1874, of Persia, Tenn. (m
Emphers Wright, dau of James and Nancy (Smith) Wright, at
Greeneville, Tenn. and had ch b nr Persia, Tenn.; 1, Walter Lester
Tunnell b Apr. 28, 1892, m Grace Carter, dau of James and Anne
(Venable) Carter, June 7, 1914, and had ch b nr Persia; (aa) Victor
Tunnell b Jan. 13, 1918; d Jan. 18, 1918; (bb) Ina Pauline Tunnell b
Oct. 7, 1922; 2, Lee Tunnell b Oct. 8, 1896, m Rufus Ball and had ch
b Greene Co., Tenn.; (aa) Gladys Ball b June 6, 1912; (bb) Nelson
Ball b Tenn.; d in Calif.; (cc) Charlie Ball died Greene Co., Tenn.;
3, Callie Tunnell b Sept. 27, 1901, m Gordon Carter, brother of Grace
Carter, Dec. 20, 1918 and had no ch.; 4, Elmer Dale Tunnell b Sept.
28, 1909; d May 11, 1911); (d) Maria Frances Tunnell b July 12,
1875, of Persia, Tenn. (m Joe R. Russell Mar. 11, 1896 Hawkins Co.,
Tenn. (b July 1875; d Mar. 15, 1923) and had ch b nr Slide, Tenn.; 1,
James Dewey Russell, m Velma Douglas Tunnell, doubly related, (b
Apr. 2, 1903, dau Joe Oliver and Callie Jane (Rowan) Tunnell; gdau
David Carter and Mary Elizabeth (Ball) Tunnell; ggdau Edward
Tate and Mahala (Bussell) Ball; gggdau William Ball; ggggd Moses
and Mary (Harden) Ball) and had no ch.; 2, Virgil D. Russell b May
1, 1902 of Slide, Tenn., m Mary Bailey and had; (aa) Della Russell b
July 20, 1922; 3, Clemmie Joe Russell b Nov. 6, 1904, m a relative, a
brother of Velma Douglas Tunnell, Oliver Lee Tunnell, Nov. 1922,
and had; (aa) daughter b and d Nov. 1923; 4, Sarah Montie Russell
b May 12, 1907; 5. Bettie Kate Russell b Jan. 1910; 6, Earl Carson
Russell b June 7, 1913; 7, Sylvia Russell b July 18, 1916; 8, Stella
Russell b June 1919); (e) Samuel Seaton Tunnell b May 16, 1879, of
Persia, Tenn. (m Laura Jane Smith May 28, 1900 (b Nov. 18, 1883,
dau Tony and Linda (Brown) Smith and had ch b nr Persia; 1,

Selmer Tunnell b Feb. 21, 1901; d Apr. 8, 1901; 2, Mack Ross Tunnell b Aug. 5, 1902; 3, Burley Robert Tunnell b Apr. 10, 1905; 4, Lou Taff Tunnell b Mar. 17, 1908; 5, Mable Bell Tunnell b July 18, 1910); (f) Orville Benjamin Tunnell b June 2, 1881, of Persia, Tenn. (m first, Kate Maynes, in Hawkins Co., Tenn. and had no ch.; and m second, Myrtle Wright, in Hawkins Co., Tenn. and had no ch.; and m third, Vena Presley, dau of Sherman and Ella (Bailey) Presley; gdau John and Nancy (Jones) Bailey, and had; 1, Jessie Tunnell b Jan. 18, 1910; d Jan. 2, 1911; 2, Sallie Tunnell b Dec. 9, 1911; 3, Bethel Tunnell b Apr. 10, 1914; 4, Bessie Tunnell b Aug. 2, 1916; 5, Roxie Tunnell b Oct. 17, 1918; 6, Luther Tunnell b Aug. 5, 1921); (g) Joseph Bruce Tunnell b Aug. 15, 1883, of Persia, Tenn. (m first, Lissie Brown and had no ch.; and m second, Ida Pearl West, dau William and Mollie (Russell) West, Feb. 4, 1906 (b Feb. 8, 1890 Slide, Tenn.) and had ch b nr Persia; 1, Cecilia Opal Tunnell b Apr. 13, 1907; 2, James Kelsie Tunnell b May 27, 1909; 3, Oliver Fatten Tunnell b June 6, 1912; 4, Cretia Lue Tunnell b May 19, 1915; 5, Sylvia Mae Tunnell b Sept. 22, 1917); (h) Mahala Lucrecie Tunnell b Oct. 25, 1885; d Sept. 1887.

Seven. Martha Tunnell b abt 1844; d May 11, 1922 nr Baileyton, Tenn.; married a kinsman, Wesley Ball, known as Dock Ball, son of Spencer and Polly (Lucas, Ball; gs of Wesley and Nancy (Bailey) Ball; ggs Moses and Mary (Harden) Ball, and had ch b Hawkins Co., Tenn.; (a) Nelia Ball, died Aug. 1, 1911 (m John Caldwell, now of Kingsport, Tenn. and had; 1, Nora Caldwell, of Persia, Tenn., m Landon Richards and had (aa) Lee Richards, m Brownlow Collins and had two ch., Avanel Collins and Mary Margaret Collins; (bb Maxie Richards; (cc) Grace Richards; (dd) Lunie Richards; (ss) Ethel Richards; (ff) Charles Richards; (gg) Infant died unnamed; 2, Charles Caldwell, m Ada Gallyon and had five ch; 3, Debbie Caldwell, m John Gallyon and had six ch.; 4, Pattie Caldwell, m Oscar Delaney and had three ch.; 5, Gib Caldwell; 6, Clyde Caldwell); (b) Emma Ball, of Van Hill, Tenn., m Nathan Hale and had; 1, Emery Hale; 2, Lucy Hale; 3, Henry Hale; 4, Albert Hale; 5, Elden Hale; 6, Henry Hale); (c) "Bud" Ball, of Van Hill, Tenn. (m first, Nelia Hawkins and had; 1, Audery Ball; 2, Clarence Ball; and m second, Cora Jones and had; 3, Minnie Ball; 4, Baxter Ball; 5, Carsie Ball; 6, Gib Ball; 7, Ray Ball; 8, Drex Ball; 9, Oscar Ball); (d) Sallie Ball, of Baileyton, Tenn. (m James McAmis (deceased) and had; 1, Audrey McAmis; 2, Cecil McAmis); (e) Orgie K. Ball, of Van Hill, Tenn. (m Nola McAmis sister of James McAmis, a daughter of half-brother of Malinda Jane McAmis who m Thomas W. Tunnell, and had 1, Ober Ball; 2, Elmer Ball; 3, Delmer Ball).

Eight. David Carter Tunnell b Oct. 18, 1847; d Aug. 30, 1910 nr Rogersville, Tenn. At one time he lived on farm entered by James Tunnell senior. He married a relative, Mary Elizabeth Ball, Aug. 1869 in Hawkins Co., Tenn. She was born Mar. 31, 1850 nr Rogersville, Tenn., and lives nr Persia, Tenn. She was the dau of Edward Tate (Ned) and Mahala (Bussell) Ball; gdau of William and Sara Ann (Wyatt) Bussell; same of William and Nancy (Tate) Ball; ggdau of Moses and Mary (Harden) Ball; same of Edward (revolutionary soldier) and Sarah (McMullen) Tate; gggdau of David (b 1759) and Catherine (Thornton) Tate, who were married in Botetourt Co., Va. The compiler of the Tunnell record acknowledges here the courtesy of Mr. P. H. Gardner, an attorney, of New York and Johnson City, Tenn., a descendant of Moses Ball, in furnishing many names and dates on the family of Rev. James and Jane (Ball) Tunnell. Children of D. C. and Mary Elizabeth Ball Tunnell b nr Rogersville

Tenn.; (a) Ella Tunnell b Dec. 27, 1871, of Morristown, Tenn. (m first, Andrew J. Gilly, son of Elcanah and Sallie (Shephard) Gilly, Mar. 29, 1905 nr Rogersville, Tenn. (b Mar. 1, 1865 Wise Co., Va.; d July 31, 1914 nr Rogersville, Tenn.); and m second, Greene Berry Cope, Sept. 22, 1916 in Rogersville, Tenn. (b July 13, 1851 Hancock Co., Tenn.; d Mar. 29, 1924, Morristown, Tenn.) and had no ch.); (b) Joe Oliver Tunnell b July 6, 1873, of Estacada, Ore.(m Callie Jane Rowan, dau of William and Elizabeth (Wright Rowan, 1893 Slide, Tenn. (b July 4, 1875) and had ch b nr Rogersville, Tenn.; 1, Earnest Carson Tunnell b Sept. 25, 1894; d Oct. |27, 1896; 2, Otis Totsy Tunnell b July 13, 1896; d Jan. 21, 1910; 3, Jeannette Pearce Tunnell b July 12, 1899, of Kingsport, Tenn., m John Newberry and had ch. b Slide, Tenn.; (aa) Carl Newberry; (bb) Irene Newberry; 4, Oliver Lee Tunnell b Feb. 5, 1901, of Persia, Tenn., m a relative, Clemmie Joe Russell, (dau Joe R. and Maria Frances (Tunnell) Russell; gdau James Harvey and Maria (Caldwell) Tunnell; ggdau Thomas and Maria Caldwell; same of Wesley and Rebecca (Ball) Tunnell; gggdau John Ball; same of James and Jane (Ball) Tunnell; ggggdau Moses and Mary (Harden) Ball) and had a daughter b and d Nov. 1923; g, Velma Douglas Tunnell b Apr. 2, 1903, m James Dewey Russell, brother of Clemmie Joe Russell, and had no ch.; 6, Joseph Carter Tunnell b Sept. 2, 1906; 7, George Franklin Tunnell b Dec. 27, 1909); (c) Charles Edward Tunnell b 1875 (m Sallie Mayfield and had ch b Knoxville, Tenn., save youngest; 1, Mable Tunnell, d in inf.; 2, Chester Brown Tunnell b 1905; 3, Burl Edward Tunnell b 1907; 4, Lena May Tunnell b 1909; 5, Virgie Tunnell b 1913 Slide, Tenn.); (d) Maggie May Tunnell b Jan. 2, 1877, of Meredian, Idaho (m Joseph Henry Fleenor junior, son of Joseph Henry and Sarah (Smith) Fleenor, and had; 1, Verlin Cain Fleenor b Nov. 17, 1893 nr Morristown, Tenn.; d Nov. 14, 1894 Persia, Tenn.; 2, Raymond Fleenor b Sept. 15, 1897 Hawkins Co., Tenn., of Minnidaka, Ida.; 3, Sarah Pearce Fleenor b July 22, 1899 Persia, Tenn., of Twin Falls, Ida., m George Bremmer in Neb. and had; (aa) Edna Bremmer; (bb) Marie Bremmer; (cc) ——— Bremmer b 1925 Twin Falls, Ida.; 4, Elcer Fleenor b Feb. 5, 1903 Mitchel, Ore., of Twin Falls, Ida., m Pearl Thorp Aug. 31, 1924 Twin Falls, Ida.; 5, David Joe Fleenor b Oct. 25, 1906 Persia, Tenn.; 6, Mary Vadie Fleenor b Dec. 17, 1908 Twin Falls, Ida.; 7, Jim Kate Fleenor (dau) b Mar. 29, 1911 Persia, Tenn.; 8, Stella Owens Fleenor b Oct. 11, 1913 Persia, Tenn.; 9, Dorothy Fleenor b May 30, 1916 Wendell, Ida.; 10, Velma Fleenor b Apr. 17, 1919 Wendell, Ida.)

Nine. William Fletcher Tunnell, b abt 1850, of Baileyton, Tenn. had a twin sister, who died in inf. W. F. Tunnell married a relative, Rhoda Tunnell, who died 1922 Baileyton, Tenn. She was the dau of John and Thuriza (Williams) Tunnell; granddau of Spencer and Rhoda (English Tunnell); ggdau of James and Jane (Ball Tunnell. Ch. b Hawkins Co., Tenn.; (a) James C. Tunnell, of Van Hill, Tenn. (m Mary White and had; 1, Claude Tunnell, of Baileyton, Tenn., m Flora Underhill and had; (aa) George Tunnell; (bb) Delbert Tunnell; (cc) Francis Tunnell; 2, Herman Tunnell, of Kansas, m Lectie Moore and had; (aa) Blanche Tunnell; (bb) James Tunnell; (cc) Vernon Tunnell; (dd) Bernadine Tunnell; 3, Hassie Tunnell, of Pittsburg, Pa., m Bryan Colston and had; (aa) Herman Colston; (bb) Robert Colston; 4, Lee Tunnell, of Baileyton, Tenn., m Ellen Colston; and had; (aa) Charles Tunnell; (bb) J. D. Tunnell; 5, Gertie Tunnell, m James Colston and had; (aa) Thelma Colston; (bb) George Colston; 6, Wilma Tunnell, m Orval Armstrong and had; (aa) Thurman Armstrong; 7, Guy Tunnell, unm.); (b) John Tunnell, of Burem, Tenn., m Nettie Alvis and had no ch.; (c) William Tunnell, of Van Hill, Tenn. (m

Tennessee Richards and had; 1, Grady Tunnell, m Mary Cook and had; (aa) Ruby Elizabeth Tunnell; (bb) William Kermit Tunnell; 2, Susie Tunnell, unm.; 3, Gertie Tunnell, unm); (d) Creda Tunnell, of Vaan Hill, Tenn. (m Jane Snyder and had; 1, Gilbert Tunnell b 1912; 2, Jessie Tunnell n 1915; 3, Sallie Tunnebb b 1917; 4, Steven Tupper Tunnell; 5, Bessie Tunnell); (e) Byrd Tunnell (m Mae Luster and had; 1, Opal Tunnell; 2, Virgil Tunnell); (f) Nettie Tunnell, died at 6 years.

V. James Tunnell junior, son of James and Jane Ball Tunnell, was born Sept. 8, 1809 and died Mar. 7, 1854. He married Mary Ann Starns, dau of Lenard and Barbara Starns, Nov. 19, 1827 (b Jan. 16, 1807; d May 18, 1872) and had an only child;

One. Alfred Sawyer Tunnell b Aug. 16, 1829 nr Nashville, Tenn. raised in Sullivan Co., Mo.; d Aug. 16, 1899 Browning, Mo.; married a relative, Martha Ann Tunnell, dau of David and Elizabeth (McClure) Tunnell; granddau Stephen and Kezia (Money) Tunnell, Mar. 27, 1856 Morgan Co., Ill. She was born June 15, 1834 nr Murrayville, Ill and died Feb. 1, 1903 Brookfield, Mo. For record see family of Rev. David Tunnell.

VI. Kizzie Tunnell, dau of James and Jane Ball Tunnell lived in Hawkins Co., Mo. She married her first cousin, Daniel Bailey, son of John and Nancy Tunnell Bailey, and had ch b in Tenn. Names may not be in order of birth.

One. Sadie Bailey married G. P. Jones and had; (a) Cordie Jones; (b) John Jones; (c) Jean Jones; (d) Rosa Jones; and others.

Two. Julia Bailey, m —— Mowell.

Three. James Bailey, of Burem, Tenn.

Four. Pearl Bailey, m John Hundley.

Five. Rosa Bailey, m Newt Bailey.

Six. Clarence Bailey.

Seven. John Bailey.

Eight. Eugene Bailey.

VII. Polly Tunnell, dau of James and Jane Ball Tunnell, is said to have married John Long. Nothing known of her family. She may have married twice as some say she married —— Robinson and once lived at Sweetwater, Tenn.

VIII. Jesse Tunnell, son of James and Jane Ball Tunnell, died after 1845 in Mo. He was born in Tenn. and moved 1842 to Mo. and lived in Daviess Co., at one time. He married Catherine Murphy, who was known as Polly, in Tenn. and had 3 ch.

One. James Tunnell b abt 1836 in Tenn.; d in Mo.; married Colgate Billingsly, abt 1861 and had ch b Mo.; (a) William Henry Tunnell b Apr. 12, 1862 nr Pattonsburg, Mo. (m Sarah Catherine Conaway Mar. 31, 1887 nr Coffey, Mo. (b Oct. 5, 1868 nr Coffy, Mo., dau of Acquilla and Rebecca (Read) Conaway) and had ch b nr Pattonsburg, Mo.; 1, William Cross Tunnell b Apr. 11, 1888, of Warrensburg, Mo., m Eunice Willis (b 1890) and had; (aa) Omar Gale Tunnell b Jan. 7, 1909; (bb) Opal Catherine Tunnell b Aug. 26, 1910; (cc) William Hadley Tunnell b Dec. 10, 1913; 2, Charles Clayton Tunnell b Oct. 5, 1890, of Pattonsburg, Mo., m Julia Saul and had; (aa) Doris Marie Tunnell b May 17, 1923; 3, Pearly May Tunnell b Jan. 7, 1892, m C. E. Williams, of Patttonsburg, and had; (aa) Vergil Clifford Williams b Aug. 11, 1909; (bb) Wyvonna Williams b Mar. 8, 1916; 4, Elizabeth Ann Tunnell b Oct. 20, 1894, of Pattonsburg, m William Scott Hoover and had; (aa) Leta Lila May Hoover b Nov. 19, 1911; (bb) William Leo Hoover b Sept. 24, 1913; (cc) Alanson Commodore Hoover b Jan. 23, 1917; 5, Addie Rebecca Tunnell b Oct. 7, 1900, m Harley Rice and had; (aa) Harley Clayton Rice b Mar. 19, 1919; (bb) Juanita Lorraine Rice b May 23, 1922; d Oct. 28, 1922; (cc) Paul Junior Rice b Nov.

17, 1923; 6, Joseph Cortes Tunnell b Dec. 9, 1904); (b) Louisa Elizabeth Tunnell b Oct. 25, 1865; d 1883; (c) Martha Jane Tunnell b Sept.
2, 1867 (m J. A. Blair 1886 and had; 1, Bertha Blair; 2, Della Blair,
m —— Fisher; 3, Dorotha Belle Blair ;4, Topsy Rosalee Blair; 5,
William Russell Blair; 6, Forest Blair; 7, Lyle Blair); (d) Mary
Belle Tunnell b 1869; d 1871; (e) Lucy Ann Tunnell b Jan. 14, 1874,
of Smithville, Mo. (m Hernando Hoover June 9, 1895 and had; 1,
William Roy Hoover; 2, Virginia Adilene Hoover; 3, George Hoover.;
4, Frederick Hoover; 5, Myrtle Hoover; 6, Molly Rosalee Hoover); (f)
Sarah Minnie Tunnell b Mar. 10, 1876; d Dec. 18, 1913 (m Edmond
Severe, (son James and Sarah (Hoover) Severe, of Pattonsburg; gs
John and Mary (Thompson) Severe, of Mo.; ggs James Severe, who
went from Mt. Vernon, Ohio to Mo.) and had; 1, Eva Annie Severe;
2, Ethel Lorena Severe; 3, Daisy Dileta Severe; 4, John Edmond
Severe; 5, Mildred Ione Severe); (g) James Benjamin Tunnell b May
15, 1878; d 1889; (h) John Sherman Tunnell b Apr. 6, 1880 (m Judie
Thompson 1907 and had; 1, Leland Tunnell b 1908; 2, Guy Tunnell b
1910; 3, Melvin Tunnell b 1913; 4, Hues Tunnell b 1916; 5, Leona
Tunnell b 1919; 6, Lucille Tunnell b 1920); (i) Frederick Newton
Tunnell b June 1, 1882, of Pattonsburg, Mo. (m Lavanchie Severe
Dec. 24, 1904 and had; 1, Mable Tunnell; 2, Dola Beatrice Tunnell;
3, Bernice Marie Tunnell; 4, Mary Dorcas Tunnell).

　　Two.　Catherine Tunnell b abt 1838; d before 1865 in Mo., unm.
　　Three.　William Henry Harrison Tunnell b Nov. 8, 1840 nr Nash-
ville, Tenn.; d Sept. 5, 1910 St. Joe, Mo.; married Martha Alice Prail
1863 in Iowa (b 1836; d 1882 Daviess Co., Mo.) and had; (a) James
Henry Tunnell b Jan. 6, 1865 Barnes City, Iowa., of Pattonsburg, Mo.
(Ida America Conaway. dau of William P. b 'Ill., served in War
Between the States with Co. C. second Mo. Cav.) and Maria Jane
Hoover Conaway Jan. 2. 1887 in Mo.; (b Sept 5, 1867 Daviess Co.,
Mo.; d Mar. 7, 1905) and had ch b Daviess Co., Mo.; 1, Margaret Ann
Tunnell b Jan. 5, 1888 unm., of Pattonsburg, Mo.; 2, Martha Belle
Tunnell b Mar. 19, 1890; d Nov. 6, 1918 St. Joe., Mo., a few days
after her husband, m Charles Emmet Mays Dec. 14, 1910 Pattonsburg,
Mo. (b Sept. 25. 1890; d Oct. 29. 1918 St. Joe, Mo.) and had; (aa)
John Edgar Mays b Oct. 3, 1912 St. Joe; (bb) Dean Jerome Mays b
July 21, 1915 Pattonsburg; 3, William Parker Tunnell b Apr. 8, 1892,
unm served in World War and was wounded; 4, Harvey Edward
Nichols Tunnell b May 10, 1895, unm.; 5, Daisy Dorcas Lydia Allison
Tunnell b Apr. 20, 1897; d Dec. 9, 1898; 6. Henry Thomas Benton
Tunnell b Jan. 6, 1899; d Mar. 14, 1889; 7, Russell Harrison Tunnell
b Nov. 23. 1901. unm., 8, child b Nov. 21. 1903, d in inf., 9, child b
Feb. 28. 1905: d in inf.); (b) William Thomas Tunnell b Apr. 17,
1875. unm., of Pattonsburg, Mo.; (c) Delila Lacell Tunnell, deceased,
m John Burge).

　　IX. Isaac Tunnell, son of James and Jane Ball Tunnell, was
born 1816 and died Dec. 1869 in Sullivan Co., Tenn.　For a number
of years he lived in Greene Co., Tenn., moving from there abt 1860.
He married first, Malinda English and had five children, the young-
est only a few hours old when her mother died on Mar. 6, 1844.　He
married second. Margaret Britt, Oct. 18. 1846 in Greene Co., Tenn.
She died Oct. 26 1851. leaving two children, one a few days old.
He married third, Barbara Ann Ford, who died Jan. 10. 1914 nr
Jonesboro, Tenn.　There were eight children by this marriage.
　　One.　Alexander Tunnell b 1835; d Sept. 22, 1885; unmarried.
　　Two.　Mary Jane Tunnell b abt 1837; d in inf.
　　Three.　Otanza Tunnell b abt 1840; d in inf.
　　Four.　James Martin Tunnell b abt 1842; d in inf.

Five. Malinda Tunnell b Mar. 6, 1844; d 1921 Jonesboro, Tenn.; married William Pickens Mar. 17, 1861 and had ch b in East Tenn.; (a) Mattie Pickens b Jan. 27, 1862; d Oct. 20, 1910 (m J. H. Cox June 2, 1889 and had; 1, Hary Hazel Cox b aug. 1, 1890; 2, Nellie Cox b Jan. 11, 1892; 3, John Spencer Cox b Nov. 24, 1895; 4, Cue Cox b June 8, 1897; 5, Fred Cox b Jan. 22, 1899; 6, Luk Cox b Mar. 6, 1911; 7, Rolland Cox b July 20, 1903; 8, Frank Cox b Nov. 8, 1906. J. H. Cox married second, Sarah Ellen Tunnell, a half-sister of his first wife's mother, abt 1917); (b) Mary Pickens b July 2, 1864; (c) Elizabeth Pickens b Sept. 4, 1866 (m Samuel Strictler May 25, 1893 and had; 1, Mollie May Strictler b May 23, 1897); (d) John Pickens b May 27, 1868; (e) Emma Pickens b Nov. 25, 1870 (m Samuel B. Cox June 16, 1897 and had; 1, Hal M. Cox b Nov. 9, 1899); (f) William D. Pickens b Nov. 2, 1873; (g) Samuel E. Pickens b July 5, 1876 (m Amanda Cox Aug. 1, 1902 and had; 1, Mary Lee Pickens b May 31, 1903; 2, John B. Pickens b Aug. 11, 1907); (h) Clida D. Pickens b Aug. 3, 1878 (m William Ford Jan. 10, 1898 and had; 1, Emma Ford b Jan. 3, 1898; 2, Roy Ford b Oct. 28, 1900); (i) J. Cecil Pickens b Oct. 27, 1880; (j) daughter b and d same day.

Six. Martha Tunnell b Apr. 11, 1849, of Jonesboro, Tenn.; married Charles Cox Sept. 6, 1866 and had ch b East Tenn.; (a) J. Emery Cox b May 25, 1867 (m Mary Fink May 11, 1888 and had 1, Martha Addie Cox b July 1889; 2, C. M. Cox b 1893, m Walter Chase Aug. 13, 1911; 4, S. E. Cox b 1903; 5, Roxie Cox b July 11, 1907; d Dec. 17, 1910); (b) Mary Frances Cox b Feb. 2, 1870; d July 1907 (m S. J. Blakely Sept. 1 1895 and had; 1, Bethel Blakely b June 6, 1896; 2, B. B. Blakely b Apr. 2, 1898; 3, J. F. Blakely b June 1903); (c) Isaac B. Cox b July 9, 1872 (m Ellie Snodgrass 1897 and had; 1, W. O. Cox b 1898; 2, May Cox b 1900; 3, Mary Sue Cox b 1903; 4, Vergie Ellen Cox b 1900); (d) Ezekiel D. Cox b Sept. 26, 1874 (m Ida Ford Oct. 6, 1901 and had; 1, H. D. Cox b Aug. 3, 1902; 2, Martha Nara Cox b May 23, 1908); (e) Sally Cox b Jan. 29, 1877 (m W. M. Banan June 1898 and had; 1, C. T. Banan b May 2, 1899; 2, Ida Pearl Banan b 1900; 3, Cecil Banan b Sept. 12, 1902; 4, Gladys Banan b 1904; 5, Raymond Banan b 1906; 6, Myrtle Banan b Aug. 1908); (f) W. Pickens Cox b May 3, 1880 (m Sallie Hutton 1904 and had; 1, Pearl Cox b Dec. 15, 1905; 2, Margie Cox b Dec. 26, 1907; 3, Martha Cox b May 1910; d Feb. 1911); (g) S. Cleveland Cox b Aug. 12, 1882, m May Carroll Dec .10, 1911.

Seven. Mary Ann Tunnell, second by the name of Mary, b Oct. 23, 1851, of Newmarket, Tenn., married James Thomas Carroll, son of George and Nancy (Hale) Carroll, Dec. 19,, 1868, who died Jan.. 28, 1919, and had ch b in East Tenn.; (a) Nancy Jane Carroll b Sept. 29, 1870 (m S. L. Northern Dec. 22, 1907 and had; 1, Margaret Pearl Northern b Aug. 26, 1908; 2, Thomas Adam Northern b Dec. 2, 1910); (b) Sarah Amanda Carroll b July 5, 1872, of London, Ky. (m J. G. Herbert and had;' 1, Hazel May Herbert b Jan. 4, 1894, m Charles G. Pearl Nov. 15, 1915; 2, Sarah Herbert b Nov. 21, 1896; d Nov. 30, 1896; 3, Bessie Forest Herbert b Dec. 4, 1897, m Woolford D. Patton 1922; 4, Gracie Golden Herbert b Aug. 18, 1899, m Daniel Crawford 1921 and had one son; 5, George Herbert b Sept. 2, 1901, served in World War; 6, Mary Elsie Herbert b Dec. 5, 1905, m ———— ———— June 1924; 7, Carl Edward Herbert b Jan. 24, 1910); (c) William Isaac Carroll b Nov. 10, of Newmarket, Tenn. (m Mary Northern and had; 1, James Thomas Carroll b Apr. 23, 1900; 2, Nellie May Carroll b Feb. 23, 1902; d Jan. 15, 1904; 3, Bessie Dallice Carroll b Jan. 21, 1904, of Rutledge, Tenn. m Joe Calloway Dec. 24, 1921; 4, Mattie Pearl Carroll b Mar. 29, 1906; d Nov. 4, 1907; 5, Martha

Elizabeth Carroll b Sept. 26, 1908; d May 16, 1909; 6, Mary Elizie Carroll b Feb. 12, 1911; 7, Earnest Carroll; 8, Harold Carroll; 9, Grace Carroll; 10, Helen Carroll b 1920); (d) Martha Ann Carroll b Nov. 11, 1876, of Knoxville, Tenn. (m Dudley Fielden, who d Feb. 1921, and had; 1, Luster Lendus Fielden b Aug. 22, 1902; 2, Mary Esther Fielden b Feb. 25, 1904, m Frank Carroll 19222 and had; (aa) Edward Carroll b1923; 3, Ethel Elizabeth Fielden b Aug. 24, 1905; 4, Lydia Ray Fielden b May 7, 1907, m James Wood and had; (aa) Francis Wood b May 1924; 5, Reuba Ruth Fielden b Aug. 11, 1910; 6, Bertha Fielden b 1912; 7, Carroll Fielden, dead); (e) Eldora Sophia Carroll b Dec. 31, 1878 (m Jud Fielden, cousin of Dudley Fielden, Nov. 29, 1899 and had ch b nr Newmarket, Tenn.; 1, Earl Horner Fielden b June 15, 1901, m Irene Hawk 1921 and had; (aa) Geneva Fielden b 1922; 2, Rosa Caldona Fielden b Jan. 18, 1904; 3, William Clifford Fielden b July 8, 1906; 4, Woodsy H. Fielden b Mar. 28, 1909; 5, Anna May Fielden b May 15, 1911; 6, Pauline Fielden b 1913); (f) Lydia Emeline Carroll b Mar. 31, 1881; d Aug. 17, 1913 nr Newmarket, Tenn. (m Andrew Marion Free, son of Samuel Howard and Mary Elizabeth Free, June 18, 1900 Newport, Tenn. (b Apr. 28, 1881) and had; 1, Howard Raymond Free b Sept. 16, 1901 Newport, Tenn.; d Oct. 4, 1901 Newport, Tenn.; 2, Paul Everett Free b May 24, 1903 Knoxville Tenn.. of Ware Shoals, S. C. m Arrie Maud Bowen Apr.1, 1920 Ware Shoals and had; (aa) Mildred Louise Free b May 9, 1924; 3, Fairy Belle Free b June 27, 1905 Knoxville, Tenn., m Grady C. Walker Mar. 6, 1922 and had; (aa) Grady Eugene Walker b Apr. 3, 1923 Ware Shoals, S. C.; 4, Floyd Emmet Free b Oct. 31, 1907 nr Newmarket, Tenn.; 5, Carroll Lockard Free b Sept. 30, 1910 nr Newmarket, Tenn.   Andrew Marion Free married second, Josephine Arrington, July 10, 1915 and lives Ware Shoals, S. C.); (g) Georgie Alexander Carroll b Jan. 8, 1884; d Feb. 25, 1884; (h) Mary Annabell Carroll b Apr. 11, 1885 of Newmarket, Tenn. (m John Groseclose July 24, 1910 and had ch b nr Newmarket; 1, James Garfield Groseclose b Sept. 23, 1911; 2, Henry Raymond Groseclose b Aug. 13, 1914; 3, Carl Wilson Groseclose b Mar. 5, 1917; 4, Rhoda May Groseclose b Mar. 5, 1920; 5, Mary Edna Groseclose b Nov. 26, 1922); (i) Ray Emmet Carroll b June 27, 1887, of Wichita, Kan., m _____ _____ 1912 and had no ch.; (j) Ida May Carroll b Nov. 28, 1890 (m G. C. Cox Dec. 10, 1911 and had;1, Woodrow Wilson Cox b Mar. 6, 1913; 2, Martha Anna Cox b Apr. 16, 1917; 3, Pauline Frances Cox b June 9, 1922).

Eight. John Wesley Tunnell b May 1, 1853 Greene Co., Tenn.; d at age of nine, in Sullivan Co.

Nine. Thomas Nelson Tunnell b Oct. 28, 1854 Greene Co., Tenn., of Dallas. Tex.; married first, Sarah Ratliff, Jan. 25, 1884 Washington Co., Tenn. (d July 27, 2897 Dallas Co., Texas, dau of Eli (b Dec. 8, 1830; d Apr. 6, 1921) and Sarah Malinda (Bays) Ratliff) and had; (a) William Elmer Tunnell b Oct. 25, 1889, of Mesquite, Tex. (m Bessie Matilda Taylor and had an only child; 1, daughter b and d Jan. 4, 1908; and married second, Martha Albertine Tosch, dau of August Frederick and Albertine Mollie (Runge) Tosch, July 9, 1911 in Texas and had; (b) Barbara Vivian Tunnell b Feb. 26, 1915.

Ten. Susanna Tunnell b 1857; unmarried.

Eleven. Eliza Frances Tunnell b Dec. 14, 1858, unmarried, of Jonesboro, Tenn.

Twelve. Rev. William Milburn Tunnell b Jan. 18, 1861, died unmarried. He was a Baptist minister and pastor of the Double Springs church, his grandfather's "old church" at the time of his death.

Thirteen. Rev. Spencer Tunnell b Feb. 27, 1863, of La Grange, Ga.; married Callie Dean Copeland (b 1868), dau of John M. Copeland, Oct. 8, 1890 and had; (a) Barbara Madison Tunnell b Sept. 27, 1891, unmarried, of La Grange, Ga.; (b) Spencer Tunnell Jr. b Oct. 19, 1892, who served as Major, with overseas service, in the World War; unmarried; (c) Trenton Robinson Tunnell b Mar. 20, 1900 Florence, Ala., of Atlanta, Ga., (m Constance Cone, dau E. H. and Caroline (Douglas) Cone; ʳdau George Douglas, Mar. 24, 1925 Atlanta, Ga.) Rev. Spencer Tunnell has served a number of pastorates. He was pastor of Mansfield, Mass. 1892; Columbia, Tenn. 1906; Florence, Ala. 1908 and from 1909 until July 1919 he was pastor of the First Baptist Church at Morristown, Tenn. He has been in La Grange, Ga. since 1919. Rev. J. J. Burnett in his book "Pioneer Baptist Preachers" says of Rev. Tunnell's work in Morristown; "he has signalized his present pastorate by building and paying for a magnificent house of worship and baptised in Holston River, in May 1913, ninty-six newly made converts in fifty-eight minutes·'.

Fourteen. Sarah Ellen Tunnell b Nov. 7, 1865, of Jonesboro, Tenn.; married Jerry/H. Cox, the son-in-law of her half-sister, abt 1917.

Fifteen. George W. Tunnell b May 30, 1868, of Jonesboro, Tenn.; unmarried.

WILLIAM TUNNELL

B. William Tunnell, son of Stephen and Kezie Money Tunnell, died 1846 nr Loudon, Tenn. "quite an old man". He may have been b abt 1779. He married Rebecca Rorex and their ch. were born nr Loudon, Tenn. Rebecca R. Tunnell moved to Mo., after her husband's death, and lived with children there. She died abt 1850. Names of ch. may not be in order of birth;

I. Kezia Tunnell b Dec. 27, 1807.
II. Letitia Tunnell b Dec. 10, 1809.
III. James M. Tunnell b May 15, 1811.
IV. Harrison Tunnell.
V. Emeline Tunnell.
VI. Francis Asbury Tunnell.
VII. William David Tunnell.
VIII. Jane Matilda Tunnell.
Of the foregoing;

I. Kezia Tunnell, dau of William and Rebecca Rorex Tunnell was born Dec. 27, 1807 Hawkins Co., Tenn. and died May 17, 1866 Roane Co., Tenn. She married William Yates Huff Sept. 29, 1829 Roane Co., Tenn. (b Aug. 25, 1809 Washington Co., Va.; d Dec. 5, 1870 Roane Co., Tenn., eldest son of John Huff, who was agent for the King Salt Works, and his wife, Mary Huff) and had eight ch b Roane Co., Tenn.

One. James Whit Huff b Aug. 22, 1830; d Nov. 7, 1894 Loudon Co., Tenn.; married Elizabeth M. Anderson (b Jan. 16, 1840; d Feb. 23. 1881, dau of ⌐ᴏᴏ⌐ˡ and Elizabeth M (Rhea) Anderson; gd Major Robert and Elizabeth (Rhea) Rhea. See Vol. Two Notable Southern Families, by Miss Zella Armstrong, for Rhea history). Ch. b Loudon Co., Tenn., save eldest b Roane Co.; (a) Elizabeth Huff b Mar. 26, 1868, of Lenoir City, Tenn., m J. R. Jump Nov. 1895 (deceased) and had no ch.; (b) William E. Huff b Aug. 7, 1872, of Rossville, Ga. (m Lucy Gallaher Oct. 20, 1897 and had; 1, James Huff; 2, Hugh McCrosky Huff); (c) James Anderson Huff b Apr. 29, 1875, general manager of Rockwood Mills, Rockwood, Tenn. (m Mable Clare Wilson Jan. 2, 1907 (b May 14, 1882) and had ch b Rockwood; 1, James Alexander Huff b Sept. 29, 1907; 2, Florence Elizabeth Huff b Feb. 21,

1909; 3, Woods Wilson Huff b Dec. 15, 1911; 4, Mable Clare Huff b June 7, 1915· Margaret Ann Huff b Feb.11, 1917; 6, Isabelle Rhea Huff b Oct. 21, 1920); (d) Mamie Eliza Huff b Oct. 3, 1877 (m J. F. Littleton and had ch b Roane Co. ,Tenn.; 1, Elizabeth Littleton b Aug. 18, 1904; 2, Mabel Huff Littleton b Apr. 22, 1909); (e) Joseph Rhea Huff b Sept. 4, 1880; d Sept. 21, 1881 Loudon Co., Tenn.

Two. Mary Angeline Huff b Oct. 18, 1832; d Jan. 17, 1884 Knoxville, Tenn.; married Hiram Bogart, son of Henry Bogart, Jan. 9, 1853 Loudon, Tenn., (b May 17, 1826; d May 3, 1869) and had ch b Loudon, Tenn., save youngest; (a) Allein Bogart b Aug. 31, 1854; d young; (b) William Henry Bogart b Oct. 25, 1856 (m Fannie Ebough Jan. 15, 1883 and had; 1, Benjamin Hope Bogart b Dec. 10, 1883; d Apr. 4, 1884; 2, Charles Parker Bogart b Mar. 17, 1885, m Hazel Stoots May 1921); (c) Mary Kezia Bogart b May 13, 1858 (m Benjamin Franklin Smith Dec. 2, 1879 Loudon Co., Tenn. (b May 29, 1855 Campbell Co., Tenn.; d Aug. 20, 1900) and had ch b Knoxville, Tenn.; 1, Charles Henry Smith b Dec. 3, 1881, attorney, Knoxville, m Maud Keller Nov. 6, 1907 and had; (aa, Charles Henry Smith the second b Feb. 6, 1910; (bb) Keller Smith b Apr. 1, 1915; 2, John Otey Smith b Aug. 20, 1884, sales manager Stonega Coal Co., of Charlotte, N. C., m Caroline Ragsdale Oct. 11, 1906 (b Feb. 20, 1886) and had ch b Knoxville, Tenn.; (aa) Robert Smith b May 20, 1911; (bb) David Benjamin Simth b July 29, 1914; 3, Mamie Lenoir Smith b Feb. 21, 1887, unm., of Knoxville, Tenn.; 4, Lida Allen Smith b July 4, 1889, of Knoxville, Tenn., m Frank C. Newman Oct. 17, 1916 (b Jan. 20, 1889 Alpha, Tenn., traveling storekeeper for Southern Railway) and had; (aa) Charlotte Allein Newman b Feb. 19, 1919 Knoxville); (d) Robert Bruce Bogart b May 22, 1860 (m Mary Maxey Dec. 22, 1881 Knoxville, and had; 1, John Hiram Bogart b Feb. 16, 1884; d Sept. 15, 1919, who m Bessie McCammon and had; (aa) John Hiram Bogart the second b Jan. 21, 1912 Birmingham, Ala.; (bb) James Randall Bigart b Nov. 21 1915 Birmingham, Ala.; 2, Walter Edward Bogart b Nov. 3, 1885; d Jan. 9, 1914 Knoxville, Tenn., unm.; 3, Ralph Kent Bogart b May 30 1887, of Cushing Okla., m Bessie Seivers June 30, 1910 Knoxville, Tenn. and had; (aa) Ralph Kent Bogart the second b Oct. 8, 1911; 4, Robert Bruce Bogart the second b Jan. 24, 1890, clerk for Southern Railway, of Knoxville, Tenn., m Margaret Green Dec. 31, 1912 Knoxville, Tenn. and had; (aa) Robert Bruce Bogart the third b Dec. 7, 1914 Knoxville, Tenn.; 5, Mary Reese Bogart b Dec. 26, 1891, of Albany, Ga., m Moultrie M. McLaughlin Sept. 13, 1908 Sevierville, Tenn. (b May 8, 1888) and had; (aa) Dorothy Louise McLaughlin b Apr. 9, 1909 Knoxville, Tenn; (bb) Moultrie McLaughlin the second b Apr. 27, 1914 Albany, Ga.; (cc) Edwin Bogart McLaughlin b Oct. 7, 1919 Albany, Ga.; (dd) Lucile Elizabeth McLaughlin b July 11, 1923 Albany, Ga.); (e) Joseph Looney Bogart b Aug. 16, 1862; d at Memphis, Tenn.; (f) Lida Bogart b June 19, 1867 Red Clay, Ga., of Knoxville, Tenn. (m J. E. Thompson Nov. 6, 1889 and had twin sons b Sept. 27, 1890 Knoxville, Tenn.; 1, Albert Ashley Thompson, served as sergeant in 157 D. B. Inf. during World War, salesman, of Knoxville, Tenn., m Mae Mullins July 27, 1916 and had; (aa) Albert Ashley Thompson the second b Nov. 9, 1923 Knoxville, Tenn.; 2, Harry Granville Thompson, served as Capt. of 81st Div. in World War, with Southern Railway, Birmingham, Ala., m Mary Elizabeth Harkleroad June 10, 1921).

Three. Emily Jane Huff b Nov. 18, 1834; d Oct. 8, 1923; married Robert R. Anderson, brother of Elizabeth Anderson, Oct. 20 1859 (b 1832; d 1895) and had; (a) Elizabeth Anderson; (b) Ada Anderson; (c) Rhea Huff Anderson; (d) Emily Jane Anderson b 1871, m Oscar

THE TUNNELL FAMILY 305

Everett Mahoney and had; 1, Robert Rhea Mahoney b 1894; 2, Martha Emily Mahoney b 1896; 3, Oscar Everett Mahoney the second, b 1899, of Johnson City, Tenn.

Four. Eliza Rebecca Huff b Oct. 29, 1837; d Jan. 1, 1913; married James Mahoney (b Oct. 30, 1833; d Aug. 19, 1903) and had no ch.

Five. Hannah Elizabeth Huff b Mar. 23, 1840; d June 17, 1864; unmarried.

Six. William Ebenezer Huff b Oct. 14, 1842, of Loudon, Tenn.; married Rachel Ann Johnston Feb. 17, 1876 Loudon, Tenn. (b Mar. 14, 1849, Hamilton Co., Tenn.) and had ch b Loudon, Tenn. (b Mar. 14, Joseph Yates Huff b Apr. 3, 1877; (b) child, twin of Joseph Yates Huff b Apr. 3, 1877; d Sept. 3, 1877; (c) Mary Jane Huff b July 30, 1887; (d) William Ebenezer Huff the second b Dec. 9, 1879 (m Ada Frances McCroskey Dec. 2, 1912 and had ch. b Loudon Co., Tenn.; 1, Rachel Elizabeth Huff b Dec. 10, 1913; 2, Henry McCroskey Huff b Oct. 22, 1915; 3, William Ebenezer Huff the third, b July 18, 1918; 4, James Robert Huff b Mar. 3, 1921); (e) Linna Bell Huff b Oct. 6, 1881, unm., of Loudon, Tenn.; (f) Sallie Tunnell Huff, twin of Linna Bell Huff, b Oct. 6, 1881; d Aug. 15, 1901 (m Will L. Kline Nov. 14, 1900 (b July 31, 1879).

Seven. Margaret Lutacia Catherine Huff b July 30, 1845; d Dec. 6, 1915 Loudon, Tenn.; married Samuel Anderson, brother of Elizabeth and Robert Anderson, Apr. 28, 1867 Roane Co., Tenn. (b July 6, 1845 Roane Co., Tenn.; d July 1, 1900 Loudon Co., Tenn.) and had; (a) Emily Anderson b Mar. 3, 1868 Roane Co., of Sweetwater, Tenn. (m Sam O. Henley July 23, 1890 Monroe Co., Tenn. and had; 1, Margaret Jane Henley b June 28, 1891; d Nov. 6, 1891; 2, Lena Henley b June 12, 1893 Monroe Co., Tenn., m J. P. Stepp and had; (aa) J. P. Stepp Jr. b Jan. 24, 1917; 3, Marshall Henley b Oct. 25, 1895 Loudon Co., of Sweetwater, Tenn., unm.; 4, Frances Henley b Oct. 19, 1899; d Nov. 24, 1900; 5, Maud Henley b Nov. 25, 1902, of ,Sweetwater); (b) Joseph Marshall Anderson b Oct. 9, 1869 Roane Co., Tenn., farmer, Sweetwater, Tenn., (m first, Lucy A. Cook Apr. 19, 1893 Loudon, Tenn. (d Aug. 1896) and had; 1, Myrtle Adaleen Anderson b Mar. 1894; d Aug. 1895; and second, Mary Belle Blair Mar. 14, 1906 Loudon, Tenn. (d July 15, 1920); (c) Addie Dorcas Anderson b Nov. 3, 1871 Loudon Co., unm., of Sweetwater, Tenn.; (d) Reese Anderson b Aug. 20, 1873 Loudon Co.; d Dec. 8, 1895 Loudon Co., unm.

Eight. Sarah Ellen Augusta Huff b July 9, 1848; d Nov. 24, 1918 Bradley Co., Tenn.; married Samuel Reese Dec. 23, 1866 (b May 7, 1843 Wheeling, Va.; d June 10, 1921 Bradley Co., Tenn.) and had an only child; (a) Ella May Reese, unm., of Cleveland, Tenn.

II. Letitia Tunnell, dau of William and Rebecca Rorex Tunnell, was born Dec. 10, 1808 in Tenn. and died Sept. 13 1893 Ray Co., Mo. She married Jacob Messimer Oct. 6, 1831 Tenn. (b Oct. 28, 1807 Tenn.; d Aug. 12, 1860 Mo. and had eight children, two of whom were born in Tenn., others in Mo. and all married in Ray Co., Mo.

One. Child b Aug. 1832; d Sept. 1832 in Tenn.

Two. John Alexander Messimer b Nov. 12, 1833; d Feb. 6, 1922 Kansas City, Mo.; married Serena Ann Moss Jan. 1857 (died May 19, 1919 Polo, o.) and had; (a) Millard Messimer b Nov. 7, 1857 Ray Co., Mo., farmer, of Polo, Mo. (m first, Lucy Bassett (d May 23, 1905) and had; 1, Wilma Messimer b July 9, 1903; and m second, Bessie Shamblin Apr. 8, 1912); (b) Alice Messimer b Apr. 10, 1860 Ray Co., Mo., of Polo, Mo. (m James Petty 1875 (d Apr. 1, 1905) and had; 1, Oha Dan Petty b Feb. 25, 1876, of Polo, Mo., m Lucy Clevinger; 2, Ida May Petty, m Clarence Emery; 3, Lula Petty, of olo, Mo., m James Emery; 4, Mettie Petty, of Polo, Mo., m Val Wilkerson; 5, David Petty, of

Cowgill, Mo., m Willie Hatfield; 6, Charity Petty, of Richmond, Mo., m ——— Alexander; 7, John Petty, of Excelsior Springs, Mo.; 8, Fowler Petty, of Kansas City; 9, Benah Petty of Knoxville, Mo., m ——— Pryor; 10, Thomas Petty, of Liberty, Mo., m ——— Brimer; 11, Venus Petty b 1903, of Polo, Mo., m ——— Butts; 12, child died in inf.); (c) Louisa Ann Messimer b June 29, 1867 Ray Co., Mo., of Kansas City ,Mo., (m Taylor Arnote 1887 Ray Co., Mo. and had; 1, Harry Arnote b July 30, 1888, unm. of Kansas City, served in World War; 2, Floyd Arnote b Aug. 9, 1895, unm., of Kansas City, served in World War); (d) Perry Messimer b July 30, 1873 Caldwell Co., Mo., of Polo, Mo. (m Grace Brown and had; 1, Helen Messimer; 2, Verle Messimer b Mar. 18. 1906 Caldwell Co.. Mo.; 3, Mary Messimer b July 29, 1918; 4, Gertrude Messimer; 5, Woodrow Messimer; 6, Joan Messimer).

Three. William F. Messimer b Feb. 26, 1837; d Okla.; lived at one time Moberly, Mo.; married first, Mart Real 1861 (d 1867) and had (a) Elmer Messimer b abt 1863, of Calif., m ——— ——— and had one ch. and m second, Ellen Carleton Jan. 1872 (d 1873); and third, Rosa Haines 1878 (d 1882) and fourth, Mrs. Ann Helms.

Four. Matilda Jane Messimer b Jan. 13, 1840; deceased; married John P. Thompson and had; (a) George Thompson, of Polo, Mo.; (b) Frank Thompson, of Polo, Mo.; (c) Louisa Thompson; (d) Marsh Thompson; (e) Flora Thompson, of Polo, Mo., m ——— Pinkerton; (f) Letta Thompson,, dead; (g) Cora Thompson twin of Letta Thompson; (h) Dave Thompson; (i) Carrie Thompson, twin of Dave Thompson. It is said some of these live in Texas.

Five. Henry Marshall Messimer b Sept. 17, 1842; married first, Rebecca Linvill and second, Mary Smith, and lived in Dent Co., Mo..

Six. Robert F. Messimer b Feb. 3, 1846; married first, Mary J. Crenshaw Nov. 4, 1869 (b Ray Co., Mo., d Apr. 23, 1900) and had ch b Ray Co., Mo.; (a) Walter P. Messimer b Sept. 14, 1872, of Lone Wolf, Okla.; (b) Lena Leota Messimer b Sept. 22, 1875 of Lone Wolf. Okla.. m Ellery L. Burdick Jan. 16, 1907. Robert F. Messimer m second Sarah E. Andrew (b Salem Center, Indiana) and lived at one time in San Diego, Calif.

Seven. Louisa Ann Messimer b Feb. 3, 1849 of Elmira, Mo.; married S. J. Crowley Feb. 12, 1869 and had; (a) William K. Crowley b Aug. 1, 1870; b Jan. 5, 1871; (b) Nannie B. Crowley b May 21, 1872 (m Clayton Whitsett Dec. 10, 1910 and had; 1, Samuel Chestine Whitsett b Dec. 2. 1912; (c) Franklin P. Crowley b Mar. 24, 1876; d May 16, 1909; (d) Missie Lettie Crowley b Dec. 17, 1880, m Charles Ora Clark Dec. 25, 1904 and had; 1, Ota Price Clark b Oct. 29, 1906; d July 29, 1907; (e) Samuel B. Crowley b Dec. 9, 1883, m Ruth Baker Feb. 23, 1911 (b Jan. 21, 1893; (f) Lota Crowley b Aug. 12, 1886; d Apr. 5, 1888.

Eight. Evaline C. Messimer b Dec. 20, 1852, of Lawson, Mo.; married William S. Crowley Feb. 1, 1872 (b Feb. 6, 1848) and had; (a) Ella Crowley b Mar. 18, 1873, m Oliver A. Pollard Feb. 1, 1894 Caldwell Co., Mo. and had a child b Feb. 20, 1895; d Jan. 30, 1896; (b) Thomas M. Crowley b June 1, 1876 Clinton Co., Mo. (m Pearl M. Osbern Mar. 3, 1897 and had; 1, Lena Eva Crowley b Mar. 3, 18M98; 2, Esther Crowley b Oct. 2, 1903; 3, Eula Crowley b Sept. 9, 1905; 4, Lucy R. Crowley b Dec. 8, 1907); (c) William Crowley b Mar. 17, 1880 (m first, Maud Taggart, Mar. 23, 1903, who d Oct. 16, 1906 and had; 1, Hazel D. Crowley b Feb. 20, 1905; and m second, Effie Mellon, Dec. 25, 1907 and had; 2. Joseph W. Crowley b Nov. 28, 1918; 3, Leta P. Crowley b Feb .2, 1911).

III. James M. Tunnell, son of William and Rebecca Rorex Tun-

nell, was born May 15, 1811 and died Nov. 13, 1905.   He married
Catherine M. Houston, dau of Samuel and Elizabeth (Ray) Houston,
Aug. 7, 1834 Roane Co., Tenn. (b Nov. 5, 1811; d Nov. 5, 1882) and
had thirteen children, names of three that died in infancy not given.

One.   Eliza Jane Tunnell b May 4, 1837; d in Mo., m John Hutchins Aug. 5, 1857.

Two.   Margaret A. Tunnell b Aug .10, 1839; d West Plains, Mo.;
m James Milstead and had: (a) Albert Milstead, m ——— ——— and
had ch· (b) Alice Milstead, m first, ——— Cook and had; 1, Pearl
Cook: and m second, ——— Green.

Three.   William David Tunnell b Aug. 29, 1841; d in Mo., married twice, the first wife being Hannie Hutching, who d in Mo.

Four.   Martha Ann Tunnell b Sept. 27, 1843; d Mo., m first, Will
Vinsant and second, ——— Benedict.

Five.   Mary C. Tunnell b July 13, 1846; d Mo.; m first, George
Browdy and second, Henry Odell.

Six.   Samuel Washington Tunnell b Nov. 10, 1848; deceased; m
Mary York.

Seven   James Tunnell, twin of Samuel Washington Tunnell, b
Nov. 10, 1848; m Zula Browning.

Eight.   Sarah R. Tunnell b and d Apr. 2, 1850.

Nine.   Frances Tunnell b Nov. 22, 1852, deceased, m Charley
Waite and at one time lived at Nampa, Idaho.

Tenn.   Robert Franklin Tunnell b Feb. 1, 1858, unmarried, lived
for years at Knoxville. Mo. and later at West Plains, Mo.

IV.   Harrison Tunnell, son of William and Rebecca Rorex Tun-
nell, died in Mo.; married Nancy Milstead and had ch., including; 1,
William Tunnell m Rosa Gibson; 2, Sarah Tunnell, m Riley Switzer;
3, Jane Tunnell, m Charley Burnson; 4, Margaret Tunnell, m Tom
Estes; 5, James Tunnell m first, Mary Ann Vancort, and second,
Zula Siders; 6, George Tunnell, m ——— ———.

V.   Emeline Tunnell, dau of William and Rebecca Rorex Tunl
nell, was born nr Loudon, Tenn. and was buried in Bradley Co., Tenn.
She m John Huff, brother of William Yates Huff, and had; 1, daughter
d young; 2, James David Alexander Huff, of Dalton, Ga. (m Sallie
Brooks and had three daughters, Nettie Huff, Rosa Huff, and Mary
Helen Huff.

VI.   Francis Asbury Tunnell, son of William and Rebecca
Rorex Tunnell, was born abt 1816 and died June 1844.   He married
Anne Houston, sister of Catherine Houston, Apr. 1339 (b Oct. 28,
1820 Blount Co., Tenn.; d Feb. 23, 1870 in Mo.) and had three ch.;

One.   Sarah Rebecca Tunnell b June 9, 1840 Ray Co., Mo., of
Millville, Mo.; married Hiram McBee Nov. 15, 1859 (b Feb. 5, 1839
Ray Co., Mo.; d Nov. 6, 1905 Ray Co., Mo.) and had ch b Ray Co.
Mo.; (a) Octavia Belle McBee b Jan. 2, 1861 (m John Henry Penny
Mar. 8, 1881 and had ch b Ray Co., Mo.; 1, Luther James Penny ɔ
Sept. 1882, of Richmond, Mo., m first cousin, Ida Magnolia Kincaid
Nov. 28, 1906 and had; (aa) Edrie Belle Penny b May 1908 nr Elk
City, Okla.; 2, Mary Belle Penny b July 1884, of Richmond, Mo.; 3,
Milo Dimitte Penny b Aug. 1886, of Richmond, Mo., m Beulah Elnora
Petree Mar. 1907 and had; (aa) Leola Frances Penny b July 1910;
(bb) Orville Clyde Penny b Apr. 1912; 4, Oscar Hiram Penny b May
1890, of Richmond, Mo., m Oleva Nora Bright Nov. 1911); (b) Laura
Augusta McBee b Jan. 31, 1863, of Cuba, Mo. (m W. E. Parsh Mar. 8,
1891 and had; 1, Samuel Olin Parsh b July 1892; 2, Virgil Olga Parsh
b June 1894; d Apr. 1913); (c) Missouri Elvira McBee b Feb. 14,
1865, of Republican City, Neb. (m W. J. McBee Nov. 26, 1885 and had
ch b Bostick, Neb..; 1, Essie Maude McBee b Aug. 1888; 2, Della

Marie McBee b Mar. 1890; 3, Nellie G. McBee b Mar. 1892; 4, Ira
Ray McBee b Dec. 189b); (d) Lucy McBee b Mar. 16, 1869; d June
1909 (m Charles T. Pinkerton Jan. 1, 1888 Ray Co., Mo. and had; 1,
Nannie Lee Pinkerton b Oct. 1894; 2, Vivian Frances Pinkerton
Feb. 1899; 3, Joseph McBee Pinkerton b Dec. 1901; 4, Charles Ralph
Pinkerton b Mar. 1903); (e) Ella Frances McBee b June 29, 1872 (m
Virgil C. Lewis Dec. 19, 1899 and had; 1, Charles A. Lewis b July
1901 in Oklahoma; 2, Harold Walter Lewis b Nov. 1902 in Mo.; 3,
Ruth Lewis b Nov. 1904 in Mo.); (1) Walter James McBee b Sept.
20, 1876; d Aug. 17 1887; (g) Vivian Salome McBee b Dec. 24, 1878
(m Clarence O. Wilson Feb. 25, 1903 Ray Co., Mo. and had ch b Ray
Co. Mo.; 1, Madarene Wilson m May 1904; 2, Gertrude Wilson b Oct.
1907; 3, Kenneth McBee Wilson b Oct. 1909; 4, Charles Melvin Wilson b Nov. 1911).

Two. Elvira Tunnell b July 31, 1842 in Mo.; d Feb. 15, 1890 in
Mo.; married John Sharp Kincaid Sept. 20, 1860 (b Jan 25, 1839; d
July 12, 1913) and had ch b Ray Co., Mo.; (a) Mary Ellen Kincaid
b July 22, 1861; d May 22, 1893 (m W. A. Waters 1881 (b Nov. 17
1903) and had; 1, Robert Elmer Waters b Aug. 17, 1882; 2, Sarah
Evena Waters b Sept. 16, 1884; d June 2. 1908, m Earl Wall Dec. 1905
and had; (aa) Mary Ellen Wall b Dec. 6, 1906; 3, Charles Monroe
Waters b Jan. 10, 1887; 4, Ray Kincaid Waters b Aug. 11, 1893); (b)
Thomas Asbury Kincaid b Sept. 11, 1865, of Elk City, Okla. (m
Idella Josephine Grimes Apr. 23, 1889 and had ch b Ray Co., Mo.; 1,
John Asbury Kincaid b May 1891, of Elk City, Okla., m Florence
Ditzler Edgar Dec 25, 1912; 2, Thomas Ely Kincaid b Oct. 1894); (c)
Louisa Ann Kincaid b June 10, 1866; d Mar. 4, 1889 (m Commodore
Porter Mansur and had; 1, Commodore P. Mansur b Jan. 26, 1888 Ray
Co., Mo.; d July 26, 1888); (d) John Irvin Kincaid b Sept. 4, 1868, of
Elk City,Okla., m Mollie Wilson Nov. 1907;   (e)   Augusta   Elvira
Kincaid b Aug. 23, 1871, of Elk City, Okla., m Charles Wall Feb. 11,
1903; (f) Sarah Elizabeth Kincaid b Nov. 6, 1874; d May 11, 1875; (g)
Madora Evaline Kincaid b Mar. 21, 1876, of Elk City, Okla. (m Charles
Henry Barham Jan. 14, 1903 and had; 1, Elvira Elizabeth Barham b
Oct. 1903 in Mo.; 2, Charles Raymond Barham b Feb. 1905 Okla.; 3,
Balaam K. Barham b Dec. 1906 in Okla.; 4, Rilla Kathleen Barham
b Feb. 1911; 5, Linnie Lucile Barham b May 1912); (h) Carrie Rose
Kincaid b Aug. 25, 1878 (m Theodore Berry Feb. 21, 1906 and had;
1, Nellie May Berry b Dec. 1, 1906; 2, O. J. Berry b Mar. 1911); (i)
Ida Magnolia Kincaid b Nov. 29, 1880 (m Luther J. Penny, first
cousin; (j) Binner Mason Kincaid b Dec. 25, 1884 (m Nancy Rebecca
Barham Dec. 9, 1908 and had; 1, Inez Aleene Kincaid b Sept. 17, 1910
Ray Co., Mo.)

Three. Frances Mary Tunnell b May 11, 1844 Caldwell Co., Mo.,
of Okla.; married Melvin Moses Carleton Oct. 13, 1869 Ray Co., Mo.
(b Apr. 2, 1836 Haverhill, Mass.; d Feb. 11, 1878 Ray Co., Mo.) and
had ch b Ray Co., Mo.; (a) Alpha O. Carleton b Nov. 27, 1870; d Sept.
5, 1923 (m William O. Cowherd Mar. 20, 1895 Ray Co., Mo. and had
1, Roy Buford Cowherd b Dec. 24, 1895 Ray Co., Mo., of Canute, Okla.,
served in World War, m Myrtle Matthews; 2, Vincil Melvin Cowherd
b May. 11, 1898, m Blanche Mayberry; 3, Earl Carleton b Apr. 13,
1901; 4, Virgil Cowherd b Aug. 26, 1904); (b) Leslie Carleton b July
8, 1872, of Fay, Okla., m Pauline Sims June 30, 1907 Custer Co., Okla.;
(c) Virgil F. Carleton, of Clinton, Okla. (m Olga M. Smallwood Feb.
5, 1896 Ray Co., Mo. and had; 1, Rogela V. Carleton b Sept. 5, 1905,
in Okla.); (d) G. Moses Carleton b Jan. 13, 1878, of Chillicothe, Mo.
(m Lucy Ellen Jackson Feb. 27 1898 Ray Co., Mo. and had; 1, Guy
Evans Carleton b Jan. 6, 1899, Ray Co., Fo., of Kansas City, m Clara

Alexander May 4, 1924).

VII. William David Tunnell, son of William and Rebecca Rorex Tunnell, was born Dec. 15, 1818; d Feb. 26, 1890 Polo, Mo. He married Eliza Kollock, sister of Alexander A. Kollock, Mar. 20, 1852 (b Aug. 17, 1836 nr Loudon, Tenn.; d Aug. 22, 1902 Polo, Mo.) and had six ch b Polo, Mo.

One. William Tunnell b Dec. 13, 1857, of Polo, Mo.; married Sylvia Hyder Mar. 4, 1880 (b Nov. 15, 1858 Polo, Mo.) and had ch b Polo, Mo.; (a) Henry Allen Tunnell b Sept. 29, 1881 (m Mary Keen June 12, 1901 nr Lawson, Mo. and had ch b Polo; 1, Junior Reed Tunnell b Oct. 24, 1904; 2, Esther Fern Tunnell b Oct. 9, 1905, m Estal Tait Sept. 23, 1923 and had a son b Sept. 1924; 3, W. Bryan Tunnell b Sept. 29, 1908; 4, Dena Tunnell (daughter) b Apr. 12, 1911); (b) Luella Tunnell b Oct. 20, 1890, of Barnsdall, Okla. (m Herman N. Hogg, son of Samuel Harper and Mary Flora Hogg, Oct. 8, 1910 (b Dec. 13, 1888 Gibbons, Neb.) and had; 1, Olen Ray Hogg b June 25, 1911 Polo, Mo.; 2, Mary Elizabeth Hogg b Mar. 10, 1917 Barnsdall, Okla.; 3, Norman Francis Hogg b June 28, 1920).

Two. E. Jane Tunnell b Feb. 6, 1860, of Okmulgee, Okla.; married first, James H. Green, who died abt 1891 and second, Woodford Mallory and had no ch.

Three. John Franklin Tunnell b Feb. 20, 1862; d May 23, 1923; married Flora Belle Hyder, sister of Sylvia Hyder, daughter of Joseph and Elizabeth Hyder, Feb. 21, 1888 Excelsior Springs, Mo. (b June 13, 1873 Polo, Mo.; d May 3, 1917 Kansas City, Mo.) and had; (a) Stella aude Tunnell b May 1, 1890, of Polo, Mo. (m John V. Mayes Sept. 30, 1908 (b Sept. 2, 1888 nr Polo) and had an only ch.; 1, Oletha Tunnell Mayes b July 8, 1909 Polo, Mo.); (b) Rose Ethel Tunnell b May 30, 1892; d Jan. 18, 1919 Polo, Mo. (m first, Earl Stansberry Nov. 28, 1906 and had no ch., and second, Ezra Cox, Apr. 7, 1909 Richmond, Mo. and had; 1, Olivia Y-Vetta Cox b Aug. 13, 1910 Polo, Mo.; married Eugenia Bell and had no ch. Eugena Bell Tun-Cox m second, Fay Phillips) (c) Flossie Della Tunnell b Nov. 23, 1894 Polo; d Mar. 25, 1895 Polo.

Four. Maryline Tunnell b May 1, 1864; d abt 1888 Polo, Mo.; married James Cummins May 26, 1880 Polo, Mo. (b 1859 Ray Co., Mo.) and had; (a) Lu Zetta Cummins b Dec. 6, 1886; d Sept. 5, 1919 Ochiltree, Tex. (m Sam Castleberry Oct. 23, 1902 and had; 1, J. Kern Castleberry b 1904 Depew, Okla., of Perrytown, Tex.; 2, Annis Castleberry b 1906 Bristo, Okla., of Hollister, Calif.) James Cummins m second, Catherine Hill, 1889 Richmond, Mo. and lives Perrytown, Texas.

Five. Benjamin Onie Tunnell b June 17, 1869; d May 21, 1910 Polo, Mo.; married Eugenia Bell and had no ch. Eugenia Bell Tunnell m second, Bert Applegate.

Six. Malissa Florence Tunnell b May 10, 1873, of Tulsa, Okla.; married first, Joseph Thompson Nov. 18, 1896 Richmond, Mo. and had; (a) Cleta Marie Thompson b 1900; (b) Joe Blair Thompson b 1911; and m second, Roscoe D. Kale 1916 Tulsa, Okla. (d 1919 Vinita, Okla.) and had no ch by this marriage.

V. I. Jane Matilda Tunnell, youngest child of William and Rebecca Rorex Tunnell, died in Tenn. She married Alexander A. Kollock, brother of Eliza Kollock and moved to Mo. where their little daughter died. They moved back to Loudon Co., Tenn. It is said they had one child named Myers Kollock. Alexander A. Kollock married a second time and lived at Lenoir City, Tenn.

NANCY TUNNELL

C. Nancy Tunnell, only daughter of Stephen and Kezia Money

Tunnell, was born abt 1782, in Va. and died 1866 at the home of a granddaughter, Mrs. Minter Bailey, Harlan Co.; Ky. She moved with her parents, to Washington Co., Tenn. 1788 and at one time lived in Greene Co., Tenn. She married John Bailey, known as "Thumby John" to distinguish him from several other John Baileys, Sept. 1799 Greene Co., Tenn. The marriage bond, dated Sept. 24, 1799, was signed by her father. John Bailey was born 1873 in Va and died Nov. 1850 in Lee Co., Va. They moved, shortly after marriage, to Harlan Co., Ky. and their children were born in that county and state. Nancy Tunnell Bailey was the mother of ten sons and one daughter and ten sons and one daughter were given to her parents. She had sons in both the Federal and Confederate States armies. Names of ch. may not be in order of birth.

I. William Bailey b 1800.
II. John Bailey b abt 1802.
III. Stephen Bailey
IV. Brittain Bailey.
V. Andrew Bailey.
VI. James Bailey.
VII. Daniel Bailey.
VIII. Carr Bailey b Apr. 4, 1819.
IX. Sally Bailey.
X. David Bailey b 1824.
XI. Jonathan Abschire Bailey b 1827.

Of the foregoing;

I. William Bailey, oldest son of John and Nancy Tunnell Bailey, was born 1800 and died about 1871 in Ky. He was a Methodist minister for fifty years. He was a Union man during the War Between the States, while his brothers were Southern sympathizers. He married first, ——— Chance and had six children; and m second, Ritter Brown and had two children.

. One Isaiah Bailey b abt 1837; served in the Fourteenth Kentucky and died in service; unmarried.

Two. Annie Bailey, b abt 1837; d in Ky.; married James Ball, who died Aug. 29, 1860, son of Moses (b 1800 Lee Co., Va.; d Harlan Co., Ky.) and Ella (Richardson) Ball, and g-s of Moses Ball, who lived at one time nr White Chapel, Va. Annie Bailey Ball had ch b in Ky.; (a) Moses Ball b 1854, of Baxter, Ky., (m a relative, Sally Bailey, dau of Jonathan Abschire and Louise (Howard) Bailey, and had ch b Ky.; 1, Floyd Ball, of Harlan, Ky., m Mary Harris and had; (aa) Harold Ball; (bb) Thelma Ball; 2, Dillard Ball, of Baxter, Ky., m Maude Banks and had; (aa) Glenn Ball; 3, Leslie Ball, of Harlan, Ky., m Mary Coleliron and had; (aa) Mildred Ball; (bb) Mabel Ball; (cc) Lucy Ball; (dd) Leslie Ball, Jr.; 4, Rosco Ball, of Baxter, Ky., m Maggie Hensley and had; (aa) Fish Ball; (bb) Moses Ball; (cc) Dilliard Ball; (dd) Gladys Ball; (ee) Curtis Ball; 5, Mossie Ball, of Concord, Tenn., m William Hobbs and had; (aa) Agnes Hobbs); (b) Ella Ball b 1856; (c) John Ball b 1858, once of Clarksville, Ark.; later of Baron, Okla.

Three. Larkin Bailey b abt 1839; married ——— Spurlock and had an only child; (a) George W. Bailey, of Va.

Four. John Carr Bailey b abt 1841; killed at Battle of Seven Pines; unmarried.

Five Zachariah Bailey b abt 1843; served in the Fourteenth Kentucky and died in service unmarried.

Six. Sarah Bailey, lived near Harlan, Ky; married a relative Minter Bailey, and had no children.

Seven. Lizzie Bailey, lived nr Harlan, Ky.

Eight. Fannie Bailey. It is not known whom these daughters by second wife married.

II. Capt John Bailey, son of John and Nancy Tunnell Bailey, was born about 1802 and died 1893 Harlan Co., Ky. He married first, Hannah Smith, dau of Henry Smith, Revolutionary soldier, and wife, Bettie Ledford Smith, about 1820 Harlan Co., Ky. Hannah Smith Bailey died Harlan Co., Ky. He married second, Patsy Clarkston, who died in Harlan Co., Ky. Names of children may not be in order of birth.

By First marriage;
One. Nancy Bailey b 1822.
Two. John S. Bailey.
Three. James Bailey.
Four. Charles Bailey.
Five. Robert Bailey.
Six. Andrew J. Bailey.
Seven. Sallie Stacy Bailey.
By second marriage;
Eight. Louisa Bailey b Feb. 20, 1845.
Nine. Silas W. Bailey.
Ten. Alexander Baailey.
Eleven. Susan Bailey.
Twelve. Polly Bailey.

Of these;
One. Nancy Bailey b 1822; d 1907 Clay Co., Ky.; married first, William Nantz, abt 1840 (d 1860) and had nine ch; and m second, Eli Vanover and had two ch, all b Harlan Co., Ky.

a. Benjamin Nantz b 1841; d 1843.

b. Sallie Nantz b 1843; d 1900; married a relative, Harrison Bailey, and had ch b Harlan Co., Ky.; 1, John Bailey, of Perry Co., Ky. m Susan Adams; 2, Hannah Bailey, m Bige Campbell (d 1914) and had; (aa) Pearl Campbell, of Richmond, Ky., m Bettie Harrison 1916 and had two ch.; (bb) Elihu Campbell, m Mary Sparks and had one child; (cc) Mollie Campbell, m ——— ———; (dd) Stella Campbell; 3, William A. Bailey b Aug. 25, 1874, of Hurley, Ky., m Lizzie Bird Oct. 25, 1896 (b Feb. 18 1875) and had 3 ch b Laurel Co., others Jackson Co., Ky.; (aa) Elbert Bailey b Nov. 11, 1897, m Clista Isaacs Aug. 2, 1923 and had, James Bailey b Aug. 7, 1924; (bb) Ethel Bailey b May 8, 1900, of Hamilton, Ohio, m William Burk Oct. 17, 1919 Jackson Co., Ky. and had, Effie Burk b Feb. 6, 1921 and Pauline Burk b Mar. 1, 1923; (cc) Ida Bailey b Feb. 2, 1902, of Hurley, Ky., m Arban Lakes Aug. 9, 1924; (dd) Ellen Bailey b Oct. 2, 1904, of Hurley, Ky., m Ben Gabbard Apr. 16, 1920 Jackson Co., Ky. and had; Junior Gabbard b Jan. 6, 1922 in Mich. and Loraine Gabbard b June 3, 1924 Hamilton, Ohio; (ee) Albert Bailey b Dec. 5, 1906; (ff) Stanley Bailey b June 2, 1909; (gg) Edna Bailey b Mar. 14, 1911; (hh) Robert Bailey b Oct. 5, 1912; (ii) Loyd Bailey b Dec. 20, 1913; (jj) Boyd Bailey b Apr. 4, 1915); 4, Nancy Bailey, m Levi Garrison and had; (aa)Froma Garrison, of Richmond, Ky., m Henry Hurst; (bb) Holla Garrison, of Richmond, Ky., m George Grimes and had one ch. (cc) Ona Garrison; (dd) Carrie Garrison; 5, Martha Bailey m Daniel Bowling and had; (aa) Charles Bowling; 6, Mary Bailey; 7, Elijah Bailey, m Lottie Brown; 8, Lillie Bailey m ——— Morgan; 9, Florence Bailey, m Isaac Daniel; and perhaps others.

c. Hannah Nantz b 1845; married James Lewis, who d 1906 in Texas.

d. John Nantz b 1847, of Chester, Ky.; married Sally Wooten and had; 1, William Nantz, m Lizzie Lewis; 2, Hannah Nantz (d

1914) m William Napier (d 1923); 3, Martha Nantz, of Perry Co., Ky.,. m first, William Sizemore, and second, ——— ———; 4, Dan Nantz, of Texas, m Rebecca Napier; 5, Nancy Nantz, m John Maggard; 6, Emma Nantz, m John Feltner and had children; 7, Susan Nantz, m Hyden Brewer; 8, Polly Nantz, m Eli Boyer; 9, Calvin Nantz, of Mc Whorter, Ky., m Eva Roberts; 10, Albert Nantz, m Mollie Maggard; 11, Mary Nantz, m Roy Melton; 12, Alexander Nantz; 13, Bettie Nantz, m Wilson Feltner.

e. Bettie Nantz b 1849, m William Hignight and had; 1, Hannah Hignight b Mar. 19, 1870, of Hamilton, Ohio, m Sam Howard Aug. 11, 1889 and had; (aa) Theresa Howard b July 15, 1890, m Thomas Brumback and had; Fred Brumback b Dec. 2, 1906; (bb) Minnie Howard b Jan. 23, 1894, m William Carter and had no ch.; 2, Serelda Hignight, of McKee, Ky., m John Halcomb and had; (aa) Hannah Halcomb; 3, Sarah Hignight, m James Robbins and had; (aa) Minnie Robbins; (bb) Earnest Robbins, m Tussie Ramsey; (cc) Joseph Robibns; 4, Mitchell Hignight, of McKee, Ky., m Rebecca Ann Thompson and had; (aa) Leonard Hignight, of Gray Hawk, Ky., m Rachel Halcomb and had, Ermon Hignight, Elvin Hignight, and others; 5, Robert Hignight, of McKee, Ky., m first, Kate Towles and had; (aa) Lucy Hignight; (bb) Marie Hignight; and m second, Eva Clemmons and had one ch.; 6, Nancy Hignight, of McKee, Ky., m first, Daniel Wilson nad had; (aa) Grace Wilson, m Frank Sparks and had; Macie Sparks and Rosa Sparks; (bb) Sarah Wilson; (cc) Rosa Wilson, and m second, John Sparks; 7, Martha Hignight, of McKee, Ky., m Miles Sparks and had; (aa) Alice Sparks; (bb) Alva Sparks; (cc) Evelyn Sparks; (dd) Nina Sparks.

f. Calvin Nantz b 1851, of Loudon, Ky.; married first, Martha Davidson, second, Bettie Brewer and third, Fannie Casteel, and had no children.

g. Alexander Nantz b 1853, of Teges, Ky., m Jane Moberly and had; 1, Lizzie Nantz, m Rutherford Allen; 2, Laura Nantz, m Logan Murrell and had; (aa) Bessie Murrell, m Walter Byrd; (bb) Gilbert Murrell, m Mattie Links; 3, Hattie Nantz, m George Nantz and had; (aa) Georgia Nantz; (bb) Lois Nantz; (cc) Albert Nantz; (dd) Elizabeth Nantz; 4, Lucy Nantz, m Carlos Byrd and had; (aa) Donald Byrd; (bb) Hubert Byrd; (cc) Jessie Byrd; (dd) Shirley Byrd; 5, William Nantz, m Lucy Combs and had; (aa) Calvin Nantz; (bb) Elmer Nantz; (cc) Hazel Nantz.

h. Mary Nantz b 1855, of Algers, Ky., m Sam Peters.

i. Martha Nantz b 1857; d 1875 Perry Co., Ky.; unmarried.

Two. John S. Bailey, son of Capt. John and Hannah Smith Bailey b abt 1824; d July 1886 Harlan Co., Ky.; married Polly Robbins, of Lee Co., Va. and had ch b Lee Co., Va.; (a) William Minter Bailey (d abt 1920) (m Rebecca Yeary and had; 1, Mary Bailey, of Dellvale, Va., m first, A. J. Garrison and had two daughters; and m second, James Shuler; and m third, Fletcher Carter; 2, John C. Bailey; 3, Sherman Bailey, of Keokee, Va.; 4, Jane Bailey of Keokee, Va., m Joseph Robbins; and others); (b) James Marion Bailey (m Susan Moore and had; 1, John S. Bailey, d abt 1923; 2, Harvey Bailey; 3, Sally Bailey; 4, Charles Bailey; 5, Tilman Bailey; 6, Russell Bailey, deceased), (c) Jane Bailey (deceased) (m Benjamin F. Parsons and had; 1, Martha Parsons; 2, Sarah Parsons; 3, Eliza Parsons; 4, Harvey Parsons; 5, John Parsons); (d) Sarah Bailey, of Keokee, Va., (m John Silas Holmes and had; 1, Floyd Holmes; 2, John B. Holmes; 3, Cora Holmes and others); (e) Martha Bailey, deceased, m Jehu Holmes, brother of John Silas Holmes and Susan Holmes, and had no ch.; (f) Tilman Bailey, deceased, (m Susan Holmes and had several children); (g) Bennett Bailey, of Pennington Gap., Va., m ———— ———— and had children, including; 1, E. L. Bailey; (h) Bascom Bailey, deceased, m ———— Clarkson; (i) Tipton Bailey, of Ky.; (j) Burner Bailey, m Abbie Clay; (a) Annias Bailey, d young in Harlan Co., Ky.

Three. James Bailey, son of Capt. John and Hannah Smith Bailey, died abt Nov. 1864. He married Nancy Wilson and had ch. b Harlan Co., Ky.; (a) Simeon Bailey, m first, Nancy Howard and had three ch., and second, Lucy Cooper; (b) John Bailey, m Pauline Buckhart; (c) Andrew J. Bailey m first, Catherine Farmer, and seccom Bailey, deceased, m ———— Clarkson; (i) Tipton Bailey, of Ky.; Crab Orchard, Ky.; (d) Ben Franklin Bailey b Aug. 30, 1864, of Viva., Ky. (m Sallie Garrison Feb. 20, 1884 and had; 1, John M. Bailey b Oct. 6, 1888, m Amanda Bowling and had; (aa) Rogers Bailey; (bb) Ben Bailey; (cc) Burton Bailey; (dd) Ruth Bailey; 2, Della Bailey b Jan. 26, 1890, m Taylor Bowling and had; (aa) Beatrice Bowling; (bb) Taylor G. Bowling; (cc) Evelyn Bowling; (dd) John Bowling; (ee) Loretta Bowling; 3, Orpha Bailey b Feb. 7, 1892, m Oscar House Nov. 26, 1913 and had; (aa) Cloyd House; (bb) Colemen House; (cc) Donald House; (dd) Glen House; 4, Martha Bailey b Jan. 5, 1895, m James Hunley Feb. 29, 1916 and had; (aa) Thelma Hunley; (bb) B. F. Hunley; 5, Myrtle Bailey b Aug. 24, 1897, m John Lewis Mar. 5, 1914 and had; (aa) James B. Lewis; (bb) Viola Lewis; (cc) Alice Lewis; (dd) Arnold Lewis; 6, William Bailey b Nov. 6, 1900, m Ethel Westedfield Nov. 18, 1920 and had; (aa) Jessie Bailey; (bb) B. F. Bailey; 7, Cora Bailey b Aug. 11, 1903, of Viva, Ky., m J. L. Cloyd Apr. 20, 1921 and had; (aa) Wilma Cloyd; (bb) Elwood Cloyd; 8, Earl Bailey b June 17, 1909; 9, Verlie Bailey b Oct. 9, 1910); (e) Nancy Bailey, m Noah Howard; (f) Sallie Bailey, m Wilson Howard.

Four. Charles Bailey, son of Capt. and Hannah Smith Bailey, died in McGoffin Co., Ky. He married ———— Salyers and had no children.

Five. Robert Bailey, son of Capt. John and Hannah Smith Bailey, born 1840, died Apr. 20, 1865 Harlan Co., Ky. He married Margaret Smith, dau of Colonel Jonathan Smith (soldier in Mexican War) and Christine (Jenkins) Smith, 1858 Harlan Co., Ky. (b 1840; d abt 1920 Harlan Co., Ky.) and had ch b Harlan, Ky.; (aa) John Sommerfield Bailey b Nov. 22, 1859, of Hamilton, Ohio (m first, Addie Jones Sept. 27, 1884, who died Sept. 8, 1889; and m second, Sallie Ann Barron July 15, 1890 and had; 1, Margaret Janet Bailey b Sept. 27, 1892, in Va., of Dooley, Va. m Fred Troy, in Va., and had; (aa) Fred Troy, the second, b Aug. 1922; and m third, Mollie Ball (d Sept. 24, 1905) and had; 2, Eunice Ethelyn Bailey b Aug. 27, 1894 in Va., of Somerset, Ky., m W. F. Morris, in Ohio, and had no children. Public acknowledgement of assistance is due John S. Bailey who has supplied most of the record of Nancy Tunnell Bailey); (b) Nancy Bailey b 1861 (m Elihu Estridge in Leslie Co., Ky. and had; 1, John S. Estridge b Laurel Co., Ky., of Bond, Ky., m Flora Johnson and had; (aa) Hugh Estridge; (bb) Paul Estridge; 2, Flora Estridge b Sept. 28, 1883, of Viva, Ky., m Elias Smith Jan. 8, 1903 and had; (aa) Dexter Smith b Oct. 30, 1904; (bb) Mable Smith b Feb. 17, 1906; (cc) Marvin Smith b May 6, 1907; (dd) Evelyn Smith b Mar. 25, 1909; (ee) Charles Smith b July 12, 1910; (ff) Murrell Smith b Oct. 3, 1912; (gg) Hugh Smith b Dec. 25, 1914; (hh) Lucy Smith b Sept. 6, 1916; (ii) Edwin Smith b May 1, 1920; 3, Joseph Marion Estridge b 1885 Leslie Co., Ky., of Stanford, Ky., m Laura Watkins 1908 and had; (aa) Nancy Alabama Estridge b 1910; (bb) Arnold Estridge; (cc)

Lorain Estridge; (aa) Joseph Marion Estridge Jr.; (ee) Earnest Estridge; 4, Addie Estridge b Feb. 5, 1889 Lestie Co., Ky., of High Knob, Ky., m Henry Noe Apr. 20, 1915; 5, Pearl Estridge b July 26, 1890 Jackson Co., Ky., of High Knob, Ky., m Sarah Bowman and had; (aa) Zethyl Estridge b Mar. 11, 1918 Owsley Co., Ky.; (bb) Albert Estridge b Jan. 29, 1922 Jackson Co., Ky.; 6, Clarence Estridge, m Ruth Wilson and had; (aa) Elihu Estridge; (bb) Wilson Estridge; (cc) Veda Gay Estridge; (dd) Doris Jean Estridge; (ee) Nancy Estridge; 7, Belle Estridge); (c) Charles Bailey b 1863; d Mar. 1865 Harlan Co., Ky.

Six. Andrew J. Bailey, son of Capt. John and Hannah Smith Bailey, died in Texas. He married Nancy Smith, sister of Margaret Smith, and had ch b in Virginia; (a) John M. Bailey, of Hindman, Ky. m first, Mollie French and second, ——— Gearhart; (b) Carr Bailey, m Nancy Huff; (c) Greene Bailey; (d) Henry Bailey; (e) James Bailey; (f) Susan Bailey; (g) Jonathan Bailey.

Seven. Sallie Stacy Bailey, dau of Capt. John and Hannah Smith Bailey, married James Turner, once county judge of Perry Co., Ky., and had ch b Perry Co., Ky.; (a) Mary Turner, deceased (m Samuel Creech, of Berea, Ky. and had; 1, Harry Creech; 2, Sarah Creech; 3, Ben Creech; 4, Nannie Creech; 5, Fannie Creech; 6, Mollie Creech; 7, Roy Creech; 8, Clarence Creech); (b) Louisa Turner, m ——— Bowens; (c) Nancy Turner, m ——— Polly; (d) David Turner, m Jane Combs.

Eight. Louisa Bailey, dau of Capt. John and Patsy Clarkston Bailey, b Feb. 20, 1845, married Joseph Miniard Jan. 3, 1859, who was born Aug. 14, 1837. Both living Nov. 1924. Children b Harlan, Ky.; (a) Polly Ann Miniard b 1862 (m Puss Turner and had; 1, See Turner, 2, Alice Turner; 3, John Turner); (b) John B. Miniard b 1865, of Hyden, Ky. (m Nancy Maggard and had; 1, P. C. Miniard b 1892; 2, Carrie Miniard b 1894; 3, Hobart Miniard b 1896; 4, Joe Miniard b 1898; g, Nannie Miniard b 1900; all of whom are married); (c) William Miniard d young; (d) Jane Miniard b 1870, m ——— ———; (e) Susan Miniard b 1873 (m Silas Boggs and had; 1, Carrie Boggs; 2, Bish Boggs; and others); (f) Nancy Miniard b 1876 (m Barn Blanton and had; 1, Francis Blanton; 2, Matilda Blanton; and others); (g) Matilde Miniard b 1883, m Sam Maggard and had; 1, Herschel Maggard b 1916; 2, Eliza Maggard b 1917; (h) Elizabeth Miniard b 1889; 5, Nannie Miniard b 1900; all of whom are married); Nine. Silas W. Bailey, son of Capt. John and Patsy Clarkston Bailey, married Bettie Griffith and had; (a) William Bailey; (b) Juda Bailey, m John McDaniel; (c) J. K. Bailey.

Ten. Alexander Bailey, son of Capt. John and Patsy Clarkston Bailey, died 1886 Harlan, Ky.; married first, Hettie Gross and had; (a) Lee Bailey; (b) John Bailey; (c) Richard Bailey; and perhaps others. Alexander Bailey m second, Sallie Ann North.

Eleven. Susan Bailey, dau of Capt. John and Patsy Clarkston Bailey, married George Nantz and had; (a) Alexander Nantz, of Helton, Ky.; (b) Silas Nantz, of Helton, Ky.; (c) John Nantz; (d) Rebecca Jane Nantz; (e) Louisa Nantz; (f) James Nantz, of Helton, Ky.

Twelve. Polly Bailey, dau of Capt. John and Patsy Clarkston Bailey, married Elijah Toliver and had; (a) James Toliver; (b) John Toliver; (c) Arthur Toliver; (d) Grant Toliver; (e) Elbert Toliver; (f) Susan Ann Toliver; (g) Louisa Toliver; (h) Nancy Toliver; (i) Ollive Toliver.

III. Stephen Bailey, son of John and Nancy Tunnell Bailey, married ——— ——— and had at least one child; (a) Jonathan

Bailey born before his uncle, Jonathan Bailey.   Stephen Bailey lived, it is said, at one time in Hawkins Co., Tenn. and at another in Arkansas.

IV.   Brittain Bailey, son of John and Nancy Tunnell Bailey, is said to have gone to New Orleans and later "to the West". No further details.

V.   Andrew Bailey, son of John and Nancy Tunnell Bailey, lived in Greene Co., Tenn. nr Lass Mountain.   He married Nancy Ball, dau of William Ball and granddau of Moses and Mary (Harden) Ball, and had; (a) Jasper Bailey; (b) Andrew Bailey Jr.; (c) George Bailey (m ——— Rowan and had; 1, Marion Bailey; 2, James Bailey; 3, Alvis Bailey; 4, Augusta Bailey; 5, Bell Bailey, all of whom are dead, and perhaps other children); (d) Jane Bailey; (e) Mary Bailey; (f) Sallie Bailey; (g) Eliza Bailey; (h) Riggs Bailey; (i) Kemy Bailey; (j) Baxter Bailey; (k) Rebecca Bailey b Oct. 12, 1859, only one living, 1924, of Persia, Tenn. (m Robert Thacker (b July 19, 1850) and had; 1, John Thacker; 2, Riggs Thacker; 3, Ida Bell Thacker; 4, Martha Jane Thacker unm., of Persia, Tenn.; 5, Robert Thacker; 6, Nancy Thacker).

VI.   James Bailey, son of John and Nancy Tunnell Bailey, died in inf. in Harlan Co., Ky.

VII.   Daniel Bailey, son of John and Nancy Tunnell Bailey, died in Hawkins Co., Tenn.   He married Kizzie Tunnell, a first cousin, the dau of James and Jane Ball Tunnell; grandau of Moses and Mary (Harden) Ball, and Stephen and Kezia (Money) Tunnell, and had; (a) John Carr Bailey, who visited in Kentucky during the War Between the States; (b) Julia Bailey m John Mowell; (c) James Bailey; (d) Sadie Bailey (m G. P. Jones and had; 1, Cordie Jones; 2, John Jones; 3, Jessie Jones; 4, Rosa Jones, and others); (e) Pearl Bailey, m John Hundley; (f) Bosa Bailey, m Newt Bailey; (g) Clarence Bailey; (h) John Bailey; (i) Eugene Bailey.   Some descendants at Burem, Tenn.   Daniel Bailey may have married twice as it is said he married ——— Henard.

VIII.   Carr Bailey, son of John and Nancy Tunnell Bailey, was born Apr. 4, 1819 Harlan Co., Ky. and died Dec. 28, 1898 Lee Co., Va. In the War Between the States he served in C. S. A.   He was county judge and surveyor of Lee Co., Va.   He married first, Frances (Ely) France, 1839, who died 1876, who was the mother of his children; and married second, Alpha C. Hart, 1883, who died 1890.   He had seven children.

One.   Peter H. Bailey b Aug. 2, 1840; d 1863; unmarried.

Two.   Louisa Bailey b 1842; d 1870; married David Crockett Flanary, who served in C. S. A., the son of Harvey L. Flanary, and had (a) Paris C. Flanary; (b) Martha Flanary (m James Maxwell and had; 1, Elbert Maxwell; 2, David Maxwell; 3, Sarah Jane Maxwell; 4, Cora Maxwell, twin of Sarah Jane Maxwell); (c) Mary Lettie Flanary, of Pennington Gap., Va., m Javin A. Shufflebarger and had; 1, Sallie Zack Shufflebarger).

Three.   Henry Clay Bailey b Sept. 4, 1844; married Timpy Johnson 1875 and had; (a) Fanny Bailey b 1876, of Olinger, Va., (m David W. Lawson and had; 1, Willard Lawson; 2, John B. Lawson; 3, Will Lawson; 4, Pat Lawson, and others); (b) John Henry Bailey b 1879 (c) Phoebe Susan Bailey b 1881 (m Robert Williams and had; 1, Bailey Williams; 2, Bernalda Williams; 3, Earnest Williams); (d) Vesta Bailey b 1884 (m Grover Sharp and had; 1, Christine Sharp; (e) Charles Carr Bailey m Addie Reasor; (f) Thomas Bailey, dead; (g) Thumby Bailey; (h) Shelly Bailey b 1895.

Four.   John Marshall Bailey b Feb. 2, 1847 Olinger, Va.; married

Susan Reasor Aug. 15, 1872 Turkey Cove. Va. (b Aug. 25, 1854 Turkey Cove, Va.) and had ch b Olinger, Va.; (a) John Reasor Bailey b Aug. 20, 1873, of Olinger, Va. (m a relative, Mattie Lunie Slemp, dau of Capt. Henry C. and Melissa (Habern) Slemp, June 7, 1896 Olinger, Va. (b Sept. 18, 1877 Big Stone Gap, Va.) and had ch b Olinger, Va., save one; 1, Vivian Gertrude Bailey b Apr. 30, 1897, of Louisville, Ky., m Marion Stallard Smith June 2, 1920 and had; (aa) Eleanor Richmond Smith; (bb) Agnes Marie Smith; 2, Laura Maye Bailey b Dec. 31, 1898, of Big Stone Gap, Va., m Earl Morris June 6, 1922 Knoxville, Tenn. and had; (aa) William Ralph Morris b June 6, 1923; 3, Ulysses Slemp Bailey b Jan. 10, 1900; 4, Willie Marie Bailey b Nov. 15, 1902 Appalachia, Va.; d Sept. 10, 1919 Olinger, Va.; 5, John Marshall Bailey, the second, b Jan. 2, 1905; 6, Helen Melissa Bailey b Sept. 17, 1908; 7, Susan Janette Bailey b Mar. 11, 1911; 8, Anna Elizabeth Bailey b Nov. 6, 1913; 9, Margaret Louise Bailey b Feb. 23, 1916; 10, Donald Wise Bailey b Oct. 9, 1917; 11, Mary Lunie Bailey b Oct. 4, 1920); (b) William Milton Bailey b Jan. 18, 1876, of Olinger, Va., (m Minerva Dorthula Orlinger Nov. 9, 1912 Orlinger, Va. and had; 1, Theodore Richard Bailey b Sept. 27, 1913; 2, Kermit A. Bailey b Feb. 17, 1915; 3, Mary Susan Delia Bailey b Oct. 7, 1918); (c) Nettie Mae Bailey b Jan. 8, 1878, of Clovis, New Mexico (m first, Harvey Lee Flanary July 4, 1896 Bristol, Va.-Tenn. who d in Texas and had; 1, Thomas Flanary; 2, Virginia Lee Flanary; and m second, J .P. Pierce, and had; 3, Ralph Pierce; 4, Nettie Mary Pierce); (d) Judge Carr Bailey b July 24, 1882, of Colorado Springs, Colo. (m Nervesta Slemp, dau Capt. Henry C. and Melissa (Habern) Slemp, and had; 1, Harold Clinton Bailey, dead; 2, Kenneth Bailey; 3, Annie Teresa Bailey; 4, John Marshall Bailey); (e) Charles Wise Bailey b Feb. 19, 1885, of Middlesboro, Ky., m Mary Nice June 8, 1921 and had; no ch.; (f) Laura Rose Bailey b June 26, 1888, of Corbin, Ky.; (g) Thomas Dewitt Talmadge Bailey b Aug. 14, 1890, unmarried, of Harlan, Ky.; (h) Ross Jackson Bailey b Jan. 22, 1893, of Middlesboro, Ky. (m Geneveva Morgan Nelson and had; 1, Ross Jackson Bailey, the second, b July 24, 1918; 2, Charles Nelson Bailey b Mar. 28, 1921; 3, Edgar Allen Bailey b 1922); (i) Joseph Weldon Bailey b Jan. 30, 1897, unmarried, of Kenova, West Va.

Five.   Jane Symth Bailey b 1849; d 1908; m Henry Barker and had; (a) Ida Barker, m James J. Orr and had one ch.; (b) Sally Barker, m Elhannon Howard; (c) Benjamin Harrison Barker b Mar. 4, 1889, m Jane Parsons and had one ch.; (d) Kitsey Barker, m Eurasmus Asberry and had one ch.

Six.   Sally Bailey b 1851, m Zachariah Cecil and had no ch.

Seven.   Charles Daugherty Bailey b Oct. 19, 1855, of Olinger, Va.; married first, Hannah D. Legg, dau of Thomas N. and Naomi (Reasor) Legg, a relative of the Slemp family, Sept. 15, 1875 Lee Co., Va. (b Feb. 9, 1861; d Nov. 3, 1887 Lee Co., Va.) and had ch b Lee Co., Va.; (a) Minnie Naomi Bailey b Nov. 4, 1876, of Olinger, Va. (m Dr. James Prichard and had an only ch.; 1, Allen Bailey Prichard b Jan. 17, 1901, of Olinger, Va., who enlisted for service in World War at Big Stone Gap July 17, 1917, sailed for France June 2, 1918, discharged from duty May 29, 1919, m Corinne Yeary at Cumberland Gap, Va. and had ch b Olinger, Va.; (aa) Helen Bernice Prichard b Dec. 15, 1922; (bb) Naomi Ruth Prichard b Jan. 3, 1924); (b) Ina Jane Bailey b Feb. 9, 1879; d 1886 Alachua Co., Florida; (c) Sallie Elizabeth Bailey b Aug. 31, 1881, of Big Stone Gap, Va. (m first, Joe Cox 1907 (d 1909 New Mexico) and m second, Claude Kelley and had; 1, Christine Kelly b 1914 Olinger, Va.; 2, Claude Winfield Kelly b 1916; 3, Charles Bailey Kelly b 1918; 4, Virginia Jee Kelly b 1912,

last 3 b Big Stone Gap); (d) Henry Carr Bailey b¹ June 24, 1884, of
Olinger, Va. (m Cordie Reasor and had ch b Olinger, Va.; 1, Dorthula Bailey b Feb. 29, 1912; 2, Earnest Hopkins Bailey b Sept. 21,
1913; 3, Edward Lee Bailey b June 5, 1916; 4, Ruba Josephine Bailey
b Aug. 23, 1920); ¹Charles Daugherty Bailey married second, Flora
A. Sword, dau of John W. and Nancy Sword, Aug. 16, 1897 Lee Co.,
Va. (b 1870; d Aug. 10, 1900) and had; (e) Charles Dewey Bailey b
June 13, 1898, unmarried (f) Judge Clay Bailey b Jan. 26, 1900, unmarried.   Charles Daugherty Bailey married third, Mary A. Sword,
niece of Flora A. Sword, dau of James T. and Martha Sword, Jan. 6,
1980 Lee Co., Va. (b Dec. 16, 1877) and had; (g) Dean Sword Bailey
b Dec. 8, 1908; d July 19, 1909 Lee Co., Va.; (h) Harold Daugherty
Bailey b Jan. 5, 1911; (i) Everett Howard Bailey b Dec. 20, 1912; d
Dec. 26, 1912; (j) Leslie Wilmer Bailey b Mar. 5, 1914.

IX.   Sally Bailey, only dau of John and Nancy Tunnell Bailey
died in Hawkins Co., Tenn.   She m John Light and 'd a year after
marriage.   One child, born the day its mother died, is supposed to
have died in inf.

X.   David Bailey, son of John and Nancy Tunnell Bailey, died
abt 1900 Texas Co., Mo.; married first, ——— Howard; and second,
——— Leford.   He had children, including; (a) Nancy Bailey, m
Peter Tuttle and lived in Mo.   No further details.

XI.   Jonathan Abschire Bailey, youngest child of John and
Nancy Tunnell Bailey, was born 1827 and died 1918 in county where
he was born .   He m Louisa Howard (b 1838; d 1903 Harlan Co., Ky.)
and had eleven ch b Harlan Co., Ky.

One.   Chadwell Bailey; married Louisa Priace and had; (a)
Charles Bailey, of Blanche, Ky., m Maud Miller; (b) Cleveland
Bailey, of Blanche, Ky., m ——— Jett; (c) David Bailey, of Wallin's
Creek, Ky., m Mary Blanton; (d) Custer Bailey, unm.; (d) Bertha
Bailey, of Pineville, Ky., m Bob Vanbevers; (e) Orphia Bailey, of
Blanche, Ky., m ——— Rawlings.

Two.   David Bailey, m Lizzie Howard and had; (a) William
Bailey of Baxter, Ky., m Rebecca Ball; (b) Sallie Bailey, of Wilhoit,
Ky., m Henry Lewis; (c) Mary Bailey, of Wallin's Creek, Ky., m
Nathan Maiden; (d) Mossie Bailey, of Evarts, Ky., m ——— Asher.

Three.   Samuel Bailey, m Bettie Brumet and had; (a) Louisa
Bailey of Wallen's Creek, Ky., m Floyd Ball; (b) Jefferson Bailey, of
Wallin's Creek, Ky.; (c) James Bailey, of Baxter, Ky., m Chil Glad-
dis; (d) John Bailey, unm., of Baxter, Ky.

Four.   William L. Bailey b Nov. 9, 1877, judge of Harlan Co.,
Ky., of Harlan; married Vestina Howard and had; (a) Claude Bailey
died Nov. 2, 1900; (b) Bertha Bailey b Dec. 27, 1900 (m Daniel Y.
Smith and had; 1, Billie Smith b Dec. 20, 1921; 2, Peggy Ann Smith
b Sept. 6, 1924 Knoxville, Tenn.); (c) Lora Bailey b Dec. 31, 1903,
unmarried; (d) Curtis Bailey b Nov. 11, 1911.

Five.   Narcissus Bailey, of Elcomb, Ky.; married George Ball
and had ch. including; (a) Louisa Ball, dead; (b) William Ball b 1892.

Six.   Addie Bailey, married Ewel Unthank and had; (a) William
Unthank; (b) Martha Unthank; (c) Doxie Unthank; (d) Pearl
Uuthank; (e) Una Unthank.

Seven.   Matt Bailey died at six.

Eight.   James Bailey, m Maggie Woodward.

Nine.   John Bailey, unm.

Tenn.   Anna Bailey, m Bobert Blanton and had; (a) Grover
Blanton; (b) Sallie Blanton; (c) Louisa Blanton; (d) Moses Blanton;
(e) Jonathan Blanton; (f) William Blanton.

Eleven.   Sally Bailey b 1856, of Baxter, Ky.; married Moses Ball, son of James and Annie (Bailey) Ball; gs Moses and Ella (Richardson) Ball and of Rev. William Bailey; ggs of John and Nancy (Tunnell) Bailey. See record of Rev. William Bailey.

PERRY TUNNELL

D.   Perry Tunnell, son of Stephen and Kezia Money Tunnell, was born 1787.   He was a Methodist minister.   In the summer of 1826 when "he only turned thirty-nine he attended a camp meeting in Alabama, preached the morning sermon, started home and died before reaching home only a few miles away."   He married Catherine Self about 1807.   She was of Indian lineage, a granddaughter of John Gunter, of Gunter's Landing in northern Alabama.   She married second, ——— Little, and moved to Texas where she died.   Children of Rev. Perry Tunnell, all born in Alabama, moved, with exception of the eldest, to Texas in 1850.

I.   Jesse Tunnell b abt 1808.
II.   Mahulda Tunnell b abt 1810.
III.   James Tunnell b June 18, 1812.
IV.   Elisha Tunnell b Apr. 13, 1814.
V.   Enoch Tunnell b abt 1816,
VI.   Josiah Allen Tunnell b Feb. 3, 1818.
VII.   Stephen Tunnell b abt 1819.
VIII.   Nancy Tunnell b Sept. 27, 1821.
IX.   John Wesley Tunnell b Sept. 28, 1822.
X.   Mary Tunnell b abt 1824.
XI.   Elizabeth Tunnell b abt 1826.
Of the foregoing;

I.   Jesse Tunnell, son of Perry and Catherine Self Tunnell was born abt 1808 and died, in Alabama, unmarried.

II.   Mahulda Tunnell, dau of Perry and Catherine Self Tunnell, was born abt 1810 and died in Van Zandt Co., Tex.   Sme married Wilson Berry and had ten ch b in Tex.

One.   Hugh Berry, dead; married Caroline Kirkpatrick (dead) and had an only child; (a) Eunice Berry.

Two.   Enoch Berry died in service during Civil War.

Three.   Catherine Berry, dead; married ——— Palmer and had; (a) Julia Palmer (m Will Mayne and had; 1, Orin Mayne, m John Kellis, of Canton, Tex., and had 2 sons; 2, Minard Mayne; 3, Arthur Mayne; 4, Rosie Mayne, m Willie Geddie and had ch.; 5, Burnell Mayne, m Minnie Oliver and had a ch.) (b) Octavia Palmer.

Four.   Eliza Jane Berry, dead; married James High and had; (a) John High; (b) Zona High; (c) Ambrose High; (d) Izzy High; (e) Eula High; (f) Webb High; (g) Mary Righ.

Five.   Elisha Berry died in Tex.; married Brusilla Hanks and had six ch. including; (a) Elizabeth Berry (m Charles H. Blackwell and had; 1, Jesse Blackwell; 2, Winnie E. Blackwell, m Harry Rumbleow and had one child, dead; 3, Percy Blackwell, of Ben Wheeler, Tex., m Sarah Wilson and had; (aa) Lucile Fern Blackwell; (bb) Sallie Patricia Blackwell; 4, Arona Blackwell; 5, Mary Blackwell; 6, Stanley Blackwell); (b) Christie Berry (m Rosie Johnson and had; 1, Mertie Berry, m Everett Wright; 2, Hiram Berry; 3, Christi Berry; 4, Ruth Berry; 5, Winton Berry; 6, Ogden Berry); (c) Addie Berry (m Elmer Davidson and had; 1, Horace Davidson; 2, Yevan Davidson; 3 Marie Davidson); (d) Exer Berry (m Alexander Norton and had; 1, Carroll Norton; 2, Wayne Norton).

Six.   Vestal Berry died in Tex.; married Martha Cooper and had; (a) Thomas Berry, m Sallie Blue and had ch; (b) Jackson Berry, m Lois Loyd and had; 1, Clarence Berry; 2, Grace Berry; 3, Ruby Berry;

and 3 others; (c) Ella Berry, m Bud Ballard and had; 1, Robena Ballard; 2, Gertie Ballard; (d) Oma Berry, m Cullen McMahon and had ch.; (e) Addie Berry; (f) Mary Berry, dead.

Seven. James Berry ,living in Tex. 1924; married Cynthia Slaughter (deceased) and had ch b Texas; (a) Herschel Berry, m Willie Large and had three ch.; (b) George Berry, m Lula Large and had three ch.; (c) Will Berry; (d) John Berry; (e) Sam Berry; (f) Frances Berry, m Clarence Cline and had two ch; (g) Meredity Berry, m Ballie Cumbie and had two ch.

Eight. Prather Berry, died Van Zandt Co., Tex.; married first, Addie Wood, and second, Neely House and had two ch.; (a) Mois Berry; (b) Dexter Berry m Leonard Wright.

Nine. Stuart Berry, died in Tex.; married Jane Loper (deceased) and had; (a) Vicie Berry, m Tom Drinkard; (b) Pearl Berry, dead; m Nora Goode and had; 1, Carson Berry; 2, Fredda Berry; (c) Kebbie Berry.

Ten. Elizabeth Berry died in Tex.; married Wallace Kirkpatrick and had; (a) Jane Kirkpatrick, m Sam Mayne and had one ch.; (b) Kate Kirkpatrick (m Leslie Large and had; 1, David Large; 2, Lula Large; 3, Willie Large; 4, Ola Large, dead); (c) John Kirkpatrick (m Margaret Slaughtter and had 1, Lennie Kirkpatrick, m V. B. Cozby and had 3 ch.; 2, Janie Kirkpatrick, m Jamez Cozby and had 3 ch.; 3, Andrew Kirkpatrick, m Clara Rusk and had 2 ch.; 4, Virgil Kirkpatrick); (d) Nan Kirkpatrick, m William Rushing and had; 1, Gay Rushing; (e) Martha Kirkpatrick (m Lewis Hall and had; 1, Walter Hall; 2, Henrietta Hall; 3, Addie Hall; 4, Nannie Hall; 5, Ben Hall); (f) Amzie Kirkpatrick, m Maggie McPhail; (g) James Kirkpatrick (m Louise Slaughter and had; 1, Oll Kirkpatrick; 2, Etta Kirkpatrick; 3, John Kirkpatrick; 4, Lonnie Kirkpatrick); (h) Hugh Kirkpatrick (m first, Sophrona Godsey and had; 1, Bertha Kirkpatrick,m Jim Box; and m second, Florence Bostick); (i) Robert Kirkpatrick.

III. James Tunnell, son of Perry and Catherine Self Tunnell, was born June 18, 1812 Blount Co., Ala. and died May 10, 1861 in Texas. He married Elizabeth Ellis, dau of Rev. Jesse Ellis, 1834, in Ala. (b June 4, 1815; d Sept. 7, 1899 Tex.) and had ten ch.

One. Eliza Jane Tunnell b July 1, 1835 in Ala.; d 1907 Garden Valley, Tex.; married first, Colonel Isaac Cozby, who d in Tex.,a and had ch b nr Garden Valley; (a) Victoria Cozby, m ———— ———— and had no children.; (b) Bell Cozby, dead (m Thomas Thompson and had; 1, Jennie Thompson, of Garden Valley m ———— White; 2, Will Thompson; 3, Nannie Thompson m ———— ———— ;4, Tony Thompson; 5, Horace Thompson; 6, Ellis Thompson, of Grand Saline, Tex.) (c) Chapman Cozby (m Sallie Wynne and had; 1, Bascom Cozby, of Grand Saline, Aex.; 2, William Cozby); (d) Beauragard Cozby, d unm. Eliza Jane Tunnell married second, George W. Childers (d bef 1911) and had; (e) Josiah Childers, m Ida Clark and had a large family; (f) Araminta Childers, dead, m ———— McGraw and had ch; (g) Lycurgus Childers d at 14; (h) Ada Childers m William Jacobs and had a large family; (i) Eula Childers, dead (m Ambrose Clark and had; 1, Linnie Clark; 2, Preston Clark); (j) Sallie Childers m Charles Wright and had several children, some dying in infancy.

Two. Josiah Taylor Tunnell b May 3, 1873 in Ala.; d Feb. 13, 1911 Comanche Co., Tex.; married first, Kittie Stewart, Dec. 23, 1867 (d May 24, 1906) and second, ———— ————, abt 1909 and had no ch.

Three. Perry Wesley Tunnell b Aug. 20, 1839 Calhoun Co., Ala.; d Mar. 20, 1911 Bridgeport, Tex.; served as C. S. A. soldier; married first, Ellen Perry Dameron May 29, 1859 (d Feb. 1880 in Tex.) and had ch b in Tex.; (a) child d in inf.; (b) child d in inf.; (c) Reuben Wesley Tunnell b Dec. 3, 1865; d 1911 Mountain Home, Idaho, unm.; (d) Mary E. Tunnell b Jan. 10, 1868, once of Lewis, Kan., m Henry Drake and had eight ch; (e) William Tunnell b Jan. 5, 1870; (f) Bearon Asbur Tunnell b Jan. 30, 1872, m ——— ———; (g) Ida May Tunnell b Apr. 1874, of Bridgeport, Tex., m William Simpson and had six ch; (h) Robert Tunnell. Perry Wesley Tunnell married second, Sarah Creed, Sept. 15, 1880 and had; (i) Sarah Elizabeth Tunnell b Jan. 13, 1882 (m Hugh M. Smith Mar. 27, 1904 and had; 1, Carl Wesley Smith b Mar. 19, 1905; 2, Lawrence Chapman Smith b Feb. 20, 1907); (j) Sanford Perry Tunnell b Mar. 20, 1883, of Ft. Worth, Tex.; (k) Robert Pierce Tunnell b Sept. 29, 1884; (l) Jesse Ross Tunnell b July 25, 1886, m Ruth Angeline Papineau Sept. 8, 1913 Omaha, Neb.; (m) Eva Pauline Tunnell b, Apr. 26, 1888, of Eagle City, Okla., m F. Paul Middleton and had a son; (n) Thurmon Cornelius Tunnell b May 8, 1891; (o) Catherine Leona Tunnell m Ernest Koontz; (p) Fleeta Maxine Tunnell b Nov. 9, 1898; (q) child d in inf. P. W. Tunnell had at time of his death, 26 grandchildren and 2 great-grandchildren.

Four. Hannah Catherine Tunnell b June 10, 1842 in Ala.; d Jan. 1918 in Tex.; married Oliver H. P. Thomas, son of Stephen and Maria (Rogan) Thomas, Sept. 19, 1858 in Tex. (b Dec. 25, 1832; d June 14, 1899 Tex.(and had ch b Texas; (a) Cora C. Thomas b Apr. 8, 1800; d 1886 (m ——— Wade and had; 1, Bert Wade; 2, Floyd Wade; 3, Icie Wade, m ——— Rawlings, all of Temple, Tex.); (b) Flora Thomas b Oct. 8, 1862 d June 15, 1864; (c) Julius M. Thomas b Nov. 14, 1865, of Marshall, Tex. (m ——— ——— and had; 1, Wanda Thomas, of Rolla, Ala.; 2, Raymond Thomas, of Marshall, Tex.); (d) Theophilus H. Thomas b Oct. 1, 1867, of Lubbock, Tex. (m ——— and had; 1, Battle Thomas, of Paul's Valley, Okla.; 2, Pearl Thomas, m ——— Pool; 3, Lottie Thomas, of Lubbock, Tex.); (e) Fannie E. Thomas b Dec. 4, 1869; d Jan. 1919 (m ——— White and had; 1, Mabel White, m ——— O'Riley, of Beeville, Tex.; 2, Charles White); (f) Cyrus L. Thomas b Nov. 14, 1871, of Hot Springs, Ark. (m ——— ——— and had; 1, Oliver Thomas; 2, Ethel Thomas; 3, Martin Thomas; 4, Ruby Thomas; 5, Lilburn Thomas; 6, Wade Thomas); (g) May E. Thomas b Dec. 19, 1873, of Lindale, Tex. (m ——— Ellison and had; 1, Francis Ellison; 2, Earl Ellison; 3, Joe Ellison; 4, Harold Ellison; 5, L. J. Ellison); (h) Edgar O. Thomas b Dec. 9, 1875, of Garden Valley, Tex. (m ——— ——— and had; 1, Roland Thomas); (i) Hattie Thomas b Feb. 25, 1878, of Long View Tex. (m ——— Browning and had; 1, Merl Browning; 2, Morris Browning; 3, J. Oscar Browning; 4, Noel Browning; 5, Robert Browning); (j) Linch Thomas b Apr. 25, 1880; d Oct. 17, 1881; (k) Emma K. Thomas b May 31, 1882, of Garden Valley, Tex. (m ——— Dunn and had; 1, Ruby Dunn; 2, Henry Dunn; 3, Willis Dunn; 4, Douglas Dunn; 5, Luther Dunn; 6, Alma Dunn; 7, Mildred Dunn); (l) Charles Thomas b Apr. 12, 1886, of Garden Valley, Tex.

Five. Jesse Ellis Tunnell b Aug. 13, 1845 nr Jacksonville, Ala. of Whitney, Tex.; married Frances Ann Thomas, dau of Stephen and Maria (Rogan) Thomas, July 27, 1869 Smith Co., Tex. (b Jan. 27, 1849 Knoxville, Tenn.) and had ch b Comanche, Tex., save two; (a) Edna Ella Tunnell b June 14, 1870, of Whitney, Tex. (m first, Edward Benton Walker June 24, 1891 Dublin, Tex. (d May 16, 1918 Whitney, Tex.) and had no ch.; and m second, Dr. William Treat Mar. 7, 1921 (b Sept. 30, 1864 Sparta, Ill.); (b) Gaius Tunnell b Sept. 21, 1871, of Quitaque, Tex. (m Mary Hairston Aug. 7, 1901 Whitney, Tex. and had; 1, Ernest Benton Tunnell b June 7, 1902 Whitney, Tex., m Mai-

zine Graddy Nov. 3, 1924 Memphis, Tex.; 2, Clyde Alonzo Tunnell b
Dec. 29, 1904); (c) Judson Thomas Tunnell b June 18, 1873, of
Quitaque, Tex. (m Alice Lows Nov. 30, 1902 Electra, Tex. and had; 1,
Jesse Tunnell b Dec. 1903 Electra; 2, Curtis Tunnell b Aug. 7, 1905
Electra; 3, Edna Tunnell b Jan. 8, 1907 Eldorado, Tex.; 4, Doyle Tun-
nell b Jan. 21, 1909; 5, Cora Tunnell; 6, William Tunnell); (d) Cyrus
Alonzo Tunnell b Feb. 10, 1875, of Blackwell, Okla. (m Cartha
D'Spain, Apr. 27, 1898 and had; 1, Lloyd Tunnell b Mar. 7, 1899 De
Leon, Tex.; 2, Mary Elizabeth Tunnell b Sept. 11, 1911 Brownwood,
Tex.); (e) Maria Elizabeth Tunnell b Nov. 11, 1876; d 1878; (f)
Emmet Tunnell b Jan. 9, 1879, of Electra, Tex. (m Lizzie Greene Oct.
16, 1905 Electra, Tex. and had; 1, Edgar Tunnell b Jan. 6, 1907 Whit-
ney, Tex. and others b Electra; 2, Leola Tunnell b July 12, 1908; 3,
Alma Tunnell b Nov. 29, 1909; 4, E. B. Tunnell b June 13, 1911; 5,
Ruth Tunnell; 6, Robert Tunnell; 7, Dorothy Nell Tunnell; 8, Ray
Tunnell; 9, Loveta Tunnell); (g) James Lynn Tunnell b Feb. 18,
1881, of Quitaque, Tex. (m Beatrice Boll Dec. 8, 1907 and had; 1,
Olga Tunnell b Dec. 16, 1911; 2, Amelia Tunnell); (h) Effie Jane
Tunnell b May 22, 1883; d Aug. 19, 1913 Dallas, Tex. (m Jesse Whit-
field Harris June 25, 1905 Whitney, Tex. and had; 1, Florrie Harris b
July 24, 1907 Midland, Tex.; 2, J. W. Harris b July 13, 1911 Dallas,
Tex.); (i) Ivy Tunnell b May 14, 1885, of Whitney, Tex. (m Francis
Erastus Russell May 10, 1903 Electra, Tex. and had; 1, Frances
Russell b June 2, 1904 Vernon, Tex.; 2, Myrtle Russell b Oct. 8, 1906
San Angelo, Tex.; 3, Bernice Russell b June 12, 1910 Chapin, Tex.; 4,
Dorothy Russell b Aug. 1, 1913 Whitney, Tex.; 5, Frank Edwin Rus-
sell b Feb. 2, 1916 Whitney, Tex.); (j) Myrtle Tunnell b Feb. 6, 1887,
of Waco, Tex., m W. H. Billington July 2, 1922 Whitney, Tex.; (k)
Jesse Franks Tunnell b Aug. 6, 1889 Dublin, Tex., of Quitaque (m
Emma Strawn Oct. 1, 1911 Electra, Tex. and had 1, Jack Tunnell b
Aug. 1912 Electra; 2, Robbie Joe Tunnell b Oct. 1916 Electra; 3,
James Franks Tunnell b June 10, 1918 Whitney, Tex.); (l) Amber
Tunnell b Oct. 18, 1891 De Leon, Tex., of Whitney, Tex. (m Thomas
Basham Sept. 30, 1907 Whitney and had ch b Whitney; 1, Eugene
Basham b Feb. 12, 1909; 2, Thomas Frederick Basham b Nov. 16,
1913; 3, Charles Tunnell Basham b June 14, 1915; 4, William Francis
Basham b Dec. 2, 1916; 5, Nell Basham b July 8, 1923).

Six.   John Blue Tunnell b Mar. 8, 1848 Ala.; d June 1913 Comanche, Tex.; married first, Sarah Frances Indiana Albin Dec. 8, 1871
in Tex., who d abt 1880, and had; (a) Ira Otis Tunnell b 1873, of
Comanche, Tex., m Minnie McDomott; (b) Ada Leah Tunnell b 1876
(m E. Drake and had; 1, Vernon C. Drake b 1900; d July 1910; 2, J.
B. Drake b 1903; 3, Bob E. Drake b 1908). John Blue Tunnell married
second, Jennie Hawkins Brodie Feb. 20, 1883 and had; (c) Clara
Edith Tunnell b Mar. 22, 1885 (m Jabez M. Smith Feb. 1, 1905 and
had; 1, Jennie Margaret Smith Aug. 15, 1907; 2, Mina Louise Smith
b Sept. 22, 1908); (d) Merline Kent Tunnell b Sept. 18, 1886; (e)
Jennie Blue Tunnell b Dec. 4, 1888, of Ft. Worth, Tex.; (f) William
Brodie Tunnell b 1891; d Jan. 15, 1904 Comanche, Tex.

Seven.   Gideon Asbury Tunnell b Nov. 26, 1850 Smith Co., Tex.,
of Gustine, Tex.; married Bettie Briscoe Dec. 25, 1873 and had ch b
Comanche Co., Tex.; (a) Flora B. Tunnell b Feb. 11, 1876, of Gustine,
Tex. (m J. D. Couch Nov. 1899 Comanche Co. and had; 1, Virgil
Couch; 2, Walter B. Couch; 3, Imogene Couch; 4, Jesse H. Couch; 5,
Sanford Couch; 6, J. D. Couch; 7, Blanton Couch); (b) Edgar S.
Tunnell b Feb 19, 1879, of Stephensville, Tex. (m ——— ——— Dec.
1896 and had; 1, Amaret Tunnell; 2, Fleda Tunnell; 3, Teresa Tun-
nell); (c) Emma A. Tunnell b Nov. 12, 1881, of Gustin, Tex. (m R. H.

Ashmore Dec. 1901 and had; 1, Lucile Ashmore, of Ft. Worth, Tex., m W. R. Upham June 1921 and had; (aa) Clayton Upham; 2, Helma Ashmore b Dawson Co., Tex.; 3, Pauline Ashmore b Comanche Co., Tex.); (d) Ada E. Tunnell b Sept. 18, 1887. of Comanche, Tex. (m J. O. Allen Sept. 1904 and had; 1, Lurline Allen; 2, Bessie Allen; 3, G. A. Allen); (e) Lavora Tunnell b Sept. 21, 1890, of Georgetown, Tex. (m P. J. Parker and had; 1, Tom Jack Parker b Dec. 6, 1912).

Eight. Narcissa Emeline Tunnell b June 8, 1853 in Tex.; d Apr. 15, 1854 in Tex.

Nine. Rev. James Sanford Tunnell b Apr. 12, 1855 Smith Co., Tex. d Mar. 9, 1910 at Methodist parsonage, Ranger, Tex. He joined the Northwest Texas Conference Nov. 1879 and served a number of pastorates. He married Nellie Marbry Dec. 25, 1881 Burnet, Tex. (b Jan. 16, 1858 Caldwell Co., Tex., now of Cisco, Tex.) and had; (a) Gladys De Maris Tunnell b Nov. 11, 1882 Burnet, Tex., of Strawn, Tex. (m Granville Lee Rice Apr. 7, 1901, Gordon, Tex. and had; 1, Gladys Cleo Rice b Mar. 21, 1902 Gordon, Tex.; 2, Esma Lee Rice b July 21, 1903, m Victor Echholm June 19, 1924 Strawn, Tex.; 3, Granville Lee Rice, the second, b Sept. 22, 1905 Strawn, Tex.; d Apr. 12, 1907 Strawn; 4, Otis Tunnell Rice b Sept. 15, 1907); (b) Avis De Loris Tunnell b Dec. 13, 1884 Liberty Hill, Tex., of Valley Mills, Tex. (m Robert Hiram Bruce Feb. 20, 1907 Morgan, Tex. and had ch b Valley, Mills; 1, dau b and d Feb. 26, 1911; 2, Robert Hiram Bruce, the second, b Sept. 17, 1916); (c) Florrie Alva Tunnell b Feb. 26, 1887 Burnet, Tex., of Ranger, Tex. (m John Shelby McDowell June 1, 1913 Strawn, Tex. and had; 1, Cecelia Shellene McDowell b Nov. 15, 1921 Ranger, Tex.); (d) Sanford Bishop Annis Tunnell b Oct. 6, 1892 Boonville, Tex., of Dallas, Tex. (m Leone Pedigo Oct. 19, 1917 Ft. Worth, Tex.); (e) Buford James Alvan Tunnell b Dec. 8, 1896 Mineral Wells, Tex., of Ranger, Tex.; (f) Olin J. S. Tunnell b Feb. 28, 1902 Gordon, Tex., of Cisco, Tex.

Ten. Miles Columbus Tunnell b Apr. 25, 1858 Smith Co., Tex.; d Apr. 1859 Smith Co., Tex.

IV. Elisha Tunnell, son of Perry and Catherine Self Tunnell, was born Apr. 13, 1814 in Ala. and died Mar. 15, 1884 Comanche Co., Tex. He married Nancy Ellis, sister of Elizabeth Ellis, Dec. 25, 1833 (d Nov. 1890 in Tex.) and had 9 children;

One. Caroline Melissa Tunnell b July 19, 1834 Ala.; d July 1870 Smith Co., Tex.; married Robert Greer Stewart 1852 Smith Co., Tex. and had ch b Smith Co.; (a) Levi Franklin Stewart b Aug. 7, 1855; d Aug 9, 1893 Red River Co., Tex. (m Mrs. Irene Stephenson 1882 and had; 1, Elbert Stewart, dead; 2, Offie Stewart; 3, Effie Stewart; 4, Levi Stewart; 5, Melissa Stewart; 6, Victoria Stewart); (b) Nancy Letitia Stewart b Aug. 6, 1857, of Potosi, Tex. (m Thomas Chappell Cox June 20, 1877 nr Tyler, Tex. and had; 1, Nellie Cox b July 7, 1879, of Blythe, Calif. m Walter Prather Aug. 17, 1898 Potosi, Tex. and had; (aa) Jessie Esther Prather b Apr. 16, 1900, m A. Knolly Feb. 19, 1919 Peora, Arizona; (bb) Leona Bethel Prather b Mar. 4, 1902 Potosi, Tex., m Holly Smith Dec. 1922 Blythe, Calif. and had, Leona Evelyn Smith b Aug. 22, 1923; (cc) Flora Mae Prather b Dec. 24, 1903 Potosi, Tex., (m Joe Mead Mar. 13, 1924 Blythe, Calif.; (dd) Oscar Julian Prather b Dec. 30, 1905 Fisher Co., Tex.; (ee) Ray Prather b Aug. 17, 1907 New Mexico; (ff) Walter Ralph Prather b Oct. 24, 1909; (gg) Buford Prather b 1912 Howard Co., Tex.; (hh) Glen Upton Prather b June 5, 1914 Howard Co., Tex.; (ii) Otis Ford Prather b June 26, 1916 Howard Co., Tex.; (jj) Bonnie Nell Prather b May 18, 1918 nr Sulphur, Okla.; (kk) Marian Lois Prather b Oct. 5, 1922 Peora, Ariz.; 2, Mary Malissa Cox b Aug. 17, 1883 Potosi, Tex., m Walter Brooks

Oct. 20, 1912 and had; (aa) Chalmo Lee Brooks b Sept. 9, 1913; (bb)
Easter F. Brooks b 1914; (cc) Faris Caldwell Brooks b Feb. 19, 1916;
(dd) Roy Cullen Brooks b May 1919; (ee) Lelia Dorothea Brooks b
Feb. 12, 1921; (ff) Walter Quinton Brooks b May 23, 1923; 3, Robert
Franklin Cox b June 28, 1885 Potosi, Tex.; 4, Marvin Chappell Cox b
Aug. 18, 1887, of Cuthbert, Tex., m Emma Reed Dec. 1920 and had;
(aa) Thurman Lee Cox b Sept. 27, 1921; (bb) General Calvin Cox b
Feb. 27, 1923; (c) Emma Audell Cox b Nov. 3, 1924; Stephen Blake
Cox b Mar. 21, 1889, served overseas in 36th Division in World War;
6, Thomas Greer Cox b Mar. 7, 1891, served overseas in World War;
7, Ernest Lee Cox b Jan. 30. 1893, served in 36th Div. Supply Co.
overseas in World War, m Willie Clements Dec. 10, 1922 and had; (aa)
Hester Ada Cox b Jan 28, 1925; 8, Chole Camilla Cox b Mar. 31, 1895,
of Potosi, Tex., m Fay Brooks Oct. 24, 1915 and had ch b nr Potosi,
(aa) Jessie Fay Brooks b Aug. 9, 1916; (bb) Stephen Lee Brooks b
Nov. 8, 1917; (cc) Augusta Letitia Brooks b Sept. 17, 1919; (dd)
Donald Stewart Brooks b Nov. 15, 1921; (ee) Willard Wayne Brooks
b Aug. 21, 1923; 9, Mattie Lois Cox b Mar. 19, 1897, of Potosi, Tex.,
m Henry Etheredge May 28, 1915 and had ch b nr Potosi; (aa) Edgar
Earl Etheredge b Feb. 27, 1916; (bb) Glenn L. Etheredge b July 17,
1917; (cc) Winnie Dell Etheredge b Aug. 23, 1920; (c) Stephen
Ellen Stewart b May 5, 1861 Smith Co., Tex., of Garden Valley, Tex.
(m Ella Sanders Feb. 22, 1887 Van Zandt Co., Tex. (b Apr. 2, 1866)
and had ch b Van Zandt Co.; 1, Robert Franklin Stewart b Dec. 22,
1887, minister, of Dodge, Tex., m Cora Reynolds in V. Z. Co. and had;
(aa) Juanita Stewart b Mar. 16, 1916; (bb) Ouitah Stewart b Feb. 21,
1919; 2, Ammie Vida Stewart b Jan. 30, 1890; d Nov. 1, 1918 (m
Hamp Keahy Dec. 22, 1907, of Garden Valley, Tex. and had ch b
V. Z. Co.; (aa) Coy Ivan Keahy b Mar. 18, 1909; (bb) Stephen Orville
Keahy b Aug. 2, 1910; (cc) Woodrow Cornelius Keahy b Sept. 13,
1912; (dd) Royce Keahy b Aug. 14, 1914; (ee) Eulis Hamp Keahy b
Jan. 20, 1917; 3, Winnie Cleophas Stewart b Sept. 16, 1892; d June
28, 1913; 4, Ethel May Stewart b Nov. 28, 1894, unm., of Garden
Valley, Tex.; 5, Nancy Melissa Stewart b Jan. 25, 1897, of Corpus
Christi, Tex., m Karl Dove Nov. 1917 Van Zandt Co., Tex. and had;
(aa) Ernestine Dove b Sept. 13, 1919 V. Z. Co.; (bb) Joe Randall
Dove b Mar. 26, 1922 V. Z. Co.; (cc) Dee Dove b Sept. 9, 1924 Corpus
Christi, Tex.); (d) Melissa Stewart b Sept. 9, 1866; d Mar. 30, 1885
V. Z. Co., m Robert Beggs and had no ch.; (e) Samuel Martin
Stewart, of Grady, New Mexico (m first, Lizzie Geddie (b Oct. 18,
1877; d Nov. 28, 1902) and had; 1, Uel Stewart b Oct. 31, 1896; d Mar.
30, 1898; 2, Urie Stewart b Mar. 14, 1899; d July 18, 1900; 3, Lennie
Stewart b Jan. 24, 1901; d Oct. 20, 1902; and m second, Katie Newbill,
and had; 4, Ruby Stewart; 5, Winnie Stewart; 6, Buren Stewart)

Two. Reuben Smith Tunnell b Dec. 11, 1837, served in C. S. A.
as Lieut.-Colonel, from Smith Co., Tex. and was killed at the battle
of Franklin; unmarried.

Three. Martin Luther Tunnell b Sept. 22, 1842; d Mar. 1863, in
Arkansas; unmarried.

Four. Rosa M. Tunnell b Apr. 6, 1846; d Nov. 1865 in Tex.; married T. M. Presley May 1865 in Tex. and had no ch.

Five. Stephen Bailey Tunnell b Sept. 24, 1849, of Grand Saline,
Tex.; married Mary Louise Turner Feb. 28, 1871 (d Oct. 28, 1909)
and had ch b Garden Valley, Tex.; (a) Oscar A. Tunnell b Nov. 18,
1871, of Ada, Okla. (m first, Fay Niblack (deceased) and had; 1,
Bruce Tunnell, dead; 2, Fay Tunnell, dead; and m second, Rosa
Shields, and had; 3, Alvis Tunnell, m ———————; 4, Sarah Tunnell;
5, Frances Tunnell); (b) Mattie Ophelia Tunnell b Feb. 26, 1873, of

Dallas, Tex. (m Jerome M. Stone 1887 (d Jan. 31, 1923 Garden Valley, Tex.) and had; 1, Mabel Earl Stone b Apr. 29, 1889; d Sept. 24, 1889; 2, Jerome Percy Stone b Sept. 18, 1890, of Dallas, Tex., m Inez Edwards Jan. 1915 Tyler, Tex. and had; (aa) Lois Evelyn Stone b Nov. 8, 1915 Tyler, Tex.; 3, Clota Stone b Aug. 18, 1892; d Oct. 6, 1911, m Edwin B. O'Quinn Nov. 6, 1910 and had no ch; 4, Julia Stone b July 26, 1894, of El Paso, Tex m Leonard C. Barrow Jan. 31, 1920 Tyler, Tex. and had no ch.; 5, Horace Bailey Stone b Oct. 8, 1896, of Dallas, Tex., served in World War, m Elizabeth Copeland Apr. 23, 1919 and had; (aa) Mary Beth Stone b Aug. 1, 1922; 6, Clyde Turner Stone b Sept. 26, 1898, served overseas in World War, of El Paso, Tex., m Thelma Coats Oct. 21, 1921 and had no ch.; 7, Fay Stone b Sept. 16, 1900, m R. Irvin Wright Dec. 18, 1920 Winnsboro, Tex. and had; (aa) Martha Ellen Wright b Mar. 25, 1924; 8, Melvin Russell Stone b Apr. 15, 1904, m Zera Boxx July 18, 1924 Nevada, Tex.); (c) Harry Matthews Tunnell b Sept. 1, 1876, of Dallas, Tex. (m Laura Bail.ff at Garden Valley, Tex. and had; 1, Frank Tunnell; 2, Harry Neill Tunnell; 3, Jack Tunnell; 4, Joe Tunnell); (d) Joseph Russell Tunnell b Sept. 27, 1878, of Dallas, Tex. (m Mittie Veasey at Garden Valley and had; 1, Maurine Tunnell b Sept. 15, 1900; 2, Mary Louise Tunnell b 1915; 3, Nell Douglass Tunnell); (e) Nancy Louisa Tunnell b Mar. 6, 1883; d abt 1886 Garden Valley, Tex.; (f) Eugene Bailey Tunnell b Aug. 2, 1885, of Tyler, Tex. (m Frances Jackson May 1913 Fort Worth, Tex. and had; 1, Frances Eugenia Tunnell b Sept. 24, 1915 Garden Valley); (g) Lillie Maud Tunnell b Oct. 28, 1887, of Grand Saline, Tex., m John E. Caldwell Apr. 21, 1918 Grand Saline, Tex. and had no ch.)

Six. Commodore Washington Tunnell b Dec. 28, 1852 Smith Co., Tex., of Garden Valley, Tex.; married Harriet Rebecca Rusk, dau of Capt. John C. Rusk and granddau General Thomas J. Rusk, for whom Rusk Co., Tex., was named, Dec. 5, 1875 Nacoydoches Co., Tex. (d June 12, 1924 Garden Valley) and had ch b Garden Valley; (a) Edward Cicero Tunnell b Mar. 23, 1877, of Colorado, Tex. (m Maggie Green Oct. 19, 1902 Van Zandt Co., Tex. and had; 1, Maggie Arl.ne Tunnell b Feb. 24, 1916; 2, Iris Rebecca Tunnell b Jan. 3, 1915); (b) Leonard Tunnell b Nov. 7, 1878 (m Lillie Mae Germany Mar. 26, 1905 Van Zandt Co. and had ch b that county; 1, Lois May Tunnell b Dec. 16, 1905; 2, Jennie Rebecca Tunnell b Dec. 17, 1907; 3, Wilson Tunnell b June 30, 1910; 4, Maxwell Leonard Tunnell b Jan. 21, 1913; 5, Marian Dorothy Tunnell b Nov. 27, 1915; 6, Perry Russell Tunnell b Oct. 8, 1919; 7, child b Jan. 7, 1923 d Jan 10, 1923; 8, Lillie Annie Tunnell b Apr. 22, 1924)· (c) Martin Luther Tunnell b May 2, 1881 (m Maud May White Dec. 25, 1901 Van Zandt Co. and had; 1, Cleo White Tunnell b Nov. 14, 1902, m Evelyn Dawson Sept. 3, 1923; 2, Commodore Nobel Tunnell b Oct. 14, 1905; 3, Andrew Bridges Tunnell b Dec. 14, 1907; 4, Luther Bryce Tunnell b Sept. 10, 1910; d Feb. 1912); (d) Homer Elisha Tunnell b Apr. 5, 1883 (m Bertha Olive Cade Sept. 21, 1902 Van Zandt Co., Tex. and had ch b that county; 1, Dee Roy Tunnell b Sept. 9, 1903; 2, Helena Florine Tunnell b July 2, 1905; 3, Commodore Seldon Tunnell b July 18, 1907; 4, Harry Cade Tunnell b Nov. 27, 1909; 5, Ruth Tunnell b Jan. 5, 1912; 6, Richard Tunnell b Aug. 28, 1913; 7. Clora Maud Tunnell b Mar. 26, 1916; 8, Joe Tunnell b June 4, 1918; 9, Marnell Tunnell b Aug. 1, 1920); (e) Nancy Helena Tunnell b Aug. 1, 1885, of Edgewood, Tex. (m Oscar William Pitts Dec. 24, 1905 V. Z. Co., and had; 1, Oscar William Pitts Jr. b Aug. 17, 1906; 2, Martin Lewis P tts b June 12, 1908; d Feb. 20, 1912); (f) Marian Argen Tunnell b Feb. 28, 1888; d Dec. 17, 1888; (g) Henry Cullen Tunnell b Nov. 3, 1889, m Dora

Bailey May 3, 1914 and had; 1, Dora Grace Tunnell b Apr. 18, 1915; 2, Cullen Bailey Tunnell b Oct. 11, 1917; 3, Chlocilia Tonita Tunnell b Dec. 21, 1919; 4, Birdie Rebecca Tunnell b May 13, 1922); (h) Clarence Rusk Tunnell b Apr. 24, 1897, (m Nannie Olive Woods Dec. 27, 1914 and had; 1, Forest Truman Tunnell b Oct. 6, 1915; 2, Corinne Rebecca Tunnell b Feb. 19, 1917; 3, Margie Laverne Tunnell b Feb. 11, 1919; 4, Mary Lou Tunnell b Dec. 15, 1920); (i) Commodore Forest Tunnell b Oct. 15. 1896 (m Ruth Skiles and had; 1, Nancy Christine Tunnell b Oct. 24, 1917; 2, Brady Virgil Tunnell b Oct. 23, 1919; 3, Helen Bernice Tunnell b Nov. 25, 1922); (j) Birdie Eulacia Tunnell b Jan. 23, 1898, of Garden Valley, Tex. (m Robert Farris Wilson Mar. 19, 1919, who d May 10, 1924, and had; 1, Bobbye Rebecca Wilson b Dec. 31, 1919); (k) Harriet Ann Tunnell b July 27, 1900; d Dec. 28, 1900; (l) Mary Rebecca Tunnell b Apr. 13, 1903.

Seven. David Fisher Tunnell b Feb. 26, 1856, of Dallas, Tex.; married Nancy Ann Jordan Feb. 23, 1883 and had; (a) Fisher Ethan Tunnell b Sept. 5, 1884, once of San Antonio, Tex., m Lillian Mae Money Apr. 10, 1910; (b) Ommie May Tunnell b Oct. 22, 1887, m Charles E. Uglow Dec. 6, 1904 and had; 1, Florabel Uglow b June 18, 1910; (c) Cammie Lee Tunnell b Mar. 17, 1890; (d) Miriam Janie Tunnell b Sept. 29, 1893; (e) Gordon Birdwell Tunnell b July 17, 1898.

Eight. Mariam Easter Tunnell b Apr. 24, 1859 Smith Co., Tex.; d Oct. 22, 1893 nr Canton ,Tex; married John Stephen Thorn Aug. 3, 1876 (d Aug. 16, 1849 Nacoydoches, Tex.; d Dec. 24, 1922) and had ch b nr Canton, Tex.; (a) Annie Thorn b July 7, 1877, of Grand Saline, Tex. (m Dr. William Henry Terry July 22, 1894 and had; 1, Floyd Terry b June 5, 1897; d Sept. 26, 1918 Great Lakes Training Station, Chicago, Ill.; 2, Chloe Terry b July 7, 1900, of Waxahachie, Tex., m Dr. W. M. Ray Dec. 19, 1920 and had; (aa) Floyd Ray b Sept. 23, 1922; 3, Cecil Terry b July 17, 1906; d Oct. 9, 1908; 4, Albert Early Terry b Sept. 21, 1909; 5, Henry Hal Terry b Aug. 27, 1912); (b) Charles Thorn b Aug. 3, 1879, of Tyler, Tex. (m Epsie Gentry and had; 1, Virginia Thorn; 2. Lula Thorn); (c) Reuben Thorn b Jan. 28, 1882, of Dallas, Tex. (m Etta Castleberry and had; 1, Child, dead; 2, Margie Thorn, m ———— ————; 3, John Thorn, twin of Margie Thorn; and another.); (d) Pearl Thorn, of Tyler, Tex. (m Ocie C. Kidd and had ch.); (e) Carlie Thorn b Jan. 13, 1889, of Canton, Tex. (m J. H. Fortune and had ch b Colfax, Tex.; 1, Ruth Ellena Fortune b Dec. 11. 1907, of Waxahachie, Tex., m Graydon McPhail Aug. 30, 1924 at Colfax, Tex.; 2, Clyde Henry Fortune b June 4, 1914; 5, Anith Fadine Fortune b Jan. 26, 1917; 6. Lula Bernice Fortune b Dec. 1, 1920; 7, Margery Eva Joe Fortune b Oct. 3, 1924.)

Nine. Amphias Seaton Tunnell b Nov. 25, 1862, of Tyler, Tex.; married first, Sallie Rosenbam (deceased); and second, May Petty (deceased); and third, Mrs. Zola Johnson, and had no children.

V. Enoch Tunnell, son of Perry and Catherine Self Tunnell, was born abt 1816 in Ala. and died in Tex.   He married Louisa Clark in Ala., who d in Tex. and had eight ch., oldest b Ala., others Texas.

One. William R Tunnell, of Grand Saline, Tex.; married Bettie Rose and had ch b Texas; (a) Riley Tunnell, of Garden Valley, Tex. (m Ollie Hentley and had ch b Texas; 1, Hubert Tunnell, m Randa Petty; 2, Onie Mae Tunnell; 3. Woodrow Tunnell; 4, Clota Tunnell; 5, Mary Tunnell); (b) Frank Tunnell, unm., of Garden Valley, Tex.; (c) Alice Tunnell, of Clovis. New Mex., m H. D. Reeves; (d) Leila Tunnell, of Garden Valley. Tex.. m T. J. Land; (e) Lucy Tunnell, of Grand Saline, Tex.. m J. N. Rhodes, (f) Myrtle Tunnell, of Garden Valley, Tex., m J. F. Elliot; (g) Sidney Tunnell.

Two. Riley Tunnell, of Tyler, Tex.; married Dodie Dowis and had ch b Texas; (a) Bunyan Tunnell, merchant, Garden Valley, Tex. (m Lora George and had; 1, Preston Tunnell, m Jessie Busby; 2, Haskell Tunnell, m Golda Swain and had; (aa) Kerney Tunnell; 3, Homer Tunnell m Ivy White and had; (aa) Marie Tunnell; 4, Myrtle Tunnell, m Rufus Welmaker; 5, Ruby Tunnell; 6, Merle Tunnell, all of Garden Valley); (b) John Milton Tunnell b Sept. 18, 1875 Smith Co., Tex., merchant, Paducah, Tex. (m Montie Kidd Dec. 22, 1895 and had; 1, Delphia Lavonia Tunnell b Nov. 20, 1895, of Denver, Col., m W. W. Latham, with Col. Nat. Bank, and had; (aa) Dorothy Janet Latham b Nov. 6, 1923 Denver, Col.; 2, Holland Bloomer Tunnell b July 18, 1902 Van Zandt Co., Tex., m Ruby Higby Oct. 20, 1922 Tyler, Tex. and had; (aa) Charles Holland Tunnell b June 22, 1923 Tyler, Tex.); Ezra Tunnell, of Dallas, Tex. (m Ola Crimm and had; 1, Dodie Tunnell; 2, Exa Tunnell; 3, Perry Tunnell; 4, Elvie Tunnell); (d) Vannie Tunnell, Methodist minister, Waco, Tex. (m Ida Swindall and had; 1, Coma Tunnell; 2, Leta Tunnell; 3, Lucille Tunnell); (e) Chester Tunnell, of Tyler, Tex. (m Zora White and had; 1, Perry Tunnell; 2, Wilson Tunnell; 3, Alphonso Tunnell); (f) Della Tunnell, of Grand Saline, Tex., m R. E. Collatt; (g) Willie Tunnell, of Garden Valley, Tex., m T. J. Howell).

Three. Perry Tunnell, a Methodist minister, died in Tex.; married Henrietta Zorn, now of Tyler, Tex., and had no ch.

Four. Wilson B. Tunnell, of Garden Valley, Tex.; married Emma Gilliam and had ch b Tex.; (a) E. R. Tunnell, of faculty of Lindale, Tex. schools (m Pearl Haddock and had ch b Tex.; 1, Gladys Tunnell, of Tyler, Tex., m Leo Prater; 2, Alton Tunnell; 3, Daphne Tunnell); (b) Fisher Tunnell. merchant of Myrtle Springs, Tex. (m Lora Paschall and had; 1, Winnie Tunnell, of Terrell, Tex., m Floyd Cleveland; 2, Merle Tunnell; 3, Opal Tunnell; 4, Loyd Tunnell; 5, Lavon Tunnell); (c) Grover Tunnell m Ora Wells and had no ch.

Five. Arthur Tunnell, of Garden Valley, Tex.; married Jimmie Henry and had; (a) Harvey Tunnell (m Lola Maxfield and had; 1, Chloe Tunnell; 2, Coy Tunnell; 3, Cleon Tunnell; 4, Doyle Tunnell; 5, Winifred Tunnell; 6, Astor Tunnell; 7, Teddy Tunnell); (b) Bon F. Tunnell b Jan. 7, 1890 Van, Tex. Supt. Lewisville, Tex. schools (m Edna Bracken Sept. 24, 1913 and had; 1. Bon F. Tunnell, the second, b Dec. 22, 1920); (c) Eldon Tunnell, of Grand Saline, Tex. (m Lillian Dickard and had three ch. (d) Osie Tunnell, of Grand Saline, Tex., m —–––– Carter; (e) Lillie Tunnell, of Terrell, Tex., m George Mayo; (f) Lattie Tunnell, of Garden Valley, Tex.. m Sherdy Jackson; (g) Roland Tunnell; (h) Virgie Tunnell; (i) Marvin Tunnell.

Six. Joshua Tunnell died in Tex.; married Cynthia Morgan and had; (a) Ollie Tunnell, of Grand Saline, Tex., m James McKinzie; (b) Effie Tunnell, of Lindale. Tex.. m J. J. Brawner; (c) Dempsey Tunnell, of Crandall, Tex. (m Ludie Hancock and had; 1, Alta Tunnell; 2. Cleo Tunnell; 3. Dempsey M. Tunnell; 4, Howard Tunnell); (d) Mack Tunnell of Garden Valley, Tex (m Emma Davis and had; 1, Guy Tunnell; 2, Mildred Tunnell); (e) Sterling Tunnell, m Dussie Jarman; (f) Pierce Tunnell (m Lora Fowler and had; 1, Gloy Tunnell; 2. Olga Lee Tunnell, 3, Eva Tunnell; 4, Park Tunnell; 5, Billy Tunnell)

Seven. Martha Tunnell died in Tex.; married Arthur Gilliam, who d in Tex.

Eight. Mary Tunnell died in Tex.; married C. E. Neill, who d in Texas.

VI. Josiah Tunnell, son of Perry and Catherine Self Tunnell, was born Feb. 3, in Ala. In 1911 he lived in Garden Valley, Tex. and died there. He married Nancy Welch Dec. 27, 1838, who d in Texas, and had 5 ch b in Tex., all dead but one in 1911. He had grandch.; 1, Harriet Winston Tunnell b 1841, m William Wade 2, daughter b 1843; d in inf.; 3, William I. P. Tunnell b 1845; 4, Thomas M. Tunnell b 1849, m Mary E. Mosley 1868; 5, Mollie E. Tunnell b 1855, m Newton Wade.

VII. Stephen Tunnell, son of Perry and Catherine Self Tunnell, a Methodist minister, was born abt 1819 in Ala. and died abt 1900 in Tex. At one time he lived Bridgeport, Tex. He married Elizabeth ——— and had ch.

VIII. Nancy Tunnell, dau of Perry and Catherine Self Tunnell, was born Sept. 27, 1821 Ala. and died Jan. 1894 in Tex. She married Samuel Prather abt 1841 in Ala. (b Feb. 9, 1817; d abt 1866 Dallas Co., Tex.) and had seven ch.

One. Catherine Prather b Nov. 4, 1842, dead; married first, Dr. J. B. Morris 1861 ('d 1865) and had; (a) John Morris died in Okla. m Ann Wise and had a son, who d young; and m second, Hamilton Jones.

Two. Rev. J. Ellis Prather b Feb. 15, 1845; d abt 1922 New Mex. married ——— ——— now of Alamagordo, N. Mex. and had; (a) S. T. Prather; (b) J. A. Prather; (c) Mattie Prather; (d) Maggie Prather; (e) Owen Prather; (f) Jennie Prather.

Three. C. R. Prather, died unm.

Four. Riley Benton Prather b Mar. 10, 1848 Smith Co., Tex.; d Apr. 30, 1918 Van Zandt Co., Tex.; married first, Alva Ophelia Darnell Mar. 10, 1869 (d Apr. 6, 1886) and had; (a) Eugene F. Prather b July 11, 1873, of Tabler, Okla. (m first Lelia Cumbie Nov. 25, 1900 (d Sept. 25, 1901) and had; 1, child b and d same day; and m second, Floy Duncan and had: 2, Lee Neil Prather b Oct. 8, 1904; 3, Nett'e Ophelia Prather b Mar. 8, 1910; 4, Fay Prather b Dec. 14, 1912; 5, Noble Prather b Dec. 5, 1914. all in V. Z. Co.; 6, Riley Thomas Prather b July 4, 1916; 7, Eugene Victor Prather b Oct. 11, 1918; 8, Samuel Benton Prather b Sept. 18, 1920; 9, Dorothy Bernice Prather b Oct. 28, 1922, all in Dallas Co.; Ark.; 10, son d in inf.); (b) Maggie Prather b abt 1875 (c) Tom E. Prather, of Altus, Okla., m Mae Bailey and had four sons; (d) Nelia Prather, of Altus, Okla. m Wilk Muse and had six ch.; (e) Luther Prather died 1910; (f) Zora Prather b 1884, of Edgewood, Tex. (m William Stephens and had; 1, William Stephens Jr. b May 31, 1905; 2, Thelma Stephens (son) b Apr. 24, 1907). Riley Benton Prather married second, Mrs. Elvira Davis Mar. 17, 1895, now of Tabler, Okla., and had; (g) Artie Prather b Jan./9, 1898; (h) Samuel Joseph Prather b Dec. 25, 1905.

Five. S. Bowden Prather b Mar. 16, 1852, of Luther, Tex.; married Josie Wallis (d Feb. 10, 1919) and had; (e) Walter Prather, of Blytheville, Calif. (m Nellie Cox, dau Thomas Chappell and Nancy Letitia (Stewart) Cox, Aug. 17, 1898 and had; 1, Jessie Esther Prather b Apr. 16, 1900, m A. Knolly Feb. 19, 1919 Peora, Ariz.; 2, Leona Bethel Prather b Mar. 4, 1902 Potosi, Tex., m Holly Smith Dec. 1922 Blythe, Calif. and had; (aa) Leona Evelyn Smith b Aug. 22, 1923; 3, Flora Mae Prather b Dec. 24, 1903 Potosi, Tex., m Joe Mead Mar. 13, 1924 Blythe, Calif.; 4, Oscar Julian Prather b Dec. 30, 1905 Fisher Co., Tex. 5, Ray Prather b Aug. 17, 1907 New Mex.; 6, Walter Ralph Prather b Oct. 24, 1909; 7, Buford Prather b 1912; 8, Glen Upton Prather b June 5, 1914; 9, Otis Ford Prather b June 26, 1916, all in Howard Co., Tex.; 10, Bonnie Nell Prather b May 18, 1918 Sulphur, Okla.; 11, Marian Lois Prather b Oct. 5, 1922 Peora, Ariz.) (b) Ara Prather, of Big Springs, Tex. (m Will Solomon 'and had; 1, Pauline Solomon; 2, Frank Solomon; 3, Richard Solomon; 4, Willie Solomon; 5, Robert Solomon; 6, Naomi Solomon; 7, Lois Solomon; 8, Jack

Solomon); (c) Samuel B. Prather b 1879; d 1892; (d) Obed Prather, of Luther, Tex. (m Mable Guthrie and had; 1, Cyril Prather; 2, Caroline Prather); (e) Irene Prather (m Buck Bridges and had; 1, Lucille Bridges; 2. ⌐ ˙ h Bridges; 3, Sybil Bridges; 4, Jack Bridges; 5, Ros-Bridges; 2, Ralph Bridges; 3, Sybil Bridges; 4, Jack Bridges; 5, Rosdred Brown and had; 1, Dorothy Lou Prather); (g) Nora Prather b 1889; d Oct. 1889; (h) Omar Prather, of McCaulley, Tex. (m Minnie Mustain and had; 1, Leroy Prather; 2, Nellie Prather); (i) Eunice Prather, of Amarillo, Tex. (m Fred Bremer and had; 1, Norvill Bremer); (j) Lon Prather, of Big Springs, Tex. (m Rose Kerns and had; 1, Lloyd Prather; 2, Eunice Prather); (k) Della Prather (m Tom Stayner and had; 1, Askelin Stayner; 2, Randall Stayner); (l) Dolph Prather, of Biσ Springs, Tex. (m Ruth Malone and had; 1, Nookie Prather; 2. Etta Prather).

Six. Texana Prather; married Ed Barbee 1876 and had ch including; (a) Fannie Barbee m three times; (b) Effie Barbee; (d) Ada Barbee, m ――― Huffman.

Seven. Samuel Prather, of Big Springs, Tex.; married first, ――― ――― and had several children; and married second, Hattie Barbee.

IX. John Wesley Tunnell, son of Perry and Catherine Self Tunnell, was born Sept. 28, 1822 in Jefferson, Ala. and died Mar. 20, 1892 in Texas. He married Martha Clark, sister of Louisiana Clark, 1841, who died Nov. 6, 1906 in Tex. and had six ch.

One. T. Adolphus Tunnell b Oct. 26, 1844 Ala.; d Apr. 30, 1892 Comanche, Tex.; married first, Tirza Amanda Stewart Feb. 16, 1869 (d Apr. 19, 1873) and had; (a) Oscar J. Tunnell b Apr. 7, 1871 Comanche Co., Tex.; d Nov. 2, 1915 Hico, Tex. (m Frances Wagner Mar. 16, 1893 Navarro Co., of Hico, Tex. and had; 1, Lillie Tunnell b Dec. 5, 1894 m J. A. Johnson June 13, 1912 and had; (aa) J. A. Johnson Jr. b Sept. 28, 1918 Farris, Tex.; 2, Garland Tunnell b Sept. 2, 1897, served in U. S. N., m Elsie A. Lankford Oct. '6, 1920 Waco, Tex. and had; (aa) Dorothy Helen Tunnell b Sept. 25, 1922 Waco, Tex.; 3, Cecile Amanda Tunnell b Aug. 29, 1899, of San Francisco, Calif.; 4, Fay Wagner Tunnell b Aug .11, 1901, of San Francisco, Calif.; 5, Erlyn Tunnell b Dec. 26, 1907); (b) Louella Tunnell b Jan. 28, 1873 Comanche, Tex.; d Apr. 8, 1912 Comanche, Tex. (J. M. Bruce Dec. 22, 1892 Greenville, Tex. and had; 1, Isla Bruce b Nov. 12, 1893; 2, Marshall E. Bruce b Nov. 27, 1896, of Loraine, Tex., served in World War, m Beatrice Wilson and had; (aa) Weldon Bruce, d at 18 months; (bb) Marshall E. Bruce Jr.; 3, Worth R. Bruce b Aug. 20, 1899; 4, Oscar G. Bruce b Mar. 1, 1905; 5, Eva Bruce b Mar. 21, 1909; 6, Robert T. Bruce b Apr. 8, 1912, day his mother died. J. M. Bruce married second, Mrs. Minnie McDonald at De Leon, Tex.); T. Adolphus Tunnell, b Oct. 26, 1844, married second, Ora Matwiler 1881, who d in Tex. and had; (c) Theodore Adolphus Tunnell b July 3, 1883, of Loraine, Tex. (m Ida Weiser Sept. 9, 1914 Hico, Tex;.and had; 1, Theodore Adolphus Tunnell Jr. b Sept. 20, 1915; 2, Rose Mary Tunnell b Dec. 30, 1916); (d) Jay F. Tunnell b Dec. 26, 1884, in U. S. Navy.

Two. Missouri Tunnell lived in Comanche Co., Tex.; married first, William Watson and had; (a) George F. Watson (m first, Elizabeth Criswell, and second, Lily Munger, and had; 1, Melvin Watson; 2, Edith Watson); (b) Erasmus Watson, m Sadie Brock and had four ch.; (c) Mattie Watson (m Walter Roberts and had; 1, Truett Roberts; 2, Emma Roberts). Missouri Tunnell married second, N. B. Franklin and had; (d) Lee Franklin (m G. P. Stewart and had; 1, Ola Stewart, dead; 2, Ernest Stewart); (e) ――― Franklin, m ―――

W,ay; (f) Sallie Franklin m Felix Dean; (g) Sledge Franklin, m ——— Isom; (h) Clara Mae Franklin; (i) Ruth Franklin, m Walter Beam. Some descendants live in Comanche Co., Tex.

Three. James W. Tunnell, once of Rising Star, Tex.; married first, Sally Redwine and second, Mary Busey. His ch were; (a) J. Nelson Tunnell (m Jessie Wagner and had; 1, Lessie Tunnell; 2, Roy Tunnell; 3, Fred Tunnell; 4, Mable Tunnell; 5, Erama Tunnell; 6, Joseph Tunnell); (b) Dora Tunnell (m Will Taylor and had; 1, Arthur Taylor; 2, Lizzie Taylor; 3, Beulah Taylor); (c) Cora Tunnell, m D. A. McGuire; (d) Mamie Tunnell (m M. R. Campbell and had; 1, Clarence Campbell; 2, Libas Campbell; 3, Robert Lee Campbell; 4, Christine Campbell); (e) Elizabeth Tunnell (m J. W. Kearney and had; 1, Golda Lee Kearney; 2, Ruby Kearney 3, Seth Kearney); (f) Fannie Tunnell m William Humphrey and had; 1, Cyril Humphrey; (g) Edna Tunnell; (h) Earl Tunnell; (i) Lillian Tunnell; (j) William Tunnell.

Four. Thomas B. Tunnell b Feb. 27, 1855, of Stamford, Tex.; married first, Matt Coker Mar. 15, 1875 (d abt 1879) and had ch b Tex.; (a) Leonard L. Tunnell b Mar. 5, 1876 (m Hattie Wagner Sept. 5, 1897 and had; 1, Floy Tunnell b Nov. 16, 1898; 2, Harvey Tunnell b July 27, 1900; 3, Essie Tunnell b Jan. 3, 1904; 4, Ralph Tunnell b May 4, 1908; 5, Inez Tunnell b Aug. 13, 1911); (b) Pearl Tunnell b Aug. 26, 1878 (m Dave White Oct. 6, 1895 and had; 1, Jesse White b Sept. 1, 1896; 2, Ollie White b Jan. 31 1898; 3, Eargle White b Feb. 26, 1900; 4, Leslie White b Mar. 21, 1902; 5, Lurline White b June 5, 1904; 6,Hylton White b Dec. 5, 1906; 7, Ovis Hazel White b Mar. 19, 1910). Thomas B. Tunnell, b Feb. 27, 1855, married second, Bettie Bruce Mar. 16, 1881 and had; (c) Coleman Tunnell b Dec. 25, 1881 (m Amanda Cooper Dec. 22, 1905 and had ;1, Ruth Tunnell b Oct. 5, 1906; 2, Charles Tunnell b Dec. 3, 1907; 3, Lana Tunnell b Feb. 16, 1912); (d) Bascom H. Tunnell b Apr. 26, 1883; (e) Ethel Tunnell b Feb. 1, 1885 (m Hammie Copeland Dec. 24, 1905 and had; 1. Thelma Copeland b Oct. 8, 1906; 2, Wynnett Copeland b Aug. 8, 1911); (e) Blanche Tunnell b Sept. 4, 1886 (m Fred Taylor Nov. 21, 1907 and had; 1, Eunice Taylor b Apr. 27, 1909; 2, Clarence Taylor b Oct. 15, 1910); (f) Benjamin Tunnell b Jan. 5, 1889; (g) Ollie Anthony Tunrell b Oct. 4, 1892; (h) Myrtle Tunnell b Sept. 17, 1894.

Five. Addison C. Tunnell b Jan. 31, of Stamford, Tex.; married Belle Cooper Jan. 31, 1888 and had; (a) Beulah Tunnell b July 11, 1889 (m Lewis Johnson Apr. 21, 1907 and had: 1, Lillie May Johnson b Aug. 18, 1908; 2, Lester Johnson b Nov. 23, 1909; 3, Florris Bell Johnson b Nov. 13, 1911); (b) Ida Tunnell b Oct. 16, 1890, m Will Hellum Apr. 17, 1911; (c) Bertha Tunnell b Sept. 16, 1892, m James Rodgers Mar. 10, 1911; (d) Minnie Tunnell b Sept. 29, 1894; (e) Annie Tunnell b Jan. 12, 1898; (f) Addie Tunnell b June 10. 1901; (g) Furgus Tunnell b Mar. 27, 1904; (h) Maynor Tunnell b Nov. 13, 1908.

Six. Louisana Tunnell married J. H. Williams and had; (a) Felix Williams, (m Leah Jones and had; 1, Erma Williams and others); (b) Minnie Williams (m F. C. Williams and had; 1, Dewey Williams; 2, Hugh Williams); (c) Troy Williams (m Vesta Griffin and had; 1, Golda Williams); (d) Charles Williams (m Mollie Black and had; 1, Preston Williams; 2, Grady Williams. and others); (e) Oma Williams, m Walter Black and had one ch.; (f) Alpha Williams, m Andy Bowman; (g) Horton Williams; (h) Robert Williams; (i) Myrtle Williams. Some of these lived in Comanche Co., Tex.

X. Mary Tunnell, dau of Perry and Catherine Self Tunnell, was b abt 1824 and d abt 1900 in Tex. She married first, Greene or George White, who died during the War Between the States; and married second, ——— Gray, with no issue by last marriage. Ch. b

Tex.; 1, Elisha White m ——— ——— and had ch.; 2, Henrietta White, m ⟍——— Henderson and had no ch.; 3, George White, of Wichita Falls, Tex., m ——— ——— and had ch.; 4, Joanna White, m ——— Gray and had; (a) Obed Gray, of Ft. Worth, Tex.; 5, Green White, m ——— ——— and had a dau., who m Inman Malone, of Handley, Tex.; 6, Fanny White, m Hard Gunnells and livel in Okla.

XI. Elizabeth Tunnell, dau of Perry and Catherine Self Tunnell, b abt 1870 in Tex.; married Joseph Swain and had; 1, Caroline Swain, d in Tex., m Henry Shaffitt and had a large family; 2, Taylor Swain, m Rebecca Rusk and had; (a) William Swain; (b) Rosa Swain, m ——.— Bonner; (c) Oscar Swain; 3, Ann Swain, m Louis Sharp and had large family, including; (a) Lena Sharp; 4, John Swain, m ——— ——— and had; (a) John Swain Jr.; 5, Celia Swain, d in Tex., m first, Isaac Gilbert and had 4 sons; and m second, James Blackstock; 6, Emma Swain, m Thomas McDow and had ch.; 7, Beulah Swain, m ——— Hacker and had ch; 8, Witcher Swain d in inf.; 9, Mattie Swain, m Charles Blackstock and had ch.; 10, Lee Swain, m Rena Young and had ch.

JOHN TUNNELL

E. John Tunnell, son of Stephen and Kezia Money Tunnell was born in Greene Co., Tenn. and died near Athens, Tenn., abt 1843. Court records, at Greeneville, Tenn., show a marriage license was issued to John Tunnell and Esther Essman on Sept. 8, 1807. She is called Easter by her descendants. They moved to Hopkinsville, Ky. in 1808. About 1821 they moved to McMinn Co., Tenn. and entered land which a granddaughter, Mrs. Hamilton, was living on in 1913. Esther Essman Tunnell lived to be 72 and died at Athens, Tenn. Names of children may not be in order of birth.

I. Lydia Tunnell b Aug. 3, 1808.
II. Sarah Tunnell b Oct. 29, 1810.
III. James Tunnell b Jan. 11, 1813.
IV. Jesse Tunnell b Aug. 8, 1817.
V. Wesley Tunnell.
VI. William Tunnell.
VII. Margaret Tunnell.
VIII. Nancy Tunnell.
IX. Kezia Money Tunnell.
X. Catherine Tunnell
XI. Betsy Tunnell.

Of the foregoing;

I. Lydia Tunnell, oldest child of John and Esther Essman Tunnell, was born Aug. 3, 1808 nr Sparta, Tenn. as the parents were on their road to Ky., and died Dec. 5, 1893 Spring City, Tenn. She married Bennett C. Franklin, son of Gillis and Susan (Logan) Franklin, May 4, 1826 nr Athens, Tenn. (b Aug. 17, 1804 nr Athens, Tenn.; d June 8, 1882 nr Rhea Springs, Tenn.) and had nine ch b McMinn Co., Tenn.

One. Martha Jane Franklin b Dec. 5, 1828; died "years ago"; married Porter Bayless and had; (a) Viola Bayless, once of Ft. Worth, Tex.

Two. Nancy Ann Franklin b Nov. 5, 1830; d Nov. 22, 1903 Harlan, Iowa; married Philip L. Melton Dec. 24, 1853 (b July 1, 1829 Greene Co., Ky.; d Feb. 3. 1897 Harlan, Ia.) and had; (a) William F. Melton b Feb. 22, 1856 Cedar Co., Ia.; d 1876, unm.; (b) Susan E. Melton b Nov. 13, 1857 Linn Co., Ia.; d July 7, 1859; (c) Edmund Tate Melton b June 22, 1859 Cedar Co. Ia.; d abt 1881 (m Jessie E. Rowley Nov. 2, 1878 and had; 1, Lawrence Melton, m ——— ——— and had 2 ch.); (d) L. Anderson Melton b June 8, 1862 Cedar Co., Ia., whose wife, Lucy died leaving 2 ch b Shelby Co., Ia.; 1, Eunice Irene Melton b June 22, 1891, of San Francisco, Calif.; 2, Edmund Franklin Melton b Aug. 21, 1897, shipping clerk General Battery Co., Moline, Ill.; enlisted in Navy at 19, stationed at Great Lakes six months, transferred to Charleston, S. C. for six months; in Miami, Florida two years; transferred to Aviation corps; mustered out July 1919; married Elva F. Gillilan Oct. 11, 1923 Linn Co., Ia. (b May 26, 1904 and had; (aa) Edmund Franklin Melton, the second, b July 19, 1924 Rock Island, Ill.) (e) John Arthur Melton b Jan. 9, 1865 Cedar Co., Ia., of Manilla, Ia. (m Mary Alice Copeland Aug. 28, 1890 Harlan, Ia. (b Aug. 1, 1873 Lancaster Co., Neb.) and had; 1, Margaret Pearl Melton b Oct. 2, 1893 Shelby Co., Ia.; d May 25, 1901; 2, Blanch Edith Melton b Oct. 11, 1895 Shelby Co., Ia., of Manila, Ia., m Lloyd L. Myers at Albert Lea, Minn.; 3, William Raney Melton b Sept. 6, 1897 Shelby Co., Ia., of Manilla, Ia., m Alvina Danman 1917 Dakota City, Neb. and had; (aa) Margaret May Melton b ay 26, 1920; 4, Bonny Ilo Melton b Mar. 11, 1902; d Mar. 26 1902; 5, Kenneth Arthur Melton b June 21, 1911); (f) Addie H. Melton b June 25, 1869 Jones Co., Ia., of Cedar Rapids, Ia. (m first, Monroe E. Butler Oct. 22, 1888 Marion, Ia. (b Aug. 15, 1866 Springfield. Ia.) and had an only ch.; 1, Nellie M. Butler b Dec. 19, 1892 Linn Co., of Ames. Ia., m John A. Lodestein 1910 Marion, Ia. and had; (aa) Ethel Lillian Lodestein b 1912; (bb) Edward Arnold Lodestein b 1916; (cc) Lawrence Lee Lodestein b 1920. Addie H. Melton m second, John F. Brenerman, 1909 Davison, Ia.)

Three. Edmund L. Franklin b Dec. 29, 1831, left McMinn Co., Tenn. at age of thirteen and lived in Jones Co., Ia. He enlisted in the 13th Iowa Volunteers and was in Sherman's march to the sea. After the War Between the States he returned to Iowa and shortly after he and Tate Melton went to Calif. with an ox-team though they walked most all the way. He returned to Iowa and died Dec. 3, 1910. He married Amanda Robinson Dec. 1, 1863 (b Oct. 24, 1842, now of Collins, Ia.) and had ch b in Iowa; (a) Lucy A Franklin b June 24, 1867; d Jan. 20, 1906; (b) Ira Franklin b Feb. 14, 1869, unm., of Collins, Ia.; (c) Acy Bennett Franklin b Dec. 23, 1871, unm., of Clinton, Ia.; (d) Lawrence E. Franklin b Sept. 23, 1873 (m Louise Vasey June 2, 1922); (e) James L. Franklin b Mar. 26, 1876, unm.. of Collins, Ia.; (f) A. Jake Franklin b June 11, 1878, of Collins, Ia. (m Rose Vasey and had; 1, Edna Franklin; 2, Eva Franklin); (g) Dolly Franklin b Jan. 8, 1881; d Mar. 2, 1882.

Four. Thomas Franklin b abt 1834; d in inf.

Five. John K. Franklin b Oct. 1836; d in Tenn.; married first, Isabel McAdoo, at Rhea Springs, Tenn. and had; (a) Mary Franklin d in inf.; (b) Amanda Franklin d in inf.; (c) Lafayette Bennett Franklin b 1886. of Anniston, Ala., m Edith Rawlings abt 1895 and had; 1, Clinton Lafayette Franklin; (d) Lydia Jane Franklin b Feb. 7, 1869 Rhea Co., Tenn., of Hebron, Neb. (m Joseph P. Baldwin 1902, (b 1869 Cookeville, Tenn., son of William and Nancy (Pearson) Baldwin) and had; 1, Robert Morton Baldwin b May 26, 1903; 2, William Orville Baldwin b Feb. 1, 1905; 3, Helen Franklin Baldwin b Jan. 5, 1908); (e) Alice Franklin d in inf.; (f) Nancy Elizabeth Franklin b 1874, of Chattanooga, Tenn., m William C. Apperson and had 5 ch.; (g) Susie Franklin d in inf. John K. Franklin married second, Blanch L. Foster, 1878 and had ch b Rhea Co., Tenn.; (i) Mabel Franklin b 1879, m ———— ————; (j) Cora Franklin b 1886, m Earl Smith 1910 and had; 1, Chester Antler Smith; (k) Meda Franklin d in inf.

Six. Susan E. Franklin b May 17, 1839; d Aug. 31, 1920 McMinn Co., Tenn.; married first, Thomas Carpenter, July 26, 1860 nr Cleveland, Tenn., who d Feb. 1863 Louisville, Ky. while serving in Union Army, and had an only ch.; (a) Lucy Alice Carpenter b July 11, 1861 Bradley Co., Tenn.; d Apr. 20, 1903 (m Thomas S. Bryson Nov. 1877 Rhea Springs, and had 5 ch, 4 of whom d in inf.; (b) Pearl Bryson d at six; (c) Thomas Lyle Bryson b June 7, 1886.   Susan E. Franklin married second, John T. Wasson July 16, 1868 Rhea Co. Tenn.

Seven.   Emily L. Franklin b Mar. 12,   1842;   d   Chattanooga, Tenn.; married Frank Duckworth, who served in C. S. A. and died at Chattanooga, Tenn. and had several children.

Eight.   Asbury Franklin b Aug. 1844, who was a Federal soldier and died in service, at Bull's Gap, Tenn.

Nine   Helen Augusta Franklin b Mar. 19, 1848, of Spring City, Tenn.; married James Henry Pearson, son of Thomas   and   Frances Pearson, Dec. 16, 1869 Rhea Springs, Tenn. (b May 21, 1840 nr Knoxville, Tenn. d Aug. 30, 1920 Spring City, Tenn.) and had; (a) James Thomas Pearson b Nov. 16, 1870 Rhea Springs; d Feb. 3, 1920 Decatur, Tenn. (m first, Anna Russell Sept. 1904 Cotonport, Tenn. and had; 1, Imogene Pearson; 2, Elizabeth Pearson d in inf.; 3, Ruby Pearson; 4, James Grundy Pearson; and m second, Anna Sherrell, in Meigs Co., Tenn. and had; 5, Helen Pearson d in inf.); (b) John Crawford Pearson b Mar. 1, 1872, of Spring City, Tenn. (m Ella Brady (d Oct. 16, 1915) and had; 1, Lillie Mae Pearson b Rhea   Springs; 2, James   Francis Pearson b Spring City; 3, Georgia Tennessee Pearson b 1903 Emerson, Ga.; d Nov. 14, 1909; 4, Louise Florence earson b Spring City, Tenn.); (c) William Asbury Pearson b Aug. 28, 1874, of Dayton, O., m Hattie Devlin and had no ch; (d) Lorena Alice Pearson b Apr. 25, 1877 Salem Tenn.; d Feb. 16, 1879 Salem; (e) Lydia Olenna Pearson b Mar. 2, 1880 Spring City, of Howard Kan. m Warren L. Tanner June 24, 1911 SSpring City, Tenn. (b Nov. 14, 1874 Sandy Lake, Penn.) and had no ch.; (f(Harvey Bennett Pearson b Rhea Springs, of Lancing, Tenn., m Maggie Serton and had; 1, Helen Mae Pearson; 2, Opal Marie Pearson; (g) Anna May Pearson b May 26, 1888 Rhea Springs, unm., of Spring City, Tenn.

II   Sarah Tunnell. dau. of John and Esther Essman Tunnell, was born Oct. 29, 1810 Hopkinson, Ky. and died at age of eighty-four in McMinn Co., Tenn.   She married Ely Cate May 14, 1835 (b Apr. 25, 1813; d Feb. 26, 1891 in Tenn.) and had ten ch. b in Tenn.

One.   Melissa Jane Cate b Feb. 28, 1836; d 1908; married John Kimbrough (d Apr. 10 1915 Knoxville, Tenn.) and had ch including; (a) John Kimbrough; (b) William Kimbrough; (c) James Kimbrough; (d) Henry Kimbrough; (e) Lizzie T. Kimbrough, of Knoxville, Tenn., (m first, ——— Mefford at Morristown, Tenn. and had ch b Morristown; 1, William Franklin Mefford b Nov. 17, 1881, m Pauline Roberts July 25, 1909 Columbia, S. C. and had; (aa) Margaret Mefford b Oct. 27, 1911; (bb) Nell Mefford b Aug. 7. 1913; 2, Lou Minnie Myrtle Mefford b May 7, 1883, m Rossie B. Watts Nov. 1902 Columbus, S. C.; 3, Lillie Maud Mefford b Dec. 23, 1884, m William J. Ussery Columbia, S. C. and had (aa) William Lee Ussery b May 28, 1909; d June 7, 1910; (bb) James Harold Ussery b Mar. 20, 1911; (cc) Mildred Ussery b Nov. 19, 1913; 4. Ollie Mefford b May 31, 1887, of Columbia, S. C., m Blanch Hazel Champion June 22, 1908 and had; (aa) Ethel Champion Mefford b Apr. 28, 1909; (bb) Annie May Mefford b May 16, 1911; (cl) Ruth Aleta Mefford b Sept. 23, 1912; 5, Ernest Mefford b Sept. 9, 1893.   Lizzie T. Kimbrough married second, B. F. Smith).

Two.   John Perry Cate b Feb. 14, 1838; d Oct. 20, 1856, unm.

Three.   James Robert Cate b Feb. 17, 1840; d Dec. 29, 1849.

Four.   Easter Catherine Cate b Oct. 29, 1842; d in Tenn.; mar-

ried Henry Amos and had; (a) John Amos (deceased); (b) Hemry
Amos (deceased), m ——— ——— and had a daughter.

Five. Lydia N. Cate b Jan. 31, 1845; d Feb. 12, 1871; married
William H. Smith Nov., 1864, a soldier in the Union Army, and had
ch b in Tenn.; (a) Lydia Martha Smith b Aug. 1865, m John B.
Thompson and has eleven children including; 1, Henry Thompson b
Aug. 13, 1882; 2, Bertha May Thompson b Feb. 4, 1885; (b) W. A.
Smith b May 21, 1968 m Cora McDaniel June 22, 1894 and had; 1,
Oscar Clifford Smith b Aug. 13, 1895; 2, Ollie Mildred Smith b Oct.
26, 1896; (c) Henry B. Smith b Oct. 4, 1870; d June 10, 1875.

Six. Mary Cate, twin of Lydia N. Cate, b Jan. 31, 1845, married ——— Gray and had fourteen children including; (a) Rufus
Gray; (b)Joe Gray; (c) Martha Gray; (d)Elbert Gray.

Seven. Charles H. Cate b May 25, 1847; married three times.

Eight. William A. Cate b Dec. 22, 1849, of Spring City, Tenn.;
married first, Sarah C. Grisham July 22, 1876 and had; (a) Mary
Cate; (b) Anna Cate; (c) Milo Cate; (d) Della Cate; (e) Hester
Cate; (f) Minna Belle Cate d young.   W. A. Cate married second,
Martha Phillips and had; (g) child b and d same day; (h) Bertha
Cate b and d same day; (i) Albert Cate; (j) Walter Cate d in inf.;
(k) Rose Cate; (l) Llyde Cate.

Nine. Sarah Martha Cate b Oct. 1, 1852; married John Stoe and
had; (a) Claud Stoe; (b) Henry Stoe.

Ten. Eli Adkins Cate b May 22, 1856; d 1878.

III. James Tunnell, son of John and Esther Essman Tunnell.
was born Aug. 8, 1817 Hopkinsville, Ky. and died Oct. 24, 1897 Chilton Co., Ala.   He married Sarah Ann Tarver, dau of Samuel Tarver,
abt 1838 (d Mar. 27, 1900 Ala.) and had nine ch b in Ala.

One. John Samuel Tunnell b Nov. 28, 1839, once of Prattville,
Ala.; married Harriet Ross June 2, 1867 (d Mar. 5, 1900) and had;
(a) James Walter Tunnell b Mar. 14, 1868, m Lizzie Phinley Nov. 27,
1902 and had no ch.; (b) Eliza Ann Tunnell b Mar. 22, 1869, m Robert
Culp Jan. 18, 1888 who d June 28, 1888; (c) William Hansford Tunnell b Sept. 5, 1870 (m Emer Gray Aug. 24, 1893 (d Mar. 8, 1907)
and had; 1, Ader C. Tunnell d in inf.; 2, Perry Tunnell d in inf.; 3,
Iuma Tunnell b Feb. 15, 1896; 4, Nelson Tunnell b Feb. 13, 1898; 5,
Cornelia Lunener Tunnell b Oct. 10, 1906); (d) John Wesley Tunnell
b May 30, 1872 (m Nancy Anderson Oct. 22, 1893, who d Dec. 31, 1907,
and had; 1, Ercey Tunnell b May 25, 1895; 2, Hatty Tunnell b July
27, 1897; (e) Josiah Thomas Tunnell b Aug. 11, 1874 (m Milly Campbell Oct. 21, 1894 and had; 1, Bessie Tunnell b Aug. 18, 1896; 2,
Clarence Tunnell b Jan. 15, 1900; 3, David Tunnell b Apr. 1903; 4,
Dolly Tunnell b Jan. 15, 1900; 3, David Tunnell b Apr. 14, 1903; 4,
Dolly Tunnell b Apr. 1907); (f) Ida Cornelia Tunnell b Aug. 4, 1876
(R. G. Skinner Apr. 7, 1901 and had; 1, Netty Lee Skinner b June
18, 1902; 2, John Edward Skinner b Aug. 8, 1906; 3, Joseph Skinner);
(g) George Alexander Tunnell b Mar. 2, 1878 (m first, Helen Misel-
din Dec. 23, 1900 (d Aug. 22, 1906) and had ch, who d in inf., and m
second, Willie Barbee June 18, 1907 and had two ch. d in inf.); (h)
Charley Tedford Tunnell b Feb. 24, 1880 (m Gertrude Miseld.n Apr.
7, 1901 and had; 1, James Tunnell b Oct. 30, 1902; 2, Oler Tunnell b
July 25, 1904; 3, Eldorado Tunnell b Mar. 1, 1906; 4, Eunice Tunnell
b Nov. 17, 1908; d July 15, 1910; 5, son b Aug. 25, 1910); (i) Martha
Emer Tunnell b Nov. 25, 1881 (m C. T. Youngblood July 27, 1903
and had; 1, Hatty Youngblood; 2, Vilomer Youngblood); (j) Salem
Luthernia Tunnell b Mar. 27, 1885 (m W. O. Minis Apr. 26, 1905 and
had; 1, John William Minis b Nov. 1, 1906; d May 9, 1908; 2, Thelma
Lee Minis b Jan. 16, 1909); (k) Mary Jane Frances Tunnell b Apr. 28,

1888 (m C. A. Allen Dec. 26, 1905 and had; 1, Hatty Bell Allen b Sept. 7, 1907; 2, Harry Herman Allen b Feb. 20, 1910).

Two. Josiah Tunnell b Feb. 3, 1842, of Mt. Sylvan, Texas; married Cornelia Percilla Limerick Dec. 12, 1866 and had no ch.

Three. Julia Ann Tunnell b Oct. 8, 1843; d Aug. 1, 1852.

Four. William Hansford Tunnell b Mar. 7, 1845; d Nov. 11, 1846.

Five. Emily Elizabeth Tunnell b Oct. 7, 1846; married Jasper Dean Dec. 1874 and had; (a) Alley Jane Dean b Dec. 15, 1875 (m Newton Moncrier and had; 1, Guthrey Moncrier; 2, Addie Moncrier; 3, Violet Moncrier); (b) Sally Dean b July 1, 1878 (William Williams and had; 1, Herbert Oliver Williams; 2, William Jasper Williams; 3, Daisy May Williams; 4, Mattie Bell Williams (deceased); 5, Henry Estis Williams); (c) Martha Ellen Dean b Jan. 7, 1882 (m Claud Thomas and had; 1, Henrietta Thomas; 2, James Paul Thomas; 3, Emer Earl Thomas; 4, Joseph Pearl Thomas; 5, Gertrude Thomas); (d) Frances Dean b Aug. 8, 1884 (m Henry Esco and had; 1, Lord Lester Esco; 2, Marvin Edward Esco); (e) Daisy Dean b Mar. 23, 1887 (m Elijah Garner and had; 1, Grady Vernia Garner; 2, Lilly Vesta Garner; 3, Boyd Lamar Garner b May 27, 1910); (f) Jasper Dean b Aug. 9, 1891).

Six. Sarah Jane Tunnell b Oct. 15, 1848; married James Fuller and had; (a) Sarah Emer Fuller b Apr. 13, 1881, m O. D. Ruff; (b) James Fuller Jr. b Sept. 14, 1882, m Dorcia Robinson; (c) Mary Fuller b Aug. 31, 1884, m John Wallis; (d) Margaret M. Fuller b Aug. 21, 1886, m ———— Baldwin; (e) Aney E. Fuller b Apr. 21, 1889; (f) John W. Fuller b Nov. 3, 1891.

Seven. James Alexander Tunnell b June 14, 1852, once of Pratt City, Ala.; married ———— ———— and had; (a) James L. Tunnell; (b) George Tunnell (d 1903); (c) Ameer Tunnell; (d) Perlee Tunnell; (e) Harvey Tunnell; (f) Houston Tunnell.

Eight. George Washington Tunnell b May 29, 1854; married ———— ———— and had; (a) Henley Tunnell b Apr. 31, 1888; (b) Nellie Tunnell b July 20, 1889, m William Downs; (c) Ellen Tunnell b June 29, 1891.

Nine. Melissa Tunnell b June 1856, d 1884.

IV. Jesse Tunnell, son of John and Esther Essman Tunnell, was born Aug. 8, 1817 in Ky. and died Feb. 14, 1902 McMinn Co., Tenn. He married Rebecca Davis Aug. 15, 1838 (b Mar. 14, 1817 N. C.; d Jan. 4, 1892 McMinn Co., Tenn.) and had fourteen children b five miles from Athens, Tenn.:

One. Nancy Jane Tunnell b July 8, 1839; d bef. 1910 Bradley Co., Tenn.; married Whit Davis.

Two. Catherine Tunnell b June 2, 1840; d bef. 1910; married F. W. Ellis 1861 (d bef. 1910).

Three. John W. Tunnell b Apr. 5, 1842; deceased.

Four. James W. Tunnell b Jan. 28, 1844; d bef. 1910; lived at one time Berry Co., Mo., later Sparks, Okla.; was a member of Co. D. and 15th Tenn. Fed. Vol. Inf. for three years and served under Sherman in the Georgia campaign; married first, Edie Calhoun 1867 Polk Co., Tenn. (d 1886 Berry Co., Mo.) and had; (a) William Tunnell b 1869, of Kiowa Co., Okla.; (b) Tenny Tunnell (m J. C. Bice in Polk Co., Tenn.); (c) Luella Tunnell, of McKinney, Tex., m James Spearman; (d) Julia Tunnell, m J. W. Boom; (e) Servilla Tunnell, m Jack Dodd in Washita, Okla. James W. Tunnell married second, Sallie Howell, 1888 Polk Co., Tenn. and had; (f) Jesse J. Tunnell b Apr. 23, 1889, of Sparks, Okla., m Inez Stills, Sparks. Okla.; (g) Ida Tunnell b 1891, m Guy Eagle July 13, 1909 Sparks, Okla.; (h) David

Calvin Tunnell b 1893; (i) Hugh Tunnell b 1896; (j) Henry Tunnell b 1899.

Five. Elizabeth Tunnell b Oct. 17, 1845; d Nov. 1, 1918 nr Athens, Tenn.; lived on farm her grandfather settled on in McMinn Co. married Brad Hamilton Oct. 10, 1872 McMinn Co. and had ch b Mc-Minn Co.; (a) Alice B. Hamilton b June 25, 1873, of Cleveland, Tenn. (m first, Henry A. Fore and had; 1, Elizabeth N. Fore b Nov. 22, 1894, deceased; 2, William L. Fore b Dec. 11, 1895, of Toledo, Ohio, m Jennie Johnson and had; (aa) Ruth Fore; (bb) William Fore; 3, Biad C. Fore b Aug. 30, 1898, of Cleveland, Tenn., m Florine Walsh and had (aa) Culvin H. Fore; (bb) Ransom A. Fore. Alice Hamilton married second, Luther Puett and had; 4, Jasper Puett b Mar. 29, 1909, dead); (b) Rebecca Hamilton b Sept. 26, 1874; deceased; m Wren Walker and had; 1, Walter Walker b Aug. 5, 1897, dead; 2, Tennie Walker b Oct. 10, 1898, of Daisy, Tenn., m ———— Burns; 3, Vesta Walker b Oct. 13, 1900, of Blanchester, Ohio, m Garland Rowland (deceased) and had; (aa) Evelyn Rowland); (c) Jesse Hamilton b Jan. 5, 1876, of Athens, Tenn. (m Grace Scarborough and had; 1, Joyce Hamilton b Mar. 25, 1906; 3, Jesse Hamilton b June 13, 1909; 4, Robert Hamilton b Mar. 6, 1912; 5, Elizabeth Hamilton b June 27, 1914; 6, Lloyd Hamilton b Mar. 26, 1919; 7, Ruth Hamilton b Oct. 16, 1921); (d) Tennie Hamilton b June 16, 1877, of Blanchester, Ohio. (m Ernest Ledford and had; 1, Elbert Ledford b June 12, 1899; 2, Glen Ledford b Dec. 29, 1900, of Chicago, Ill.; 3, Chester Ledford b Feb. 14, 1902, dead; 4, Lester Ledford, twin of Chester, b Feb. 14, 1902, dead; 5, James Ledford b Jan. 10, 1908; 6, Louise Ledford b Oct. 28, 1912, dead); (e) Laura Hamilton b Nov. 23, 1879, dead; (f) Rance W. Hamilton b Oct. 23, 1882, dead (m Gertie Long and had; 1, George Hamilton b Sept. 19, 1906, of Etowah, Tenn., m Pearl Burnett; 2, Annie Hamilton b Jan. 22, 1908; 3, Bertha Hamilton b Mar. 8, 1911; dead; 4, Dula Mae Hamilton); (g) Nancy J. Dular Hamilton b Jan. 3, 1885, dead (m Arthur Haynes and had; 1, James A. Haynes b Sept. 18, 1907, dead; 2, Hubert W. Haynes b Mar. 21, 1911, dead).

Six. Thomas M. Tunnell b Jan. 26, 1847, of Aurora, Mo.; married Sarah Jane Berry in Berry Co., Mo. and had at least one ch., a dau.

Seven. David H. Tunnell b Aug. 29, 1848, of Aurora, Mo., married Tenny Williams in Berry Co., Mo.

Eight. Sophia Tunnell b Oct. 6, 1850; d bef 1910 in Mo.; married William Joquish (dead).

Nine. Matthew C. Tunnell b Mar. 22, 1852; dead.

Ten. Julia Tunnell b July 15, 1853; married John Barker.

Eleven. Levi H. Tunnell b Sept. 14, 1854, dead; married Amanda Rogers, McMinn Co., Tenn. In 1910 lived Lincoln Co., Ark.

Twelve. William Mayfield Tunnell b May 29, 1856.

Thirteen. Carroll S. Tunnell b 1858; dead.

Fourteen. Brownlow Tunnell b 1860; d abt 1898 nr Ripley, Okla.; married Della Melton in McMinn Co., Tenn.

V. Wesley Tunnell, son of John and Esther Essman Tunnell, died unmarried, in Tenn.

VI. William Perry Tunnell (called by some William Hansford Tunnell), son of John and Esther Essman Tunnell, moved to near Plato, Mo. It is said at one time he lived in Ill., at another in Kansas.

He married Lorinda Blevins, in Tenn. and together they visited Tenn. kin in 1883.

VII. Margaret Tunnell. dau of John and Esther Essman Tunnell, married John Hunt and lived at Rome, Ga. Had at least one ch.; (a) John Hunt, Jr.

McMinn Co., Tenn.   She married Gus Eaton and had ch.

IX.   Kezia Money Tunnell, dau of John and Esther Essman Tunnell, died unmarried, Prattville, Ala. at age of 25.

X.   Catherine Tunnell, dau of John and Esther Essman Tunnell, married John Roberts and lived in McMinn Co., Tenn.

XI.   Betsy Tunnell, dau of John and Esther Essman Tunnell, married ―――― Epperson. A niece, Mrs. Pearson, mentions this aunt.

STEPHEN TUNNELL JR.

F.   Stephen Tunnell Jr., son of Stephen and Kezia Money Tunnell, was born Mar. 8, 1790 Greene Co., Tenn. and died Feb. 9, 1837 Lowdnes Co., Miss. He was ordained an elder 1824 at Tuscaloosa, Ala. by Bishop Roberts. He and his wife were charter members of Piney Grove church near Steens, Miss. He married Sarah Hamilton, dau of Abraham Hamilton, of Maryland, 1810 in Tenn. (b 1793 Sullivan Co., Tenn.; d Dec. 1871 Miss.) They moved to Monroe Co., Miss.; from there to Lowdnes Co., Miss., then to Marion Co., Ala., and again to Lowdnes Co., Miss. The land he entered near Steens, Miss. went to a son, and a grand son now owns it.   Children;

I.   Nancy Tunnell b June 1, 1811.
II.   Elijah Tunnell b Sept. 13, 1814.
III.   John Tunnell b Sept. 16, 1816.
IV.   Polly Tunnell b Oct. 24, 1817.
V.   Betsy Tunnell b Feb. 5, 1820.
VI.   Sarah Ann Tunnell b May 16, 1822.
VII.   Stephen Money Tunnell b May 31. 1824.
VIII.   Peyton Graves Tunnell b June 11, 1826.
IX.   Jane Tunnell b Oct. 13, 1828.
X.   David Parker Tunnell b Feb. 7, 1831.
XI.   Martha Kezia Tunnell b July 30, 1833.
XII.   Thomas Lloyd Tunnell b Nov. 13, 1836.

Of the foregoing;

I.   Nancy Tunnell, dau of Stephen and Sarah Hamilton Tunnell, was born June 1, 1811 and died 1887 in Miss.; married M. D. Foster 1832 (d 1861) and had ten children;

One.   Fletcher Foster, d on a battlefield during the War Between the States;   unmarried.

Two.   Stephen Foster, d in inf.

Three.   Washington Foster, a Methodist clergyman.

Four.   Sarah Jane Foster, twin, b abt 1840; d at 13.

Five.   Betty Foster; twin with Sarah Jane Foster, died 1913; married James Asbury Lewis Jan. 13. 1859 (son of Wiley, b Jan. 8, 1808 Davidson Co., Tenn., d 1885, and Martha (Summers) Lewis) and had; (a) Thomas Wiley Lewis b Jan. 15, 1860, pastor Madison Heights church, Memphis, Tenn. (1920) (m first, Mary Naomi Whitson Dec. 21, 1881 (d July 7, 1917 Memphis, Tenn.) and had; 1, Irvine Asbury Lewis b Oct. 24, 1889, attorney, Columbus, Miss. who was a member of Legislature of Miss. 1920; and m second, Maud Kink, Jan. 19, 1919; (b) Nancy Caroline Lewis b Oct. 3, 1862; deceased (m Rev. Freeman Asbury Whitson, brother of Mary Naomi Whitson, (d abt 1900) and had; 1, Leon Winans Whitson, of Detroit, Mich., m ――――
――――and had no ch.; 2, Annie Bessie Whitson, of Ft. Worth, Tex., m H. P. Stearns and had no ch.; 3, Lewis Whitson, of Jackson, Miss.; 4, Pierce Whitson, twin with Lewis Whitson); (c) Willard Newton Lewis b Sept. 1865, attorney, Davis, Okla. (m first, Lilly ――――, m second, Hattie Ruth Collins, abt 1910 and third, Bessie Woodward abt 1918 and had no ch.); (d) Edward Summers Lewis b Oct. 3, 1868, clergyman of Greenville, Miss. (m Mamie De Loach and had; 1, Edward S. Lewis, the second; 2, Virginia Lewis); (e) John Silas

Lewis b Aug. 15, 1874; deceased (m Mamie ——— and had; 1, John
Silas Lewis, the second, b 1909); (f) William Finus Lewis, twin with
John Silas Lewis, b Aug. 15, 1874; (g) Dixie Lewis, of Chattanooga,
Tenn., m Addie ——— and had three ch.
      Six. Mollie Foster, of Woodland, Miss.; married ——— Owen
and had several children.
      Seven. Thomas Foster, a clergyman.
      Eight. John Foster.
      Nine. William Foster, a clergyman.
      Ten. Jackson Foster.
      II. Elijah Tunnell, son of Stephen and Sarah Hamilton Tunnell
was born Sept. 13, 1815 and died Oct. 17, 1837 nr Ittawamby, Minn.
He married Temperance Gilmore Tunnell married second, Jonathan
Stevens, went to Arkansas and died there 1892.
      One. Mary Ann Tunnell b Oct. 1833; d Dec. 6, 1912 Carbon, Tex.
At the time of her death she had eighty-five greatgrandchildren. She
married first Calvin Dickson Weaver, Aug. 29, 1850, who died Dec. 24,
1864 Nashville, Tenn., while serving in the C. S. A.   She married
second Isaac Newton Reeves, July 3, 1885 Eastland, Tex., who died
Dec. 13, 1911 Carbon, Tex.   Ch b in Tex.;
      a.   Frederick Tunnell Weaver b Oct. 20, 1851; d Aug. 19, 1916
Carbon, Tex. (m Nancy Robinson 1869 and had; 1, daughter b and d
Oct. 12, 1870; 2, Ophelia Weaver b Mar. 5, 1872, m J. L. Wilson Nov.
30, 1888 and had; (aa) Henry Wilson, m Ola Reese and had two ch.;
(bb) Ollie Wilson, m Dora Taylor and had four ch.; (cc) Zettie Wilson, m John Taylor and had four ch.; (dd) Nettie Wilson, m Bud Key
and had four ch; (ee) Hubert Wilson, m ——— ——— and had two
ch.; (ff) Bertha Wilson, m Henry Ling and had two ch.; (gg) Jocie
Wilson, d at 17; (hh) Fred Wilson, m ——— ——— and had one
child; (ii) Sherman Wilson, unm.; 3, Mattie Weaver b Dec. 10, 1873,
m J. H. Forsythe Oct. 1891 and had; (aa) Ida Forsythe, m Loy Smith
and had four ch.; (bb) Annie Forsythe, m Joe Thorp and had one
child; (cc) Ethel Forsythe, m V. Walker and had one child; (dd)
Irene Forsythe, m Jack Winn and had no ch.; (ee) Elmyra Forsythe,
m Dewey Lang and had two ch.; (ff) Bell Forsythe, m ———
and had one child; (gg) Florence Forsythe; (hh) Viniss Forsythe;
(ii) Modell Forsythe; (jj) Weaver Forsythe; (kk) Bernice Forsythe;
4, Lee Weaver b Jan. 2, 1876, of Carbon, Tex., m Mary Brown Mar. 26,
1899 and had; (aa) Vernon, m Odell House and had one child; (bb)
Chester Weaver, unm.; (cc) Clyde Weaver, unm.; (dd) Welma Weaver, d at two; (ee) Lettie Mae Weaver; (ff) Wood Roe Weaver; 5,
Richard Weaver b Apr. 20, 1877, m Nettie Hester Jan. 3, 1901 and
had; (aa) Cecil Weaver, unm.; (bb) Lois Weaver, m Jennings Reese;
(cc) Opal Weaver; (dd) Janette Weaver; (ee) Loretta Weaver, d at 3;
(ff) Barney Weaver, d in inf; (gg) Helen Weaver, twin; (hh) Twin
of Helen Weaver, d in inf.; 6. S. S. Weaver b Dec. 11, 1878; d Jan.
12, 1879; 7, Bell Weaver b Dec. 27, 1879, m O. W. Thomason Dec. 21,
1902 and had; (aa) Earl Thomason, m Julia ——— and had one child;
(bb) Della Thomason, m J. Hoover; (cc) Aaron Thomason; (dd)
Elmer Thomason; (ee) Edna Thomason; 8, John Tunnell Weaver b
Feb. 18, 1882, of Carbon, Tex., m Ruth Jordan Apr. 2, 1904 and had;
(aa) Bessie Weaver; (b) Modena Weaver; (cc) John Tunnell Weaver,
the second; 9, Eli Weaver b Apr. 24, 1883, m Annie Nix and had (aa)
Cordie Weaver, m Clay Johnson; (bb) Clifford Weaver; (cc) Elton
Weaver; (dd) T. L. Weaver; (ee) Leona May Weaver; 10, Tennie
Weaver b Nov. 18, 1884, of Carbon, Tex., m J. N. Jordan Dec. 23,
1903 and had; (aa) Pearl Jordan; (bb) Herman Jordan; (cc) Jodie
Jordan; (dd) Virgil Jordan d in inf.; (ee) Edith Jordan; (ff) Ila

Ruth Jordan, d in inf.; (gg) Weaver Jordan; (hh) Letha Jordan;
(ii) Rufus Jordan; 11, Nannie Weaver b Apr. 18, 1886, m Grover
Thomason and had; (aa) Delma Thomason; (bb) Raymond Thomason;
(cc) Ruby Thomason; (dd) Cleo Thomason; 12, Newton Weaver b
June 7, 1887, m Celia Warren (d Apr. 21, 1925) and had; (aa) Lola
Weaver, m Gordon Parks; (bb) Jewel Weaver; (cc) Juanita Weaver;
(dd) Oscar Weaver; (ee) J. T. Weaver; (ff) Margurite Weaver; (gg)
Newton Weaver, the second, d at two years; (hh) Harlan Weaver b
1924; 13, May Weaver b Mar. 28, 1889, m Ed Collins and had; (aa)
Annie Mae Collins d in inf.; (bb) Lucile Collins; (cc) Henry Collins;
(dd) Oscar Weaver; (ee) J. T. Weaver; (ff) Marguerite Weaver; (gg)
Jack Collins; (hh) Nettie Lea Collins; 14, J. H. Weaver b Feb. 25,
1891, m Emma Rayborn and had; (aa) Loellen Weaver; (bb) J. W.
Weaver; (cc) Hazel Weaver; (dd) child, d in inf.; (ee) Delton Weaver;
15, Birdie Weaver b Oct. 10, 1893; d Apr. 7, 1894; 16, Ella Weaver b
Sept. 19, 1895, m Odus Rankin June 22, 1917 and had; (aa) Viclet
Faye Rankin; 17. Sophronia Weaver b Dec. 21, 1897, m T. H. Linders.
May 13, 1922).

  b.   Mary Weaver b 1854; d Mar. 31, 1923 (m John Rye, who d
1870, and had; 1, James Rye; 2, Lizzie Rye, of Clyde, Tex., m ———
Morman; 3, Eudora Rye; 4, Lem Rye; 5, Dessie Rye, m ——— Robertson; 6, John Rye, of Stamford, Tex.; 7, Farlie Rye, of Abilene, Tex,
m ——— Dicks; 8, Fry Rye d 1918; 9, Mart Rye d 1923; 10, Ella Rye,
of Spur, Tex., m ——— Robins).

  c.   Rachel Weaver b 1856; d Apr. 22, 1904 in Ark. (m Robert
Anglin, who d 1876, and had; 1, Mary Anglin, m ——— Blevins; 2,
George Anglin; 3, Josie Anglin, m ——— Free; 4, Ollie Anglin, m
——— Drake; 5, Lula Anglin).

  d.   Sarah Weaver b 1858, of Duster, Tex. (m Rev. H. S. Anglin,
brother of Robert Anglin, 1876, and had; 1, Beulah V. Anglin b July
14, of Cisco, Tex., m David F. Brown Jan. 29, 1895 and had ten ch
living in 1925; (aa) Lillie M. Brown, of Scranton, Tex., m S. J. Dodson
(deceased) and had no ch.; (bb) Carrie Brown b May 28, 1899, of
Brownwood, Tex., m ——— Williams and had two ch.; (cc) Dovie O.
Brown b Nov. 13, 1901, of Cisco, Tex., m ——— ——— and had one
child; (dd) Franklin O. Brown b Aug. 23, 1903, of Scranton, Tex., m
Tressie Dodson and had no ch.; (ee) Jo Brown b Apr. 4, 1907; (ff)
Cecil Brown b July 6. 1909; (gg) O. B. Brown b 1911; (hh) O. C.
Brown b May 17, 1913; (ii) Viola Brown b Nov. 1915; (jj) Christine
Brown b Dec. 25, 1918; 2, D. M. Anglin b Mar. 9, 1879, of Cisco Tex.,
m Mary Brown May 12, 1903 and had; (aa) Burtie Anglin b June 2,
1904; (bb) Weldon W. Anglin b Apr. 18, 1906; (c) Nellie Anglin b
1908; (dd) D. M. Anglin b Nov. 26, 1911; (ee) Virgil Anglin b 1913;
(ff) Graham Anglin b Nov. 6, 1923; 3, Eva Anglin b July 25, 1881,
of Gorman, Tex., m O. C. Dennis Jan. 20, 1897 and had ten ch living;
(aa) Claud Dennis b 1898, of Duster, Tex., m Minnie Lee Kirk and
had one child, Jessie Lee Dennis b 1920; (bb) Burt Dennis b 1901; (cc)
Elmer Dennis b 1903 m Lois Underwood Aug. 14, 1920 and had a
child b 1922 and another 1925; (dd) Marion Dennis b 1907; (ee) Willie
Dennis b 1909; (ff) Eulan Dennis b 1911; (gg) Oades Dennis b 1913;
(hh) Opal Dennis b 1921; (ii) Duan Dennis b 1925; 4, Arthur Anglin b
Aug. 18, 1885, of Duster, Tex., m Isia Smith June 25, 1905 and had;
(aa) Charley Anglin b 1907; (bb) Norman Anglin b 1909; (cc) Era
Anglin; (dd) Curtis Anglin b 1915; (ee) Ruth Anglin b 1917; (ff)
Erma Anglin b 1920; 5, Walter Anglin b Oct. 5, 1888, of Tahoka, Tex.,
m Fannie Teague June 25, 1905 and had; (aa) Floy Anglin b 1906;
(bb) Herman Anglin b 1910; (cc) Avel Anglin b 1913; (dd) Dammer

Anglin b 1917; (ee) child, dead; (ff) Leonard Anglin b 1923; 6, Lee
P. Anglin b Jan. 17, 1889, of Duster, Tex., m Elvira Stephens Sept.
23, 1917 and had; (aa) Terrell Anglin b 1919; (bb) Fay Anglin b
1921; 7, Maud Anglin b Mar. 1, 1893, of De Leon, Tex., m Allen Lee
Nov. 16, 1911 and had (aa) Oscar Lee b 1913; (bb) Velma Lee b
1915; (cc) —— Lee b 1918; (dd) Earl Lee b 1920; (ff) Janeva Lee b
1922; (gg) J. A. Lee b 1924; 8, Rev. J. B. Anglin b Sept. 5, 1896, of
Tebon, New Mex., m Vera Lee Aug. 1918 and had; (aa) J. B. Anglin
Jr. b May 2, 1921; 9. Callie Anglin; 10, John W. Anglin, dead; 11,
Claude Anglin, dead; 12, J. O. Anglin, dead.

    e. Calvin Weaver, died in childhood.

    Two. Sarah Tunnell b July 9, 1835; d Apr. 26, 1924 in Miss.;
married Stephen McReynolds, son of W. H. McReynolds, Jan. 25, 1854
(b July 21, 1832 Lowdnes Co., Miss.; d June 10, 1864 Va.) and had ch
b Fayette Co., Ala.; (a) William E. McReynolds b Dec. 17, 1854, of
Ethelville, Ala. (m Elizabeth Bobo Nov. 26, 1876 and had; 1, Lillie
McReynolds b Nov. 29 1877 Chickasaw Co., Miss., of Ethelville, Ala.,
m William Ferguson and had; (aa) Robert M. Ferguson; (bb) Charles
Dean Ferguson; and two children who d in inf.; 2, Minnie McReynolds
twin of Lillie McReynolds b and d Nov. 29, 1877; 2, James McReynolds b Feb. 11, 1880 Pickens Co., Ala.; 4, Jesse McReynolds b Dec.
10, 1882, of Columbus, Miss., m Frances V. Chatham Jan. 26, 1908
and had; (aa) Ruby McReynolds; (bb) Grady McReynolds, dead;
(cc) child, dead; (dd) son; (ee) Doris McReynolds; 5, son b and d
Mar. 19. 1896; 6, William D. McReynolds b Sept. 8, 1897; 7, Charles
L. McReynolds b Aug. 27, 1900, of Milport, Ala.); (b) John F. Mc-
Reynolds b Sept. 23, 1856, of Ethelville, Ala. (m Eliza J. Dawkins
Mar. 11, 1894 and had ch b Pickens Co., Ala.; 1, John W. McReynolds
b Oct. 11, 1897, of Ethelville, m Wilma Morton and had; (aa) Leroy
McReynolds; (bb) son; 2, Robert I. McReynolds b Nov. 15, 1898, of
Milport, Ala., m Mary Wheeler and had; (aa) Leon McReynolds; (bb)
son; 3, Sarah J. McReynolds b Apr. 18, 1900, of Pickensville, Ala., m
Charlie Schwartz and had four children, two of whom are dead; 4,
William S. McReynolds b Oct. 29, 1902, of Ethelville, Ala.; 5, Mary
R. McReynolds b Oct. 27, 1904, m Amos Henderson; 6, Thomas F. Mc-
Reynolds b July 29, 1906: 7, George S. McReynolds b July 8, 1908; 8,
Lydia B. McReynolds b Aug. 5, 1910; 9, Joseph Parker McReynolds);
(c) Robert McReynolds b Dec. 14, 1858, of Milport, Ala. (m Lillie B.
Spruill Dec. 24, 1888 Pickens Co., Ala. (b Jan. 21, 1872 and had ch
Pickens Co., Ala.; 1, Marinda B. McReynolds b Nov. 14, 1889, of Ken-
nedy, Ala., m James T. Smith June 23, 1912 and had; (aa) Theodore
Taylor Smith b Apr. 23, 1913 Lamar Co., Ala.; (bb) Clyde Marshall
Smith b Oct. 2, 1914 Pickens Co., Ala.; 2, Sallie M. McReynolds b
July 26, 1891, of Ft. Worth, Tex., m Rev. R. J. Shelton July 11, 1915
and had; (aa) R. Owen Shelton b Jan. 13, 1917; (bb) W. Christine
Shelton b Dec. 17, 1919; 3 Willie L. McReynolds b Dec. 25, 1892, of
Mi'nort, Ala., m H. O. Shelton Apr. 16, 1912 and had; (aa) Olivia
Shelton b May 6, 1913, dead; (bb) W. Olin Shelton b Apr. 16, 1919; 4,
Maggie L. McReynolds b Apr. 20, 1895, of Birmingham, Ala., m V. G.
Sherrill and had; (aa) Opal May Sherrill d in inf.; (bb) Mabel Leon
Sherrill b Mar. 5, 1916; 5, Jessie L. McReynolds b Nov. 6, 1897, of
Columbus, Miss., m James L. Ferguson July 16, 1916 and had; (aa)
Loyd Ferguson b July 6, 1917: (bb) Helen C. Ferguson b Jan. 18,
1919; 6, Mattie E. McReynolds b Dec. 2, 1900, of Milport, Ala., m R.
Dewey McAdams Dec. 25, 1919 and had; (aa) E. Pearl McAdams b
Oct. 2. 1920; 7, Annie K. McReynolds b June 30, 1904; 8, Effie L. Mc-
Reynolds b June 20, 1908; 9, Robert M. McReynolds, the second, b
and d Oct. 28, 1910).

Three. Elizabeth Tunnell b Mar. 10, 1837; d June 1883 in Ark. nr Magnolia; sent with her mother and step father to Ark. She married Jack Reed and had two daughters, one of whom died in childhood, and a son, William Taylor Washington Reed (deceased), who m ———— ———— and it is said has descendants in Texas.

III. John Tunnell, son of Stephen and Sarah Hamilton Tunnell, was born Sept. 16, 1816 Monroe Co., Miss. and died Sept. 8, 1865 Aberdeen, Miss. He married first, Catherine Sullivan, Dec. 1836, who died shortly after and m second, Savilla Hillyard, 1840 (b Aug. 13, 1824; d Sept. 3, 1881 Smithville, Miss.) and had five ch. b in Miss.

One. William Mack Tunnell b Jan. 11, 1843; d Apr. 26, 1858 in Miss.

Two. Stephen Calaway Tunnell b Nov. 11, 1844, Athens, Miss.; d Feb. 3, 1904 Aberdeen, Miss.; married Martha Ann (Lambeth) Morgan, Jan. 3, 1865 nr Aberdeen, Miss. (b Sept. 17, 1840 nr Aberdeen; d Jan. 20, 1915 nr Aberdeen, Miss.) The mother of Martha Ann Tunnell was, before marriage, Susan Taylor, cousin of ex-president Taylor. Ch. b nr Aberdeen, Miss.; (a) William Greene Tunnell b Nov. 10, 1870, farmer Aberdeen, Miss. (m Della Hankins Oct. 22, 1922 Aberdeen, Miss. and had; 1, Willie Boyd Tunnell b Sept. 15, 1923); (b) child b Dec. 30, 1872; d Jan. 6, 1873; (c) Eugene Sykes Tunnell b Sept. 5, 1875, farmer (m Cora Bott Dec. 28, 1895 and had ch b nr Aberdeen, Miss.; 1, Cloe Tunnell b Dec. 28, 1896, of Memphis, Tenn., m ———— ————; 2, Stephen Tunnell b Sept. 6, 1898, w.th Frisco R. R., Amory, Miss.) (d) Fannie Tunnell b Oct. 20, 1877 (m Wooden Wise May 20, 1902 and had; 1. Lillian Wise b Sept. 25, 1905); (e) Horace Greeley Tunnell b May 10, 1880, m Lena Hill Jan. 17, 1907 and had no ch.

Three. Martha Tunnell b June 1849; deceased; married ———— Gregory and descendants live Detroit, Ala.

Four. Sallie Tunnell b July 17, 1852, of Amory, Miss.; married James Weaver, son of Hue and Matilda Weaver, Nov. 18, 1866 (d Oct. 22, 1900) and had; (a) John Weaver b Mar. 10, 1869 (m Rhoda Oden and had; 1, Reba Weaver b Dec. 8, 1894; 2, Charles Weaver b Aug. 3, 1897; 3, Griffin Weaver b Jan. 23, 1906; 4, Juanita Weaver b Oct. 11, 1910): (b) Walter Weaver b Apr. 22, 1872 (m Frances Manning Mar. 7, 1894 and had; 1, Aretha Weaver b Sept. 4, 1895; 2, Ethel Weaver b Aug. 9, 1898; 3, James Weaver b Apr. 26, 1903; 4, Woodie Weaver b Oct. 13, 1905; 5, Berley Weaver b Nov. 18, 1907; 6, Roy Weaver b Dec. 11, 1911); (c) Charles Weaver b Sept. 23, 1874 (m Jennie Schurlock Dec. 19, 1907 and had; 1, Miriam Louise Weaver b Nov. 26, 1910); (d) Tressie Weaver b May 16, 1877; d Feb. 16, 1907 (m Clarence Mize Oct. 13, 1901); (e) Annie Weaver b Aug. 10, 1879; d Apr. 24, 1905.

Five. Effie Tunnell b Nov. 1858, of Sulligent, Ala.; married W. B. Lewis and had; (a) Lula Lewis (m J. H. Crump and had; 1, William Crump, m Erma Posey; 2, Lillian Crump, m Roy Furman and had; (aa) Annie Cloe Furman: (bb)Gladys A. Furman; 3, Burlie Crump; 4, Ittie Crump; 5, Orlie Crump; 6, Annie Mildred Crump; and one child dead); (b) W. Marvin Lewis, of Springfield, Mo. (m Florence Cook and had; 1, Buford Lewis; 2, M. Lewis; 3, Pauline Lewis; 4, W. M. Lewis; 5, Dorothy Winfrey Lewis); (c) W. Kirby Lewis, deceased; (d) ᵀ C. Lewis (m Lizzie Noe and had; 1, Clyde Lewis; 2, Flora Bell Lewis: 3, Verna Lewis; 4, Bernice Lewis; 5, ———— Lewis); (f) J. D. Lewis, of Ensley, Ala., m Ollie Duke and had; 1, Archie Lewis; (g) Eula Lewis (m J. W. Franklin and had; 1, Louise Franklin; 2 Connie Franklin; 3, ———— Franklin; 4, Hewitt Franklin; 5, Stanley Franklin); (h) G. L. Lewis, unm., of Akron

Ohio; (i) E. B. Lewis, m Gladys Byrns and had; 1, Aileen Lewis; (j) E. C. Lewis, Florence, Ala., m Jimmie Herndon; (k) E. T. Lewis, m Shatrula Comer.

IV. Polly Tunnell, dau of Stephen and Sarah Hamilton Tunnell, was born Oct. 24, 1817 and died 1886 nr Stone's Cross Roads, Miss. She married Rev. Stephen Gilmore 1838 Miss. (died in Miss.) and had ch b in Miss.

One. Stephen Gilmore Jr. b abt 1840; killed in Battle of Donaldsonville.

Two. Sally Gilmore b abt 1842; d nr Tremont, Miss.; m M. D. Stone and had four children, two of whom were; (a) Arkie E. Stone b Sept. 7, 1880 Stone's Cross Roads, Miss., or Amory, Miss (m E. F. Wheeler Jan. 2, 1901 and had; 1, Mildred Wheeler b Jan. 3, 1902; 2, Pauline Wheeler b May 31, 1904 Sulligent, Ala.); (b) Thella Stone b Jan. 28, 1882, of Sulligent, Ala. (m Jala Pennington Jan. 3, 1904 and had; 1 Filmore Stone b Sept. 1, 1908).

V. Betsy Tunnell, dau of Stephen and Sarah Hamilton Tunnell, was born Feb. 5, 1820 and died 1840. She m Robert Sullivan 1838 and had;

One. son d in inf.

Two. daughter, name not known.

VI. Sarah Ann Tunnell, dau of Stephen and Sarah Hamilton Tunnell, was born May 16, 1822 and died 1855, in Miss. She married Dr. B. B. Duke 1840 in Miss. (d in Miss.), who m second, Rebecca Jones, who d in Miss. Ch. of Sarah A. Tunnell Duke b in Miss.

One. Stephen Duke b abt 1842; d unmarried.

Two. Moses Duke b abt 1844; d unmarried.

Three. Hayes Duke b abt 1848; moved to Oklahoma and it is said he has descendants near Chickasaw, Okla.

VII. Stephen Money Tunnell, son of Stephen and Sarah Hamilton Tunnell, was born May 31, 1824 Columbus, Miss. and died Aug. 16, 1884 Pontotoc Co., Miss. He married Siscily Orton, dau of William and Frances Orton, Apr. 30, 1844 Columbus, Miss. (b Jan. 22, 1828; David Co., N. C; d Jan. 27, 1910 Pontotoc Co., Miss.) and had ten ch.;

One. John Parker Tunnell b Oct. 29, 1845 Columbus, Miss.; d Jan. 16, 1865 Camp Douglas, Ill., soldier in War Between the States; unmarried.

Two. Sarah Frances Tunnell b Nov. 22, 1848; d May 2, 1914 nr American Fork, Utah; married Jasper Yancey, son of Philip and Sophronia Yancey, Oct. 25, 1870 (b Aug. 19, 1848) and had ch b Miss., oldest nr Okolona; others in Monroe Co.; (a) William Elvie Yancey b Sept. 4, 1872, of Weiser, Idaho (m Marie Hyde Mar. 28, 1900 Cardston, Alberta, Canada (b Nov. 1882 Franklin, Ida., dau of Don Carlos and Sarah Ann (Thomas) Hyde) and had ch b Cardston, save youngest; 1, Elvie Hyde Yancey b Apr. 23, 1901; 2, Oliver Yancey b Dec. 6, 1902; d May 31, 1918 Weiser, Idaho; 3, Hugh Yancey b Jan. 26, 1904; 4, Rose Yancey b Sept. 12, 1906; 5, Marion Yancey b Aug. 28, 1909; 6, Ruth Yancey b Aug. 16, 1912; 7, Don Merlin Yancey b Aug. 30, 1919 Weiser, Ida.); (b) Thomas Elgin Yancey b Apr. 26, 1874, of Taylorville, Utah (m Annie Bringhurst 1906 in Salt Lake Temple and had; 1, Oren Yancey; 2, Marie Yancey; 3, —— Yancey); (c) David Odis Yancey b Aug. 29, 1875, of Pleasant Grave, Utah (m Mae Tomilson 1898 Salt Lake Temple and had; 1, Hazel Yancey; 2, Darrell Yancey; 3, Laura Yancey; 4, and 5, Eve Yancey and Evelyn Yancey, twins 6, Jasper Yancey, deceased); (d) Mary Emma Yancey b Aug. 5, 1877; d June 14, 1908 Lorenzo, Idaho (m J. H. Hardman Nov. 10, 1896 Provo, Utah and had; 1, Abraham Hardman b 1898; 2,

Virgie Hardman b 1900, m first, Alvin Ambrose (d Gooding, Ida.) and had; (aa) Helen Ambrose; and m second, Louis Fray; 3, Marelda Hardman b 1902, m Douglas Turner at Gooding, Ida. and had; (aa) child b and d same day; (bb) Edward Turner, died at 2; (cc) daughter b 1924; 4, Henry Hardman b 1904; 5, Orville Hardman b 1906; 6, David Hardman b 1908); (e) Money Lee Yancey b Jan. 27, 1879, of Thornton, Ida. (m Florence Wilcox 1915 and had; 1, Jessie Yancey; 2, James Yancey; 3, ——— Yancey); (f) Flora Edna Yancey b Aug. 9, 1881, of American Fork, Utah (m Edwin William Conder, son of Edward and Sarah Conder, Nov. 12, 1901 Provo City, Utah (b Oct. 27, 1881 American Fork, Utah) and had ch b American Fork; 1, Ethel Conder b Aug. 25, 1902, m Earl Sorenson July 29, 1920 Provo City and had; (aa) Earl Sorenson, the second, b June 21, 1921; (bb) Lamar Sorenson b May 30, 1923; 2, Lydia Conder b Apr. 6, 1904, of San Francisco, Calif. m Tom Hagerty, in Salt Lake City; 3, child b Oct. 28, 1905; d Nov. 2, 1905; 4, Erma Conder b Feb. 11, 1907; 5, Bernice Conder b June 11, 1911; 6, Edwin Conder, the second, b July 6, 1915; 7, Melvin Conder b Dec. 2, 1918; 8, Marland Conder b July 14, 1920; 9, Evelyn Conder b Mar. 21, 1924. E. W. and Flora Yancey Conder have given their name to and are rearing as their own a child of a daughter by her first marriage; 10, Norma Conder b May 26, 1920); (g) John Albert Yancey b July 18, 1886, of American Fork, Utah (m Emma Hugard in Provo City and had; 1, Kenneth Yancey; 2, Leona Yancey).

Three.   Mary Caroline Tunnell b Nov. 20, 1850 Columbus, Miss.; d Jan. 29, 1881 Pontotoc Co., Miss.; married W. R. Hood Oct. 1870 and had; (a) Edgar T. Hood b Aug. 14, 1878 Pontotoc Co., Miss.; d Oct. 28, 1899 Chickasaw Co., Miss.; (b) Louella Hood b Dec. 10, 1879; d Jan. 27, 1882.

Four.   Amanda Martha Tunnell b Dec. 13, 1853 Monroe Co., Miss., of Houlka, Miss.; married John W. Winter 1896 Houlka, Miss. and had one child, d in infancy.

Five.   James Thomas Tunnell b May 4, 1856; d Feb. 27, 1910 Monroe Co.; married first, Bettie Hood Jan. 12, 1879 (d Mar. 5, 1882) and had; (a) Willie Ann Tunnell, m Clifton E. Hodges Aug. 13, 1917 and had children.   J. T. Tunnell m second, Tempie Hood, Jan. 11, 1883 (d Sept. 1903) and had ;(b) David Atmon Tunnell; (c) Bettie Tunnell; (d) Toy E. Tunnell; (e) Lee Andrews Tunnell, dead; (f) Anton Thomas Tunnell; (g) Jessie Edna Tunnell, dead; (h) Cecil Tunnell; (i) Le Roy Tunnell; (j) Herman Tunnell, dead; (k) Jimmie Viola Tunnell, dead; (l) Tempie Tom Tunnell, dead.   J. T. Tunnell m third, Mrs. Cora Atkins, Dec. 16, 1909.

Six.   Stephen Tunnell b Dec. 17, 1858 Monroe Co., Miss.; d July 31, 1861.

Seven.   Jesse William Tunnell b Sept. 16, 1861 Monroe Co., Miss. of Pontotoc, Miss.; married first, Susie A. Armstrong, Oct. 21, 1885 (d July 27, 1900) and had ch b Miss.; (a) Mary Tunnell b Sept. 19, 1886 (m Marvin Kilgo Smith Jan. 13, 1914 and had; 1, Edgar A. Smith b Nov. 1904; 2, Louise L. Smith; 3, Loyd Keith Smith; 4, Mary Sue Smith; 5, Jessie Lee Smith, d Mar. 1918 Springville, Miss.; 6, Hulet Smith; 7, Ulysses Smith; 8, Jewel Smith; 9, Ruby Smith; 10, Laura Alice Smith); (b) David Orton Tunnell b July 18, 1888 Chickasaw Co., Miss. (m Lucy Young 1915 Dublin, Tex, and had ch b Desdemona, Tex.; 1, Jesse Carroll Tunnell; 2, William Tunnell); (c) Sam Jones Tunnell b June 21, 1890, m Oma Smith at De Leon, Texas and had three children; (d) Frank Burkett Tunnell b Jan. 25, 1892 (m first, Bessie Lawson Dec. 24, 1912 and had; 1, Vida Tunnell; 2, J. B. Tunnell; 3, Edna Mae Tunnell; and m second, Mary Young, Oct. 1921 and had; 4, Leota Lawson Tunnell); (e) Eline Curtis Tunnell b Dec. 1, 1893 (m Lillie Mae Smith and had; 1, Carrie Belle Tunnell; 2, B. Tunnell; 3, Clyde Bradford Tunnell; 4, Ada Fay Tunnell; 5, and 6, Maxine and Maxie Tunnell, twins, b Oct. 1923); (f) Elma Palmyra Tunnell b Aug. 16, 1896, m Henry J. Smith Aug. 8, 1921 and had; 1, Dorothy Alice Smith b May 24, 1922 Memphia; (g) Watson Donley Tunnell b Sept. 14, 1898, m Mary Patterson Sept. 1923 and had; 1, ———— Tunnell b July 17, 1924; (h) child b 1900; d July 25, 1900. Jesse William Tunnell b Sept. 16, 1861 married second, Alice Underwood Apr. 7, 1901 Okolona, Miss. and had; (i) Jessie Belle Tunnell b Mar. 16, 1905, m Howard Clinton Chapman Aug. 6, 1921 and had; 1, Howard Clinton Chapman Jr. b Aug. 24, 1922; 2, Mary Alleene Chapman b Mar. 31, 1924.

Eight. Polly Ann Tunnell b Sept. 12, 1864 Monroe Co., Miss; d Aug. 8, 1867 Monroe Co.

Nine. Margaret Palmyra Tunnell b Aug. 13, 1867 Monroe Co., Miss.; d Aug. 22, 1884 Pontotoc Co., Miss.; unmarried.

Ten. David Jackson Tunnell b Mar. 20, 1870; married Sallie Brown 1900 Houlka, Miss. and had; (a) Blanche Tunnell b Aug. 1903; (b) Sank Tunnell; (c) Wallace Tunnell; (d) Hal Reed Tunnell; (e) child d in inf.

VII. Peyton Graves Tunnell, son of Stephen and Sarah Hamilton Tunnell, was born June 11, 1826 in Miss. and d Mar. 1877 in Ark. He married Vina Fortune 1850 in Miss. (d Jan. 10, 1910 in Ark.) and had ten children b in Miss., save one. Names may not be in order of birth.

One. Reuben Tunnell b Dec. 14, 1852 Choctaw Co., Miss.; d aft 1915 Wickes, Ark.; married Carrie Davis 1877 Nevada Co., Ark. and had ch b Ark.; (a) Etta Tunnell b Mar. 10, 1879 (m L. T. Triplett and had; 1, Eulus Triplett; 2, Jewel Triplett, dead; 3, Reuben Triplett; 4, Irma Triplett; 5, Lester Triplett); (b) Carl Tunnell (m Ola Maie Rollins and had; 1, Lewis Tunnell; 2, Fred Tunnell); (c) Ella Tunnell (m J. E. McDaniel; and had· 1, Ruby McDaniel; 2, Delmer McDaniel; 3, Noble McDaniel; 4, Bernice McDaniel); (d) Jack Tunnell, dead; (e) Rascho Tunnell (m Lee Hunter and had; 1, Holter Tunnell; 2, Jennie V. Tunnell); (f) Olo Tunnell (m Mary Bell and had; 1, Ruby Tunnell; 2, Evelyn Tunnell; 3, Ollie Tunnell; 4, Osa Ola Tunnell; 5, Margaret Tunnell); (g) Lee Tunnell (m J. A, Gilleon at Wickes, Ark., postmaster, Wickes and had; 1, Thelma Gilleon; 2, Margaret Gilleon; 3, Alexander Gilleon); (h) Jennie V. Tunnell (m Reece Henry and had; 1, Horace Henry; 2, Lila Henry); (i) Everett Tunnell, m Reece Hunter and had 1, Estelle Tunnell.

Two. William Thomas Tunnell, died at 2.

Three. John Peyton Tunnell b Dec. 26, 1857; d Sept. 30, 1904; married Tennessee Cottingham Oct. 22, 1879 (d Sept. 5, 1897) and had; (a) Laura Tunnell b Sept. 22, 1880, once of Forest, Texas (m James Edmond Brooks Aug. 1, 1895 and had; 1, Ila Brooks b Aug. 22, 1896; 2, Arthur Brooks b Apr. 19, 1899; 3, Garland Brooks b Jan. 1, 1902); (b) Mary Tunnell, m ———— McKneelee; (c) William Tunnell, once of Sayre, Ark., (d) Alice Tunnell b Jan. 27, 1887, m Charles McCroskee and had; 1, son b May 18, 1908; d Feb. 3, 1912; (e) Gertrude Tunnell, m ———— Meaddors; (f) Ethel Tunnell b 1893, of Bluff City, Ark. (m Walter Meaddors Feb. 3, 1910 and had; 1, Audie Meaddors b Aug. 14, 1911); (g) Carl Tunnell b Mar. 22, 1894; (h) son b and d Sept. 5, 1897; and perhaps others.

Four. Sarah A. Tunnell b July 10, 1859; d Jan. 19, 1889 Sayre, Ark.; married William B. Moores Dec. 11, 1879 Sayre, Ark. (b Apr. 25, 1859 Tenn., now of Yakima, Wash.) and had ch b Sayre, Ark; (a) Claude E. Moores b Sept. 13, 1880, of Calif. (m Olive I. Sutton Jan.

17, 1904 and had; 1, and 2, Izola Moores and Willie Moores, twins, b Mar. 9, 1969); (b) Lula Moores b Apr. 12, 1883, of Elma, Wash. (m Clabe Frizzell Dec. 24, 1902 and had; 1, Roy William Frizzell b Nov. 6, 1903, m Gladys May Ford Aug. 12, 1921 and had; (aa) Roger Le Rov Frizzell b Feb. 22 1923; 2, Olive Mabel Frizzell b Nov. 22, 1904, m William Lacey and had; (aa) Shirley Ellen Lacey b June 24, 1922; 3 Lois Ramona Frizzell b Jan. 27, 1911; 4, Ruby Wilma Frizzell b June 6, 1917; d May 9, 1919; 5, Lolo Frizzell b Dec. 28, 1922); (c) Beulah Moores, twin with Lula Moores, b Apr. 12, 1883; d Apr. 29, 1884 Sayre, Ark. William B. Moores m second, Mollie M. Frizzell, of Chedister, Ark.

Five. Isaac Newton Tunnell b Sept. 18, 1861 Chickasaw Co., Miss.; farmer, Cale, Ark.; married Laura E. Irvin Mar. 10, 1885 Nevada Co., Ark. and had ch b Nevada Co., Ark.; (a) Arthur C. Tunnell b Feb. 8, 1887, of Boise, Idaho, Clergyman of Nazarene church; stationed for several years at Hutchinson, Kansas and later served as superintendent of Kansas district; (m Mary Esther Evers and had;1, Mariam Eureva Tunnell; 2, Clifford Earl Tunnell; 3, Gerald Merlin Tunnell b July 12, 1920); (b) Ruby Tunnell b Nov. 21, 1888 (m Charles Steed, farmer, Chedister, Ark. and had; 1, Letha Jecava Steed; 2, Mary Steed; 3, Aubery Steed; 4, Fielden Irvin Steed; 5, Dilcie Steed; 6, Dartis Steed); (c) Bessie Tunnell b Apr. 19, 1890; d Apr. 12, 1891 Nevada Co., Ark.; (d) Ada Tunnell b Sept. 26, 1891 (m Henry C. Hyde, farmer Bluffdale. Tex and had; 1, Joe Lindon Hyde); (e) Edna Tunnell b Oct. 12, of Theo, Ark. (m Samuel E. Chamlee, a farmer, and had ;1, Christal Chamlee; 2, Sibyl Lee Chamlee; 3, Hazel Chamlee; 4, G. W. Chamlee); (f) Viola Tunnell b July 11, 1894, of Teho, Ark., m G. B. Goodwin, in Miss.; (g) Marcia Tunnell b Feb. 12, 1896 of Bluffdale, Tex. (m Carl James Goodwin, in Ala., a farmer, and had; 1, James Willard Goodwin; 2, Milton Goodwin; 3, Autrey A. Goodwin; 4, L. E. Goodwin); (h) Drue Essie Tunnell b Jan. 2, 1898, unm., of Cale, Ark.; (i) Earnest Moore Tunnell b Sept. 25, 1899, of Ft. Worth, Texas, m Mamie Billings; (j) Jessie Clae Tunnell b Sept. 14, 1901, of Dupo, Ill. (m Ernest C. Morrow and had; 1, Vada Heloise Morrow); (k) Oliver H. Tunnell b Mar. 24, 1903; (l) Virda Tunnell b Dec. 19, 1905, of Bluff City, Ark., m Clyde Delaney; (m) Cecil Calvin Tunnell b Aug. 5, 1907; (n) Olga Eudara Tunnell b May 28, 1909; (o) Isaac Warden Tunnell b Sept. 18, 1911.

Six. Timothy G. Tunnell died in Miss.

Seven. Mary Malinda Tunnell b Apr. 1, 1865, of Sayre, Ark.; married Elijah William Barlow May 6, 1883 Sayre, Ark. and had ch b Sayre. Ark; (a) Lula Christine Barlow b Feb. 16, 1891, of Prescott, Ark., m Everett M. Davis Feb. 27, 1922; (b) William Aubery Barlow b July 18, 1893, farmer, Sayre. Ark.. m Leila Dawson Dec. 24, 1916 Bluff City. Ark. and had; 1. William Dawson Barlow b Dec. 5, 1919 Prescott, Ark.; (c) James Hugh Barlow b Feb. 15, 1898, bookkeeper, Sayre. Ark.. m Pertie Benton Mar. 26, 1921 Sayre, Ark. and had; 1. son b and d Nov. 16, 1923.

Eight. Nancy L. Tunnell, died 1872 in inf. in Pike Co., Ark.

Nine. Nathan P. Tunnell, died 1874 Pike Co., Ark.

Ten. Julia Tunnell b Jan. 13, 1875 in Ark., of Emmet, Ark.; married James Jacy Hill and had (a) Bertha L. Hill b Apr. 5. 1896; (b) Mamie O Hill b Aug. 10. 1897; d Dec. 8, 1910; (c) Vera B. Hill b Apr. 28, 1900; (d) Willie C. Hill b Feb. 5, 1902; (e) James K. Hill b Mar. 21, 1904; (f) Oleta L. Hill b Aug. 6. 1906; (g) Lacy R. Hill b Sept. 14, 1908; d Jan. 18. 1911; (h) Neva Winnie Hill b Sept 8, 1910.

IX. Jane Tunnell, dau of Stephen and Sarah Hamilton Tunnell, and had no children.

X.   David Parker Tunnell, son of Stephen and Sarah Hamilton
Tunnell, was born Feb. 7, 1831 Marion Co., Ala. and died May 24,
1924 nr Texarkana, Tex. At age of two his parents moved to Lowdnes.
Co., Miss., where they had lived some years before.   In 1853 he went
to Page Co., Iowa and about 1854 to Collins Co., Tex. In Oct. 1861
he joined the Ninth Texas Infantry and served under Sidney Johnston, then General Bragg, then J. E. Johnston.   He was mustered
out at Meredian, Miss. in May 1865.   He married Ann (Murray)
Wood Jan. 19, 1869 Fayette Co., Ala. (b May 10, 1836; d Sept. 5,
1900 Steens, Miss., dau of Richard Ivey Murray (b May 1, 1797 Dublin, Ireland) and his wife, Agnes Moore Murray (b Mar. 7, 1806, married Jan. 2, 1822) and had an only child;
   One.   Carrie Tunnell b Sept. 4, 1870 Lowdnes Co., Miss., of
Texarkana, Tex.; married Robert Elbert Leech Nov. 3, 1893 (b Apr.
23, 1869 Fayette Co., now Lamar Co., Ala., farmer, son of Elbert and
Frances Harriet (Davis) Leech; g-s of Ephriam Leech, whose father,
William Leech, was one   of the early settlers nr Columbus, Miss.)
and had ch. b Steens, Miss.; (a) Sarah Agnes Leech b Sept. 1, 1894,
of Lankersheim, Calif., m Gorman A. Charles, son of Joseph and
Florence Charles, Feb. 28, 1920 Washington, D. C. (b July 15, 1889
Pittsburg, Penn., a photographer) and had no children; (b) Rachel
Leech b Jan. 12, 1896, of Charco, Tex. (m Cyrus Reagan, son of
John E. and Mary Susie (Wallace) Reagan, May 22, 1919 (b Mar. 3,
1891 Lavaca Co., Tex. and ch b nr Charco, Tex.; 1, Cyrus Tunnell
Reagan b May 26, 1920; 2, Robert Terry Reagan b Feb. 17, 1922; d
July 13, 1923); (c) David Elbert Leech b Aug. 24, 1900 who served
in Navy during World War, now a marine engineer; (d) Robert
Bernard Leech b June 10, 1902; d Dec. 25, 1902 Steens, Miss.; (e)
Peyton Collier Leech b Apr. 3, 1904.
   XI.   Martha Kezia Tunnell, dau of Stephen and Sarah Hamilton
Tunnell, was born July 31, 1833 Lowdnes Co., Miss. and died June 10,
1889 Ittawamba Co., Miss. She married Loami Somerford, son of
William and Piety Somerford, June 30, 1853 Ittawamba Co., Miss.
(b July 30, 1833 South Carolina; d May 22, 1918 Aberdeen, Miss.) and
had 7 ch. b Ittawamba Co., Miss.
   One.   David Tunnell Somerford b May 26, 1854; d Jan. 5, 1870.
   Two.   John Wesley Somerford b May 18, 1856; d Aug. 15, 1865.
   Three.   Thomas Somerford b Feb. 8, 1858; d Oct. 8, 1859.
   Four.   Ira Milton Somerford b Mar. 26, 1860, of Ft. Worth, Tex.;
married Sarah A. Streetman (b Feb. 27, 1864, deceased) and had; (a
Mattie E. Somerford b Aug. 8, 1885; (d) Metzger E. Somerford b
Jan. 26, 1887; (c) John L. Somerford b Oct. 15, 1888; (d) Ida L.
Somerford b July 19, 1890; (e) Gertie B. 'Somerford b Sept. 21, 1893;
(f) May Somerford b Feb. 4, 1896; (g) Mary A. Somerford b June
29, 1900; (h) Morris Somerford b June 25, 1904.
   Five.   Mary Jane Somerford b Oct. 25, 1863; d Mar. 4, 1886 It-
tawamba Co., Miss., a week after her marriage to John Perry on Feb.
28, 1886, Ittawamba Co., Miss.   John Perry b Feb. 16, 1862 Lincoln
Co., Tenn., now of Wodland, Miss.
   Six.   Sallie Annie Somerford b Mar. 16, 1866, of Woodland,
Miss. married her sister's widower, John Perry, in Ittawamba Co.,
Miss. and had; (a) Lonie Belle Perry b Mar. 9, 1887 Chickasaw Co.,
Miss., of Julia, Texas, m Ed Davis June 13, 1905 Chickasaw Co.,
Miss.; (b) William A. Perry b Sept. 22, 1888 Monroe Co.. Miss., of
Aberdeen, Miss, m Lydia Greene Young in Monroe Co., Miss.; (c)
John Clarence Perry b Feb. 4, 1891 Monroe Co., of Aberdeen, Miss.
(m Berline Clemons Apr. 20. 1918 Chickasaw Co., Miss. and had ch b
that county; 1, Eula May Perry b Mar. 17, 1920; 2, Maggie Reva

Perry b Jan. 30, 1922; 3, Edgar Perry b Feb. 2, 1924); (d) Madge Sophrona Perry b Aug. 5, 1895 Chickasaw Co., Miss., of Aberdeen, Miss. (m first, her first cousin, Roy Vaughn Somerford, son of Gaines Somerford, Nov. 26, 1916 Aberdeen, Miss. (b Mar. 6, 1890; d Dec. 3, 1921) and had; 1, Roy Vaughn Somerford Jr., b Feb 16, 1921; and m second, Lewis Wilson Sept. 19, 1923); (e) Ethel Pearl Perry b Apr. 7, 1897, of Prairie, Miss. (m Lewis Smith Jan. 6, 1915 and had ch b Chickasaw Co., Miss.; 1, Connie Allen Smith b Nov. 25, 1915; 2, Daniel Johnson Smith b Apr. 17, 1917; 3, Annie Jewel Smith b July 27, 1920; 4, Oma Lewis Smith b June 30, 1922; 5, Noma Louise Smith b July 15, 1923); (f) Edgar Berl Perry, twin of Ethel Pearl Perry, b Apr. 7, 1897; (g) Louie Lee Perry b July 24, 1903, of Aberdeen, Miss., m Allen Wilson Jan. 26, 1924 Monroe Co., Miss.; (h) Dovie D. Perry, twin of Louie Lee Perry, b July 24, 1903, of Woodland, Miss.

Seven. Gaines Somerford b May 18, 1869, of Aberdeen, Miss., married first, M. A. Harmon Feb. 16, 1888 (d Nov. 21, 1911) and second, Lola Wilson, Feb. 27, 1913. He had children b in Miss.; (a) Roy Vaughn Somerford b Mar. 6, 1890; d Dec. 3, 1921 (m Madge Sophrona Perry, dau of John and Sallie Annie (Somerford) Perry, Nov. 26, 1916 Aberdeen, Miss., and had; 1, Roy Vaughn Somerford Jr. b Feb. 16, 1921); (b) Elzie Somerford b 1896, m Leomer Easter and had no ch.; (c) Irene Somerford b 1908; (d) Ruth Somerford.

XII. Thomas Loyd Tunnell, son of Stephen and Sarah Hamilton Tunnell, was born Nov. 13, 1836 and died on the farm his father entered about 1828 nr Steens, Miss., on Aug. 15, 1914. He was a soldier in the War Between the States. He married Martha Frances Stone Aug. 30, 1860 (b Oct. 22, 1837; d Feb. 20, 1915 Steens, Miss.) and had five ch. b nr Steens, Miss.

One. Sarah Jane Tunnell, b July 2, 1861; lives on the old home stead, Steens, Miss.; married first, Boothe Franklin Brownlee Jan. 1, 1879 (b Jan. 16, 1855 New Hope, Miss.; d July 7, 1903) and second, O. P. Brown, Jan. 14, 1914. Ch b Miss.; (a) Willie Quinn Brownlee b Sept. 19, 1880, of Steens, Miss. (m James Oscar Green Aug. 12, 1898 and had; 1, Jesse Wheeler Green b Oct. 8, 1899; d Oct. 6, 1917; 2, David Trouper Green b July 21, 1901, engeneer, Steens, Miss., m Adell Cline Aug. 28, 1922 and had; (aa) David Trouper Green, the second, b Aug. 1, 1924; 3, Margie Lee Green b Jan. 1903; 4, James Oscar Green, the second, b June 1904, merchant, Birmingham, Ala., m Annie May Reed Feb. 11, 1924; 5, Polly Green b Oct. 6, 1906, m Arvin Cline Aug. 1923; 6, George Burton Green b Aug. 28, 1908; 7, Alice Tunnell Green b Oct. 29, 1909; 8, Virginia Green b Oct. 8, 1911; 9, Frank Green b 1913; d July 1915; 10, dau b and d 1914; 11, Sarah Ellen Green b Dec. 18, 1921); (b) Thomas Byington Brownlee b June 27, 1882, of Isola, Miss. (m Mary Harris May 12, 1912 Columbus, Miss. and had; 1, John Harris Brownlee b Feb. 15, 1913; 2, James Edward Brownlee b July 1916); (c) Carrie Lee Brownlee b Aug. 5, 1884, of Vernon, Ala. (m William Wallace Cobb Nov. 7, 1906 Vernon, Ala. and had; 1, Roland Tunnell Cobb b Sept. 1, 1907 Vernon, Ala.; 2, Sarah Chapell Cobb b Dec. 11, 1908 Vernon, Ala.; 3, Martha Stone Cobb b Dec. 12, 1912; 4, Mary Wallace Cobb b Sept. 11, 1914); (d) John Tunnell Brownlee b Aug. 28, 1886; d New Hope, Miss.; unmarried.

Two. Mary Loyd Tunnell b Aug. 12, 1862; d Sept. 25, 1868 Steens, Miss.

Three. Alice Lee Tunnell b Nov. 30, 1864; d Oct. 20, 1887 Steens, Miss.; unmarried.

Four. William Albert Tunnell b May 9, 1867; d Oct. 8, 1869 Steens, Miss.

Five.   Charles Thomas Tunnell b Aug. 2, 1870; d Sept. 5, 1876 Steens, Miss.

NICHOLAS MONEY TUNNELL

G.   Nicholas Money Tunnell, son of Stephen and Kezia Money Tunnell, was born Apr. 30, 1792 Greene Co., Tenn. and died, after 1865, near Bethel, Morgan Co., Ill. He lived for several years in Ky., it is thonght in Hardin Co. He married at an early age. He married first, Sarah Gentry (died in Morgan Co., Ill.) and second, Martha Jones Wilcox, dau of Ambrose and Permelia (Wilson) Jones. She had been married twice before her marriage to N. M. Tunnell. She m first, Alexander Watt and second, Joshua Willcox. At this time there are less than one dozen descendants of Nicholas Money Tunnell who bear the name of Tunnell. Children may not be given in order of birth.

By first marriage;
I.   Nancy Tunnell b 1810.
II.   Martin Luther Tunnell.
III.   Kizzie Tunnell b 1815.
IV.   Susan Tunnell.
V.   Perry Tunnell b Feb. 21, 1821.
VI.   Stephen Andrew Tunnell b Dec. 17, 1823.
VII.   Hannah B. Tunnell b Oct. 9, 1824.
VIII.   Jesse Tunnell.
IX.   Sarah Tunnell.
By second marriage;
X.   Polly Tunnell.
XI.   Huldah Jane Tunnell.
XII.   Manerva Caroline Lemmons Tunnell b Mar. 17, 1839.
XI'I.   John Wesley Tunnell b Sept. 14, 1842.
XIV.   Hettie Ann Tunnell b July 9, 1846.
XV.   Jonathan Hardin Tunnell b July 20, 1847.
Of the foregoing;
I.   Nancy Tunnell, dau of Nicholas Money and Sarah Gentry Tunnell, born 1810 in Ky., died 1844; married Jonathan Watson (d Sept. 25, 1881) and had eight ch.;
One.   David Watson b 1826; d 1902; m ——— ——— and had ch.
Two.   Cephas Watson b 1828; d Feb. 17, 1862.
Three.   Susan J. Watson b Abt 1830; d Sept. 24, 1898 Itasca, Tex. married first, William A. Patton (d abt 1863) and had; (a) Cephas S. Patton b Dec. 25, 1856; d July 21, 1902 Mangum, Okla. (m his first cousin, Margaret J. Wooldridge Oct. 20, 1884 and had; 1, Constance E. Patton b Aug. 16, 1885, m Litchfield G. Townsend Dec. 27, 1908 and had; (aa) Jonnie Galon Townsend b Nov. 1, 1909 Snyder, Okla.; (bb) Garland Patton Townsend b May 26, 1911 Mangum, Okla.; (cc) Paul Litchfield Townsend b Jan. 20, 1913 Mangum, Okla.; (dd) Clara Florence Townsend b Feb. 4, 1915 Mangum, Okla.; (ee) Francis Mark Townsend b Oct. 19, 1919 Clinton, Okla.; (ff) Murrel Clyde Townsend b Mar. 14, 1922 Purcell, Okla.; 2, Florence A. Patton b Dec. 6, 1887; d Oct. 12, 1915 Mangum, Okla.; 3, Clara J. Patton b Apr. 7, 1890, m Louis A. Rushing Oct. 24, 1916 and had; (aa) Louis Rushing b June 16, 1919; (bb) Ralph P. Rushing b Nov. 4, 1922; 4, William A. Patton b May 25, 1892, unm.; 5, Dewitt I. Patton b Apr. 25, 1896, m Jessie Lee Thompson June 18, 1918 and had; (aa) Ross Dewitt Patton b June 10, 1919; 6, Dewey C. S. Patton b Sept. 1, 1898, m Leon Eaton Sept. 17, 1920 and had no ch.; 7, Dwight L. M. Patton b June 2, 1901, m Opal Hembree June 3, 1923); (b) Belle Patton b Oct. 20, 1860; d Nov. 20, 1891 Dade Co., Mo. (m Thomas Lawrence Aug. 6, 1880 and had; 1, Althea Lawrence b May 6, 1888, of Dallas,

Tex., m R. L. Robinson May 3, 1911 Dallas, Tex. and had one ch);
Susan J. Watson married second, B. F. Simons 1869 Parsons, Kan.
and had; (c) Ella Simons b Jan. 24, 1870, of Cleburne, Tex. (m first,
E. J. Daniel, Nov. 18, 1886 and had; 1, Edda Daniel b Jan. 5, 1888
Itasca, Tex.; d Mar. 19, 1923 Itasca, Tex., m Claud Wakefield Mar. 13,
1907 Waxachie, Tex. and had; (aa) Loreta Tyson Wakefield b Dec.
17, 1915; and m second, James Haby Brockette Oct. 2, 1904 Itasca,
Tex. (b Nov. 27, 1861) and had; 2, A. B. Brockette b Aug. 27, 1907
Itasca, Tex.); (d) Mellie Simons, twin of Ella Simons, b Jan. 24, 1870;
died young; (e) Will Edmonds Simons b Nov. 17, 1871 Montana, Kan.,
of Yuma, Ariz. (m Mary Louise Simpson Jan. 15, 1896 Hill Co., Tex.
(b Mar. 30, 1880 Ala.) and had; 1, Fred E. Simons b Nov. 5, 1896
Itasca, Tex., of Somerton, Ariz., m Ada Lucile Morton Apr. 6, 1923
and had; (aa) Fred E. Simons Jr., b Sept. 6, 1924 San Diego, Calif.;
2, Dewey Marshall Simons b Feb. 10, 1899 Itasca., Tex., of Cahoma,
Tex., m Eunice Packett Dec. 25, 1921 Winters, Tex. and had; (aa)
Billie Weldon Simons b Feb. 1, 1925 Winters, Tex.; 3, Roy Edmond
Simons b Dec. 6, 1902 Hillsboro, Tex. of Yuma, Ariz., m Addalissa
Morton Oct. 6, 1924 Yuma, Ariz.; 4, Susie Celestia Simons b May 29,
1906 Herford, Tex.; 5, Willis Marion Simons b June 21, 1913 Winters,
Tex.); (f) Pearl Simons b Nov. 17, 1874 Montana, Kan., of Ballinger,
Tex. (m Miller Black Dec. 2, 1900 and had ch b Itasca, Tex.; 1, Otha
Audney Roosevelt Black (dau) b Sept. 25, 1901; d Aug. 3, 1904; 2,
Lela Blanch Black b Sept. 13, 1904; 3, Autye Ople Black b Nov. 17,
1908).; (g) Earl Simons, b and d same day.

Four.   Rachel Watson b 1836; d 1844.

Five.   Samuel Watson b Dec. 13, 1838, of Lamar, Mo. 1911; d
Mo.; m Rebecca Sims Sept. 14, 1860 (d after 1911) and had; (a)
Wesley Watson b Nov. 11, 1861; d 1898 (m Emma Lingle 1890 and
had; 1, Clyde Watson b 1892; 2, Charles Watson b 1891; 3, Earl Wat-
son b 1896; 4, Dewey Watson b 1898); (b) Lizzie Watson b Sept. 17,
1868; d Aug. 26, 1903 (m James W. Trout June 29, 1890 and had; 1,
James Trout b July 29, 1891; d Oct. 23, 1891; 2, Leonard Trout b
July 25, 1892); (c) Jennie Watson b Dec. 20, 1868; d Jan. 2, 1907; (d)
Linnie Watson b Jan. 18, 1872; d Sept. 27, 1900.

Six.   Jane Watson b Jan. 5, 1840; d Mar. 1, 1911 Vinson, Okla.;
married Robert T. Wooldridge Oct. 22, 1862 (b Jan. 23, 1837; d Aug.
4, 1913 Vinson, Okla.) and had; (a) Cephas N. Wooldridge b Aug. 16,
1863 Dade Co., Mo.; d July 22, 1887 Lockwood, Mo. (m Mattie Marshall Nov. 28, 1886 and had; 1, Willa Wooldridge b July 20, 1887,
unm., of Kansas City); (b) Margaret J. Wooldridge b July 9, 1865,
of Harrah, Okla. (m Cephas S. Patton. See record of William and
Susan Watson Patton); (c) Peach M. Wooldridge b Feb. 22, 1867, of
Dallas, Tex. (m James A. Donham June 14, 1884 (deceased) and had;
1, Della Donham b May 16, 1885, m Joe Austill Dec. 24, 1901; 2,
George Donham b Mar. 6, 1887; 3, Odessa Donham b Feb. 8, 1889; d
July 25, 1891; 4, Esther Donham b May 22, 1892; 5, Ruth Donham b
Jan. 13, 1898; d Aug. 9, 1899; 6, Lorane Donham b Nov. 7, 1900; d
July 27, 1902; 7, Robert Donham b May 19, 1905); (d) Edmund Grant
Wooldridge b Mar. 12, 1869 Dade Co., Mo., of Vinson, Okla. (m first,
Jennie D. Vanlear Nov. 8, 1892 (d Sept. 3, 1903) and had ch b nr
Vinson, Okla.; 1, Jessie D. Wooldridge b Aug. 12, 1896, m G. C. Cham-
bers Dec. 30, 1914 Hollis, Okla. and had; (aa) Jessie Novella Cham-
bers b Feb. 4, 1916; (bb) Jennie Loretta Chambers b June 12, 1919;
(cc) G. C. Chambers Jr. b Apr. 12, 1922; 2, Cora May Wooldridge b
Apr. 14, 1900. E. G. Wooldridge m second, Maggie V. Ellis Aug. 13,
1905 Vinson, Okla. and had; 3, Hazel Inez Wooldridge b Sept. 3, 1907;
4, Winston Oliver Wooldridge b Apr. 29, 1909; 5, Alma Oceil Woold-

ridge b Aug. 5, 1917); (e) Jonathan Colfax Wooldridge, twin of Edmund Grant Wooldridge, b Mar. 12, 1869 Dade Co., Mo., of Vinson, Okla. (m Mamie E. McCain Aug. 19, 1891 Pluto, Tex. and had; 1, Clara Ethel Wooldridge b and d June 25, 1892 Pulto, Tex.; 2, Rushie Corra Wooldridge b Dec. 16, 1893 Pluto, Tex., m Raphael A. Fanning Mar. 5, 1911 Reed, Okla. and had ch b Vinson, Okla.; (aa) Dorothy Olettie Fanning b Aug. 16, 1912; (bb) Lowell Colfax Fanning; (cc) Alma Geraldine Fanning b Sept. 17, 1919; 3, Alva Eugene Wooldridge b Apr. 8, 1896 Pluto, Tex., m Bertha Lee Cox Aug. 11, 1917 and had ch b Vinson; (aa) Alva Eugene Wooldridge Jr. b Aug. 2, 1918; (bb) Teddy Colfax Wooldridge b Apr. 14, 1923; 4, Ercie E. Wooldridge b Aug. 27, 1898 Itasca, Tex., of Vinson, Okla., m T. L. Francis June 29, 1918 Vinson and had; (aa) Jonnie Lavelle Francis b Apr. 19, 1918; ɔ, Bessie Alma Oceil Wooldridge b Nov. 30, 1902 Pluto, Tex.; d Mar. 1, 1913 Vinson, Okla.; 6, Katie Mae Wooldridge b Nov. 23, 1905, m Alval Worthen Dec. 30, 1922 Vinson, Okla. and had; (aa) Rodney L. Worthen b Oct. 4, 1923 Vinson); (f) Rushie Ann Wooldridge b Sept. 14, 1871; d Nov. 30, 1893 Itasca, Tex. (m Eugene Duncan June 12, 1888 Sylvania, Mo. and had; 1, Hattie Duncan b July 16, 1890, m —— —— 1924 Waco, Tex); (g) Robert B. Wooldridge b May 21, 1875; d small; (h) Albert N. Wooldridge, twin of Robert B. Wooldridge, b May 21, 1875; d small; (i) Alda May Wooldridge b June 10, 1876, of Wheeler, Okla. (m Alexander S. Mathis Dec. 27, 1892 Pluto, Tex. and had; 1, Earnest Mathis b Nov. 17, 1897; d Sept. 12, 1899; 2, Okla Mathis (dau) b Aug. 11, 1902, m —— —— 1924; 3, Opal Mathis b Aug. 5, 1908, m —— —— 1924; 4, Alpha J. D. Mathis); (j) Alva George Wooldridge b Apr. 12, 1879; d 1880; (k) Horace Edgar Wooldridge b May 28, 1881, of Vinson, Okla. (m Alice Pruett Oct. 4, 1903 Vinson, Okla. and had ch b Vinson; 1, Alford Wooldridge b Sept. 1, 1906; 2, Bernie Wooldridge b Jan. 9, 1908; 3, J. T. Wooldridge b Apr. 21, 1910; dead; 4, Loraine Wooldridge; (l) Edna Gertrude Wooldridge b Oct. 20, 1883 Dade Co., Mo., of Willow, Okla. (m Gouley F. McSpadden Apr. 7, 1901 Greer Co., Okla. and had; 1, Orah Belle McSpadden b Mar. 20, 1902 Greer Co., m Garvin Lee Hill Dec. 26, 1923; 2, Peachie Alta McSpadden b Dec. 30, 1903 Greer Co.; 3, Cuba Maye McSpadden b Apr. 23, 1906 Harmon Co., Okla.; 4, Sherman Boyd McSpadden b Aug. 16, 1910; 5, Iva Lurleen McSpadden b 1913, Harmon Co.; 6, Edna Lonell Kathleen McSpadden b 1920 Harmon Co., Okla.)

Seven. Nicholas Watson b 1842; d Apr. 18, 1876; married Anna Wyatt and had no ch.

Eight. Kizziah Watson b 1844; d 1904 Dade Co., Mo.; married Jacob McKanna and had ch. including; 1, John McKanna; 2, Mattie McKanna; 3, Maggie McKanna; 4, Peachey McKanna; 5, Gilbert McKanna.

II. Martin Luther Tunnell, son of Nicholas Money and Sarah Gentry Tunnell, b abt 1812 in Ky.; d after 1847; married Barbara —— and had no ch. He lived nr Bethel, Ill. Is said to have served in the Black Hawk war.

III. Kizzie Tunnell, dau of Nicholas Money and Sarah Gentry Tunnell, was born 1815, in Ky., and died nr Murryville, Ill. She married Richard Wilson, who d nr Murryville, Ill., and had children b nr Murryville.

One. Zibbah Wilson b Sept. 30, 1838, of Manchester, Ill.; married William Greenwalt Apr. 17, 1855 (d Jan. 10, 1897 Manchester, Ill.) and had ch b nr Manchester, Ill.; (a) George Greenwalt b June 14, 1856 d Feb. 21, 1909 Manchester, Ill. (m Sarah Neal, dau of John Terry Neal (d Feb. 1917 Manchester, Ill.) and Caroline Lemon Neal

(b Nov. 3, 1833; d Mar. 1921), on Oct. 29, 1878 nr Murrayville, Ill.
(b Aug. 2, 1856 nr Manchester, Ill.) and had; 1, Ethel May Greenwalt
b Feb. 1h, 1883 Manchester, Ill., of Manchester, m Edward E. Rousey
Sept. 14, 1904 Manchester, Ill. and had; (aa) Ruth Rousey b July 11,
1914 Manchester; 2, Jessie Greenwalt b Sept. 16, 1885 Manchester, of
Roodhouse, Ill., m Theodore Drennan Feb. 15, 1905 and had ch b Manchester; (aa) George Neal Drennan b Nov. 23, 1905; (bb) Paul William Drennean b Jan. 12, 1911); (b) Charles Greenwalt b Nov. 11,
1860, of Jacksonville, Ill. (m Ella Neal, sister of Sarah Neal, Oct.
20, 1881 and had; 1, Edward Greenwalt, of Jerseyville, Ill., m Eva
McCracken and had; (aa) Charles Samuel Greenwalt; (bb) Lucille
Greenwalt; (cc) Ralph Edward Greenwalt; 2, Bida Greenwalt, m
Rebecca Baker and had; (aa) George Howard Greenwalt b Apr. 30,
1912; 3, Stella Greenwalt, of Murrayville, Ill., m T. B. Beadles and had;
(aa) Wilbur Beadles b Oct. 26, 1913; (bb) Margaret Ellen Beadles b
Nov. 3, 1916; (cc) Robert Beadles b Apr. 27, 1919; (dd) John Paul
Beadles b Oct. 15, 1922); (c) Eddie Greenwalt b Nov. 25, 1862; d Apr.
18, 1863; (d) Albert Greenwalt b Apr. 26, 1865, of Manchester, Ill.
(m Agnes Wagstaff Feb. 20, 1895 and had ch b Morgan Co., Ill.; 1,
Maude Greenwalt, of Rochester, Minn., m Samuel Hauck and had;
(aa) Samuel Hauck Jr.; 2, Sidney Ross Greenwalt, of Manchester,
Ill., m Susie Windsor; 3, Ada Greenwalt, of Jacksonville, Ill., m Lennie Goocher and had; (aa) Helen Goocher; 4, Gertie Greenwalt, of
Roodhouse, Ill., m Charles Garner and had; (aa) Elinore Garner;
(bb) Cloe Garner; 5, Hazel Greenwalt, unm.; 6, May Greenwalt, twin,
unm.; 7, Fay Greenwalt, twin of May Greenwalt, m John Thady and
had no ch.; 8, Mildred Greenwalt, twin, unm.; 9, Mabel Greenwalt,
twin of Mildred Greenwalt, of Greenfield, Ill., m Harley Short); (e)
Hattie Greenwalt b Sept. 10, 1875, of Bloomington, Ill., m J. H. Pike
Feb. 18, 1904 and had no ch.; (f) Ernest Greenwalt b May 26, 1877;
d July 24, 1913 Pekin, Ill. (m Mary Parks June 25, 1904 and had an
only ch; 1, Donald Parks Greenwalt).

Two. Cephas B. Wilson b Aug. 17, 1845; d Jan. 20, 1894; married Sarah Angie Billings, dau of Abram and Nancy Terry Billings,
Nov. 12, 1872 (b Oct. 21, 1848 nr Manchester, Ill., of Manchester) and
had no ch.

Three. George Wilson (deceased married first, Amanda Patterson and second, ———— ———— in Kansas City and had ch. by first
marriage; (a) Birdie Wilson; (b) Effie Wilson, m ———— Wyly; (c)
Cora Wilson, of Valparaiso, Ind., m ———— Petts; (d) Lola Wilson,
m ———— ————.

Four. Lewis Wilson, of South Dakota; married Angie Irving
and had 5 ch. including; (a) Chester Wilson, of Port Angeles, Wash.;
(b) Oliver Wilson; (c) Burl Wilson; (d) Harry Wilson.

IV. Susan Tunnell, dau of Nicholas Money and Sarah Gentry
Tunnell, married Thol Farris and moved from Illinois. She is said
to have lived at one time in Oregon and another in Florida.

V. Perry Tunnell, son of Nicholas Money and Sarah Gentry
Tunnell, was born Feb. 21, 1821 and died Oct. 24, 1847 Morgan Co.,
Ill. He married Anna Eliza Whitlock, dau of Charles and Martha
(Wilson) Whitlock, gdau Moses Wilson, Revolutionary soldier of Ky.,
Feb. 25, 1841 nr Athensville, Ill. (b Mar. 6, 1823 Adair Co., Ky.; d
Sept. 22, 1890 Morgan Co., Ill.) and had four ch b nr Athensville, Ill.

One. Mary Ann Tunnell b Jan. 22, 1842; d Sept. 7, 1898.

Two. Elizabeth Tunnell b Sept. 30, 1843, of Murryville, Ill.;
married Thomas Entrikin, son of Thomas and Millicent (Carlisle)
Entrikin, Nov. 24, 1870 Morgan Co., Ill. (b July 27, 1839 Lancaster,
Penn.) and had ch b nr Murryville, Ill.; (a) Thomas Perry Entrikin

b Apr. 16, 1873, unmarried, of Murrayville, Ill.; (b) Virginia Isabella
Entrikin b May 24, 1876, unmarried, of Murrayville, Ill., who supplied
many names and dates on family of Nicholas Money Tunnell; (c)
Charles Wilson Entrikin b June 27, 1879, of Murrayville, Ill. (m
Stella Norton Sept. 12, 1902 and had ch b Margan Co., Ill.; 1, Faith
Florecia Entrikin b Apr. 10, 1904; 2, Martha Mildred Entrikin b Mar.
2, 1906; 3, Charles Wayne Entrikin b Aug. 4, 1907; 4, Helen Lucille
Entrikin b Jan. 10, 1910; 5, Albert Clare Entrikin b July 6, 1911; d
July 8, 1911; 6, Lillian Alice Entrikin b Oct. 19, 1913; 7, Cayle Gilbert
Entrikin b Aug. 12, 1915; 8, Marjory Frances Entrikin b Aug. 22,
1917; 9, Mary Eloise Entrikin b June 27, 1919; 10, Harold Keith Entri-
kin b Feb. 23, 1M921; 11, Gerald Kent Entrikin b Oct. 3, 1922; 12,
Ruth Pauline Entrikin b May 29, 1924).

Three. Joseph Francis Tunnell b Sept. 28, 1845; d July 9, 1894;.
married first, Jane Dadisman, abt 1863, who d Apr. 25, 1880, the
mother of his children; and second, Serelda Edwards, 1882, who d
Apr. 1912. Ch. b Morgan Co., Ill.; (a) son b abt 1865; d in inf.; (b)
Ida E. Tunnell b Dec. 22, 1867, m Newt Sorrells; (c) Laura Tunnell
b Aug. 24, 1869; d Apr. 24, 1924, Jacksonville, Ill. (m Frank Tribble,.
of Franklin, Ill. and had; 1, Una Tribble b 1894, m Leslie Clayton; 2,
Elsie Tribble b 1896, m Grover Caldwell); (d) Olivia Tunnell b Oct.
17, 1773, of Havana, Ill. (m ——— England and had; 1, Teddy England; 2, Ethel England); (e) Sarah E. Tunnell b Apr. 27, 1879, m
George Seymour.

Four. Charles Wilson Tunnell b Oct. 10, 1847; d Aug. 18, 1850.
VI. Stephen Andrew Tunnell, son of Nicholas Money and Sarah
Gentry Tunnell, was born Dec. 17, 1823 and died Oct. 23, 1889 Bethel,.
Ill. He married Sarah Ann Rall, who was born in Paris, France,
who died nr Bethel, Ill. and had eleven ch.

One. Rachel Elizabeth Tunnell b June 22, 1848 Athensville, Ill.;
d Mar. 16, 1922 Jacksonville, Ill.; married Thomas Blair Oct. 1865 nr
Meredosia, Ill. (of Quincy, Ill. 1924) and had ch b Bethel, Ill.; (a)
Frank E. Blair b Oct. 24, 1866, of Chapin, Ill. (m Georgia Bloyd and
had; 1, Opal M. Blair b June 2, 1893, of Chapin, Ill., m Marie Frye
Apr. 20, 1918 Springfield, Ill. and had no ch.; 2, Blanche E. Blair b
Nov. 15, 1895; d Jan. 28, 1924 Chicago, Ill., m Harold Woodward
1913 Springfield, Ill. and had; (aa) Odell Woodward b Feb. 20, 1915
Chapin, Ill.; (bb) Janice Woodward b Nov. 2, 1917 Chicago; (cc)
Barbara Jean Woodward b Jan. 19, 1924 Chicago); (b) Ida B. Blair
b Nov. 13, 1868, of Barrow, Ill. (m James Beddingfield and had an
only ch.; 1, Bessie Beddingfield b Jan. 1894 Chapin, Ill., m ———
Bowman, St. Charles, Mo. and had; (aa) Bernard Lynn Bowman b nr
Hillview, Ill.); (c) William S. Blair b Oct. 30, 1870, of Versailles, Ill.
(m Meda Festler and had; 1, Hazel Blair b Sept. 1893, m Howard
Taylor and had; (aa) Beryl Taylor, son b Versailles; 2, Floyd Blair,
m ——— ——— and had; (aa) Forest Blair, b Kewanee, Ill.; (bb)
William Blair b Versailles).

Two. Delia Tunnell b Aug. 13, 1849; d Aug. 14, 1849 Athensville, Ill.

Three. Mary E. Tunnell b Sept. 18, 1851 Bethel, Ill., of Galesburg, Ill.; married John W. Sargent, son of James Berry and Mary
Jane (Carter) Sargent, soldier in the War Between the States, Feb.
14, 1868 Bethel, Ill. (b July 18, 1836 nr Jacksonville, Ill.; d July 14,
1915 Kewanee, Ill.) and had ch b Morgan Co., Ill.; (a) Ella Sargent
b 1870; (b) Edward Sargent b Sept. 7, 1871; d Nov. 27, 1915 Kewanee,
Ill.; (c) Minnie B. Sargent, m Horace L. Bridgman; (d) Lourinda
Sargent b Aug 1878; d Nov. 5, 1920 Galesburg, Ill. m first, Louis
Wells Nov. 30, 1901 (d 1913 and second, A. L. Richmond. 1915; (e)

Martha C. Sargent, m ——— Nolen; (f) Rachel Elizabeth Sargent, m Eugene Simms, son of Edward Chatham and Emily Catherine (McCutchen) Simms, Oct. 1, 1904 Kewanee, Ill.; (h) Ida Sargent, m Frank Heiser and had ch.; (i) James Sargent, m ——— ——— and had ch.; (j) Albert Sargent; (k) Mary Sargent, m Clarence Reed; (l) Enoch Sargent.

Four.   Nancy Ann Tunnell b Apr. 3, 1853; married first, ——— Hale, Mar. 13, 1873 (d 1892) and second Du Jones, and had ch.

Five.   son died in inf.

Six.   Martha Jane Tunnell b Oct. 8, 1855, m William Libbey and had ch.

Seven.   Luvesta Etta Tunnell b Aug. 10, 1857; d in inf.

Eight.   Dora Tunnell b May 3, 1859, m Hiram Ethel Nov 27, 1879 and had no ch.

Nine.   Minnie Tunnell b abt 1861; d 1865.

Ten.   Charles Tunnell b June 17, 1866, of Kewaneee, Ill.; m Martha Cowart 1904 and had no ch.

Eleven.   daughter b and d in inf. abt 1868.

VII.   Hannah Boone Tunnell b Oct. 9, 1824 in Ky.; d Nov. 22, 1905 nr Athensville, Ill.; married Sampson Wood, who died Aug. 5, 1879 Athensville, Ill. and had;

One.   William Wood, of Athensville, Ill.; m first, ——— ——— and had; (a) Pearl Wood, m Will Hubbell; and m second, Mahala ——— and had; (b) Laura Wood b Mar. 31, 1887; d July 22, 1925 Virden, Ill., m Robert Atkinson JMuly 3, 1905 and had an only child; 1, Robert Atkinson, junior, b 1907; d July 31, 1925 Chatham, Ill.; (c) Peter C. Wood, of Franklin, Ill.; (d) Charles Wood, of Virden, Ill.; (e) daughter, m L. Oliver Barnett, of Virden, Ill.

Two.   Mary Elizabeth Wood, died bef. 1905, m Henry Barnett, deceased.

Three.   George Wood, of Athensville, Ill.; married ——— ——— and had at least two children; (a) Victor Wood, of Jacksonville, Ill., m Elsie Dryden; (b) Chester Wood, m Pearl Dryden, sister of Elsie Dryden.

Four.   Richard S. Wood, of Kansas; m ——— ——— and had at least one ch.; (a) Ida Wood, of Roodhouse, Ill., m Charley Floranel.

Five.   Nannie Wood, of St Louis, Mo., m ——— Hodge.

Six.   Thomas Tilman Wood (dead); m Annie McBride.

Seven.   Kizziah Wood died 1891 nr Athensville, Ill.; married William G. Sortor and had; (a) Vivian Leasley Sorton b nr Wrights, Ill.; d nr Kansas City; (b) Sampson Boone Sortor b Norwood, Mo. of Granite City, Ill. m ——— ——— Edwardsville, Ill. and had; 1, Henry Sortor; 2, Harold Sortor; 3, Margaret Sortor; 4, Mable Sortor; 5, Vensene Sortor; 6, Junie Sortor); (c) Mary Josephine Sortor b 1883, of Roodhouse, Ill. (m Ed Drury at St. Louis, Mo. and had; 1, Carl William Edward Drury b Granite City, Ill.; m second, Robert Ruyle and had; 2, Loyal Hall Ruyle b nr Roodhouse, Ill.); (d) Mable Sortor b nr Athensville, Ill.; d nr Colorado Springs, Mo., m Earl Kissell in St. Louis, Mo. (d Granite City) and had no ch.; (e) Leora May Sortor b Indian Territory, of Chicago, Ill., m Frank Cantow.

Eight.   Martin Wood.

Nine.   Sibia Wood, dead; m Walter Strawmatt, now of Manchester, Ill. and had at least one ch.; (a) Carry Strawmatt, of Manchester, m ——— Lasson.

VIII.   Jesse Tunnell, son of Nicholas Money and Sarah Gentry Tunnell, died in early childhood.

IX.   Sarah Tunnell, dau of Nicholas Money and Sarah Gentry Tunnell, lived at Chapin, Ill.   She married John Rice and had ch.

X. Polly Tunnell, dau of Nicholas Money and Martha (Jones) Watt Willcox Tunnell, moved from Illinois. It is not known whom she married.

XI. Hulda Jane Tunnell, dau of Nicholas Money and Martha (Jones) Watt Willcox Tunnell, married first, James Riley Pruitt and second, John H. Pickett, a soldier of the War Between the States, son of Rev. Thomas Pickett, Apr. 12, 1867. Ch.; 1, Alice M. Pruitt, of Des Moines, Iowa, m ———— Castleberry; 2, John W. Pruitt, d in inf.; 3, William S. Pickett b July 12, 1869; 4, Anna L. Pickett b Oct. 3, 1871; 5, Washington Pickett b Dec. 14, 1873; 6, Walter L Pickett b Dec. 16, 1876; 7, Vena B. Pickett b June 12, 1878; d June 24, 1878; 8, Charles E. Pickett b Feb. 28, 1881.

XII. Minerva Caroline Lemons Tunnell, dau of Nicholas Money and Martha (Jones) Watt Willcox Tunnell, was born Mar. 17, 1839 Morgan Co., Ill. and died Aug. 19, 1924 Van Alystyne, Tex. She married Amos Nichols Apr. 17, 1856 (b Aug. 6, 1832 Knox Co., Ohio; d Feb. 8, 1896 Van Alystyne, Tex.) and had eight ch.

One. Jesse T. Nichols b Mar. 30, 1857 Powsheik Co., Iowa; d Sept. 21, 1862 same county.

Two. Martha A. T. Nichols b Apr. 4, 1859 Powsheik Co., Iowa; married first, Edwin N. Buford July 25, 1881 Denton Co., Tex. (b Feb. 25, 1861 Ky.; d Oct. 24, 1887 Collin Co., Tex.) and had; (a) Jesse E. Buford b Apr. 30, 1882 Grayson Co., Tex.; (b) Alvie Edwin Buford b Feb. 13, 186 Collin Co., Tex. (m first, Nellie Maud Senior May 26, 1907 (b Aug. 29, 1890) and had; 1, Elton Elmer Buford b Dec. 28, 1908; and m second, Ida Ruth Digman Oct. 24, 1916 (b Mar. 7, 1900 Collin Co., Tex.) and had 2, Francis Buford b Aug. 2, 1917; 3, Edwin Newton Buford b Sept. 4, 1919; 4, Cleople Buford b Dec. 28, 1921; 5, Ruth Delila Buford b Feb. 3, 1924). Martha A. T. Nichols m second, Henry D. Miller, May 5, 1890 Grayson Co., Tex. and had; (c) Lelah G. Miller b Feb. 18, 1891; d Apr. 27, 1893; (d) Ira Ray Miller b Dec. 28, 1892 Collin Co., Tex. (m first, Susa Bell Digman Oct. 16, 1910 (b Mar. 26, 1894 nr Crowell, Tex.; d June 7, 1923) and had; 1, Willie Belle Miller b July 29, 1911; 2, Floy Leonard Miller b Mer. 28, 1913; 3,Ethel Pauline Miller b Nov. 22, 1914; 4, Ida Mozell Miller b Apr. 13, 1916; 5, Martha Hazel Miller b Mar. 13, 1918; 6, Ina Ray Miller b Aug. 24, 1920; 7, John Willford Miller b Mar. 4, 1923; and m second, Beatrice Josephine Holmes Apr. 22, 1924 (b June 4, 1904 nr Piedmont, Ala.); (e) Lillian Miller b July 8, 1894 (m Oscar C. Hansard May 17, 1913 Collins Co., Tex. and had; 1, son b and d Feb. 18, 1914; ,2 Lloyd A. Hansard b May 22, 1915; 3, James Hansard b Sept. 1, 1917; 4, Melba Christine Hansard b Jan. 26, 1920; 5, Oscar Clifford Hansard b Aug. 18, 1921; 6, Glenda Ann Hansard b Dec. 11, 1923); (f) Vallie Miller b July 18, 1897 (m Noah Keeling Sept. 13, 1914 and had; 1, Lawrence Alonzo Keeling b Aug. 17, 1915; 2, Beatrice Henrietta Keeling b Apr. 26, 1918; 3, Agnes Gavonna Keeling b Aug. 17, 1921; 4, Lillie Marie Keeling b Nov. 4, 1924); (g) Bonnie Fay Millard b July 16, 1899 (m Jesse Garrett Hansard (b July 17, 1886) and had; 1, Mable Marie Hansard b Jan. 28, 1917; 2, Jesse Julian Hansard b Feb. 5, 1922).

Three. Jacob T. Nichols b Feb. 7, 1861; d Mar. 28, 1896, unm.

Four. John E. Nichols b Mar. 17. 1863, contractor, Van Alystyne, Tex.; married Rosa J. Brown Oct. 27, 1884 Grayson Co., Tex. (b June 3, 1866 Collin Co., Tex.) and had ch b nr Van Alystyne, Tex.; (a) Frank A. Nichols b Nov. 25, 1885; (b) John L. Nichols b June 29, 1888; d Mar. 12, 1892; (c) Roy E. Nichols b Sept. 6, 1891; (d) Zetta Nichols b May 2, 1895; (c) Sallie V. Nichols b Jan. 9, 1898; (f) Charles A. Nichols b Dec. 17, 1900; d Sept. 24, 1902.

Five. Jonas N. B. Nichols b Apr. 17, 1864; married Ella F. Bartee Oct. 18, 1890 Grayson Co., Tex. and had; (a) Claude Nichols b Oct. 19, 1891 Grayson Co.; d Nov. 3, 1891 Grayson Co.; (b) Charles Nichols b Nov. ., 1892 Grayson Co.; d July 27, 1893 Grayson Co.; (c) Otis Nichols b Apr. 5, 1894 Grayson Co.; (d) William Nichols b June 10, 1896 Grayson Co.; (e) Myrtie Nichols b Nov. 7, 1897 Fannin Co., Tex. d June 22, 1898; (f) Eunice Nichols b Nov. 4, 1900 Choctow Nation.

Six. Mary Ella Nichols b Apr. 22, 1869, of Weston, Tex.; married R. F. Miller Mar. 11, 1894 in Tex. (b Feb. 22, 1869) and had ch b Tex; (a) Cecil Miller b Jan. 22, 1895; (b) Ross Miller b Apr. 19, 1869; d Mar. 9, 1897; (c) Stella May Miller b Nov. 20, 1897 (m Joe Marion Wilson Sept. 15, 1915 Grayson Co., Tex. and had; 1, Ancil Leland Wilson b July 1, 1916; 2, Lester Carlile Wilson b Oct. 22, 1917; 3, Mary Ida Wilson b Apr. 1, 1921; 4, Joe Alton Wilson b Jan. 22, 1923); (d) Amy Miller b Mar. 5, 1902, of Weston, Tex. (m Jim J. Wilson Dec. 25, 1912 and had; 1, Irene Wilson b Oct. 16, 1917; 2, Bobbie Jim Wilson b Oct. 5, 1924); (e) Lucile Miller b Dec. 13, 1904.

Seven. Amos M. Nichols b Mar. 28, 1876 Grayson Co., Tex., of Van Alystyne, Tex.; married Cora Bertha Cooper Mar. 28, 1909 and had; (a) Amos Buford Nichols b Sept. 1, 1910; (b) Esther Juanita Nichols b June 22, 1913; (c) Nora Caroline Nichols b July 30, 1914; (d) Frances Elizabeth Nichols b Jan. 31, 1919; (e) Joseph Samuel Nichols b June 25, 1922, all b nr Van Alystyne, Tex.; (f) Martha Pauline Nichols b Oct. 8, 1924 nr Weston, Tex.

Eight. Oscar B. Nichols b May 8, 1880, Van Alystyne, Tex., of Sherman, Tex.; married Winnie Ellen Tipton May 19, 1920 (b Nov. 23, 1899) and had; (a) Clyde E. Nichols b Apr. 14, 1921 Van Alystyne; (b) Nettie Caroline Nichols b Dec. 15, 1923 Sherman, Tex.

XIII. John Wesley Tunnell, son of Nicholas Money and Martha (Jones) Watt Willcox Tunnell, was born Sept. 14, 1842 Morgan Co., Ill. and died June 13, 1901 at Robert Lee, Tex. He married first, Jane Wells and had several children, all of whom died in infancy; and married second, Frances C. Doyle, Feb. 18, 1877 and had six ch.

One. Callie Tunnell b Mar. 3, 1878 Fannin Co., Tex.; d Mar. 4, 1878.

Two. James Hardin Tunnell b Oct. 21, 1879 Fannin Co., Tex., unm.; was postmaster at Brownwood, Tex.

Three. Mary Frances Tunnell b July 8, 1881 Honey Grove, Tex.; married Walter Green Dec. 26, 1900 Robert Lee, Tex. and had ch b Robert Lee; (a) Ezra Green b Nov. 6, 1901, m Mamie Hawling 1921 San Angelo, Tex.; (b) Addie Green b July 31, 1904, m Luther Dunnam at San Angelo, Tex.; (c) Beulah Green b Jan. 14, 1908; (d) Walter B. Green; (e) J. R. Green; (f) Dorothy Sue Green.

Four. Frank Tunnell b June 7, 1884 San Angelo, Tex.; married Emma Caudle Aug. 31, 1902 Robert Lee, Tex. and had; (a) Walter Lee Tunnell b Feb. 1, 1904 Robert Lee; (b) James Clifton Tunnell b Jan. 9, 1906; (c) George Elzy Tunnell b May 17, 1909 Robert Lee, Tex.; (d) Estella Frances Tunnell b Aug. 7, 1917 Merrill, Ore.; (e) Jocelyn M. Tunnell b Aug. 24, 1919 Klamath Falls, Ore.; (f) Margaret Ellen Tunnell b Oct. 19, 1921 Klamath Falls, Ore.; (g) Emma Louise Tunnell b June 15, 1923 Klamath Falls, Ore.

Five. John W. Tunnell b Apr. 16, 1889 Honey Grove, Tex.; married Alice Carter June 6, 1915 San Angelo, Tex. and had no ch.

Six. Mattie May Tunnell b Oct. 15, 1892 Robert Lee, Tex., of Compton, Calif., m Erman Collett July 2, 1921 Wichita, Kan. and had no ch.

XIV. Hettie Ann Tunnell, dau of Nicholas Money and Martha

(Jones) Watt Willcox Tunnell, was born July 9, 1846 and lives Athensville, Ill. She married William Perry Rigg, son of Archibald and Elizabeth (McLane) Rigg, Nov. 15, 1866, who served in War Between the States in Co. C. 6th Ill. Cav. (b Apr. 8, 1839 Waverly, Ill.; d 1923 Athensville, Ill.) and had 8 ch b nr Athensville.

One. Edwin Rigg b Sept. 14, 1867, m Lillian Frances Edwards Apr. 1, 1894 and had; (a) Mabel Eugenia Rigg b Feb. 13, 1895; (b) Wilfred Alonzo Rigg b Mar. 21, 1896.

Two. Charles Rigg b Dec. 28, 1868, m Laura Ann Ferguson and had; (a) William Stanley Rigg b Jan. 22, 1891; (b) Jesse Lee Rigg b Dec. 21, 1892; d Jan. 24, 1893; (c) Gracie Edna Rigg b Dec. 25, 1893; (d) Etna Rigg, twin of Gracie Edna Rigg, b and d Dec. 25, 1893; (e) Nellie Viola Rigg b Oct. 5, 1896; d Sept. 12, 1902; (f) Opal Lucile Rigg b Oct. 8, 1898; d July 3, 1903; (g) Jewel Gladys Rigg b Jan. 24, 1901; (h) Ruby Pearl Rigg b Oct. 11, 1903; (i) Emerald Elijah Rigg b Feb. 11, 1906.

Three. Wilfred Alonzo Frederick Augustus Ferdinand Rigg b Oct. 29, 1870, Baptist minister of Gillespie, Ill., m Margaret Modena Stamper Aug. 11, 1900 and had; (a) Hazel Irene Rigg b Nov. 21, 1903.

Four. Luella Sonora Rigg b Mar. 4, 1873, unm. of Athensville, Ill.

Five. Samuel Archibald Rigg b Mar. 9, 1876; d 1924 in Ark.

Six. Emma Angeline Rigg b Apr. 19, 1878, m first, Greenville M. Weaver, Nov. 5, 1900 and had; (a) Arber Gordon Weaver b July 2, 1902; (b) Beryl Weaver b and d Aug. 10, 1904; (c) son b Aug. 1906; and m second, ——— ———.

Seven. Dora Ellen Rigg b Aug. 24, 1880, m Andrew Jackson Covey Dec. 27, 1903 and had; (a) Samuel Archie Covey b Apr. 25, 1905.

Eight. Nannie Laura Ann Pixie Edith May Rigg b Apr. 21, 1884, m Henry Strahan Oct. 11, 1902 and had; (a) Kenneth Donovan Strahan b Nov. 3, 1902; (b) Inez Gertrude Strahan b Mar. 20, 1905.

XV. Jonathan Hardin Tunnell, son of Nicholas Money and Martha (Jones) Watt Willcox Tunnell, was born July 20, 1847 and died June 14, 1907 Houston, Tex. He married Frances Emily Mitchell, dau Anderson and Elzira (Whitlock) Mitchell; gd of Charles and Martha (Wilson) Whitlock; ggdau of Moses Wilson, Revolutionary soldier, of Ky., Apr. 14, 1870 in Ill. (b abt 1850 nr Murrayville, Ill.; d after 1908 Houston, Tex.) and had; 1, Martha E. Tunnell b Mar. 18, 1871; d Sept. 2, 1896, married first, Thomas S. Knith and had two sons, who died in inf., one named Robert Emmett Knith; and m second, George Granger and had no ch. 2, Emily Louise Tunnell b Jan. 3, 1873; d Oct. 2, 1873; 3, John J. Tunnell b July 8, 1875, of Houston, Tex. in 1908, who m Dovie ——— and had no ch.; 4, Ernest Nicholas Tunnell b 1878; lost in the Galveston, Tex. flood Sept. 1, 1900; 5, Emmett Eugene Tunnell b 1880; d 1881; 6, Jessie Belle Tunnell b Feb. 1882; d 1882.

WESLEY TUNNELL

H. Wesley Tunnell, born about 1797, son of Stephen and Kezia Money Tunnell, was born in East Tenn. He may have been born about 1794 or 1796, or earlier. He died after 1854, in Morgan Co., Ill. He married Elizabeth ——— born 1798, it is supposed in Tenn. A few years after their marriage they moved to Alabama to be near his brothers, Stephen and Perry Tunnell. Later they went to Independence, Mo. for a time and abt 1830 moved to Morgan Co., Ill. where his brothers, Jesse, Nicholas Money and David Tunnell lived. Elizabeth Tunnell, whose maiden name has not been learned, died in Illinois. Names of ch. may not be in order of birth.

I. Lizzie Tunnell b 1834.

II. Stephen S. Tunnell b Dec. 29, 1820.

III. Perry Tunnell b abt 1822.
IV. James Russell Tunnell b abt 1824.
V. William Tunnell born 1830.
VI. David Tunnell.
VII. Nicholas Tunnell.
VIII. Enoch Tunnell.
IX. Mary Tunnell.
X. Lucinda Tunnell b 1839.
Of the foregoing;

I. Lizzie Tunnell, dau of Wesley and Elizabeth Tunnell, died at Franklin, Ill. after 1901; married Ambrose Ham, who d at Franklin before his wife, and had an only child; (a) Charles Ham, who d abt 1915 nr Waverly, unmarried.

II. Stephen S. Tunnell, son of Wesley and Elizabeth Tunnell, was born Dec. 29, 1820 in Tenn.; came to Morgan Co., Ill. 1830; d Feb. 9, 1904 Morgan Co., Ill. He had at one time, the Bible of his grandfather, Rev. Stephen Tunnell. He married Emeline Ferguson, dau of Benjamin and Susan Ferguson, Apr. 2, 1840 Morgan Co., Ill. who d Sept. 2, 1902 Morgan Co., and had ten ch. b Morgan Co.

One. Jane Tunnell b Feb. 9, 1841, once of Oak Mills, Kan.; married William H. Morrison Dec. 8, 1858 and had; (a) Horace Morrison b Nov. 1, 1859; (b) Walter Morrison b Dec. 11, 1861; (c) Lillian Morrison b Apr. 26, 1863, m ———— Byrd; (d) Willie Morrison b Apr. 12, 1868; (e) Mabel Morrison b Aug. 18, 1871, m ———— Johnson.

Two. Lizzie Tunnell b Jan. 3, 1843; d unmarried.

Three. daughter, died in inf.

Four. Martha Tunnell b May 28, 1847; d in inf.

Five. Anna Tunnell b May 14, 1849; d Jan. 1, 1895; married W. O. Dresbach Nov 1, 1866 and had; (a) Harry V. Dresbach b Aug. 31, 1867, of Joplin, Mo. (m Minnie E. Kelsey Dec. 18, 1894 and had; 1, Helen Kelsey Dresbach b Nov. 1, 1897); (b) Alice Dresbach b Nov. 9, 1868; d July 25, 1899; (c) Florence Dresbach b Aug. 28, 1870; d Aug. 24, 1898; (d) John Dresbach b Oct. 10, 1872; d Mar. 11, 1892; (e) Pearl Marie Dresbach b July 27, 1874, m Wilbur Damack Sept. 1, 1900; (f) Thomas Dresbach b Nov. 29, 1877; d Feb. 7, 1907; (g) Clyde Dresbach b Dec. 15, 1880; d Nov. 17, 1903.

Six. Jouisa M. Tunnell b Mar. 3, 1853, of Jacksonville, Ill.; married William H. Ketner, son of Henry and Mahala (Crouse) Ketner, settled in Morgan Co., 1834, from North Carolina, Aug. 3, 1876 (b Aug. 29, 1894; d Sept. 3, 1924) and had ch b nr Woodson, Ill.; (a) Fred Ketner b May 13, 1878, of Woodson, Ill. (m Maggie Fitzsimmons May 24, 1905 and had; 1, Clarence Ketner b Oct. 20, 1905; 2, Bernice Ketner b July 19, 1908); (b) Georgia M. Ketner b Sept. 7, 1880, of Jacksonville, Ill. (m Homer Anthony Jan. 1905 and had; 1, Herbert Cecil Anthony b Jan. 22, 1907; d Feb. 7, 1907; 2, Emily Louise Anthony b July 1908; 3, ———— Anthony); (c) Herbert Ketner b Aug. 9, 1883; d Aug. 18, 1883; (d) Wilbur Ketner b Sept. 30, 1885, of Lamar, Mo. (m Fay Henry, dau of John Henry, and had; 1, Harold Ketner b Nov. 20, 1907); and others.

Seven. Will Tunnell b Aug. 31, 1856, of King City, Mo.; married May Sheppard July 4, 1880 nr Woodson, Ill., dau of Albie and Sarah (McAlister) Sheppard, and had; (a) Edgar Tunnell b Aug. 21, 1882, of King City, Mo. (m Mayme Moore Oct. 26, 1906 King City, Mo. and had ch b King City; 1, Charles Tunnell b June 20, 1907; 2, Clifford Marion Tunnell b Apr. 25, 1910; 3, Earl Maxwell Tunnell; 4, Mary Madeline Tunnell b Feb. 29, 1916); (b) Dr. Henry Tunnell b June 13, 1884 Woodson, Ill., of Clyde, Kan. (m Ida Pratt Oct. 27, 1906 King City, Mo., and had; 1, Henry Lewis Tunnell b Nov. 1917

Clyde, Kan.; 2, Willis Earl Tunnell); (c) Orville Tunnell b Aug. 5, 1886 Woodson, Ill., m Vera Black Nov. 1908 King City, Mo.; (d) Eva Belle Tunnell b Oct. 16, 1891 King City, Mo., m Willis H. Hammer Aug. 5, 1916 Savannah, Mo.; (e) Louise Tunnell b Apr. 4, 1894 King City, Mo., of Jacksonville, Ill. (m Harry Hofmann, son of J. Eckhardt and Jennie (Morrison) Hofmann; g-s of John G. and Rebecca (White) Hofmann, Sept. 30, 1914 Jacksonville, Ill., and had ch b Jacksonville; 1, Harry Fletcher Hofmann b Aug. 16, 1915; 2, William Arlington Hoffman b Apr. 4, 1920, Easter Day.

Eight. Charlie Tunnell b July 5, 1858; d young.

Nine. Florence Tunnell b Feb. 2, 1861; d 1885; married Dr. Mc-Beth and had; (a) Dudley McBeth b Oct. 4, 1884, of King City, Mo. (m Lizzie Ball 1905 and had; 1, Clarence McBeth b July 18, 1906; 2, Florence McBeth b July 28, 1907; 3, Strausie McBeth b Jan. 10, 1909.

Ten. Clarence Tunnell b Jan. 21, 1867, of King City, Mo.; married Maggie Colville and had; (a) Claude Tunnell b June 1, 1892; (b) Florence Tunnell b Feb. 19, 1895; (c) Lena Tunnell b Jan. 1, 1888; (d) Flossie Tunnell b July 5, 1900.

III. Perry Tunnell, son of Wesley and Elizabeth Tunnell, was born about 1822 and died abt 1848 in Missouri. He married Margaret Elizabeth Crockett, of the well-known Tennessee Crockett family, abt 1842, who died abt 1850 in Texas, and had two ch.

One. James Albert Tunnell b Apr. 27, 1844 at Independence, Mo., of Clyde, Tex.; married Nancy Melvina McKenzie June 1870 Youngsport, Tex. and had; (a) Margaret Elizabeth Tunnell b Apr. 13, 1871, of Ranger, Tex. (m Robert Howton Oct. 30, 1889 and had; 1, Elzaphan E. Howton b Oct. 12, 1890, of Ranger, Tex., served over seas in World War, m da Herrington and had a daughter; 2, Onan L. Howton b May 1892 Blanket Tex.; d Apr. 13, 1896 Blanket, Tex.; 3, Alpha T. Howton b Jan. 26, 1895, of Tahoka, Tex., m Ernest Lawler May 20, 1911; and had; (aa) Truman Lawler; (bb) Alvera Lawler; and two others; 3, Aaron E. Howton b July 10, 1897 Blanket, Tex., of Lacasa, Tex.. m Lily Bradford and had two sons; 5. Louisa T. Howton b Apr. 12, 1900 Blanket, Tex., of Deming, New Mex., m Dennis Rutland and had three ch.; 6. Malvina M. Howton b Sept. 17, 1903 Brown-v Tex., of Zephyr, Tex., m Sam Dupree and had; (aa) Homer Eugene Dupree; (bb) ———— Dupree; 7, Viola Howton b Oct. 29, 1908); (b) Mary Jane Tunnell b Mar. 6, 1873, of Clyde, Tex., (m Ivo R. Keele Aug. 8. 1889 and had; 1, Bessie L. Keele b July 17, 1891 Killeen, Tex.. of Los Angeles, m Haney Harlow July 1910 and had; (aa) Evans Howard Harlow b Sept. 2, 1912; 2, Lillie R. Keele b June 25, 1893 San Saba, Tex.; d June 2, 1914; 3, Orion A. Keele b Sept. 15, 1895 Killeen, Tex.. who was First Lieutenant in World War and died Nov. 4, 1918, in service; 4, Arthur J. Keele b Dec. 4, 1899 Killeen, Tex., of San Antonio, Tex.. served in U. S. N. a year, m Mabel Walker Feb. 7, 1919 and had; (aa) Helen Ernestine Keele b Nov. 24, 1919; 5, Ora M. Keele b July 3, 1900 Killeen, Tex., of Big Springs, Tex., m Dr. Guy Longbotham Oct. 9, 1921 and had a son; 6, Louise E. Keele b Apr. 9, 1903 Blanket, Tex., of Dallas, Tex., m Roy Hensley Sept. 21, 1921 and had two ch.; 7. Theodore F. Keele b Dec. 8, 1905 Clyde, Tex., in war service in Hawaii; 8, Velma I. Keele b May 10, 1908; 9, Eldon Keele b Nov. 22, 1912 Clyde, Tex.); (c) J. Perry Tunnell b Oct. 25, 1875. of Winters. Tex. (m Maggie Mitchell Dec. 24, 1893 and had; 1, James F. Tunnell b Sept. 4, 1896; 2, Clyde Tunnell b Nov. 8, 1898, m Jimmie Walker; 3, Bonnie F. Tunnell b Feb. 24, 1901; 4, Ray A. Tunnell b July 14, 1903; 5. Rena M. Tunnell b 1906; 6, Ruth M. Tunnell b Oct. 30, 1908; 7, Reayd Tunnell b Sept. 16, 1910; d Dec. 22, 1910); (d) Sarah Louisa Tunnell b May 31, 1878, of Van Nuys, Calif. (m Thomas

Magill Sept. 29, 1900 Leonard, Tex .(d Oct. 3, 1908 Stamford, Tex.) and had; 1, Norman O. Magill b July 8, 1901 Blanket, Tex., of San Francisco, Calif.; 2, Homer E. Magill b May 5, 1903 Brownwood Tex.; d Nov. 25, 1908 Clyde, Tex.; 3, Lyle Ira Magill b June 12, 1906 Brownwood, Tex.; 4, Albert R. Magill b Apr. 20, 1907 Dublin, Tex.); (e) Thomas Henry Tunnell b June 27, 1880 Newberg, Tex., of Dexter, New Mex. (m Alice Wolfe Dec. 11, 1903 and had; 1, Eva E. Tunnell b Mar. 4, 1905 Clyde, Tex., of Dexter, New Mex., m Everett Davis; 2, Seth Tunnell b Aug. 6, 1906 Clyde, Tex.; 3, Olan H. Tunnell b Oct. 19, 1910 Clyde, Tex.; 4, R. C. Tunnell b Aug. 1913 Clyde, Tex.; 5, Vera Tunnell b Dec. 29, 1915 Winters, Tex.; 6, Audice Tunnell b 1918 Clyde, Tex.; 7, Nina May Tunnell b Oct. 1920); (f) John William Tunnell b Dec. 6, 1883 Newburg, Tex., of Zephyr, Tex. (m Jennie Dupree Nov. 1902 and had ch b Zephyr, Tex.; 1, William Tunnell b Sept. 17, 1903, of Blanket, Tex. m Velma Parsons; 2, Burgess Albert Tunnell b June 1907; d Apr. 1908; 3, Raymond Tunnell b Aug. 1910; 4, Lilas Tunnell b Aug. 1913); (g) Nancy Vandalia Tunnell b Feb. 18, 1885; d Sept. 1891; (h) Jesse L. Tunnell b July 17, 1890, of Van Nuys, Calif. (m Katie Graham and had ch b Clyde, Tex.; 1, Murmon Tunnell b Jan. 15, 1915; 2, Von Tunnell b May 1916); (i) Clara Lunena Tunnell b Dec. 25, 1894 Blanket, Tex., of Clyde, Tex. (m Bert Stone Dec. 1909, who d Apr. 9, 1922 Clyde, Tex., and had ch b Clyde, Tex.; 1, Lola Olive Stone b Nov. 3, 1910; 2, Doward Stone b 1912; 3, Ione Stone b Apr. 1914; 4, Helen Stone b 1917).

Two. Louise Adaline Tunnell b Nov. 7, 1847; d July 9, 1884 nr Lampassas, Tex.; married Thomas R. Brauscum 1865 (b Oct. 29, 1843; d July 10, 1884) and had; (a) Franscisco Vandalia Brauscum b Nov. 13, 1866; d very young; (b) James Wilson Brauscum b Oct. 18, 1868; d very young; (c) Thomas Henry Brauscum b Nov. 20, 1870; d 1913 Callahan Co., Tex., unm.; (d) John Walton Brauscum b Mar. 11, 1873, of Indiahoma, Okla. (m Ida Rollins and had; 1, Roy Brauscum; 2, Harry Brauscum, dead; 3, Claud Brauscum; 4, Thelma Brauscum; 5, Jewell Brauscum; 6, Joe W. Brauscum; 7, Irie Brauscum); (e) Jones Dempsey Brauscum b Jan. 19, 1875, of Brady, Tex. (m first, Etta Wall, Brady, Tex., who d Oct. 20, 1913, leaving a dau; 1, Hazel Allen Brauscum b abt 1915; and m second, Blanche Davenport); (f) George Nathaniel Brauscum b Mar. 10, 1878, of Duncan, Okla. (m Mary Simons and had; 1, Othel Brauscum; 2, Addie May Brauscum; 3, Georgetta Brauscum); (g) Albert Alfonso Brauscum b Apr. 28, 1880, of Olden, Tex. (m Susan Mary Peel Oct. 11, 1899 Llano, Tex. (b Aug. 6, 1880) and had; 1, Florence Elizabeth Brauscum b July 12, 1900 Field Creek, Tex.; 2, Floyd Henry Brauscum b Mar. 2, 1904 Kingsland, Tex.; d July 16, 1921 Wichita, Kan.; 3, Lola Pearl Brauscum b July 13, 1907 Floydada, Tex.; 4, Walton Alfonso Shultz Brauscum b Feb. 19, 1909 Hillcrest, Tex.; 5, Bonnie Lee Brauscum b Mar. 28, 1911 Salt Gap, Tex.); (h) Jessie Brauscum b July 8, 1884; d in inf.

IV.   James Russell Tunnell, son of Wesley and Elizabeth Tunnell, was born 1824 and died Oct. 30, 1898 in Tex. At one time he lived in Morgan Co., Ill. He moved to Mo. where he enlisted in the C. S. A. and moved to Texas 1865. He married first, Louisa McDaniel, of Mo., who died in Tex. and had five ch., names of but two known, others dying in infancy. He married Elizabeth Langley, in Mo., who lived at Pride, Tex. a few years ago and had seven ch by this marriage. He is said to have married three times.

One.   Mary Jane Tunnell, dau of James Russell and Louisa McDaniel Tunnell, b Mar. 27, 1848, of Phoenix, Ariz.; married Frame W. Stegall Feb. 20, 1868 and had; (a) Mary Louisa Stegall b Nov. 20, 1868, m R. G. McLendon Dec. 20, 1882; (b) Florence Martha Stegall b Mar. 4, 1870, dead; (c) James William Stegall b Mar. 13, 1875, m Isabella Durbin Nov. 3, 1898; (d) Stephen LeRoy Stegall b Nov. 23, 1876, m Beatrice Tutt Dec. 24, 1894; (e) Clara Arrie Stegall b June 20, 1880, dead, m R. H. Smith June 16, 1898; (f) Enoch Marvin Stegall b Apr. 1, 1882, of Brant, Tex., m Ethel Tutt Dec. 13, 1905; (g) DeWitt Talmadge Stegall b Apr. 10, 1884, m Mabel Middleton May 22, 1901; (h) Ophelia Frame Stegall b Feb. 23, 1888; (i) Hester Grace Stegall b Oct. 22, 1891.

Two.   Stephen C. Tunnell, son of James Russell and Louisa McDaniel Tunnell, died 1879 in North Dakota. He was unmarried.

Three.   John Bell Tunnell, son of James Russell and Elizabeth Langley Tunnell, b abt 1860, of Pride, Tex.; married Isabella Bradford Jan. 11, 1903 and had; (a) James Russell Tunnell b Oct. 28, 1903; (b) Walter Otis Tunnell b Nov. 18, 1905; (c) William Cullen Tunnell, twin of Walter Odis Tunnell, b Nov. 18, 1905; (d) Jessie May Tunnell b June 7, 1908; (e) Zada Naomi Tunnell b Dec. 6, 1910; (f) Ruth Tunnell.

Four.   James Sterling Tunnell, son of James Russell and Elizabeth Langley Tunnell, b Nov. 11, 1862 in Mo., of Ballinger, Tex.; married Elizabeth Brown Dec. 17, 1882 (d Dec. 25, 1865 Gonzales, Tex.) and had ch b Blanco, Tex.; (a) Sterling Tunnell b Jan. 15, 1884; d Jan. 17, 1884; (b) Malcolm Tunnell b Feb. 8, 1886; d Mar. 8, 1914 Tulsa, Okla.; (c) Gordon Tunnell b Jan. 16, 1889, of Hye, Tex. (m Eula Page Apr. 7, 1907 and had ch b Hye, Tex.; 1, Sterling Tunnell b Aug. 31, 1908; 2, Lola Marie Tunnell b Aug. 24, 1910; 3, Georgia Gardine Tunnell b June 20, 1919); (d) Shuford Tunnell b Jan. 13, 1891, of Bradshaw, Tex. (m Alfa Strigler Oct. 20, 1918 and had; 1, Laura Helen Tunnell; 2, Gloria Tunnell); (e) Ruth Tunnell b July 8, 1897, of Hye, Tex. (m Robert Crider July 4, 1917 and had; 1, Vernon Crider; 2, Byron Crider); (f) Georgia Tunnell b Mar. 6, 1900, of Hye, Tex.; (g) Stephen Tunnell b Sept. 8, 1903, of Hye, Tex.

Five.   Wesley Lee Tunnell, son of James Russell and Elizabeth Langley Tunnell, b Nov. 30, 1866, of Tahoka, Tex.; married Dora Moore June 5, 1895 and had; (a) John Hansford Tunnell b May 11, 1896, of Tahoka, Tex., m Lenore B. ——, of Gonzales, Texas and has; 1, Mary Margaret Tunnell; (b) Howard Tunnell b Oct. 24, 1897; (c) Charles Tunnell b Oct. 1, 1904; (d) Roy Tunnell b Apr. 15, 1911; (e) Hythan Tunnell.

Six.   Carrie Tunnell, dau of James Russell and Elizabeth Langley Tunnell, of Ballinger, Tex.; married John Nixon and had; (a) Grace Nixon; (b) Edna Nixon; (c) Alice Nixon; (d) Luther Nixon.

Seven.   Alice Tunnell, dau of James Russell and Elizabeth Langley Tunnell, of Lubbock, Tex., married John Fred and had; (a) Felix Fred; (b) Clara Fred; (c) Noma Fred; (d) Russell Fred; (e) Gibbs Fred; (f) Nolan Fred; (g) Odis Fred.

Eight.   Felix Calvin Tunnell, son of James Russell and Elizabeth Langley Tunnell, b Oct. 30, 1873, of Ajo, Ariz., married Laura Betty Barker Aug. 17, 1916 Johnson City, Tex. (b Aug. 14, 1886 Johnson City, Tex.) and had; (a) Carlotta Mabel Tunnell b Sept. 30, 1920 Glendale, Ariz.; (b) Felix Maxwell Tunnell b Sept. 22, 1922 Ajo, Ariz.; (c) Elnora Elaine Tunnell b Sept. 4, 1924 Ajo, Ariz.

Nine.   Frame Wood Tunnell, son of James Russell and Elizabeth Langley Tunnell, b Oct. 30, 1873, of Ajo, Ariz., married Laura Betty Page Sept. 16, 1902 (b Mar. 24, 1887 Blanco Co., Tex.; d July 18, 1922 Kerrville, Tex.) and had; (a) Thelma Irene Tunnell b Jan. 22, 1904 Blanco Co., Tex. (m Stanley Jones July 10, 1923 Florence, Ariz. (b Dec. 7, 1904 Oswestry, England) and had; 1, Malcolm Stanley Jones b July 6, 1924); (b) Gladys Elizabeth Tunnell b May 14, 1905 Runnels

Co., Tex.; (c) Joseph Weldon Tunnell b May 6, 1907 Midland Co., Tex.; (d) J. P. Tunnell b July 10, 1910.

V. William Tunnell, son of Wesley and Elizabeth Tunnell died unmarried Morgan Co., Ill.

VI. David Tunnell, son of Wesley and Elizabeth Tunnell, enlisted Aug. 9, 1862 in the 101st Illinois Volunteer Infantry and died June 1, 1863 at Millikan's Bend. He was not married.

VII. Nicholas Tunnell, son of Wesley and Elizabeth Tunnell, was born abt 1828 and died 1895. He married Elizabeth Smith, who died 1897 Broken Arrow, Okla. and had fourteen children; names may not be in order of birth;

One. Clarinda Tunnell, died young.

Two. Mary Tunnell, died young.

Three. George Tunnell, died young.

Four. Emma Tunnell, died abt 1896; married Albert Church and had; (a) Ollie Church, m ——— Miller; (b) Goldie Church; (c) Lula Church.

Five. Annie Tunnell, m first, John Lankford and had; (a) Clara Lankford, of Oilton, Okla. (m Wallace Doolin and had ch., names may not be in order of birth; 1, Vera Doolin, d small; 2, Stella Doolin; 3, Walter Doolin; 4, Raymond Doolin; 5, and 6, twins, Bernice and Beulah Doolin; 7, Vesta Doolin; 8, Fern Doolin b Oct. 1907; 9, Wallace Doolin, the Second, b Oct. 1909; 10, Edwin Doolin); and m second, John N. Robison and had; (b) Edward Robison, m Annie ——— bef. 1906; (c) George Robison, m Clara ———; (d) Leora Robison; (e) Clarence Robison).

Six. James Albert Tunnell b Feb. 12, 1850 Ill.; d June 26, 1916 Jennings, Okla.; married first, Sarah Johnson Mar. 1881 Gainesville, Tex .and had; (a) Cazzie Mae Tunnell b Jan. 26, 1882 in Tex.; d Feb. 1, 1901 Jennings, Okla. (m John Brannan abt 1896 Pawnee, Okla. (d 1912) and had; 1, George Brannan b May 5, 1899, m Mary Barker and had; (aa) Goldie Brannan b May 1920); (b) Albert Warren Tunnell b Aug. 15, 1884 Gainesville, Tex., of Jennings, Okla. (m Jennie Will June 23, 1907 Terlton, Okla. and had; 1, Verona Tunnell b Jan. 24, 1909 2, Saydee Esther Tunnell b Nov. 7, 1911; 3, Dollie Alberta Tunnell b Feb. 1, 1916; 4, Albert Carlos Tunnell b May 31, 1918; 5, Audrey Ruth Tunnell b Dec. 21, 1920; 6, Elsie Naomi Tunnell b Aug. 25, 1924); (c) Mary Tunnell b June 24, 1886 Ind. Ter. (m Joe Myers July 22, 1902, of Jennings, Okla. and had; 1, Owen Liberal Myers b Aug. 20, 1907; 2, Stella May Myers b June 24, 1909); (d) Myrtle Tunnell b Mar. 29, 1889; d Sept. 1890. James Albert Tunnell m second Mrs. Arena Knapp Apr. 1903 and had; (e) Carrie Tunnell b Feb. 21, 1904.

Seven. Everette Tunnell, married Mrs. Minerva Isabell and had; (a) Ina Mae Tunnell b Sept. 4, 1897, of Bristow, Okla., m J. C. Stevens 1920; (b) Albert Willard Tunnell b Jan. 1, 1900, unm.

Eight. William Tunnell, married Laura Bunch and had an only ch.; (a) Manda Tunnell, m ——— ———.

Nine. Lizzie Tunnell died Apr. 29, 1900 in Kan.; m G. W. Morgan and had; (a) Randa Morgan, died 1919, (m Carlos Foster and had three sons); (b) Edith Morgan, of Bristow, Okla.

Ten. John Basil Tunnell, m ——— ——— and left Okla. abt 1881.

Eleven. Amanda Tunnell, m Robert Sardin and had; (a) Robert Sardin Jr., of Bristow, Okla.; (b) Jessie Sardin, unm., of Bristow; (c) William John Sardin m Goldie ———.

Twelve. Miranda Tunnell, died abt 1894, m Sam Smith and had no ch.

Thirteen. Sylvia Tunnell, of Bristow, Okla., m Sam Smith and had an only ch.; (a) Fay Smith, of Bristow, Okla., m ——— ———.

Fourteen. Charles Tunnell, of Jennings, Okla.; married Mattie Cordelia McAlister Sept. 8, 1911 nr Webber's Falls, Okla. (b May 25, 1888 nr Vian, Okla.) and had; (a) Thomas Everette Tunnell b June 6, 1913 Webber's Falls; (b) Warren Elzie Tunnell b Sept. 5, 1916 nr Haskell, Okla.; (c) Heber Leonidas Tunnell b May 5, 1919 nr Jennings; (d) Charles William Tunnell b Dec. 2, 1922 nr Jennings (e) Raymond Lee Tunnell b Aug. 14, 1924 nr Jennings, Okla.

VIII. Enoch Tunnell, son of Wesley and Elizabeth Tunnell, died a young man.

IX. Mary (Polly) Tunnell, dau of Wesley and Elizabeth Tunnell, married ——— Happy and is said to have moved to Oregon.

X. Lucinda Tunnell, dau of Wesley and Elizabeth Tunnell, was born 1839 and died 1905 nr Alexander, Ill. She married Anthony Ferguson, son of Benjamin and Susan Ferguson, and a brother of Emeline Ferguson, who married Stephen Tunnell, Nov 1, 1855. He was born 1836 Morgan Co., Ill and died May 22, 1917 Jacksonville, Ill. He married second, Mrs. Grace F. Curtis, b Jan. 5, 1844, who d Aug. 9, 1920 Kansas City, Mo. Anthony Ferguson enlisted in Co. D. 101st Ill. Vol. Inf. and was at the Siege of Vicksburg. Ch. b Morgan Co., Ill.

One. William Ferguson b Aug. 4, 1857; d Aug. 1901 nr Alexander, Ill.; married Anna Bell Harvey nr Alexander, Ill. (b Oct. 20, 1862 nr Warsaw, Ill., dau of Edward Harvey, b in England; Capt. of steambooat on Miss.; d on Miss. river) and Mary Powell Harvey (b nr Quincy, Ill.; d Quincy, Ill.); gd George Harvey, of Eng; same John Powell, of Delaware, the grandson of a Scotch nobleman) and had ch. b nr Alexander, Ill.; (a) Jessie Ferguson b Feb. 22, 1883, of Woodson, Ill. (m Howard Henry, son of John and Clara (Marsh) Henry, Mar. 1907 Jacksonville, Ill. and had ch b Woodson; 1, Orville Henry; 2, Mardell Henry; 3, Lester Henry; 4, Wayne Henry, dead; 5, Edrie Pauline Henry; 6, John Mervin Henry); (b) Earl Ferguson b Nov. 2, 1884; d Nov. 9, 1897; (c) Edward Ferguson b July 14, 1886, of Rantoul, Ill. (m May Wilson Feb. 1906 St. Louis, Mo. and had; 1, Helen Ferguson b Jacksonville, Ill.; 2, Grant Ferguson b Champaign, Ill.; 3, Verne Ferguson b Champaign, Ill.); (d) Grant Ferguson b Mar. 30, 1890, of Jacksonville, Ill. (m May Birdsell and had ch b Jacksonville; 1, Violet Ferguson; 2, Melvina Ferguson; 3, Grant Ferguson Jr.; 4, Annadell Ferguson; 5, Lee Edward Ferguson); (e) Etta Mae Ferguson b July 3, 1893, of Jacksonville, Ill., (m first, Floyd S. Suiter, son of J. B. Suiter, June 19, 1913 Jacksonville, Ill. (b 1891; d Feb. 12, 1920 Peoria, Ill.) and had; 1, Evelyn Suiter b Peoria, Ill.; 2, Eleanor Suiter b Peoria, Ill.; and m second Walter Ahlquist in Jacksonville, Ill. and had 3, Gladys Lucille Ahlquist b 1923); (f) Della Ferguson b Apr. 29, 1896; d Oct. 15, 1918 Jacksonville, Ill. and had no ch.); (g) Ruth Ferguson b Apr. 19, 1898, of Jacksonville, Ill. (m her sister's widower, D. O. Floreth and had; 1, Earl Henry Floreth); (h) Lulu Irene Ferguson b Feb. 19, 1901, (m Baird Gunn, son of John T. Gunn, Feb. 19, 1921 Jacksonville, Ill. and had; 1, Margaret Irene Gunn; 2, James Baird Gunn b Mar. 17, 1925).

Two. Albert Ferguson, of Murrayville, Ill.; m Minnie Barnes Sept. 16, 1880 Parsons, Kan. and had ch b Morgan Co., Ill.; (a) Lloyd Ferguson, of Peoria, m Julia ——— and had no ch.; (b) Lee Ferguson; dead; (c) Drucy Pearl Ferguson, of Peoria, m Otto Woods and had 4 ch.; (d) Homer Ferguson, unm.; (e) Alene Ferguson b May 2, 1896 (m Charles Heber Austin Dec. 3, 1914 (b Apr. 19, 1893, son of Charles Arthur and Ada (Newton) Austin; gs Rev. John Henry and Agnes (Seymour) Austin; ggs John E. and Sarah (O'Brien) Seymour;

-same John and Margaret (Barrett) Austin) and had one son.

Three. Susie Ferguson, m Butler Benson nr Alexander, Ill. and had ch b Morgan Co., Ill.; (a) Willie Benson, m Lizzie Olroy and had; 1, William Benson); (b) Claude Benson, m ———— ———— and had -sev ch.; (c) Lula Benson, unm .

Four. Lizzie Ferguson, of Alexander, Ill., m Clay Ewen and had ch b Morgan Co., Ill.; (a) Edna Ewen, of Waverly, Ill., m ———— Rohrer and had 3 ch.; (b) May Ewen, m George Rone and had 3 ch.; (c) Roy Ewen; (d) Lena Ewen, of Bearnstown, Ill., m ———— Peak and had no ch; (e) child, dead; (f) child, dead.

Five. Ida Ferguson, of Buffalo, Ill., m first, Fred Evans and had no ch. and m second, Milt Todd and had; (a) Ronald Todd, dead; (b) Lucinda Todd, m ———— ————; (c) Raymond Todd, m ———— ————.

Six. Benjamin I. Ferguson; m Drucy Todd and had ch b Morgan Co., Ill.; (a) Otto Ferguson, m Birdie ———— and had 3 ch.; (b) Harold Ferguson, m Dorothy Deatherage Aug. 1922; (c) Hal Ferguson, unm.

Seven. Edith Ferguson, of Jacksonville, Ill.; m Fred B. Six, Morgan Co., and had ch b Morgan Co., Ill.; (a) Ronald Six, d in inf.; (b) Harriet Maud Six, m Edward Leonard June 28, 1924 and had; 1, John Edward Leonard b May 11, 1925.

Eight. Horace Ferguson died at two.

Nine. Maud Ferguson, of Jacksonville, Ill., m Jack Walsh and had ch b Morgan Co., Ill.; (a) Donald Walsh, m ———— Foster and had 1 ch.; (b) Clifford Walsh; (c) son, d in inf.; (d) Catherine Walsh; (e) Anthony Walsh.

JESSE TUNNELL

I. Jesse Tunnell, son of Stephen and Kezia Money Tunnell, was born abt 1798 in East Tenn. He moved to Kentucky, it is thought Hardin Co., abt 1825 and later to Morgan Co., Ill. He died July 1, 1835, Morgan Co., Ill., leaving a wife and three children. (Court record). His wife was Mary Snow, who married, for second husband, ———— McLaughlin and was living in Winchester, Ill. in 1850. It is said by relatives of Mary Snow that her name was Mary (Polly) Parker, of Ky. She may have been a widow when she m Jesse Tunnell. There are no descendants of Jesse Tunnell bearing the name. Ch.;

I.   Marcus Tunnell b 1827.
II. Nancy Ashley Tunnell b Aug. 12, 1828.
III. Jane Tunnell b abt 1830.

Of the foregoing;

I. Marcus Tunnell, son of Jesse and Mary Snow Tunnell, was born 1827 in Ky. and died abt 1900 Rockdale, Tex. He was a minister, first of the Congregational church and later of the Methodist church. He moved to Texas in the 1850's and was for a time, a chaplain in C. S. A. and a Confederate blockade runner at Galveston, Tex. He married first, Martha Strong, dau of Prince Albert Strong, of Ky., Jan. 10, 1853 Jacksonville, Ill. (b 1836, now living, Dec. 1924, San Jose, Calif.) and had one son. He married second, Martha Adams, abt 1858 in Tex., who died abt 1868, and had three ch. by his marriage. He married third, Anna Rhodes, Oct. 1869, in Tex., who died Feb. 10, 1910 Marlin, Tex., and had two children.

One. Robert Jerome Tunnell b Dec. 25, 1853 Manchester, Ill., (name changed to Byron Jerome Tunnell 1855), went to Calif., with his mother 1859. He was a civil engineer and went to Guatamala in 1893. For some years he lived at Salina Cruz, Isthmus of Tehuantepec, Mexico and died July 8, 1920 Oxaca, Mexico. He m Isabel Vioelt Smith, of West Point, Calif., dau of John Richardson and Isabel (Affleck) Smith, Apr. 24, 1894, Guatamala, and had no children. Mrs. Tunnell was born Feb. 17, 1873 and lives Cia, Mexicana de Petrolea "El Aguilla".

Two. Mary Tunnell b abt 1860; d in inf., Leon Co., Tex.

Three. Daughter b abt 1862; d in inf., Leon Co., Tex.

Four. Jessie L. Tunnell b 1864, of San Antonio, Tex.; married T. W. Patton 1882 and had; (a) Willie Mac Patton b Jan. 1884; d May 1885; (b) Eunice Lee Patton b Sept. 1885; d 1888; (c) Winifred Lee Patton b July 31, 1889, of San Antonio, Tex. (m J. E. Jackson Aug. 9, 1907 and had; 1, Winifred Lee Jackson b Dec. 23, 1909); (d) Audrey B. Patton b Mar. 12, 1894, of San Antonio, Tex. m C. D. Shaw Mar. 3, 1910.

Five. Idella Tunnell b Nov. 13, 1870 nr Cameron, Tex., of Orange, Tex.; married first, George A. McBryde Dec. 9, 1891 Rockdale, Tex. (d Sept. 9, 1911 Ardmore, Okla., son of Malcolm and Margaret McBryde) and had; (a) Willie Mabel McBryde b Sept. 28, 1892 Cameron, Tex., of Port Arthur, Tex., (m first, George Nicholson and had; I, George Albert Nicholson b Apr. 30, 1913 Marlin, Tex.; and m second, W. G. Salling, Feb. 10, 1925); (b) Frank Carlton McBryde b May 1, 1895; d June 18, 1895; (c) Margaret Leona McBryde b Oct. 29, 1900 Wooten Mills, Tex.; (d) Annie McBryde b and d Mar. 1902 Wooten Mills, Tex.; (e) Benjamin Fisher McBryde b July 16, 1906 Strawn,Tex.; d May 2, 1909; (f) Doris Esther McBryde b Apr. 9, 1908; d Apr. 30, 1909, shortly before her sister. Idella Tunnell married second, Leon Frank Campbell July 16, 1913 Galveston, Tex.

Six. Fisher Tunnell b Mar. 30, 1876 Rockdale, Tex.; d Aug. 4, 1882 Rockdale, Tex.

II. Nancy A. Tunnell, dau of Jesse and Mary Snow Tunnell, was born Aug. 12, 1828 in Ky. and died July 5, 1885 Emporia, Kansas. She married first, in Ill., Henry McLaughlin, who served in the War Between the States, was wounded in battle at Peach Creek and died in service. He was born Scioto Co., Ohio and came to nr Winchester, Ill. with his parents in the 1830's. Nancy Ashley Tunnell married second, John Orr, Dec. 14, 1865 nr Murrayville, Ill. He was born Jan. 24, 1819 Green Co., Ky. and died Apr. 16, 1886 Reading, Kan. He was the son of James Orr (b Jan. 10, 1782; d Sept. 10, 1823) and Margaret Greer Watt Orr (b Aug. 29, 1793; d Aug. 11, 1871).

One. Daniel Webster McLaughlin b May 1, 1847 nr Murrayville, Ill.; d May 15, 191, Rose Hill, Kan.; was a soldier in the War Between the States as one of the "hundred day men", under command of Col. Fox of Jacksonville, Ill. He married Mary J. Gosnell Oct. 17, 1867 nr Greenfield, Ill. (b Nov. 28, 1848 nr Wilmington, Greene Co., Ill.; d Feb. 26, 1924 Rose Hill, Kan.) and had; (a) Willie Crary McLaughlin b Apr. 24, 1870 in Ill.; d Aug. 14, 1870 Ill.; (b) Linnie Belle McLaughlin b May 27, 1871 in Ill.; d Jan. 25, 1896 Rose Hill, Kan., unm. (c) Jessie McLaughlin b Mar. 6, 1873 Ill.; d Apr. 7, 1873 Ill; (d) Georgie McLaughlin b Feb. 4, 1874 Ill.; d Aug. 1, 1874 Ill.; (e) Carrie Edith McLaughlin b June 4, 1876 Ill.; d Jan. 7, 1910 Wichita, Kan. (m Albert F. Bushnell Nov. 23, 1899 Wichita, Kan. and had ch b Wichita, Kan.; 1, Harmon Bushnell b Mar. 27, 1902; d May 20, 1915 Wichita; 2, Clarence Bushnell b Apr. 13, 1907, of Wichita); (f) Katie McLaughlin b June 24, 1878 Ill.; d Feb. 18, 1896; (g) Olive McLaughlin b Apr. 23, 1880; d Dec. 3, 1885; (h) Blanche McLaughlin b July 31, 1882 Ill.; d Jan. 17, 1887; (i) Florence May McLaughlin b May 24, 1884 Maroa, Ill. of Clearwater, Kan. (m Verlin C. Hinshaw Apr. 13, 1904 Wichita, Kan. and had; 1, Vivian Ruth Hinshaw b Aug. 16, 1905 Rose Hill,

Kan.; d Jan. 9, 1909 Rose Hill; 2, Leslie Delbert Hinshaw b Feb. 23, 1909 Rose Hill; 3, Cecil Eugene Hinshaw b Apr. 12, 1911; 4, Helen Marie Hinshaw b Jan. 9, 1913; 5, Max Merle Hinshaw b July 16, 1914; 6, Loyd Chauncey Hinshaw b June 16, 1918, all nr Wellington, Kan.; 7, Donald Lee Hinshaw b July 17, 1921 Rose Hill, Kan.; 8, Harold Neal Hinshaw b Apr. 10, 1923 Rose Hill, Kan.); (j) Mary Edna Mc-Laughlin b June 21, 1887 Rose Hill, Kan., of Rose Hill (m Alonzo Baker Feb. 28, 1906 Wichita, Kan. and had ch b Rose Hill; 1, Esther Baker b Nov. 25, 1906; 2, Fern Baker b June 16, 1908; 3, Marjorie Baker b Oct. 30, 1910; d Jan. 19, 1912; 4, Wilbur Baker b Aug. 1912); (k) Ruth McLaughlin b Oct. 28, 1889 Rose Hill, of Rose Hill, Kan. (m Carl Smith Jan. 26, 1911 nr Rose Hill and had; 1, Naomi Smith b Sept. 9, 1917 Rose Hill, Kan.)

Two. Elizabeth Jane McLaughlin b Apr. 20, 1853 Murrayville, Ill.; d abt 1901 Denver, Col.; married Theodore Deal, at Maroa, Ill., of Oakland, Calif. 1924, and had; (a) Norman Hugh Deal b Maroa, Ill., of Indianapolis; (b) Winona Deal b Maroa, Ill., of Denver, Col. (m Frank Rogers and had; 1, Loren Deal Rogers b Mar. 1899); (c) Lela Deal, b Carthage, Mo., of Calif., m ———— ————; (d) Ethel Deal b in Carthage, Mo., of Calif., m ———— ————.

Three. Willie McLaughlin d in inf. nr Murrayville, Ill.

Four. Charlie McLaughlin d in inf. nr Murrayville, Ill.

Five. Mary Edna McLaughlin d in inf. nr Murrayville, Ill.

Six. Jessie McLaughlin d in inf. nr Murrayville, Ill.

Seven. John Tunnell Orr b Aug. 31, Maroa, Ill.; d July 31, 1898 Carendon, Ark.; married first, Verda M. Willis, Oct. 12, 1887 Columbus, Ohio and had no ch.; and married second, Erneze Baker, July 23, 1890 in Wis. (d Aug. 10, 1898) and had an only child; (a) Geneva Louise Orr b July 6, 1894 in Wis., of Plymouth, Kan. (m Ralph Lambert Sept. 30, 1916 Newton, Kan. and had; 1, Edith Irene Lambert b Jen. 4, 1918 Plymouth, Kan.)

Eight. Ora Ella Orr b Mar. 17, 1875, of Strong Hill, Kan.; married Joseph Elmer Gordon, son of Thomas and Betsey (Crape) Gordon, at Reading, Kan. (b Aug. 21, 1871 Reading, Kan.) and had; (a) Ray Kenneth Gordon b Apr. 12, 1899 Allen, Kan., of Strong City, Kan., unm.; (b) Edgar Elmer Gordon b Aug. 16, 1906 Reading, Kan.; (c) Verna Lorene Gordon b Feb. 9, 1914 Reading, Kan.

III. Jane Tunnell, dau of Jesse and Mary Suow Tunnell, was born abt 1830 and died abt 1853 . She married first, Mart Masters, who died abt 1850. She married second, a cousin of her first husband, John Orr, abt 1852. He was born Jan. 24, 1819 Green Co. Ky. and died Apr. 6, 1886 Reading, Kan. He was the son of James Orr (b Jan. 10, 1782; d Sept. 10, 1823) and Margaret Greer (Watt) Orr (b Aug. 29, 1793; d Aug. 11, 1871). John Orr, a number of years later than his marriage to Jane Tunnell Masters, married her sister, Nancy Ashley Tunnell McLaughlin. John Orr was one of the eleven members who founded the M. E. Church in Maroa, Ill in 1857i Jane Tu..-nell had no children.

MARTIN LUTHER TUNNELL

J. Martin Luther Tunnell, son of Stephen and Kezia Money Tunnell, died, it is said while young. It is not known whether he was born in Va., or Tenn.

DAVID TUNNELL

K. David Tunnell, son of Stephen and Kezia Money Tunnell, was born Nov. 25, 1800 Washington Co., Tenn. and died in the early 1850's near Murrayville, Ill. He moved to Kentucky and was an itinerant Methodist minister there for eight years. In 1826 he was "admitted on trial" in the Kentucky Conference. The "Minutes" show he was stationed at Christian in the Green River district in 1827. He was admitted into full connection and had a charge at Liberty in the Augusta district in 1828. He married Elizabeth McClure May 4, 1829 in Hardin Co., Ky. who died 1866 nr Murrayville, Ill. She was of Scotch-Irish descent, a cousin of Dr. John Logan, the father of General John Logan. Rev. David Tunnell and wife moved to Morgan Co., Ill. shortly after their marriage and lived a few miles north of Jacksonville. In 1830 he entered land nr Murrayville, Ill. on which his daughter, Jane Wyatt, lived in 1886. Children born Morgan Co., Ill.

I. Robert McClure Tunnell b Oct. 17, 1830.
II. Jane Stuart Tunnell b May 10, 1832.
III. Martha Ann Tunnell b June 15, 1834.
IV. Mary Harrison Tunnell b Nov. 17, 1837.
V. Arabelle Holderman Tunnell b Jan. 20, 1841.

Of the foregoing;

1. Robert McClure Tunnell, son of David and Elizabeth McClure Tunnell, was born Oct. 17, 1830 north of Jacksonville, Ill. and died Nov. 25, 1904 in Kansas. He was a distinguished minister of the Congregational church and served as pastor, at Manhattan, Kansas, from Jan. 1883 until 1889. He was principal of Fairmont Institute in 1892. He was greatly interested in his lineage and furnished valuable information concerning the first settlers of the Tunnell family in America. (See History of Holston Methodism, p 177, by Rev. R. N. Price, of Morristown, Tenn.) During the War Between the States Rev. R. M. Tunnell served in recruiting service and was discharged from service, by special order of the war department at Washington, on Aug. 15, 1867. He had an affection for the name of McClure, for it was his mother's maiden name, his own name and two of his children bore the name. He married first, Peachy Ann Randall, Feb. 24, 1857 Upper Alton, Ill., who died July 30, 1862, and had three children. He married second, Sophie Chapin, Sept. 6, 1870 in Springfield, Ill., and had two children.

One. David Blackman Tunnell b Mar. 10, 1858, lived in St Louis, Mo. 1886 and was unmarried. Later he went to Calif.

Two. Robert McClure Tunnell, the second, b June 10 1860; d in inf.

Three. Charles Francis Tunnell b Jan. 23, 1862; d in inf.

Four. Jane Chapin Tunnell b July 7, 1871, unm., of Chicago, Ill.

Five. Elizabeth McClure Tunnell b July 8, 1876, unm., of Pacific Beach, Calif.

II. Jane Stuart Tunnell, dau of David and Elizabeth McClure Tunnell, was born May 10, 1832 nr Murrayville, Ill. and died May 27, 1895 nr Murrayville, Ill. She married James Lee Wyatt Nov. 17, 1853 Morgan Co., Ill., who served in the Mexican War and in 101st Ill. Vol. Inf. in the War Between the States (b Aug. 26, 1824 Ky.; d Apr. 30, 1881 Morgan Co., Ill., son of Edward Wyatt (b abt 1796; d 1878) and Anna Kennedy Wyatt (b 1800 N. C..; d 1866 nr Murrayville, Ill., m in Todd Co., Ky.) and had ch b nr Murrayville, Ill.

One. Edgar Allen Wyatt b Oct. 10, 1854, of Los Angeles, Calif. married Alice McEvers Oct. 6, 1881 (b Nov. 28, 1862 Murrayville, Ill.) and had; (a) Willard Wyatt b Mar. 18, 1883 (m Lorena Swarthout June 10, 1903 (b Jan. 1, 1886 Kan.) and had; 1, Marie Wyatt b Aug. 30, 1906; 2, Lucile Wyatt b Apr. 10, 1909; 3, and 4, twins, Floyd Wyatt and Lloyd Wyatt, b Oct. 17, 1911); (b) Harrison Lee Wyatt b Sept. 29, 1888 (m Edith Elston Sept. 4, 1912 (b May 12, 1890 Iowa) and had; 1, Edith May Wyatt b June 16, 1913; 2, Alice Wyatt b Apr. 10, 1915; 3 Elston Wyatt b June 14, 1919).

Two. Anna Bell Wyatt b Aug. 11, 1856, d Aug. 16, 1872.
Three. Robert Lincoln Wyatt b Apr. 3, 1858; d abt 1918, un-
married.
Four. Mary Elizabeth Wyatt b Feb. 17, 1860; d Sept. 28, 1911;
married S. A. D. Curtis Nov. 26, 1879 (b Nov. 22, 1858 Manchester,
Ill.) and had; (a) Marguerite Curtis b Dec. 26, 1880 Manchester, Ill.
of Fullerton, Calif. (m Garland Lish Nov. 2, 1909 Pheonix, Ariz. (b
Sept. 9, 1878 Silverdale, Kan.) and had; 1, Charles Douglas Lish b
Apr. 7, 1911 Winslow, Ariz.; 2, Sarah Elizabeth Lish b Oct. 13, 1912,
Winslow, Ariz.; 3, Philip Lish b Aug. 25, 1914 Allison, New Mex.);
(b) James Lee Curtis b Dec. 9, 1882 Manchester, Ill., of Winslow,
Ariz. (m Helen Hubbard June 9, 1912 and had; 1, Samuel Curtis b
Mar. 16, 1913; 2, Ruth Helen Curtis b June 26, 1914; 3, James Lee
Curtis, the second, b Apr. 10, 1916; 4, Barbara Curtis b Sept. 8, 1920);
(c) Edward Everette Curtis b July 16, 1885 Manchester, Ill.; d Jan.
29,1920 Wichita, Kan.; served over seas in Infantry greater part of
the World War (m first, Sallie Annie Elliott, first cousin of Emory
E. Elliott, who m Florence Belle Curtis, on Apr. 22, 1908. She d Sept.
19, 1908. He m second, Rhoda Carr Elliott, who is not a relative of
his first wife, May 28, 1914 Rincon, New Mex. (b Jan. 28, 1885,
Humphrey, Ky.) and had; 1, Mary Elizabeth Curtis b July 15, 1915);
(d) Florence Belle Curtis b Jan. 6, 1888 Manchester, Ill., of Dallas,
Tex. (m Emory E. Elliot Dec. 18, 1906 La Monte, Mo. and had; 1,
William Curtis Elliott b Apr. 4, 1909; 2, Floriet Maxine Elliott b Mar.
3, 1912; 3, Mary Nadine Elliott b June 19, 1914. Mr. and Mrs. Elliott
have given their name to and are rearing a niece of Mr. Elliott's; 4,
Mabel Adeline Elliott b June 17, 1921); (e) Maurice Bennett Curtis
b July 27, 1890 Manchester, Ill. of La Monte, Mo. (m Harriet Pearl
Chaplain Dec. 25, 1912 and had; 1, Emma Pearl Curtis b Nov. 19, 1913;
2,Flossie Elizabeth Curtis b Mar. 2, 1915; 3, Robert Clay Curtis b Oct.
13, 1917; 4, Lloyd B. Curtis b July 11, 1919); (f) Emma Marie Curtis
b Oct. 15, 1892 Manchester, Ill., of La Monte, Mo. (m Elbert F. Rissler Dec. 18, 1912 Sedalia, Mo. and had ch b La Monte, Mo.; 1, Mary
Louise Rissler b Oct. 23, 1914; 2, Charles Kenneth Rissler b July 27,
1918); (g) Robert Lester Curtis b Jan. 21, 1896, Edna, Kan., of Sedalia, Mo.,who served as Corporal in World War, with nine months
overseas service; left Sedalia, Mo., Oct. 4, 1917 for Camp Funston,
transferred to Camp Cody, N. Mex. Oct. 20, 1917, and Aug. 24, 1918
to Camp Dix, N. J.; sailed Oct. 13, 1918 with Co. E. 134th Inf. for
Cherbourg, France. Left St. Medard, nr Bordeaux, Nov. 6, 1918 for
front, arrived Le Mans Nov. 7th; re-equipped and assigned as re-
placement to 4th Div. Alsace-Loraine, Nov. 12th. Was in Co. C. 47th
Inf. Div. Placed in Army of Occupation. Returned to the States, sailing from Brest, July 16, 1919. Discharged at Camp Taylor, Ky. Aug.
4, 1919. He married Muriel Irene Burke Dec. 23, 1920 and had; 1,
Edgar Everett Curtis b Dec. 26, 1921 La Monte, Mo.; 2, Robert Lester
Curtis the second, b Oct. 28, 1923 Sedalia, Mo.); (h) Mary Elizabeth
Curtis b Oct. 26, 1900 Edna, Kan., of Dallas, Tex., m Levi Frank
Harper Oct. 17, 1921 Dallas, Tex.
Five. John Edward Wyatt b Feb. 20, 1862, of White Hall, Ill.;
married Margaret Strang, dau of C. F. Strang, Nov. 8, 1882 and had
no ch.
Six. James Lee Wyatt b Feb. 17, 1874, of Murrayville, Ill.;
married Letitia Marshal Chittick (b Oct. 4, 1866) and had an only
child; (a) Jane Wyatt b Sept. 16, 1899; d Feb. 3, 1907.
Seven. Son b May 24, 1866; d May 29, 1866.
Eight. Martha Jane Wyatt b Nov. 8, 1867, of Kansas City, Mo.;
married George Edward Hughes Nov. 12, 1885 (b Apr. 14, 1864 Mur-

rayville, Ill.) and had; (a) Elmo Leone Hughes b Jan. 12, 1887 Mur-
rayville, Ill.; d Feb. 21, 1907 Kansas City, Mo.; (b) Edrie Rhea
Hughes b July 24, 1889 Kansas City, Mo., of Kahoka, Mo. (m Dr. Olin
Thompson Murphy June 28, 1911 (b Mar. 1884 New Haven, Mo.) and
had ch b Kahoka, Mo.; 1, George Leland Murphy b Apr. 14, 1912; 2,
Virginia Elizabeth Murphy b Sept. 7, 1913; 3, Robert Earl Murphy b
Sept. 4, 1915; 4, William Olin Murphy b Jan. 28, 1917; 5, Dorothy
Jane Murphy b Mar. 13, 1919; 6, Virgil Dean Murphy b May 1, 1923);
(c) Edna Loraine Hughes b Dec. 31, 1893 Kansas City, Mo. (m first,
George Henry Clinton Feb. 20, 1915 Kansas City, who served in Navy
during World War, and had; 1, Dixie Lee Clinton b Aug. 28, 1916;
and m second, Carroll F. Andrada Aug. 31, 1921).

Nine.   Linnie Belle Wyatt b May 24, 1871; of Yorba Linda, Calif.;
married I. Leroy Taylor Sept .7, 1887 and had; (a) Ralph Taylor b
July 28, 1888; d in inf.; (b) Grace Stewart Taylor b Sept. 20, 1891
(m Edgar V. Hayworth and had; 1, Vera Marie Hayworth b Mar. 25,
1910; 2, Margaret Bell Hayworth b Dec. 10, 1912; 3, Edgar Wyatt
Hayworth b Apr. 14, 1915); (c) Blanche La Verne Taylor b May 25,
1893; (d) Verna Margurite Taylor b Mar. 31, 1896, m Joseph T.
Hamm; (e) Leroy Wyatt Taylor b Oct. 17, 1898; (f) Maud Alice
Taylor b Aug. 30, 1901; (g) George Edward Taylor b Aug. 6, 1905.

III.   Martha Ann Tunnell, dau of David and Elizabeth McClure
Tunnell, was born June 15, 1834 nr Murrayville, Ill. and died Feb. 1,
1903 Brookfield, Mo. She married Alfred Sawyer Tunnell, a son of
her first cousin, James Tunnell junior, on Mar. 27, 1856 Morgan Co.,
Ill.   Alfred Sawyer Tunnell was born Aug. 16, 1829 nr Nashville,
Tenn. and died Aug. 16, 1899 Browning, Mo. He was the son of James
and Mary Ann (Starns) Tunnell; grandson of Rev. James and Jane
(Ball) Tunnell; same of Lenard and Barbara Starns. See record of
Rev. James Tunnell . Ch. b in Mo.

One.   Robert McClure Tunnell b Dec. 25, 1856 Scottville, Mo.; d
Sept. 6, 1909 Brookfield, Mo.; attorney; married Flora Shrock Jones,
dau of P. D. Shrock, and had no ch. Flora Shrock Jones Tunnell married second, ——— Dell and lives at Browning, Mo.

Two.   Alpha Alice Tunnell b Dec. 30, 1858, of Browning, Mo.;
married Dr. David Lafayette Whaley Sep. 5, 1880 (b Dec. 20, 1851; d
Dec. 11, 1910; and had; (a) Dr. Roy Wallace Whaley b June 6, 1881,
m Alpha Lorene Haymaker and had no ch.; (b) Claude Lafayette
Whaley, of Macon, Mo. (m Clara Gooch and had; 1, Drummond Lafayette Whaley b Mar. 16, 1909); (c) Lillian Gladys Whaley b June 28,
1892, of Hume, Mo. (m M. E. Duncan, dentist, June 28, 1921 and had
no ch.); (d) Alfred Byron Whaley b June 24, 1896, Chiropractor,
unm., of Browning, Mo.

Three.   Jane Bell Tunnell b Nov. 11, 1861; d Sept. 10, 1862.
Four.   Wallace Victor Tunnell b Dec. 29, 1864; d Mar. 26, 1876.
Five.   Dr. James David Tunnell b Dec. 11, 1866, of Reger, Mo.;
married Ida Rogers and had no ch.
Six.   William Enlow Tunnell b May 25, 1869 nr Scottville, Mo.;
d July 19, 1916; married Minerva A. Warren Jan. 1, 1891 Scottville,
Mo. and had ch b nr Scottville, Mo.; (a) Roy Earle Tunnell b Oct. 1,
1891 d Aug. 22, 1892; (b) Alpha Alice Tunnell b Jan. 12, 1893, m
Davie Lovell; (c) William Frederick Tunnell b Apr. 3, 1896, served
two years with A. E. F. overseas, m Gladys Myers; (d) Robert Mc-
Clure Tunnell b Nov. 4, 1901, served overseas, in active service.
wounded and gassed in World War; (e) Veda Margaret Tunnell b
Aug. 26, 1910; d Sept. 26, 1911; (f) James David Tunnell b Jan. 27,
1912; (g) Donna Gertrude Tunnell b Jan. 12, 1914.   Minerva A.

Warren Tunnell married second, Fred G. Dell, Aug. 29, 1917 Trenton, Mo.

IV. Mary Harrison Tunnell, dau of David and Elizabeth Mc-Clure Tunnell, was born Nov. 17, 1837 nr Murrayvil⁻, Ill. and died 1895 in Mo. She married Rev. William Fogle and had; (a) Charles Fogle; (b) John Fogle; (c) daughter. At one time the family lived at Brookline.

V. Arabell Holderman Tunnell, dau of David and Elizabeth McClure Tunnell, was born Jan. 20, 1841 nr Murrayville, Ill. and died May 10, 1915 Murrayville, Ill. She married Robert Lee Wyatt, a brother of her sister's husband, Mar. 29, 1860 nr Murrayville, Ill. He was born Feb. 1835 nr Murrayville, Ill. and died Oct. 24, 1912 Murrayville, Ill. In the War Between the States he served in Co. F., 101st Ill. Inf. Vol. He enlisted Aug. 7, 1862 and was mustered out, as Sergeant, June 7, 1865. Ch. b nr Murrayville, Ill.

One. Peachy Ann Wyatt b Jan. 8, 1861; d young; unm.

Two. Robert Logan Wyatt b Sept. 21, 1863, of Kildare, Okla.; married Nettie Kingsley, dau Jeremiah and Elizabeth (Sharp) Kingsley, (b Aug. 31, 1867 Mintral Point, Mo.) and had; (a) Elvin Wyatt b Apr. 15, 1888 nr Murrayville, Ill., of Kansas City, Mo., m Ora Butterfield Aug. 3, 1907; (b) Howard Earl Wyatt b Jan. 15, 1890 nr Murrayville, Ill.; of Kansas City, Mo., m Ludy Hale Aug. 5, 1914; (c) Maud Wyatt b Sept. 30, 1892 nr Murrayville, Ill., of Shawnee, Okla. (m Charles E. Van Bebber Nov. 3, 1920 and had; 1, Helen Marie Van Bebber b May 3, 1922); (d) May Alice Wyatt b Dec. 25, 1894 Murrayville, Ill.; d Jan. 28, 1895; (e) Bessie Wyatt b July 5, 1896; d Nov. 13, 1898; (f) Grace Wyatt b Feb. 25, 1898 Kildare, Okla., m John D. Cobler Feb. 26, 1916 Newkirk, Okla.; (g) Robert Wyatt b Mar. 28, 1900 Kildare, Okla.; d Apr. 28, 1900; (h) Edith Wyatt b Mar. 15, 1901 Kildare, Okla., of Anderson, Mo.; (i) Wilburn Wyatt b May 5, 1903 Kildare, Okla., of Los Angeles, Calif.

Three. William E. Wyatt b Apr. 28, 1866; d young.

Four. Mary Elizabeth Wyatt b Aug. 10, 1868; d Feb. 10, 1904 nr Murrayville, Ill.; married Marion M. Crouse (b May 25, 1868; d Aug. 12, 1910) and had ch b nr Murrayville, Ill.; (a) Harry Leroy Crouse b 1890; d 1922 Los Angeles, Calif., m Charlotte Ruth Windrick Oct. 15, 1915 and had no ch.; (b) Ethel Mae Crouse b 1892, of Albuquerque, N. Mex. (m Clare Lyman Gay Oct. 16, 1912 Murrayville, Ill. and had; 1, Helen Frances Gay b Barry, Ill; 2, Marjorie Marie Gay b Barry, Ill.; d Springfield, Ill.; 3, Clarence Eugene Gay b Springfield, Ill.); (c) Helen Elizabeth Crouse b 1894; d 1915 Jacksonville, Ill. unm.; (d) Ralph Wyatt Crouse b 1897; d 1924 Denver, Col., unm.; (e) Robert Oland Crouse b 1899; d 1924 Tuscon, Ariz., unm.; (f) Mary Eleanor Crouse b 1901, of Albuquerque, N. Mex., unm.

Five. Walter Lee Wyatt b Feb. 8, 1870; d 1924 Los Angeles, Calif., m Hettie Seaver and had no ch.

Six. James Albert Wyatt b Dec. 27, 1872; married Myrtle Mitchell and had; (a) Hilda Wyatt b 1895; (b) Harold Wyatt b 1897; (c) Edna Wyatt b 1899; (d) Eva Wyatt b 1901.

Seven. Horace Wyatt b Sept. 3, 1875, of Colby, Kan.; married India Self, dau George and Eliza (McAlister) Self, and had; (a) Hazel Bell Wyatt b 1900; (b) Mary Esther Wyatt b 1902, m ——— ——— and had one ch.; (c) and (d), twins, Florence Wyatt and George Wyatt, b abt 1908; (e) Lambert Hastings Wyatt b bef. 1915.

Eight. David Wyatt b Mar. 6, 1878; d young.; unm.

THE TUNNELL FAMILY

Rev. John Tunnell, son of William and Ann Howard Tunnell, was born 1755 nr Fredericksburg, Va. and died July 1790 at the Sweet Springs in Va., now in West Va. He was never married.

Of the four sons this one was the best known. He was an eminent minister, credited with doing wonderful work, one of the first itinerants in America, and greatly loved and respected as an orator and a Christian. His name has been preserved in many of the histories of Methodism. He was admitted into the traveling connection "at a preaching house at the Conference which began May 20, 1777 nr Deer Creek, Maryland." At the Christmas Conference of 1784, when American Methodism was separated from the British and organized as a distinctly American Church, Rev. Francis Asbury was ordained a Bishop and Rev. John Tunnell was elected to an eldership. Mr. Tunnnell attended the first Conference held west of the Alleghanies. He spent some months in the West India Island of St. Christopher's but had no charge there. He was elder of the district embracing East Jersey, Newark, New York and Long Island in 1786; of the Holston and Nollichucky, known now as East Tenn. 1787; of Tar River, Bladen, New River, Roanoke, Caswell, New Hope, Guilford, Salisbury, Yadkin and Halifax in 1788. He was the presiding elder of the district embracing Holston, West New River, Greenbrier and Botetourt, 1789, his last appointment.

In Bishop Asbury's writings are references to Mr. Tunnell. Of his death Bishop Asbury wrote; "Sat. 11, 1790. Brother Tunnell's corpse was brought to Dew's Chapel. I preached his funeral sermon. It is fourteen years since Brother Tunnell first knew the Lord and he had spoken about 13 years and had traveled through 8 of the 13 states. Few men as public ministers were better known or more beloved. He was a simple-hearted, artless, child-like man. For his opportunities he was a man of good learning; had a large fund of Scripture knowledge; was a good historian, a sensible, improving preacher, a most affectionate friend and a great saint". Stevens says; "He takes historical rank amoung the founders of Methodism in the great valley of the West, its most important arena". He moved, melted and charmed his audiences. It might seem almost as if the life and adventures of Rev. John Tunnell were inextricably interwoven with the history of pioneer Methodism in the United States.

NOTABLE
SOUTHERN FAMILIES

Volume IV

The Sevier Family

To my uncle
Robert A. J. Armstrong
This book is affectionately dedicated

The Sevier Family

IN SIX PARTS

FOREWORD

THE history of John Sevier and his family is interlocked with the history of thousands upon thousands of citizens of Tennessee and every other Southern State. A speaker said not long ago that no where else in the United States than in the mountains of Tennessee can a man address a crowd of two or three thousand people with not a foreign born hearer, or a hearer whose parents are foreign born. No where else are traditions so deeply ingrained of the pioneers who won the land. The ancestors of every man and woman in the section participated with Sevier in the Winning of the West and were on more or less intimate terms with the Great Commander.

Many of the things that are here set down will therefore be twice told tales, as around every fireside in the mountains stories are still told of the prowess and courage of the Good Governor, Nollichucky Jack, of the beauty of Bonny Kate or the sweetness and bravery of Sarah Hawkins, who was the first Madame Sevier; of the charm of the Sevier girls and the bravery of the sons; of the heroic fortitude of Valentine Sevier III, and his sorrow of six sons and daughters killed by Indians; of the almost king-like reign of John Sevier in Tennessee and of the fact that, had he so desired, perhaps he might have truly reigned, a king, for the Spanish proposals were many and various. Yet, lest the knowledge of these things should pass as the generations go and lest the dates and names should become confused, these facts are gathered from many sources.

Before closing the chapters of this History of the Sevier Family I take this opportunity to thank Charles Lyman Sevier, Robert A. J. Armstrong, Mrs. Eugene Coile, Miss Kellogg, of the Wisconsin Historical Society, Custodian of the Draver papers, Mrs. Sessler Hoss, Elston Luttrell, Miss Augusta Bradford, of the Chattanooga Library, A. N. Turner, A. V. Goodpasture, William Drane, Miss Lucy M. Ball, Mrs. Sophia Hoss French, Charles Sevier, Mrs. Florence Underwood Eastman, John Trotwood Moore, Tennessee State Librarian, A. P. Foster, Assistant Tennessee State Librarian, Miss Cora Sevier, Mrs. Theodore Francis Sevier, Mrs. Louise Sevier Giddings, Mrs. Gray Gentry (Evelyn Sevier), the late Charles Bascom Sevier, Mrs. John Trotwood Moore, Daniel Vertner Sevier, Jr., Benjamin F. Wyley, W. H. Waddell, Mrs. Ruth Catherine Hoyt, Mrs. N. B. Pearman, Samuel Sevier Kirkpatrick, Fain Anderson, Miss Kate White, J. J. Brown, Mrs. G. L. Wing, Mrs. Ida Barclay Tucker, Mrs. William P. Bowdry, Mrs. M. W. Barney, Seldon Nelson, Mrs. Sabine, Miss Lucy M. Ball, and many other members of the family whose information and interest contributed so largely to the value of the record.

ZELLA ARMSTRONG

GOVERNOR JOHN SEVIER

BIBLIOGRAPHY .

Not all of the hundreds of books studied during the preparation of the Sevier Family History can be listed here but some of the important volumes whose contents contributed valuable information should be mentioned. Among them are:

Ramsey's Annals of Tennessee

Ramsey's History of Lebanon Church

Wheeler's History of North Carolina

Wheeler's Reminiscences of North Carolina

Goodspeed's History of East Tennessee

Waddell's Annals of Augusta County

Chalkley's Abstracts of Augusta County

White's King's Mountain

Draper's Heroes of the Revolution

Haywood's History of Tennessee

Ellett's Pioneer Women of the West

North Carolina Colonial Records

North Carolina State Records

Roosevelt's Winning of the West

Putnam's History of Middle Tennessee

Taylor's Historic Sullivan

Sumner's History of Southwest Virginia

Turner's Life of General John Sevier

Heiskall's Andrew Jackson and His Times

Lenoir's History of Sweetwater Vally

Lineage Books D. A. R.

Lineage Books S. A. R.

Gilmore's John Sevier

Thompson's Life of Loyola

Allison's Dropped Stitches

PART ONE

Antecedents and Emigration

The Sevier Family

ANTECEDENTS AND EMIGRATION

THE Sevier family name, originally Xavier, had its earliest history in the Kingdom of Navarre, an independent monarchy until its sovreign, Henry III, succeeded to the throne of France as Henry IV. He ruled Navarre and France in a romantic period and as Henry of Navarre is one of the best known characters in history. The "White Plume of Navarre" was a rallying cry and is one of the famous phrases of history and literature.

Navarre lay on two sides of the Western Pyrenees. The territory is now in Spain and France; it is now the Spanish province of Navarra and a part of the French Department of Basses-Pyrenees. Pamplona is the capitol of Navarre.

Henry IV, (Henry III, of Navarre) was born in Castle Pau, Bearne, in 1553. He was the third son of Antoinne de Bourbon and Jeanne d'Albret, daughter of Henry II of Navarre and Margaret, sister of Francis I, of France, and succeeded to the throne of France through Margaret, after Francis' grandsons had died without heirs. Henry III had married his cousin Margaret of France, grand-daughter of Francis.

This brief understanding of Navarre and its rulers is necessary to the story of the Xaviers, as they were prominent in the history of the country and intimate friends and kinsmen of the royal family.

The first mention I have seen of the Xaviers is in the time of King Jean III, known as Jean d'Albret, King of Navarre. One of his counselors was Don Juan de Jassu. Don Juan married, doubtless with the King's full approval and assistance, the King's ward, the orphan Marie de Xavier and Azpileuta. This young girl was sole heiress to the houses of both her father and her mother, Xavier and Azpileuta. The Xavier castle and estate lay in what is now Spain. At that time both estates were of course in Navarre.

It is frequently said in family traditions and records that the Xaviers were close kin to the reigning family and that they were of Bourbon descent through Charles of Orleans. That is indication

1

of very close kinship and the loyalty of the family through a long and stormy period of time is proof that a close tie of some sort certainly existed.

In later years a King of France had among his several names Xavier. Louis Stanilaus Xavier, Count of Provence, became King of France as Louis XVIII, but I think it is possible that he was given a complimentary name of Saint Francis de Xavier, perhaps however, partly because Saint Francis was a kinsman.

Marie de Xavier, heiress of that name and title, who was also heiress of the Spanish name Azpileuta, was a matrimonial prize in the court of Navarre in the latter part of the fifteenth century. Don Juan de Jassu, upon his marriage to her, assumed her titles. The marriage took place about 1485. When a large family was born to them, one half the children took the name Xavier and one half Azpileuta. It is said that the eldest children assumed Azpileuta and the youngest children Xavier, from which I conclude the Spanish name was more important and that probably the fortune was larger, since the eldest born children took it.

Among the children born to Marie and Don Juan Xavier and Azpileuta whose names we know are:

Phillip de Xavier.
Miguel de Xavier.
Juan de Xavier.
Valentine de Xavier.
Francis de Xavier.
Magdalen de Xavier, a nun in the convent of St. Clare and Gandia.

These all took the name de Xavier and were therefore according to history and tradition among the younger children.

Among the youngest, and said by many to be the youngest child, was Francis de Xavier. He was born April 7, 1506, and it is by his birth that I predicate the probable marriage of his parents, since he was the youngest or nearly the youngest of a large family. It is shown on the above list that at least five sons were born in the "younger half" of the family since these five took the name of Xavier. Francis Thompson's Life of Loyola mentions Esteban and Diego d'Equia as first cousins of Francis Xavier.

Francis was born, as were his brothers and sisters, in the Castle de Xavier, eight leagues from Pamplona, the capitol of Navarre.

Francis studied for the priesthood and became one of the greatest missionaries of the world. He was subsequently pronounced a saint by the Catholic Church. As Saint Francis de Xavier he is the best known member of his family with the exception of his many times great nephew John Sevier, First Governor of Tennessee.

Francis de Xavier was born April 7, 1506, in the Castle de

Xavier, eight leagues from Pamlona, close to the little village of Sanguesa. His full name was Francois de Jassu de Xavier, which shows that for a generation the children used their father's name with their mother's. His mother was sole heiress of the Spanish House of Azpileuta and her father was heir to the house of Xavier, or Xavarro. She herself was an only child and much sought at the Court of Navarre. The King of Navarre was her guardian and over-lord and doubtless by his wish she was betrothed to his chief Counselor of State, Don Juan de Jassu.

Upon his marriage Don Juan dropped his name which does not appear again in the family annals except in the first name, Juan which in the Anglicized form of John is many times repeated.

Francis de Xavier is said by many to be the youngest child of the couple, while all historians concur in saying he was one of the youngest. I conclude that all the children who took the Azpileuta name were born in the latter part of the fifteenth century 14——, and that some of the Xaviers were also born in that century. The history of St. Francis de Xavier is interesting and dramatic and is given in full in the Cathollic Enclycopedias. Many biographies have been written also, and from his life, details of his family history can be gathered.

"From his infancy he was of a complying, winning humor, and discovered a good genius and great propensity to learning to which of his own notion he turned himself, whilst all his brothers embraced the profession of arms," is a quaint quotation from one Life of Saint Francis.

His studious inclination determined his parents to send him to Paris in the eighteenth year of his age where he entered the College of Saint Barbara. He took his degree as Master of Arts in 1530, and taught philosophy as Beauvais College, although he still lived at Saint Barbara. Saint Barbara was headquarters for Spanish and Portuguese students.

St. Ignatius came to Paris in 1528 intending to finish his studies. Francis de Xavier was then twenty-two years old. Ignatius had conceived a plan to organize a society which we know now as the Society of Jesuits. At St. Barbara he formed an intimate friendship with Francis de Xavier and Peter Faber, a Savoyard, who was a school mate and friend of Fancis. Peter Faber yielded almost immediately to the influence of Ignatius and fell in with his plans. But to quote the old books, "Francis de Xavier, whose head was full of ambitious thoughts, made a long and vigorous resistance."

However in time, through the influence of St. Ignatius he became a devoted convert to religion and his life thereafter was given to apostolic work. In 1534 he was of the seven persons who first took the oath of the Society of Jesuits. He became one of the great missionaries of the world and traveled far and wide teaching the gospel. Much space could be filled with his life and works, but as he is not a direct ancestor of the Sevier family the information will be condensed.

After many years of evangelical work in India and Japan, Francis de Xavier turned to Sancian, an island off the south Chinese coast, to wait for a favorable moment to enter China to pursue his missionary work. He died there December 2, 1552, before he had made his entry into China. A shrine has been erected to his memory on this island where he died. It is an interesting fact that recently (March, 1924) American Catholics have been given charge of the Island of Sancian and the little shrine, devoted to the memory of Francis de Xavier.

Announcement was made in March, 1924, from Rome that the French priests of the Paris-Foreign Missions had relinquished the island to the care of the Catholic Foreign Missionary Society of America. The island was made a "prefecture apostolic" at the same time. The chief point of interest on the island is the shrine of St. Francis.

Francis was beatified two years after his death, canonized ten years after his death, and now, nearly four hundred years after his death, the scene of his last days comes into the possession of American Catholics.

St. Francis' life was written in Latin by Turselin in six books and was first published in Rome in 1594. The same author translated into Latin and published in 1596 his Letters in four books. His Life was also written by Orlandino and was written in Italian by Bartoli, in Portuguese by Luzena and in Spanish by Garcia. See Nierenberg's Illustrious Men, Histories of India, Histories of Japan, etc. His History was published in French and in English by Dryden in 1688.

Interesting details of the Sevier family are revealed in Henry Dwight Sedgwick's Life of Ignatius Loyola. Francis Xavier was one of the early converts to Loyola's Society of Jusus, and all histories of Loyola mention Xavier. Dr. Sedgwick says:

"Loyola's second disciple, Francois de Jassu et de Xavier, was of the same age as Lefevre, (the first disciple)_ but from a different social class. An official document declares him to be a hijodalgo, a gentleman according to feudal standards. His people dwelt in the kingdom of Navarre, which at that time lay on both sides of the Pyrenees. His father's family had lived to the north of the mountains, his mother's to the south, at Xavier, the family castle and estate where Francois was born some twenty-five miles southeast of Pamplona. The parents resided at Xavier and had been prosperous until King Ferdinand invaded and annexed Southern Navarre in 1512, when they, as partisans of the French claimants, were dispossessed of a part of their estates, at least, and left camparatively poor. Four years later on Ferdinand's death, there was a rising on behalf the old royal house, but this was quickly put down, and Cardinal Ximenes, at that time regent for young King Charles, ordered all the strongholds throughout Spanish Navarre to be destroyed. The castle of Xavier shared the common fate, its towers and fortifications were torn down, leaving it defenseless, almost a ruin. As the duke of Najera, viceroy of Navarre, executed these orders, it may be that Loyola had a hand in the demolition. Besides the injury to the castle the family were stripped legally and illegally of various rights; their former tenants, finding them outside the pale of royal favor, denied rents and feudal dues; drivers taking cattle across their land refused to pay toll howerer long established; and later on at the time of the French invasion, neighboring farmers occupied their fields and lawless peasant cut down their timber. For these latter doings there was some excuse, since Xavier's two elder brothers, Miguel and Juan, were among the inhabitants favorable to the old royal house who took arms and declared for their former allegiance. So it came to pass that while Loyola, in the Spanish army, was fighting to defend the citadel at Pamplona, Xavier's brothers were serving with the French troops.

"The insurrection, if it may be called, came to an end in 1524; the two fighting brothers made their peace with the Spanish government and returned home to find the family affairs in a pitiable condition. Francis, in the meantime, had stayed with his mother. He was only six years of age in 1512 and ten years of age in 1516, and had acquired enough schooling to prepare himself for the course in Philosophy at Saint-Barbe. and to Paris he went in time for the October term in 1525, where he had the good fortune to fall in with Pierre Lefevre. While studying philosophy of the schools under Juan Pena, so his biographers say, he was applying himself with great fervor to a better philosophy of a different kind, the knowledge of self and the service of God. This better philosophy he owed at first to Pierre Lefevre and only afterward to Loyola; for it seems that Xavier, in the beginning at least, was less impressionable than Pierre to Loyola's persuasion. Perhaps the yong nobleman entertained more pleasureable visions of the worldly life than the young peasant, and was less disposed to renounce them; possibly the fact that Loyola had served under the Spanish colors in Navarre, against what Xavier regarded as the patriotic party, may have put some barrier between them, And besides, it seems certain that the new ideas of religious and ecclesiastical matters, that were spreading in Paris, at first possessed some attraction for Xavier; but all obstacles and causes of separation, whatever they may have been, were swept away by Loyola's passionate purpose, and Xavier became his second disciple. Xavier is the prototype of modern Christian missionaries, sans peur et sans reproche. Like Bayard on Sir Phillip Sidney, he is renowned for his modesty as for his dauntless courage."

PHILLIP DE XAVIER
AND VALENTINE DE XAVIER

Phillip de Xavier, said to be the eldest of the second half of the children of Don Juan and Marie de Xavier de Azpileuta, was born in the last year of the fifteenth century, say about 1493. It is said that Phillip was a close friend and devoted follower of the young King of Navarre, Henry, who succeeded to the throne of France as Henry IV and it is further said that Phillip married a close kinswoman the young King, thus tightening the cord of intimacy; but I think the marriage must have been of a son or a grandson of Phillip, as Phillip, son of Marie and Don Juan was born about 1495 and King Henry of Navarre was born in 1553 The King's intimate friend and contemporary therefore, must have been a grandson of the original Phillip. The repetition of the name of Henry in the royal line and of Phillip, Valentine and Juan, in the Xavier family, is of course confusing and, when tradition is the basis of anecdote, even hopelessly confusing. Tradition tells of this marriage of a Phillip to a kinswoman of the king and it is doubtless to be relied upon. As will be seen the generations are confused also in family annals when Valentine becomes the subject of relation.

Valentine is said in some records to be the youngest son of Don Juan and Marie and this is the first time I have seen the name Valentine de Xavier, although it may have been a frequent name in the family of the heiress de Xavier and Azpileuta. The name is in frequent use to this day. John is, of course, a popular name in the family and it is interesting to observe the continued use of these names through four centuries.

Valentine and Phillip de Xavier, probably grandsons of Don Juan and Marie, espoused the Protestant cause with their friend the King of Navarre, and it is said that upon the very morning of the Massacre of St. Bartholomew, August 24, 1572, Valentine Xavier, being apprised by some friends of danger,fled from France. Other family traditions give 1685, more than a century later as the year in which Valentine Xavier escaped from France to London and the occasion, the Revocation of the Edict of Nantes. It is true that in that year also many Huguenots fled to London for safety, so, to which ever tradition you are inclined, there is much interesting evidence.

Whatever the date it was evidently a Valentine Xavier who fled from France to London, and there took up his residence. Valentine Xavier married Mary Smith in London about the year 1700, but this is obviously not the Valentine who was born to Don Juan de Jassu and Marie de Xavier de Azpileuta about the year 1503, although it may conceivably be the Valentine who fled from France in 1685 because of the Revocation of the Edict of Nantes.

Valentine Xavier, the Refugee from France, we will call Valentine Sevier I because he is really the first of the English and American

Family as we know it and because he was first to assume the English form of the name Sevier, although he was perhaps the fourth or fifth Valentine in direct line.

Having arrived in England and having assumed the name Sevier, Valentine married Mary Smith about the year 1700.

They had among other children:

Valentine Sevier, II.

William Sevier.

Some family records say that Valentine, II, was born in London in 1699, others give 1702 as the date and still others 1704 and some 1722. I think the 1699 date is several years too early and the 1722 much too late. His birth probably took place in 1702. He died in America when he was a very old man in 1803 and he was then by all accounts about one hundred and one or two years of age.

Whatever the actual date of his birth, the sons, of Valentine Sevier I, and Mary Smith Sevier were Valentine II, and William Sevier. The name was already Anglicized and from this time is always Sevier.

There is a family tradition, and it has been repeated by learned historians again and again, that the two sons, William and Valentine II, ran away from home and "took ship to America about 1740." This is repeated sometimes in the very paragraph which gives the approx.mate date of their birth as 1702 or even 1699. Now, either they were born later than the date 1702, as is most often given, or they did not run away from home, as we cannot imagine men of forty or thereabouts running away! Perhaps they ran away when they were quite young men and spent the years that followed before they sailed to America in some place in England, or perhaps they "took ship" much earlier than 1740. Ramsey says they emigrated to America before 1740. It is pretty certain that they "took ship" as there was no other way to arrive in America at that date, so we can be sure that a part of the family tradition is correct: "They ran away from while still young men and took ship to America."

Bishop E. E. Hoss, a descendant of Valentine II, says the emigration took place sometime in the decade between 1730 and 1740. George Washington Sevier, a grandson of Valentine II, in writing to Dr. Lyman C. Draper, says the emigration took place in 1730.

One family record referred to above, says they were born in London in 1720 and 1722. the marriage of their father, Valentine having taken place in 1715. This is completely disproved , however, by the record of Valentine Sevier II which has been carefully preserved. He died in America, December 1803, and he was then one hundred and one years old. This establishes his birth about the year 1702.

Shortly after landing in Baltimore, where the ship upon which they took passage come to port, Valentine and William each married. William Sevier married a Catholic lady, Miss———O'Neil and her name has been preserved in the family nomenclature to this day.

William Sevier and his descendants will be found in Part Two of this book. His family remained in Maryland for sometime, though later many of his descendants migrated to Tennessee, where the family of his brother Valentine II, had become established and famous.

.Valentine Sevier II married Joanna Goode, and his descendants exclusive of the descendants of his eldest son, Governor John Sevier, will appear in Part Three of this book.

PART TWO

William Sevier and His Descendants

WILLIAM SEVIER AND
HIS DESCENDANTS

WILLIAM Sevier, son of Valentine Sevier I and Mary Smith Sevier was born in London in 1702 or shortly thereafter, and sailed for America in company with his brother Valentine Sevier II. It is of them the story is told that they ran away from home and took ship for America in 1740. However the dates of birth or of running away must be wrong for it is not probable that young men of thirty eight and forty "ran away." Bishop Hoss notes the date of emigration to America as somewhere in the decade between 1730 and 1740, while George Washington Sevier, in a letter to Dr. Lyman Draper says they emigrated in 1730. This matter is fully discussed in Part One.

William Sevier shortly after his arrival in Baltimore married———— O'Neil, said to be of a prominent Catholic family of Maryland.

They had at least one son————Sevier ,who married ———————— and had at least four children, namely:

(1)   Theodore Francis Sevier who died at sea unmarried.

(2)   Ann Sevier, who married Frederick Seyler and had no children.

(3)   Sarah Sevier, who died unmarried.

(4)   William Pierre Sevier, born January '9, 1793.

WILLIAM PIERRE SEVIER

William Pierre Sevier, born January 19, 1793, died December 10. 1846, ran away from home when he was still quite young and fought in the war of 1812. He was captured and taken to Dartmoor prison in England and was there at the time of the Massacre.

A family tradition is that in the massacre that his best friend Granville Sharpe Townsend was shot and that William Pierre Sevier caught his wounded friend in his arms. His devotion to this friend is proven by the fact that he named a son for him and it is interesting to note that the name is still used in the family, Colonel Granville Sharpe Townsend Sevier, United States Army, bearing it in full.   William Pierre Sevier married in 1820, Lucretia Williams Weller, born———— died 1776.   They lived in Russellville, Kentucky.

William Pierre Sevier and Lucretia Williams Weller Sevier had twelve children:

(1)   Granville Sharpe Townsend Sevier, born February 1, 1822.

(2)   Benjamin Miller Sevier, died young, born March 21, 1824.

(3)   Frederick Seyler Sevier, born 1828.

11

(4)   William Pierre Sevier, born 1830.
(4)   Theodore Francis Sevier, born 1830.
(6)   John Williams Sevier, born May 14, 1834.
(7)   Elizabeth Ann Sevier, born October 6, 1836.
(8)   Sara Louisa Sevier, died young, born 1838.
(9)   ————————Sevier, died young.
(12)   Kate Sevier } twins, born 1844.
(10)   Jane Sevier }

Granville Sharpe Townsend Sevier, born February 1, 1822, died in California in 1852 of cholera. He went west as a physician and established a hospital. He died in the service of others.

Benjamin Sevier died young.

Frederick Seyler Sevier, born August 16, 1851, was executed during the Lopez Expedition in Cuba.

Theodore Francis Sevier, born February 22, 1832, died in Sabucal, Texas, in 1915, leaving a widow who now resides (1924)_ with her daughter, Mrs. Frederick Giddings, in St. Elmo, Tennessee. Theodore Francis Sevier will be the subject of the last paragraph.

John Williams Sevier, born————, died of pneumonia during the War Between the States.

Sarah Sevier died young.

Louise Sevier died young.

Ann Elizabeth Sevier, born—————,died in Chattanooga in 1913.

THEODORE FRANCIS SEVIER

Theodore Francis Sevier, son of William Pierre Sevier and Lucretia Williams Weller Sevier, was born February 22, 1832. He died in Sabucal, Texas, 1915. He married Mary Benton Douglas November 2, 1855. Colonel Sevier is best known as Colonel Frank Sevier. He served with distinction in the Confederate Army as a Colonel of Ordnance. He as on the staff of General Albert Sidney Johnston. Mary Benton Douglass was the daughter of Kelcey Harris Douglass. She was born in the Republic of Texas in 1839.

The children of Theodore Francis Sevier and Mary Benton Douglas Sevier were:

(1)   Henry Douglass Sevier, died in infancy.
(2)   Theodore Francis Sevier, Jr., died in New York City, unmarried, in 1904.
(3)   Louise Sevier.
(4)   Granville Sharpe Townsend Sevier.
(5   Mary Douglas Sevier, died young.
(6)   Frederick William Sevier, died young.
(7)   John O'Neil Sevier, living in Baltimore.
(8)   Jessie Benton Sevier.
(9)Hal (Henry Hulme) Sevier.
(10)   Lucretia Weller Sevier.

Of the foregoing:

Frank Sevier, Jr., died in New York City in 1904.

Granville Sharpe Townsend Sevier is a Colonel in the United States Army. He is unmarried.

John O'Neil Sevier, married Frances——————.They have no children.

Jessie Benton Sevier married Joseph Edward de Belle, and lives in Jacksonville, Florida. They had two children; Joseph Edward de Belle, Jr., and Jessie de Belle. Edward de Belle, Jr., died young. Jessie de Belle married Eugene Hodson Drew and had two children, Eugene Hodson Drew, Jr., who died in infancy and Edward de Belle Drew.

Louise Sevier married Frederick Giddings and had six children, namely, Elizabeth Marshall Giddings, Mary Douglas Giddings, (who died unmarried in 1923) Helen Marshall Giddings, (who died young), Louise Sevier Giddings, Rose Haines Giddings, and Frederick Giddings, Jr.

Hal (Henry Hulme) Sevier married Clara Driscoll and lives in Austin Texas.

Lucretia Weller Sevier married Kingston Pickford and died in Texas, June, 1904, a few weeks after her marriage.

PART THREE
Valentine Sevier, II
The Emigrant
AND HIS DESCENDANTS
EXCLUSIVE OF GOVERNOR JOHN SEVIER
AND HIS DESCENDANTS

VALENTINE SEVIER, II, THE EMIGRANT

VALENTINE SEVIER the Emigrant is known throughout this book as Valentine Sevier II, to distinguish him among the many Valentines. His father is Valentine Sevier I, of definite record, although he may have been the fifth or sixth Valentine in direct succession. Valentine Sevier I married Mary Smith in London, as noted in Part One of this volume.

Valentine Sevier II, son of Valentine Sevier I and Mary Smith Sevier, was born in London in 1702. Historians and members of the family conflict in regard to the date, varying from 1699 to 1722, but he died in 1803 at the age of one hundred and one years. With his brother William Sevier, (see Part Two of this volume), he emigrated to America about 1730 or later, landing in Baltimore. He died at his home twenty-five miles from the home of his son, Governor John Sevier, December, 1803, at the age of one hundred and one years. This establishes his birth in 1702. His death is recorded in Governor Sevier's Journal, December 14, 1803.

The family tradition that is frequently quoted by historians claims that Valentine and William Sevier "ran away from home and took ship for America in 1740." Many grave historians give the statement in the same paragraph, which gives the birth of William and Valentine as taking place in 1700 and 1702, not conscious, apparently, of the unusualness of men of thirty-eight and forty running away from home at that mature age. It is quite possible of course that they ran away from home at an earlier period spending the intervening years elsewhere in England before they "took ship" to America in 1740, if that is the year in which they sailed.

It is fairly certain that they "took ship" in 1730 or 1740, or between those dates, and that they landed in Baltimore. Bishop Hoss says that they emigrated some time in the decade between 1730 and 1740, giving no definite year, and George Washington Sevier, son of Governor John Sevier, says that they emigrated in 1730. Ramsey's Annals says they emigrated in 1730.

Valentine Sevier II married shortly after he landed in Baltimore, by the family tradition, but he evidently did not marry Joanna Good until about 1744. The tradition is that he married a "Baltimore Lady" which is a bit indefinite for genealogical records. Other statements indicate that he moved on from Maryland to Virginia before his marriage. However he married Jonna Goode or Goade (the

17

name is frequently spelled Goade). She was the grand daughter of John Goode or Goade who had emigrated to America by way of the Barbadoes in 1650. Bishop Hoss says that Valentine II met his future wife in Augusta or Culpepper County, Virginia. The marriage took place, I think, about the year 1744.

Sometimes a tradition is more nearly right that we understand. Perhaps Valentine Sevier did marry a "Baltimore Lady" shortly after landing. Perhaps his marriage to Joanna Goode in 1744 (about), when he was at least forty-two years of age, was a second marriage.

Valentine Sevier II and Joanna Goode Sevier settled shortly after their marriage in Culpepper County, Virginia, moving later to Rockingham County, (Augusta) Virginia, where John Sevier, their eldest child and the most famous member of their family, was born September 23, 1745.

Valentine Sevier was a member of Scholl's Military Company in 1742, (Waddell's Annals of Augusta County, pages 45 and 47). This clearly proves that he was already in Augusta in the year 1742. Also it is an indication that he met Joanna Goode in Virginia as claimed by Bishop Hoss, because, although he was in Virginia in 1742, the marriage probably did not take place until 1744.

The home of Valentine Sevier II, in Rockingham County, was directly on the line of travel and so great became the burden of entertainment that he presently applied to the County Court for permission to keep an Inn, declaring that he was so "infested with travellers" that it was necessary. Permission was granted and the amount to be charged for man and beast was fixed.

Valentine Sevier was a very large man, almost a giant, if we may believe tradition. His grandson, George Washington Sevier, writes to Dr. Lyman Draper that his "grandfather was a very large man and that his mind and memory at the age of one hundred years were bright and active."

In the year 1773, it is supposed after Joanna Goode Sevier's death, since no further mention of her occurs, Valentine Sevier moved from Virginia to "the mountains," arriving on the Watauga Settlement, December 25, 1773. He was accompanied "by five sons and three daughters" to join one son already there (Valentine III) leaving one daughter in Virginia. This wholesale moving from Virginia without mention of Joanna clearly indicates that she was not living. Also the fact is clear that he had six sons and four daughters living at that date.

After he reached the Watauga Settlement, although I have no means of knowing the date, Valentine Sevier II married a second time and by this marriage to Jemima, who survived him, it is presumed that he had at least two children. Descendants of his second wife may be able to furnish the name of the second wife and the names of other children. He established a home twenty five miles from the site of Governor John Sevier's home on the south side of the Holston River, probably two or three miles below the present site of Kingsport near the old Fort Patrick Henry.

He evidently reared a family in Tennessee, though the name of no child of the second marriage is positively known to me. Governor Sevier in his Journal mentions "my brother G. Sevier," whom he visited in Nashville. I have never seen any other reference to G. Sevier. It is possible, of course, in transcribing the Journal a mistake may have been made and G. is in reality C. and an abbreviation for Charles Sevier, who was probably the sixth son by the first marriage.

Valentine Sevier II after arriving in Tennessee took no active part in public affairs. He was indeed already advanced in life, although he lived thirty years after his migration to "the mountains." He arrived in Tennessee Christmas day 1773. He died in December, 1803 in Carter County, Tennessee. In the brief mention made in Governor Sevier's Journal of his father's passing, no wife is mentioned as surviving.

There are many earlier notes in the Journal, however, which show that Valentine Sevier II maintained a separate household for many years and that it was about twenty-five miles from the Governor's home, "Plum Grove."

There is probably no way at this date to secure a complete statement of the names of the children of Valentine Sevier II. I shall therefore give the name of every child as I have heard it and the authority therefor. There were six sons by the first wife and the names of five of these sons are positively known. Also there were four or more daughters by the first marriage. Of the six sons, John, Robert, Valentine, Joseph and Abraham are known, all having participated in the Battle of King's Mountain. The name of the sixth son is uncertain but in a copy of Abraham Sevier's Bible record the name of a brother Charles appears. He may be the sixth son and I will so list him.

As for the daughters of the first marriage, many discrepancies appear in mention of them. George Washington Sevier, for instance, in writing to Dr. Draper, says that his father, John Sevier, had only two sisters. This letter is now in the Draper collection in Madison, Wisconsin. He says that Polly and Catherine are his father's only sisters. This statement can be accounted for in several ways, for instance he may have meant only surviving sisters at the date of his letter; or some of the sisters may have been half sisters and not considered sisters by the rest of the family. Bishop Hoss, says that in 1773 Valentine Sevier II migrated from Virginia to Tennessee accompanied by five sons (to join one son already in Tennessee) and three daughters, leaving one daughter in Virginia. This clearly mentions ten children, four of them daughters. I think there was another daughter by the first wife, so I conclude that George Washington Sevier meant two surviving sisters at the date he wrote to Dr. Draper.

CHILDREN OF VALENTINE SEVIER II AND JOANNA GOODE SEVIER

(The sons in this list are given first. There is no conflicting data concerning them, and no uncertainty regarding the names of the first five. I have no information as to the exact order of birth. The daughters of the first marriage I will list and I will give all the information possible concerning each, even where the data is conflicting.)

I   John Sevier
II   Robert Sevier
III   Valentine Sevier III
IV   Joseph Sevier
V   Abraham Sevier
VI   Charles Sevier
VII   Catherine Sevier
VIII   Polly Sevier
IX   Bethenia Sevier
X   Elizabeth Sevier
XI   Sophia Sevier

BY SECOND WIFE JEMIMA

XII   "G" Sevier

I do not try to follow the order of birth, although John, Robert and Valentine were the first, second and third sons. Abraham was thirteen years of age in 1773, which establishes the date of his birth, and Charles, if he were the sixth son, was probably much younger The daughter who was left in Virginia may have been grown and married in 1773 or she may have been very young and therefore left with kinspeople or friends.

Abraham Sevier, the fifth son, left a Bible record in his family Bible and in it is mention of Charles Sevier, a brother. This is the only mention by that name I have ever seen of this son, although it is quite clear there were six sons at the time of the migration in 1773. The record of Abraham Sevier's Bible has been preserved by Mrs. Dulcinia Gragg Swift, of Jacksonville, Illinois.

She has what she believes to be an exact copy of Abraham's Bible record, but this record includes the children of the first wife only, as neither Rebecca nor "G" Sevier, is mentioned. Mrs. Dulcinia Gragg Swift, is a descendant of Abraham Sevier.

Mrs. Sophia Hoss French, of Morristown, Tennessee, as sister of Bishop Hoss, and a descendant of Governor Sevier, through his son

John Sevier, Jr., has furnished me with a list of the children of
Valentine Sevier as follows:

    I   John Sevier
    II   Valentine Sevier
    III   Robert Sevier
    IV   Joseph Sevier
    V   Abraham Sevier
    VI   Bethenia Sevier
    VII   Elizabeth Sevier
    VIII   Sophia Sevier
    IX   Polly Sevier

As will be seen, all lists agree as to the names of five of the
sons, discrepancies only occurring in the names of the other sons and
in the names of the daughters. I will however, take up the history of
each name and give all the information possible, even conflicting
statements.

John Sevier, eldest child of Valentine Sevier II and Joanna Goode
Sevier, will appear in Part Five of this book and his descendants
in Part Six.

WILL OF VALENTINE SEVIER, THE EMIGRANT

The will of Valentine Sevier II is on record in the court house at
Elizabethton, Carter County, Tennessee. In it he mentions his loving
wife Jemima and three children, Catherine Abraham and Joseph.
Whether Jemima Young, to whom he gives a "sadle and fether bed,"
is a married daughter, we have no means of knowing.

In the name of God Amen. I. Valentine Sevier of Carter County,
and State of Tennessee, being low in body tho of sound mind and
memory do make ordain and constitute this my last Will and
Testament, and first, I give and bequeath my Soul to God who gave
it and my body to be buried at the discretion of my executors.
Secondly, after the discharge of all my just debts, I leave my dear
and loving wife Jemima Sevier a Sufficient Maintainance to be paid
her yearly by my Executor, and to Jemima Young I give and bequeath
one women's sadle and one Fether Bed to be paid to the said Jemima
Young after my decease, and all the Residue of my goods, lands
Tenements to be equally divided between my two sons Abraham and
Joseph Sevier, Abraham Sevier paying Catherine Matlock wife of
William Matlock fifty pounds unyon Currency and Joseph Sevier
paying said Catherine forty pounds like money. I also appoint
Pharoah Cobb and John Hendricks my sole executors to this my last
Will and Testament Revoke and Disannulling all Wills by me here_
tofore made declaring this to be my last Will and Testament in
witness whereof I have set my hand and Seal this the 12th day of
March, 1799.   VALENTINE SEVIER
    John Dunlap (Jurat)
    John Hendricks (Jurat)
    I hereby certify that the foregoing is a true, full and correct
copy of the Will of Valentine Sevier now on file in this office This
August 29, 1924.   GEO. F. YOUNG
        Deputy County Clerk of Carter County, Tenn.

Valentine Sevier, III

VALENTINE SEVIER, III

VALENTINE SEVIER III, second child and second son of Valentine Sevier II, the Emigrant, and his wife, Joanna Goode Sevier, was born in Rockingham County, Virginia, in 1747. Entering the service of the colonies at a very early age, he was engaged in many Indian skirmishes and campaigns before the Revolution. In accounts of Dunmore's War there is mention of Valentine Sevier and his service. He was a sergeant at Point Pleasant, 1774, and in company with James Robertson discovered the attack about to be made on that Point. At Cedar Springs he commanded a company and he also commanded a company at Musgrove's Mill. He was one of the earliest settlers in Tennessee (the territory which is now Tennessee) making his settlement in 1772, the year preceeding the date that his father's entire family removed from Virginia to "the Mountains." This family arrived December 25, 1773. He was Colonel of Militia and First Sheriff of Washington County. He was Justice of Peace of Washington County. He was one of the five Sevier brothers who fought in the Battle of King's Mountain and one of the seven Seviers in the battle as two of Governor Sevier's sons also participated.

Colonel Valentine Sevier shared with his brothers, John Sevier, Robert Sevier, Abraham Sevier and Joseph Sevier, the hardships of pioneer life, as well as the glory of King's Mountain and dozens of other battles, but unlike them he lost dearly beloved children, four sons in the prime of young manhood and two daughters, in the awful struggle with the Indians, and he saw another daughter scalped before his eyes. His infant grandchildren who were murdered are literally unacounted as the names of only two are known, though we know that others fell victim to the tomahawk or were destroyed in the flames. In the Winning of the West, as President Roosevelt called the great campaign in which the Seviers, the Shelbys, the Wears and hundreds of other heroes participated, no man gave so much, not even those who gave their own heart's blood. Indeed, I know of no other record equal to this, six children killed, a seventh scalped and more than two grandchildren destroyed!

George Washington Sevier said to Dr. Draper that his uncle Valentine Sevier III, was a very large man, "larger than Valentine Sevier II, and he was very bold and gallant." A. W. Putman, in his history of Middle Tennessee, describes Colonel Sevier in this way:

"He had been a hunter in his youth, with figure erect as an Indian's, spare of flesh with a clear skin and a bright blue eye."

A. V. Goodpasture says of Colonel Sevier: "His father was a Virginian of French extraction, from whom he inherited something of the Cavalier spirit so prominent in the character of his brother, Governor John Sevier. Spare of flesh, with an errect commanding, soldierly presence, a bright blue eye and quick ear, he was at once ardent, brave, generous and affectionate.

"He had served his country faithfully, both in the Indian wars and the War of Independence. He was sergeant in Captain Evan Shelby's company at the battle of Point Pleasant, and was distinguished for vigilance, activity and bravery. He entered the Revolutionary War as captain, and commanded a company at Thicketty Fort, Cedar Springs, Musgrove's Mill and Kings Mountain.

"He was the first sheriff of Washington County, a justice of the peace, and Colonel of the County Militia. He took an active interest in the establishment of the State of Franklin, and soon after its fall in 1788, he emigrated to Cumberland, and erected a station near the mouth of the Red River, opposite the town of Clarkesville, where the extinct town of Cumberland was afterwards established, between Clarksville, and New Providence."

It was in 1789 that Colonel Sevier decided to move to the Cumberland country. He sold his land in the Watauga and in the fall of 1789, he established himself on the Red River near the present site of Clarkesville, Tennessee. He was doubtless influenced in this removal by his early friendship with James Robertson who had moved to the Cumberland Country. General Robertson settled in Nashville and became the founder of that city. Valentine Sevier established his station on the beautiful eminence overlooking the present site of Clarkesville. His location is known as Fort Sevier. It commands a magnifient view of the River and of the entire settlement. During the War Between the States its location attracted the immediate attention of military authorities and it became a fort. It was first used by the Confederate Army and later by the Federal troops. The fortifications are plainly to be seen and the property is known as Fort Sevier. This shows that though the location had long been in other hands the fact of its having been the Valentine Sevier station was familiar. Probably when the fort was built remains of the block house and palisades covered the hill, though now there is no trace of these. They were doubtless destroyed when the fort was built. An old negro man, claiming to be ninety-four and looking it, is now living nearby. His name is Sam Washington. He told me that he moved to the section about the beginning of the War, that he helped build the fortifications for the Confederates, that he was a young man at that time and that he helped later when the Federals took it for a fort. He took me to an old graveyard which he said

was very old when he helped build the fort and which he said had
not been used since as a graveyard. The stones are old and not in
regular shape, being merely rocks brought from the river bluff a few
yards away. No marking of any sort is indicated, these graves atedat-
ing by many years the formal stones with marking (in that section.)
One stone is carefully cut and shaped and is marked 1844, but a difference of at least fifty years is apparent.

Undoubtedly the victims of the massacre were buried in this
plot, probably in one large grave or perhaps in two or three open-
ings. At least ten people seem to have been killed in the massacre
and as there were few men left for work, I think it unlikely that
separate graves were dug.

The number of these rough head stones can be accounted for if
other members of Valentine Sevier's family died about that time and
were buried there. Also it may contain some of the bodies of neighbors and fri nds, as all the settlement went to the Block House in time
of trouble, according to the traditions of the neighboorhood now.
Colonel Sevier died February 23, 1800, and it is possible that he is
buried there also.

The bodies of the three sons, Valentine Sevier IV, Robert and
William who were killed by Indians in 1792 were destroyed and
therefore are not buried in this plot. It is possible that the body of
Ann Sevier's first husband, Thomas Grantham, who was the first
member of the family group to be sacrificed, may be in this plot.

Only eleven names of the fourteen children of Valentine Sevier III,
and Naomi Douglass Sevier are known and if the other three died
young they too may be buried in this graveyard.

After July 29, 1800 Valentine Sevier's son John Sevier who was
administrator, removed his mother to East Tennessee where he married Susannah Conway. No more Seviers are therefore laid away in
that plot of ground. The graveyard is plainly a part of the residence property and was probably included in the palisades. It lies in
what was undoubtedly the rear of the premises.

The "Station" included the homes of the married daughters,
Elizabeth Sevier, the eldest child who was married to Charles Snyder
and Ann, the second daughter, who married first Thomas Grantham
and married second John King. Probably both Elizabeth and Ann
married before the removal from East Tennessee to the Clarksville
site as Elizabeth was twenty-one years of age and Ann eighteen at
that time Thomas Grantham was killed shortly after the Seviers arrived in their new home. This was the first one of the dreadful
calamities that befell the family. He was killed in 1790. Thus Ann
was left a widow when she was nineteen.

Other heart breaking bereavements came in quick succession.
General James Robertson had become alarmed at the war-like demon-
strations of the Cherokees and he sent a call for volunteers "for spies

and rangers." Valentine IV, Robert and William Sevier desired to offer themselves for this service and, despite the weakness of his own station in the wilderness, Colonel Sevier gave them his permission and his God speed. They were killed almost within sight of the home and the father and mother never saw the three stalwart sons again. They had not even the scant comfort of burial for their beloved as the bodies were utterly destroyed.

The story is tragically short and details are few. They left their home in January 1792 for the journey to Nashville, having been joined by John Curtis, John Rice and two or three others. They started up the river in canoes as horses were scarce in the settlement. The Cumberland River above Clarksville makes a horseshoe curve to a place called Seven Mile Ford. Double Head, the Indian Chief, having discovered the purpose of the young men, crossed the country to Seven Mile Ford and lay in wait or the party. As the boats came around the bend the murderous Indians fired, killing John Curtis and Robert and William Sevier. The remainder of the party got their boats across the river and attempted to return to the station, hugging the opposite shore. Seeing that he had failed to kill all the members of the party, Double Head and his followers recrossed the isthmus made by the river. The canoes by this time had been abandoned and Double Head took the boats,clothes and other possessions. Early next morning Double Head found and killed John Rice and Valentine Sevier and it was some time before the father knew of the terrible tragedy. Robert and William Sevier were killed in the afternoon of January 15, 1792, and Valentine Sevier IV was killed January 16, 1792.

Scarcely had the family recovered from the shock of losing these three young Seviers in the prime of their young manhood, when Nov. 11, 1794, without the slightest warning, the Station was attacked by forty Creek Indians from a town called Tuskeya, and the rest of the family was almost destroyed. Every history of Middle Tennessee mentions this tragic story, but after all we have few details of the massacre. Fifty years after, Dr. Draper secured interviews with Hugh Bell, a neighbor; and a letter from Valentine Sevier III, to Governor John Sevier telling the story very simply had been preserved. He had previously written to his brother telling of the loss of his sons, Robert, William and Valentine, but saying that he had other sons "small ones." at the massacre another son, Joseph, was killed and two daughters, Elizabeth and Ann, were killed.

The letter to Governor Sevier is dated five weeks after the massacre.

Clarksville, Tennessee
December 18, 1794

Dear Brother:

The news from this place is desperate with me. On Tuesday 11th of November last,, about 12 o'clock, my station was attacked by about forty Indians. On so sud-

den a surprise they were in almost every house before
they were discovered. All the men belonging to the
Station were out, except Mr. Snider and myself. Mr. Snider, Betsy, his wife, his son John and my son Joseph
were killed in Snider's house. I saved Snider so
the Indians did not get his scalp, but they shot and
tomahawked him in a barbarous manner. They also
killed Ann King and her son James, and they scalped my
daughter Rebecca; I hope she will recover. The Indians
have killed whole families about here this fall. You may
hear the cries of some persons for their friends daily.
The engagement commenced at my house, continued
about one hour the neighbors say. Such a scene no man
ever witnessed before; nothing but screams and roaring
guns and no man to assist me for some time. The Indians
have robbed the goods out of every house and have
destroyed all my stock. You will write our ancient father
this horrid news, also my son Johnny. My health is
much impaired. The remains of my family are in good
health. I am so distressed in my mind that I can not
write.

Your affectionate brother until death,

Valentine Sevier.

Some historians in quoting this letter give Mr. Snider's name
as William doubtless reading the "Mr." as "Wm." However there
was no William Snider in the settlement at that time. Charles
Snider's estate was settled two years after his death.

Two other contemporary letters give gruesome details of the
event. Anthony Crutcher, a neighbor, wrote his brother William
Crutcher, living in Nashville, and John Easton, a neighbor, wrote
to General James Robertson. Both those letters were written the
day following the massacre.

ANTHONY CRUTCHER'S LETTER

Clarksville, Tennessee

November 12 1794

Dear Brother:

Yesterday I was spectator to the most tragical scene
that I ever saw in my life. The Indians made an attack
upon Colonel Sevier's station, killed Snyder, his wife
and child, one of Colonel Sevier's children and another
wounded and scalped which must die. On hearing the
guns four or five of us ran over. We found the poor
old Colonel defending his house, with his wife. It is
impossible to describe this scene to you. Mr. James, who
goes to you was an eye witness, and can give you the
particulars. The crying of the women and children in
town, the bustle and consternation of the people, being
all women and children but the few that went to Col.
Sevier's, was a scene that cannot be described. This
is a stroke that we have long expected, and from intelli-
gence, we hourly expect this place to be assailed by
the enemy. Col. Sevier is now moving, and the town
will not stay longer than Mr. James' return. My wife

now lies on her bed so ill that it would be death to move her; thus are we situated. This place will, no doubt, be evacuated in a day or two unless succor is given by the people of the interior part. Pray ask the influence of Major Tatum, Douglass and all our friends, with General Robertson, to guard us, or, at least, to help us get away.

The discrepancy between Valentine Sevier's statement that forty Indians were in the party of marauders and John Easton's "fifteen" is easily accounted for. Colonel Valentine Sevier fought them alone for sometime and they accomplished their murderous design before men from the neighborhood arrived. They probably slipped quietly away, one by one, as they saw help approaching.

JOHN EASTON'S LETTER TO BRIGADIER GEN. ROBERTSON:

Clarksville, Tennessee
November 12, 1794

Dear Sir:

I flatter myself that the contents of this letter will be as seriously considered as the premises demand Yesterday about eleven o'clock in the morning, a heavy firing commenced at Colonel Sevier's by a party of about fifteen Indians. The Colonel bravely defended his own house and kept the savage band from entering; but they cruelly slaughtered all around him. Three of his own children fell dead. Charles Snyder and two small children also fell. Unfortunately for us in this place, we were not prepared to go to their assistance, for the want of men. However, I was on the ground the first man, and was the first spectator of the horrid sight—some scalped and barbarously cut to pieces; some tomawked very inhumanly, and the poor helpless infants committed to the torturing flames. However, without entering further into the horrors of this barbarous massacre, suffice it to say that, we consider ourselves in most imminent danger. Indian signs in almost every quarter, which lead us to think that we stand in great need of protection. This is the object of this letter, favored by Mr. Daniel Jones, who goes mostly on this particular business, and I hope his journey, or the cause of his journey, will be attended to; if not I am confident that Clarksville will be evacuated; But I flatter myself a protection will be willingly and speedily granted.

Charles Snyder was the husband of Valenntine Sevier's daughter, Betsey, or Elizabeth Sevier. Ann King was his daughter, married to John King, who escaped death. "Johnny" was Colonel Sevier's eldest son, who was then in East Tennessee. Rebecca, who was

---

The discrepancy in the spelling of the name Snyder will be noted. Names were not unalterably spelled at the time and Snider appears quite as often as Snyder, for the young man who married Elizabeth Sevier. Colonel Sevier in his letter spells the name both ways, as will be seen.

scalped, recovered as her father hoped she would. She wore a sort of tarred cap all of her life and was remembered by some of the elder people in the family because of that unusual distinction. She married John Rector and lived to a good old age.

Many historians in relating the story of the massacre say that the only surviving child of Colonel Valentine Sevier was the son "Johnny" who was in East Tennessee, but this is not correct as Rebecca survived, James survived, Alexander survived, and it is also believed another daughter, Joanna, survived.

James Sevier who was a lad of about seventeen, was working in the field with Ann King's husband, John King. They escaped, as before they heard the shots and screams and could reach the station the massacre was over. Hugh T. Bell told Dr. Draper that Colonel Valentine's son, Alexander Sevier, a child of about twelve, was out rabbit hunting and thus escaped the disaster.

At least one child of Charles Snider and Elizabeth Sevier Snider survived, though many children whose names are not recorded are said to have been killed.

In Dr. Draper's interview, Hugh Bell, who was the nearest neighbor, relates that he heard the noise and was among the first to reach the scene, though too late to be of assistance. In mentioning the survivors he speaks of a little boy, a grandson about four, whom Dr. Draper puts down with a question mark after his name—Alexander Green (?).

Colonel Valentine's son, Alexander Sevier, is said by Rebecca to have been almost twelve and out rabbit hunting, but as a matter of fact, he used G. as his middle initial. However, I have wondered if this child with the question mark after Greene might be a child of Ann King, whose first husband, Thomas Grantham, was killed by Indians in 1790. This is only supposition and could only be verified in case some descendants of this line have information. Dr. Draper it is understood, copied his notes after he returned to Michigan, many months after he made his historic trip through Tennessee, interviewing Tennesseeans. He was not seeking genealogical information primarily, but history, and moreover the interviews were secured fifty years after the massacre.

Hugh Bell says that the little four year old boy in the Block House, referred to in Dr. Draper's interview with Rebecca Rector, was a little grandson. Draper's notes of the interview seem to make him Colonel Sevier's son and that is the reason Draper seems uncertain of the name.

After the massacre Colonel Sevier removed his family to Nashville to live. After the killing and robbery, he had little left with which to withstand the winter. However he did not go immediately, as his letter is dated several weeks after the massacre, when he was still in the station. Several letters to his brother John written from Nashville are extant. In them he explains that he is making his home in Nashville. Later, 1798, in a letter to his brother, he says he is leaving Nashville to return to Clarksville to live. He did not, however, return to the station, as I understand, but to a town lot and house in Clarksville itself, fronting on what has been known for many years as the Square. There he lived and shortly afterwards, died.

Colonel Valentine Sevier III, while he was still in Virginia in 1767, when he was twenty years of age, married Naomi Douglas. She was called Amy. She survived him many years, dying in 1845. In her application for a pension she said that she was married to Valentine Sevier in Shenendoah County, Virginia, by a minister named Anderson. At her death in 1845, she was one hundred and one years of age. This would put her birth in 1744 and make her three years the senior of her husband who was born in 1747. In the Pension Record is the statement: "Naomi Sevier, living with John Rector (a son-in-law) aged 97," Pension List 1840. If Naomi was 97 in 1840, then she was born in 1743, and was four years her husband's senior. Her daughter, Rebecca Sevier Rector swore in her pension application that her mother, Naomi Douglas Sevier, who died July 17, 1845, was 101 years six months and ten days old. By that statement she was born Jan., 7, 1744. In the Bible of a descendant, Charles Rector Sevier, her birth is recorded as April, 1743.

Colonel Valentine Sevier III, died February 23, 1800. He was only fifty-three years of age. His estate is inventoried by his son, John Sevier, who was his executor, July 29, 1800. The Inventory includes a lot in Clarksville and some household goods and a "house Bible," which I presume means a family Bible. In the sale of the effects the widow, Naomi Douglass Sevier, bought the Bible.

Naomi bought the Bible for fifty cents from which I conclude that she valued it very much as fifty cents was probably a great deal to her at that time. Her son John Sevier, bought for ten dollars, the brass blunderbuss which when discharged, the day of the massacre, knocked Valentine Sevier down and knocked out three of his teeth. It is a curious circumstance that the Bible, for which Naomi paid her pitiful little fifty cents is in existence now and has been a help in the preparation of this chronicle, whereas the blunderbuss for all its brass and its supposed ten dollar value is no more!

Colonel Sevier is buried in Clarksville. I visited the old City Cemetery in which there are many graves, but I am inclined to think that his body was interred in the plot on the Block House site, where his children were buried after the massacre.

The D. A. R. Chapter, of Clarksville, recently placed a handsome marker in the Court House Square to the memory of Colonel Valentine Sevier ,"The First Citizen of Clarksville." The bronze tablet calls attention to the massacre and the dreadful hard ships endured by this family and is a splendid testimonial to Colonel Sevier. Mrs. H.

A. Leach, of Clarksville, was chairman of the committee in charge of the work and it is largely because of her efforts that the testimonial was erected.

CHILDREN OF VALENTINE SEVIER

Valentine Sevier III, and Naomi Douglass Sevier had at least ten or eleven children whose names are positively known. It is said that he had fourteen children. So far as I am able to give the names are:

1. Elizabeth Sevier, born in Virginia, February 13, 1768, the eldest child.

2. John Sevier, born in Virginia, September 1769, named for his uncle, Governor John Sevier.

3. Ann Sevier, born March 23rd 1771.

4. Valentine Sevier IV, born 1772.

5. Robert Sevier, born 1775, twin to William.

6. William Sevier, born 1775, twin to Robert.

7. James Sevier, born August 31st, 1777. He was aged 17, November 11, 1794.

8. Joseph Sevier, born September 1778.

9. Alexander G. Sevier, born November 6, 1782.

10. Rebecca Sevier, born 1783.

11. Joanna Goode Sevier, born February 14, 1784.

The children of Colonel Valentine Sevier III will now be taken up under their individual names.

ELIZABETH SEVIER

(1.) Elizabeth Sevier, called Betsy, daughter of Colonel Valentine Sevier III and Naomi Douglass Sevier was born in Virginia, February 13, 1768, and was their first child. She accompanied her parents when they made their second migration to Middle Tennessee after the Revolution. As she was then past twenty she was possibly married at that time and probably her husband accompanied the party.

She married Charles Snider, or Snyder.

Some historians quote the letters from Colonel Valentine Sevier to his brother, Governor John Sevier, as saying that her husband was William Snider, but this is evidently a mistake on the part of the copyist who mistook the "Mr." for "Wm". Rebecca Sevier told Dr. Draper that her sister's husband was named Charles Snider and other evidence exists to show that he was Charles. John Montgomery Snider continually appears in land records with the Seviers, but he was probably a brother or perhaps the father of Charles Snider.

Elizabeth Sevier Snider was killed in the massacre, November 11,

1794. Her husband and little son John Snider were killed at the same time. No reference is made by Colonel Sevier, in his letter to his brother, to other children but Rebecca Sevier Rector says, "her son, John, and other little ones were killed." There must have been at least one surviving child for a descendant of Elizabeth has joined the D. A. R., giving the name of a surviving child, Susannah Snider, who married Thomas Stanley Warren. Their son Thomas Jefferson Warren maried Elizabeth Guthrie. Their daughter, Lelia Warren married Theodore A. Kline and joined the D. A. R. on this record.

The known children of Elizabeth Sevier Snider and Charles Snider therefore were:

(A) John Snyder, killed by Indians November 11, 1794
(B) Susannah Snider, married Thomas Stanley Warren.
Others killed in infancy.

JOHN SEVIER
Son of Colonel Valentine Sevier III

(2) John Sevier, son of Colonel Valentine Sevier III and Naomi Douglass Sevier, was born in Virginia, September, 1769. He was named for his uncle John Sevier. He accompanied his family to "the Mountains" when he was still a child and later, it is said, when the family moved to Middle Tennessee in the fall of 1769, he went with his parents, returning almost immediately for some reason to the home of his uncle, John Sevier, in East Tennessee. He thus escaped the Indian massacres. He seems, however, to have been in the Red River district at times. For instance, John Sevier and John Montgomery Snider bought land in Montgomery County in 1793 and 1749, showing that he was there at that time. He was apparently not in Clarksville when his three brothers, Valentine IV, Robert and William, were killed. Also he was absent when the dreadful massacre of November 11, 1794, took place. He served, however, as executor of his father's will, July 29, 1800. I imagine that his own marriage had taken place or was about to take place, for he completely closed up his father's affairs in Montgomery County, disposed of all the household possessions and moved his mother and the surviving children to East Tennessee. His only purchase in the sale of effects is the brass blunderbuss, for which he paid ten dollars.

He married and a large posterity traces through him. He was of a somewhat roistering disposition if his nick-name, "Devil Jack," is to be taken as evidence. The name distinguishes him from his uncle, Governor John Sevier, from his cousin, John Sevier, junior, and from the numerous other Johns. So I have adopted it in this record in places where merely "John Sevier" is not sufficiently distinctive.

His wife was Susannah Conway, born June 9, 1776; died May 4, 1816, the daughter of Colonel Henry Conway and Sarah Hundley Conway. The marriage took place in 1800. The name Hundley frequently appears in Sevier annals, as three sisters, Susannah, Nancy and Elizabeth, married Seviers. Nancy Conway married James Sevier, second son of Governor John Sevier. Elizabeth Conway married John Sevier, junior, third son of Governor John Sevier, and Susannah married "Devil Jack" Sevier. Susannah was called Susan by her father and Ann by her son, Senator Ambrose Hundley Sevier. In reading references to her therefore this fact of her seeming to have three names must be borne in mind.

The marriage bond of Devil Jack Sevier and Susannah Conway is dated 1800 and is now in Greeneville, Tennessee. They had seven children, but the marriage proved an unhappy one and Susannah Conway divorced her husband. This was at a time when divorce was uncommon and I imagine that Susannah's grievances were many before she took the step. Having secured her divorce she married September 30, 1812, Hugh Maloney. Hugh Maloney was born in Ireland in 1781, died in Tennessee, October 8, 1840. Hugh Maloney and Susannah Conway Sevier Maloney had two children, namely: William Conway Maloney and Thomas Fleming Maloney. Descendants of these Maloney children married, as will be seen, descendants of the first marriage of Susannah Conway. Susannah died in Greene County, Tennessee, in 1816. Her second husband survived her many years. Devil Jack Sevier volunteered for the War of 1812 and served with conspicuous bravery with General Jackson at New Orleans. It is said that on his way home he died and was buried at sea. He was General Jackson's color bearer at New Orleans.

The children of Hugh Maloney and Susannah Conway Sevier Maloney:

(A) William Conway Maloney, born July 13, 1813; died June 5, 1882. He married Louise Cureton. He had children:William Cureton Maloney, Hugh D. Maloney, born 1842, June 6; and Nannie Maloney. Nannie Maloney married Hal Herring as his first wife. William Cureton Maloney married ——————————— and had a daughter, Louise Maloney, who married Hal Herring as his second wife.

(B) Thomas Fleming Maloney, born January 3, 1815, died July 22, 1841.

The children of Devil Jack Sevier and Susannah Conway Sevier were:

(I do not know that they should be in this order).

(A) Ambrose Hundley Sevier, born 1801.

(B) Henry Sevier.

(C)   Sarah Sevier.
(D)   Mariah Sevier, born 1803.
(E)   Narcissa Sevier.
(F)   Nancy Sevier.
(G)   A daughter, ———————— Sevier.

Ambrose Hundley Sevier

(A)   Ambrose Hundley Sevier, son of Devil Jack Sevier and Susannah Conway Sevier, was born in Greene County, Tennessee, November 10, 1801. He was named Hundley in honor of his mother's family. I do not know where Ambrose was obtained, although it was a frequently used name at that period, Ambrose being noted among several well-known families. Ambrose Hundley Sevier moved west while still a young man. At the time of his mother's death he was only fifteen and he may have decided then to emigrate to the western country. He became very prominent in his new home and was elected Senator from Arkansas. Later he was appointed by President Polk, Peace Commissioner to Mexico at the close of the war with Mexico. While he was in Mexico on this mission he contracted fever at Vera Cruz and died at his home in Arkansas, December 31, 1848, at the age of forty-seven years.

He married August 26, 1827, Juliette Johnson, daughter of Judge Benjamin Johnson. Juliette Johnson was born October 12, 1812, and died March 16, 1845.

The children of Ambrose Hundley Sevier and Juliette Johnson Sevier were:

(a)   Mattie J. Sevier.
(b)   Michael Sevier.
(c)   Annie Maria Sevier.
(d)   Elizabeth Sevier.
(e)   Ambrose Hundley Sevier, Jr.

(a)   Mattie J. Sevier, daughter of Ambrose Hundley Sevier and Juliette Sevier, was born ————————. She married John Shelby Williams, son of David and Priscilla Shelby Williams (see Shelby and Williams families in Notable Southern Families, Volume II).

The children of Mattie Sevier Williams and John Shelby Williams were:

(1)   David Shelby Williams.
(2)   Juliette Sevier Williams, who died young.
(3)   Maude Johnson Williams.
(4)   Anna Fassman Williams.
(5)   Ambrose Sevier Williams.

Of the foregoing:

(1)   David Shelby Williams married May Lawson McGhee, of

Knoxville, and had no children and married for his second wife ———
——————.

(2) Juliette Sevier Williams died young.

(3) Maude Johnson Williams married Robert P. Bonnie, of Louisville, and had children: Shelby Williams Bonnie, Mattie Sevier Bonnie
and Robert P. Bonnie, Jr.

(4) Anna Fassman Williams married Wentworth P. Johnson, of
Norfolk, Virginia, and had Wentworth P. Johnson, Jr., and Shelby
Williams, a daughter. Also there were three children who died in
infancy.

(5) Ambrose Sevier Williams. Of him I have no record.

(b) Michael Sevier, son of Ambrose Hundley Sevier and Mattie
Sevier, was born June 23, 1822. He married Sarah E. Bayless, Octo-
ber 14, 1854. She was born June 18, 1822. They had three children,
Elbridge Gerry Sevier, born August 22, 1846, died 1923; Robert Edgar
Sevier, born May 26, 1856, died December 30, 1898. He lives in Little
Rock, Arkansas. He married Beulah Henderson and had two chil-
dren, namely, Shelby H. Sevier and Mrs. Walter Morris. A daughter
of Michael Sevier and Sarah E. Bayless was living in 1923.

(c) Annie Maria Sevier, daughter of Ambrose Hundley Sevier
and Juliette Johnson Sevier, was born —————. She married,
July 31, 1849, Thomas J. Churchill, Governor of Arkansas, born
March 10, 1824, died 19—.

(d) Elizabeth Sevier daughter of Ambrose Hundley Sevier and
Juliette Johnson Sevier, was born —————.

(e) Ambrose Hundley Sevier, Jr., son of Ambrose Hundley Sevier and Juliette Johnson Sevier, was born —————.

Henry Sevier

(B) Henry Sevier, son of Devil Jack Sevier and Susannah Conway Sevier, was born 18—.

Sarah Sevier

(C) Sarah Sevier, daughter of Devil Jack Sevier and Susannah
Conway Sevier, was born 18—. It is said by some that she married
————— Smith.

Mariah Sevier

(D) Mariah Sevier, called "Nannie," daughter of Devil Jack
Sevier and Susannah Conway Sevier, married twice, her first husband being Lewis Broyles. They had a daughter, Mary Broyles,
who married W. J. Mhoon. They had a daughter, Lucy Mhoon, who
married M. Wilkerson. After the death of Lewis Broyles, Mariah
Sevier Broyles married for her second husband, her cousin, Joseph
Sevier, son of Valentine Sevier, of Greeneville, Tennessee, son of

Captain Robert Sevier, killed at King's Mountain. Joseph Sevier was killed in the War Between the States. Her children by Joseph Sevier were Dr. Robert Sevier, now deceased, Lewis Sevier, now living in Savannah, Tennessee, and Miss Nannie Sevier, living in Savannah.

Narcissa Sevier

(E) Narcissa Sevier, daughter of Devil Jack Sevier and Susannah Conway Sevier, was a twin to Nancy Sevier. They were born in Greene County, Tennessee, October 30, 1810. Narcissa Sevier married William J. Harding, whose mother was Esther Marian Herring, a sister of General Francis Marian. William Herring and Narcissa Sevier Herring had at least two children, namely:

(a) Sarah Herring.

(b) John Henry Herring.

Of these:

(a Sarah Herring married John Nelson Kendall and had two daughters, Blanche Kendall, who married J. W. Ridgeway and had a daughter, Mary Ridgeway, who married A. P. Wood and has a daughter, Anette Wood); and ——————— Kendall who married J. H. Happy and has five children, ——————— Happy, married Melvin Albutton; Miss Ina Happy, James H. Happy, J. Kendall Happy and Samuel Roberts Happy.

(b) John Henry (Harry) Herring, who married Julia Williams had a son, John Henry (Hal) Herring, who married twice, both times a kinswoman, descendants of his great-grandmother, Susannah Conway, by her second husband, Hugh Maloney. Hal Herring's first wife was Nannie Maloney, daughter of William Maloney and granddaughter of Hugh and Susannah Conway Sevier Maloney. By this marriage he had one son, Henry William Herring, who lives in Oregon. Hal Herring married for his second wife, Louise Maloney, granddaughter of William Maloney and great-granddauhter of Hugh and Susannah Conway Sevier Maloney. By this marriage Hal Herring has two sons, ——————— Herring and Lewis Broyles Herring.

Nancy Conway Sevier

(F) Nancy Conway Sevier, daughter of Devil Jack Sevier and Susannah Conway Sevier, was a twin to Narcissa. They were born on the Chucky River, near Warrensburg, Greene County, Tennessee, October 30, 1810. Shortly after their birth their mother divorced Devil Jack Sevier and when they were two years old, she married Hugh Maloney. When Nancy Sevier was eighteen years old, Dec. 18, 1828, she married James Irwin, of Murfreesboro, Tennessee.. In 1830 they moved to McMinnville to reside and a year later to Savannah, Tennessee, where Nancy Sevier Irwin died in 1885, being

seventy-five years of age. Her death took place October 7, 1885.
She had ten children, eight of whom lived to maturity and were
living when she died.

The information of the family of Nancy Sevier was secured
partly from the following obituary notice which appeared in the
Savannah (Tennessee) Courier, October 22, 1885, a copy of which
was recently sent me.

"Mrs. Nancy Sevier Irwin

"Mrs. Nancy Sevier Irwin, daughter of John Sevier and Susannah
Conway Sevier, was born on the Chucky River, near Warrensburg,
Greene County, Tennessee, October 30, 1810. Her father was a
nephew of John Sevier, first Governor of Tennessee. Her paternal
grandfather was Valentine Sevier, a Colonel in the Revolutionary
War. She had three brothers and three sisters. Her brother Ambrose Hundley Sevier was for a number of years United States
Senator from Arkansas and was sent to Mexico by President Polk
as Peace Commissioner after the War of 1848. She married James
Irwin, of Murfreesboro, Tennessee, December 18, 1828, and moved
to McMinnville about 1830, and to Savannah, Tennessee, about 1831.
She died October 7, 1885. Her ten children all grew up except the
youngest, Hundley Irwin. Her daughter, Juliet, died March 22, 1864."

Children of Nancy Sevier Irwin and James Irwin:

(a)   Anne Maria Irwin.
(b)   Susannah Elizabeth Irwin.
(c)   Juliett Sevier Irwin.
(d)   Hattie Louise Irwin.
(e)   Mary Dinwiddie Irwin.
(f)   Cornelia L. Irwin.
(g)   John Sevier Irwin.
(h)   Dr. Louis B. Irwin.
(i)   James William Irwin.
(j)   Hundley Irwin.

Of the foregoing:

(a) Anna Maria Irwin, daughter of Nancy Sevier and James
Irwin, married William H. Cherry, of Nashville. They had two
children, Minnie Cherry (who married James M. Head, of Brookline, Massachusetts, and William Irwin Cherry (who married Florence Wilkes and lives in New York City).

(b) Susannah Elizabeth Irwin, daughter of Nancy Sevier Irwin
and James Irwin, died unmarried.

(c) Juliette Sevier Irwin, daughter of Nancy Sevier Irwin and
James Irwin, died unmarried.

(d) Hattie Louise Irwin, daughter of Nancy Sevier Irwin and

James Irwin, married William H. Cherry, of Nashville. They had
two children: Minnie Cherry, (who married James M. Head, of Brookline, Massachusetts.) and William Irwin Cherry, (who married
Florence Wilkes and lived in New York City.)

(b) Susannah Elizabeth Irwin, daughter of Nancy Sevier
Irwin and James Irwin, died unmarried.

(c) Juliette Sevier Irwin, daughter of Nancy Sevier Irwin and
James Irwin, died unmarried.

(d) Hettie Louise Irwin, daughter of Nancy Sevier Irwin and
James Irwin, married Dr. Robert A. Hardin. They have four children:
Nancy Elizabeth Hardin, who married R. Mahlen Stacey and lives
in Pulaski, Tennessee, and has one child Rebecca Louise Stacey, who
married Ernest Keller and lives in Knoxville; Robert A. Hardin, Jr.,
who married Irene Barlow and lives in Birmingham, Alabama. They
have four children, Hettie Louise Hardin, who married Robert Lee
Jordan and lives in Memphis, Tennessee. They have two chilren,
Elizabeth Irwin Jordan and Robert Hardin Jordan; and Charles W.
Hardin, who married Ida Isinger and lives in New York City. They
have one child, Mary Florence Hardin.

(e) Mary Dinwiddie Irwin, daughter of Nancy Sevier Irwin
and James Irwin, married Edgar Cherry, of Savannah, Tennessee, and
had four children, mong them Juliette Irwin Cherry, who married
Webb W. Crawford and lives in Birmingham, Alabama. They have
two sons, Webb W. Crawford, Jr., and Cherry Crawford.

(f) Cornelia L. Irwin, daughter of Nancy Sevier Irwin and
James Irwin, married Daniel A. Welsh. They had two sons who died
in infancy.

(g) John Sevier Irwin, son of Nancy Sevier Irwin and
James Irwin, married Fannie Church. They lived in Savannah, Ten-
nessee, and had three children, Dr. James Irwin, Annie Irwin and
Eliza Irwin.

(h) Dr. Louis B. Irwin, son of Nancy Sevier Irwin and James
Irwin, married Mary Bailey. They had no children.

(i) James William Irwin, Jr., son of Nancy Sevier Irwin and
James Irwin, married Cornelia Browles. They had four children:
Louise Irwin, Gertrude Irwin, James, Irwin and ————— Irwin.

(j) Hundley Irwin, son of Nancy Sevier Irwin and James Irwin,
died young.

(k) —————Sevier.

(G)—————Sevier, daughter of Devil Jack Sevier and
Susannah Conway Sevier, was born 18———. I have no record of
her name or birth. In the obituary of Nancy Sevier who married
James Irwin is the statement that she had three brothers and three
sisters. I therefore have set down the number of seven children.
This daughter, was of course, older than the twins, who were the
youngest children of "Devil Jack."

ANN SEVIER

3. Ann Sevier, daughter of Colonel Valentine Sevier III and
Naomi Douglass Sevier, was born in Virginia in 1771. She accompanied her parents to the mountains of Tennessee when she was
very small and later in their second emigration to Middle Tennessee,
near the present site of Clarksville. She married twice. Her first
husband was Thomas Grantham. He was killed by Indians in 1790.
Her second husband was John King. At the time of the massacre of
the Valentine Sevier Station, November 11, 1794, John King was
working in the fields some distance from the houses with Ann's
brother, James, a lad of about seventeen. They heard the shots and
screams but could not arrive in time to give assistance. Ann Sevier
and her little son, James King, were killed in the massacre. She
was but twenty years old. Several children were killed whose
names are not recorded and also several survived whose names are
not known. It is a matter of record, however, that several grandchildren of Valentine Sevier were in the station. It is a
part of Rebecca's testimony and Hugh Ball's that Rebecca tried to
rescue a child whom the Indians placed in a blazing fire and that
because of this effort to save the child they scalped her. It is not
known whether she saved the life of the baby. Hugh Ball, the nearest
neighbor, who came to the assistance of Colonel Sevier when he
heard the firing, in an interview with Dr. Draper, says that a little
"grandson" about four years old survived, but does not mention
his name. It is in notes of an interview with Rebecca Sevier that
Dr. Draper calls him Alexander G. or Greene and seems uncertain
which, but lists him as Colonel Sevier's son. This child was in the
Block House with Naomi Douglas Sevier when Colonel Sevier shut
the door and fired the blunderbuss which knocked him down and
knocked out three of his teeth. This child, born in 1790, would not
be Naomi's child, I imagine, but if Dr. Draper's "Greene," with a
question mark, can be translated into Grantham, he could be Ann
Sevier's child by her first husband, Thomas Grantham. In 1790
when this child was born, since he was about four in 1794, Ann
Sevier was nineteen years of age and the wife or the recent widow
of Thomas Grantham, who was killed by Indians in 1790. I know
nothing, however, of this child Alexander and place him here merely
on supposition. This cannot be Alexander who was about twelve and
was out rabbit hunting.

The children of Ann Sevier Grantham King:

(A)   Alexander Grantham (?).

(B   James King, killed by Indians in infancy.

VALENTINE SEVIER IV

(4)   Valentine Sevier IV, son of Colonel Valentine Sevier III

and Naomi Douglas Sevier, was born in 1773, after his parents had removed from Virginia to the Mountains. He was the fourth Valentine Sevier in direct succession, and perhaps many times that number, as we have no record of the generations that preceded "Valentine Xavier" who fled from France to London and established the English branch of the family and the name as we know it: Sevier. Valentine Sevier IV is said to have been unmarried when January 16, 1791, he was killed by Indians near Clarksville, near the mouth of the Red River. His body and that of John Rice, who was killed at the same time, were burned by Captain Solomon White.

ROBERT AND WILLIAM SEVIER

(5 and 6) Robert and William Sevier, twin sons of Colonel Valentine Sevier III and Naomi Douglass Sevier, were born in "the Mountains" in 1775. They accompanied their parents to Middle Tennessee and were killed by Indians near the mouth of Blooming Grove Creek, January 15, 1791. They were on their way to join General James Robertson at Nashville. Hugh T. Ball found the body of William Sevier, but the body of Robert, who jumped into the water, was never found. A skeleton was found a year later a mile away and it was thought that Robert ran a mile before he died. They were just nineteen years of age and were unmarried.

JAMES SEVIER

7. James Sevier, son of Colonel Valentine Sevier III and Naomi Douglass Sevier, was born August 30, 1777, in the Mountains of East Tennessee. He accompanied his parents in their migration to Middle Tennessee and participatd with them in the dreadful hardships and sorrows that came to them. In 1794, when the massacre took place, James was a lad of seventeen. He was working in the fields at some distance from the houses when the Indians surprised the station. His brother-in-law, John King, was with him. They heard the noise and screaming but reached the house too late to be of any assistance.

In 1798, James Sevier married Susan or Susannah Warren, of Greene County, Tennessee. The marriage bond is dated November 29, 1798, and is signed by his brother, John Sevier. It is for $1,200. This is two years before his father died, but he was witness to a deed in Clarksville, July 30, 1798.

The marriage bond attracted quite a deal of interest when it was exhibited in 1924 by Judge J. T. Phillips, of Kingsport, who has kept it in his possession for many years.

The bond is signed by James Sevier as principal, and his brother, John Sevier, as security, and is given as a guarantee of the legal consummation of the marriage, and to insure that there is no impediment to the act existing. The bond is drawn in favor of John Sevier, Esq., Governor of Tennessee, and is for the sum of $1,200. It is witnessed by Dave Warren, clerk of the court, and the fee for its issuance is shown to be 75 cents.

The document is written in pen and ink, is perfectly preserved, and perfectly legible after a lapse of 136 years.

Senator Ambrose Hundley Sevier says that James Sevier moved to Kentucky and that when he last heard from it was 1843. Rebecca Sevier Rector testified that she was living at the time of their mother's death in 1845.

James Sevier died at his home in Kentucky in 1865.

James Sevier and Susannah Warren Sevier had twelve children:

(A) Elizabeth Sevier.
(B) Rebecca Sevier.
(C) Sarah Sevier.
(D) Mary Sevier.
(E) Charles Sevier.
(F) Thomas Sevier.
(G) Valentine Sevier.
(H) Alexander Sevier.
(I) John Rector Sevier.
(J) Martha Sevier.
(K) Robert Sevier.
(L) Samuel Sevier.

Of the foregoing:

(A Elizabeth Sevier, daughter of James Sevier and Susannah Warren Sevier, was born March 25, 1801. She married ————.

(B) Rebecca Sevier, daughter of James Sevier and Susannah Warren Sevier, was born March 27, 1803. She married ———— Brown and had one child, Douglas Brown, and he had one child, ———— Brown.

(C) Sarah Sevier, daughter of James Sevier and Susannah Warren Sevier, was born May 21, 1805. She married John Farris. They had a daughter, Martha Ann Farris, who married James Madison Adkin, and their daughter, Ella Nene Adkin, married James Edgar Lynch.

(D) Mary Sevier, daughter of James Sevier and Susannah Warren Sevier, was born July 27, 1807.

(E) Charles Warren Sevier, son of James Sevier and Susannah Warren Sevier was born July 21, 1810.

(F) Thomas H. Sevier, son of James Sevier and Susannah Warren Sevier, was born February 12, 1812.

(G) Valentine Sevier, son of James Sevier and Susannah Warren Sevier, was born Februaary 14, 1814. He married Margaret Smith.

(H) Alexander Sevier, son of James Sevier and Susannah Warren Sevier, was born March 15, 1816.

(I) John Rector Sevier, son of James Sevier and Susannah Warren Sevier, was born March 15 ,1818. He died 1865. He married Nancy Ewing and had five children: (a) Alexander Sevier; (b) James Sevier; (c) Douglas Sevier; (d) Charles Sevier; and (e) Susan Sevier. Of these (a) Alexander Sevier married Nancy Sawyers and has four children: Cora Sevier, Alexander Sevier, Jr., Marena Sevier and John Sevier.

(J) Martha Sevier, daughter of James Sevier and Susannah Warren Sevier, was born January 21, 1820. She married Tyre Gibson and had six children: James Gibson, Susan Gibson, Jane Gibson, Amelia Gibson, Ellen Gibson and Kitty Gibson.

(K) Robert Sevier, son of James Sevier and Susannah Warren Sevier, was born October 28, 1823. He married Margaret Beatty.

(L) Samuel Sevier, son of James Sevier and Susannah Warren Sevier, was born October 28, 1825. He married Amelia Hibbard.

JOSEPH SEVIER

8. Joseph Sevier, son of Colonel Valentine Sevier III and Naomi Douglass Sevier, was born in 1778 in East Tennessee. He accompanied his parents in their migration to Middle Tennessee and was killed by the Indians in the massacre November 11, 1794. He was very young, fifteen or sixteen at most, and was, of course, unmarried.

ALEXANDER G. SEVIER

9. Alexander G. Sevier, son of Colonel Valentine Sevier and Naomi Douglass Sevier, was born about 1782. At the time of the massacre in 1794 he was a lad of about twelve and was out rabbit hunting. He thus escaped the massacre. Hugh Bell, the neighbor who came to the help of the station, mentions Alexander, a lad of twelve, out rabbit hunting. He married about 18— Elizabeth A————. He is frequently mentioned in Governor Sevier's Journal. He died, according to Senator Ambrose Hundley Sevier, about 1828.

Senator Ambrose Hundley Sevier, in a letter dated 1843 (in the Draper manuscript), says, "My grandfather, Valentine Sevier, left three sons, John (my father), who died about thirty years ago; Alexander and James. Alexander died fifteen years ago. James went to Kentucky an I lost track of him."

He says at another time that in 1890, at the death of Colonel Valentine Sevier III, only three sons were living, John, James and Alexander. At the death of Naomi Douglass Sevier in 1846, her daughter says that only one son, James, was living.

Major Alexander G. Sevier in the War of 1812 and thus gained his title. He was commended for bravery and is mentioned many times in current histories and documents. He died in 1828. His widow, Elizabeth A. —————— Sevier, applied for a pension, and mentioned three children, but did not give their names.

REBECCA SEVIER.

10. Rebecca Sevier, daughter of Colonel Valentine Sevier II and Naomi Douglass Sevier, was born in East Tennessee in 1783. She was eleven years of age when, having accompanied her parents to Middle Tennessee, she suffered with other members of her family in the dreadful massacre. It is said that when the murdering Indians threw a child into the fire that Rebecca rushed to rescue the baby. For this deed she was scalped and left for dead. Some historians state that she was scalped three years earlier when her brothers were killed but Colonel Valentine Sevier's letter, quoted in full in the first part of this chapter, settles the question of the date. She wore a tarred cap all her life after this experience.

She married John B. Rector about the year 1800. Much of the information of this part of the Sevier history is obtained from her statements either in pension papers or in interviews with Dr. Lyman Draper. Her mother, Naomi Douglass Sevier, made her home for many years with Rebecca and drew a pension. One pension record shows Naomi Douglass Sevier living with John Rector (son-in-law), age 97, Pension List 1840."

Rebecca Sevier Rector, in her interview with Dr. Draper in 1844 in Greene County, Tennessee, tells him about the forty* Indians who surprised her father's station in 1794, killing her sister, Ann King and scalping her (Rebecca) and leaving her for dead. Ann King's husband escaped because he was in the field. (Ann's first husband, Thomas Grantham, had been killed by the Indians in 1790). In 1791 her twin brothers, Robert and William, were killed by the Indians near the mouth of Blooming Grove Creek and the next morning her brother, Valentine Sevier IV, was killed the same place.

She says that her sister, Elizabeth Snyder, born 1768, the first born, was killed, also her husband Charles, in the blacksmith shop, and "their son John and little ones." Rebecca's brother, Joseph, born 1788, was also killed under a work bench in the shop. Rebecca states that her brother James, a lad of 17 years (born 1777)

---

*Either Hugh Bell was mistaken in the number of Indians who carried out this frightful deed or Valentine Sevier and Rebecca were mistaken. Hugh Bell says that about fifteen Indians massacred the Station. Colonel Sevier and Rebecca say forty Indians.

was in the field pulling corn and that Alexander,† four years of age, born 1790, was in the block house with her mother when Colonel Valentine Sevier shut the door and fired the blunderbuss that knocked out three of her teeth.

Rebecca Sevier Rector and John Rector appear in the Greene County (Tennessee) census of 1850. John Rector's age is given as 86, establishing his birth in 1764. A descendant furnishes the exact date, March 10, 1764. This makes him much older than Rebecca, whose age is given in the census as 67, born in Tennessee. This agrees with the foregoing record of her birth in 1783 John Rector died February 5, 1856, according to entry in the Bible record of Charles Sevier Rector.

In 1851, Rebecca Sevier Rector applied for an increase of pension allowed her mother for her father's services in the Wars. She sets out that only she and her brother James were living at the time of her mother's death in 1845, (not 1844, she says, as the Pension Department had made a mistake).

The census of Greene County, Tennessee, of 1850 gives the names of John Rector and his wife, Rebecca Sevier Rector, and the names of four persons in their household, namely:

George Rector, age 33, born 1817.
Valentine Rector, age 16, born 1834.
Jane Rector, age 24, born 1826.
——————— Rector, age 7, born 1843. This last name could not be deciphered, but the child is too young to be a child of Rebecca and John Rector and may have been a grandchild.

In the census of Greene County, Tennessee, for 1870, Valentine Sevier Rector is given, aged 37. This puts his birth about 1833 and shows that he is the Valentine named above. Rebecca evidently gave him her father's full name. The census gives his children as:

a. Charles T. Rector, born 1859.
b. James Rector, born 1861.
c. Barbary E. Rector, born 1863.
d. Louisa Jane Rector, born 1865.
e. Frances Rector, born 1869.

Charles Sevier Rector, who is now (1924) living in Mohawk, Greene County, Tennessee, says he is the son of Jacob F. Rector, born January 29, 1844, died October 13, 1904, who was the son of John J. Rector, born ———————, died ———————, who was the son

————————————————————

†The Alexander mentioned by Rebecca as four years old was very evidently the little grandson mentioned by Hugh Bell, as her brother Alexander who was twelve was out rabbit hunting.

of John B. Rector and Rebecca Sevier Rector. Charles Sevier Rector has the Bible which the widow of Colonel Valentine Sevier III bought at the sale in Clarksville for fifty cents. He has given me many names and dates from this Bible, for instance, the birth of Naomi Douglass Sevier, April, 1743, and the birth and death of John B. Rector (March 10, 1764, February 5, 1856). These were not previously known to me.

From his record the only name we know positively as the child of Rebecca Sevier Rector and John B. Rector is John J. Rector, but I think from the dates of the people living with Rebecca and John in 1850 that George Rector, born in 1817, and Jane Rector, born in 1826, may have been their children. The other two, Valentine Sevier Rector and the child whose name is not given, are probably grandchildren.

The names, then, of the children of Rebecca Sevier Rector and John B. Rector:

a. John J. Rector.
b. George Rector.
c. Jane Rector.

a. John J. Rector, son of Rebecca Sevier Rector and John B. Rector, was born ————. He married Barbara Dearstone, born December 11, 1806, died July 17, 1872. They had a son:

Jacob F. Rector, born ————, died ————, married November 23, 185—, Louisa Jane Howell, born June 15, 1847, died March 15, 1879. Louisa Jane Howell was herself a descendant of the Sevier family. She was the daughter of ———— Howell and his wife, Sarah Jane Sevier Howell (born May 30, 1820, died March 29, 1896), whose father was "John Sevier," she said to her grandson, but I have not been able to determine which of the many Johns was her father. This was not Governor John Sevier, as her birth is given five years after his death.

Jacob F. Rector married after his first wife's death, Mary Kincer, December 9, 1879.

Their child was.

e. Charles Sevier Rector, born ————, 1878, in Greene County, Tennessee, now living in Mohawk, Tennessee.

JOANNA SEVIER

11. Joanna Goode Sevier, said to have been the eleventh child of Colonel Valentine Sevier and Naomi Douglass Sevier, was born ————. Miss Mary Ross Headman is authority for the statement that she was their eleventh child. In writing to Governor John Sevier in 1799, Colonel Sevier says, "the rest of my family is well, excepting Joanna, who is ill of a fever, but not serious."

Therefore, it may be accepted that Valentine Sevier III had a daughter, Joanna.

Whether this Joanna is the Joanna Goode Sevier who married Younger Landrum, Jr., November 8, 1800, I am unable to say.

See Part Four.

CHAPTER THREE

Captain Robert Sevier

CAPTAIN ROBERT SEVIER

ROBERT SEVIER, third son of Valentine Sevier II and Joanna Goode Sevier, was born about 1750, in Rockingham County, Virginia. He accompanied his father and four brothers to "the Mountains" in 1773. He there married, probably in 1777, Keziah Robertson, daughter of Charles Robertson and Sarah Nichols Robertson. They had two sons, Charles, aged two years, and Valentine, aged four months, when the call for the Mountaineers to assemble came and they marched to King's Mountain, where the British force engaged them. Captain Robert Sevier, commanding a company, was mortally wounded in the battle and was at first thought to be dead. He lived for a short time, however, and was carried from the battlefield toward his home. He died nine days after the battle, when he was almost within sight of his home, it is said. His contemporaries give him credit for being as brave and as handsome as his distinguished brother, Governor John Sevier, and it is thought by many that except for his early death he would have had a great part in the annals of Tennessee. As it is, his name remains one of the literal heroes of King's Mountain.

John Sevier was appointed administrator of Captain Robert Sevier's estate and guardian of the two children. Their mother married, shortly after the death of Captain Sevier, ————— Tipton. The enmity existing between the Seviers and the Tiptons probably caused friction after this marriage, as it must have been awkward having a Tipton for a step-father and John Sevier for a guardian.

There is a tradition among the descendants of Charles Sevier that he and his brother, Valentine, ran away from home because their uncle, Governor John Sevier, was unkind to them and because he apprenticed them to a hatter! However Valentine's son, Charles Sevier, who is now living (1925), in Bristol, Tennessee, told me that the two boys were treated cruelly by their mother's second husband, ————— Tipton. He did not mention any cruelty of his great-uncle, John Sevier, and as he is nearer in generation to the actual incidents than any other living person, his evidence is good. He had the information from many members of his family. He told me that Keziah Robertson Sevier Tipton joined her husband in unkindness and cruelty to the two orphan children of Captain Robert Sevier, and that the Seviers, all of them, including Governor Sevier, deeply resented her attitude and her husband's to the two orphan children. Of course, the feud between the Seviers and the Tiptons is well known and I can imagine that Governor Sevier would resent any bad treatment of the orphans. Mr. Charles Lyman Sevier said that the resulting family estrangement has lasted to the present time. Keziah Robertson Sevier Tipton had children by her second husband, but according to Mr. Sevier there has never been any friendliness between the two branches of her descendants. I think this story is more credible than the other and the evidence is certainly more direct. It is difficult to believe that Governor John Sevier would be deliberately unkind to the fatherless children of his favorite brother. I am inclined to think that if anything, he would have aided them to escape from home and that he probably did! The Sevier-Tipton feud, which was raging at this time, would lend excuse to Tipton (Keziah's second husband)for disliking the Sevier children.

Captain Robert Sevier died nine days after the batttle of King's Mountain, that is, October 16, 1780. He was about thirty years of age.

The children of Captain Robert Sevier and Keziah Robertson Sevier were:

1. Charles Robertson Sevier, born 1778, died 1855.
2. Valentine Sevier, born June 1780, died March 24, 1854.

MAJOR CHARLES ROBERTSON SEVIER

Charles Roberton Sevier, the elder son of Captain Robert Sevier and Keziah Robertson Sevier, is known as Major Charles Sevier. He was born in what is now known as East Tennessee, Greene County, in 1778, two years before the Battle of King's Mountain. His father was mortally wounded in that battle and died, leaving two infant children. Charles, the elder, had evidently been named in honor of Keziah's father. He is usually called Major Charles Sevier, but I have seen his name given in full, Charles Robertson Sevier. He went to Overton County when many of the Sevier family went there, early in the years of 1800 and in the organization of the county he was given in the military department of the county a commission as Second Major. This was May 13, 1806. His cousin, Charles Matlock, received a commission as Captain at the same time. Charles Matlock was, presumably, a son or grandson of Governor John Sevier's sister who married William Matlock and was then living in Overton County. A daughter of Governor Sevier, (Joanna) and her husband, Joseph Hawkins Windle, were living in Overton County at that time, where Joseph Hawkins Windle was keeping a store on the John Sevier property. After the death of the Governor his widow, Bonnie Kate, joined the rest of the family in Overton and resided there until a few months before her death. Evidently, therefore, Charles Sevier was on exceedingly good terms with several

members of the John Sevier family. Although in 1806 he was twenty-
eight years old and too old to be "running away," there is no evidence
to show how long he had been in the county with other members of
the Sevier family. Perhaps he did leave his step-father's house when
he was a young boy.

It is said that Governor Sevier apprenticed him to a hatter
about the year 1790 and that he did not like the job and left to go to
live with his mother's brother, Charles Robertson, on the Chucky
River. That shows friendliness with the mother's family.

Later he went to Overton County to make his home and there
many of the Seviers gathered preceeding or following Bonnie Kate's
removal after the Governor's death. The fact that Charles Robertson Sevier joined them disposes of the story that he resented the
cruelty and unkindness of his paternal relatives.

When West Tennessee was opened to settlers Charles Robertson
Sevier went to Madison County and bought a farm four miles from
the city of Jackson, Tennessee.

Charles Robertson Sevier married Elizabeth Witt, who was born
about 1786. She was the daughter of Joseph Witt and Sarah Kimbrough Witt and the granddaughter of Charles Witt and Lavinia
Harbor Witt, of Halifax County, Virginia. Elizabeth Witt was a
first cousin to Preston Jarnagin, whose son, Dr. C. P. Jarnagin, married Catherine Anne Hale, also a descendant of the John Sevier family. See Chapter III, Part Six.

The marriage of Major Charles Robertson Sevier to Elizabeth
Witt took place in 1802, in Greene County, Tennessee. In 1806,
Charles Sevier was commissioned second major of Overton County.
After a few years, the exact date not being known, he emigrated
to Brownsville, Tennessee, where he reared a large family.

Major Charles Sevier served with General Andrew Jackson. It
is said that he secured his military title in the War of 1812, and
that he was promoted by General Jackson, but, as has been seen,
he was commissioned Major in 1806, so he probably went into the
war as a Major. He was living May 15, 1854, when his son, John
Sevier, wrote to Dr. Lyman C. Draper that his father was "suffering
from a bad memory due to old age."

Major Sevier was a very large man and was greatly interested
in politics. It is told of him that he espoused the cause of James K.
Polk and that on the day of the election in 1844, he rode into town
on a white bull stained with poke berry juice.

In 1832, the sons of Major Sevier felt that General Jackson had
not shown proper appreciation of their father's service. They declared, therefore, that they would not support him for President.
This infuriated their father and he bade them never again darken
his door! They voted for the opposition and left for Texas. This

story seems to account for the wholesale migration of the family to the then new state of Texas, but evidently amity was restored, for the father moved out to join his sons a few years later. In 1854 he came to this decision, but the long, hard trip (he was then seventy-six years of age), seriously injured his health, and in a year's time, 1855, he died, at the home of his son Valentine Sevier, near Milford, Ellis County, Texas. His wife's death occurred within a few weeks.

Children of Major Charles Sevier

Major Charles Robertson Sevier and Elizabeth Witt Sevier had fourteen children, among them six sons:

(These are not given in the order of birth.)

A. Robert Sevier.
B. Valentine Sevier.
C. John Tinturff Sevier.
D. Mary Sevier.
E. Keziah Sevier.
F. Bathenia Sevier.
G. Catherine Sevier.
H. Elizabeth Sevier.
I. Nancy Sevier.
J. ———— Sevier, a daughter.
K. Joseph Sevier.
L. Charles Wallace Sevier.
M. Elbridge Sevier.
N. Adam H. Sevier.

Robert Sevier

A. Robert Sevier, son of Major Charles Sevier and Elizabeth Witt Sevier, married ———————— and had children, all of whom died young.

Valentine Sevier

B. Valentine Sevier, son of Major Charles Sevier and Elizabeth Witt Sevier, was in the Tennessee legislature for two or three terms. He married Anna Murray. He moved to Texas in 1850 and lived to be about ninety years of age. It was in his home in Milford, Ellis County, Texas, that his father and mother died in 1856. He had eight children, namely:

a. John Tinturff Sevier, Jr.
b. Bailey P. Sevier.
c. F. A. Sevier.
d. Mary F. Sevier, married ———— MacDonald.
e. Charles H. Sevier.
f. ———— Sevier.

g. ——————— Sevier.
h. ——————— Sevier.

Of the foregoing:

a. John Tinturff Sevier, Jr., son of Valentine Sevier and Anna Murray Sevier, was born October 29, 1831, at Brownsville Tennessee. He married and had thirteen children, namely: 1, George Wallace Sevier of Brandon, Texas, born at Milford, Texas 1871; 2, Oscar Sevier; 3, Charles Sevier; 4, Helen Norwood Sevier; 5, William Sevier; 6, Jane Sevier; 7, Lona Sevier; 8, May Sevier; 9, John Sevier; 10, Guy Sevier; 11, James Sevier; 12, Eddie Sevier and 13, Ernest Sevier.

b. Bailey P. Sevier, son of Valentine Sevier and Anna Murray Sevier, married ——————— and lived at Carter City, Mills County, Texas.

c. F. A. Sevier, son of Valentine Sevier and Anna Murray Sevier, married ——————— and lived at Cheatham, Texas.

d. Mary F. Sevier, daughter of Valentine Sevier and Anna Murray Sevier, married ——————— MacDonald and lived at Anson, Jones County, Texas.

e. Charles H. Sevier, son of Valentine Sevier and Anna Murray Sevier, married ——————— and lived at Sherman, Texas. He had a son, Charles S. Sevier, who was postmaster at Sherman.

John Tinturff Sevier

C. John Tinturff Sevier, son of Major Charles Robertson Sevier and Elizabeth Witt Sevier, was born January 23, 1807. He died 1866. He was sheriff of Haywood County for fourteen years. He married three times. His first wife was Maria Henderson, sister of Congressman Thomas J. Henderson, cf Princeton, Illinois. Six of the Sevier children left Major Charles Sevier's home, all going to Texas, as will be seen by reading their histories. John Tinturff Sevier, however, though leaving at the same time and perhaps for the same reason, did not go to Texas but to Brownsville, Tennessee, only twenty miles from Jackson. By his first wife he had one child, Mary Ann Amanda Sevier, who married ——————— Link and lived in Brownsville. By his second wife, ——————— Brickle, he had one son, Valentine Brickle Sevier, who moved back to Jackson and made his home with his grandfather, Major Charles Sevier. Valentine Brickle Sevier died 1905. He married first, ——————— Westbrook and had one son John Sevier, and married for his second wife, Mollie Whitehead, and had five children: Elizabeth Sevier, who married H. W. White and had a son, H. W. White, Jr.; Minnie Sevier, who married Finnis Lack, of Paducah, Kentucky, and has one son Frederick Lack; James Sevier, who married Pauline Houston and lived in Paducah, Kentucky; Charles William Sevier, who married

Nellie Steele and had a son, Charles Bertrand Sevier; and Robert Sevier, who married Gladys Spence and has three sons, Robert Sevier, Jr., James M. Sevier and Charles Wallace Sevier.

John Tinturff Sevier married for his third wife Sarah Sangster, by whom he had nine cildren, namely:

c. Charles Henry Sevier.
d. John Brickle Sevier.
e. James Sevier.
f. Robert Wallace Sevier.
g. ———— Sevier, died in infancy.
h. Jane Sevier.
j. Mary Catherine Sevier.
k. William Sevier.
l. Laura Sevier.

Of the foregoing:

c. Charles Henry Sevier, son of John Tinturff Sevier and Sarah Sangster Sevier, was born in 1839, in Jackson, Tennessee. He died September 21, 1898. He married Cora Edwin Anderson, born July 26, 1839, died July 14, 1911. They had children namely: 1, Cora Amanda Sevier, born April 2, 1858, now living in Brownsville Tennessee, unmarried; 2, Dr. John Henry Sevier, born August 11, 1862, lives in Brownsville, Tennessee. He married Lee Wagner and has twin sons, both honor men at Johns Hopkins Medical School in Baltimore, neither of whom is married. John Alston Sevier is located at Colorado Springs, Charles Edwin Sevier is in Lausanne, Switzerland; 3, Laura Sevier, died young; 4, Julia Sevier, married James M. Livingston and lives in Detroit, Michigan. She has three children, Edwin Sevier Livingston, Cora Livingston and Charles Livingston; 5, Sue Sevier, died about 1910. She married Thomas F. Harolson and had children, Thomas Sevier Harolson, Hazel Sevier Harolson, William Harolson and Sallie Rose Sevier Harolson; 6, Charles A. Sevier, born August 13, 1870, lives in Jackson, Tennessee. He married Ida Matthews Sutherlin, of Paris, Tennessee, April, 1899. They have two children, Jane Sutherlin Sevier, born May 13, 1902, and Charles Henry Sevier, born September 20, 1906.

d. John Brickle Sevier, son of John Tinturff Sevier and Sarah Sangster Sevier, married Katherine Henderson, of Cedar Rapids, Iowa. He died without children, January 1, 1908.

e. James Sevier, son of John Tinturff Sevier and Sarah Sangster Sevier ————————

f. Robert Wallace Sevier, son of John Tinturff Sevier and Sarah Sangster Sevier, married his cousin, Edith Anna Sangster. They left three children, Robert Wallace Sevier, Jr., Mary Sevier and Elder Sevier. Robert Wallace Sevier, Jr., is unmarried and lives in New York City; Mary Sevier married John A. Rose and has a daughter, Jeanne Adele Ross; they live in Clarksdale, Miss.; Elder Sevier married Hattie Yelovington and lives in Paris, Tennessee, and has two children, Gene Sangster Sevier and Mary Edith Sevier.

g. ───────── Sevier. This child died in infancy.

h. Jane Sevier, daughter of John Tinturff Sevier and Sarah Sangster Sevier, married Eph Clay. She died leaving no children.

i. Mary Catherine Sevier, daughter of John Tinturff Sevier and Sarah Sangster Sevier, married Dr. Thomas Potter, of Brownsville, Tennessee. They died leaving two children, a son, ─────── Potter, of Brownsville, and a daughter, Mary Potter, who married Fred Price, and has a daughter, Viola May Price.

k. Elizabeth Sevier, daughter of John Tinturff Sevier and Sarah Sangster Sevier.

l. Laura Sevier, daughter of John Tinturff Sevier and Sarah Sangster Sevier.

Mary Sevier

D. Mary Sevier, daughter of Major Charles Robertson Sevier and Elizabeth Witt Sevier, was born ───────────. She married ─────────── Anderson and lives in Missouri.

Keziah Sevier

E. Keziah Sevier, daughter of Major Charles Robertson Sevier and Elizabeth Witt Sevier, was born ───────────. She married ─────────── Simonton. The fact that Charles Robertson Sevier named a daughter for his mother, Keziah Robertson, seems to refute the statement that he resented her treatment of himself and his brother when they were children. Keziah Sevier Simonton lived at Purdy, Tennessee.

Bethenia Sevier

F. Bethenia Sevier, daughter of Major Charles Robertson Sevier and Elizabeth Witt Sevier, proves by her name that her father kept in close touch with his family,, for the name Bathenia is identified with Sevier. It was borne by a sister of Governor John Sevier. Bethenia Sevier, daughter of Major Charles Sevier, married ─────── Brown and went to Texas to live.

Catherine Sevier

G. Catherine Sevier, daughter of Major Charles Sevier and Elizabeth Witt Sevier, was born ───────────. She was also given a family name. She married ─────────── Sanford and went to Texas

Elizabeth Sevier

H. Elizabeth Sevier, daughter of Major Charles Robertson Sevier and Elizabeth Witt Sevier, was born —————. She was given her mother's name. She married ————— Holt and went to Texas.

Nancy Sevier

I. Nancy Sevier, daughter of Major Charles Robertson Sevier and Elizabeth Witt Sevier, was born —————. She married Jesse Russell, of Jackson, Tennessee. They had two sons, Robert Russell and Jesse Russell, Jr. Robert Russell was in the Mexican War and later in the Confederate Army. Jesse Russell, Jr., married ————— ————— and had five children, namely: Charles Russell, Lucy Russell, Leighton Russell, Milborn Russell and Betty Russell.

————— Sevier

J. ————— Sevier, a daughter of Major Charles Robertson Sevier and Elizabeth Witt Sevier, died young.

Joseph Sevier

K. Joseph Sevier, son of Major Charles Robertson Sevier and Elizabeth Witt Sevier, was born —————. He went to California.

Charles Wallace Sevier

L. Charles Wallace Sevier, son of Major Charles Robertson Sevier and Elizabeth Witt Sevier, was born —————. He went to Texas.

Elbridge Sevier

M. Elbridge Sevier, son of Major Charles Robertson Sevier and Elizabeth Witt Sevier, was born —————. He went to Texas.

Adam H. Sevier

N. Adam H. Sevier, son of Major Charles Robertson sevier and Elizabeth Witt Sevier, was born —————. He went to Texas.

VALENTINE SEVIER, SON OF CAPTAIN ROBERT SEVIER

Valentine Sevier, son of Captain Robert Sevier and Keziah Robertson Sevier, was born June, 1780. He was about four months old when Captain Robert Sevier fell mortally wounded at King's Mountain. Valentine was the second child, his elder brother, Charles Robertson Sevier, being but two years of age in 1780. Their mother married ————— Tipton for her second husband.

The two Sevier children grew to maturity in East Tennessee,

where Valentine, reaching his majority, became Clerk of the Court at Greeneville, a position which he held fifty-two years until his death. He married twice and had fifteen children, thirteen by his first wife and two by his second wife. His elder son by the second wife, Charles Lyman Sevier, is now living in Bristol, Tennessee, and is one of the few men, if not the only man in America who is a grandson of a Revolutionary soldier who was killed in the Revolution. Mr. Sevier is also a grandson of a Colonial hero, as Captain Robert Sevier was an officer, as were his brothers, Valentine and John, in the Colonial Army.

Valentine Sevier married first Nancy Dinwiddie and second Vinerah Cannon. The first marriage took place when he was twenty-four years of age in 1804, in Greeneville, Tennessee. The second marriage took place April 26, 1846, also in Greeneville, Tennessee. Nancy Dinwiddie came of a Tennessee family. Vinerah Cannon, however, was of a Wallingford, Connecticut, family, and was visiting in Greeneville when she met and married Valentine Sevier.

Valentine Sevier died ——— 24, 1854.

The children of Valentine Sevier, son of Captain Robert Sevier, from a list found among his papers:

By his first wife:

A. Isabel Sevier, born January 10, 1805.
B. Keziah Sevier, born March 22, 1806.
C. Robert Sevier, born October 13, 1807.
D. Betsy (Elizabeth) Sevier, born October 13, 1809.
E. Susanna Sevier, born March 3, 1812.
F. James Sevier, born February 17, 1814.
G. Charles Sevier, born April 30, 1816.
H. Jane Sevier, born August 24, 1818.
I. David Sevier, born October 6, 1820.
J. William Robertson Sevier, born September 7, 1822.
K. Mary Sevier, born December 21, 1824.
L. Edward Sevier, born July 20, 1826.
M. Joseph Sevier, born March 30, 1830.

By the second wife:
N. Charles Lyman Sevier.
O. Henry Valentine Sevier.

Isabel Sevier

A. Isabel Sevier, daughter of Valentine Sevier and Nancy Dinwiddie Sevier, was born January 10, 1805. She married Frank A. McCorkle and had two children:

a ——————— McCorkle.
b. Nancy McCorkle.

a. ————————————— McCorkle, son of Isabel Sevier McCorkle and Frank A. McCorkle, married ————————— and had a son, Rev. Samuel McCorkle.

b. Nancy McCorkle, daughter of Isabel Sevier McCorkle and Frank A. McCorkle, married Cornelius Coffin and had Isabella Coffin who married Thomas Lanier Williams (see Williams Family, Vol. II, Notable Southern Families) and had Ella Williams, who is not married; Isabel Williams, who married William Gannaway Brownlow II (see Volume I, Notable Southern Families) and lives in Knoxville, Tennessee, and Cornelius Coffin Williams, who married ———— ———————— and has two children, Rose Isabella Williams and Thomas Lanier Williams II, and lives in St. Louis.

Keziah Sevier

B. Keziah Sevier, daughter of Valentine Sevier and Nancy Dinwiddie Sevier, was born March 22, 1806. She married George Jones, of Greeneville, Tennessee. She had at least one child, Mary Jones, born April 13, 1826 who, married August 7, 1852, Thomas A. Nelson, who died 1873. Their children are; Selden Nelson, of Knoxville; Lizzie Nelson, (who married John Williams and had a daughter, Mary Nelson Williams); Charles Nelson, (who married Mattie Chappell);Mary Nelson. (called Mollie, who married Charles E. McTeer); Lieutenant Commander Nelson, (who married Catherine McDonald); and Judge Thomas A. R. Nelson.

Robert Sevier

C. Robert Sevier, son of Valentine Sevier and Nancy Dinwiddie Sevier was born, October 13, 1807. He was educated at West Point. He entered West Point in 1824 and graduated in 1828 in the class with Jefferson Davis. He served for some years in the United States Army and participated in the Black Hawk War in 1837. He died in Missouri. He married Ann Hopkins Sibley.

Their children were:

(A) Charles Sevier, married Emma Denis and had Doctor Robert Sevier, born December 1, 1869; Reverend George F. Sevier; ———————————— Sevier, married Charles Zaeger; Ann Sevier married ———————————, Gras; M. ————————Sevier, married George F. Maitland and Charles D. Sevier.

(B) Robert Sevier, M. D., married Virginia Elizabeth Woodson, June 14, 1893 and had Robert Woodson Sevier, born March 23, 1894 and Virginia Elizabeth Sevier, born April 27, 1905.

(C) Robert Sevier married Ann Sibley and had Charles Sevier, born September 30, 1832, at Fort Leavenworth, Kansas. Now living at 1481 Adams Street, Denver, Colorado.

Elizabeth Sevier

D. Elizabeth Sevier, daughter of Valentine Sevier and Nancy Dinwiddie Sevier, born October 13, 1809, died June 14, 1882. She married Reverend John Whitfield Cunningham, of Kentucky, in 1831. John Whitfield Cunningham was a uncle of Martha Ellen Cunningham, who married William Robertson Sevier, and a brother of Samuel B. Cunningham. John Whitfield Cunningham and Elizabeth Sevier Cunningham had ten children, five of whom died in infancy.

The surviving children were:

a. Nancy Jane Cunningham, born 1834, died Minneapolis, Minnesota, 1909. She married Herman Knickerbocker.

b. John Cunningham married but had no children.

c. Katherine Mitchell Cunningham, born 1835, died Fort Scott, Kansas, 1916. She married Cheney M. Castle, Minneapolis, Minnesota. She had no children.

d. Jane Isaac Cunningham, died young.

e. Lucy Isbell Cunningham, born 1845, Jonesboro, Tennessee, died Fort Scott, Kansas, 1909. She married Doctor William C. Porter, of English birth, in 1867.

Their children: Katherine Elizabeth Porter, born 1868, died 1884; John William Porter, born 1870, married Maud Taylor, of Chicago, and has four children: John William Porter, Jr., died young; Robert Taylor Porter, born 1903 in Chicago; Knight Cunningham Porter, born 1905 in Chicago; Alice Sarah Porter, born 1872, died 1916; Caroline Belle Porter, born 1874, married Dudley Featherstone 1919 and has no children; and Lucy Porter, born 1886, married John Robinson McCurdy, in New York City in 1920. They have one child Jean McCurdy, a daughter born October 1924.

Susan Sevier

E. Susan Sevier, daughter of Valentine Sevier and Nancy Dinwiddie Sevier was born March 3, 1812. She never married. She lived to a very great age.

James Sevier

F. James Sevier, son of Valentine Sevier and Nancy Dinwiddie Sevier was born February 17, 1814. He married twice, first Jane Simpson, who died in 1863. He had a son Charles Sevier, who lived in Savannah, Tennessee, and a son George Jones Sevier, whose widow lived at one time in Oxford, Mississippi. James Sevier's second wife was Mrs. Eva Brewer Neil.

Mrs. Theodore Francis Sevier told me, (in 1924), that she and her husband Colonel Sevier, visited this cousin, James Sevier, in Rogersville, Tenn., in 1868 and that his wife had died three months earlier and that his sons were: Valentine, George and another who was in the Confederate Army. That there was another son, the youngest, named John, who was too young for military service. his father thought, but later he too joined the Confederate Army.

Charles Sevier

C. Charles Sevier, son of Valentine Sevier and Nancy Din-widdie Sevier was born April 30, 1816. He married Elizabeth Briscoe and had two children, Thomas Sevier and Nannie Sevier. He died in Mississippi in 1844.

Jane Sevier

H Jane Sevier, daughter of Valentine Sevier and Nancy Din-widdie Sevier, was born August 24, 1818. She married August 26, 1832, her second cousin, James Harvey Vance, of Kingsport, Tennessee, see Vance Family, Volume II, Notable Southern Families. The marriage took place at Warm Springs, North Carolina. James Harvey Vance died at Kingsport, Tennessee, July 7, 1893. James H. Vance and Jane Sevier were cousins, both being great-grand-children of Charles Robertson.

They had nine children, namely:

a. Charles Robertson Vance, who was born August 22, 1833, at Jonesboro, Tennessee. He married Margaret Newland, October 16, 1860 and had five children. James Isaac Vance, (born September 25, 1862 at Arcada, Tennessee, married December 22, 1866, at York-ville, South Carolina, Mamie Currell. They have six children, Margaret Vance, Agnes Vance, James Isaac Vance, Jr., and Charles Robertson Vance); Dr. Joseph Anderson Vance, (born November 17, 1864); Charles Robertson Vance, Jr.; Margaret Vance, (born January 20, 1877); and Rebecca Vance, (born January 20, 1877.)

b. Maria C. Vance, who married Reverend John King, of Leesburg, Virginia.

c. Anna Elizabeth Vance, died young.

d. Keziah Vance, died unmarried.

e. James Harvey Vance, Jr., who married Easton or Faston Paddock.

f. William Kirkpatrick Vance, who married Fannie Miller, of Union City, Tennessee.

g. Nannie Vance, died unmarried.

h. Joseph Vance, who married Mattie Fain and had two sons, James Fain Vance and Charles Robertson Vance.

i. Jane or Jennie Vance.

David Sevier

I. David Sevier, son of Valentine Sevier and Nancy Dinwiddie

Sevier, was born October 6, 1820. He died May 22, 1890. He was Clerk and Master at Greeneville, Tennessee, for many years. He married Anne Netherland. They had six children, five daughters and one son. He married a second wife, Annis Rutledge and had one son by the second marriage. I have the names of only two daughters and the one son by the second marriage who was David Rutledge Sevier. One daughter Nellie Sevier, married William Roller, of Kingsport, Tennessee and died several years ago. A daughter Nannie Sevier, born August 6, 1849, married Reverend Alexander N. Carson June 15, 1875. She died September 21, ——— in San Francisco. Her four children were: Harry Carson, Frank Carson, Nannie Carson and Charles Carson.

William Robertson Sevier

J. William Robertson Sevier, son of Valentine Sevier and Nancy Dinwiddie Sevier, was born September 7, 1822, died August22, 1882. He married twice, first in 1844, Martha Ellen Cunningham, daughter of Dr. Samuel B. Cunningham, first President of the East Tennessee and Virginia Railway, now the Southern Railway, and married second, in 1864, Lucy Evans. Lucy Evans was the daughter of Hamilton Evans, of Tazewell, Claiborne County, Tennessee. His mother was a Holt and his grand-mother a Hampton. By the first wife William Robertson Sevier had two children, a son Samuel D. Sevier, who died young and a daughter, Nannie Sevier, who married Guy Ellis Sabin, and by the second wife William Robertson Sevier had a son, William Robertson Sevier, Jr., of the United States Navy.

Nannie Sevier, daughter of William Robertson Sevier and his first wife, Martha Ellen Cunningham, was born in Jonesboro, Tennessee, in 1856. She married Guy C. Sabin, September 13, 1876. They had six children, one of whom died in infancy. Mabel Sabin, the only daughter, died at seventeen years of age. The sons: Albert Sevier Sabin, born 1877, married Emily Maud Raysor, of South Carolina, and has seven children, six sons and one daughter, Archibald Raysor Sabin, Albert Sevier Sabin, Katherine Margaret Sabin, William Robertson Sabin, Cornelius Ayre Sabin, Ellis Sabin and Donald Gavin Sabin, Guy Earl Sabin, who is unmarried. William Robertson Sabin, died unmarried, and Archibald D. Sabin, died unmarried.

Mary Sevier

K. Mary Sevier, daughter of Valentine Sevier and Nancy Dinwiddie Sevier, was born December 21, 1824.

Edward Sevier

L. Edward Sevier, son of Valentine Sevier and Nancy Dinwiddie Sevier, was born July 20, 1825. He married Mary Nelson Garrett and resides in Asheville, North Carolina.

Joseph Sevier

M. Joseph Sevier, son of Valentine Sevier and Nancy Dinwiddie Sevier, was born, March 30, 1829. He married his cousin Nannie Sevier Broyles, widow of Lewis Broyles and a daughter of Devil Jack Sevier and Susannah Conway Sevier.

They had children namely: Dr. Robert Sevier, deceased; Lewis Sevier, married and lives in Savannah, Tennessee, and has three children and Miss Nannie Sevier, all of Savannah, Tennessee.

Joseph Sevier was killed in the War Between the States at Peach tree Creek, Atlanta, July 22, 1864.

Charles Lyman Sevier

N. Charles Lyman Sevier, son of Valentine Sevier and his second wife, Venerah Cannon Sevier, was born 1847. It will be noted that the name Charles was used in the family of the first wife and also in the family of the second. Charles Lyman Sevier married Julia Brown.

Their children are:

a. Wilbur Lyman Sevier, who married Leta Montague.
b. Henry Brown Sevier, who married Etta ——————.
c. Dr. Joseph Ramsey Sevier, who married Edith Love.
d. Eloisa Venerah Sevier, who married H. H. Shelton.

Henry Valentine Sevier

O. Henry Valentine Sevier, son of Valentine Sevier and his second wife, Vinerah Cannon Sevier, was born 1849. He died —————— He married Isabelle C. McGaughey, daughter of Samuel McGaughey.

Their children are:

a. Samuel Valentine Sevier.
b. Lyman Cannon Sevier.
c. Victor Sevier.

CHAPTER FOUR

Joseph Sevier, Sr.

JOSEPH SEVIER, SR.

JOSEPH SEVIER, son of Valentine Sevier II, the Emigrant, and Joanna Goode Sevier, was born in Rockingham County, Virginia, in 1751. He moved to Tennessee in 1773, arriving on Chris'mas Day, 1773, accompanying his father and four brothers, to join Valentine Sevier III, who was already there. Three sisters were in the party and one sister had been left in Virginia. Joseph Sevier was then twenty-one years of age. His father made a settlement in the Watauga District.

Joseph Sevier served in the Battle of King's Mountain and is mentioned in many histories, including Draper's Kings Mountain and Its Heroes. He is frequently confused with Governor Sevier's oldest son, Joseph Sevier, Jr., who was his namesake. Joseph Sevier, Jr., also served at King's Mountain and in the various Indian campaigns in which Joseph Sevier, Sr., participated. In addition to the service at King's Mountain Joseph, Sr., is mentioned in the Draper Manuscript as in the Indian campaign in the fall of 1778 and he was one of the men who rescued Colonel John Sevier from the hands of General McDowell who held him under arrest, in the absence of the sheriff, at Morgantown, North Carolina. Joseph Sevier, Sr., and his nephew John Sevier, Jr., had a very exciting escape from Indians at one time.

It is said by some that Joseph Sevier, Sr., died in 1826, but even in death he may be confused with his nephew Joseph Sevier, Jr., who died in 1826.

He was only eleven years older than his nephew Joseph and the fact that they were so nearly the same age adds to the constant confusion concerning them. When only the name "Joseph Sevier" appears it is frequently impossible to know which Joseph is meant. Only other circumstances, text and date can solve the riddle, and it cannot always be solved.

Joseph Sevier, Sr., married Charity Keewood. This information as to his marriage was given me by his grandson, Alfred Windle Sevier. However, Bishop Hoss says that Joseph Sever, Jr., married Charity Keewood for his first wife. There is probably an error in this statement, as it seems incredible that two Joseph Seviers married two Charity Keewoods. And yet from various references I think it is quite possible that both of them married into the Keewood family. The Keewoods live not far from the home of Valentine

Sevier II, and were prominent people. Governor Sevier refers in his Journal to his brother Joseph and the Keewoods showing plainly that there was a close connection of some sort. And again in mentioning his son "Joseph and wife" he adds names of the Keewood family , as will be seen in the chapter in this book devoted to Joseph Sevier, Jr., Chapter One of Part Six.

It will be recalled that when the Sevier family moved from Virginia, they arrived in Tennessee, Christmas Day, 1773, at the Keewood Settlement. The family of Valentine Sevier II, remained in that neighborhood, though later John Sevier moved to another location.

Joseph Sevier, Sr., and his wife are buried three miles east of Willow Grove, Tennessee, on Obey River, in Clay County, Tennessee. I do not know whether there is a tombstone or whether there are dates upon it. I have seen his death date given as 1826, but I have no certain knowledge of this and he may have lived much longer. His father willed to Joseph and Abraham Sevier his estate after maintenance to the widow was paid.

Joseph Sevier and Charity Keewood Sevier had at least one son, namely:

Alfred C. Sevier.

Alfred C. Sevier, son of Joseph Sevier, Sr., and Charity Keewood Sevier, was born —————. I do not know for what name his middle initial stood, but Keewood was as frequently spelled Cawood and Caywood as it is spelled Keewood. Alfred C. Sevier married his cousin, Mary Hawkins Windle, daughter of Joseph Hawkins Windle and Joanna Goode Sevier Windle who was the daughter of Governor John Sevier by his second wife Catherine Sherrill Sevier (See Chapter Fourteen of Part Six, this book).

Alfred C. Sevier and his wife, Mary Hawkins Windle Sevier, are buried at Monroe, Tennessee. They had at least two children namely:

A   Joseph Windle Sevier.
B   Amanada Sevier.

Joseph Windle Sevier

A   Joseph Windle Sevier, son of Alfred C. Sevier and Mary Hawkins Windle Sevier, was born —————. He is now living (1924) at Livingston, Tennessee. He married and has five daughters, namely:

Mrs. Lillian Sevier Stewart, Livingston Tennessee.
Mrs. A. E. Speck, Sheridan, Arkansas.
Mrs. J. S. Arms, Celina, Tennessee.
Mrs. John Lee Bowman, Crawford, Tennessee.
Miss Leuce B. Sevier, Livingston, Tennessee.

Amanda Sevier

B   Amanda Sevier, daughter of Alfred C. Sevier and **Mary Hawkins** Windle Sevier, was born _____.._____. She married ————— **Abston** and lives at Willow Grove, Tennessee.

Joseph Windle Sevier gave me this information. He and his sister Amanda are by this record, grandchildren of Joseph Sevier, Sr., which is very close in generation, and his information should therefore be reliable.

CHAPTER FIVE

Abraham Sevier

ABRAHAM SEVIER

ABRAHAM SEVIER, son of Valentine Sevier, the Emigrant, and Joanna Goode Sevier, was born in Rockingham County, Virginia, February 14, 1760. He died June 18, 1841. He went with his father and four brothers to the "Mountains" in 1773, where his elder brother, Valentine Sevier III, had preceded the family.

When he was just twenty years of age he fought in the Battle of King's Mountain and was the youngest of the five brothers who participated in that famous encounter. They were: John Sevier, Valentine Sevier III, Robert Sevier, Joseph Sevier, Sr., and Abraham Sevier. There were two other Seviers in the battle, namely: Joseph Sevier, Jr., and James Sevier, sons of Governor John Sevier.

Valentine Sevier II willed to his sons Joseph and Abraham Sevier his estate after maintenance to the widow was paid.

Abraham Sevier was living in Overton County, Tennessee, in 1832. His pension declaration was made there in 1832 and he died there in 1841. He is on the pension list of 1840, aged 80 years. That agrees with this record of his birth in 1760.

Abraham Sevier married about 1785, Mary Little, of Augusta County, Virginia. She was the daughter of Major-General Little and was born May 14, 1770. She died March 14, 1839.

Abraham and Mary Little Sevier had nine children. It is said they were all born in Overton County, Tennessee.

1. Elizabeth Sevier.
2. Mary Ann Sevier.
3. John Sevier, born January 13, 1795, died September 2, 1795.
4. Jemima Douglass Sevier.
5. Joanna Goode Sevier.
6. Valentine Sevier.
7. Rebecca Richards Sevier.
8. Abraham Rutherford Sevier.
9. Catherine Sherrill Sevier.

Of the foregoing children of Abraham Sevier:

ELIZABETH SEVIER

1. Elizabeth Sevier, daughter of Abraham Sevier and Mary Little Sevier, was born November 12, 1790. She died November 21,

1805. She married ————— Scroggins and left no children, dying at the age of fifteen years, soon after her marriage.

MARY ANN SEVIER

2. Mary Ann Sevier, daughter of Abraham Sevier and Mary Little Sevier, was born December 9, 1792. She died November 21, 1813. She married ————— Hatterman. She died shortly after her marriage, leaving no children.

JOHN SEVIER

3. John Sevier, son of Abraham Sevier and Mary Little Sevier, was born January 13, 1795. He died in infancy, September 2, 1795.

JEMIMA DOUGLASS SEVIER

4. Jemima Douglass Sevier, daughter of Abraham Sevier and Mary Little Sevier, was born August 27, 1786. She died July 3, 1822. It is believed that she died unmarried.

JOANNA GOODE SEVIER

5. Joanna Goode Sevier, daughter of Abraham Sevier and Mary Little Sevier, was born April 5, 1799. She died December 29, 1839. She married Alfred C. Robinson and lived in Tennessee. She left children.

VALENTINE SEVIER

6. Valentine Sevier, son of Abraham Sevier and Mary Little Sevier, was born November 10, 1801. He died January 25, 1842. He married Elizabeth Arnett, in Tennessee, and is said to have had six sons, one of whom died young. The five who lived to maturity were:

A. John Sevier.
B. Annias Sevier.
C. Abraham Sevier.
D. George Sevier.
E. Valentine Sevier, Jr.
F. ————— Sevier, died young.

Of these:

A. John Sevier, son of Valentine Sevier and Elizabeth Arnett Sevier, married ————— and is said to have raised a family in Calhoun County, Illinois.

B. Annias Sevier, son of Valentine Sevier and Elizabeth Arnett Sevier, was born about 1827 and died in Illinois. He married Cornelia Caroline Gunnells, January 9, 1845, Morgan County, Illinois, and had children, among them:

a. Daniel A. Sevier, of Waverly, Illinois, who married ————
and had children, among them: 1 Marian E, Sevier (who married
Frederick E. Deatherage, son of Charles W. Deatherage, September
21, 1904, Morgan County, Illinois); 2, Elizabeth Caroline Sevier
(who married Wayne Leslie Carter, January 1, 1908, Morgan County,
Illinois); 3, John W. Sevier (who married Genevieve Peebles, daughter of William and Bertha Thomas Peebles, February 15, 1915, Morgan County, Illinois); 4, Nellie E. Sevier, of Rushville, Illinois
(who married Morris Hargrove Demaree Fe' rux y 21, 1917 Morgan County, Illinois, and had a son, born April 8, 1822).

b. John D. Sevier, deceased, who married Lizzie Clayton, daughter of Frank and Alpha Jane Clayton, and had several children, one
of whom was Edith Sevier (who married Peter Dawson, son of
Richard and Rebecca Kessler Dawson, November 20, 1901, Morgan
County, Illinois).

c. Charles D. Sevier, who married Margaret Carter, daughter
of N. and Nancy Masters Carter, December 9, 1880, Morgan County,
Illinois.

d. Nathan Sevier, who married Eliza McKay, November 24, 1878,
Morgan County, Illinois, and had several children, including: 1, Nora
Sevier (who married James M. Thompson, son of G. R. and Lydia
Hart Thompson, December 24, 1901, Morgan County, Illinois); 2,
Harriet Pearl Sevier (who married William Sitton, son of James
and Mary Patterson Sitton, November 25, 1905, Morgan County,
Illinois); 3, Vol (Valentine) Sevier (who married Maude Brown,
daughter of Charles and Lucretia Ryman Brown, August 30, 1911,
in Jacksonville, Illinois, and had a son, Charles Brown Sevier).

e. William Sevier, who married Mary Robson, August 3, 1892.

f. Don Manuel Sevier, who married Lilla B. Jones, daughter of
Albert and Luzetta Jones, November 8, 1893, Morgan County, Illinois.

g. Mary Sevier.

h. Nannie E. Sevier, born 1850, died May 12, 1924, Waverly,
Illinois, who married Charles Scott, April 28, 1874, Morgan County,
Illinois. Charles Scott died 1893.

i. Hattie Sevier, married William M. Miller, April 17, 1884, in
Morgan County, Illinois.

C. Abraham Sevier, son of Valentine Sevier and Elizabeth
Arnett Sevier, was born September, 1830, Overton County, Tennessee. He died in battle at Dallas, Georgia, May 25, 1864. He
served in the Union Army. Though born in the South, he had lived
for a long time in Illinois, where he had removed when he was a
boy, when he enlisted in the Union Army. He married Eliza Jane
Asbaugh, January 17, 1848, in Morgan County, Illinois. They had
two children:

a. Christopher Monroe Sevier, born May 19, 1856, married Madge Lee Cou tas, Apr l 29, 1885, and had: 1, Olive A. Sevier, born March 14, 1886; 2, Lois Aileen Sevier, born September 9, 1887 (known as Eva. She married Adolph Seymour, March 1904, Jefferson City, Mo., and had Lucile Seymour, born 1906, Jefferson City, Mo.); Annias Sevier, born January 11, 1890, (known as Nike G .Sevier. He married Margaret Freeman and had no children); 4, Lee Coultas Sevier, born March 8, 1891 (who married Nellie Wagoner in 1916 and had: Nellie Lee Sevier, born 1920); 5, Bertha Emma Sevier, born April 1, 1893, (who married first William Cook, 1909, who died in 1913, leaving William Cook, Jr., born 1911; and married second Ellis Elliott, in 1914, and had James Elliott, born 1916).

b. John H. Sevier, of Waverly, Illinois.

D. George Sevier, son of Valentine Sevier and Elizabeth Arnett Sevier, lived in Morgan County, Illinois.

E. Valentine Sevier, Jr., son of Valentine Sevier and Elizabeth Arnett Sevier, lived in Morgan County, Illinois.

REBECCA RICHARDS SEVIER

7. Rebecca Richards Sevier, daughter of Abraham Sevier and Mary Little Sevier, was born October 20, 1804. She died July 6, 1822, unmarried.

ABRAHAM RUTHERFORD SEVIER

8. Abraham Rutherford Sevier, son of Abraham Sevier and Mary Little Sevier, was born January 12, 1807. He died February 1 / , 1870, near Clinton, Henry County, Mo., at the home of his daughter, Elizabeth Jane Sevier. Abraham Rutherford Sevier marri d about 1830 in Tennessee, Mary Colson, who was born 1808. She died November 16, 1861, in Clinton, Missouri.

Their children were:

A. Mary Susan Sevier.
B. Eliza Jane Sevier.
C. William Palmer Sevier.
D. George Allen Sevier.
E. Rebecca Catherine Sevier.

A. Mary Susan Sevier April 18, 1834, in Tennessee. She died 1917, in Nevada, Missouri. She married John Sartorious, younger brother of the Earl of Sartorious. They had only one child, Anthony Sartorious, who lives at Rich Hill, Missouri. He is married and has children.

B. Eliza Jane Sevier was born December 16, 1835, in Tennessee. She died May 2, 1912, at Clinton, Missouri. She married three times. She married first ———— Sweet, by whom she had two children. She married second Henry Gragg, by whom she had four children. Henry Gragg was born January 27, 1820. He died May 12, 1892. She married third ———— Woods, by whom she had no children. He died shortly after their marriage. Her children were:

a. William Sevier Sweet.
b. Mary Sweet.
c. Catherine Lee Gragg.
d. George Washington Gragg.
e. Dulcenia Gragg.
f. Amos Gragg.

Of these:

a. William Sevier Sweet is unmarried.

b. Mary Sweet married William Walsh and has five chidren: 1, Belle Walsh (who married ————— M Daniel and lives at Rich Hill, Missouri, and has William McDaniel, Lorena McDaniel and John McDaniel); 2, Maggie Walsh (who married Dr. Joseph McDonald, lives at Rich, Missouri, and has four children); 3, Catherine Walsh, who married ————— Jenkins, lives in Oklahoma and has three children); 4, Ora Walsh (who married Roy Pulliam, lives in Sedalia, Missouri, and has three children); and 5, Jeffrey Walsh, who married ————— and has two children).

c. Catherine Lee Gragg was born January, 1865. She married Wylie Alexander and lives at Clinton, Missouri. She has six children, namely: 1, Naomi Elizabeth Alexander (who married ———— ———— and has one child); 2, Mary Ann Alexander (who married ————————); 3, Herbert Alexander; 4, Nina Alexander; 5, Ralph Alexander; and 6, Margaret Alexander.

d. George Washington Gragg, was born December 20, 1867, in Missouri. He married Minnie Roach and had five children, namely: 1, Esther Gragg; 2, Emmett Gragg; 3, Edmund Gragg; 4, Ethel Gragg; and 5, Elbert Gragg.

e. Dulcenia Gragg, called Della, was born October 14, 1870, at Clinton, Missouri. She married Charles Otis Swift, June 16, 1897. They live in Jacksonville, Illinois, and have five children, namely: 1, William Frederick Swift, born August 21, 1900, and 2. Lillian Elizabeth Swift, born March 2, 1902. (She married Roy G. Blauvelt, June 14, 1924, at Springfield, Illinois).

f. Amos Gragg was born July 26, 1879, at Hutchinson, Kansas. He married Leona Waggoner and they live at Apple on, Mo. They have two children, namely: Herbert Gragg, born June 4, 1900, and Maurine Gragg, born November, 1902.

C. William Palmer Sevier, son of Abraham Rutherford Sevier and Mary Colson Sevier, was born February 17, 1843. He l ves in Bu ler Mo. He married Mary Lilly and had four children, namely:

(a) Lucille Sevier.
(b) Minnie Sevier.
(c) John Se ier.
(d) Charles Sevier.

Of these:

(a) Luc lie Sevier, born 1860, lives at St. Joseph, Mo., and has been married twice. She has the Bible of Abraham Rutherford Sevi r.

(b) Minnie Sevier, died in infancy.
(c) John Sev er, died in infan y.
(d) Charles Sevier, died at twenty-thre e.

D. George A len Sevier, son of Abraham Rutherford Sevier and Mary Colson Sevier, was born June 12, 1845, in Overton County, Tennessee. He died April 13, 1874, in Clinton, Missouri. He married Mary Frances Dunn, January 4, 1866. Mary Frances Dunn was born October 8, 1847. She and her husband were among the first settlers in Henry County, Missouri. She married, after George Allen Sevier's death, A. V. Clary and lives (1923) in Henry County, Missouri. George Allen Sevier had four children, namely:

a. James William Sevier.
b. Rose Ellen Sevier.
c. Dora Sevier.
d. Edward Franklin Sevier.

Of these:

a. James William Sevier, was born October 21, 1866, in Henry County, Missouri, died October 11, 1921, in Clinton, Missouri. He married February 15, 1892, Lucella Patt, daughter of J. M. and Martha Patt. Their children are: Walter Franklin Sevier, born January 2, 1894, died in infancy; Mary Sevier, (married Walter Goodman and has one child, Willard Sevier Goodman); Lee Sevier and Bessie Sevier.

b. Rose Ellen Sevier was born June 11, 1868, in Henry County, married William Williams and had two children, John Sevier Williams, deceased, and Sarah Williams, married ———————— Wilson.

c. Dora Sevier, born October 23, 1870, in Henry County, Missouri, now living (1924) in Springfie d, marr ed November 3, 1897, W. G. Martin. Their children are Ray Paul Martin and Ruth Martin, who married William Harbstreet and has William L. Harbstreet and Lula Ray Harbstreet.

d. Edward Franklin Sevier, born November 2, 1872, 'n Henry County, Missouri, lives in Urich, Missouri. He married Clara Barth. Their children are: Arlie May Sevier, born December 5, 1906; Wi l'am Harold Sevier, born October 4, 1908; Ruby Ellen Sevier, born May 21, 1910, and Paul Eugene Sevier, born April 4, 1912.

E. Rebecca Catherine Sevier, daughter of Abraham Rutherford Sevier and Mary Colson Sevier, was born April 6, 1848. She died 1918 in Gridley, California. She married three t'mes. She married first Richard Watson. They had one ch ld, Harriet Wa'son, who was known by her step-father's name, Jeffrey. Harriet married George Daniels and had children. Rebecca Catherine Sevier married second ———————— Jeffrey and had no children, and married th rd ———————— Taylor and had no children.

CATHERINE SHERILL SEVIER

9. Catherine Sherill Sevier, daughter of Abraham Sevier and Mary Little Sevier, was born March 17, 1809. She died September 18, 1861. She married ———————— MacFarland. She lived in Tennessee. Once again the complimentary but confusing habit of naming children for the "in-laws" in the Sevier family has an example. Catherine Sherill Sevier was evidently named for her father's brother's second wife. Governor John Sevier married Catherine Sherill for his second wife and thereafter the Catherine Sherill Seviers are numerous.

MORGAN COUNTY, ILLINOIS, SEVIER MARRIAGES

So many Sevier descendants live in Illinois that the following list of marriages in Morgan County, which has been furnished me by Miss Lucy M. Ball, will prove of value. These persons doubtless are all descendants of Abraham Sevier and Mary Little Sevier.

Sevier, Annias and Mrs. Amanda Louise Weatherford, February 1, 1885.

Sevier, Albert Earl, son of Dan and Lela Jones Sevier, and Mary Bryan Morris, daughter of Richard and Lydia Dennis Morris, November 1, 1915.

Sevier, Mrs. Eliza J., and Wilson Mitchmer, October 14, 1871.

Sevier, Elizabeth, and Charles Hagen, August 9, 1872.

Sevier, Ella E., daughter of Valentine J. and Luvina Lassiter Sevier, and Ananias G. Thompson, son of Sylvester and Minerva Sample Thompson, January 14, 1892.

Sevier, Elizabeth Caroline, daughter of D. A. and Lillie Mills Sevier, and Wayne Leslie Carter, January 1, 1908.

Sevier, Ida, daughter of William T. and Delilah Johnson Sevier, and Frank Graham, son of John and Emily Sevier Graham, April 19, 1875.

Sevier, James, son of Archibald and Emily Medlen Sevier, and Lula Kidd, daughter of John and Mary Joiner Kidd, April 8, 1860.

Sevier, John A., and Amelia Burns. License granted August 28, 1841.

Sevier, John W. and Permelia A. Burns Sevier, and Mattie Timmons, daughter of William and Lucinda Burns Timmons, March 6, 1890.

Sevier, John M., and Charlotte Whitlock, February 21, 1866.

Sevier, John W., son of D. A. and Lillie Mills Sevier, and Bertha Thomas Peebles, February 11, 1915.

Sevier, Martha Ann, and James William Doulton, September 21, 1857.

Sevier, Mary E., and Henry Burch, November 23 ,1869.

Sevier, Laura, and John Austin, July 2, 1884.

Sevier, Nancy M., and James Brown, September 4, 1872.

Sevier, Roy D., son of N. S. and Mary Brown Sevier and Della Wetherbee, daughter of Walter and Nancy Dennis Wetherbee, March 9, 1905.

Sevier, Sarah Frances, and George W. Large, March 13, 1862.

Sevier, Valentine and Mrs. Lavinia Dennis, March 24, 1870.

Sevier, William T., and Delilah T. Johnson, June 4, 1874.

Sevier, W. A., son of John and Parmelia A. Burns Sevier, and Ella M. Ketcham, daughter of Samuel and Mary J. Osborn Ketcham, March 2, 1890.

CHAPTER SIX

Charles Sevier

CHARLES SEVIER

CHARLES SEVIER, son of Valentine Sevier, the Emigrant, and his wife, Joanna Goode Sevier, was born about 1768. I have found only two references to him by name. Mrs. Swift, of Jacksonville, Illinois, who has a copy of Abraham Sevier's Bible record, says that Abraham (son of Valentine II, the Emigrant) mentions a brother Charles. Otherwise the list which she has in the copy of Abraham's Bible record of the children of Valentine Sevier II corresponds with the list of children as given in other records I have found. Her list, however, does not mention either Rebecca or "G. Sevier," who is mentioned by Governor Sevier as being in Nashville, where he visited him. It is of course, possible that the transcriber from the original notes of Governor Sevier's Journal may have changed "C" to "G" and that the apparent reference to a brother named "G." in reality meant for "C." and means Charles.

Records show that Valentine Sevier, the Emigrant, was accompanied to the "Mountains" in 1773 by his five sons, to join his other son, Valentine Sevier III, who was already established there. Four of the five sons were John, Robert, Joseph and Abraham. The other son I have never seen mentioned by name. He was probably young, as Abraham, who was youngest of the five mentioned above, was only thirteen years of age in 1773. It is possible that Charles was the other brother and at that time, being only eight or ten years of age, was not important enough to mention by name. He was evidently too young in 1780 to serve in the Battle of King's Mountain.

February 8, 1794, Governor Sevier says in his Journal, "Charles lay here all night." This reference to an intimate member of the family circle suggests a brother.

In records of the Witt family, collected by Miss Lucy M. Ball, "Bathenia Witt, who was also called Thenia, married Charles Sevier, said to be a brother of Governor John Sevier." Miss Ball, however, has not been able to trace this couple or find whether they had any children. However, a marriage record in Grainger County, Tennessee offers possible clew to this family. The record is Thomas Hart to Nance Sevier, January 11, 1798, and the bond is signed by Charles Sevier. Bathenia is a family name.

As Governor John Sevier's daughter, Nancy, married Walter King, this "Nance" is without a doubt a niece of the Governor and very probably a daughter of Charles.

CHAPTER SEVEN

Catherine Sevier

CATHERINE SEVIER

CATHERINE SEVIER, daughter of Valentine Sevier the Emigrant and Joanna Goode Sevier, appears on some lists of Valentine's children and not on others. George Washington Sevier says that his "father's only sisters were Polly and Catherine," which seems to be sufficient proof that Catherine existed, although he palpably ignored the other sisters. This may be accounted for if he did not include "half-sisters" (for it is quite possible that Valentine Sevier II married and had children before his marriage to Joanna Goode) or he may have meant only living sisters at the time he wrote to Dr. Draper.

Also Catherine may have had a double name and may have been Catherine Elizabeth, for I find both Catherine and Elizabeth as married to William Matlock. (Certainly they may both have married him as first and second wife). William Matlock was living in Elizabethton in 1797. The April term of Court, Carter County, Tennessee. met in the home of William Matlock. In 1797, William Matlock applied for license to keep a tavern. The Matlocks moved to Overton County and were there in 1806.

Valentine Sevier II. in his will dated March 12, 1799, directs his sons, Abraham and Joseph, to pay, one of them forty pounds and one fifty pounds current money to Catherine. wife of William Matlock.

In the Life of Jefferson D. Goodpasture. written by his sons, mention is made of "Governor Sevier's sister, Mrs. Matlock, who was the mother of Valentine Matlock, one time sheriff of Overton County." She evidently named her son for her father, Valentine Sevier II.

The Borden Genealogy, states that John Borden married for his second wife in 1824, Catherine Sevier, daughter of Governor Sevier, (this is manifestly an error, as Governor Sevier's daughter was a generation older) and that his first wife was Catherine Matlock, daughter of William Matlock. It is probable that both wives were of the Sevier blood and that the first wife, Catherine Matlock, was a granddaughter of Catherine Sevier and William Matlock and that the second wife was a granddaughter or a grand niece of the Governor.

Catherine Sevier Matlock and William Matlock had probably four children whose names we know, namely: Valentine Matlock (the sheriff of Overton County); William Matlock, Jr., (whose daughter Catherine must have married John Borden); possibly George Matlock and Charles Matlock.

1. Valentine Matlock.

2. William Matlock, Jr.

3. George Matlock.

4. Charles Matlock.

VALENTINE MATLOCK

1. Valentine Matlock, born possibly about 1780, was sheriff of Overton County, Tennessee.

WILLIAM MATLOCK, JUNIOR

2. William Matlock, Jr., born about 1782, married ——————— and had a daughter, Catherine Matlock, who married John Borden as his first wife about 1818. (See Borden Genealogy below).

GEORGE MATLOCK

3. George Matlock was a deputy sheriff in Overton County.

CHARLES MATLOCK

4. Charles Matlock was a captain in the military department of Overton County at its organization, May 13, 1807.

FROM THE BORDEN GENEALOGY

The Borden Genealogy says:

John Borden, son of John and Mary Echols Borden and great-grandson of Benjamin Borden (to whom Governor Gooch of Virginia granted the 100,000-acre tract of land known as Borden's Manor), married first, Catherine Matlock, daughter of William Matlock, and second, Catherine Sevier, daughter of Governor John Sevier.

They had nine children, namely:

1. Rebecca Borden, born June 26, 1817, married ——————— Alexander.

2. George H. Borden, born October 24, 1819, died 1865.

3. Ann Borden, born September 8 1821, died December 22, 1888, married ——————— Alexander.

4. Elizabeth Borden, born November 5, 1825, died September 5, 1851.

5. Euphemia Borden, born January 4, 1828, died September 16, 1866.

6. William Joseph Borden, born in Benton County, Alabama, May 14, 1830; married Emma Gabriel Gossom, of New Orleans.

Residence, Oxford, Alabama.   Their children were:

a.   Edwin Gosson Borden, born August, 1858, married January 26, 1884, Caroline Moench.   Residence, San Francisco,   Their children are:

(1)   Fredrick William Borden.

(2)   Henry Forney Borden.

(3)   Emma Claudine Borden.

b.   Willie C. Borden, born August, 1859, married ———————— Treadway, of Newman, Georgia.

c.   Malbert Troupe Borden, married December 16, 1890, Mildred A. Harris, daughter of James M. and Mildred A. (McCulloch) Harris,, of Lynchburg, Virginia.   Residence, Cedartown, Ga.   They had Christine Borden.

d.   Pelham Borden, born 1864, married ———————— Harper, of Corsicana, Texas.

e.   Ann Borden, married ———————— Frey, of Newman,Ga.

f.   Ermine B. Borden, married ———————— Martin, of Newman, Ga.

g.   Joseph Borden, born in 1871, died in infancy.

h.   Francis Borden, born in 1871, died in infancy.

i.   Benjamin Borden, born November 8, 1875.

7.   Mary Catherine Borden, born May 2, 1833, married ———————— Bacon (s. p.)

8.   Andrew Campbell Borden, born November 15, 1835, married (1) January 1, 1856, Frances Knighten, (2 December 1, 1859, Frances Buford.   Residence, Dallas, Texas.   Their children were:

a.   Lydia Catherine Borden, born April 26, 1858, died in infancy.

b.   Henry Allen Borden, born October 25, 1860, married Martha Buckingham.   Their children are:

(1)   Adelaide Louise Borden.

(2)   Alberta Lake Borden.

(3)   Henry Grady Borden.

c.   Nancy Lorena Borden, born February 9, 1865, died May 5, 1865.

d.   Lulu Ellen Borden, born March 19, 1866, died June 9, 1867.

e.   Charles Lewis Borden, born June 21, 1868.

f.   Dora Louise Borden, born January 29, 1871, married in Italy, Texas, J. M. D. Trammel.   They had Chesley Trammel.

g.   Euphemia Tate Borden, born October 24, 1873.

h.   John Pickins Borden, born August 30, 1876.

9.   Joel E. Borden, married ———— ————————, of Hope Arkansas, born August 12, 1838 died 1891.   They had Patrick Donnelly Borden.

CHAPTER EIGHT

Polly Sevier

POLLY SEVIER

POLLY SEVIER, daughter of Valentine Sevier the Emigrant and Joanna Goode Sevier, was born in Rockingham County, Virginia, in 1755. She possibly married Robert Rutherford. One of Governor Sevier's sisters married him, I believe.

In Madison, Wisconsin, are letters from George Washington Sevier, son of Governor Sevier, in which he mentions his aunts, "Polly and Catherine."

CHAPTER NINE

Bethenia Sevier

BETHENIA SEVIER

B ETHENIA SEVIER, said to be the daughter of Valentine Sevier, the Emigrant, and Joanna Goode Sevier, was born in Virginia about 17—. She is said not to be one of the three daughters who accompanied Valentine Sevier the Emigrant to "the Mountains" in 1773, but to have followed the family party "after 1773." She married James Hawkins, doubtless of the family of Sarah Hawkins, who was the first wife of Bethenia's brother, Governor John Sevier.

This information concerning Bethenia Sevier came from Mrs. Sophia Hoss French, of Morristown.

CHAPTER TEN

Elizabeth Sevier

ELIZABETH SEVIER

E LIZABETH SEVIER, daughter of Valentine Sevier the Emigrant and his first wife, Joanna Goode Sevier, was born in Rockingham County, Virginia, about 1757. She was possibly named Catherine Elizabeth, as I find both names listed as having married William Matlock. (Of course, two sisters may have married the same man as first and second wife).

In the life of Jefferson D. Goodpasture, written by his sons, mention is made of "Governor Sevier's sister, Mrs. Matlock, who was the mother of Valentine Matlock, one time sheriff of Overton County." She had evidently named her son for her father, Valentine Sevier II.

The Borden Genealogy (see Chapter Seven) states that John Borden married for his second wife in 1824, Catherine Sevier, daughter of Governor John Sevier, (this is manifestly an error, as the Governor's daughter Catherine was a generation older) and that his first wife was Catherine Matlock, daughter, of William Matlock. It is very probable that both wives were of the Sevier blood and that the first wife, Catherine Matlock, was granddaughter of Catherine or Eli abeth Sevier, sister to the Governor, who married William Matlock, and that the second wife was a granddaughter of Governor Sevier instead of a daughter, or possibly a grand-niece of the Governor.

Catherine or Elizabeth Sevier Matlock and William Matlock had, then, very probably, chidren as follows: Valentine, whom we know positively, and William Matlock, Jr., and possibly another, George Matlock. There was also a Charles Matlock.

1. Valentine Matlock, born about 1780.
2. William Matlock, Jr., ——————.
3. George Matlock, ——————.
4. Charles Matlock, ——————.

Valentine Matlock was born about 1780 He was Sheriff of Overton County.

William Matlock, Jr., married —————— and probably had a daughter, Catherine Matlock, who was the first wife of John Borden, marrying him about 1818. See Borden Genealogy in Chaper Seven.

George Matlock was a deputy sheriff.

Charles Matlock was a captain in the military department of Overton County at its organization May 13, 1807.

"William Matlock" was a resident of Elizabethton in 1797. This was probably the husband of John Sevier's sister, either Catherine or Elizabeth.

It is an interesting fact that Valentine Sevier II in his will directed his two sons, Joseph and Abraham, who inherited the residue of his estate, to pay to Catherine Matlock, wife of William Matlock, one forty pounds and the other fifty pounds.

CHAPTER ELEVEN

Sophia Sevier

SOPHIA SEVIER

S OPHIA SEVIER, daughter of Valentine Sevier, the Emigrant, and Joanna Goode Sevier, was born in Rockingham County, Virginia, about 17—. She is said to have married ——————— Peters.

CHAPTER TWELVE

G. Sevier

G. SEVIER

I HAVE found only one reference to "G." Sevier, and that is the reference made by Governor John Sevier in his Journal under date of Sunday, May 7, 1797, in Nashville, Tennessee, when he says: "I met with my brother, G. Sevier." It is, of course, possible that in transcribing the Journal, "C." was mistaken for "G.", and that this reference is intended for Charles Sevier as mentioned in Chapter Ten, Part Three, of this volume.

However, G. Sevier is perhaps the son of Valentine Sevier, the Emigrant, by his second wife, Jemima, as he is not included in any list of Valentine's children by Joanna Goode Sevier.

PART FOUR

Joanna Goode Sevier
Who Married
Younger Landrum, Jr.

JOANNA GOODE SEVIER

Who Married Younger Landrum Jr.

JOANNA GOODE SEVIER was the name, according to several members of the family, of the eleventh child of Colonel Valentine Sevier III and Naomi Douglas Sevier. A descendant writes that she copied the list of children from the family Bible of Colonel Valentine Sevier III, then in possession of his granddaughter, and that Joanna Goode Sevier was the eleventh child. She gives her birth as February 14, 1784. She says, "I know nothing further concerning her." In a letter to Governor John Sevier in 1799, Colonel Valentine Sevier speaks of Joanna when he says. " The rest of my family is well, except Joanna, who is ill of a fever, but not serious."

In Greene County, Tennessee, November 8, 1800, a Joanna Goode Sevier married Younger Landrum, Jr. I have no positive information as to whether she is the Joanna who was the daughter of Colonel Valentine Sevier III. Possibly some other member of the family can give a connecting link that will establish her identity.

I will set down first all the facts relative to her birth and paternity, and then give her record from her marriage to Younger Landrum, from which point everything is clear concerning her.

Joanna is evidently a descendant of Joanna Goode, who married Valentine Sevier II, as she has that full name. Some of the Landrum descendants think that she was the daughter of Governor John Sevier, but that is not possible, as he had a daughter by that name who married Joseph Hawkins Windle and whose full history is given in Chapter Seventeen, Part Six, of this book. The other sons of Joanna, who married Valentine II, are Abraham, Joseph, Robert, Valentine III and a possible Charles. Abraham Sevier had a daughter, Joanna Goode, who married Alfred C. Robertson. Captain Robert Sevier, who was killed at King's Mountain, left two sons only. This leaves it possible that Joseph Sevier, Sr., Valentine Sevier III or Charles Sevier named a daughter Joanna Goode Sevier who grew to maturity and married Younger Landrum, Jr., in 1800. I know nothing of the children of Charles Sevier, if there were any. Of Joseph Sevier, Sr., I know of only one son, Alfred Sevier.

This leaves Colonel Valentine Sevier, who did have a daughter, according to some descendants. named Joanna, who was his eleventh child. As has also been noted, he mentions a Joanna who was a member of his household in 1799.

113

The Secretary of the Historical Society of Missouri, quoting a sketch of Judge Richard Hundley Landrum (1821-1915) by Walter B. Stevens, says that Richard Hundley Landrum's grandmother was Joanna Goode Sevier Landrum, a niece of Governor John Sevier.

However, Rebecca Sevier Rector, in her interviews with Dr. Lyman Draper, never seems to have mentioned a sister as having survived the massacre of 1794, or as living in the same county as Rebecca lived (Greene County, Tennessee), and there rearing a large family; but neither does Rebecca mention her brother John Sevier (Devil Jack), who was in East Tennessee at the time, so he can hardly be said to have literally survived it. Hugh Bell does not mention John and he does not mention Joanna.

Dr. Draper, who was evidently profoundly interested in the massacre and in securing information concerning it, makes no effort, apparently, to interview Joanna's sons and daughters who were living in Greene County when he interviewed Rebecca Sevier Rector. Hugh Bell, who gave a full account of the massacre to Dr. Draper, does not mention Joanna, but he also omits any mention of James, who is mentioned by Rebecca. Senator Ambrose Hundley Sevier, who gives the list of surviving sons when Colonel Valentine Sevier III died in 1800, does not mention either Rebecca or Joanna, although Rebecca was still living in 1848 when he wrote Dr. Draper.

Joanna, if born in 1784, would have been ten years old at the time of the massacre. If she had been merely out of the station, as James and Alexander were, it seems that fact would have been mentioned. If present and surviving that frightful calamity, it seems that she would have been mentioned by someone. Of course, there is the possibility that she was visiting some of the kinspeople, perhaps in East Tennessee, as was the eldest son, John, who is mentioned by Bell and others, though Rebecca, his own sister does not refer to him once in her interview with Dr. Draper.

Joanna's daughter, Elizabeth Landrum Scully, says her mother "died December 4th, 1841,, being in the fifty-fifth year of her age from the fourteenth of February last." This gives the same day of the month as indicated by other descendants, with a discrepancy of two years, an error which may have occurred in transcription.

She named her children some of the Valentine Sevier III family names. Of her six children, four were given names that suggest that family, for instance, "Elizabeth," "Rebecca," "Alexander Sevier" and "William Douglas." I have made an effort to locate among her descendants her family Bible which might give definite information.

Her children and grandchildren were familiar with the details of the massacre, which is an indicaton that Joanna was associated with it. Also her granddaughters, Rebecca Scully Adams and Sarah Turnbull, said their great-grandmother lived to be one hundred years of age. This seems to indicate Naomi Douglass Sevier. Also, Joanna's grandson, Charles K. Hale, said his mother said that her mother, Joanna Goode Sevier Landrum, was reared in Colonel Valentine Sevier's home.

Personally I have no doubt that she was the daughter of Colonel Valentine Sevier III and Naomi Douglass Sevier, but I have no proof to offer.

Joanna Goode Sevier was born February 14, 1784. She died at Warrensburg, Greene County, Tennessee, December 4, 1841, at the home of her daughter, Rhoda Landrum Turnbull. She is buried near by, in the Hawkins cemetery, and her daughter Rebecca Hale is buried beside her.

She married Younger Landrum, Jr., November 8, 1800. (That is the date of the marriage bond; sometimes the ceremony was delayed until later). The marriage took place at Lick Creek Church in Greene County, Tennessee. Younger Landrum, Jr., was the son of Captain Younger Landrum of the Revolution. Another son of Captain Landrum, James Landrum, served under him guarding prisoners of Burgoyne. James Landrum was afterwards a Presbyterian minister. Captain Landrum's company was in Lawson's Brigade of Colonel John Malccmb's Regiment, which assisted in the Guildford Expedition. This information is obtained from the pension declarations of Henry Caswell, Allen Blair and William Turner, who served under Captain Landrum. After the close of the Revolution Captain Landrum and his two sons moved from Amherst County, Virginia, to Greene County, Tennessee, to reside. Captain Landrum died in Greene County.

During the Revolution Younger Landrum Jr. became famous for an exploit that all his descendants know of through family legend. When his company was following the Indians in the Chickamauga Campaign and was located near where Chattanooga is now, several sentries were killed one after another, with apparently no enemy near at hand. Younger Landrum, Jr., volunteered to take the place of the next man assigned to the post. He declared before going out to his duty that he would shoot anything that moved. He kept his word and when a hog came rooting near him shot, with the result that an Indian warrior disguised in a hog's skin went to his happy hunting ground. The adventure made Younger Landrum famous, but his own death followed very soon. He left six children, the youngest being born in 1812, it is said the very year his father died.

The marriage bond of Joanna Sevier and Younger Landrum Jr., is now in the County Clerk's office in Greeneville, Tennessee, and in view of the discussion concerning her, is particularly interesting.

It is dated November 8, 1800.

State of Tennessee:

Greene County

> To any licensed minister of the Gospel regularly called, having care of Souls, or to any Justice of the Peace for said County, etc.

Whereas: Younger Landrum hath this day given bond and security agreeable to an act entitled "an act to establish rules to be observed in Solemnizing the Rites of Matrimony," by the same act being empowered and authorized, I do hereby License you, or any of you, to celebrate the Rites of Matrimony between the said Younger Landrum, and Joanna Sevier, of this County, according to the ceremonies of your respective Church, and agreeable to the rules prescribed in the said act.

> Given under my hand at office the eighth day of November, 1800.

It is said that the marriage took place in Lick Creek Church. It is possible that records of that church, if they have been preserved, would yield further information.

The Greene County census of 1830 gives Joanna Landrum, widow of Younger Landrum, Jr., between forty and fifty years of age. This agrees with the record of her birth in 1784 or 1786.

She died December 4, 1841, and is buried a quarter of a mile from Warrensburg, Tennessee.

Joanna Goode Sevier and Younger Landrum, Jr., had six children, all of whom were born in Greene County, Tennessee. They were:

1. Elizabeth Landrum, born September. 1801.
2. Mary Landrum, called Polly, born January 22, 1803.
3. Rebecca C. Landrum, born December 9, 1805.
4. Rhoda Landrum, born September 7, 1810
5. Alexander Sevier Landrum, born October 24, 1811.
6. William Douglass Landrum, born 1812.

ELIZABETH LANDRUM

1. Elizabeth Landrum, daughter of Joanna Goode Sevier Landrum and Younger Landrum, Jr., was born in Greene County, Tennessee, September 1, 1801. She married October 21, 1824, in Greene County, William Scully. She died December 15, 1859, at Warrensburg, Tennessee. John Scully, the father of William C. Scully, moved from Virginia to Tennessee. William C. Scully died September 25, 1868, the year that his son, William A. Scully, died.

Elizabeth Landrum Scully and William C. Scully had six children, namely:

a. Rebecca Scully.
b. Naomi Scully.
c Ann Elizabeth Scully.

d. William A. Scully.

e. George Scully.

f. Robert Scully.

Of these:

a. Rebecca Scully, daughter of Elizabeth Landrum Scully and William C. Scully, was born about 18—, in Greene County, Tennessee. She married Ezekiel Adams. Their children were: Elizabeth Adams, who married William Francis Robinson and has Lula de Bush Robinson, Anna Mae Robinson, married W. D. Cobble; and Willie Emma Robinson.

b. Naomi Scully, daughter of Elizabeth Landrum Scully and William Scully, was born in Greene County, Tennessee, 18—. She married 18—, Jacob Luttrell. They had a son, William Luttrell, now living (1924) in Morristown, Tennessee.

c. Ann Elizabeth Scully daughter of Eilzabeth Landrum Scully and William C. Sculy, was born 18—.

d. William A Scully, son of Elizabeth Landrum Scully and Wiliam C. Scully, was born in Greene County, Tennessee, July 18, 1827. He died in Greene County in 1868, the same year his father died. He was a Confederate soldier. He married Donna M. Collier and they had at least one daughter. Mary (Mollie) Scully, who married ———————————— Haworth.

e. George Scully, son of Elizabeth Landrum Scully and William C. Scully, was born in Greene County, Tennessee, in 18—.

f. Robert S. Scully, son of Elizabeth Landrum Scully and William C. Scully, was born in Greene County, Tennessee. 18—. He married twice, first Frances Murray and second Jane Williams.

Mary Landrum

2. Mary Landrum, daughter of Joanna Goode Sever Landrum and Younger Landrum, Jr., was called Polly. She married July 15, 1822, Nicolas Hayes Davis. (born in Jefferson County, Tennessee, 1797, died September 20, 1840) son of Nicolas Davis. Mary Landrum Davis died in Jefferson County Tennessee, April 26, 1862. Nicholas Hayes Davis was the son of Lieutenant Nicholas Davis, of Prince Edward County, Virginia, who served three and one-half years in the Revolutionary Army, enlisting twice. He was a British prisoner at Charleston for fourteen months. From Charleston he marched to old Jamestown, where an exchange of prisoners was made. He died in Tennessee in 1843. He married Mary Hayes and his son was given Hayes as a middle name in her honor. He made his pension declaration in Jefferson County in 1823. He came to Tennessee after the Revolution. His wife, Mary Hayes Davis, survived him.

The children of Nicholas Hayes Davis and Mary Landrum Davis were:

a. Miranda Elizabeth Davis.
b. Sarah Jane Davis.
c. Elbert Sevier Davis
d. Samuel Alexander Davis.
e. Margaret Narcissa Davis.
f. Mary A. C. Davis.
g. Rebecca Landrum Davis.
h. James Hayes Davis.

Of the foregoing:

a. Miranda Elizabeth Davis, daughter of Mary Landrum Davis and Nicholas Hayes Davis, was born June 12, 1823. She married John McMillan in 1836. They had at least one son, Horace McMillan, who lives in Knoxville.

b. Sarah Jane Davis, daughter of Mary Landrum Davis and Nicholas Hayes Davis was born November 11, 1824. She married ———————— Parker.

c. Elbert Sevier Davis, son of Mary Landrum Davis and Nicholas Hayes Davis, was born January 23, 1827. He married———————— Campbell.

d. Samuel Alexander Davis, son of Mary Landrum Davis and Nicholas Hayes Davis, was born June 27, 1829, in Greene County, Tennessee. He married Sarah Chaney in 1854. He moved to Illinois to live in 1855 and died in Spring Garden, Illinois, January, 1902. His children were: James Davis, a Methodist minister, married Effie Hoskinson; Mary Davis, married Loyd Browning; Samuel Davis, married Ida Watson; Emma Davis, married Frank Springfield.

e. Margaret Narcissa Davis, daughter of Mary Landrum Davis and Nicholas Hayes Davis, was born in Greene County, Tennessee, August 17, 1831. She died in Jefferson County, Tennessee, in 1918. She married Daniel Carter and had no children.

f. Mary A. C. Davis, daughter of Mary Landrum Davis and Nicholas Hayes Davis, was born September 25, 1833. She married Martin Bennett and had two children who died in infancy.

g. Rebecca Landrum Davis, daughter of Mary Landrum Davis and Nicholas Hayes Davis, was born March 17, 1836. She married in Jefferson County, Tennessee, in 1858, James Duncan Cox, born 1832 died 1889. She died March, 1876. They moved to Jefferson County, Illinois, to reside in 1860. They had six children, namely:

Charles Andrew Cox.
Mary Jane Cox.
Sarah Lavinia Cox.
William Martin Cox.
Albert Franklin Cox.
Samuel Walter Cox.

Of these: Charles Andrew Cox son of Rebecca Landrum Davis Cox and James Duncan Cox was born in Jeffe son County Tennessee, December 24, 1859. He married Alice Clinton, near Spring Garden, Illinois. Their children are Nettie Cox, who married Lycurgus Page and has Valora Page, married to William Cooper, Comaletta Page and Wastenia Page; Vivian Cox, who married Frank Fowler; Tarzel Zoe Cox, who married Asa Kelly and has one son, Stanton Kelly; Ivan Cox, who married Gertrude Wyrick, who died April, 1924, and left a daughter, Betty Jane Cox.

Mary Jane Cox, daughter of Rebecca Landrum Davis Cox and James Duncan Cox, was born February 5, 1861, near Spring Garden, Illinois. In this township she married Thomas Averett Turner, February 8, 1877. He was born in Henry County, Virginia, October 18, 1856. His father, Monroe L. Turner, was a Confederate soldier and died in the Confederate hospital at Richmond, December 24, 1863, at the age of 33. His widow, Martha Leah Turner, came to Belle-rive, Illinois, to her father, Archibald Grant, in 1865, with her family of five children.

The children of Mary Jane Cox (called Janey) and Thomas A. Turner are:

Alva Nola Turner, born February 1, 1878.

Lena Turner, died in infancy.

Rosa Lee Turner, born September 30, 1880, died at the age of twenty-two years.

Charles Andrew Turner, born October 22, 1883, in California.

Sadie Myrtle Turner, born December 1, 1886, in Illinois.

Theodore Turner, born August 11, 1889.

Eva May Turner died at the age of six years.

Evie Forest Turner, born April 3, 1894.

Vara Fay Turner, born August 10, 1896.

Duward Bellmont Turner, died in infancy.

Alva Nola Turner, son of Janey Cox Turner and Thomas A. Turner, was born February 1, 1878. He married Amy E. Neal, Frisco, Iilinois, March 14, 1906, divorced November, 1919. Their children are: Mary Lee Turner, born Waco, Texas, May 5, 1907; Frank Theodore, born Spring Garden, Illinois, May 6, 1909.

Charles A. Turner, son of Janey and Thomas Turner, married Lois Hall at Effingham, Illinois, October 22, 1913. They have a daughter, Dorothy Jane Turner.

Sadie Myrtle Turner, daughter of Janey and Thomas Turner, married Fred Campbell, of Ewing, Illinois. They have one son, Clyde Campbell.

Sargeant Theodore Turner, son of Janey and Thomas Turner. married Ethel (Peggy) Daugherty. He served overseas in the World War.

Evie Forest Turner, daughter of Janey and Thomas Turner, married Dail Johnson.

Sarah Lavinia Cox, daughter of Rebecca Landrum Davis Cox and James Duncan Cox, was born 1867, near Spring Garden, Illinois. She married John Judson Monroe, of Mount Vernon, Illinois. Their children were: James Oliver Monroe, who married Fredda Kosch, and has children: John Judson Monroe, Oliver Monroe, Jr., and Thomas Warren Monroe; Blanche Monroe, who married Cleve Hester; Shelton Monroe, who died young; Raymond Monroe, who married Lucia Fisher; Floy Monroe, Ruth Monroe and Olive Monroe.

William Martin Cox, son of Rebecca Landrum Davis Cox and James Duncan Cox, was born 18—. He married Zettie Hammond. Their children are: Leo Cox, who married Ruth Dial; Otto Cox, who married Lura Lawson; Aline Cox, twin to Irene, married Joseph Kelly; Irene Cox, twin to Aline, married Dr. Harvey Wade; Aud Cox and Claude Cox.

Albert Franklin Cox, son of Rebecca Landrum Davis Cox and James Duncan Cox, was born ——————. He married first Marie Hubbard and married second —————— Howard. He has two sons, Howard Cox and —————— Cox.

Samuel Walter Cox, son of Rebecca Landrum Davis Cox and James Duncan Cox, is in the regular army.

h. James Hayes Davis, son of Mary Landrum Davis and Nicholas Davis, was born February 23, 1839. He died in Jefferson City, Tennessee, in 1917. He married Belle Rannin. Among their children were: John Davis, Dr. Elbert Davis, Fanny Davis, Bert Davis and Christopher Davis.

REBECCA C. LANDRUM

3. Rebecca C. Landrum, daughter of Younger Landrum, Jr., and Joanna Goode Sevier Landrum, was born December 9, 1807, in Warrensburg, Greene County, Tennessee. She married Captain Joseph Hale, (born 1796,) of the War of 1812, as his second wife. They both died in the year 1873. Their children were:

a. James Hale.
b. George Sevier Hale.
c. Charles Keith Hale.
d. Younger Hale.
e. John Hale.

Of these:

George Sevier Hale who was a Confederate soldier, son of Rebecca Landrum Hale and Captain Joseph Hale, married first, Nancy Jones, and second, Catherine Smith. He has a son, Joseph Hale.

Charles Keith Hale, son of Rebecca Landrum Hale and Captain

Joseph Hale, married Margaret Evans. They had at least two children, Dr. Walter Keith Hale and Dr. Emma Hale. Charles Keith Hale died in Spartanburg, South Carolina, July 3, 1923.

Younger Hale, son of Rebecca Hale and Captain Joseph Hale, married Jennie Scruggs.

RHODA LANDRUM

4. Rhoda Landrum, daughter of Joanna Goode Sevier Landrum and Younger Landrum, Jr., was born in Greene County, Tennessee. September 7, 1810. She died May 7, 1889. She married James Turnbull, called Turnbill by some of his descendants. They had five children:

a. John Turnbull.

b. Joseph Turnbull.

c. James Turnbull.

d. Rebecca Turnbull.

e. Sadie Turnbull.

ALEXANDER SEVIER LANDRUM

5. Alexander Sevier Landrum, son of Joanna Goode Sevier Landrum and Younger Landrum, Jr., was born 1811, in Greene County, Tennessee.

Alexander Sevier Landrum died in Tennessee in Jefferson County August 19, 1848, being only 37 years old. His wedding suit was made by Andrew Johnson, then a tailor of Greeneville, afterwards President of the United States.

Alexander Sevier Landrum married Anna Reams. Their children were:

a. William Bartlett Landrum, born 1832.

b. Richard Hundley Landrum, born 1834.

c. James Landrum, died young.

d. Durthulia Landrum, born 1842.

e. David Landrum, born 1844.

f. Rebecca Landrum, born 1847.

Of these: William Bartlett Landrum, son of Alexander Sevier Landrum and Anna Reams Landrum was born 1832, died 1903. He married twice, first ————————— and second Louisa Matilda Ryan. Their daughter, Olive Elizabeth Landrum, married Norman B. Pearman, who was a Major in the Army overseas, during the World War.

Richard Hundley Landrum, son of Alexander Sevier and Anna Reams Landrum, was born 1834. He died in Missouri, where he was very prominent, a Judge and for many years in the legislature.

WILLIAM DOUGLAS LANDRUM

6. William Douglass Landrum, son of Joanna Goode Sevier Landrum and Younger Landrum, Jr., was born in Greene County, Tennessee, March 1812. His name indicates descent frcm Naomi Douglass Sevier, and recalls also one of her twin sons, Robert and William, who were killed by Indians. William Douglass Landrum was only three months old when his father volunteered for the War of 1812. William Douglas Landrum married Martha Ann Owens. Both died and are buried in Nashville, Tennessee. Martha Ann Owens Landrum, died in 1866. Their children were:

a. Richard Alexander Landrum.
b. William Nicholas Landrum.
c. Thomas Irwin Landrum.
d. James Younger Landrum.
e. Cornelius Valentine Landrum.
f. George Henry Landrum.
g. Robert Houston Landrum.
h. Mary Catherine Landrum.

Of these: Richard Alexander Landrum, son of William Douglass Landrum and Martha Ann Owens Landrum, married ——————— Rowe, in Talledega, Alabama. They had a large family.

Willam Nicholas Landrum, son of William Douglass Landrum and Martha Owens Landrum, married ——————— Seahorn. His children live near Morristown, Tennessee.

Thomas Irwin Landrum, son of William Douglass Landrum and Martha Owens Landrum, served in the Confederate Army. He married ——————— Morgan. After her early death he married Elizabeth Broadus, of Louisville, Kentuckey. They both died there in 1921. They had seven children:

(1) Henry Landrum, deceased; (2) Mattie Landrum, who married Reverend A. V. Sizemore; (3) John Thomas Landrum, who married Jennie Elizabeth Nenenirk and has one daughter Dorothy Landrum; (4) Robert Owen Landrum, who married first——————— Blankenbaker and had one son, Robert Owen Landrum, Jr., and married second ——————— and has no children; (5) William Clarence Landrum, who married ——————— Tigh, and has several children; (6) Oscar Broadus Landrum; (7) ——————— Landrum, who married Robert S. Weaver in Sterling, California and has one child.

James Younger Landrum, son of William Douglass Landrum and Martha Ann Owens Landrum, never married.

Cornelius Valentine Landrum, son of William Douglass Landrum and Martha Owens Landrum, was born in 1844. He is the only living (1924) grandchild of Joanna Goode Sevier Landrum and Younger

Landrum, Jr. He married tw'ce, first Annie E. Netherland, who lived three years only, leaving a son, Rufus E. Landrum, who lives in Nashville. Cornelius Valentine Landrum married for his sec nd wife Lovinia Parker, who lived less than five years. Her children were Mabel Landrum, married ——— ——————— ——— and died at twenty-four, and George H. Landrum.

George Henry Landrum, son of William Douglass Landrum and Martha Ann Owens Landrum, married ——————————.

Robert Houston Landrum, son of William Douglass Landrum and Martha Ann Owens Landrum, married ——— Stone. They had two children, a son and a daughter. The son married and died. His widow and a daughter live in Missouri.

Mary Catherine Landrum, daughter of William Douglass Landrum and Martha Ann Owens Landrum, married ——————— Talbot and had two children.

PART FIVE

Governor John Sevier

His First Wife
Sarah Hawkins Sevier

and

His Second Wife
Catherine Sherrill Sevier

CHAPTER ONE

Governor John Sevier

GOVERNOR JOHN SEVIER

P IONEER, soldier, statesman, and one of the founders of the Re-
ublic; Governor of the State of Franklin; six times Governor of
Tennessee; four times elected to Congress; the typical pioneer
who conquered the wilderness and fashioned the State; a projector and
a hero of King's Mountain; thirty-five battles, thirty-five victories."

John Sevier, first child of Valentine Sevier I and Joanna
Goade Sevier, was born September 23, 1745, in what was then known
as Augusta County, Virginia, and is now Rockingham County, about
six miles west of New Market on the old stage road between Staunton and Lexington, Va. He was sent to Staunton to school and
there he acquired a fair education, and he learned also in his youth
the outdoor sports and skill that stood him in good stead in after
years. While he was still a youth at school in Staunton, he began
the romantic career which he followed during all his years, for he
fell into a mill race and was rescued by a young lady, Miss Anne
Paul, who afterwards became the second wife of Governor George
Matthews, of Georgia.

When he was sixteen, he left school, married and set up for
himself. His wife was a school mate, Sarah Hawkins, and only
fifteen years of age. They went immediately to housekeeping and
very soon after their marriage John Sevier purchased land and laid
out a village which he called New Market. He resided there for a
period of ten years. At the close of the French and Indian War he
saw military service and was given a Captain's commission in 1772,
by Lord Dunmore, the last royal Governor of Virginia. He is said
to have survived, with his usual romantic good fortune, death in an
ambuscade at this time.

With a gift for success in any line, John Sevier prospered as a
merchant in the town which he had built, and had accumulated a
comfortable fortune when he felt the lure of the "Mountains" and,
after two trips to the country we now know as Tennessee he decided
to move his family to the new land. He made his first trip in 1770.
In 1772, he attended a horse race at Wautauga Old Fields. His
brother, Valentine Sevier III, was already settled in the "Mountains" and enthusiastic about the country. After the trip of 1772, John

Sevier decided to settle in the new country and he persuaded his father's family to journey with him. I imagine that Joanna Goode Sevier had passed away before this time, as no mention is made of her in the wholesale removal of the two families. She was alive in August 1773, however, as she is mentioned as a witness in the Augusta County, Va., Abstracts.

The group included John Sevier, his wife and several children, Valentine Sevier II and four other sons, Abraham, Joseph, Robert and Charles (?) and four daughters whose names are not recorded. The statement is made that one of Valentine's daughters remained in Virginia. One son, Valentine III, was already in the "Mountains."

The caravan arrived in Keewood settlement in the "mountains" on Christmas day, December 25, 1773, after a tiresome wagon trip of three hundred miles. Keewood is variously spelled, Keewood, Keywood, Cawood, and Caywood. Francis Turner's Life of John Sevier says that upon arrival each family went to its own cabin. The settlement was six miles from Shelby's. Later the Seviers abandoned the Keewood Settlement and moved to Washington County.

Sarah Hawkins Sevier lived just a few weeks more than seven years in the new country. She died in January or February 1780. Several historians, including Wheeler of North Carolina, give 1779 as the date of her death, but I believe 1780 is right. George Washington Sevier, the first son by John Sevier's second marriage, says that she died in "Washington County, (East Tennessee) 1780."

In 1776 John Sevier moved his family to the north bank of the Watauga, three miles above Elizabethton, and in 1778 to the south bank of the Nolichucky, about ten or twelve miles from Jonesboro.

John Sevier was at the time of his removal to Tennessee, comparatively a rich man for the period and place. He might have continued his successful business career. Instead he gave himself almost wholly from that time to public service, and though he died a poor man, he died a great man, and he gave to us, who follow after, a great state, and to his country a great territory, for all historians unite in yielding him great credit for the Winning of the West.

Even before his permanent settlement in the new country he had been chosen as one of the leaders, for in 1772 he was elected one of the thirteen commissioners of the Watauga Aassociation and one of the five judges. This was the first free organized government in the world.

In the first military movements in which Tennesseans took part, the expedition to Point Pleasant, 1774, John Sevier was not present. His brother, Valentine Sevier III, was conspicuous, and his brother Robert Sevier was also a participant.

The first general outbreak of the Cherokees occurred in midsummer, 1776. The Battle of Long Island Flats, near Kingsport, Tennessee, took place July 20, 1776, and Fort Lee was assaulted July 21, 1776. Fort Lee is near Elizabethton. It was at Fort Lee and on this date that the famous incident of Catherine Sherrill having a hairbreadth escape from the Indians took place, when she leapt the stockade and was caught in the arms of John Sevier.

In 1776, the inhabitants of the Watauga District, after repelling the Indians, but having suffered severe losses, prayed the Government of North Carolina to annex the district. The petition was received at Raleigh, August 22, 1776. John Sevier prepared the paper according to Dr. Ramsey, who found the document in the North Carolina archives. He says: "It appears to be in the handwriting of one of the signers, John Sevier, and is probably his own production."

November 12, 1776 the Provincial Congress of North Carolina met at Halifax and among other delegates were John Carter, John Haile and John Sevier as elected delegates from the "across the Mountain" territory, already called Washington district, though it received later the formal title of the County of Washington. A year and a half later the first session of the Court of Washington County was held, February 23, 1778, with twently-three justices present. Colonel John Carter was elected chairman. Valentine Sevier III (he is called Jr. in the record, but in this history, owing to there being many Valentines he is distinguished as Valentine III) was elected Sheriff and John Sevier clerk. John Sevier retained the clerkship of Washington County until he was elected Governor of Franklin, when his second son, James Sevier, became the Clerk of Washington County and retained that office for the extraordinary term of fifty-seven years. Some records say that he was clerk for forty-seven consecutive years but either number establishes a record.

John Sevier was the first citizen in the community. He was the leader in all enterprises and his Indian warfare was making him famous. In the summer of 1780, a part of his regiment, under the command of Major Charles Robertson, Captain Valentine Sevier III, and Captain Robert Sevier, accompanied Colonel Isaac Shelby to the aid of the patriots in South Carolina. This regiment served in the Battles of Thicketty Fort and Musgrove's Mills. Major Patrick Ferguson of the British Army was incensed by this action on the part of the Mountaineers and he sent word to them that if they did not immediately lay down their arms he would burn the country clean and hang the leaders!

The message served but to inflame them against the British commander instead of intimidating them as he had intended. The word was carried by Samuel Phillips, a parolled prisoner, to Shelby, who was living in Sullivan County. Shelby rode at once forty or fifty miles to John Sevier's residence to consult with him, and the result of that conference was the assembling of the Mountain men at Sycamore Shoals and the march to King's Mountain.

The credit of the first plan for the campaign of King's Mountain is due to Shelby and Sevier. All historians unite on this point.

The story of King's Mountain fills us with unspeakable admiration. Every man in the mountains responded to the call of Shelby and Sevier and the first draft in American history had to be resorted to, not to determine which men should go to battle, but to decide which men should stay at home as the women and children could not be left unprotected.

Of the battle itself we have not space here to tell the story in full. Campbell, Shelby and Cleveland made an official report of it a few days later, Sevier leaving immediately after the battle for a raid against the Indians who took that opportunity of course to threaten the settlement. The report says that the right wing of the American forces commanded by Col. Sevier was first to reach the summit of the Mountain and "obliged the enemy to retreat along the top of the mountain to where Col. Cleveland commanded."

Whole families participated in the King's Mountain Battle. It is not surprising that there were seven Seviers in it when one thinks of the military spirit of their blood and the history of their participation in war and military operations for centuries. John Sevier was a Colonel; Robert Sevier was a Captain and was mortally wounded; Valentine Sevier III was a Captain. Abraham Sevier was a private and Joseph Sevier Sr., brother of Governor Sevier, was a private. John Sevier's two eldest sons, Joseph Sevier, Jr., and James Sevier were privates. In addition John Sevier's brothers-in-law were present and several of the young men who were either then or later married to his daughters, were present. So King's Mountain for the Seviers was quite a family party!

After the successful close of that engagement John Sevier went out immediately on an Indian campaign. Upon arriving at his home from King's Mountain, he had only one hour's rest out of the saddle! His sons and many of the men of the regiment followed him in this campaign, also.

In August, 1781, Sevier and Shelby and their men crossed the Mountains again, at the insistence of General Nathaniel Greene, who sent a request for help. They joined Francis Marion and participated in the military operations in South Carolina for several months. Ramsey's Annals says:

"A large number of negroes and a vast amount of other property were taken from Georgia and South Carolina and carried away. But to the honor of the troops under Sevier and Shelby no such captives or property came with them into the country of their residence; their integrity was as little impeached as their valor. They came home enriched by no spoils, stained with no dishonor, enriched only by an imperishable fame, an undying renown and an unquestionable claim to the admiration and gratitude of their countrymen and posterity. This has been accorded to them by a consent almost unanimous. The authorities of the states in whose service they were employed conceded it to them. The officers who commanded them asserted it for them."

John Sevier's Indian Campaigns are a part of Tennessee history; their full story would require a volume, and it required for him almost his whole time for twenty years. This includes the time of his arrival in "the Mountains," to permanently reside at the close of the year 1773, to the Etowah Campaign, in 1793. He was always victorious. There is no other commander in any war who was always victor. He served in so many campaigns that it would be impossible to really name or number them and he actually fought thirty-five battles with the Indians and never lost a battle. His plan was to be always aggressive, to strike quick and hard. Roosevelt says of him:

"For many years he was the best Indian fighter on the border. He was far more successful than Clarke, for instance, inflicting greater loss on his foes and suffering much less himself, though he never had anything like Clarke's number of soldiers. His mere name was a word of dread to the Cherokees, the Chickamaugas and the upper Creeks. He combined a cool head with a dauntless heart; he loved a battle for its own sake, and was never so much at ease as when under fire; he was a first class marksman and as good a horseman as was found upon the border. He was almost the only commander upon the frontier who ever brought an Indian War of whatever length to an end, doing a good deal of damage to his foes and suffering very little himself."

Tradition is authority for the belief that John Sevier was the handsomest man on the frontier. His son, George W. Sevier, describes him to Dr. Draper: "He was five feet, nine inches high, well proportioned and straight. He weighed one hundred and ninety pounds. He had a long face, and a broad, high forehead. He had deep blue eyes, an aquiline nose and a fair complexion.

He had the extraordinary power of winning the multitude and was simply adored in the Mountain country. He made few enemies; those few, however, were powerful and mighty: Andrew Jackson, Archibald Roane, John Tipton. Someone writing of him says: "He knew how to be gracious and condescending, but he possessed at the same time a reserve of personal dignity upon which no one ventured to trespass. His courage was indisputable; he fought every fight to a finish. But for all that he was essentially a man of peace, hating strife and loving quietness and ease. From his youth up, in spite of all statements to the contrary, he was strictly temperate in his habits, never touching tobacco in any form and rarely making use of any liquor."

The historian Phelan has thus summed up Sevier's attainments:

"John Sevier is the most prominent name in Tennessee history. And within these limits and upon this field he is the most brilliant military and civil figure the state has ever produced. Jackson attained a larger fame in a broader field of action, and perhaps his mental scope may appear to a wider horizon to those who think his statesmanship equal to his generalship. But the results he accomplished affected the history of Tennessee only in so far as it formed a part of the United States. Sevier, however, was purely a Tennessean. He fought for Tennessee, he defended its boundaries, he watched over and guarded it in its beginning, he helped form it and he exercised a decisive influence on its development. The basis of Sevier's character was laid in sincerity, in truth, and in honor. He was loved because he had a loving heart. The gentle word, the quick sympathy, the open hand, the high purpose, the dauntless courage, the impetuosity, the winning suavity, were the wings and the turrets and the battlements of a magnificent and harmonious structure. Energy, ability, and determination can accomplish many feats, and cunning can simulate many effects. But the tender and the true and the loyal heart is beyond their power. This may not be counterfeited, and its deficiency cannot be supplied. The most beautiful trait of Sevier's character was the exquisite sweetness of his disposition."

Roosevelt, who is not too enthusiastic about Sevier, nevertheless pays him a remarkable tribute which deserves to be quoted in full. He says:

"Sevier, who came to the Watauga early in 1772, nearly a year after Robertson and his little colony had arrived, differed widely from his friend in almost every respect save high-mindedness and dauntless, invincible courage. He was a gentleman by birth and breeding, the son of a Huguenot who had settled in Shenandoah valley. He had received a fair education, and though never fond of books, he was, to the end of his days, an intelligent observer of men and things, both in America and in Europe. He corresponded on intimate terms and equal terms with Madison, Franklin, and others of our most polished statesmen; while Robertson's letters, when he had finally learned to write them himself, were almost as remarkable for their phenomenally bad spelling as for their shrewd common sense and straight forward honesty. Sevier was a very handsome man; during his lifetime he was reputed to be the handsomest man in Tennessee. He was tall, fair-skinned, blue-eyed, brown haired, of slender build, with erect military carriage and commanding bearing; his lithe, finely proportioned figure being well set off by the hunting shirt which he almost invariably wore. From his French forefathers he had inherited a gay, pleasure-loving temperament that made him the most charming of companions. His manners were polished and easy, and he had great natural dignity. Over the backwoodsmen he exercised an almost unbounded influence, due as much to his ready tact, invariable courtesy, and lavish, generous hospitality as to the skill and dashing prowess which made him the most renowned Indian fighter of the South West. He had an eager, impetuous nature, and was very ambitious, being almost as fond of popularity as he was of Indian fighting. He was already married and the father of two children when he came to Watauga, and, like Robertson, was seeking a new and better home for his family in the West. So far his life had been as uneventful as that of any other spirited young borderer; he had taken part in one or two unimportant Indian skirmishes. Later he was commissioned by Lord Dunmore as Captain in the Virginia Line."*

To detail the history of John Sevier would require volumes and involve the whole history of Tennessee, and indeed all of that history so aptly called by Roosevelt "The Winning of the West." Only a few opinions of the Great Tennessean and a few salient facts in his life can be recorded here. A leader, the foremost citizen in the community, he was elected Governor of the State of Franklin at its inception and remained its guiding influence throughout its life. As its term of existence shortened and a lesser domain was included in its boundaries he became Captain General of Franklin. When Franklin no longer existed and he was an outlaw and debarred by the great State of North Carolina from holding office, the people elected him to the North Carolina Legislature, a piece of bravado which must have shocked the North Carolinians, though it was justified when the Legislature repealed its former act and permitted the late Captain General and Governor of the Lost State of Franklin to take his seat.

He was elected to Congress and served two terms.

When Tennessee became a state in 1796, John Sevier was looked upon by the whole populace as the coming Governor. He was elected and was twice re-elected, serving three terms of two years each. Being then ineligible by the constitution to another term he retired to private life. Archibald Roane served a term of two years as Governor. At the close of Governor Roane's administration,

---

*Roosevelt is in error regarding the number of children, for John Sevier and Sarah Hawkins Sevier had five or six children at this time. The date of Lord Dunmore's commission to John Sevier, was given in 1772, before he removed to "The Mountains," not afterwards.

John Sevier, having become eligible again, was re-elected to the office and once again served three terms—six years, making twelve years in the chair as Governor of Tennessee, with a previous administration of the Governorship of Franklin for a period of four years. Few men have received such an extraordinary mark of the appreciation and confidence of a people.

He was re-elected to Congress in 1811 and served four years. In 1815 he was re-elected to his seat in Congress without his knowledge, being then in Alabama as a Commissioner to establish the Creek Boundary Line.

President Madison had appointed him one of the Commissioners for the Creek Boundary Line in 1815 and on that service he died. He was buried where he died on the east bank of the Talapoosa River near Fort Decatur, with honors of war, by Captain William Walker.

John Sevier was never wounded in all his remarkable career, but at Boyd's Creek he had what might be called a close shave, for a lock of his hair was cut off by a rifle ball, at the Battle of Boyd's Creek.

John Sevier is identified with the religious and educational life of the South as well as with its military history and civil government, for he contributed to Church and School in a large way. He gave three acres for the site for a Baptist Church in the new town of New Market, which he established, and built the Church. He was then scarcely more than a boy in years, for he established the town of New Market shortly after he was sixteen years old. In Tennessee he built a Presbyterian Church near the site of his home.

He was one of the incorporators of Blount College, now the University of Tennessee, and introduced the bill for its establishment. He was a trustee of Washington College. These two institutions were the first institutions of learning west of the Alleghany Mountains.

He died in 1815, September 24, in Fort Decatur, Ala., being one day past his seventieth year. He was buried there but later his body was removed to the Court House Square in Knoxville, where a tall shaft stands to mark the spot for all time.

CHRONOLOGY
LIFE OF
John Sevier

1745 September 23, born in Virginia.

1761 Married Sarah Hawkins.

1761 Established town of New Market, Virginia.

1772 Lord Dunmore gave him a Captain's Commission.

1772 Elected one of thirteen Commissioners and one of five judges of Watauga Association, though not then a resident of Watauga.

1773 Christmas Day. Arrived in Watauga to make his home in what we now know as Tennessee.

1776 July 21. Fort Lee was assaulted. He saved Catherine Sherrill. The famous incident resulted in her nick-name, Bonny Kate.

1776 August. Watauga Association prayed North Carolina to annex the territory. John Sevier prepared the paper.

1777 Represented Watauga in North Carolina Territory.

1779 Aggressive Indian Campaigns.

1780 January (or February) Sarah Hawkins Sevier died.

1780 August 14, Married Catherine Sherrill.

1780 October 7. Battle of King's Mountain.

1780 Important Indian Campaigns, Chickamauga, Lookout Mountain.

1784 August 23. Presided at Jonesboro Convention.

1784 November. Appointed Brigadier General of Militia for Washington District.

1784 State of Franklin organized.

1784 Elected Governor of Franklin.

1785 March 1. Took Oath as Governor of Franklin.

1785 Fall of year. Concluded Indian Treaty

137

1786   September. United with Georgia against Creeks.

1787   Made member of Society of Concinnati.

1787   June 24. Asks mediation of Georgia between North Carolina and Franklin.

1788   Warrant issued by North Carolina for High Treason. Arrested at Jonesboro. On trial at Morgantown, North Carolina. Dramatic rescue at Morgantown. Returned with his rescuers to Tennessee.

1788   November 21. Debarred from Office by the North Carolina Assembly.

1788   Captain-General of State of Franklin.

1788   Fall of the State of Franklin.

1789   Elected to Assembly of North Carolina.

1789   November. North Carolina repealed act of November 1788 and Sevier took his seat in Assembly and was reinstated Brigadier General.

1790   March. Elected to Congress from Washington District, embracing all present State of Tennessee.

1790   April 2. United States having accepted deed from North Carolina, what is now Tennessee ceased to be a part of North Carolina.

1790   June 17. John Sevier took his seat in Congress.

1790   William Blount having been appointed Governor of the United States Territory South of the Ohio, recommended Sevier as Brigadier General of Washington District and President George Washington made the appointment.

1796   May 6. He was admitted to the Bar by Gov. William Blount.

1796   Tennessee becomes a State.

1796   Sevier having been elected Governor of Tennessee takes Oath March 30. Serves three terms, (six years) all that is allowed by Constitution.

1803   Re-elected Governor of Tennessee; again serves six years, limit of Constitutional eligibility.

1811   Elected to Congress. Serves four years.

1815   Re-elected to Congress without his knowledge.

1815   Appointed by President Madison one of the Commissioners to establish the Creek Boundary line.

1815   September 24, died at Fort Decatur, Ala.

CHAPTER TWO

Sarah Hawkins

SARAH HAWKINS

S arah Hawkins, who was the first wife of John Sevier, was born about 1746 in Virginia. She was the daughter of Joseph Hawkins and his wife, Anneke Jane Edwards Hawkins.

She married John Sevier in 1761 when she was only fifteen years of age. They went immediately to housekeeping and John Seiver soon established a township called New Market. Their first child, Joseph Sevier, was born in 1762. He was named for Sarah Hawkins' father. John Sevier's brother, Joseph Sevier, was only ten or eleven years older. Much confusion has resulted because of the similar names of these two young Seviers.

After they had lived in the village of New Market for about ten years, John Sevier became interested in the new country to which his brother, Valentine Sevier I.I, had removed and he made two trips to visit this brother and inspect the country. In 1772 on the second of these trips he had evidently decided to make his home there for he was elected a Commissioner of the Watauga Association in that year. In 1773 he removed his family and they arrived in the new settlement, Christmas Day, 1773. Roosevelt says they removed with two children, but there were then more than two children, perhaps five or six.

Sarah Hawkins lived a short seven years in the new country, dying in January or February, 1780, in Washington County. Several historians give her death in 1779, and some historians say she never moved to Tennessee from Virginia, but George Washington Sevier, her stepson, said she died in January or February 1780, in Washington County, in what is now East Tennessee. I imagine that she is buried in one of the old graveyards near Jonesboro, though it would be impossible at this time to identify the grave.

When the dust of Bonny Kate was removed from Alabama where she had lain for nearly ninety years, to lie beside her husband in the Knox County Court House grounds, where were many who thought that Sarah Hawkins should also be moved and the same honor paid to her. The circumstances, however, were very different, for Bonny Kate's grave had been marked at her death and her grave place was well known. Sarah Hawkins died more than fifty years earlier than Bonny Kate, and the grave was not known. Removal under the circumstances would have been literally impossible.

The following interesting data concerning the early history of the Hawkins family has been compiled by Mrs. Sessler Hoss (Irene Ewing Morrow) of Muskogee, Okla. Mrs. Hoss found this valuable information in the course of her research work. She calls attention to the fact that the record as here printed gives Joseph Hawkins' daughter who married John Sevier as "Susan" Hawkins, whereas, all Sevier records mention her as Sarah. In this record Sarah is mentioned as having married Mr. Graham, of Winchester, Virginia. This is quite probably an accidental transposition made by the early chroniclers. It is somewhat curious that Mr. A. W. Putnam, the eminent historian, who was a grandson-in-law of Governor John Sevier, (having married the daughter of George W. Sevier,) gives the name of Governor Sevier's first wife as Susan Hawkins. Otherwise all historians agree upon her as Sarah Hawkins. He may have had a copy of this Hawkins genealogy and have been misled by it.

The marriage of Jane Hawkins to Col. Richard Campbell is interesting as it gives the parentage of Richard Campbell, who married Catherine Sevier, daughter of Governor John Sevier by his second wife, Bonny Kate Sherrill. Richard Campbell Jr., was thus first cousin to Catherine's half brothers and sisters, and they were first cousins also to Tennessee's famous hero, who gave his life in the Alamo, Davy Crockett.

The record supplied by Mrs. Hoss is as follows:

Three brothers, Joseph, Benjamin, and Samuel Hawkins came to America from England in 1658, settling in Gloucester and Matthew Counties, Va., which were then a part of Maryland. Another brother, John, followed in 1691 and settled in Massachusetts. The fifth came the same year but died shortly afterwards.

Samuel Hawkins had three sons:

Joseph
Benjamin
Samuel

Joseph (son of Samuel, the emigrant) was born in 1712 and married the Quakeress, Anneke Jane Edwards, in 1739. All four of their sons served in the Revolution.

Their children were:
Benjamin
Joseph
Richard
Samuel
Jane, married Col. Richard Campbell.
Susanna, married John Sevier, first Governor of Tennessee.
Rebecca, married John Crockett. "Davy" was their son.
Sarah, married Mr. Graham, of Winchester, Va.
Mary, married John Byrd, of Virginia.
Caroline, married Mr. Wyndall, of Virginia.

Samuel, son of Joseph and Anneke J. Edwards Hawkins, married Christian Worthington and had nine children, all five of the sons serving in the War of 1812.

Joseph
Benjamin
Samuel
Byrd
John J.
Lydia
Sara
Rebecca
Eleanor

John J. Hawkins, son of Samuel and Christian W. Hawkins, had six children:

Samuel, born 1811
Benjamin, W., born 1816
Christiana, born 1816
Joseph C., born 1818.
Nathan B., born 1812.
Elizabeth Caroline, born 1819

Philemon Hawkins was born in England in 1690. Came to Virginia and settled at Todd's Bridge, about 1815. Married 1815, Ann Eleanor Howard, daughter of Col. Howard, of Plymouth, England. Children:

Philemon, II.
John, moved to North Carolina, and then back to Virginia.
Ann, died unmarried.

Philemon II married Delia Martin in 1743 and had the following children:

John
Philemon III
Benjamin
Joseph
Ann
Delia

Philemon Hawkins III married Lucy Davis in 1775 and had the following children:

Eleanor, married Sherwood Haywood.
William, married Ann Boyd.
John D. married Jane Boyd.
Delia, married Stephen Haywood.
Sarah, married Col. William Polk.
Joseph, married Mary Boyd.
Benjamin, married Sally Pearson.
Lucinda, married Louis B. Henry.

Another correspondent says that Sarah Hawkins, daughter of Joseph Hawkins, was a descendant of Sir John Hawkins and his wife, Katherine Conson. Sir John Hawkins was Admiral of the Port during the fight with the Spanish Armada.

A very interesting account of the Hawkins family appears in Wheeler's Reminiscences. This is too long to quote here. Hawkins County, in Tennessee is not named for Sarah Hawkins, first wife of Governor Sevier, as many have supposed, but for Benjamin Hawkins, who appears in the foregoing table as the son of Philemon Hawkins. So far as I know, Governor William Blount's wife, Mary Grainger Blount, is the only one of our early Tennessee women pioneers for whom a county is named. Grainger County bears her family name, and she has the additional honor of having Maryville named for her.

Sarah Hawkins Sevier had ten children, all of whom lived to maturity. One, Richard Sevier, died a young man, however, and he was then unmarried. Each of her other nine children was married and left children, and the descendants of these are literally thousands of well known people residing now in all parts of America.

George Washington Sevier, the first son of Governor John Sevier by the second wife, Bonny Kate Sherrill Sevier, gave the full list of Governor Sevier's children to Dr. Lyman C. Draper, in a letter which is now on file in the Draper Collection in Madison, Wisconsin. Other authorities agree on the list, although we have no knowledge of the exact order in which these children were born. In the chapter concerning each of these children I will give the date of birth where it is known, and I have arranged the names in the order that seems probable from the information at hand. George Washington Sevier, in his letter, groups them, giving first the five sons and then the names of the five daughters of the first marriage.

James Sevier also mentions his brothers and sisters in his letters and they are mentioned in Governor Sevier's Journal. Though no list is given in the Journal, he refers many times to his children, even mentioning Richard, the young boy who died, giving in full the dream of seeing in Heaven "my son Dickey."

This statement is made because several early historians say that John Sevier had only six children by his first wife. Roosevelt follows these historians and says particularly that in 1793, at the close of the year, they moved to the new country, "then having two children." As a matter of fact they then had several children (the dates of birth of the three sons, Joseph, James and John, are a matter of record), probably three sons and two daughters. The

THE SEVIER FAMILY

rest of ten children were born between Christmas Day, 1773, and January or February, 1780, when Sarah Hawkins Sevier died.

It is a remarkable fact, showing a patriotic spirit that probably has not an equal, that all of her five sons, all under age, served in the Revolution and the campaigns that immediately fol'owed.

Joseph and James Sevier at eighteen and sixteen were in the Battle of King's Mountain and the Indian Campaigns. James says that he was in "all of his father's campaigns except one." John Sevier, Jr., is said, upon good authority, to have served in the Revolution, although he was too young (fourteen) to go to King's Mountain. He joined his father later, before the Revolution was over. Valentine Sevier, at fifteen, in 1788, was serving in the Indian campaigns. He was, of course, entirely too young for Revolutionary service. Richard Sevier, her fifth son, is also said to have seen military service with his father, although very young.

THE CHILDREN OF SARAH HAWKINS SEVIER

Joseph Sevier

James Sevier

John Sevier

Elizabeth Sevier

Sarah Hawkins Sevier

Mary Ann Sevier

Valentine Sevier

Richard Sevier

Rebecca Sevier

Nancy Sevier

CHAPTER THREE

Catherine Sherrill
"Bonny Kate"

CATHERINE SHERRILL

Catherine Sherrill was born in 1754, in North Carolina. Her family resided on the Yadkin and with other pioneers moved to the Mountains we now know as East Tennessee. Her father was Samuel Sherrill and the family consisted of several sons and two daughters. One of the daughters, Susan Sherrill, married Col. Taylor, "a gentleman of considerable distinction," to quote the account in Mrs. Elizabeth F. Ellett's book, Pioneer Women of the West. Mrs. Ellett, in the preface of this book, says that the article on Catherine Sherrill was prepared by A. W. Putnam, the distinguished historian of Middle Tennessee. A. W. Putnam married Catherine Sevier, daughter of George Washington Sevier, who was the eldest son of Catherine Sherrill Sevier and Governor John Sevier. The account of "Bonny Kate" in Mrs. Ellett's book is the fullest known of the vivacious lady who so greatly influenced her state and time, and I have therefore relied upon Mr. Putnam's statements for the detail of this sketch. The one or two small errors in his article are such as might easily occur in setting type from hand-written manuscript. The book was published in 1852 and the article was prepared probably some time before that date. This was less than twenty years after Bonnie Kate's death, and, as Mr. Putnam knew her well and talked to her many times I conclude his statements are correct.

Samuel Sherrill settled upon the Nollichucky, and his home was called "Daisy Fields." He was "well to do in the world for an emigrant of that day." He served in the Revolution and he was in the Battle of King's Mountain. Three of his sons. Adam, George and Samuel, Jr. were also in the Battle of King's Mountain. George Sherrill was very young. Adam Sherrill was born on the Yadkin, in North Carolina, in 1758. He died in Russellville, Ala., where he had accompanied his sister, "Bonny Kate." Adam Sherrill married Mary McCormack, or Carmack. It is said that the other sons of Samuel Sherrill were Uriah Sherrill and John Sherrill. Someone has written me that Bonny Kate's father was Uriah Sherrill, but practically every historian gives her father as Samuel Sherrill. Governor Sevier in his Journal speaks once of Acquila Sherrill and several times of William Sherrill.

Although the Sherrills came to Watauga Settlement quite early and the Seviers in 1773, it is said that John Sevier and Catherine Sherrill had not seen each other until the historic occasion in June, 1776, when the Fort was attacked and the famous incident of his christening her "Bonny Kate" took place. Old Abraham and a party of braves besieged the station Fort, into which the people of the settlement had gathered for protection, as for some weeks the Indians had been threatening the settlers. James Robertson and John Sevier were in the Fort and in command with some thirty fighting men. Some of the women went out of the enclosure thinking the Indians had withdrawn. The savages, however, approached stealthily and attacked the party. The women screamed and ran toward the Fort, some of them reaching it in time to enter. Catherine Sherrill succeeded in almost reaching the gates, but the Indians intercepted her direct path, and she made a circuit, resolving to scale the palisades in the rear. Someone inside the wall tried to help her, but slipped, falling within the enclosure while she fell to the ground without. The savages were almost upon her, firing and shooting arrows at her. She said, in telling the story: "The bullets and arrows came like hail. It was now—leap the wall or die! For I would not live a captive." She managed to get to her feet and then leapt to the edge of the palisades into the arms of Captain John Sevier, who was calling to her "Jump! My Bonny Kate Jump!" He reached toward her, caught her and swung her to safety.

The Sherrill family had moved into the Fort only the day before the attack by the Indians, according to A. W. Putnam's account, which makes it quite possible that historians are correct in saying that John Sevier had never seen Catherine Sherrill until she started toward the enclosure. Some of the men within the Fort had desired to sally forth to the protection of the women, when the attack was first discovered, but the commanders advised against this, as it would endanger the entire group and it was already too late to be of any assistance. Some of the other women in the party reached the Block House safely, one was killed, one or two were captured.

The incident is one of the most famous in Southern History, and any one will acknowledge that the introduction of the intrepid girl and the soldier was romantic. Four years later, after the death of his wife, Captain Sevier married Bonny Kate, whom he had saved and christened.

Catherine Sherrill is credited by tradition and written history as being the handsomest young woman of her time, at least in her vicinity. A writer declares that she could "out run, out jump, walk more erect, and ride more gracefully than any other female in the mountains 'round about or on the continent at large."

She certainly gave ample proof of her ability to run and jump, and as for her carriage, "she bore herself jauntily even in old age."

It is rather an interesting fact that Putnam does not once in his account of her in Mrs. Ellett's book refer to her sobriquet, Bonny Kate, or tell the story of Captain Sevier so calling her or of his actually saving her on that day, although every other historian of that time gives the story in full. Putnam says she was over and within the defences and quotes her as saying she found herself 'by the side of one in uniform,' and "I could gladly undergo that peril and effort again to fall into his arms and feel so out of danger, but then it all of God's good Providence." So perhaps he simply neglected to tell the story merely through too great familiarity.

I think she proved her courage by her marriage, quite as much as by the many feats attributed to her, for she became stepmother to ten young Seviers of ages varying from eighteen years to not as many months. She was equal to the emergency however, and raised them all to maturity. Richard Sevier, a young boy when she married his father, died at eighteen, unmarried.

Catherine Sherrill Sevier and Governor John Sevier had eight children, all of whom survived to maturity and marriage, and they evidently also raised four of the Governor's grand-children, as Elizabeth Sevier, the eldest daughter by the first marriage, died early and left four children to the care, apparently, of Governor and Mrs. Sevier. Also several of Catherine's nephews and nieces were raised by her, and in my research into Sevier records, I am continually finding a niece or nephew of John Sevier, who claims to have been raised in the Governor's home by Bonny Kate. She must have had a heart of gold and she certainly had her hands full. Some one may say that a stepson of eighteen—Joseph Sevier was eighteen—could not have been of much care to the bride, but in the few weeks between her marriage and the Battle of King's Mountain, (seven in all) Catherine is said to have made the homespun suits which her husband and his two sons wore to the Battle. So the honey-moon was evidently not an idle one. It is said that when some one complimented her on this she answered that if all of Governor Sevier's ten children had been boys and all of them old enough to go to the Battle she could have outfitted them all!

Her athletic habits must have stood her in good stead, after her marriage, for she managed her husband's estate, farmed it and marketed the products.

Modern wives express resentment sometimes when husbands bring home "a friend to dinner." "Bonny Kate's" husband was apt to bring his whole company home, as he says, "to dine and lodge!" And it is gravely said in history that he never let an old comrade leave in the morning on an ancient, tired nag, but always urged him to go to the stables and choose one of the blooded horses in exchange!

We can imagine that Bonny Kate must have been sorely strained to retain her title as "Bonny" under such circumstances, that is, if "Bonny" described her disposition as well as her beauty. General Sevier did not confine his hospitality apparently to his friends, for it is told that on one occasion, having taken thirty Indian prisoners, he had no place to take them, so he took them to his home! They loved that and settled down to stay and thereafter nothing could make them stir from the plantation. They seem to have been there for years; at least no one has set down the time of their departure, if it ever happened. They did nothing, and Bonny Kate, with her energetic disposition, must have been tried by the arrangement, however much the Indians enjoyed it. Their only contribution to life, I gather, was the teaching of their language and other Indian languages to Catherine's second daughter, Ruth Sevier. The result of this teaching, which was probably more the effect of companionship than actual intention, was that before she was ten, she could chatter like a magpie in several tribal tongues. This ability served her afterwards on many occasions, for she acted as official and unofficial interpreter several times. In the meanwhile the little tribe of thirty adopted her and made her a princess, and prophesied that she would marry a great chief of their people, which was little enough to promise in return for overlong hospitality. How this prophesy was fulfilled is an interesting part of the history of Ruth Sevier, which appears in Chapter XII. Part Six of this volume.

Bonny Kate's step daughters were all married from her home, each of them, it is said, being married by Dr. Doak. John Sevier mentions the minister, Dr. Doak, in giving accounts of the weddings of his daughters.

Putnam says that Governor Sevier's first wife died in 1779, that date being given also by Wheeler's History of North Carolina and several others. Other historians say that she died in January or February, 1780. It is also a rather curious fact that Putnam says her name was Susan Hawkins. This coincides with a genealogy of the Hawkins family, although every other authority gives her name Sarah Hawkins.

The marriage of John Sevier and Catherine Sherrill took place August 14, 1780, and was performed by Joseph Wilson.

Bonny Kate was left alone, often for weeks at a time, to manage the estate and take care of the children and servants, for the grown sons by the first marriage were with their father in practically every campaign—James Sevier in his pension declaration says he was in every campagn with his father except one—but she seems not to have been afraid. She refused to go to the Block House in time of danger, saying, "The wife of John Sevier knows no fear," and "I neither skulk from duty or danger." The Indians seem to have respected this fearlessness and perhaps to have admired her and protected her because of it; but the Tories were serious enemies. It is said that at one time some Tories came to her demanding to be told her husband's whereabouts, intending to hang him, but offering her and her childen safety in return for information. When she refused to give them any information one man drew his pistol and threatened to kill her. "Shoot, shoot!" was her answer, "I'm not afraid to die." The leader of the party told the man to put up his pistols, saying, "Such a woman is too brave to die."

Since no picture survives to tell of Catherine Sherrill's beauty, this quotation from Putnam is particularly interesting:

"We have seen her in advanced age—tall in stature, erect in person, stately in walk, with small piercing blue eyes, raven locks, a Roman nose, and firmness unmistakable in every feature. She was able to teach her children in the exercises conducive to health and usefuless, to strength of nerve and of action. None could, with equal grace and facility, placing a hand upon the mane of a spirited horse, and standing by his side, seat themselves upon his back or in the saddle. She had the appearance and used the language of independence, haughtiness and authority, and she never laid these entirely aside. Yet was not her pride offensive, nor her words or demeanor intended heedlessly to wound. It could be said of her without any question, that she 'reverenced her husband,' and she instilled the same scriptural sentiment into the minds of his children. The very high respect and deference which one of her dignified appearance ever paid him, no doubt had a favorable influence upon others; for though he was a man of remarkable elegance of person, air and address, and of popular attraction, yet it must be confessed that she contributed much to all these traits, and to his usefulness and zeal in public service. She relieved him of his cares at home, and applauded his devotion to the service of the people.

"Her reply to those who urged her 'to fort,' or to take protection in one of the station, was 'I would as soon die by the tomahawk and scalping knife as by famine! I put my trust in that Power who rules the armies of Heaven, and among men on earth. I know my husband has an eye and an arm for the Indians, and the Tories who would harm us, and though he is gone often, and for weeks at a time, he comes home when I least expect him, and always covered with laurels. If God protects him whom duty calls into danger, so will He those who trust in Him and stand at their post.'

"This was the spirit of the heroine—this was the spirit of Catherine Sevier. Neither she nor her husband seemed to think there could be any danger or loss when they could encourage others to daring to duty, and usefulness.

"She embraced the religious sentiments of the Presbyterians, and her life throughout was exemplary and useful. In this faith she lived and died. A favorite expression of hers was 'I always trust in Providence.' She always taught her children that 'Trust in God, with a pure heart, is to be rich enough; if you are lazy your blood will stagnate in your veins, and your trust will die.' She would never be idle. Knitting often engaged her fingers, while her mind and tongue were occupied in thought and conversation. She always wore at her side a bunch of very bright keys."

"During the twelve years in which he officiated as Governor of Tennnessee, his wife made his home delightful to him, his children, and his friends. It was the rest of the weary, the asylum of the afflicted, well known as the 'hospitable mansion of the First Governor, the people's favorite.'

"After the death of Governor Sevier in 1815, his widow removed to Overton County, Tennessee, where Governor Sevier had 57,000 acres of land. Several of her children and other kinspeople had preceded her to this location and practically all her family resided there. She selected a romantic and secluded spot for her residence and named it 'The Dale.' It was on a high bench or spur of one of the mountains a few miles from Obed River. Her sons erected log cabins for bedroom, dining-room, and kitchen, and others for stable and crib. Here she resided for years attended by the Governor's body servant, Toby, who had accompanied him in all his Indian campaigns; Toby's wife, Rachel, and one other female servant, Susy, and a boy. Seldom did she come down from her eyrie in the Mountain. The aged eagle had lost her mate."

Among the treasures she had transported from the Governor's mansion was a carpet which admirers had presented to Governor Sevier. This was the first article of its kind west of the Alleghanies, and it was an object of greatest curiosity. When distinguished company was expected it was carefully spread upon the floor, only to be dusted and re-rolled, boxed and put away, when the visitors departed. It is said that only one one occasion was it ever left on the floor over night, and that was during the visit of the Princes of Orleans. It can be easily imagined that its splendor failed to impress the palace bred youngsters!

"She was remarkably neat in her person, tidy and particular, and uniform in her dress, which might be called half-mourning—a white cap with black trimmings. She had a hearth rug the accompaniment of the favorite carpet, which was usually laid before the fireplace in her own room, and there she was commonly seated, erect as a statue, her feet placed upon her rug, her work-stand near her side, the Bible ever there or on her lap, the Governor's hat upon the wall; such were the striking features of that mountain hermitage."

Late in her life, June 10, 1836, her favorite son, Samuel Sevier, removed to Alabama to reside, and Bonny Kate decided to go to him to spend her remaining days. She was then already eighty-two and but a few months were vouchsafed to her in that son's society, for she passed away, October 2, 1836, in his home at Russellville, Ala. She was buried there and her body lay for many years beside that of her son and other members of the family. In June, 1922, it was determined by patriotic Tennesseans to bring back her ashes to the home of her youth. Mr. Samuel Heiskell, of Knoxville, secured permission from the authorities and relatives. July 27, 1922, he brought the remains to Tennessee to re-inter her ashes beside her husband in Knoxville. The occasion was made a patriotic one and hundreds of people gathered from all parts of the South.

THE CHILDREN OF CATHERINE SHERRILL SEVIER

Catherine Sevier

Ruth Sevier

George Washington Sevier

Samuel Sevier

Polly Preston Sevier

Eliza Conway Sevier

Joanna Goode Sevier

Robert Sevier

PART SIX

Descendants of
Governor John Sevier

CHILDREN OF GOVERNOR JOHN SEVIER

By the First Wife, Sarah Hawkins Sevier:

By the Second Wife, Catherine Sherrill Sevier:

It is not possible to give the foregoing names in the exact order of birth, as authorities differ widely regarding this. In the chapter devoted to each child the date of birth when known will be given, or the approximate date and the reason for considering it the approximate date.

The list of children has been carefully compiled from statements by George Washington Sevier and James Sevier, checked carefully with Governor Sevier's Journal, other historical documents and later statements by descendants, Bishop Hoss, Mrs. Sophia Hoss French, Mr. Charles Bascom Sevier, Mr. Samuel Sevier, and many others.

CHAPTER ONE

Joseph Sevier

JOSEPH SEVIER

Joseph Sevier, Jr., son of Governor John Sevier by his first wife, Sarah Hawkins Sevier, was their eldest child. He was born in Rockingham County, Virginia, in 1762, as shown by the fact that at the Battle of King's Mountain, October 7, 1780, he was eighteen years of age. Joseph was named for his mother's father, Joseph Hawkins, and his uncle, Joseph Sevier, Sr.

Joseph Sevier went with his father to "the Mountains" in 1773. At the Battle of King's Mountain he was the last man to cease firing, disobeying the order to cease, crying out, "They have killed my father, they have killed my father!" He was mistaken, however, as it was Captain Robert Sevier, his uncle, who fell mortally wounded. This same story is told of James Sevier, who was sixteen years of age, and evidently happened to one or both of them.

Joseph Sevier, when he was only nineteen years of age, was employed to keep watch on hostile movements of the Indians. This probably began the long association with the Indian people which he later cemented by marrying an Indian girl. He was almost continually employed to conduct Indian affairs from the time he was nineteen years of age and during the entire administration of Governor Blount he was a trusted agent. Like several other Seviers he was fluent in the Indian tongues and this made his services very valuable. His second marriage took him evidently entirely from his own people, for Governor Sevier, in writing to George Washington Sevier, alludes to Joseph rather sadly when he begs his son Washington not to go West, as so many young men were doing. He says, "I have already lost one son to the savages."

This Joseph Sevier is frequently confused with his uncle, for whom he was named, and many historians are misled by the name "Joseph Sevier." There is, indeed no way of distinguishing them when so named except by the date or the text of the article, and frequently no way whatever.

They were nearly the same age, at least the difference was not radical, a matter of eleven years at most. Joseph Sevier, Sr., was the fourth son of his father and that indicates his birth about 1751, though if daughters were born to Valentine Sevier II and Joanna Goode Sevier before Joseph Sr. was born, then his birth was later than 1751 and he was even nearer the age of his nephew and namesake. Joseph Sevier, Jr., who was born in 1762.

Even in the matter of marriage they are almost hopelessly confused by the family historians. Each of them is said to have married "Charity Keewood" and certainly one of them did marry Charity Keewood, but the oc-incidence of two Joseph Seviers marrying two Charity Keewoods seems too extraordinary! Bishop Hoss gives the information that Joseph, Jr., married Charity Keewood, but I am inclined to think that he, too, was confused by the Joseph Seviers. The descendants of Joseph Sevier, Sr., give his marriage positively to Charity Keewood.

It is very probable they both married into the Keewood family and perhaps they married cousins of the same name. Many references indicate the possibility of two Keewood marriages. The Keewood plantation was not far from the Seviers' and the exchange of visits and courtesies was frequent. It will be recalled that when the Sevier family moved from Virginia they arrived at the Keewood Settlement Christmas Day, 1773. The intimacy with the Keewoods evidently continued. Governor Sevier in his Journal makes mention of the Keewoods in connection with his brother, Joseph, denoting some relation, and again mentions his son Joseph and the Keewoods. He several times sets down the visit of Mr. and Mrs. Joseph Sevier (son) and Miss Sallie Keewood.

Governor Sevier in his Journal dated February 2, 1794, mentions "son Jo., wife and Sally Keewood came here."

February 4, 1794, "Self, wife. Jos., wife, Miss Sallie Keewood Mary Ann and Ruth went to Jonesboro."

Therefore Joseph, Jr., was married before 1794.

Joseph Sevier. Jr., married evidently rather young as did his father, and there is a record that he had two sons by his first marriage. Their names were John Finley Sevier and Richard Cunningham Sevier. John is evidently named in compliment to Governor Sevier. Joseph, Jr., had a brother, Richard and that name is perhaps a compliment to that brother who died about the time the younger Richard was born. This leaves the names Finley and Cunningham unaccounted for and it may be that the mother of these two sons was a Finley or a Cunningham. A John Findlay, or Findley, served in the Revolution and is given as one of the participants in the Battle of King's Mountain. The name may have been in compliment to him, whether he was a relative or friend only. I have no record of their descendants, and little mention of them except in documents in Washington giving power of attorney to their uncle George Washington Sevier, to collect their inheritance of their father's part of Governor John Sevier's estate.

They testify that they are the only heirs of their father, Joseph

Sevier, Jr. Their Uncle, George Washington Sevier, also so testifies.
William Matlock, their great uncle by marriage, also so testifies. This document is dated 1826. This statement plainly ignores
the second marriage of Joseph Sevier, Jr., and the children
by the second marriage.

Joseph Sevier's second wife was Elizabeth Lowry, the Indian
girl, and it is because of this Indian connection that the sons Richard and John refused to recognize the marriage.

Of John Finley Sevier and Richard Cunningham Sevier I have
no further information after their declaration in 1826 that they
are the only heirs of their father, Joseph Sevier, son of Governor
John Sevier.

It is the irony of fate that the descendants of John Finley
Sevier and Richard Cunningham Sevier, if there are any, are not
known, whereas the descendants of the other children are known.

Joseph Sevier, Jr., married for his second wife, Elizabeth Lowry, daughter of George Lowry, a Scotchman, and Ocatlootsa, who
was a daughter of the great chief Oconstoto. A few years after
this marriage Joseph Sevier died, and his widow, Elizabeth Lowry,
married for her second husband, John Walker, supposed to be an
Englishman, although Governor Blount calls him a half-breed. A
son of this marriage was John Walker, Jr., who became famous
for his elopement with Elizabeth Meigs.

THE CHILDREN OF JOSEPH SEVIER
By the First Wife, Charity Keewood (?) Sevier:

1.   John Finley Sevier
2.   Richard Cunningham Sevier

By the Second Wife, Elizabeth Lowry Sevier:

3.   Margaret Sevier
4.   Eliza Sevier

MARGARET SEVIER

Margaret Sevier, daughter of Joseph Sevier, Jr., and Elizabeth
Lowry Sevier, was born about ————. She married Gideon Morgan about ———— and had at least three children:

(a). Gideon Morgan, II
(b). Elizabeth Lowry Morgan
(c). Cherokee America Morgan

(a). Gideon Morgan, II, son of Gideon Morgan and Margaret
Sevier Morgan, was living in 1920, in Tip, Oklahoma. I know
nothing further of him.

(b) Elizabeth Lowry Morgan, daughter of Gideon Morgan
and Margaret Sevier Morgan, married Hugh McDowell McElrath.

They had a son, John Edgar McElrath, who married Eliza Ann Alden. They had a daughter, Bertha McElrath Alden, who married Benjamin Bakewell.

(c). Cherokee America Morgan, daughter of Gideon Morgan, and Margaret Sevier Morgan, married Andrew Lewis Rogers. They had seven children, namely:

  A. Andrew Lewis Rogers, Jr.
  B. Connell Rogers
  C. Hugh Morgan Rogers
  D. John Otto Rogers
  E. Lucy Rogers
  F. Paul Rogers
  G. Clifford Rogers

A. Andrew Lewis Rogers, Jr., married Josephine Howard and has four children, namely: Andrew Lewis Rogers III, Partricia Rogers, Josephine Rogers and Kenneth Rogers. Paul Rogers died in infancy. Andrew Lewis Rogers and his family live on Garrison Hill, Fort Gibson, Okla.

B. Connell Rogers, married for his first wife, Florence Nash, and had Ella Nash Rogers and Gertrude Whitman Rogers and married for his second wife Kate Cunningham and had Marion Sevier Rogers, Lewis Byrne Rogers, Howard Cunningham Rogers, and Connell Rogers, Jr. Of these: Gertrude Rogers married a Persian, Dr. Georgivus Shimoon, a prominent dentist of Muskogee, and had one daughter. Mrs. Shimoon died in the summer of 1916. Ella Nash Rogers married David Castle and had two sons, David Castle, Jr., and Connell Rogers Castle, who live in Kansas City. Marian Sevier Rogers married ————.

C. Hugh Morgan Rogers married twice but had no children by his first wife. He married for his second wife, Bertha ————. They had one daughter, Bertha, who was born January, 1910, two weeks before her father's death.

D. John Otto Rogers married ———————— and has two children, Lucy Rogers and John Otto Rogers, Jr. He lives at Eagle Lake, Texas.

E. Lucy Rogers.

F. Paul Rogers.

G. Clifford Rogers married ——————————— and has two sons, Clifford Rogers, Jr., and ——————————Rogers. He lives at Fort Gibson, Okla.

Mrs. Cherokee America Morgan Rogers made her home with

her eldest son, Andrew Lewis Rogers, Jr., and died in the spring
of 1919.

ELIZA SEVIER

Eliza Sevier, daughter of Joseph Sevier, Jr., and Elizabeth
Lowry Sevier, was born about ————. She married about ————
Templin Ross, of Pennsylvania, and had two children, Hugh Ross
and Joseph Ross. Templin Ross and Elizabeth Sevier Ross died
of cholera at the time of the Indian emigration in 1838. Their
children were cared for by some people in Arkansas.

CHAPTER TWO
James Sevier

JAMES SEVIER

James Sevier, second son of Governor John Sevier by his first wife, Sarah Hawkins Sevier, was born in Virginia, in Rockingham County, October 25, 1764. He was still a small boy when his father moved to the "Mountains." He participated in Governor Sevier's Indian Campaigns, writing to Dr. Lyman Draper, in a letter which is now in the Draper Collection in Madison, Wisconsin, that he was in every Indian Campaign with his father except one. His elder brother, Joseph, was only a little older and the two lads went with their father to the Battle of King's Mountain, as many histories testify. James was not quite sixteen when the forces were gathering for the King's Mountain Campaign. He was too young to be included in the list of men to go or stay to protect the homes and women and children, a vitally important duty, but his stepmother, Bonny Kate, called out, "Mr. Sevier, here is another of your sons who wants to go with you." The Governor then decided to permit him to accompany the party and found a horse for the boy. He was thus one of the two youngest participants in the Battle, the other being William Isbell, who was only fifteen. James Sevier was within three weeks of being sixteen. Bonny Kate, whose marriage had taken place a few weeks before, made the homespun suits which Joseph and James wore in the Battle.

The story is told of him and of his brother Joseph that he was the last man to cease firing, disobeying the order to cease firing when the Battle of King's Mountain was over, crying, "They have killed my father, they have killed my father." It was, however, his uncle, Captain Robert Sevier, who was mortally wounded. The incident may have occurred to both boys as a matter of fact, and evidently did occur to one or both. Governor Sevier gave the field glass which Patrick Ferguson, the English Commander, carried, to his son, James Sevier. The glass remained in the family for some years and was presented to the Tennessee Historical Society by a grandson of James Sevier, who was also James Sevier. During the World War, when a request was made by the Government of the United States for field glasses, this historic instrument was loaned to the government. I do not know its present location.

James Sevier, starting so early in life upon a successful career at war, followed his distinguished father and was in all but one of the thirty-five battles with Indians. He had a long and honorable

171

life in the service of his state and country. He was Clerk of the
Court of Washington County, Tennessee, for forty-seven years,
some histories even say fifty-seven years. He lived with his father
and stepmother, Catherine Sherrill Sevier until his own marriage
in 1789 and then established his own home a few miles from theirs.
This was near Jonesboro, Tennessee. He died on his place, January
21, 1847, aged eighty-two years.

JAMES SEVIER'S PENSION DECLARATION
Draper Mss. 100247-254

James Sevier—Washington County, Tennessee: Declaration—
11th Sept. 1832: aged 68 years served in 1780, in his uncle Robert
Sevier's Company, in his father, Col. John Sevier's regiment, in
the Battle of King's Mountain—that Capt. Robert Sevier was mortally wounded in that battle and died a few days after—that immediately after, the regiment collected at a place called the Swan
Ponds, now in Greene County—Col. John Sevier commanded,
Jesse Welton & Jonathon Tipton were the Majors: Affiant was in
Captain Landon Carter's Company: Left home the last of Nov.—
met the Indians in force on the South side of French Broad, on
Boyd's Creek, & had a pretty severe engagement with them, in
which we were pretty successful—must have been more than two
months on this tour.

Shortly after Gen. Green's battle with the British at the Eutaw
Springs, there was a request made for men from this side of the
mountains—who were to serve three months—after they joined
Gen. Greene. My father, Col. John Sevier, & Lt. Colonel Charles
Robertson, commanded the Washington troop—Valentine Sevier
& Jonathon Tipton were Majors—commenced our march for South
Carolina in September, 1781, we passed through Morgantown &
Charlotte, N. C. & through Gen. Gates' battle ground—joined
Gen. Greene, at the High Hills of Santee, where he was recruiting
his men after the severe service at Eutaw: we were sent on to join
Gen. Marion in the Swamps of Santee; while with Gen. Marion,
declarant was one of a party that took a British post below Monk's
Corner, consisting of about a hundred men. They had fortified a
large brick tenement, belonging to a Mr. Colleton: The officers
commanding the Americans were Cols. Sevier, Mayhem, Oree
(Horry) or Horre, & Maj. Valentine Sevier. We made some attempt
to take more of their outposts, but found them all evacuated—I
suppose called in by the British General. Having served out the
time, we returned home, although Gen. Marion expressed a great
desire that we remain a few weeks longer. My father, Capt. Carter,
and most of his company, did stay for some considerable time longer
& were then discharged; believes he was upwards of 4 months
from home on this service.

Shortly after his return home from S. C.,—he thinks in Feb. 1782, there was an Indian alarm, & call for men; that himself & an elder brother who had returned from Virginia that fall, equipt themselves as volunteers & went about 50 miles to the place of rendezvous on Holston River; that shortly after they got there, & before many men had collected, the weather became extremely cold & a deep snow fell, so that it was thought the Indians would not disturb the frontier people at that time, & that it would be advisable to break up and return home—we did so. Who was the officer that ordered the men out at that time, I do not recollect, unless it was Col. Charles Robertson, as my father and Capt. Carter had not returned at that time from S. C. My brother and myself joined no company, & I think were not more than two weeks from home. That through the summer of 1782, the lower Cherokees near the Lookout Mountain & on Coosa River were very troublesome: As soon as their crops were matured, my father raised an army of men—set out the last of August or first of September & went & destroyed all the Lower Towns on the the waters of the Tennessee, & two towns on Coosa River—one called Estanaula, the other called Spring Frog's Town; two villages on the waters of Coosa. On this campaign we had no fighting. The body of Indians kept out of our way. We took some 7 or 8 prisoners (warriors)—with a number of women & children. After remaining some length of time in the Nation, & having destroyed everything that came within our grasp, on which they could support. An Indian countryman by the name of Rodgers came in with a flag for peace—the Indians were requested if they wanted peace to go up to Old Chota town, on Tennessee River, & there a peace talk would be held with them. They did so; a peace was made & the prisoners restored to their friends. Maj. Valentine Sevier was all the Major that was out at that time, as I believe. Declarant served in Capt. Alex Moore's company—there was Capt. Sam Weare & Capt. Robert Bean who commanded companies—the other captains now forgotten. I believe we were upwards of two months on that campaign.

In August, 1780, a campaign was ordered against the Middle Settlements Indians—the place of meeting was beyond the limits of the settlements, on a creek called Indian Creek, that he was one of the men that met to go on said tour. While at the place of rendezvous, & waiting for others to collect, a man by the name of Hill went into the mountains to hunt, & was shot at by an Indian before he discovered him, but being missed, & seeing the Indian, he fired on & killed him. This circumstance caused a mutiny amongst the men. They were afraid their families would be killed in their absence, broke for home, & the campaign fell through. I mention this to show that I was twice called out to go on campaigns that fell through. My father, in this atter instance, was to have commanded—there was no major that I recollect. I believe we were not more than 10 days or 2 weeks from home.

Early in the summer of 1781, the frontier inhabitants became much alarmed about the Indians. My father, who was Colonel of the County, ordered out a company of Rangers—or what was then called a scouting party—this declarant was one of that party, & went out, & James Hubbard was the Captain, as well as he recollects—were out about 2 weeks.

Was born in 1764. Col. Richard Campbell, who was killed at Eutaw Springs was said declarant's uncle.

March 29, 1789, James Sevier married Nancy Conway, whose sisters, Elizabeth and Susannah also married into the Sevier family, Elizabeth marrying James' brother, John Sevier, Jr., and Susannah marrying their first cousin, "Devil Jack Sevier," son of Valentine vier III. The three Conway sisters were daughters of Colonel Henry Conway, who was also a distinguished Revolutionary soldier. Nancy Conway, who married James Sevier, was born March 22, 1772. She died July 15, 1743, aged seventy-one years.

James Sevier and Nancy Conway Sevier had eleven children, namely:

1. Elizabeth Conway Sevier, born July 9, 1790.
2. Sarah Hundley Sevier, born July 22, 1792.
3. Maria Antoinette Sevier, born May 12, 1794, died two years later.
4. Minerva Grainger Sevier, born May 30, 1796.
5. Pamelia Hawkins Sevier, born March 15, 1798.
6. Susannah Brown Sevier, born June 25, 1800.
7. Elbert Franklin Sevier, born September 17, 1802.
8. Elbridge Gerry Sevier, born March 19, 1805.
9. Clarissa Carter Sevier, born April 9, 1807.
10. Louisa Maria Sevier, born December 16, 1811.
11. Mary Malvina Sevier, born April 14, 1814.

ELIZABETH CONWAY SEVIER

1. Elizabeth Conway Sevier, first child of James Sevier and Nancy Conway Sevier was born, July 9, 1790. She was named in honor of her mother's sister, Elizabeth Conway, (who married John Sevier, Jr., and died in a very short time after the marriage). Elizabeth Conway Sevier married March 8, 1810, James S. Johnston.

SARAH HUNDLEY SEVIER

2. Sarah Hundley Sevier, second child of James Sevier and Nancy Conway Sevier was born July 22, 1792. She married January 11, 1810, Hugh Douglas Hale, born August 12, 1787, in Far-

quahr County, Virginia. He was a son of Phillip and Catherine
Douglas Hale. The children of Hugh Douglas Hale and Sarah
Hundley Sevier Hale were:

a. James W. Hale
b. Phillip Perry Hale
c. Eliza Jane Hale
d. Catherine Anne Hale
e. William Dickson Hale
f. Lemuel Johnson Hale
g. Sarah Amanda Hale
.h. Laura Evelyn Hale
i. Hugh Douglas Hale, II.
j. Franklin Sevier Hale.

Of the foregoing:

a. James W. Hale, son of Hugh Douglas Hale and Sarah Hundley Sevier Hale, died September 9th, 1842, unmarried. It is told
that he was engaged in his young manhood to Miss Taylor, an aunt
of Robert L. Taylor, former Governor of Tennessee, and that she
was struck by lightning at a Camp Meeting and instantly killed.
This is said to have grieved him so deeply that shortly afterward
he died.

b. Phillip Perry Hale, son of Hugh Douglas Hale and Sarah
Hundley Sevier Hale, married Caroline Susan Gullege. Their
children were: (1) Sarah Hale, who married L. B. Snyder and died
without issue; (2) Thomas Hale, who died young; (3) Elizabeth
Hale, who died young; (4) Franklin Sevier Hale, who died young;
(5) Laura Hale, who married Lieutenant Hundley Maloney and
died without issue; (6) Fred Douglas Hale, who married first Theo-
dosia Bell and had: Fred P. Hale, Harriet Susan Hale, John Weller
Hale, Josephine Hale and Annie Lee Hale; and married second,
Mary Neal and had: Ruth Sevier Hale, Annie Lee Hale and Eliza-
beth Hale, and married third Minnie Edwards and had: Phillip Hae,
Mildred Hale, Hugh Douglas Hale and James Hale; (7) Anna Eliza
Hale, who married Frank Gottsseilig; (8) Joseph Hale, who married
Laura Beaucamp and had children: William Hale, Joseph Hale, F,
and Carolina Susan Hale; (9) Hugh Lemuel Hale, who married
Emma Wilkinson and had three children: Phillip Hale, Douglas
Hale and Eugenia Hale; (10) Phillip Thomas Hale, who married
Lena Lyle Bolinger and had six children: Thomas Farris Hale, Wil-
liam Roy Hale, Phillip Theodore Hale, David Ward Hale, Earl
Douglas Hale and Franklin Sevier Hale.

c. Eliza Jane Hale, daughter of Hugh Douglas Hale and Sarah
Hundley Hale, married David Wendel Carter and had eight children:
(1) James William Carter, who married Mary Lou Tindal and had
among other children, Mary Carter, who married Robert Augustine

Burne; Mary Weller Carter, Janie Carter and John Tindal Carter; (2) Alfred Moore Carter, who married first Chassie King and had one daughter, Maud Carter, who married Ellis Crymbel and had two sons, Carter Crymbel and Ellis Crymbel, II; Alfred Moore Carter married for his second wife, Nannie Zimmerman, by whom he had no children; (3) David Wendal Carter, II, who married Cornelia Keith and had children: Lieutenant Keith Carter, David Wendal Carter, III, Annie Frazier Carter, Hugh Sevier Carter, Stanley Carter, who married Nettie Lee Hill; (2) Franklin Alexander Carter, who married Annie Laird and has three children: Annie Laird Carter, David Wendell Carter and Robert Cowden Carter; (3 Ella Douglas Carter, who married Dr. Samuel W. Rhea and has two sons, Joseph Carter Rhea, (who married Troupe Davis and has Ellen Douglas Rhea and James Wendel Rhea, who married Helen Haynes and has two sons, James Wendel Rhea, II, and Haynes Rhea).

(d) Catherine Anne Hale married Dr. Charles Tenant Porter Jarnagin, in Jefferson County, Tennessee. Dr. Jarnagin was born April 6, 1812, died about 1894. He was born and died in Jefferson County, Tennessee. Dr. Charles Tenant Porter Jarnagin was the son of Preston Bynum Jarnagin and his wife, Elizabeth Conway Jarnagin, who were married December 20, 1810. Preston Bynum Jarnagin was born August 13, 1791, near Witt's Foundry, then in Jefferson, now Hamblen County, Tennessee, died July 28, 1828, in Jefferson County. He was the son of Captain Thomas and Mary (Witt) Jarnagin. Thomas Jarnagin was born July 25, 1747, in Virginia, died February 26, 1802, near Witt's Foundry, Tennessee. He was the son of Capt. John and Mary Jarnagin. Mary Witt, born April 4, 1753, Virginia, died December 14, 1829, near Witt's Foundrey, Tennessee, the daughter of Charles and Lavinia Witt, who lived in Halifax, Virginia.

Elizabeth Conway Jarnagin married, December 20, 1810, Preston B. Jarnagin, and died July 14, 1816. She was the daughter of General Joseph Conway.

The children of Catherine Anne Hale Jarnagin and Dr. Charles Tenant Porter Jarnagin were: (1) Ann Eliza Jarnagin, who died young; (2) Charles Jarnagin; (3) Douglas Jarnagin, who married ——————— and had at least one child, Beatrice Jarnagin; (4) Catherine Jarnagin, who married Dr. Britt Watkins; (5) Mary Jarnagin, who married David Swaggerty and their child, Katie Swaggerty, married Lon McSwain; Mary Jarnagin married for her second husband, Joseph Carty, and had no children; (6) John Sevier Jarnagin, married Kate D. Hubbard May 23, 1872, at Jefferson City, Tennessee. They had four children, (Estelle Jarnagin, married Blair Neff; Mary Kate Jarnagin, married Walter Harris; Henry

Porter Jarnagin, died young; and Ruth Jarnagin, died young); (7) Dr. Joseph Conway Jarnagin, married Ida Bass, July 4, 1876, in Montezuma, Georgia. Their children were: Mamie Vinson Jarnagin, who married Clifford Corbin Farmer and has, Mary Farmer, Joseph Jarnagin Farmer, Clifford Corbin Farmer, Jr., William Hawes Farmer, and Catherine Hale Farmer; Annie Kate Jarnagin, who married Daisy Cason; Caroline Chapman Jarnagin, who married William Edward Markwalter, and has Edward Markwalter, Jr., and Rebecca Markwalter; Joseph C. Jarnagin, who died young; and Ida Bass Jarnagin, who married Milton Randolph Lufborrow and has Carolina Lufborrow and Charmion Lufborrow; (8) ———— Jarnagin, a daughter, who died in Georgia. She married ———— Yates and left two children, William Yates and Eliza Yates. By the will of Dr. Jarnagin she is mentioned as a child of his first wife, Catherine Anne Hale and therefore a Sevier descendant. There are some people, however, who say she was the daughter of Dr. Hale's second wife.

(e). William Dickson Hale, son of Hugh Douglas Hale and Sarah Hundley Sevier Hale, married Martha Powell and had children: Mary Hale, Catherine Hale, Sarah Hale, and Leila Hale, who married Joseph Green.

(g) Sarah Amanda Hale, daughter of Hugh Douglas Hale and Sarah Hundley Sevier Hale, married Charles W. Meek. Their children were, James Hale Meek, who married Jennie Hensley and had one son, James W. Meek, who married Caroline Corinne McWilliams and has one son, James W. Meek, Second; Daniel Kenny Meek, who died young; William Blain Meek, who married Martha Powers and has two daughters, Vesta Sevier Meek, who married Robert Lee Davis and has one child, Katherine Davis; Iva Douglas Meek, who is unmarried; Florine Cornelia Meek, who married James P. Evans and has one son, Hubert Evans, who married Clara Theresa Hill, and a daughter, Lula Evans who married William James for her first husband and for her second husband married Dr. Paul Gheering and died at the birth of a daughter; Ida Sevier Meek, who married Jacob Orville Lotspeich and had children: Claude Meek Lotspeich, (who married Helen Gibbons and has five children, Henry Gibbons Lotspeich, Margaret Sevier Lotspeich, Edgar Hale Lotspeich, William Douglass Lotspeich and James F. Lton Lotspeich); Roy Douglass Lotspeich, who married Ethel Weir and has children, Katherine Mildred Lotspeich, Jacob Orville Lotspeich, Second, Helen Sevier Lotspeich. Douglass Weir Lotspeich; Edgar Sevier Lotspeich married Ruth Moore and has children: Caroline Lotspeich, Edgar Sevier Lotspeich and Robert Orville Lotspeich; Ella Douglas Meek married Charles E. Lothrop and has two children, Ida Meek Lothrop and Douglass B. Lothrop, who married Ruth

Dooley and has two sons, Douglass B. Lothrop Second and Clinton Dooley Lothrop; Charles W. Meek married Adah Jariel and had two children: Joseph Meek and Sarah Meek. Franklin Hale Meek married Almena McG. Smith and had two children, Charles W. Meek, who died young, and Bathurst Lee Meek (who married Grace Tarver and has Bathurst Lee Meek, Jr.; Joseph M. Meek married Alma Burt Hughes and has two children, James Hughes Meek and Sarabel Meek.

(h). Laura Evelyn Hale, daughter of Hugh Douglas Hale and Sarah Hundley Sevier Hale, married Thomas E. Gosnell and had children: Lemuel Ward Gosnell (who married Mary Elizabeth Hill and had children: Myroyn Aydlett Gosnell, Katherine Lisserand Hill Gosnell, Clara Douglass Gosnell and Munsey Ward Gonell. Katherine Lisserand Gosnell, married Dr. Sterling P. Martin, Second, and had two daughters; Clara Douglass Gosnell, married first Samuel McLaughlin, and second William Silverthorne, and has two sons, Harry Douglass Silverthorne (who married Caroline M. Rocs) and Carl Douglass Silverthorne. Lemuel Ward Gosnell married for his second wife, Mrs. Cullie Oglesby; Matthew Gosnell, who died young; and Franklin Gosnell, who is unmarried.

(i). Hugh Douglas Hale, Second, son of Hugh Douglas Hale, First, and Sarah Hundley Sevier Hale, married Sarah Vance, a sister of Governor Zebulon Vance, of North Carolina, and had three children: Margaret Hale, Sarah Hale and Franklin Hale.

(j). Franklin Sevier Hale, son of Hugh Douglas Hale and Sarah Hundley Sevier Hale, was killed in the Battle of Franklin in The War Between the States.

MARIA ANTOINETTE SEVIER

3. Maria Antoinette Sevier, daughter of James Sevier and Nancy Conway Sevier, was born May 12, 1794. She died 1796.

MINERVA GRAINGER SEVIER

4. Minerva Grainger Sevier, daughter of James Sevier and Nancy Conway Sevier, was born March 15, 1796. She married April 30, 1816, John Nelson, who died in 1830.

PAMELIA HAWKINS SEVIER

5. Pamelia Hawkins Sevier, daughter of James Sevier and Nancy Conway Sevier, was born March 15, 1798. She died in 1842. She married May 6, 1817, Alexander M. Nelson, who was probably a brother to John Nelson, who married her sister, Minerva. She had a son, Alexander M. Nelson, Jr., who was born July 23, 1820.

SUSANNAH BROWN SEVIER

6. Susannah Brown Sevier, daughter of James Sevier and Nancy Conway Sevier, was born June 25, 1800. She married, November 26, 1818, Richard Purdom. They had a son, Alexander Purdom, who was born, November 12, 1819.

ELBERT FRANKLIN SEVIER

7. Elbert Franklin Sevier, son of James Sevier and Nancy Conway Sevier, was born September 17, 1802. He married twice. He first married Matilda Powell. The marriage took place August 9, 1832. They had two children, Elbert Powell Sevier, who married and had a son, James Sevier; and Sarah Sevier, who died with her mother in Knoxville of cholera in 1854. Elbert Franklin Sevier married for his second wife, Eliza James, a daughter of Reverend Jesse James, of Chattanooga. They had a son, James Sevier, who became a minister.

ELBRIDGE GERRY SEVIER

8. Elbridge Gerry Sevier, son of James Sevier and Nancy Conway Sevier, was born March 19, 1805. He married November 13, 1827, Mary Caroline Brown, born February 27, 1810, died ————. daughter of Thomas Brown and his wife, Mary McElwee Brown.

Elbridge Gerry Sevier and Mary Caroline Brown Sevier had twelve children, namely:

a. Thomas Brown Sevier
b. Henry Clay Sevier
c. Rowena Jane Sevier
d. James Sevier
e. Elbert Franklin Sevier, born January, 1836, lived a few days only.
f. John Elbridge Sevier
g. Elbert Franklin Sevier, (second child by this name).
h. Mary Caroline Sevier
i. Charles Bascom Sevier
l. William Hazleton Sevier
j. Conway Sevier, and (twins).
k. Ann Elizabeth Sevier

a. Thomas Brown Sevier, son of Elbridge Gerry Sevier and Mary Caroline Brown Sevier was born September 16, 1828. He was never married.

b. Henry Clay Sevier, son of Elbridge Gerry Sevier and Mary Caroline Brown Sevier, was born July 16, 1831, died in Liberty, Mo., 1918. He married, December 19, 1853, Mary Jennie Tipton, born Mobile Alabama, 1831, died Liberty, Mo., 1920. Their children were:

A. Elizabeth Sevier
B. William James Sevier
C. Robert E. Sevier
D. Charles Sevier

Of these:

A. Elizabeth Sevier, born 1856, died ————.

B. William James Sevier, born 1858, Bates County, Mo. He married Mary McGuinness, born Missouri City, Mo.,1864. They had eight children: (1) Herbert Eugene Sevier, born 1885 (who married Grace Muir and lives in Windham, Mont. They have six children, Jean, Alice, May, John Woodrow, Mary Elizabeth, Hazel, Madeline and Parker Sevier); (2) Roy Sevier, born 1887 (who married Lois Froman and lives in Liberty, Mo.); (3 Oscar Sevier, born 1899, (who married Vivian Ritter and lives in Liberty, Mo. Oscar Sevier served in the 91st Division 316 Military Police in France); (4) Ethel Sevier, born 1891 (who married Keller Bell and has two children, Keller Bell, Jr., and Anna Margaret Bell, and lives in Liberty, Mo.); (5). Stella Sevier, born 1892 (who married Frank Jackson and lives in Edgerton, Mo.); (6) Robert Earl Sevier, born 1895 (who married, 1920, Virginia Isabell Kendrick, born 1898, daughter of Edgar and Effie Kendrick. They live in Liberty, Mo., and have one child, Marilyn Sevier, born 1924. Robert Earl Sevier enlisted December 5, 1917 in Coast Artillery Corps and was in Camp at Fort McArthur, Calif., until May 13, when he was sent to France, where he served in 52nd Ammunition Train. He was discharged February 14, 1919); (7) Anna Bernice Sevier, born 1897; (8) Hazel Madeline Sevier, born 1899.

C. Dr. Robert E. Sevier, born 1860, married May Wadded. They have two children, (1) Helen May Sevier, and (2 Roberta Ann Sevier.

D. Charles Sevier, born 1865, married Elizabeth Taboy. They have two sons, (1) Charles Henry Sevier; and (2) Robert Fields Sevier.

c. Rowena Jane Sevier, daughter of Elbridge Gerry Sevier and Mary Caroline Brown Sevier, was born May 14, 1832. She married H. W. Von Aldehoff. They had five children: Florence Caroline Von Aldehoff, Alice Eugenia Von Aldehoff, John Sevier Von Aldehoff, Blanche Von Aldehoff, and John Sevier Von Aldehoff. Florence Caroline Von Aldehoff, daughter of H. W. Von Aldehoff and Rowena Jane Sevier Von Aldehoff, was born July 2, 1851. She married Thomas Augustus Hurt and had at least one child, Augusta Hurt, who married Frederick Trabue Mosely. John Sevier Von Aldehoff first son of H. W. Von Aldehoff and Rowena Jane Sevier Von Aldehoff, was born September 2, 1852. He died October 23, 1859. Alice Eugenia Von Aldehoff, daughter of H. W. Von Aldehoff and Rowena Jane Von Aldehoff, was born January 3, 1855. John Sevier Von Aldehoff, second son of H. W. Von Aldehoff, and second son to bear the name, was born September 14, 1855. Since he was born four years before his older brother of the same name died, I conclude that his name was changed after that brother's death. He is married and lives in Dallas, Texas. Blanche

Von Aldehoff, daughter of H. W. Von Aldehoff and Rowena Jane Sevier Von Aldehoff, was born April 10, 1859.

d. James Sevier, son of Elbridge Gerry Sevier and Mary Caroline Brown Sevier, was born August 1, 1835. He made his home in Kingston, Tennessee, and was a distinguished and learned man. He never married. He died in 1908.

e. Elbert Franklin Sevier, son of Elbridge Gerry Sevier and Mary Caroline Brown Sevier, was born in January, 1836, and lived only a few days.

f. John Elbridge Sevier son of Elbridge Gerry Sevier and Mary Caroline Brown Sevier, was born January 24, 1839.

g. Elbert Franklin Sevier, son of Elbridge Gerry Sevier and Mary Caroline Brown Sevier, was born December. 25, 1843. He was the second child to be given the name as the first child of the name died in infancy. He married Bettie Taylor and had five children, one son and four daughters, namely: Taylor Sevier, Evelyn Sevier, Edith Sevier, Ethel Sevier and Hazel Sevier. Of these: Evelyn Sevier married Gray Gentry, son of Fenton Allen Gentry and has one son, Fenton Allen Gentry, Jr.; Taylor Sevier is unmarried. Edith Sevier, Ethel Sevier and Hazel Sevier died young.

h. Mary Caroline Sevier, daughter of. Elbridge Gerry Sevier and Mary Caroline Brown Sevier, was born July 18,. 184—.

i. William Hazleton Sevier, son of Elbridge Gerry Sevier and Mary Caroline Brown Sevier, was born October 15, ————.

j. Conway Sevier, son of Elbridge Gerry Sevier and Mary Caroline Brown Sevier, was a twin to Ann Elizabeth Sevier and was born November 7, 1848. He was christened Conway, but as a child was nicknamed Samuel, and lived and died known by that name. He died in 1923. He never married.

k. Ann Elizabeth Sevier, daughter of Elbridge Gerry Sevier, and Mary Caroline Brown Sevier, was a twin to Conway (known as Samuel) and was born November 7, 1848. She married Noah Lybarger and had no children. Being left a widow she returned to the family home in Kingston and kept house for her bachelor brothers James Sevier and Samuel Sevier, until her death, about 1915.

l. Charles Bascom Sevier, son of Elbridge Gerry Sevier and Mary Caroline Brown Sevier, was born November 12, 1856. He married Alice Zedder and lived in Harriman, Tennessee, until his death in 1920. He had one daughter, Mary Katherine Sevier, who married Thomas Francis Reimer

CLARISSA CARTER SEVIER

9. Clarissa Carter Sevier daughter of James Sevier and Nancy Conway Sevier, was born April 9, 1807. She married May 7, 1822,

John Jones, and had at least one son, ————— Jones, who married ————— and had a son, Thomas E. Jones, of Knoxville,. Tennessee. He married and has a son, Derrell E. Jones.

Carissa Carter Sevier Jones and John Jones had probably several children. In the family Bible, (from which I secured most of the information in this chapter), which is now in possession of Mrs. Gray Gentry, two children are entered as "Jones" but it is not stated which of these children are Clarissa's and which her sister's, for it will be noted that her sister, Louisa Maria Sevier, also married a J nes. However, by the date of birth of two of her children, Sevier James Elbridge Jones, born February 20, 1823, and Sarah Ann Jones, born January, 1825, they were evidently Clarissa's children, as Louisa Maria Sevier was not married until 1827.

LOUISA MARIA SEVIER

10. Louisa Maria Sevier, daughter of James Sevier and Nancy Conway Sevier, was born December 16, 18 1. She married James Houston Jones, O tober 16, 1827. They had children, namely:

a. Sue Purdom Jones
.b. Ann E i a Jones
c. George Jones
d. Mary Louise Jones

a. Sue Purdom Jones, daughter of Louisa Mar a Sevier Jones and James Houston Joues, married in 1841, Gibson Allen Duckworth. They had thirteen chidren, only six of whom survived to maturity, namely: E la Louise Duckworth, who was their first child; (9) Susan Duckworth; (10) Harry Duckworth; (11) Maria Duckworth; (12) Minnie Duckworth and (13) Kate Duckworth. Ella Louise Duckworth, the first child of Sue Purdom Jones Duckworth and Gibson Allen Luckworth, married December 16, 1879, Valentine John Kindel E la Louise Duckworth Kind l and Valentine John Kindel had five children, namely: Eva Lois Kindel, married 1907, John Robert Boxley and has John Robert Boxley, Jr.; William Allen Kindel, married September 1, 1905, Lineta Rogers and has Wil iam Allen Kindel. Jr., and Martha Louise Kindel; Cher y Maud Kindel married Carey C. Orr, 1914, and has Dorcthy Jane Orr and Cherry Sue Orr.

b. Ann Eliza Jones, daughter of Louisa Maria Sevier Jones and James Houston Jones, born July 5, 1829, marri d Felix G. Lee.

c. George Jones, son of Louisa Maria Sevier Jones and James Houston Jones, born September 7, 1838, died April 11, 1922. He married Catherine —————————. They had a daughter, Nannie Sevier Jones, who married John M. Bishop.

d. Mary Louise Jones, daughter of Louisa Maria Sevier Jones and James Houston Jones, married Thomas J. Lane. Their children were Annie Lane, who married Clarence Carter Trim and has an only child, Louise Trim, who married Charles Donaldson, and has an only child, Geraldine Trim Donaldson; Jessie Lane, who married twice, first ——————— Drummond, and second ——————— Stamps, and has two sons, Fleming Drummond and Bowie Drummond; and Henry Lane, who is not married.

THE JONES CHILDREN ENTERED IN THE JAMES SEVIER FAMILY BIBLE

There are five children named Jones whose births are recorded in the Family Bible belonging to Major James Sevier, now in possession of his great-grand daughter, Mrs. Gray Gentry. There is no indication as to the parents of the five Jones children, but as noted above by the date two of them, Sevier James Elbridge Jones and Sarah Ann Jones are evidently children of Clarissa and John Jones, whose marriage preceded that of Louisa Maria and James H. Jones.

The five entries are:

Sevier James Elbridge Jones, born February 20, 1823.
Sarah Ann Jones, born January 1825.
Ann Eliza Jones, born July 5, 1829.
William Elbert Franklin Jones, no date given.
James Sevier Jones, born September 1830.

MARY MALVINA SEVIER

11. Mary Malvina Sevier, daughter of James Sevier and Nancy Conway Sevier, was their youngest child. She was born April 4, 1814. She married James Stuart July 2, 1829. She had a daughter, Mary Stuart, who married John Howard, of Knoxville.

CHAPTER THREE
John Sevier, junior

JOHN SEVIER. JUNIOR

Major John Sevier, Jr., as he was known, was third son of Gov John Sevier and his first wife, Sarah Hawkins Sevier. He was born June 20, 1766, at New Market, Virginia, and given his father's full name. He died April 26, 1845.

John Sevier, Jr., was too young to participate in the Battle of King's Mountain, though he accompanied his father on several of the later Indian Campaigns, and it is said by his daughter, Mrs. Thomas Price, (Martha Ann Sevier, that he fought in the Revolution. He was only seventeen when the war was over, but his brother, James, was fighting at sixteen. It is probable that he accompanied his father in the campaigns of the last two years of the Revolutionary war and later in the Indian warfare.

He was elected recording and engrossing clerk of the first Convention held in the State of Tennessee.

He married three time and had eighteen children. He married first Elizabeth Conway; second, Sarah Richards, and third, Sophia Garoutte.

His first wife, Elizabeth Conway, was the daughter of Colonel Henry Conway, of the Revolution. Her sisters, Nancy and Susannah Conway, also married into the Sevier family. Nancy married James Sevier, (John Sevier, Jr.'s, brother) and Susannah married John Sevier, son of Valentine, called Devil Jack to distinguish him among the Johns. He was first cousin to James and John.

The marriage bond of John Sevier Jr., and Elizabeth Conway, is dated July 8, 1788. He was just twenty-two years of age. His bond was for $1,250, and it was signed by his father. It is said that his wife died in childbirth with her first child. A list of the children of John Sevier, Jr., prepared by his grand-daughter, Mrs. George French, a sister of Bishop Embree Hoss, from whom she secured her material, does not show the name of any child by the first wife. She gives seventeen children, beginning with the first child by the second wife. She told me that if there was a living child by Elizabeth Conway Sevier that she never heard of it. On the other hand, Bishop Hoss himself says there were eighteen children.

John Sevier Jr., married for his second wife Sarah Richards, of Philadelphia. They had seven children:

1. William Sevier
2. Samuel Sevier
3. James Sevier
4. Eliza Sevier
5. Sarah Sevier
6. John Sevier, III.
7. Thomas Sevier

John Sevier, Jr., married for his third wife Sophia Garoutte, of a French family of distinction. They had ten chi'dren, namely:

8. John Garoutte Sevier
9. Elizabeth Conway Sevier
10. Sophia Smith Garoutte Sevier
11. Louisa Rebecca Sevier
12. Michael Robert Sevier
13. George Washington Sevier
14. Anna Maria Sevier
15. Sarah Hundley Sevier
16. Archibald McAfee Sevier
17. Martha Ann Sevier

Sophia Garoutte was the daughter of Michael Garoutte, a Frenchman and his wife, Sophia Smith Garoutte. They had thirteen children, of whom Sophia, who married John Sevier, was the sixth. Michael Garoutte was born April 12, 1750 He married October 23, 1778. His parents were Antoine Garoutte and Lady Anne De Lascour. Antoine Garoutte was born January 19, 1695 He lived in Marseilles, Frances, and was Attorney General for that section of France. His son, Michael Garoutte, was a Captain of many vessels, and was very wealthy and was an admiral in the French Navy.

WILLIAM SEVIER

1. William Sevier, son of John Sevier, Jr., by his second wife, Sarah Richards Sevier, is given as their first child. No information.

SAMUEL SEVIER

2. Samuel Sevier, son of John Sevier, Jr., and his second wife, Sarah Richards Sevier. No information

JAMES SEVIER

James Sevier, son of John Sevier, Jr., by his second wife, Sarah Richards Sevier, was evidently named for his father's bother. He went to Indiana. In an old letter, now in possession of the family, written by Robert E. Sevier (son of Michael) to his uncle, John Garoutte Sevier, he says: "I have found some new kinspeople, James Thompson Sevier, son of your brother James

who went to Indiana." This letter is dated 1871. This James
Thompson Sevier lived at Russellville, Ark.

ELIZA SEVIER

4. Eliza Sevier, daughter of John Sevier, Jr., by his second
wife, Sarah Richards Sevier, married Joseph W. Throckmorton,
of Philadelphia. No further information.

SARAH SEVIER

5. Sarah Sevier, the daughter of John Sevier, Jr., by his second wife, Sarah Richards Sevier, received her mother's name and
her grandmother's name, as John Sevier, Jr., was the son of Sarah
Hawkins Sevier.

JOHN SEVIER, III.

6. John Sevier, III, was the son of John Sevier, Jr., by his
second wife, Sarah Richards Sevier. He received his father's and
his grandfather's name. I have no further data.

THOMAS SEVIER

Thomas Sevier, son of John Sevier, Jr., and Sarah Richards
Sevier, was born about 1803. He never married. He lived almost
all his life with a sister, probably Eliza, in Philadelphia. In 1860
Thomas Sevier came South to visit his niece, Elizabeth, in Union
City, Tennessee. He was too old for service in the Army but he
sympathized strongly with the South. He was about sixty years
old when he went to Corinth to see his friend of many years, General Albert Sidney Johnston. This was just before the Battle of
Shiloh. General Johnston sent him up the Tennessee River in charge
of Commissary boats. The boats were captured by Federal troops,
and he was never seen or heard of again.

JOHN GAROUTTE SEVIER

8. John Garoutte Sevier, son of John Sevier Jr., and his third
wife, Sophia Smith Garoutte Sevier, was born April 28, 1810. It
will be observed that a son by the second wife is also named John
Sevier. To add to the confusion, each of these is referred to at
times as John Sevier, III.

John Garoutte Sevier was educated for a lawyer. In 1831 when
he was twenty-one years of age he married Mary N. Mayfield. They
had ten children, only five of whom lived to maturity, namely:

    a. Elizabeth Evelyn Sevier

    b. Henry DeCab Sevier

    c. William J. Sevier

    d. John Michael Sevier

    e. James J. Sevier

John Garoutte Sevier and his family, including his brother,

Michael Sevier and his sister, Martha Ann Sevier, who had made her home with her brother, John Garoutte Sevier, since the death of their father, John Sevier, Jr., moved about 1845, to Obion County Tennessee, near Union City, Tenn. In 1859 John and Michail again felt the call of the frontier and they went to Conway County, Arkansas. They were there only a few years when John Garoutte Sevier lost his wife and a young daughter. The War Between the States divided his family, one son going to the Northern Army. The remaining three sons joined the Confederate Army. After the War he went back to Union City to make his home with h's only surviving daughter, Elizabeth Evelyn Sevier, who had married in 1854 Thomas Ransom Curlin, son of Samuel Curlin. Thomas Ransom Curlin was descended from the Curlins and Coopers, of North Carolina, the Coopers being descended from Sir Ashley Cooper, the first Earl of Shaftsbury.

a. Elizabeth Evelyn Sevier Curlin and her husband, Thomas Ransom Curlin had eight children, one of whom died in infancy. The seven surviving children were:

A. Robert T. Curlin, born April 22, 1852.
B. Sarah Eliza Elizabeth Curlin, born August 5, 1854.
C. Laura Sophia Curlin, born July 21, 1857.
D. Mary Rebekah Joanna Curlin, born December 12, 1858.
E. Nancy Alida Curlin, born September 11, 1861.
F. John Edward Allen Curlin, born July 4, 1864.
G. James Lemuel Curlin, born January 27, 1867.

Of these:

A. Robert Curlin married Virginia Watson, and had one child, who died in infancy. He has made his home in Union City, Tenn.

B. Sarah Eliza Elizabeth Curlin married Lycurgus Hall. They had five children, one dying in infancy. The other four are (1) Dr. Horace Curlin Hall, born September 12, 1873, residence Laredo, Texas, married Carmilla Scott. They have three children, Mary Hall (who married Captain William H. Colburn, U. S. A., and has one daughter, Mary Beverly Colburn; Horace Curlin Hall, Jr., and Beverly Scott Hall. (2). Ioma Hall, born August 5, 1876, married George DeBoe Lauderdale, resides in Dallas Texas and has one child, Edward Kirk Lauderdale. (3). Nell Kirk Hall, born 1887, married first James Merrin, and had one daughter, Minda Merrin. Her second marriage was to William B. Kellogg. Their residence is at Houston, Texas. (4). Elizabeth Sevier Hall, born 1890, married Jack M. Little and has two children, Jack M. Little, Jr., and Mary Elizabeth Little, residence, Dallas, Texas.

C. Laura Sophia Curlin married George B. Sower, of Christianburg, Va. They resided at Wanchula, Florida, and had two children one dying young. The remaining son, Curlin Brook Sower, married

Harriet Edwards, and has one son, George Bruce Sower, born September 30, 1907.

D. Mary Rebekah Joanna Curlin married James E. George and had two children, one dying in infancy and the remaining one, Gertrude Sevier George, residing at Union City, Tennessee.

E. Nancy Alida Curlin married Martin Walker Barney. They have two children, Earle Sevier Barney, born July 17, 1890, and Pauline Curlin Barney, born Jan. 9, 1890, residence Union City, Tenn.

F. John Edward Allen Curlin married Dorothy Bain, residence Dallas, Texas. They have four daughters: (1) Laura Earl Curlin (married first Lucius Earl McBride, and had one son, Lucius Earl McBride, Jr., who married Louise Barr; Laura Earl Curlin married, second, to Alfred M. Daniel, and had one child, Elizabeth Daniel). (2) Nina May Curlin, married William Ford Nolan, and has two children, Emma Catherine Nolan, and Wilford Allen Nolan, residence Dallas, Texas. (3) Irene Ethel Curlin married Marshall William Beedle, and has three children, Edward Marshall Beedle, Charles William Beedle, and Claude Allen Beedle. Their residence is in Dallas, Texas. (4) Pauline Belle Curhad no children.

G. James Lemuel Curlin, residence Dallas, Texas, is unmarried.

b. Henry DeCab Sevier, son of John Garoutte Sevier and Mary Mayfield Sevier, married ——————— and had a son, William Henry Sevier, who lives at Mayflower, Ark.

b. William J. Sevier, son of John Garoutte Sevier and Mary Mayfield Sevier married ——————— and had two daughters, Laura Sevier and Drucilla Sevier, who live at Joplin, Mo.

d. John Michael Sevier, son of John Garoutte Sevier and Mary Mayfield Sevier, married ——————— and had one son, Elbridge Sevier, who lives at Dexter, Mo.

e. James J. Sevier, son of John Garoutte Sevier and Mary Mayfield Sevier, was killed in the Battle of Vicksburg 1863 in the Confederate Army.

ELIZABETH CONWAY SEVIER

9. Elizabeth Conway Sevier, daughter of John Sevier, Jr., and her grandmother. She married ——————— Byers.

SOPHIA SMITH GAROUTTE SEVIER

10. Sophia Smith Garoutte Sevier was the daughter of John Sevier, Jr., and his third wife, Sophia Smith Garoutte Sevier. She was named Sophia for her mother and grandmother, Sophia Smith, wife of Michael Garoutte. She was born 1815.

LOUISA REBECCA SEVIER

11. Louisa Rebecca Sevier, daughter of John Sevier Jr., and his third wife, Sophia Smith Garoutte Sevier, was born November 21, 1816. She married Major Byrd Brown (born October 20, 1801; died March 24, 1886). She died May 20, 1842, leaving two children,

    a. John Jacob Brown

    b. Sophia Louisa Sevier Brown

a. John Jacob Brown, son of Louisa Rebecca Sevier Brown and Major Byrd Brown was born February 23, 1840. He married January 1, 1866, Esther Eliza Wilson. They had ten children, namely:

    A. Thmoas Jefferson Wilson Brown

    B. Byrd Brown

    C. Embree Sevier Brown

    D. Nolachucky Brown, died in infancy

    E. Martha Rebecca Brown

    F. William Franklin Brown

    G. John Jacob Brown, Jr.

    H. Charles Vestal Brown

    I. Mariah Louisa Brown

    J. Ella Star Brown.

Of these:

A. Thomas Jefferson Wilson, born Oct. 2, 1867, married Genevieve Arnold, of Western West Virginia, August 14, 1907. No children.

B. Byrd Brown, born March 19, 1869, married Chloe Clark, of Nance County, Nebraska, February, 1904. One daughter, Mollie May, born 1905, married Dean Huddart, January, 1823. One son, Dean Duane.

C. Embree Sevier, born May 30, 1870, married April 2, 1919, Harriet Margaret Shields, daughter of David Shields, of Washington County, Tennessee. Their children, Nancy Esther, born December 1920, Jacob Embree, born Jan. 20, 1923; David Shelby, born January 28, 1924.

D. Nola Chuckey, born February 2, 1872. Died August 26, 1873.

E. Martha Rebecca, born October 6, 1873. Died March 27, 1901.

F. William Franklin Brown, born June 24, 1875.

G. John Jacob Brown, Jr., born March 26, 1877, married Oct. 1, 1901, to Nelia Fondren, of Washington County, East Tennessee. No children.

H. Charles Vestal, born July 25, 1881, married October 20, 1907, to Lillian Miller, of Washington County, Tennessee. Their children—Thomas Sherrill, born Oct. 18, 1909.

1. **Mariah Louisa**, born Jan. 19, 1883, married June 9, 1909 **Herman** Pierce of Sullivan County, Tennessee. Their children, **Ella Rowena**, born April 14, 1921 and Esther Louisa, born Feb. 10, 1924.

J. **Ella Star**, born July 10, 1887, married April 16.1919 **Hugh Miller** Cox of Sullivan County, East Tennessee.

(b.) Sophia Louisa Sevier Brown, daughter of Louisa Rebecca Sevier Brown and Major Byrd Brown, was born January 14, 1842. She married Shelby McDowell Deaderick (see Deaderick Family Volume 1 Notable Southern Families) Her second husband was George Columbus Ward and her third husband was John A. Graham. Sophia Louisa Sevier Brown had children by each of her marriages. Her children were:

A. John Wallace Deaderick
B. Mary Louisa Ward
C. Nellie Ward died unmarried
D. Esther Ruth Ward, died in infancy
E. William Ward, died in infancy

The only surviving children of Sophia Louisa Sevier Brown were the son of her first husband and a daughter by the second husband.

Mary Louisa Ward, daughter of Sophia Louisa Sevier Brown Ward and George Columbus Ward (whom she married December 20, 1857) married a kinsman of her mother's third husband (John A. Graham) Mary Louisa Ward married Jonathan Summerfield Graham August 5, 1870, several years before her mother's marriage to John A. Graham took place. Mary Louisa Ward Graham and Jonathan Summerfield Graham had eleven children, namely:

1. Roxie Inez Graham
2. Henry Jackson Graham
3. Sarah Lou Graham
4. Elizabeth Emmetta Graham
5. Esther Ruth Graham
6. John Wallace Graham
7. Shelby Franklin Graham
8. Jessie May Graham
9. Mary Lillian Graham
10. Girtrude Graham
11. Orlena Graham
these last children being twins.

Of the foregoing: Roxie Inez Graham married William Clyde Dishner, April 27, 1920. (their children are William Clyde Dishner, junior, Nola State Dishner and Harry Lee Dishner); Henry Jackson Graham married Jessie Eva Smith, September 10, 1922 (their children are John Smith Graham and Jackson Dale Graham); Sarah Lou Graham married Charles Andrew Dillow, July 1, 1923 (their child is Charles Graham Dillow.

MICHAEL ROBERT SEVIER

12.   Michael Robert Sevier, son of John Sevier, junior and his third wife Sophia Smith Garoutte Sevier, was born June 18, 1822. He was named after his grandfather Michael Garoutte and for his paternal uncle Captain Robert Sevier who was killed at King's Mountain.   Michael Robert Sevier accompanied his brother and sister, John Garoutte Sevier and Martha Ann Sevier to Obion County in 1845.   In 1859 he moved with them to Conway County Arkansas.

He married, probably before he left East Tennessee, Sarah E. Bayless, of Jonesboro, Tennessee.   They had several children some of whom died young.   Their children were:

    a.   Elbridge Gerry Sevier, died about 1922
    b.   Sophia T. Sevier, born about 1850
    c.   Samuel Sevier, died about 1900
    d.   Robert E. Sevier, died about 1898
    e.   Abraham Sevier, died about 1884
    f.   John Sevier, died young
    g.   Archibald Sevier, died young
    h.   Anna M. Sevier, died young
    i.   Mary L. Sevier, died young
    j.   Martha E. Sevier, died young
    k.   Leonidas A. Sevier, died about 1878
    Of the foregoing:

Elbridge G. Sevier, son of Michael Robert Sevier and Sarah E. Bayless Sevier married Elizabeth Compton.   They had ten children, namely, Elbert E. Sevier, Oliver Sevier, Thomas R. Sevier, Mike Sevier, Archibald Sevier, Katherine Sevier, Caroline Sevier, John Sevier, Arthur Sevier and Joseph Sevier.

Sophia T. Sevier, daughter of Michael Sevier and Sarah T. Bayless Sevier, married twice.   She first married William A. Lavendar and had four children, namely Joseph M. Lavendar, Sarah M. Lavendar, Benjamin L. Lavendar, and Ada L. Lavendar.   She married for her second husband Albert A. Mosely and had six children, namely John Mosely, Robert Mosely, Lee Mosely, Lillian Mosely, Emma Mosely and Charles Mosely.

John S. Sevier, son of Michael Robert Sevier and Sarah E. Bayless Sevier, married Cynthia M. Hall.   They had six children, namely, Laura Sevier, Frank Sevier, Beulah Sevier, Lilly Sevier Emory Sevier and Charles Sevier.

Robert E. Sevier, son of Michael Robert Sevier and Sarah E. Bayless Sevier, married Beulah Harrison and had two children namely: Ethel Sevier and Shelby Sevier.

The record of this branch of the family has been furnished by Mrs. ,Sophia T. Moseley, the only surviving child of Michael Robert Sevier and Sarah E. Bayless Sevier.

GEORGE WASHINGTON SEVIER

13. George Washington Sevier, the son of John Sevier, junior, and his third wife Sophia Smith Garoutte Sevier, was born about 1823. He received the name of his paternal uncle, George Washington Sevier, first son of Governor Sevier by Catherine Sherrill Sevier.

ANNA MARIA SEVIER

14. Anna Maria Sevier, daughter of John Sevier, junior and his third wife, Sophia Smith Garoutte Sevier, was born about 1824. She married Henry Hoss, of Jonesboro, Tennessee. They had six children namely:

1. Amanda Fadora Hoss
2. Elijah Embree Hoss
3. Archibald Hoss
4. Sophia Hoss
5. John Isaac Hoss
6. Mattie Hoss

Of the foregoing:

(1.) Amanda Fadora Hoss married Samuel J. Kirkpatrick and had ten children, namely: Minnie Kirkpatrick, (who married Charles Kirkland, and had five children, Isabel Kirkland, Winifred Kirkland, Jesse Kirkland, Mollie Kirkland and William Kirkland); Hugh Henry Kirkpatrick, (who married Nina Bell Murphey and has two children, Mildred Kirkpatrick, married Max Maloney and has a daughter, Anna Bell Maloney, and a son, Hugh Henry Kirkpatrick, junior); Paul White Kirkpatrick, (who married Vesta Pennington and has one child. Mary Harris Kirkpatrick); Samuel Sevier Kirkpatrick (who married Anna Maria Panhurst and has no children); Jessie Eugenia Kirkpatrick (who married John Henry Bowman and has two children William Bowman and John Henry Bowman, junior); Archibald Hoss Kirkpatrick (who married Bessie Cruikshanks and has four children Anna Kirkpatrick, William Kirkpatrick, Dorothy Kirkpatrick and Bessie Kirkpatrick); William Reeves Kirkpatrick (who died unmarried. Anna Kirkpatrick (who died unmarried); Mary Kirkpatrick (who died young): and Charles Prescott Kirkpatrick (who married Essie Annie Schuessler).

(2.) Elijah Embree Hoss, son of Henry and Anna Maria Sevier Hoss was born in Washington County, Tennessee, April 14, 1849. He married Abbie Bell Clarke, daughter of Edwin R. Clarke and Mary Ann Sessler Clarke. He became a distinguished Bishop of the Methodist Episcopal Church South. Died at the home of his son, Dr. Sessler Hoss, at Muskogee Oklahoma, April 23, 1919. He had three children;

a. Mary Muriel Hoss was born at Santa Ross California in 1870. She married John Headman and has two children, Francis Headman and Embree Headman.

b. Embree E. Hoss, junior, married Blanche Divine of Chattanooga and has one son, E. E. Hoss III.

c. Sessler Hoss, a physician of Muskogee Oklahoma, married Irene Ewing Morrow of Nashville Tennessee (see Armstrong, Luttrell, McAdoo, Cockrill, Ewing, in Notable Southern Families Vol. I and III).   Dr. Hoss died at his home in Muskogee, Oklahoma Dec. 29, 1921.   He had two children, Sessler, junior, who died in infancy and Irene Ewing Hoss.

3. Archibald Hoss, son of Henry Hoss and Maria Sevier Hoss, married Allie Susong and has three children, Henry Hoss, Anna Hoss and Dorothy Hoss.

4. Sophia Hoss, daughter of Henry Hoss and Anna Maria Sevier Hoss, married George D. French, of Morristown, Tennessee and had four daughters, Virginia French, who married E. R. Taylor and has one son, E. R. Taylor, junior; Josephine French, who married W. C. Kreger, of Abingdon, Virginia and has three children, Jean Sevier Kreger, W. D. Kreger, junior, and George French Kreger; Mattie French who is unmarried; and Dora French, who married———— Barrow and has no children.   She lives in Morristown.

5. John Isaac Hoss died unmarried.

6. Mattie Hoss born March 24, 1855, married P. H. Prince June 11, 1878 and lived in Arkansas.   She had two children, Anna Prince and William Prince.

SARAH HUNDLEY SEVIER

15. Sarah Hundley Sevier was the daughter of John Sevier, junior, by his third wife, Sophia Smith Garoutte Sevier.   She was born in 1826.   It will be observed that there was also a Sarah by the second wife.   Hundley was a name in the Conway family and is a favorite middle name to the present time among descendants. Sarah Hundley was the name of John Sevier.junior's first wife's mother.   He named one daughter for the first wife Elizabeth Conway and one for her mother.   Sarah Hundley Sevier married first, Robert E. Humphries, and second, Shelby Currey.   In documents in Washington concerning the Sevier estate, Emmetta Humphries, administratrix of the John Sevier Estate, says that she is the child of Sarah Hundley Sevier.

ARCH'BALD MCAFEE SEVIER

16.   Archibald McAfee Sevier, son of John Sevier, junior, and his third wife, Sophia Smith Garoutte Sevier, was born August 2, 1829.   He assumed the maintenance and education of his youngest sister Martha, while he was still quite young.   He moved to Missouri in 1856.   He lived in Neosha Mo. until his death.   He married Paulina Belle Sutton but had no children.

THE SEVIER FAMILY

MARTHA ANN SEVIER

17. Martha Ann Sevier, daughter of John Sevier, junior, and his third wife, Sophia Smith Garoutte Sevier, was born November 3, 1831. She married Thomas P. Price in 1850 in West Tennessee where she had accompanied her brother John Garoutte Sevier with whom she made her home after the death of their father, John Sevier, junior. She removed with her husband to Neosho Mo. They had eight children among them:

- a. Frank J. Price
- b. Albert H. Price
- c. Henry T. Price
- d. (a daughter) who married C. M. Harland of Memphis
- e. (a daughter who married B. P. Armstrong of Neosho, Mo.

Mrs. Martha Ann Sevier Price lived until a few years ago. She resided in Memphis with her daughter, Mrs. C. M. Hart'and, after the death of Thomas P. Price in Neosho in 1905.

CHAPTER FOUR
Elizabeth Sevier

ELIZABETH SEVIER

Elizabeth Sevier, daughter of Governor John Sevier and his first wife Sarah Hawkins Sevier, was their eldest daughter. Her birth took place in Virginia about the year 1768. She came to the "Mountains" with her parents in 1773, arriving at the new home on Christmas day. Her marriage to William Clark said to be a veteran of King's Mountain and certainly a participant in other military expeditions of the time, took place about 1786. Her eldest child, Elizabeth Clark was born, according to 'family records, July 20, 1787.

William Clark was in Governor Sevier's Regiment at King's Mountain it is said and served at other times in Governor Sevier's Regiment. He was born in Shenandoah County Virginia, April 7, 1757. He lived in Pendleton District, South Carolina, but moved late in life to Hall County, Georgia, where he died June 4, 1843. It was while he was a resident of Washington County, North Carolina (now Tennessee) that he served with Governor Sevier and that his marriage to Elizabeth Sevier took place.

It is said that Elizabeth Sevier Clark died at For. Madison South Carolina and that all of her children were born in South Carolina. She died before 1792, for February 14, 1792 William Clark married Ruth Goodwin in Franklin County, Georgia.

Elizabeth Sevier Clark and William H. Clark had three children who are positively known and probably a fourth child. Documents in Washington concerning the Sevier estate mention her three children, Elizabeth, Sarah and John and omit the fourth child, Ruth. But family records give the name of this child and I therefore include her here. There may be an error in the list or Ruth may not have been living when the list was prepared. There are some errors and some omissions in the Washington documents.

I do not know the order in which these names should be p'aced but Elizabeth Clark it is said by descendants, was the eldest child.

Children of Elizabeth Sevier Clark and William H. Clark:
1. Elizabeth Clark
2. Sarah Hawkins Clark
3. John Clark
4. Ruth Clark

Elizabeth Sevier Clark probably died shortly after the birth of her last child as Major Clark married his second wife February 14, 1792.   It is said that at least one of Elizabeth's children, Sarah Hawkins Clark, was reared by Gov. Sevier and that she married from his house.   It is possible that all of Elizabeth's children lived with Gov. and Mrs. Sevier and that the little boy called "Sevier" by Gov. Sevier in his Journal was Elizabeth's son, John, who may have had Sevier as a middle name.   (Major Clark had a son however by his second wife named Sevier and also one named John).

January 25, 1795: Gov. Sevier in his Journal speaks of the "horses that ran away with Sevier and Ruthy"! Ruthy was his daughter. "Sevier" may be the son of Mary Ann Sevier who was a widow and seems to have made her home with her father, or he may be John (Sevier) Clark son of Elizabeth.

William Clark who married Elizabeth Sevier was born April 7, 1757 in Shanandoah County, Virginia.   While a resident of Washington County, North Carolina in 1777 he enlisted in Captain Thomas Price's Company. Col. John Sevier's Regiment.   In 1778 he served in Col. Valentine Sevier's Regiment.   June 1780 he served in Captain Asher's Company and in 1781 in Captain Williams' Company, Col. John Sevier's Regiment.

About 1785 he married Elizabeth Sevier who died) sometime before February 14, 1792.

February 14, 1792 he married in Franklin County, Georgia, Ruth Goodwin born May 14, 1771.   He died in Hall County, Georgia June 4, 1843.

The children of Major Clark and Ruth Goodwin Clark were:
John Clark born November 5, 1792.
Oliver Clark born October 5, 1794
Sevier Clark born September 11, 1797
Sabra Clark born March 3, 1799

"Major and Mrs. William H. Clark" were present at the wedding of Catherine Sevier to Richard Campbell, December 24, 1795. and at other times they were in the household of Gov. and Mrs. Sevier for visits, but this Mrs. Clark is evidently Major Clark's second wife.   Major Clark's widow, Ruth Goodwin Clark, was granted a pension in her application executed April 2, 1844.

ELIZABETH CLARK

Elizabeth Clark daughter of Elizabeth Sevier and William H. Clark was born in South Carolina, July 20, 1786.   She married John Elston in 1801.

The information which follows regarding the descendants of

Elizabeth Clark Elston and John Elston was furnished by Mr. Elston Luttrell and is used in the form in which he prepared it.

John Elston and Elizabeth Clark Elston reared a family of eleven children, the first six born in Pendleton District, South Carolina, and the last five born in Habersham County, Georgia. They lived near the South Carolina and Georgia line. on the Tugaloo River, first on the South Carolina side in what was then the Pendleton, District, later Oconee County, until 1815-16, then on the Georgia side in Habersham County until 1834, at which date they moved to the Creek nation and settled in the upper Choccolocco valley in Benton (afterwards Calhoun) County, Alabama. Five of their children, namely, Sevier, William, John Clark, Ruth and Martha, came with them to Alabama.

The children of John and Elizabeth Clark Elston were eleven in number, as follows:

1. Allen Elston, born May 25, 1802.
2. Sally Elston, born August 8, 1805.
3. Neaty Elston, born June 29, 1807.
4. Nancy Elston, born September 16, 1809.
5. Sabra Elston, born April 8, 1812.
6. Sevier Elston, born December 27, 1814.
7. William Elston, born April 6, 1817.
8. Elizabeth Elston, born October 23, 1819.
9. John Clark Elston, born July 4, 1822.
10. Ruth Elston, born July 18, 1825.
11. Martha Elston, born April 17, 1831.

John Elston and his sons were among the pioneer settlers of old Benton County, Alabama. They bought and entered large plantations of valuable land around the old Corn Grove postoffice in the upper Choccolocco Valley. John Elston died July 11, 1853; just seven days after signing his last will and testament. His wife Elizabeth died November 11, 1845. They lie buried side by side in the family burying ground, on the Allen Elston home place near the house. Several of their children and grandchildren are also buried there.

I—ALLEN ELSTON

Allen Elston, the eldest child of John Elston and Elizabeth Clark Elston, and grandson of David Elston, of New Jersey, was born in Pendleton District, South Carolina, May 25, 1802. He married Martha Humphreys of the same place in 1822. Martha Humphreys was born in South Carolina October 23, 1806. They emigrated to the Choccolocco valley in Alabama about 1836, and settled in Benton (now Calhoun) County, near the Corn Grove postoffice. Here he died May 21, 1879, age 77 years.

Martha Humphreys Elston, wife of Allen Elston, died January 2, 1855.   Mr. Elston afterwards married a second wife, Mrs. Minerva Gibson.   The children of the first wife Martha Humphreys Elston, were ten in number, as follows:

1. Nancy Elston, born June 23, 1823.
2. Sabra Elston, born May 6, 1825.
3. Martha Elizabeth Elston, born June 8, 1827.
4. William Clark Elston, born March 6, 1829.
5. Sarah Elston, born June 17, 1831.
6. John Humphreys Elston, born June 18, 1835.
7. Kitty Hudson Elston, born October 31, 1837.
8. Susan Frances Elston, born February 14, 1840.
9. Eva Borders Elston, born Septeber 18, 1842.
10. Ann W. Elston, born October 24, 1844; died in infancy.
For further account of these see later.

II—SALLY (OR SARAH) ELSTON EDDINS

Sally Elston, second child of John Elston and Elizabeth Clark Elston, was born in Pendleton district, South Carolina, August 5, 1805. Her name is written "Sally" in the family Bible, but in her father's will she is mentioned as Sarah. She married James Eddins, of Franklin County, Georgia; died in Pickens District, South Carolina, in 1831 or 1832, leaving four daughters and one son. James Eddins afterwards married Salina Trimmer, of Toxaway Creek, South Carolina, and moved to Pickens County, Alabama, in 1835. He died December 22, 1877.

III—NEATY ELSTON DENMAN

Neaty Elston, the third child of John Elston and Elizabeth Clark Elston, was born in Pendleton District, South Carolina, June 29, 1807. She was married to Blake Denman near Cherokee Mountain, Habersham County, Ga. They lived there several years and then moved to Alabama and settled on a farm near Jacksonville. Here she died about 1852. Blake Denman died at the same place about 1886. They had seven or more children, whose names are not known.

IV—NANCY ELSTON

Nancy Elston, fourth child of John and Elizabeth Clark Elston, was born September 16, 1809. She is supposed to have died young.

V—SABRA ELSTON YOWELL

Sabra Elston, fifth child of John Elston and Elizabeth (Clark) Elston, was born in Pendeleton dist., S. C., April 8, 1812. She was married to James Allen Yowell, of Lincoln County, Tennessee. They had perhaps nine or ten children. She died there 1855-60.

VI—SEVIER ELSTON

Sevier Elston, sixth child of John Elston and Elizabeth (Clark) Elston, was born in Pendleton dist., S. C., December 27, 1814. He went to Alabama with his father in 1834. He married in S. C., Elizabeth B. Davis, of Pickens District, in 1847. They settled in Benton County, with others of the family, and acquired large agricultural interests. They had an only son, Harvey Davis Elston, born August 3, 1861, died July 11, 1869. Sevier Elston was postmaster at Corn Grove postoffice from 1842 to 1852. He died September 26, 1885.

VII—WILLIAM ELSTON

William Elston, seventh child of John Elston and Elizabeth (Clark) Elston, was born in Habersham County, Georgia, April 6, 1817; came to Alabama with his parents in 1834. He married there Miss Jane Worthington near White Plains, Calhoun County, Alabama, 18—. Had one daughter, Eleanor Elston, and an infant that died young. He died in 1854 of pneumonia. In 1857 his widow Jane and daughter Eleanor went out to Texas with some relatives. There Mrs. Elston married a second husband, name not known, and then a third named Broadus. They were yet living there in Burleson County, in 1881. The daughter Eleanor (later spoken of as Annie Elizabeth) married twice in Texas; 1st to A. Judson Jones, of Virginia. 2nd in 1879 to William Elston Taylor, her half-cousin from Talladega, Ala., he being a grandson of Allen Elston, Sr., of S. C. There were two sons by this union: (1) William Elston Taylor, Jr. (2) Andrew Law Taylor.

VIII—ELIZABETH (ELSTON) WEIR

Elizabeth Elston, eighth child of John Elston and Elizabeth (Clark) Elston, was born in Habersham County, Georgia, October 23, 1819. Was married to Dr. John R. Weir, of Blount County, Tenn., in about 1835. Had several children. About 1842 moved to Washington County, Texas Elizabeth died there April 20, 1851. Dr. Weir also died there in 1878-9. Two or three of their children were living in Texas in 1881. We find the following record of some of the children in the family Bible of John Elston, Mrs. Weir's father: (1) Mary Weir, born July 17, 1836, (2) Cullen Weir, born March 27, 1838. (3) Third child born February 26, 1840.

IX—JOHN CLARK ELSTON

John Clark Elston, ninth child of John Elston and Elizabeth (Clark) Elston, was born at Owl Swamp, in Habersham County, Ga., July 4, 1822. Moved with his parents to Alabama in 1834 He married January 21, 1846, Selina Jones, of Pendleton dist., S. C., a first cousin of James M. Jones, husband of his niece Nancy Elston. They lived in Benton (Calhoun) County, Alabama, till about 1869, then wɐnt to Johnson County, Texas, where he died March 19, 1896, Grandview postoffice. They had four children. For record of these and the grandchildren see later.

X—RUTH (ELSTON) MATTISON

Ruth Elston, tenth child of John Elston and Elizabeth (Clark) Elston, was born in Habersham County, Georgia, July 18, 1825. Migrated with parents to Alabama in 1834. Was married to Glover Mattison, in Alabama, about 1838. Reared four children. They moved to Denton County, Texas, in about 1866, and Ruth (Elston) Mattison died there July 8, 1870. Two of her children were living there in 1881. We have no further record of the children.

XI—MARTHA (ELSTON) HOLLINGSWORTH

Martha Elston, eleventh child of John Elston and Elizabeth (Clark) Elston was born in Habersham County, Georgia, April 17, 1831. Came to Alabama in 1834; was married at home about 1846 to Stephen P. Hollingsworth, of Rusk County, Texas, and they went at once to Texas to make their home, settling in Johnson County. Mr. Hollingsworth died there in the fall of 1879. Mrs. Hollingsworth was living there in 1881. They had three children.

CHILDREN OF ALLEN AND MARTHA (HUMPHREYS) ELSTON OF CALHOUN COUNTY, ALABAMA

I—NANCY (ELSTON) JONES

Nancy (Elston) Jones, daughter and first child of Allen and Martha (Humphreys) Elston, born in Pendleton District, S. C July 23, 1823; came with her parents to Alabama in 1836; was married to James Martin Jones, of Tennessee, July 3, 1838. They lived a few years in Petersburg, Tennessee; then came to Benton (now Calhoun) County, Alabama, and lived out their days in this county. James Martin Jones was born in Maury County, Tennessee, September 12, 1812; died in Jacksonville, Alabama, January 16, 1875, and was buried in Oxford, Alabama. Nancy (Elston) Jones died in Jacksonville, December 28, 1875, and was buried in Oxford cemetery. The children of this couple were seven in number. For further account of the children see later.

II—SABRA (ELSTON) HAYS

Sabra (Elston) Hays, daughter and second child of Allen and Martha (Humphreys) Elston, was born in Pendleton dist., S. C., May 6, 1825; came to Alabama with her parents in 1836; was married February 11, 1841, in Tennessee, to John B. Hays of that state while on a visit to her sister, Nancy Jones. John Hays was born Nov. 28, 1816. They settled at White Plains, Alabama. John Hays died April 9, 1863. Mrs. Hays died Sept., 26, 1886. They had nine children as follows, all born at White Plains:

1. Martha J. Hays, born January 14, 1842.
2. Allen A. Hays, born August 7, 1843.
3. Clifton C. Hays, born Dec. 6, 1845.
4. Infant daughter, born and died in 1847.
5. Alice V. Hays, born July 22, 1849.
6. Clara C. Hays, born December 24, 1852.
7. John Knox Hays, born March 4, 1855.
8. James W. Hays, born January 28, 1858.
9. Addie L. Hays, born Nov. 9, 1862.

III—MARTHA ELIZABETH (ELSTON) 1, DENDY; 2, DOYLE; 3, LUTTRELL

Martha Elizabeth (Elston) 1, Dendy; 2, Doyle; 3, Luttrell; third child of Allen and Martha (Humphreys) Elston, was born in Pendleton District, S. C., June 8, 1827. Moved to A'abama with her parents in 1836. Was married at home February 25, 1847, to James W. Dendy, of South Carolina. They had two children, one of whom died in infancy. The other child, James Allen Dendy, was born May 27, 1848; went out to Texas when a young man and reared a family there; was still living there in 1918 near Weatherford. James W. Dendy (the husband and father) was born March 21, 1823, and was a first cousin to his wife Martha E. Elston, their mothers being sisters.

Mrs. Martha E. (Elston) Dendy married in 1860 a second husband, Dr. James A. Doyle, a widower with several grown children. They lived in Fort Madison, Oconee County, S. C., until Mr. Doyle's death about 1887. Mrs. Doyle then went to live with her son, James Allen Dendy, in Texas, where she remained until 1898. She then went to Oxford, Ala., where she was married to her widowed brother-in-law, Harvey W. Luttrell. They lived happily there until his death which occurred July 26, 1899. She again returned to Texas to make her home with her son, James A. Dendy, near Weatherford. Here she died October 8, 1916, aged 89 years. She had no children by her second and third marriage.

IV—WILLIAM CLARK ELSTON

William Clark Elston, son and fourth child of Allen and Martha (Humphreys) Elston, was born in Pendleton District, S. C., March 6, 1829; came to Benton County, Ala., with the family in 1836. He married Adline Findley, of Benton County, Alabama, in 1848. Adline was born Nov. 23, 1829. They moved to Arkansas in 1870 and settled in the Red River Valley near the Texas line. Here the mother Adline, died February 19, 1877. Mr. Elston later moved over into Oklahoma, leaving most of his children (now grown up) in Arkansas and Louisiana. He died in Oklahoma in 1899.

The children of William Clark and Adline (Findley) Elston were nine in number, six sons and three daughters. The sons came to be very successful business men in and around Shreveport, La. For further account of these see later.

V—SARAH (ELSTON) BOWLING

Sarah (Elston) Bowling, daughter of Allen and Martha (Humphreys) Elston, was born in S. C. June 17, 1831; came to Alabama with her parents in 1836. She married February 25, 1847, Dr. William E. Bowling, of Georgia. They settled near the Corn Grove postoffice where they lived out their lives. Dr. Bowling was a farmer, school teacher and practicing physician. He died March 6. 1899. His wife died June 4, 1904. The children of this union were six in number. For further account of them and their offspring see later.

VI—JOHN HUMPHREYS ELSTON

John Humphreys Elston, son and sixth child of Allen and Martha (Humphreys) Elston, was born in S. C. June 18, 1835. He lived on the old home place with his father all his life. He was a leading and highly esteemed citizen and served in the Confederate States army in the War Between the States. He married Mollie Reagan, of Talladega County, Alabama, about 1876. They had two children: 1, Janie Elston, daughter, born March 16, 1878. 2, Louie Elston, son, born November 9, 1879. In the year 1880 Mr Elston went on a tour through Texas and died there May 10, 1880.

VII—KITTY HUDSON (ELSTON) HUDSON

Kitty Hudson (Elston) Hudson, daughter and seventh child of Allen and Martha (Humphreys) Elston, was born in Benton County, Alabama, October 31, 1837. She was married to J. Gip Hudson at home in 1868. She died November 5, 1874, leaving two or three small children.

VIII—SUSAN FRANCES (ELSTON) LUTTRELL

Susan Frances (Elston) Luttrell, daughter and eighth child of Allen and Martha (Humphreys) Elston, was born in Benton County, Alabama, February 14, 1840. She grew up intellectually active and was favored with good academic education. Her religious and moral ideals were high. She moved in cultured and refined circles of society. She was married December 14, 1856, to Harvey Wilkerson Luttrell, formerly of Knox County, Tennessee, but then of Oxford, Alabama. They lived in and near Oxford to the end of their lives. Mrs. Luttrell died at Oxford April 25, 1897. Mr Luttrell died same place July 26, 1899. The children of this union were eleven, as follows:

1. Corrie Luttrell, dau. born April 1, 1858.

2. Oscar F. Luttrell, son, born June 14 1859.

3. Elston Luttrell, son, born May 26, 1861.

4. Chester M. Luttrell, son, born October 8, 1862.

5. Bruce F. Luttrell, son, born July 13, 1868.

6. Rush Luttrell, son, born December 7, 1870.

7. A son, not named, born Jan. 14, 1872. Died 1872.

8. Katie Luttrell, dau., born July 4, 1875. Died 1875.

9. Marcy Luttrell, son, born January 16, 1877.

10 and 11. Frank and Fred Luttrell, twin sons, born March 28, 1879. Frank died Aug. 24, 1879. Fred died Aug. 14, 1879.

For further account of these children see later.

IX—EVA BORDERS (ELSTON) DeARMAN

Eva Borders (Elston) DeArman, daughter and ninth child of Allen and Martha (Humphreys) Elston, was born in Benton (later Calhoun) County, Alabama, September 12, 1842. She was married to James T. DeArman of the same county December 24, 1865. They lived out their lives in this county at different locations. Mrs. De-Arman died in Anniston, Ala., February 10, 1905. Mr. DeArman died same place a few years later. Of this union there were six children, as follows:

1. Alma Newell DeArman, daughter, born Nov. 14, 1866.

2. Cleff Elston DeArman, son, born June 21, 1869.

3. Kittie Turnipseed DeArman, dau., born July 20, 1873.

4. Louie DeArman, son, born October 31, 1876.

5. Retha DeArman, daughter, born July 9, 1878.

6. Pearl DeArman, daughter, born May 15, 1883.

For further account of these children see later.

X—ANN W. ELSTON

Ann W. Elston, daughter and last child of Allen and Martha (Humphreys) Elston, was born in Benton County, Alabama, October 24, 1844; died March 9, 1845.

CHILDREN OF JOHN CLARK ELSTON AND SELINA (JONES) ELSTON

1. Mary (Elston) Keith, daughter and first child, was born in 1847-8; was married to a Mr. Keith; died in Tennessee.

2. Roxie Carolina (Elston) Snow, daughter, and second child, was born August 14, 1849. She married in Oxford Alabama, Nov. 26, 1868, Clark Snow, youngest son of Dudley and Priscilla (Mounger) Snow, of Oxford. Here also they lived out their days. Roxie died in Oxford July 4th, 1909. Clark Snow died July 19th, 1919. They had seven children. See account of the children later.

3. Brazora (Elston) Heath, daughter, born————; was married to Chester Heath. Died in Cleburne, Texas; left children, one of them Arthur Heath of Artesia, New Mexico.

4. John Jabez Elston, son, born at Corn Grove December 24, 1853. Died January 24, 1856. Buried on the Allen Elston home place.

CHILDREN OF ROXIE CAROLINA (ELSTON) SNOW AND CLARK SNOW, OF OXFORD, ALABAMA

1. Kate Corinne Snow, daughter, born in Oxford, Alabama, Jan. 28, 1870; was married to Thomas Daniel Jackson June 17, 1896; died June 10, 1915. She left one daughter Joyce Elston Jackson born Dec. 5, 1904.

2. Ada Elston Snow, daughter, born December 8, 1871; was married to Charles Caleb Morgan November 17, 1897. To this union were born two sons: 1, Marechal Clark Morgan; 2, Norman Snow Morgan.

3. Ruth Snow, daughter, born in Oxford, Alabama, February 17, 1876; was married to Samuel Hallman December 15, 1910. Residence Oxford, Alabama. No children.

4. Julius Fane Snow, son, born March 22, 1878. Died January 13, 1879.

5. Maxie Snow, daughter, born July 19, 1879; was married to Joe L. Montgomery January 4, 1920.

6. Norman Lee Snow, son, born June 7, 1883. Not married.

7. Mary Winnifred Snow, daughter, born October 11, 1885; was married to James N. Griffin December 19, 1907. To this union one son, Jim Snow Griffin, born January 25, 1918.

CHILDREN OF NANCY (ELSTON) JONES AND JAMES MARTIN JONES

1. Mary Elizabeth (Jones) Hames,, daughter and first child, was born in Petersburg, Tennessee, April 18, 1843. Was married in Jacksonville, Ala., in 1866, to Captain William M. Hames and is yet living there. Had six children. Captain Hames died Feb. 8, 1908.

2. Joseph A. Jones, son, born in Alabama April 28, 1845. Married and had family of several children. Residence, Birmingham Ala.

3. Abner Gregory Jones, son, born in Alabama December, 1846. Died September 16, 1863.

4. Rowena (Jones) McClurkin, daughter, born 1848. Was married November 6, 1866, to James McClurkin. He lived near Oxford, Ala. for a number of years and raised a family of seven children. Husband died and she now lives in Jacksonville, Florida. The seven children are:

a. Curtis McClurkin, son, born 1867. Died in Anniston, **Ala.**

b. Joseph J. McClurkin, son, born December 10, 1868.

c. Burt McClurkin, son, born October 25, 1870.

d. Florence McClurkin, daughter, born August 30, 1875. Died———.

e. Walter McClurkin, son, born 1877.

f. Avery McClurkin, son, born October, 1881.

g. George P. McClurkin, son. born ————. Died————.

5. Mattie (Jones) Lester, daughter, born December 1, 1851. Was married February 4, 1885, to a Mr. Lester. Died in Jacksonville, Ala.

6. Alice (Jones) Camp, daughter, born December 2, 1862. Married.

7. Walter Jones, son, born June 1, 1864. Died in Anniston.

POSTERITY OF WILLIAM CLARK ELSTON AND ADLINE (FINDLEY) ELSTON OF ALABAMA

(1) FANNIE LEE (ELSTON) 1, HARRIS; 2, HARRIS

Fannie Lee (Elston) 1, Harris; 2, Harris, daughter and first child, was born in Alabama, in 1849; was married to Walter Harris, of Texas, and to this union were born two children, George and Walter O. Walter Harris died and then his widow Fannie Lee married a second husband, George Harris, brother of her first husband, and to this union was born one daughter, Golda. The mother died in Texas about 1878. For account of these children see later.

(2) (3) (4) (5) HENRY WORD ELSTON, WALTER ELSTON, HORACE ELSTON AND MARTHA ELSTON, four children of William Clark Elston are all mentioned as having died in childhood.

(6) JOSEPH WALKER ELSTON

Joseph Walker Elston, son, born in Alabama **November 3,** 1860. Went to Arkansas with his father's family about 1870. When reaching maturity began service as station agent with the V.S.&P. Railway in Louisiana. Was in this service a number of years and also engaged in mercantile business and was quite successful. He married at Haughton, La. December 8, 1886, Emily Ogilvie Moore, a school teacher from Georgia. To this union were born in Haughton, La., nine children. See later. The father moved to Shreveport, La and prospered with his brother-in-law until the family jointly were possessed of several large river bottom plantations, oil land, an interest in one several large river bottom plantations, oil land, an interest in one of the city banks, and the commercial business of Elston, **Prince &** McDade, (wholesale grocers and cotton factors) and seventeen producing oil wells, all located in the vicinity of Shreveport. **Joseph W.** Elston died September 16, 1900.

(7) PERCY PELHAM ELSTON

Percy Pelham Elston, son, born in Alabama, March 30, 1867. Lived most of his life in Haughton and Shreveport, La., where he was associated with his brothers in business. Died in 1898 at the age of 31. Was never married.

(8) ROSA PEARL (ELSTON), 1, ALLEN; 2, PRINCE

Rosa Pearl (Elston), 1, Allen; 2, Prince; daughter, born Jan., 5, 1870. She married first Pleasant D. Allen, of New Orleans, a railway trainman, and by him had two sons, Lawrence Elston and Joseph William. Mr. Allen was killed in a railway accident. Rosa Pearl later married a second time Joseph Wilson Prince. No children by this union. They lived on their two-thousand-acre plantation a few miles from Shreveport, La. For account of the Allen children see later.

(9) CHARLES H. ELSTON

Charles H. Elston, son, born April 5, 1873. Married Mamie Boone, and to this union was born one son, Charles Joseph Elston, April 21, 1898, at Doyline, La., and he married Peggy Eva Green February 18, 1921, and had one son.

CHILDREN OF FANNIE LEE (ELSTON) HARRIS

1. George Harris, son, by first husband Walter Harris, was born in Texas.

2. Walter Campbell Harris, born in Texas__———; married and had four children: (1) Fannie Lee Harris; (2) Juanita Harris; (3) Margaret Harris; (4) Walter Campbell Harris, Jr.

3. Golda Harris, daughter by second husband, George Harris, born in Texas————; m. George Frank Brooks and had two daughters: (1) Fannie Lee Brooks; (2) Margaret Brooks. The mother Golda (Harris) Brooks died in Temple, Texas.

CHILDREN OF JOSEPH WALKER ELSTON, OF LA

1. Julia Moore Elston, daughter, born in Haughton, La., Sept. 26, 1887. Married Buford Dean Battle in Shreveport, La., Aug. 27, 1919.

2. Dudley Clark Elston, son, born February 13, 1889. Married first Myrtle Lawrence April 29, 1907. To this union were born three children: (1) Ruth Elston, b. July 27, 1909. (2) Dudley Clark Elston, Jr., b. April 4, 1911. (3) Paul Lawrence Elston, b. June 7, 1912. Dudley Clark Elston married a second wife Una Lee Harrell, and to this union have been born three children: (1) Joseph Harrell Elston, b. September 28, 1918. (2) Robert Douglas Elston, b. March 2. 1921. (3) Evelyn Claire Elston, b. January 28, 1923.

3. Ethel Earl Elston, daughter, born at Haughton, La., September 12, 1890. Was married to Ross E. McDade May 24, 1911, and to this union have been born three daughters: (1) Ethel Elston McDade, (2) Emily Sarah McDade, (3) Juliet Adeline McDade.

4. Parks Moore Elston, son, born at Haughton, La., January 26, 1892. Married Lucy Nicholson, and to this union have been born three daughters: (1) Eleanor Earle Elston, b. May 7, 1917. (2) Ethel Lemerle Elston, b. January 5, 1920. (3) Dorothy Lilian Elston, b. March 28, 1922.

5. Joseph Walker Elston, Jr., son, born at Haughton, La., Nov., 9, 1894. Married Wilhelmina McDade. She was born January 22, 1893. To this union have been born four children: (1) Margaret Lindsey Elston, b. July 12, 1917. (2) Joseph Walker Elston (III), b. Nov., 22, 1919. (3) Mamie Elizabeth Elston, b. November 19, 1921. (4) Wilhelmina Elston, b. September 4, 1923.

6. William Word Elston, son, born December 27, 1894. Not married.

7. Robert Lee Elston, son, born February 15, 1897. Not married.

8. Harry Paul Elston, son, born July 15, 1899. He finished his education with A. B. degree at Washington University, St. Louis, Missouri, in 1923. Married Mildred Gibbons of St. Louis April 12, 1924. She was raised in London, England, and came to St. Louis with her parents in 1919. H. P. Elston is one of the managing heads of the large wholesale grocery and cotton business of Elston, Prince & Mc-Dade, of Shreveport, La.

9. Emily Elizabeth Elston, daughter and last child of Joseph Walker Elston, Sr, and Emily O. (Moore) Elston, was born in Haughton, La., September 5, 1901. She was married June 12, 1924, to Floyd Reynolds Hodges. Residence, Shreveport, La.

CHILDREN OF ROSA PEARL (ELSTON) 1, ALLEN

1. Lawrence Elston Allen, son, born in New Orleans, Nov., 12 1897. Not married. Lives in California.

2. Joseph William Allen, son, born in New Orleans Jan., 11, 1904. Married Mildred Love January 3, 1923, at Shreveport. Resides in California.

CHILDREN OF SARAH (ELSTON) BOWLING AND DR. WM. E BOWLING OF CALHOUN COUNTY, ALABAMA

(1) MARTHA ELIZABETH BOWLING BARKER, the first child, was born December 29, 1847; was married to Abiah Morgan Barker September 26, 1865, in Alabama, but went at once to Texas, where the family afterward lived. She died in DeLeon, Texas, in 1922; husband yet living there in 1924, age 81. Their cihldren were five in number as follows:

a. George Ephraim Barker, b. July 20, 1866, married Cora Womble. Has several children and grandchildren. Residence, Waco, Texas.

b. Alban Eustace Barker, b. March 5, 1868. Married and has children. Residence, DeLeon, Texas (1924).

c. William Barker, b. September 26, 1869. Married and has children. Residence, DeLeon, Texas (1924).

d. Mollie Barker, b. ————. Married first a Ross; second a Hammett. Residence, DeLeon, Texas (1924).

e. Evan Barker, b. ————. Residence, DeLeon, Texas.

(2) GEORGE W. BOWLING, son, b. June 29, 1849. Died April 1861.

(3) VIRGINIA CUNNINGHAM (BOWLING) EVANS, third child born October 10, 1850; was married to Josephus M. Evans, October 19, 1871. They lived at Heflin, Alabama. The mother died there January 8, 1919. The children of this union were nine in number as follows:

a. Lena Georgia Evans, b. July 18, 1872; was married to W. Jack Vaughn November 24, 1892; Has two children. Residence, Heflin, Alabama.

b. Ewell Kirkham Evans, son, b. December 1873; d. 1875.

c. Jesse Evans, son, b. September 20, 1875; married Susie Belle Ingram, of Opelika, Alabama, December 23, 1902; has four children; residence Anniston, Alabama.

d. William Evans, son, b. 1877; died young.

e. Alex Olin Evans, son, b. July 23, 1880; married Minnie Lee Harris January 1, 1907; died March 30, 1914; had one child that died young.

f. Cynthia Elston Evans, daughter, b. February 11, 1883; died May 1, 1885.

g. Martin Josephus Evans, son, b. March 14, 1885; residence, Heflin, Alabama.

h. George Bismarck Evans, son, b. October 3, 1887; married Onnie Lou Black October 8, 1913; one child; wife died 1920. Residence, Heflin, Alabama.

i. Bruce Knox Evans, son, b. March 5, 1890; married Nellie Mae Grant November 3, 1914; one son; residence Anniston, Alabama.

(4) CYNTHIA BORDERS (BOWLING) WRIGHT, fourth child, was born Sept. 7, 1856; was married to Eli Martin Wright Dec. 17, 1874. Mr. Wright died within a few years. She died at Heflin, Ala., 1919. The children were two, as follows:

1. Lizzie Martin Wright, daughter, born July 9, 1880; married Ulysses Vaughn; has two children, Ruth and Martin. Lives at Heflin, Ala.

2. Elijah Allen Wright, son, born 1882; married ——————. Wife deceased. Two children, Flora and Allen. Residence, Heflin, Ala.

(5) SALLY JACKSON (BOWLING) FAULKNER, fifth child, was born December 10, 1861. Was married January 30, 1879, to John Thomas Faulkner. Residence, (1924) 1801 Copeland Avenue N, Birmingham, Ala. J. T. Faulkner was born in Cobb County, Ga., Feb. 7, 1856, and died in Birmingham March 23, 1912. The children of this union were eleven in number, as follows:

1. John Thomas Faulkner, Jr., born and died November, 1879.

2. Maud Virginia Faulkner, da., b. May 26, 1861; died May 28, 1882.

3. Thomas Byron Faulkner, son, b. April 9, 1883; married Katherine Gossett Dec. 2, 1906; one son, Thos. B., Jr., b. Oct. 12, 1909

4. Sarah Blanche Faulkner, da., b. Dec. 12, 1886, was married May 12, 1909, to Walter Douglas Miles; has one dau., Sallie Blanche, b. April 29, 1916.

5. William Ralph Faulkner, son, twin to Blanche, b. Dec. 12, 1886; married Nov. 20, 1910, Margaret Kathleen Saunders; has one da., May Christine, b. Aug. 12, 1912.

6. Jacob L. Faulkner, son, b. July 26, 1889. Not married.

7. Frank Elston Faulkner, son, b. Oct. 10, 1891; married April 2, 1910, Dora Williams; has one da., Hazel, b. Nov. 26, 1911.

8. May Faulkner, dau., b. May 6, 1894; died Nov. 30, 1898.

9. Ruth Elizabeth Fulkner, dau., b. May 20, 1896; was married June 10, 1916, to Melvin D. Jones; has one dau., Dorothy Elizabeth, b, Mar. 23, 1919.

10. Fred L. Faulkner, son, b. Mar. 4, 1900; married Nov. 10, 1920, Louise S. Collins, of Biringham, Ala.

11. George Randolph Faulkner, son and last child, b. Nov. 16, 1902.

(6)__WILLIAM BISMARCK BOWLING, son and last child of Sarah Elston and Dr. William E. Bowling, was born in Calhoun Co., Ala., Sept 24, 1870. Received high school education. Taught school, studied law, was elected to Congress several terms and is now (1924) serving. Married June 2, 1896, at LaFayette, Ala., Frances Steele Collins, whose parents were from London, Eng. Their children are four in number, as follows:

1. George Randolph Bowling, son, b. March 7, 1897; married Dec. 7, 1922, Sally Susan Dowdell; has one son, George Randolph Bowling, Jr., b. May 12, 1924. Residence, LaFayette, Ala.

2. Marian Elston Bowling, dau., b. Mar. 28, 1899; married to George Luckie Jenkins June 12, 1824. Residence, LaFayette, Ala.

3. Sarah Frances Bowling, dau., b. Jan. 18, 1901; not married.

4. Elizabeth Bowling, dau., died in infancy, 1904

CHILDREN OF SUSAN FRANCES (ELSTON) LUTTRELL AND HARVEY WILKERSON LUTTRELL, OF CALHOUN CO., ALA.

(1) CORRIE LUTTRELL SOWELL, daughter and first child, was born in Oxford, Ala., April 1, 1858. Was married to Charles L. Sowell, of Brewton, Ala., Oct. 22, 1885. Died May 8, 1903. Had no children.

(2) OSCAR FOWLER LUTTRELL, son, b. June 14, 1859. In 1889 he and others organized the Bank of Brewton, at Brewton, Ala., and he served as cashier of this institution for a period of twenty-four years. He married April 12 ,1893, Mollie Magill Oden, daughter of John P. Oden of Syllacauga, Ala. He died in Brewton, Ala., July 23, 1922. The children were four in number, all sons, as follows:

1. A son, not named, born May 20, 1895. Died in infancy.

2. John Oden Luttrell, born Sept. 10, 1896. Married. Residence, Denver, Colorado (1924).

3. Oscar Forney Luttrell, born June 13, 1899. Married in Atlanta, Ga., Aug. 23, 1922, Eliza M. Fariss. Residence, Atlanta.

4. Frank Alex Luttrell, born Dec. 16, 1901. Not married. Lives with his mother in Brewton, Ala.

(3) ELSTON LUTTRELL, third child, born near Oxford, Ala., May 26, 1861. Married in Florida July 15, 1886, Lucy Barber, daughter of James L. and Ellen M. Barber, of Kentucky. Lived some years in Oxford, Ala. Later located in Brewton, Ala., where he has since been engaged in mercantile business. The children of this union are five in number, as follows:

1. Randolph Luttrell, son, born in Oxford, Ala., May 29, 1888. Married Georgia Binion, daughter of J. T. Binion, of Dothan, Ala., July 4, 1907. Residence, Brewton, Ala., since 1897. The children of this union are: 1, Lucile Luttrell, born July 9, 1909. 2, Randolph Binion Luttrell, born March 26, 1912. 3, Joe Bell Luttrell, born March 1, 1918. 4, Clarence Reid Luttrell, born Feb. 1, 1923.

2. Corrie Luttrell, daughter, born in Oxford, Ala., June 7, 1889. Married Clarence M. Reid, of Fort Deposit, Ala., Dec. 16, 1908. Residence, 509 Finley Avenue, Montgomery, Ala. They have only one child, Lucy Olivia Reid, born Dec. 2, 1911.

3. Annie Laurie Luttrell, daughter, born in Oxford, Ala., December 15, 1891. Married in Brewton, Ala., Aug. 25, 1908, to William Marshall Strong. The children of this union are four: 1, Laurie Barber Strong, born June 23, 1916. 2, George Elston Strong, born Jan. 29, 1918. 3, Lutie May Strong, born Jan. 20, 1920. 4, Marshall Rush Strong, b. June 3, 1923.

4. Harvey Haynes Luttrell, born near Brewton, Ala., April 19. 1894. Served in the World War 1918-19. Married Mary Jane Adams, daughter of John A. Adams, in Montgomery, Ala., Sept. 24, 1919. Residence, Montgomery Ala. No children.

5. Alton Luttrell, born near Brewton, August 24, 1895. Died July 21, 1896.

(4) CHESTER McAULEY LUTTRELL, son, born Oct. 8, 1862. Followed mercantile pursuits all his life. Married October 5, 1886, Augusta Harwell, Oxford, Alabama. Present residence, Bradford, Pennsylvania. Their children are four in number, all daughters, as follows:

1. Juliet Luttrell, born July 31, 1887. Married to the Rev. Royal K. Tucker, of Mobile, Alabama, 1908. Residence (1924) Louisville, Kentucky. They have five children, all girls: (1) Lael Tucker, born March 28, 1909. (2) Ruth Tucker, born April 21, 1911. (3) Lucile Tucker, born October 29, 1912. (4) Juliet Tucker, born November 20, 1914. (5) Royal Leigh Tucker, born December 10, 1919.

2. Kattie May Luttrell, born January 18, 1900. Was married to Dr. Ernest E. Tucker, of Mobile, Alabama, ————. Residence (1924) New York City. They have two children: (1) Ernest Tucker, born March 20, 1921. (2) Katherine Tucker, born December 12, 1922.

3. Elizabeth Lynn Luttrell, born March 9, 1893. Was married to Lowell S. Langworthy, of Bradford, Pennsylvania, ————. There they yet live and have three children: (1) Mary Lynn Langworthy, born October 20, 1915. (2) Richard Langworthy, born May 21, 1919. (3) Lucile Langworthy, born October 20, 1921.

4. Ethel Lucile Luttrell, born April 28, 1898. Not married. Lives with her sister, Katie May Tucker, in New York City.

(5) BRUCE FRANCIS LUTTRELL, son, born near Oxford, Ala., July 13, 1868. Married at Evergreen, Alabama, August 4, 1896, Lena Crumpton, daughter of B. H. Crumpton. Has fo'lowed mercantile pursuits and is at present located in Tampa, Florida. The children are nine in number, as follows:

1. Suelston Luttrell, daughter, born July 26, 1897. Married October 10, 1920, to Charles A. Barker. Residence, Philadelphia, Pa.

2. Ralphine Luttrell, born January 28, 1899. Married July 22, 1915, to Ellis H. Till. No children. Residence, Tampa, Forida.

3. Rush Luttrell, son, born January 17, 1900. Died July 28, 1900.

4. Lucy Grace Luttrell, daughter, born September 12, 1901. Married December 16, 1918, to J. H. Fisher, of Virginia. Has one daughter, Bernadette, born April 1, 1921. Residence, Tampa, Florida.

5. Marcie Luttrell, daughter, born August 3, 1903. Married in Tampa, Florida, June 29, 1921, to Willis W. Henderson. Has two children: (1) Dorothy, born 1922. (2) Geraldine, born 1923.

6. Bruce Luttrell, Jr., son, born August 6, 1905. Not married.

7. Boardman Luttrell, son, born November 28, 1906.

8. Ernestine Luttrell, daughter, born August 17, 1908. Married in Tampa, Florida, May 10, 1924, to Barney Tapp, of Tampa.

9. Lena Luttrell, daughter, born December 25, 1912.

(6) RUSH LUTTRELL, son, born near Oxford, Ala., December 7, 1870. Spent his life in railroad train service. Married in Calera, Alabama, Lutie Blevins. Died May 13, 1924. No children.

(7) A son, not named, born January 4, 1872. Died July, 1872.

(8) KATIE LUTTRELL, daughter, born July 4, 1875. Died August 18, 1875.

(9) MARCY LUTTRELL, son, born January 16, 1877. Was an electrical and mechanical engineer. Electrocuted by accident in Selma, Alabama, December 14, 1903. Not married.

(10 & 11) FRANK and FRED LUTTRELL, twin sons, born March 28, 1879. Fred died August 14, 1879. Frank died August 24, 1879.

CHILDREN AND GRANDCHILDREN OF EVA BORDERS (ELSTON) DeARMAN AND JAMES T. DeARMAN OF CALHOUN COUNTY, ALABAMA

(1) ALMA NEWELL (DeARMAN) BORDERS, daughter, born Nov. 14, 1866. Was married to William C. Borders, Jan. 23, 1884. Died June 14, 1891, in Anniston, Alabama. She had two children, as follows:

1. Sam J. Borders, son, born June 14, 1885. He is an R. F. D. mail carrier and resides at DeArmanville, Alabama.

2. Salie Borders, daughter, born May 2, 1887; was married —— —— to W. O. Chitwood. Residence, DeArmanville, Ala.

(2) CLEFF ELSTON DeARMAN, son, born June 21, 1869. Married Lucy Methvin, of Senoia, Ga., December 28, 1898. Cleff Elston died April 28, 1901, and his wife Lucy died April, 1911. They had no children.

(3) KITTIE TURNIPSEED (DeARMAN) METHVIN, daughter, born July 20, 1873. Was married to D. R. Methvin, of Senoia, Ga., December 27, 1894. Present residence, Anniston, Alabama. There were six children to this union, as follows:

1. Eva Lucile Methvin, born October 4, 1895. Married a Mr. Dye. Residence Anniston, Alabama.

2. D. T. Methvin, born August 12, 1897.

3. Cleff Leon Methvin, born September 26, 1899. Married and resides in Anniston, Alabama.

4. Roy Methvin, born April 22, 1901.

5. Paul Methvin, born September 3, 1903.

6. Kittie Ruth Methvin, born October 14, 1909.

(4) LOUIE JONES DeARMAN, son, born October 31, 1876. Married Ida Rosila Brightmon, of Anniston, Ala., June 27, 1899. Residence Fairfield, Alabama. Their children are seven in number as follows:

1. Hubert Pryor DeArman, born October 29, 1900.

2. Evelyn Louise DeArman, born September 18, 1902; was marred to James Newton Smith, February 15, 1922; has one son, James Newton Smith, (Jr.) born October 3, 1924.

3. Cleff Elston DeArman, (Jr.) born December 15, 1904.

4. Retha Gertrude DeArman, born November 3, 1906.

5. Ida Margaret DeArman, born April 6, 1911.

6. Louie Jones DeArman, (Jr.) born April 6, 1911. (Twin).

7. Virginia Loraine DeArman, born June 29, 1913.

(5) RETHA EVELYN (DeARMAN) McCLURKIN, daughter, born July 9, 1878. Was married to James Walter McClurkin, Anniston, Alabama, April 4, 1906. They resided in Anniston and have four children as follows:

1. James Avery McClurkin, born June 7, 1907.

2. Evelyn Pearl McClurkin, born May 31, 1910.

3. Louie Walter McClurkin, born January 14, 1918.

4. Sarah Retha McClurkin, born May 10, 1918.

(6) PEARL (DeARMAN) OWENS, daughter, born May 15, 1883; married December 20, 1910, to Foster Pierce Owens, of Heflin, Alabama. They now reside at Heflin and have three children as follows:

1. Foster Pierce Owens (Jr.), born August 25, 1913.

2. Retha Eva Owens, born November 18, 1916.

3. Annie Pearl Owens, born January 14, 1920.

FAMILY OF ALLEN ELSTON, SR., OF SOUTH CAROLINA
AND ALABAMA

Allen Elston, one of the younger sons of David Elston, of New Jersey, was born in Eizabeth, New Jersey, January 13, 1782. He naturally followed the fortunes of his father's family in their migrations, first to Wilkes County, North Carolina, then to Tennessee and Kentucky. The father David Elston seems to have finally located in Kentucky near Lexington, possibly then embraced in "The State of Franklin", and ta have lived out his life there. But the two sons, John and Allen, in about 1798, being then 24 and 16 years of age respectively, went on further southward and settled in upper South Carolina, in Pendleton District, on the Georgia line. We find these two brothers and their families lived quite close together for several succeeding generations. About 1815 John Elston crossed over the line into Habersham county, Georgia. Allen Elston may have done likewise. They both developed large and valuable agricultural and mercantile interests. Later they decided to try their fortunes further west and in a yet newer country. Accordingly in 1833, "the year the stars fell," Allen Elston moved to the Creek nation and located in the Choccolocco valley in Tal'adega county. His brother, John Elston, followed him in 1834 and located in the same valley in Benton county. Here their good fortunes followed them. Allen and his sons amassed valuable agricultural and mercantile properties and all lived out their lives in this county. The father, Allen Elston, Sr., died December 9th, 1868, aged nearly 87 years.

Allen Elston (Sr.) of South Carolina, son of David Elston of New Jersey, as best we can determine from the evidence before us, which however is not absolutely conclusive, married in South Carolina, a first wife who was Ruth Clark, a daughter of Major William H. Clark and a grand-daughter of Governor John Sevier, of Tennessee. We have no record of any children by this marriage, and the probabilities are that Ruth did not live long after the marriage. Allen married a second wife, Mrs. Annie Blair Terrell, a widow with one daughter, Elizabeth Terrell. This daughter afterwards married William Johnson and had children, one of them Harriet Johnson, who married Charles J. Cooper, of Oxford, Ala., and had a large family.

This completes the record of the children of Elizabeth Clark who married John Elston and Ruth Clark who married Allen Elston which was furnished by Elston Luttrell a descendant of Elizabeth Clark Elston and John Elston. This splendid record has been of material assistance in the compilation of the Sevier Family History.

SARAH HAWKINS CLARK

2. Sarah Hawkins Clark, daughter of Elizabeth Sevier Clark and Major William H. Clark was born about 1788. She seems to have spent much time in her grandfather, Gov. John Sevier's, home and is certainly very frequently mentioned by him as "Sally Clark".

She married possibly about 1804 in Knoxville in the Governor's mansion. She married General James Rutherford Wyly, a grandson of Colonel Benjamin Cleveland of King's Mountain fame. Descendants of this couple have therefore three lines to King's Mountain. (John Sevier, Major Clark and Col. Cleveland) General Wyly was also a distinguished officer of the war of 1812. He was the son of James and Jamima Cleveland Wyly, Jamima Cleveland Wyly being the daughter of Col. Benjamin Cleveland and Mary Graves Cleveland.

Sarah Hawkins Clark Wyly and General James Rutherford Wyly had twelve children. eight sons and four daughters, namely:

1. William Clark Wyly

2. Oliver Cromwell Wyly

3. Benjamin Cleveland Wyly

4. John Henry Wyly

5. James Rutherford Wyly, junior

6. Robert Wyly

7. Walton Wyly

8. Augustine Clayton Wyly

9. Elizabeth Wyly

10. Louisiana Wyly

11. Mary Ann Wyly

12 Sarah Catherine Wyly

13. Florence Wyly

Of the foregoing:

1. William Clark Wyly, son of Sarah Hawkins Clark Wyly and General James Rutherford Wyly was born————. He married———— Amelia Starr and had two children.

A. Robert Wyly

B. Eliza Hanna Wyly lived and married in the West. She died some years ago. She married William Tipman Trammell, son of Jehu and Elizabeth (Fain) Trammell. Jehu Trammell was the son of William Trammell.   Elizabeth Fain the daughter of Ebenezer and Mary (Black) Fain.   Ebenezer Fain was a soldier in the Revolution.   According to D. A. R. Books Eliza Hannah Wyly had at least four daughters, all of whom belong to D. A. R., as follows

1. Augusta Josephine Trammell, born Georgia, married John William McWilliams.

2. Anna Eliza Trammell, born in Georgia, married Charles Parmelee Beeks

3. Rosalind Clark Trammell, born in Georgia, married Benjamin Rush Blakely.

4. Amelia Elizabeth Trammell, born in Georgia, married Charlie Reed Johnson.

2. Oliver Cromwell Wyly, son of Sarah Hawkins Clark Wyly and General James Rutherford Wyly was born about 1808.   He married for his first wife Lucy Edins in 1828 and had three daughters and five sons, namely: Newton Cromwell Wyly, born 1829; Benjamin F. Wyly, born 1830; James A. Wyly; Carolyn M. Wyly; Sarah Amelia Wyly; Louise Wyly; Robert A. Wyly and William Sevier Wyly.

Newton Cromwell Wyly, born 1829, married in 1849, Malinda Townsend and had one son, Homer Virgil Miller Wyly.

Benjamin F. Wyly, born in 1830, married in 1858, Sallie Williams and had three sons, Eugene Wyly, Newton Wyly and ———Wyly.

James A. Wyly married for his first wife a Miss Williams and had no children and married for his second wife Miss Verner and and had a son and a daughter.

Carolyn M. Wyly married Henry Alexander Fuller and had three sons, Oliver Clyde Fuller (who married Kate Fitzhugh Caswell and has Edythe Fuller, Elizabeth Fuller, Inez Fuller, Lytie Fuller, and Robert Fuller); Henry Walter Fuller; Clarence Paul Fuller; and Annie Raily Fuller (deceased).

Sarah Amelia Wyly married Henry Lamar Smith and had two sons; Victor Lamar Smith (who married Carolyn Johnson); and Alexander Wyly Smith (who married Ida Kendrick and has Alexander Wyly Smith. junior, married Hellen Hill Payne and has three children and was a Captain in the United States Army; Kendrick Smith was in the United States Aviation Corps; and Ester Smith).

Lula or Louise Wyly married Colet Carter and had a daughter, Florence Carter, who married Judge Frank Carter of Asheville North Carolina.

Robert A. Wyly married———Hatchett and has six sons.

William Sevier Wyly married ———Hatchett, a sister of his brother Robert Wyly's wife, and had two sons of whom only one is now living.

2. Oliver Cromwell Wyly married for his second wife, Ade'ine Byrd, a daughter of Colonel Thomas Byrd and had four children, **two** sons and two daughters.

Oliver Cromwell Wyly married for his third wife———————— and had ten children, all but one of whom were living in Texas **in** 1918.

3. Benjamin Cleveland Wyly, son of James Rutherford **Wyly** and Sarah Hawkins Clark Wyly, married first Ann McGee and **had** one son, John McGee Wyly, who married Amelia Forney and **had** four children; Annie McGee Wyly (who married David Lowe **and** has a daughter Annie Wyly Lowe, married Walker Willis); Benja**min** F. Wyly (who married Ellie Peck and has three children, Lottie **Wyly,** Catherine Wyly, married————————, and Forney Wyly); Sadie Swo**pe** Wyly (who married F. M. Billings and has Wyly Billings and F. **M.** Billings, junior; and Henry Forney Wyly (who married Sallie **Dunlap** and has two children, Henry Forney Wyly, junior, and Sallie **Dunlap** Wyly.)

Benjamin Cleveland Wyly married for his second wife **Eliza** Snow and had Samuel Snow Wyly; Frank Wyly (a daughter) **who** married Tom Garlington; Ella Wyly married ————————Brothers; Ida Wyly married Joe Clay King, and Jennie M. Wyly **married** William Murrary Davidson.

4. John Henry Wyly, son of Sarah Hawkins Clark Wyly, **and** General James Rutherford Wyly was born 18————————.

5. James Rutherford Wyly, junior, son of Sarah Hawkins **Clark** Wy'y and General James Rutherford Wyly was born 18————————.

6. Robert Wyly, son of Sarah Hawkins Clark Wyly **and** General James Rutherford Wyly was born 18————————. He **married** unmarried.

7. Walton Wyly, son of Sarah Hawkins Clark Wyly **and** General James Rutherford Wyly was born 18————————. He **married** Mary Johnson and had no children.

8. Augustine Clayton Wyly, son of Sarah Hawkins Clark **Wyly** and General James Rutherford Wyly, was born 18————————. **He** married Josephine Taylor Hamilton and had three children, Made**line** Wyly, Nell I. Wyly, who married Montagu Gammon and **Thomas** Hamilton Wyly.

9. Elizabeth Wyly, daughter of Sarah Hawkins Clark **Wyly** and General James Rutherford Wyly, was born 18————————. **She** married Thomas Sparks.

10. Louisiana Wyly, daughter of Sarah Hawkins C'ark **Wyly** and General James Rutherford Wyly, was born 18————————. **She** married————————Byrd.

11   Mary Ann Wyly, daughter of Sarah Hawkins Clark Wyly and General James Rutherford Wyly was born 18————. She married 18————. Judge William Henderson Underwood and had Helen Underwood (who married M.A. Nevin and had William Henry Nevin, beceased; James Banks Nevin (who married first Alace Wells and is deceased); Thomas O'Connor Nevin, deceased; Sarah Hawkins Nevin, deceased; James Banks Nevin (who married first Alace Wells and married second Mary Bryan); Mary Michell Nevin (who married Randolph Wright); Wyatt Holmes Nevin, deceased); Annie Lou Underwood (who married Captain C. Rowell and had William Sinclair Rowell; Neal Rowel', deceased; Mary Wyly Rowell; Martha Cheatham Rowell, deceased; Elizabeth Clifton Rowell, deceased; and Annie Lou Rowell, deceased); Florence Wyly Underwood (who married E. M. Eastman and has Zoe Eastman, married Charles Robin Pitner, John Eastman married Laura Hume, Helen Eastman, unmarried, and Guy Eastman married Emma Hume); Mary Corde'ia Underwood (who married D. D. Plumb and had Rosa Milledge Plumb, married J. H. O'Neill); Ida Underwood (who married George H. Snyder and had Wyly Snyder, George Snyder and Clifford Snyder; Wilhemina Underwood (who married John H. Pitt and has no children); Rose Underwcod who married C. R. Clark and has one son, Charles Richard Clark, junior); John James Underwood (who died young); Charles Walton Underwood (who married Martha Moore and has John Underwood, Charles Walton Underwood, junior, William H. Underwood, Robert Wyly Underwood, Valentine Xavier Underwood; Mary Underwood, married William Anderson and Evelyn Underwood, married Ralph Tanner.)

12.   Sarah Catherine Wyly, daughter of Sarah Hawkins Clark Wyly and General James Rutherford Wyly was born 18————. She married William Addison Rogers and had two daughters, Zoe Rogers, who married William Clifton Mansfield and A'ah Rogers, who married———— Daniel.

The chi'dren of William Clifton Mansfield formerly of Cleveland and Sweetwater, Tennessee, but now of Atlanta, Georgia, and his wife, Zoe Sevier (Rogers) Mansfield are as follows:-

1. William Mansfield, died in infancy
2. Zoe Sevier Mansfield, died 1914, unmarried
3. Katherine Louise Mansfield,who married Samuel Tipton Jones of Sweetwater, Tennessee and had four children:-
    a. Clifton Martin Jones
    b. Florine Mansfield Jones
    c. Sevier-Tipton Jones, who died in infancy
4. Felice Mansfield who died unmarried in 1918 of influenza.
5. Eston Sevier Mansfield who married Ellie Patterson of Atlanta.   They were the parents of three children:-
    a. Sevier Mansfield who died in infancy
    b. Marian Mansfield
    c. William Denton Mansfield

In the marriage of these two are united the families of the two bitter political opponents, John Sevier and Colonel Tipton and the erroneously called "Tipton-Sevier feud" comes to a happy end, Samuel Tipton Jones being a lineal descendant in the sixth generation from Col. John Tipton while Katherine Louise Mansfield, his wife, is, likewise in the sixth generation, a lineal descendant of Governor John Sevier.   In recognition of this union one of their children bore the name Sevier-Tipton Jones.

13. Florence Wyly.   It appears that another child of Sarah Hawkins Clark Wyly and General James Rutherford Clark was Florence Wyly, born 18————. She married Dennis Joseph O'Callagham and had a daughter, Mary Lilly O'Callagham, born in Clarksville, Ga., who is a member of the D. A. R. through this record.

JOHN CLARK

3. John Clark, son of Elizabeth Sevier Clark and Major William H. Clark, was born ————. By accounts that some members of the family have sent me he married———— and had at least one daughter who was called by descendants of this family "Cousin Kittie Clark".   However this may be a mistake.   If he died young, it would account for his father naming another son John Clark.

RUTH CLARK

4. Ruth Clark, daughter of Major William H. Clark, was born————.   In the records in Washington concerning the Sevier estate, Elizabeth Sevier Clark is mentioned as having three children and the names are given: Elizabeth, Sarah and John.   But an error may have been made.   Ruth may have been accidentally omitted or Ruth may have been deceased when the list was prepared. Some errors in regard to other heirs do occur in these records, some names being repeated and some omitted.

Ruth Clark married, Allen Elston, brother of her sister's husband, John Elston, by family tradition and by the record prepared by Elston Luttrell, see page 220.   By Mr. Elston's account she was the first wife of Allen Elston and probably died young without issue.

Allen Elston and Ruth Clark Elston settled about 1834 in the Choccolocco valley in Talladega County, Alabama, where he lived until his death, surviving his first wife by many years.

CHAPTER FIVE
Sarah Hawkins Sevier

SARAH HAWKINS SEVIER

Sarah Hawkins Sevier, daughter of Governor John Sevier and his first wife, Sarah Hawkins Sevier, was born in Rockinkham, Virginia, July, 1770. She received her mother's full name. She was about ten years of age when her mother died in January or February 1780, and she was raised after her father's second marriage by Catherine Sherrill Sevier, her step-mother. She married early as all the Sevier girls did, probably about 1787, when she was seventeen years of age. The Sevier girls married from fourteen and fifteen up. Their mother, Sarah Hawkins, married John Sevier when she was about fifteen and John Sevier was sixteen.

Sarah Hawkins Sevier married Benjamin Brown, known as and usually called, Judge Benjamin Brown. She died before 1839. In letters from some members of the family she is called Dolly Sevier and she evidently had that diminutive.

In 1818 she must have been a widow as in the Sheriff's Bill of Sale for her father's property she is mentioned alone, while the other daughters are all mentioned with the names of their husbands.

A Benjamin Brown aged 87 was a pensioner in the 1840 list. This puts his birth in 1753, and would make him seventeen years older than Sarah Hawkins Sevier Brown, so I presume this Benjamin (who is not called Judge) was her husband's kinsman.

Mr. and Mrs. Benjamin Brown are frequently mentioned by Governor Sevier in his Journal. They are recorded as dining and lodging in the Sevier household and they evidently lived not too far away for frequent visits.

Sarah Hawkins Sevier Brown and Judge Benjamin Brown had ten children but I have not the names of any of them.

CHAPTER SIX

Mary Ann Sevier

MARY ANN SEVIER

Mary Ann Sevier, daughter of Governor John Sevier and his first wife, Sarah Hawkins Sevier, was born in Virginia. By the authority of Mrs. Sophia Hoss French she was born in 1771 or 1772. I have no other record of her birth date and therefore place her as the sixth child. Governor Sevier in his Journal refers to her as Mary Ann, while the other older daughters, (his Journal. so far as it has been preserved, begins in 1790), are called by their married names. Mrs. Benjamin Brown, Mrs. Walter King, etc. He does not mention Mary Ann's wedding and therefore if she were born in 1771 or 1772, I conclude that she was married before the first recorded date in the Journal, but became a widow early and was an inmate of his household. This would account for his reference to her as "Mary Ann"; and for less frequent references than he bestows upon the comings and goings of Mr. and Mrs. Benjamin Brown, who frequently dine or "lodge" with him. Only once, later in his Journal, (September 1812) does he call the name of "Mrs. May". So her marriage to her second husband, John Corland, took place after that date.

According to the record of Mrs. French, Mary Ann Sevier married for her first husband, Samuel May. There are few references to this marriage and I conclude that Samuel May died very young. Samuel May appears on the tax list of Greene County, Tennessee, in 1783. This may have been her first husband or his father. She is better known by the name of her second husband, who was Joshua Corland.

The name of her second husband is sometimes given as Joshua Corlin and sometimes Joshua Corland. As will be noted in other instances, the spelling of many names varied. Her brother, George Washington Sevier, speaks of her as living July 23, 1739, when he writes to Dr. Draper.

I do not know the names of her children. There is, however, a reference in Governor Sevier's Journal———— to a child named "Sevier", that could only be a grandchild and, of course, only the child of a daughter. As the other married daughters certainly did

not make their home in his home, it is possible that this child "Sevier", who was evidently about the age of his daughter Ruth, was **the** daughter of Mary Ann who was then, or later, the widow of **Samuel** May. This is only supposition. Some of the descendants **may** have data that will link "Sevier" to the family tree. He may **have** been the son of Elizabeth, who named her son John Clark **for** Governor Sevier. He may have been named John Sevier Clark **and** called by his middle name.

In the bill for the Sheriff's Sale, February 10, 1818, are mentioned "Joshua Corland and Mary Ann his wife".

CHAPTER SEVEN

Valentine Sevier

VALENTINE SEVIER

Valentine Sevier, son of Governor John Sevier and his first wife, Sarah Hawkins Sevier, was born in Virginia in 1773. He was a child when he accompanied his family to the "Mountains", now Tennessee, arriving Christmas day, 1773. Valentine Sevier was born in 1773 which was the year his father's entire family moved from Virginia to "the Mountains". He received the name Valentine which is identified with his family for centuries, but the result is almost hopeless confusion to students of the family history as at least four of his first cousins, his grandfather, and his uncle had exactly the same name. The two older men can be identified as they appear in the records, because of their age or other circumstances, but the five young men all about the same age and all named Valentine Sevier offer a puzzle that is frequently not to be solved. Even in his marriage this Valentine is confused with Valentine, the son of Abraham Sevier, for it is said that Valentine the son of Governor John married————Arnott (Arnett?), while it is established that Valentine, the son of Abraham, married Elizabeth Arnett. Whether these two Valentines married sisters or cousins of the same surname, or whether descendants have merely confused one Valentine with the other is more than I can say.

In the absence of information to the contrary however I will say that Valentine Sevier, son of Governor John Sevier, married, according to statements made to me,———— Arnott. His marriage took place about 1795, when he was about twenty-two years of age.

Valentine Sevier went to Overton County, Tennessee, where Governor Sevier had immense holdings, fifty-four thousand acres at least. Joanna Sevier Wendell and John Wendell were I think the pioneers of the family in opening up this new territory and possibly Valentine Sevier accompanied his sister and brother-in-law. This was several years before his father's death. After that event, "Bonny Kate" and other members of the family joined the Overton

237

County colony . In the meanwhile many Seviers had moved to Overton and among them were Abraham Sevier and his family, including his son Valentine. Therefore the location of Valentine Sevier records in Overton County is not conclusive. Valentine Sevier, son of Ayraham, was however younger than Valentine, son of Governor John Sevier.

Valentine Sevier was living in 1818 when the Sheriff's Bill of Sale was published, and George Washington Sevier in a letter to Dr. Draper in 1839 says that he was living then.

I think it probable that Valentine Sevier (subject of this chapter) married in East Tennessee about 1795. A descendant of Martha Sevier, who was I think his daughter, says that Martha was born in 1799. This would put her father's marriage about the date 1795.

Joseph Sevier in a letter to Bishop Hoss in 1916, said that he was a descendant of Henry Sevier, son of Valentine Sevier, son of Governor John Sevier. I have not been able to hear from this man.

Mrs. Martha Sevier Price, of Memphis, a grand daughter of Governor Sevier (daughter of John Sevier, junior) wrote in 1907 that her brother Michael Sevier raised a great-grand-daughter of Valentine Sevier. She was the daughter of a Federal soldier———— Sevier, who died in Little Rock, Arkansas, during the War Between the States. In his last hours he begged Michael Sevier to get his little motherless girl and raise her. Michael Sevier agreed to do this and as soon as peace was declared went for the child. (Mrs. Price does not say in her letter where he went, so we have not that clew). This child was named Mary Sevier and she was raised in the family of Michael Sevier.

Mrs. Price's letter also says that at one time a grandson of Valentine Sevier, Samuel Sevier, was living in Camden Arkansas. He was possibly the father or grandfather of Joseph Sevier who wrote to Bishop Hoss in 1916, but who has answered no recent letters.

From the foregoing information, the children of Valentine Sevier were:

1. Henry Sevier
2. Martha Sevier, born about 1799
   and others.

THE SEVIER FAMILY

HENRY SEVIER

Henry Sevier, son of Va'entine Sevier, was born about 1797. He must have grown up in Overton County with his sister Martha Sevier and other young kinspeople. He married about 1715 and had a son Joseph J. Sevier, who had a son Joseph J. Sevier, who wrote to Bishop Hsos from Rockford Mo., in 1916, giving this information. He has answered no recent letters however.

MARTHA SEVIER

Martha Sevier, born about 1799, was probably the daughter of Valentine Sevier.

She must have grown to maturity in Overton County with dozens of her young kinspeople. Her step grand-mother "Bonny Kate was domiciled in Overton County in what must have been a handsome home for the period and this home probably provided a meeting place for the young people of the entire neighborhood.

Martha Sevier married——— Poindexter about 1815. Mrs. F. A. Birdsall of Yazoo City, Miss. is her descendant.

CHAPTER EIGHT

Richard Sevier

RICHARD SEVIER

Richard Sevier, son of Governor John Sevier and his **first wife,** Sarah Hawkins Sevier, was born in 1775.

A list of **Governor** Sevier's children prepared by **Mrs. Sophia** Hoss **French, of Morristown, a** descendant of Governor **Sevier** through **his third son,** John Sevier junior, gives Richard as **dying in** December, **1792.** He would then have 'been less than **twenty years** of age.

In **another reference** it is said that he died of a fever **contracted** in an Indian **Campaign when** he was eighteen years of age, **this would** p'ace his **death in the fall** or winter of 1793.

His death **while** still a youth accounts, of course, **for only brief** mention **of him.**

Governor John Sevier makes but one reference to **his son** Richard **in the Journal.** Under date of January 14, 1794,he **gives** details **of a dream of** being in an unknown country, **evidently** Heaven, **and his** son "Dicky" meeting him there. The **dream shows** that his **father's** mind was still deeply concerned with **his recent** sorrow.

CHAPTER NINE
Rebecca Sevier

REBECCA SEVIER

Rebecca Sevier, daughter of Governor John Sevier by his first wife, Sarah Hawkins Sevier, was born in Virginia probably about the year 1777. She died November 17, 1799, just four and one half years after her marriage, while still a young woman.

Young women at that period married as a rule at an early age and I judge therefore that at her marriage in 1795, she was not more than seventeen or eighteen years old. It is for that reason that I place her birth about 1777. Several of Governor Sevier's daughters were married even before they were seventeen, two of them at fifteen, which was at that time a frequent custom. Rebecca Sevier was a small child if not a baby when her mother died in 1780 and she was raised by her step-mother, Bonny Kate Sevier. She married John Waddell, or Waddle, as it was sometimes spelled, Thursday, February 26, 1795, just one week after her sister, Nancy Sevier, married Walter King.

Governor Sevier mentions the marriage in his Journal as follows:

(1795, February)

"Thursday, 26, Rebecca's wedding to John Waddle.

Friday cold. Saturday very cold. Came home from

Rebecca's wedding."

Rebecca, it seems from that record, was married away from home, presumably in Jonesboro, as that is the point most frequently mentioned when the family journeyed forth. No reason is given or suggested by any information that I have for the marriage to take place away from the family residence. It would seem that John Waddle was an accepted visitor to the house as he was among the guests at Nancy Sevier's wedding to Walter King, just one week earlier.

John Waddell was born in Philladelphia about 1765.   He was
the eldest of ten children of John Waddell I and his wife, Rachel
Quee Waddell.   John Waddell I was born of Scotch parents in
County Donegal, Ireland, in 1736.   He emigrated to America and
settled near Philadelphia where he married Rachel Quee, the
daughter of a Scotchman and his wife who was Hester Rittenhouse.
They soon emigrated to what we now know as Tennessee and
settled in Washington District.   They were Presbyterians and
educated their son John Waddell II to be a Presbyterian minister.
He did not however follow this profession.   He was too young to be
in the earlier part of the Revolution, but he served, it is said in the
later campaigns with the young Seviers, whose neighbor he was,
under Col. John Sevier who was later his father-in-law.
He survived his wife Rebecca Sevier, more than half a century,
dying in 1855 in Hot Springs, Ark.   He married a second time and
had children, who have descendants but these do not come in the
Sevier line and so they are not included in this history.

Rebecca Sevier Waddell died November 17, 1799, just four and
a half years after her marriage to John Waddell II, leaving two
children namely:

1   Sarah Rebecca Sevier Waddell

2   John Sevier Waddell.

SARAH REBECCA SEVIER WADDELL

Sarah Rebecca Sevier Waddell, daughter of John Waddell II
and Sarah Rebecca Sevier Waddell, was born April 25, 1796.   She
was given her mother's name and Rebecca's mother's name, Sarah
(Hawkins).   She died May 1883.   She married about 1815, or a
little earlier, Abram Hair and has numerous descendants.   It is
said that the children of Abram Hair and Sarah Rebecca Sevier
Waddell Hair were:

Martha Hair

Mary Hair

Minerva Hair

Elizabeth Hair

I do not know if there were other children of if these came in
this order.

Elizabeth Hair, daughter of Sarah Rebecca Sevier Waddel Hair and Abram Hair, was born 18———.   She married about 18———, — ——— Chandley and had a daughter, Nancy Chandley, born 18———, who married——— Weed.   They had a daughter, Opal Weed, born 18———, who married George A. Sprinkle and lives now in Weavers-ville, North Carolina.

JOHN SEVIER WADDELL

John Sevier Waddell, only son of Rebecca Sevier Waddell and John Waddell II, was born February 14, 1799.   His mother died when he was nine months old.   He and his sister, Rebecca, went to live with their paternal grandparents, John Waddell II and Rachell Quee Waddell, who lived near Jonesboro, Tennessee.   John Sevier Waddell married January 6, 1831 Sophia Doak, daughter of John Doak and Jane Montgomery Doak and grand-daughter of Dr. Samuel Doak, founder of Washington Cllege.   In 1838 John Sevier Waddell with his wife and two children, Samuel Waddell and Rebecca Jane Waddell emigrated to Henry County, Missouri.   He purchased land near Calhoun, Missouri and there he spent the remainder of his life. He died February 11, 1864.   He married twice.   His first wife, Sophia Doak Waddell, died June 27, 1843.

They had three sons and one daughter, namely:

a.   Samuel Whitefield Waddell, born December 5, 1831 in Tennessee, died out west November 1877.

b.   Rebecca Jane Waddell

c.   Alexander Nelson Waddell

d.   James Newton Waddell

Of these:

a.   Samuel Whitfield Waddell, son of John Sevier Waddell and Sophia Doak Waddell, born December 5, 1831 in Tennessee, died out west November 18, 1877 unmarried.

b.   Rebecca Jane Waddell, daughter of John Sevier Waddell and Sophia Doak Waddell, was born March 13, 1835 in Tennessee, died in Coronodo, California, October 1, 1918.   She married, October 6, 1853, James Monroe Duncan.   They had nine children but of these only three daughters lived to maturity, namely:

Ella May Duncan, born September 12, 1864, died December 26, 1919 in California, married Dr. Joseph P. Gray and had a daughter, Rebecca Gray, born in Nashville, Tennessee, who married Arthur

Lowell Endicott July 7, 1914, and they have a daughter, Margaret Elinor, born April 5, 1925. They make their home in Pasadena, California.

Jennie Doak Duncan born September 4, 1867 in Henry County, Mo., married Rev. Sterling Price Brite, August 30, 1893, in Windsor, Mo. Their children are: Mary Louisa Brite, born November 17, 1898; John Duncan Brite, born march 4, 1901; Joseph Landes Brite, born July 9, 1903, married Cordelia Metcalf; Katherine Duncan, born October 7,1879 near Windsor, Mo.

c. Alexander Nelson Waddell, son of John Sevier Waddell and Sophia Doak Waddell, born December 21, 1838 near Calhoun Mo., died February 15, 1913 near Windsor, Mo. He married January 5, 1868, Eliza Frances Carter in Missouri. She was born in Virginia and went with her parents, Thomas Carter and Eliza Carter, to Missouri in 1861. Alexander Nelson Waddell and Eliza Carter Waddell had six children, three sons and three daughters, namely:

Robert Doak Waddell, born near Windsor Mo., July 22, 1869, married October 12, 1904. They had no children. He lives at Bartlesville, Okla.

John Carter Waddell, born August 27, 1871, died August 27, 1915.

Eliza Jane Waddell, born April 16, 1873, near Windsor, Mo., married Avery Finks, of Calhoun, Mo., in 1902. They have Frances Avery Finks, born 1912.

Alice Nelson Waddell, born January 8, 1875 near Windsor, Mo., died in St. Louis, Mo., December 14, 1918. She married December 19, 1919, Arthur J. England. They had one child, Frances Hall England, born February 1915.

Annie May Waddell, born October 21, 1876, near Windsor, Mo., died at Liberty, Mo., August 26, 1918. She married March 3, 1915, Dr. Robert E. Sevier, son of Henry Sevier of Liberty, Mo. She left two children, Helen May Sevier, born January 4, 1917 and Robert Ann Sevier, born August 8, 1918.

Alexander Thomas Waddell, born October 26, 1882 near Windsor, Mo., married Doris Mathews, of Sedalia, Mo. They have one child, Alice Lee Waddell, born January 20, 1908.

d. James Newton Waddell, son of John Sevier Waddell and Sophia Doak Waddell, was born, May 1, 1843 near Calhoun, Mo. He died January 28, 1915, in Henry County, Mo. He married

Martha Box.   They had one daughter Bettie Waddell, born 1884.

John Sevier Waddell, after the death of Sophia Doak Waddell, married **Mary Ann Pinkston, November** 1,1844.   She was born in Estell, Ky., November 19, 1823, and moved with her parents, Bassel Lee Pinkston and Elizabeth Norland Pinkston, to a farm near Calhoun, Mo.   Mary Elizabeth Pinkston Waddell died October 1, 1866 leaving seven children, namely:

     e.   Thomas Jefferson Waddell

     f.   Sarah Elizabeth Waddell

     g.   John Franklin Waddell

     h.   William Wilson Waddell

     i.   Isora Waddell

     j.   Medora Waddell

     k.   Mary E. Waddell

Of these:

e.   Thomas Jefferson Waddell, son of John Sevier Waddell by his second wife, Mary Ann Pinkston Waddell, was born August 20, 1845, died April 4, 1862, near Calhoun, Mo.

f.   Sarah Elizabeth Waddell, daughter of John Sevier Waddell by his second wife, Mary Ann Pinkston Waddell, was born August 13, 1850, near Calhoun, Mo.   She died July 2, 1909.   She married August 31, 1871, Thomas Preston Kairns, of Canada.   They had no children.

g.   John Franklin Waddell, son of John Sevier Waddell by his second wife, Mary Ann Pinkston Waddell, was born January 13, 1852, near Calhoun, Mo., he married in Brownsville, Texas about 1883.

h.   William Wilson Waddell, son of John Sevier Waddell by his second wife Mary Ann Pinkston Waddell, was born March 10, 1854, near Calhoun, Mo.   He married Augusta Florence Duncan March 20, 1878.   She was the daughter of John Duncan and Mary Frances Crews Duncan.   William Wilson Waddell and his wife had six children though only four lived to maturity, namely:

    Leslie Waddell

    Clay Duncan Waddell

    Marie Elizabeth Waddell

    Augusta Florence Waddell

Of these:

Leslie Waddell, born August 30, 1879 near Windsor, Mo.   **He** married Virginia Bohn, of Brighton, Ill., December 24, 1907.   **They** had two children: Eleanor Louisa Waddell, born November 8, 1909 and William Clay Waddell, born March 23, 1911.   Their **mother,** Virginia Bohn Waddell, died November 29, 1921.   She was **born** February 14,1880.   Dr. Leslie Waddell married, December 25, 1922, for his   second   wife,   Alice   Corinne   Power   of   Kansas,   born September 16, 1892.   Dr. Leslie Waddell is located in Pittsburg, **Pa.,** and is a member of the faculty of the University of Pittsburg.

Clay Duncan Waddell, born near Windsor, Mo., April 28, 1885. He married Lydia   Peak,   of   Nevada,   Mo.,   September   21,   1911. Lydia Peak was born, January 4, 1893, in Boon County, Missouri. She was the daughter of Judson Davis Peak and Emily Jane **Ford** Peak.   They had three children, Mary Frances Waddell,born October 20,   1913;   Virginia Nadene Waddell,   born   May   14, 1916,   died December 14, 1922 and Clay Peak Waddell, born November 20, 1918.

Marie Elizabeth Waddell was born near Windsor, Mo., September 24, 1894 .

Augusta   Florence   Waddell   was   born   near   Windsor,   **Mo.,** October 19, 1897.   She married Cleveland S. Cotter, March 11, 1917, in Jefferson City, Mo.   They had   one   child,   William   Waddell Cotton, born May 10, 1918.

i.   Mary Isora Waddell, daughter of John Sevier Waddell **and** his second wife Mary Ann Pinkston Waddell, was a twin to **Medora** Waddell.   They were born May 20, 1856, near Calhoun Mo., Isora Waddell married November 6, 1872, Alexander Brame of **Kentucky.** They had five children, three of whom grew to   maturity, **namely:**

Gertrude Brame, born April 21, 1875, died in Visalia, **Cal.,** married March 25, 1902 in Clinton, Mo., Henry Taylor.   They had **one** son, Richard Taylor.

Bessie Brame, born near Windsor, Mo., March 12, 1880, **married** Claude B. Hall, September 27, 1906, died March 24, 1910 in Portland, Oregon.

Ruth Brame born December 29, 1891, married   Noel   **Sheats,** October 26, 1918 in Seattle, Washington.

j.   Medora Waddell, daughter of John Sevier Waddell and **his** second wife Mary Ann Pinkston Waddell, was a   twin   to   **Isora**

Waddell. They were born, May 20, 1856 near Calhoun, Mo. She married September 29, 1875, Earhart, son of Dr. Earhart, of Texas. They had six children, only five of whom lived to maturity: namely:

William Earhart, born near Nevada, Mo., August 1876.

Ethel Earhart, born near Nevada, Mo., August 1882, died in Nevada, Mo., November 1, 1915

Murry Earhart, born near Nevada in 1882

Frank Earhart, born in Nevada, Mo., 1890

k. Mary E. Waddell, youngest child of John Sevier Waddell, and Mary Ann Pinkston Waddell, was born, August 15, 1858 near Calhoun, Mo., and died, April 10, 1872.

CHAPTER TEN
Nancy Sevier

NANCY SEVIER

Nancy Sevier, the daughter of Governor John Sevier and his first wife, Sarah Hawkins Sevier, was born about 1779. She lived in the household of her step-mother, Bonny Kate, until her marriage. She is frequent'y mentioned in her father's Journal and her marriage to Walter King is noted as taking place, February 19, 1795. After that date she and her husband are very often mentioned in the Journal. Walter King owned and operated the Iron Works near the Sevier plantation and frequent trips are made to the Works by various members of the family.

Nancy's marriage was quite a social event many relatives and neighbors assembling for the ceremony. The Journal gives this entry concerning it:

"February 19, 1795.
Thursday, 19, Mr. King and Nancy married. Jimmy Weir's family here. Mr. Harril', Mr. Waddell, Mr. Claiborne, Mr. Weir's family here, Cousin Jack and Mr. Doak."

"Mr. Weir" refers to Colonel Samuel Weir. Jimmy Weir was another neighbor. Mr. Waddell is John Waddell or Waddel, who married Rebecca Sevier a week later. Mr. Doak was doubtless the officiating minister. "Cousin Jack" may be the nephew of the Governor, known in this record and familiarly at that period as Devil Jack. "Cousin" was used interchangeably with "nephew" for many years, or the Governor may have called the young man by the name by which he was called by the young Seviers. I do not know of any real Cousin Jack that Governor Sevier possessed.

I understand that descendants of Nancy Sevier King and Walter King lived in Knoxville and that a Walter King, who must be IV or V, in Knoxville has their family Bible. Nancy Sevier King was living in 1818, as she is listed in the Sheriff's Bill of Sale. A son of Nancy Sevier King, Austin King was Governor of Missouri and was living in Missouri in 1853. A letter from him is on file in the New York City Library.

"The Encyclopedia of the State of Missouri" says: "Austin A. King, lawyer, legislator, Governor of Missouri and member of

Congress, was born in Tennessee, September 21, 1801. He died in Richmond, Missouri, April 22, 1870. His father was a soldier in the Revolutionary War, and from him he inherited a strong national spirit. While a young man he came to Missouri and settled in Columbia, where he practiced law with success. In 1837 he removed to Richmond, Ray County, and was appointed circuit judge and served on the bench for eight years. In 1848 he was chosen Governor'.

If Walter King, father of Austin served in the Revolution, as stated in the foregoing paragraph from "Encyclopedia of the State of Missouri," he must have been considerably older than his wife. I have no confirmation of his Revolutionary service and am inclined to think this biographical note is in error as he was probably too young. It was probably his father who served.

Mrs. Emma King Turner, wife of Emmitt Turner, joined the D. A. R. on the record of Gov. Sevier and her lineage is given in the D. A. R. Lineage Books as follows: She is a daughter of Thomas Benton King and Clara Bingham, grand daughter of Austin Augustus King and Nancy Roberts, great grand daughter of Walter King and Nancy Sevier and great great grand daughter of Governor Sevier.

From the foregoing information Nancy Sevier and **Walter King** had at least two sons.

Walter King, junior.

Austin Augustus King.

WALTER KING, JUNIOR

Walter King, junior, son of Nancy King and Walter King married and had descendants who lived in East Tennessee.

AUSTIN AUGUSTUS KING

Augustus King, son of Nancy Sevier King and Walter King, was born September 21, 1801. He died in Richmond, Mo., September 22, 1870. He was Governor of Missouri and was a member of Congress from Missouri. He married Nancy Roberts.

CHAPTER ELEVEN

Catherine Sherrill Sevier

CATHERINE SHERRILL SEVIER

Catherine Sherrill Sevier, was the daughter of Governor John Sevier and his second wife, Catherine Sherrill Sevier. In the list of Gov. Sevier's children, prepared by George Washington Sevier (son of the Governor) for Dr. Lyman C. Draper, Catherine is given as the second child of her mother and she appears in practically all lists in this order. However Mrs. Ellett, author of Pioneer Women of the West , says in her sketch of Ruth Sevier that Ruth was the second child of her mother, leaving the first place for Catherine. Also, Ruth's marriage took place two years after Catherine's, indicating that Ruth was the junior, for marriage took place early in life at that period and from the time a girl was fifteen she was considered ready for marriage. I therefore place Catherine Sherrill Sevier before her sister, Ruth, in this record placing her as the first child of her mother and the eleventh child of her father Gov. John Sevier.

She grew to womanhood on her father's plantation, "Plum Grove", near Jonesboro, Tennessee. She is frequently mentioned in her father's Journal. He has various endearing names for her, calling her Catty, Cattery, Kitty and the like.

She married twice. Her first marriage is recorded in Governor Sevier's Journal, with considerable detail. He gives the officiating minister's name and the list of guests present. He sets down the groom as "R. Campbell", but we know from other records that he was Richard Campbell, son of Richard Campbell, senior, and that he was a first cousin to the elder Sevier children, as their mother, Sarah Hawkins, was a sister to the elder Richard Campbell's wife, Mary Hawkins. Also a letter from George Washington Sevier to Dr. Lyman Draper confirms this knowledge for he states that his sister, Catherine married Richard Campbell.

The marriage of Catherine Sherrill Sevier to Richard Campbell took place, Thursday 24, 1795, which was quite a marrying year for the Seviers, Nancy and Rebecca having married in February, 1795. Dr. Samuel Doak officiated and evidently the ceremony was an event of general interest in the neighborhood. Governor Sevier records many guests present, among them: Major John Sevier and his wife (this was the third son of the Governor), Mrs. Waddell (this was the daughter, Rebecca), Mr. Harrill, (he was also a guest at Nancy's wedding), Mr. J. A. Anderson, Mr. McKee and his lady, Miss Peggy, Mr. Sherrill, (this was the father or brother of Bonny Kate), Mr. and Mrs. Wear (Col. Samuel Wear and his first wife Mary Thompson Wear), Major James Sevier and his lady (this was the Governor's second son, his wife was Nancy Conway), Mrs. William Clarke (this was Major Clarke's second wife. He married first, the Governor's eldest daughter, Elizabeth), Benjamin Brown and his wife, (this was the daughter, Sarah Hawkins Sevier), Josiah Allen and John Ficks. (The inclosures are mine. Ed.)

This makes quite a social item. If the Governor had only been thoughtful enough to describe the bride's costume and to name the members of the household who were present there would be nothing left to sigh for. I should so like to know what children were living in his home, as well as these names of the sons and daughters who evidently came from their own homes to be present.

Catherine Sherrill Sevier Campbell and Richard Campbell had one son, of record. Whether there were other children by this marriage I do not know. If so none lived to maturity probably. The one son was named George Washington Campbell in compliment to Catherine's brother, George Washington Sevier.

George Washington Campbell married —————— and has descendants, one of whom, George Washington Campbell, was Lieutenant Governor of Missouri in 1903.

Governor Sevier in his Journal makes frequent mention of Mr. and Mrs. R. Campbell. He goes to a ball at their home in Knoxville, Christmas evening, 1799. In June 1800, he makes the last reference to R. Campbell, when he goes to "a little hop at R. Campbell's". Evidently the Campbell's were socially inclined and evidently the Governor saw them frequently. Shortly after this last date there is a break in the Journal and afterwards frequent breaks. After several years, in 1808, the name of A. Rhea begins to appear. Richard Campbell had died and Catherine's second marriage had taken place in the interim.

Thursday, December 12, 1799 Mrs. R. Campbell is mentioned in the Journal and Pater Campbell. Pater may be her son although I have record of only one son, George Washington Campbell. "Pater" may be a nickname for him.

Catherine Sherrill Sevier Campbell married Archibald Rhea, junior, about 1803. His sister, Jane Rhea, married Catherine's brother, Dr. Samuel Sevier. Archibald Rhea, junior, is mentioned many times in Chalkley's Abstract of Augusta Records. He received land October 21, 1771. (Page 516, Volume III.) This Archibald Rhea, junior, however, I consider a generation older than the Archibald, junior, who married Catherine Sevier. He was possibly father to Archibald who married Catherine There were evidently many successive members of the family ....d Archibald Rhea.

I have not the exact date of the second marriage, but as the third child by Archiabald Rhea was born January 1, 1809, I conclude that the marriage took place about 1803. Catherine Sevier Campbell Rhea died May 1, 1827. Archibald Rhea died January 25, 1833.

The children of Catherine Sevier Campbell Rhea were:

1. George Washington Campbell
2. James White Rhea
3. John Sevier Rhea
4. Ann Eliza Rhea.

Further records of Catherine Sevier's children have been sent to me by Mrs. Ida Barclay Tucker as this chapter is going to press. They will be found in full in the appendix, though received too late for inclusion here. By Mrs. Tucker's record Catherine Sevier had two other Rhea children, one of whom, Mary Rhea was her grandmother. The names supplied by Mrs. Tucker are:

5. Mary Rhea
6. Jane Rhea

GEORGE WASHINGTON CAMPBELL

George Washington Campbell, son of Catherine Sevier Campbell and Richard Campbell was born in East Tennessee, about 1797, the marriage of his parents taking place Christmas eve, 1795. He received his name in compliment to his mother's favorite brother who was himself quite young (fourteen) in 1796. This was George Washington Sevier, eldest son of "Bonny Kate".

George Washington Campbell married and had children, though I do not know their names. A grandson of one of them was George Washington Campbell, who was Lieutenant Governor of Missouri in 1903. Mr. C Schiller Campbell of Lincoln, Nebraska writes that he is the son of James C. Campbell, born August 19, 1834, who was a grand son of Catherine Sevier Campbell and Richard Campbell

JAMES WHITE RHEA

James White Rhea, son of Catherine Sevier (Campbell) and Archibald Rhea, junior, is said to be the first son by Catherine's second marriage. He was born in East Tennessee. He died in Galveston, Texas.

JOHN SEVIER RHEA

John Sevier Rhea, son of Catherine Sevier (Campbell) Rhea and Archibald Rhea, junior, was born in East Tennessee. He was named in compliment to Gov. John Sevier.

ANN ELIZA RHEA

Ann Eliza Rhea, daughter of Catherine Sevier (Campbell) Rhea, was born January 1, 1809. She married Thomas Hooper Merrill, —————— 18——. They had eight children. Ann Eliza Rhea Merill, died September 7, 1887, and is buried in Courtland, Alabama.

The children of Ann Eliza Rhea Merrill and Thomas Hooper Merrill:

    a. Angelina Merrill

    b. Orlando Merrill

    c. Edwin Merrill

    d. Ellen Merrill

    e. Emma Merrill

    f. William Merrill

    g. Thomas Merrill, junior

    h. Laura Merrill.

MARY RHEA AND JANE RHEA

The history of Mary Rhea and Jane Rhea will be found in the Apendix.

CHAPTER TWELVE

Ruth Sevier

RUTH SEVIER

Ruth Sevier, daughter of Governor John Sevier and his second wife, Catherine Sherrill Sevier, was their second child. She is usually given as the first child of the second marriage, but Mrs. Ellet, in Pioneer Women of the West, says she was the second.

She was raised at the beautiful Plum Grove residence of her parents and enjoyed a very novel life for a young girl even in that interesting period. She learned in her childhood to speak the Indian tongue and could, in fact, converse in several dialects with the chiefs of the various nations. At one time her father had taken prisoner thirty Indians and having no place to take them, he brought them home! They so thorough'y enjoyed the Plum Grove plantation that they refused to leave, and little Ruth became their adoration. They taught her all they knew of woodcraft and legend and they christened her "Chuckey's Rutha", Chuckey being their name for John Sevier, while Rutha was his pet name for his small daughter whom he seems to have especially adored. The Indians called her a princess and prophesied that she would marry a Chief and be one of them, a prophesy which was singularly fulfilled, for she did marry a young man who, though of the white people, had been raised by Indians, adopted into their tribe and made a Chief.

Ruth Sevier was so adept in the Indian tongues that on several occasions she acted as interpreter and was consulted very frequent y in important matters even when she was not absolutely the offi.ial interpreter.

She married twice. Her first marriage was to the young man who had grown up with the Indians. He was Richard Sparks. He had been captured at four years of age and was given the name of Shawtunte. He was a childhood playmate of Tecumseh and The Prophet, two of the great chiefs and two of the most dangerous. He was reared in the family of Tecumseh until he was sixteen. He was then released and he went to the Kentucky settlements and later into East Tennessee and to the settlement on the Holston and Nollachucky Rivers. His mother, seeing him, recognized him instantly by a mark. He took the name Richard Sparks after his release from Indian captivity, and under that name Governor

267

Sevier took him into his family and made use of his knowledge of Indian character and his familiarity with the country. Governor Sevier obtained for him an appointment in the United States Army. In the meanwhile Rutha had taken great interest in the newcomer with his romantic history, being at first the only one who could communicate with him. She taught him to read and write and gave him in fact the benefit of all her own schooling.

They were married about the time that Governor Sevier obtained an appointment for him in the Army. Governor Sevier very frequently mentions "Rutha" in his Journal, and "my daughter, Mrs. Sparks". Richard Sparks was a Colonel and was stationed at Fort Pickering on the Mississippi River in 1801 and 1802. He was afterwards sent with his regiment to New Orleans, Baton Rouge and Fort Adams. Ruth Sevier Sparks accompanied him and made loyal friends. She seems to have inherited her father's faculty of acquiring friendship. Colonel Richard Sparks died at Staunton, Virginia, in 1815.

Ruth Sevier Sparks married for her second husband, Daniel Vertner, of Mississippi, near Fort Gibson. He is said to have been a wealthy planter. In 1834, Ruth Sevier Sparks Vertner was visiting friends or relatives in Maysvil'e, Kentucky, when she died.

She had no children. She has many namesakes, however, among the descendants of her brothers and sisters, the name Ruth occuring frequently in the family annals. Her second husband was also extremely popular with the Seviers and his name is perpetuated as "Daniel Vertner Sevier," the name having been used for several generations.

CHAPTER THIRTEEN

George Washington Sevier

GEORGE WASHINGTON SEVIER

George Washington Sevier, son of John Sevier and **Catherine** Sherrill Sevier, was born February 1, 1782. He was **John Sevier's** thirteenth child. After his father's death he removed to **Overton** County, Tennessee with his mother and he was Clerk of the **Circuit** Court in that county for several years. His military record is **as** follows: Ensign of the Second Infantry, March 26, 1804; **Second** Lieutenant, August 22, 1805; First Lieutenant, May 31, 1807; **Captain** of Rif'e Company, May 3,1808; Lieutenant Colonel, July 6, **1812;** Colonel, January 24, 1814. His descendants are eligible to **the** Societies of 1812.

Much of the early history of the Sevier family is based **upon** his letters to Dr. Lyman G. Draper. These are now in the **Draper** Collection in Madison, Wisconsin. He was employed by **Governor** Claiborne, of Mississippi, and died in Mississippi while in his **service.**

He married Catherine Weatherly Chambers, by whom he **had** eleven children, namely:

(1) George Washington Sevier, junior

(2) Catherine Anna Sevier

(3) William C. Sevier, never married

(4) Thomas K. Sevier, never married

(5) Cornelia V. Sevier

(6) John Vertrees Sevier, never married

(7) E iza M. Sevier

(8) Marion F. Sevier, never married

(9) Laura J. Sevier

(10) Putman M. Sevier, never married

(11) Henry Clay Sevier, never married.

Of the foregoing:

DR. GEORGE WASHINGTON SEVIER, JUNIOR

Dr. George Wash'ngton Sevier, junior, married Sarah **Knox,** of Nashville, niece of Mrs. Andrew Jackson, who was raised at **the** Hermitage by President and Mrs Jackson. They had six **children,** namely: George Washington Sevier, III, William Sevier, **Andrew**

Jackson Sevier, Mary Catherine Sevier, Eliza Donelson Sevier and Jennie Vertner Sevier. Andrew Jackson Sevier married Columbia Dobys, and they had seven children: Columbia Sevier (who married Willard H. Utz, of Louisiana); Andrew Jackson Sevier, Second, (who married J. S. Agee, of Alabama); Jennie Vertner Sevier (who married T. F. Young, of Vicksburg); Mary Catherine Sevier (who married W. J. Ward, of Arkansas); and Ada Elizabeth Sevier (who married A. C. Williamson, of Arkansas); one daughter, Sarah Knox, died unmarried many years ago. Mary Catherine Sevier married Robert Dunbar, leaving two children, Robert Dunbar, Second, and Nannie Bells Dunbar, both living in Missouri. Jennie Vertner Sevier married George Clarke for her first husband and for her second husband married Adolphus Harris, of Virginia. They had one daughter, Sarah Knox Harris, who married Captain George Sager, of Port Gibson, Mississippi. Eliza Donelson Sevier married W. T. Jefferies, of Port Gibson, Mississippi, and left two children, Mary Sevier Jefferies and Evan Shelby Jefferies. Mrs. Jefferies and Mrs. Utz are the only living children of Dr. George W. Sevier and his wife, who was Sarah Knox, and are among the oldest descendants of Governor John Sevier, and the nearest to him in point of relation, being great-grand daughters. They also represent other early Tennessee families in their relation to the Jackson, Shelby, Knox, and Donelson families.

CATHERINE ANN SEVIER

Catherine Ann Sevier, married Albigence Waldo Putman, a grandson of General Israel Putman. They had two children: Julia (who married William O'Niel Perkins, lived in Nashville for many years and had no children) and Waldo Washington Putman (who married Eliza Jane Smith and had three daughters: Emma, Agnes and Caroline. Misses Emma and Agnes Putman are not married. Miss Caroline Putman married Robert Morrison, of Chattanooga, and had four children, Kenneth Morrison, who died young. Harold Morrison, who married Sterling Milne, Louise Morrison, who married Roy L. Baker and has one child, Roy L. Baker, junior, and Putman Morrison, who married Elizabeth Venneble and has five daughters: Elizabeth, Agnes, Mary, Esther and Ruth.

3. William C. Sevier, never married

4. Thomas K. Sevier, never married

5. Cornelia V. Sevier

6. John Vertrees Sevier, never married

7. Eliza M. Sevier, married John F. Donald

8. Marion F. Sevier, never married

THE SEVIER FAMILY

LAURA J. SEVIER

9. Laura J. Sevier married Henry L. Norvell and had Joseph A. Norvell (who married Mary Slinkard and had Louise Norvell and Nita Norvell, of Colorado, neither of whom is married ; Cornelia Sevier Norvell, (who married Albert B. Payne and had Albert B. Payne, Second, never married; Ida Payne, married Minor Scovel, Amy Payne married Charles Rosse and Douglas Payne married Annie Alexander); Aduella B. Norvell (who never married); Sarah Woods Norvell (who married N. W. Leonard); Moselle Norvell (who married Frank Porterfield Elliott. and is now living in Nashvil'e.   Her children are Laura Norvell Elliot and Elizabeth Porterfield El iott

10. Putman M. Sevier, never married

11. Henry Clay Sevier married twice, first Mary Clark and second Mary Nash.

CHAPTER FOURTEEN

Samuel Sevier

SAMUEL SEVIER

S amuel Sevier, son of Governor Sevier and his second wife Catherine Sherrill Sevier, was born in East Tennessee, June 26, 1785. He died October 25, 1844. Governor Sevier in his Journal makes frequent mention of Samuel. On 28th of September,1795, which by the Journal, fell on Monday, an oratorical contest was held at Martin Academy. The prizes were $3.00, $2.00 and $1.00 and they were captured by James Anderson, James Trimble and Samuel Sevier. Governor Sevier fails to record the amount of the prize, which I find mentioned elsewhere, however, and though he says there were three winners in the contest, he apparently gives the names of but two, "James Anderson Trimble, and Samuel Sevier". This is only a seeming error, he merely forgot the first name of the Trimble boy, who was James Trimble, and punctuation was not the Governor's strong point.

Odd that after a hundred and thirty years we find recorded in history and the Governor's Journal the prowess of three little boys in oratory!

Samuel Sevier became a physician and moved to Alabama to reside. His mother, late in life, went to his home to live with his family near Russellville, Alabama, and there she died and was buried. It is said that Samuel was her favorite son. He had settled on a large grant of land made to Gov. Sevier and several members of the Sherrill family also went to that section.

Dr. Samuel Sevier married in 18——, Jane Rhea, whose brother, Archibald Rhea married Samuel's sister, Catherine Sevier as her second husband. About the time of his marriage Samuel Sevier moved to Alabama to a plantation near Russellville and there he lived until his death, in 1844. He was buried in the old cemetery near that place and his mother was buried beside him. In 1922, through the efforts of Colonel S. G. Heiskall, of Knoxville, the body of Catherine Sherrill Sevier, widow of Governor Sevier and mother of Dr. Samuel Sevier, was moved from the Russellville cemetery to Knoxville and reinterred beside her husband.

Catherine Sherrill Sevier had moved from Tennessee in June

1836, to spend the "rest of her life" with this favorite son, but she lived only a few months, passing away in October of the same year.

Dr. J. G. M. Ransey, of Annals of Tennessee fame, is authority for the statement that Samuel Sevier married a sister of Archibald Rhea, who married Catherine Sevier. He makes reference to this in his history of Lebanon Church.

Dr. Samuel Sevier and Jane Rhea Sevier had ten children, namely:

1. John Sevier, who married Mildred Merrill

2. Catherine Ann Sevier, who married Branham Merrill

3. Margaret Sevier, who married Charles B. Tenant

4. Joanna Sevier, who married Hugh Dickson

5. Archibald Rhea Sevier, who married Malinda Chisholm

6. Benjamin Brown Sevier, who married Drucilla Ewing

7. Daniel Vertner Sevier, who married Sophronia Chisholm

8. Branham Merrill Sevier, who married a Spanish girl in Mexico

9. Jane Sevier, who married Lewis C. Chisholm

10. Samuel Sevier, who married Jane Desprey.

Once again the family habit of naming children for various in-laws is illustrated. Benjamin Brown Sevier, for instance, is evidently named for Sarah Hawkins Sevier's husband and Daniel Vertner Sevier is named for Ruth Sevier's second husband and Archibald Rhea Sevier is named for Catherine Sevier's husband, though in this instance, Archibald Rhea was also maternal uncle to the namesake and Mrs. Samuel Sevier (Jane Rhea) was a daughter of Archibald Rhea, senior.

JOHN SEVIER

John Sevier, son of Dr. Samuel Sevier and Jane Rhea Sevier, married Mildred Merrill. Their children were:

a. Ruth Sevier, who married ———— Wilder, and for her second husband ———— Colins and lived in Louisville, Kentucky.

b. Mary Sevier, who married ———— Knight. She died in Memphis.

c. "Tib" Sevier, who married ———— Wiggins. She died in Memphis.

d. John Sevier, who lives in Wasihngton.

e. Sallie Sevier, who lives in Louisville.

f. Edgar Sevier, who died.

CATHERINE ANN SEVIER

2. Catherine Ann Sevier, daughter of Dr. Samuel Sevier and Jane Rhea Sevier, married Branham Merrill. Their children were:

   a. John Merrill, who married Miss Fannie Hopgood

   b. Branham Merrill, Junior.

   c. Mildred Jane Merrill, who married ———— Didlake.

DR. DANIEL VERTNER SEVIER

7. Dr. Daniel Vertner Sevier, son of Samuel Sevier and Jane Rhea, was born 18——. He married twice, first, Mary Sophronia Chisholm and second, Catherine Keelen. By his first marriage he had four children:

   a. Adelia Sevier, who married Joseph Baumer.

   b. Cullen Sevier, who died in infancy.

   c. Daniel Vertner Sevier, junior, who married Media Watkins.

   d. Dr. Samuel Gillington Sevier, born December 19, 1854, who married M. J. Benson, January 19, 1885. Their children were Bessie Cordelia, died in infancy; Annie Esther, died in infancy; Mary Sophronia, married W. T. Kirk; Samuel Prentice, who married Cathleen Morris; James Henry, Edgar and Tommie Camille, a daughter.

Dr. Daniel Vertner Sevier married for his second wife, Catherine Keelen and had three daughters:

   e. Katie Sevier, who married Dr. Caterbury.

   f. Nancy Sevier, who married Thomas Hyde.

   g. Jennie Sevier, who died in young womanhood.

Daniel Vertner Sevier, junior, has in his possession a beautiful miniature painting by Peale, of Governor John Sevier. It was given by the widow, Catherine Sherrill Sevier to her son Dr. Samuel Sevier and by him to his son, Dr. Daniel Vertner Sevier and by him to his son, Daniel Vertner Sevier, junior. He loaned this miniature to the Tennessee Historical Society in 1924.

JANE SEVIER

9. Jane Sevier, daughter of Dr. Samuel Sevier and Jane Rhea Sevier, married Lewis C. Chisholm and had Joanna Chisholm, who married G. Lueddemann.

SAMUEL SEVIER, JUNIOR

10. Samuel Sevier, junior, son of Dr. Samuel Sevier and Jane Rhea Sevier, was born 18——. He moved to Aberdeen, Mississippi,

to reside and became a dentist. For many years he was the most prominent dentist in that whole section of the country. He married Josephine Desprez, daughter of William Desprez, a prominent physician and surgeon of his time. Dr. Samuel Sevier, junior, and Josephine Desprez Sevier had four children, namely:

a. Samuel Sevier III, born February 16, 1874, who married Mary Louise Fogarty and has three daughters, Josephine Desprez Sevier, Susan Rhea Sevier and Mary Louise Sevier.

b. William Rhea Sevier, who is a druggist and lives in Birmingham, Alabama. He married ———— ———— and has three children, Nell Davidson Sevier, Anne Rhea Sevier and William Kearney Sevier.

c. Susan Gaffney Sevier, of Birmingham, Alabama, who is unmarried.

d. Jane Desprez Sevier, who married W. H. Clarke, of Aberdeen, Mississippi, and has four daughters and one son, namely: Evelyn Willoughby Clarke, Josephine Etheridge Clarke, who married W. L. Watkins; Louise Desprez Clark and Susan Elizabeth Clarke, all of Aberdeen, Mississippi, and the one son, Rufus Gordon Clarke, who makes his home in Columbus, Mississippi.

CHAPTER FIFTEEN

Polly Preston Sevier

POLLY PRESTON SEVIER

Polly Preston Sevier was the fifteenth child of Governor John Sevier and the fifth child of his second wife, Bonny Kate Sevier. Polly is not a nickname for Mary in this case, as it frequently is, as she had an older sister named Mary Ann Sevier. Governor Sevier had a sister Polly and he probably named his little daughter for this sister. The name Preston compliments some favorite "in-law", doubtless, as the Sevier family habit is to name children for in-laws into the third and fourth generation.

Polly Preston Sevier was born about 1789 in East Tennessee. She married William Overstreet, junior, September 18, 1806, and it was the custom of the period for girls to marry about sixteen, not much later, at least, and frequently earlier. She was living in 1818, as she is mentioned as an heir, in the Sheriff's Bill of Sale. According to information furnished by a descendant, Mrs. J. R. White, of Glasgow, Kentucky, she had several children, at least four, three daughters and a son.

These children were:

1. Rebecca Burden Overstreet

2. Ruth Sparks Overstreet

3. Catherine Overstreet

4. George Overstreet

Nancy Overstreet, possibly a sister of William Overstreet, married Robert Neilly, December 29, 1797.

These names all show the usual tendency toward naming children for the in-laws. Rebecca Burden shows the connection with John Borden, (for Burden is Borden differently spelled), whose two wives were of the Sevier blood, the first, Catherine Matlock and the second, Catherine Sevier. Rebecca Sparks Overstreet was named for her aunt, Ruth Sevier, whose first husband was Richard Sparks.

REBECCA BURDEN OVERSTREET

Rebecca Burden Overstreet, daughter of Polly Preston Sevier Overstreet, and William Overstreet, junior, was born 18——. She married Micajah Armstrong, sometimes spelled Misija. They had at least one daughter, Mary Ann Armstrong, who married D.. Lemuel Hughes and had a son, W. B. Hughes.

W. B. Hughes married———— ———— and had six children, namely:

a. Grace Hughes, who married J. Robert White, of Glasgow, Kentucky, and has five daughters, Elizabeth White, who married Guy C. Miller, Julia White, Mary Hope White, Ruth Sevier White and Grace Roberts White.

b. Mary F. Hughes, who married E. B. Trigg and has two children, Catherine Sevier Trigg and Anne Ballard Trigg.

c. Robert Bonner Hughes, who married———————— and lives in Portersville, California. He has three children, Frank Hughes, Dorothea Hughes and ————— Hughes.

d. Dr. James Lemuel Hughes, who married— ·————. ———— and lives in Madera, California. He has four children.

e. Dr. W. C. Hughes, who married————————·— ·– and lives in Madera, California. He has two children.

f. Cora Hughes, who is unmarried and lives in Dinuas, California.

RUTH SPARKS OVERSTREET

Ruth Sparks Overstreet, daughter of Polly Preston Sevier Overstreet and William Overstreet, junior, was born 18————. She married William Dill Jourdain as his first wife. She had five sons and one daughter. She died in 1849. Dr. Jourdain married for his second wife her niece, the daughter of her sister Catherne Overstreet who had married Absolom Holman. I do not know the names of the children of Ruth Sparks Overstreet Jourdain.

CATHERINE OVERSTREET

Catherine Overstreet, daughter of Polly Preston Sevier Overstreet and William Overstreet, junior, was born 18————. She married Absolom Holman of Salina, Tennessee. They had two daughters, Catherine Holman and ————— Holman. Catherine Holman married Dr. William Dill Jourdain as his second wife, his first having been Ruth Sparks Overstreet, her mother's sister. Catherine Holman Jourdain had by her marriage to Dr. Jourdain, two children, namely: Ruth Catherine Jourdain and Robert Lee Jourdain. Ruth Catherine Jourdain married ————— Hoyt and lives in California. Robert Lee Jourdain lives in St. Louis, Missouri.

William Dill Jourdain, who married twice into the Sevier-Overstreet connection was born in the Greeneville District, South Carolina, January 31, 1799. He moved with his parents to Smith County, Tennessee, in 1808. He began to study medicine at twenty years of age at Murfreesboro, Tennessee. After graduating from the Nashville School of Medicine, he practiced medicine in Nashville for two years and then removed to Glasgow, Kentucky. He married twice, first Ruth Sparks Overstreet, by whom he had five sons and one daughter. After her death in 1849, he married her niece, her sister Catherine's daughter, Catherine Holman, daughter of Absolom Holman, of near Salina, Tennessee.

Dr. Jourdain subsequently removed to Missouri and entered the ministry of the Christian Church. He died in Norbonne, Missouri, January 21, 1889.

GEORGE OVERSTREET

George Overstreet, son of Polly Preston Sevier Overstreet and William Overstreet, junior, was born 18——. He married————— ———— and lived in Overton County, Tennessee, He left a large family. He was given Power of Attorney by several heirs, May 5, 1857, and his post office address was then Locust Shades, Tennessee.

CHAPTER SIXTEEN
Eliza Conway Sevier

ELIZA CONWAY SEVIER
(also called Betsey)

Eliza Conway Sevier, daughter of John Sevier and his second wife, Catherine Sherrill Sevier, was born in East Tennessee, November 11, 1790. She married, August 9, 1810, Major William McClellan of the United States Army. They lived for a while in Knoxville and later at various Army posts. Mrs. Ellet, in "Pioneer Women of the West", speaks of her as living in the year in which the book was published in Van Buren, Arkansas. George Washington Sevier says in his letter to Dr. Draper that Eliza Conway Sevier McClellan was living in 1839. When John Sevier was inaugurated Governor of Tennessee, in 1803, his son-in-law, Major McClellan "was living in his brick house in Knoxville". Eliza Conway Sevier McClellan, died June 26, 1860.

Governor Sevier, in his Journal, frequently mentiones "Betsey" and "my daughter Betsey" when he evidently means a child. At this time (the dates of the Journal), his eldest daughter Elizabeth, who is frequently called Betsey, was married and had children of her own. I conclude that the Governor used Betsey as a dimunitive for Eliza Conway Sevier.

Eliza Conway Sevier McClellan and Major William McClellan had five children, namely:

1. John McClellan
2. Ann McClellan
3. Catherine McClellan
4. Mary Jane McClellan
5. Lida McClellan

Of the foregoing:

JOHN MCCLELLAN

John McClellan married a Miss Gregg and lived in Texas. He had no children.

ANN MCCLELLAN

Ann McClellan married Judge Brown and had children. She lived in Marshall, Texas.

MARY JANE MCCLELLAN

Mary Jane McClellan married Captain Gabrial Rains, United States Army, afterwards General Gabriel Rains, Confederate States Army. He was a son of General Gabriel Rains. Captain Rains was a distinguished officer of the Army and a graduate of West Point. Immediately upon the breaking out of the War Between the States he resigned from the United States Army and offered his services to the Confederacy and became a Brigadier General. General Gabriel Rains and Mary Jane McClellan Rains had six children, namely: Stella Rains. (who died unmarried); Leila Rains (who married first,——————— Randall and had a son, Charles Rains Randall, died unmarried, and married second, Judge William Watkins Smythe, of Augusta, and has four children, James Haris Smythe, died young, Bonita Smythe, married Lee Hankinson and has four children, and Josephine Smyth, who married James Welborn Camak, and died, leaving one child, a son); Sevier McClellan Rains (who was killed in the West in an engagement with Indians. He was an officer in the United States Army and was unmarried); Catherine McClellan Rains (who married Kirby Tupper, a Captain in the United States Army); and Fanny May Rains (who married Colonel Walter Chatfield, of the United States Army)

LIDA MCCLELLAN

Lida McClellan married John Gregg, a planter in Texas and had three children, Willie Gregg (who was killed in Battle in the War Between the States); Alla Gregg (who died unmarried) and Nola Gregg (who married ——————— Nelson).

CHAPTER SEVENTEEN
Joanna Goode Sevier

JOANNA GOODE SEVIER

●anna Goode Sevier, daughter of Governor John Sevier and his second wife,Catherine Sherrill Sevier, was born November 11, 1792. She had at least two cousins of exactly the same name and possibly other young kinswomen of the same name and she is therefore continually confused with namesakes. Her uncle,Abraham Sevier, named a daughter Joanna Goode Sevier and another uncle, Colonel Valentine Sevier III, seems to have had a daughter of the same name. Histories of these Joannas will be found in other chapters of this book.

Queerly enough in one list of Governor Sevier's children two Joannas appear. This is thought by some members of the family to be merely an accidental error. Others claim that a grand-daughter lived in the home of Governor Sevier, while still others think that the second Joanna is a niece, possibly the daughter of Colonel Valentine Sevier III. The additional Joanna in the list mentioned, gives John Sevier nineteen children, but it is well known that there were only eighteen. The same list makes two other errors, though these can be explained. Elizabeth is given twice and Mary is given twice. The explanation of these apparent errors is simple, Elizabeth was the oldest daughter. A younger daughter Eliza, was nicknamed Betsey. Someone, in preparing the list has translated "Betsey" into Elizabeth and, omitting Eliza entirely, has given two children as named Elizabeth   There was also a daughter named Mary Ann in the first group of children, while Polly is one of the younger daughters. Polly is frequently a nickname for Mary and the person who prepared this record, probably so construed it, giving two Marys and omitting Polly. Polly however, was evidently a name given in compliment to Governor Sevier's sister Polly.

Governor Sevier mentions his daughter Joanna many times in his Journal. Mrs. French, of Morristown, who has collected much information, gives Joanna's birth as occuring November 11, 1794. She died July 31, 1823. Her obituary now in possession of her grand-son,Joseph Windle Sevier, gives the date of her death "July 31, 1823, in the thirtieth year of her age", thus placing her birth in 1792. The date, November 11, 1794, as given by Mrs. French, seems to me to be wrong for this reason   Governor Sevier's Journal gives full, if crisp information concerning the happenings of November 11, 1794 and the days before and after. He would not have failed to mention the birth of a daughter, and particularly one to whon he gave his mother's full name. He says: "Tuesday 11, November, Rain. Finished halg. corn. Frank ran away." Frank was one of the slaves. He is mentioned at other times. Early in the next year, 1795, Joanna is mentioned as going to meeting with the Governor "and wife", so she must have been larger than a babe in arms. I conclude therefore, that she was born in 1792 but probably on November 11, as Mrs. French indicates.

She married about 1810, when she was possibly sixteen or seventeen. She married Joseph Hawkins Windle, who was the first cousin of the elder Sevier children, whose mother was Sarah Hawkins, before her marriage. Joseph was the son of Caroline Hawkins, who married Joseph Windle.

Joseph Hawkins Windle prepared a statement of his children's names which is dated February 2, 1826. In it he says that his wife is deceased.

The eight children of Joanna Goode Sevier Windle and Joseph Hawkins Windle by the father's statement were:

1. Daniel S. Windle
2. Juliet Windle
3. Robert A. Windle
4. Samuel W. Windle
5. Catherine Windle
6. Mary Windle
7. Ruth V. Windle
8. Joanna Goode Sevier Windle

With one exception, Mary Windle, I have not the descent of these children, but I will list them here in order that dates and names can be added by descendants who have the information.

DANIEL S. WINDLE

Daniel S. Windle, son of Joseph Hawkins and Joanna Goode Sevier Wind'e, was born 18——. His middle initial doubtless stands for Sevier.

JULIET WINDLE

Juliet Windle, daughter of Joanna Sevier Windle and Joseph Hawkins Windle, was born 18——.

ROBERT A. WINDLE

Robert A. Windle, son of Joanna Goode Sevier Windle and Joseph Hawkins, was born 18——.   A power of attorney was given to a Robert A. Windle by several Sevier heirs, May 5, 1857.

SAMUEL W. WINDLE

Samuel W. Windle, son of Joanna Goode Sevier Windle and Joseph Hawkins Windle, was born 18——.

CATHERINE WINDLE

Catherine Windle, daughter of Joanna Goode Sevier Windle and Joseph Hawkins Windle, was born 18——.

MARY WINDLE

Mary Windle, daughter of Joanna Goode Sevier Windle and Joseph Hawkins Windle, was born 18——.   She received the name Hawkins, according to records in the family of her descendants, her full name being Mary Hawkins Windle.   Mary was of course, for Joanna's sister.   She married in 18——, her second cousin, Alfred C. Sevier, son of Joseph Sevier, Sr., son of Valentine Sevier II.

Alfred C. Sevier and Mary Hawkins Windle Sevier had at least two children:

1. Joseph Windle Sevier
2. Amanda Sevier

Of these:

Joseph Windle Sevier, son of Alfred C. Sevier and Mary Hawkins Windle Sevier, was born 18——.   He is now living, (1923), at Livingston, Tennessee, and has furnished this part of this record.   He had five daughters, namely: Mrs. Lillian Sevier Stewart, of Livingston; Mrs. A. E. Speck, of Sheriden, Arkansas; Mrs. J. S. Arms, of Celina, Tennessee; Mrs. John Lee Bowman, of Crawford, Tennessee; Miss Leuce E. Sevier, of Livingston, Tennessee.

Amanda Sevier, daughter of Alfred C. Sevier and Mary Hawkins Windle Sevier, was born 18——.   She married ———————— Abeton, and lives at Willow Grove, Tennessee.

RUTH V. WINDLE

Ruth V. Windle, daughter of Joanna Good Sevier Windle and Joseph Hawkins Windle, was born 18——.   She was given the name Ruth in compliment to her mother's sister, Ruth, whose second husband was Daniel Vertner.   I conclude that Ruth V. means Ruth Vertner.

JOANNA GOODE SEVIER WINDLE

Joanna Goode Sevier Windle was the daughter of Joanna Goode Sevier Windle and Joseph Hawkins Windle, and was born 18——. She was given her mother's full name.

CHAPTER EIGHTEEN
Robert Sevier

ROBERT SEVIER

Robert Sevier, son of Governor John Sevier and his second wife, Catherine Sherrill Sevier, was born in East Tennessee, about 1789. He was living in 1818 when the Sheriff's sale of his father's property took place. Also his brother, George Washington Sevier, mentions him as living July 23, 1839, when G. W. Sevier writes to Dr. Draper. I have no other information concerning him.

Appendix

APPENDIX

EXPLANATION OF TITLES USED

Valentine Sevier I, refers to the first Valentine Sevier of direct record. He emigrated from France to England and there married Mary Smith.

Valentine Sevier II, refers to the son of Valentine I. He was the Valentine who emigrated to America and married Joanna Goode.

Colonel Valentine Sevier, brother of Governor John Sevier, is usually called Colonel Valentine Sevier in histories and always in this book. In this book he is always given the suffix III, also, as he was the third Valentine Sevier in direct line.

Governor John Sevier is usually called Governor John Sevier. However, he appears in various histories, sometimes as General, sometimes in his earlier years as Captain and Colonel.

Nollichucky Jack, refers to Governor John Sevier. It was a name bestowed upon him by Indians and taken up by his friends and admirers.

James Sevier, son of Governor John Sevier, is usually called Major Sevier.

John Sevier, junior, means the son of Governor John Sevier. Though there are many Johns, all historians unite in giving Governor Sevier's son the suffix "Junior".

"Devil Jack" Sevier, refers to Governor John Sevier's nephew, John Sevier, son of Valentine Sevier III.

Bonny Kate Sevier, refers to Governor John Sevier's second wife, who was Catherine Sherrill.

ADVERTISEMENT OF THE SHERIFF'S SALE

An advertisement in the Knoxville Register, February 10, 1818, by the Sheriff of Knox County, John Callaway, is interesting as it gives the names of fifteen of the eighteen children of Governor John Sevier. as living at that date. This advertisement is often referred to in the foregoing pages.

"I expose for public sale on Saturday the 14th of March next, at the Court House in Knoxville, all the right and title that Joseph Sevier, James Sevier, John Sevier, Joshua Corland and Maryann,his wife, Sarah Brown, Valentine Sevier, Walter King and Nancy his wife, Daniel Vertner and Ruth his wife, Archibald Rhea and Catherine his wife, George W. Sevier, Joseph H. Wendell and Joanna his wife,

303

LAST RECORD OF JOANNAH SEVIER

Samuel Sevier, Wm. Overstreet, junior, and Polly his wife, and Robert Sevier, the heirs of John Sevier deceased, have in a tract of land containing 290 acres on the South side of the Holston River on the waters of Stock Creek known by name as the Marble Spring Place".

This advertisement proves that only three of the children of Gov. Sevier, namely: Elizabeth, Richard and Rebecca, had passed away before February 10, 1818.

Joannah Sevier was a witness in court August 20, 1773, Vol. I, Page 174 Abstracts of Augusta County, Virginia. This is the last record concerning her in Virginia. The family moved to the "Mountains" in a short time arriving Christmas day 1773. I have never seen any reference to her in accounts of the moving or thereafter. Her name is spelled Joana, Joannah and Joanah, while her family name is spelled Good, Goade and Goode.

THE BORDEN GENEALOGY

Hattie Borden Wells in the Borden Genealogy, gives John Borden, son of John and Mary Borden and great grandson of Benjamin Borden, to whom Gov. Gooch, of Virginia granted Borden's Manor, as marrying for his second wife "Catherine Sevier, daughter of Gov. John Sevier". about 1824. This is manifestly impossible, as Governor Sevier's daughter Catherine was a generation older and had been married twice long before this date. She first married Richard Campbell and later married Archibald Rhea.

John Borden married twice and probably his two wives were cousins. The first wife was "Catherine Matlock, daughter of William Matlock". I think she was a grand daughter of Catherine Sevier (sister of Governor Sevier, who married William Matlock), and that his second wife, Catherine Sevier, was a grand daughter instead of a daughter of Governor John Sevier.

In case this supposition is correct she was probably the daughter of Robert Sevier, (son of Gov. Sevier). I have no data of his family, though it is said that he married and left children. He lived near the family of Matlock, so that the widowed John Borden would very likely have known Robert Sevier's family. However the same statement applies to Valentine Sevier (son of Governor Sevier) for he also married and lived near the Matlocks and I have very little record of his family.

NICHOLAS SEVIER

Volume II, Page 383, of Chalkley's Abstract of Augusta, Virginia Records, shows that Nicholas Sevier entered land, February 22, 1750.

MICHAEL SEVIER

Michael Sevier is refered to in Governor Sevier's Journal as M. Sevier. Michael Sevier is mentioned in Chalkley's Abstract of Augusta Records, Volume II, Page 381. One Michael Sevier was killed by Indians June 26, 1792, near Ziegler's station, two miles from Bledsoe's Lick, Sumner County, Tennessee. In Governor Sevier's Journal under date, December 14, 1794, he says, "M. Sevier's wife delivered of a son".

"TOBY"

A history of John Sevier would not be complete without mention of Toby, who was evidently his body servant. Toby is very frequently spoken of in the Journal and he accompanies his master on every occasion. No doubt he participated in many of the dramatic events of the period and he too should be remembered as a pioneer, for "they also serve who only stand and wait."

One quotation from the Journal is an example of many.

(July 1798)

Wed. 11, Myself, Washington and Toby set out for Tellico Block House to the treaty—staid that night at Maryville—Pd expenses 12.

Toby was a trusted servant and was sent to and fro on many missions in addition to accompanying his master as will be seen by the reference to Willam Sevier.

LUCINDIA SEVIER

Mrs. Effa Pegram Carter Breed, of Ithaca, New York, writes:

"My mother, Ann Eliza Carter, was born November 17, 1825, at Scotland Neck, Surry County, Virginia, opposite the place of. Jamestown Settlement. Scotland Neck, being the name of the homestead, named in honor of Scotland Neck, North Carolina. She was the daughter of William Carter and Lucy, or Lucindia Sevier. Lucy, or Lucindia Sevier, died when her daughter, Ann Eliza was a small girl and William Carter married a second wife. Therefore she knew very little of her ancestry, but was told she was a granddaughter of Governor John Sevier. She remembers that in her childhood, an old lady lived at her home who was called Aunt Winnie Sevier. She does not know whether this was her deceased mother's sister or aunt.

Records both at the homestead and in Surry County, Virginia, were burned during the War Between the States.

"Ann Eliza Carter married Ebenezer Thompson, of Portsmouth, Virginia, about 1849. He was born August 6, 1817, and died March 7, 1912. She died December 24, 1895. They had five children, namely:

1. Emma Thompson, born 1850, died 1852.

1. Carter Sevier Thompson, born December 6, 1855 died September 7, 1912. He married Miriam McWilliams, of Philadelphia. They had no children.

3. Effa Pegram Thompson, born July 6, 1861, married Arthur M. Breed, April 8, 1896. He died October 3, 1919. They had four children, Paul Thompson Breed (born January 14, 1897); Monroe Thompson Breed, (born July 18, 1898); Ebenezer Thompson Breed, (born March 1, 1903.)

4. Lozier Thompson, born July 28, 1863, died March, 1908. He married Eva Alexander about 1895. They had one child, Lozier Thompson, junior, born July, 1897, who married Helen————— about 1919. They have one child, Lozier Thompson III, born February 1921.

5. Ellie Wilson Thompson, born May 30, 1868,
(Editor's Note: Lucindia or Lucy Sevier was not the daughter of Governor John Sevier as he had no daughter by that name. She was possibly a grand-daughter or niece. Zella Armstrong)

DESCENDANTS OF REBECCA SEVIER WHO MARRIED JOHN RECTOR

(See Page 45)

Robert D. Hull of Moshiem, Tennessee, furnishes me with the following information of Rebecca Sevier (daughter of Valentine Sevier II) who married John Rector.

Rebecca Sevier Rector and John Rector had several children, among them:

1. George Rector

2. Frank Rector

3. Susan Rector

Of these:

1. George Rector, son of Rebecca Sevier Rector and John Rector

2. Frank Rector, son of Rebecca Sevier Rector and John Rector

3. Susan Rector, daughter of Rebecca Sevier Rector and John Rector, married Isaac Dearstone and had nine children namely:

a. John Dearstone

b. Crist Dearstone

c. Robert Dearstone

d. Isaac Dearstone, Jr.

e. Mattie Dearstone

f. Martha Dearstone

g. Rachel Dearstone

h. Margaret Dearstone

i. Elizabeth Dearstone

Of the foregoing:

a. John Dearstone married Nannie Hull. They had five children, George, Robert, Nannie, Bertha, and Lona.

d. Isaac Dearstone, junior, married Linda Sevier. They had o sons, John Dearstone and Charles Dearstone.

e. Mattie Dearstone married Alfred Roberts.

f. Mattie Dearstone married ——————Susong and had one aughter, Hattie Susong.

g. Rachel Dearstone married Gabriel Susong. They had six children, John, Melvin, Carl, Ella and Nannie.

h. Margaret Dearstone married—————— Bullen. They had three children, Charles, Guy and Etta.

i. Elizabeth Dearstone, married David M. Hull. They had six children, Robert D. Hull, George Hull, John Hull, Kittie Hull, Maggie Hull and Cora Hull. Of these: Robert D. Hull married Mary Ellen Kelton, and has two daughters, Samantha Hull and Arnold Guy Hull. George Hull died when a young man. John Hull married Bess Wright. They have four children: Daniel Hull, Robert Hull, Luella Hull and Loreine Hull. Kittie Hull died young. Maggie Hull married John Wampler. They have three children: Earl Wampler, Pearl Hull Wampler and Viola Hull Wampler. Cora Hull married John Gray. They have no chidren.

ABRAHAM SEVIER FAMILY
(See Page 73)

Mrs. G. L. Wing of Browning, California, has sent a list of children of Abraham Sevier which is not exactly like the list furnished me earlier. She is a great grand daughter of Abraham Sevier. She writes: "The following is recorded in my father's Bible." She then gives the names as they appear on Page 73 with the following changes:

Elizabeth Sevier, born November 12, 1790, married Mr. Scriggins November 21, 1805.

Mary Ann Sevier married ————— Holterman, November 21, 1813.

Joanna Goode Sevier born April 3, and died December 29, 1836. She married Alfred Robison January 5, 1823.

Valentine Smith Sevier, born November 20, 1801, married Elizabeth Arnett August 25, 1819.

Abraham Rutherford Sevier, born January 12, 1807, married Mary Coulston January 31, 1833

Catherine Sherrill Sevier, born March 17, 1809, married Jasper Rowland 1842.

Mrs Wing adds one child not given in the other record, namely:

Robert B. Sevier, born July 7, 1812, died 1821.

CHILDREN OF VALENTINE SEVIER AND ELIZABETH
ARNETT SEVIER
See Page 74

Valentine Sevier, junior, son of Valentine Sevier and Elizabeth Arnett Sevier, was born August 3, 1841, Morgan County, Illinois and died April 2, 1891. He was a minister of the Southern Methodist Church. He married three times. It is said that he had three children by one marriage, and that he had a son Charles. Mrs. George L. Wing gives this record: Valentine Sevier, junior, married Rebecca Jenkins, August 3, 1876 in Shelby County, Illinois and had:

a. Elbert V. Sevier, born September 5, 1878, died August 31, 1879.

b. Daisy Sevier, born October 13, 1880. Lives in Banning California, and married George L. Wing in 1904, in Nevada, Missouri. They have one son Fredrick Sevier Wing, born 1906.

c. Mina Sevier, born November 1884, married Charles L. Bell, 1908 in Nevada, Missouri, and had no children.

d. Buford V. Sevier, born June 2, 1887, married Virgie Middleton, 1919 and had Robert Jean Sevier and Betty Jane Sevier.

e. Earl J. Sevier, born August 23, 1889, married Alberta Flory, 1918.

LAURA EVELYN HALE
(See Page 178)

After the chapter concerning James Sevier and his children was printed Mrs. Clara D. Silverthorne sent me the names of the nine children of Laura Evelyn Hale and her husband Thomas T. Gosnell, namely:

Frances Elizabeth, died at eighteen

William, died young

Douglass, died young

Emma Josephine, died young

Mathew, died at twenty-six

Lemuel

Frank

Clara Douglas

Clara Douglass Gosnell married first Samuel McLaughlin and had no children and married second, William Custis and had Harry Douglass Silverthorne (who married Caroline M. Raffo and has no children), Carl Douglass Silverthorn, (who is a Lieutenant in the Army and is not married).

JAMES SEVIER

The following record is furnished by M. R. Woodland, of Rahway, New Jersey, who is descended from James Sevier, one of four brothers born in Virginia early in 1800.   I do not know the names of their parents.   The four brothers as given by Mr. Woodland:

I.   James Sevier, born 1811 (?)

II.   Bethel Sevier, born 1818 (?)

III.   George Sevier, born

IV.   John Sevier, born

I.   James Sevier, born 1811 (?), died 1881, married in Virginia about 1840, Mary Ann Boiles, or Bi'es.   Her brothers and sisters were Gilbert Boiles, Peggy Boiles, (who married William Waggoner) Eddie Boiles and Sally Boiles.   Mary Ann Boiles Sevier (born 1812 ?) died 1875.

The children of James Sevier and Mary Ann Boiles were:

1.   Mary Sevier

2.   Sarah Sevier

3.   Elizabeth Sevier

4.   Nancy Sevier

5   Joseph Best Sevier

6.   John Wes'ey Sevier

7.   Perry Sevier

8.   Isaac Sevier

1.   Mary Sevier, daughter of James Sevier and Mary Ann Boiles Sevier, was born in Virginia, 1841 (?).   She died July 1, 1903.   She married Edward Paterson, born 1838, died 1894.   Their children were:

a.   Ann Paterson, born 1868, died 1921, married William Sayer.

b.   James Paterson, born 1870, died

c.   Lucy Paterson, born 1872, died 1888

d.   George Paterson, born 1876

e.   Joseph Paterson, born 1880, died 1898.

2.   Sarah Sevier, second daughter and second child of James

Sevier and Mary Ann Boiles Sevier, was born in Virginia in 1843 (?), She died 1861.

3. Elizabeth Sevier, daughter of James Sevier and Mary Ann Boiles Sevier, was born in Virginia in 1844. She married, January 25, 1866, William Thomas Woodland (born 1846, died 1911) a Veteran of the War Between the States.

Their children:

a. John William Woodland, born December 12, 1866, married twice, first Hulla Shank, by whom he had no children, and second Maggie Gunning, by whom he had one child, Catherine Woodland, born June 19, 1903, who married Harold Fox and has two children, William Thomas Fox, born 1920 and Roy Franklin Fox, born 1922.

b. Manford R. Woodland, born May 3, 1868, married Luna May McCormack, August 30, 1891.

c. Jasper Newton Woodland, born December 5, 1870, married Grace ——————. Their children are Manford Woodland and —————— Woodland.

d. Lillie Ann Woodland, born February 28, 1872, married Elmer E. Orice, December 30, 1899.

4. Nancy Sevier, daughter of James Sevier and Mary Ann Boiles Sevier, was born in Virginia, in 1846. ?. She married —————— Cupp.

5. Joseph Best Sevier, son of James Sevier and Mary Ann Boiles Sevier, was born in Virginia in 1847 (?). He was a Veteran of the War Between the States. He married Emma Linn. Their child, Bessie Sevier, married George Perry. They had four children, namely: Tollis Perry, born October 1, 1901, who married Glen Ruby, and had Margaret Ruby, Paul Ruby, Pauline Ruby and —————— Ruby. Ruth Perry, born April 3, 1903; John Perry, born June 18, 1905 and Russell Perry, born February 2, 1907.

6. John Wesley Sevier, son of James Sevier and Mary Ann Boiles Sevier, was born in Virginia, in 1849. He died in prison at Andersonville during the War Between the States.

7. Perry Sevier, son of James Sevier and Mary Ann Boiles Sevier, was born in Virginia, in 1850. He died November 29, 1908, He married twice, first Jennie Miller and second Matilda Bull. By his first wife, Jennie Miller (born 1855, died 1884) he had two children:

a. Mamie Sevier, born August 26, 1879, who married Frank Nugent and had a daughter, Bessie Nugent, born 1900, who married John Schwartz in 1921. They have one child, Genevieve Rose Schwartz, born 1921, died young.

b. Orie Sevier, born February 5, 1882, married Pearl Roney, and has two children, Manford Sevier, born 1907 and Orrie Sevier, junior, born 1904.

Perry Sevier by his second wife, Matilda Bull has three children:

c. Easter Sevier, born May 21,1899, married **Frank** Cultiflower, and had children.

d. Joseph Ray Sevier

e. Dale Sevier, born, —————. Married Pearl Howard.

8. Isaac Sevier, son of James Sevier and Mary Ann Boiles Sevier, was born in Virginia in 1852. He died in 1882 (?).

LOULA SEVIER

Mrs. F. M. Gibson, Harlem, Ky. P. O. Box 548 writes:

"My grandmother was Loula Sevier, who married a Methodist minister by the name of ————— Bijreo, (my mother's father). They had a daughter, Cornelia Sevier Bijreo and a son,Robert Bijreo. Cornelia Sevier Bijero married ————— and has a daughter ————— who married F. M. Gibson of Harlan, Ky.

ISAAC SEVIER

Mrs. Mary C. Green of Danville, Ky., has written me that her grandfather:

Isaac Sevier, born November 3, 1789 was a first cousin of Governor John Sevier. Isaac Sevier was the son of ————— Sevier and Elizabeth Taylor Sevier. Isaac Sevier married————— and had a daughter, Agnes Sevier, who married ————— and had a daughter, Mary————— who married ————— Green and lives in Danville, Ky.

(Editor's Note. Isaac Sevier born November 3, 1789, is too young to be the first cousin of Gov. John Sevier, He was possibly a son of a first cousin and in that case he is a grand son of the Emigrant William Sevier.) See Part Two.)

SOME "SEVIERS"

Mrs. John M. Combs, of Cambridge, Ohio is deeply interested in a branch of the Sevier family, spelling the name Seviers with a final **s**. She has sent the following interesting information:

"—————Seviers married Jane Hultz. She was born 1743, died 1824. At her death she had one hundred and six descendants. —————Seviers and Jane Hultz had only one son, John Seviers, born 1764, died 1884. He married Elizabeth or Betsy Vlery. She died 1853. They settled in Beaver Dam, Pensylvania and had twelve children:

1. Charles Seviers
2. Polly Seviers
3. Jesse Seviers
4. John Seviers, born July 30, 1800
5. Jane Seviers, who married James Sankey
6. Cyrus Seviers
7. Henry Seviers
8. Betsy Seviers

9. George Seviers

10. Rebecca Seviers

11. Milton Seviers

12. Hiram Seviers

Of the foregoing:

John Seviers married Nancy Huffman and settled in Ohio. They had six children: Jacob Seviers, Elizabeth Seviers, Mary Seviers, John Seviers and Sarah Seviers.

It is said that George Seviers the ninth child of ———— Seviers and Jane Hultz Seviers visited his kin in Virginia, (Note by editor.   There were not any of the Sevier family living in Virginia when George would have been of age to visit.   He may have visited his mother's kin).

Mrs. Combs thinks that residence among Pensylvania Dutch people caused the spelling Seviers with the final s.

(Note by editor.   If this ————————Seviers who married Jane Hultz was born about the same year as his wife, 1743, he was a little older than Gov. John Sevier who was born 1745.   ———— Seviers could be a possible first cousin to Gov. Sevier (in that case the son of William Sevier) or he could be a half brother to Gov. John Sevier, if Valentine Sevier the Emigrant married before he married Joanna Goode.   Valentine Sevier in some of the records is said to have married a Baltimore lady shortly after his arrival in America, but his marriage to Joanna Goode took place in Virginia, about 1744,, when he was forty-two years of age.   At that period marriage took place early in life and I think it very probable that he did marry "a Baltimore lady" before his marriage in Virginia to Joanna Goode .

FROM LIFE OF GOODPASTURE

In the Life of Jefferson D. Goodpasture, written by his two sons will be found this in reference to the children of Governor John Sevier who lived on the Governor's 57000-acre tract of land in Overton County where "Bonny Kate" also lived, to-wit:

"Among his sons and daughters there were Catherine Campbell, whose second husband was Archibald Rhea; Joanna Windle, and Valentine Sevier who lived on Iron's Creek; Mary Overstreet who lived on Obed's River; George W. Sevier who lived on Sulphur Creek and afterwards removed to Nashville; Sarah Brown, who lived at the James McMillan place, and Ann Corlin who lived on Ashburn's Creek."

The same authority says that Abraham Sevier lived ten miles north of Livingston, and that Joseph Sevier (brother of Gov. Sevier not the son) lived near the mouth of Ashburton's Creek.

VERA FAY TURNER

(See Page 119)

Vera Fay Turner married, 1925, Dr. I. G. McCutcheon of St. Louis.

ANOTHER JOHN SEVIER

This interesting record has been sent to me but I have no means of knowing where this branch of the Seviers should be placed.

John Sevier, born in Tennessee, lived at one time in Kentucky, then in Brown County, Illinois and later in Missouri. Date and place of birth not known, though he may have been born as late as 1800. The name of his first wife, by whom he had seven children, is unknown. His children by first marriage, (names may not be in order of birth):

a. Archibald Sevier, b. Sept. 18, 1820, in Kentucky

b. Helen Sevier

c. Lucinda Sevier

d. Jane Sevier

e. John Sevier

f. Will Sevier

g. Valentine Sevier.

Children by second marriage; (names may not be in order of birth):

h. Moses Davis Sevier born, Mt. Sterling, Illinois

i. Frank Sevier

j. Newton Sevier

k. Jasper Sevier

l. Sarah Sevier.

Of the foregoing:

a. Archibald Sevier, oldest child of John Sevier and his first wife, was born Sept. 18, 1820, in Kentucky. He moved to Brown County, Illinois and in April 1887 was living at Indian Grove, Chariton County, Missouri. He died 1901. He married Emily Medlin about 1839. She was born about 1822 and died Aug. 1900, in Missouri. Names of their children and dates of births from the Bible of Archibald Sevier:

A.   Catherine Sevier, b. Oct. 30, 1840

B.   Sally Sevier b. July 4, 1843

C.   Emily Josephine Sevier, b. Sept. 7, 1844

D.   John Wesley Sevier, b.Feb. 18, 1847

E.   Elizabeth Jane Sevier b. Feb. 12, 1849

F.   Nancy Minerva Sevier b. Feb. 14, 1851

G.   Lou A. Sevier b. Jan. 9, 1853

H.   William Thomas Sevier b. Jan. 28, 1855

I.   ————————— Sevier, twin, b. Dec. 28, 1856

J.   ————————— Sevier, twin, b. Dec. 28, 1856

K.   James Madison Sevier, b. Oct. 7, 1858.

Of these:

A.   Catherine Sevier, daughter of Archibald Sevier and Emily Medlin Sevier, was born Oct. 30, 1840.

B.   Sally Sevier, daughter of Archibald Sevier and Emily Medlin Sevier, was born July 4, 1843 and died about 1922, at Clayton, Illinois.   She married ————————— Stiffey and had three children, namely; Alva Stiffey, of La Grange, Missouri; Oliver Stiffey, of Clayton, Illinois; Mary Stiffey, of Timewell, Illinois, who married John Woodworth.

C.   Emily Josephine Sevier, daughter of Archibald Sevier and Emily Medlin Sevier, was born Sept. 7, 1844 and died about 1922 at Clayton, Illinois.   She married John Graham and had two children; Frank Graham, who married a cousin, Ida Sevier, the daughter of William T. and Delilah Fannie Johnson Sevier, on April 19, 1895 in Morgan County, Illinois (they had a daughter, Letha Graham, who is unmarried, and another child .   The second child of Emily Josephine Sevier Graham is Fred Graham.

D.   John Wesley Sevier, son of Archibald Sevier and Emily Medlin Sevier, was born Feb. 18, 1847 and died at Precept, Nebraska. He married Mary Elizabeth Beckman, Nov. 10, 1868, Mt. Sterling, Illinois.   She now lives at Beaver City, Nebraska.   Their children; 1. Hettie Sevier, born April 25, 1871, Timewell, Illinois, lives at Forest Grove, Oregon; married Leo Umscheid, who is deceased, and had children; Clarence Umscheid, who is married and has three children; Margaret Umscheid, who is married and has two children; Myrtle Umscheid, who is married and has two children; Guy Umscheid, Ralph Umscheid, Alice Umscheid and Robert Umscheid.

2, William Henry Sevier born Oct. 1, 1873, Alexander, Illinois, lives Beaver City, Nebraska, married Sarah Malone; 3, Guy Lee Sevier, born April. 27, 1875, Exeter, Illinois, lives Beaver City, Nebraska, married Edith Garrett and had four children; Ruby Sevier, Marie Sevier; Irene Sevier and Lucille Sevier; 4, John Sevier born June 6, 1877, Exeter, Illinois, who lives at Hudson, Colorado and is not married; 5. Robert Sevier, born April 28, 1879, Alexander, Illinois, who lives Chicago, Illinois and is unmarried; 6. Rose May Sevier, born Oct. 5, 1881, Elk Creek, Nebraska, lives Beaver City, Nebraska, married Ben W. Hardin and had nine children: Harold Hardin, Gerald Hardin, Nellie Hardin, Warren Hardin, Wayne Hardin, Maxine Hardin, Dorothy Hardin, Donna Hardin and Doris Hardin; 7. Emma Sevier, born Sept. 27, 1883, Elk Creek, Nebraska, lives Beaver City, Nebraska, married Fred W. Shafer and has Fred W. Shafer, junior; 8. Katherine Sevier born July 29, 1885, Beaver City, Nebraska, lives at Cook, Nebraska, married Guy Hall and has a daughter, Hazel Hall; 9. Mable Sevier born Nov. 4, 1889, Burlington, Colorado, lives on Grand Island, Nebraska, married Grove O'Neil and has two children, Althea June O'Neil and Cecil James O'Neil.

E. Elizabeth Jane Sevier, daughter of Archibald Sevier and Emily Medlin Sevier, was born Feb. 12, 1849, Brown County, Illinois and died on her birthday, Feb. 12, 1925, Alexander, Illinois. She married Charles Hagen, Aug. 17 1870 at Alexander, Illinois. He was born April 21, 1843, Strasburg, Germany. Their children: 1. Rose Hagen, born Nov. 24, 1871 in Sangamon County, Illinois, lives at Arcadia, California, married Ellis Martin Mawhinney, the son of Joseph and Amy C. (Wiley) Mawhinney, Brunswick, Missouri. He was born Jan. 12, 1864, Parkersburg, West Virginia. Their children, a son and a daughter, born at Brunswick, Missouri, died in infancy; 2. Minnie Hagen, born May 1873, Sangamon County, Illinois, lives at Sims, Illinois, married, I. N. Sumner, who died June, 1924 at Sims, Illinois and had seven children: Charles Sumner, unmarried, of Lone Pine, California; Florence Sumner, of Little Rock, Arkansas, married Billy Milam and had two children, Billy Milam, junior. and Jaunett Milam; Ellis Sumner, of Little Rock, Arkansas, married Lillian ————— and has no children; Rose Sumner, of Little Rock, Arkansas, married Henry Mines and has an only child, Ruby Mines; Earl Sumner, married ————— ————— and has two sons, one of whom is William Sumner; Robert Sumner, unmarried; Clarence Sumner; 3, Catherine Hagen, born April 30, married Fred R. Wallbum, a prominent farmer of Morgan County, Illinois, April 26, 1905, Morgan County Illinois. He was born Feb. 8, 1870, Morgan County, Illinois and is the son of Fred and Barbara (Reiser) Wallbum. Their five children were born near Alexander, Illinois; Charles Fredrick Wallbum, b. Feb. 9, 1906,

Barbara Elizabeth Wallbum, b. March 2, 1908; Catherine Marguerite Wallbum, b. April 3, 1911, d. April 10, 1911; George Elder Wallbum b. Feb. 28, 1913; Nellie Rose Wallbum b. Aug. 1, 1916; 4. Elizabeth Hagen born and died the same day, in 1880, near Alexander, Illinois; 5. Charles Hagen, junior, born 1881, Sangamon County, Illinois, lives at Quincy, Illinois, married Hattie Whorl and had three children: Carl Hagen, who married Mary ———— and had a daughter Mary; Helen Hagen and Catherine Hagen; 6. Nell Hagen, born April 7, 1885, Morgan County, Illinois, lives at Lynnville, Illinois, married Earl Landis and has an only child, Maxine Landis; 7. Will Hagen, born 1887, Chariton County, Missouri, lives at Canton, Illinois, married Amy Cooper and has four sons: Basil Hagen, Lewis Hagen, Robert Hagen, George Hagen.

F. Nancy Minerva Sevier, daughter of Archibald Sevier and Emily Medlin Sevier, was born Feb. 14, 1851 and died Nov. 20, 1920 in Springfield, Illinois. She married James Brown Sept. 4, 1872 in Morgan County, Illinois and had no issue. Mr. Brown lives near Alexander, Illinois.

G. Lou A. Sevier, daughter of Archibald Sevier and Emily Medlin Sevier, was born Jan. 9, 1853 and lives near De Kalb, Illinois. She married Henry Ferguson Nov. 15, 1868, Mt. Sterling, Illinois and had six children: 1. Artie Ferguson born Dec. 28, 1869, lives Kingston, Illinois, married Guy Gossett, 1917, Rockford, Illinois and had no children. Their adopted son is Lowell A. Dearinger; 3. Mary Ferguson, born March 29, 1876, lives, Wichita, Kansas, married Ezra Henry, 1894, Wichita, Kansas and has an only child; 4, Marguerite Ferguson, born March 16, 1878, lives, De Kalb, Illinois, married John H. Cooper Oct. 1, 1893, Quincy, Illinois and has an only child, Hazel Cooper born Oct. 2, 1896, St. Louis, Missouri, of De Kalb, Illinois, who married Leslie Cutlip July 5, 1918; 5. Joe Feruson born Oct. 31, 1880, lives at Sparland, Illinois, married Laura Beaumont 1903, Sparland, Illinois and has four children: Edward Ferguson, who married ———— ———— and has one child, George Ferguson; Denny Ferguson; Anna Ferguson; 6. Della Ferguson born Aug. 4, 1885, lives, De Kalb, Illinois, married first, Jesse Kindhart 1910 in Oklahoma and had an only child, Keith Edward Kindhart, born May 25, 1912, Molin, Illinois. She married second, James Thornton, June 20, 1919, Sycamore, Illinois.

H. William Thomas Sevier, son of Archibald Sevier and Emily Medlin Sevier, was born Jan. 28, 1855 and died in Missouri. He married Delilah Fannie Johnson, June 4, 1872, Morgan County, Illinois and had seven children: 1. John Sevier, of Triplett, Missouri; 2. Will Sevier; 3. Lou Sevier, lives, Springfield, Illinois, married Patsy Ryan and had five children, including Carl Ryan, Ethel Ryan and Mamie Ryan; 4. Mary Sevier married Mike Rustenmeyer;

5. Ethel Sevier married ———— ————; 6. Ida Sevier died near Triplett, Missouri, married her cousin, Frank Graham, April 19, 1895; 7. Cora Sevier, of Ashland, Illinois, married ———— ————.

I. ———— Sevier, twin child of Archibald Sevier and Emily Medlin Sevier, born Dec. 28, 1856, died 1856.

J. ————Sevier, twin child of Archibald Sevier and Emily Medlin Sevier, born Dec. 28, 1856, died 1856.

K. James Madison Sevier, Son of Archibald Sevier and Emily Medlin Sevier, born Oct. 7, 1858, married Lula Kidd, daughter of John and Mary (Joiner) Kidd, April 8, 1880, Morgan County, Illinois.

b. Helen Sevier, the daughter of John Sevier and his first wife.

c. Lucinda Sevier, the daughter of John Sevier and his first wife.

d. Jane Sevier. The daughter of John Sevier and his first wife.

e. John Sevier, the son of John Sevier and his first wife, lived, at one time, near Champaign, Illinois. He married ———— ———— and had at least one child, a daughter, Minnie Sevier.

f. Will Sevier, son of John Sevier and his first wife, moved out West and was never heard from.

g. Valentine Sevier, son of John Sevier and his first wife, lived near, Champaign, Illinois. He married ———— ———— and had several sons and at least one daughter, Kate Sevier.

h. Moses Davis Sevier, son of John Sevier and his second wife, Mary Bass Sevier, was born at Mt. Sterling, Illinois. He married ———— ———— and had a son, Daniel or David Sevier, who lived in Kansas.

i. Frank Sevier, son of John Sevier and his second wife, Mary Bass Sevier.

j. Newton Sevier, son of John Sevier and his second wife, Mary Bass Sevier.

k. Jasper Sevier, son of John Sevier and his second wife, Mary Bass Sevier.

l. Sarah Sevier, daughter of John Sevier and his second wife, Mary Bass Sevier, lived at Hiawatha, Kansas. She married ———— Quigley. She is credited by some of the Seviers, as being the daughter of Moses Davis Sevier. Others say she was the daughter of his father.

ARCHIBALD SEVIER

Descendants have furnished me with the following information concerning Archibald Sevier, thought to be a son of John Sevier, junior, but his approximate birth antedates John Sevier, junior's son, Archibald's, birth by forty years.   Also Archibald Sevier, son of John Sevier, junior, though married, died without children.   This information is valuable and it is printed in full as some descendant may be able to place this Archibald Sevier.

Archibald Sevier was born about 1789 and died near Burksville, Kentucky, when his children were small.   He married Hannah Webb, who married for her second husband, Elmond Brezee, of Barzee, and there were four children of her second marriage.   She is said to have died in Washington or Oregon.   Archibald Sevier and Hannah Webb Sevier had two children:

a.   Moses Webb Sevier born 1809

b.   George Washington Sevier, born Jan. 5, 1816.

Of the forgoing:

a.   Moses Webb Sevier, son of Archibald Sevier and Hannah Webb Sevier, was born 1809, near Burksville, Kentucky and died Sept. 11, 1877 in Texas.   For a number of years he lived near Clinton, Henry County, Missouri, where others of the Seviers lived.   He married Susan Glum Hibbler in 1846, born 1819 in St. Louis, Missouri, died Oct. 15, 1886, Seagoville, Texas.   Their children:

A.   Hannah Melissa Sevier, born Sept. 24, 1848

B.   Margaret Ann Sevier, born Jan. 19, 1851

C.   Nancy Jane Sevier, twin of Margaret Ann Sevier

D.   Charlotte E. Sevier born Feb. 19, 1854

E.   Susan Laura Sevier born March 18, 1856

F.   Martha Pauline Sevier born March 9, 1858

G.   Fieldon Moses Sevier born March 11, 1861

H.   George Washington Sevier born Jan. 20, 1866

I.   Rosa Lee Sevier born Feb. 14, 1870.

Of these:

A. Hannah Melissa Sevier, daughter of Moses Sevier and Susan G. Hibbler Sevier, was born Sept. 24, 1848 in Osage County, Missouri.   She lives at Urich, Missouri.   She married first, Archibald Bethel Colson June 24, 1863, in Henry County, Missouri, who died in that county Nov. 15, 1908, and had children born in Henry County, Missouri: 1. Dr. J. R. Colson born Dec. 11, 1865, of Schell City, Missouri, married Ara Morrison, 1894 and has four children, none of whom is married; Eugene Colson, who served in World War with overseas service; Archie Colson; Wilbur Colson; Cassell Colson; 2. Martha Jane Coleson born Jan. 16, 1867, lives, Clinton, Missouri, married first, Meredith Anderson and had four children; Arthur Anderson married Gertrude ————; Earl Anderson married Alpha Coontz; Archie Anderson married Mary Middleton; Rhote Anderson married Mollie Warner; and married second, ———— Angle; 3. Laura Susan Colson born March 2, 1869 married Dr. T. L. Crissman and had two sons; Archie Chrissman, of Fayetteville, Arkansas, served as musician in the Navy during the World War, married first, Alice ————, who died; and second, Nina Strong; Harry Crissman, of Dallas, Texas, married Mary ————; 4. Mary Charlotte Colson born July 7, 1871, married first, Tom Clyer, and second ———— Biggs. Her children; Eugene, of Pueblo, Colorado, served in the 35th Division in the World War overseas, married Georgia Salmon; Melissa, of Clinton, Missouri, married Glenn Knouse; 5. Gertrude Colson born March 27, 1873, lives, Montrose, Missouri, married Joseph Harness Oct. 18, 1893 and has; Glum Harness, who served in World War, and Richard Preston Harness, namesake of his uncle; 6. Boss Colson born April 19, 1875, lives Nevada, Missouri, married Maud Frost and had; Byrle Colson, of Calhoun, Mo., served in 35th Division Overseas in World War, married Ida Brockway; Archie Colson, who died when about eight; Sevier Ellen Colson, of Kansas City, Missouri; 7. Richard Preston Colson born Sept. 21, 1880, unmarried. Hannah Melissa Sevier married second, Archibald Byrum Redford Aug. 28, 1913.

B. Margaret Ann Sevier, daughter of Moses Sevier and Susan G. Hibbler Sevier was born Jan. 19, 1851, Osage County, Missouri and died a number of years ago. She was a twin.

C. Nancy Jane Sevier twin with Margaret Ann Sevier, daughter of Moses Sevier and Susan G. Hibbler Sevier, was born Jan. 19, 1851, Osage County, Missouri and died in Kaufman, Texas. She married Thomas Wess at Kaufman, Texas and had no children.

D. Charlotte E. Sevier, daughter of Moses Sevier and Susan G. Hibbler Sevier, was born Feb. 19, 1854, in Henry County, Missouri and died in Bonham, Texas. She married Lum Thomas at Kaufman, Texas and had three children who lived, at one time, at St. Charles, Missouri.

E. Susan Laura Sevier, daughter of Moses Sevier and Susan G. Hibbler Sevier, was born March 18, 1856 in Henry County, Missouri and died at Kaufman, Texas. She married William Anderson and had an only child, Fannie Lee Anderson, who is dead.

F. Martha Pauline Sevier, daughter of Moses Sevier and Susan G. Hibbler Sevier, was born March 9, 1858 near Clinton, Missouri and lives at Seagoville, Texas. She married Curtis Hanes son of William and Mary Jane (Hawthorn) Hanes, at Kaufman, Texas, was born June 2, 1858, and has children, born, Seagoville, Texas; 1. Claude Hanes born March 6, 1882, lives Fredrick, Oklahoma, married Susie Ayres May 17, 1803, Kaufman, Texas and had eight children born, Manitou, Oklahoma; Vaughn Hanes, Dean Hanes, Carroll Hanes, Maupane Hanes, Reba Hanes, Therman Hanes, Evelyn Hanes and C. C. Hanes; 2. Flora Hanes born June 28, 1885, lives Dallas, Texas, married John J. Fletcher April 17, 1902 Dallas, Texas and had children born Vinyard, Texas; Curtis C. Fletcher born 1905; John J. Fletcher, junior, born 1910; Patrick Fletcher born 1912; Paul Burnett Fletcher born 1915; 3. Sula Hanes born May 19, 1888, lives Tulsa, Oklahoma, married C. B. Fallis Feb. 29, 1906, Seagoville, Texas and has; Frances Fallis born 1907, Jacksonville, Texas and Sevier Fallis born 1911 Dallas, Texas; 4. Bsyan Hanes born Oct. 29 1897, lives Seagoville, Texas, married Ethel Farr July 29, 1920, Clinton Missouri and has Betty Jo Hanes born 1923 Seagoville, Texas.

G. Fieldon Moses Sevier, son of Moses Sevier and Susan G. Hibbler Sevier, was born March 11, 1861, Henry County, Missouri and died near Mesquite, Texas. He married Annie Bodine, of Savoy, Texas and had: 1. Glynn Sevier; 2. Connie Sevier, living near Bonham, Texas.

H. George Washington Sevier, son of Moses Sevier and Susan G. Hibbler Sevier, was born Jan. 20, 1866, Dallas County, Texas and died in Texas. He was not married.

I. Rosa Lee Sevier, daughter of Moses Sevier and Susan G. Hibbler Sevier, was born Feb. 14, 1870 in Texas and died, unmarried in Kaufman County, Texas.

b. George Washington Sevier, son of Archibald Sevier and Hannah Webb Sevier, was born Jan. 5, 1816 near Burksville, Kentucky and died Sept. 4, 1893. He moved to Missouri when a small boy. He married Jane Catherine Tolle Sept. 24, 1840. She was born Sept. 21, 1822 and died Feb. 27, 1902. Their children were born in Missouri.

 A. George Archibald Sevier born Aug. 20, 1841

 B. Moses N. Sevier born Feb. 8, 1844

 C. Chloe H. Sevier born Oct. 29, 1845

 D. Parmenas Sevier born May 24, 1847

 E. Sagisman M. Sevier born Jan. 27, 1851

 F. Milton L. Sevier born Nov. 27, 1853

 G. Robert E. L. Sevier born Jan. 27, 1864

Of these:

A. George Archibald Sevier, son of George Washington Sevier and Jane Catherine Tolle Sevier, was born Aug. 20, 1841 in Missouri.

B. Moses N. Sevier, son of George Washington Sevier and Jane Catherine Tolle Sevier, was born Feb. 8, 1844 and died May 19, 1902.

C. Chloe H. Sevier, daughter of George Washington Sevier and Jane Catherine Tolle Sevier, was born Oct. 29, 1845, and lives at Monrovia, California. She married F. M. Monroe.

D. Parmenas Sevier, son of George Washington Sevier and Jane Catherine Tolle Sevier, was born May 24, 1847 and died Nov. 14, 1847.

E. Sagisman M. Sevier, son of George Washington Sevier and Jane Catherine Tolle Sevier, was born Jan. 27, 1851 and lives at Monrovia, California. He married Ellen ————.

F. Milton L. Sevier, son of George Washington Sevier and Jane Catherine Tolle Sevier, was born Nov. 27, 1853 and lives at Los Angeles, California. He married Helen C. Mefford.

G. Robert E. L. Sevier, son of George Washington Sevier and Jane Catherine Tolle Sevier, was born Jan. 27, 1864 in Marion County, Missouri and lives at Rosamond, California. At the age of four he moved to Southeast Iowa for four years, then returned to Marion County, Missouri and later to Monroe County, Missouri where he lived for a number of years. He married first, Annie M. Christian Oct. 1, 1891 and had; 1. Roger Walter Sevier born July 27, 1893 in Missouri; and married second, Lucile D. Colson, a niece of Archibald Bethel Colson, May 3, 1905 in Missouri and had children born in California: 2. Robert M. Sevier born Feb. 20, 1906; 3. Lucile M. Sevier, twin with Earl M. Sevier, born Sept. 26, 1911; 4. Earl M. Sevier, twin with Lucile M. Sevier, born Sept. 26, 1911; 5. Donald C. Sevier born Oct. 31, 1914; 6. Betty Lee Sevier born June 1, 1917; 7. John H. Sevier, twin with George Bryan Sevier, born Jan. 30, 1920; 8. George Bryan Sevier, twin with John H. Sevier, born Jan. 30, 1920.

MARY RHEA
(See Page 263)

Mrs. Ida Barclay Tucker writes that Catherine Sevier and Archibald Rhea had a daughter, Mary Rhea and a daughter Jane Rhea.

Mary Rhea born —————— died 1858, married William Barclay and had two sons, Archibald Rhea Barclay and Hugh G. Barclay. Archibald Rhea Barclay married but had no children. Hugh G. Barclay married Margaret Chilton. Their children were:

1 Frances Barclay

2. Alice Barclay

3. Septima Barclay

4. Hugh G. Barclay, junior.

Of these:

Frances Barclay married Joseph Davidson.

Alice Barclay married Henry Hammond of Mobile, Ala. Their children: Hugh G. Barclay, III, Lucile, Alice, Louise, Helen and Hugh.

Septima Barclay married Philip Huston, of Louisville, Ky. Their children: Chilton, Ellen, Philip, Edith, Rowland, Margaret and Cecil.

Hugh G. Barclay, junior, married Carrie Brannon. Their Children: Hugh G. Barclay, III, Lucile, Alice, Louise, Helen and Lee.

Ida Barclay married Thomas Tudor Malcolm Tucker. Their Children:

a. Margaret Chilton Tucker, who married William Fitzgerald, Mayor of Toledo, Ohio.

b. Lucy Glover Tucker, who married Richard Crays, Effingham, Ill.

c. Allene Platt Tucker.

d. Mary Chilton Tucker.

e. Hugh Barclay Tucker, who married Lucy Cory and lives in Little Rock, Ark.

f. Douglass M. Tucker.

g. Philip Tucker.

MARTHA SEVIER
(See Page 237)

Martha Sevier, said to be a granddaughter of Governor Sevier and thought by descendants to be a daughter of his son Valentine

Sevier, married ————— Poindexter. She had a daughter Sarah Poindexter who married Hugh Cowan and they had a daughter Josephine Cowan who married G. W. Dorsey.

SARAH CATHERINE WYLEY

See Page 224

Sarah Catherine Wyly and William Addison Wily Rogers had four children, Zoe, Minnie, Ada and Walter. Walter died unmarried about 1890. Minnie married Stanley Owen of Yadkin College, and had one child, William Mansfield Owen. Minnie died about 1895. Ada married Mathew Daniels. They have four children, Katie Wyly, Vera, William and Zoe.

Elston Sevier Mansfield married Frances Langston, in 1920, his first wife dying soon after the birth of William.

Florine Mansfield Jones, married Harry Avis Hall of Charlston, West Va., October 19, 1924.

Samuel Tipton Jones and Katherine Louise Mansfield Jones had a fourth child, Samuel Tipton Jones, junior.

WILLIAM SEVIER

William Sevier is mentioned by Gov. Sevier many times in his Journal, though at no time in a way that he can be identified. For instance:

(March 1797 (He was then in Knoxville and was Governor of Tennessee) "Tues. 28, cool, sent Toby home to assist Wm. Sevier down; also sent with him 6 crowns and four dollars to Mrs. Sevier, a muslin pattern to Joanna and a dimity one to Polly."

That seems a very human touch for the great warrior and statesman, thinking of his little daughters (they were about twelve and fourteen) and sending them a "pattern" of goods for new frocks from the great metropolis and trading center of Knoxville. I can imagine they were wild with delight over the muslin and dimity!

WILLIAM VALENTINE BAXTER

William Valentine Baxter said to be a descendant of the Seviers was born in Greene County. His grand daughter says he was a grandson of Governor John Sevier. He was killed in the War Between the States.

NANCY SEVIER

(See Page 257)

Nancy Sevier who married Walter King had a son not listed on Page 257 who was called for her father John Sevier. John Sevier King was born May 30, 1815 in Roane County, Tenn. and died April 15, 1884 in Louden, Tenn. The date of his birth in Roane County shows that Nancy Sevier King and Walter King had moved to Roane County by that date. John Sevier King married Martha Earnest (born April 1, 1814, died May 30, 1880). The marriage took place December 2, 1834. They had eight children, among them W. H. King who was the third child. I do not know the names of the other seven children. W. H. King was born in Kingston, Roane County, Tenn. August 31, 1843. He married November 27, 1864, Cynthia P. Fryar. They had six children, namely:

W. H. King, Jr.

Charles W. King

Martha Earnest King

Ann M. King

Nancy Sevier King

————— King died young

W. H. King married October 7, 1874 for his second wife, Sarah E. Foster.

Kingston the County seat of Roane County, Tenn. was established in 1799 on land belonging to Robert King.

Mrs. Clara King Bowdry of Fort Worth, Texas sends me further information of the descendants of Walter King and Nancy Sevier King. She writes:

Walter King and Nancy Sevier King had several sons and daughters who removed to Missouri:

Dr. Thomas A. King

Amanda King, who married ————— Brazeale

Martha King, whose second husband was Major Robert Sevier.

Austin Augustus King.

Other sons remained in Tennessee.

Austin Augustus King was Governor of Missouri from 1848 to 1853. He was born in Sullivan County, Tenn (1801). He married in Jackson, Tenn., later removing to Richmond, Mo. He was twice married. He first married Nancy Harris Roberts. His second marriage was to Mattie Woodson.

His children by his first marriage were:

1. Walter King who married Annie Miles

2. Elizabeth King who married three times, ———— Moore, ———————— Lackey, and ———————— Richberg.

3. William A. King who married twice, Theodora Pence, and Kate Denley Clark

4. Edward King who married Jennie Lule

5. Thomas Benton King who married Clara Bingham

6. Henry King who died in infancy

7. Austin Augustus King, Jr. who married Dorothy Lyle.

His child by his second marriage was:

8. Mary Bell King who married Harry Toole.

Of the foregoing:

William A. King removed to Texas in 1873 settling in Stephenville, Erath County.

Mrs. Elizabeth King Richberg went to Chicago to reside.

Mrs. Mary Belle King Tootle resides in New York City

Thomas Benton King removed to Texas to reside in 1873, settling in Stephenville, Erath County. He married Clara Bingham, daughter of George Caleb Bingham, a noted artist of Missouri and his first wife Elizabeth Hutchinson of Booneville, Mo.

Thomas Benton King had ten children namely:

a. Horace B. King married Stella Pitts

b. Alice King married E. S. Newton

c. Emma C. King married Emmett Turner

d. George Bingham King married Florence Morris

e. Austin A. King, deceased

f. Thomas Benton King, Jr. died in infancy

g. Clara Louise King married W. P. Bowdry

h. Donald King married twice, Berta Davis and Elizabeth Jones

i. Laura Rollins King

j. Frances R. King married J. P. Burt, Jr.